More Praise for
MORGAN: AMERICAN FINANCIER
BY JEAN STROUSE

"In this engrossing story—an extraordinary accomplishment, filled with the vitality of the biographer and the fascination of her subject—Morgan has finally met his match."
—Michael Holroyd

"Strouse is in full command of Pierpont Morgan's personal life, his financial operations, his collecting, and his benefactions, and presents a rich, vivid picture of the background against which they took place.... She has written a magnificent biography, which illuminates her subject and his world."
—Robert Skidelsky, *New York Review of Books*

"[A] brilliant new study of J.P. Morgan."
—James Grant, *Times Literary Supplement* [London]

"By uncovering the big-government impulses of capitalism's patron saint, Strouse gives us a generous sense of Morgan's contradictions. She peers thoughtfully behind the myth of an economic despot to discover a more nuanced figure."
—*Fortune*

"The Morgan that Jean Strouse has brought to life in her masterful, long-awaited biography is deeply human, the most intricate and integrated portrait we have yet had. . . . Her storytelling [has] the richness and penetration of a novel."
—David Michaelis, *New York Observer*

"Strouse . . . uses marvelous detail . . . to breathe life into a 19th century icon. And she makes plain and readable for the layman the . . . financial controversies of Morgan's day."
—*USA Today*

"A thoroughly documented, conscientiously nonpartisan, and rounded life of the financial colossus. . . . More completely than those who have labored over this gigantic figure before, Strouse exposes the whole man."
—*Boston Globe*

"Based on painstaking research on sources perhaps never tapped, including the Morgan family papers, this study is likely to be definitive for a hundred years."
—*Baltimore Sun*

"She is the first to integrate the very personal biography of a man previously seen as stock villain or hero [and] to set this complex character in the context of richly reported social history."
—*Chicago Sun-Times*

"[Jean Strouse's] command of the varied and complex aspects of Morgan's life and work is nothing short of dazzling, and her writing is exemplary, even in passages dealing with the complexities of high finance."

—*Houston Chronicle*

"[Written] with uncommon intelligence, maturity, and psychological insight, *Morgan: American Financier* is that rare masterpiece biography that enables us to penetrate the soul of a complex human being."   —*Philadelphia Inquirer*

"Strouse is no apologist for Morgan, but she finds much in him to admire and goes far past the stereotypical robber baron image to which muckrakers and their heirs reduced him. . . . It is, in the end, the largest accomplishment of this ambitious book that it gives us not a myth, but a man."

—*Washington Post Book World*

"Elegant, impressively researched. . . .With a sure command of her narrative and an instinct for the telling detail, Strouse has created a subtle, shaded portrait."   —*Chicago Tribune*

"Strouse has amassed a huge amount of information about Morgan. . . . Her style brings clarity to 19th century financial matters and her storytelling is riveting."   —*Hartford Courant*

"Nobody . . . has captured Morgan's life, death and influence after death as well as Jean Strouse. . . . It is hard to imagine a biographer coming any closer to perfection."   —*St. Louis Post-Dispatch*

"Through Strouse's use of new sources and her exceptional ability to tell a riveting, intricately detailed story, she has scored a resounding triumph."

—*New York Post*

"A superbly researched, well-written biography of a great—and in the author's view, somewhat misrepresented—figure in American history."

—*Kirkus Reviews*

"J. Pierpont Morgan has, in Strouse, finally been accorded a biographer whose talents match his enormous legacy. Strouse (whose *Alice James* won the Bancroft Prize) seamlessly weaves Morgan's exploits as America's leading banker with his frenetic social life, in the process vividly evoking the spirit of the Gilded Age."   —*Publishers Weekly*

"Enormously entertaining."   —*New York Daily News*

MORGAN

ALSO BY JEAN STROUSE

Alice James: A Biography
(winner of the Bancroft Prize)

MORGAN

American Financier

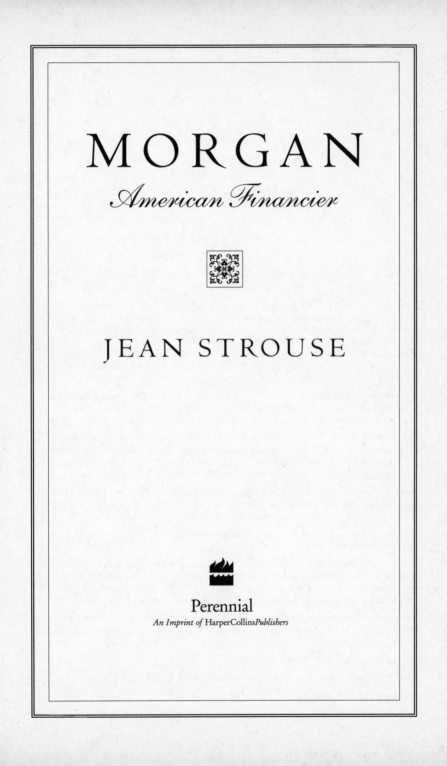

JEAN STROUSE

Perennial

An Imprint of HarperCollins*Publishers*

Grateful acknowledgment is made to the following for permission
to reprint previously published material:

Harvard University Press: Excerpts from *The Letters of Henry Adams*, by J. C. Levenson et al. (eds.)
(Cambridge, Mass.: Harvard University Press, 1988). Copyright © 1988 by the Massachusetts His-
torical Society; excerpts from *The Letters of Theodore Roosevelt*, selected and edited by Elting R. Mori-
son (Cambridge, Mass.: Harvard University Press, 1952). Copyright © 1951, 1952 by the
President and Fellows of Harvard College; brief quote from *The Morgans: Private International
Bankers, 1854–1913*, by Vincent Carosso (Cambridge, Mass.: Harvard University Press, 1987).
Copyright © 1987 by Vincent P. Carosso. Reprinted by permission of the publisher.

Northeastern University Press: Excerpts from *The Letters of Bernard Berenson and Isabella Stewart
Gardner, 1887–1923*, edited and annotated by Rollin van N. Hadley. Copyright © 1987 by Rollin
van N. Hadley. Reprinted by permission of Northeastern University Press.

Random House, Inc., and Chatto and Windus: Excerpts from *The Letters of Roger Fry*, edited by Denys
Sutton. Copyright © 1972 by Pamela Diamond. Rights throughout the world excluding the United
States are controlled by Chatto and Windus, a division of Random House UK, London. Reprinted by
permission of Random House, Inc., and Chatto and Windus.

Simon and Schuster, Inc.: Excerpts from *J. Pierpont Morgan: An Intimate Portrait* by Herbert L. Satterlee. Copyright © 1939 by Herbert L. Satterlee and copyright renewed 1967 by Mabel Satterlee
Ingalls. Reprinted by permission of Simon and Schuster, Inc.

This book was originally published in 1999 by Random House, Inc. It is here reprinted by arrangement with Random House, Inc.

HarperCollins books may be purchased for educational, business, or sales promotional use. For information please write: Special Markets Department, HarperCollins Publishers Inc., 10 East 53rd
Street, New York, NY 10022.

First HarperPerennial edition published 2000.

Library of Congress Cataloging-in-Publication Data has been applied for.

ISBN 0-06-095589-9 (pbk.)

06 07 08 ❖/RRD 10 9

CONTENTS

INTRODUCTION

When Pierpont Morgan died in 1913, at seventy-five, he was the most power-ful banker in the world. He had organized giant railroad systems and corporate "trusts," presided over a massive transfer of wealth from Europe to the United States, and, at a time when America had no central bank, acted as monitor of its capital markets and lender of last resort. In the process, he helped transform a largely agrarian society into a modern industrial state—and entered into a struggle over the nature of the country's identity that dates back to Jefferson and Hamilton.

Anyone who occupied that contested ground would have drawn political fire, and it is not surprising that Morgan was exalted by the right as a hero of economic progress and vilified by the left as an icon of capitalist greed. Yet a hundred years later the terms of the argument have not appreciably changed.

The best of the Morgan biographers, Frederick Lewis Allen, suggested some of the reasons why: sparse information about a deeply reticent man, dry finan-cial reporting, ambiguous facts, and passionately held opinions. "There were legends and anecdotes galore," Allen concluded in 1949, "but many of them were of uncertain veracity. . . . [W]hat evidence had accumulated about Pier-pont Morgan was strikingly divided between the one-sidedly laudatory and the one-sidedly derogatory."

On the laudatory side, a Yale professor conferring an honorary degree on Morgan in 1908 compared him to Alexander the Great, then invoked a higher power: " 'Unto whomsoever much is given, of him shall much be required; and to whom men have committed much, of him they will ask more.' " Switching Testaments eight years later, B. C. Forbes, the founder of *Forbes* magazine, called Morgan "the financial Moses of the New World." Morgan's authorized biographer, his son-in-law Herbert Satterlee, gathered useful information but offered no analytic appraisal, left out large pieces of the public and private life, and got important facts wrong. Intent on answering Morgan's critics by em-phasizing his patriotic spirit and jolly Christmas parties, Satterlee drained all vitality from the tale.

The critics drew sharper pictures. Wisconsin's Republican Senator Robert W. La Follette described Morgan in 1910 as "a beefy, red-faced, thick-necked financial bully, drunk with wealth and power, [who] bawls his orders to stock markets, Directors, courts, Governments, and Nations." In the thirties, the banker appeared in John Dos Passos's novel *1919* as the "boss croupier of Wall Street," a "bullnecked irascible man with small black magpie's eyes," famous for "suddenly blowing up in a visitor's face and for that special gesture of the arm that meant, *What do I get out of it?*" Matthew Josephson, in his history *The Robber Barons* (1934), portrayed Morgan as " 'imperiously proud,' rude and lonely, intensely undemocratic . . . equal to throwing articles of food or clothing at his servants when they nodded and forgot his wants." Half a century later, in E. L. Doctorow's *Ragtime*, Morgan figured as "a burly six-footer with a large head of sparse white hair, a white moustache and fierce intolerant eyes set just close enough to suggest the psychopathology of his will."

When I first considered writing about Morgan in the 1980s, at the urging of my editor, Jason Epstein, I thought the story would be worth trying to tell again if new evidence made it possible to see past the legends and anecdotes—and then I learned that the Pierpont Morgan Library in New York had vaults of uncatalogued biographical documents, including Morgan's childhood diaries and schoolbooks, his adult letters and cables, volumes of business correspondence, hundreds of photographs, and extensive files on his purchases of art. Only Satterlee had seen this material, and used it selectively; Allen saw some of it, but drew a well-crafted three-hundred-page sketch, not a full-scale portrait.

Over the next several years I found additional documents in private hands, at the Morgan Grenfell archives in London, and in other repositories on both sides of the Atlantic.* Eventually I began to write, and got about halfway through a draft before I saw that it wasn't working. Months later I realized why. From the outset I had found Morgan's detractors more convincing than his champions: they were better writers, they reflected popular American assumptions (including my own) about the "robber baron" chapter of our history, and their bracing hostility gave the story force. The advocates, by comparison, seemed defensive and fawning. As a result, I had been looking for a modified, human-scale version of the "boss croupier" of Wall Street—the cynical tycoon who subjected the entire U.S. economy to the "psychopathology of his will"—and that was not what I found. The evidence didn't support the picture I had preemptively drawn, and I hadn't been noticing what it did suggest.

---

* Three valuable financial histories appeared while I was working on this project—Vincent Carosso's *The Morgans*, an excellent academic study of the firm's activities up to Pierpont Morgan's death; Ron Chernow's livelier, more accessible account, *The House of Morgan*, which tells the story of the bank from its origins through the 1980s; and Kathleen Burk's *Morgan Grenfell*, a concise profile of the British house from 1838 to 1988.

For example: Matthew Josephson in *The Robber Barons* reported that after Morgan precipitated the "peculiarly atrocious and wanton" panic of 1901, which "ruined thousands of people" and "was felt in all the financial capitals of the world," he "swore at 'idiots' and 'rascals' who sought to interview him, and . . . threatened one reporter with 'murder.' " Asked if some statement was not due the public, the banker announced, "*I owe the public nothing.*" This story turns out to be largely fiction. Briefly: a group of Morgan's rivals tried to take over one of the railroads he controlled, the Northern Pacific, by secretly buying its stock while he was in France. When his partners in New York caught on, they cabled him for instructions, then began to buy up the remaining shares. They quickly acquired what they needed, which drove up the price of NP and incited speculators to "short" the market—to sell stock they didn't own, expecting to make a profit by buying shares for delivery as the price came down. But the price did not come down, because no one was selling. Instead the "shorts," desperate to buy stock they had to deliver, drove NP from $146 to $1,000 a share. To raise cash for these preposterous prices, they dumped their other stocks, the market crashed, and the panic of 1901 was on. Morgan, knowing that the crisis could ruin thousands of people and unhinge the U.S. economy, arranged by cable for his partners and the raiders to postpone receipt of stock they had bought, and to sell enough shares at $150 to allow the shorts to cover. He then went to London and stopped a nascent panic there by offering roughly the same terms—not the actions of a man who thinks he owes the public nothing.

Josephson cites as his source Lewis Corey's antagonistic biography, *The House of Morgan* (1930), and Corey cites Joseph Pulitzer's *World* for May 11, 1901. In fact on May 11 the *World*—competing with William Randolph Hearst's *Journal* for crowd-pleasing sensationalism, and noted for its antipathy to plutocrats—described Morgan arriving in Paris and working around the clock to stop the panic: one headline reads, MORGAN WINS IN NP FIGHT AND STOCKS REBOUND. The banker had declined at first to give an interview to the *World*'s correspondent, saying he did not yet know very much. Several hours later he told the press, "The situation looks a little better." On May 12, the *World* reported not that Morgan swore at " 'idiots' and 'rascals' who sought to interview him," but that he denounced the men who had started the panic as idiots and rascals for "tangling themselves up in a situation which he had particularly warned them to avoid." He had, the paper went on, worked until 3:00 A.M. and risen at 7:00 to take a quiet drive in the Bois de Boulogne. As he sat alone on a bench, "lost in thought," the *World*'s correspondent asked again for an interview, "but the magnate threatened murder and re-entered the carriage." He said, "I can't be interviewed now. I am leaving tomorrow morning for London." End of story. All these dispatches are datelined Paris. Then at the bottom of the column an odd second ending to the article appears, datelined London. In this version, a reporter (the writer who filed from Paris? a new one? an imaginary one?) approaches the banker saying "you told me yesterday to come again," and asks whether, since Morgan is being blamed for the panic, some statement is not due the public. It is in this dubious context that the *World* has him say, "I owe the public nothing"—yet historians since the 1930s have relied on Josephson's account.

Born into a wealthy family, Morgan had a patrician sense of noblesse oblige and unusual motivations: he could have made a lot more money than he did, if that had been his primary aim, and unlike many sons of rich men, he worked hard all his life. He spent half of his fortune on art. About his collecting, as about his financial career, the experts disagreed: the German-educated scholar William Valentiner called Morgan "the most important art collector I ever met," while the British critic and curator Roger Fry announced that "a crude historical imagination was the only flaw in his otherwise perfect insensibility [to art]."

Even Morgan's personal appearance gave rise to legend. He had a skin disease called rhinophyma that in his fifties turned his nose into a hideous purple bulb. One day the wife of his partner Dwight Morrow reportedly invited him to tea. She wanted her daughter Anne to meet the great man, and for weeks coached the girl about what would happen. Anne would come into the room and say good afternoon; she would not stare at Mr. Morgan's nose, she would not say anything about his nose, and she would leave. The appointed day arrived. Mrs. Morrow and Mr. Morgan sat on a sofa by the tea tray. Anne came in, said hello, did not look at Morgan's nose, did not say anything about his nose, and left the room. Sighing in relief, Mrs. Morrow asked, "Mr. Morgan, do you take one lump or two in your nose?"

The problem here is that Dwight Morrow did not join the firm until after Morgan died. Still, I checked with Anne Morrow Lindbergh. She wrote back: "This ridiculous story has not a grain of truth in it," but "is so funny I am sure it will continue."

As Morgan slowly came into focus in my imagination, I learned more about the staying power of the stories. Associates as well as biographers complained that he was difficult to know. His British partner Edward C. Grenfell reported in 1906 that "JPM" was "an impossible man to have any talk with. The nearest approach he makes is an occasional grunt." Brusque, publicity-shy, and neither introspective nor articulate, Morgan had no coherent philosophy and never explained his decisions. The high-stakes business of merchant banking required strict confidentiality, but he carried that ethos further than most. After a dinner in his honor in Chicago one night, the *Tribune* ran the headline MONEY TALKS BUT MORGAN DOESN'T. On the mantel in his private study, he kept a white enamel plaque that read, in blue Provençal script: *Pense moult, Parle peu, Écris rien* (Think a lot, Say little, Write nothing).

He is said to have observed, "A man always has two reasons for the things he does: a good reason—and the real reason," yet when it came to his own behavior he acknowledged not the slightest difference between "good" and "real" reasons. Asked why he had merged a group of railroads or bought a controlling interest in an insurance company, he said, "I thought it was the thing to do"—at once shutting out inquisitors, displaying his Olympian self-assurance, and telling the partial (in both senses of the word) truth. He was, as Henry Adams said of Theodore Roosevelt, "pure act."

At times he seemed made of contradictions. Conservative by nature and reverential toward tradition, he had meritocratic instincts and an astute receptivity to new ways of doing things. Though physically robust—he outlived and outworked several younger partners—he worried constantly about his health. He was sociable and shy, deliberate and impulsive, ingenuous and shrewd, domineering and flexible, exuberant and depressive, extravagant and frugal, worldly and religious, inscrutably reserved and deeply sentimental.

He actually left many more records in his own voice than previous biographers have found, and a huge cast of characters supplies testimony as well—including U.S. presidents, European statesmen, art scholars, business associates, his father, rector, physicians, and son, his first and second wives, his favorite daughter and his rebel daughter, and his delightfully indiscreet librarian, Belle da Costa Greene.

A woman in her nineties, whose family knew him well, told me that when Morgan entered a room "you felt something electric. He wasn't a terribly large man but he had a simply tremendous *effect*—he was the king. He was *it*." William Lawrence, the Episcopal bishop of Massachusetts, noted that a visit from Morgan left him feeling "as if a gale had blown through the house." Belle Greene pronounced her "Big Chief" "the most *exhausting* person I know. He often tells me he 'likes my personality,' and yet when I leave him I feel utterly divested of it—as of a glove one draws off and gives to a friend because he likes it."

E. C. Grenfell, who had complained about Morgan's conversational skills in 1906 ("the nearest approach he makes is an occasional grunt"), saw something else three years later. He wrote to a friend at the end of 1909: "[T]he popular idea of this man is very wide of the truth. He is neither hard nor cunning. Outwardly he is rough because he is very strong & yet very shy & has no command of words. . . . He has made big mistakes & even when his schemes are well conceived, he runs big risks of being tripped up or attacked in flank by meaner or smaller men. . . . His shortcomings are so patent that they almost add to his attraction."

Though cast as the high priest of modern capitalism, Morgan did not really believe in free markets. All his adult life he tried to stabilize the emerging U.S. economy, to discipline speculative profiteers and bring the market's destructive forces under control. With his eye on the lenders of capital (the United States was a net debtor until 1914), he took personal responsibility for maintaining the dollar's value and coaxing economic adversaries to the bargaining table—workers and managers as well as warring railroad and steel barons—while urging Washington to modernize the country's antebellum banking system. He privately subsidized social reformers who worked with the urban poor, and prominent labor leaders considered him singularly fair. Still, people suffered under policies he supported, especially farmers squeezed by falling crop prices and the rising cost of debt. And by 1900 much of the United States was horrified at the power of the trusts. Convinced that he was guiding the country toward a spectacularly prosperous future, Morgan made no distinction between his own interests and the national interest, although he was not an objective arbiter in the long-standing struggle over America's identity but an active partisan representing people who had billions invested in the outcome.

As Grenfell noted, Morgan made "big mistakes" and had "patent shortcomings." Had he been more concerned with the social costs of industrialization, he might seem more sympathetic now, and had he been able to explain himself, he would have been easier for me to write about—but biographers aren't supposed to speculate about what might have been.

Although the proponents of big business secured political ascendancy at the end of the nineteenth century, it was the opposition—populists, Progressives, and their intellectual heirs—who won the battle over how the story would be told. They depicted Morgan as a ruthless predator who robbed America's farmers and workers to line his own pockets. Offered that scenario, most of us would side with the farmers and workers, but it does the democratic tradition an injustice not to see other dimensions of the story now.

Many people have known a more complex version all along. Leading critics of big business during Morgan's lifetime, including Lincoln Steffens, Ida Tarbell, and Theodore Roosevelt, recognized that the demonization of capitalists had gone too far, but their revision did not trickle down (or up) into popular opinion. Steffens's disciple Walter Lippmann observed in 1914 that muckraking exposés had tapped into deep and legitimate dissatisfactions—otherwise, a "land notorious for its worship of success would not have turned so savagely upon those who had achieved it." Still, Lippmann mocked the "sense of conspiracy and secret scheming" in which " 'Big Business,' and its ruthless tentacles, have become the material for the feverish fantasy" of people whose lives had been radically altered by economic change: "all the frictions of life are readily ascribed to a deliberate evil intelligence, and men like Morgan and Rockefeller take on attributes of omnipotence, that ten minutes of cold sanity would reduce to a barbarous myth."

Nearly a century later, as fresh evidence and historical distance make it possible to take a more realistic look at Morgan, the questions his life raises are once again at the center of national debate—only now the markets are global, the emerging economies are Asian, and the corporations under scrutiny are Microsoft and Intel rather than railroads and U.S. Steel. Can central bankers effectively "manage" the business cycle? In economic crises, which tottering governments or banks ought to be bailed out, and which allowed to fail? What is the best way to control inflation? Does industrial competition naturally lead to consolidation? Are big corporations inherently bad? How can affluent societies offset economic inequality? How and when should government intervene in commercial markets?

At the end of the twentieth century, responsibility for sorting out answers to those questions rests with the Treasury and Justice departments, the Federal Reserve, the SEC, the FTC, the Group of Seven, the IMF, and the World Bank. At the end of the nineteenth, with predictably mixed and controversial results, Morgan acted largely on his own.

August 1998

PART I

CHARACTER

No human being, whose life has been the subject of a biographer, has been so differently estimated, both in the popular mind and in elaborate memoirs. One historian lavishly praises him. Another indiscriminately condemns him; and we are called upon to form our opinion of his life and character from their writings.

> J. Pierpont Morgan,
> high school essay
> on Napoleon, 1854

Pierpont Morgan arriving for the Pujo Committee hearings in Washington, D.C., with his daughter Louisa and son, J. P. Morgan, Jr.
(Archives of The Pierpont Morgan Library, New York)

Chapter 1

MONEY AND
TRUST

Pierpont Morgan's arrival took the quiet chamber by surprise. It was 2:00 P.M. on a mild Wednesday in December 1912, and the congressional committee did not expect its star witness until the following day. Politicians, lawyers, clerks, reporters, and the casual visitors who had come to watch these proceedings on Capitol Hill stopped what they were doing. All eyes followed the seventy-five-year-old banker and his party as they filed slowly toward seats near the center of the hall.

Morgan's matronly daughter, Louisa, stayed close to his side. His son, J. P. Morgan, Jr., walked a step behind. Next came two young partners from Morgan's Wall Street bank—Thomas W. Lamont and Henry P. Davison, with their wives—and a couple of lawyers. From a distance, the two J. P. Morgans looked very much alike. Each stood six feet tall, weighed over two hundred pounds, carried a velvet-collared Chesterfield topcoat, and walked with a tapered mahogany cane. People standing nearby could see the same broad planes in both faces, but the son's hair was dark and his features trim, while the father wore a drooping, grizzled mustache, what hair he still had was white, and his overgrown eyebrows arched up like wide-angled Gothic vaults. It was hard not to stare at the elder Morgan because of the rhinophyma—excess growth of sebaceous tissue—that deformed his nose. No one stared for long. Edward Steichen, who had taken the old man's photograph a few years earlier, said that meeting his gaze was like looking into the lights of an oncoming express train.

Once the New Yorkers had found seats, the afternoon's witness—a statistician named Philip Scudder—resumed his testimony, and Mr. Morgan heard his name mentioned several times. Mr. Scudder was describing, with the help of tables, charts, and diagrams, how eighteen financial institutions effectively controlled aggregate capital resources of over $25 billion—comparable to two thirds of the 1912 gross national product.

There is no precise way to measure the value of a 1912 dollar nearly a century later, but using a rough equivalent to the consumer price index and adjusting for inflation, $25 billion from 1912 would be worth about $375 billion in the 1990s. A more revealing comparison comes from the percentage of gross national product: two thirds of the 1998 GNP would be about $5 trillion.

For months in 1912 this House Banking and Currency subcommittee, headed by Louisiana Representative Arsène Pujo, had been trying to establish that a "money trust" ruled over America's major corporations, railroads, insurance companies, securities markets, and banks. The investigation served as climax to more than two decades of intense popular antagonism to "big money" interests—an antagonism that traced back to the founding of the American colonies. And now here under subpoena was the dominant figure behind all the recent financial consolidations, "the Napoleon of Wall Street."

Morgan by 1912 could not cross the street, much less the Atlantic, without arousing speculation in the stock market and the press. He managed to enter the Pujo Committee hearing room with minimal fanfare on Wednesday, December 18, because of a schedule change. The committee's counsel, Samuel Untermyer, had telephoned the Morgan bank on Tuesday morning to say that he would not be ready to examine the financier on Wednesday as originally planned, but would start on Thursday, December 19, instead. Morgan took a private train to Washington on Tuesday anyway, bringing with him an imposing array of counsel that included Joseph Hodges Choate, one of the country's leading corporate lawyers, a former U.S. ambassador to Britain's Court of St. James, and past president of the Bar Association of the City of New York; former Senator John Coit Spooner, once Wisconsin's preeminent railroad attorney; Richard V. Lindabury, who was defending the Morgan-organized U.S. Steel Corporation against a government antitrust suit; De Lancey Nicoll, former district attorney for the City of New York; William F. Sheehan, former lieutenant governor of New York; George B. Case of the New York law firm White & Case; and Francis Lynde Stetson of Stetson, Jennings & Russell, known as "Morgan's Attorney General." None of these men would be allowed to advise the banker as he testified, but they provided weighty political support.

The party reached Washington early Tuesday evening and went directly to the Willard Hotel at 14th and Pennsylvania. Morgan was gloomy and irritable. He had a bad cold. After dinner, too tired for any more talk with lawyers, he sat up late smoking his favorite cigar—a large Pedro Murias JPM made especially for him in Havana—and playing solitaire.

He disliked everything about these hearings. For years he had worked closely with politicians he trusted, and thought U.S. markets would continue to thrive if the government let financial experts alone to conduct business in the nation's best interests. Neither the government nor the press had left him alone lately, however, and neither seemed willing to take his word about what constituted the country's best interests. Pretty soon, he ruefully told a friend, business would have to be conducted with "glass pockets." The Pujo Committee apparently wanted to go through his pockets, and to score political points with the proceedings.

Morgan had some grounds for thinking that the country ought to leave its financial affairs to him. Over the past half century, his bank had helped transform the United States from an economic neophyte into the strongest industrial power in the modern world. In the 1850s, when America needed much more capital than it could generate on its own, the Morgans and their associates had funneled money from Europe to build railroads and float government bonds. By the turn of the century, Pierpont Morgan was organizing giant industrial corporations, largely with American money, and the vital center of world finance had shifted from London to New York.

The risks involved in funding the emerging U.S. economy were as enormous as the potential rewards, but investors regarded the Morgan name on issues of stocks and bonds as a warranty. It is a maxim on Wall Street that cash chases performance, and the house of Morgan established its reputation by backing properties that yielded steady profits and long-term growth. Moreover, Morgan personally took on the job of financial disciplinarian, acting as mediator between the owners and the users of capital. His clients, largely foreign at first, were putting up money to build railroads, steel mills, farm equipment, and electrical plants, and when things went wrong with one of those operations, Morgan fired the managers, restructured the finances, and set up a board of trustees to supervise the company until things went right. He was building internationally competitive financial and industrial structures, and his power came not from his own wealth but from a record that led other bankers and industrialists to trust him.

It is another Wall Street maxim that markets hate uncertainty. Wars, panics, crashes, and depressions punctuated Morgan's professional life, disrupting the flow of capital toward the future he had appointed himself to guard, and over time he had managed to impose a measure of order on America's turbulent economic development. He reorganized the nation's railroads (the process came to be known as Morganization), put together the world's first billion-dollar corporation (U.S. Steel), and had a hand in setting up International Harvester and General Electric—all on the principle that the combination of rival interests into huge, stable systems was preferable to the boom-and-bust cycles, price wars, waste, and speculative recklessness of internecine competition. The "Napoleon of Wall Street" advocated a kind of managed competition, in which the managing was done not by government bureaucrats but by experienced professionals who understood the complexities of high finance—in other words, by him. Given the arcane nature of capital markets, a private banker with transatlantic authority, access to accurate information, and a high sense of stewardship was able to exercise extraordinary power.

Under Morgan's direction, New York's major financial houses in 1912 were serving in effect as a central bank. Andrew Jackson had terminally crippled the Second Bank of the United States in 1836, shortly before Morgan was born, and Woodrow Wilson signed the Federal Reserve System into law in 1913, just after Morgan died. Between 1836 and 1913 there was no central bank to regulate the supply of money and credit in the United States, no official lender of last resort, no federal recourse in times of acute turbulence or panic. America's antiquated banking system had been devised before the Civil War, for a decentralized agricultural society. When the federal government ran out of gold in 1895, Morgan raised $65 million and made sure it stayed in the Treasury's coffers. When a panic started in New York in 1907, he led teams of bankers to stop it.

For a moment in 1907 he was a national hero. Crowds cheered as he made his way down Wall Street, and world political leaders saluted his statesmanship with awe. The next moment, however, the exercise of that much power by one private citizen horrified a nation of democrats and revived America's long-standing distrust of concentrated wealth. Morgan's critics charged that he had made huge profits on the rescue operation—even that he had engineered the crisis in order to scoop up assets at fire-sale prices. The 1907 panic convinced the country that its financial welfare could no longer be left in private hands. It led to the setting up of a National Monetary Commission, to the "money trust" investigation, and eventually to the founding of the Federal Reserve.

———

As Morgan played out rounds of solitaire late Tuesday night at the Willard Hotel, he had several things on his mind besides the approaching congressional ordeal. He was due to leave in January on his annual trip to Egypt, where he was underwriting archaeological excavations as president of New York's Metropolitan Museum of Art. He planned early in 1913 to visit the expedition house he had commissioned for museum field-workers at Deir el-Bahri, the magnificent temple complex within the ancient city of Thebes. After Egypt, he would stop to see the new buildings he had funded at the American Academy in Rome, then go on to take the waters at Aix-les-Bains in southeastern France.

He could, he said, do a year's work in nine months but not in twelve, and accordingly visited Aix every spring. Though he had exceptional physical stamina, Morgan periodically collapsed in depression and "nervous" exhaustion, and tried to ward off these breakdowns with foreign travel and spa cures.

His wife, who also suffered from depression, did not figure in his travel plans. The marriage had been over in all but form for thirty years. He sent her to Europe for months each summer and fall with a chauffeured car, one of their daughters, and a paid companion; when she returned, he took troops of friends, often including his mistress, abroad. Mrs. Morgan was heading home on the Atlantic in December 1912 as he prepared to leave.

He had spent increasing amounts of time in Europe as he turned the focus of his attention from business to collecting art. The scope of his 1901 acquisitions had prompted one of his British partners, Clinton Dawkins, to wire the New York firm (referring to Morgan in code)—"I hope, though we cannot hint it, that Flitch will not buy the National Gallery at the end of the year." The following summer, as "Flitch" dined with Edward VII in London and entertained Kaiser Wilhelm on board his yacht, *Corsair,* at Kiel, Dawkins complained: "We never see him and it is difficult to get hold of him. He spends his time lunching with Kings or Kaisers or buying Raphaels."

The Raphael, an altarpiece known as the *Colonna Madonna,* was about to go on exhibition at the Metropolitan Museum in 1912, along with other highlights of the painting collection Morgan had been shipping over from London all year. Among the canvases that would be shown together in the United States for the first time were Rembrandt's *Nicolaes Ruts,* Vermeer's *A Lady Writing,* Gainsborough's *Duchess of Devonshire,* Lawrence's *Miss Farren,* and works by Turner, Rubens, Van Dyck, Reynolds, and Greuze. A set of Fragonard panels called *The Progress of Love,* which had occupied a special room in Morgan's London house, would not be shown until a similar room could be constructed for them at the Met. In December 1912 Morgan was in the process of buying for $200,000 an altarpiece attributed to Filippo Lippi from the chapel of the Villa Alessandri, Fiesole—*St. Lawrence Enthroned with Saints and Donors.*

As a private collector and as president of the Metropolitan Museum, Morgan was stocking America with the world's great art. His purchases included not only Old Master paintings and drawings but sculpture, majolica, tapestries, Regency furniture, bronzes, jewelry, watches, ivories, coins, armor, portrait miniatures, seventeenth-century German metalwork, Carolingian gold, rare books and illuminated manuscripts, Gutenberg Bibles, medieval reliquaries, Limoges enamels, Gothic *boiserie,* Chinese porcelains, ancient Babylonian cylinder seals, Assyrian reliefs, and Roman frescoes from Boscoreale.

By 1912 he had spent about $60 million on art (roughly $900 million in the 1990s), and had given many important objects away. What would happen to the collections after his death was not clear. The Metropolitan Museum hoped to receive them as a gift, but Morgan wanted the museum to build a new wing, and New York City officials had not come up with the requisite funds. To accommodate his rare books, manuscripts, and drawings, he had built an Italianate marble library, designed by Charles McKim, next to his house in Murray Hill. The London *Times*, reporting on the library's treasures in 1908, said of millionaire collectors: "One out of ten has taste; one out of a hundred has genius. Mr. Frick, Mr. Altman, Mr. Widener in America, and the late Rodolphe Kann in Paris, come under the former category; but the man of genius is Mr. Pierpont Morgan."

Few Americans had been as magnanimous as the London *Times*, either toward Morgan's collecting or the career that made it possible. The federal government had begun at the turn of the century to enforce the Sherman Antitrust Act, a law passed in 1890 to curb private economic power, prohibit monopolization, and proscribe agreements that had the effect of restraining trade. When Theodore Roosevelt's Justice Department won a celebrated antitrust suit against a railroad holding company organized by Morgan, James J. Hill, and E. H. Harriman, Morgan's British partner Mr. Dawkins observed that to use "the blessed word 'combination' . . . in America causes as much disturbance now as the singing of the Marseillaise under the Third Empire."*

Combination, monopoly, merger, consolidation, trust: to Morgan and his colleagues, these forms of industrial organization made practical and financial sense. They had grown out of new mass-production and distribution capacities that were radically reducing operating costs, increasing efficiency, and creating immense national wealth. Elsewhere in America, however, the new industrial leviathans' subjugation of labor, stifling of free-market competition, and concentration of financial and political power were widely seen as a threat to the country's fundamental ideals.

Popular hatred of the trusts, along with a split in the Republican Party between Roosevelt's Progressives and William Howard Taft's Old Guard, had helped elect Woodrow Wilson in November 1912. The new chief executive would take office with Democratic majorities in both houses and a clear mandate for reform. He immediately declared war on monopoly concentration, promising to protect American farmers and workers from big business.

As if all that weren't enough to keep Morgan awake on the eve of his appearance before the Pujo Committee, a number of his consolidations were in trouble. U.S. Steel, the largest jewel in his crown, had been charged with violating the Sherman Act. The New York, New Haven, & Hartford Railroad, on which he had hoped to base a New England transportation empire, was nearly bankrupt and under political attack. And the securities of his 1902 shipping

---

* There was no Third French Empire: The *Marseillaise* called for war on tyranny in 1792, during the French Revolution.

combine, the International Mercantile Marine, had never sold at all. The disaster that hit the IMM's White Star Line in April 1912 was not an antitrust suit but an iceberg. After the loss of the *Titanic*, people joked that the IMM stock held more water than the sunken ocean liner.

As the Pujo Committee began looking into Morgan's "trustification" of banking and credit in March of 1912, J. P. Morgan, Jr., called "Jack," hoped that Congress might "behave quite decently" about the inquiry, but his optimism collapsed when the committee appointed Samuel Untermyer—an experienced corporate lawyer and a strident critic of the "money trust"—as its chief counsel. "Investigation will probably proceed now on as unpleasant lines as can be arranged," Jack had warned his father in April.

———

It was late by the time Morgan finished his last cigar at the Willard on Tuesday night, put away his cards, and went to bed. When his party arrived at the hearing room in the House Office Building on Wednesday afternoon, he looked worn-out, and was having difficulty breathing through his cold. Louisa and counselor Lindabury sat next to him on one side, the Davisons on the other, with Jack, the Lamonts, and former DA Nicoll directly behind them. They found Mr. Untermyer surprisingly accommodating. He quickly completed his examination of the statistician, and called Morgan to the witness stand at 3:00.

Untermyer's opening questions were routine, establishing for the record the general organization of J. P. Morgan & Co., its connections to affiliated banks in Philadelphia, London, and Paris, the names of its partners, and the kind of business it conducted. He brought out that the firm accepted deposits and issued securities for its corporate clients. (The functions of commercial and investment banking were not separated until 1933, by the Glass-Steagall Act.) Morgan confirmed information prepared ahead by his partners that as of November 1, 1912, seventy-eight corporations had nearly $82 million on deposit at his bank, and that the total assets of those companies amounted to nearly $10 billion.

After half an hour, Chairman Pujo interrupted to say that the members of the committee had been called to the House: the proceedings would resume in the morning. Before the politicians left, Morgan told them he hoped his testimony could be taken as quickly as possible, since he was planning to go abroad.

At 9:00 A.M. on Thursday, he returned to find several hundred spectators packed into the committee hall, with reporters and photographers competing for space up front. He was accompanied, this time, by Joseph Choate, John Spooner, William Sheehan, and George Case, as well as Louisa, Jack, Davison, and Lamont. And this time he looked rested and alert.

As the questioning resumed he asked to move up to the committee table on a raised dais, within arm's reach of Mr. Untermyer, "So I can hear better. I am a little hard of hearing: you know, I'm getting old." When his voice grew hoarse, he turned to Louisa for throat tablets, and at one point Untermyer asked if he wanted a glass of water. "No, thanks," said Morgan.

"If you get tired, don't hesitate to say so," the lawyer offered.

"I'm not tired," Morgan replied.

The first light moment of the day came when Untermyer asked if his witness was not a large stockholder in another powerful bank, the National City. "Oh no," answered Morgan, "only about a million dollars' worth." He seemed surprised when general laughter greeted this response, but after a minute he joined in.

Untermyer wanted to show that New York's five leading banks—J. P. Morgan & Co., National City, the First National, Bankers Trust, and Guaranty Trust— had a stranglehold on the country's capital and credit. The hearings brought out that officers of these five banks held 341 directorships in 112 U.S. companies—in banks, public utilities, insurance, transportation, manufacturing, and trade; the Morgan partners alone sat on 72 boards. Nonetheless, Morgan wanted to show that there was no such thing as personal control in the complicated business of money.

To dozens of questions he replied that he did not know or could not remember. Though he had once mastered every number on every piece of paper that came through his office, he *was* getting old, as he reminded Mr. Untermyer, and had been delegating the detail work to younger men for years. To other questions his answers were incomprehensible. As his partners and close friends knew, his intelligence was not verbal or analytic but perceptual and concrete: it dealt in numbers, objects, action. At times the exchanges between Untermyer and Morgan had the edgy/comic quality of absurdist drama, as if the two men were speaking different languages and earnestly pretending to understand each other.

On the question of free market competition versus monopoly concentration, Untermyer suggested: "You are opposed to competition, are you not?"

Morgan declined the suggestion: "No. I do not mind competition. . . ."

Untermyer pressed: "You are an advocate of combination and cooperation, as against competition, are you not?"

Morgan chose the less incendiary word: "Yes: cooperation I should favor."

"Combination as against competition?"

"I do not object to competition, either," Morgan said. "I like a little competition."

Then he asked if he might continue for a moment on a "sensitive" subject which he really did not "want to talk of. . . . This is probably the only chance I will have to speak of it."

"Certainly," Untermyer nodded. "You mean the subject of combination and concentration?"

"Yes." Perhaps thinking of the consolidations that had failed, and the competitive pressures that had given rise to the trusts, Morgan went on: "the question of control. Without you have control, you cannot do anything."

Untermyer did not understand. "Unless you have got control, you cannot do what?"

"Unless you have got actual control, you cannot control anything," Morgan enigmatically repeated.

Untermyer: "Well, I guess that is right. Is that the reason you want to control everything?"

Morgan: "I want to control nothing. . . ."

Untermyer: "What is the point, Mr. Morgan, you want to make, because I do not quite gather it."

Morgan did not see himself as *wanting* control. All his life he had observed what happens to money as it moves through international markets, changing direction as swiftly as a school of fish. He had worked with it in cycles of expansion and contraction, through panics, depressions, competitive price wars, speculative gambles, and government defaults. When a Morganization succeeded, stock prices rose; when a combination failed, all his financial and political efforts could not keep share prices from falling. Asked to predict what the stock market would do, he invariably replied, "It will fluctuate." Necessity, in his view, had drafted him to do what he could to police the markets and keep the U.S. economy on track, but in the end no one could *control* money, and it is in that context that his opaque, clumsy testimony makes some sense.

Urged to clarify his point, he went on: "What I say is this, that control is a thing, particularly in money, and you are talking about a money control—now, there is nothing in the world that you can make a trust on money."

Plausibly enough, Untermyer found this statement difficult to follow: "Your idea is that when a man has got a vast power, such as you have—you admit you have, do you not?"

Morgan demurred: "I do not know it, sir . . ."

Untermyer: "Well, assuming that you had it, your idea is that when a man abuses it, he loses it?"

Morgan: "Yes: and he never gets it back again, either."

Shortly after this exchange, Untermyer asked whether the witness would like to stop for lunch. Morgan: "I do not want to stop at all. I am ready to go right on. I would like to get through. That is all. . . . I wanted to have you understand my views about the thing. I will stop any remarks on my side, however." The committee recessed for lunch.

———

The old man seemed at times to be enjoying the chance to say things he had long thought about, noted New York's *Evening Post,* but then "suddenly, he would look about and discover the presence of the crowd, as if he had not seen the people before. A quick change would pass over his face; he would shrink visibly, and become again the man he has been so long, a hater of publicity and self-disclosure. Nothing more interesting could be imagined than this constant shift of personality, from the great power in finance, dominating, direct, and courageous, to the man of artistic tastes and retiring habit, shrinking before the faces of strangers."

After lunch, Untermyer again tried to establish the reach of Morgan's empire and again met with denials. "Your power in any direction is entirely unconscious to you, is it not?"

Morgan qualified his assent: "It is, sir, if that is the case."

Circling around another way, Untermyer tried to get at the reasons behind the consolidation of railroad systems, steel plants, and banks. And this time he succeeded in drawing out of his witness a peremptory (and to democratic ears, an outrageous) assumption of political prerogative. Behind Morgan's cryptic replies lay his conviction that the process of industrial concentration was a virtual force of nature—irresistible, certainly not invented by him, and better off in his hands than it might have been in others', though he was also denying that it was by any stretch of the imagination in his hands at all.

Asked why he had amalgamated large corporations, Morgan replied, "If it is good business for the interests of the country to do it, I do it."

"But Mr. Morgan," objected Untermyer. "Is not a man likely, quite subconsciously, to imagine that things are for the interests of the country when they are good business?"

"No sir," said Morgan.

Untermyer: "You think that you are able to justly and impartially differentiate, where your own interests are concerned, just as clearly as though you had no interest at stake, do you?"

Morgan: "Exactly, sir."

Untermyer: "And you are acting on that assumption all the time, are you not?"

Morgan: "I always do, sir."

Untermyer: "Of course, there is a possibility of your judgment being mistaken, is there not?"

Morgan gave a disarming reply: "Oh, I may be wrong in my judgment, but I do not think it lies in that direction."

Untermyer: "Does it not go somewhat on the theory that the wish may be father to the thought?"

Morgan: "What is your question?"

Untermyer: "That the wish to bring these interests together may lead you to believe that the country is not injured by that sort of concentration?"

Morgan: "I do not think so."

Finally, in what has become the most famous exchange in the hearings' thousands of pages of testimony, the two men returned to the question of controlling money and credit. Untermyer said, "The basis of banking is credit, is it not?"

Morgan: "Not always. That is an evidence of banking, but it is not the money itself. Money is gold, and nothing else."

There was in 1912 a significant difference between actual metal coin and loans represented by pieces of paper (banknotes, bonds, bills). When Morgan repeated yet again that money could not be controlled, Untermyer asked him whether credit was not based on money—that is, did not the big New York banks issue loans to certain men and institutions "because it is believed that they have the money back of them?"

Morgan: "No sir. It is because people believe in the man."

Untermyer: "And he might not be worth anything?"

Morgan, with less than perfect regard for grammar: "He might not have anything. I have known a man to come into my office, and I have given him a check for a million dollars when I knew they had not a cent in the world."

Untermyer: "That is not business?"

Morgan: "Yes, unfortunately it is. I do not think it is good business, though."

Untermyer did not, apparently, think much of this answer, for he repeated his proposition: "Is not commercial credit based primarily upon money or property?"

Morgan: "No sir; the first thing is character."

Untermyer: "Before money or property?"

Morgan: "Before money or property or anything else. Money cannot buy it"—and he elaborated, after a few more questions—"because a man I do not trust could not get money from me on all the bonds in Christendom."

———

After the committee adjourned on Thursday afternoon, Morgan and his party went directly to Union Station and from there by private train to New York. Stock prices, which had dropped at the beginning of the week in what Wall Street analysts called a Pujo market, rose on Friday in a jubilant "Morgan market." One trader told *The New York Times*, "We are wearing the Morgan colors to-day. He has helped us to get our nerve back." Jack Morgan cabled the London partners that his father's testimony had been "quite extraordinarily successful, perfectly frank, very helpful to situation. He himself is delighted and very well, and whole country appears to be very pleased and satisfied."

With somewhat less enthusiasm, the *Times* reported that though the old man had not changed many people's views about the questions under investigation, still, "If impressions gleaned the day after from conversation with Senators and Representatives count for anything, J. P. Morgan lost no prestige through his appearance. . . . On the contrary, his willingness as a witness and his evident sincerity and frankness seem to have created a distinctly favorable impression."

An editorial in the *Evening Post* praised his "uncommon ability," bowed to his expertise, and scolded those who were attacking the methods of high finance, yet found several of his positions "contrary to all that is settled in regard to the nature of man. . . . It will never do to say that unchecked power is a good thing because it is in the hands of good men."

Two weeks later, Morgan left for Egypt with his daughter Louisa and several friends. On the Nile in early February he slid into a delusional depression. He could not eat, had "horrid" dreams, asked constantly about conspiracies, subpoenas, and citations for contempt of court, and felt, reported Louisa, that "the country was going to ruin, that his race was run, and his whole life work going for naught!"

The party retreated to Cairo, then to the Grand Hotel in Rome. The Pope, the Kaiser, and the King of Italy sent messages of concern. Morgan rallied for a drive up the Janiculum to see the new buildings at the American Academy. He attended Easter services on March 23 at St. Paul's American Church. On March 31, just shy of his seventy-sixth birthday, he died in his sleep.

———

Two days later, a headline in the Paris *Herald* asked, HOW WEALTHY WAS HE? Toward the end of April, after the funeral and burial in Hartford, after memorial services in London, Paris, and Rome, there was a surprising answer. Morgan's fortune seemed to be less than $100 million. When his estate was finally settled in 1916, his American banking interests, securities, and real estate were valued at approximately $58 million, and his art collections at $20 million.* He left another $2.5 million worth of property in England.

The total value of the estate came to about $80 million (roughly $1.2 billion in the 1990s). Morgan had made plenty of money, but not nearly as much as people had imagined. In buying out Andrew Carnegie to put together U.S. Steel in 1901, the Morgan syndicate had paid $480 million, of which Carnegie personally received nearly half. John D. Rockefeller, already worth nearly a billion

---

* Those assessments were low. The federal government had no inheritance tax in 1913, but New York State did: the tax on Morgan's estate in 1916 came to about $3 million. On the art collections, he himself thought he had spent $50 million to $60 million. Not everything he had bought turned out to be "right," but a rough calculation of his costs and the prices paid for some of the art objects shortly after his death puts the value in 1913 somewhere between $60 million and $80 million—which would mean that the collections were worth more than all the rest of his estate. An approximate equivalent to 1913's $70 million in the 1990s would be $1 billion, but the increase in the value of art cannot be gauged by a consumer price index; many of the objects Morgan bought for thousands of dollars would now be worth millions.

dollars by 1913, reportedly learned of Morgan's net worth from the newspapers, shook his head, and said, "And to think he wasn't even a rich man."

Tributes to Morgan that spring centered on his "rugged honesty and rock-ribbed integrity." Theodore Roosevelt praised his "sincerity and truthfulness," *The Wall Street Journal* his "first-class mind," the London *Times* his "distinctly wholesome" influence on the stability of international finance. Others called him an uncrowned monarch and the "embodiment of the heroic age in American industrial history."

Even some of Morgan's critics said he was a builder and conservator, not a wrecker, liar, or cheat. Joseph Pulitzer's *World* called him the "commanding figure" of a moribund financial feudalism: "Never again will conditions of government make it possible for any financier to bestride the country like a Colossus. . . . Having greater force, greater character, greater intellect and greater vitality than any other man in Wall Street, he naturally became the leader, and he remained the leader. . . . The system he built up with so much skill and effort is doomed to crumble. . . . In time little will remain except the feeling of bewilderment that a self-ruling people should ever have allowed one man to wield so much power for good or evil over their prosperity and general welfare, however much ability and strength and genius that man possessed."

Samuel Untermyer told the press: "Whatever may be one's view of the perils to our financial and economic system of the concentration of the control of credit, the fact remains, and is generally recognized, that Mr. Morgan was animated by high purpose and that he never knowingly abused his almost incredible power."

Morgan's famous remark before the Pujo Committee—that credit in the conduct of the world's business was based primarily on character and trust—came directly out of his own experience and applied above all to himself. By 1912, however, it was too late for a private banker to wield so much public power, and it was too late for Morgan to change.

Pierpont and his sisters Sarah (left) and Mary, in 1847.
(Archives of The Pierpont Morgan Library, New York)

Chapter 2

PIERPONTS
AND MORGANS

U nlike most of the Americans who made large fortunes in the last third of the nineteenth century, Morgan traced his lineage back to the early settlement of New England. Both sides of his family had arrived before the Revolution. Two hundred years of American heritage, however, was about all the intellectual, ecclesiastical Pierponts and the enterprising, managerial Morgans had in common.

Descended from French Pierreponts who crossed the English Channel with the Norman conquest, John Pierpont emigrated to Boston from London in 1640. His son, James, a Harvard graduate and pastor of the Congregationalist First Church of Christ in New Haven, was a founder of Yale College, where he taught moral philosophy and wrote a book on *Congregational Churches in Connecticut*. James's daughter, Sarah, married the young theologian Jonathan Edwards, and their daughters brought other eminent men into the family: Mary married the merchant Timothy Dwight, and gave birth to another Timothy (author, Congregational clergyman, president of Yale) and Theodore (lawyer and leading Federalist); Esther Edwards married the Reverend Aaron Burr, a founder of Princeton—it was their son who served as Thomas Jefferson's Vice President, shot Alexander Hamilton, and stood trial for treason.

Down the Pierpont line came two more generations before the birth, in 1785, of Pierpont Morgan's grandfather, John, in Litchfield County, Connecticut. He graduated from Yale in 1804, when his distant cousin Timothy Dwight was president, then went to work in South Carolina as private tutor to the children of a wealthy planter. Appalled at the contrast between slavery and the extravagant style of plantation life, he told a friend that "the vinegar of poverty renders disgustful to the taste every other pleasure and embitters even the cup of Friendship." This incipient reformer came back north to study law, and was admitted to the Essex County (Massachusetts) Bar in 1812, but spent all his time writing poetry. Soon he gave up law to try the retail dry goods business. His firm went bankrupt in 1816.

Mr. Pierpont married his fourth cousin, Mary Sheldon Lord, in 1810, and the couple had three children while he continued to search for a calling. He pawned the family silver in 1816 to publish a volume of poetry called *The Airs of Palestine*. More notable for its nationalist sentiment and romantic animation of nature than for literary quality, the book nonetheless captured the imagination of a young country in need of homegrown cultural heroes. John Pierpont was briefly hailed as America's leading poet.

Next he took up the study of theology, first in Baltimore, then at Harvard's new Divinity School, where Unitarianism reigned. Unitarians, in the liberal wing of Congregationalism, rejected the Calvinist doctrines of predestination and original sin; they believed instead in free will, spiritual democracy, and the possibility of universal salvation. Making no distinction between religious and secular concerns, they urged all men to act in the interests of individual freedom and social reform. The historian Sydney Ahlstrom has characterized the denomination as "perfectabilitarian."

John Pierpont turned out to be well suited to the moral climate of Harvard and the Unitarian cloth. He studied privately with William Ellery Channing, and boarded with the Divinity School's founder, Henry Ware. On being ordained in 1819, he was appointed minister of Boston's Hollis Street Church, at a salary of $2,200 a year. Finally at thirty-four, in poetry and the pulpit, he had found his life's work.

The Reverend John Pierpont was six feet tall, with intense blue eyes and a flaming red nose caused by a mild version of the rhinophyma that afflicted his grandson. He preached with such conviction that audiences noticed only his passionate intensity: "his eyes fairly blazed and made you forget his nose and everything else."

He and Mary now had six children—William, Mary, Juliet, John Jr., James, and Caroline—and not enough money to go around. The Reverend Pierpont supplemented his clerical salary by writing and lecturing. He also took up a roster of radical causes, including temperance, the abolition of slavery, prison reform, the education of girls (not including his own), the disbanding of the state militia, and phrenology—the study of mental faculties based on the physiognomy of the skull. His dedication to his ideals bordered on the fanatical, and when his temperance lectures brought him into conflict with wealthy rum merchants who rented storage space in his church basement, his employers arranged for him to take a sabbatical in Europe and the Middle East to ease the antagonisms at the church.

His family stayed in Boston. Mrs. Pierpont suffered from mysterious ailments—a combination of emotional instability and "an irritating cutaneous affection" (possibly scabies), which her husband described as a "careless and utterly desperate [disease] . . . that must have worn out the patience of Job, and soured the temper of any one short of an angel." The angel in his house was unable to perform the duties of mother and wife, he went on, "and when, at times, she has appeared irritable, I have marveled not that she was so, but that she was not more so."

Nonetheless, he left her for a year in 1835–36. She took in boarders for income. The younger children were still in school, but Mr. Pierpont hoped the two older girls, Mary and Juliet, would "do all to aid you that lies in their power."

Juliet had other things on her mind besides helping her mother run a boardinghouse. She had been engaged for a year to a young merchant from Hartford, Connecticut, named Junius Spencer Morgan. Early in 1836, Junius wrote to the traveling Reverend Pierpont to say that he had just joined a wholesale dry goods firm in Hartford called Howe, Mather & Co., and could now offer his fiancée the prospect of a good living and a home. He named the first of May as their wedding date, "as I think the quicker these things are settled after we are ready the better. I hope this arrangement will meet your approval, & regret exceedingly that I cannot receive her from a Father's hand, but I hope her parents will never have cause to repent of her choice."

Little is known about the young Juliet Pierpont except that she helped take care of her mother and chose a man whose interests and abilities could not have been more unlike her father's. Junius later referred to the "beautiful countenance of her early years," but from her father she inherited the skin disease rosacea, which runs in families, tends to be more common in women but more severe in men, and is sometimes, as it was with her son, a precursor of rhinophyma.

The man she was about to marry was by all accounts "a perfect beauty." With prominent cheekbones and eyes full of intelligent light, Junius Morgan looked as though he could charm a salon or command an army with equal ease. An American journalist who visited the Morgan estate outside London some years later surveyed its attractive decor and described his host as "the most beautiful thing in the house . . . a man used to giving orders and having them obeyed; taking decisions quickly and taking the right ones." Junius at twenty-one had mastered the material world from which Dr. Pierpont had turned away in distaste and defeat.

Junius's first American ancestor was Miles, a Welshman who sailed to Boston in 1636. (Morgans were so abundant in Wales that many women never changed their names: Miles's grandmother, Bridget, was the daughter of one Anthony Morgan and the widow of another—her full name was Bridget Morgan Morgan Morgan.) When twenty-year-old Miles reached Boston, he joined a party headed by Colonel William Pynchon and set off to explore the Connecticut River Valley. At a place they named Springfield, Miles staked claim to land that stayed in his family for two centuries. Though he was the youngest member of the party, he quickly became second in command. He farmed his land, raised cattle, bought more acres, took on civic and religious office, and had nine children—the youngest, Nathaniel, when he was fifty-five. Nathaniel's grandson, Joseph, fought as a captain in the Revolutionary War and fathered another Joseph, the paternal grandfather of Pierpont Morgan.

Born in 1780, this Joseph moved from Springfield and yeoman farming into the wider world of commerce and capital that opened up with the nineteenth century. In 1807 he married Sarah Spencer of Middletown, with whom he had three children: Mary, Lucy, and Junius Spencer, born in West Springfield—now Holyoke—in April 1813. Beauty was not among the attributes of the Morgan women; Junius got his handsome features from his father.

Joseph was working the family land and dealing in real estate when his father died at the end of 1813, leaving him property worth $15,000.* Two years later he spent $10,000 on a stagecoach line and tavern, then in 1817 moved his family down the Connecticut River to Hartford, where he acquired another tavern—the Exchange Coffee House—that served as a meeting place for travelers, politicians, and the local gentry. The Morgans lived at the Exchange Tavern until 1829, when Joseph traded it up for the fifty-room City Hotel. He sent his son to boarding school at Middletown, and his daughters to the Emma Willard School in Troy, New York.

A new urban culture was taking shape in early-nineteenth-century America, with taverns and hotels at its center, and Joseph turned out to have instincts perfectly suited to the transition from country to town. His early innkeeping enterprises were small enough to be owned and managed by him, but with his accumulating capital he moved into every important aspect of the country's market revolution: he helped organize banks to finance Hartford's economic boom, and was a founder of the Aetna Insurance Company; he invested in steamships, railroads, bridges, and canals—large-scale enterprises that reached beyond the physical boundaries of Hartford, were financed by

---

* The equivalent of that sum in the 1990s would be roughly $225,000. Joseph had recently bought 36 acres of land for $370, and a house on 18 acres for $750; he paid his farmhands $6 to $12 a month.

selling shares of stock, and operated by hired managers. Most of Joseph's ventures succeeded. He bought one hundred shares of stock in the Hartford & New Haven Railroad when the books opened in 1835, and noted in his diary on December 14, 1839: "Locomotive first came to [Hartford] Engine House on N. Haven Rail Road." The Aetna's stock, worth $150,000 in 1819, grew to $4 million by 1881.

Politically, Joseph supported the nationalist programs of John Quincy Adams and Henry Clay, ideological descendants of Alexander Hamilton. As the country's first Treasury Secretary, Hamilton had set out to free the newly independent states from economic dependence on England. He sought to build a national economy by structuring into the new state as much favoritism for business as he could; and in 1791, aiming to rationalize the country's financial markets and facilitate the growth of interregional trade, he set up a central bank—the First Bank of the United States. His efforts met with fierce opposition, especially in the agrarian South.

Americans brought to their political philosophy a deep-seated fear of big government and concentrated wealth. The Jeffersonian republicans who challenged Hamilton's vision of the future looked to an economy based not on a strong federal government and national commercial markets but on decentralization, individual freedom, and agriculture. They believed that a relatively weak government would foster local autonomy and egalitarian democracy; the country's natural economic order would be ruled not by aristocratic elites in distant cities but by the self-sufficient farmer on his rural acre. "Those who labor in the earth are the chosen people of God, if ever he had a chosen people," Jefferson wrote in 1781: ". . . generally speaking the proportion which the aggregate of the other classes of citizens bears in any state to that of its husbandmen, is the proportion of its unsound to its healthy parts, and is a good enough barometer whereby to measure its degree of corruption."

Carrying the commercial/industrialist position forward into the 1820s, Kentucky Congressman Henry Clay proposed an American System in which tariffs would protect U.S. industry against competition from European manufacturers, federal funds would maintain and improve public roads and canals, and a central bank would provide the country with a stable supply of money and credit. John Quincy Adams, President from 1824 to 1828, adopted Clay's system and made its author his Secretary of State.

Joseph Morgan stood firmly on the side of the Clay/Adams economic policies and against their outspoken critic, the popular 1812 war hero, Andrew Jackson. "Old Hickory" attacked the Adams administration as aristocratic and elitist, charging that it catered to the special privileges of plutocrats while ignoring the farmers and workers whom Jackson, following Jefferson, saw as the true constituents of a democratic government. In the 1828 presidential campaign, the general from Tennessee ran on his military record and plebeian origins, promising to stand up for ordinary Americans.*

Joseph lost a beaver hat betting against Jackson, who won 56 percent of the popular vote in 1828. Once in office, the anticentrist, broadly populist new President turned the "Monster" Second Bank of the United States into a symbol of the eastern moneyed interests that he would bring down. Early in 1832, as the next election campaign got under way, Joseph Morgan made a trip to Washington. He talked with the charismatic Henry Clay, listened to speeches about South Carolina's threat to nullify the notorious Tariff of Abominations that helped the manufacturing North and hurt the agricultural South, and met the President: "Was introduced to Gen. Jackson found him very polite & dressed very well upon the whole he appeared better than I expected."

Jackson easily defeated Clay that fall, with 219 electoral votes to his opponent's 49. Joseph wrote in his diary: "Abroad the Political Horizon is overcast, disunion threatens us from the South, there is danger of the Manufacturers losing a protective tariff[.] Jackson is again re-elected President everything looks squally."

The President immediately took up his promise to destroy the Second Bank of the United States. Hamilton's charter for the First Bank had not been renewed in 1811, after an intense debate over whether a national bank violated the Constitution by giving too much power to the government; state-chartered banks resented having to compete with and be regulated by the federal institution. In 1816, however, the financial chaos created by the War of 1812 and the explosive growth of state banks led Congress to charter a Second Bank for twenty years. Headquartered in Philadelphia under the direction of an arrogant patrician named Nicholas Biddle between 1823 and 1832, the Second Bank proved no less controversial than the First.

Biddle's bank—like its predecessor, a private corporation operating with quasi-governmental authority—served as a cautious, reasonably effective regulator of the growing economy. It issued banknotes, lent money, sold government bonds, held federal reserves, stabilized domestic and foreign exchange, tried to control the international balance of payments, disciplined state banks by requiring them to maintain adequate reserves—and made more enemies than friends. Its anti-inflationary credit restrictions helped lenders in the money centers of the East, and hurt borrowers—speculators as well as farmers, workers, shopkeepers, and mechanics in the South and West. State bankers denounced it as a government-sponsored monopoly that stifled private

---

* Adams, Clay, and Jackson were all Democratic Republicans in 1824. Four years later, Jackson ran as a Democrat, while Clay and Adams called themselves National Republicans. In the 1830s the National Republicans became Whigs in opposition to what they saw as Jackson's virtually monarchical power.

enterprise. Wall Street resented its location outside New York. Southern states-rightists saw it as an unconstitutional usurpation of local authority. House Democratic leader James K. Polk said it had set itself up as a rival to the government and asked "whether we shall have the republic without the bank, or the bank without the republic." The maladroit Biddle magnified the bank's "Monster" image by telling Congress it could destroy state banks at will, even though he pointed out that it did not, and his payments to politicians and journalists confirmed his critics' worst fears.

Early in 1832 Jackson vetoed a bill to renew the bank's charter, warning of the evils that "might flow from such a concentration of power in the hands of a few men irresponsible to the people." When Biddle came out for Henry Clay in the 1832 election, Jackson told Martin Van Buren: "The Bank . . . is trying to kill me, *but I will kill it.*" He had to get rid of two Treasury secretaries to do it, but over the next four years he effectively dismantled the bank.

———

While Joseph Morgan worried about the political and economic climate, he was preparing his son for a commercial career. As soon as Junius graduated from school at sixteen, he went to Boston to clerk for a merchant and banker named Alfred Welles. He stayed five years. By the time he completed his apprenticeship in 1834 he was twenty-one and engaged to Juliet Pierpont. Joseph secured him a partnership with a banker named Morris Ketchum at 40 Wall Street in New York; the new firm would be called Morgan, Ketchum & Co.

Business was booming in New York's markets and harbors. The Erie Canal, completed in 1825 to link the city by water to the Great Lakes, had increased the speed and reduced the cost of transport in both directions. By the time Junius arrived, Manhattan had become the major "money center" in the United States, handling 40 percent of the country's foreign trade.

Speculation on Wall Street was wild, however, and the national financial weather dangerously "squally" in 1834. Railways, roads, bridges, and canals were opening up vast new markets in the West. Local land prices soared at the hint of a new railroad line; factories and towns were sprouting like weeds on the open plains. The United States had 329 banks in 1829, and more than twice that number by 1837. Most of them made loans almost as readily as they accepted deposits, with minimal security requirements: between 1829 and 1837 the amount on loan jumped from $137 million to $525 million. With no federal braking mechanisms after the crippling of the Second Bank, gambling and inflation surged out of control.

Junius had planned to start his married life in New York, but after eighteen months, prudence won out over ambition. Early in 1836 he accepted a partnership with the dry goods firm of Howe, Mather & Co. in Hartford, telling the Reverend Pierpont, "altho' I may not realise a fortune as soon, yet it seems safer" than Wall Street. He put $10,000 into the business (probably borrowed from his father), and hoped to move it to New York "as soon as we feel a little stronger & have added to our capital."

He finished up the last of his New York work and returned to Hartford early in March. Joseph had finally built his family a house, at No. 26 Asylum Street on Lord's Hill just west of downtown.* At the beginning of May, Junius went to Boston, where the Reverend Samuel K. Lothrop married him to Juliet Pierpont at her father's church. The couple took a ten-day honeymoon in Providence. Joseph wrote in his diary on May 11: "Junius came home with his new wife." The new wife's sister, mother, and grandmother came to stay with the Morgans that summer. By mid-August, Juliet was pregnant.

Joseph's diary does not mention an impending grandchild. It lists Aetna losses, Junius's business trips, a visit from the returned Reverend Pierpont, the purchase of a pew at Hartford's Center (Congregational) Church, farming details, local deaths, and political news: Democrat Martin Van Buren ran against four Whigs in 1836 and won. At the beginning of March 1837 Andrew Jackson announced in his last address as President: "I leave this great people prosperous and happy." Joseph was delighted to see him go: "This day Andrew Jackson retires to Hermitage. We ought to rejoice."

Then on April 17, Joseph wrote: "Junius 1st child a son born 3 a.m." Junius and the Reverend Pierpont had birthdays in April. The young couple chose not to make their firstborn a junior. They named him John Pierpont Morgan.

Three weeks later the bill for the 1830s' expansion came due. Set off by a chain of events that included credit restrictions imposed by the Bank of England, domestic crop failures, an adverse trade balance, and a fall in the price of cotton, the panic of 1837 started in New York and was followed by one of the worst depressions in American history. The nineteenth century would see a new economic crisis every 10 to 20 years: in 1819, 1837, 1857, 1873, 1884, and 1893. According to John Kenneth Galbraith, the intervals between panics corresponded "roughly with the time it took people to forget the last disaster."

———

Junius stayed in Hartford for two weeks after the birth of his son. In early May, as the financial crisis threatened Howe, Mather clients with default, he went south to collect on precarious debts. "Don't give out!" Mather urged him. "Stick to them for good." Junius's mail from the firm that spring included cheerful

---

* In the 1840s, other wealthy families seeking to escape the crush of urban commerce would follow Joseph's lead, making Lord's Hill—also called Asylum Hill—the city's premier residential site. Asylum Street, laid out as the Litchfield Turnpike in 1800, took its name from the Connecticut Asylum for the Education and Instruction of Deaf and Dumb Persons, built in 1821 on the north side of the road; its first principal was Thomas Gallaudet.

news about his family: "Your wife & baby is fine & write today," and "Your wife was at the store yesterday looked very smart & she said young Mr. Morgan was also doing nicely."

The store was doing nicely as well, under the circumstances. "Our own affairs look better than when you left," reported the partners on May 8, "& we feel confident we shall stem the tide." The news from New York was "*Bad. Bad—Bad.*" In mid-May, New York's banks stopped payment in specie—metal coin with a fixed value—and banks throughout New England followed suit. "We are after all in a devil of a stew without any basis to our currency," Howe and Mather told Junius, instructing him to collect the southern debts in cotton or the notes of strong banks. By the time Junius came home in late June he had secured most of the money owed to the firm in the South.

Three generations of Morgans now lived under Joseph's ample roof. Junius paid his father $9 a week in board for "Self & Family," and there was a constant stream of guests. Juliet's sister Mary came from Boston to help with the baby; Junius's sister Lucy, who had married into Hartford's prominent Goodwin family, often brought her children over for the day. The Morgans had a large staff of white and "coloured" help—farmhands, gardeners, cooks, serving girls, chambermaids. For Juliet, life as Mrs. Junius Morgan in this affluent Hartford household was radically different from the straitened circumstances of her life as Miss Pierpont in Boston.

She took her son to be baptized by her father at the Hollis Street Church in July 1837. The baby's cumbersome name gave rise to several alternatives. Family letters and diaries refer to "Junius Child," "Junius Boy," "young Mr. Morgan," and "Master J.P." His parents nicknamed him "Bub." Schoolmates later called him "Pip." As soon as he was old enough to write, he signed himself "J. Pierpont Morgan," and was known as Pierpont Morgan for the rest of his life.

Illness descended on his childhood with the unpredictable regularity of bad weather. Two months before his first birthday, in February 1838, "young Mr. Morgan" began having convulsions. Joseph wrote in his diary on the nineteenth: "Junius Child had a fit." Early in March: "Junius Boy has had a sick week better to day no fits for several days Mary Pierpont came here from Boston." And on March 24: "Junius Boy worse has many fits."

Then Juliet came down with scarlet fever. When she took the baby with a nurse to see her parents at the end of April, Joseph noted: "Child very unwell I fear I never shall see him again." Mother, son, and nurse stayed in Boston for six weeks, then moved to Guilford on the Connecticut shore to escape the city heat. Junius came from Hartford whenever he could get away. "Boy far from being well," wrote Joseph in late July.

Next, Junius developed a fever that kept him in bed for two months. Late that fall the child's convulsions finally stopped. "Master J.P. improves daily," Junius told his father-in-law in November, and in December, "Bub very well & an astonishing boy."

The specter of infant mortality haunted mid-nineteenth-century parents. Three of Lucy Goodwin's children died before the age of three. Pierpont's terrifying seizures left his parents extremely solicitous about his "delicate" health, and as he grew older, vague, unnamed maladies often kept him out of school. He retained a hypochondriacal sense of frailty all his life. Some mysterious affliction seemed to have him permanently in its grip, and he feared that if it disappeared in one form, it would come back in another.

"Whatever the nature of the [seizure] illness," wrote his son-in-law in an unpublished recollection, "it left a strong impression of anxiety and concern on the family even after it appeared to have been entirely outgrown. This accounts for a sort of tradition about the facial infirmity that later appeared"—Morgan's grotesque nose—"that it was another manifestation of the early trouble. It was believed that the growth could very easily have been removed. This was, in fact, the opinion of several eminent physicians. But a cure was never attempted. The supposed reason was that Mr. Morgan had an idea that if he should have the growth removed from his nose the other trouble might come back."

———

The contrast between Morgans and Pierponts sharpened during the childhood of the boy with both names. The competent, close-knit, energetic Hartford relatives were exacting and somewhat stern. The Bostonians—feckless, impecunious, at odds with one another, plagued by physical and psychological troubles—were a mess; they were also, for a child, more fun.

The Morgan grandparents played an integral role in Pierpont's daily life, serving in effect as a second set of parents. Junius and Juliet moved into a rented house in 1838, and when they went away for a month's vacation in June of 1839 (Juliet was pregnant again), their two-year-old stayed with Joseph and Sarah on Asylum Street. Joseph, busy managing the construction of his wedding present to Junius—a house near his own on Lord's Hill—wrote to the traveling pair that "your *beautiful* Dog breathed his last" and "Pierpont makes us no trouble, he behaves like a man."

That Christmas, Juliet's parents visited Hartford. Junius reported that for several days after their departure, "Bub" was "quite troubled because no plate was put upon the table for Mama P and Papa P – & he now often talks about them." Mama and Papa P. had brought a new puppy for Christmas, and it was the boy's "great favorite."

One of the Reverend Pierpont's admirers wrote that "he had not the limitations, either in character or thought, of the old Puritan mind," but a "child-like character, one in which the direct sense of truth and right outran all other considerations." Listening intently to the dictates of truth and right sometimes made Mr. Pierpont deaf to the world around him. Giving a lecture at Hartford's Young Men's Institute in 1838 on his travels in Constantinople, he described, among other things, the astonishing fertility of Ottoman women—one had married before the age of twelve and died at forty-seven, having given birth to twenty-seven children. The rural Connecticut River Valley subscribed to a more conservative Puritan orthodoxy than Boston did in the late 1830s, and Hartford's nose was too blue for this sort of talk. Joseph reported the lecture "very long & not very well liked. Gave some displeasure to some of our *very* modest Ladies in speaking of the Fecundity of the Turkish ladies, etc . . ."

For all Mr. Pierpont's zeal on behalf of truth and social justice, he had little empathy with the troubles in his own family. His wife's father and brother were alcoholics, and when his own son William started down the same path, John Pierpont turned away in disgust. William died mysteriously in his late forties. His sister Mary told their father that "he was a thoroughly honest upright loving spirit . . . 'Charity for others faults' he had. Would, my Father, you had more of it."

Mr. Pierpont's second son, John, Jr., followed more closely in the paternal footsteps. After graduating from Harvard, he joined the Unitarian ministry, then took a preaching job in Savannah, Georgia. The elder John Pierpont worried about the younger's ability to keep faith with abolitionist orthodoxy while in the South, to which his son replied, "My ideal of duty is not as high as yours." In 1854 John, Jr., could speak fearlessly from the southern pulpit on any topic except slavery—the one topic on which his father would have wanted him to speak out: "Dear Father," he tried to explain, "I am different from you in much. I look not upon life with your eyes. . . . But I trust that I am honest, even tho I am weak."

The youngest son, James, had a penchant for trouble. He married at twenty-four, had two children, then headed off to the California gold rush leaving his father to look after his family. Failing to strike it rich, he tried and failed at several jobs. After his wife died in 1856, he deposited their children with her father and moved to Georgia to be near John, Jr., and their sister Caroline, who had married a southern businessman. James composed music, played the organ at John's church, and far surpassed his brothers in the realm of Pierpont heresy by riding with the Confederate cavalry in the Civil War. He eventually outbid his father for literary immortality by writing a song called "Jingle Bells."

———

John Pierpont's sabbatical had not moderated his visionary fervor. In the fall of 1839, after he stepped up his attacks on slavery and "demon rum," the Hollis Street proprietors censured him for "too busy interference with questions of legislation," for lacking "discretion, moderation, charity and Christian meekness and humility," and for his "unkind and excited manner of preaching." They voted to fire him, 63 to 60.

Junius told his father-in-law that though "indignant" at the way the matter had been handled, he was glad it was over. It was not over. Mr. Pierpont refused to resign. Claiming that his adversaries had rigged the censure motion by having wealthy rum sellers buy up pews and cast more votes than they were entitled to—they had—he fought back for the freedom of the Unitarian pulpit in what became known locally as the Seven Years War. He demanded to hear the specific charges against him. When his accusers said he had entered into "*every* exciting topic that the ingenuity of the fanatic . . . could conjure up to distract & disturb the public mind, such as *Imprisonment for Debt*, the *Militia Law*, *Anti-Masonry*, *Phrenology*, *Temperance*, and . . . above all, the *Abolition of Slavery*," Mr. Pierpont declared himself "*Guilty, Guilty, Guilty!*" Engaged in what he saw as a holy fight for the spiritual health of a nation threatened by economic materialism and the widespread worship of Mammon, he invoked Daniel Webster—"If the pulpit be silent . . . *the pulpit is false to its trust*"—and took his case before a Unitarian Ecclesiastical Council.

Popular sentiment throughout New England ran strongly in Mr. Pierpont's favor, although Ralph Waldo Emerson held off: writing about the fracas to Theodore Parker, the Sage of Concord observed, "I think the people almost always right in their quarrels with their ministers, although they seldom know how to give the true reason of their discontent."

Junius, trying to rein his father-in-law in, recommended a good lawyer and kept an eye on the proceedings. When he learned from a Hartford newspaper that Mr. Pierpont was considering running for Congress on the antislavery Liberty Party ticket early in 1842, Junius dispatched a lecture in which he either failed to see or chose to ignore the fact that the older man cared more for his moral rectitude than for his career: "I hope you have not given your assent to any such measure but will come forward *at once* & put a stop to it," Junius ordered—". . . if you allow such use of your name you lose at once all respect as a Christian minister, & it will be such an injury to you as can never be remedied. . . . I write for *your sake* not mine, & trust you will excuse, but I could not keep still."

John Pierpont declined the nomination, but not because of Junius's warnings: the loyalists at the Hollis Street Church wanted him to save his energies for his own fight. The case of the church proprietors versus John Pierpont turned into an "ecclesiastical circus," with more testimony about book publishing, phrenology, and the price of courtesans in ancient Corinth than about slavery or temperance. When the Unitarian elders finally reached a verdict in 1845, ending the Seven Years War, they hedged—finding that the proprietors had insufficient grounds for dismissal, yet feeling called on to express "disapprobation of Mr. Pierpont's conduct on some occasions." The verdict amounted to exoneration with censure. Mr. Pierpont resigned from the Hollis Street Church in a rage, and accepted a Unitarian ministry in Troy, New York.

———

Joseph Morgan, approaching sixty, showed no signs of slowing down. Between April and August 1839, he recorded the progress on Junius's wedding present: "Setting out Peach Trees on Junius Lot . . . Staked out the ground for Junius New House . . . raised Barn . . . digging cellar . . . began to lay cellar wall . . . raising Junius House." Juliet had her baby—Sarah Spencer, named for her paternal grandmother—in December. Three months later the younger Morgans moved into 108 Farmington Road, a two-story wood building with dormer windows in a gambrel roof, a wide bay on the second floor, two chimneys, and views of downtown Hartford and the surrounding farms. Junius hired a gardener to take care of the grounds and a black woman named Mary Ann to help in the house. Joseph worked on the place all spring, putting up fences, grading the land, planting strawberries and more trees.

He remained loyal to Henry Clay, whom he visited on a trip to Kentucky in 1844 and supported as the Whig candidate for President that fall. Clay lost to James K. Polk—a southern slaveholding Democrat who promised to lower tariffs, annex Oregon and Texas, and oppose a national bank. On March 4, 1845, Joseph mourned: "James K. Polk of Tennessee takes the helm of Government to day. Dreadful."

Junius agreed. In politics and business, he was following in his father's footsteps. Howe, Mather & Co. continued to prosper, and when the depression finally ended in the mid-forties, Junius bought an additional $25,000 share in the firm with Joseph's help. He also bought stock in banks, insurance companies, and railroads, and served on their boards. In religion, however, he chose a different path.

As the revolutionary struggle against England receded into the past, wealthy urban New Englanders in the middle of the nineteenth century gravitated to the Anglican Church. In part they were reacting against a revival of Puritan orthodoxy, the radical social activism of Unitarians and Transcendentalists, and fundamentalist extremes. The sumptuous architecture of Anglican churches and cathedrals, with vaulting arches, monumental columns, elaborate stained-glass panels, and neo-Gothic spires, stood in sharp contrast to the white clapboard meetinghouses on New England town squares. Junius turned in the 1840s from his father's ascetic Congregationalism and his father-in-law's strenuous Unitarianism to the liturgical, ritualized worship of the Episcopal Church. By 1853 the affiliation of Episcopalianism with wealth and social prestige was so pronounced that its clergymen worried about presiding over a "church . . . only for the rich."

Pierpont Morgan was growing into a serious, good-looking boy with his father's dark brown hair, hazel eyes, and confident gaze. Ill health continued to trouble him—he came down with "lung fever" in the winter of 1841, and scarlet fever six months later—but he managed to do physical chores alongside Joseph in Hartford and to pay long visits to John Pierpont in Troy as soon as he was old enough to travel alone. His mother gave birth to a second girl, Mary Lyman, in 1844, and two years later to another boy, Junius Spencer, Jr. That fall Pierpont, age nine, went away to school at the Episcopal Academy in Cheshire, between Hartford and New Haven. He came home three months later because his Morgan grandfather was ill.

Joseph, who rarely mentioned his own health in the hundreds of pages of his diary, now complained of back pains and chronic dyspepsia. "Without I get relief soon, this frail earthly tenement of mine will soon wear out," he wrote shortly before his sixty-seventh birthday. "God grant that . . . I may find a dwelling not made with hands, eternal in the Heavens, there to go no more out forever." After Christmas, Pierpont was sent away to board at the Pavilion Family School on the outskirts of Hartford. Joseph in early April reported himself "Quite unwell I feel my race is almost run. . . . making my will." He invited his grandchildren to tea for Pierpont's tenth birthday on April 17, and at the end of June finished hoeing potatoes and shipping his hay to market. He died on July 23 at home, surrounded by his family.

Joseph left an estate worth roughly $1 million—about $90,000 in real estate, the rest in stocks of banks, canal companies, steamship lines, railroads, bridges, and the Aetna. When Pierpont began to keep a diary three years later, he marked significant events ("Father's birthday," "my birthday") on a printed list of days in the front. Next to July 23, he wrote, "Grandfather died 1847."

A MORAL
EDUCATION

Between the ages of seven and twenty, Pierpont changed schools nine times. He boarded at Hartford's Pavilion Family School, his third, for nearly two years. Early in 1848 he recited in class a poem called "Warren's Address to the American Soldiers," which hundreds of American schoolboys had delivered to the sound of cheers and stomping feet. It began,

> Stand! the ground's your own, my braves!
> Will ye give it up to slaves?

and had been written for the laying of the cornerstone at the Bunker Hill Monument in 1825—by John Pierpont.

That night, orator reported the event to author in a playful tone he used with no other adult. His grandfather had just sent him a gold pen—"the very [thing] I was wanting this long time"—but "I am sorry to say I shall not like Santa Claus any more because he did not do as you wanted him to do about getting it to me on New Years day . . . therefore if I was in your place I would not trust Santa Claus any more to bring presents."

Looking forward to visiting the Reverend Pierpont in upstate New York for his spring vacation, the boy wrote again in March: "I am almost ready to think that April will never come I think so much of going to Troy." He teasingly refused to disclose what day he would arrive, since he wanted it to be a surprise—"but perhaps Mother will write you what week." And he had an assignment for his famous literary progenitor. He needed an essay to recite for an exam, "and I don't know any good ones so I would be very much obliged to you if you can to write me a piece not a very long one in prose." After concluding with news of his family and his own health (not good), he added a postscript: "Please answere [*sic*] this letter as soon as possible and send that piece."

If he did receive an original essay from his grandfather's pen, no record of it has survived. He made the trip to Troy on April 11. Whenever he left home, his parents reached across the distance with anxious, admonitory notes. Junius warned his father-in-law: "Pierpont goes tomorrow to make you a short visit. I think he needs some restraining, & hope you will [have him]* devote a certain part of each day to reading & study. I hope he will be a good boy & [not] give his grand mother nor yourself any trouble." A week later, writing on Pierpont's eleventh birthday, which he did not mention, Junius repeated those directives to his son and scolded: "I noticed some words in your last letter not correctly spelt which I hope will not occur in the next."

Though the boy was hoping to spend his entire month's vacation in Troy, his parents summoned him home after two weeks. Juliet thought he should not stay so long as to make his grandparents "twice glad" at his departure. Besides, Junius had signed him up for an entrance exam at the Hartford Public High School.

Junius was intensely invested in Pierpont's moral and practical education. Holding adamant views about the proper way to raise a son, he chided the Reverend Pierpont for failing to guide Juliet's brothers in the "right path," and moralized after the death of the alcoholic William, "It only shows the importance of bringing up children in such a way that they may either prove a blessing or a curse."

Like most mid-nineteenth-century American Protestants, Junius saw male childhood not as a time for exploration and play but as training ground for the serious business of adult life. Some of the moral lessons he directed at his son addressed specific behavior, but most of them prescribed the Yankee virtues of industry, prudence, restraint, veracity, thrift—qualities summed up in the term *character*. When Pierpont started yet another school at thirteen, Junius warned him to be "very careful with what boys you associate not to get intimate with any but such as are of the right stamp & whose influence over you will be good. You must bear in mind that *now* is the time for you to form your character & as it is formed now so it will be likely to remain. You cannot have this too strongly impressed upon you."

Junius kept disrupting his son's life with moves to new schools and hectoring

---

* Junius left "have him" out of the sentence, then added it in above the line. He was so accustomed to issuing instructions to both John Pierpont and John Pierpont Morgan that this omission—which has him telling the older man to devote a certain part of each day to reading and study—seems a funny but not surprising mistake.

Junius Spencer Morgan.
(Courtesy of Robert M. Pennoyer)

him with unsolicited advice, yet much of his surveillance had a positive cast. He took Pierpont on stockholders' excursions, assigned him tasks at Howe, Mather, taught him about history, great men, commerce, and books. One night in Hartford the two spent hours going over an arithmetic problem until they proved that the boy's answer, which did not agree with the text, was correct.

There were fewer congenial notes in Pierpont's relations with his mother. A decade into her marriage, Juliet Morgan had lapsed into cranky self-absorption. Her letters to her son alternated cautionary platitudes with complaints about her own troubles, and offered far more criticism than motherly comfort. When he left for school one winter, at age thirteen, she wrote: "I think you will continue to be [happy and well] if you are true to yourself, and do what you can for the good of others, keep to the right path. Be open—correct & never swerve from the truth on any consideration." He had been gone only a week, and was homesick: "Don't write *too* often to multiply postage," Juliet scolded— "if you write home once a week I think it will answer." She sent love from the family, then issued another long-distance reprimand: "10½ o'clock is rather too late a bed hour for you."

As the term went on, she forgot to send things he requested, reproached him for not liking what she did send, and corrected his spelling. Informing him that some pigeons he had been keeping at home had been stolen, she reflected that it would be a loss to Junius and a disappointment to the neighbor taking care of them, but not that it might be painful to her son.

The adult Morgans augmented their lessons with books. When Pierpont was seven, Junius gave him a story called *Marco Paul's Adventures and Travels in the Pursuit of Knowledge: On the Erie Canal*. The lessons in this well-thumbed volume have to do with commerce, credit, and profit as the just reward of special intelligence. One day as Marco and his cousin Forester watch trains go by, Marco says he would rather collect fares than drive the locomotive. Forester points out that the man in charge of the locomotive gets better pay. Why? Marco asks. "Because," Forester explains, "it requires patience and skill and steadiness of mind. Those employments which require high mental qualifications are always better paid than others. There is great responsibility attached to them usually."

On the subject of great responsibility, Juliet presented her son with a biography of George Washington by Jared Sparks for Christmas in 1845. Sparks, a Unitarian clergyman educated at Harvard with John Pierpont, looked at America's first President through the lens of his own time and saw a model of hard work, self-discipline, and common sense.* Pierpont checked off chapters in the table of contents as he read them.

---

* Called the American Plutarch, Sparks taught history at Harvard, and edited a series called the *Library of American Biography*, on America's great men. His *Writings of George Washington* took up twelve volumes, the last of which was a biography. Juliet gave her son an abridgment.

A book called *Young Men Admonished,* on the dangers of drinking, gambling, extravagance, and straying from the truth, came from Junius's sister, Lucy Goodwin. *Character* counts "more than any other possession" as security against dishonesty, declared the author: "It is worth more than any stock in Wall-street." Pierpont said much the same thing to the Pujo Committee sixty years later.

A more entertaining form of instruction came from John Pierpont, who gave his grandson for Christmas in 1847 *The Youth's Historical Gift . . . containing familiar descriptions of civil, military, and naval events by the Old English chroniclers, Froissart, Monstrellet, and others, and also the history of Joan of Arc and her times.* The cover featured a charging mounted knight stamped in gold.

———

Pierpont transferred to the Hartford Public High School in the fall of 1848. The steady stream of parental stricture had not brought him into line. A Hartford classmate later recalled him as "full of animal life and spirits . . . and not renowned as a scholar"—he "never got a lesson if [he] could help it." Told of that recollection in old age, Morgan agreed, "Never," with a look of "grim humor in his face."

Humor got him thrown out of class one day, but there was nothing funny about his response. He sent a formidable letter of protest to the teacher, indicating on the envelope that it came from "a persecuted *pupil,*" and was "very important in my mind."

"Miss Stevens," he began: "I should like to enquire of you the reasons why you as a teacher and of course over me only a scholar should treat me in such an inhumane manner as to send [me] out of the class for laughing a little too loud which I can assure you I am perfectly unable to control and which no punishment will cure me of." She could not deny, he went on (undermining his point with a double negative), "that I have not tried to behave better in class lately. If I wanted I could sit still (without saying a word) in a corner." However, if the other students followed suit, "would not you think that all the class were very stupid indeed and you would have to do all the talking[?]" Who would look stupid then?

Sounding more like an exasperated parent than a mischievous twelve-year-old, he warned that if Miss Stevens did not change her ways he would go to another class or skip it altogether: "I do not say this hastily in anger but you cannot say but what I have stood it a great while and I think that upon reflection you cannot say but what I have been treated unjustly. . . . Going into [a different class] is a long contemplated step. J. Pierpont Morgan."

J. Pierpont Morgan's partner in adolescent crime was his cousin James Junius Goodwin, two years ahead of him at the high school. Jim's father was president of the Connecticut Mutual Life Insurance Company and also, like

Pierpont's father, a neo-Federalist, an Episcopalian, and a Whig. The boys spent most of their free time contriving to see the girls at a nearby school called Miss Draper's Seminary. At first they watched from a distance as "the Drapers" took a carefully chaperoned group walk every afternoon. Then one day Jim pretended he had left his lessons in a house along the route. Cutting through the column of girls, he managed to introduce himself to several of them. Every afternoon after that the boys intercepted the promenade with flowers, candy, and notes. Once in a while a benevolent teacher allowed them to walk a little way beside the line. When the cousins encountered sterner guards, they split up, one proceeding down the right side of the procession and the other the left, to elude simultaneous capture—then raced around the block or cut through a yard to make a second pass, trying not to appear out of breath.

Pierpont occasionally climbed a tree next to what he called Drapers Convent, and from those "lofty summits" managed to "converse with the fair damsels in the third story." Reflecting to Jim on these capers a few years later, he found it surprising that the girls still liked them "after all the lectures &c &c we caused them to receive."

On the flyleaf of his Hartford High geometry text he wrote to a friend: "I promised Miss Dina I would go home with her to-day." He had something special to tell her—"I will say it tomorrow in recess or before or after school." In the back of the book, this nascent connoisseur of feminine attire wrote, "I can't say that I *do* like that dress much. It is rather old womanish, I think. How do you like Miss P's dress?" These engaging matters took up more of his attention than the text: "Tell Miss Peabody that Gertrude has gone and ask her if we cannot wait and say the geometry tomorrow for I don't know mine."

Some notes he wrote backward, to be read only with the help of a mirror. On the flyleaf of his Virgil text he asked a friend in reverse script to "write as soon as possible telling about the first girl who you have seen naked etc." and then "Mary Doyle – ditto – I should like to have seen." It cannot have been easy in Hartford in the 1850s to see girls naked. Perhaps the boys caught glimpses of servants with Irish names like Mary Doyle through keyholes at home—or maybe they commandeered the "lofty summits" of the Draper trees at night to do a little spying.

———

In the spring of 1850, Junius went to England for three months. Now a senior partner in his firm, which changed its name to Mather, Morgan & Co., he had joined the ranks of New England's mercantile elite. He was probably the first Morgan to cross the Atlantic since Miles sailed the other way in 1636, and he sent Pierpont detailed accounts of his trip. He went first to the Lake District, where he saw the residence of "the celebrated Rev. Dr. Arnold" and Harriet Martineau's cottage at Ambleside. Wordsworth had just died. Visiting the poet's fresh grave at Grasmere, Junius told his son: "If you will look in the works of Wordsworth & Southey, you will see frequent mention of the places I have described."

Proceeding to London, this Connecticut Yankee was powerfully moved by England's history, institutions, and traditions. He saw the chair in which generations of monarchs had sat for coronation, and attended a debate on the Corn Laws in the House of Lords—between Earl Grey (for) and Lord Stanley (opposed): "as they are both men of whom I had heard a great deal, I was much interested in seeing & hearing them," he told Pierpont. By mail he guided the boy through the City, London's financial district, describing Baring Brothers, the Bank of England, and the Royal Stock Exchange (much like "the Exchange which you saw in New York, but . . . in some respects much handsomer"). The American minister in London, Abbott Lawrence, had a "fine house near the Duke of Wellington & lives in considerable style." The English generally dined at "6½ o'clock, rather later than we dine in Conn."

At home Junius had a picture of Arthur Wellesley, Duke of Wellington. In London he went to see Apsley House, the residence of the Duke—"who you remember conquered Napoleon at Waterloo," he reminded his son—and the carriage taken from Napoleon in defeat. In May he spotted the Tory "Iron Duke" himself near the House of Commons, "the man I wanted to see more than any other in England—he was on horseback & stopped to speak to persons just opposite where I stood so that I had a good opportunity of seeing him, the likeness we have is very good."

Junius addressed Pierpont as the lieutenant in command while the captain was away: "I expect much from you as you are now old enough to take charge of affairs somewhat yourself." By return mail, the boy kept his father up to date on business, the family strawberry garden, and local politics.

Just as Joseph had moved with America's urbanizing markets from Springfield to Hartford in 1817, Junius by 1850 was ready for a larger venue than Hartford. In London that spring he met international bankers and leading figures in world trade. Four months after returning home, he dissolved Mather, Morgan and went into business in Boston with the owner of an import wholesale house that had sold $2 million worth of dry goods in 1849. J. M. Beebe, Morgan & Co. opened for business on January 1, 1851.

Junius's family moved in with his mother on Asylum Street while he made arrangements for them in Boston. Pierpont stayed home from school much of that term with earaches and boils on his face, ears, and neck. In February 1851 he transferred to the Episcopal Academy at Cheshire, which he had attended briefly before Joseph died. This time he boarded with the principal, the Reverend Seth Paddock. Though plagued by sore throats, headaches, and ulcerated chancres on his lip, he played football and chess, studied Latin and Greek, and in the spring spent his free time fishing, frogging, riding, sailing rafts, hunting wildflowers, and planting a garden.

For all his "animal spirits" and disinclination to study, he had at fourteen some solemn interests. He attended temperance lectures at Cheshire, and kept track of the proceedings at Episcopal conventions the way boys a hundred years later would follow baseball—even collecting autographs of the bishops. He also collected presidential autographs, scoring a coup with a letter from Millard Fillmore, the free-soil Whig who succeeded to the White House in 1850 when Zachary Taylor died. Home from school for spring vacation in 1851, he attended Whig meetings at City Hall, and spent the state's election day at the offices of *The Hartford Courant*, getting news the minute it came in.

He began to keep diaries in 1850—small "Line-a-Day" books. Like most masculine journal writers of his time and social class, he was far more interested in registering what happened than in exploring subjective responses or ideas. "Sleighing, skating; beat father in backgammon," he wrote in early January 1850. The next day, "wound 7 skeins of cotton for mother. A man fell off one of the towers of the new depot & killed." He rarely mentions his siblings. Over the following months he recorded: "Dancing school. Ladies to tea." "Father did not come home." "Mother ill." "Bought shad for 25¢." "No school on account of bile [boil] on my neck which was very painful." "Finished 3rd Book of Virgil. Picked some cherries." Not even death evoked a comment: "Mr. S. B. Paddock [with whom he was living] died at 10 o'clock aged 56. In evening staid at home and read."

Once in a while emotion breaks the surface. After a long illness he wrote, "Glad to get back to school again." In March of 1851, after not hearing from home for several weeks: "Think it strange mother don't write." In Hartford one night, "Very lonesome at home with no one here."

What the diaries chiefly portray is a young mind intent on order and control. Next to the day and date printed on each page, Pierpont entered the number of days gone by and remaining for the year—on October first, for instance: "Days past, 274," "To come, 91." At the end of 1851 he tabulated "Places Resided" between January and July—there were seventeen—and the diary pages covering each place. He kept lists of his income, expenses, the initials of girls he liked, and all the letters he sent and received, including postage paid.

His evasion of emotion and meticulous attention to detail probably served several ends at once. To be stoical, prudent, and self-controlled was to be the upright "little man" Joseph and Junius urged him to become, *not* an impractical wastrel of the Pierpont line. Making lists and keeping track of things may have provided a sense of mastery he did not have over larger areas of his life, such as family conflict, his mother's moods, changes of address, friends, and schools, a grandfather's death, and his own illnesses. It is hard to imagine a more terrifying loss of control than suffering a seizure.

Jared Sparks, writing about George Washington's early interests, observed: "It is singular that a boy of 13 should occupy himself in studying the dry and intricate forms of business, which are rarely attended to till the affairs of life call them into use." Pierpont also took a singular early interest in business. At his father's store he learned to keep books and copy letters, and the math problems he worked on at school amounted to practice sessions for a life in finance. He converted dollars to pounds sterling, calculated interest rates, and worked out divisions of partnership profits. One day he had to "calculate the cost of an inland bill of exchange at Boston on New Orleans for $15,265.85 at 1% advance." Also, "78 oz. avoirdupois pure gold will yield me what value in coin if from the proceeds 1/10 of 1% be taken for coinage." Another day, given a capitalist's annual income of $2,940—the interest on property four fifths of which paid 4 percent interest, while the remainder paid 5 percent—he had to calculate the amount at interest. (The answer is $70,000.)

Pierpont was fourteen when he left Cheshire in July 1851. That August his family moved to a Boston town house that Junius had rented from the merchant/philanthropist Amos Adams Lawrence at 15 Pemberton Square. Pierpont set out at once to explore his new surroundings. He spent hours watching ships in the harbor, sailed a kite on the Common, and took his little brother, nicknamed the "Doctor," to the Bunker Hill Monument. After evenings at the theater, he pronounced *The Hunchback & How to Settle Accounts with Your Washerwoman* "very good," but had no comment on *Hamlet.* He heard President Fillmore speak at the State House, and Dr. Oliver Wendell Holmes on "Love of Nature." In Cambridge he secured the autograph of Jared Sparks, now president of Harvard. And he went out to Medford to visit the Reverend Pierpont, who had recently moved back to the Boston area from Troy.

In September, Pierpont passed the entrance exam for Boston English, a high school that specialized in math to prepare young men for commercial careers. (Boston Latin offered a more scholarly education in the classics.) After a few days, he noted, "Begin to like school very well." He placed eleventh in a class of thirty-three the first term, and got an "excellent" mark for character. In math he worked on second degree equations, infinite decimals, and the multiplication of radicals.

Someone saved several of his essay assignments. In *Thoughts and Resolutions on Entering the English High School,* he said he intended to go straight into business after graduation, "to act and think in all cases for myself." In order to obtain "a good situation in a store or office . . . I must have a good character in the school I last attended as no one will want a clerk who is not strictly correct and gentlemanly in his conduct and attentive to his business. . . ." In a paper on *Industry:* "perhaps the most essential" of virtues can "raise a person from the lowest stages of poverty and misery to wealth and an honorable station in society." Elsewhere Pierpont proudly compared primitive means of transport to railroad trains "drawn by the 'iron horse' " at thirty to forty miles an hour, and reflected that in 1652 America had been all forest and wilderness—two hundred years later, with cities studding the continent, "Commerce comes in to aid us . . . bringing the wares of other shores to us and taking ours to them."

Indirectly striking a more personal note, he worried about young men forced to leave home—"the poor sailor" who braves deadly storms to bring back goods for wealthy merchants, and soldiers who enter "the bloody contest, not knowing, whether it is the will of God that they should breathe out their last expiring breath, away from home, and all who could pity them." On the subject of slavery, he wrote in 1852 about "free and inoffensive negroes . . . snatched" from their "much loved home and country" by "cruel and heartfelt" (more likely, *heartless*) enslavers who drag the captives to "other shores, where no friend watches over or preserves them from the cruel lash."

Slavery "has shook the pillars of this vast republic," he continued, as "one by one the admission of Texas, the boundary of slave rule and the Fugitive Slave Law have issued from the capitol of the nation." The Compromise of 1850 had postponed direct conflict between North and South, but sectional battle lines were etched into the nation's consciousness. Several prominent northerners—including Junius but *not* the Reverend Pierpont—worried more about preserving the Union than about abolition, and Pierpont Morgan echoed their concern. "If the North refuse the entreaties of the South the 'Flag of our Union' must inevitably fall," he declared. ". . . The proud eagle which for less than a century has spread his wings over a free and independent nation will fly away with disgust. Our national pennant will fall into disgrace and the Republic of the United States will be known no more for ever."

———

In moving to Boston, Pierpont had left his childhood, extended family, and best friend behind. He and Jim corresponded weekly, setting up a mock partnership called "Goodwin Morgan & Co." Pierpont ordered items available in the big city—shoes, engravings, books—and sold them to his cousin at no profit. In return, he asked for detailed news about Hartford, especially "the Drapers," and volumes of genealogy: he was updating the family tree.

Though two years younger than Jim, he assumed command, dispensing autographs among their friends and issuing orders like a sergeant at arms: "Did you deliver to W.R. Lawrence the autograph of O.W. Holmes which I asked you to. If you did why didn't you ask him for R.C. Winthrop's. Go & ask him for it, and he will give it to you. I told him to." He reported on the anomalies of transportation costs (it was cheaper to take a train from Boston to New York—two dollars—than from Hartford, even though the distance was twice as great). And he had become quite the authority on art. Sending to England for a special set of *Illustrated London News* covers, he advised Jim to order them as well: "I would if I was in your place for they are so much handsomer" than the ordinary issues; "you will want them unbound."

Illness interrupted the business of "Goodwin Morgan & Co." in the spring of 1852. Pierpont came down with rheumatic fever, which caused such painful inflammations of his hip and knee that he could not walk. He missed twenty-nine days of school between March and May, and stayed home most of the summer. He went out to Medford to visit his grandfather in October "to see what good the pure air of the country would do me," he told Jim. He had "a first rate time," and soon felt well enough to "wish I was back again in Hartford. How about the Drapers?"

Country air and the company of Mr. Pierpont improved his spirits, but he was still too sick to go back to school. At the end of October his parents decided that a more radical "change of air" would do him good. Junius arranged for Charles W. Dabney, a shipowner/businessman and U.S. consul in the Portuguese Azores, to take Pierpont with him when he sailed. Although the boy had planned to go straight through high school into business, ill health forced a detour. On November 8, 1852, he left home for a rest cure in the sun.

———

Pierpont had to be carried on board the square-rigged bark *Io* in Boston Harbor. Before this illness he weighed 150 pounds; now, fifteen years old and five feet ten inches tall, he weighed 126. As the ship left Boston he noted in his journal: "Wind NW . . . Passed Cape Cod Light at 8 p.m.," and the next day, "On the broad Atlantic out of sight of land for the first time in my life."

Rough weather kept the seven other passengers belowdecks, but not Pierpont or Mr. Dabney. The young man's health improved dramatically at sea: "I did not feel neuralgia [nerve pain] at all," he wrote to his parents in Boston. Heading off into the unknown, leaving home and family like the soldiers, sailors, and slaves of his high school essays, he kept closer track than usual of exactly where he was in place and time. His journals record daily measures of latitude, longitude, barometric pressure, wind direction, and distance traveled.

With strong westerly winds, the *Io* reached the Azores—three island groups about nine hundred miles west of Portugal—in eleven days, sailing into the port of Horta on the island of Faial. Pierpont took a hotel room overlooking the harbor. At home, November meant bare trees and cold, gray days. Winter temperatures in exotic, sun-splashed Faial ranged from 55 to 70 degrees. Gardens bloomed with hydrangea, azalea, japonica. Pierpont sent oranges and local wine home for the Morgan family Christmas, hoping that "Santa Claus wont forget me in his annual visitation to Pemberton Square."

He soon made a friend at his hotel, a consumptive English physician named Cole who had also come to Faial for reasons of health. The invalids ate together, played chess after dinner, and took long walks through Horta's narrow streets. Still, Pierpont was lonely. He told his parents: "I don't believe I should live . . . if Mr. Dabney's family were not here."

Three generations of Dabneys represented American interests in Faial between 1807 and 1892. Pierpont went to the consular residence and the Dabney mansion for dinners and private Sunday services (there was no Protestant church on the Catholic island), and had free run of the family's libraries, billiard tables, gardens, stables, and grounds.

As his health slowly improved he spent hours at the Faial harbor learning about ships—who owned them, what they carried, how fast they traveled, how they were repaired. He mastered this information not only out of an inveterate fascination with commerce and transport, but also because he was entirely dependent on these vessels for news from home. In involuntary exile, trying to keep his attachments alive by mail, he sent letters, journals, and presents by every departing ship, ordered five American newspapers, and expected to hear from home once a week. Even the smallest details would interest him, he promised. Every time a ship came in he raced down to search her hold for items addressed to himself. Week after week found him "woefully disappointed."

His pleas for mail grew more intense as the silence from Boston grew more protracted. Dispatching a stack of letters by the *Io* in mid-December, he wailed, "O! how anxiously I shall look for her return," and when a gale came up he consoled himself that it would speed her round-trip passage. Seven weeks after he left Boston, an American schooner brought his first letter from home, on Christmas Day. The Pemberton Square Santa Claus *had* forgotten him, or else had failed to send packages to Faial in time. Putting the best face on the situation, Pierpont declared the letter "a very good Christmas present," making the day "very happy . . . indeed."

Why his parents did not write more is not clear. Some of the silence had to do with vagaries of weather and transport. Steamships were just beginning to replace sailing packets in the 1850s, and most mail went via England; sailing from Liverpool to Faial could take twenty-eight days, which, added to the transit time from the United States, meant that letters might spend two or three months en route. Still, Pierpont had reached Faial in eleven days, and several clippers arrived direct from Boston with mail for the Dabneys but none for him. Perhaps his parents thought that frequent contact with home would diminish his self-reliance.

He bought canaries and a blackbird "in order to have something to take care of and to make the time pass pleasantly," but it didn't help. Stormy weather in December brought several "lame duck" ships back to the harbor and long days indoors. Pierpont tried to occupy himself with billiards, whist, letter-writing, and reading—a book on the queens of England, and James Fenimore Cooper's appropriately titled *Homeward Bound.* He was too anxious to read: after an hour "I get so nervous and twitchy . . . there is no pleasure in it."

As always, he kept close track of expenses. His hotel room cost five Spanish dollars a week, plus 40¢ to 50¢ for laundry. And he was learning about foreign exchange. He concluded that he should not have brought American quarters, since they were worth only 24¢, while American dollars fetched $1.10 in Spanish currency, and English sovereigns $5.40 to $5.60—"according to the wants of the jews here to send money to England."

Though he attended a few Portuguese ceremonies and dances, Pierpont took little interest in the local population. His sympathy for sailors and slaves had to do with the idea of separation from home, not with social compassion. If, as he had been taught, industry and initiative promised prosperity, the poor had only themselves to blame. "The people here are very poor indeed," he told his parents, and "very lazy. They go around begging and it is very difficult to get through the street with out being accosted . . . for money and food." Another day, surveying ruined houses and crumbling streets, he concluded: "These lazy Portuguese haven't the pride enough to keep any thing in repair."

Early in January he came down with influenza. Dr. Cole kept him company. "I don't know what I should do if it were not for him," the invalid sighed. "We can amuse ourselves together very well. He intends if nothing happens to go to America in the spring." *He* wanted to go to America sooner than that. At the end of January, "very lonesome and unhappy," he asked permission to return by the next Liverpool steamer, and repeated his familiar complaint: "I wish I received letters as often as you do. I have received but one in 10 weeks."

Just as he recovered from the flu, one of his toes swelled up until once again for a few days he couldn't walk: "It seems," he moaned, "as though as soon as I get over one thing another comes." Still, his health was improving. He ate twenty oranges a day, and was so fat he couldn't button his pants "within at least an inch and a half."

One night in February a flag went up in the harbor to signal the *Io*'s arrival from Boston. Racing to the consul's residence, Pierpont found the Dabneys "jumping and dancing in high glee. Until it has been experienced I don't think the pleasure can be imagined of a vessel coming into a place like this bringing letters &c from your friends when you can only receive them every two or three months." He boarded the ship as soon as she anchored, and found a letter from Junius. With Mr. Dabney's help he brought the rest of the mail ashore, and when "no more could be found for me then I began to feel very bad indeed. . . . I thought perhaps they had been left behind and all those kind of sad foreboding. That night I slept very little." Early the next morning he went back to search again, and found a packet of letters from relatives and friends. Another foray the following day produced still more. He had been gone three months; this mail was his first substantial contact with home.

Packages had to clear customs, and he waited in agony as days went by with nothing further landed from the *Io*. Then early one morning, shouting voices woke him up. People were calling to the bark's captain, who was staying in the hotel room just below his, to look out at the harbor. Pierpont jumped out of bed to see the beach strewn with the wreckage of ships driven ashore overnight by a storm. The *Io*, still afloat, had been converted from a three-masted barkentine into a sloop, her crew having cut away two masts to keep her from running aground. Pierpont ran down to the beach to inspect the damage. Two days later—ten days after the *Io*'s arrival—he got his packages, which included new pants, slippers, molasses candy, and a watch.

While the ship was being repaired he felt more cut off than ever. "Franklin Pierce I suppose was this day inaugurated President of the United States of America," he reflected on March 4, 1853, underlining his sense of isolation with a flourish: "Should like very much to know who composes his cabinet but on this lone island on the broad Atlantic's bosom news is very old ere it reaches us & especially when the messenger lies here at anchor dismasted."

During the early weeks of his "cure" he tried to keep a certain amount of starch in his upper lip, but by February he had had enough: "I continue to like Fayal as much as ever I did," he told his parents, "which is not much." Only the Dabneys and Dr. Cole made his stay bearable. Then in mid-March, Cole suffered a lung hemorrhage. Pierpont sat up with him most of the night. On March 29 he reported: "My poor friend here Dr. Cole died last evening at 5 o'clock he was a very nice gentleman and was a great source of pleasure to me. . . . He is to be buried tomorrow morning." A few days later he added, "I miss him very much, for he was a very agreeable person."

After four months in the semitropics his health was restored. He could now walk "as fast as anybody," he told Boston, and had gained back all the weight he lost the previous fall: "The object of my coming here being accomplished, I think it is about time to turn my face homeward." His parents finally agreed that he was cured. Instead of bringing him home, however, they arranged to meet him in England for a new phase of his—and their—cultural education.

———

Pierpont left Faial on April 15, 1853, on the steamship *Great Western*. Eight days later, having turned sixteen en route, he reached London and put himself up at the Castle & Falcon Hotel in the City. He did errands for Mr. Dabney, visited Lloyds, and in one day took in Buckingham Palace, Westminster Abbey, Apsley House, Hyde Park, and the House of Lords. At the end of April he met his parents in Manchester. He took his mother walking and shopping; with Junius he made professional calls. The Americans toured Stratford-on-Avon, Warwick Castle, and Oxford before heading in mid-May to London.

Junius's firm, J. M. Beebe, Morgan & Co., had posted $7 million in gross annual sales for 1852, and England's leading traders knew it. At the beginning of 1853 George Peabody, the most prominent American banker in England, had invited Junius to join his London firm—an offer the latter declined with regret on account of his obligations to his Boston partners. On May 18, Mr. and Mrs.

Junius Morgan attended a dinner Mr. Peabody gave for the new American minister in London. Pierpont had to miss it because he was sick.

He got some recompense the next day when he and his father toured the Bank of England, the leading financial institution in the world, set behind a massive, Corinthian-columned facade built by Sir John Soane at the end of the eighteenth century. Pierpont wrote in his diary that night: "I held £1,000,000 in my hand."

The American trio set off for the Continent at the end of May, sped through Belgium and Germany (catching sight of the Prussian King Frederick William IV in Dresden), then spent two leisurely weeks in Paris. Staying at a hotel in the Rue Saint-Honoré, they went to the Opéra, the Louvre, Notre Dame, the Luxembourg Palace, and the Jardin des Plantes. Pierpont noted excellent dinners at the Palais Royal and the Café de Paris. One day he saw Napoleon III and his Empress, Eugénie. Another, he visited Napoleon's tomb at the Invalides, rode in "the woods of Boulogne," and toured Versailles.

Back in London in June, he continued his royalty watch, spotting Queen Victoria (who had been crowned the year he was born) and Prince Albert early one morning at Cobham. The next night he saw them again at the opera. He took a day trip to Windsor, and heard the archbishop of Canterbury preach at St. George the Martyr in Bloomsbury. His journals note visits to the Crystal Palace at Sydenham and the Duke of Devonshire's residence, Chatsworth. In July the Morgans made a quick trip through Wales, Ireland, and Scotland—where they visited Abbotsford, home of Sir Walter Scott—before sailing home.

———

Pierpont had been away for nine months. After a cursory stop in Boston he went straight to Hartford and spent most of August visiting the Goodwins, "the Drapers," and his Morgan grandmother. In a diary note about one day's outing he sounds positively rhapsodic: "Had 1st rate time. Helen Wells rode with me. Most splendid in every respect." When he returned to Boston in September, he told Jim: "Father thinks we had better be joined like the Siamese twins don't you think it would be a good plan." Also, "I do wish I knew some first rate girls here to wait upon to Lectures Concerts &c." At Boston English he rejoined his class even though he had missed an entire year: "Have to study pretty hard to keep up."

Keep up he did, in Astronomy, Theology, Moral Philosophy, and Evidences of Christianity (all "very dull"), complaining that he studied from 8:00 A.M. till 12:00 P.M. and had "hardly . . . a single moment that I can with truth call my own." He did manage to find moments to attend Whig meetings at Faneuil Hall and lectures by Wendell Phillips, Edward Everett, Henry Ward Beecher, and Oliver Wendell Holmes—all increasingly preoccupied with questions of slavery and sectional conflict—and to see a stage production of *Uncle Tom's Cabin*. Partisan politics did not keep him from writing to Mississippi Democrat Jefferson Davis, then Secretary of War, for an autograph: "it would give me great pleasure to add yours . . . to the already numerous collection of your illustrious predecessors in office."

The only allusion in his diaries to the "peculiar institution" of slavery appears in June 1854. An escaped slave named Anthony Burns had been arrested in Boston under the Fugitive Slave Act and held in federal custody for his master. Antislavery Bostonians did everything they could to prevent Burns's extradition. A biracial group led by the prominent abolitionist T. W. Higginson tried to rescue him by force, which led President Pierce to call in the cavalry and marines. On June 2, federal troops escorting Burns to Boston Harbor had to march through a lamentation of church bells, past buildings draped in black and displays of Old Glory hanging upside down. "We went to bed one night old fashioned, conservative, Compromise Union Whigs," wrote the Morgans' landlord, A. A. Lawrence, "& waked up stark mad Abolitionists." William Lloyd Garrison burned a copy of the Constitution, calling it a covenant with death. If Pierpont shared New England's moral outrage, he left no record of it. "Great excitement in Boston on account of the slave Burns who was remanded today," he wrote in his diary. "Beautiful day."

The subjects he discussed in letters to Jim Goodwin included sartorial trade (caps, coats, boots), comparative religion (Hartford's Christ Church versus Boston's St. Paul's), a pretentious acquaintance ("I should present him with a few beans some evening and see whether he knows beans or not"), and the opposite sex. He warned Jim about a Hartford belle named Ellen Terry (no relation to the British actress) whom he "positively disliked," explaining: "she is all self. She thinks everything must be done for her that she desires and when you do it she seems to think it is nothing but what you had to do." Still, he asked Jim to talk to Miss T. "and see if you cannot get something out of her about me."

He had finally met some "first rate girls" in Boston, whom he referred to by their initials. One in particular—"E.D."—accompanied him to concerts, parties, lectures, and museums. She was Elizabeth Darling, a former "Draper," three years older than her admirer. He walked her home whenever possible, and made friends with her father and brother. He called on other girls in Boston and Hartford as well, but Lizzie Darling appears to have been his favorite.

In the early summer of 1854 he divided his attention between Lizzie and an essay he was writing for graduation. On July 22 he announced in his diary: "Thus ends school with me." And on the twenty-fourth, Exhibition Day, he read his essay aloud before an audience of teachers, students, their families, and friends.

Other graduating seniors spoke on "Eloquence," "Is Conscience Paramount to Human Law?" and "Effects of Intellectual Pursuits upon the Character." Pierpont had chosen to discuss a historical figure. "In the year 1769," he began, with an almost audible roll of drums, "when the wicked and profligate Louis XV, goaded by his own guilty conscience and laden with the execrations of his subjects, was sinking into his grave, in the little island of Corsica, the most remarkable being of his age made his appearance on the arena of life."

Napoleon galvanized the nineteenth-century imagination. Books about him coursed off the presses decades after his defeat. "*Empire*" defined fashions in clothing, architecture, furniture, and art. Mental patients claimed to be the Man of Destiny. Military leaders celebrated Napoleon's strategies, statesmen studied his rise to power, schoolboys fought for the right to play him in mock battle. To Ralph Waldo Emerson's dismay, the French Emperor held Americans in singular thrall.

Pierpont bowed to the legendary stature of his subject: "The name and fame of Bonaparte have spread from one extremity of the earth to the other, and glowing delineations of his unequalled bravery, his consummate genius, and his indomitable perseverence [*sic*], have been drawn by the master spirits of every civilized land." His own portrait highlighted the great man's humble start: "Descended, as he was ever proud to own, from no princely progenitor, Napoleon Bonaparte was, in an extraordinary degree, a self-made man." Any boy might imagine himself setting off on the same path. What especially interested this one was the general's indomitable will: "No obstacles fell in his way which seemed to him insurmountable. . . . He might be defeated, as he sometimes was, but he shrunk from no hardship through impatience, he fled from no danger through cowardice."

Pierpont's parents had offered him other kinds of heroes: Sparks's George Washington was a model democratic leader—honest, industrious, self-abnegating—while Junius's Duke of Wellington stood for the hallowed power of military and aristocratic tradition. Yet to the junior Morgan, as to generations of Americans, the morally ambiguous Corsican adventurer had far more appeal than the virtuous father of the American Revolution or the conservative British Duke.*

The seventeen-year-old author returned repeatedly to Bonaparte's place in history—to the measure ultimately taken of a controversial man and his myth—in overblown passages that eerily prefigure the mixed assessments of his own career. "No human being, whose life has been the subject of a biographer, has been so differently estimated, both in the popular mind and in elaborate memoirs," he wrote. Though one historian "lavishly praises" and another

---

* A. L. Guérard found in 1924 that Harvard freshmen, asked to name their favorite historical character, repeatedly gave Napoleon first place. "Indeed," noted Howard Mumford Jones and Daniel Aaron in the 1930s about the Napoleonic legend in America, "the 'Child of Destiny' was more interesting than the Olympian Washington, who was neither besmirched nor humanized by Napoleon's horrible but fascinating feats."

"indiscriminately condemns" the Corsican, none doubted his courage or genius. The experts failed to agree largely on the question of *motive.*

Pierpont took skeptical yet admiring exception to Napoleon's claim that he had worked only for "the prosperity of France": "Unmitigated personal ambition led him to prefer his own private advancement to the future welfare of his country." It was ambition plus "preeminent genius" that "made him master of many surrounding countries which yielded to his victorious sword."

Not long after his own exile on a lonely island, Pierpont imagined Napoleon at St. Helena: "What must have been his feelings, on finding himself no longer his own master, surrounded on all sides by the ocean, and closely watched by sentinels placed there by his enemies? And when, after many many years, he lay upon his death bed, his spirits crushed, his hopes of liberation vanished, and his body languishing away with severe sickness, how often must his thoughts have reverted to those brighter days in his existence, when he was the idol of France and the conqueror of the world!"

The essay concludes with a nod to the historical long view: "No human tribunal can yet settle the main points in Napoleon's life satisfactorily to all." Nonetheless, the writer has settled some points himself, since "bigotry and hatred" characterize Bonaparte's critics, while "admiration of genius and bravery" distinguish his fans. In the end, "time, that great modifier of political sentiments and opinions, must glide along many years more before a correct estimate can be made of Napoleon's motives. Private animosities and private attachments must be buried in oblivion. The personal enemies and friends of the conqueror must pass away. The institutions of France which were commenced during his reign must be more fully developed.

"When this shall have been accomplished; then, and not till then, can a just judgment be given of the life and motives of NAPOLEON BONAPARTE."

—

Chapter 4

FOREIGN AFFAIRS

George Peabody, the American banker in London who wanted Junius to join his firm, had not given up. He renewed his offer at the end of 1853. Junius went to England to discuss it. His Boston partnership agreement was about to expire, and early in the new year he agreed to join Peabody's Anglo-American bank as of October 1.

Peabody's rise to the position he held in 1854 had been steep. It was commonly said around Salem, Massachusetts, that "you were either a Peabody or a nobody," but young George was both. Born into a poor branch of the family in South Danvers (now Peabody), Massachusetts, in 1795, he left school at eleven to work in a general store, fought in the War of 1812, then went into the wholesale dry goods business in Washington, D.C. By 1827 he was no longer a nobody: his firm had branch offices in Philadelphia and New York, and he was worth $85,000. In 1837, trading $700,000 worth of goods a year with England, Europe, India, and China, he moved to London and opened an office in the City.

There he watched London's premier investment houses finance international trade without actually buying or selling goods, and made the lucrative transition from merchant to merchant banker. He began to supply commercial credit for a fee to U.S. farmers, cotton planters, and foreign buyers, and to manage international currency exchanges for export-import markets, becoming a specialist in short-term trade. He financed long-term investment as well, channeling European capital to the United States.

America's booming 1830s went bust just as Peabody set himself up in London. By 1842 British capitalists held roughly $100 million in defaulted U.S. state bonds, and as a result not even the federal government could sell new paper in London. The bonds had been issued for just the kinds of enterprises Joseph Morgan financed—railroads, turnpikes, canals, and local banks. Like Joseph, Peabody believed that careful investment in the emerging American market would ultimately pay. The problem was that the Europeans who held the money the United States needed had no way to gauge the caliber of ventures three thousand miles away.

Capital markets are essentially the organized processes through which money for long-term investment is raised, distributed, traded, and above all *valued*, and Peabody made it his business to certify value. He minimized the risk to his clients' capital by vouching, insofar as possible, for the quality of the securities he underwrote—chiefly, bonds for railroads and states. He also waged an effective campaign from London to get state governments out of default, since legislatures that reneged on their debt jeopardized all U.S. access to foreign capital. Working through reporters, politicians, clergymen, and other bankers, Peabody helped persuade the governments of Maryland and Pennsylvania to resume servicing their debt. His personal interest, as a banker taking responsibility for properties he represented, coincided with America's interest in reopening channels through which money flowed westward across the Atlantic.

Within a few years foreign anxiety about American defaults had subsided, and wealthy Europeans, uneasy about the 1848 upheavals on the Continent, were once again looking for investment opportunities in the United States. Six thousand new miles of railroad track were laid down in the 1840s. Peabody's reputation for backing "sound" ventures brought him ample business, and as the new construction boom created a large demand for rails, he moved into the iron trade as well. In the spring of 1852, commenting on the English market for American securities and speaking for his firm, he told friends: "We believe *we* pretty much regulate prices & are the principal controlers of the Market."

The world's *haute banque* investment houses such as Rothschilds and Baring Brothers did not solicit clients or steal one another's business. They waited for kings, states, and entrepreneurs to come to them. To compete in this market without violating Old World rules, Peabody discreetly promoted his services through financial acumen and statesmanship.

In 1851, the U.S. government failed to finance American participation in Prince Albert's international exhibition of industrial products at the Crystal Palace. The U.S. displays consisted of a few wineglasses, a pair of saltcellars, and a square of soap—until George Peabody put up $15,000. As a result, between May and October 1851 six million people saw Cyrus McCormick's reaper, Samuel Colt's revolvers, and Richard Hoe's printing press. Congress

Pierpont in Switzerland, 1856.
(Archives of The Pierpont Morgan Library, New York)

eventually paid Peabody back for an act that had earned him diplomatic standing and the permanent affection of Albert's wife, the Queen.

That Fourth of July he gave a banquet in honor of Anglo-American friendship. Abbott Lawrence, the American minister in London, had advised him
against it, since the Fourth celebrated England's defeat at American hands. Un-
deterred, Peabody invited the eighty-four-year-old Duke of Wellington, and
once Wellington accepted, social London followed. A thousand people attended
the party at Almack's in St. James's Street, under portraits of George Washington and Queen Victoria decorated with Union Jacks and American flags. When
Wellington arrived at 11:00 P.M., the band played "See, the Conquering Hero
Comes." Peabody presented him to Mr. Lawrence in quiet triumph.

By 1852 the bachelor Peabody had a thriving business, an international
reputation, and nearly $3 million. He did not, at age fifty-seven, have an heir,
which was why he needed Junius Morgan. The great nineteenth-century international banks were family dynasties with offices all over Europe. In the high-
risk business of raising and lending large amounts of money across great
distances for long periods of time, they chose to work through affiliates related
by blood or marriage. The Rothschilds, beginning with Mayer Amschel in eighteenth-century Frankfurt, had built an empire on hereditary ties: family members headed branches in Paris, London, and Vienna. Jewish, multilingual,
politic, private, the Rothschilds occupied a unique place in the upper echelons
of European culture, and their allegiance to the bank transcended all other
claims. Partly because they had few peers and partly to keep the business and
the assets in the family, sixteen of Mayer Amschel's eighteen grandchildren
married relatives.

While the princely Rothschilds lived surrounded by art in sumptuous town
houses and on large country estates, the abstemious George Peabody rented
rooms at the Regent Street Hotel and had little interest in culture. He worked
ten hours a day, did not drink, smoke, or take vacations, and stood for half an
hour one day with a head cold in the London rain passing up a twopenny bus
to wait for one that cost a penny. Pierpont sketched him for Jim Goodwin as "a
very agreeable gentleman and very full of wit, but a regular old bachelor if you
could have seen the quantity of nic-nacs which he carried with him to America . . . stored away in his trunks with the greatest precision you would most
certainly have thought that he was going to Central Africa or to some other un-
explored regions."

The "regular old bachelor" was fastidious about his appearance: he wore
custom-tailored clothes, and dyed his hair as it began to turn gray. He also had
a mistress and a daughter in "a secluded but dignified and permanent establishment" in Brighton. According to his biographer, Franklin Parker, Peabody
did not marry the woman because of "class and background" and the rigid
Victorian code: "a gentleman did not, as a rule, marry his mistress no matter

how fond he may have been of her." The gentleman's own social stature, if that was the ground of his delicacy, had been recently acquired.

George Peabody could not know that the dynasty he started by bringing in Junius Morgan would surpass Rothschilds and Barings, the reigning lords of world finance. He did know that the economic future lay in America, and through Morgan he staked a claim to it. As word of the new partnership got out, an English friend told Junius that with Peabody nearing retirement, "we naturally look to you as the future representative of American credit in this country." Barings' American agent wrote to his London office: "If Mr. Peabody was safe before, he will be much safer now with Mr. Morgan at his side"—and the competition for Barings in America would be considerably "more formidable than before."

Conscious of the social limitations imposed by his bachelor habits and tastes, Peabody wanted his new partner to live in style. A mutual friend found "a splendid palace for you in Grosvenor Square," he wrote to Junius in May 1854: "I certainly like the location. What think you and Mrs. M. of it at [£]1,000 [$5,000] a year?" Junius thought he had better wait till they arrived.

He spent his last half year in the United States winding up old business and preparing for his family's move. Pierpont helped out once he finished school in June. He was chafing to start his own career—he had his eye on the East India shipping trade—but his father decided he should go to school in Europe first to learn French and German. Junius spoke no foreign language, and told Jim Goodwin that "the advantage [of knowing French] . . . cannot be overstated. I regret so much that I am deficient that I don't intend my children shall have the same cause for regret."

In early September, Pierpont made rounds of farewell visits to family and friends. Boston's leading merchants honored Junius with a dinner on September 12—testimony to their collective esteem and the prodigious Victorian appetite. The elder Morgan later recalled that as he began to realize the enormity of the step he was taking, "my heart failed me." The words of encouragement he received from his Boston colleagues "nerved me for the work I had to do." Perhaps the repast did as well, though not everyone ate every course. It began with raw oysters, two soups, baked bass, and boiled cod, followed by "Removes" (leg of South Shore mutton, caper sauce; Westphalian ham, champagne sauce; filets of beef with mushrooms), "Ornamental Dishes" (boned turkey with truffles, oyster aspic, "Pattie of Liver in Jelly"), entrées (calf's head with turtle sauce, pigeon cutlets in olive sauce, "Vol au Vent, of Birds, à la Financier," larded sweetbreads with green peas), game (black ducks, plover, partridges, woodcocks, teal), desserts (omelette soufflé, meringue baskets, charlotte russe, champagne jelly, blanc mange), ornamental sweets (pineapple, bonbons glacés, vanilla and lemon ice creams), coffee, and liqueurs. The next morning, the Morgans sailed for England.

Having decided against the "splendid palace" on Grosvenor Square, Junius settled his family temporarily at a hotel. On October 2, George Peabody & Co. officially announced its partnership with Mr. J. S. Morgan of Boston. Pierpont wrote in his diary, "Father commenced business in London." The firm started with £450,000 (roughly $2.25 million) in capital, of which Peabody put up £400,000, Junius £40,000, and their English partner, Charles Cubitt Gooch, £10,000. Each would earn 5 percent interest on his share. Of the net profits and losses, Peabody would take 65 percent, Morgan 28 percent, Gooch 7 percent. Morgan would have an additional £2,500 (about $12,500) a year for entertaining, an integral part of his work. That fall the firm moved into new quarters at 22 Old Broad Street.

Pierpont showed his brother and sisters the town, and looked at houses with his parents: they took a short-term lease on one in Gloucester Square, just north of Hyde Park. The older girls, Sarah and Mary, soon left for a boarding academy in Westbourne Terrace near Lancaster Gate. Eight-year-old Junius ("Doctor") went to school in Twickenham, twelve miles from London on the Richmond Road. English boys mercilessly teased him at first, calling him Boston and Yankee Doodle, but the youngest Morgan soon learned to hold his own. The Twickenham headmaster described him as "docile—instantly obedient—exceedingly intelligent frank & affectionate. . . . He is entirely at his ease with his companions & his Masters. . . . This is mutually delightful, & must produce the best results."

For Pierpont, Junius had chosen a Swiss school near Vevey on Lake Geneva. When the seventeen-year-old departed for the Continent on November 1, 1854, only little Juliet (called Sis to distinguish her from her mother) remained at what now, three thousand miles from New England, constituted home.

———

Pierpont left London with a mixture of impatience at the delay of his career and excitement about impending foreign adventures. At the last minute, the American minister in London, James Buchanan, asked him to deliver a packet of government papers to Paris. The junior diplomat wrote to the Reverend Pierpont: "Imagine your senior grandchild taking his departure from the London Bridge Terminus for Calais and Paris as Bearer of Government Despatches on a foreign tour." Dense fog kept the other passengers on board the steamer at Calais, "whilst I in my official capacity was whizzing along towards Paris." After delivering the papers, he headed south and east, stopping at the top of the Jura Mountains along the French-Swiss border for "the finest view which I ever had in my life"—the snowy peak of Mont Blanc against a cloudless sky, "below me the lake of Geneva with its magnificent scenery and villages in one of which was to be for a little time at least my residence." From Geneva a four-hour sail took him to Vevey. His school, Bellerive, was about a mile from the village.

Run by M. Edouard Sillig, Bellerive had eighty-five students in the autumn of 1854, many of them English and American. Pierpont took private lessons in German and French to help him catch up. He made friends with twins named Payson from Boston, and quickly found a lot to complain about.

Breakfast consisted of coffee and dry bread. Clothes were meted out like provisions once a week. Too many students and too much spoken English interfered with his learning French. "In a room about the length of our parlors in Boston but much narrower," he griped, "15 boys find accommodations for the night." When the headmaster asked him not to smoke, he told his parents: "This is no place for boys over 15." The Paysons boarded in town—"generally the way those do who know how to take care of themselves."

Junius had asked M. Sillig to treat Pierpont as he would his own son, and the headmaster at first reported that "dear Pierpont" with his "rather advanced intelligence" would quickly adjust to "little privations" and find "real happiness" at the school. Soon, however, Sillig's running notes confirm the boy's sense of a mismatch. "Adapts himself very slowly," he wrote after a week, and as time went on: "Makes fun of things. Smokes . . . Restless at his lessons . . . Talks after the lights are out . . . A joker. A talker . . . Does not behave well. 'Answers back.' . . . Sulky. In a dreadful temper."

Pierpont's health began to trouble him—he came down with sore throats, stiff necks, "lung fevers," acne outbreaks, and a corn on one of his toes that required minor surgery. Blaming these illnesses on the "perfectly terrible" climate of "this uncivilized country," he grumbled to his parents, "I never expect to be well while I am here."

Yet his diaries and letters to Jim Goodwin and Mr. Pierpont were not nearly as gloomy as reports he sent home. To the London authorities he exaggerated his misery, reproaching them for condemning him once again to deprivation and exile, while admitting to his chums that he was having a pretty good time. As soon as he moved out of the dormitory to a chalet on the road to Chillon, his rooms became headquarters for the American students at Vevey. He pooled their allowances, and under his jurisdiction the Yankees played whist and billiards, smoked, went sleighing, skating, hiking, and sailing, ate sweet sausages with sour champagne, shared American newspapers—and once in a while worked on their studies.

Pierpont at eighteen was no less outraged by the injudicious exercise of authority in Switzerland than he had been at thirteen in Hartford when Miss Stevens threw him out of class for laughing. One Sunday, M. Sillig authorized local celebrants of the Fête de la Sainte Barbe, the patron saint of artillery, to fire cannons into Lake Geneva from school grounds. The first explosions woke Pierpont up at 5:00 A.M. ("the very morning when we are allowed to sleep a little later than usual"), and a change in the scheduled festivities caused him to miss lunch after church. Crowning these indignities was a grand ball held "in town on *Sunday* night," he exploded to Jim. "I think that take it altogether it was the most disgraceful affair which ever occurred in a Christian country. . . . I gave Mr. Sillig pretty plainly my opinion of his conduct in permitting the sons of Christian parents who had been brought up to look upon the Sabbath as a day which belongs to God attending any such meetings. He took it very well and thanking me said that he thought he had done wrong in having anything to do with it."

Whether or not Sillig was humbled by this tirade (it seems to have been the interference with his sleep and lunch that brought on Pierpont's denunciation of the "most disgraceful affair" in Christian history), he cannot have liked facing down six feet and 160 pounds of sanctimonious American boy.

———

On the subject of religion itself Pierpont said little, but a diary entry at the end of 1854 reflects his sense of personal connection to a discriminating Savior and his faith in divine guidance toward the mercy and reward he will ultimately deserve: ". . . it has pleased Almighty God to preserve my life to the opening of another [year]. May it please him to forgive all my sins of thought, word and deed and lead me to lead in future a life more devoted to His service . . . and if it should please the Almighty Father to preserve my life may I so live [that] at the last day I shall receive from thy dear son, 'Well done good and faithful servant.' "

His appreciation of this world's pleasures was in no way blighted by fear of punishment in the next. The account books he kept as he traveled in the 1850s reflect his tactile, visual sensibility and mandarin tastes. In Paris he bought himself leather boots, white kid gloves, a coat (115 francs—$23), a vest, "pantaloons," collars, a beaver hat, and a stash of cigars. He noted the entrance fees at Versailles, Napoleon's tomb, the Gobelin tapestry factory, the École Nationale des Beaux Arts, and the Louvre. He sent his mother furs. Occasionally he gave money to beggars—2 francs one day "by mistake for one sous." At Vevey he paid 10 francs ($2) for a Jenny Lind concert, 6 francs for confectionery, 2.50 for cologne, 17.50 for bouquets. He bought Mme. de Staël's *Corinne* and a volume on the *Guerre de Trente Ans.* And he balanced his accounts in pounds sterling, francs, scudi, florins, Austrian gulden, Neapolitan ducats, and Tuscan pauls.

He also listed frequent payments for medicines and doctors' fees. In July 1855 he told Jim that "an eruption" had appeared on his face "which injures my looks very considerably." The Bellerive physician sent him for a cure to Loeche-les-Bains in the Valais, where sulfurous waters boiled out of the ground into vats. Spa guests of both sexes wore long shirts to soak in the baths. Pierpont rose at five and bathed until ten, taking breakfast and playing dominoes and whist on floating trays; then he went back to bed for half an hour ("a necessary penalty for each bath"), had a second breakfast, and exercised (mandatory) from noon until two. The cure exceeded his expectations, he reported, thanks to a Baltimore family named Hoffman, "plenty of excursions, plenty of dancing &c &c &c &c, flirting into the bargain."

He quickly indicated what the four etceteras referred to: an eighteen-year-old Italian whom he pronounced "one of the handsomest and most unpretending young ladies I think I ever saw," with "dark hair & eyes & beautiful skin." The eruption on his face did not keep him from speaking to the girl (in French), but her "horrid old brother in law" did: this jailer made every effort "to vex her and prevent her talking with any one."

One afternoon, as Pierpont was reading aloud to Mrs. Hoffman, an earthquake sent chairs skidding across his hotel room and knocked chimneys off the roof. A few nights later a second tremor shook the guests awake at 2:00 A.M. Dressing quickly, Pierpont raced to the Hoffmans' rooms and had "hardly been in there three minutes," he told Jim—excitement turning him into a poet—"when who should make her appearance but Miss Rolaris, the young Italian, in her night dress, panting and pale as marble with fear. . . . I never had seen such a beautiful expression before. She took a chair and sat for about an hour, totally unconcerned as to her dress, or the position in which she was. Although as beautiful as she well could be, there was not the least affectation or coquettry about her. But enough for Loeche and its belles," he broke off in midstory, and did not mention the Italian beauty again.

He teased Jim constantly about girls. "In every letter you mention some new feminine angel who is far handsomer than anyone else you ever saw," he wrote. "To speak plainly old fellow you are going to fast altogether and need some correction." And, "If . . . Cupid *has* shot his dart into your heart let me advise you to have the wound attended to immediately, for fear that Mortification should ensue and the hole remain in its present state."

When one of the Drapers announced her engagement, he mused: "don't it make you feel old, old fellow to see all these girls that we used to carry on with, going the way of all the world and splicing themselves for life in this manner?" He dropped his jocular tone the minute he guessed that Cupid *had* dealt his cousin a wounding blow: "Why in thunder when you were writing about being in such low spirits didn't you make a clean breast of the matter and write me the whole cause of your sadness? *Has* any young female been treating you badly Jim? I admire your coolness."

Coolness was not one of his own attributes in these matters. When Jim accused him of being fickle, he protested: "it is no such thing. I never was so, you very well know, in any of my affections, and sometimes I think it is a very great disadvantage that I am not a little more so, for once I have taken a liking to a person it is very difficult for me to get over it." The volume of his correspondence with female friends at home and his responsiveness to young women he met abroad suggest that he was capable of taking a liking to several persons at once.

——

In August 1855 he met his family for a brief holiday in Paris (as chief linguist, "I was compelled to do all the talking"), then returned to Bellerive to put the finishing touches on his French. That fall he placed first in his class. In the humanities he studied *The Aeneid* and Louis XVI, read *Robinson Crusoe* in French, translated Mme. de Sévigné into German, and wrote out in three languages maxims that echo what he had been taught on the other side of the Atlantic. "In all labor there is profit: but the talk of the lips leads only to penury." "The crown of the wise is their riches: but the foolishness of fools is folly." His facility with numbers impressed everyone at Bellerive. A fellow student recalled him as "little short of a prodigy," able to calculate cube roots in his head. Pierpont advanced quickly through algebra and geometry to trigonometry and physics.

The Baltimore Hoffmans were spending the winter in Vevey, and he often called on Mrs. Hoffman for tea and confidential talk. "How pleasant it is," he reflected to Jim after one visit, "to be surrounded with persons who are always glad to see you and with whom you always feel perfectly at home." His own home was too far away, and his mother too absorbed in her own troubles, to afford him any sort of haven. The Hoffman household gained a further attraction that winter—an American niece who had come to Vevey for her health. Pierpont the expert on illness found in this young lady none of "that uneasiness so common for the generality of persons in the same condition. I tell you what Jim she is a trump and I begin to feel a little queer." In matters of romance he constantly swore his confidant to secrecy: maybe Hartford was reading over Jim's shoulder, or maybe Jim had a tendency to gossip; more likely, these warnings reflect Pierpont's rather grandiose sense that all eyes were trained on him. "I find her (remember this is all strictly between you and me) exceedingly comme il faut. She has the best disposition of any young lady I know, she is lively, agreeable, & although not *exceedingly* handsome is very pleasing. Dont you breath a word of this to a living soul. I'll tell you how I get along in that quarter. Being exceedingly intimate with her uncle & aunt I can see as much of her as I wish which makes it very nice."

Taking his father's advice about association with the "right" sorts of people, he joined "the tip top young men of Vevey" in organizing a series of private balls for "very choice and select" company. "It costs me about $1.75 a night," he told Jim, "but that is dog cheap when you can laugh, talk and dance with such a beautiful girl as Miss Hoffman as much as you choose."

Pierpont's acne did not spoil his social life, but it did make him self-conscious. Having a series of photographs taken early that winter, he notified Hartford (mangling his grammar): "Grandmother will be rather surprised . . . to hear that anyone with such an eruption on my face should have had their portrait taken." To his delight the pictures showed "no defects of the kind." Instead, they show an attractive young man with light brown hair slicked across his forehead and flashy sartorial taste: in a huge bow tie, dotted waistcoat, and double-breasted jacket with wide lapels, he looks warily amused, as if not sure this self-display will turn out well. He stopped in Paris later that spring "to see if anything can be done for my face." Apparently, nothing could.

———

During his time at Vevey, Pierpont watched Britain, France, and Austria defend Turkey against Russia in the Crimean War with a distinctly American eye. A jingoist two decades before the term was coined, he thought European imperialism should confine itself to the eastern side of the Atlantic and leave America's nascent expansionism alone. When Sebastopol fell to the Western allies in October 1855, he told Jim: "The whole western part of Europe is in one blaze of triumph & joy occasioned by the victories of the allied armies in the east." He did not join the cheering. "To tell the truth I am rather sorry." He feared that England and France, finding they could handle powerful Russia, would "stick their fingers in our affairs at home as respects Cuba or the Sandwich Islands [Hawaii] . . . I have also the idea that if they attempt it John Bull & Johnnie Crapeau combined will find their match."

Junius decided early in 1856 that his son had completed half of his scholarly assignment: he was fluent in French. Next, he would go to the university at Göttingen to "starch up" his German.

For all Pierpont's early dislike of the Swiss school, he was sorry to leave his friends, especially the Hoffmans, who had "for eighteen months through sickness and through health . . . done all for me that any but a parent could do," he confessed to Jim. Distancing himself from a painfully familiar subject with conventional wisdom, he went on: "When one leaves home or relations, as I have so often been obliged to do, it is with the satisfaction of knowing that it is only for a season, that not many months will elapse before we shall again be able to take our accustomed seat at the table and our old places among our friends, and it robs parting of its deepest sting." He had no such consolation now. "When it comes to taking leave of friends and true friends at that, whom in all probability we shall never meet again, then it is hard too hard to part." He apologized to his cousin for his melancholy mood: "Jim you will hardly thank me for writing to you thus sadly, but I feel to tell the truth rather sad, and if you dont want to read it just skip it over."

———

At the end of April 1856, he and Frank Payson arrived at Göttingen, a small university town south of Hanover "situated upon a dead plain about an hundred miles from the Rhine," he told Jim, with "bookstores and libraries in every street." (Frank's twin, Charles, disappeared from Pierpont's letters after the first few weeks at Vevey.) A railroad under construction would soon disrupt the provincial peace, predicted the student of modern transport, but for the moment "silence reigns supreme." The university—"the greatest and finest in Germany"—had special strengths in chemistry and math, as well as some of the leading professors in Europe, including Friedrich Wöhler, "considered with [Justus Von] Liebig the greatest living Chemist."

The German students at the university divided into scholars and dilettantes. Pierpont charted a path between the two: he took advanced trigonometry, chemistry with Professor Wöhler, and daily German lessons—and spent his free time at bowling alleys, billiard halls, garden concerts, beer fests, operas, fencing lessons, and dances.

Pronouncing German "awful to learn," he swore he would master it in six months ("sink or swim, live or die") or not at all. He worried about flirting in a new tongue, and was agreeably surprised to learn that "nothing delights a German damsel more than to get hold of a partner who is a raw recruit in the language." When he wanted to make a "remarkably witty remark I usually dive into French," he told Jim—but quickly concluded that "there is no way as good to learn a language as to converse with and have your faults corrected by a pretty girl."

He and Frank fitted out their rooms in "royal splendor and eastern magnificence." They hired a servant for two thalers a month (the price of fifty good cigars), entertained often, and—personal preference conforming to paternal dicta—made friends with the families who formed the "*first society,* or in other words, the aristocracy of Göttingen."

Junius came to visit in the spring of 1856. Father and son talked about U.S. politics and international trade. President Franklin Pierce, a Jacksonian Democrat from New Hampshire with close ties to the South, was failing to keep the pro-slavery forces in check. Pierpont told Jim in disgust that if the country managed to avoid a civil war, no thanks would be due to Pierce, "for he has certainly done his part to create one."

Democrats had occupied the White House for twenty of the twenty-eight years since Andrew Jackson's victory over John Quincy Adams, and southern Democrats in Congress had consistently defeated northern proposals for protective tariffs, homestead laws, a transcontinental railroad, and land-grant colleges—effectively relegating the Whig heirs of Hamilton and Clay to the sidelines. In 1854 the fight over the Kansas-Nebraska Act destroyed the ailing

Whigs, and redefined national party politics along sectional lines. The act essentially repealed a ban on slavery in the western territories: southern Whigs voted with the Democratic majority to pass it over the violent objection of northern Whigs. Northern Democrats bolted in protest, and opponents of slavery from dissident groups and both major parties in the North gradually drew together into a new party that took the name "Republican." Its members began to unite around the neo-Hamiltonian ideas that the Union should take precedence over states' rights, and that local powers posed more threat to individual liberty than the centralized power of the state.*

The Morgans voted Republican—in a mock election at Göttingen in November 1856 Pierpont backed the losing John Frémont against Democrat James Buchanan—but were less concerned with slavery than trade. Cotton accounted for more than half of all U.S. exports in the 1850s, and Peabody & Co. was trading on its own account as well as handling cotton sales for clients. Pierpont proudly quoted to Jim an English admiral who said that while the British fleet was "a capital weapon for a war with most any nation . . . unfortunately the United States have a ship which we cannot take and which will render our navy useless, i.e., The Ship 'Cotton.' " No one connected with the Peabody firm wanted the United States to sink that ship in a civil war.

———

Writing to Jim, Pierpont generally had less to say about affairs of state than affairs of the heart. When he suspected his cousin of a serious attachment in the spring of 1856, he delivered a lecture on the subject, sounding very much like his own father. "Although younger, I have seen much more of the world and society than you have," he began, ". . . so pray don't think that it is entirely unadvisedly that I write this." Jim's recent letters showed "too plainly that you are really much more interested" in a certain young lady ("I won't mention names for fear the letter may fall into other hands") "than you are willing as yet to own to yourself." Pierpont warned Jim to "look out . . . that it does not . . . lead you to commit yourself to such a degree that your honor will be compromised and force you to an act which will be your deepest regret through life."

As an example, the nineteen-year-old guardian of feminine virtue and masculine honor cited a situation in which he had recently been "compelled to have a hand." (He uses the word "compelled" three times in this brief sketch:

---

* The Reverend Pierpont urged his sons William and James to join the ongoing fight for free-soil Kansas in 1855. Both had failed at everything else, and their father figuratively threw up his hands: "I can do no more for either of them," he told John, Jr., "except . . . in a pinch, to furnish each of them with money enough to take them to Kansas, and there let them find—above ground or under it—a habitation for themselves." The brothers did not go to Kansas. They persuaded their father to buy them sewing machines, and earned meager livings doing piecework.

strong forces were at work.) A fellow student at Vevey, with no thought of marriage, had paid such "very decided" attentions to a "fine young lady, highly educated and very attractive," that the girl had fallen "desperately" in love. Her
parents favored the match. Pierpont, seeing that his friend's honor was about
to become "so compromised that he would have been compelled by public opinion to marry the girl in spite of himself," had been "compelled to interfere."
Hence his unsolicited advice: "if I felt it my duty in that case how much more is
it for me to warn *you* in time."

Furthermore, he felt called on to correct his cousin's "decidedly erroneous
ideas" about marriage. The "fair damsel" in question had a gift for music, and
Jim was urging her to study abroad. A life on the stage would not do for the wife
of James Junius Goodwin, Pierpont explained: "Your career in life, like mine depends on our own individual exertions, our courses . . . will both be in the mercantile sphere and from this cause it becomes our duty to select for our wives
those who, when we go home from our occupations, will ever be ready to make
us happy and contented with our homes."

This pontifical account makes a mercantile career sound like a spiritual calling—which, in Junius' eyes, it virtually was. The fact that Pierpont's vision of
conjugal bliss did not match the situation in his own home (though not because his mother had a career) did nothing to detract from his conviction: a
wife should "be *domestic*," he concluded, "her heart must be at home with her
husband and children, not in the world." Jim would not be "happy with a wife
who was ever individually before the public, or who in society held any position
not connected with yours."

Jim did not much like this "dull sermon." He promised to talk the whole
thing over in person next time the cousins met.

———

Pierpont learned German in six months with the help of the obliging Fräuleins,
but had to postpone his start in business yet again when his father directed him
to spend one more winter on the Continent. In August 1856 he took the waters
at Wiesbaden, then went home to London.

His family had finally settled at No. 14 Princes Gate, a five-story town house
in Knightsbridge facing Hyde Park.* It was set well back from the road, with
Ionic columns framing a portico entrance, Corinthian pilasters under a neoclassical pediment on the first floor, and swags of fruit and flowers decorating
the cornice. In the back, French doors opened onto a terrace, and stone stairs

---

* The two rows of attached houses built on this stretch of Kensington Road in 1849–50
were called "Prince's Gate" (with an apostrophe) because they stood opposite the 1848 gate-
way to the park named for the Prince of Wales, later Edward VII. The Morgans did not use the
apostrophe, and most street signs, guidebooks, and architectural historians refer to the address as "Princes Gate."

led to a large lawn and gardens shared by all the houses in the block. Just a short walk down the Exhibition Road was the South Kensington Museum (later the Victoria and Albert), built after the 1851 Crystal Palace Exhibition to educate the British public about industrial arts and innovative design.

Pierpont found his mother in a state of collapse. Everything about the transatlantic move had agreed with Junius, who was fully engaged with his work and Anglo-American social life, but Juliet's depressions and physical complaints had grown steadily worse. She had left a close-knit world of relatives and friends for the vast, drafty reaches of a foreign capital that made no effort to welcome Americans. Speaking the language did not help her penetrate the dense thickets of English reserve, and a scant education had not prepared John Pierpont's daughter for the wider sphere of cultural reference she found abroad. She possessed none of the self-confident charm that enabled scores of American women to "conquer" London a little later in the century. With her husband preoccupied, four of her children away at school, and no interests of her own, Juliet took to her bed with vague, protean symptoms, just as her mother had done.

There was probably a genetic basis to the depression that turned the Pierpont family into a sad roster of instability, alcoholism, suicide, and "nerves." After Juliet's mother died in 1855, the Reverend Pierpont described how completely her suffering had vitiated their marriage: she had contributed "little toward making our home the scene of confidential and affectionate intercourse which constitutes one's *beau ideal* of a truly happy Christian home." In the next generation, Juliet contributed little to the affectionate intercourse in *her* household, and her negative example may have helped shape Pierpont's ideal of the generously domestic woman "ever . . . ready to make us happy and contented with our homes." Juliet's brother, John, Jr., drew an explicit parallel between her diseases and her mother's—he thought their "constitution and temperament . . . the same"—and suspected that Juliet's ailments were "imaginative, not real"—he no doubt meant "imaginary." Juliet consulted London's best physicians, but no one ever found an organic illness or a cure.

She decided to spend the winter of 1856–57 in the United States, hoping to leave her indispositions in London with her husband and children. In mid-September, Pierpont escorted her to Liverpool and saw her off on the *Baltic.*

From Princes Gate that fall he groaned to Jim in mock complaint that his siblings "consider me as a kind of 'valet de place' whenever I come home." He squired them around town until the older three went back to school. Mary was his favorite: active and curious, "she does not care about keeping very still for a long time at once." Neither did he. Once the "children" left, he found the house too quiet. Visits from Frank Payson and the "exceedingly" agreeable Miss Hoffman from Vevey promised to relieve the "monotony."

That Miss Hoffman was passing through London with her father on her way home to be married did not diminish Pierpont's regard. He took her, with her father and Frank, to dinners, theater, Madame Tussaud's, the Royal Mint, the Queen's Stables and Mews, and, when the autumn rains let up, on carriage drives. "Between you and I Jim," he whispered, "Miss H. is one of the finest girls I ever met in delicacy of feeling & taste, in sweetness of disposition & in fact in every charm. . . . I never may meet her again but if I should live many years I am very sure I shld not see her equal." Though there seemed no chance now of his winning primary place in her affections, he would be "only too happy if I thought I had such an object to look forward to."

Frank left at the end of September to start work with one of Junius's former partners from Boston, Levi P. Morton, now head of a wholesale house in New York. Pierpont went riding every morning in Hyde Park, and spent his afternoons at Peabody & Co. organizing twenty years of correspondence.

The London firm was buying and selling American securities for its clients, offering brokerage and general banking services to select friends, trading on its own account, and promoting a few promising new ventures, one of which in 1856 was a transatlantic cable. Cyrus Field, a wealthy New York paper merchant who recognized what Samuel Morse's telegraph could do for international communications and trade, had secured a charter to lay a cable between the western point of the British Isles and the eastern tip of North America. George Peabody & Co. agreed to help finance the project in July of 1856.

Four months later Junius reported to Mr. Peabody that the Atlantic Telegraph Company was getting along "famously" and would be a "great property," sure to *"pay largely"* once the cable was working. He asked his senior partner, traveling in the United States, to lobby quietly for a federal subsidy: "There can be no doubt that, as a matter of policy, our Government should do something in aid of the enterprise, & . . . a word from you would have much weight with those in Washington who could bring this forward in a proper way." He also persuaded Peabody to sit on the company's board in order to keep its management "honest": "Our connection with America & its business makes it very desirable that we should have an influence on the organisation of a Co. which is to have so much influence either for good or evil." The politics of influence and the strict supervision of management would be hallmarks of Morgan banking for over half a century.

Solving the physical and financial problems of transatlantic communication took ten years, even with government subsidies from Britain and the United States. Fires, broken cables, dropped wires, financial panics, storms at sea, and the Civil War intervened. The value of the stock rose and fell like the surface of the Atlantic. Issued at £1,000, the shares fell to £300 in July 1858, then rose to £900 that August when twenty-nine hundred miles of primitive cable first connected the continents. Queen Victoria's congratulatory message to President Buchanan took sixteen hours to transmit. Peabody imagined that Field must feel like "Columbus in the discovery of the new world." Junius told Pierpont: "None of us can properly estimate the effect of this success upon the world, nor do we really grasp in our minds the magnitude of what has been accomplished." Three weeks later the cable broke, as did the price of the stock.

The operation finally succeeded in July 1866, when the gigantic S.S. *Great Eastern* finished laying a redesigned, heavily armored ductile cable across the ocean floor from Valentia, Ireland, to St. John's, Newfoundland. Only then did the property, reorganized as the Anglo-American Telegraph Company and substantially refinanced, begin to pay. Despair often swamped Junius's hopes in the intervening decade. When Field at one low point accused Peabody & Co. of having caused his ruin, Junius replied, "You do not seem to recollect that we have been *large* losers by an enterprise undertaken by yourself and into which we entered at your earnest solicitation." The Atlantic cable changed the way the world worked, making it possible for the United States to communicate with Europe in a matter of minutes rather than weeks. Moreover, after 1866, financiers such as Peabody and Morgan could move quickly in and out of markets, easily trade in foreign currencies, and anticipate the effects of international news. Peabody & Co. gained access to essential information, as well as prestige and profits, from backing this ambitious venture.

———

Pierpont went back to Göttingen for three months in October 1856. "Lonesome" without Frank Payson, he joined a student society called the Hannovera, and was soon reporting on "capital" Saturday suppers of roast goose and beer, Wednesday-night card games, and balls. In his farewell speech he delighted his German friends by mixing up the words *Dauer* (length, duration) and *Bedauern* (regret, pity): he wished them "great sorrow" instead of "long life." One of his university professors had asked him to stay on and make a career in math, but Pierpont had other plans for his facility with numbers.

Early in 1857, finished at last with school and reasonably fluent in German and French, he headed south. He spent a month in Rome wandering through churches, galleries, and ruins, buying mosaics, jewelry, perfumes, bronze vases, reproductions of Canova's *Hebe* and *The Dying Gladiator*. "It is very pleasant indeed travelling about & seeing the world," he wrote to Jim, "but the truth is I have been so long unsettled & obliged to make my own arrangements for comfort that I shall not be sorry to settle down once more at home. Besides I am anxious to get to work, it seems to me high time."

Not quite. He came down that spring with a sore throat, cough, and chest pains. Junius told Jim that his son's illness had "interfered so much with my plans for him that I don't know exactly how he is to be situated." Pierpont asked Jim to find out what plans Junius had in mind; *he* wanted to go to China.

Jim crossed the Atlantic in June for a foreign education of his own. He started with a Pierpont-guided tour of Europe—the cousins had not seen each other in three years—but Junius cut the trip short in early July, summoning his son home.

Pierpont found Princes Gate full of the "children" and their friends. His mother, still in the United States, had been gone nearly a year, but was not too ill to veto his latest dream: "Mother objects most strenuously to my going to China," he told Jim in mid-July. Junius had rented a summer house in Barnet on the northern outskirts of London. The entire household moved there shortly after Pierpont arrived.

By 1857 America had fully recovered from the depression of the 1840s, and business, particularly the railroad business, was booming. Junius proudly told a friend that spring: "We none of us realise the wonderful increase of capital in the United States. The day is not far distant when they will cease to watch with solicitude the rate of [the Bank of England on] Threadneedle Street." The British *Economist* had made the case even more strongly in 1851, predicting that "the economic superiority of the United States to England is ultimately as certain as the next eclipse."

The center of this "wonderful increase of capital" was no longer Philadelphia or Boston but Wall Street. The exuberant growth of a market for railroad securities in the 1850s had brought trading and speculation to the New York Stock Exchange on a grand scale: about a thousand shares had traded on the exchange in a high-volume week during the 1830s; twenty years later a million shares a week could change hands. This boom led several investment firms to specialize in railroad finance, and among the best was a New York house called Duncan, Sherman & Co.

One of its senior partners, William Watts Sherman, was living abroad in 1857. He often called on Junius in London and Barnet, and wrote to Mr. Peabody in July: "It was a lucky fortune or astute sagacity my dear sir that guided you when you fell upon such a man as partner. I know not where you could have found his superior."

Peabody had watched Duncan, Sherman & Co. with an approving eye ever since its inception in 1851. Sherman's partner, Scotsman Alexander Duncan, had been introduced to him as having "sound and enlarged views and . . . one of the most beautiful fortunes" in America—about $4 million. Peabody told Junius in 1854: "I look upon this house as almost the only one in the United States who at present have the necessary capital, enterprize & talent to manage successfully a very large money business." He gave Duncan, Sherman the right to draw on him for unlimited credit, favored it over other New York banks, and considered appointing it to manage his firm's affairs in the United States.

In the ebullient markets of 1857, however, the New Yorkers were not willing to act as subsidiary agents for Peabody & Co.; they wanted the opposite arrangement, with the London firm as agent of the American. That July, Junius

Morgan and Watts Sherman made a decision that sidestepped the question, created a strong link between their firms, and solved Junius's problem about what to do with his son. Pierpont would go to work as an unsalaried clerk at Duncan, Sherman, "for some schooling in *American Banking*," Mr. Sherman told Peabody by mail. "I think him a *very* promising young man."

Junius had left Wall Street with regret in the chaos of 1836. He had hoped to return to New York, but his career took him instead from Hartford to Boston to London. Now, twenty years after giving up the prospect of making a fortune on Wall Street, he sent his son to apprentice there. At the end of July the "*very* promising young man" sailed for America with the Shermans. Once again, he carried important letters and documents—this time from his father. Junius dispatched an anxious note to his son on board the *Persia* just before she sailed, asking him to double-check on the safety of the papers, and urging: "I want you to realise the importance of the step you are now taking & the influence it is to have on your future life. *Be true to yourself* & all is well. Kind regards to Mr. & Mrs. Sherman. Goodbye. God Bless & keep you is the prayer of Yr aff[ectionate] Father."

Pierpont on August 1, 1860.

(Archives of The Pierpont Morgan Library, New York)

Chapter 5

NEW YORK

For Pierpont, itching to get into the thick of things, New York in 1857 *was* the thick of things—the largest, most interesting city in the United States. Settled by the Dutch and populated early on by a mix of Huguenots, English, Germans, and Jews, New Amsterdam had always been the most culturally diverse of the European colonies in North America. Because its Knickerbocker aristocracy had to share power with the British, neither group managed to dominate the city as definitively as the Brahmins did Boston, old-line families Philadelphia, or southern planters Charleston. Vital, polyglot Manhattan with its thriving commercial markets remained wide open and in turbulent flux, holding out the promise of whatever generations of outsiders wanted to find. They came by the thousands—immigrants, pirates, gamblers, fugitives, visionaries, artists, strivers, crooks. As New York's money markets fueled the explosive expansion of the U.S. economy, Wall Street by all authoritative accounts was on its way to becoming the financial capital of the world. Pierpont at twenty had already lived in more cultures than most people would ever see. He took to New York as soon as he settled in, and made it his home for the rest of his life.

Shortly after the *Persia* docked he went briefly to Newport, Rhode Island, which was just beginning to become a fashionable resort, then on to Boston and Hartford. He found his mother, staying with Sarah Morgan on Asylum Street, little changed. The slightest exertion upset her for days.

Returning to New York in early September, he moved into a house at 45

West 17th Street with Joseph Peabody, a relative of his father's partner, and a third young man called Vose. Jim Goodwin's sister, Sally, described the trio that fall as living in "fine style."

Forty-five West 17th was in New York's most fashionable residential area, a designation that had been moving steadily north since the beginning of the century. After the Revolution, merchants, shipowners, and traders had built Federal town houses along unpaved roads near the seaport at the lower tip of Manhattan. When commerce took over Wall Street in the 1820s, converting private residences to banks and office buildings, Manhattan's wealthy elite built new houses in what had been a rural village called Greenwich on the North (Hudson) River two miles farther up. And as trade brought traffic and noise to the Washington Square vicinity in the 1840s, those who could afford to move fled north again, this time building Italian Renaissance mansions and row houses on quiet, tree-lined streets around Union Square, where Pierpont and Joe Peabody settled.

Their neighbors in 1857 included Cyrus Field at 84 East 21st Street, Junius's former partner Morris Ketchum at 60 East 23rd, and Levi P. Morton—another of Junius's former partners, now Frank Payson's boss—at 15 West 17th. Along Fifth Avenue were Watts Sherman, August Belmont (the American representative of the Rothschilds), and City Bank president Moses Taylor. The *New York Herald* pronounced the mansion of merchant/shipowner Moses Grinnell at 14th and Fifth, "one of the most majestic piles in that *distingué* neighborhood." From 17th Street, Pierpont walked or took a horse-drawn omnibus down Broadway every morning to the offices of Duncan, Sherman & Co. at 11 Pine Street on the corner of Nassau. Just east of his office, on William Street, was the New York Stock and Exchange Board, founded in 1817, now trading shares in forty railroads, ten canals, eight coal and mining companies, three gaslighting firms, and four banks. A block to the west, the 284-foot spire of Richard Upjohn's Gothic Revival Trinity Church towered over the buildings along Wall Street.

Duncan, Sherman & Co. paid its new clerk no salary; he had $200 a month from his father. His first assignment was copying out letters in the correspondence department. Junius approved: "There is I believe no place where so much general information can be had of the working of the business as at the correspondence," he told his son. Pierpont studied bookkeeping with Charles H. Dabney, the partner in charge of accounting and a cousin of his host at Faial. And he served as confidential New York agent for George Peabody & Co., running informal credit checks, executing orders on the Exchange, handling interest and dividend payments for the firm's clients and partners. He sent his father news of American finance by every steamer that left New York.

In 1857, nine years before the Atlantic cable went into operation, London bankers depended entirely on mail for information from the United States. Junius that fall praised Pierpont's reporting: "I am much pleased with the zeal & activity you have evinced in all these matters. . . . that is the way to do every thing, be wide awake, know what is going on soon as any one & make use of the information. It has pleased Mr. Peabody also that you have been so prompt."

The content of news from America in the fall of 1857 pleased Junius less than the manner of its delivery. Twenty years had passed since the 1837 panic—time enough for most people to forget the dangers of inflation and overconfidence. Not Junius Morgan. He vividly recalled the squalls that had driven him from Wall Street in 1836, followed by panic and depression.

Railroad companies in the "miraculous" fifties had laid down the beginnings of a national transportation system—twenty-two thousand miles of track running through the heavily populated states of the Atlantic coast and west to the Great Lakes. It now took three days to ship freight from Chicago to New York, where in the thirties it had taken three weeks. Unlike steamboats and canal barges, railroad cars could go almost anywhere—over mountains, across prairies, through forests—on relatively predictable schedules in all kinds of weather. Rail lines, and the telegraph system that grew alongside them, were on the way to making one economic unit of the sprawling North American continent; they were already stimulating production and creating huge domestic markets by linking eastern cities to the Mississippi River and the farms and prairies of the Midwest. Feeding the headlong growth of the fifties were fresh supplies of California gold, easy credit policies, rising prices, a roaring bull market, and wild speculation in stocks and land. Relatively high yields on U.S. securities attracted foreign capital: British investors were earning 10 percent on American railroad bonds, compared with 5 percent at home.

The U.S. economy remained highly dependent on foreign money and conditions overseas. Europeans in 1853 held about $222 million in American securities—19 percent of all outstanding U.S. stocks and bonds; three years later, the Treasury Secretary estimated that foreign investment in U.S. railroads alone amounted to nearly $83 million.

Then suddenly in 1856 European demand for U.S. produce plummeted as the end of the Crimean War brought Russian grain back on the market. At the same time, the Bank of England hiked its short-term rate to stop an outflow of money to India and China, which drew capital out of the United States as well: foreign investors sold off American holdings to earn higher returns in London. The selling wave knocked down American securities prices, which reduced the assets of banks holding securities as collateral. Junius predicted a new "season of trial" for the world's financial markets that fall, and warned a colleague: "he is wisest who has out least canvas when the storm commences." In September 1857 a New York–bound ship carrying $1.6 million in California gold sank in a hurricane off Cape Hatteras, bringing on a sharp contraction in the U.S. money supply.

The tempest Junius had anticipated struck in early October. Stock prices collapsed, railroads went bankrupt, creditors demanded repayment of loans, overextended borrowers could not cover their debts, and banks and businesses failed. The Western Blizzard quickly crossed the Atlantic. On October 7, Junius assured the traveling Mr. Peabody: "We are easy & strong & shall keep so. Nothing will tempt us out of the most conservative course, for we believe that in the end will give us the most profit as it certainly will comfort." The next day he advised Pierpont by mail: "You are commencing your business career at an eventful time, let what you now witness make an impression not to be eradicated. In making haste to be rich how many fall, *slow & sure* should be the motto of every young man."

Watching closely as the Bank of England took charge of the British crisis by lending money to reputable merchants and banks, Junius bemoaned the absence of financial leadership in the United States: "What a pity that the [American] Banks could not earlier have seen the wise course & with a bold but judicious help to the merchants have carried those who deserved it before they themselves were obliged to give way." His fondness for meteorologic imagery accommodated the nautical as well: the "ship" of finance would not sail easily "out of such a storm into smooth seas," he predicted—especially with no one at the helm.

As several of Peabody & Co.'s American clients failed, its British creditors began calling in their loans. Duncan, Sherman & Co., with many of *its* debtors defaulting, owed money to the Peabody firm—the credit agency R. G. Dun & Co. suspected as much as $2.5 million.* By November Junius had lost his equanimity: with outstanding obligations amounting to £2.3 million ($11.5 million), Peabody & Co. would be forced to suspend unless it could borrow from the Bank of England.

In Manhattan, Watts Sherman was expecting news of this situation by wire from a ship scheduled to dock at Halifax, Nova Scotia. When no bulletin arrived, he sent Pierpont down to the New York telegraph office to "hunt it up." There the young man learned that confidential messages were being held in Halifax for fear of the press, which had access to the wires. He went straight to Cyrus Field, builder of the recently completed Halifax–New York telegraph, and reported to Junius: "I . . . asked him what he had got & he showed me a dispatch. 'G.P. & Co have rec'd 1000 m. from Bank & all is OK.' " Before Pierpont reached his office with this news, the papers printed rumors that Peabody & Co. had suspended payment, and brokers came swarming into Duncan, Sherman full of new fears. A statement to the press quickly set the record straight. The Bank of England credit actually amounted to £800,000, or $4 million. Mr. Peabody had arranged for thirteen English banks to guarantee the advance.

---

* R. G. Dun merged with its chief rival, the Bradstreet Company, in 1933.

Pierpont was outraged that Sherman had not confided in him sooner. Had he known a wire was expected he could have had the news much earlier, he told his father, since Field had promised "whenever he could do anything for me in line of telegraphing it would give him the greatest pleasure to do it." The incident brought out his contempt for people in positions of authority who did not take him seriously enough, such as Miss Stevens and M. Sillig. It also reinforced his conviction that he had to take charge of important matters himself, and underscored the value of accurate information.

The near failure of Peabody & Co. plunged the naturally alarmist Junius into despair. He thought his own reputation had been irreparably tarnished and twenty-two years of work destroyed, he told his son—who tried to buck him up: "It pained me exceedingly to see how severely the panic now raging on your side has affected your spirits," Pierpont wrote, but Wall Street had taken the news of the Bank of England's action in just the "right manner, & I can assure you that it has tended to strengthen rather than weaken the character & credit" of the London house. He forwarded "good toned & complimentary" newspaper articles, and dismissed less favorable stories as "ridiculous." To pick up gossip on the Street, he quietly stepped outside: "No one knew me & consequently I could hear everything said"—all of it favorable to Peabody & Co.

Then, turning the tables, the twenty-year-old had some fatherly advice: "I must repeat my entreaty that you will now break off for a little & go off somewhere & seek relief from business—do go where you will be entirely free from its anxieties for if you dont you will be sure to suffer more than any amount of money can repay you for."

Junius did not take a vacation. By the end of 1857, barely a month after the Bank of England's action, Peabody & Co. had met over half its £2.3 million in liabilities, using less than half (£300,000) of the Bank credit. It repaid that loan in March 1858, having met all outstanding obligations. The experience left the house shaken and watchful—especially about accepting credits through correspondent firms—but not broke. After covering expenses and setting aside a £33,000 "suspense account" (temporary carrying) fund, the partners netted £50,000 profit (roughly $250,000) for 1857. That was considerably less than they had made in 1856 (£87,469), and the decline continued in 1858, to £43,043. Earnings recovered to £60,000 the next year, and reached £76,437 in 1860.

Duncan, Sherman recovered as well, but sustained more damage to its reputation. At the end of 1857 R. G. Dun & Co. thought the house ought to close. Pierpont, patrolling Wall Street incognito again, overheard mostly negative talk. Still, by April 1858, the firm's standing had been restored and its credit rated "reliable & Sound."

In the depression that followed the 1857 panic, big cities in the Northeast fared worst. Two hundred thousand people were suddenly unemployed, nearly forty thousand of them in New York City. During the harsh winter of 1857–58, enraged mobs broke into coal yards to steal fuel, and rallies to protest the loss of jobs turned into riots. Religious leaders called helplessly for calm; revivalist sects enlisted thousands to atone for the nation's sins and pray for an end to hard times. Much of the press blamed the crash not on the business cycle, an inadequate banking system, or foreign markets but on Wall Street. The contraction continued until December 1858, after which the economy began once again to expand. Railroad building resumed; $26 million in foreign capital returned to U.S. markets in 1859. Industrial output rose as prices fell, which helped American products compete abroad.

———

Pierpont's features still retained the slight blur of late adolescence, but with his cosmopolitan manners, foreign languages, and European clothes he moved easily into the upper reaches of New York society. The names in his first New York address book include a few old Knickerbocker families but chiefly the city's mercantile and banking elite. The northernmost listing belonged to the banker Isaac Newton Phelps, at the corner of Madison and 36th. Above 42nd Street, Manhattan stretched off into swamps, rocky ledges, and open fields dotted with shantytowns, slaughterhouses, taverns, hospitals, and garbage dumps. An aqueduct system piped water from the Croton River through miles of masonry conduit to a holding lake at 86th Street, then on to a distributing reservoir at 42nd and Fifth. City officials had recently bought 843 acres of land above 59th Street for a central park. Construction of the "Greensward," designed by Frederick Law Olmsted and Calvert Vaux, began in 1856.

During his first months in Manhattan Pierpont surveyed the city's cultural fare: he went to the theater, the opera, Philharmonic concerts, and an exhibition of banker August Belmont's collection of paintings at the new National Academy of Design—a redbrick building at 51 West 10th Street, with studios for artists as well as exhibition space—noting in his diaries the initials of young women who accompanied him.

Wealth and poverty resided much closer together on this narrow island than they did in Hartford or Boston, and not far from the elegant town houses off Union Square were the tenements of the Lower East Side. Pierpont did not reflect on this disparity in the few letters from this period that survive, nor on the protests of the unemployed during his first winter in New York. He gave $10 one day to the Five Points Mission in the notorious slum at the intersection of Baxter, Worth, and Park streets off the Bowery. The church he joined had been one of the first to set up mission chapels for the poor on the Lower East Side.

St. George's Episcopal Church, on Stuyvesant Square at Second Avenue and 16th Street, occupied a geographical middle ground between New York's mansions and slums. Its rector, Stephen H. Tyng, was such a charismatic speaker—called "the prince of platform orators"—that his rival, Henry Ward Beecher, refused to follow him on a stage. In the historic Protestant/Catholic tension within the Anglican Church, which dated back to its split from the Vatican under Henry VIII, Dr. Tyng was resolutely in the Protestant camp. He had been trained in the Low Church Evangelical tradition that emphasized verbal inspiration, the authority of the Bible, and personal conversion over holy sacraments and the authority of the bishops, and he became a leading opponent of the High Church movement that was moving, in the middle decades of the nineteenth century, intellectually and theologically toward Rome. Under the fiercely partisan Dr. Tyng, St. George's served as the outpost of the Episcopalian Evangelical position in New York.

Pierpont would have friends in both the High and Broad (social-reformist) Church factions within Episcopalianism, but he remained all his life a devout adherent of the Low Church. Where the Reverend Pierpont looked on life as a perpetual quest for moral and social improvement, Dr. Tyng saw it as a search for refuge from sin in God: individuals would be saved not through good works, moral striving, or sacramental rites, but *only* through faith in the atoning death of Christ. At Pierpont's confirmation in 1861, Tyng urged new communicants to "come with a deep sense of your own guilt, and trust in that Gracious Savior, without a doubt or a fear. In him the Gospel reveals to you entire forgiveness. . . . Look upon your salvation as now accomplished."

———

During the crisis of 1857 Pierpont visited his mother in Hartford just for the day at Thanksgiving and Christmas. She remained deeply unhappy, and for months had been begging her father to write or let her come see him, as she was "in great need of council and advise [sic]." Mr. Pierpont did not have much contact with Juliet during her long sojourn in the United States. At the age of seventy-two, he had, much to his descendants' surprise, fallen in love.

To his son John, Jr., he described Harriet-Louise Campbell Fowler, a forty-six-year-old widow, as "much the most splendid woman, in her appearance, that Medford can show." It should surprise no one that he loved her "most truly": the miracle was that "at my age, she should love me." Splendid appearance aside, Louise Fowler had a qualification that appealed to him above all others—she was a "picture of *health* . . . having never been confined to her bed for a day, except in *accouchement*." He married her in December 1857, and reported that all he now lacked for "perfect happiness" was enough work to get him out of debt.

A month after the wedding, Juliet proposed to spend part of the winter with her father and stepmother, who was just five years her senior. Mr. Pierpont replied that he could not add the expense of a boarder to his household's straitened circumstances—particularly, he implied, one with extravagant tastes. The exchange touched raw nerves. Juliet responded with a barrage of self-justification and insult, declaring it "strange" that "knowing & feeling this weight of anxiety you should have thought best to add another to suffer, as she must, if only by seeing you suffer, if she has entered into the connection blindly—if not & she was fully aware of your situation, she can have nothing to say."

Juliet had not seen her own husband or four younger children for eighteen months when Junius in March of 1858 sent an alarming report. Little "Doctor," approaching his twelfth birthday, was seriously ill. He had been complaining of pain and numbness in one leg for months. In February, doctors found an infection in the socket of his hip, and ordered the leg immobilized. "The poor little fellow has to lie in one position and be carried from one room to another," his father reported; the child would probably have to stay off his feet for six months, but bore his suffering "most patiently," crying only when he thought of the cricket games he was missing. "He is a good boy & I feel will bear with resignation whatever is appointed him."

Over the next few weeks the pain and weakness increased. Junius remained constantly at his son's bedside, feeding him with a spoon, cheered at the feeblest sign of recognition. It was no use. At 5:15 A.M. on March 12, the boy died. His exhausted father wrote to Pierpont that night: "his gentle spirit took its flight, as quietly as if going into a sweet sleep. . . . Our dear little Junius the idol of our little household has been taken from us almost in an instant."

Juliet was packing for London when Pierpont arrived from New York with this news. She collapsed. All thought of returning to England was indefinitely postponed.

Junius, "worn out with anxiety and grief," told Pierpont he was trying to "bow in submission to His will who allowed it, but my heart was too much bound up in the dear boy and I cannot be reconciled." Pierpont had been away from home for most of this child's life: "You my dear son have lost an only brother," Junius went on, "& altho you have been much separated I know your love for him must have been strong—who that knew that gentle, unselfish, affectionate child could help loving him. . . . May you . . . lay this admonition to heart & so live that whenever you shall be called you may be found ready."

Later that month, Junius took little Juliet and her governess to Brighton for a change of scene. "I cannot tell you how lonely I feel and how stricken down by this heavy blow," he wrote to Pierpont from the seaside. "Nor can I realise that it is really so that I am not again here to see the dear one who was so entwined about my heart." He had no interest in work—"it seems to me the anxieties, trials, afflictions & disappointments of the last year have been too much for me and that I never shall be in business what I once was."

Grief for his younger son did not preclude a lecture to the elder, and Junius abruptly changed the subject. Pierpont had bought five shares of stock in the Pacific Mail Steamship Company, at $63 a share. Founded in 1848 by New York merchant William Henry Aspinwall, the company ran ships from San Francisco to South America and Asia, with a large government subsidy for mail.* Junius scolded: "I do not like your buying stocks or having your mind turned in that direction. How many have been shipwrecked on that one thing—speculation in stocks. I want you to bring your mind quietly down to the regular details of business . . . [and resolve] never to buy any stock on speculation." He took up the subject again three weeks later, after consulting Mr. Aspinwall: "I judged he thought it a risky stock to hold. If it pays 10% div. in May had you not better sell & put it into something else?"

Pierpont ignored this advice. He was considerably less averse to risk than his father, and bought 10 more shares of Pacific Mail that June at 76¼ (the company did pay a 10 percent dividend in May), and kept on buying as the price went up. A year later he reported a loss of $1,467.30 on 150 shares purchased at $81 to $82 and sold at $72 to $73.† He fared better on a smaller speculation: he bought one share of the Michigan Central Railroad Company for $31.25 in January 1858 and sold it a month later for $65, over 100 percent profit.

Duncan, Sherman promoted him out of correspondence in March 1858 (still paying no salary), and Junius congratulated him on his unspecified new duties. "Be true to those responsibilities and to yourself," wrote the indefatigable Polonius. "Never under any circumstances do an act which could be called in question if known to the whole world. Remember that there is an Eye above that is ever upon you & that for *every act—word & deed* you will one day be called to give account."

Junius insisted that bankers handling large amounts of other people's money had to put themselves beyond reproach, their authority and expertise unequivocally untainted by greed. The reward for this high detachment was the freedom to work in a well-protected market. A reputation for integrity would earn material as well as moral profit, while abusing a privileged position for personal gain would guarantee the loss of both. Wealth dishonorably acquired was "worse then useless when you consider the awful cost," continued

---

* Aspinwall and his associates had built a 47½-mile railroad across Panama in the 1850s. Before the completion of this line, merchandise, mail, and passengers had to travel 13,000 miles around the Horn from San Francisco to New York; the railroad cut the trip to 5,000 miles. Aspinwall's railroad company earned more than $7 million in its first six years. It was the first essential "path between the seas," and led to the building of the Panama Canal.

† The Pacific Mail directors were fighting Cornelius Vanderbilt, who wanted his Atlantic and Pacific Steamship Company to run the trans-Isthmus traffic through Nicaragua. Pierpont could have sold the stock at a profit had he held on to it; Pacific Mail prospered over the long run, and was one of the stocks listed in the first Dow Jones average in 1884.

Junius. He had the highest hopes for his only remaining son: "I depend much upon you and feel that you will not disappoint my expectations—be wise, considerate, thoughtful, ever keeping in mind the great end of your being."

Pierpont turned twenty-one in April, and for the occasion Junius again sounded the theme of avarice: "Do not let the desire of success or of accumulating induce you ever to do a single action which will cause you regret. Self approbation and a feeling that God approves will bring far greater happiness than all the wealth the world can give."

———

When Juliet finally returned to London in May, Junius found "little improvement in [her] case." She was "still a great invalid and I fear may long continue so," he told her father: "The effect of this upon the happiness & comfort of a family your own sad experience will enable you fully to appreciate."

Though Pierpont left no report of its effect on him, he cannot have taken much pleasure in the company of his depressed and demanding mother. Perhaps he found some solace in being able to take care of her as if he were the parent rather than the other way around—managing her finances, making her travel arrangements, trying without much success to cheer her up. All his adult life he would be drawn to people he could take care of, and also to those—doctors, clergymen, sympathetic women—who in one way or another took care of him.

Junius had given up on finding "happiness & comfort" in his marriage. Soon after Juliet arrived in England he made plans to visit the United States that fall with his eldest daughter, Sarah. He had not been home in four years. In August he bought the house at No. 13 Princes Gate, next door to the one he was renting. It would not be ready until November, and his family had to move out of No. 14 by September 1. He and Sarah would be in the United States all fall. Since Junius ordinarily dictated arrangements for everyone in his family (and a good many others besides), his shrug to Pierpont about his wife's autumn accommodations testifies further to their estrangement: "I don't know what will be her plans," he wrote. At the end of August he sailed with Sarah to New York.

———

Pierpont had been spending weekends that summer at Cozzens' Hotel near West Point on the Hudson, visiting a family named Osborn. Like most of his friendships, this one mixed business with pleasure. William Henry Osborn was president of the Illinois Central Railroad, whose securities Peabody & Co. had been underwriting since the early 1850s. Osborn and his wife, Virginia, had two small children and an appealing variety of guests. One guest in particular attracted Pierpont's attention: Virginia Osborn's sister, Amelia, whom he had met at Newport the summer before.

Called Memie (pronounced "Mimi"), Amelia Sturges had qualities Pierpont had been drawn to in the past—the "unpretending" femininity of the Italian girl at Loeche-les-Bains, and the "lively, agreeable" disposition of Miss Hoffman at Vevey. Small, with a heart-shaped face framed by thick brown hair parted in the middle and knotted at the nape of her neck, Memie had been crowned beauty queen at a New York ball early that winter. One admirer described her as "the most charmingly self-possessed and natural sovereign that imagination could conceive," concluding with a flourish: " 'Loyalty to such a Queen ceases to be a virtue.' "

Memie was twenty-three in the summer of 1858—two years older than Pierpont. She studied singing and piano, spoke German and French, and taught sewing to young women at the Wilson Industrial School for Girls on the Lower East Side. At thirteen she had joined the Old North (Dutch Reformed) Church on Fulton Street—her family followed—and in 1858 was translating into English a little tract called *La Vraie Croix*. She told her mother she enjoyed the work "even if it should not prove good enough to be published."

Her father, Jonathan Sturges, had started out in the wholesale grocery business as partner to Luman Reed, one of New York's leading merchants and early art collectors. After Reed died in 1836, Sturges carried on the older man's commercial and cultural work.* He managed a prospering tea and coffee trade, became a director of the New York, New Haven, & Hartford Railroad, helped found the National Bank of Commerce, and organized a group of men to buy and preserve Reed's art collection, which eventually formed the core of the New-York Historical Society.

By 1850, Jonathan Sturges had enough capital to invest in enterprises other

---

* In the 1830s, after a brief flirtation with European Old Masters—high costs and the difficulty of authentication made the market too risky—Luman Reed turned his attention to contemporary American artists. He sent Thomas Cole, the country's first popular landscape painter and "father" of the Hudson River School, to study art abroad, and subsidized Cole's famous five-canvas *Course of Empire*. He also supported Cole's disciple Asher B. Durand. Reed converted the third floor of his Greenwich Street house into an art gallery open to the public one day a week, and hosted meetings of the Sketch Club, a small group of artists and writers who met to draw and talk over supper. Early members of the club included Cole, Durand, Samuel F. B. Morse, James Fenimore Cooper, William Cullen Bryant, Washington Irving, Reed himself, and Jonathan Sturges.

In 1846 several Sketch Club members decided to form a larger group of men interested in the arts. The first meeting of the Century Association, named for its hundred initial members, took place in January 1847 in rented rooms on lower Broadway. The Century moved to 15th Street off Union Square in 1858—it was a Century Association ball that elected Amelia beauty queen that year—and in 1891 to a clubhouse designed by Stanford White, at 7 West 43rd. Among its first members were Jonathan Sturges, Frederic Church, John Kensett, George Inness, Henry James, Sr., John Jay, Richard Morris Hunt, William Aspinwall, Frederick Law Olmsted, George Templeton Strong, and Joseph Choate.

than his own, and like many other wealthy men at midcentury, he turned to railroads. Illinois had been trying since the 1830s to build a rail line from Galena to Cairo at the junction of the Ohio and Mississippi rivers to link midwestern traffic to the South, but political fights, competing groups of speculators, and the collapse of the state's credit in the forties had made it impossible to raise the necessary funds. In 1850 Illinois Senator Stephen Douglas persuaded Congress to make its first large federal land grant—about two and a half million acres in the Mississippi River Valley—to this railroad. Douglas stood to profit from the venture, since he owned property along the proposed route; he also hoped to ease the antagonism between North and South by engaging both sides in building a continental network of roads. Early in 1851, the state legislature turned over the land grant and charter to a group of eastern capitalists that included Jonathan Sturges and William Aspinwall, to build the Illinois Central.

In April, eighteen-year-old Virginia Sturges wrote in her diary: "Father was out till half past twelve last evening consulting over a railroad in Illinois 600 miles long, which twelve gentlemen are to build. Mother sighs over it sometimes & I . . . long to look into the future and see if this great enterprise will succeed." Four years later it had not succeeded. Less than half the track had been laid, land sales had dried up, and the company was nearly bankrupt. Its president, Robert Schuyler, had been involved in an unrelated fraud, which led investors to sell their IC holdings. At the end of 1855 the gentlemen proprietors appointed a new president, William H. Osborn, a native of Salem, Massachusetts, who had made a fortune in the Philippine shipping trade. Osborn had met the Sturges family on vacation at Saratoga Springs in upstate New York, and married Virginia in 1853. Amelia teased her father for years about being afraid to take her anywhere after he "lost" Virginia at Saratoga.

Osborn rescued the Illinois Central by reviving land sales, hiring new officers and engineers, and working with the road's outside counsel, Abraham Lincoln. He raised fresh capital by assessing stockholders for cash and selling bonds abroad, and so effectively restored the confidence of the road's London bankers, including Peabody & Co., that by 1856 foreign investors controlled the company. Traffic fell off dramatically after the 1857 panic, as did the value of Illinois Central securities. That both eventually recovered was due partly to Osborn, who used his own money and credit to keep the company solvent, and partly to external circumstances: the railroad carried Union troops and supplies through the Mississippi Valley during the Civil War.

Pierpont probably renewed his acquaintance with Amelia while helping Osborn in the aftermath of the panic. He saw her as often as he could in the summer of 1858, and that fall called regularly at her parents' house in New York—a large brownstone at 5 East 14th Street. With four boys and Amelia still living at home, the family spent summers and weekends at an American

Gothic "cottage" Mr. Sturges had built in Fairfield, Connecticut. Unlike the well-traveled Morgans, the Sturgeses had never been to Europe, but they lived in more intimate relation to the arts—to literature and music as well as painting, and to contemporary American works as well as reproductions of famous Old Masters.

Frederic Church, a student of Thomas Cole, had produced his panoramic *Niagara* after visiting the Osborns on vacation at the Falls in the summer of 1856. Memie, also there that July, told her mother: "Our cottage is now decorated by a charming sketch of Niagara from Mr. Church's brush. He is intoxicated . . . rises at sunrise, and we only see him at meal times. He is so restless away from the Falls that he cannot keep still, always feeling as if he were losing some new effect of light."*

Pierpont brought his father, sister, and cousin Sally Goodwin to visit the Sturges household on East 14th Street in the fall of 1858. Junius discussed railroad matters with Jonathan Sturges, and was enchanted with Memie.

In January she reported to an aunt that the elder Mr. Morgan had asked her "in a laughing way, if I would not go out [to London] with him should he stay [in New York] till February. I said, 'Oh yes if Father will let me.' So the very next day he went to Father with his petition and it has ended in [Father's] giving his consent."

Pierpont would have to stay in New York while his father took Memie abroad. This arrangement would deprive him not only of her company but also of the chance to introduce her to London and the pleasures of foreign travel himself. He knew better than to object to the dictates of paternal plans. Still, this one effectively cut him out in a new situation—a private affair of the heart—and made more explicit than ever just who in the family had seigneurial rights.

Junius was about to turn forty-six. Fearing that a high-spirited young woman half his age might find Princes Gate and the London winter season dull, he promised Memie a tide of pictures once the galleries opened in March,

---

* *Niagara*, now at the Corcoran Gallery in Washington, D.C., made Church famous. Measuring 42½ by 90½ inches, it places the viewer at the edge of the falls in a rush of water and spray under a brooding, rainbow-highlighted sky. The Williams, Stevens and Williams gallery bought it for the then extraordinary sum of $4,500, and crowds paid to see the "Great Picture" on exhibition. One European critic said it provided "an entirely new and higher view both of American nature and art." Church had an even greater success in 1859 with *The Heart of the Andes*, which he began on a trip he took to Latin America with Cyrus Field. Exhibited at the Tenth Street Studio Building in New York for three weeks, it attracted twelve thousand viewers, and sold for $10,000—a record price for an American landscape painting. After its New York showing, *The Heart of the Andes* traveled to England, toured the United States, and was widely reproduced in steel engravings. Pierpont bought a print for $60 in 1863. The painting now belongs to the Metropolitan Museum of Art.

and invited Sally Goodwin to come with her. Mrs. Sturges confided her own sense of excitement to her sister as Memie packed to leave: "We feel as if Amelia's time is drawing near. . . . [The Morgans] live at the corner of Hyde Park & Kensington Gardens and have their own horses carriages and every luxury of a well appointed English establishment!"

On February 2, Pierpont and the Sturgeses took a tugboat into the Hudson off Jersey City to see Memie, Junius, Sarah Morgan, and Sally Goodwin off on the SS *Persia*. The winter Atlantic was rough, with high seas the first few days and ice storms farther out, but Memie's stomach proved as strong as her sense of adventure. One night she wore Junius's cloak to walk on deck with the captain in a storm: "Sea a sight never to be forgotten," she wrote in a journal she kept throughout the trip. "Deck seemed perpendicular at times. . . . Shipped two seas passed partly over our heads but drenched me pretty well." She read Tennyson, played backgammon, and toured the ship's engines with the captain. Sally Goodwin described her as "full of fun and life."

As soon as Memie had unpacked at Princes Gate, Junius took her for a drive through Hyde Park and London's famous streets. She pronounced it a "smashing day," and over the next several weeks proceeded—all fresh American energy—to discover the Old World. With Mr. Peabody she attended the theater and the opera; she toured the National Gallery and Sir John Soane's museum, rode in Rotten Row, saw French Academy pictures, English landscape paintings, the Duke of Wellington's funeral car, and Queen Victoria. In quiet moments she played the grand piano Junius had just bought (probably for her pleasure), and wrote to the junior "Mr. Morgan" in New York.

Junius's preoccupation with his guest did not rule out supervising his son's digestive system by mail: "You are altogether too rapid in disposing of your meals," he scolded in March, "and then there is the great irregularity in the matter I so often spoke to you of when in New York. You may depend upon it you can have no health if you go on in this way. I would *urge* of you to correct it at once—If you do not, dyspepsia with all attendant evils is sure to be upon you."

Juliet, "low-spirited" when her husband and guests arrived, stayed in her room. "We young people have to entertain the company with Uncle Junius," Sally Goodwin reported. Junius entertained often, serving French food, champagne, and strawberries he raised under glass. Pierpont kept him supplied with American apples, wild turkeys, oysters, Havana cigars, buckwheat, and water from the Congress spring at Saratoga. Amelia was a great asset at the Princes Gate dinners. "She is pretty and agreeable, and has plenty of confidence," observed Sally. "I think it is a blessing that those who have do not appreciate."

Memie's parents and younger brothers, Arthur and Henry, met her in London for a grand tour that spring. As it was their first trip abroad, Pierpont had drawn up an itinerary. "Having been carefully over most of the ground myself several times," he wrote with orotund gravity to Mr. Sturges, "I am convinced that you will find the order in which I have arranged your visit to the various cities best conducive to the pleasure of the present trip & to the satisfaction of future retrospection." He offered just a general outline and a few personal opinions, assuming the travelers would find details in guidebooks. They would see some of Rubens's greatest paintings in Antwerp, pay dearly in Brussels for lace, find the Berlin Museum "very fine," and need two weeks for Paris—"tell all the milliners, dressmakers, &c that you must positively have your purchases at least a week before you really do." The route along the corniche from Marseilles to Genoa was "the finest ride in the world." Rome would reward "as much time as you can possibly grant it," as would everything in the vicinity of Naples.

The Sturges letters and diaries from this trip offer a Jamesian picture of novice American aesthetes abroad. In London the travelers went to the Royal Academy and Thomas Baring's art collection (Memie noted "an excellent Claude. Fine Murillos, very fine Teniers"), heard Dickens read from *The Pickwick Papers,* and attended a lecture by Charles Kingsley, author of *Hypatia* and *Westward Ho!* They crossed the Channel to France in late May, worried that war between Austria and Italy might interfere with their plans, then more or less followed the itinerary Pierpont had drawn up. Memie described her father's "raptures" among gems of Dutch and Flemish art at The Hague, yet after weeks of looking at pictures found herself, like many another first-time visitor to Europe, "surfeited" with galleries—"one fairly gets an art dyspepsia."

At Verona, crowded with Austrian soldiers, she located Juliet's tomb in a "miserable little garden, with . . . tumbling down walls & dying grape vines," and Romeo's house looking over a market "where the odor of cheese bologna sausages & onions combined fills the air & mingles most unpleasantly with dreams of rope ladders midnight serenades & tales of love." In early November her family made its way back through Paris to London.

———

While the Sturgeses traveled, Pierpont worked. Jim Goodwin, who had completed *his* European tour and moved to New York, read him Sally's London reports; Sarah Morgan kept her brother posted as well. In September Junius decided that his son had spent enough time (two years) as an apprentice at Duncan, Sherman. Pierpont resigned. In a formal letter of farewell, the firm's partners thanked him for his "voluntary and unpaid services," and praised his "untiring industry . . . earnestness, zeal and fidelity of a rare character." That he had learned a great deal about business and shown himself "practically capable of discharging the duties of any desk in our office" should gratify not only him but also "our Esteemed friend your Good Father."

Yet in wishing the junior Morgan every future success, his employers had "one word of advice," which they hoped he would not take amiss. Pierpont had a quick temper and no patience with other people's mistakes. From his father he had learned an astringent perfectionism, but not the smooth urbanity that eased the workings of Junius's iron will. Messrs. Duncan, Sherman, and Dabney warned him politely ("instigated by the attachment you must know we feel for you") that on taking his place in the ranks of commercial life he ought to bear in mind that "*liberality* in views and acts generally brings better returns than can be hoped for from a course which others can possibly regard as sharp or contracted. —Suavity and gentle bearing toward those with whom we deal goes also a long way towards making up the capital which ensures success."

Accustomed as he was to reproof, Pierpont met this one with elaborate deference: "I cannot allow your very kind note of today to be received and laid aside," he replied, "without expressing to you my grateful and heartfelt thanks for the very kind feelings towards me which you have voluntarily expressed, especially for the advice which your interest in my welfare has led you to give and which I fully appreciate." He could have "no prouder satisfaction than the reception of such a note as you have handed me," and would attribute any future success he might have to "the counsels which you have given me during the first two years of my business life which I cannot but think will be the happiest."

Four days later he took the *Persia* to London, where he spent quiet weeks discussing his future with his father and waiting for Memie to return from the Continent. He had not seen her in nine months.

The Sturgeses reached their hotel late at night on November 10. The next morning right after breakfast "in walked Pierpont and Sarah Morgan . . . and Sally Goodwin," wrote Memie's brother Henry in his diary: "Then the way there [*sic*] tongues went answering questions and asking them. Soon after . . . Mrs. Morgan came too so I had a chance of seeing [her] for the first [time]. . . . I do not think she is good looking at all."

For the next two weeks Pierpont saw Memie every day. He took her to the National Gallery, the South Kensington Museum, the Crystal Palace, and out shopping. "Returned after dark to dinner," she wrote in her diary one night. "Had a charming time." Her enthusiasm over touring the Duke of Devonshire's Chatsworth may have had as much to do with her companion as the weather: a "delicious day like spring[,] soft shadows on the grassy slopes!!!!!"

At the end of November, having designed the Sturgeses' European tour, Pierpont escorted them home. He went down to Liverpool the day before they sailed to arrange for his party to dine at the captain's table on the *Persia*. He booked the chief officer's room for himself.

A new, teasing tone in Memie's diary as they crossed the Atlantic suggests that Pierpont was reading over her shoulder. He never traveled light, and turned up at their Liverpool hotel with a "*small* quantity of luggage," she noted. The day of departure she was "Up bright and early. More than some of my *friends* can say for *them*selves." Turbulent seas kept most passengers in their rooms. Not Pierpont and Memie. "Breakfasted at 10," she wrote the third day out: "Mr. Morgan & myself the only ones at table of the party." At lunch, "Mr. Morgan imitating the example of the Good Samaritan ran up & down with roasted apples, crackers, & *rugs*! until we were all very comfortable. Driven by the rain into our parlour (i.e. Chief Officer's room)"—i.e., Pierpont's room.

The following day, "*Most* of us were disagreeable to ourselves & everybody else. Sat in our *cheerful* parlour most of the day." And the next: "One of my friends very *blue* all day. Disappeared from dinner very suddenly. No cry of Man Overboard so concluded he was all right."

Though she does not guess at the cause of Pierpont's "blues," it may have been the presence of a rival—the ship's captain, who showed Memie his engine room and private quarters, and often joined their party for tea. Still, she spent most of her time with Pierpont. The day after she detected no cry of "Man Overboard," she and her suitor strolled the deck in the morning, spent the afternoon at backgammon, went out after dinner to watch the play of phosphorescence on the water, and stayed up over more backgammon till eleven. Memie reported herself "awfully beaten. Mr. M. decidedly under the weather (not seasick)." He stayed in his room all the next day, appearing only for backgammon after dinner—this time she won, and began referring to him in her diary as "my *adversary*."

One stormy night as they approached New York, Memie organized an after-dinner walk: "The air cold and bracing. Captain took one arm Mr. M. the other so there was no fear of slipping on the snowy decks." When the weather cleared, people came up "like turtles to sun themselves." The travelers reached home on December 8.

Memie had been away nearly a year, and friends flocked to see her. Pierpont called the day after they arrived, then again the next day, and the one after that. In Memie's diary the phrase "Mr. Morgan spent the evening" now appears as a regular refrain.

Amelia Sturges.
(Archives of The Pierpont Morgan Library, New York)

A HOUSE DIVIDED

Nothing had been decided about his future when Pierpont left London in November 1859. From a desk at Duncan, Sherman he did odd jobs for Peabody & Co. while his father considered the options. Then in late December he got word from London that he was to tour the South, to report on the railroads, banks, and cotton merchants with whom the London firm was doing business. Junius no doubt did need an eyewitness report as the conflict between North and South intensified, and professional demands clearly took precedence over romance. Still, if the senior Morgan was promoting an attachment between his son and Amelia Sturges, he had an odd way of going about it. Having separated the pair from February to November 1859, he now decreed another lengthy parting.

Pierpont's interest in Memie was apparently not exclusive. On a "tremendously cold night" at the end of December, he left New York in such a rush that he did not have time to call on "some of my lady friends up town," he told Jim Goodwin, who was living with his brother, Frank, on Irving Place: "I was nearly frozen when I reached the cheerful fire at the maiden establishment of our old friends the Misses Peters" in Philadelphia.

The thermometer registered zero when he went on the next day to Baltimore: "I much preferred chatting before a pleasant fire with the charming young ladies of B. than running the risk of being obliged to continue my trip southward minus a nose & ears which would most certainly have required amputation had I ventured out sleighing." The two days he had allotted for Baltimore turned to four. His old flame Miss Hoffman ("of whom you *may* have heard") was about to be married: "I saw her intended but cannot say that I fell into raptures over him as some have done. I hope he is all right for he will have *one* of the sweetest women for a wife this world ever produced."

When Jim reported a rumor—probably of a Morgan/Sturges engagement—making the rounds in New York, Pierpont denounced it as containing "no truth . . . *whatever.*" If there should be any such news, his cousin would be the first to know. And he went on, in a less than romantic vein: "Now that you have become acquainted with the Sturges' I would advise you to nourish the acquaintance. Should you see any of the family, please remember me most kindly to them. You will find . . . that there are few if any more desirable families to be on intimate terms with in the City of N.Y. This between us and the post."

He "tore" himself away from Baltimore on January 4 to attend a session of Congress, where Democrats were blocking the nomination of Ohio Republican John Sherman to be Speaker of the House. Sherman had endorsed a book (*The Impending Crisis,* by Hinton Rowan Helper) that blamed "all the shame, poverty, ignorance, tyranny and imbecility of the South" on the slave system, and urged nonslaveholding whites to overthrow it. Southern extremists threatened to secede. Politicians came to the Capitol that January armed with knives and guns, and fistfights broke out on the House floor.

After watching several hours of this bitter dispute, Pierpont pronounced the House of Representatives a "disgrace." Like his federalist father, he hated the prospect of internecine war. Also like Junius, he was quick to see the worst in a difficult situation. Saying nothing about the moral and ideological issues at stake for America's embattled democracy, he thundered to Jim: "Of all the legislative bodies which I have seen in this country & in Europe never did I see so little dignity." He left Washington after one day, "completely disgusted & disappointed with everything."

Intense cold weather followed him to Richmond—he had to go over the Virginia mountains, since the Potomac was frozen. In North Carolina he noted "1000 slaves on train." He stayed for ten days in Charleston with Peabody's local agent, H. W. Conner, studying the cotton trade, then proceeded to Savannah, where he met with bankers and merchants, toured cotton presses, and saw a production of *Othello* ("very poor"). At Macon, Georgia, he called on his uncle, John Pierpont, Jr. Traveling by steamboat from Montgomery to Mobile took three days: "On the River all day," he noted in his diary. "Stopped every few moments to take on cotton. Novel sight to me."

In New Orleans, the major port of the South, he set himself up in the branch office of H. W. Conner & Son, called on businessmen in the commercial district along Corondelet Street, attended church with Mr. Conner, drove out to Lake Pontchartrain, and escorted Conner's daughter to *Il Trovatore.* Every few days he reported to his father on prices and shipments of cotton, bonds of the Mississippi Central Railroad, and conditions in southern markets.* The 1860 cotton crop—almost four million bales—sold abroad for $191 million, more than half the value of all U.S. exports that year.

Turning back north in April, Pierpont stopped in Charleston for the Democratic convention. Junius expected he would find Watts Sherman there, "& others desirous of having a hand in making the new President"—assuming that the next president, like six of the last eight, would be a Democrat. The convention turned out to be so bitterly divided between northern supporters of Stephen Douglas, still hoping for peace based on states' rights, and southern radicals looking for provocation to secede, that the delegates could not agree on a candidate; they adjourned to try again in June.

The Republicans met in Chicago in May. Both their leading candidates opposed the expansion of slavery—William H. Seward, the powerful New York senator, and Abraham Lincoln, the articulate but relatively little-known Illinois lawyer. Running for the Senate against Stephen Douglas in 1858, Lincoln had made his famous argument for national union, citing the Gospel according to Mark: " 'A house divided against itself cannot stand.' I believe this government cannot endure, permanently half *slave* and half *free*." It would have to become "*all* one thing, or *all* the other." Four months later Seward explicitly connected the struggle over slavery to economic centralization. Though separate systems of free and slave labor had long coexisted within the Union, Seward declared, changes in commerce, transport, and population had brought the states "into a higher and more perfect social unity or consolidation," and set the two systems on a collision course: "an irrepressible conflict between opposing and enduring forces" would require the country finally to choose between loosely coordinated sectionalism and federal union.

After much horse-trading and tumult, the Republicans in 1860 nominated Lincoln on a platform that opposed any extension of slavery and promised to increase the tariff, pass homestead laws, and build a transcontinental railroad. The Democrats, meeting again in June, failed to reach a consensus: they split into sectional factions, the northerners putting up Stephen Douglas, the southerners John Breckinridge of Kentucky.

Pierpont reached New York in late May, having been away five months. He spent most of his time that summer with Memie in Fairfield. Junius fretted by

---

* He carried a letter of introduction from one of President Buchanan's advisers, the Yankee lawyer Samuel Barlow, to Judah P. Benjamin, the conservative Louisiana senator who was trying to prevent secession, but his diaries do not record that he used it. Junius, thanking Mr. Barlow for the letter, offered a cynical reflection on the struggle over slavery: he hoped his son would not "get taken up for 'a white man' in a country where Blacks seem to be thought of so much more importance."

mail about cotton, and even more about not being able to find his son the right job on Wall Street. Perhaps he was defining the "right" connection too narrowly, or perhaps Pierpont had a reputation for the "sharp . . . contracted" behavior Duncan, Sherman had warned him about. By July, Junius was considering the China trade: "I feel so much solicitude to have you well settled & it is now time," he wrote, "but if nothing offers then I think your time will be more profitably employed in travelling East than in remaining in New York without occupation."

The junior Morgan had longed to go to China in 1857, when his mother weighed in with a veto. Now, as his father reconsidered the proposition, Pierpont had a compelling reason to stay in New York. Early in August, just before he went to see his family in England, he asked Memie to marry him, and she gave him the answer he wanted.

She wrote to her youngest brother, Henry, with whom she had been planning another trip abroad: "something has happened which will be likely to cut our plans short. I hope one of these days that you will have for a brother Mr. Morgan, & a good kind one I am sure you will find him, so you see I have engaged another courier for life . . . [And] now I want you to write to me, & tell me if you are pleased with the choice I have made."

Both families were pleased—and under the circumstances, Junius agreed not to dispatch his son halfway around the world. "You see," he teased Memie from London early in the new year, "I sent your young friend back to New York instead of to *China* as you seemed to prefer, but I don't seem to have offended either party by so doing."

Pierpont bought Memie a locket in Paris and a ring at Tiffany's as soon as he returned to New York. They planned a year's engagement; the wedding would take place in October 1861.

Virginia Osborn told one of her aunts in mock complaint that no one in the family went to parties that winter, "for Memie has become very domestic in her tastes and prefers talking to Pierpont in her comfortable home to doing the same thing in the midst of a crowd." At the beginning of January, Memie came down with a severe cough that hung on for weeks. Pierpont hovered in constant attendance, taking her out for walks whenever she felt strong enough.

He was so delighted with her and their engagement that he had "some difficulty in coming down to things below," noted his father. "Things below" meant work, and with the question of his affiliation still unresolved, Pierpont took a one-room office at 53 Exchange Place. "We are sending him something to do," Junius told Memie, "no great profit in it to him, but much better than being idle." The elder Morgan found a silver lining in his son's professional limbo: "I think he is most fortunate in being out of business in such times. . . . he ought to be thankful that the present is not his first year's experience in business on his own account."

There had never before been "such times" in America's history. A Republican coalition elected Abraham Lincoln in November 1860, with the hopelessly divided Democrats splitting their vote. The victory of a President and party avowedly hostile to slavery brought the long-standing sectional conflict to a head. In the four months between Lincoln's election and inauguration, seven southern states left the Union: South Carolina led the way in December 1860, followed by Mississippi, Florida, Alabama, Georgia, Louisiana, and Texas.*

Junius found "nothing short of sacrilege" in the idea of "dis-union." To a colleague that January he denounced the "pitiable" President Buchanan who had proved himself "entirely incapable . . . & imbecile at a time when the blood of every true patriot & lover of his country is boiling with indignation against those who are threatening its dissolution." A number of northern businessmen hoped to conciliate the South, since war would cut off cotton supplies, close factories and textile mills, curtail the transatlantic shipping trade, disrupt European markets for American securities, and stop southern purchases of northern manufactured goods. Junius, however, thought there could be no temporizing with rebellion: "I trust the North will make no concessions or propose any compromise which their good judgement will not approve after the excitement of the moment is over." And he predicted that secession would prove "suicidal" for the South: "The day which dawns on a Southern Confederacy will see 'the beginning of the end of Slavery' in those states."

When delegates from the seven seceding states drew up a Confederate constitution in early February, Junius told Memie he was glad to be so far away from the "terrible state of things . . . on your side of the water," and concluded on a familiar note of disgust: "Whatever may be the result of the present troubles, I look upon the reputation of our country as gone. We have shown to the world how little real strength it has & how powerless for good is our government. Hereafter we must take our stand before other nations on the same level with the petty states of Central America. I cannot tell you how I mourn all this."

Lincoln passed through New York at the beginning of March on the way to his inauguration. Mrs. Sturges, watching as he rode along 14th Street in an open barouche, found him a "bright pleasant looking" man who appeared younger than she expected, with "a hard lot before him." On March 4, the new President promised in his inaugural address not to interfere with slavery where it already existed but to preserve the Union at any cost. Confederates took the speech (which had been considerably toned down by Lincoln's advisers) as a declaration of war. Southern troops fired on Fort Sumter, a Union garrison on an island off Charleston, South Carolina, on April 12. Two days later a Confederate flag flew over the fort. The Civil War had begun.

---

* Inaugurations took place in March of the year following a presidential election until 1933. Franklin Delano Roosevelt was the first president to be inaugurated in January.

———

Henry Adams, looking anxiously for some sign of Lincoln's character at the inaugural ball, saw "a long, awkward figure; a plain, ploughed face; a mind, absent in part, and in part evidently worried by white kid gloves; features that expressed neither self-satisfaction nor any other familiar Americanism . . . ; above all a lack of apparent force." Shortly after the firing on Fort Sumter, Virginia Osborn told a friend in California that "it would be hard to find any one anywhere who has confidence either in Mr. Lincoln or Mr. Seward [the Secretary of State]." Even to members of Lincoln's own cabinet, the rawboned novice in the Executive Office seemed indecisive, excessively cautious, and appallingly unprepared to deal with the national crisis.

Still, patriotic fervor ran high. Henry Sturges, age fifteen, saw "the Gallant Seventh Regiment off to the WAR" at New York's Cooper Institute on April 19, and attended a rally in Union Square the next day: "Everybody wears Union cockades—thousands of people—splendid speeches—the greatest time I ever saw." His twenty-one-year-old brother, Edward, left for Washington with the regiment's next detachment. The Seventh took with it "one out of almost every family of standing and respectability," noted Virginia: many "delicately nurtured, fastidious boys" were volunteering to fight.

Not Pierpont, who apparently shared Junius's feeling that the American form of government had failed. Virginia was still arguing with him several months later in defense of the Constitution. He spent the spring and summer of 1861 handling cotton sales, railroad bonds, and Southern state bonds for Peabody & Co., and forwarding loans from London to the War Secretary in Washington. At a sale to raise money for the Union he bought copies of Asher B. Durand's *Sketches from Nature*, Henry Inman's *Black Your Boots Sir*, and James Suydam's *Moonlight*.

In Medford, Massachusetts, that spring, an exultant John Pierpont turned out sheaves of poetry urging the North to victory in bloody battle, and over the summer persuaded Massachusetts Governor John Andrew to get him a job as a Union army chaplain. At age seventy-six, the old crusader—whose second marriage had turned out to be everything he hoped—marched off to war. "Well done! hero of 76!" cheered his son John.

Chaplain Pierpont of the 22nd Massachusetts Volunteers did not prove to be much of a soldier. From a tent pitched at Hall's Hill on "the 'seceded soil of Virginia,' " he described his camp life to John, Jr.: "alone by day and night, in a cotton cloth tent, without window or floor other than the ground, without a seat beside my camp bed, without a light . . . without a fire . . . with the most jejune of all possible diet [boiled potatoes, hard biscuit fired in salted swine fat, less than two ounces of meat in two weeks]. But *n'importe*. There is employment connected with it, useful employment, *work* to which while in camp, I feel myself competent, and by which I have some faint and forlorn hope that my country may be served." Even that faint hope gave way as the temperature dropped and the aged warrior found himself "tramping and puffing up and down Hall's Hill" at 3:00 A.M. to keep warm. Concluding that it was not his duty to self, family, or country to "get my *living* by freezing myself to *death*," he resigned his commission and took a desk job in the Treasury Department under Secretary Salmon P. Chase. Reunited with his wife, he crowed to John from Washington: "I am here in the service and *pay* of the United States at $100 a month."

His youngest son, James, was in the service and pay of the other side. Now married to Eliza Jane Purse, the daughter of a Savannah businessman who kept him in line with an "iron rod," James signed up with the 1st Georgia Cavalry and rode off to war. He would never know the fate of the little song he had composed in 1850 called "One Horse Open Sleigh." Published in Boston in 1857, then again as "Jingle Bells, or the One Horse Open Sleigh" in 1859, it did not gain widespread popularity until the twentieth century, and James died in 1893. Locally, he earned renown for the tunes he wrote to cheer on the Confederacy in the early 1860s—"We Conquer or Die" and "Strike for the South."

———

Late in the summer of 1861, Pierpont took part in a business deal that provoked years of controversy. In the wake of the Union defeat at Fort Sumter in April, the ill-prepared Northern army urgently needed guns. A man named Arthur Eastman, who later described himself as not in any regular business but "familiar with firearms and ordnance," had located five thousand breechloading rifles called Hall Carbines, left over from the Mexican War, in a federal warehouse on Governors Island off the southern tip of Manhattan. In May, Eastman offered to alter the obsolete guns for the army and bring them up to modern standard. Ordnance Chief James W. Ripley considered them worthless and turned him down, observing that alterations generally made things worse. Eastman then proposed to buy the carbines outright, and Ripley agreed to sell the lot for $3.50 each—but Eastman did not have the necessary $17,500.

After the Union suffered a second defeat, at Bull Run on July 22, Lincoln ordered his armies in the west to take the offensive. General John C. Frémont, the new commander of the Western Department (and Buchanan's 1856 opponent for the presidency), began buying arms for his troops from anyone who had them to sell. One of his agents, a New York lawyer named Simon Stevens, learned that Eastman had five thousand carbines at his disposal, and contracted to buy them for $12.50 each ($62,500), with an advance of $20,000. Like Eastman, however, Stevens did not have ready cash.

He telegraphed General Frémont on August 5, offering to sell him five thousand 58-caliber carbines—altered and brought up to government standard—for $22 each. When Frémont agreed to these terms by return wire and ordered the guns sent to Missouri at once, Stevens had to admit that the rifles were not *yet* up to standard: he could send them right away for $21 each, or have them fixed and send the first lot, as originally priced, in ten days. Frémont told him to proceed with the alterations, and "hurry up."

Eastman had agreed to pay the government $17,500 for guns that Stevens would buy from him for $62,500 and sell back to the government for $110,000. But neither man had the means to set the deal in motion.

In early August, Stevens applied to Pierpont Morgan, who lent him $20,000 on the security of General Frémont's purchase order.* On August 7, Morgan went with Eastman and Stevens to the arsenal on Governors Island. He made out a draft to the officer in charge for $17,486, in exchange for 4,996 carbines, and a second draft to Eastman for $2,514—a total of $20,000. He would lend Stevens the remaining $42,500 due Eastman in twenty days, *if* he had begun to receive government payments. The guns would remain in the federal warehouse in his name, as security for his loan, until Eastman could have them altered.

The alterations took longer than expected. The first shipment of 2,500 guns went off to Frémont in St. Louis at the end of August. Morgan then decided to remove himself from the deal, and Junius's former partner Morris Ketchum agreed to take his place. On September 10, Frémont's ordnance officer in St. Louis paid Morgan $55,550 for 2,500 re-rifled carbines ($22 each plus packing and freight). Morgan deducted $26,344 to cover his own advances, interest, and commission, and sent the balance to Messrs. Ketchum, Son & Co. He had earned about 9 percent interest ($156) on his $20,000 loan, and a commission of $5,400—more than 25 percent.

An interest rate of 9 percent was not unusual in the late summer of 1861. A 25 percent commission was. Morgan knew that Stevens desperately needed financing and stood to earn substantial profit. Probably no commercial bank would have issued the loan that summer, since money in the North was tight. Under the circumstances, the two men probably agreed to a profit-sharing reward for the banker who financed the deal.

By the time Morgan released the rest of the arms for shipment in mid-September, he was no longer part of the transaction. Stevens sent the guns to Frémont with a bill for $58,175. On September 26, the general certified that

---

* Stevens probably knew Morgan through family connections. His brother, Henry, was an American book dealer in London who worked for George Peabody and Junius Morgan, and their sister was the Sophia Stevens who had thrown Pierpont out of class in Hartford for laughing. In 1854 George Peabody hired Henry Stevens to set up a library for his hometown of South Danvers, Massachusetts. The dealer offered to supply books at either a shilling or a pound per volume. Peabody chose the shilling-a-volume selection. Stevens reported that Peabody often asked him, "How are books today?"—as if their value fluctuated like the price of cotton or shares in the Illinois Central.

the guns had arrived "in good order," but the bill could not be paid "for want of funds." By early October, when Ketchum presented Frémont's certificate of indebtedness to the War Department, a congressional committee was investigating profiteering in military supplies, and all arms payments had stopped.

The committee's 1862 report concluded that "no public functionary of sane mind" would have had the government buy for $110,000 arms that it had just agreed to sell for $17,500—and that even exigencies of war did not justify a charge of $22 for these rifles.

Simon Stevens and Morris Ketchum did not agree. Ripley, thinking the guns worthless, sold them for $3.50; Frémont, a thousand miles away and fighting, thought them worth $22 when brought up to standard. Differing perceptions of value are the basis of all free trade, and when the War Department offered a settlement of $11,000 in June 1862, Ketchum and Stevens sued for the full $58,175. Ketchum argued that bankers in wartime had to rely on vouchers such as Frémont's agreement to buy guns from Stevens, and that no one would risk lending to the war effort if such contracts could be annulled or altered after funds had been advanced. The Supreme Court ruled in December 1867, on an appeal from the Court of Claims, that the government was bound to honor Frémont's telegraphed contract with Stevens. The War Department paid Stevens $58,175, plus accrued interest.

Pierpont Morgan never explained his decisions to take part in or get out of this deal. Morris Ketchum testified that in late August 1861 "Mr. Morgan had not sufficient funds under his control to continue his advances"—which may have been true temporarily, but he surely had access to more. Morgan, like Ketchum, probably saw the loan in purely commercial terms, as involving some risk and reasonably assured reward. The moral question that outraged those who considered it profiteering most likely did not enter his calculations.

R. Gordon Wasson, a vice president at J. P. Morgan & Co., Inc., who wrote a book about these events in 1941, claimed that Pierpont had not realized Stevens was selling the government its own arms, and that once he found out, he could no longer stomach the deal. Since Morgan made his loan based on the security of the Frémont telegrams, and since he accompanied Eastman and Stevens to buy the guns from the federal arsenal, he clearly knew the nature of the transaction from the outset. And Morris Ketchum was an old family friend. If Morgan had developed a sudden distaste for the sale, he would not have handed it over to this associate.

The most likely explanation for his withdrawal from the Hall Carbine affair in September 1861 is that he was about to marry Memie and leave for Europe, and wanted to settle his accounts before he left. If the deal had been completed as planned, he would have earned his fees and been free of obligation by the end of August. When the alteration work dragged on, delaying the government's payment, it probably seemed a good idea to get out.

Once clear of the Hall Carbine loan, Pierpont focused all his attention on Memie, who had come down with one respiratory ailment after another. She divided her time that summer between Fairfield and the Osborns' new house in Garrison, determined to conquer her "dreadful debility." At the end of August, racked by chills, fevers, chest pain, and a relentless cough, she told Pierpont she was too sick to marry him. He dismissed her fears: after the wedding, he would take her to the Mediterranean to rest in the sun and get well.

Jonathan Sturges, also wondering whether the marriage should proceed, consulted Junius by mail. The senior Morgan had not been expecting his son to leave New York. He replied that an absence "at this particular juncture would be a sacrifice to [Pierpont] and also some inconvenience and disappointment to us in view of the different matters which he has in charge." Still, he thought the two fathers should not see the matter only in that light. Pierpont's future was clearly "bound up" in Memie—"she of all others possesses those qualities of heart and mind best calculated to make his life happy." In view of Memie's health and the "future welfare and happiness of our children," Junius gave his "cheerful assent to the marriage"—not without touching again on its cost to him—"even though it should involve greater sacrifice than is now supposed." Jim Goodwin would handle Pierpont's work while the young couple took their therapeutic honeymoon.

A week before the wedding, Memie's fits of paroxysmal coughing were followed by turns of "violent retching worse than any seasickness I ever had," she told her mother from Garrison. She slept badly, took long naps during the day, and felt queasy from the porter (dark beer) her doctors prescribed. She worried about how she would look for the ceremony, since "my face in repose is so very very thin." When Virginia suggested she keep the veil over her face, Memie was delighted: it would be such "a relief not to have so many eyes upon me."

Juliet Morgan came from London with Sarah for the wedding—they would spend the winter in the house Pierpont had rented for himself and his bride, at 42 West 21st Street, while the newlyweds traveled. Goodwins trooped down from Hartford, and the Reverend Pierpont came from Boston on his way to active duty in Virginia. The day before her wedding, Memie took Communion with Pierpont at St. George's Church. He wrote on the flyleaf of her Book of Common Prayer, "Memie from Pierpont. St. Georges. Communion Sunday. Octo. 6, 1861."

Monday, October 7, was sunny and clear. A small wedding party gathered in the Sturgeses' flower-filled front parlor at 10:00 A.M. Pierpont had grown a mustache, which added a couple of years to his appearance. Memie looked pale and fragile in a dress of ivory-colored, watered ribbed silk, hand-sewn in Paris, with wide "pagoda" sleeves, a full skirt, bustle, and train. Its fitted, high-necked bodice came to deep points in front and back, emphasizing her tiny waist. She did keep the veil over her face throughout the brief service, occasionally leaning on Pierpont's arm for support. Everyone watched her for signs of strain.

Her parents gave a party that afternoon, and Memie rested most of the next day. On October 9, as John Pierpont's Massachusetts regiment marched down 14th Street, Mr. and Mrs. Pierpont Morgan and a maid named Anna McAfferty sailed from New York Harbor on the *Persia*. Pierpont sent Mr. Sturges a note by pilot boat from Sandy Hook: "Memie is very bright & cheerful—& rabid for lunch. She is very much better than I feared & has borne the partings remarkably well. Love to all from herself and myself. Yours in great haste . . ."

———

Crossing the turbulent autumn Atlantic, Memie felt better than she had in months. She slept through the night without coughing, and was the only woman on board to appear at every meal. The couple stopped briefly in London to consult the eminent physician Sir Henry Holland. Junius said Pierpont's mustache made him look as if he ought to get up early and call the roll.

In Paris, Memie was examined by lung specialists Armand Trousseau and Jules A. Béclard, who told Pierpont she had tuberculosis. This news "came upon me most unexpectedly," he told Mr. Sturges, and he did not share it with his wife. Her left lung seemed worse than the right. There was no cure, but the doctors hoped she might improve with rest, a remedial diet, and warm air.*

Knowing without a diagnosis that she was extremely ill, Memie dutifully followed the experts' instructions. She took a small pellet of turpentine after every meal—"quite tasteless," she reported to her mother, "until melted in the stomach & then I *like* the slight flavor." Turpentine was supposed to "lessen the great accumulation of mucus which I almost vomit (so loose & abundant is it) night & morning"—and also to calm the "feverishness which follows my internal shakes." In addition, she swallowed cod liver oil, a teaspoon of "nice jelly" twice a day, and asses' milk whenever she could get it. The one prescription she objected to was painting her left shoulder with iodine: she often forgot, and soon let it go, trusting to "the lovely air, nourishing food, the above medicines & most loving care."

She had only praise for the provider of this loving care. Pierpont carried her up seven flights of stairs one day in Paris. "It is an anxious charge for him," she told her parents, "& at present I can do but little to repay him." Another day: "I wish you could see his loving devoted care of me, he spares nothing for my

———

* Scientists did not discover the rod-shaped tubercle bacillus until 1882, and did not find an effective cure until the 1950s.

comfort & improvement." He took solitary walks through the romantic city, and brought back flowers, her favorite foods, and a foot warmer lined in velvet.

In early November the honeymooners proceeded south to Algiers, where the Mediterranean sun glinted off turrets and whitewashed walls. Memie loved sitting in the open French doors of their bedroom at the Hôtel de la Régence, watching the street life in the square below, reading and writing letters in air "soft as July." The proprietor sent up fresh fruit and flowers every day.

Her menstrual periods had stopped that summer, probably because she had lost so much weight. From Algiers five weeks after her wedding she confided to her mother that though her "*visitor*" had not returned, the Paris physicians thought it just as well, given the state of her health. "Now don't beloved Mother *fancy anything else* for such is not the case." Memie's certainty that she was not pregnant suggests that her marriage may not have been consummated: perhaps doctors had advised the couple to wait until the rest cure restored her strength.

Pierpont went out riding every day, jumping fences and "scouring" the Algerian countryside. At the beginning of December, Memie's health took a sharp turn for the worse. She came down with intestinal trouble, and "nervous" fevers set in every afternoon. Having felt better crossing the ocean than at any point since leaving home, she now longed for the sea: "I think oh if some one only would take me in their arms & lay me down upon a ship at sea."

Someone did take her in his arms and carry her down to the town square every morning to sit in the sun, then back upstairs to rest. He ordered special foods from Marseilles, brought home roses, geraniums, and mignonette, took her for drives in the afternoons, roasted apples in their fireplace, and, as he had done for himself in the Azores, bought birds to keep her company—two nightingales and three canaries. Memie could have enjoyed all this if she were well, she told her mother, "but I believe that when anyone has a nervous fever upon them everything looks dark and sometimes one's spirit even rebels against the dispensation of a loving all wise God." Though having a "kind and loving husband makes me happy in spite of many adverse circumstances," she missed her family intensely, being so ill so far from home: "it is only 9 weeks today since we were married & it seems a year."

Mrs. Sturges had offered to join them if Pierpont thought it necessary. He hesitated to have her cross the winter Atlantic, but Memie was now too weak to stand or get dressed—he and Mrs. McAfferty had to help her walk across the room—and so thin that lying down made her bones ache. In late December, certain at last that she needed her mother's care, he asked Mrs. Sturges to come, telegraphing Junius to write for him, since the message would reach New York faster from London than Algiers. Jonathan Sturges was deeply worried about his daughter, but questioned the urgency of the situation in light of

Pierpont's hypochondria: "*he* is very easily alarmed when *he* is sick or any one else[;] so is his Father."

As if in answer to this charge, Pierpont followed Junius's letter with a long explanation of his own: "I do not wish to alarm you," he told Mr. Sturges, "nor do I think there is any immediate danger but I should not think I was doing right to hide from you the true state of her health. I can but feel that she is very sick." He blamed her rapid deterioration on the Algerian climate—and himself: "The greatest mistake I ever made was coming here at all. I fear it will take all winter to bring our dear Memie back to where she was when she arrived. . . ."

Sharing her hopes for a sea cure, he booked passage for three on a steamer to Marseilles. When his party arrived at the Algiers harbor, however, the ship's captain took one look and refused to let them board; he did not think Memie would survive the trip. The trio returned in defeat to the hotel, and Pierpont resumed his sad report to Mr. Sturges: "I cannot hide from myself that Memie is very *very* sick." The disease in her left lung had progressed with "fearful rapidity"—acute consumption such as Memie's was said to "gallop"—and a local homeopath said the right lung had worsened as well: "I need not tell you what a blow it is to me & I know it will be to you & yours. We can only trust & hope although it may be against hope that our Heavenly Father may yet let the cup pass with out our drinking. . . . I hope I may say His will not ours be done."

At last he informed his wife of the Paris doctors' diagnosis. She was too ill to be much affected by the news, he told her father, and continued "most hopeful and happy, although the tears frequently come into her eyes when she thinks of herself so sick away from you all." He anxiously awaited Mrs. Sturges's arrival. "I don't know what we would do without Mrs. McAfferty—she nurses Memie most devotedly & as Memie is now so weak that she requires such tender nursing as only women can give I am compelled most reluctantly to yield my place."

Mary Sturges left New York on January 15 with her son Edward, who was on military leave. At Queenstown (now Cobh, the seaport on the southwest coast of Ireland) they found a letter from Junius saying the younger Morgans had somehow crossed the Mediterranean to Nice. Mary and Edward went quickly through London and Paris to Marseilles, where they caught a steamer to Nice. On February 2, Pierpont met them at the dock and drove them up a winding, stone-walled road to their Niçoise residence, the Villa St. Georges. Set amid groves of olive, orange, and lime, it had a spectacular view of the snow-covered Maritime Alps. Canaries flew around freely in a plant-filled conservatory off Mrs. Sturges's room, and the pair of nightingales lived in a little salon adjoining Amelia's. On warm days Pierpont had been wheeling his wife out to the gates of the villa in a Bath chair, then back through rose gardens and shady lanes of trees. When it was colder, he built wood fires indoors. By the time her mother arrived, Memie rarely felt up to going out. Her cough kept her awake most nights; she slept during the day.

Junius had been urging his son to come to London to discuss business, and four days after the Sturgeses arrived, Pierpont left. Mary Sturges wrote to him daily, reporting on the alternating good and bad spells to which he had become all too accustomed. "We miss him very much," she noted in her diary.

The news from New York was largely about the war. "Whenever we are not absorbed in anxiety about our dear absent ones," wrote Virginia in February, "our country's troubles take up all our thoughts." The North had just had its first real triumph: General Ulysses S. Grant and Flag Officer Andrew Foote had blocked the advance of the rebel army up the Mississippi River, and captured two Confederate forts on the Kentucky-Tennessee border. Encouraged by strong expressions of Union feeling in Tennessee and northern Alabama, Virginia continued: "What a feeling of thanksgiving will thrill through our country if we see a prospect of *soon* quelling this terrible rebellion."

She had a special message for her brother-in-law: "Tell Pierpont I begin to hope that I shall be able to prove to him that the Constitution is *not* a failure but a very good thing to live under, that we *have* a government strong in the affections of the people, wherever its present representatives may stand, and that before you all return from Europe you may be proud to call yourselves citizens of the United States."

Most people expected the fighting to be over by spring. Jonathan Sturges asked his wife to "tell Ed he'll miss all the glory if he don't get back soon."

———

Memie lost what little strength she had during the ten days of Pierpont's absence. Her cough grew worse, and her mouth so sore she could eat only egg whites and bouillon with rice. In London, Junius urged his son to stay a few more days, but Pierpont was desperate to get back to Nice. He made the journey in forty-eight hours, arriving, exhausted, early Sunday morning, February 16. Memie "threw her wasted arms around his neck and kissed him so lovingly," reported her mother.

He sat with his wife all day, yielding his place to Mrs. Sturges and Anna only when he went to bed. At midnight, Memie ordered her mother to sleep. Six hours later Mary was back. "Oh Mother," said Memie, "Annie and I have had a hard night." Mary sent Anna to bed, and fed her daughter fresh eggs, warm barley water, and her own special tea.

"As I knelt by her side and bent over her hand she said, 'Oh Mother you are praying for me it is so sweet to think so.' " Memie then seemed to sleep, although she kept opening her eyes. Suddenly, at 8:30, she began to breathe strangely, and her expression changed. "I tried to raise her," continued Mrs. Sturges, "and called Anna; as soon as she looked at her she said death was in her face. I ran to call Pierpont he got down just in time to see her breathing her last. Eddie did not get into the room till after she was gone. Poor Pierpont knelt by her in an agony of grief calling upon her only to speak to him once more."

It rained all day. Pierpont went out to telegraph the news to his father.

No one slept much that night at the Villa St. Georges. On Tuesday, a nurse embalmed the body—"Mr. Morgan not very well," wrote Mrs. Sturges in her diary—and on Thursday an Anglican Reverend C. Childers came to conduct a private funeral service. He read from Saint Paul's Epistle to the Philippians (1:21–24): "For to me to live is Christ, and to die is gain. But if I live in the flesh, this is the fruit of my labour: yet what I shall choose I wot not. For I am in a strait betwixt two, having a desire to depart, and to be with Christ; which is far better: Nevertheless to abide in the flesh is more needful for you."

Pierpont marked this passage in Memie's Bible. At the beginning of its New Testament he wrote, "Amelia S. Morgan. Died at the Villa St. Georges near Nice France at 8:30 a.m. Monday February 17, 1862. 'Her end was peace.' " In the prayer book he had inscribed to her the day before their wedding, he now added: " 'I go to prepare a place for you.' "

———

Junius wrote as soon as he received his son's wire. "I cannot tell you how much I am grieved by the sad, sad intelligence conveyed in your telegram. . . . I have, as you know, taken a gloomy view of our dear Memie's case, but was wholly unprepared for the sudden termination of it. It is a hard blow for you my Dear Son—but I feel sure you will resign the precious one into her Saviour's arms without a murmur. He gave her to you and has taken her away."

Knowing that Pierpont blamed himself for having taken Memie to Algiers—and for having failed to save her—Junius resumed the next day: "It is not my Dear Son well to go back to second causes in such cases." Nothing could have made the outcome different. He had just seen Sir Henry Holland, who said he knew in October that Memie's case was "hopeless," and her early death therefore a blessing. "We know that our lives and all that we have are in the hands of a kind Heavenly Parent who never afflicts but for our good."

Junius took consolation in thinking of "the great comfort to Memie that her Mother was with her during the last weeks of her life." He did not mention that his own demands had kept her husband from being with her during her last days. He offered to come to Nice at once if he could be "of any service"—an offer his son declined. Pierpont was not ready to resign his wife to her Saviour without a murmur, nor to submit to the Heavenly Parent who never afflicts but for our own good—and he may not just then have felt up to his earthly parent's moral cheerleading.

It took nearly three weeks for news of Memie's death to reach New York, and three more for condolences to return. While they remained in Nice, her husband, mother, and brother had the sad task of reading hopeful letters from home, many addressed to her.

From the rooms Pierpont had prepared for his bride on 21st Street, his mother joined the chorus of those who urged him to take comfort in Memie's release from suffering—"We would not call her back for she is with the blessed loved ones who have gone before." Then in mid-condolence she placed a shopping order: "I wish you could get Sarah & myself some of Bondier's Gloves Black double buttons—I cannot find a pair my number here—6 3/4 long fingers—Sarah's 6 1/2 short fingers—and what there are, are 1.50 per pair."

At the Villa St. Georges, Pierpont, Edward, Mary, and Anna McAfferty packed up their own and Memie's belongings. Memie's body lay in a vault at the Church of the Vaudois until Edward took the coffin and all their trunks down to Marseilles and sent them on, with a courier, to New York. The mourners left Nice early on February 26 in the pouring rain. For weeks they traveled slowly through Italy and France, united in grief. Pierpont was twenty-four years old.

PART II

—

HEIR
APPARENT

On the whole . . . [Henry Adams] thought he had done as well as his neighbors. No one could yet guess which of his contemporaries was most likely to play a part in the great world. A shrewd prophet in Wall Street might perhaps have set a mark on Pierpont Morgan, but hardly on the Rockefellers or William C. Whitney or Whitelaw Reid. No one would have picked out William McKinley or John Hay or Mark Hanna for great statesmen. Boston was ignorant of the careers in store for Alex. Agassiz and Henry Higginson. Phillips Brooks was unknown; Henry James was unheard; Howells was new; Richardson and LaFarge were struggling for a start. Out of any score of names and reputations that should reach beyond the century, the thirty-year-olds who were starting in the year 1867 could show none that was so far in advance as to warrant odds in its favor.

The Education of Henry Adams

Pierpont in mourning, 1862.
(Archives of The Pierpont Morgan Library, New York)

Chapter 7

QUESTIONS OF CONTROL

Pierpont planned to stay abroad until April with Mary and Edward Sturges when Junius sent word in March that his presence in New York was "absolutely necessary." Jim Goodwin seemed about to break down under the strain of business he was trying to handle alone. Pierpont took reluctant leave of his mother-in-law—she would wait until the winter Atlantic calmed down—and promised Jim by mail: "together I think we shall make matters work nicely." He hoped "constant occupation" would keep his mind from "dwelling on the sad, sad scenes of the past few months."

When he reached New York, he moved in with Jim and Frank Goodwin on Irving Place. His mother and sister were still in the house he had rented for himself and Memie on 21st Street, which was just as well: living there that spring would have been too painful a daily reminder of his loss. Photographed in widower's black shortly after his return, he looks solemn, Byronic, and slightly stunned.

Memie's burial service took place in Fairfield on May 3, a bright spring day with magnolias and pear trees in bloom. Pierpont had ordered a pink-marble gravestone in Italy, inscribed "Not Lost But Gone Before." Juliet and Sarah left for England shortly after the service. "Pierpont took tea here, very sad & desponding," reported Mary Sturges in mid-May. The next day, "Heard Pierpont sick, went to see him, bad cold and sore throat." A week later his body was covered with sores. His physician, suspecting smallpox, ordered him quarantined. As the sores began to clear up, the doctor changed the diagnosis to varioloid, a

mild form of smallpox. By mid-June Pierpont was back at his office and spending weekends in the country with his in-laws. Probably at Jonathan Sturges's
urging, he joined the Century Association, the group of artists, writers, and
patrons that had begun as the Sketch Club.

At the beginning of September 1862 he formed a partnership at 53 Exchange Place with Jim. Ten years earlier the cousins had conducted mock deals
as the fictional Goodwin, Morgan & Co. Now, in an accurate reflection of their
relative professional stature, they called the new firm J. Pierpont Morgan & Co.
(Jim said later, "I was the Co.") Their work consisted chiefly of trading government bonds and foreign exchange, and reporting to London on American
prices and politics. The war had suspended cotton exports, curtailed iron imports, and led foreign investors to dump American securities. Railroad construction declined from 1,500 miles in 1860 to 574 in 1864. Client defaults
and the perils of wartime finance made Junius more cautious than ever; he
would handle only reputable accounts and heavily collateralized loans.
Peabody & Co.'s stock and bond business, having earned £36,493 profit in
1860, showed £13,910 in losses the following year, and £5,771 more in 1862.

With the patronage of the federal government and the boost of wartime demand, however, certain kinds of business were booming in the fall of 1862.
Feeding the Union army stimulated Chicago's meatpacking industry, slaughterhouses, and banks. Textile mills stepped up production to meet military demand, as did makers of boots and shoes. The price of wheat went up. Pierpont
reported to London on the "tremendous traffic" and abundant earnings of the
Illinois Central, the Erie, and the New York Central railroads, as they ferried
troops and supplies, and he characterized stocks after the Union victory at
Antietam that September as "rampant." European investors began returning
to the market.

Pierpont accompanied New York Republican boss Thurlow Weed to Washington in mid-September to see Treasury Secretary Salmon P. Chase about securing the right to issue government bonds. Chase had been raising money by
auctioning bonds to small groups of brokers and bankers, but as the cost of the
war escalated he needed a larger, more efficient system. Pierpont reported to
Junius that his visit proved useless—"Chase was as firm as it was possible to
be." In October the government chose the Philadelphia house of Jay Cooke &
Co. to sell its securities on commission. Cooke organized the first mass-market,
national bond-sale campaign, pricing some of the issues low enough for ordinary people to buy. By 1864 he had floated over $360 million of government
bonds. Peabody & Co. traded heavily in the secondary market for these bonds
between 1862 and 1866, chiefly through Pierpont in New York. They did
£229,200 (just over $1 million) worth of business in U.S. loans, earning a
profit of £16,600 ($83,000).

The hard work that Pierpont hoped would keep his mind off Memie's death wore him out. Late in the summer of 1862 he came down with such severe headaches that his friends and doctors urged him to take a vacation. Trying the water cure at Saratoga Springs in September, he found his anxiety at being away "worse than when on the spot." The problem, he explained to his father in a rare moment of self-examination, lay not in external circumstances: "The wear & tear upon me does not arise from deficiency in help the fault is with myself & myself only—it is my nature & I cannot help it. When I have responsibility laid upon me I cannot throw it upon anyone else however competent the party may be. I am never satisfied until I either do everything myself or personally supervise every thing done even to an entry in the books. This I cannot help—my habit since I have been in business has been so & I cannot learn to do otherwise." This "habit," though Pierpont complained about its toll, served him well as he learned about the business of finance. His minute attention to detail and inability to delegate had to do with both his own desire for control and Junius's exacting surveillance. They also reflected his perfectionism and instinctive assumption of command. Later commentators would disagree as to whether he was a "detail" or a "big picture" man. He was both. In these early years he made himself master of every penny on the ledger and every aspect of every deal he made. As the range of his affairs grew too wide for one man to manage, he would be forced to delegate technicalities to lieutenants—although he complained of finding mistakes in the books, and once said he could sit down at any desk in the office and take up wherever the clerk had left off.

Pierpont's own health problems had markedly subsided during his years with Memie. After she died, his troubles returned, and he began to have mysterious "nervous" breakdowns, periodically collapsing with headaches, depressions, and exhaustion. For all his prodigious energy, he felt unable during these episodes to carry the weight of responsibility he had assumed. That the limits to what he could do were set by these troubles paradoxically took a certain kind of control out of his hands. It was no failure of will but his refractory health (always an effective card to play with Junius) that kept him from doing more. "My place I know & feel is at my post," he told his father in September 1862. "I have no desire to leave it so long as I hold out in strength or ability to attend to its duties."

Pierpont went to Fairfield for his wedding anniversary in October to put flowers on Memie's grave. In private, he copied out poems about love and loss. One, called "Fading," begins:

> Once a lovely flower grew near me
> And entwined around my heart
> But it withered, and in sadness
> I was doomed from it to part . . .

Late that fall he moved into 42 West 21st Street with Jim Goodwin. He had bought furnishings from the young German cabinetmaker and decorator Gustave Herter, who was beginning to adapt European styles of interior design for affluent New York. The Sturgeses came for dinner just before Christmas, to "the sweet little home prepared for our darling child," mourned Mary. Pierpont had mementos everywhere. "Poor fellow!" his mother-in-law continued: "he cherishes everything belonging to *her*."

———

Between 1862 and 1865 Abraham Lincoln presided over a consolidation of federal power that would have delighted the ghost of Alexander Hamilton. Free of opposition from the Democratic South, the Republican administration and Congress enacted measures that encouraged economic expansion and transferred political power from the states to the federal government. They gave away huge tracts of public land to facilitate railroad construction, encouraged immigration, passed a homestead act, established a system of land-grant colleges, imposed tariffs to protect Northern industry from foreign competition, levied taxes, issued millions of dollars in paper currency, borrowed millions more by selling government bonds, and created a national system of federally chartered banks answerable to the Treasury.*

The Morgans would be among the primary beneficiaries of this profound transformation, but like most of their contemporaries, they did not see it coming in the early years of the war.

Union armies suffered terrible losses in the summer of 1862. Pierpont reported to Junius that fall as the government floundered: "Dissatisfaction with the Administration at Washington continues to increase – distrust as to the capability of the cabinet is very generally felt & a change is loudly clamored for." Junius attributed the "disasters" of the Northern cause to "the most flagrant incapacity on the part of those in power both in the Army and at Washington."

Henry Adams, serving as private secretary to his father, the American minister in London, found English society "demented" and "altogether beside itself" on the subject of the American President. After the Republicans lost quite badly in the 1862 elections, Mary Sturges reported: "All are against the Administration." An agonized Lincoln told a friend in December: "If there is a worse place than Hell, I am in it." Not until the spring of 1863 did Americans begin to feel, according to Adams, that "somewhere behind the chaos in Washington, power was taking shape."

---

* The government set up a Bureau of Internal Revenue and taxed income for the first time, at 3 to 5 percent, in August 1861; the tax was phased out in 1872 and not imposed again until 1914.

On January 1, 1863, Lincoln issued the Emancipation Proclamation. In March, Congress passed a Conscription Act requiring able-bodied men aged twenty to forty-five to serve in the Union army. Only a couple of Pierpont Morgan's letters from 1863 have survived, and in them he says nothing about these events. There was no question of his going to war. Junius considered his son's presence on Wall Street essential to the conduct of their joint business. Like many of his contemporaries, Pierpont paid a substitute $300 to go in his place. Other draft-age Northerners who did not see military service included Theodore Roosevelt, Sr., John D. Rockefeller, Andrew Carnegie, Elihu Root, Philip Armour, Jay Gould, Jim Fisk, Collis P. Huntington, and Jay Cooke. Dozens of young men in the Morgans' social vicinity *did* fight, among them Memie's brothers Edward and Fred, Oliver Wendell Holmes, Jr., Charles Russell Lowell, Robert Gould Shaw, Thomas Wentworth Higginson, Charles Francis Adams, Jr., and Robertson and Garth Wilkinson James. Yet not all the potential soldiers even in Boston abolitionist families went to war: William and Henry James stayed home; Henry Adams did not fight, but served as secretary to his father, the American minister in London.

When Republican conscription officers began drawing names for the New York draft in July 1863, the men most likely to be called—predominantly the Democratic Irish poor—went on a rampage. They attacked draft offices, federal buildings, Republican newspaper offices, and abolitionists' houses. Spotting prosperous-looking men on the street, they shouted "Down with the rich" and "There goes a $300 man." Henry Sturges wrote in his diary on July 15: "Fearful and disgraceful riot in New York. Colored people burnt alive [in the Colored] Orphan Asylum." There is no record of Pierpont's thoughts on the draft riots or his status as a $300 man.

Eighteen months after Memie's death, Pierpont was returning to fuller engagement with life. At the end of July 1863, he organized an expedition with several friends, including Arthur and Henry Sturges and Edward Ketchum, Morris's son. The party started at West Point, proceeded by train and stagecoach to Lake George in the Adirondacks, and continued mostly by sailboat to Lake Champlain. From Burlington, Vermont, they drove across the state to New Hampshire's White Mountains. Pierpont swam, sailed, rode, and one day climbed both Cannon Mountain and Mount Lafayette. Another day, he won a race up Mount Washington, beating Henry Sturges by a neck.

In business he was flourishing—conducting joint-account operations with his father's firm and, on his own, issuing short-term loans, trading foreign exchange, brokering securities, and financing commodity trades. His share of the net profits at J. P. Morgan & Co. rose from $30,000 in 1862 to $58,000 in 1863. A special account on the firm's books lists $300 he spent on cigars for himself and his father in 1863—exactly the cost of a substitute soldier.

His earnings nearly doubled at the height of the war. Others around him fared even better. There were said to be twenty millionaires in America in 1843, and two decades later over a hundred in New York alone.* Junius continued to preach and practice caution, but Pierpont was not listening. In the fall of 1863 he took part in a market manipulation that brought down the paternal wrath.

To help finance the enormously expensive war, Congress had passed a Legal Tender Act early in 1862 authorizing paper dollars called "greenbacks" to circulate as currency; the first modern fiat money issued by the U.S. government effectively put the North on a double monetary standard of paper and gold. There was no official link between the greenback dollar and gold, and neither currency traded at a fixed price. Still, gold was always worth more than paper: it was a relatively scarce precious metal, and served as the medium of foreign trade, which meant that international markets determined its value. Paper dollars had no intrinsic value, and could be printed whenever the government needed more.† As a result, the exchange rate between gold and greenbacks was highly sensitive to political events. If the Northern armies did badly, investors bought gold in a "flight to quality," driving up the price. When good news from the front brought hopes of peace, hoarders sold gold and the price fell.

Pierpont was ideally situated to follow these fluctuations as he traded domestic and international exchange. He had reported to Peabody & Co. in the fall of 1862 that gold, "which governs in a great measure the exchange market, has now become a speculative value at the Stock Exchange and is consequently as variable as the most speculative shares upon the list. . . . Favourable news from the seat of war naturally makes the price fall while the contrary produces the opposite result."

Late in the summer of 1863 he began quietly buying gold on joint account with Edward Ketchum, a member of his expedition to the mountains that July. By early October they had accumulated a cache worth over $2 million, financing the venture by borrowing against the gold, and betting on being able to sell it for enough to clear the debt and make a profit. In mid-October, they shipped $1.15 million of their hoard to England, which took the markets by surprise,

---

* In 1863 Alexander T. Stewart, the country's leading dry goods distributor, reported an annual income of over $1.8 million, William B. Astor $838,525, and Cornelius Vanderbilt $680,728.

† Since America's chief trading partner was England, and since the price of the British pound was pegged to gold, the price of gold in greenbacks was essentially the dollar price of £1 sterling. A pound at the beginning of the war was worth $4.86 in gold, but after 1862 the greenback price of gold fluctuated widely. It reached a peak in 1864, when a U.S. trader who wanted to buy £1 worth of gold had to pay $12 in greenbacks.

created a temporary gold shortage in New York, and drove the price up. They sold the rest as the price climbed, netting $132,407—over $66,000 each.

The New York Times reported that the shipment had been made by "a young house in Exchange-place, respectably connected on the other side" of the Atlantic, and went on: "Though shrewdly conceived, this manoeuvre is not wholly new to the market"—a similar attempt by other parties had failed earlier in the year. Wall Street regarded the "manoeuvre" as a clever coup in turbulent times that did not seriously disrupt the markets; those who lost out were chiefly other speculators. The gold corner did no appreciable damage to Pierpont's reputation.* R. G. Dun & Co. a few months later characterized the partners at 53 Exchange Place as able bankers conducting a "first-rate" business.

Pierpont's gambling so outraged Junius, however, that he threatened to sever their professional connection. He objected not to the fact that the gold operation took advantage of the Union's monetary troubles for private gain—which was what other critics charged—but because it constituted evidence of character flaws: willful disobedience, recklessness, and greed.

He was, Junius told Jim Goodwin early in the new year, "disappointed & pained to learn that P. continues his speculations on such a scale notwithstanding my repeated admonitions. His head seems to have been turned by the position he has been able to attain & he thus goes on disregarding any opinion but his own."† Junius examined the New York profits and losses for 1863—together the cousins had earned almost $90,000: Jim $29,000, Pierpont $58,000—and fumed: "Is it not surprising that persons having such a snug good business—giving them without risk or trouble all the profit they ought to desire are willing thus to jeopardise every thing for the purpose of speculating to make a little more[?]" Pierpont's $66,000 extracurricular windfall amounted to a lot more.

Junius said he had felt for some time that his son was neglecting the London business in favor of his own, and that "People who put themselves in position to lose twice their capital by speculation are not safe people to be entrusted with the business of others—to say nothing of their ability to protect & look after such interest." He would not rely on such people—"I decide therefore to transfer from you all our business on the 1st of April"—and closed this tirade to Jim: "I have been made most unhappy by the course your business has taken

* He and Ketchum had bought most of their hoard at around $146 to $147 an ounce. Gold was trading at 148¾ on Saturday, October 10, the day of their shipment. It rose steadily all week to a high of 156⅞, then settled back down to the 140s.

† Junius dated this letter "January 31, 1863," but from internal evidence it appears to have been written in 1864. At the beginning of a new year it often takes weeks to change the force of habit and write the date correctly.

& that P. has so utterly disregarded my warnings. I feel that I have done my duty & shall leave him in the future to act without any such hindrance."

The senior Morgan did not withdraw the London accounts, and did not leave the junior for long without the "hindrance" of paternal advice. Instead, in 1864 and for the next two decades he made sure there was a senior partner in New York keeping a firm hand and eye on his headstrong son.

The elder statesman he brought in that fall was Charles Dabney, the banker who had taught Pierpont accounting at Duncan, Sherman. Pierpont got along well with Mr. Dabney, whose daughter had married his friend Frank Payson. On November 15, 1864, the firm of J. Pierpont Morgan & Co. dissolved, and Dabney, Morgan & Co. opened for business at 53 Exchange Place.

Of the new firm's $350,000 capital, Pierpont and Junius put up $100,000 each, Jim Goodwin and his father $75,000 and $50,000, respectively, and Dabney $25,000. Pierpont and Dabney would each have 40 percent of the profits, Jim 20 percent. Dabney's name and prestige apparently counted for so much that he did not have to contribute a significant share of cash. Junius told the senior Goodwin in December with a practically audible sigh of relief that the new arrangements in New York seemed "*just* right & if they don't make money it is their own fault. All they want is to exercise sound judgement & patience—not to be too eager for business or profits. . . . I don't know of a man better suited for Pierpont & James than Mr. Dabney, or one in whom we all can place more entire reliance."

———

In a message to Congress at the end of 1862, Lincoln had predicted that this "fiery trial through which we pass, will light us down, in honor or dishonor, to the latest generation." Pierpont gave no indication that he felt any sense of dishonor about his actions during the nation's fiery trial. His son-in-law later claimed that Morgan had been exempted from military service by ill health— that fainting spells followed by varioloid in the winter preceding the draft led his doctor to declare him unfit. There is no mention of fainting spells in the Morgan or Sturges papers from this period, and Pierpont had varioloid, from which he recovered completely, in the early summer of 1862. The first draft calls took place a year later. If he had a medical exemption, he would not have been required to hire a substitute, although he might have done it anyway. In the summer of 1863 he was well enough to race Henry Sturges up Mount Washington, and win.

Perhaps it was his son-in-law and not Morgan himself who felt it necessary to "excuse" his nonparticipation in the war on grounds of health. As to Morgan's business activities, Wall Street regarded the Hall Carbine deal and gold speculation as standard transactions in trade, and Junius condemned the latter on practical rather than moral grounds. Both Morgans considered themselves patriots high above the political fray, their sights trained on the nation's long-term economic progress. Only in retrospect did they come to see Lincoln as having presided over a federalist consolidation that was integral to the future they had in mind.

Pierpont eventually viewed everything connected with the Civil War in a sentimental light—particularly its commander in chief. As the conflict receded he collected documents on the death of John Brown, Walt Whitman's war diaries, autographs of leading generals, and battle-scene illustrations by the artists Edwin Forbes, A. R. Waud, and Thomas Nast. He also acquired dozens of documents relating to Lincoln—portraits, letters, legal papers, speech drafts, an 1863 message to Congress about the Freedman's Aid Society, and the manuscript of a twenty-two-stanza poem Lincoln wrote in 1846 called "The Bear Hunt." He bought plaster casts of Lincoln's hands, and in 1910 was offered a letter written by Lincoln in March 1863 to New York's Governor Horatio Seymour. His librarian replied that the letter would be an important addition to the library's collection of Lincoln materials—"As you may know, Mr. Morgan is a great admirer of Lincoln."*

Morgan contributed to private pension funds for Generals Sherman and Grant. In 1873 he joined the Union League Club, founded in 1863 (by Jonathan Sturges, among others) to support the Northern cause; after the war it played an active role in Republican politics, military affairs, and the fine arts. And in 1877, when Congress adjourned without appropriating funds for army and navy salaries, Morgan told the Secretary of War that in view of the government's failure to perform this "obvious and sacred duty," he wanted to prevent "loss and distress" to "a class of men whose interests should in our judgment, command the greatest and most earnest solicitude of the Government and of the Country." He organized a syndicate to furnish the army with $550,000 a month for four months. Congress authorized funding for the military that fall, and repaid the syndicate's $2.2 million with interest. Like Mr. Peabody's underwriting of the American exhibits at the 1851 Crystal Palace fair, Morgan's diplomatic gesture enhanced the reputation of his firm. His great admiration for Lincoln and sense of "sacred duty" to support the men responsible for the nation's defense significantly revised his wartime views.

———

In Junius's ten years with Peabody & Co. the partners had shared £444,468 (roughly $2.2 million) in profits. They suffered their only losses in the first two years of the Civil War; by 1863 earnings were back up to £61,217. George Peabody retired in the fall of 1864. Having spent his entire life making money,

---

* The letter to Seymour turned out to be a copy. The manuscript of "The Bear Hunt" is at the Pierpont Morgan Library.

he directed his energies in retirement to giving it away—nearly $9 million.* On October 1, 1864, his firm was reorganized as J. S. Morgan & Co.

While Junius restructured the Morgan firms in London and New York, Pierpont was making some changes of his own. Early in 1864 he and Jim moved out of the 21st Street house and rented another from Levi P. Morton, on Madison Avenue just north of 38th Street, for $4,500 a year. He hired the firm of Herter Brothers (Gustave had been joined by his half brother, Christian)† to help furnish the interior, though he himself bought $700 worth of bronzes at an auction and various items at the department stores A. T. Stewart and W. & J. Sloane. For domestic help in their bachelor quarters, the cousins had a housekeeper, waitress, and cook.

And toward the end of 1864 Pierpont began to court a young woman named Frances Louisa Tracy, whom he had probably met at St. George's Church. Her father, Charles, had graduated from Yale, read law with the Honorable Joseph Kirkland in Utica, married Kirkland's daughter Louisa, and come to New York to practice law in 1849. Living at 81 East 17th Street, the Tracys had five pretty daughters and a son.

"Fanny" Tracy was taller and larger-boned than Memie Sturges, with a slight underbite and wide-set blue eyes that seemed to take the world in with timid trust. Though not as imaginative or high-spirited as her predecessor in Pierpont's affections, she had a sober, appealing sweetness. She was twenty-two, and he twenty-seven, when they met.

Over the next few months he became a regular caller at 17th Street, and escorted Miss Tracy to concerts, the opera, and church. The day before he left on a trip to the South in March of 1865, he sent her a note saying he would call that evening, since he could not go "without seeing you once more." When he

---

* In London he set up a $2.5 million fund to build public housing for the "industrious poor," later called the Peabody Estates. Queen Victoria offered him a baronetcy to acknowledge England's gratitude; when he declined the honor on the grounds of his U.S. citizenship, she wrote a personal letter thanking him for his "princely munificence," and sent him a portrait miniature of herself. Peabody gave $150,000 to Harvard for a museum of archaeology and ethnology, $150,000 to Yale for a museum and chair in natural history, $140,000 for a museum of science in Salem, Massachusetts, and smaller sums to other U.S. institutes, libraries, and historical societies. After the Civil War he set up a Peabody Southern Education Fund, with $2 million to provide free public schools and improved teacher training in the South. His hometown of South Danvers, Massachusetts, was renamed Peabody in 1868. Also that year, his figure in bronze, by the sculptor William Wetmore Story (an old friend of the Morgans from Hartford), was placed behind London's Royal Exchange. When Peabody died in 1869, the British gave him a funeral at Westminster Abbey, and sent his remains to the United States on the ironclad HMS *Monarch*.

† This Christian Herter was the grandfather of the Massachusetts governor and Secretary of State Christian A. Herter.

appeared after dinner, the Tracys granted the couple a few minutes alone. Pierpont proposed marriage, and Fanny accepted.

They decided to keep the engagement secret until his return, but he imagined that his evident excitement as he said good night "must have left a good many very curious people at No. 81." In Baltimore two days later he started a letter to "My own dear Fannie"—spelling her name his own way: "How strange it seems to be able to write this: to feel that I have a right to say so & to know that it is true, *so* true." He had not heard a word of that morning's sermon in church: "My thoughts Fannie dear were with you and of you as I looked back over the past few months and saw how you have entwined yourself around me, how essential you have become to me, how little happiness I have in any associations except those of which you are the center. I can hardly believe it, but still it is true. I can only throw myself in humble gratitude before Him who has showered upon my poor unworthy head a cup so full, so overflowing with blessings."

People attuned to words tend to find conventional language inadequate for intense emotion, but Pierpont used the standard forms with no apparent unease. He had been so conditioned by Memie's death, Junius's pessimism, and long observation of an unhappy parental marriage that he had more to say about the difficulties this new love would face than about its pleasures. "Oh Fannie do you realize the solemnity of the scene we went through on Friday night," he went on—"do you realize that henceforth our lives are to be as one to each other – that we are to bear one another's joys & sorrow for sorrow will come Fannie, that we are to sustain each other in every difficulty and that our hearts must always be as an open book to the other, no doubt no fear unknown & unshared by the other[?]" Although such union was a "fearful mistery" [*sic*], it alone could "satisfy a love like mine for you & like the love I know & feel you have given me in return."

The next day found him at Hampton Roads in southeastern Virginia. He was traveling with Frank Payson, but did not confide his secret to this friend whose "curiosity" was "very much excited" by his mysterious correspondence. The correspondence discloses nothing about the purpose of his trip except that it had to do with the army. Looking out his bedroom window at streets filled with troop transports, Pierpont wrote: "I cannot tell you how calm and happy I feel. . . . Oh Fannie, you ought to be very grateful for having the power of making any human being as happy completely happy as you have me—can I ever do enough for you to repay you for it all[?]"

He was headed for the front, as Union forces surrounded Lee's deteriorating army at Petersburg, Virginia, and he hoped the fighting would not delay his return to his fiancée's side: "These separations are very trying dearest but we ought to be thankful that it is no worse."

Newly in love, he appears intoxicated less with the object of his affections than with aspects of his own experience—his right to claim Fanny as his own, the curiosity aroused by their secret, the shower of God's blessings on his head. He thought his fiancée ought to be grateful for having the power to make him so happy, and saw the war chiefly as an impediment to his return.

The war was in fact drawing to an end. Its last great battles took place at the beginning of April in Virginia, not far from Hampton Roads. Lee surrendered on April 9. Five days later John Wilkes Booth assassinated Lincoln. By the end of May Jefferson Davis was in custody and the last of the Confederate troops had surrendered. The surviving Morgan correspondence mentions none of these events. On March 31 Pierpont wrote to Junius about his engagement to Fanny, and Junius on April 11 and 15 sent back his "warmest and fullest approval of what you propose. . . . I cannot doubt that you have acted wisely, and altho' the event will bring up sad thoughts of the past yet you must not dwell upon them."

In New York for his twenty-eighth birthday on April 17, Pierpont wrote out a promise "to allow Frances to attend the opera at least once in three weeks during the opera season and I further agree to accompany her thither provided she prefers said escort to any other."

That spring, as the Union mourned Lincoln, Andrew Johnson moved into the White House, and the country began adjusting to the end of the war, Pierpont's chief concerns were domestic. He had known Memie for three years before they got married, during which time she contracted a fatal disease. This time he was in a hurry. He had proposed to Fanny on March 17, and set their wedding date for the first of June. When the government declared June 1 a national day of mourning for Lincoln, he moved the ceremony to May 31. It took place at St. George's Church. None of his immediate family attended, but Goodwins, Tracys, Ketchums, Dabneys, Peabodys, Sturgeses, and Paysons joined the celebration. The couple took a two-week tour of New England, then sailed for Europe on the *Persia*.

Pierpont had made this honeymoon passage before. In October 1861 Memie had rallied in cold ocean air. On calmer seas in June of 1865 Fanny was miserably sick. Her husband spent his time "being nurse" and heartily enjoying five meals a day. His high spirits did not abate once they landed. He introduced his wife to his family and friends in London, showed her the principal sights, then took her to Paris, where she spent most of the time in her room.

Virginia and William Henry Osborn met the Morgans in Paris, and a letter from Virginia to her mother explains Fanny's discomfort and Pierpont's good cheer: the new Mrs. Morgan had been pregnant since early June. "She has been almost totally deprived of sightseeing," wrote Virginia, "and I fancy will find the happiest moment she has had since leaving home will be that in which she returns to it. Pierpont has selected her the most exquisite toilette money can buy . . . but she is too miserable to enjoy [it]."

Pierpont's sisters, Sarah and Juliet, returned with the couple to New York. Jim Goodwin had moved out of the Madison Avenue house he and Pierpont had shared. At the beginning of September nearly half the Morgan family moved in.

———

While Pierpont traveled that summer, Edward Ketchum, his partner in the 1863 gold maneuver, was arrested. Ketchum had stolen $3 million in securities from his father's bank—unhappily called Ketchum Son & Co.—and forged $1.5 million in gold certificates, some of them in Pierpont's name. *The New York Times* reported on "startling scoundrelism" at the foot of Trinity Church, and described Wall Street as "agitated beyond anything" since Grant took Lee. Edward's felonies bankrupted his father. Morris Ketchum repaid several of the victims, and eventually moved to Georgia.

Junius, horrified, called this filial betrayal "the most astounding news I ever heard." He told Jim Goodwin that Edward's conduct "would almost lead one to fear he was at heart bad. How else could he keep up such appearances when he knew he had at that moment brought ruin and disgrace upon his father?" Who, the elder Morgan wanted to know, "are the parties interested with him in these enormous speculations?"

One of them was his own son. Pierpont had continued to do business with the junior Ketchum after their lucrative corner, advancing money for stock purchases and investing in some of his friend's ventures. After Edward's arrest, Wall Street whispered that Dabney, Morgan, like Ketchum Son & Co., would soon be forced to suspend. The loss to Edward Ketchum on the Dabney, Morgan books at the end of 1865 amounted to about $50,000, which Pierpont transferred to his private ledger.

At the peak of the crisis, Charles Dabney instructed Jim Goodwin: "Nothing will be done to give publicity to our loss by [Ketchum] – it will be much better for us to lose the whole than to stir the matter now, we shall gradually recover public confidence which is absolutely essential, much more than any money we can hope to recover from altering our course." The firm's policy should be public silence, and a discreet word in private: "It will be well to caution E.K. not to speak of his debt to us to any one who may call on him. . . . *We must keep still.*" They did keep still. Ketchum went to Sing Sing.

———

Pierpont in his twenties had come to resemble his stolid, square-jawed mother more than his finer-featured father. His Pierpont heritage seemed to entail nothing but trouble—skin problems, a "nervous" constitution, susceptibility to extreme mood swings—and he was almost completely estranged from his mother's family, including the eccentric old man to whom he had once been devoted. When Juliet, returning to New York in 1864, invited her father to visit, the Reverend Pierpont complained that he would have to call on her "where she is—at Pierpont Morgan's," but "*he* has never invited me to his house."

Trouble with his descendants aside, John Pierpont was having the time of his life in Washington, D.C. He headed a lecture association that brought famous speakers to the capital (including Horace Greeley and Ralph Waldo Emerson), and ran a weekly French study group with another white-bearded government clerk, Walt Whitman. When Whitman managed to get an early proof of Victor Hugo's *Les Miserables*, the two poets took turns reading it aloud to the group, trying to translate on their feet. Mr. Pierpont celebrated his eightieth birthday in April 1865, read elegiac poetry on the White House lawn after Lincoln's assassination, then went to work on a digest of U.S. Supreme Court decisions touching on revenue questions. In August 1866 he died in his sleep.

———

In the aftermath of the war, as industrialists began to organize U.S. commercial operations on a vast new national scale, Junius Morgan was building a banking dynasty capable of financing whatever the future might hold. Two of his daughters helped. In June of 1866 Sarah married a banker—George Hale Morgan, the son of banker George Denison Morgan and nephew of former New York Governor (now U.S. Senator) Edwin Denison Morgan. Though also originally from Wales, this family was not related to her own. Sarah's husband joined Dabney, Morgan & Co. in the fall of 1866. Neither she nor the firm had to change names.*

Early in 1867 the Morgans' middle daughter, Mary, married Walter Hayes Burns, a banking partner of Levi P. Morton's. (Morton had founded a Wall Street firm in 1863, after unpayable Southern debts caused his wholesale business to fail.) The newly wed Mr. and Mrs. Walter Burns settled in London, where he headed the house of Morton, Burns & Co.

Pierpont's youngest sister, Juliet—the most troubled of his siblings, and the most like her mother—fell in love with an Ecuadorian named Flores, to her parents' acute dismay. She eventually gave him up, and though she failed to secure another banker, she did manage to find a husband with the right name—John Brainerd Morgan, an Episcopal minister and the younger brother of Sarah's husband, George.

Pierpont was doing his part to extend the Morgan domain. On March 10, 1866—nine months and ten days after her wedding—Fanny gave birth to a girl. Both parents had wanted a son but instantly fell in love with the baby, whom they named Louisa Pierpont after her grandmothers. Charles Dabney,

---

* The division of profits was reconfigured so that Dabney and Pierpont took 39 percent each, Jim Goodwin 12 percent, George 10 percent.

traveling abroad that spring, said he hoped Pierpont would write "when his parental excitement has somewhat subsided." Junius told Jonathan Sturges that he longed to see his son "in his new relation of Father of which he seems so proud."

Pierpont *was* proud of being a father, and by January 1867 his wife was pregnant again. He loved presiding over a house full of people—children, relatives, guests—the corollary of which was that he hated to be alone. In February, when Fanny took Louisa to visit the Hartford relatives, he came home from work the night they left to find their chef preparing dinner, but "didn't want to eat alone," so went out to a neighbor's, where he dined, played cards till 11:30, then returned to a "dismal" empty house. He ate out or had friends in every night. After serving saddle of mutton and playing cards with guests till 10:00 one evening, he took the men to play billiards at the Union League Club, then returned home, he told Fanny, "thoroughly disgusted with its loneliness."

For all his complaints about desertion, he was hardly ever alone. "Important engagements" prevented him from joining his wife in Hartford for the weekend—in the evenings he attended dinners, a musicale, and a ball. On Sunday he went to St. George's in the morning, dined midday with the Tracys, returned to church in the afternoon, called on Fred Sturges and his wife, Mary, who had just had a boy ("I condoled with Fred on the sex of the new baby"), and stopped at Virginia Osborn's for tea before calling on the elder Sturgeses and Dabneys. The next morning he had breakfast at the Levi Mortons', and expected to dine at his club "unless someone takes pity on me."

In their first year of marriage, he and Fanny had discovered some distinct incompatibilities. He thrived on the activity and stimulation of the city, and had an inexhaustible appetite for new experience and legions of acquaintance. Fanny liked the country, quiet evenings at home, reading, and intimate talks with old friends. Her husband's pace was hard on her "nerves," and from time to time she needed to get away, which he experienced as abandonment.

He resumed his protests in July, when she visited a sister in Providence: "You don't know how awful lonely the house seemed without you and Louisa. . . . I don't care to have the dose repeated oftener than reasonably. It rained pitchforks all night. . . . I feel very well but *so* lonely. Kisses to Louisa ad libitum [as much as you like]. Tell her to say 'dear Mama.' " Two days later he came down with such a severe headache that he could not write or sit up; it faded in the evening but left him weak all the next day. He remonstrated: "It will be a long time before I let you off again for so long a time it is lonely enough."

Though he appeared robust as he turned thirty, Pierpont was more anxious than ever about his health. No longer the slim, romantic figure who had returned in mourning from Nice in 1862, he now weighed two hundred pounds, and his girth had joined the list of symptoms he fretted about—headaches, poor digestion, intermittent inertia and "blues." Both he and Fanny suffered from depression, but where her remedy was retreat, he sought social distraction and the curative waters at health spas.

The couple did agree on spending summers out of the hot city, and in 1867 they rented a large house at Irvington, high on the east bank of the Hudson. Pierpont commuted to Wall Street by boat, inviting friends up nearly every weekend. His domineering habits were not to everyone's taste. Fred Sturges brought his wife and son to stay with Fanny for a week in August while he and Pierpont commuted to town. He liked the house, the views, the servants, and his host's guided tours of neighboring sites and estates, but not the schedule: the household retired every night exactly at ten, "as the bell was to be rung at six, breakfast at seven and boat at eight—which programme was promptly carried out," Fred told his brother Henry. "After breakfast Pierpont had prayers and at eight minutes of eight we stepped into the wagon for the boat and at a quarter before ten I was in my office." Every afternoon at four they returned: "It certainly was very delightful all this week to have a cool sail up and down the river instead of dusty cars," continued Fred, "but I could not stand being tied to run as I had to every day at exactly twenty minutes of four in order to catch Pierpont's carriage which he has to carry him to the boat."

As soon as the Sturgeses left, Pierpont went to Saratoga Springs to take the waters. Fanny, now eight and a half months pregnant, and Louisa, who had the measles, stayed with the Tracys, who had rented a cottage on the west bank of the Hudson just below West Point, at Highland Falls. Pierpont found fewer friends at the fashionable resort/retreat than he expected—only Delafields, Stuarts, Alsops, Bartletts, Brookses, Griswolds, Phelpses, Blisses, Goodridges, Cornings, and the Reverend Tyng. He stayed at the Clarendon Hotel ("fearfully lonely"), and described the cure to his wife: "Sleep Water Breakfast Bowling Dinner Bowling Supper & Sleep." The routine worked "like a charm"—he lost three pounds in five days.

In daily letters to Fanny he worried about her exertions and their daughter's health, lamenting: "I need not tell you how lonesome how very lonesome it is without you & Louisa. I feel like a ship without a crew or rudder and were it not that I feel that I am deriving benefit from the waters I should scarcely be able to keep myself from joining you at West Point without delay." With no crew or rudder he was finding ample entertainment: at the Clarendon was a Miss Marshall of Natchez—"the most lovely looking girl in the house," he told his wife. ". . . I expect to be very devoted if I can get time aside from bowling."

His concern for his health had taken on the status of a *duty*: to forestall breakdown and nervous collapse, he was obliged to coddle himself. At Saratoga in 1867 it was not free choice—he would of course rather be with the pregnant wife and sick child he clamorously missed—but the benefit he derived from the waters that required him to endure this lonely exile (surrounded by friends). His anxieties about his health were real, even though doctors found nothing organically wrong. Yet his packaging of what he wanted to do in the language of high moral necessity recalls his lecture to Jim Goodwin in 1856 on the duty of choosing a helpmeet wife.

Many years later, in another context, Junius offered an ironic reflection on this kind of self-assigned motivation: "I have no doubt that there is a satisfaction in doing one's duty, even if is spelt with a large *D*," the elder Morgan told a friend at the end of 1885, "but don't you think it is a word whose definition can be made to conform to almost anything which one *wants* to do?"

If Pierpont perceived a gap between what he said and what he did—between duty and desire, his own "good" reasons and the "real" ones—he never let on. He stayed at Saratoga for two weeks in 1867.

On September 7, a few days after he returned to Irvington, his wife gave birth to a son. The baby had no name for three weeks. Fanny described Pierpont as happy but not elated the way he had been at Louisa's arrival—his first child would always be his favorite—and unwilling to name his son after himself, though she was urging him to. Perhaps he was thinking of Morgan family tradition—neither Joseph nor Junius had given his firstborn son his own name. Or perhaps he did not really want to give up his singularity, to see himself as a point on a line of succession. Intently focused on what lay ahead of him, he paid surprisingly little attention to what, or who, would come after. In the abstract, before Louisa was born, he had longed for a son; now that he had one, he was not rejoicing. Yet Fanny won out. They named the boy John Pierpont Morgan, Jr., and called him "Jack."

———

While Pierpont fathered a family, worried about his health, managed Junius's transatlantic business, and traded for his own firm and its clients in gold, cotton, iron rails, Peruvian guano, foreign exchange, government securities, and commercial paper, the country was engaged in bitter political struggles. Andrew Johnson had squared off against Radical Republicans who wanted the newly powerful federal government to guarantee suffrage and political equality for blacks. According to the historian Eric Foner, the struggle over slavery had convinced Republican reformers that freedom stood "in greater danger of abridgment from local than national authority"—which was "a startling reversal of the founding fathers' belief, enshrined in the Bill of Rights, that centralized power posed the major threat to individual liberties."

Johnson was ideologically closer to the founders than to Reconstructionist reformers. He turned out to be an obtuse, impolitic states-rightist who tried to conciliate the white South by granting amnesty to former Confederates; he vetoed measures to establish a Freedmen's Bureau and a Civil Rights Act, and opposed the Fourteenth Amendment, which would extend full citizenship and voting rights to blacks. The Radicals were trying to impeach the President in December 1867 when Morgan went to Washington.

Far more concerned with economic stability than the politics of Reconstruction, Morgan wanted the government to promote sound currency and industrial productivity, and thought a disruptive impeachment the last thing the country needed as it recovered from war. He listened to the debates in Congress, and cheered the Radicals' defeat, "happily squelched by a vote of 2 to 1."* He also attended debates on the nation's finances.

Immediately after the war, with inflation rampant and a $2.8 billion national debt, the public had favored a return to the prewar gold standard, which meant that the government had either to eliminate fiat money entirely or to increase the value of all paper currency (greenbacks and banknotes) until it was convertible into gold, dollar for dollar. In April 1866 Congress authorized Treasury Secretary Hugh McCulloch to begin retiring greenbacks—$10 million in the six months following passage of the law, and $4 million a month after that—but popular sentiment soon changed. The economy was contracting sharply after the wartime boom. It reached its low point in December 1867, just as Morgan visited Washington. In that context, tightening the money supply seemed cruel.[†]

For farmers, small merchants, and working people, the availability of "easy" paper money is good. It stimulates production and creates jobs. And for bor-

---

* Two months later, Republican moderates joined the Radicals to bring charges against Johnson for "high crimes and misdemeanors in office." He was the only president subjected to impeachment proceedings until December 1998. The Senate acquitted him by one vote.

[†] "By the time of the Civil War," writes John Kenneth Galbraith, "the American monetary system was, without rival, the most confusing in the long history of commerce and associated cupidity." Before the advent of greenbacks in 1862, the main form of paper money in the United States had been notes issued by state-chartered banks. In 1860 there were seven thousand different kinds of banknotes in circulation—and five thousand counterfeit issues—with no central regulation or control. The wartime National Banking Act of 1863 had tried to straighten out some of the confusion. It set up a system of nationally chartered banks that loaned money to the government in exchange for U.S. bonds, then issued notes worth up to 90 percent of the value of the bonds. That system created a uniform currency of national banknotes; it also provided some insurance against bank failures—the bonds could be sold to redeem a defaulting institution's notes—and it boosted the market for wartime government bonds. In 1865 Congress killed off the state notes by taxing them 10 percent. National banknotes remained an important form of currency until the Federal Reserve System was set up in 1913, but they had two major drawbacks. Since most of the issuing banks were in the Northeast, the notes tended to concentrate there, creating shortages in the South and West. And the issuing of national notes based on the banks' holdings of U.S. bonds meant that this currency was pegged to the federal debt rather than to economic demand.

rowers of all kinds, it makes debts easier to repay. A farmer can take out a loan for $1,000 in the spring, and pay it back after his harvest with dollars worth *less* than those he borrowed. The dollars are worth less because "easy" money leads to inflation: with plenty of cash chasing relatively few goods, prices go up and the value of a dollar goes down.

Lenders of money hate inflation for exactly the reason borrowers like it: they do not want their loans repaid in depreciated currency. Roughly $486 million in long-term U.S. federal debt was held abroad in 1867. The foreigners who owned the bonds had a potent weapon if the government let the value of its legal tender decline—they could sell the bonds and refuse to buy more, which would seriously debilitate American capital markets. The Treasury and the private bankers who saw themselves as guardians of those markets wanted the country back on the gold standard in order to maintain the flow of foreign money to the United States.

To international bankers and traders, a gold dollar was far more than a medium of exchange. Gold stood as the ultimate guarantor of value, a universally sanctioned measure that provided people making economic decisions with reliable information about what things were worth. In an era of wild financial instability, it was "the rule of law applied to money"—a disciplinary force that could regulate currency markets, forestall inflation, keep purchasing power relatively constant, and assure America's trading partners that their financial commitments would hold steady over time: the government would repay its debts in full. The gold standard also promised to keep control over the U.S. economy in the hands of men who had these concerns in mind.

This new sectional conflict, with eastern bankers and foreign traders taking one view of fundamental monetary questions and western farmer/debtors another, would divide the United States for the next three decades.

Morgan ardently supported government action to restore the gold standard, and he denounced do-nothing politicians who hoped that time and economic growth would bring the nation back to "sound" money. From Washington in 1867 he told Fanny that Republican Representative Justin Morrill of Vermont, though sympathetic to the hard-currency view, "seemed to be of the opinion that Congress could safely take the position regarding the laws of finance and political economy that the ancient Emperor did when he thought by standing on the shore he could command the waves to advance or recede at his pleasure. My own impression is that in many of his predictions Mr. Morrill will find himself equally disappointed." It was Morgan who was disappointed when, early in 1868, Congress rescinded authority for the Treasury's contraction.

That election-year summer, the Republicans nominated Union war hero Ulysses S. Grant, whose acceptability to the Radicals made Morgan uneasy.

When the Democrats turned to former New York Governor Horatio Seymour, Morgan pronounced himself disgusted. He had hoped for a Democrat who, "though he might not be elected, would still create some anxiety in the minds of the rabid radicals now carrying everything with such a high hand." The fact that Seymour had addressed the violent mob during New York's 1863 draft riots as "my friends" should have been enough to "sink him forever," Morgan told his wife—"for Seymour personally I have the most supreme contempt." Secretary of State Seward thought the Democrats "could have nominated no candidate who would have taken away fewer Republican votes."

The Republicans, now unmistakably the party of the new industrial interests, pledged themselves in 1868 to protectionism and the gold standard, while the Democrats tried to resuscitate the South and attract the small businessmen, farmers, and workers who had been left out of the Republican coalition.

———

Though Morgan would play a major role in the long-term fight against "easy" money, his anxieties about his health in 1868 took precedence over economic politics. Having been so eager for a career in finance as a boy, and so impatient to get started as a young man, he now seemed conflicted over what he actually wanted to do.

Attributing his "nervous" breakdowns to overwork, he took off the entire summer of 1868 and went to Europe—alone. His wife's parents again rented a cottage on the Hudson at Highland Falls. He installed Fanny and the children in a house on adjoining property called Stonihurst. When he reached London, he consulted Sir Henry Holland, who had seen Memie in 1861, and who recommended the hot springs at Carlsbad for Pierpont's gastrointestinal trouble. In Paris, worried about his lungs, he called on one of the pulmonary specialists who had diagnosed Memie's TB—was he experiencing her symptoms in an unconscious attempt to bring her back?—before proceeding with his parents and sister Juliet to Carlsbad.

He had expected the town to be dreary, and found himself "most agreeably disappointed." Carlsbad was situated in a narrow, winding valley surrounded by thick woods, with hot springs jetting out of the rocks. A spa physician named Ganz ("by no means a goose so far as his profession is concerned") found nothing wrong with Morgan's lungs, but diagnosed a "torpid" liver. He prescribed long walks and several glasses of Carlsbad water a day.

The other spa guests included pretty girls, handsome ladies, several Russians, some French, "Jews almost without number and of course many Germans," Pierpont told Fanny. Soon he was feeling "as well as a lark" and losing weight: no two scales agreed, but the fit of his clothes showed that "the circumference is not as great as when I was in New York. I can button my shoes with less difficulty, which to say the least is a satisfaction." His head was "clearer & freer from all pressure than for many years past. . . . I don't believe I ever felt better, only one thing is needful & that I shant tell for fear it might make you feel too important." Full of "impatient longings to see you and the children," he urged his wife in letter after letter to "Kiss Louisa & Jack for their paternal relative – I fear they may forget they have one."

After four weeks at Carlsbad, the Morgan quartet went on to Vienna, where Pierpont and Junius spent their evenings in the public gardens listening to Strauss waltzes over coffee and cigars, and their afternoons looking at art. Pierpont pronounced the paintings in the Belvedere Palace "very mediocre," but approved of Prince Lichtenstein's Raphaels, Correggios, Murillos, and Guidos. As usual, his tastes ran to the imperial and the Napoleonic. He wandered among Maria Theresa's paintings and tapestries in Schönbrunn Palace— Bonaparte had stayed there while negotiating with Austria after the Battle of Wagram in 1809, and Napoleon II had died in one of the palace rooms. Touring the private apartments of Emperor Franz Joseph, Pierpont pronounced them "in no way superior to those of less prominent mortals." In the Church of St. Augustine, he studied urns and sarcophagi containing two hundred and fifty years of Hapsburg family remains, and paused before the body of Franz Joseph's brother, Ferdinand Maximilian Joseph, named Emperor of Mexico in 1864 and executed by followers of Benito Juárez in 1867: "One's mind could not but be filled with the saddest thoughts as one stands by a tomb where so many hopes lie withered," he told his wife.

In Munich he visited the Neue Pinakothek (he called it the Gallery of Modern Pictures) to study a "great picture of the destruction of Jerusalem" by Wilhelm von Kaulbach, "which I have so long desired to see." Kaulbach (1804–1874), a painter of huge, dramatically lit scenes in the German Romantic style, dominated the Bavarian academy in the 1850s and 1860s, and was enormously popular in America. He had been court painter to Ludwig I when he completed the idealizing *Destruction of Jerusalem* in 1846; Ludwig built the Neue Pinakothek expressly to house this 20- by 23-foot canvas, the most expensive nineteenth-century painting yet commissioned.

Calling on Kaulbach in his Munich studio, the Morgans found him working on "a beautiful picture of 'Charity' for Mr. Probasco of Cincinnati," Pierpont reported to Fanny, and about to start another—of the meeting of Queen Elizabeth and Mary, Queen of Scots—for George Peabody Wetmore in New York: "Father was very much taken with his paintings, & finally contracted with him for a beautiful one of which he had just finished the cartoon. It will certainly be a great acquisition." Junius gave Pierpont the cartoon—*Vogelgesang* (The Bird Song), based on a Schiller poem—in 1873. It depicts a pretty shepherdess, barefoot and bare-breasted, lying in the grass beside a pond; she is listening to a wandering minstrel and leaning into his embrace, though pretending to push him away.

After Munich, the Morgan party went through Paris to London. Pierpont returned to New York early in September.

———

In the aftermath of the Civil War, as the ebullient culture of American enterprise turned to the enterprise of culture, scores of wealthy families began touring European cities—the Morgans had begun in the 1850s—and came home full of excitement about the visual arts. The United States, breathing what the critic Robert Hughes has called "thin aesthetic air," had no tradition of royal collecting, no great public repositories such as the Louvre, the British Museum, or the Vatican, nothing like the major private collections of pictures, church treasure, decorative arts, manuscripts, and books that had been assembled by European dukes and merchant princes. Americans interested in the serious study of art still had to go abroad, but in a mood of aesthetic nationalism, affluent postwar families took it upon themselves to bring culture home.

At first, most of them bought contemporary paintings of the Barbizon and Düsseldorf schools, and lionized storytelling artists such as Kaulbach. According to the art historian Nicholas Hall, "every important American collector active before 1914" started out with "at best a Corot, as often a Daubigny, or a Diaz." A notable exception was James Jackson Jarves, guided by Ruskin and the Brownings, who bought Italian paintings of the thirteenth to the early fifteenth centuries.* Not until the 1890s did collectors such as Morgan, Isabella Stewart Gardner, Peter Widener, and Benjamin Altman move on to Old Masters.

Jarves predicted in 1855 that private individuals would form America's great public collections, and that the United States would soon "rival the 'Old World' in art treasures." Henry James described the spirit in which the New World was taking possession of the Old in 1867: "I think that to be an American is an excellent preparation for culture," he told a friend. "We have exquisite qualities as a race, and it seems to me that we are ahead of the European races in the fact that . . . we can deal freely with forms of civilization not our own, can pick and choose and assimilate and in short (aesthetically etc.) claim our property wherever we find it."

———

* Jarves's taste for works by Simone Martini, Pollaiuolo, and Sassetta, though widely shared by European connoisseurs, ran far ahead of his compatriots'. Critics assailed the collection when it went on exhibition in New York, the Boston Athenaeum turned it down, and Yale acquired it in 1871 for $22,000—less than a quarter of the $100,000 Jarves thought it was worth. A Yale undergraduate said in the college paper at the time that "one hour's study of Bierstadt's *Yosemite Valley* would for me be worth more than all this collection."

The New York Morgans had outgrown No. 227 Madison Avenue, and while Pierpont traveled in the summer of 1868, Fanny proposed by mail that they move to Englewood, New Jersey. He had no interest in leaving Manhattan. Although living in the suburbs might be pleasant, he replied, he could not be tied to train schedules or "compelled" to spend winters out of town—as things stood, "I get quite enough of that by Oct. or November." Nor was he willing to sever his ties with friends, city associations, clubs, or church: "My attachment to Dr. Tyng is so strong & my satisfaction in the services at St. Georges so great that I should not willingly place myself in a locality where I should be prevented from going there." Knowing how much his wife wanted a different kind of life, he pleaded external obligation and adopted a tone of regret: "So long therefore as I have means, and the necessity remains as great as now for my being in the city, I think we shall have to stay there, pleasant as it would be at Englewood."

Shortly after returning to New York that fall, he rented a large house two doors from the Sturgeses on 14th Street. It was "*far* more downtown than I like," he told Fanny, but he had seen nothing better. At $5,000 a year, it seemed "not high as rents go." They moved in November, just as Ulysses Grant won the presidential election. The Republican victory, with majorities in both houses of Congress, did not end the struggle over Reconstruction, but to the Morgans' relief it inaugurated a period of relative fiscal calm. The Treasury tried to stabilize the nation's money markets, and assumed some of the functions of a central bank.

Frances Tracy Morgan, about 1875.
(Courtesy of Robert M. Pennoyer)

Chapter 8

NEW DIRECTIONS

Between the Civil War and the end of the century—a period that came to be known in Mark Twain's sardonic phrase as "the Gilded Age"—Americans added thousands of track miles to the largest rail network in the world, settled the western half of the continent, harvested natural resources, developed immense domestic markets, and hugely increased the country's industrial productivity. John D. Rockefeller built a giant oil monopoly, Andrew Carnegie put together an empire in steel, Philip Armour and Gustavus Swift revolutionized the meatpacking business. Boston bankers financed Bell's telephone. New Yorkers raised capital for Edison's electric light. All these economic and technological changes dwarfed traditional politics—no President of real stature occupied the White House between Lincoln and Theodore Roosevelt—and radically altered the nature and pace of American life.

They were also making the country rich. The U.S. population more than doubled between 1870 and 1910, while estimates of national wealth increased fourfold, and consumer prices on average fell by 40 percent. Per capita income grew almost 3 percent a year between 1874 and 1879. A rapidly growing labor force helped drive this expansionary surge, as did a dramatic rise in "capital formation"—money withheld from consumption for long-term investment in machinery, factories, refineries, and mills. For the latter half of the nineteenth century the annual rate of increase in physical plant and equipment was 5.4 percent, almost twice the yearly increase in the size of the workforce (2.8 percent) and the supply of land (2.9 percent). During the seventies and eighties, roughly a quarter of the gross national product went into building industrial facilities.

The task of organizing financial markets to mobilize vast amounts of money for long-term ventures fell to bankers such as the Morgans. Junius in 1857 had proudly described "the wonderful increase of capital in the United States," and predicted that soon Wall Street would "no longer have to watch with solicitude the rate of [the Bank of England on] Threadneedle Street." Still, it would be some time before Wall Street did not have to keep an eye on Threadneedle Street. Foreign investors owned about $1 billion worth of U.S. government securities by 1869, and the country would remain a net debtor until 1914. In the immediate post–Civil War years, without an American central bank, the financiers responsible for raising investment capital tried to maintain U.S. credit abroad, prevent panics, stabilize domestic markets, and devise ad hoc solutions to the problems created by all this turbulent growth.

As the satiric sobriquet suggested, not everyone in the Gilded Age was getting rich. The period from the 1860s to the 1890s saw the longest price decline in U.S. history, and farmers' crop income steadily fell as the cost of debt rose. Workers' wages did not keep up with the growth of national wealth: between 1873 and 1910 money wages rose by just a third, and "real" wages only 20 percent. It was partly the armies of post–Civil War immigrants—14 million between 1885 and 1910—that kept wages from rising more rapidly. Largely Catholic and Jewish, from southern and eastern Europe, these newcomers were more distinctly "foreign" than earlier, northern European workers, and less easily integrated into the American melting pot. They settled in crowded cities where they hoped to find jobs, their dreams of prosperity dissipating in the struggle to survive.

The stark discrepancy between booming national economic growth and the troubles in farm towns, factories, and slums raised familiar Jeffersonian-Hamiltonian questions about the nature of the American dream—agrarian or commercial?—that came up most urgently in the contractions following the panics of 1873, 1884, and 1893.

—

After the successful laying of the Atlantic cable in 1866, the great commercial event of the early postwar years was the completion of the transcontinental railroad that Lincoln had imagined would finally make one nation of the disparate states. On May 10, 1869, the Central Pacific line building eastward from California and Union Pacific tracks heading west across the Great Plains met at Promontory Point near Ogden, Utah. Two months later Mr. and Mrs. Pierpont Morgan set off across the country.

Morgan had an avid personal interest in this excursion: though he traveled to Europe the way other New Yorkers went to Boston, he had never seen the western half of the United States. He had a professional interest as well: most of the money his bank was channeling from savers to users now went into railroads. As the roads created a national mass market by providing cheap, quick all-weather long-distance transport for enormous quantities of freight, they were also carving up the country's wilderness, galvanizing its industrial imagination, stimulating technological innovation, spurring production of coal, iron, and steel, and fueling capital growth. In the 1860s they overshadowed all other American enterprise. The Pennsylvania Railroad was the largest private company in the world by 1865, with thirty thousand employees, 3,500 miles of main track, and a capital investment of $61 million.

Railroads consumed money on an altogether colossal new scale. Textile mills, America's largest manufacturers in the 1850s, rarely cost $1 million to build, whereas the four big east–west trunk lines—the Pennsylvania, Erie, New York Central, and Baltimore & Ohio—were initially capitalized at between $17 million and $35 million each. Building canals between 1815 and 1860 had cost $188 million, much of it raised through sales of state and municipal bonds, the rest from individuals and local institutions such as Joseph Morgan's Hartford banks. Investment in private railroad securities amounted to $1.1 billion by 1859, not including the value of government land grants and loans.

The Morgan transcontinental expedition—Pierpont, Fanny, her sister Mary Tracy, and his cousin Mary Goodwin—left Jersey City at 5:00 P.M. on July 5, 1869. They were traveling under the escort of John Crerar, an officer of the Pullman Palace Car Company and a director of Chicago railroads and banks. They woke up on July 7 in Chicago.

Fanny's journals give a running account of the trip, though not of her husband's observations. For ten days the foursome visited friends in Chicago, went to dinners and the opera, toured stockyards, and took a quick trip with Mr. Crerar down the St. Louis Road to Lexington, Kentucky, and back. Minus Crerar, they continued west in a Pullman Palace car called the *Minnesota*. George M. Pullman's luxurious sleeping coaches *were* palatial, with plush carpets and seats, glass chandeliers, heavy curtains, elaborate marquetry, and wood-paneled ceilings and walls. "Such comfortable rooms surely never were on a rail road before," exclaimed Fanny. Pullman comforts did not include dining facilities. The travelers brought along sandwiches and cakes, and stopped at "eating houses" along the route. Pierpont rustled up fresh provisions wherever he could.

The rail lines crossing the country in 1869 had been built by competing companies in disconnected patches, with no standard track gauge and no national plan. Each company ran its own cars on its own tracks, which meant that passengers had to change trains—and carloads of freight had to be unpacked and reloaded—at each new stretch of road. Though the Morgans were getting the royal treatment, they had to wait for hours between trains like everyone else. They crossed the Mississippi at Fulton, Illinois, on a "fearful look-ing bridge resting on one or two islands," noted Fanny, and were ferried across the Missouri from Council Bluffs, Iowa, into a Nebraska aspen forest. Waiting at Omaha for the Union Pacific train, the easterners spent an afternoon gath-ering wildflowers and weighing themselves: Mary Goodwin registered 112 pounds, Fanny and Mary Tracy 140 each, Pierpont 200.

Fanny shuddered at a band of Pawnees "just in from a fight with other Indi-ans, riding the horses they had captured" in Columbus, Nebraska—"horrid looking wild creatures with no clothes to speak of—blankets & shivs & spears. . . . One came up and spoke to Pierpont, who, not understanding him, retired to the train immediately." At Uinta, Utah, the Morgan party took a stagecoach to Salt Lake City: Fanny pronounced the Mormons "well and neat and prosperous" but the town "horribly dirty" and the hotel beds apparently "stuffed with chips of granite." Pierpont and the Marys met "the old sinner" Brigham Young, who to their amusement seemed taken with Miss Tracy. Con-tinuing by rail to Promontory Point, the travelers changed to the Central Pa-cific line, which took them across Nevada and California to Sacramento.

In Northern California they spent several days touring farmlands, coastal mountain ranges, and mines, surprised by cool weather. In San Francisco they stayed at the "palace" of Milton Slocum Latham, a pro-slavery senator during the Civil War, now manager of the London & San Francisco Bank. Fanny was delighted to be where there were doctors, fresh fruit, no mosquitoes, and full-dress dinner parties. Dining at the mansion of William C. Ralston, who had re-cently organized the Bank of California with Darius O. Mills, she noted a mechanical piano and "quantities of beautiful roses." Another day, Ralston took her out in his four-horse charabanc. Pierpont went off on business with Mr. Latham.

Fanny's diaries have none of Memie's sparkle or sense of adventure, and myriad ailments curtailed her participation in her husband's life. When their party went to Yosemite in early August, she was suffering from corns and diar-rhea ("P. kept plying me with medicine"), and found the others' activities "pretty severe for a nervous person." Pierpont and "the girls" rode horses through Tuolumne Meadows, ate wild blackberries, and hiked up a ravine. After getting caught in a rainstorm one day, they dried their clothes before a log fire; Pierpont wandered around all afternoon in seersucker long johns, looking as if he'd been "spooned" into them, noted his wife. The two Marys washed their blackened skirts in the river. Fanny couldn't wait to leave "this dirty place" and return to civilized life at the Lathams'.

In his last few days on the West Coast, Pierpont saw San Francisco's China-town, the Almaden Mines, Napa Valley, Sonoma, and Vallejo. His party left Sacramento on August 21 with hampers of food. At Omaha, the end of the Union Pacific line, they dined "sumptuously" in a local hotel. John Crerar met them at Cedar Rapids in a Pullman car for the segment to Chicago. Men lined the platforms at small towns along the route to stare at the elegant coach; Fanny thought they were "delighted to see our two specimen California pears." The travelers stopped in Chicago for three days, then headed home along the Lake Ontario shore.

———

Pierpont had just traveled six thousand miles on the "iron horse" he had applauded as a boy, and seen at firsthand both the promise and the difficulties of the roads his bank was helping build.

The money to be made in railroads had stimulated a frenzy of competitive construction. Anyone who could grab a land grant and hawk securities could promise to lay down a road. Some promoters issued phony stock and pocketed the proceeds; others built shoddy tracks over circuitous routes, since the government issued new loans based on mileage completed. One midcentury wit noted dryly that speculators were building lines that ran from nowhere in particular to nowhere at all. The well-run roads that did earn profits invariably attracted competition: rivals built parallel tracks, sometimes aiming to steal traffic, sometimes just to force the original line to buy them out. Buccaneer managers manipulated their own roads' securities, plundered the capital reserves, bribed politicians for grants and loans, and formed construction companies to charge exorbitant fees that they themselves—as directors—willingly paid. It was classic free-market economics: a boom in demand led to overbuilding, which in turn led to cutthroat fights for survival.

The financial structure and competitive nature of this industry in the late 1860s presented the roads' bankers, managers, and investors with novel problems. For one thing, railroads had to buy land, dig track beds, pay workers, buy and lay track, and purchase engines and cars long before they were earning anything at all—which meant that they had to keep borrowing money at interest, adding to their costs. Selling stock instead of borrowing would have required no fixed payments, but stocks in America's fledgling capital markets were still considered highly speculative, and cautious investors wanted bonds—mortgages on the road's property, issued at high rates of interest. Most U.S. roads were capitalized primarily with bonded debt.

For another thing, once a road was operating it could carry lots of passengers and enormous loads of freight for only slightly more than it cost to carry a single passenger or bushel of wheat. Since every additional item transported brought down the average cost, it made economic sense for the roads to use long trains, loaded full and run fast. This principle, called economies of scale, operated in many industries: if it cost less per unit to make or carry a lot of something than a little, large companies organized accordingly could operate far more cheaply and efficiently than small ones. In most of these industries the economies reached maximum efficiency (lowest cost) at a point that left room for several firms to remain in the competitive field. Business-cycle upturns might lead to overbuilding, excess capacity, and price wars, but competition sorted out the more efficient firms, the others eventually failed, and the market regulated the prices the survivors could charge.

The economic problem for railroads was peculiar, however. The roads required huge initial capital investments, and operated with an unusually high ratio of fixed costs (mainly interest payment on debt) to variable costs (engine fuel, workers' wages). Before the development of trucking, railroads were "natural monopolies" in their own territories—one railroad could do the job more cheaply than two. Yet that road needed large volumes of traffic to stay in business because of its high fixed costs. By running big trains loaded full, line A could keep its operating costs low, and earn enough money to service its debt and turn a profit. If a parallel line B slashed prices to siphon off A's traffic, A would have to match the price cuts in order to maintain some volume and income. As a result, competition between parallel roads was singularly fierce.

Passengers and shippers, forced to pay high rates on routes where one road had a monopoly, welcomed this kind of competition since it forced prices down. Eventually, however, by drastically cutting prices and dividing the available traffic, neither line A nor line B could earn enough to cover its fixed costs, and both would operate at a loss until one or the other defaulted on its debt and went bankrupt. Paradoxically, bankruptcy brought a competitive advantage: since a road in default did not have to service its debt, it could operate with lower costs than its rivals and charge lower rates. The logical outcome of this struggle seemed to be bankruptcy for all—which was why competition among capital-intensive railroads seemed "ruinous" to their owners and managers. And the failure of enormously expensive roads, financed largely by foreign capital, affected the entire U.S. economy.

The Morgans hated this kind of warfare, which played havoc with national financial markets and left their client-investors holding worthless paper. Hoping to transform railroad securities from high-risk speculations into stable, long-term investments, they and a few other bankers—chiefly the New York house of Winslow, Lanier & Co.—attempted to discipline the industry. The fact that railroads continually needed huge infusions of capital put the bankers in a powerful position.

Although competition effectively regulated consumer prices in industries with many participants—including railroads on long-distance routes, where the markets could support more than one major carrier—there had to be some form of external regulation for the "natural monopolies" the railroads had on local routes. Toward the end of the century, the states and the federal government began to regulate rates, but in the seventies and eighties railroad managers and their bankers had little external supervision.

As soon as Pierpont returned to New York at the beginning of September 1869 he was drawn into a fight over a small road in upstate New York called the Albany & Susquehanna. The A&S ran just 142 miles between Albany and Binghamton, but connected with four larger roads leading south to Pennsylvania's coalfields. One of the four was the Erie, run by the "Mephistopheles of Wall Street," Jay Gould. A small, driven, meticulously groomed man of few words and clever instincts, Gould cast a covetous eye on the A&S as soon as it was completed in December 1868.* He wanted this valuable link between New England's markets and Pennsylvania's coal supplies for the Erie empire, and did *not* want his competitors—chiefly, the New York Central—to control it.

Pierpont had a professional interest in the A&S. In May of 1869 he had helped negotiate a $500,000 third mortgage for the road and been appointed a co-trustee. That summer, as the Morgans headed across the continent, Gould and "Jubilee" Jim Fisk had begun buying stock in the A&S. Once they owned a controlling interest, they planned to elect their people to the board, install new officers, and take charge. They met a resolute opponent in A&S president Joseph H. Ramsey.

Gould bought up as many A&S shares as he could, and tried to bribe local stockholders for more. Ramsey retaliated by issuing to his allies thousands of shares that had been sitting on the company's books; then he smuggled the books out of his office and buried them in the Albany Cemetery. Gould and Fisk had Ramsey suspended as president of the road by a judge they controlled on the New York State Supreme Court—George G. Barnard, a Tammany crony of "Boss" Tweed's. Ramsey quickly applied to Albany judge Rufus W. Peckham

---

* Gould had gained control of the Erie in another competitive battle. Cornelius Vanderbilt, former steamboat magnate and principal owner of the New York Central Railroad, had in the early 1860s built a regional rail system up the Hudson River from New York City to Albany, and after the Civil War he had begun extending it west along the Great Lakes to Chicago. He decided to take over the Erie in 1867, when it threatened to steal some of the Central's traffic. "Commodore" Vanderbilt was a tough old bird who played by his own rules and generally got what he wanted. In 1867, however, he underestimated Erie president Daniel Drew, a seasoned pirate who had made a fortune manipulating the road's shares. "Uncle Daniel" called in Jay Gould and "Jubilee" Jim Fisk, another marauder whose ebullient spirits, street-fighter tactics, and flashy tastes masked a shrewd intelligence. This trio secured control of the Erie by bribing state officials and issuing millions of dollars in phony stock. Drew, thinking he had extracted all the profit he could, resigned from the presidency and left the Erie to Gould, who immediately added William M. "Boss" Tweed, leader of New York City's corrupt Democratic machine, to the road's board of directors.

A piece of fraud perpetuated by Drew may be the source of the term "watered stock." As a young cattle drover bringing herds from Putnam County to market in New York, he fed his cows salt just before they reached town, then let them drink as much as they could hold. The profitable difference between their real weight and their weight at the moment of sale was pure water.

(who later served on the U.S. Supreme Court), and both sides tried to force the A&S into the hands of a partisan receiver: Peckham got his order in first by a matter of minutes.

Over the next few days the battle escalated from stock raids and legal disputes to slapstick and physical combat. Fisk stormed the A&S office in Albany with a gang of New York City thugs, only to find himself marched off to jail by a man who turned out to be an A&S employee posing as a policeman. As soon as he was free Fisk retreated to Manhattan, then returned with restraining orders from Judge Barnard and fresh recruits. He and his "troops" took over the A&S station at Binghamton, appropriated a train, and headed down the line toward Albany, annexing stations as they went; A&S men flipped a switch to derail the cars. The two sides later met in a tunnel near Harpursville and went after each other with sticks, rocks, knives, and guns until the governor ordered the state militia to take charge of the road.

It was a long way from gunfights in Harpursville to the boardrooms of London's merchant banks. Jim Goodwin reported to Junius in late August, with Pierpont en route from California, that Gould and Fisk were "carrying things with a high hand but they have found their match in Ramsey." Dabney, Morgan had feared that Gould's hostile takeover would succeed, but Judge Barnard was now being threatened with impeachment—this was not his first display of injudicious alliance with Gould—and the public was siding with Ramsey. Jim thought "G[ould] & F[isk] are losing their power somewhat, & if vigorous steps were taken there is a fair chance of getting rid of them—they are a shame and disgrace to the country."

Morgan reached New York on September 1 and was immediately drafted by Ramsey allies. After consulting his lawyer father-in-law, who had trained upstate, he hired an Albany attorney named Samuel Hand (father of the future Court of Appeals judge Learned Hand), and entered the fray. In Dabney, Morgan's name he bought six hundred shares of A&S stock (the books had been retrieved from the Albany Cemetery). Then he contacted all the stockholders who were guaranteed to back Ramsey, and made sure they or their proxies attended the annual meeting in Albany on September 7. He personally presided over the voting, and was elected a vice president and director of the road.

In a separate election, the Gould-Fisk forces voted in men of their own. Two months later the New York State Supreme Court upheld the Ramsey group's victory. Morgan leased the A&S to a coal carrier, the Delaware & Hudson Canal Company, for ninety-nine years, which took the company out of play.*

---

* Immediately after the "Susquehanna War," Gould cornered the gold market and brought on the crash that came to be known as "Jay Gould's Black Friday." Spending most of his time on his gold maneuver late that summer, he had left the A&S work primarily to Fisk.

Although his own speculations five years earlier had provoked his father to outrage, the junior Morgan was coming around to the senior's point of view, and this first venture into a railroad war bore what would become his professional signature. On behalf of the company's bondholders, he managed to out-maneuver corporate raiders and stow the road where he considered it safe. *The New York Times* a few years later declared that the A&S contest, "waged not only by litigation but by force of arms," had "made Mr. Morgan universally respected as an able financier."

Mr. Morgan was doing well in many ways—a confidential R. G. Dun & Co. report estimated his net worth at $600,000 to $700,000 (and Junius's at $8 million to $10 million)—but he did not yet have the unalloyed admiration of Wall Street. The credit agency described him as "consd. of excellent char., extra ability, shrewd, quick of perception, but oftentimes close & sometimes erratic in minor details which with his peculiar brusqueness of manner has made him & his house unpopular with many." Still, the house had "rich & strong bus. friends & relations. Do a conservative, paying bus. & are safe for their engts."

The Dun & Co. estimates were high—Junius by this time had a net worth of roughly $5 million, Pierpont about $350,000. The last part of the credit report would have pleased Junius, but the first part, which echoed Duncan, Sherman's warning about the younger Morgan's "sharp and contracted" dealings with colleagues, was also true. As if to illustrate the point, Pierpont was not getting along with his partners. He wanted to ease his brother-in-law George out of the firm—they disagreed on just about everything—and he no longer had much use for Charles Dabney. Even Jim Goodwin complained that since Pierpont kept his professional correspondence with his father private, the others often had no idea of the elder Morgan's views. Jim was so troubled by this state of affairs that he wrote to Junius about it at the end of 1869.

Dabney, now sixty-three, felt he had "lost his influence" with Pierpont, reported Jim, and that his former apprentice did not treat him "with enough respect." When the five-year term of the partnership expired in 1871, Dabney planned to resign. Jim did not think Pierpont could run the firm alone: Dabney's "moral influence in our favor" had been "very great with the public at large," but there was "no use denying" (here Jim practically quoted from the Dun report) that "Pierpont's brusque manners have made him personally unpopular with a great many—all this has had a damaging effect upon us."

Both Dabney and Jim wanted to bring in Frank Payson's partner, Emil Heinemann (another Dabney son-in-law: Heinemann's wife and Payson's wife were sisters), but Pierpont did not. In prose that stutters with self-justification, Jim repeated to his uncle that while their house had attained a "very good position" under Dabney, "Pierpont alone could not retain [it]. . . . *All* admit his great executive abilities – but *and I say it in all kindness* – many (I have good reason to believe it) object to his impulsiveness and manners, and *I* have not sufficient force to control him." Pierpont's "quick comprehension and fondness for detail" would match up nicely with Heinemann's "tact and judgment for planning and originating business," urged Jim.

Nothing came of the Heinemann plan, and Junius did not appreciate his nephew's frankness. Jim apologized: "Please do not say *anything* to P. or any one *else* about these letters I wish them forgotten." Junius left the problems of his New York affiliates unresolved for the time being, although he continued to worry about unsecured credits and to advise "masterly inactivity" in times of the slightest financial unease.

———

As Pierpont worried his partners and tried to prevent speculators from gambling with his clients' securities, Junius began to take some calculated risks. In March 1870 the elder Morgan met Andrew Carnegie, who had emigrated from Scotland to Allegheny, Pennsylvania, at age twelve, and worked his way up through the ranks of the Pennsylvania Railroad Company to become head of its Pittsburgh Division by the time he was twenty-four, in 1858. Ten years later, this son of a Scottish weaver owned $400,000 worth of securities and partnerships in railroads, banks, iron mills, and telegraph lines; he also owned a bridge-building company called Keystone.

Carnegie decided in 1869 to build a railroad bridge across the Mississippi River—something more substantial than the "fearful looking bridge resting on one or two islands" that Pierpont and Fanny crossed. With the help of his mentors at the Pennsylvania Railroad, Carnegie won the construction contract for a bridge at St. Louis, to be designed by former army engineer James B. Eads. The plans called for three metal arches resting on masonry piers sunk into rock ninety-three feet below the river's surface. Skeptics predicted it would take $7 million to build the bridge—and seven million years.

Hoping to raise money (less than $7 million) in London, Carnegie presented his plans to Junius in the spring of 1870. He had been preceded by an enthusiastic letter of introduction from Pennsylvania Railroad president J. Edgar Thomson. At J. S. Morgan & Co., Carnegie described a span that would put U.S. technological ingenuity on display, generate lucrative iron sales, and serve as a "toll-gate on the continental highway." Junius wondered at first how the public would view such a "novel" project—"a mortgage bond upon a *Bridge*"—but agreed to take $1 million of Illinois and St. Louis Bridge bonds at 85 percent of their face value, after making some changes in the wording to protect his firm from risk.

Accustomed to the work of managing iron foundries and railroads, Carnegie was enthralled by the lofty methods of Old Broad Street. Careful discussion, a few adjustments, a simple agreement—"that was all it took," writes his biographer Joseph Wall, "to move into the market the necessary gold to heat the foundries in Pittsburgh and put iron beams across a muddy river 5000 miles away. Here was capitalism in its most powerful form, and Carnegie would never tire of watching its quiet, smooth operation." The bonds for the bridge sold so well that when Dabney, Morgan asked for a share, Junius said no: his own firm's allotment was "already smaller than what we want or ought to have." Building the bridge did not take seven million years, but the Morgan banks had to keep advancing money as construction deadlines passed. Fifteen men died working underwater in pneumatic caissons filled with compressed air, and many more were crippled by a mysterious ailment not yet known as the bends. Eads wanted to use steel for parts of the structure; Carnegie still favored iron. By the time the bridge finally opened in July 1874 the United States was in the midst of a depression. Little rail traffic moved across the new "toll-gate on the continental highway," and the company had to borrow again from its bankers to pay interest on its bonds.* Still, the St. Louis Bridge was a brilliant piece of engineering, and the Morgans did not hold Carnegie responsible for its problems. More accustomed to the vicissitudes of long-term projects than they had been with the Atlantic cable, they helped finance Carnegie's other bridge and railway enterprises, and also a steel-rail rolling mill he began to build in 1873 several miles south of Pittsburgh on the Monongahela River. As soon as Carnegie was convinced that iron would be superseded by more versatile, durable steel, he moved quickly. He named his new mill the Edgar Thomson Steel Works, after the president of the Pennsylvania Railroad. The E.T. plant went into operation in September 1875. Its first order, for two thousand steel rails, came from the giant Pennsylvania.

Having made a close study of railroad economics, Carnegie realized there would also be scale economies in making steel. He built big, efficient, technologically up-to-date mills and ran them at full capacity, which kept his production volume high and his costs low. In the summer of 1876, he crowed to Junius: "we have made a wonderful success—every sanguine prediction I have made is more than verified & we are making . . . steel rails for less than $50 per ton." With the lowest costs in the industry, he could "scoop" the market by underselling his rivals anytime he wanted. Although government tariffs protected this new industry, Carnegie told Junius proudly that "even if the tariff were off entirely, you couldn't send steel rails west of us."

Carnegie had access, partly through Junius, to the capital he needed for this propitious start, but unlike the railroads with their ongoing need for money, his steel operations soon proved so profitable that he no longer had to depend on

---

* By 1878 the company was bankrupt, and the Morgans reorganized it to protect their bondholder-clients: they set up a new corporation to buy the bridge, refinance its debt, and issue new stock. In 1881 Pierpont leased the bridge to Jay Gould, whose Wabash and Missouri Pacific railroads were now its principal customers.

bankers. In 1876 he built half the exhibition space for America's hundredth birthday party, the Philadelphia Centennial Exposition; two years later he secured the contract for the Brooklyn Bridge; in 1885 he was producing most of the steel that built America's tools, factories, tall buildings, ships, streetcars, and machines. With his tremendous economies of scale and the daunting amounts of money that would be required for anyone to build competing facilities, Carnegie had seized and consolidated his "first mover" advantage. He *loved* competition—he knew he could always win—and from 1875 to 1901 he reigned over American steel.

———

Junius also ventured in 1870 into a form of finance that had proved extremely successful for Europe's *haute banque* firms, the funding of government loans. The Rothschilds had financed Wellington's peninsular campaign, the first issue of Prussian bonds in 1818, and the Crimean War. Baring Brothers had underwritten the Louisiana Purchase and France's indemnities after Waterloo. Serving as bankers to states brought these houses political influence as well as profits and prestige. "There are six great powers in Europe," announced the Duc de Richelieu in 1818: "England, France, Prussia, Austria, Russia and Baring Brothers."

The Morgans had tried without success to break Jay Cooke's hold on the primary market for U.S. government securities in 1862. Over the next few years Junius had sponsored bond issues for the governments of Chile, Peru, and Spain, watching for larger opportunities to put his flourishing but not yet first-rank firm on a par with the world's great banks. He found an opening in 1870. War between France and Prussia broke out that summer when the moribund Second Empire of Napoleon III took on Otto von Bismarck's powerful North German Confederation. Junius thought the ambitious French Emperor (Bonaparte's nephew) had "signed his own death warrant." Four weeks later Napoleon III surrendered, but French republicans seized Paris and refused to give up.

As Prussian armies attacked Paris, officials of the fallen French government appealed to London for financial aid. Neither Rothschilds nor Barings would have anything to do with a loan under these circumstances. Lowering their sights to the next echelon of bankers, the French tried J. S. Morgan & Co. Junius made a quick survey of French financial history, he later told a reporter, found that no government since 1789 had failed to repay its debts, and contracted for a syndicated loan of £10 million ($50 million).

In retrospect, Junius claimed he had been sure of success, but in fact he took a large gamble at a moment of extreme political turbulence. Paris surrendered to the Iron Chancellor at the end of January 1871. When the French accepted Germany's harsh terms for peace (including a punitive $1 billion war indemnity) and elected a National Assembly dominated by monarchists, the republicans set up a revolutionary Commune and launched a civil war. The value of the "Morgan" bonds plummeted. Junius held on to the certificates he had not sold, bought others back at a steep discount, and helped France raise money in England to pay Bismarck's indemnity. In 1875 France redeemed the entire 1870 issue at par. J. S. Morgan & Co., having taken the bonds at 80 and bought back many more as the price fell, earned £1.5 million ($7 million) in commissions and redemptions on this loan—15 percent of its total value—as well as the respect of the international banking world.

———

Pierpont had not solved his problems with his partners, but in other respects he seemed to be thriving. In the fall of 1869 he moved his family uptown to a large house with a high front stoop at 6 East 40th Street, next door to the Fifth Avenue mansion of William Henry Vanderbilt (the Commodore's son) and diagonally across from the Croton Reservoir, whose Egyptian-styled walls rose fifty feet above the street. Herter Brothers furnished the new Morgan house in relatively modest style—they were doing far more elaborate work for the Vanderbilts and for Ulysses Grant's White House. The following summer, Pierpont and Fanny again rented Stonihurst at Highland Falls. Their third child, another Juliet Morgan, was born there in July 1870.

As wealthy Americans eager to emulate Europe set out to build cultural institutions of their own, Pierpont began to play a prominent role in New York's civic life. He helped found the American Museum of Natural History in 1869, along with Theodore Roosevelt (the father of the future president), Levi P. Morton, and several other friends. And when a group of prominent New Yorkers at the Union League Club announced plans to build an art museum in 1869, Morgan was among the first subscribers; he became a patron of the Metropolitan Museum of Art, with a contribution of $1,000, in 1871.

His professional situation was causing him such discomfort, however, that at thirty-three he decided to retire. When Charles Dabney announced at the beginning of 1871 that he would resign from the firm on July 1, Pierpont told George Morgan and Jim Goodwin in an awkward formal note that he wanted out as well—invoking familiar dictates of external necessity and health: "I feel it is my duty towards you to say to you thus early that I feel that I must reserve to myself the right to avail of this opportunity to withdraw from active business and liquidate." Having been "strongly urged to adopt such a course & take a respite at least for a time from the responsibilities of business life," he would comply, though "with great reluctance & not without grave doubts."

Just who had "strongly urged" him to withdraw from business is not clear—his doctors? his family?—but he was acutely conflicted over how much and with whom he wanted to work. He did not *have* to work. Other sons of wealthy men in the Gilded Age spent their time (and their fathers' money) hunting, sailing, traveling, drinking, racing horses and yachts. It was generally "new" men from more modest backgrounds who were building America's corporate commonwealth and making large fortunes. Though Pierpont had too strong a work ethic for a life of conspicuous leisure, as well as too much urgent pressure from London, he did not seem able to harness himself to his job, and depression periodically took the struggle out of his hands. Nervous troubles released him from all responsibility and constraint.

Junius had no intention of letting his son quit. If the junior Morgan's health required a leave of absence, the senior would grant it. But in establishing a position among the world's leading international bankers, Junius was looking to expand his base in the crucial U.S. market, not contract it, and his prince regent in New York was an essential part of the plan. If he had to sacrifice the disappointing George and the loyal but ineffectual Jim, he would. The real problem was finding a replacement for Dabney. Much as Junius had disliked Jim's report of Pierpont's unpopularity on Wall Street, he knew he needed a competent senior counselor on the far side of the Atlantic.

By fortuitous circumstance, Junius's requirements early in 1871 neatly coincided with those of the prominent Philadelphia banker Anthony J. Drexel, at Drexel & Co. Private financiers of Austrian Catholic descent, the three Drexel brothers were doing a large business in international trade through affiliated partnerships in New York (Drexel, Winthrop & Co.) and Paris (Drexel, Harjes & Cie.); they also had good connections in Germany. The brothers were worth approximately $7 million, and their American firms averaged $350,000 a year in profits.

At the end of 1870 forty-five-year-old Tony Drexel had won the account of the Pennsylvania Railroad away from his Philadelphia rival, Jay Cooke, and was looking for more dynamic leadership than he had in Paris or New York. Having done business with J. S. Morgan & Co., including transfers of funds for the 1870 French loan, he turned to Junius for advice. The senior Morgan at once suggested combining the houses of Drexel and Morgan. With their strong positions in Philadelphia and London, the two banks could "largely and profitably" increase their joint business in Paris. Junius's son would supply the necessary force in New York.

On March 8, 1871, Pierpont called on Tony Drexel, twelve years his senior, at home in West Philadelphia, Pennsylvania. In the course of a long talk, the two men agreed (subject to Junius's approval) that Pierpont would serve as senior partner in a New York firm called Drexel, Morgan & Co. This arrangement promised him more autonomy than he had under Dabney, with authority over Drexel's younger brother, Joseph, and another banker named J. Norris Robinson. He would work closely with Tony Drexel and his elder brother, Francis, in

Philadelphia, but still answer ultimately to Junius. First, however, he would take a year off.

When he returned to New York, he told Jim and George that he planned to retire and liquidate their firm. That was not the whole truth. Without mentioning his commitment to the Drexels, he reminded his partners of the "timely notice" he had given them two months earlier, and again justified his departure on grounds not of choice but of obligation. He had come "with the greatest reluctance" to the decision to withdraw—not for his own sake but for "those most near and dear to me and whose interests I feel bound to respect and protect." Did he mean his father and their banking business? His wife and children? Tortured syntax underlined his discomfort: he needed rest "at the risk of any personal sacrifice (even if necessary to the extent of sacrificing a business and position to build up & create which my labor of the past ten years has been devoted together with your own)." His renunciation deserved praise, not blame: "Our career together has been a long and most successful one and it takes a great deal of courage to bring it to a close." As he looked with "great anxiety" to the future, he doubted he would ever again be able to "give to business the close attention which I have done in the past." In fact he had promised his closest attention to the business of Drexel, Morgan & Co. in a year's time.

Junius approved of Pierpont and Tony Drexel's plans. George Morgan took a job with the firm of Heinemann & Payson. Jim Goodwin, accepting his dismissal like a good soldier, agreed to manage the New York office while Pierpont took his year off. In the end it was Jim, not Pierpont, who retired from Wall Street; he married Sarah Lippincott of Philadelphia in 1873, then divided his time between Hartford and New York, serving on corporate boards at Pierpont's invitation, and helping his brother, Frank, manage their Hartford real estate.

Drexel, Morgan & Co. opened for business on July 1, 1871, at 53 Exchange Place. A few days later, Pierpont set off with his family for a year abroad.

Pierpont in his early thirties.
(Archives of The Pierpont Morgan Library, New York)

ILL WINDS

Morgan's entourage in 1871 consisted of his wife, three children, two nursemaids, and Fanny's sister Mary. They stopped to see Junius and Juliet in England, then went on with a courier named Cesar through Germany, Austria, and Switzerland. At Vevey, Pierpont showed the children his old school. He had planned to spend the winter in Italy, but in Rome, feeling restless and "blue," he decided to take everyone to Egypt.

They sailed from Brindisi to Alexandria in the middle of December 1871, crossing the immense cultural distance that separates West from East. Morgan did not record his first impressions of this ancient, mysterious land, but he would return to what he called "my beloved Egypt" for the rest of his life.

Foreign rulers had been conquering Egypt and commandeering its cultural treasure for thousands of years. Herodotus, writing in the fifth century B.C., supplied the standard occidental text on Egypt until Napoleon's invasion in 1798 opened the country to modern European study and to further appropriation of artifacts and art. Between 1809 and 1828, the French produced an encyclopedic nineteen-volume *Description de l'Égypte*, and the English Orientalists John Gardner Wilkinson and Edward W. Lane followed with detailed studies of their own. (Morgan, engaged more by immediate experience than by scholarship, bought these books long after he began traveling to Egypt.) In the 1820s, Jean-François Champollion deciphered the hieroglyphics inscribed on the black basalt Rosetta Stone, which brought about a revolution in knowledge of ancient Egypt.

Regular steamship passage between Marseilles and Alexandria started in 1835, and by midcentury Cairo had become a major stop on the grand tour. The French diplomat Ferdinand de Lesseps organized efforts to dig a canal across the Suez isthmus in 1859. Ten years later, a few months after the completion of America's transcontinental railroad, Empress Eugénie sailed from Port Said to Suez for the formal opening of the canal. Among the other dignitaries who attended were the Prince and Princess of Wales, Emperor Franz Joseph, and an envoy from the Pope. Verdi, commissioned to write an opera for the event, failed to complete it in time: *Aïda* premiered in Cairo in 1871.

Thomas Cook took his first organized expedition up the Nile shortly after the opening of the canal, and in 1870 three hundred Americans registered at the consul general's office in Cairo. Seasoned travelers made fun of the "Cooks and Cookesses," to whom the locals referred as "Kukiyyeh."

Morgan chartered a private boat to sail up the Nile from Cairo in early January 1872, but when the unwieldy craft with its native crew and huge triangular sails proved too slow, he exchanged it for a Cook's steamer.* For three weeks the New Yorkers cruised through the lush Nile Valley past sights that had not changed for millennia—mud villages, date palms, fields of clover and barley, flocks of ducks and geese, men quarrying limestone in the blazing sun. They stopped at Giza, Memphis, Karnak, and Thebes, touring ancient pyramids and the remains of palaces and temples, then turned back north at Aswan. Their courier, Cesar, kept track of purchases en route—tea, chocolate, coffee, oranges, biscuits, tomatoes, medicines, cold cream, wine, tobacco, charcoal, an antique knife, ostrich eggs, bran for baths, "silk for Madame."

In mid-January the travelers returned to Rome, where Pierpont called on the American sculptor William Wetmore Story, an old Hartford friend now living in Renaissance splendor at the Palazzo Barberini on the Quirinal. Story had cast the bronze figure of George Peabody for the City of London, and his villa served as a salon for the colony of expatriate American artists in Rome. At the Palazzo Barberini the Morgans met the sculptor Harriet Hosmer, the painters Eugene Benson and Luther Terry, the composer Francis Boott, and Story's son, Waldo, also a sculptor. Henry James, who regularly stayed with the Storys, thought his host more likable than talented; in a book on *William Wetmore Story and His Friends* (1903), he called the sculptor's career "a sort of beautiful sacrifice to a noble mistake."

On April 17, the Morgans celebrated Pierpont's thirty-fifth birthday at the Hôtel Bristol on the Place Vendôme in Paris.† The Bristol had the first entry in

---

* Ancient Egyptians called their country "The Two Lands," referring to the southern portion between Aswan and Asyut as Upper Egypt and to the northern region as Lower. Parties sail up the Nile heading south and down returning north.

† The old Bristol, at No. 3-5 Place Vendôme, has been demolished. The current Hôtel le Bristol, on the Faubourg Saint-Honoré, appropriated the name after World War I.

Baedeker's "Hotels of the Highest Class," and its bedroom suites included dining room, drawing room, and (not the usual nineteenth-century hotel fare)
private bath. After this visit, Pierpont stayed at the Bristol whenever he was in
Paris.

At the beginning of May he left his family in France and went on to London
alone. His months of travel had had the desired effect—he was in high spirits,
reporting to Fanny that he had not bought anything at the opening of the
Royal Academy of Art, since "my pocket book for that purpose needs replen-
ishing." She was now ailing, however. He warned her from London not to
"overdo it and break down again," and found her a nurse, "Hanoverian—
Protestant—not bad looking, nothing stunning however," with good manners
and recommendations: "Shall I bring her over?" In June he accompanied his
father to Germany for a final tune-up at the Wildbad spa, then in August took
his party home.

———

Just before he left New York in the early summer of 1871, Pierpont had learned
that a large farm in Highland Falls, half a mile south of the house he had been
renting, was for sale. Since he would be abroad all year, he authorized Fanny's
father to negotiate for the property in his name. In April 1872 Mr. Tracy
bought the place, called Cragston, for $60,000 ($58,000 cash). In July he reported that "Pierpont's new barony" looked "radiant" in the summer sun.

The large wooden farmhouse on a hill overlooking the Hudson had been built
for a family named Baldwin in 1859. It was not on the fashionable east bank of
the river known as Millionaire's Row, where the Osborns and Secretary of State
Hamilton Fish had estates, but on the less stylish western side, near West Point.
Before the final papers were signed, both Morgans began imagining what they
would do with their new house. Pierpont had a thousand ideas for remodeling,
while Fanny wanted everything "*very* simple," with mats on the floors and furniture covered in chintz. Well aware that she and her husband had sharply divergent tastes—and that his usually prevailed—she hoped he would not make
the place too grand: "We each have our ambition," she wrote to Mary Sturges
from Europe, "and mine is *not* elegant furniture. I prefer to spend the money on
books and pictures and permanent things that thieves will not be tempted to
break through and steal." That she considered pictures less vulnerable to theft
than furniture seems odd. In any case, her husband wanted both.

The Morgans took possession of their new "barony" in the fall of 1872. It
had been a 368-acre working farm, with cattle barns and a dairy. Fanny got
her way about the chintz, but over the next several years Pierpont turned his
Hudson highlands acreage into an English country estate. He cleared away
rocks and woods to open the view, with wide lawns sweeping down to the river.
He filled the house with paintings, Chippendale, flowering plants, potted

palms, and Persian rugs. Outdoors there were tennis courts, stables, dog kennels, ponds, root cellars, greenhouses, vineyards, fruit trees, several gardens, and a Georgian carriage house. His gardeners planted thousands of daffodils along the Hudson shore and rhododendrons around the house. On his summer travels after 1872, Morgan brought along his own Cragston strawberries, tomatoes, and fresh cream.

————

Anthony Drexel left for a sabbatical of his own that fall. Pierpont worked out of his old office on Exchange Place until construction of a new building for the bank was finished at 23 Wall Street, on the corner of Broad, early in 1873.* Facing the New York Stock Exchange to the west and the Doric temple of the U.S. Subtreasury Building to the north, the six-story white marble Drexel building came to be known as "the Corner." Junius's old friend Levi P. Morton rented the ground floor for his banking firm, Morton, Bliss & Co.

In his first major undertaking as head of Drexel, Morgan & Co., Pierpont acquired the U.S. government as a client. Jay Cooke's success at selling Civil War bonds had earned him exclusive contracts for federal loans after 1865, but rival bankers, including the Morgans and Levi Morton, wanted to break his hold on this prestigious, lucrative business. Competition and monopoly were not restricted to railroads and steel mills, and the Morgan allies found an opening when the government began to refinance its Civil War debt.

The Treasury had made war bonds attractive by paying a relatively high interest rate of 6 percent. The bonds were mostly "5-20s"—twenty-year obligations that the government could pay off in five. Five years after the war, Treasury officials eager to reduce the $2.8 billion national debt decided to replace the wartime obligations with new ones bearing lower rates. In July 1870 Congress voted to refund $1.6 billion of the outstanding "5-20s" at 4 percent and 5 percent interest.

Proceeds from the sales of new bonds would be deposited in national banks, and when the deposits reached a certain amount—say, $5 million—the secretary would use the money to buy back $5 million of old 6 percent bonds. An 1869 Public Credit Act required that all these transactions be conducted in gold. The refunding loans were designed to reduce interest payments *and* help build up the country's gold reserves in preparation for return to a single monetary standard.

* The Drexel, Morgan records are incomplete, and there is no statement about the initial division of profits. The new firm started out with $1 million in capital, $900,000 of which was put up by the Drexel brothers as a "special bills payable" fund. Of the remaining $100,000, $61,000 came from the Philadelphia partners Tony Drexel, Francis Drexel, and J. Hood Wright, and $39,000 from New York ($15,000 each from Pierpont and Joseph Drexel, $9,000 from J. Norris Robinson).

When the first loan, offered through hundreds of disparate agencies and banks, sold poorly, Treasury Secretary George Boutwell called in Jay Cooke, who put together a transatlantic syndicate to share the selling and the risks. Cooke handled the issue so well that it put his house "head and shoulders above any American house in Europe," Levi Morton admitted to President Grant.

Still, Drexel, Morgan and Morton, Bliss wanted a share of the loans, and they had strong connections in Washington. Junius and Levi Morton had known Secretary Boutwell in Boston. Grant had been a trustee of the George Peabody Southern Education Fund since 1867, Tony Drexel managed Grant's personal finances, and Morton entertained the President and his wife at Newport.

The November 1872 election returned Grant to the White House (he defeated the Democratic editor of the New York *Tribune*, Horace Greeley) and sent Boutwell to the Senate. When the Secretary decided to issue another $300 million refunding loan before leaving the Treasury, Cooke proposed to take the entire issue in conjunction with London's Seligman Brothers and N. M. Rothschild & Sons. Pierpont called on Boutwell at the beginning of January 1873 to offer the services of a rival syndicate—Drexel, Morgan and Morton, Bliss in New York, with J. S. Morgan & Co., Baring Brothers, and Morton's English firm.

The junior Morgan commuted to Washington for weeks, and by the end of January he and Morton had worked out a compromise with Boutwell, Grant, and Cooke: the two banking groups would form a "super-syndicate" to sell a $300 million 5 percent loan. Pierpont and Morton kept London posted on the negotiations by cable, but at the last minute had to commit themselves without consultation. Junius scolded: "While we feel your action well intended, should not have been taken without all parties consent. Doubt whether Rothschild will ratify in which case Baring probably adopt similar course. If so, very embarrassing."

Junius was wrong. Rothschild (who was in any case Cooke's responsibility) and Baring both ratified the agreement. Morgan *père* seemed more annoyed at the New Yorkers' failure to get his final consent than interested in the fact that his son, at thirty-five, had just negotiated with the President, the Treasury Secretary, and the government's leading banker, and gained for the house of Morgan a prominent share in the federal loans.

A few months later Junius demanded to know why Drexel, Morgan allowed syndicate documents to issue from Cooke's office and bear that firm's signature first. He was eager to establish his bank as *primus inter pares*, but Morgan *fils*, in a reversal of their usual roles, made a pragmatic argument for deference to traditional rules: Cooke had legitimate leadership of the loan, since his group had signed the contract first, and there was "no questioning the fact that Cooke can do much better with the Clerical force of the Treasury Dept than anyone else can, particularly as they have got a house in Washington. We got everything we want that it is possible to get."

The 1873 loan did not sell well: when the subscription books closed in late February, the super-syndicate had placed less than $50 million of the $300 million issue. The general economy was showing signs of strain, and investors could buy comparable securities paying higher interest elsewhere. It took three years for the markets to absorb the bonds.

————

To keep communications secret once the Atlantic cable was completed, international bankers sent their messages in code. The Morgans used various systems and names over the years: Pierpont was "Vienna," "Charcoal," "Flintlock," and "Flitch"; at one point his New York firm was "Floatage," J. S. Morgan & Co. "Flutists," N. M. Rothschild & Sons "Forefather." A cable from Pierpont to Junius in the 1870s read in part: "amber despise maliciously fawn whisper shank plainness rediving absconding apish quicksand forcing smelting your comma whereupon meanly . . . repeats zealot," which meant "am desirous make negotiations which shall place Delaware & Hudson Canal Co. above any question for 3 years come what may . . . requires $5 million." Clerks did the decoding unless a cable was labeled "Denkstein," which meant it had to be read only by the person to whom it was addressed.

————

The postwar boom had paused for eighteen months in 1869–1870, then resumed, but by early 1873 money was tight, new construction had fallen off, and the stock market had the jitters. Pierpont, learning that Jay Cooke & Co. was having trouble, began calling in Drexel, Morgan's loans and building up cash reserves to prepare for a storm. He told Junius in April that he was handling only bonds "which can be recommended, without a shadow of a doubt, and without the least subsequent anxiety, as to payment of interest." Joseph Drexel wanted to hold on to the firm's risky, high-interest loans, but Pierpont overruled him.

Even as he took these precautionary steps, Pierpont was looking out for promising new prospects. He urged Junius in March to let him negotiate for bonds of Commodore Vanderbilt's New York Central Railroad, and continued to argue the point after his father refused: though the price seemed high, the value was "true"—just the sort of security with which the Morgan name ought to be connected—and as the price rose, Pierpont pointed out that had they moved in time, they could have had the entire issue to themselves.

He was feeling "remarkably well" in the spring of 1873—"never better," in fact, even though stocks were "very sick." Events justified his prudence. The Vienna stock market collapsed in May, and the trouble spread to Berlin, Amsterdam, Paris, and London. British investors stopped buying American securities.

Pierpont moved his household to Cragston for the summer in May. He commuted by steamboat, leaving the office every day at three. Fanny gave birth to their fourth child, Anne Tracy, in July. Highland Falls had "never looked so beautiful before," Pierpont told his father in an expansive mood. "I only wish all my investments turned out as favorably." He attributed his good spirits to his new partnership, and breathed a sigh of relief in June when Tony Drexel returned from his year off to take an "immense responsibility off my shoulders." The business was working "well and smoothly," Pierpont continued to Junius in July. In marked contrast to his final years with Dabney, Morgan, he found "nothing harassing or disturbing."

The economic crisis he had prepared for struck that fall, setting off one of the worst depressions in U.S. history. In early September a couple of defaulting railroads brought down banks that had lent them money. Then on September 18 Jay Cooke & Co. failed. Wall Street was stunned.

Cooke, the government's leading private banker, had also been ruined by a railroad—the Northern Pacific, chartered in 1864 to run from the Great Lakes to the Pacific Northwest. Just about everything had gone wrong for this road. It started with a huge grant of federal land, but the parcels did not sell. Cooke entered the picture in 1869, agreeing to underwrite $100 million of Northern Pacific bonds—just before the Franco-Prussian War curtailed European investment. The road's construction costs ran much higher than predicted, and the tracks reached only as far as Bismarck, North Dakota, when the NP defaulted. Cooke tried to keep it in funds with short-term loans, but by September, hugely overextended, he could no longer meet his own obligations, and went bankrupt. Investors panicked. Stock prices collapsed. Fifty-seven investment firms failed. On September 20 the New York Stock Exchange closed for the first time in its history.

The panic touched off by Cooke's failure exposed the weaknesses in the economy as a whole. With no central bank, the country had no way to increase its currency supply or make cash available to faltering firms. The recent boom had been fueled by too much unsecured debt, and speculation had driven stock prices far beyond rational valuations. Moreover, the United States still depended heavily on capital that could vanish overnight—European investors held $1.5 billion of American securities in 1873. The day after Cooke's suspension, Pierpont cabled Junius: "Affairs continue unprecedented bad large failures Phila NY." He described the panic to a colleague as far worse than those of 1837 and 1857—a "cyclone, which came upon us without an hour's warning."

He *had* taken warning, however, and his own affairs were in good shape thanks to his early defensive measures. "Everything satisfactory with us with ample margin," he continued to his father. "Impossible foresee future consequently important prepared for any emergency." A few days later, at the height of the panic, he and Drexel reported proudly: "No anxiety whatever as to selves

NY Phila. Had over in Bank last night nearly 1½ millions." Assured of their firms' safety, they turned to the larger picture: "Our anxiety is to prevent disaster spreading."

The two bankers could not keep the disaster from spreading, though they tried to function as an unofficial central bank, providing other firms with cash and importing money from England to ease the sudden contraction. President Grant authorized the Treasury to pump $26 million of retired greenbacks back into circulation, which brought some relief. The Stock Exchange reopened after ten days. Nonetheless, the economy slid into a crippling six-year decline that would be known until the 1930s as the Great Depression.

Demand dried up. Businesses contracted, cut wages, and laid off employees. Railroad construction dropped from 7,500 miles in 1872 to 1,600 in 1875; by the following year over half the roads in the country were bankrupt. Coal production fell off by five million tons between 1873 and 1875, pig iron by half a million. Investment capital disappeared; foreigners lost $600 million in the United States between 1873 and 1879. By 1878, 327 banks had suspended payment. Ten thousand companies were wiped out that year, with assets worth over $250 million.

The depression brought about major structural changes in American politics, business, and finance. It sharpened conflicts between interest groups in a stratified and increasingly pluralistic society, signaled the end of the country's preoccupation with slavery, union, and civil rights, and put monetary questions once more in the forefront of daily life.

The postwar boom in productivity led everywhere to the problem of excess capacity. Even before the contraction, industries across the country had been struggling to cope with periodic imbalances of supply and demand. Too many goods flooding the market with no increase in the money supply had driven prices down, and the depression cut them further: wholesale prices, which had doubled during the Civil War, fell 30 percent between 1873 and 1879.

Adam Smith noted in 1776 that "People of the same trade seldom meet together, even for merriment and diversion, but the conversation ends in a conspiracy against the public, or in some contrivance to raise prices." The impetus to fix prices increased in the late nineteenth century in direct proportion to the size of potential profits and losses. "The tendencies Smith observed seemed mild indeed when compared with the manic compulsions stimulated afterward by the revolution in productivity"—writes the historian Thomas K. McCraw— "which made the potential rewards of industrial success far greater than anything possible in Smith's era. It had the same magnifying effect on the potential cost of failure: the immense capital investment represented by a large modern factory or string of factories raised the penalty for failure beyond anything Smith could have contemplated."

Rising productivity after the industrial revolution had created overcapacity problems all over Europe as well. European governments, playing an active role in their countries' economic affairs, gave legal sanction to cartels that set prices and limited production. In making these agreements enforceable, foreign states curtailed free-market competition, promoted the growth of loose horizontal associations, mediated industrial conflict, and imposed a certain amount of stability on the marketplace. The price they paid for "managing" competition this way tended to be reduced productivity and fewer innovative gains. In the United States, by contrast, national commitment to individual initiative and unfettered market forces, matched by ideological opposition to central planning, ensured that the "state" had no power to control industrial overcapacity or modulate fluctuations in the business cycle. Competition red in tooth and claw was animating U.S. economic growth, as private capital in search of profit built giant modern enterprises, and powerful industrialists devised private solutions to the problems they faced.

Individual railroad managers struggled to stabilize their markets and earn enough to meet fixed costs. Forced to keep rates low where they faced competition—usually on long routes between major cities—they raised prices on short hauls in rural areas where they had monopoly control. And they gave discounts to large shippers who promised steady business. These discriminatory policies outraged farmers and other small-scale shippers, who formed cooperative organizations called Granges in self-defense, and demanded external regulation of the roads.

The railroads, too, tried cooperation in self-defense. As early as 1854 the Big Four trunk lines had met in New York with their western allies to set prices, coordinate through traffic on connecting roads, and agree on "general principles which should govern Railroad Companies competing for the same trade, and preventing ruinous competition. . . ." Incentives to compete proved stronger than the inclination to cooperate, however. With no enforceable sanctions, these peace treaties invariably fell apart.

As the long depression of the seventies reduced traffic and increased competition on roads across the nation, the heads of the trunk lines tried again to divide up traffic in the West. John W. Garrett of the Baltimore & Ohio, a long-term Morgan client, reported to Junius in March 1877 that they had agreed to act upon one "great principle"—"to earn more and to spend less, to fix a system under which reasonable and equitable rates between all points can be established and maintained." This attempt at confederation also failed.

What did seem to work was consolidated ownership of regional systems that could maximize efficiency, minimize costs, coordinate information, and restrict competition—and the strong roads were moving in that direction. By 1874 the giant Pennsylvania controlled six thousand miles of road (8 percent of all U.S.

mileage) between the Atlantic seaboard, the Great Lakes, and the Mississippi River. Jay Gould in the seventies acquired control of the Union Pacific Railroad, the Wabash Railroad, and Western Union, building a transportation and communications empire in the West.

In different ways, Andrew Carnegie and John D. Rockefeller took command of other wildly competitive industries in the seventies, creating huge, low-cost, high-volume enterprises organized to take advantage of technological innovations, administrative rationalization, and tremendous economies of scale. Carnegie dominated the steel market by relentlessly underselling less efficient rivals, and by running his mills at full blast to maintain high production volumes even if he wore the mills out in the process. It was, he knew from careful cost accounting, cheaper to build new mills than to cut production runs. And he did not hesitate to scrap old methods when a new discovery promised to lower his costs. He had installed expensive Bessemer converters at his E.T. plant in 1873–75, but as soon as he was convinced that an amateur English chemist had found a way to make steel better and more cheaply with open-hearth furnaces, he ordered open-hearth equipment and switched to the new technique. Small savings per ton at very high volumes quickly justified the cost.

The depression enabled Carnegie to buy up competitors and raw-material suppliers at fractions of their values. By 1881 he had consolidated steelworks, iron mines, coke plants, and coalfields into the tightly organized Carnegie Bros. & Co., Ltd., capitalized at $5 million. He himself held 55 percent of the new partnership, which earned $2 million profit its first year. With his immense competitive advantages, this master strategist had no use for cooperative cartels. "The market is mine whenever I want to take it," he told a rival. "I see no reason why I should present you with all my profits."

John D. Rockefeller by 1873 owned the largest consolidated oil-refining complex in the world, Standard Oil of Ohio. During the depression he expanded his facilities, improved the quality of his products, kept a hawkish eye on costs, stockpiled cash, bought out rivals, and began the process of vertical integration—acquiring raw materials such as ore lands and timber as well as distribution facilities such as tank cars, ships, and warehouses—to protect his enterprise from the fluctuations of the market. His tactics were not genteel. He forced competitors to sell out by spying on them, depriving them of raw materials he controlled, and slashing prices until they had to operate at a loss. Because he shipped the huge volumes of freight the railroads needed for income, he could force the roads' managers not only to give him discounted rates but also to kick back a portion of the higher fees his rivals had to pay. By the end of the seventies the Rockefeller partnerships controlled 90 percent of America's oil-refining capacity, as well as pipelines, gathering facilities, and transportation systems. In 1882 the partnerships reorganized as the Standard Oil Trust, which held the securities of forty constituent companies worth $70 million.

These shrewd, aggressive, single-minded "captains of industry" were operating not according to grand plans but on pragmatic instinct. Trying to harness the tremendous productive capacities unleashed by new technologies and huge domestic U.S. markets, they built companies that came to dominate world trade and earned them immense personal fortunes.

Before the industrial revolution, Adam Smith described how the invisible hand of market forces governed economic activity: individual firms invariably tried to grow faster and make more money than their rivals, but competition ensured that all earned roughly equal profits, and none could dominate the market. That model of "perfect" competition represented the American ideal, but with the rise of large-scale, capital-intensive enterprise it became possible for a few giant firms to overcome competitive restraints and control significant portions of their markets.

The great size, ruthless efficiency, and sometimes brutal tactics of these companies aroused fierce political opposition. Yet the firms that succeeded over the long run did so largely because their operational strategies—making use of scale efficiencies, new technologies, vertical integration, and rationalization of the production process—made economic sense. As the "visible hand" of management, in Alfred Chandler's potent phrase, took over from the market, the country entered into a debate about competition and regulation that would continue for over a hundred years.

The successful entrepreneurs of the late nineteenth century rarely concerned themselves with the political or social consequences of their actions, and few had moral qualms about their work. They saw themselves building a great industrial empire and making America rich. "To imagine that such men did not sleep the sleep of the just would be romantic sentimentalism," reflected Richard Hofstadter decades later. "In the Gilded Age even the angels sang for them."

Not all the angels. To farmers caught in the vise of falling prices and the rising cost of debt, to small businessmen ruined by corporate giants, and to workers who earned minimal wages laboring long hours under hazardous conditions with no job security, the consolidation of large-scale, mechanized production in the hands of men such as Carnegie, Rockefeller, and the railroad barons represented everything their antecedents had fought a revolution against. The opponents of big business had little political leverage in the 1870s, however, and no expectation of government help.

Reviewing a French book about the United States in 1876, *The New York Times* criticized the author for failing to realize how *unimportant* Americans considered their government: "Its powers are more limited, its functions less extensive, its relations to the people and to other Governments of less consequence than in the case of European Governments." The *Times* went on proudly: "The American citizen of to-day can pass a busy or a leisurely life of great or of moderate prosperity, and have very little personal occasion to know or to care what sort of men fill the offices. . . . Our Government nowhere touches our purse or our pride as that of France does those of its citizens. It is not a dispenser of special honors of any kind; it does not stand guard for us against the encroachments of socialism . . . it cannot greatly help or hinder us in any of our ordinary interests and ambitions."

The government also did not stand guard against the economic power of big business, and it *was* dispensing special favors to those who could afford them. Political parties in the post–Civil War period operated more on the basis of patronage than principle—according to Hofstadter, "they divided over spoils, not issues"—and the corporate bank accounts of the Gilded Age fueled the politics of patronage.

Party leaders at all levels of government brokered deals, handed out offices, and managed the money that supported their increasingly complex organizations and expensive election campaigns. Legislators from both parties accepted cash, stock, free passes, directorships, and other financial favors from railroad promoters, and voted for bills that favored the roads. At one point four different roads were paying Republican National Committee chairman William E. Chandler. Liberal Republican Lyman Trumbull sat in the Senate while on retainer from the Illinois Central. Jay Cooke before his failure took out a mortgage for House Speaker James G. Blaine, and sold land at a steep discount to Ohio Governor Rutherford B. Hayes. One Gilded Age reformer quipped that Rockefeller had done everything imaginable to the Pennsylvania State Legislature except refine it—and that the Pennsylvania Railroad ran the State Supreme Court "as if it were one of its limited trains." Job Stevenson of Ohio characterized the House of Representatives in 1873 as "an auction room where more valuable considerations were disposed of under the speaker's hammer than in any other place on earth."

The Grant administration proved to be the most corrupt of the century, with financial scandal tarring nearly every member of the cabinet. Both of Grant's vice presidents were implicated in the 1872 Crédit Mobilier fraud, in which a construction company set up by Union Pacific Railroad profiteers issued stock to congressmen who authorized federal subsidies and looked the other way, until the arrangement was exposed by the New York *Sun*. The Navy Secretary took bribes from naval suppliers, the Interior Secretary's son sold surveying contracts, the Secretary of War got kickbacks from Indian trading posts, the President's private secretary was involved in a whiskey-tax scam, and Grant's brother-in-law helped Jay Gould corner gold.

Pierpont championed one of the few honest officers in Grant's cabinet— Benjamin Bristow, Treasury Secretary from 1874 to 1876—and was disgusted by Washington corruption. Still, the Republican commitment to monetary stability mattered more to the Morgans than any individual figure or scandal. In 1874 Grant vetoed a moderately expansionist Inflation Bill that would have increased greenback circulation by $64 million. Wall Street was delighted with the veto, as were liberal reformers and western bankers who saw the bill as an unhealthy expansion of the government's power to regulate the money supply.

The Republicans suffered huge losses in that fall's midterm elections, chiefly because of the economic crisis. Democrats won governorships in eight states and control of the House for the first time since the war. Samuel J. Tilden, the reformist new governor of New York, called the outcome "not merely a victory but a revolution." It was not quite the revolution Democrats had in mind: for most of the next two decades the parties split control of the Senate, House, and White House, which meant that few strong initiatives emanated from Washington. Since the federal government had no clear fiscal or monetary policy, leadership on economic questions came largely from the nation's financial capital—New York.

—

The Morgan bank was doing well in all this tumult. For 1873, the year of the panic, the Philadelphia and New York houses netted over $1 million (Philadelphia roughly $580,000, New York $460,000), after deducting $200,000 to cover possible bad debts. "I don't think there is another concern in the country can begin to show such a result," Pierpont told his father, whom he was beginning to echo. "Profitable as the year was, it has been attended by hard work and great anxiety during the panic, and the satisfaction is greatest from the enhanced position accorded us by the public generally which is very marked."

His definition of "the public" did not include many people west of the Hudson or east of Lexington Avenue, but his social world also acknowledged his "enhanced position." After he saw one of his wife's friends off on a steamer to Europe at the end of 1873, the woman gushed: "Fanny how I do love him—I can't help saying so he is now on such a grand noble scale."

The depression-era cutback in commercial activity increased the stakes and the conflicts on Wall Street. "The competition for the best business is getting very strong & the margins consequently less," the junior Morgan told the senior early in 1875, but "we have been very successful thus far in getting our share." There was competition even within the Morgan/Drexel alliance, as New York surpassed Philadelphia: Drexel, Morgan earned nearly $600,000 in 1874, reported Pierpont, "pretty good for a dull year," and "Phila. netted about 400,000. New York carried the palm."

In August of 1875, the failure of his first employer, Duncan, Sherman & Co., brought his own firm "a great many new accounts," Pierpont told a colleague, "so it is an ill wind that blows nobody good." Still, those who wanted the "best" business had to go after it. Bankers who could sell government bonds in Europe, especially during a depression when domestic capital was tight, would gain not only profit and prestige but a voice in the direction of U.S. monetary policy—and Jay Cooke's failure left the government's business open to competition.

After corruption charges forced Boutwell's successor at the Treasury to resign in 1874, Grant appointed Benjamin H. Bristow, a liberal Kentucky Republican and Union army veteran who had argued most of the government's Reconstruction cases between 1870 and 1872, when he served as U.S. solicitor general. Bristow was physically imposing at six feet, 225 pounds, and the *New York World* thought the firm "sweep" of his jaw promised "aggressive perseverance" at the Treasury. Secretary of State Hamilton Fish said Grant had finally done something to redeem himself by appointing the trustworthy Bristow.

The Morgans took no part in Bristow's first refunding loan, but secured a share of the second early in 1875, with Rothschilds in the lead. Junius told Bristow by cable of his "pleasure in thus responding your wishes & in being associated with negotiations bringing us into more intimate relations yourself." Pierpont followed up with a call on the Secretary, whom he found "clearheaded [and] reliable . . . very different from his immediate predecessors," but unlikely to stay at Treasury for long since he was "evidently ill at ease" with the corruption around him. The new loan sold well, but Pierpont resented the arrogance of Rothschild's U.S. agent, August Belmont: "So far as we are concerned," he complained, "we are entire nonentities—we are never consulted or informed [by Belmont] & have no more idea of what is being done than if we had no interest or liability in the matter."

Over the following year, Pierpont strengthened his alliance with Bristow. He told the Secretary in February 1876: "I am entirely at your service at any time and if you want to see me, I will go on to Washington whenever you like"—to which Bristow replied, "I need not assure you that, should refunding operations be resumed, I should very much hope to have the benefit of the services of Mr. Drexel and your house in the negotiations."

Two weeks later, an investigation launched by Bristow established that Grant's private secretary had helped the Whiskey Ring avoid paying millions in federal taxes—a finding that infuriated the President, and prompted rumors that the Treasury Secretary would have to resign. From New York, Pierpont wrote Bristow "to beg you on behalf of all those who desire an honest and capable control of the Treasury Department to stand by your colors at any personal sacrifice." Bristow replied, "I beg to express my gratitude for your words of sympathy and confidence—and to say that it looks now as if matters had assumed a different shape. At any rate the discomfort of my position is not as great as it has been for a few weeks past."

Wall Street, noting the warmth of feeling between the Secretary and 23 Wall Street, speculated that Bristow would leave the government to join Drexel, Morgan. When Bristow did resign—forced out by Grant that June—it was not to join the Morgan bank but to make a bid for the Republican presidential nomination. He had the support of liberal reformers, but the combined opposition of Grant and the party bosses shut him out.

———

Pierpont had been relatively free of depression in his new partnership, but in the spring of 1875 his mood once again turned blue. Fighting off a head cold in early March, he told Junius he felt "as if I could bite 10-penny nails with pleasure . . . I feel way down & would sell myself for [a] small sum."

As before, feeling "way down" coincided with difficulties in his office—this time, over Drexel's younger brother, Joseph. Pierpont was fed up with this partner, who had resisted calling in their loans before the 1873 panic. "He is *very* sensitive," the junior Morgan complained to the senior, "and I have to study his whims constantly to avoid any questions." He did not hide his dislike, and other people noticed: a colleague described him that spring as a "rough, uncouth fellow, continually quarreling with [Joseph] Drexel in the office."

To ease the tension, Drexel partner J. Hood Wright came up from Philadelphia. Pierpont found Wright the exact opposite of Joseph—competent, quick, accurate, and "a capital negotiator"—and would have liked to continue with him alone but did not see how he could jettison Tony Drexel's brother. He felt as trapped as he had at Dabney, Morgan five years before. And as he had then, he decided "the best thing would be for me to give up myself—I don't feel good for much anyway."

Joseph Drexel himself decided to retire in the fall of 1875: he wasn't getting along with his brothers *or* Morgan, and cannot have liked this situation any more than they did. Still, Pierpont felt "strongly disposed to give up." Since he tended to see things as black or white, discord with one partner undermined everything else, and the plunge in his mood after three internally tranquil years prompted thoughts of drastic change.

He did not have the single-minded absorption in his work that other barons of the Gilded Age did. Carnegie didn't even pause to get married until 1887, when he was fifty-two (after his ambitious, possessive mother died). Rockefeller, the son of a con man from western New York State, had started out with none of Morgan's sense of patrician entitlement; everything about the founder of Standard Oil—his thin straight line of a mouth, ascetic habits, Baptist piety, hard bargains—spelled diligence and thrift. The only time a colleague ever saw him enthusiastic was when Rockefeller learned that one of his buyers had bought a cargo of oil far below market price: "He bounded from his chair with a shout of joy, danced up and down, hugged me, threw up his hat, acted so like a madman that I have never forgotten it."

Living well mattered to Morgan as much as doing well. He supervised the plantings at Cragston as carefully as he did the wording of government bonds: one Sunday in the fall of 1875 he proudly cut 278 of his own roses, and later stipulated while ordering new bushes from the head of a British nursery that he wanted no Standards unless they had "extra stout stems and 2–3 year old heads and roots," the stems not less than "an inch to 1½″ in diameter," and "*half,* not full Standards." In his late thirties he was drawn to many things besides banking—travel, society, the Episcopal Church, history, art—although as always it was his delicate health, not deliberate choice, that dictated respite.

Disposed to "give up" in September 1875, he deferred to his father: the decision "must depend in a great measure on what your plans may be for next year." It can hardly have surprised him that those plans did not include the demise of Drexel, Morgan. Junius instructed his son to find a new partner.

Pierpont canvassed the field and found it wanting: the reputable figures on Wall Street seemed dull, the disreputable a dime a dozen. To Junius he complained about how few businessmen seemed "unexceptionable in character, ability, and experience. . . . The longer I live [he was all of thirty-eight] the more apparent becomes to me the absence of brains—particularly evenly balanced brains." Still, he did find a new partner, an Italian-born international shipping merchant named Egisto P. Fabbri, who had done business with Junius for years.

Fabbri was an unusual choice. When Junius raised questions about working with a foreigner, Pierpont pointed out that their new colleague was a naturalized American, the Drexels Austrian, and Wright a Scot. The house of Morgan would have a blue-blood Yankee reputation for the next hundred years, but Pierpont's surprisingly meritocratic instincts did not confine him to the Anglo-Saxon Protestant American elite. Fabbri joined Drexel, Morgan on January 1, 1876—he was just then sequestered on the jury that sent "Boss" Tweed to jail—and took to banking, Pierpont reported, "like a duck to water."*

Pierpont's assessment of the "absence of brains" on Wall Street did not endear him to colleagues, and those who did not know him well continued to be put off by his lofty manner. Yet attentive observers might have seen that he was surrounding himself with men of integrity and professional skill. In choosing to work with Tony Drexel, Benjamin Bristow, J. Hood Wright, and Egisto Fabbri—and *not* with Charles Dabney, George Morgan, Jim Goodwin, or Joseph Drexel—he strengthened his position for the future.

---

* In the new partnership 45 percent of the profits went to Morgan, 40 percent to the Philadelphia house, 15 percent to Fabbri. Each partner left half his share of the annual earnings on deposit at the firm, to assure it adequate capital.

Junius remained in command. Late in 1875, on the other side of the Atlantic, he decided that his son was spreading himself too thin, and instructed him to resign from several corporate boards. Pierpont complied, but protested that he had refused ten directorships for every one he accepted, and never took one he did not think "advantageous" to their firm. He sat on the boards of the National Bank of Commerce, the Central Trust Company, the Delaware and Hudson Canal Company (to which he had leased the Albany & Susquehanna), the Pullman Palace Car Company, Carnegie's Illinois and St. Louis Bridge, and several railroads. Some of these commitments took considerable time, others less ("although I attend to the duties—I will never be a dead head"), and he justified the work on grounds to which his father could hardly object, as "of great service to our business beside being associated with gentlemen of recognized position and influence." He joined more boards over the next decade. What seemed to the elder Morgan a waste of time became in the younger's hands a crucial instrument of financial oversight and control.

———

Persuaded for the second time not to retire, Pierpont took his family to Europe for the summer of 1876 as the United States celebrated its centennial. Six Morgans sailed from New York in June, and on arriving in England went straight to Dover House, an estate Junius was leasing in rural Roehampton (he bought it two years later). Seven miles from London—twenty-five minutes by carriage from Princes Gate—Dover House stood on the ridge of a hill overlooking Wimbledon Common and Putney Heath. The New Yorkers drove up a winding carriage road from Putney Park Lane, through wide stone entrance gates and handsome old trees and lawns, to the columned porticoes of a large Regency villa. Junius showed them through its octagonal entrance hall, glassed-in conservatory, skylighted staircase, sixteen bed and dressing rooms, two kitchens, and separate cellars for coal, beer, and wine. Outside, he had stables, flower gardens, a dairy, and a lawn-tennis court; he put in strawberry and asparagus beds, and greenhouses for orchids, peaches, melons, and figs.

Junius at sixty-three was aging well. He had a full head of white hair, and his air of wise distinction seemed clarified by time. Still vigorous and trim, he rode daily, and challenged his sons-in-law at tennis. (Pierpont now avoided all exercise more vigorous than walking.) The years had been less kind to Juliet, who had withdrawn further than ever into invalidism and complaint. She no longer traveled, and rarely left her room. Dover House reflected her presence not at all.

It did reflect Junius's interest in art—he had begun buying landscape paintings and portraits. Luigi Palma di Cesnola, appointed director of New York's Metropolitan Museum in 1879, later described Junius as a "liberal patron" who had "no pretensions to making a picture gallery, but bought many paintings simply to decorate his London house and his beautiful country seat." In the spring of 1876, shortly before Pierpont's family arrived, a spectacular theft deprived Junius of a portrait he was about to buy—of Georgiana, Duchess of Devonshire, by Thomas Gainsborough.*

Georgiana had posed for Gainsborough in a white dress with a blue silk petticoat and sash, masses of elaborate curls, and a huge plumed hat. Half pouting, half smiling, she regards the viewer with a coy combination of innocence and surmise, one hand holding a delicate pink rosebud, the other a full-blown rose. The dealer William Agnew bought the portrait from Christie, Manson, and Woods in May 1876 for a little over £10,000 ($51,540)—the highest price yet paid for a picture at auction—and put it on display at his Bond Street gallery. Junius contracted to buy it for an undisclosed sum, estimated by outsiders at £14,000 to £15,000.†

Crowds lining up to see the Duchess attracted the attention of an American thief named Adam Worth. A German Jew who emigrated to Boston as a child, Worth had made a distinguished career of crimes against property, never people. In 1869 he stole $1 million from a Boston bank, then moved to Europe calling himself Henry J. Raymond, the just-deceased founder of *The New York Times*. At the time of Agnew's *Duchess* exhibition, he needed something to ransom his less-talented brother from Newgate Prison, and decided the painting would be perfect. Late one night he climbed through a gallery window, cut Georgiana out of her frame, and escaped—a coup that captured headlines on both sides of the Atlantic. Agnew's offered a £1,000 reward, but before Worth opened negotiations with Scotland Yard his brother was released on a technicality, which left Adam with a world-famous white elephant, and Junius Morgan bereft.

Worth eventually smuggled the portrait to the United States in the false bottom of a trunk. For the next twenty-five years he corresponded with Agnew's, partly through the personal columns of the London *Times*, claiming that his heist had made the painting even more valuable than it was in May of 1876. He demanded £15,000 for Georgiana, and referred, in an odd version of the Pygmalion story, to their "elopement." Junius never saw his lost Duchess again.

---

* The daughter of John, first Earl Spencer, Georgiana had married the fifth Duke of Devonshire when she was seventeen in 1774. (She was the great-great-great-great-aunt of Diana, Princess of Wales.) Her celebrated beauty and libertine ways made her the talk of late-eighteenth-century England, and nineteenth-century *modistes* copied her extravagant style.

† There were questions about its authenticity. It had been sliced down to three-quarter length, allegedly by an English schoolmistress to fit the space over a mantel. The painter John Everett Millais inspected the canvas at Christie's and announced, "I don't believe Gainsborough ever saw it."

The younger Morgans stayed at Dover House for the month of July 1876. Pierpont went to London with Junius for meetings and dinners—saving the menu (all in French) from an American centennial celebration at the Westminster Palace Hotel on July 4—and watched the boat races at Henley. He discussed business with two new partners Junius had imported from Boston, Jacob C. Rogers and S. Endicott Peabody, a distant relative of George. With Fanny he spent a weekend in Kent at the country house of Henry Riversdale Grenfell, an MP and a director of the Bank of England, and another nearby in Seven Oaks with the Peabodys. Touring Kent, the Morgans visited Sir Philip Sidney's Penshurst, Lord Sackville's Knole Park, and "another beautiful place belonging to the inventor of some hair-dye," reported Fanny.

Alone, Pierpont went to Paris for a few days on business, reporting to his wife in a buoyant mood: "The King of Greece & myself arrived safely at Hotel Bristol this morning. He took the swell apartments au premier – I 'au troisieme' – at same time I had rather be myself than the King." Fanny had opposed this separation. He urged her to "Keep good courage – it won't last always and you will have the satisfaction of doing your duty & you know I love you dearly & am with you always." Finally, after eleven years of marriage, he spelled her name with a *y*.

She cheered up when they took the children to Scotland in August and she had her husband more to herself. "After dinner P. & I walked off over the bridge . . . home before dark," she wrote in her diary, and "Pierpont and I walked off a little way down the river and came back for a quiet evening in our room." Pierpont (who could take only so much peace and quiet) went back to London on business after a week.

Tony Drexel was in Washington that August negotiating for a new government loan. The leading contender this time was Joseph Seligman, a close friend of and financial adviser to President Grant. Seligman had emigrated from Bavaria to the United States in 1837, at nineteen. By 1862, when he and his brothers started the New York banking firm of J. & W. Seligman & Co., they had built a merchandising empire worth nearly $1 million. Their German-Jewish bank with offices in London and Frankfurt had sold U.S. bonds in Germany during the Civil War, and in the summer of 1876 former Treasury Secretary Bristow warned Drexel in "strict secrecy" that Seligman would have the "inside track" on the refundings as long as Grant remained in office. At Bristow's urging, Drexel went with Seligman in July to meet with the President and his new Treasury Secretary, Lot Morrill.

Election-year politics loomed over these negotiations. Both parties were so mired in corruption that they had to promise reform. The Republicans rejected House Speaker James Blaine, whose hands were deep in the railroad tills, and settled on the pallid but respectable Rutherford Hayes, a hard-money conserv-ative and three-term governor of Ohio—Henry Adams called him "a third-rate nonentity."* The Democrats countered with New York's wealthy Governor Tilden, also a sound-money man, who had helped break up the Tammany Hall ring of "Boss" Tweed. With his commitment to gold and years of experience as a railroad attorney, Tilden had the support of prominent Wall Street Demo-crats, including the Rothschilds' American agent, August Belmont.

Belmont, as former chairman of the Democratic National Committee, had attacked the Republicans at his party's convention in June, and as a result Seligman and Grant wanted to cut the Rothschilds out of the next syndicate. Tony Drexel conferred from Washington by cable with Junius and Pierpont in London, while Fabbri in New York reported "*very great* discontent" with the ad-ministration: Grant had been acting "injudiciously, if not recklessly, removing from mere personal motives men of excellent standing & record" (among them, Bristow), and causing trouble for the Republicans "at a juncture when unity & concentration of forces are of vital importance." The politically astute Fabbri was not sanguine about the outcome of the election, and warned that if the Democrats won, Belmont would be a useful ally. In any case, given the Roth-schilds' powerful international position, "it would be a mistake to ignore" them.

Day after day, Pierpont postponed his return to Scotland. Finally in late Au-gust the bankers and the Treasury agreed to terms for a $200 million 4½ per-cent loan, with Rothschilds in the lead.† While Seligman had started out with an "inside track," the Drexel, Morgan group had pulled even. The loan sold quickly in London and New York.

When Pierpont rejoined his wife and children on August 29, he brought startling news: they were going to stay abroad all winter. His American part-ners were managing well enough in his absence that he could take another full year's leave.

This radical change of plans cannot have been easy for a large family that had planned and packed for a summer. Louisa, traveling with her father in Eu-rope years later during the worst depression of his life, reflected to Fanny that his nervous anxieties and black despair were "just such as you were meeting during those years that you spent over here, only worse!" The Morgans spent the autumn of 1876 in Paris.

* Adams had backed Bristow, as had Henry Cabot Lodge and Samuel Bowles, editor of the Springfield *Republican*, who wrote in February 1876: "Bristowism . . . is breaking out now on all sides." After the Republican convention, Democrats published a paper saying that in re-jecting Bristow the GOP had demonstrated its indifference to real reform.

† Belmont's signature appeared at the top of the contract, and the Rothschilds took 41.25 percent of the first $40 million pledge. Drexel, Morgan and J. & W. Seligman, with their Lon-don associates, split 33.75 percent. Morton, Bliss took the other 25 percent.

In the United States, the Democrats were playing up the specter of Grant-era corruption and straddling the fence on finance—they had paired Tilden with an easy-money vice presidential candidate on an inflationist platform—and seemed likely to win. Drexel, Morgan contributed $5,000 to Hayes's struggling campaign in September, cabling its London partners: "Such contributions most advantageous for the future Syndicate business and facilities," and urging London to contribute as well, since "Defeat means inflation." Junius doubted the wisdom of this policy, "looking our position" as foreign bankers interested in U.S. government finance, but agreed to subscribe $5,000 through Drexel, Morgan "for the purpose mentioned. JSMCo's name must not appear." In November neither candidate earned enough electoral votes to win, though Tilden got 51 percent of the popular vote. With each side claiming victory in several disputed southern states—and each accusing the other of fraud—Congress appointed a commission to determine the outcome. This group awarded the victory to Hayes after a long, bitter fight, two days before the inauguration.

From Paris in December the Morgan family went on to Egypt. They stayed at Cairo's palatial New Hotel, then took a Cook's steamer, the *Beni Souef,* up the Nile. Pierpont had no interest in roughing it or going native. His party traveled in regal style with a dragoman (interpeter/guide), a French physician, several Egyptian servants, a nurse, a maid, a French waiter, their regular courier, Cesar, and Fanny's cousin Mary Huntington. On the Nile they had hot baths, western beds, French cuisine, and Sunday religious services conducted by Pierpont. Just below Sohag they peered into a primitive mud hut—"Oh!" exclaimed Fanny in her journal. In the evenings the doctor taught Pierpont to play piquet. One night the travelers entertained the American consul and the governor general of the district on the *Beni Souef.* "Though the talk had to pass through the dragoman, the dinner was a success," Fanny wrote. "They were enchanted with the children's collection of Scotch views, and my family pictures."

The next day the entourage took a picnic to Karnak and posed for a photograph against monumental columns of stone—servants in turbans and robes, ladies in gloves, jackets, and heavy skirts, with hats and parasols for shade. Jack and his father wore three-piece knicker suits, starched wing collars, pith helmets, sturdy boots, and bow ties. Leaning on a walking stick, Pierpont looks as though he is about to lead an expedition into the desert for the Royal Geographical Society.

Instead, he led his family on to Aswan and Philae (where they watched Nubians shoot the Cataract on logs), then back downriver to Cairo: he bought jewelry, scarabs, and rugs, and attended a production of *Aïda.* His party spent the rest of the winter in Rome, then met up with the entire Morgan clan in Paris at the Hôtel Bristol. They celebrated Junius's sixty-fourth birthday on April 14 at the Café Anglais on the Boulevard des Italiens, and Pierpont's fortieth at the Bristol three days later.

When Pierpont traveled on his own, he ordered confections of satin, crepe, silk, and lace for Fanny and the girls from French couturiers—chiefly, Charles Frederick Worth (who was actually English) in the Rue de la Paix. With his family in tow in the spring of 1877, he had seven different seamstresses come to their hotel room one morning for fittings, and in the afternoon took Fanny to Worth's to present her formally to "that potentate." The New Yorkers crossed the Channel at the end of April, stopped in London for a last round of dinners, museums, and country weekends, and in mid-May sailed home.

Chapter 10

—

"THE FUTURE IS
IN OUR OWN HANDS"

Pierpont and Fanny celebrated their twelfth anniversary in New York at the end of May 1877. His hair and walrus mustache were flecked with gray. She still had a pretty face at thirty-five, but had steadily put on weight as she entered early middle age, and the strains in their marriage had begun to show.

She tolerated the visitors he brought home, and the companions, usually female, he engaged for their travels, but he so rarely came up to Cragston by himself in the late seventies that the event was worth noting in her diary: "Pierpont brought no one with him."

Even more than most couples in their circle, the Morgans lived in different worlds. He spent long days immured at 23 Wall Street, which allowed women in only once a year (on New Year's Day, when the bank was closed; a new partner some years later who insisted on keeping his female secretary had to install her in an office across the street). Several nights a week Pierpont went out to meetings, dinners, or his clubs. And he did not discuss business with his wife. According to a family friend, Fanny once made the mistake of mentioning at a party something he had told her in confidence, and he never again trusted her with private information. Her days were taken up with supervising the household staff and the activities of her children. She served on charitable committees, exchanged calls with friends, and went out occasionally to operas, lectures, and concerts. She remained close to her own family—in 1874 her parents bought Stonihurst, the house just north of Cragston that she and Pierpont had rented. But she was discontented and increasingly depressed.

Complaining of dyspepsia and "oppression" after returning from Europe in June of 1877, she went off in August to stay with her friends Fred and Adele Stevens in Newport. She had known the former Adele Livingston Sampson, daughter of a wealthy manufacturer, as a child. Adele had married Frederic W. Stevens, an attorney, Yale graduate, and grandson of Jefferson's Treasury Secretary Albert Gallatin; though Stevens was not wealthy, Adele became one of the richest women in America after her father's death. The couple had four children (one named after Fanny), and summered in a Newport villa designed for them by the architecture firm of McKim, Mead & Bigelow. In town they had just built a Romanesque mansion on Fifth Avenue at 57th Street. Visiting them at Newport in August of 1877, Fanny noted in her diary that Fred liked to discuss "all the high questions of race and development and moral responsibility about which he thinks so much"—implying that her own husband did not. Adele for her part found Fred dull, and greatly admired Pierpont: it was she who had said, after he saw her off on a steamer to Europe, how much she loved him now that he was "on such a grand noble scale."

When Pierpont joined the party for a weekend in Newport, Fanny left to spend the day with her sister Clara. Back in New York he wrote: "I hope with all my heart that you will feel brighter & brighter which however is scarcely to be expected as long as you bear the load of such a brute of a husband." He celebrated her return a week later by filling 6 East 40th Street with flowers.

It is not clear what transgression elicited his amends, but Pierpont at least in this case acknowledged his faults and was eager to make up, while Fanny tended to nurse her sense of wrong. Each had, in various ways, begun to criticize the other. In the summer of 1878, Louisa, age twelve, went to spend a few days in Warwick, Rhode Island, with the elderly William Warner Hoppin and his wife. Hoppin had been governor of Rhode Island in the 1850s, and Fanny's sister Clara was married to his son, Fred. Fanny had promised to stop for a visit when she picked Louisa up, but sent her father instead. Pierpont scolded her from Saratoga: "I wish it had been arranged for [Louisa] to stay a little longer & for you to go for her—Old Mr. & Mrs Hoppin I could see were hurt [by] your not going & you might stand it for a day or two to give those who have always been most kind to us a little pleasure if they feel so strongly about it."

Fanny had spent much of that winter in bed with headaches. In March, though she rarely commented on her husband's taste, she noted in her diary that he had bought at a picture sale "a hideous Toulmouche for $950."*

---

* Auguste Toulmouche (1829–1890), who depicted the lives of elegant Parisians, was quite popular in America after the Civil War and known as "the painter of boudoirs." Pierpont had bought a canvas called *Waiting*.

Thomas Alva Edison, 1878.
(U.S. Department of the Interior, National Park Service,
Edison National Historic Site)

Morgan had returned in May 1877 to a country in political and economic turmoil. As far as he was concerned, the most important action of the Hayes administration was the appointment of Ohio Senator John Sherman to the Treasury. This adroit politician, brother of Civil War general William Tecumseh Sherman, had years of experience with government finance. He had been chairman of both the Senate Finance and the House Ways and Means committees. Like the Morgans, he had watched European investors pull money out of U.S. markets after the 1873 panic, and he firmly believed that returning the country to the gold standard would bring back foreign confidence and capital. Accordingly, at the urging of then Secretary Bristow, Sherman in the Senate had drafted a bill that would put the United States back on gold for the first time since 1862. Called the Specie Resumption Act and passed by the lame-duck Republican Congress early in 1875, it authorized the Treasury to resume paying all its obligations in gold—at the prewar price of $4.86 to the British pound—by January 1, 1879.

Designed as a compromise, this vaguely worded act had two essential, related problems. The first was financial—how to bring the value of a greenback dollar up to equivalence with gold by the target resumption date. As long as gold, pegged to the pound sterling, was worth more than greenbacks on the market, people would spend the paper and hoard the gold, causing the latter to disappear from circulation (Gresham's law: Bad money drives out good). To solve this problem, the act proposed to make greenbacks scarce and gold more abundant: it set a limit of $300 million on greenback circulation, which required the Treasury to withdraw $82 million in paper dollars, and it authorized the Secretary to build up a gold reserve from sales of U.S. bonds.

By deliberately reducing the money supply, however, this plan led to the second problem. More than ever in the long 1870s depression, people in the crippled rural economies of the South and West wanted "easy" money, and they violently opposed any further currency contraction. Several dissident groups formed an independent Greenback Party in 1875: seeing the move back toward gold as a malignant plot by eastern and foreign capitalists, they demanded *more* greenbacks, abolition of the "money monopoly," an end to foreign investment in the United States, reduction of the federal debt, and repeal of Sherman's Resumption Act—which Ohio's Democratic Governor William Allen denounced as a conspiracy of the "money power" to "drain the life-blood of the American people." The Greenbackers ran a third-party candidate for president in 1876—the eighty-five-year-old former industrialist turned reformer, Peter Cooper—and won about 1 percent of the vote.*

---

* Cooper had built the country's first locomotive, the *Tom Thumb*, for the Baltimore & Ohio Railroad in 1830. In 1859 he founded Cooper Union on New York's Lafayette Street just

Morgan, like most eastern bankers and international traders, did not see any way to free the United States from dependence on foreign money except through the mechanisms he was promoting—the growth of domestic capital markets and careful reduction of the Civil War debt. Intently focused on the ability of a debtor nation to keep borrowing abroad, he never wavered in his long-term commitment to gold. Cheapening the currency by printing more greenbacks promised to accelerate the flight of foreign capital and increase borrowing costs, since inflation would erode the value of dollar-denominated assets. While monetary easing might provide temporary relief in Iowa and Kansas, Morgan was convinced it would destroy U.S. credit in international markets, and damage the domestic economy even further.

Passage of the 1875 Resumption Act had reassured Europe that U.S. obligations would ultimately be paid in gold, and foreign investors had eagerly taken up the Rothschild/Morgan/Seligman syndicate's 1876 refinancing loan. Most of the bonds sold at a premium, up to four points above the bankers' contract price. In the midst of ferocious conflict over the currency, reports of the profits on this $200 million issue heightened western antipathy to the "money power." The syndicate earned over $3 million—$1 million in commission (one half of 1 percent), plus the spread between their buying and selling price.

Treasury Secretary Sherman began in 1877 to build up a gold reserve through bond sales as authorized by his own Resumption Act. That June he contracted with private bankers for another $235 million re-funding issue, as well as a $40 million loan just for gold. Wall Street's critics in and out of Congress began demanding that the Treasury sell its bonds directly to the public rather than through banking syndicates, and that the debts be payable in greenbacks or silver rather than gold.

Silver added yet another tangle to the monetary confusion. In the 1830s, Andrew Jackson's Treasury had defined the silver–gold ratio as 16 to 1—there was sixteen times as much silver in a silver dollar (371.25 grains) as gold in a gold dollar (23.22 grains). For various reasons, not much silver had been coined after 1848, but the discovery of large lodes in Nevada after the Civil War raised the prospect (on the plains) of more cheap money, and (on Wall Street and in Washington) of another threat to the sound dollar. Congress had "demonetized" silver in 1873, voting no longer to mint it into coin and eliminating it for the moment as a factor in the currency wars. In retrospect, demonetization would be called the "Crime of '73."

Pressure to restore silver as legal tender mounted during the seventies depression, especially after the Resumption Act tied the greenback to gold, limit-

below Astor Place, to provide a public forum and education in art and technology for working people. Lincoln gave the speech that won him the Republican nomination at Cooper Union in 1860.

ing its inflationary potential. Silver had wider popular appeal than greenbacks, probably because it seemed like "real" money in a way that paper certificates did not. And the silver coming out of the West drove the price down until a silver dollar was worth only 90¢ in gold—exactly as the inflationists hoped. Support for remonetization was running so high by the fall of 1877 that the House easily passed (163 to 34) a bill proposing "free and unlimited coinage of silver" introduced by Missouri Representative Richard Bland.

August Belmont warned Secretary Sherman that the Bland bill would completely stop sales of the current refunding loan—and in fact the price of the bonds quickly fell below par: the syndicate bought back $750,000 worth to keep the market from collapsing, then suspended sales. A delegation of bankers, including Morgan, called on Sherman in Washington to make the case against silver.

Speaking for the group, Belmont argued that Europe would take the remonetization of silver as an act of repudiation by the federal government. Foreigners had bought hundreds of millions of dollars in U.S. bonds on the assumption that they would be redeemed for gold. Changing the contracts now—substituting silver, worth 10 percent less than gold—would be tantamount to theft. Belmont's rhetoric identified gold with the national honor: Treasury Department records showed the history of "a nation's faith kept inviolate with a most punctilious and chivalrous spirit." At this crucial moment, "sound financial policy and love of our country's fair name alike" demanded from the administration "the most uncompromising hostility to the *blind* and *dishonest* frenzy which has taken hold of Congress."

The bankers made their case in language of high moral necessity, setting "discipline," "sound" money, "inviolate" faith, and America's integrity off against "wild" inflation, a "corrupt" currency, "blind and dishonest frenzy," and "reckless booming anarchy." Despite their Olympian assumptions, they were not neutral observers of this debate but intensely interested participants who represented millions in foreign investment and held substantial wealth of their own. The long-term postwar deflation was *increasing* the value of those assets, while inflation would have exactly the opposite effect. Speaking as experts in international capital markets, the bankers had a powerful point, but the fact that they were also profiting from the course they advocated made it hard for their opponents to see any legitimacy in their claims.

The anticapitalist Greenback Party drew most of its strength from the rural West and South. With agricultural productivity on the rise while prices declined worldwide, small farmers slipped further than ever into debt, tenant farmers could not buy land, and agricultural wages fell. Grange cooperatives continued to press for easier money and regulation of railroad rates, and state legislatures in the Midwest passed laws setting freight rate ceilings in the 1870s. The railroads challenged the power of states to regulate private property, but the Supreme Court ruled in a landmark case, *Munn v. Illinois* (1877), that private enterprises operating in the public interest ought to be subject to public regulation.

The overall number of workers employed in manufacturing actually rose during the depression of the seventies, and real wages on average declined only slightly, since falling prices offset cuts in pay. Still, sixty-five months of economic contraction produced pockets of severe unemployment in cities and nominal wage cuts across the country. Many people worked twelve-hour days, seven days a week, for a few cents an hour. In January 1874 New York City police broke up a throng of seven thousand protesters who were demanding "Work or Bread" in Tompkins Square, and sent dozens to jail. A year later a secret order of militant Irish American coal miners called the Molly Maguires waged guerrilla warfare against the owners of Pennsylvania's anthracite coalfields. The miners had been forced to accept medieval living and working conditions, and the owners—chiefly Franklin B. Gowen, head of the Philadelphia & Reading Railroad—fought all attempts to form a trade union. In 1873 Gowen hired a Pinkerton detective to infiltrate the Irish "terrorists," and when, as a result, the Mollys were brought to trial, Gowen served as both a prosecutor (he had a law degree) and a witness. Twenty of the group's leaders were eventually executed. They blamed Gowen.

In the summer of 1877, with railroad income still declining, the Baltimore & Ohio cut wages for the second time in a year. On July 16 B&O workers went out on a strike that quickly spread to other lines and industries across the country. Skilled and unskilled workers joined to demand an eight-hour day, an end to child labor, restoration of wages to predepression levels, and nationalization of the railroads. General strikes shut down Chicago and St. Louis. State governments called out citizen armies. When militiamen shot protesters gathered in the Pittsburgh rail yards, the crowd set fire to engines and cars. Over a hundred people were killed, hundreds more injured, and millions of dollars in property destroyed. President Hayes sent federal troops to restore order, and by July 29 the nationwide Great Strike—the most violent Americans had known—was over. It left widespread fear of class warfare in its wake, and laid bare the country's deep-seated hatred of the railroads.

———

Americans were not entirely preoccupied with politics and economics in this turbulent decade. In 1873 Mark Twain published the satirical novel that he wrote with Charles Dudley Warner, *The Gilded Age*, and *The Adventures of Tom Sawyer* three years later. Louisa May Alcott wrote *Eight Cousins*, *Rose in Bloom*, and *Under the Lilacs*, while Emily Dickinson was quietly composing poems in

Amherst. William Dean Howells edited *The Atlantic Monthly* in the seventies, and published novels and essays of his own. Charles W. Eliot, the new president of Harvard College, appointed Henry Adams an assistant professor of history; from Cambridge Adams edited the literary/political quarterly *North American Review*. Henry James moved permanently to England, where he began to explore his great theme of the American encounter with Europe in *The American* (1877), *Daisy Miller* (1878), and *The Europeans* (1878); he published his first real masterpiece, *The Portrait of a Lady*, in 1880–81.

"It takes an endless amount of history to make even a little tradition," James later wrote, "and an endless amount of tradition to make even a little taste." Looking back on one hundred years of its own history in 1876, the United States did not yet have much aesthetic tradition or taste; it did have ardent cultural nationalism, and its cities were becoming vital centers for the arts. The careers of John Singer Sargent, Thomas Eakins, Winslow Homer, John La Farge, and Augustus St. Gaudens were getting under way, as were those of the architects Henry Hobson Richardson, Ralph Adams Cram, Richard Morris Hunt, Charles Follen McKim, and Stanford White.

Several of the institutions built by America's wealthy elite to endow the country with cosmopolitan culture were completed in the 1870s. The banker William W. Corcoran created the Corcoran Gallery in Washington, D.C., in 1870, to house his private collection of American paintings (by Cole, Bierstadt, Remington, Durand), and Boston's Museum of Fine Arts opened on the Fenway in 1876. In New York the architectural firm of Calvert Vaux and Jacob Wrey Mould was designing the building that would house the Metropolitan Museum on the eastern edge of Central Park (which Vaux had also designed). The museum installed its collections in temporary headquarters during the seventies—first in a dancing academy on 53rd Street and Fifth Avenue, then in a private brownstone called the Douglas Mansion at 128 West 14th Street. Henry James pronounced the Met's early collection not brilliant but useful: "it contains no first-rate example of a first-rate genius; but it may claim within its limits a unity and a continuity which cannot fail to make it a source of profit to students debarred from European opportunities."

Directly across the Park at 77th and Central Park West, President Grant laid the cornerstone for the American Museum of Natural History building in 1874. This five-story red-granite structure, also by Vaux and Mould, was so far from the center of the city that its superintendent found the prospect "desolate and forbidding . . . my only companions were scores of goats. . . . [S]outh of us there was no building near, except the 'Dacotah,' a fine apartment hotel at the corner of Central Park West and Seventy-second Street."

The Morgans played supporting roles in the early lives of these New York institutions—Pierpont as a founding trustee of the Museum of Natural History and a patron of the Met. Junius helped finance one of the art museum's important early acquisitions, a collection of Cypriot antiquities unearthed by the American consul in Cyprus (and the Russian consul as well), the Italian-born General Luigi Palma di Cesnola. The museum's president, John Taylor Johnston, paid $60,000 for the Cesnola collections through J. S. Morgan & Co. in 1872–73, and another $60,000 for a second installment three years later. Cesnola was excavating in Cyprus at the same time that Heinrich Schliemann, a self-made German American millionaire, was looking for the sites and objects described by Homer in the *Iliad* and the *Odyssey*. To great public fanfare, Schliemann found the legendary cities of Mycenae and Troy in 1873 (although the materials he discovered actually antedated the Trojan War by almost one thousand years). Cesnola made no such dramatic discovery, but ultimately sent about 35,000 objects to New York—sculpture, vases, bronzes, jewelry, sealstones—dating from prehistoric to Roman times, roughly 3000 B.C. to A.D. 200.

Lax laws in the eastern Mediterranean allowed foreign excavators to take much of what they found, and with the Cesnola purchase New York's Metropolitan Museum secured a wide-ranging collection that remains the finest body of Cypriot antiquities outside Cyprus. The Met repaid Johnston for his advances through donor subscriptions, to which Pierpont contributed $2,500 in 1877. Cesnola, who knew more about these objects than anyone else, was appointed the museum's first director two years later.

In New York in the autumn of 1877, a year after America's centennial jubilee, several of the men who had the most to celebrate met for a dinner in honor of Junius Morgan. The Morgan men alternated transatlantic trips, with Pierpont going to England every spring and Junius to America in the fall. On November 8, 1877, ninety-four of America's leading politicians, businessmen, and bankers gathered at Delmonico's Restaurant on Fifth Avenue at 26th Street to pay tribute to "the great service" Junius had rendered his country "in upholding its credit and its honor in the commercial capital of the world."

The guests that Thursday night included the governors of New York, Massachusetts, Connecticut, and Pennsylvania, former Treasury Secretary Hugh McCulloch, railroad presidents Thomas Scott (of the Pennsylvania) and John W. Garrett (the Baltimore & Ohio), along with Cyrus Field, George M. Pullman, Jesse Seligman (Joseph's brother and head of the New York firm), Levi Morton's partner George Bliss, Charles Tracy, A. A. Low, August Belmont, and General Cesnola. Among the Morgan partners were Tony Drexel, Egisto Fabbri, J. Hood Wright, and S. Endicott Peabody, who had just retired from the London bank. Seated together at one end of the M-shaped table was the younger set, including Pierpont (age forty), Jim Goodwin (forty-two), Theodore Roosevelt, Sr. (forty-six, just appointed collector of customs for the Port of New York by President Hayes), Henry Adams (thirty-nine), the bankers Charles Lanier and

Morris K. Jesup, and railroad attorney George MacCulloch Miller. *The New York Times* the next day called the event "one of the most extraordinary testimonials ever offered to a private citizen": "the wealth and brains of the Union . . . turned out a representation that has probably never before been equaled at any gathering of the sort in the history of the Metropolis."

An orchestra played as the guests assembled in an upstairs parlor under British and American flags. Promptly at seven, New York's Democratic Governor Tilden led the party in to dinner with Junius on his arm. Flowers adorned tables, balconies, and wall brackets. Elaborate sugar sculptures showed the American journalist H. M. Stanley traveling through Africa to rescue the British explorer David Livingstone, and a locomotive and cars passing through a tunnel under a mountain of candy. The dinner included oysters, a "timbale à la Périgourdine" (foie gras in a pastry shell), filets of beef, woodcock, canvasbacks, partridge with truffles, baby hens, a "gelée Orientale," "Charlotte Doris," apple pudding, vintage wines and Champagne.

Governor Tilden, who but for a roll of the political dice might have been President Tilden, rose to address the group over coffee and cigars. With an odd mix of irony, sanctimony, flag-waving, and economic acumen, he glancingly acknowledged the country's depression-era conflicts, and referred in wry amusement to his audience's collective wealth.

He opened by assuring the gathering that "every man who, by any effort, reduces the cost or increases the fruits of any service demanded by society, to that extent enlarges the productive capacity of human labor and increases the results of its exercise [Applause]." Although the "owners of colossal capitals and managers of colossal capitals" before him might be under the illusion that they were working for themselves, he—only partly tongue-in-cheek—had "the satisfaction to be able to claim, on behalf of the general public, that they are chiefly working for that public [Applause]." Had they not brought about the nation's great transportation revolution? Tilden remembered when bringing crops to market cost more than the crops. Now, produce from all over the country could be shipped to the East Coast cheaply enough to compete in international markets.

At this moment of intense democratic hostility to private wealth, Tilden repeatedly congratulated his listeners for the noble public service they were performing. Though they might seem "to all human eyes" to be seeking selfish gain, there was "a wise and beneficent over-ruling Providence which directs events so that nearly all they do in lessening the cost of these [transport] services results, not in enlarged profits, but in diminished charges; and thus inures to the benefit of the mass of the people [Applause]." As long as the railroads reinvested the "comparatively small share" of income that did count as profit, they created "better machinery, better processes, and more competition—all resulting in cheaper service to the public." Whatever fraction of profit *was* taken out for personal use would do its beneficiaries no good at all "when they go on that long journey to the bourne from which no traveller returns [Laughter and applause]."

Tilden then recalled a visit he had paid the previous summer to Junius Morgan at Dover House in Roehampton. While being shown over the estate, "inspecting with pleasure the appliances of comfort and luxury" in its mansion, gardens, stables, dairies, and lawns, the governor had found himself "thinking how much, after all, [Mr. Morgan had] got for himself out of his great wealth and great business [Laughter]." He had remarked to his host at the time, "I don't see but what you are a trustee here; you get only your food, your clothing, your shelter"—and added to the Delmonico's assembly: "Of course, a man may have some delight in a sense of power, in a sense of consequence; but I rather thought his hostler beat him in that particular [Laughter]."

In closing, Tilden saluted Junius's quarter century of service as America's economic standard-bearer in London. He trusted that Morgan, like everyone else in the room, had discovered there was something finer than money—"the merited esteem of their fellows"—and something finer even than that: "a consciousness that human society is better because we have existed."

Junius stood, nodding his white head to quiet the long ovation. As the applause died down he told his hosts that receiving this assurance of their respect and friendship was full compensation "for a life of labor, of responsibilities and of anxieties; a compensation beside which mere money results sink into insignificance. It is the proudest moment of my life."

Paying warm tribute to his mentors, partners, and colleagues, he noted that he had been received in England with such cordiality and confidence "that I should be the most ungrateful of men, if I did not repay it by endeavoring to create the kindest feelings between the two countries." The "three and twenty years" of his London career had begun when few American securities were quoted on any European bourse. Then came the Civil War and a huge national debt. In a first-person plural that accurately reflected his sense of personal responsibility for guiding U.S. economic affairs, Junius described how the country had reduced that debt "with resolution and determination, and with a sound financial intelligence, which enabled us to lighten some of its burdens within an almost unprecedented space of time." Postwar America still needed European funding, but "those who controlled that capital responded liberally to our requirements, because they believed in the ability, in the honor, and in the integrity of our people"—and, Junius did not have to add, because they believed in the bankers who represented American interests abroad. By 1877 U.S. bonds were quoted on almost every exchange in Europe, ranking "side by side with those of the oldest and most wealthy of those countries."

Junius owned a letter that George Washington wrote to an English friend in 1788, just as the States were forging their confederation. He now brought it out and read aloud: "If this people continue to be animated by the same feelings of patriotism," Washington had predicted, "if they shall continue true to themselves, no power on earth can prevent their becoming a *great, a commercial, and a powerful nation.*"

That forecast had been "wonderfully" fulfilled, Junius Morgan concluded in New York nearly a hundred years later. Would not a similar prediction in 1877 be just as sure to come true? If the nation's legislators were careful to pass only laws that promoted the "honor and integrity of this country in its highest sense" and preserved our "good name pure and unspotted"—that is, if they returned the country to the gold standard—"no power on earth can prevent our continuing to be a free, a powerful, and a respected people." Thanking his hosts again for "the honor you have done me to-night," Junius closed by acknowledging his high sense of stewardship and its even higher source: "A kind Providence has been very bountiful to us, and under this guidance, the future is in our own hands."

It is impossible, another hundred years later, to hear the self-righteousness, jingoism, and presumption in these speeches without a measure of late-twentieth-century cynicism. Even at the end of the Victorian century, Henry James characterized this kind of American triumphalism as "the Eagle's scream." Yet where Tilden winked at democratic doubts about the integrity of the rich, Junius spoke from heartfelt conviction. He saw himself piloting the U.S. economic ship through turbulent seas (his favorite metaphor), and earnestly believed that a republican noblesse oblige had placed the country's future in his hands.

The speakers who followed him that night extolled the nation's "measureless" natural resources, great manufacturing capacity, enterprising people, and infinite prospects. Several addressed the question that was haunting them all—the Bland silver bill recently passed by the House—but former Treasury Secretary McCulloch, now a merchant banker in London, took it up directly.* If ratified, he warned this audience of the converted, the bill would deal a "dangerous, if not fatal blow" to the national credit Junius Morgan had done so much to uphold. It would check the tide of returning prosperity, disrupt business in general, break the pledge under which federal bonds had been sold, and bring debt reduction to a halt. There could be no such thing as a "*double* standard" of gold and silver: silver would drive gold out of circulation and leave the country with a currency "subject to constant and most injurious fluctuations [Applause]." McCulloch concluded with the hope that the Senate would defeat

---

* McCulloch had been comptroller of the currency in 1863–64, and worked closely with Jay Cooke, who was selling government bonds to national banks. On leaving the Treasury in 1869, McCulloch had gone into partnership with Cooke, and continued their London business alone after Cooke failed in 1873.

the Bland bill, "and that our distinguished friend, soon after his return to his English home, will receive the glad tidings that the national honor is to remain inviolate [Great applause]." The party broke up at midnight.

———

Early in the new year, former Treasury Secretary Bristow, now practicing law in New York, told Pierpont he had seen nothing like the "fever" over the probable success of the Bland bill in the pro-silver South and West since the secessionist frenzy at the outbreak of the Civil War. Pierpont reported to Junius in mid-January that the press and the public were attacking the refunding syndicate as "interested opposers of the Silver legislation."

The syndicate members *were* interested opponents of the Bland bill—more than ever after Congress passed a resolution at the end of January 1878, authorizing payment of the interest and principal on U.S. bonds in silver. Investors panicked and sold American securities for gold. The bond market collapsed. In early February Pierpont and several associates went to see Treasury Secretary Sherman.

Under the circumstances, Sherman was willing to let them out of their contract to take a new allotment of bonds that March, but he warned that the question of their liability was likely to be brought up and adjudicated in public: the bankers had to decide whether they wanted to take that risk. They unanimously did not. In the current political climate "we should certainly be attacked from one end of the country to the other," Pierpont told Junius, and "I had rather make a loss than have anyone have the right to say that we did not come right up to the scratch in meeting the obligations we had assumed." In fact, when he made this trip to Washington, "it was reported that we had gone there expressly to get rid of our liability for the 6th March call—and it made quite a stir." From now on, the Morgans would take public scrutiny into account.

Later that month the Senate passed a modified silver bill called the Bland-Allison Act, which provided not for unlimited coinage of silver but for $2 million to $4 million a month. Though President Hayes vetoed it, Congress rallied enough votes to override the veto. Pierpont reported to Junius on the "alarming spirit" in Congress: silverites were "elated" at even this limited "victory over Eastern hard money men."

The victory proved hollow. Sherman issued only the minimum amount of silver the law required—$2 million a month—and by slightly expanding the money supply in the six months between March and December 1878 the Bland-Allison Act eased the country back toward the gold standard without a drastic social upheaval, which ultimately helped the hard-money men.

In April Sherman contracted with the Rothschild/Morgan syndicate for a $50 million loan specifically payable in gold, the proceeds to go into the Treasury to prepare for the return to hard currency on January 1, 1879, as dictated by the 1875 Specie Resumption Act. The issue sold quickly, and with its success the country returned to the single standard of gold.* Through a combination of the depression, long-term postwar deflation, and the Treasury's gradual tightening of the money supply, prices had fallen to prewar levels, and by the end of 1878 the reduced volume of paper currency was roughly equal to the expanded gold reserve. In mid-December, two weeks before the official target date of January 1, greenbacks were quoted at the same price as gold for the first time since their issue in 1862. When resumption day finally came, banks along Wall Street draped their facades in bunting, and the Drexel Building hoisted an American flag. The banks, prepared for a run on gold, were delighted when it did not occur: since holders of greenbacks knew that they could exchange their paper dollars for gold, they didn't have to.

Levi Morton congratulated Secretary Sherman, who replied: "Thanks for your congratulations, which I heartily reciprocate; for the syndicate are entitled to a large portion of the merit now given to me. As I got more than my share of the abuse, it is probably thought that I should get more than my share of the credit."

———

At the beginning of 1879, there was a change in the English house of Morgan. Jacob Rogers returned to the United States as Boston agent for the bank, and Pierpont's brother-in-law Walter Burns took Rogers's place in London. After a few years as Levi Morton's London partner, Burns had been appointed European director of the U.S. Mortgage Company in Paris—he was fluent in French—and served as Junius's translator during the negotiations for the 1870 French loan. Pierpont had been urging Mary's husband to enter the family firm for years, and as soon as the new plans were definite, told him, "I never was a party to or interested in an arrangement to which I gave my approval more willingly or with stronger convictions that it was 'the thing to do.' " As always when powerfully moved, he was at a loss for words: "So far as regards my feelings toward you personally, you ought by this time to know them thoroughly. If not I cannot put them on paper." Burns became a partner in J. S.

---

* The syndicate's work with the Treasury on this loan went so smoothly that the bankers rewarded a key government official for his "kind offices." Compensating useful civil servants was clearly not a new idea. Drexel, Morgan & Co. told J. S. Morgan & Co. in September that the syndicate had saved large amounts of money through the exertions of Daniel Baker, chief of the Treasury's Loan Division, and suggested that a "suitable return should be made to him"—particularly since other government officials had "received such large sums heretofore." The syndicate set aside $10,000 of its 0.5 percent commission "for distribution among various parties in the Dept. who have done so much to facilitate the working of the Syndicate Account."

Morgan & Co. the same day the United States returned to the gold standard, January 1, 1879.

———

The long depression was coming to an end. Farm prices began to pick up in the middle of 1879, when disastrous weather in Europe created demand for American produce, but Wall Street had felt the recovery earlier. In February Pierpont reported to Jacob Rogers that since the first of the year business had been "such that I haven't seen for many many years," and "negotiations of great magnitude follow each other with great rapidity."

He was involved in a negotiation of relatively small magnitude but enormous potential. On October 20, 1878, he had written to Walter Burns about having been "very much engaged for several days past on a matter which is likely to prove most important . . . to the world at large [and] to us in particular in a pecuniary point of view. Secrecy at the moment is so essential that I do not dare to put it on paper. Subject is Edison's electric light."

Thomas Edison was known by 1878 for his work on the telegraph, telephone, and phonograph. He had taken out his first patent, for a telegraphic stock ticker, in 1869, and over the next forty years registered 1,092 more, averaging a new license every two weeks. In 1876 he built a small laboratory for industrial research at Menlo Park, New Jersey, and a year later found a way to record and reproduce sound. He demonstrated the first "talking machine" to a skeptical assistant by shouting "Mary Had a Little Lamb" into a hand-cranked recorder that scratched sound waves onto a revolving cylinder covered with foil. Then he replaced the cutting stylus, turned the crank again—and later said he was "never so taken aback in all my life" as when the song came crackling out: "I was always afraid of things that worked the first time." People flocked to Menlo Park to see the amazing machine, and Edison took it to Washington in April 1878 to show to the American Academy of Sciences, several congressmen, and President and Mrs. Hayes.

That fall he turned his attention to light. Gas lamps and candles lit most interiors at the time (society aesthetes preferred candles, complaining that gas made diamonds look dull), but city streets and big public spaces were illuminated by arc lighting—electrical arcs that sparked a brilliant discharge between two carbon electrodes. Arc lights were too intense for commercial and domestic use, however, and after Edison toured a Connecticut arc-light plant early in September, he set out to subdivide electrical energy into smaller units. A few weeks later he produced a brief incandescence by passing an electric current through a platinum-wire filament in a partially evacuated bulb. England's Lord Kelvin, asked later why no one else had figured out how to do it, said, "The only answer I can think of is that no one else is Edison." On September 16, the New York *Sun* ran a story about EDISON'S NEWEST MARVEL, SENDING CHEAP LIGHT,

HEAT AND POWER BY ELECTRICITY. Edison crowed, "I have it now!" and promised to illuminate downtown Manhattan with a single five-hundred-horsepower engine. He also promised to have a complete system in a few weeks—and to make electricity cheaper than gas. The price of gas-company stocks promptly fell 25 to 50 percent.

Developing electric-light systems was going to require money, and Edison authorized his attorney, Grosvenor P. Lowrey, to organize financing for the project: "All I want at present," he said on October 3, "is to be provided with funds to push the light rapidly." Lowrey served as general counsel for Western Union, and had a long-standing friendship with Egisto Fabbri—his law office was on the third floor of the Drexel Building. On October 15, 1878, thirteen men incorporated an Edison Electric Light Company; among them were Edison, Lowrey, Fabbri, three of Lowrey's partners, and several Western Union officials. Fabbri was appointed to the board, the five-man executive committee, and the position of company treasurer. In return for funding the development of incandescent lighting, the company would own, sell, and license the use of Edison's electrical inventions. It issued 3,000 shares of stock at $100 each, for a nominal capitalization of $300,000. Edison retained half the shares. The other half was taken by a small syndicate of investors, among them Fabbri and two other Morgan partners, Tony Drexel and J. Hood Wright. The syndicate paid for 500 shares right away, to provide Edison with $50,000.

The thirty-one-year-old inventor, entirely self-taught and so preoccupied with his work that he rarely bothered to comb his hair, change his coat, or go home to sleep, was not the sort of man with whom the Morgans generally did business. Moreover, they did not ordinarily get in on the ground floor of new ventures, tending to wait until commercial value had been established. Pierpont once told a colleague that his strengths lay more in the consolidation of existing projects than in the promotion of new ones. Still, in October of 1878, he had instantly seen the value of Edison's project "to the world at large [and] to us in particular in a pecuniary point of view," and urged his London partners to join him in backing it: "I fear Father will think it all imaginary," he told Burns, "but am sure he will change his mind."

He had to move quickly. News of the invention brought inquiries from financiers all over the world. At the time of Pierpont's top-secret letter to Burns, Lowrey was urging Edison to assign all his foreign business to Drexel, Morgan: the English patents would provide "enough money not only to set you up forever but to . . . really endow a working labratory [*sic*] such as the world needs and has never seen," argued the lawyer; if the enterprise was to succeed, it must be represented by "sober business men of the highest commercial standing," with "an amount of [financial] skill and power which neither you nor I possess." The Morgan bank had the contacts and experience to organize the business all over the world, as well as the ability to raise the "hundreds of thousands of dollars" the Light Company was going to need. In sum, Lowrey told his client, "you are introduced to a new class of men," with "all the means which may ever be required" to promote the development and management of "what we all think is to be a great property."

On November 19, Pierpont cabled Burns—"extreme secrecy essential"—that the business was "assuming desirable shape[.] Have secured one third whole thing with complete control and management our idea is offer London joint account for Great Britain if satisfactory."* Drexel, Morgan would serve as Edison's banker on both sides of the Atlantic. The risk would be "nominal," Pierpont promised his London partners, requiring little money until "success demonstrated by actual trial here." On the side of potential reward, "impossible overestimate result if such success attained."

Junius was evidently unimpressed. His skeptical response has not survived—perhaps he shared the views of the British trade journal *Engineering,* which sniffed that Edison's scheme might prove "good enough for our Transatlantic friends" but was clearly "unworthy of the attention of [England's] practical or scientific men." Pierpont tried to answer the paternal objections by mail, writing and tearing up several letters about "the Edison business," then gave up in frustration and decided to make his case in person when he went to London in the spring. "I cannot however allow another mail to go by," he wrote at the end of 1878, "without saying to you from my heart that I appreciated the feelings which prompted your letter. . . ." Deeply troubled by his father's doubts, he went on: "If there is one thing which is dear to me in life it is the interest which you take in me and mine, & consequently I should never think of questioning the spirit in which you might write even if I could not agree with your views on all points. . . ." He felt sure that "if you understood what was proposed [about the Edison matter] you would look at it with a different light." He did not appear to notice his apt double entendre.

Without his father's backing, Pierpont proceeded to finance the Edison project. (See Chapter 12.)

———

In the midterm elections that fall, a new Greenback-Labor Party won more than a million votes, sending fourteen representatives to Congress. New York's

* The agreement for Great Britain, Ireland, and parts of the dominions, signed on December 31, 1878, provided for the bank to assign and manage Edison's patents in those areas at its own expense for five years. Drexel, Morgan would reimburse Edison for prior expenses on British patents, and if it had not disposed of the principal patents after three years Edison could demand their return. By "have secured one third whole thing" Morgan may have meant the terms on which his bank contracted for the business in Portugal, New Zealand, and parts of Australia in March 1880: Edison would get 65 percent of the net proceeds, and Drexel, Morgan 35 percent, with Lowrey taking one third of the bankers' share.

residential Upper East Side—the wealthiest constituency in the country—elected the Morgans' syndicate partner Levi Parsons Morton to the House.

Descended from New England Puritans, Morton was the son of a Vermont pastor. He had begun his career as a storekeeper in New Hampshire, worked with Junius at J. M. Beebe, Morgan & Co. in Boston, and founded his New York bank in 1863. His London partnership had been headed by a former Canadian finance minister, Sir John Rose, ever since Walter Burns left for Paris. With fair hair, small appraising eyes, a florid complexion, and invariably elegant attire, Morton looked like a cross between a curate and a country squire. His first wife died in 1871; two years later he married the former Anna Livingston Reade Street, of Knickerbocker stock. The couple had five children and lived in a six-story brick mansion with tall arched windows at 85 Fifth Avenue, on the northeast corner of 42nd Street. Edith Newbold Jones, later Wharton, made her debut in their ballroom in 1879. The second Mrs. Morton disliked her husband's Old Testament name and called him L.P. They named their only son Lewis Parsons Morton.

Junius sent Morton congratulations after the 1878 election, as did former Treasury Secretary Boutwell, current Secretary Sherman, Anthony Drexel, and Pierpont Morgan. In office, Morton remained intimately involved with the Treasury's refinancing operations. No law prohibited him from serving as lawmaker in the federal government and as banker negotiating with that government, but critics in the public and press objected that his dual role gave unfair advantage to Wall Street. Congressman Morton, like his Morgan friends, acknowledged no distinction between Wall Street interests and the national interest: two months into his term he told the House that if the country maintained its "honor and good faith" by maintaining the gold standard, "in my opinion the day is not far distant when the City of New York will be the clearing-house for the commercial exchanges of the world."

———

Before Pierpont turned his full attention to the "negotiations of great magnitude" that followed the economic recovery and return to the gold standard, he wanted to secure the last of the Civil War refunding loans. The struggles over these final bond issues marked a turning point in an awkward, halting transfer of power—from Old Guard to New, London to New York, Rothschilds to Morgans, Junius to Pierpont.

Junius still insisted on treating the house of Rothschild as sovereign—a deference Pierpont thought it no longer deserved. Counting on the prerogatives of their position, the Rothschilds took precedence on deals they did not initiate, withheld information from syndicate partners, and let Drexel, Morgan do much of the actual work. Early in 1879 Pierpont told Walter Burns that Baron

Rothschild's treatment of "all [our] party, from Father downwards is such as to my mind no one would stand."* Moreover, he considered the Baron's imprimatur no longer essential to the bond issues' success. Every Treasury Secretary he worked with had urged him to "drop" Rothschilds, he reported, largely because of "strong antipathy" to Belmont.

In January 1879 the Morgan/Morton group outmaneuvered the Rothschilds, Seligmans, and a syndicate led by a new domestic competitor, the enormously successful First National Bank, for the right to sell a new 4 percent issue abroad. Congressman Morton was in Sherman's office when he learned that the Secretary was about to give the loan to the First National: its vice president, Harris Fahnestock, was cabling his London associates for approval. Morton contracted for the entire issue on the spot. Just as he finished speaking, a messenger handed Sherman a wire from Fahnestock in New York agreeing to terms. Morton had cinched the deal by seconds.

Junius was furious at his associates—just as he had been in 1873—for committing themselves without consulting London, especially the Rothschilds. Pierpont, bristling, replied that if Morton hadn't moved so quickly the business would have been lost, and "It seemed to me that JSM Co. ought to be more bound to *us* than to the Rothschilds." Nonetheless, Junius granted Baron Rothschild management of the loan.

Four months later Pierpont took the initiative on another matter that made his father even angrier. Secretary Sherman, impatient to finish up the refundings, opened bids on April 4 for $40 million of 4 percent bonds to replace the last of the old 6 percents. Pierpont urged his London partners to enter a large bid, and when they called for only $1 million he persuaded the National Bank of Commerce, whose board he had sat on since 1875, to make an offer for the entire $40 million. Sherman awarded the Bank of Commerce the whole loan by mistake: thinking it had put in for $4 million rather than $40 million, he accepted the bid, then felt bound to honor his commitment.

Junius read his forty-two-year-old son the riot act in a cable Pierpont called the most "cutting and severe" he had ever received—which was saying a lot. Levi Morton's New York partner, George Bliss, found the junior Morgan in such a state of "nervous excitement" that he could barely speak: "I have rarely been more sorry for any person than I was for Mr. Morgan." Fabbri feared that Pierpont would have one of his "attacks."

Instead, Pierpont cabled detailed explanations to London, secured J. S. Morgan & Co. a share in the Bank of Commerce contract, and received what

* Lionel de Rothschild's title was Austrian—he had refused a baronetcy from Queen Victoria. His son, Nathan Mayer, became the first Lord Rothschild, and the first Jewish member of the House of Lords, in 1885.

amounted, from Junius, to an apology: "We accept your explanations which modify our views. . . . We accept with many thanks $1,500,000 in Bank of Commerce subscription"—and wanted $2,500,000 more.

Although Junius had seen that the economic future belonged to the western side of his transatlantic alliance, he was not ready to yield authority to his heir apparent, even as Pierpont began to emerge as a forceful presence on Wall Street, exercising sage instincts and reasonable caution. As the dust from the National Bank of Commerce fracas settled, Tony Drexel and Egisto Fabbri sent London warm praise of "our Mr. Morgan, to whose personal management and prompt action alone the Syndicate is entirely indebted." Pointing out the healthy growth in America's capital markets, Pierpont's U.S. partners thought the source of recent misunderstandings had been the "extreme reluctance on your side of the water to believe that a large and legitimate demand existed here for this loan." Only men with "direct, personal experience on the spot" could now gauge the markets and politics of the United States, concluded Drexel and Fabbri.

In May of 1879 both Morgan houses took part in one last refunding contract, for $150 million, led by the First National Bank—the first national bank chartered in New York City under the 1863 Banking Act. Combining the functions of a bank and brokerage house, First National took large accounts and small risks: it made traditional loans, worked with other national banks across the country, acted like a federal reserve in lending money at moments of crisis, and did a large business buying and selling bonds. Under its conservative president, George Fisher Baker, the First had secured participation in the government refunding loans; at the end of 1877, an awed bank examiner reported to Washington that First National had "turned over" $225.5 million in bonds that year, and earned $670,000. Baker's bank proved such a staunch defender of sound currency during the years leading up to Resumption, and handled the Treasury's final bond issues so well, that it came to be known on Wall Street as Fort Sherman.

The May 1879 syndicate signaled the end of the Morgans' dependence on the house of Rothschild and the beginning of a long, close alliance between Pierpont and George Baker. Unlike Junius, the Rothschilds had not accurately gauged the American future, and their reliance on Belmont alone to keep them in touch with U.S. affairs led to their eventual eclipse as a financial power in the New World. They had no share in this final contract, and failed to gain participation after the negotiations had closed. George Bliss crowed to his London partners, "We have no doubt the Baron chafed a good deal under the loss of the business." The Baron died a week later, at seventy-one.

By the end of the 1870s, the Treasury and the bankers had refinanced $1.4 billion of Civil War debt, saving the government $20 million a year in interest. The work done by the Morgans on these loans established their professional efficacy and earned them freedom to choose strategies and friends. In June of 1881, as Pierpont put together a syndicate for a new project, he told Burns that their group should be able to "undertake and control among selves sufficient good business without dividing as heretofore with others," creating "a combination which would defy competition."

The refunding loans also drew attention to Pierpont as a financial adviser to the government—a mixed blessing in light of popular antipathy to Washington/Wall Street collusion. Answering a question from Fernando Wood of the House Ways and Means Committee at the end of 1880, Morgan urged Congress to "secure what is almost indispensable, looking to the future of our financial institutions, i.e. an elastic currency" that could expand and contract according to seasonal demand. Congress did not take that advice for thirty-three years.

In the meantime the syndicate system, under which groups of bankers shared selling, profits, and risks, came to serve as the prototype for underwritings of large securities issues. Looking back on the 1870s in 1910, the financial analyst John Moody wrote that through the "single monumental success" of the refundings, the Morgans had reopened the United States to capital investment. After 1879, noted Moody, the "aggregation of great sums of money was absolutely essential for the conduct of human affairs . . . and the head of the syndicate—the man with the resources and temperament capable of conducting them—was about to concentrate the greatest financial power in the history of the world."

Pierpont in London, 1881.

(Archives of The Pierpont Morgan Library, New York)

Chapter 11

FAMILY AFFAIRS AND PROFESSIONAL ETHICS

Women had been letting Pierpont down all his life. Before he finished school his mother had withdrawn from the family into depression and reproach. Death had deprived him of Memie in his early twenties, inscribing her forever in his memory as an image of stolen promise. He had begun his marriage to Fanny with exhilaration and sober warnings about inevitable sorrow; fifteen years later, the couple were finding more pain than joy in each other's company.

For a wedding one summer Pierpont ordered dresses from Worth's for his wife and daughters. He and Fanny quarreled the day before the event. In revenge, she appeared with the girls in well-worn clothes, leaving the Paris designs in the closet. "He was powerless to protest before so many guests," recalled one of Fanny's nieces, "and he simply glowered all day and puffed his eternal cigar—his childlike pleasure absolutely ruined, and deeply hurt. She had a real talent for wounding him, though she probably had . . . ample provocation."

In the spring of 1879 he took Louisa, now thirteen, along on his annual trip to Europe. While they were gone Fanny came down with "nervous" headaches. "Felt forlorn all day," she wrote in her diary, and as the days went by: "Still forlorn." "Very miserable—bed at 8 with sick headache." Pierpont closed a letter to her from London (he had dropped her nickname), "Good bye Frances dear—I love you dearly. Perhaps you don't know it but it's true."

Louisa had always been his favorite child, and she now became his preferred traveling companion. She did not have to conform to any schedule but his, since all the girls were tutored at home. He loved her sunny temper and un-questioning adoration. Unlike her mother and his own, she never demanded anything of him, nor did she retreat the way they did into illness and finding fault. Part child, part woman, part *him,* she seemed effortlessly to understand his moods and desires. She was constantly available—and she knew when to leave him alone.

He indulged her extravagantly on the 1879 trip, abandoning all the rules of home. As they crossed the Atlantic she dined with the adults and stayed up late. In London he took her to concerts, art museums, and flower shows. When she couldn't find a hat she liked, he ordered one made up from parts of several *he* liked best. In Paris he showed her the Opéra, the Louvre, and the Palais Royal, bought her dresses at Worth's, and hired a carriage to let her explore the city with a friend. "I wish you could see the very fascinating way Louisa carries herself & the very pleasant impression she makes in all quarters," he told Fanny proudly. The girl took after both parents in one respect: she weighed 142 pounds at age thirteen.

When Pierpont took his second daughter, Juliet, abroad the following year, he wrote to Louisa: "Everything that I have seen and done recalls to my mind our trip of last year so that you are constantly in my mind to say nothing of my heart & at times it is very difficult to realize that you . . . must not very soon be coming into the room." He enlisted her in his battle with her mother over style, hoping she would like the dresses he had bought "altho' I fear the displeasure of the head of the house for getting them of Worth." Crossing to Europe late one December alone, he imagined the family getting ready for Christmas with-out him, and told Louisa, "it makes the tears come into my eyes that I cannot be with you in person but you know that I will in spirit. . . . How my heart aches to see you – I have had many sad hours since I left you on the dock."

He had no such special fondness for his son, whom he found awkward, diffi-cult, shy—and inordinately attached to Fanny. In the fall of 1879, twelve-year-old Jack had an illness that kept him out of school for several weeks, and former Rhode Island governor William W. Hoppin (Fanny's sister's father-in-law) in-vited the boy to Providence for a change of scene. Pierpont in his own sickly adolescence had gone to stay with his maternal grandfather in Medford, then off to lonely exile in the Azores. He told Governor Hoppin in 1879 that he was "touched" and flattered by "your loving solicitude in the boy," but feared the sojourn would be "quite impracticable"—first, because Jack was almost ready to go back to school, and secondly, "because his Ma! is scarcely willing to have him out of her sight." Pierpont had wanted to send his son abroad, to strengthen his character and "give him for a few years the advantage of the En-glish schools," but had "cheerfully" renounced that desire in the interests of family peace: "In order to escape a domestic imbroglio I have abandoned years ago all attempts to separate Mother & Boy."

From the first the Morgans had formed these intense father-daughter, mother-son pairs. The younger girls, Juliet and Anne, had more freedom to fend for themselves.

In the early winter of 1880 Fanny seemed unusually well. She began giving teas at 6 East 40th Street, and was disappointed when only one hundred people came to her first reception; to her relief, 246 showed up a week later. She went with friends to lectures and plays, and sat behind W. S. Gilbert and Arthur Sullivan at a Mendelssohn Glee concert. Her reading included George Eliot's just-published *Impressions of Theophrastus Such*, Jane Austen's *Pride and Prejudice*, Charles Kingsley's *Hypatia*, Phillips Brooks's *Influence of Jesus*, letters of Horace Walpole and Prosper Merimée, and several novels by Henry James— *The Europeans*, *The American*, and *An International Episode*. She noted the titles in her diary, without comment.

By February she was exhausted. When eight-year-old Anne came down with scarlet fever, Pierpont insisted that her mother, who had never had the disease, go to Florida for a rest. Fanny took Jack along. The girls stayed with their father, a nurse, and a new governess named Florence Rhett. Morgan kept his wife up to date on their lives by mail. He had been out to dinner so often he had had no chance for "tête-à-tête larks" with Miss Rhett "*as yet* but the time will come." The older girls were thriving, Anne convalescing nicely, and household affairs proceeding "*à merveille.*" He closed with a joke about his already famous reticence: "Don't tell any one I have written so long a letter—it would hurt my reputation which you of all others should hold most dear."

Three weeks later Fanny sent him a surprising piece of news: she was pregnant. He fired off an exultant telegram—"Jubilate"—and followed up by mail: "I can scarcely yet make myself believe that it is not a false alarm." He was forty-two, his wife thirty-seven. He loved having children, and also the idea of himself as paterfamilias with a large, clean, well-mannered brood tumbling around in town and country houses. Besides, he wanted another boy. His own parents had had three daughters and two sons.

Fanny was decidedly less rapturous. She believed no mother had enough attention for more than four children—a theory drawn from experience, since her own mother had seven. Moreover, she did not like being pregnant. Pierpont commiserated by mail and tried to cheer her on: "I dread for you the inconveniences and uncomfortable feelings, aches & pains. However darling if it is to be so let us remember that everything has always gone well—that the children have always been wonderful specimens & an unceasing joy & delight—and if it *should* be a boy—just think what a satisfaction."

Shortly after his wife returned from Florida, Pierpont left for Europe with his daughter Juliet. As the British White Star Line's SS *Germanic* pulled out of New York Harbor, he sent Fanny a note: ". . . I felt very badly to go off & leave you feeling so down & so forlorn – it made my heart ache." Yet he apparently did not consider rescheduling his trip. Disconsolate as Fanny might be at the prospect of bearing him another child (and since she did not really want it, this one did seem to be uniquely *his*), he could/would not vary his routine.

Hoping to infuse her with some of his own excitement, he had a tender if impracticable idea on the subject of childbearing: "I only wish I could do it for you—I should be only too happy." And he urged his wife to concentrate on "what is at the end of the journey – won't it be lovely. Just think of a duplicate of Jack or Louisa – it's worth days of discomfort I only regret that the discomfort cannot be more equally divided – but I think my heart aches quite as much for you & I love you dearly for it all."

Juliet had cried a little as they left New York, but quickly turned "quite chippy," running about the deck "joyful at the idea of being my escort." They were traveling with the Charles Laniers and David Eglestons, and a maid for Juliet. Morgan had met Lanier shortly after he moved to New York. The same age and in the same business—Winslow, Lanier, founded by Charles's father, specialized in railroad finance—they had been friends ever since. Egleston worked in the iron trade, and his sister, Sarah, was married to Lanier. Pierpont's forty-third birthday took place on the Atlantic. Sarah Lanier gave him a little gold Tiffany compass for his watch chain at breakfast on April 17. At lunch the entire dining room applauded as the steward presented him with a bouquet of vegetables. That evening there was another public salute when the chef brought out an immense cake with "JPM 43" written in pink icing.

Morgan loved this kind of attention to personal detail, and the luxurious SS *Germanic*, crossing the ocean in eight days, was as great an improvement over the bark *Io* he had taken to the Azores thirty years earlier as plush Pullman Palace cars were over the rickety Hartford & New Haven trains he had ridden as a boy with his father. He and his friends "enjoyed ourselves to the utmost," he told Fanny, "& all came to the conclusion that the only way to go to sea was by White Star Steamer."

In London he found his father well but his mother so ill with stomach trouble, headaches, and "neuralgic spasms" that he was afraid to let her namesake see her and stayed at a hotel. He took little Juliet to *Aïda* ("which also gave me great pleasure") and visited various London friends, then went to Paris. There he stayed as always at the Bristol—he had the Prince of Wales's rooms this time—with the Laniers, Eglestons, Jim Goodwins, Walter and Mary Burns, and George and Sarah Morgan. He ordered maternity dresses at Worth's, and reported to Fanny that the entire Morgan family was rejoicing at the news of child "No. 5—I told you so!"

Fanny alone was not rejoicing, and on April 29 she had a miscarriage. Her mother cabled Pierpont the news. His own sorrow was at first "swallowed up in my anxiety about your dear self," he wrote to his wife. Only after learning by cable from Fabbri that she was cheerful and out of danger—and that she did not want him to cut his trip short—did he talk of his feelings about losing the child: the "disappointment I feel will increase from day to day with no end. It is a new experience for both of us & we must accept it as for the best altho it is hard *so* hard." He wanted to know what had caused the miscarriage—a question that was never answered.

Still, he was enjoying the Paris spring. Lanier gave a dinner for the entire party at the Café Lion d'Or, and Pierpont gave another at the Café Anglais. Driving out to Bourg-la-Reine just south of the city one day, he ordered roses for Cragston. Juliet seemed in "seventh heaven" with Burns and Morgan cousins to play with and a cascade of dresses ordered by her papa: "they are . . . extremely becoming to the puss," he told Fanny. "I have all varieties – some very plain to gratify your maternal instincts & some a *little* more elaborate to please my own vanity." In closing, he returned to their loss: "And darling now good bye. I am so sorry not to be with you at this time but you know how I love you & how I sympathise with you in your disappointment even if it is not as great as my own."

When he returned to London in mid-May, his mother had an "attack" that left her unable to speak or use her left arm—possibly a mild stroke. Though the symptoms cleared up quickly and the doctors seemed optimistic, she often failed to recognize her son, who feared he might not see her alive again.

Heading home with his daughter on the White Star's *Britannic* at the end of May, he caught a vivid glimpse of his own mortality. As the ship crossed the Atlantic the water temperature plunged from 56 degrees to 40 to 34. Pierpont, on deck under the bridge one evening in a dense fog, heard the first mate suddenly shout "Hard a port!" and as he felt the liner veer off course he saw looming up out of the mist a hundred feet ahead an enormous iceberg, "green as an emerald," he told Junius—he could "easily have tossed a biscuit" onto its surface. This huge floating mass was as tall as the ship's funnels: "had we hit it . . . little would ever have been heard of the 'Britannic.' " The ship stopped for the night, and the next morning her passengers saw an even larger iceberg two hundred feet away, its height obscured in the fog.

Shortly after Pierpont reached home in June, Fanny took the children to Newport to visit her pregnant sister, Mary, now married to Alfred Pell; his family owned the land between Cragston and the Tracys' Stonihurst, called Pellwood. Pierpont went to Cragston by himself midweek, and told his wife he felt like "loneliness personified when I opened the door"—"silence reigned supreme." They had argued just before she left, possibly about the miscarriage, and he apologized for not having been "more agreeable": "I certainly had no idea of making any criticisms – I only desired to ask questions for my information. I thought afterwards I should probably have been more acceptable in my absence than presence."

On the subject of Mary Pell's pregnancy, he trusted that Alfred would be "spared the bitter disappointment I experienced" and Mary "the harrassing illness which you experienced." He hoped his wife would have a "merry" time at Newport, and "come back to the sorrows and trials of home invigorated & courageous." That fall, Fanny's account books began to list purchases of opium and morphine.

———

Pierpont was now making well over half a million dollars a year—his 45 percent share of Drexel, Morgan's net earnings in 1880 came to $800,000, roughly equivalent to $12 million in the 1990s. For 1879 his profit share was $672,000, in 1881, $948,000, and in 1882, $739,000. He had other income as well, from the associate firms and private investments.

He had been renting 6 East 40th Street for a decade, and was ready to buy a house of his own. Both he and Fanny wanted to live in Murray Hill, which extended from 34th to 40th Streets between Madison Avenue and Third. With its spacious brownstones, brick carriage houses, and quiet, tree-lined streets, the neighborhood had an understated elegance. Most of the Morgans' close friends lived in the vicinity. The Sturgeses and Osborns had moved in 1871 to twin brick town houses faced with stone on Park Avenue just south of 36th Street, designed for them by Richard Morris Hunt. Jim Goodwin and his wife owned 45 West 34th, although they spent most of their time in Hartford. George Baker of the First National was building on Madison near 38th. The Laniers lived at 30 East 37th, the Eglestons at 8 East 35th, Morris K. Jesup at 197 Madison, Frank Payson at 45 West 36th. The neighborhood might as well have been called Morgan Hill.

When Pierpont first arrived in New York in 1857, he had made the acquaintance of Mr. and Mrs. Isaac Newton Phelps, who lived on the corner of Madison at 36th. Early in 1880 he decided to buy the Phelps mansion, one of three Italianate brownstones that took up the east side of the block between 36th and 37th streets, and wired his father for permission.* Set on a 67- by 175-foot lot, the house would cost $225,000—which Pierpont acknowledged might be a "little high but we think situation unequalled. Cable your views."

Junius cabled negative views. Pierpont replied, "I certainly am not willing to undertake anything unless you think it wise," and put the negotiations on

---

* Anson Greene Phelps (1781–1853), a New York merchant specializing in the iron and copper trade, had founded Phelps, Dodge, & Co. in 1832 with his sons-in-law, William Earl Dodge and James B. Stokes. He built the Madison Avenue houses in 1852 for himself and his children, but died before the work was completed. The northernmost brownstone, No. 229 Madison, belonged to the Stokes family, the one in the middle (No. 225) to the Dodges, and No. 219 to Isaac Newton Phelps. The families shared a stable that ran behind all three lots.

hold. Two months later, when he visited London, he secured his father's "entire approval" of the purchase. He wrote to Louisa as Fanny recovered from her miscarriage: "Tell Mama that I have cabled Mr. Phelps today that I would take his house on the N.E. corner of Madison Avenue & 36th Street so you will have room for your dog & cat—and the rest of the Museum of Natural History."

Though Junius thought the property too expensive, Pierpont told Fanny he hoped they would find 219 Madison Avenue "just the house we desire and if we don't we can tear it down and build again." He would have preferred something "more modern," but had seen nothing else that would satisfy them both in Murray Hill.

In the end, he decided to modernize the house rather than tear it down. Since the Stokes and Dodge families wanted to preserve the uniform look of the block, Morgan changed the exterior only slightly—he had the entrance moved around the corner from Madison to 36th, replacing the original door with a wide bay, and left the grounds and brick stables much as they were. Over the next two years, however, he changed almost everything about the inside of the house. The firm of Herter Brothers did the structural and decorative work. Christian Herter, who had studied design in Paris, now led the firm—he became the leading cabinetmaker and interior designer of the Gilded Age. Fanny made suggestions about fabrics and colors, but Pierpont took charge of all decisions as to layout, furniture, and architectural design. During the two years of renovations, he often stopped by to consult as Herter tore out the 1850s interior at 219 and started over.

———

After the Morgan/Drexel firms moved out of government finance, they devoted most of their time and energy to railroads. U.S. railroad construction boomed as the long depression came to an end—75,000 miles of new track were laid in the 1880s, more than in any previous decade anywhere in the world. The capital invested in American railroads rose from $2.5 billion in 1870 to $10 billion by 1890. Only a few banks could mobilize this kind of money, and they divided into two groups: Yankee houses such as Drexel, Morgan; Winslow, Lanier; Kidder, Peabody; and Lee, Higginson—and the German-Jewish firms, Kuhn, Loeb and J. & W. Seligman.

Financiers played a far more active role in railroad affairs than bankers earlier in the century had in the small-scale enterprises owned and managed by men like Joseph Morgan. By 1880 a few privately owned giants such as Carnegie Steel and Standard Oil were generating so much profit that they did not need the capital markets, but the railroads depended on bankers who could tap repeatedly into investor savings. Unlike Carnegie and Rockefeller, the thousands of widely dispersed stock- and bondholders who "owned" railroad companies did not run them, and had no effective control over the managers who did. The bankers stepped into that breach. Morgan allegedly once reminded a recalcitrant railroad president that "*your* roads belong to *my* clients."

Answerable to their still largely foreign clientele for billions of dollars in long-term investment, the Morgans kept watch over the users of this money. In practice, their guardianship came to mean everything from giving financial advice and bailing out bankrupt roads to firing and hiring managers, appointing new directors, fighting off hostile takeover attempts, and trying to control duplicate building and "ruinous" competition. For a railroad the name of a respected banker on its finance committee meant continued access to funds. In a period of explosive economic growth and spectacular risk, the bankers' power—and profits—derived from a combination of expertise and pragmatic principle. If they abused their authority for private gain, they could not function in this specialized market—which is what Junius had been saying all along, and what Pierpont meant years later when he identified "character" as the basis of investment banking.

The Morgans' work with the Cairo & Vincennes Railroad was an early case in point. J. S. Morgan & Co. had sponsored £700,000 of first-mortgage bonds for this Illinois road in 1872, and a year later rescued the company from default. The C&V had been run into bankruptcy by its president, former Civil War general Ambrose Burnside (whose tonsorial habits gave rise to the term "sideburns"), and the bankers, acting for their client/bondholders, reorganized the company entirely. When they installed a new board of directors, Junius insisted on a majority of "our friends" to ensure "our absolute control which must be undoubted." The new board consisted of Pierpont (president), Tony Drexel, their partner J. Norris Robinson, Jim Goodwin, railroad banker Morris K. Jesup, Solon Humphreys of E. D. Morgan & Co., and three men from Illinois. Fanny's father was appointed New York attorney for the road. Burnside stayed on in the "nominal presidency always acting under control our friends," and voting "according our instructions."

Over the next eight years, the banker-dominated board settled lawsuits, retired the floating debt, and authorized the purchase of connecting lines and new equipment (including a locomotive called the *J.S. Morgan*). An ethical question arose in 1875. The European board of directors wanted to set up a fund with which to control the market for C&V securities. Pierpont, outraged, warned Junius that if their colleagues persisted in this folly the American directors would resign: "We all know that if it was announced that the directors had appropriated a fund to be used for operating in the stocks and bonds of the company – the credit of the company would be entirely destroyed."

The C&V was a long-term headache, and in 1881 the bankers leased it to Jay Gould's Wabash, St. Louis, & Pacific Railway. For their efforts they had lost £472,500—over $2 million. Pierpont's work with this road taught him more than he might have wanted to know about bankruptcy, mismanagement, and how *not* to run a railroad, but it also strengthened the investing community's perception that his house would "stand by its goods" and look out for the interests of its clients.

Morgan tried wherever he could to prevent the unnecessary building that escalated competitive warfare. His bank had issued hundreds of thousands of dollars' worth of bonds for the Chicago & Alton Railroad in the early 1870s, and when the road's directors wanted to issue $3 million in new stock to pay for an extension through Illinois and Missouri to Kansas City, he argued against it: there were three lines already covering that route, he told a C&A official, none of them paying a dividend. "We have had for several years past a fever for building and extending competitive lines," he went on, "and nearly every company that has undertaken it has suffered accordingly. If the lesson of the last few years is to be disregarded and it is the desire of the Alton stockholders to allow themselves to be saddled with an encumbrance of $3 million more – then I say only let them do it and they will suffer in consequence by the decline of their stock." If the directors went ahead with the plan—which Junius considered "suicidal"—Pierpont threatened to "sell my stock and retire" from any further responsibility for its welfare. The C&A did not build the Kansas City extension.

This kind of meticulous supervison maintained the Morgans' access to European capital markets, and it won them a major new client at the end of 1879. William Henry Vanderbilt, Pierpont's 40th Street neighbor, had inherited nearly 75 percent of the stock in the New York Central Railroad when his father, the Commodore, died in 1877. The Vanderbilts were the last single-family owners of a great American trunk line.

Before his death, the swashbuckling old Commodore had added extensive branching lines to the New York Central system, which now covered 4,500 miles and was the major carrier between New York and Chicago. Much of his empire-building had come in response to competitive threats from his old enemy Jay Gould, who by this time controlled the Union Pacific in the West, the Wabash in the Midwest, and several smaller roads in the East. Probably only death could have ended the Commodore's fight with Gould, but his son decided in the fall of 1879 to give up the costly struggle and sell most of his New York Central stock—in part because he wanted to cash in his fortune (William was fifty-eight), but also because a bill before the New York State legislature threatened to make single-family ownership of major transport lines illegal. Vanderbilt's lawyer, Chauncey Depew, advised him to sell. Hoping to keep his exit a secret so as not to depress the stock price, Vanderbilt asked Pierpont to take the company public.

The Morgan bank quietly organized an international syndicate to buy 150,000 shares of Vanderbilt's stock at $120 per share, with an option on another 100,000 within two months. Public subscriptions opened in New York and London at $131 in January 1880—$11 over the syndicate's cost—and the price immediately fell. Pierpont blamed market bears who "attacked" the transaction because "we did not use the customary . . . manipulation of bidding up the price and then saddling the stock upon the public at the fictitious value." He tried but failed to steady the market. In March a subsyndicate bought the unsold stock, and slowly placed Vanderbilt's 250,000 shares.*

Taking the New York Central public transferred control of the road from the Vanderbilts to the board of directors, and as a condition for handling the underwriting Morgan took a seat on the board. He also secured seats for two Gould allies he trusted, Cyrus Field and Solon Humphreys—their inclusion was seen on Wall Street as a declaration of peace between warring giants. Vanderbilt said he had made a choice "between continuing the competition for western connections and making its members my friends. I thought it wise to do the latter." The New York *Tribune* hailed the alliance as "the most powerful railway combination ever known."

The most powerful railway combination ever known could not control the price of New York Central shares, but Pierpont hoped it might curb competition. In February 1880, just a month after the initial stock offering, the heads of the New York Central, Wabash, and Erie roads met in New York, he reported to Junius, "with a view of making permanent running arrangements"—that is, agreeing to divide up traffic rather than wage war. As part of this mediated peace, he wanted an exclusive contract between Gould's Wabash system—just about to reach Buffalo from the Midwest—and the New York Central (which he now, as its banker and director, referred to as "we").

That summer, Gould contracted with a New York Central rival to build a competing line upstate. Pierpont was disappointed but not surprised: "I had thought I could gradually bring about such an understanding between them all as to secure for the New York Central the traffic which will now go elsewhere," he told Junius. He did not blame Gould alone: Vanderbilt had "irritated

---

* Pierpont patiently ignored the vicissitudes of the market. He told Junius in March 1880 that "we did not expect a quick turn when we commenced—and we have no reason to be disappointed at the result so far." A month later he advised George Bliss not to sell shares, since the price was likely to go higher. By June, Drexel, Morgan showed a net profit of $12 a share, and J. S. Morgan & Co. had earned $514,000 on its 41,300 shares. Four years later, when S. Endicott Peabody asked about New York Central during a panic, Pierpont demurred—"I never advise anybody to buy stocks"—but he indirectly gave the advice requested: "I, myself, would much rather buy than sell." At the end of 1885, when a competitive struggle with the Pennsylvania drove the New York Central stock price down to $90, the London bank's holdings showed a paper loss of over $11 million, and the Morgans stepped in. (See Chapter 13.)

and harrassed" men he ought to be coming to terms with, and engaged in "legal quibbles which would be disgraceful to any Bowery lawyer." Pierpont was "not very anxious, myself, to have much to do with either one or the other."

———

At the beginning of 1881 a bank panic roiled the markets and threatened to reverse the economic recovery. The junior Morgan tried "navigating the ship thro' the storm," he told the senior (using the preferred paternal trope): "I have been through several severe times here – but I never saw anything look as black as it did on Friday . . . as I telegraphed Mr. Drexel, I saw but one thing to do, and that was to haul in sail and await developments." His friend George Baker once said there was nothing so bad about a panic—"you just have to keep your head and you can make a lot of money"—but Pierpont in 1881 pointedly chose not to take advantage of the situation. "We could, probably, have made a good deal of money by buying stocks and Exchange," he continued to his father, "but I think you will agree with me that in such times, no profit pays for the anxiety and the uncertainty attending all such transactions." From the speculator who had manipulated the gold market with Edward Ketchum during the Civil War, this was a radical change.

The panic of 1881 proved relatively short-lived, but the attendant anxiety and uncertainty, plus a bad head cold, had Pierpont once again thinking of quitting Wall Street. He felt "about as depressed and worn out as . . . possible," he told Junius, and was longing to give up. This time, however, it was his own sense of obligation rather than paternal stricture that kept him at his post. Where in the past he had invoked dictates of duty to his health or family to justify whatever he chose to do, he now defined his responsibility in the larger terms Junius had always urged. Sounding a solemn note that underlined his sense of calling, he sighed to Jim Goodwin: "If it were simply my own affairs that were concerned, I would very soon settle the question and give it up, but with the large interests of others on my shoulders it cannot be done. . . . I often think it would be very desirable if I could have more time for outside matters."

If, as Junius observed, duty was a word whose definition could be made to conform to almost anything one wanted to do, Pierpont's problem from now on would be that he wanted both time for "outside matters" *and* the large responsibilities of his job.

———

At the end of 1881, Morgan shrugged out of harness and went abroad for six months without his family. He sailed from New York on the Cunarder *Servia*, which he liked much less well than the White Star ships—after this trip, he took the White Star line whenever he could.

He spent Christmas with his parents in London—Juliet was as wretched as ever—then went off early in January with Junius to cruise the Mediterranean on a chartered steam yacht, the British Royal Squadron's *Pandora*. Their party consisted of Colonel and Mrs. Stanley Clarke (she was the daughter of Levi Morton's London partner, Sir John Rose), a Scots couple named Balfour, Pierpont's favorite sister, Mary Burns, and a beautiful American widow named Alice Mason.

A Beacon Hill Bostonian, Alice Mason had lost her first husband, William Sturgis Hooper, in the Civil War, which left her alone at twenty-five with a small daughter. She stayed in Boston for two years, then went to live with her father-in-law, Massachusetts Congressman Samuel Hooper, in Washington. Alice had blue eyes, flawless skin, silky brown hair, a slender figure, and ample means furnished by her husband's wealthy family and her own. A circle of admirers soon surrounded her in Washington, among them the Speaker of the House, Schuyler Colfax, and the chairman of the Senate Foreign Relations Committee, Massachusetts Senator Charles Sumner.

Sumner had had a distinguished career as an antislavery senator, adviser to Lincoln, and, after the war, as a Radical Republican leader. He was, however, nearly three decades Alice's senior—a portly fifty-five-year-old bachelor—and when the couple announced their engagement in the summer of 1866, their friends were surprised. They were married quietly in Boston that fall. In Washington, they entertained politicians, foreign diplomats, and intellectuals ("Mrs. Sumner is remarkable for her genius as a leader of this kind of society," reported the Boston *Transcript*), and were the center of attention whenever they went out. "Sumner and his beautiful wife are themselves history and romance," wrote one enchanted spectator: "they ought to be handsomely bound and opened a page at a time." The fable quickly lost its magic.

Sumner spent long hours on Capitol Hill early that winter, hoping to unseat President Johnson and get on with Reconstruction. Alice found him boring—"always reading, writing and snoring," she complained—as well as rigid and self-righteous, with no sense of humor and no idea how to live with a young wife and a child. Sumner's mind was "a pathological study," said Henry Adams—". . . it contained nothing but itself." Others noted the senator's "unmanly and brutal" treatment of Alice, and complete lack of "natural feelings and sympathies." His defenders said she was dictatorial and foul-mouthed.

In February 1867 Mrs. Sumner began to be seen around town with an elegant Prussian diplomat, Baron Friedrich von Holstein, which generated gossip and humiliated her husband. In April Holstein was recalled to Berlin (Alice thought Sumner had arranged it, an accusation he denied). In June she took her daughter away for the summer to Lenox, Massachusetts. She and Sumner never spoke again.

Victorian America might ignore flirtation carried out under cover of marriage, but it did not countenance leaving a respectable husband. Boston society closed ranks against Alice: "Ladies of standing do not call upon her," Samuel Gridley Howe told Sumner. Her Hooper father-in-law cut her out of his will. Alice Mason Hooper Sumner eventually got a divorce, took back her maiden name (calling herself "Mrs. Mason"), and moved, like Countess Olenska in Edith Wharton's *Age of Innocence,* to Europe. Emerson visited her, Sargent painted her,* Henry Adams looked back fondly on her "outrageous youth." Henry James admired "her great beauty (which on horseback is enormous)," and also her "honesty, frankness and naturalness."

In 1879 Alice's daughter, Isabella Hooper, married Edward Balfour, a young man in the Liverpool foreign trade whose family came from Balbirnie, Scotland.† And at some point in her European travels, Alice met Junius Morgan. He was sixty-eight and she forty-three—a year younger than Pierpont—when she accompanied him on the Mediterranean cruise, with her daughter's in-laws, at the beginning of 1882. By all measures except social convention this match made sense. Alice was engaging, worldly, interested in art, more alone than ever after her daughter's marriage, and though she had resources of her own, probably not insensible to the allure of a handsome fortune. Junius, still extremely attractive, did not subscribe to Boston's rigid moral codes, and his marriage had been a vacant shell for twenty-five years. In the manner of European aristocrats, he traveled openly with "Mrs. Mason," often in the company of his son and understanding friends.

In January 1882 the Morgan Mediterranean tour started at Nice. Pierpont drove alone one morning to the Villa St. Georges, the site of Memie's death.

---

* Alice sat for Sargent in Paris early in 1885, and her portrait was shown that summer at the Grosvenor Gallery in London. Violet Paget, a friend of Sargent's who wrote novels and essays under the pseudonym Vernon Lee, told her mother in July that ever since Sargent's unflattering portrait of Madame Virginie Gautreau (a picture later known as *Madame X*), "women are afraid of him lest he should make them too eccentric-looking. A certain Mrs. Mason, an ex-beauty, has got up quite a storm against him" over her portrait, "which I think very dignified & beautiful." Alice thought it made her look "like a murderess," and stored it unceremoniously in an attic.

† He was apparently not related to the future Prime Minister. After Isabella's marriage, Henry James found Alice "intrinsically as attractive as ever" but "less interesting since she has become a kind of appendage or satellite to a little Scotch squirearchy. She seems immensely fond of young Balfour, who strikes one as an ordinary youth; and it is hard to interest one's self in her daughter, who, though sweet and maidenly, is unfinished and uncultivated. In this respect she resembles Mrs. Mason herself, who is redolent of American civilization. In no other country could such beautiful material have remained so unwrought."

"There it lay just as quietly and retired as it did 20 years ago," he wrote to Fanny. "It seems hardly credible that so many years and such happy years too have gone by since those sad days, which must ever make that spot full of tender sadness to me." He picked pansies in the garden, enclosed them with his letter, and asked Fanny to give them to Mary Sturges "with my love."

Two days later he and his companions set off under clear skies to cruise down the west coast of Corsica, past Napoleon's birthplace at Ajaccio, and through the Strait of Bonifacio to Sicily. Pierpont's original letters from this trip have not survived, but Fanny copied out forty-two pages of extracts in what amounts to a running journal. Palermo, he wrote, was "protected on all sides by mountains, so that it lies in a sort of amphitheatre," its streets paved with large blocks of stone. The Sicilian capital had endured centuries of foreign conquest. The Normans after 1072 made it the center of trade between Europe and Asia, and its architecture reflected its polycultural history—Sicily was called the archaeological museum of Europe. Pierpont especially enjoyed the cathedral, erected in the twelfth century by an English archbishop on the site of an older church—"one could walk for hours outside admiring the carvings, twisted columns, capitals, &c." Inside, he liked only a chapel containing richly carved porphyry sarcophagi of medieval kings and queens: Frederick II, King of Sicily and Holy Roman Emperor (1215–50), was wrapped in sumptuous robes with Arabic inscriptions.

At nineteen Pierpont had outfitted his student rooms in "royal splendor and eastern magnificence"—qualities he found everywhere in Sicily. Returning to the cathedral early the next morning, he was taken into the sacristy to see more carvings and a screen embroidered with "real pearls and a ruby of rare color and size." From there he went to the royal palace, where he singled out another "rare old chapel," with solid porphyry columns, walls "emblazoned with the most perfect old mosaics similar to those in St. Marks, Venice," and marble wainscoting inlaid with mosaic—the most highly valued of Middle Byzantine art forms. That afternoon he drove out to Monreale to see *its* Byzantine church, which he considered "if possible, superior to St. Marks." He spent two hours examining the mosaics, and would gladly have stayed until dark, but fear of local "brigands" dictated an early return: "we arrived in Palermo all safe, without having to pay any ransom for any of the party."

He was in high spirits. What this apostle of America's economic future most wanted to do, once he got free of professional and familial obligations, was to immerse himself in the cultures of the past. He had been looking at European art for nearly thirty years, and though he would never be an intellectual aesthete on the order of Henry Adams or Henry James, these letters show him making more discriminating observations than he had before. What they convey above all, however, is his energy for exploration. He took a quick side trip to

Mount Aetna with Mary and the Clarkes, then waited for the others at Messina, telling Fanny, "My next letter will go from my beloved Egypt."

At Shepheard's Hotel in Cairo five days later, he announced in mock solemnity: "Man intends, woman expects, but the elements frequently interfere." His promise of daily letters had failed to "appreciate the fact that one cannot write very well when one is flying around like a jack out of a box." *Pandora* had left Messina on a calm afternoon, steaming between Calabria and Sicily "with Mt. Etna rising in all its grandeur" and the mountain range "tinged with that pink light so common in these latitudes." The first dinner bell at 6:30 sent everyone belowdecks to dress. Before the second bell the yacht rounded the southern tip of Italy, "and the vessel began to pitch around in the most extraordinary manner." Only the writer and Mrs. Balfour made it to dinner—"the others were seen no more that night." Pierpont spent most of the next twelve hours "holding on with both hands, for fear of being propelled" into a collision from which "either my body or the sides of my state room would suffer."

In all his ocean travels he had not imagined "any vessel could fly about so easily" as *Pandora* did on the Ionian Sea. He had a specific interest in her performance: before leaving New York he had taken an option on a yacht of his own. This crossing convinced him that "there is no limit to the gymnastics which a ship may go thro' and still be entirely safe."

At Alexandria port officials gave an elaborate welcome to the Morgan party. Egypt was in acute political turmoil that winter. Its debt had soared in the sixties and seventies as the country Westernized, expanded its cotton and shipping trades, and encouraged foreign capitalists to build railroads and the Suez Canal. By 1879 the government was bankrupt, and its European creditors forced the ruling Khedive to abdicate in favor of a puppet regime headed by his son, Tawfiq. At the time of the Morgans' arrival in January of 1882, Egyptian nationalists were in open rebellion against Tawfiq and foreign dominion. Most tourists stayed away. Cook's steamers had carried eight hundred foreigners up the Nile in 1881; in the winter of 1882, a journalist saw only three privately rented boats at Luxor, all American—"it would seem that the English are very much scared." Pierpont's letters from this trip (or the portions Fanny transcribed) do not mention the political situation.*

---

* In July of 1882, a few months after the Morgan visit, British troops landed at Alexandria and Suez, defeated the nationalist rebels, turned Egypt into a British protectorate, and occupied the country until 1922. The resident British administrator of Egypt from 1882 to 1907 was Evelyn Baring (later the Earl of Cromer—known as "Over-Baring"), who installed British officials in virtually every branch of the Egyptian government, enforced a stringent reorganization of the economy, and ensured regular payment of interest to foreign holders of Egyptian bonds.

The travelers stopped at Alexandria for lunch, then went on to Cairo, reaching Shepheard's—a rambling Victorian palace with pharaonic aspirations, built in the 1840s—late that night. Pierpont's companions called him an "Egyptomaniac" as he showed them citadels, minarets, mosques, and bazaars. One day he organized a picnic expedition to the Pyramids at Giza, securing the use of a house that had been built for the Empress Eugénie. After lunch some of the party climbed the Great Pyramid, built by the Old Kingdom Pharaoh Khufu, known to the Greeks as Cheops. Those who made it to the top, led by Pierpont, descended to see the Sphinx and its temple on the other side. He reported his friends delighted with the excursion, though "by to-morrow, when they try and walk, they may not be so joyful."

Though these tourists were more intrepid than most in a politically turbulent year, they shared the colonial view of Egypt as exotic spectacle to be taken in with little sacrifice of Occidental custom or comfort. On Sundays they attended Cairo's English Church, although Pierpont found the music and sermons "fearful." After dinner one evening with the American consul, he professed "great relief" that the man had "a European cook and mode of serving, so that, instead of being obliged to eat Arab dishes, with our fingers, we had knives and forks and passable food."

At the Boulaq Museum, founded by the French in the late 1850s, they saw objects from the time of Rameses II—part of a cache of royal mummies and burial equipment that had been recently discovered by Gaston Maspero, director-general of the Antiquities Service and the museum. Rameses the Great, who ruled Egypt from about 1290 to 1224 B.C., was then widely thought to be the Pharaoh in the Book of Exodus, and had built some of the most impressive monuments in the Nile Valley—the temples at Abu Simbel, the Hall of Columns at Karnak, the great forecourt at Luxor, the Ramesseum, and a glorious tomb for his wife Nefertari in the Valley of the Queens. Morgan declared these finds more important than anything the museum had had before: "I put my hand on [Rameses'] skull," he told Fanny, "his hair is still attached."

The Morgan party sailed up the Nile in February, going straight to Luxor and the Valley of the Kings. Pierpont showed his friends "glorious" Karnak at night—as they wandered under a full moon among the ruins and columns of the Great Hall, "I almost wished that I myself had never seen it before." Across the river the next day the group lunched in the Temple of Rameses at Medinet Habu, toured Tombs of the Kings in windswept cliffs above the plain, then headed back downriver.

On reaching Cairo, Junius and Alice Mason took a couple of days to recover, but Pierpont wanted no rest. He had arrived in Egypt during Ramadan, the holiest of Muslim holidays, honoring the revelation of the Koran to Mohammed. Processions and music filled the streets as thousands of people streamed back into Cairo after making the pilgrimage to Mecca. One night

Pierpont drove out to see the crowds on the outskirts of the city, and several days later he attended the ceremony marking the end of Ramadan at the foot of Citadel Hill. He described fifteen thousand Egyptians "of every conceivable color" thronging into the square, along with "distinguished notables," royal harems, "dervishes of all kinds . . . yelling and dancing, crying Allah, Allah." Cannons fired throughout the city as the Khedive arrived to receive a holy carpet from the pilgrims in "one of the most gorgeous and imposing spectacles I have ever seen."

Some of what drew Morgan so powerfully to Egypt was his fascination with sacred places and objects—from the rituals and pageantry of contemporary Islam to remnants of Coptic Christianity, Old Testament landscapes, and the ancient religious cultures of the pharaohs. In mid-February, his party returned to *Pandora* and made a holy pilgrimage of its own.

Disembarking at Jaffa on February 17, the travelers set off in open wagons for Jerusalem. Pierpont thought he spotted the house of Simon the Tanner and the place where David fought Goliath. He reached the entrance to the Holy City after dark. "I must leave you to imagine, for I cannot describe the sensations with which I entered that gate," he told Fanny. "I shall not soon forget it."

Early the next morning he made his way to the Church of the Holy Sepulcher. "As you enter the door, directly in front of you is a slab of marble covering the stone said to be the one upon which the Saviour was anointed for burial, after the Crucifixion," he wrote. "Turning to your left you ascend stairs and you find yourself in a vaulted Chapel, built upon what is supposed to be the summit of Calvary. A death like silence pervades, the distant sounds of an organ in a distant part of the Church are heard. Awestruck and impressed you stand almost breathless upon what must always be the most sacred spot on earth. I cannot attempt to describe my feelings. Words fail me entirely. I could only say to myself, It is good to be here."

Descending to the church, he wandered through chapels built by Greeks, Catholics, Armenians, and Copts until he found himself under a large dome with a small chapel in the center. "Entering through a door about four feet high into a vestibule," he continued, "you pass through another door and you are in the Sepulchre of our Lord. There is the slab on which He was laid. Impelled by an impulse impossible to resist you fall on your knees before that shrine."

The Morgans returned to London in early March, and from there Pierpont cabled New York that he would buy the yacht he had optioned—a 185-foot black-hulled steamer called *Corsair*. She and a twin vessel, *Stranger*, built by William Cramp & Sons in Philadelphia in 1880, were the largest, most technically sophisticated yachts in the United States, with schooner rigs, graduated screw propellers, compound two-cylinder engines, raked stacks, and elliptical sterns. They were also the most elegantly appointed: the main saloon in *Corsair*'s forward bulkhead had black and gold silk upholstering, quilted plush divans, twin sideboards, and a tiled fireplace. In March of 1882, Pierpont ordered *Corsair* fully commissioned and ready for his use by June: he would keep her staff of officers and crew.

The Laniers and Eglestons met him in Paris in May. His bill for a party of five staying eight days at the Hôtel Bristol, including meals, came to 1,900 francs—about $380. He sailed for home from Liverpool at the end of May, having been gone since December; on the passenger list of the White Star's *Britannic* are Laniers, Eglestons, and, mysteriously, "Mr. J. Pierpont Morgan and Friend."

Morgan joined the New York Yacht Club shortly after he arrived, and built a large L-shaped dock into the Hudson just below his country house. He wrote in the Cragston guest book on June 17: "Steam yacht Corsair left 23rd St. N[orth] R[iver] @ 2:30 p.m. Saturday June 17, 1882 and arrived at Cragston dock at 6 pm. against strong ebb tide." He spent most of his free time that summer cruising the East Coast with parties of friends. Fanny went to Europe with the girls.

Yachting became extremely popular with the American gentry in the early 1880s. A few members of the New York Yacht Club sailed their own boats, but most hired skippers and were drawn to this pastime for other reasons, including the example of aristocratic Europe and the extravagant competitions of the Gilded Age. *Corsair*, when Morgan acquired her, far surpassed her nearest rivals in size—the 146-foot *Jeannette*, owned by the playboy proprietor of the *New York Herald*, James Gordon Bennett, Jr. (who *was* a sailor), and the 145-foot *Sappho*, successful 1871 defender of the America's Cup, belonging to William Proctor Douglas. In 1883 Bennett raised the bar by building a 226-foot steamer called *Namouna*, with interior work by Stanford White: "Fairylike in form, Oriental in the splendor of her decorations, and cosy and comfortable as an old English home in the plan of her appointments," this yacht required a fifty-man crew and $150,000 a year to run. Bennett's *Herald* staff dubbed her "Pneumonia." Not to be outdone, Jay Gould launched a 230-foot, white-hulled, three-masted floating palace called *Atalanta* in 1883; the New York Yacht Club refused to admit him, citing his "robber baron notoriety."

As Morgan's wealth and renown increased, people began to credit him with oracular remarks, the most famous of which, on the subject of how much it costs to own a yacht, is "if you have to ask you can't afford it." Recorded instances of what he actually said are less breezily succinct, the two most likely being "You have no right to own a yacht if you ask that question" (to oil baron Henry Clay Pierce) and "If it makes the slightest difference to you what it costs, don't try it" (to W. P. Bonbright, head of a New York securities firm).

As to the actual costs, Morgan sold the first *Corsair* for $70,000 (cash) when he built a larger yacht in 1891, but there are no accounts recording her annual upkeep. His own yacht proved well worth whatever she cost. After 1882, *Corsair* served as his second summer home, liberating him from railroad schedules, an inquisitive public, and family obligations. He often spent nights on the yacht as she lay at anchor off West 23rd Street, away from the heat and noise of the city. Between April and November he conducted meetings on board and took friends cruising, with total jurisdiction over accommodation, itinerary, and cuisine. Ocean travel had always relaxed him and improved his health. Early in 1883 he organized a Corsair Club of six men (including Lanier, Egleston, and Fred Sturges—the number later expanded to twelve) who sailed with him in the summer and met for dinners during the winter.

The yacht had public benefits as well. In London in the 1850s George Peabody had burnished his reputation with elaborate banquets and large acts of unofficial diplomacy. On the other side of the Atlantic thirty years later, the black-hulled *Corsair,* immediately recognizable as Mr. Morgan's, testified to healthy profits, princely privilege, and safe navigation through turbulent economic seas.

———

In the summer of 1882, while Pierpont worked and tried out his yacht, Junius spent most of his time at Dover House. One night in July he gave a small dinner for the British Prime Minister, William Ewart Gladstone. His guests included Alice Mason, Sir John and Lady Rose, Fanny Morgan, and her brother, Charley Tracy. Gladstone, reported Fanny, saluted his host's good looks, keen insight, and "great decision of character."

Junius, almost seventy, was winding down. Though he continued to tend his transatlantic business, he had begun to cede authority and to rely with expansive affection on his son. "I can't tell you how much I have enjoyed your visit," he told Pierpont one spring in the early 1880s: "It has really 'set me up' & I feel more like myself than I have done for a year past."

Powerful men are often so preoccupied with their own affairs that they pay little attention to their sons. Not Junius Morgan. He had assiduously drawn Pierpont into his world from the start, teaching the boy about business, helping him with homework, monitoring his reading habits and pocket change, imparting first glimpses of European history and culture, ordering up the acquisition of foreign languages, standing militant watch over the shaping of his character. He had chosen Pierpont's teachers, employers, associates, partners—even, in effect, his first wife. From London Junius had dictated the terms of New York deals, and called his son to task for every minor infraction as well as for major lapses in judgment.

Pierpont, taking all this paternal surveillance in stride, had never been cowed by his father's or anyone else's rebuke. On the contrary, he displayed high confidence in his own abilities and prerogatives, and an astonishing lack of self-doubt. The speculations of his early twenties that had outraged his father and his repeated attempts to quit Wall Street in his thirties were the only signs of conflict over whether or not he would fulfill the paternal decree. Though occasionally distressed by Junius's hectoring, he seems in the end to have shrugged off its negative content and derived strength from the searchlight trained at all times on his performance. If there was something hollow in being valued so exorbitantly as the consummation of paternal ambitions, it showed chiefly in his disinclination to father his own son.

He never directed that kind of heat and light at Jack. He had complained to Governor Hoppin that Fanny would not let the boy out of her sight, but Jack did leave home at thirteen—for St. Paul's School in Concord, New Hampshire, and bitterly missed his mother. Long after he had adjusted to being away, in the spring of his junior year, he begged her: "Please come up as soon as you can for I . . . want you very badly," and the following fall, "O you dearest I keep thinking all the time that so many minutes or hours have gone by and that there are only so many more before I see you again and it makes me feel nice all over." Writing to Louisa, he imagined "How nice it must be to be a girl and be educated at home."

As Fanny moved further to the margins of her husband's life in the 1880s— the miscarriage seems to have marked a definitive turning point in their marriage—she drew her children close around her, especially Jack. He responded to her moods and anxieties like a tuning fork. Gallantly solicitous, he warned her not to go to Cragston alone ("you will be so blue and lonely that you will be sick"), and begged her to take good care of herself ("I wonder why I should be so foolish and nervous about you but it cannot be helped"). When she seemed happy he hoped "the cheerfulness is not put on to comfort me and keep me from feeling anxious about you," and when she did not he offered to take her sadness on himself: "I hope you'll keep cheerful while Papa's away but if you're blue remember that you said one could get cheerful by cheering up someone else who was blue. . . . I will promise to be as blue as I can when you come up."

This last gesture was only partly a joke. Like both of his parents, Jack suffered from depression, and he told Fanny: "The most peculiar thing about it is that when I am not blue I wonder how I possibly could ever be troubled that way, and when the disease comes on I don't see how anyone could ever have been cheerful."

Jack's relations with his father included no such intimate confidences. Longing for paternal notice ("Do you think there is any chance of Papa coming up here?" he asked Fanny one spring from St. Paul's—"I don't suppose he can but don't you think there may be some chance?"), he tried not to be disappointed when promised visits were canceled or cut short.

Most transactions between father and son in these years involved money. Jack needed permission for everything he bought, even collars and hats, and approached each negotiation with dread: "Papa hates so to have me come to him about money matters," he told his mother, and "I don't want to do anything . . . Papa wouldn't like." Hoping to join the St. Paul's Racket Club in 1883, he braced himself for refusal: "Of course if Papa thinks it is too expensive a luxury there is nothing more to say." "Papa" gave permission, Fanny sent thirty dollars, and Jack became an avid tennis, squash, and racquets player. Pierpont in fact granted most of Jack's requests, when he found time to listen to them, but the boy invariably expected him not to.

During his own school years, Pierpont had had freer charge of his own purse, and been so impatient to do his father's work that he formed a mock partnership with Jim Goodwin. He collected autographs of famous men, carried diplomatic papers to Paris for James Buchanan, and avidly studied history, languages, Europe, and girls.

Jack, commenting to his mother on an editorial in New York's *Evening Post*, reflected: "I cannot see that a protective tariff is necessary or beneficial but then I am not old enough to have thought very profoundly on the subject." Elected editor of the St. Paul's paper, he hoped it would teach him "to act for myself on my own responsibility. You see, I am very deficient in self-reliance." On receiving a scolding from the St. Paul's headmaster, he reported that "the only thing it has done is to make me think that perhaps I had better have died a very small boy." He was slated to go to Harvard after St. Paul's, but contemplating the entrance exams, he moaned, "I wish there were no such place as Harvard." He and his mother decided he would not be ready in the fall of 1884, and persuaded Pierpont to let him put off "the evil day" for a year. In January 1885 Jack moved to Boston for tutoring in science, writing, English, and Greek, and entered Harvard that fall with the class of 1889.

———

Visiting her son at Harvard one spring, Fanny wrote to Louisa that she found Boston with its "plain living and high thinking" more congenial than New York, "for I do not feel here as if the place were too big for me, and my training not sufficient to teach me how to fill it!" Pierpont, who did not share his wife's fondness for plain living and high thinking, had long since ceased objecting to her absence. By the mid-eighties, she was spending several months each summer and fall in Europe with a daughter and a paid companion; her husband went abroad in the winter and spring.

Fanny sought emotional solace from Louisa as well as Jack, but her daughter's ministering talents were already spoken for, which put Fanny in an awkward position. She approved of Louisa as Pierpont's companion whenever the adult Morgans were on opposite sides of the Atlantic—which by now was most of the time—probably because she did not want the job to fall to anyone else: "[I] trust you to keep your Father's life as cheerful as it can be, while you are at home with him," she wrote one July on her way to Europe with the other girls. Still, she resented being deprived of her favorite daughter's company—especially once Jack went away to school—and continued a month later, "You do not know how much I wish you were with us—yet how glad I am you stay to make 'home' for your Father." Fanny's tyrannical dependence on Louisa suggests some of what her husband may have been seeking to escape.

She complained bitterly of loneliness whenever she was separated from Louisa, to whom she insisted that neither Juliet nor Anne could make up the difference: they were too young, and "I do not want them to feel with me as you would do naturally, if you were only here. And yet it is wrong to sadden your youth any more than it must be saddened." Her message had the intended effect—it made Louisa cry, and reply, "I wish I could have been at home to help you as you say I could have done. I felt reproached to have been having a good time while you were really suffering."

If Fanny did not hear from Louisa as often as she liked, she scolded, "When you are so silent I get a feeling that you are not real, and that I have imagined the close friendship between us!" Then a letter full of "loving thoughtfulness" cleared off her "blues": "It was worth having them to have brought out from you such tender sympathetic expressions." One night she wrote: "Goodnight my precious daughter, how I would love to take you in my arms, lay my head on your shoulder, and have about five minutes of cry! Your shoulders are so soft, and your clasp so tender and loving!"

She reflected indirectly on her marriage after a minor episode at Dover House one summer. Feeling a "little chill" from Junius, she confessed to Louisa that it made her "horribly blue and disappointed," and concluded, "I suppose . . . I look for more love than I have any right to expect, and that is the trouble." Her children's love had not failed her so far, but "later it may be that you also will find me sometimes a dull and unsatisfactory companion, for though I have the power of winning love I do not seem to have the power of keeping it. That time (of your all finding me out) has not come yet!"

Fanny's sad reproaches worked less well with her husband than with Louisa, but one autumn they elicited an extraordinary response. She had been traveling all summer, pelting him with complaints about his failure to write, and was at Dover House in September when he finally took up a pen. He led off with local news—a Cragston ball had gone well; William Henry Osborn was ill—then addressed her grievance: "I note all you say . . . about writing and wish I could make you understand my feelings on that subject."

As often when caught between demands of desire and duty, his conflict took physical form: it was not that he *would* not comply with Fanny's wishes—for some mysterious reason he *could* not. The problem was "the difficulty of writing the principal one being writing one word when I mean another these constant mishaps throw me into such a state of depression that I get quite exhausted and after I have written I am completely used up and unfit for anything else for hours."

He continued, "I would gladly give all I have of this world's goods and commence anew if I could only sit down and write as I would so gladly do even every day." He did not understand his bizarre condition, "nor do I want to worry as it seems confined to writing but I cannot bear to be misunderstood or be considered [he left out the adjective—*derelict?*] by anyone, beyond everyone either you or Father. I don't know as I make it intelligible now but I write this in justice to myself. If I can over come it which I shall try to do I shall be I think the happiest mortal living."

He never again mentioned this problem, which seems singularly well designed to get him out of something he didn't want to do.

Louisa genuinely cared for both her parents, and accepted her unusual obligations to them both. If she preferred one to the other she never let on. Nonetheless, she had to be nursemaid-parent-confidante to her mother, keeping her shoulders and sympathies ready twenty-four hours a day. For her father she served as filial consort, traveling through Europe's cultural capitals, meeting eminent people, tending to his domestic needs in New York. Only in the privacy of her diary did she indicate the difficulty of her situation. A long talk with Fanny late one night left her exhausted—"Of course it was mostly apropos of the old sore subject. *Perhaps* she is right that I brood over it until I exagerate [*sic*] it to myself. Still it is not imagination on my part and the position of judge is too often forced upon me for me to forget it for any time. It is very hard to be so helpless to do anything for those you love best in the world!"

Whenever she went to London with her father she saw another wretched marriage up close. In April of 1883, Pierpont's mother asked him and Louisa to stay with her at Princes Gate, but he chose Junius and Dover House instead. Louisa and Mary Burns called on Juliet one afternoon. They found her wandering downstairs in her nightgown, her hair in crimping pins, saying she had gone to bed because "she was so lonely and no one had been to see her." Mary asked her to go back upstairs or at least put on a dressing gown in front of the servants, which infuriated Juliet: "she told Aunt Mary not to interfere with her," Louisa reported, "and that if any one had paid her any attention . . . she would not have had to go to bed." The threesome sat in the library for fifteen minutes, until Juliet went back upstairs. Frightened and shocked, Louisa told her mother: "Grandma is as queer as she can be and does nothing but complain of our neglect of her, whenever I see her. Poor old lady I am sorry for her, and yet she is so selfish in it all, and so cruel to Grandpa."

———

Junius now spent three months every winter in Rome. He was there on February 22, 1884, when Juliet woke up at Princes Gate with her arms and face twitching. Several hours later she had a seizure, and never regained consciousness. She died the next day with Mary Burns at her side.

It took her husband forty-eight hours to reach London by Rapide Train-de-Luxe. He told Pierpont that all traces of suffering had disappeared from Juliet's face, which made death seem "like the peaceful holy sleep of a child." She had regained the "beautiful countenance of her early years," and that was the image he wanted to remember. The funeral took place in the dining room at Princes Gate, and ended at the Brompton Cemetery, where Juliet was buried next to her second son.

In New York, Pierpont described himself to a family friend as "very much upset" by this news, and "incapable of doing anything very satisfactorily." Juliet had decided near the end of her life to honor her father with a stained-glass window in Boston's Hollis Street Church. John Pierpont had never forgiven the Hollis Street officials for forcing him out in their bitter Seven Years War, and probably would not have wanted his memorial embedded in those particular walls. Nonetheless, Pierpont Morgan completed his mother's commission that March, dictating the inscription: "To the glory of God: and in memory of the Revd John Pierpont. Born Litchfield, Conn., April 6, 1785. Died Medford, Mass. (   ). Minister of this church from (   ) to (   ). Erected by his daughter, Juliet Pierpont Morgan." Someone else filled in the dates.

When Pierpont took Louisa to London a few weeks later, the background of his life had changed. Juliet's existence had been an insoluble problem for everyone, not least for Juliet herself, and though her husband and children had given up trying to help her, she had always simply been there—ailing, demanding, aggrieved. Now she was gone. What affection her son once bore her had long since turned to pity, and his grief, like his father's, was for someone he had known in the distant past.

Junius had been careful while Juliet lived to see Alice Mason mainly outside London—on the Mediterranean cruise, in Paris and Rome, at Dover House with other guests. As a widower, however, he could spend time with her freely, and London began to gossip. Louisa was appalled at hearing rumors about "Grandpa and Mrs. Mason" that spring, and rose indignantly to his defense. It seemed "disgusting that a man of 71 can not have a friend without its making this kind of talk," she declared to her mother. "Especially when his wife has not been dead two months. . . . It makes me sick." Still, Louisa did not like Alice

Mason, who was coming for dinner that night: "I don't know how I can be civil to her. From what I hear it is the way she speaks that has made most of the talk." Alice probably assumed a tone of intimacy with Junius that suggested they were lovers. "She would probably like nothing better," continued Louisa. "Nasty thing. Cousin Lucy told *Papa* about it." Her "Papa" had known about it for years.

The drawing room at 219 Madison Avenue, 1882.
(Archives of The Pierpont Morgan Library, New York)

Chapter 12

—

"THE GILDED AGE"

The tumultuous final third of the nineteenth century has generated more divergent interpretations than any other period in American history. It has been written about as *The Gilded Age, The Age of Innocence, The Age of Excess, The Age of Reform, The Age of Energy, The Age of Enterprise, The Mauve Decade, The Brown Decades, The Populist Moment, The Confident Years, The American Renaissance, No Place of Grace*—and its most conspicuous figures have been characterized as *The Robber Barons, The Lords of Creation,* and *The Vital Few.* Much of the dissension about it, at the time and since, has had to do with money.

U.S. national wealth rose from $30 billion in 1870 to nearly $127 billion by 1900, and the size of individual private fortunes soared. William Henry Vanderbilt inherited $70 million when his father died in 1877, and more than doubled that sum in seven years—largely by selling his New York Central stock—leaving $200 million at his own death in 1885. John D. Rockefeller by 1892 had a net worth estimated at more than $800 million (roughly $12 billion in 1990s dollars).

A magazine article on "The Owners of the United States," published in 1889, claimed that the average annual income of the country's hundred wealthiest men was between $1.2 million and $1.5 million—dwarfing the incomes of European royalty—while 80 percent of U.S. families earned less than $500 a year. Few of the new millionaires came from New England, none from the South: the huge fortunes of the late nineteenth century were made in railroads, industry, and finance, in New York, Pennsylvania, Illinois, Ohio, and the West. According to the author of the article, attorney Thomas G. Shearman,* the Americans worth more than $100 million by 1889 included John D. Rockefeller, the Vanderbilts, Jay Gould, and the California railroad magnate Leland Stanford. Among those with over $30 million were various Astors, Russell Sage, P. D. Armour, Henry Flagler, William Rockefeller, Collis P. Huntington, Darius Ogden Mills, Claus Spreckels, and August Belmont—for some reason Shearman did not include Carnegie. At the low end of the list, with $20 million to $30 million, were Marshall Field, Oliver Hazard Payne, H. O. Havemeyer, Anthony Drexel, and Junius and Pierpont Morgan. Shearman estimated the two Morgans' and Tony Drexel's net worth at $25 million each, which was high: Junius and Pierpont together were probably worth about $30 million in 1889.

This tremendous concentration of private affluence had powerfully unsettling effects not only on the vast majority of Americans who were not rich but also on the nation's Old Guard elites. Boston's Brahmins, New York's Knickerbockers, and the residents of Philadelphia's Rittenhouse Square still had ample bank accounts and distinguished lineage, but power, and wealth in previously unimaginable amounts, now belonged to "new" men. Henry Adams regarded the inexorable advance of capitalists, bankers, "goldbugs," and Jews (he used the terms interchangeably) with a scorn fueled by his own sense of eclipse. A character in Edith Wharton's *Age of Innocence* complained that with the country in the hands of crass political bosses and unwashed immigrants, "decent people had to fall back on sport or culture."

Members of the old Yankee gentry who did not simply fall back on sport and culture devised new ways of reinforcing social boundaries. They joined private clubs, founded patriotic and genealogical societies, sent their sons to exclusive schools,† drew up the *Social Register*, moved to restrictive suburban communi-

---

* With his partner John W. Sterling, Shearman specialized in railroad reorganizations and managing large estates, and served as counsel to the National City Bank. He represented Jay Gould in the Erie wars, and also in the Albany & Susquehanna takeover attempt—against Pierpont Morgan, Joseph Ramsey, and Samuel Hand—and his penchant for tearful appeals to juries on behalf of his clients earned him the nickname Weeping Tommy. In 1881, Shearman joined the social reformer Henry George to argue for a "single tax" to offset the economic advantages of monopoly and redistribute wealth from rich to poor.

† Only a few New England boarding schools qualified for the training of America's Protestant elite when Jack Morgan left home in 1880—St. Paul's, founded before the Civil War, and Exeter and Andover, which dated to the eighteenth century. As increasing numbers of newly successful men wanted their sons to have the education and social imprimatur conferred by these preparatory academies, the schools came to play an important role in the definition of a national upper class, and several new ones were founded between 1880 and 1905— Groton, Choate, Taft, Hotchkiss, St. George's, Middlesex, Deerfield, Kent. They came to be known collectively as St. Grottlesex.

ties, and exhibited a newly virulent anti-Semitism. A few successful German Jews had already been accepted into Protestant society, but rising xenophobia suddenly turned them out of suburbs, hotels, resorts, and clubs: Joseph Seligman, who worked with the Morgans on the government refundings and had helped found New York's Union League Club during the Civil War, was stunned to find himself refused admission to the Grand Union Hotel at Saratoga Springs in 1877.

Pierpont occupied a distinctive place on this shifting social ground, since he qualified for membership in both the old and new elites. Educated on two continents, fluent in two foreign languages, he had spent his life among wealthy, powerful people, lived in the best neighborhoods, joined the most prestigious clubs, earned a listing in the first *Social Register,* sent his son to St. Paul's and Harvard, and felt equally at home in Manhattan, Boston, Newport, London, Paris, Cairo, and Rome. He had nothing to prove in the glittering drawing rooms of the nouveaux riches, and looked more to Europe than to old New York for models of behavior and style. Yet his professional drive and multiplying fortune were more characteristic of the arrivistes than of the Old Guard. Few men his age who assumed patrician status as a birthright spent their days trying to curb railroad wars or market government bonds.

A casual remark by professional socialite Ward McAllister to the effect that "only about 400 persons living in New York had any claim to be called 'society' " produced a catalogue of the top "400" names (actually, counting spouses and adult children, about 550) running from Astor to Vanderbilt. McAllister announced in his introduction to the published list that he was including "only those . . . who are now *prominently* to the front, who have the means to maintain their position, either by gold, brains, or beauty, gold being always the most potent 'open sesame,' beauty the next in importance, while brains and ancestors count for very little." The Morgans qualified, as did the Levi P. Mortons, William Butler Duncans, W. W. Shermans, Charles Laniers, August Belmonts, and several Vanderbilts.

Henry Adams, generously endowed with ancestors and brains, sneered at the stature accorded to mere gold: "Scarcely one of the very rich men held any position in society by virtue of his wealth, or could have been elected to an office, or even into a good Club," he wrote in his *Education.* Yet Adams made an explicit exception of Morgan, "whose social position had little to do with greater or less wealth."

Perhaps because of his prominent standing in both worlds—he had status in the old and power in the new—Morgan was less intent than many plutocrats on barricading the enclaves of privilege. He had refused in 1868 to leave the disheveled metropolis for tidy suburban New Jersey, and complained to his father a few years later about the dearth of brains on Wall Street. Drawn to talent, energy, and competence, he had rejected partners whose qualifications were only dynastic, and made unconventional choices in hiring Egisto Fabbri and backing Thomas Edison. About the "tight little citadel" of old New York, he might have said, with one of the most socially self-confident characters in *The Age of Innocence,* "we need new blood and new money."

His meritocratic instincts did not lead him to Jews. Early in the next century he would decline participation in a deal that seemed "a little too Jewish," and refer to his own house and that of Barings' American representatives as the only "white" firms in New York. Yet his derogations of Jews were infrequent and offhand, common to the world he knew; they bore none of the personal venom expressed by other Anglo-Saxon patricians, including Henry Adams and his own son, Jack.* In 1904 Morgan offered the presidency of one of his major enterprises to the man who seemed most qualified for the job—a German Jew. (See Chapter 23.)

He made another unorthodox choice when it came time to find a new rector for St. George's Church. He had remained devoted to the conservative Dr. Tyng for twenty years, but by 1878, when Tyng finally retired, the church was a shambles. Attendance and endowment had declined after the Civil War as immigrants, poverty, and "trade" encroached on the once fashionable neighborhood around Union Square, and the wealthy fled north. Only about twenty of the "old" families remained active at St. George's, including the Tracys, still on East 17th Street, and the Morgans, even though they had moved uptown. Pierpont joined the St. George's vestry, which was headed by Fanny's father. Forty churches below 20th Street relocated north in the eighties and nineties, but Charles Tracy and his son-in-law refused to seek higher ground. The problems in this parish were emblematic of what was happening in cities throughout the Northeast, and though neither Tyng nor his immediate successor had been able to solve them, the St. George's governors were determined to find someone who could.

In the autumn of 1882 they interviewed the Reverend William Stephen Rainsford for the job. The Irish-born son of an Anglican clergyman, Rainsford at thirty-two was a "deep-chested, broad-shouldered Christian athlete," reported the New York *Sun*—over six feet tall, with rugged good looks that seemed more suited to the stage than the pulpit. He was also a charismatic preacher and a pronounced social radical.

He had moved from Dublin to London in the 1860s, when his father, Marcus, was appointed rector of a chapel in Belgrave Square. In the Church's mid-century theological schism, the senior Rainsford sided with the Evangelical

---

* Morgan's youngest daughter, Anne, expressed the casual anti-Semitism of her generation when she told Fanny that she didn't feel like sharing a new sidesaddle with houseguests, "By which remark you may think I have some Jew in my pedigree even if I can get into the Colonial Dames on *both* sides of the house."

Revival against the Oxford Movement's High Church Anglo-Catholics. The junior Rainsford earned a degree at Cambridge before taking holy orders, then emigrated to Canada in 1878. He started out preaching the Evangelical gospel and urging "New Birth" through faith in Christ, but his work with the urban poor in London and Toronto turned him violently against the doctrines of his father and Dr. Tyng. Their Low Church party had taken "the wrong side" in the great social struggle of the century, Rainsford later charged, when "it turned a deaf ear to the exceeding bitter cry of Labour" and supported "the tyranny of wealth." While millions of people lived in squalid slums, their working hours "intolerably long," their wages, diets, and living conditions appallingly inadequate, organized Christianity stood by arguing over dogma. Evangelicals in particular were so intent on "saving men's souls from a distant Hell they left them to suffer in a very real present Hell."

Rainsford soon gravitated to the reformist Social Gospel movement that grew out of English Christian socialism. Its leaders, sounding more like John Pierpont than Stephen Tyng, argued that Christianity was not a private pact between man and God but an active humanitarian ideal. They rejected popular Social Darwinist ideas about economic survival of the fittest, and organized community efforts in city slums to fight for legal justice, public health, and workers' rights.

The St. George's vestry invited Rainsford to come down from Canada in the late fall of 1882, and interviewed him in Morgan's private study. The banker and the rector had not met before, but Morgan was familiar with Rainsford's views, and the clergyman knew all about St. George's decline. He had walked through the once elegant Stuyvesant Square, its dry fountains filled with dead cats and trash, and pronounced it "a dirty, neglected mockery of what a city park might be," though "not so completely fallen from grace" as its neighbor, Tompkins Square—there "you took considerable chances if you walked across it at night." Not in the least put off by these desolate prospects, he wanted to try out his ideas for social reform on a large city church.

In Morgan's study that night, Rainsford outlined the conditions under which he would accept the job, certain (he said later) that his conservative hosts would not accept them. He would put all his energy into revitalizing St. George's and making it stand for social reform; he would charge nothing for church membership, abolish all committees except the vestry, and appoint new committees himself; he wanted $10,000 a year for three years, in addition to his salary, to spend as he chose on the church.

As soon as he finished speaking a voice said, "Done." It was Morgan, who "wrung my hand, and said: 'Come to us. We will stand by you.' "

Rainsford not only had a vision of what he wanted to do, he had specific plans and saw opportunity where other people saw only crisis. Reflecting later on Morgan's swift decision, the clergyman said, "No man could more quickly or accurately size up a situation. . . . He was always looking for men fit to lead. He believed more in men than in measures. Once he found the man he was looking for, or thought he had found him, he . . . was willing to trust him far."

Although many people considered Morgan a connoisseur of character, he once told his rector, "I am not a good judge of men. My *first* choice of a man is sometimes right; my *second* choice never is." He chose people on instinct, for reasons he could not explain, and he made some big mistakes.

As promised, Dr. Rainsford turned St. George's into a "hive of Christian activity." Jack Morgan wrote home from boarding school in 1883, "Isn't it splendid about the way Mr. Rainsford is making things move along after being so stagnant for so long? It must be a continual pleasure to go to the church now instead of a sad thing as it was last year."

The rector started on the problems of the neighborhood. With immigrants and Americans from rural areas pouring into the nation's cities, New York's population had multiplied eightfold between 1825 and 1875, and grew from less than 2 million in 1880 to nearly 3.5 million in 1900. By 1898, when the five boroughs incorporated as New York City, half its residents were foreign-born. Rainsford reached out to the immigrant occupants of Lower East Side tenements with social services, and sent his assistants and deacons to recruit in the shops around Union Square: he opened a Sunday school and kindergarten on Avenue A, set up clubs, a trade school, and athletic facilities for young people, and discussion groups and drama societies for adults. His heroes in urban missionary work were the Boston Episcopal activist Phillips Brooks and the Danish journalist/photographer Jacob Riis, who published his shocking documentary study of the slums, *How the Other Half Lives*, in 1890.

For all his attention to the "other" half, Rainsford also managed to bring socially prominent families back into the St. George's fold—Laniers, Minturns, Ketchums, Oelrichs, Schieffelins, Patons, Jays. He did not convert them to radical social activism, but he enlisted their help. The men funded his projects; the women taught domestic skills to girls from the Lower East Side, visited poor families with food and gifts at holidays, and donated money of their own. Rainsford wanted the parish house to serve as a community center, and after Fanny's father died in 1885, Pierpont paid for a Charles Tracy Memorial House, with a chapel, Sunday school rooms, offices, meeting rooms, public bathrooms, and a gym.

Once a week Rainsford came uptown to have breakfast at 219 Madison. Morgan stood behind him with moral support and an open checkbook—even when they disagreed, which was often—and stood beside him at the church doors every Sunday morning, greeting parishioners as co-host and guardian of the proceedings. One year during Lent Rainsford invited laymen and clergymen from other denominations to lecture at St. George's. Morgan disliked this departure from tradition, but when it elicited public criticism he sent a letter to the press pointing out that the revitalization and "great work" going on at St. George's had "no parallel in the United States": there could be no disloyalty to the Episcopal Church and no conceivable harm, he went on, in the rector's calling on "the best writers and thinkers he could secure, both clerical and lay," to discuss subjects "which are engrossing the thought of the Christian world."

This unlikely friendship lasted nearly thirty years, during which time Morgan's liberality extended further than Rainsford knew. When the clergyman and his family left Toronto for New York at the beginning of 1883, the financier arranged with the railroads to pay for the move "so that Mr. Rainsford would not be aware but that it would be an act of courtesy on the part of the roads." Rainsford suffered from depression, and in the mid-eighties Morgan sent him on camping expeditions in the Rocky Mountains with Jack, which gave the rector an extended vacation, and Jack outdoor experience with an athletic adult male. When Rainsford broke down completely in 1889, Morgan sent him away for six months of salaried travel and rest. At the end of this furlough, the banker set up a trust fund for the rector's family, telling him: "Don't work too hard, you ought not to have to worry about money. Don't thank me, and don't speak of it to any one but your wife." Several years later he gave the Rainsfords money to build a house in Ridgefield, Connecticut.

After Morgan died, Rainsford wrote about him in two published memoirs and a private "Recollection." He noted the contradictions in his patron's character—a stubborn resistance to change combined with a "wide and deep tolerance" in religious matters: "I do not believe any of all of my teachings, in the pulpit or out of it, moved him by so much as one inch from the [Evangelical] 'plan of salvation,' the traditions of his youth which he held with vise-like tenacity," recalled Rainsford. "Of every radical proposition I advanced—ecclesiastical, social, religious—he disapproved; yet back of me, ever and always, was his firm loyalty. Without it I couldn't have accomplished what I did."

The rector found the banker "intemperate and sometimes unjust in his oppositions," but also "absolutely honest and patriotic." Behind the autocratic demeanor he saw the qualities that won people's trust: "When he chose to exercise it, there was an extraordinary and winning charm about J. Pierpont Morgan," Rainsford wrote. ". . . I have never seen any eyes quite like his. They had penetration and kindliness combined to an extraordinary degree. When he said a thing, and looked full at you as he said it, to doubt him was impossible."

As minister/confessor, Rainsford saw more of the private Morgan than most people did, and described his friend's "extraordinarily emotional" side—the "flashes of insight, call it genius or call it prophetic fire." Morgan was "more reserved than any man I ever knew," with few inner resources in times of trouble: "no scholar, no reader, [he] had not learned to care for nature, or find any rest or companionship in her high company." When the famous reserve broke down, the "profound emotionalism of his nature had its way with him. The

great deeps were broken up, and to some near one he called aloud for help."
In these hours of "despairing despondency," the banker "deeply doubted himself," and "three times in thirty years all shadow of reserve between us
was . . . swept aside. I do not know that as he thus clung to me, I was able to do
him any good, but at least I told him what I thought was the truth; and if love
and longing could help a man, he ought to have had some succor from me."*

Many of Rainsford's comments about Morgan sound a self-aggrandizing
note. Retrospectively emphasizing the superiority of his own convictions, the
rector suggests that he alone was able to meet the needs of this great, troubled
soul; entirely dependent on his benefactor's largesse, he admits to no self-
interest. And though he claims exemption from the common response to
power—"Many love to bow themselves before the strong. And so an environ-
ment of almost universal flattery and adulation, sometimes gross and fawning,
moved with [Morgan] wherever he went"—he was not immune to this effect.
Moral one-upmanship is aggressive first cousin to bowing before the strong.

Morgan's support of Rainsford had only partly to do with his affinity for men
of action. His own work, which he regarded as a noble calling, largely satisfied
his patrician sense of obligation to provide for a society that afforded him great
material privilege. After hours, he was neither inclined nor qualified to contend
with the urgent social problems of the Gilded Age, but he could give his imprimatur to a moral crusader who wanted nothing more than to take those problems on—especially when the crusader was British, Anglican, good-looking,
charismatic, and, like his patron, melancholic. Perhaps in his relations with
Rainsford, Morgan was also salvaging broken fragments of his past, indirectly
requiting the affection of another radical preacher.

———

New York in the decade surrounding the country's centennial emerged as the
center of U.S. commerce and culture, representing in concentrated form the
conflicts and achievements of the "American Renaissance." While Rainsford
tended to urban poverty and the influx of immigrants at one end of the social
scale, wealthy New Yorkers set out in an expansive, nationalist mood to turn
their metropolis into one of the cultural capitals of the world.

Artistic and scientific enterprise has always flourished in great commercial
cities—in ancient Athens, Alexandria, and Rome, Renaissance Florence,
seventeenth-century Amsterdam, eighteenth-century Paris, nineteenth-century
London—and the Yankee merchant princes regarded New York as next in line:

---

* When Rainsford published his first memoir in 1922, Jack told Fanny that it made him
"very uncomfortable," and he thought his father "would have hated" some of its revelations:
Rainsford "doesn't see that some people think their struggles and sorrows are not for the public, and that some people shun publicity for their inner feelings."

it would be a uniquely *American* place, harnessing the energies and talents of democracy to the heritage and cultural standards of the past.

New Yorkers who could afford the latest technology in the early eighties learned to use telephones, experimented with Mr. Edison's light, and rode for the first time in passenger elevators. Steam-driven elevated railroads altered the topography of the city for all social classes, and the Brooklyn Bridge, completed in 1883—the longest span ever built—seemed a triumph of American science, ingenuity, and design.

Artists and writers were taking possession of the Old World's legacy and inventing a vernacular of their own. Between November 1884 and April 1885 the illustrated *Century Magazine* ran articles on "Sculptors of the Early Italian Renaissance," "Dutch Portraiture," "The Worship of Shakespeare," and the city of Florence—along with pieces on "Recent Architecture in America" and "American Painters in Pastel." There was an essay on "The Poet Heine" by Emma Lazarus, and a review of illustrations by the American artist Elihu Vedder for a new edition of Omar Khayam's twelfth-century *Rubaiyat*, translated by Edward FitzGerald ("an American artist has joined the Persian poet and the English translator," wrote the *Century*'s critic, "and the result . . . presents the original strain in a richer, profounder harmony"). The magazine also published fiction by Mark Twain ("Huckleberry Finn"), Henry James ("The Bostonians"), William Dean Howells ("The Rise of Silas Lapham"), and Joel Chandler Harris ("Free Joe and the Rest of the World"), along with nonfiction about the Civil War (Ulysses S. Grant on "The Battle of Shiloh"), and essays on the Smithsonian, Daniel Webster, Oliver Wendell Holmes, "Phases of State Legislation" by Theodore Roosevelt, Jr., and postslavery issues of race—the "greatest social problem before the American people today."

Journals devoted to art, architecture, and interior decor began to appear around 1880, and the country's growing regard for education and the arts was reflected in new professional organizations (the American Historical Association, the Architectural League of New York), as well as in the founding of universities, schools, galleries, libraries, orchestras, opera houses, and museums.

The Metropolitan Museum of Art finally moved into its permanent home in 1880. That March, President Hayes and New York's cultural elite attended the formal dedication of Vaux and Mould's Ruskinian Gothic redbrick pavilion at Fifth Avenue and 80th Street. The principal speaker was Joseph Hodges Choate, a trial lawyer and museum trustee. In the context of increasing political conflict between rich and poor, Choate emphasized the moral and social value of the new institution, reiterating its founders' belief that a knowledge of art would "humanize, educate, and refine a practical and laborious people." The original aim had been to provide a vast "department of knowledge" for "the vital and practical interest of the working millions"—modeled on the South

Kensington Museum in London—to teach American artisans and students "what the past has accomplished for them to imitate and excel."

This marriage of commerce, aesthetics, and social virtue was going to cost a great deal of money, and Choate urged his audience of potential patrons to direct some of their resources to art: "Think of it, ye millionaires of many markets, what glory may yet be yours, if you only listen to our advice, to convert pork into porcelain, grain and produce into priceless pottery, the rude ores of commerce into sculptured marble, and railroad shares and mining stocks . . . into the glorified canvas of the world's masters, that shall adorn these walls for centuries. The rage of Wall Street is to hunt the philosopher's stone, to convert all baser things into gold, which is but dross; but ours is the higher ambition to convert your useless gold into things of living beauty that shall be a joy to a whole people for a thousand years."

The "higher ambition" of turning money into art had enormous appeal for wealthy New Yorkers, but they did not begin giving major works to the museum until later in the decade. In the early eighties the city's aesthetic attentions were focused largely on the house. A writer for *Harper's Monthly* announced in October of 1882 that "Internal Decoration" had become the consuming passion of "the present generation," and that nothing could be "more beautiful, more orderly, more harmonious than a modern New York house which has blossomed out in this fine summer of perfected art." The rage for "artistic houses" had grown so intense, she noted, that artists such as John LaFarge, Augustus Saint-Gaudens, and Lewis Comfort Tiffany were turning their attention to interior decor.

The houses of the Gilded Age served as domestic museums—private exhibitions of architecture, artifact, and art that would testify to their owners' ample means and stylish tastes. A few of these men had in fact become discriminating connoisseurs—among them Henry Marquand, John Taylor Johnston, John Claghorn, and John Wolfe—but most of the new American millionaires in the early eighties had more money and zeal than educated knowledge about the arts; awed by European culture, they imported it in bulk to the United States.

Morgan's 40th Street neighbor William Henry Vanderbilt bought up the entire west side of Fifth Avenue between 51st and 52nd Streets for $700,000 in 1879—the year he sold his interest in the New York Central—and spent another $2 million building enormous twin brownstones for himself, his wife, and two married daughters. Designed and decorated by the Herter brothers, these boxlike mansions reflected Vanderbilt's self-ascribed preference for "an almost indiscriminate assemblage" of Roman balconies, "Ghiberti" doors, English oak panels, a neoclassical library, a Japanese parlor, a Venetian frieze, Chinese screens, and mother-of-pearl on every available surface. The picture gallery—the largest in New York—was filled with French art from the Académie, and open to the public by invitation once a week.

Mr. Vanderbilt commissioned a study of his new house by the art critic Earl Shinn, who produced a multivolume paean that captures both the parochialism and exhilaration of this American moment. The country was "just beginning to be astonishing," Shinn wrote under the pseudonym Edward Strahan in 1883–84: "Re-cemented by the fortunate result of a civil war, endowed as with a diploma of rank by the promulgation of its centenary, it has begun to reinvent everything, and especially the house." The Vanderbilt mansion might "stand as a representative of the new impulse now felt in the national life. Like a more perfect Pompeii, the work will be the vision and image of a typical American residence, seized at the moment when the nation began to have a taste of its own." That this "typical American residence" had been built at a cost of $2 million, by six hundred American workers and sixty imported Europeans, was an irony lost on Mr. Shinn.

When two of Vanderbilt's sons built palaces along Fifth Avenue in the early eighties as well, the stretch of the avenue between 50th and 58th Streets came to be known as Vanderbilt Row. Cornelius II constructed a late Gothic/early Renaissance château of redbrick and white stone between 57th and 58th Streets, its courtyard facing Grand Army Plaza and Central Park. His brother William Kissam hired Richard Morris Hunt to design a limestone castle modeled on the Château de Blois and the Jacques Coeur mansion at Bourges, between 52nd and 53rd Streets. To celebrate its completion in March 1883, William K.'s wife, Alva, held a costume ball that gave free rein to the fantasies of New York's social elite: Alva dressed as a Venetian princess accompanied by live doves, her husband as the Duc de Guise; her brother-in-law, Cornelius, came as Louis XVI, and *his* wife as Edison's electric light. There were sixteen more Louis XVIs, eight Marie Antoinettes, seven Marys, Queen of Scots, one King Lear, one Queen Elizabeth, assorted Scottish lairds and Valkyries—and General and Mrs. Ulysses S. Grant in ordinary evening dress.

Edith Wharton, speaking for Old New York, sighed to her friend Ogden Codman, Jr., "I wish the Vanderbilts didn't retard culture so very thoroughly. They are entrenched in a sort of *thermopylae* of bad taste, from which apparently no force on earth can dislodge them." Another critic quipped that America's late nineteenth-century architecture was "either bizarre or Beaux-Arts."

The Morgans' friends Fred and Adele Stevens had been among the first to build a European castle in New York. On the southwest corner of Fifth Avenue and 57th Street, their redbrick Romanesque mansion, completed in 1876, had four stories, five towers, acres of Flemish and Spanish tapestries, and an entire palace ballroom shipped over from Ghent. It stood out among the rows of brownstone that Mrs. Wharton said made the city look as if it had been coated in cold chocolate sauce. Oscar Wilde, driving along Fifth Avenue one January day in the eighties and depressed by everything he saw, cheered up at the sight of the Stevens mansion with sun glinting off its gables: "That house," he said, "seems like a voice crying, in this wilderness of dark art, 'Brighter days, brighter days, brighter days.' "

To the south and east, transportation baron Henry Villard commissioned from McKim, Mead, and White a set of six linked brownstones around an open courtyard at 451 Madison between 50th and 51st Streets, behind St. Patrick's Cathedral. This Italian Renaissance palazzo had more grace and conceptual integrity than the Fifth Avenue châteaux; it also had a hydraulic elevator, electrical wiring, thirteen flush toilets, a central heating system that used a ton of coal a day—and it cost nearly $1 million.

In late October of 1882, at some geographic and financial distance from the excesses of Vanderbilt Row, the Morgans moved into their renovated brownstone on the corner of Madison and 36th. Like most of the new "domestic museums," this house was richly ornamented with Oriental rugs, ceramics, paintings, elaborate woodwork, stained glass, and bric-a-brac. Yet it made quieter, more American claims for itself than many of its contemporaries (it was not "neo-" anything), and articulated a measure of patrician restraint.

Working closely with the Morgans, Christian Herter had installed Circassian walnut doors at the new entrance on 36th Street and stained-glass sliding panels opening from a mosaic-tiled vestibule onto the front hall. Walking up a few steps to the first landing, visitors immediately faced the minstrel and maid in Pierpont's beloved von Kaulbach cartoon, *The Bird Song,* above a recessed mantel. Daylight filtered through a stained-glass dome (from the studio of John La Farge) into the central well of the house, and also through stained glass set into spandrels over triple arches on the landing. Twin white-oak staircases with densely spindled railings led from the front hall up to the family living quarters. There was an elevator off the hall, a two-story burglarproof safe in the butler's pantry, a gymnasium for the children in the basement, and a private telegraph wire connecting the house to 23 Wall Street.

On the main floor, the new drawing room took up the entire west side of the house. It centered on a seventeen-foot bay framed by Pompeiian-red columns and a gold-flecked white frieze inset with stained glass. A coved ceiling painted to look like mosaic emphasized the length of the room, and a studied arrangement of rugs, cushions, tables, chairs, Japanese embroideries, silk brocade curtains, paintings, and books managed to avoid Victorian clutter and give the space a feeling of formal balance.

The gentleman's library, a standard feature of the New York town house, was just to the right of the entrance hall, which meant that Pierpont could come in from the street and disappear into his private study without running into anyone else. He hired Dr. Rainsford in this room shortly after moving in. Its wainscoting and recessed inglenook were made of Santo Domingo mahogany, and there was an eight-foot plate-glass window facing south. Herter had covered the chairs and sofas in peacock-green plush, tiled the raised fireplace in ocher and blue, and installed allegorical figures representing History and Poetry in octagonal panels on the ceiling. Morgan proudly told visitors that Herter had painted these panels *"himself,* with his *own hands."* Stained-glass doors designed by John LaFarge led from this masculine retreat into a sunny conservatory that ran sixty feet along the eastern side of the house, filled with orchids, ferns, climbing vines, and flowering plants. Banks of potted palms lined the windows, and a lion's head framed in black marble spouted water in a fan-shaped stream.

The dining room, more stolid and Victorian than the rest, was painted dark red, with English oak wainscoting, Siena marble columns, Oriental screens and jars, a small circular table with oak and leather chairs, and a stained-glass skylight twelve feet square. Over a large sideboard hung Frederic Church's painting *Near Damascus.*

In November of 1882, Pierpont had these rooms photographed for a large-folio, four-part publication called *Artistic Houses, Being a Series of Interior Views of a Number of the Most Beautiful and Celebrated Homes in the U.S., With a Description of the Art Treasures Contained Therein* (1883–84). Bound in tooled leather and privately printed in a limited edition for five hundred wealthy subscribers, *Artistic Houses* surveyed ninety-seven buildings, including the residences of William H. Vanderbilt, George Baker, Marshall Field, Henry Marquand, John T. Johnston, Fred Stevens, Louis C. Tiffany, Samuel Tilden, and Henry Villard.*

Like Earl Shinn's tribute to the Vanderbilt mansion, it paid proud homage to America's aesthetic accomplishments and tastes. "The domestic architecture of no nation in the world can show trophies more original, affluent, or admirable," declared the anonymous author of the text, art critic George W. Sheldon. By not using their own names, Shinn and Sheldon probably hoped to protect their critical reputations while serving as paid purveyors of praise, but in the surge of excitement about the arts in the early 1880s, they may have believed much of what they said. Sheldon catalogued the "rare," "exquisite," "costly" objects that filled the "artistic" houses, and described their owners as "professional [men] of scholarly pursuits, cultivated tastes, and wealth sufficient to gratify both." Only a few of these men had the time or predisposition for scholarly pursuits, but Sheldon's hypberbole suggests how highly they valued cultivated taste, and how insulated they were from critical appraisals of their judgment. "To the Greeks there was no gulf between the useful and the beautiful," Sheldon wrote. "So one feels in Mr. J. Pierpont Morgan's mansion."

* Most of the photographs were printed backward by D. Appleton and Company in 1883. In 1987, Arnold Lewis, James Turner, and Steven McQuillin reproduced the photographs with the negatives right side up in *The Opulent Interiors of the Gilded Age;* their new text supplies invaluable historical context and aesthetic assessments.

———

Unlike many of the owners of "artistic houses," Morgan did not install a formal picture gallery at 219, but he, too, had been collecting contemporary European salon paintings. A catalogue on *The Art Treasures of America* by the busy Mr. Shinn, again as "Edward Strahan," devoted four pages to "the small but precious collection got together by Mr. J. Pierpont Morgan of New York."* Virtually all the Morgan paintings were landscapes or narrative genre scenes depicting worlds far removed from modern industrial America—an open-air Arab *Court of Justice* by T. Moragas, a flirtation on the Grand Canal by Luis Alvarez, a Spanish promenade by the popular Barbizon school painter Narcisse Diaz de la Peña, a servant of Horace forgetting his errand by Hector Leroux. There was a canvas attributed to Corot called *Le Gallais*—Shinn declared it a "magnificent specimen" of that artist's "charm of mystery and pearly tenderness," but it eventually disappeared from Morgan's walls. Someone said that Corot painted six hundred works, six thousand of which were in America.

Shinn liked the adjective "pearly." He considered Morgan's *Laundress of the Cupids*, by J. L. Hamon, to be "one of the most audacious and original of the fancies of that poet of the palette"—a "pearly scene of dawn" in which "a maiden cleanses her conscience of its loves." The "greatest rarity" in Morgan's possession, however—according to Shinn—was *The Cardinal's Fête*, painted by "the Cavaliere Scipione Vannutelli, of Rome" in 1875: "the dashes of glitter, the mixture of pomp and piety, the indulgent and complaisant clergy, the palace decked with tapestry and with sacred banners, afford an opportunity to the painter for the resources of a glittering palette."

Tastes in art change, and connoisseurship was in its infancy in the 1880s. Still, Shinn's raptures over work that now seems at best banal, his uncritical endorsement of Victorian sentimentality, his silence on the formal properties and aesthetic values of these works, and his disregard of superior artists (in the collection of Joseph Drexel, he does not mention paintings by Canaletto or Caravaggio), render the catalogue more useful as a window on the aspirations of the Gilded Age than as a source of information about art.

Morgan's taste was not entirely Eurocentric. Probably owing to his Sturges connection, he had several works by Americans—Frederic Church, Asher B.

---

* The three-volume *Art Treasures of America, Being the Choicest Works of Art in the Public and Private Collections of North America* (1879) included the collections of the Drexels, Vanderbilts, William Rockefeller, Levi Morton, August Belmont, Harris Fahnestock, A. T. Stewart, James Gordon Bennett, Christian Herter, W. T. Walters, H. P. Kidder, Leland Stanford, Charles Crocker, Milton Latham, and Darius Ogden Mills—and also the Corcoran Gallery in Washington, the Museum of Fine Arts in Boston, the New-York Historical Society, the Lenox Library, and the Metropolitan Museum of Art.

Durand (*Thanatopsis*), John F. Kensett (*Sunrise in the Adirondacks*), S. R. Gifford (*October in the Catskills*), and a scene from the *Odyssey* by Elihu Vedder that he had commissioned called *Nausicaa and Her Companions*, which Shinn found "quaint and interesting."*

While Americans were collecting academic genre scenes, the nineteenth century's great innovative artists—Manet, Monet, Cézanne, Degas, Renoir— were rejecting conventional subjects and forms to portray the life immediately around them, experimenting with light, color, texture, and composition. The first Impressionist exhibition in Paris in 1874 announced one of the most radical artistic developments of the century (the other was photography), which contemporary critics and collectors, with some notable exceptions, dismissed as insane. When Morgan and other American collectors of his generation eventually turned away from salon paintings in the late 1890s, they would look not to the modernist future of Van Gogh, Picasso, and Matisse but to the hallowed authority of the past.

———

In 1883, shortly after Morgan moved into 219, he had a catalogue of his books compiled and published by the New York dealer Joseph F. Sabin.† His early library more or less typified a New York gentleman's collection of the 1880s, with editions of famous authors in fine bindings, religious texts (Bibles, hymnals, psalters, tracts), and standard histories. Perhaps reflecting personal interests, however, Morgan owned sixty-six volumes on *Napoleon and His Generals* and Robert Burton's *Anatomy of Melancholy* (1621). The library's lighter fare included a ribald *Life of Sir John Falstaff* illustrated by George Cruikshank, a book on *Mrs. Jordan*, the English actress who was mistress to William IV, and *A Burlesque Translation of Homer*, published in 1792.

Morgan was, however, also building a reference library on art. He owned Crowe & Cavalcaselle's *Early Flemish Painters*, Vasari's *Lives of the Painters*, Michael Bryan's *Dictionary of Painters and Engravers*, books on Venice and Pompeii, several volumes on ceramics, a catalogue of the Louvre's collections before 1815, and Ruskin's *Modern Painters, Stones of Venice*, and *Seven Lamps of Architecture*. Like Ruskin and the Harvard art historian Charles Eliot Norton (though without their aesthetic and moral analyses), Morgan was drawn to the arts of the Middle Ages, and by 1883 he owned several of the books that were kindling nineteenth-century interest in medieval subjects—including Sir

———

* The Durand and the Vedder (the latter as *Greek Girls Bathing*) are now in the Metropolitan Museum of Art.
† Sabin's father, Joseph (1821–1881), had been one of the leading book men in the United States—a publisher, cataloguer, auctioneer, importer, and seller of books, and compiler of the renowned *Dictionary of Books Relating to America*.

John Froissart's *Chronicles*, published in 1868 with chromolithographic reproductions from manuscripts in the French Bibliothèque Nationale, Paul Lacroix's *Les Arts au Moyen Age*, Henry Shaw's *Dresses and Decorations of the Middle Ages*, and two volumes on *Les Evangiles des Dimanches et Fêtes de L'Année*. He also had facsimiles of manuscript illuminations by Jehan Fouquet, the great fifteenth-century French master who was equally celebrated as a panel painter.

And he had begun to acquire original literary and historical authors' manuscripts. Junius in 1881 had given him the complete holograph manuscript of Sir Walter Scott's 1815 novel *Guy Mannering*, set in eighteenth-century Scotland—the loss of this Scottish national treasure to the United States cannot have pleased the British. Pierpont himself bought an autograph letter of Robert Burns written in 1793. Junius owned the George Washington letter that he had read at Delmonico's in 1877; Pierpont by 1883 had four Washington letters, as well as a set of autographs by the signers of the Declaration of Independence, and a bound set of documents relating to the death of Alexander Hamilton. The most important item in his library of the early eighties was a copy of John Eliot's Indian Bible (Cambridge, 1663)—the first complete Bible printed in North America, in an Algonquin dialect.

———

Morgan's new house was the first private residence in New York entirely illuminated by Edison's lights. Bare bulbs, singly and in clusters, are visible in the photographs of 219 in *Artistic Houses*—they didn't need shades since the light they gave off was so dim. Engineers had installed a steam engine under the stables behind the house, and wired the building so that Morgan could light up the first floor, front hall, and cellar by turning a knob near the head of his bed. He remained resolutely committed to electric lighting, despite his father's initial opposition, and even though Edison had not been able to keep the promise he made in 1878 to have a working system ready in a few weeks; there was still no system at the end of 1882.

The wizard of Menlo Park had wanted "funds to push the light rapidly," but wanted to spend them in his own way. His attorney, Grosvenor Lowrey, had from the outset been caught between the Edison Electric Light Company directors and an autocratic prodigy who had an "easily ruffled ego," and "bristled whenever doubts of his eventual success were voiced." At the end of December 1878, just weeks after the Light Company was organized, executive-board members complained that Edison had spent nearly $20,000 on new buildings—far more than they "had been led to suppose was necessary." In the future, they wanted detailed vouchers for expenses.

One morning a month later, Lowrey stopped by the Drexel, Morgan office and learned of a setback—Edison had discovered that the platinum wire filament used in his first lightbulb wouldn't work. Morgan partners Fabbri, Drexel, and Wright, who owned EELC stock, jokingly asked Lowrey if he knew of any-one who wanted to buy their shares, but (Lowrey told Edison) "Mr. Fabbri looked serious." As Lowrey made the case for scientific trial and error, urging patience, "Mr. Morgan stood by listening without saying anything." The head of the bank had agreed to handle lighting patents in Europe, replacing Edison's foreign agent, but details had not been worked out. One of the partners noted that Edison was about to draw on his European representative for $1,800 in patent fees, and that Morgan might not want to take over advancing such sums if he was losing confidence in the project.

"Mr. Morgan spoke for the first time," reported Lowrey, and said on the con-trary, he had been waiting for just this kind of opportunity to settle with the agent on fair terms—he was quite prepared to go ahead as planned. An exul-tant Lowrey concluded that "these gentlemen" were not "to be very easily frightened away from a thing they once made up their mind to," and urged his client to be completely frank with "our friends" at 23 Wall Street about what-ever difficulties might arise: they would all learn from his experience.*

Transforming a brilliant idea into a marketable system took far longer and cost far more than anyone initially expected, and as Edison worked to solve a range of technical problems, build large central power stations, and set up fac-tories to manufacture the necessary equipment, some of his backers lost pa-tience. The EELC had been set up to hold patents; its directors never intended to get involved in manufacturing. In the fall of 1879, the board refused to raise more capital on the earlier terms, considering (Lowrey told Edison) "that you agreed to give them an electric light and that they agreed to give you Fifty thou-sand Dollars."

The company increased its capital stock several times—to $480,000 in No-vember 1880. Some of the new shares were issued to Edison in return for ex-

---

* The standard version of the early Edison business depicts the inventor as a visionary, folksy genius putting up a noble fight against ruthless capitalists (chiefly Morgan) who kept him begging for funds and used him for their own ends. Recent work in the Edison archives— most notably by Robert Friedel and Paul Israel (*Edison's Electric Light, Biography of an Inven-tion*)—and papers in the Morgan archives tell a different story.

Some of the confusion about Morgan's role in the business stems from the fact that there were three different groups involved in the project, which most histories of the subject have conflated into one. These were (1) the incorporator/directors of the Edison Electric Light Company (Fabbri, the partners in Lowrey's law firm, several Western Union men); (2) the syndicate of investors (including Fabbri, Drexel, Wright, and by early 1879, Henry Villard); (3) the company's bankers (Drexel, Morgan & Co.). There was some overlap—Fabbri be-longed to all three groups; Villard was a director and an investor—but they were not identi-cal in their actions or interests. The fact that Morgan did not initially buy stock in the Light Company has been seen as a lack of commitment, but the $50,000 put up by the first in-vestors was pocket change to Morgan; he made a much larger pledge in committing himself to the business, and by the early 1880s he was a large owner of Edison stock.

tensions of the initial patent agreements; most were sold for cash. To raise money for manufacturing companies, Edison sold much of his stock, borrowed against the rest, and tapped the savings of friends. The Morgan bank tendered informal advice. Fabbri warned his "Friend Edison" late in 1879 not to conduct public exhibitions of "your great invention" before testing them completely in the lab: though errors might be instructive for men of science, public failures were "extremely damaging" in business, and Fabbri wanted to make sure that "for your own sake as well as that of those interested with you every precaution is taken to insure the success you so well deserve."

At the end of 1880, Drexel, Morgan helped Lowrey incorporate an Edison Electric Illuminating Company, with $1 million in capital stock, to build a central power station on Pearl Street in downtown Manhattan. Pierpont took Jacob Rogers and Jack out to see Edison's Menlo Park "invention factory" in January 1881, and two months later told his friend William W. Hoppin: "I think there is a good thing in this for all parties who undertake to introduce it properly into cities—and feeling this way I was very anxious you should derive the benefit of it for Providence." Just how good a thing it was did not become widely known for a few more years. In the meantime, Drexel, Morgan held the company's deposits, arranged its loans, managed Edison's personal investments, and—just as Lowrey had predicted—effectively promoted incandescent light at home and abroad.*

Thirty years after George Peabody advanced funds to display McCormick's reaper, Colt's revolvers, and Hoe's printing press at London's Crystal Palace Exhibition, his successors helped exhibit Edison's light at world's fairs. At the Paris Electrical Exposition in 1881, the Edison display attracted the attention of a French architect who put Edison lights in the foyer of the Paris Opéra, an American naval ensign who went on to develop electric street-rail systems in the United States, and the German engineer/industrialists Emil Rathenau and Werner von Siemens. In 1882 the Edison exhibit at another Crystal Palace fair led to the building of a central power station in London's Holborn Viaduct. Pierpont had finally changed Junius's mind: J. S. Morgan & Co. organized an Edison Electric Light Company in London in 1882, and in October of 1883 merged it with its chief rival to form the Edison & Swan United Electric Light Company, Ltd.

"The greatest advantage Edison had over all rivals," conclude the historians Robert Friedel and Paul Israel, was the trust of "the wary and watchful men of

---

* At Edison's request in the spring of 1881, the bank agreed to buy half of his stock in the Edison Electric Light Company of Europe at par, and put it into a syndicate "to be managed by us for our mutual benefit, with a proportionate division of profits." A week after the bankers made this offer, the stock's value dropped, and Drexel, Morgan told Edison it would cancel the transaction "to relieve you of any embarrassment." Edison sent his thanks "for your consideration."

Wall Street," which gave him a "capability possessed by no inventor in history before him." Edison chafed at times under the obligations to meet timetables and demands that came with using other people's money, but after one round of struggle his secretary reported him "begin[n]ing again to think that DM&Co. are thorough good people to be associated with as although they may be a little hard in some things they do not make a lot of empty promises. If they undertake to do a thing they fulfill their contract not only to the letter but also in the spirit in which it was made."

Pierpont personally put Edison's invention on prominent first-class display in New York. On September 4, 1882, the inventor walked from his just-completed central power station on Pearl Street down to Drexel, Morgan & Co., which had been wired with 106 electric lamps. Edison checked the installations. Minutes before 3:00 P.M., an electrician at Pearl Street turned on the current in a generator called Jumbo, after P. T. Barnum's famous elephant. Precisely at 3:00, Edison flipped a switch at 23 Wall Street. A *New York Times* reporter noted that it was still daylight when the bulbs came on, but by 7:00 P.M., as the city grew dark, the electric light "showed how bright and steady it is . . . soft, mellow, and grateful to the eye." The *Herald* added: "From the outer darkness these points of light looked like drops of flame suspended from jets." Edison told the *Sun*: "I have accomplished all I promised."

Not quite. The cost of the Pearl Street station was nearly triple the original estimate, which made capitalists in other cities reluctant to invest in central power stations.

The electrical system at Morgan's new house got off to a less auspicious start than the one downtown. When the engineers finished the private installation at 219, Morgan asked Edison's chief lieutenant, Edward H. Johnson, to inspect it. What did he think? Touring the building slowly, checking wires, sconces, and bulbs, Johnson said, "If it was my own I would throw the whole damned thing into the street."

"That," Morgan replied, "is precisely what Mrs. Morgan says."

Not about to give up, Morgan asked Johnson to rewire the whole house before his family moved in. When the system was finally turned on, the steam-powered generator under the stables made so much noise and smoke that the next-door neighbor complained. Morgan apologized. He had taken "great pains and precautions" to avoid these problems, he wrote, and would "spare neither exertion nor expense to correct" them: "Nothing but the fact that it would leave my house in entire darkness prevents me from stopping the Engine at once."

He called for repairmen, but the Edison company had a surfeit of projects on its hands in December of 1882, and its famous banker had to wait. After three weeks, Morgan wrote to the president of Edison Electric, Sherbourne B. Eaton: "I must frankly say that I consider the whole thing an outrage to me, as well as the neighbors—& I am unwilling to stand it any longer. Please let the matter have immediate attention." In January, engineers set India Rubber supports under the engine, lined the housing with felt, and dug a trench across Morgan's yard to funnel the smoke and steam through his own chimney, farther from the neighbors.

Once these problems were solved, Morgan held a reception at 219 that introduced four hundred of his friends to Edison's electric light. Then one night while the family was at the opera, the wiring in the library set the banker's desk on fire. Johnson came to inspect the damage early the next morning. "The house was pervaded by a strong smell of wet, burned wood and burned carpet," he later recalled. The library floor had been torn up, and the desk, heavy rug, and assorted charred objects were piled in the center of the room.

Suddenly Johnson heard footsteps: "Mr. Morgan appeared in the doorway with a newspaper in his hand, and looked at me over the tops of his glasses.

" 'Well?' he said.

"I had formulated an explanation, and was prepared to make an elaborate excuse. Just as I opened my mouth to speak, Mrs. Morgan appeared behind Mr. Morgan, and as I caught her eye she put her finger on her lips and then vanished down the hall. I said nothing, but looked at the heap of débris."

Morgan finally asked Johnson what he was going to do.

Make the system safe, the engineer replied. He himself was to blame for the wiring—there was nothing wrong with the lights.

How long would it take?

Johnson: "I will do it right away."

"All right," said the banker. "See that you do."

Morgan stayed with this experiment at considerable personal inconvenience and cost. He knew from financing railroads, the Atlantic Cable, and the St. Louis Bridge how much difficulty could lie between a good idea and a working result. Not all of Edison's early supporters had similar stamina. The William H. Vanderbilts installed electricity in *their* new houses in 1882, but when crossed wires set fire to the picture gallery, Mrs. Vanderbilt gave up. Edison took the whole installation out.

Morgan's children responded in character to this venture. "Certainly this is the age of electricity," Jack told Louisa from St. Paul's in 1883. "In our reading room they take a paper called 'Scientific American' and in looking through that I saw only about three new inventions that were not connected in some way with electricity. It makes one very much ashamed of not knowing more about it than one does."

Louisa attended a costume party in the early eighties as "the spirit, it could hardly be called the ghost, of electricity," reported the *Herald*. "She was gowned in electric green satin, covered with a net work of embroidery done in electric wire." There were electric ornaments in her hair, and at the touch of a button concealed in the folds of her dress, all the tiny bulbs lit up. What kind of battery animated her electrifying appearance the *Herald* did not say.

———

The American rage for "reinventing everything, especially the house" extended to country as well as city properties in the 1880s, and with his family ensconced at 219, Morgan decided to expand and modernize Cragston. He had acquired additional land at Highland Falls, which brought the total to 675 acres, and in 1886 engaged the Boston architects Peabody & Stearns to remodel his Hudson Valley farmhouse. Like his Manhattan brownstone, this rural retreat was relatively unpretentious by the standards of the Gilded Age: George W. Vanderbilt constructed a French château called Biltmore on 130,000 acres in North Carolina at a cost of $3 million—with "league-long marble halls" and "alternate Gothic and Palladian cathedrals," reported Henry James.

Peabody & Stearns were known for respecting the contexts of their buildings and for balancing "picturesque" style with organic coherence. The firm had designed New York's Union League Club, Harvard's Hemenway Gym, and houses throughout New England, including a boxy rustic cottage in Northeast Harbor, Maine, for Harvard's president Charles W. Eliot. To the wood-frame house at Cragston, Robert Swain Peabody added asymmetrical new wings with wide bays, a Palladian window above the entrance, a conservatory, a full third story with gables and eaves, a widow's walk, and a piazza facing south and east for panoramic views of the Hudson. Inside, he rearranged walls to provide fewer, larger rooms, more bathrooms, a library, and a wine cellar—all under Morgan's close surveillance. Someone penciled on one of the architect's drawings: "These steps are not right. Mr. M. asked to have them changed," and on another, "Mr. M. does not want a bath here but thinks a slop sink is all that is required." The cost of the alterations, plus a new dairy and several cottages, came to $76,000—$16,000 more than the price of the entire farm in 1871, but probably less than an outbuilding for the "Granderbilt" palazzi.

Pierpont was not as wealthy as the industrial tycoons, and shared some of his father's concern not to give the impression that the Morgan bankers cared more for their own pleasure than for the interests of their clients. Still, he had always treated himself and his friends to whatever he considered "the best" in the way of luxury and comfort, and his indulgence increased with his means. He sent bushels of oysters, terrapins, and Cragston apples to his London partners every Christmas, and in New York took large parties to the new Metropolitan Opera House and to private Patriarchs' Balls (the fifty members of the exclusive Partriarchs' Association gave two to three balls a season). He had a saddle of Newport lamb delivered to 219 twice a week by a Rhode Island butcher, cases of whiskey sent up from Kentucky, and bottles of brandied fruit and tins of cream biscuits awaiting him at the White Star dock every time he sailed. His suits were custom-tailored in London. For his annual Fourth of July picnics at Cragston, crews of men fired torpedoes and rockets from the Hudson River shore. One afternoon in the eighties, he spent 275,000 francs ($55,000) on jewelry at Tiffany's in Paris. And one spring he sent his wife a French chef. Fanny had just fired her American cook, complaining that the woman "asks $50 per month and is worth about $25." Shipping a Frenchman across the Atlantic and setting him up in New York would cost far more, but Pierpont thought it worth the expense. Fanny did not. "A 'male foreigner' will know little about American cooking," she protested, "and less about American ways."

Morgan paid little attention to cost for things he really wanted—house, yacht, painting, necklace, dress, horse, dog—but did not like to pay more than he had to for other people's work. He knew that strangers would try to overcharge him, and when the contractors turned in a bid for the new Cragston dairy, he told Peabody & Stearns he had no intention of "going ahead on such a basis. I understand it is nearly double what Mr. Vanderbilt's dairy cost, which from all accounts is too high." A more chilling example: when a maid he brought to Europe for Louisa one year spent the entire Atlantic crossing seasick in her bunk, Louisa wanted to send the girl to Germany to recover, "but Papa says no," she told Fanny. "He says that to give her so much money for being with us eight weeks, and then after finding her perfectly useless for almost two of those weeks, to send her away for two or three more of them would be perfectly absurd."

With the rise in Morgan's means and public prominence came a dramatic increase in requests for financial help. In 1884 he put up the last $4,000 for the Groton School in Massachusetts, founded by the Reverend Endicott Peabody (called the Rector), the son of Junius's former partner, S. Endicott Peabody. He gave free investment advice to friends, including William Wetmore Story, the American sculptor in Rome, whom he advised late in 1884 not to keep all his "eggs in one basket": if Story sold some of the eggs and sent the proceeds to New York, Morgan would "invest in safe securities productive of income."

He gave hundreds of gifts each year to hospitals, museums, the Episcopal Church (over $200,000 to St. George's in 1887 alone), and individual members of the clergy; and he made personal loans, usually without expectation of repayment, to artists such as Story's son Waldo and the painter Luther Terry, to other people whose work he admired, and to some who simply needed help. One of the latter was Lizzie Darling, the "E.D." whom he had courted in Hartford and Boston years before. She had never married, and was living in Dedham, Massachusetts. In 1886 Pierpont paid some of her taxes and the interest on a loan. A year later he advised her to sell bonds to pay off the loan, and regretted not having seen her recently: "If you get in difficulty for current expenses," he offered, "let me know and I'll send you a cheque."

She did—and he did—but he was not willing to subsidize her indefinitely. Six years later he wrote kindly but firmly, "My dear Lizzie, It is true that I have received your various notes and ought really to have answered them but I did not like to say no, and in the face of your assurance that the last remittance I made would be all that you would need, and in the face of the many demands upon me from all quarters, I felt that I had gone as far as I ought; however I do not wish to leave you in the lurch and therefore enclose my cheque as you request for $300, but you will not misunderstand me when I say that this is as far as I should be willing to go. With kindest regards I am always sincerely yours. . . ."

Morgan's regal manner had also increased with his eminence and income. When the managers of the White Star Line changed their sailing schedule one winter, dictating a slight modification in his clockwork travel plans, he asked them to reconsider: "I do not want to interfere" (which was clearly not the case), he wrote, "but cannot you turn it round" so the ship would leave as usual on the last Wednesday in May? White Star did not reschedule its transatlantic traffic to suit the convenience of one peremptory passenger, who wrote again: "sorry you cannot see your way clear to make the arrangement . . . the unexpected change puts us all very much out."

Morgan and Egisto Fabbri, 1885.
(Archives of The Pierpont Morgan Library, New York)

Chapter 13

A RAILROAD
BISMARCK?

A t 23 Wall Street in the 1880s, Pierpont spent most of his time on railroad
finance. Shortly after he secured the New York Central account with the
sale of Vanderbilt stock in 1879–80, he agreed to handle a bond issue for the
Northern Pacific. This still-unfinished line, intended to run from Lake Superior
to Puget Sound, had brought down Jay Cooke & Co. when it went bankrupt in
1873. It had slowly reorganized (an appeal to the bondholders in 1875 urged,
"Your road *uncompleted* is wholly unremunerative, but *completed* it becomes
one of the great highways of the nation"), and in 1880 its president asked
Drexel, Morgan to raise money for the last section of track, from Montana to
the coast. Morgan put together a syndicate with Winslow, Lanier and August
Belmont to sell $40 million of Northern Pacific general mortgage bonds—"the
largest transaction in railroad bonds ever made in the United States," reported
the *Commercial and Financial Chronicle.*

Junius was skeptical, but after the New York partners answered all his questions—and quoted a letter from Interior Secretary Carl Schurz promising the
road's president that "Nothing can be further from the wish of this Department than to do anything which would impede or interfere with the success of
the enterprise that you have in hand"—he agreed to manage European sales.
The issue sold well on both sides of the Atlantic. "Warmest congratulations
our joint great success," cabled the London firm to New York. Drexel, Morgan
replied, "We reciprocate congratulations. Great success is general subject conversation."

Success in the financial markets guaranteed completion of the Northern Pacific, which made it a threat to other roads in the area even before the final track went down. The man most worried by the impending competition was the owner of a northwestern rail and steamship empire, Henry Villard. A German immigrant, Villard had covered the Civil War for several New York newspapers, and married the daughter of abolitionist William Lloyd Garrison. He saw the commercial potential of Pacific Northwest trade as soon as the transcontinental railroad opened access to the region in 1869, and proceeded to build a transportation network called the Oregon Railway & Navigation Company. Shortly after he joined the board of the Edison Electric Light Company in 1879, he installed an electric lighting system on one of his OR&N steamships. By 1880 he was wealthy enough to commission his million-dollar mansion from McKim, Mead & White at 451 Madison Avenue, and to buy one of the newspapers for which he had worked as a reporter, New York's *Evening Post*.

When the Northern Pacific was bankrupt in the seventies he could afford to ignore it, but once the Morgan-generated $40 million was on its way to his rival's coffers, Villard had to act. In November 1880 he bought a controlling interest in NP stock, and announced that he would bring the railroad and his OR&N together into a holding company called the Oregon & Transcontinental; it would own enough voting stock in both subsidiaries to govern and coordinate their operations. Morgan did not oppose this plan. He had no objection to Villard, and approved of running potentially competing systems under one roof. The Northern Pacific elected Villard president in September 1881, and completed its construction over the next two years with further help from Drexel, Morgan. Pierpont took a seat on the NP board in September 1883. He was immediately drawn into action.

Not only had construction costs vastly overrun company estimates, but Villard had been liberally spending money on other projects as well. Stock market bears (speculators betting against the O&T) and the beginnings of a new recession crippled the overextended system in October of 1883. By the end of the year both Villard and the O&T were insolvent.

Morgan, sounding a familiar theme, wired his London partners that he would have to step in to protect the credit of the Northern Pacific, "with which we [are] all publicly identified." When renewed attacks by the speculators in December "made radical steps essential" to put the property beyond the "machinations of those scamps," he took charge with a mix of reluctance and pride: "I certainly have no desire to be burdened with all this trouble," he grumbled to Walter Burns, "but there I am, representing interests which cannot be shirked." He was annoyed at Villard for "not having been frank and open on all points" with the NP directors, but also felt sorry for him: "he no doubt believes he has done his best."

Morgan and Fabbri persuaded Villard to resign from the presidencies of the NP, the OR&N, and the O&T. Then they bailed out the holding company by furnishing new capital in the form of loans, subscriptions for common stock, and additional bond sales. They put the proceeds of the NP second-mortgage bonds into a fund that could be paid out only under Morgan's signature, and appointed a strong committee to "hold everything with a tight rein."

By mid-December 1883—three months after he joined the NP board—Pierpont reported himself satisfied that the road's "dark days" were over and its earning capacity "secured beyond doubt." The stock market's response to the rescue had been "marvellous," but he cared less about share price than about routing the gamblers: "it is a great delight to see those fellows who have been destroying other people's property severely punished." He advised friends that the stock's real value was considerably higher than current market quotations. At the end of 1883 his firm's $40 million Northern Pacific loan showed a positive balance. The following summer, he leased the OR&N to the Northern Pacific, and reported that the company would net over $2 million in 1884.

"Whatever may be the profit of the account," he concluded to Burns, "nothing will give me greater satisfaction than the knowledge of having been able to rescue from immanent [*sic*] danger the Northern Pacific and O&T Companies, as we have been able to do the last three months – but it has been a hard fight . . . you can never know, without being here, all we went through."

Villard knew. Early in 1884 he had a nervous breakdown. His Italianate brownstones on Madison at 50th Street were still unfinished. That spring, he went to Germany with his family to recover. Two years later he returned to New York as the American representative of the Deutsche Bank, and sold his houses to Mr. and Mrs. Whitelaw Reid (Elisabeth Mills Reid was the daughter of financier Darius Ogden Mills; her husband published the New York *Tribune*). The Villards moved north, to the corner of Madison and 72nd Street, in 1886.

———

In the scandal-ridden presidential election of 1884, Morgan crossed party lines to vote for Grover Cleveland, a Democrat. Although he worked with men he trusted in Washington, the banker had little regard for politicians, and cared more about economic stability than party affiliation.

He had company in his contempt for politicans. The British journalist James Bryce, a correspondent for the liberal weekly *Nation*, observed that Americans toward the end of the nineteenth century did not say "politicians" but "the politicians," because "the word indicates a class with certain defined characteristics." "Politician" had become a term of reproach, Bryce went on, "not merely among the 'superfine philosophers' of New England colleges, but among the better sort of citizens over the whole Union. 'How did such a job come to be perpetrated?' I remember once asking a casual acquaintance who had been pointing out some scandalous waste of public money. 'Why, what can you expect from the politicians?' was the surprised answer."

There were exceptions—ambitious, practical men with strong nerves and flexible spines such as Benjamin Bristow, Lincoln's former private secretary John Hay, Henry Cabot Lodge, Albert Beveridge, and Theodore Roosevelt, Jr. The senior Roosevelt, an influential businessman of Knickerbocker descent, had turned away from politics in disgust after exposure to the corrupt Republican machine when he was customs collector for New York. His son led the reform Republicans in the New York State Assembly in the early 1880s, and later recalled the horror with which his upper-class friends had greeted the news of his interest in elective office: they "laughed at me, and told me that politics were 'low'; that the organizations were not controlled by 'gentlemen'; that I would find them run by saloon-keepers, horse-car conductors, and the like."

Morgan had raised money for the successful Republican campaign of James Garfield and Chester Arthur in 1880. He had publicly endorsed Roosevelt, Jr., for the New York Assembly in 1881, and for reelection the following year. He did not, however, support the party's 1884 presidential nominee, James G. Blaine. Called the Plumed Knight for his ornate tastes and ostentatious attire, Blaine had been Speaker of the House and Secretary of State. He freely traded favors, offices, and legislative votes for party campaign funds, and his history of dubious dealings with the railroads had deprived him of the Republican nomination in 1876. According to Richard Hofstadter, this champion spoilsman's chief contribution to American politics was "to lower its tone."

The Democrats had gained control of the House in the midterm 1882 elections, and hoped to win the presidency for the first time since 1856 by nominating New York's Governor Cleveland in 1884. An obscure Buffalo lawyer who had been elected mayor of that city in 1881 and governor the following year, the corpulent Cleveland (he weighed 250 pounds) had a reputation for integrity, political courage, and fiscal caution. Known as Grover the Good, he opposed boss politics and big government while supporting civil service reform, free trade, the rights of private property, and the gold standard. The political heir of Samuel Tilden, he was on most issues indistinguishable from a Republican, and his nominators hoped that GOP opponents of Blaine, called Mugwumps,* would ignore party affiliation and vote Democratic—which is exactly what they did. Among the bolters were Mark Twain, liberal reformers E. L. Godkin, George W. Curtis, and Carl Schurz, and a number of prominent businessmen, including Morgan. Joseph Pulitzer's *World* listed four reasons for endorsing Cleveland: "(1) He is an honest man. (2) He is an honest man. (3) He is

---

* The word meant "great chief" in the Algonquin Indian dialect, and appeared in John Eliot's Indian Bible. In politics, it characterized those who held themselves above dogmatic party loyalty, "professing disinterested or superior views."

an honest man. (4) He is an honest man." Republican insider Levi Morton did not join the Mugwumps: having been appointed U.S. minister to France by Garfield in 1881 and retained there by Chester Arthur after Garfield's assassination, Morton came home in the fall of 1884 to raise money for Blaine. Other loyalists who supported the party ticket were John Sherman, Andrew Carnegie, Jay Gould, and twenty-six-year-old Theodore Roosevelt, Jr.

Political issues played a far smaller role in the 1884 campaign than character did. When the Democrats revived charges about Blaine's shady history with the railroads and the lies he told to cover it up, Republicans disclosed that the bachelor Cleveland had fathered a child—and Grover the Good suddenly turned into a "gross and licentious man," a "moral leper," a "coarse debauchee who would bring his harlots with him to Washington." James Bryce called the election a contest over "the copulative habits of one and the prevaricative habits of the other." Mark Twain said Blaine's deceptions had so taken the wind out of his own sails that "I don't seem able to lie with any heart lately." Republicans took to chanting, "Ma! Ma! Where's my pa? Gone to the White House, Ha! Ha! Ha!" The Democrats tried to shrug off their candidate's "youthful indiscretion," and a Cleveland adviser came up with the slogan "Public Office is a Public Trust," which was about all the governor tried to say during the preelection furor.

Morgan cabled his London partners that October: "Result elections very doubtful. Vote will be close." Also, "stock market in hands of gamblers, public hold aloof—it is good time keep entirely quiet." The vote *was* close—Cleveland won by three tenths of a percentage point on the popular ballot, and by thirty-seven votes in the electoral college. The first Democrat to occupy the White House in twenty-four years promised in his inaugural address to respect sound business principles, and filled his cabinet with conservatives.

———

The U.S. economy reached the peak of its latest expansion in March of 1882, then began to contract. International trade played a large role in the downturn. Domestic prices and incomes had risen rapidly between 1876 and 1881 as U.S. exports exceeded imports, while British prices suffered abrupt declines. America's chief trading partner had been losing gold for some time. Accordingly, the Bank of England raised interest rates in 1881–82, which drew international capital out of the United States.

Furthermore—just as the Morgans had feared—railroad competition was destroying confidence in the markets. The foreign capital invested in U.S. railroads had quadrupled between 1876 and 1883, from $375 million to $1.5 billion, but the boom's new rate wars, parallel building, and mismanagement sent that flow into reverse: between 1882 and 1885 foreigners sold off U.S. railroad holdings at the rate of $25 million a year.

Declining securities values agitated Wall Street in the fall of 1883 as Morgan and Fabbri were putting the Northern Pacific on solid ground. In May of the following year the failure of several New York brokerage firms and banks touched off a more ominous crisis.* Cyrus Field cabled Junius Morgan: "Many of our businessmen seem to have lost their heads. What we want is some cool-headed strong man to lead." Junius's son did what he could to forestall widespread liquidation, buying stocks as panicked investors sold, and advising friends to do the same. With the consequences of the 1857 and 1873 panics in mind, the New York Clearing House Association stepped in to act as "lender of last resort"—a phrase coined by the British financial journalist Walter Bagehot in 1873. The Clearing House issued $25 million in loan certificates to ease the strain on the money markets and keep sound firms afloat. The panic caused severe damage in New York but did not spread to the rest of the country or bring on a prolonged depression. The worst of the trouble was over by the summer of 1885, and the economy remained relatively stable for the next six years.

The contraction that began in 1882 did have stark effects on Wall Street. Drexel, Morgan's earnings plummeted from $1.6 million in 1882 to $662,000 the following year, and the firm lost $41,000 in 1884.

Junius, always gloomy during economic reversals, was feeling worn-out and thinking about the future. In December 1884, as J. S. Morgan & Co. posted a

* The event that started it was the collapse of the brokerage house Grant & Ward. Ulysses S. Grant had traveled around the world after leaving the White House in 1877, and returned to New York without money or plans. Although Morgan had sided with Treasury Secretary Bristow against Grant in the seventies, he now helped raise money for the former President. In November 1880, Morgan, Tony Drexel, and the Philadelphia publisher George Childs asked twenty men to contribute $5,000 each to a private fund for Grant, in view of the fact that the general's income was "not sufficient to secure him in that position of comfortable independence that he should be enabled to occupy." Such a step would not be necessary "in any other great nation," the trio explained, as "all but ours provide munificently for their citizens or subjects who have done the state illustrious service." Potential donors would "be good enough to consider this note as strictly confidential." With the money raised by their wealthy friends, the Grants bought a house at 3 East 66th Street in New York. Two years later Morgan agreed to lend Grant more money—"although as I told you we are not making any time loans"—but warned: "it will be necessary that we have collaterals, that being our rule, the wisdom of which I think you will appreciate."

The unworldly Grant had gone into business in the early eighties with a rogue trader named Ferdinand Ward, who used his new partner's reputation to secure funds and attract clients. When Ward's scheme of secret speculations and phony profits collapsed in May of 1884, it brought down a prominent New York bank, set off a panic, and ruined Grant. Ward eventually went to jail. Grant, humiliated, depressed, and dying of throat cancer, began writing articles about the Civil War to earn money. With Mark Twain's help he expanded the articles into a full-length memoir, which he finished just before he died in 1885. His posthumously published *Personal Memoirs* turned out to be a great work of military history; it sold over three hundred thousand copies, and earned his heirs nearly half a million dollars.

$20,000 loss for the year, he revised the articles of his London partnership, authorizing Pierpont to continue the firm, or not, with £1 million in capital, in the event of his own retirement or death. Walter Burns wanted permission to run the firm himself if Pierpont chose not to, which Junius did not think "nice." In the meantime, the elder Morgan brought in a new British partner, Robert Gordon, to take some responsibility off his shoulders. It would be a great relief to "turn my back on Old Broad St.," he told Pierpont—"not that I do not enjoy business when I can take it easily & there is less wear & tear than now, for I do. But what I feel the want of now most of all is *rest.*"

Pierpont was also giving some thought to the future. He brought two new bankers into his New York firm in 1884. One was George S. Bowdoin, who had since 1871 been a partner in Levi Morton's house, Morton, Bliss & Co. Bowdoin had managed the purchase of *Corsair* for Morgan in 1882, and was an original member of the Corsair Club. With a genealogy that included Alexander Hamilton, Philip Schuyler, and Gouverneur Morris, he was exactly the type of patrician people came to expect at the Morgan bank. In a photograph taken in the eighties with Morgan and Lanier he looks substantial, affable, calm—like someone you would trust with your grandmother's bank account.

Morgan's other new associate was Charles H. Coster, who had been working at Egisto Fabbri's shipping and trading house. Fabbri highly recommended the thirty-two-year-old Coster, who soon proved invaluable to Drexel, Morgan. Pierpont in his first years on Wall Street had paid such close attention to detail and been so unable to delegate responsibility that he periodically collapsed in "nervous" exhaustion. Twenty years later, the business had grown far beyond even his capacity for single-handed control. Coster had what John Moody later called "a mind in a generation for detail," and over the next few years he took charge of the technicalities in Morgan's corporate work. Pale, meticulous, slight of build, high-strung, and prematurely gray, Coster traveled to railroad offices all over the country, racing from one meeting to the next, drafting reorganization plans late into the night, mastering fine points of finance and law. During a railroad foreclosure in the Middle West, an opposing lawyer pointed out that twelve hundred of the road's bonds lacked a crucial endorsement and were therefore invalid. Coster asked for a lunch break. As he and his assistant left the building, the latter asked, "Where shall we lunch?" Coster snorted, "Lunch, nothing! Is there a printing press in town?" There was—one. For the next hour and a half Coster had the missing endorsements printed on the bonds, and personally signed them all.

Morgan supplied this lieutenant with whatever he required, and spent his own time bringing in new deals and negotiating for an end to railroad warfare. Wall Street watchers credited Coster with all the bank's successful reorganizations between the mid-eighties and the end of the century. At one point he sat on fifty-nine corporate boards. Moody considered him "Morgan's right arm."

One of Coster's first assignments was to take over from Fabbri the handling of the Edison business. Six years after his first successful experiment with incandescence, Edison had come to detest the dominion of the patent-holding Electric Light Company. His original backers still had seen no return on their investment, but the independent companies he set up to manufacture lamps, engines, and tubes were earning money; when the EELC directors asked for a share of the manufacturing business in the spring of 1884, Edison was outraged that men who had refused to fund these ventures wanted some of his profits. He no longer trusted his attorney, Grosvenor Lowrey, or Light Company president Sherbourne Eaton, regarding them as tools of the EELC board. That fall, with the company's five-year contract about to expire, Edison waged a shareholder fight for control, and won: Lowrey and Eaton were voted out, along with several other directors.

The Light Company would be run by its executive vice president, Edward H. Johnson, the engineer who had rewired Morgan's house. Morgan partner J. Hood Wright stayed on the board, and Coster was elected to replace Fabbri. Coster worked so well with his predecessor's "Friend Edison" (whom he addressed as "Professor") that he also succeeded Fabbri as treasurer of the EELC. Drexel, Morgan continued as bankers to the company and to Edison, who secretly gave Morgan and Wright 155 shares of Machine Works stock each.

———

The worst of the railroad conflicts that were driving foreign capital out of U.S. markets in 1883–84 involved the two largest railroads in the United States—the Pennsylvania and the New York Central. In the fall of '84, Junius met with officers of both roads on his annual visit to New York and tried to persuade them to give up their "absurd struggle for pre-eminence." He failed.

The previous June, when a small road called the New York, West Shore & Buffalo went into receivership, the Pennsylvania had bought up its devalued securities. The West Shore had been built expressly to compete with Vanderbilt's New York Central: it ran from Weehawken, New Jersey, up the west bank of the Hudson to Albany—directly parallel to the New York Central tracks on the other side of the river—then on to Buffalo, where it connected with another line to Chicago. It also ran along the edge of Pierpont's property at Highland Falls. As workmen laid down tracks in May of 1882, Louisa had reported from Cragston to her father in London: "I don't think that the railroad is going to bother us this summer as we were afraid it would. . . . And I don't think (Mama doesn't either) that the men at work there are going to be so very bad. They will probably steal she says from the garden, but I shouldn't think they would try to enter the house."

The West Shore—financed by a syndicate that included Jay Gould, George

Pullman, Henry Villard, and the firm of Winslow, Lanier—represented exactly the kind of parallel building the Morgans wanted to stop. With the New York Central already servicing the New York–Albany route, the West Shore was superfluous: on this kind of short haul, one line could efficiently carry all the available traffic. Having gone bankrupt, the West Shore should probably have been allowed to fail.

Pierpont was surprised to find Winslow, Lanier involved. He sent a private note around the corner to his friend one night by messenger: "My dear Charlie," it began. ". . . I feel that you are surrounded by men . . . without the least particle of honor who will not hesitate to put you in a false position if by so doing they can shield themselves or secure for themselves any benefit whatever." He knew that his friend was "bothered and worried," and promised to "do anything in my power to help you." The time "may and probably will come when it will be necessary for you to take a stand against them and if so I know you will not hesitate, and I will stand by you through it all and so will everyone else that knows you. Call on me at any and all times. . . ." Lanier quit the railroad's board early in 1884.

As soon as the West Shore was acquired by the Pennsylvania it became part of the larger conflict. William H. Vanderbilt said it had been built only to threaten the New York Central: "There is not a dollar's worth of new business from one end to the other. All the business the road does is stolen from the Central. I tell you I look on the West Shore road just as I would on a man whose hand I found in my money drawer." He suspected the Pennsylvania of having backed the West Shore venture all along, but couldn't prove it.

Whether by design or chance, the Pennsylvania Railroad officials who acquired the West Shore were in fact retaliating for an incursion into *their* monopoly of traffic in the Pennsylvania coal regions. In 1883 a syndicate that included Vanderbilt, the Rockefeller brothers, and Andrew Carnegie had begun building a line called the South Pennsylvania to run from Harrisburg west to Pittsburgh. Carnegie had had the enthusiastic backing of his former bosses at the Pennsylvania when he set up his iron and steel business in the early seventies, but once he started shipping huge quantities of coal and steel rails, he locked horns with the railroad giant over its freight rates—as had Standard Oil. The steel and oil men in the South Penn syndicate wanted a road of their own to break the Pennsylvania's monopoly, and Vanderbilt joined in order to get his hand into his rival's money drawer. As soon as construction began on the new road in the summer of 1884, the Pennsylvania's freight rates dropped.

With the South Penn controlled by New York Central allies and the West Shore in the hands of the Pennsylvania, each side had a knife at the other's throat. Junius failed to talk them into laying down their weapons in the fall of

1884, but his firm was ideally situated to intercede. Pierpont sat on the New York Central board and served as the road's principal banker. The Drexels had been financing the Pennsylvania for years.

At the end of May 1885 Pierpont and Vanderbilt took the same steamer from London to New York. Junius told Vanderbilt just before they sailed that he expected a solution to the West Shore business "not very far in the future," and was "glad therefore that you and Pierpont . . . will have an opportunity for exchanging views" on the Atlantic. Pierpont liked crossing the ocean with Vanderbilt, he told Louisa, because ship captains tried to show the old Commodore's son "how fast they can go." Still, between Liverpool and New York he had time to point out that Vanderbilt's reputation was on the line along with his own—investors who had bought New York Central shares at 131 on the strength of Vanderbilt-Morgan representations had seen the price plummet to 82, thanks to this "absurd" struggle. Massive sell-offs were damaging the railroad and the U.S. economy. By the time the ship reached New York, Morgan had prevailed on Vanderbilt to negotiate. In June he and Coster went to see the officers of the Pennsylvania.

Morgan arranged for the Pennsylvania's president and vice president, George B. Roberts and Frank Thomson, to meet with the New York Central's newly elected president, Chauncey Depew (formerly Vanderbilt's lawyer), on board *Corsair.* At ten o'clock one hot July morning, Morgan and Depew picked up Roberts and Thomson at the Jersey City pier and headed north. They stayed out all day, cruising up the Hudson to Garrison, back down to Sandy Hook, then north again, while Depew—speaking for himself, Vanderbilt, and Morgan—appealed for an end to the "ruinous" competition of parallel building and rate wars.

The big trunk lines had far more to gain from acting in concert than from continuing warfare, Depew pointed out, urging his rivals to join in a "community of interest" that would divide their territories into discrete "spheres of influence." As a first step, he suggested that the two roads exchange their troublesome properties, the West Shore and the unfinished South Penn.

Morgan, smoking his signature Cuban cigars, made the bankers' case for cooperation: if the flow of foreign capital to U.S. railroads were to continue, investors had to be protected from the waste and wild market fluctuations brought on by this kind of fight. No agreements—no more money.

The *Corsair*'s crew served lunch. The discussion went on. The day waned. Thomson came around, but Roberts seemed willing to go bankrupt in order to punish his rivals. He held out in silence until the yacht pulled alongside the Jersey City pier at 7:00 P.M. Finally, as he stepped onto the dock, he shook Morgan's hand and said, "I will agree to your plan and do my part."

The Drexel, Morgan bankers immediately executed the *Corsair* agreement. They set up a committee to buy the West Shore for $24 million and lease it in perpetuity to the New York Central. Since the Pennsylvania could not purchase the South Penn directly under the state's antimonopoly law, Morgan bought a 60 percent interest in the $5.6 million road, then traded it to the Pennsylvania for the bonds of another line.

Wall Street hailed the West Shore agreement as a first step toward lasting peace in the railroad wars and Morgan as its architect. "To railroads, least of all, would our people like to see applied the principle of the survival of the fittest," declared the *Commercial and Financial Chronicle.* "Mr. Morgan conceived the first [peaceable] settlement which was the embryo of them all."

Among those not cheering were Andrew Carnegie and the thousands of other shippers who objected to the prices the railroads could charge once competition was out of the way.*

William H. Vanderbilt died in 1885, leaving most of his $200 million fortune to his sons, Cornelius II and William K., and $10 million each to his six remaining children. Cornelius took over the family interest in the New York Central. He was the only Vanderbilt the Morgans actually liked, and Pierpont worked easily with him and Chauncey Depew on New York Central affairs.

———

In addition to public acclaim and the satisfaction of ending the Pennsylvania–New York Central standoff (at least for the moment), the *Corsair* agreement brought Morgan a new lawyer. Since Fanny's father had just died, her brother, Charles Edward Tracy, did the legal work on the West Shore deal. The Vanderbilts' attorney was Francis Lynde Stetson, who handled the negotiations so effectively that Morgan began to solicit his professional advice. Drexel, Morgan retained Charles E. Tracy for a year, but early in 1887—possibly at Morgan's urging—the Stetson law firm hired him and changed its name to Bangs, Stetson, Tracy, & MacVeagh. Charles Tracy soon moved to the sidelines as counsel to the bank. Morgan worked almost exclusively with Stetson.

A prominent Democrat, Frank Stetson had helped prosecute Boss Tweed in the seventies as assistant to New York City's corporation counsel, William C. Whitney. He had supported Samuel Tilden's failed bid for the presidency in 1876 and Grover Cleveland's successful run in 1884. Offered a cabinet posi-

---

* To Carnegie's dismay, the *Corsair* agreement restored monopoly power to the Pennsylvania. He fought on for years against the "monstrous" behavior of his former employer, sometimes in alliance with the farmers, manufacturers, and merchants who were urging the states to regulate railroads, sometimes with Rockefeller, who used his market dominance to secure cheap shipping rates. Finally in 1896 Carnegie gained control of another road—the Pittsburgh, Shenango & Lake Erie—to carry his freight at lower cost and steal traffic from the Pennsylvania. This move brought Roberts and Thomson to the bargaining table at last: they cut their rates, which saved Carnegie $1.5 million a year, and he agreed not to build any more railroads.

tion in the Cleveland administration, he declined (his friend Whitney was appointed Secretary of the Navy), but served as an unofficial adviser to the President. Stetson played a leading role in the development of modern corporate law over the next thirty-five years, and became known as Morgan's Attorney General.

Junius in the early 1860s had set out to build an international network of banks based, like Rothschilds' and Barings', on family ties. Things had not worked out that way. Pierpont found fault with most of his early associates, and in the seventies and eighties had begun to build a different kind of dynasty based on merit. Of all the men assigned to work with him, he retained only Tony Drexel and Walter Burns. At the end of 1885, when Fabbri retired to Italy, Coster took his place. In selecting Frank Stetson rather than Charles Tracy, Pierpont again rated professional ability over family connections. His closest friends in the eighties were Lanier and Bowdoin—good, not brilliant bankers—but the men whose judgment he relied on were Coster and Stetson.

———

The exigencies of railroad wars did not prevent Morgan from taking his annual trip to Europe each spring. In May of 1885—shortly before he sailed home with William H. Vanderbilt—Louisa reported to Fanny from Venice that "Papa enjoyed it all, except the churches. He would sit outside & smoke, holding converse (in very broken Italian) with gondoliers and beggars," while the rest of the party "explored the interior of some 'very fine' church with praiseworthy fidelity, assisted by our fiery red copy of Baedeker."

In 1886 Pierpont and Junius celebrated their April birthdays in Rome. Egisto Fabbri came down from Florence to see them. Alice Mason was probably there as well. Louisa told Fanny that Junius wanted to stay in Rome partly on his son's account, "as here there is no office for him to go to, & he does rest." Suffering with a toothache, her Papa was not doing much sightseeing, "and not even much shopping," although he found "one or two beautiful pieces of embroidery" and several Greek terra-cotta figures.

After an American dentist took care of the troublesome tooth, the Morgans spent their days touring the city, dined out every night, and called on the William Wetmore Storys. Louisa admired the expatriate sculptor's colossal statue of *America Victrix*, which was about to be cast in bronze and sent to San Francisco, but found the work of his son, Waldo, far more "delicate and . . . poetical, if not so strong and grand. People say that the Father has talent, the son, genius." Her father bought three of Waldo's sculptures for £600: two heads—of a gladiator and Honorius, the last emperor of Rome—and a seated figure called *Phryne* holding a silver Cupid. Louisa told Fanny: "I think it quite exquisite and am sure you will admire it—especially as she has plenty of clothes on!"

At 23 Wall Street, almost before the ink on the West Shore contracts was dry, Morgan took on another kind of fight. He had just induced bitter rivals to give up a "ruinous" struggle in mutual self-interest. Once a road was *in* financial ruins, however, he had more authority to impose his rationalizing will.

The Philadelphia & Reading Railroad, an anthracite coal line in eastern Pennsylvania, had gone into receivership in 1880. Two years later its president, Franklin B. Gowen, asked J. S. Morgan & Co. to reorganize the company. Tony Drexel wanted nothing to do with it, since Gowen's financial reports had been "systematically unreliable," and the Reading's bonds were "not the kind I would care to buy or recommend."* If Junius decided to rescue this road, Drexel advised, he should control the entire transaction himself.

In the end, Pierpont rescued the Reading. The road's managers applied to Drexel, Morgan for reorganization right after the *Corsair* agreement in 1885, and the junior Morgan had his London affiliates buy $1 million of Reading general mortgage bonds to assure control. Then he issued $20 million in new bonds, which he sold through a syndicate, and took charge of the company's finances in what would become a pattern for future Morganizations.

Led by Coster, a team of men examined every aspect of the railroad's operation from the servicing of debt, maintenance and running costs, and expenses and earnings on coal properties, to rents on leased feeder lines. Next, the bankers assessed stockholders for cash to fund the short-term debt and supply the company with new working capital. Over time they cut the road's fixed costs in half—from $14 million to less than $6.5 million—by reducing its bonded debt and increasing its capital stock. They also created a reserve fund for expansion, and based the new capitalization on estimated minimum earning capacity so that even in stringent times the road should be able to meet its obligations.

To safeguard these measures, Drexel, Morgan refused to give responsibility for the reorganized company back to the men who had run it into default. They appointed a three-man management committee and a five-year voting trust. The titular head of the management committee was J. Lowber Welsh, a Philadelphia banker long associated with the Reading; the operative head was Pierpont Morgan, who also chaired the voting trust. Made up of Morgan partners and Morgan-sanctioned railroad men (including Welsh), the voting trust issued certificates to shareholders in exchange for the company's common

---

* Gowen had been counsel to the Philadelphia & Reading in 1864, and its president since 1869. He had also organized the Philadelphia & Reading Coal & Iron Company, the country's largest producer of anthracite coal. It was he who led the coal operators' refusal to recognize a miners' union in 1875 and hired a Pinkerton agent to infiltrate the Molly Maguires.

stock, which was registered in the names of the five trustees. For the next half decade the trustees would control the company, actively monitoring the railroad's management, finances, and administrative reforms.

At the news of a Morgan "rescue," American and European investors bought the Reading's new bonds and bid the stock price up. Pierpont cabled Junius in January 1886 that if everything proceeded as he hoped, this reorganization would be "scarcely second to W. Shore." His management committee negotiated agreements between the Reading and the region's dominant carrier, the Pennsylvania, to maintain rates and divide up traffic. It also brought the Pennsylvania into an anthracite coal pool which proposed to limit production and maintain coal-price minimums—quite an achievement, Pierpont reported to Junius, since the trunk line had never agreed to take part in this kind of cartel before.

Morgan ran the Reading management committee for two years and headed the voting trust for five. His biggest problem proved to be exactly the one Tony Drexel had warned Junius about: the "unreliable" Franklin B. Gowen. In March 1886 Pierpont brought into the bond syndicate Austin Corbin, an old friend of Junius's whom Gowen seemed to trust.* "We ourselves appreciate importance Corbin's alliance also his influence with Gowen," he cabled Walter Burns, "at same time doubt his or anybody's ability to control FBG."

Six months later, nobody had been able to control FBG, and the bankers decided he had to go. Morgan spent all day negotiating with Gowen's agents on September 17, 1886, and by early evening he had the resignation he wanted.

His wife was away in England with Anne, and his elder daughters were giving a ball at Cragston that night for West Point cadets. Pierpont had told the girls he could not possibly get to Highland Falls in time for the party, but he managed to catch a train right after signing Gowen's termination papers. He reached the house minutes before the guests were due, and his son helped sneak him upstairs in order to surprise Louisa and Juliet. "I created quite a sensation when after having slipped up to my room unperceived and donned my dress coat . . . I walked into the room quite unexpectedly," he reported to Fanny. The ball went off with "great éclat—girls in powdered hair—officers in full uniform—they kept it up until midnight and all seemed to have a good time." Louisa added, "The best part of the evening was Papa's coming."

Jack told his mother, "Papa is simply triumphant about this Reading business," and a week later, "I have never seen him in such good spirits and so bright and well at this time of the year."

---

* Corbin had gone into banking after graduating from Harvard College and Law School, and eventually took over and revived the ailing Long Island Railroad. He tried to develop a transatlantic steamship port at the eastern end of Long Island, hoping to cut transit time between New York and Europe, and make the LIRR a crucial land-sea link—without success.

With Gowen out of the way, Morgan installed Corbin as president of the Reading, and two years later congratulated him on accomplishing the "end we both had so much at heart." They had resuscitated the bankrupt company, let the world know it had new, capable management—under the reassuring supervision of the Morgan bank—sold its securities in foreign and domestic markets, and turned a healthy profit. Drexel, Morgan & Co. earned $1 million on the sale of new bonds (5 percent of the $20 million total), 6 percent on additional advances, and a $100,000 commission for the management committee. The London firm saw additional gains on the $1 million of general mortgage bonds it had bought to ensure control.

Pierpont considered restoring the confidence of foreign investors the most important part of the business. He concluded to Corbin: "you have brought to the support of your Company a European alliance which I am sure you will find, at all times in the future, prepared to sustain you in the wise development of the property entrusted to your care." Once again he had moved the right man into a difficult job. Gowen committed suicide in a Washington hotel room at the end of 1889, "for no apparent reason," according to the *Dictionary of American Biography.*

———

Tight supervisory control was proving far more effective at promoting the "wise development" of railroad properties than any other means the Morgans had tried. In the crisis stage of the Reading reorganization, Pierpont did not hesitate to take charge of the company's management committee and have it report to him as voting trustee; he also secured careful regulation for the future by appointing people he trusted to positions of authority. Once the emergency passed, however, he tried to avoid obvious conflicts of interest. Late in 1887 he vetoed a suggestion that Reading trustee J. Lowber Welsh be elected to the road's board of directors. Serving in that double capacity would be a clear breach of duty, he told Welsh: "I cannot agree that (consistently with a proper interpretation of the Trust) the Voting Trustees can or should vote themselves in as Directors. How can they fairly judge of the wisdom or policy of the management if they are in advance committed to its action by the presence of its members or some of them in the Board of Directors?" In any case, with Corbin in charge of the road, he did not need Welsh on the board.

Wall Street praised the Reading reorganization as the salvation of the nation's railroads and economic future, but the most significant praise came from London. At the end of December 1887 Junius wrote to "heartily congratulate" his son on the success of the Reading rescue—"a success of which you may well be proud, and of which *I* am proud for you."

He could not leave it at that. This inexhaustible well of advice urged his fifty-year-old son to "rest upon your oars" and refuse all reorganizations not "of a character as important as those you have hitherto had." Then, mixing metaphors, "I would *hold off* & let the 'small fry' go to some other Doctor." Speaking of doctors, Junius went on: "But beyond & above all this is the question of *your health.*" In the past it had been Pierpont who worried about taxing his system with too much work and bringing on nervous collapse. Now it was Junius: "No body, however strong & well he may be can stand such a strain upon his physical & mental powers as you have had the last two years without paying, sooner or later, the penalty unless he gives those powers a *real rest* & gives it to them *in season – do* I beseech of you give heed to this advice."

Pierpont ignored it. He *was* worn-out by his exacting work, and complained of headaches, fevers, and heavy colds. (Leaving for Europe one spring, he slept ten hours a night crossing the Atlantic and took morning and afternoon naps.) Still, he did not break down. No longer an apprentice, he was exactly where he had always wanted to be—at the center of a drama he found as compelling as anything in his life. Moving out from under his father's heavy thumb and serving as financial "doctor" to the largest business enterprise in the world brought about a marked improvement in his health.

Again, not everyone admired his work. Editorials in the New York *Sun* denounced the coal road consolidation as arrant price-fixing, and mocked Morgan's assurance that it would promote "peace and fraternity." The *Times* praised the Reading rescue but worried about monopoly power over traffic rates and coal prices, and wondered whether the arteries of public transport ought to be controlled by private bankers—questions that would shadow Pierpont Morgan for the rest of his life.

———

Morgan's relations with New York's major newspapers in the 1880s were for the most part cordial. He moved in the same social circles as Whitelaw Reid, the publisher of the *Tribune,* and Charles A. Dana, the owner-editor of the *Sun.* He assumed these men would respect his expertise, and when the *Sun* assailed the Reading reorganization in February 1886, he sent a note to "My dear Mr. Dana," explaining: "I am not in the habit of questioning anything that may appear in the newspapers, for I generally find them as a whole fair on any question of financial importance." The recent articles, however, had been "so unfair that I cannot but feel they found their way into the paper without your knowledge." Offering to discuss the matter in person, he asked the editor to excuse his frankness, but thought it "better not to have a transaction of such importance presented unfairly to the public in its inception."

Criticism from newspapers apparently did not lead him to the conclusion drawn by A. J. Liebling decades later—that the only guarantee of a free press is owning a press—for he did not leap at a chance to buy New York's *Evening Post* and *The Nation* when they were offered to him in 1886. Founded by Alexander

Hamilton and edited for years by William Cullen Bryant, the *Post* had been owned by Henry Villard since 1881. Villard bought *The Nation* that year as well, in order to hire its renowned editor, Edwin Lawrence Godkin, and began publishing it as a weekly supplement to the *Post*.

The Anglo-Irish Godkin was a reformist Republican who campaigned in print against silver currency, boss politics, and municipal corruption. His crusades led one reader to reflect on New York's infamous morals with a shrug: "What can you expect of a city in which every morning the *Sun* makes vice attractive, and every night the *Post* makes virtue odious?" For all the *Post*'s virtuous stands, there were no clearer lines of ethical demarcation between journalism and politics in the 1880s than between business and politics. Godkin helped lead the Mugwump support of Grover Cleveland, and after the election he lobbied the administration about appointments and policies, suggesting not very subtly that the *Post* would give full coverage to whatever trouble might result if the President did not take his advice.

Godkin tried to gain financial control of the *Post* after Villard's nervous breakdown, and asked several of his wealthy friends, including Morgan, for help. He made his case to Morgan in the spring of 1886. The banker replied that July: "I am not quite prepared to say that there is no use in again discussing the subject we talked about before I sailed for Europe. It depends in a great measure upon the magnitude of the transaction."

In September, Godkin told a friend that "Pierpont Morgan seems at present disposed to behave handsomely, *but this is strictly confidential.* The greatest difficulty with him is the fear of having it known. He thinks it might bother him in financial circles."

Owning a leading New York newspaper would no doubt have "bothered" Morgan in political and journalistic circles as well—as it was, critics accused Godkin of editing a "railroad organ" for Villard—but nothing came of these discussions. When Villard returned from Germany in September of 1886, he was furious to learn of his editor's discussions with Morgan. Still arguing over the incident several years later, Godkin protested to Villard that "no money would have induced me to 'serve under' Pierpont Morgan or anyone else. The proposed plan of purchase involved no such risk."

Although their joint newspaper venture did not materialize, Morgan continued to support Godkin with personal loans. After the editor's death in 1902, he helped endow a fund at Harvard for an annual E. L. Godkin Lecture on "The Essentials of Free Government and the Duties of the Citizen."

Putting all his professional energies into stabilizing railroad finance and maintaining the flow of investment capital from Europe, Morgan did not pay much attention to public hostility toward the railroads or to the growing discontent of the American worker. He had his eye on the country's long-term economic future. To the extent that he took the class conflicts and social problems of the present into account, he delegated them to Dr. Rainsford.

He left no record of his response to the labor militance of the 1870s—the troubles at the anthracite coal mines that led to the execution of Molly Maguires, or the great railroad strikes of 1877. In the wake of these episodes, the Knights of Labor, a national federation of unions led by Terence V. Powderly, resolved to renounce violence and negotiate for higher wages, shorter hours, and better working conditions through collective bargaining, but when peaceful tactics failed during the 1884–85 depression, the Knights resorted to strikes: successful actions against the Union Pacific and Missouri Pacific railroads brought them national respect and new members. Then on May 1, 1886, radical anarchists in Chicago called for a general strike. Chicago police attacked the strikers at the McCormick farm-equipment plant on May 3, and four people were killed. The next day someone threw a bomb into the crowd at a protest demonstration in Haymarket Square, and the police opened fire; by the time the battle was over, fifty people had been wounded and ten killed, including six policemen.

The Haymarket affair sharply divided the country. A jury convicted eight (mostly foreign-born) anarchists of conspiracy to commit murder, and sentenced seven of them to death. People sympathetic to the strike thought the verdicts draconian, but many Americans feared violence and socialism more than the police. Membership in the Knights fell from 700,000 in 1886 to less than 100,000 by 1890. The American Federation of Labor, a loose association of trade unions organized in 1886, took its place. Led by Samuel Gompers, the AFL repudiated radical tactics, aiming to improve wages and working conditions through "pure and simple unionism." Starting with 140,000 members, it grew to a million by 1900.

———

While Morgan worked on peace treaties and bankruptcy reorganizations in the 1880s, the railroad industry was imposing other kinds of order on itself—practical measures that increased efficiency and brought costs down. The problem of calculating the time across three thousand miles added to the complications of transcontinental shipping: Illinois had twenty-seven incremental measures of time, and Wisconsin thirty-eight, until the American Railway Association in 1883 divided the country into four temporal zones, shifting from "God's time" to "Vanderbilt's time." Three years later the roads settled on a national standard track gauge of 4 feet 8½ inches, which meant that they no longer had to transfer freight to new cars at each new stretch of track. Furthermore, steel rails were replacing iron, and better signals, brakes, and couplers were improving safety.

Steadily decreasing transport costs combined with intense competition for traffic and an overall decline in prices to bring passenger rates down 50 percent between 1850 and 1900. Freight charges fell even further: railroad freight revenue went from 1.88¢ per ton mile in 1870 to .73¢ by 1900. These declining revenues *heightened* the competition Morgan was trying to control, and the railroad managers' ad hoc attempts to deal with the problem—especially price-fixing pools, secret rebates, and high rates on short routes where they had monopoly control—met with escalating opposition from the farmers and other shippers who wanted *more* competition among carriers rather than less.

Huge-volume producers such as Rockefeller and Carnegie could dictate special accommodations or buy railroads of their own. Shippers who did not have that kind of market power tried to get Grange associations and state legislatures to protect them.

Across the country throughout the eighties, from very different perspectives, the consumers and the managers of railroad services were deciding that the chaotic national transportation system needed some kind of external control. In February 1887 large majorities in both houses of Congress passed an Interstate Commerce Act, which President Cleveland signed into law. It forbade railroads to discriminate among shippers, required them to publish schedules of fares, outlawed rebates, and prohibited price-fixing and traffic-allocating pools; it also established a five-member commission to determine "just and reasonable" rates.

Some railroad managers, including Chauncey Depew at the New York Central and Charles Francis Adams, Jr., now president of the Union Pacific, hoped the new law would succeed at preventing rate wars where the roads themselves had failed. Staunch conservatives regarded it with contempt. The ardently pro-business Senator Nelson W. Aldrich of Rhode Island called the act "a delusion and a sham . . . an empty menace to the great interests, made to answer the clamor of the ignorant and the unreasoning."

Junius Morgan denounced the law from London as "a disturbing cause . . . imposed by the National Will, a case of force majeure." Force majeure refers to unexpected or uncontrollable events such as hurricanes and earthquakes ("acts of God")—which apparently to Junius included acts of Congress. Pierpont did not think the government could solve the railroads' problems—he believed more in banker control than political intervention—but once the law passed, he set out to work with it. He had marginally more faith in Washington than in state legislatures that were openly hostile to the railroads and the trusts.

———

The Republicans regained the White House in 1888, in an election dominated by questions of finance. The U.S. Treasury in the late eighties had a rare *surplus* of funds. Tariffs imposed to protect American industries during the Civil War were bringing in more money than the government spent—$63.5 million more in 1885—and the parties disagreed about what to do with it. Late-nineteenth-century neo-Federalist Republicans, sounding like late-twentieth-century Democrats, favored active government spending to promote economic expansion and pay for expensive public projects. The Democrats in 1888, like free-market Republicans a hundred years later, wanted to *reduce* the government's role in the nation's life, although they divided sharply over protectionism. Cleveland sided with moderate Republicans on many economic questions, but was unequivocally for free trade: he regarded import duties as an unfair tax that would hurt American exports, and he wanted the nation's wealth distributed through unregulated commerce, not drawn out of the markets and dispensed by the Treasury.

Under pressure from powerful industrial lobbies, Congress had defeated several tariff-reform bills in the seventies and eighties, and Democratic leaders warned Cleveland that pressing the issue would split the party and lose him the 1888 election. He pressed it anyway, attacking existing trade barriers and denouncing the notion that America's "infant industries" still needed protection. Andrew Carnegie in the seventies had proudly described his production costs to Junius as so low that "even if the tariff were off entirely, you couldn't send steel rails west of us."

Cleveland's Republican opponents in 1888 were Indiana Senator Benjamin Harrison, the grandson of "Old Tippecanoe," and Levi P. Morton, the Morgans' banking colleague. Morton had repeatedly failed to win a Senate seat, largely because of his association with what Pulitzer's *World* called the "money kings" and the "Republican Corruption Fund." He secured the vice presidential nomination in 1888 with the help of New York's Republican boss, Thomas Collier Platt, called the Easy Boss because of his dandified clothes and urbane style.

The Republicans in 1888 ran a stronger and much better-funded campaign than their opponents. Led by the adroit Pennsylvania boss, Matthew Quay, they raised over $3 million—far more than had ever been spent in a U.S. election—mainly from industrial beneficiaries of the tariff. Quay's minions used some of the money to buy votes and rig elections in Indiana and New York, and distributed leaflets attacking Democrats all over the country. Cleveland refused to campaign, claiming that it was beneath the dignity of his office. Harrison invited thousands of people to Indianapolis to hear his "front porch" speeches about the dangerous Democrats and the lower wages and unemployment that would result from reducing the tariff.

Voters did not express a clear preference in this single-issue election. Cleveland won the popular ballot by 60,000 votes, but lost in the electoral college, 168 to 233. Accepting Boss Quay's congratulations shortly after the results came in, Harrison said with no trace of irony: "Providence has given us the victory." A dumbfounded Quay later exclaimed to a reporter, "Think of the man!

He ought to know that Providence hadn't a damn thing to do with it": Harrison had no idea how many Republicans had been "compelled to approach the gates of the penitentiary to make him President."

He quickly learned how many Republicans he had to reward. Having promised not to hand out patronage, he found almost every position in his cabinet pre-sold. He was forced to appoint the unsavory James G. Blaine Secretary of State, and to make one of Quay's chief contributors, Philadelphia merchant John Wanamaker, Postmaster General.

Vice President–elect Morton was more familiar with the game. To repay Mr. Platt for delivering the Empire State, Morton proposed to make him Secretary of the Navy: "The feeling is I think universal that New York saved the day at [the Republican Convention in] Chicago and in November," he urged Harrison, "and that she is entitled to proper recognition." Harrison declined to award Platt the Navy, and warned Morton in future not to "make the mistake of furnishing *a* name for *a* place."

Harrison's administrative team came to be known as the Businessman's Cabinet. The new Senate included so many wealthy representatives of industry and banking that it was called the Millionaire's Club. Republicans had won the presidency and congressional majorities in both houses for the first time since 1875. They proceeded to give away the tariff-generated Treasury surplus in the form of premiums to government bondholders, subsidies to steamship lines, extravagant pork-barrel bills, repayment of taxes paid by the North during the Civil War, and lavish pensions to anyone who claimed to have served the Union cause. In 1890 they raised import duties on a range of products by nearly 50 percent with the McKinley Tariff Act.

Morgan probably voted a straight Republican ticket in 1888—he contributed $1,000 to a Harrison/Morton inaugural fund—but he had no personal or ideological quarrel with the Democratic incumbent. When Cleveland left the White House early in 1889, he joined his friend and adviser Francis Lynde Stetson at Bangs, Stetson, Tracy, & MacVeagh—the "Morgan law firm"—in New York.

———

The vaguely worded Interstate Commerce Act, passed in 1887, was a political compromise that proved difficult to interpret, even more difficult to enforce, and failed to address a number of critical questions. Were the roads in fact suffering from too much competition, as their managers and bankers saw it, or not enough, which was what farmers and shippers thought? Could a government agency fairly arbitrate between opposing economic interests, or would it favor one side over the other? What were "just and reasonable" rates—just to carriers or to shippers? If there was a conflict between maximizing railroad efficiency and promoting competition, where did the public interest lie, and who would decide? How should the country weigh political concerns for fairness against economic incentives to rationalize its leading industry? How could this law be enforced?

The act had little impact on competition west of the Mississippi, and at the end of 1888, after a new round of rate wars, the railroad bankers Drexel, Morgan, Brown Brothers, and Kidder, Peabody summoned a dozen officers of major lines to meet at Morgan's Madison Avenue house. Those attending included Union Pacific president Charles Francis Adams, Jay Gould (who had been ousted from the Union Pacific board in 1885, and now controlled the Missouri Pacific), Chauncey Depew of the New York Central, and George Roberts of the Pennsylvania.

After seating these men around a table in his dining room, Morgan announced that the purpose of the meeting was to stop railroad managers from taking the law into their own hands whenever they felt wronged. "This is not elsewhere customary in civilised communities," he said, like a stern teacher scolding a pack of unruly boys, "and no good reason exists why such a practice should continue among railroads." The Pennsylvania's George Roberts argued that there would be no trouble at all if the bankers would stop putting up money to build competing roads—to which Morgan replied that if the railroad men would stop the rate wars, the financiers would do everything they could to prevent construction of parallel lines.

Charles Francis Adams, who had been contending with these problems for years—first as a political journalist, then on a Massachusetts regulatory commission, now as president of a major trunk line—wrote a private account of the meeting shortly after it took place. Most of the discussion the first day centered on a new rate-setting pool: the same old story, lamented Adams in his journal, with no executive power, no remedial measures, no more ability to bind the participants than a "rope of sand." The next day, Adams proposed that only an "outside compulsory force" could bring warring railroads into line, and the force he had in mind was the Interstate Commerce Commission. Any plan the railroads came up with on their own would surely "excite an insuperable popular objection," whereas exactly the same plan advanced by the ICC might meet with general favor. Adams had expected the bankers to agree. To his surprise, the railroad men assented as well. Roberts said the ICA, properly enforced, could "remove a great many of the difficulties that are now surrounding the management of the railways." Depew hoped the commission might "secure some machinery by which peace can be maintained."

In early January, Adams met with three of the five commissioners, and drew up a plan for an organization of railroad presidents: the twenty-two roads in the new "Interstate Commerce Railway Association" promised to maintain stable rates, allocate traffic, and refer all violations to the ICC. In effect, this new trade association would try to use the "machinery" of the law against cartels to enforce the terms of a new cartel. One of the commissioners with whom Adams had conferred, Aldace Walker, resigned from the ICC to head the ICRA.

Several voices outside the industry praised the agreement. The New York *Sun,* which had lambasted Morgan's Reading consolidation, called the new plan a "revolution in railroad methods," and looked forward to the substitution of "straightforward business principles for chicanery and corruption." John Moody thought every stockholder in America and Europe ought to give his proxies to the group that had met at 219, since only by concentration in a "few strong hands" could investment capital be protected against the "gigantic waste and fraud and duplication" endemic to the American railroad system.

Nonetheless, within weeks another rate war in the West made it clear that the new association did not amount—according to an officer of the first defecting road—"to a hill of beans." It had no real power to enforce rules, arbitrate disputes, or even hold on to its members. Jay Gould unofficially certified its demise early in February 1890, when he asked a colleague, "Is it worth while for us to be represented at the meeting of the President's Association in Chicago, or shall we simply send flowers for the corpse?"

Charles Francis Adams believed, like Moody, that the railroad world would be better off with fewer players—with competitors consolidated into big, stable systems under strong supervisory control. Ending the current anarchy would require "a railroad Bismarck," Adams wrote, but so far no one, himself included, had been able to impose order on this battlefield. Morgan had brought the latest adversaries to the bargaining table, as he had the Pennsylvania and the New York Central in the West Shore fight, but he could not force them to cooperate. In the privacy of his journal, Adams asked: "Will Pierrepont Morgan develope [*sic*] the needed force?" He answered, "Possibly. He has many of the elements of power needed. It remains to be seen if he is an organizer."

Junius Spencer Morgan in London, 1890.
(Archives of The Pierpont Morgan Library, New York)

Chapter 14

—

FATHERS AND SONS

The transfer of power that had gradually taken place over three decades—from the London to the New York Morgan banks, and from the senior to the junior Morgan—was nearly complete. Junius told Drexel, Morgan at the beginning of 1887 that J. S. Morgan & Co. would accept participation in a railroad syndicate without knowing the price of the bonds or the probable duration of the business: "We are quite satisfied that you have arranged all these points to your own satisfaction, & we are quite ready to join with you in anything that you think good enough for yourselves."

For thirty years he had been channeling investment capital westward across the Atlantic and watching over his country's credit in international markets. By the late eighties, though still a net debtor, the United States was the leading industrial power in the world. Junius took magnanimous pride in this state of affairs, announcing to his New York partners at the beginning of 1887 that America had the best market for its own "high-priced securities," which meant that his services were no longer as necessary as they had been: "The Americans are so rich now that they can afford & wish to pay more for their own securities than any foreigner would feel able to do," he reflected, "and this is a healthy state of things for the country, however little profitable it may be for our pockets."*

---

* To put this change in broader perspective, Americans in the eighties directed a large share of the country's gross national product into capital formation—the creation of wealth in the form of goods such as buildings, machinery, and equipment that produce other goods

Junius was no longer spending much time at 22 Old Broad Street. In the spring and summer he stayed at Dover House, where he supervised the gardening and haying, and entertained legions of guests—among them Alice Mason, Henry James, John Singer Sargent, the William Wetmore Storys, the Chauncey Depews, and Levi Morton's partner, Sir John Rose. In the winters he rented a furnished villa at Monte Carlo for $5,000 a year—a house and stables set on the side of a steep hill, with olive groves, terraced gardens, and views of the Mediterranean. Monaco had "the best winter climate that I have found anywhere," he told a friend, "and one that just suits *old age.*"

He stayed at the Villa Henrietta from November until May, attended by his London butler, Thomas Hand. Alice Mason had accommodations of her own in town. Every morning he waited for the mail to arrive at 11:00, then walked down the hill to see Alice. He lunched at 1:00, took a drive at 2:30, had tea at 5:00, dinner at 7:30, and played cards with guests until bedtime.

In April 1889 Pierpont took Louisa to Monte Carlo to celebrate Junius's seventy-sixth birthday and his own fifty-second. He drove his daughter into Nice one day to go sightseeing and shopping with friends. After lunch he went off by himself to the Villa St. Georges, where Memie had died twenty-seven years before. In her diary Louisa wrote: "I wish I could have gone with him. Still I suppose he would rather have been alone."

———

Only once during his thirty-five years abroad did Junius betray a sense of insecurity about his status in class-conscious England. When Louisa was invited to the opera one spring in the eighties by British friends who had the Queen's box, her grandfather refused to let her go: "According to him," she told her mother, "you must treat English people with reserve to give them a high idea of your importance." She privately disagreed: "I think you should accept a kindness as it is meant—but perhaps he is right."

Like the aristocratic owners of Britain's great country houses, Junius had been surrounding himself with beautiful things, including portraits of other people's ancestors. After losing the *Duchess of Devonshire* to a thief, he had acquired another Gainsborough, *Miss Wilbraham,* as well as two paintings of Emma Hamilton by George Romney and three portraits by Joshua Reynolds: *Mrs. Yates, Lady Dawson,* and *The Honorable Henry Fane with His Guardians.* Also on his walls at Dover House and Princes Gate were pictures attributed to Turner (*Landscape with Walton Bridges* and a watercolor, *Lake of Albano*),

---

and services, sustaining a high rate of economic growth. Before the Civil War, about 15 percent of GNP went into capital formation; in the 1870s the figure rose to 25 percent, and in the eighties to 28 percent.

Greuze (*A Lady's Head*), Millais, Gérôme, and the popular English artists John Opie, Sir Edwin Landseer, William Powell Frith, and George Elgar Hicks.

Next to the elegant figures in Junius's eighteenth-century portrait gallery, the pictures of his Morgan ancestors looked distinctly plain. When he decided in 1887 to have his own features committed to canvas, he chose Frank Holl, an English artist whose recent subjects included the wealthy Liberal politician Joseph Chamberlain and the Prince of Wales. Holl had specialized in genre scenes before he turned to portraiture; critics complained that he painted "nothing that was not inspired by the coffin or the gallows," and that his shapeless, colorless Academy pictures "gave everyone the creeps." His portrait of Junius gave Jack Morgan the creeps when he saw it at the Royal Academy in the summer of 1887: Jack thought it looked "lopsided," and did not "make Grandpa out as handsome as he really is."

Junius liked the picture well enough to commission another, of his son, in 1888. This painting (which turned out to be Holl's last—he died a few weeks after completing it) portrays Pierpont in black against a black background, with highlights on his head and hands. His receding hair is gray, his eyebrows and mustache still dark. His waistcoat pulls across his ample girth, and though he hooks his right arm casually over the back of his chair, he looks anything but relaxed, regarding the artist/viewer with a challenging stare.

Holl minimized what had begun, in Morgan's early fifties, to be his most recognizable physical attribute, the disfiguring growth of his nose. The painter's brushstrokes blur this feature slightly into shadow—a visual euphemism that makes it hard to tell shade from flesh. Pierpont liked the painting, and ordered photographs of it, by the "late lamented artist," to give to friends.

He had always paid fastidious attention to the details of his appearance. He favored milled soaps, colognes, silver-backed hairbrushes, and all the masculine accoutrements of collars, ascots, tiepins, watch fobs, cuff links, gloves. In ordering a captain's cap for the New York Yacht Club, he was concerned with proportion: since the size (7⅞ inches) was so large, he thought "the top should be rather full." But no amount of grooming had been able to conceal the eruptions and flushing that marked his face in adolescence, or the disease—rhinophyma—that by 1888 was deforming his nose.* His social and professional self-confidence were too well established to be undermined by this affliction, but as he became an increasingly public figure, his brusque manner and always searching gaze took on dimensions of defiance, as if he dared people to

---

* Surgeons could shave away the rhinophymous growth of sebaceous tissue during Morgan's lifetime (it is now correctable by laser surgery). Satterlee suspected that his father-in-law did not seek surgery because he feared something worse, such as a return of his infantile seizures; others said Morgan wanted to avoid public ridicule (see Chapter 26).

meet him squarely and not shrink from the sight, asserting the force of his character over the ugliness of his face.

———

Jack, miserable in his first year at Harvard, complained to his mother, "I wish the four years were over so I could get away from here." He had to force himself to return to college that fall: "It makes me sick to go away from home," he wrote. "I feel more and more how entirely I hate Cambridge and everything connected with it."

Harvard had a social hierarchy very much like that of Gilded Age New York, its upper echelons occupied by boys with large means, prep-school backgrounds, entrée to Boston society, and memberships in exclusive social clubs. Jack cheered up once he was elected to the elite sophomore "waiting" club, Delta Kappa Epsilon, and then to the Delphic, one of the "final" clubs that designated social success at Harvard. Not as prestigious as the Porcellian, the Delphic took in "stray young gentlemen not duly appreciated by their contemporaries, but interesting in themselves, some rich, others clever, still others simply agreeable," recalled one of the "clever" ones, George Santayana (Class of '86).

Where Pierpont as a young man had been drawn to lectures by famous men and classes with the leading scholars at Göttingen, Jack spent four years at Harvard without mentioning, in his copious letters home, professors William James, Charles Eliot Norton, James Russell Lowell, Josiah Royce, George Herbert Palmer, Barrett Wendell, Phillips Brooks, or Francis Peabody. He was invited to lunch with the president of the college, Charles W. Eliot, in the winter of his freshman year. Eliot was transforming Harvard from a finishing school for the blue-blooded elite into a top-flight academic university, with intellectual distinction on its faculty and a new diversity among students. Walter Lippmann several years later described Eliot striding across the campus as "a little bit like God walking around." Jack, dreading his lunch with the great man, told his mother he would "rather die than go. (Burn this letter)."

He did go and did not die, but found the academy in Cambridge, like that at St. Paul's, contemptuous of the life he was destined to lead. Eliot believed that a great university should stand for "intellectual and spiritual forces against materialism and luxury," and much of the Harvard faculty regarded commerce with scorn. When one of Jack's teachers said he was "disgusted" at the idea that the boy would go into banking after college, Jack wrote plaintively to Fanny: "I don't know why so many people chiefly those who are engaged in tuition or some literary pursuit, seem to look upon business as if it were the general sewer in which all ambition and intelligence disappear or worse get turned to 'money getting' arrangements. I must confess I don't see any harm, myself, in making a little money, provided it can be done honestly and reasonably."

There was no question of Jack's going into anything other than banking, although he might have preferred something else. Studying a strain of seaweed in the laboratory of the Harvard botanist William G. Farlow, he managed to prove a theory for the professor, and earned an A in natural history. A sense that other endeavors had more value than "money getting" was not unique to Harvard, and support for Jack's interest in science came from an unlikely quarter. Egisto Fabbri, writing from Florence, hoped the boy would "nurse and develop" his scientific inclination: "A man situated as he is and will be, can do untold good," Fabbri told Fanny, "by encouraging & following scientific pursuits, to exercise through his means and his example a most wholesome and beneficent influence and finally make for himself a far more lasting fame and page in history than the most successful business career can possibly vouchsafe."

Men of science do win more lasting public acclaim than men of business, but that argument carried no weight with Pierpont Morgan. He had no misgivings about his own career, and would maintain the patriarchal line of succession despite his lack of interest in his son.

One Saturday he sent Jack a telegram saying he would be in Boston for a few hours that night and wanted to see him: he would arrive at 6:40 and leave at midnight. Jack worked hard all day in order to be free in the evening. When the train from New York was delayed, he waited under a railroad bridge for an hour in the rain (he told his traveling mother with uncharacteristic sarcasm), "and had the delightful opportunity of driving from the Station to the Club with [Papa] in the same carriage with Mr. Bowdoin and Mr. Depew." His papa compounded the slight by neglecting to bring any of Fanny's cables, and disclosing nothing about his summer plans. Jack was more hurt than angry. To Fanny he characterized the visit as "somewhat unsatisfactory. There are certainly some drawbacks to belonging to a busy man no matter how fine he may be as I believe you have sometimes found out."

Wherever the difficulty between father and son had started, it compounded itself at every turn. Disturbed early on by Jack's too-intimate alliance with Fanny, Pierpont had withdrawn, and the boy's terror of his remote "Papa," along with his self-doubts and hunger for approval, kept widening the distance between them. Pierpont's own strongest ties had always been to the father who held him to lofty standards, sent him away to school, subjected him to decades of critical scrutiny, and taught him by relentless lecture and example what it meant to be the "right" kind of man. The negative content of Junius's preaching had been offset by the intensity of attention he directed at his son—but attention was precisely what Pierpont withheld from *his* son. He seemed not so much critical as indifferent.

At Harvard, as at St. Paul's, Jack cringed at the prospect of asking for paternal dispensations, though again, most of his requests were granted. Looking

forward one February to his summer expedition in the Rockies with Dr. Rainsford, he bowed his head in anticipatory submission—"If Papa thinks it is too
much luxury for me to spend so much every summer just on my own pleasure,
I shall have to accept his idea of course." He went to the Rockies. At the end of
the summer he asked for a horse and permission to smoke, and was astounded
by affirmative answers on both counts: "I cannot exactly understand [Papa's]
kindness about the horse," he told Fanny, but guessed it was a reward for having done well at school.

The experience of another Harvard undergraduate ten years earlier offers a
striking contrast. The junior Theodore Roosevelt wrote to the senior from Cambridge in 1876: "I do not think there is a fellow in college who has a family that
love him as much as you all do me, and I am *sure* that there is no one who has
a Father who is also his best and most intimate friend, as you are mine."

Still, Jack found compensations in being Pierpont Morgan's son. In the summer of 1887 he visited his grandfather in England with his cousin Junius, the
son of Sarah and George. Crossing on the White Star's *Germanic,* he told Fanny
that the name he shared with his father "causes all the stewards to be most attentive and obliging." He guessed this solicitude indicated "a desire for fees,"
but was "not disagreeable." Not disagreeable, either, was being treated by the
Dover House servants as his grandfather's "heir presumptive," while his
cousin, "being only a daughter's son is comparatively left out."

Insecure, snobbish, and shy, Jack displayed none of his father's early avidity
for the opposite sex. At twenty he reported to Fanny that he had kept clear of
the one young woman on board the *Germanic* who could be called a "belle," because "she struck me as being *common.* I can fancy Louisa turning up her
nose . . . and saying I am stuck up but I do like girls to seem ladylike."

In the fall of his senior year, Jack found a young woman who did measure up
to his standards. She was Jane Norton Grew, called Jessie, the seventeen-year-
old sister of his St. Paul's and Harvard classmate Edward Grew. He called often
at her family's house on Beacon Street in the winter of 1888–89, and told his
mother that Miss Grew seemed responsive to his attentions.

Terrified of what his father would think, however, the status-conscious
young lover added: "Tell Papa the Grews are very nice people. If he wants genealogy it is as follows. Mr. Grew belongs through his mother to the great Sturgis tribe here in Boston. . . . Mrs. G. was a Miss Wigglesworth, a great name in
Cambridge and Boston both. So you see they have an inherited right to be nice
if they want to." He had been attracted by the "tone of their family line" on his
visits to Ned, he assured Fanny, well "before any other feeling came in."

His "other feeling" was soon so strong that he wanted to marry Jessie, and
early in March, with Fanny abroad, he went to New York to discuss the situation with his father. Pierpont was in Washington when Jack arrived, and did
not get home until three in the morning. Over breakfast a few hours later, the

young man took a deep breath and "managed to blurt out the trouble I am in."
He told Fanny that his "Papa" seemed "naturally very much surprised, I fear
not agreeably so"—but "did not laugh at me" or seem "angry at my having let
myself go." After "getting at a few facts" over breakfast, the elder Morgan
promised to discuss the situation further that night.

Jack waited all day "in fear and trembling for the half hour before dinner," he
continued to his mother. "I shall try to obey him in what he advises if possible."
The more he saw of Jessie, the surer he was of his "wise choice," and though he
hesitated to say so in writing (he said in writing), he was "becoming more
hopeful of final success."

Pierpont was about to leave on his annual spring trip to Europe. In the half
hour before dinner that night he promised Jack he would go to Boston after he
returned, to "see what is to be done." Not quite believing that the fateful moment had passed so easily, Jack proffered Jessie's pedigree to strengthen his
case. The senior Morgan, less given than the junior to bloodline worship, said,
"I am quite willing to take her fitness and fineness for granted," and concluded
simply, "I'll help you."

Jack was delirious. "Nothing could have been sweeter or more tender than
his management and treatment of the whole matter," he told his mother: "my
head and heart are both so full of it that I can think and write of nothing else."
He was hoping to go to Europe with Ned Grew after graduation to study French
and German, and found the encouraging "attitude of Grew *père* on the subject . . . most pleasant . . . [and] flattering. I am afraid I care more for approval
than is right."

Accustomed as he was to sharing all his troubles and pleasures with his
mother, Jack assumed she would be thrilled by his romantic prospects. He was
wrong. On receiving these letters, Fanny confessed to Louisa her "sickening
disappointment" when she realized that "the son who has been so much to me,
has passed out of my home life forever!" She could not imagine that Jessie
would refuse him. Generalizing her dismay, Fanny said she disliked "these
young attachments," yet felt that Jack was "not like other men in these matters—and I think this is a deeply serious matter with him."

Jack graduated from Harvard in June of 1889 with an honorable mention in
natural history, then did go abroad with Ned Grew. When he returned late that
fall, he went to work as an apprentice to Junius's former partner Jacob Rogers.
He and Jessie announced their engagement in the winter of 1890, and were
married in Boston's Arlington Street Church at the end of the year.

———

The younger Morgan girls, Juliet and Anne, were more rebellious than Louisa
or Jack and more independent of their parents. Louisa described Anne to their
father as "irresistibly funny, in spite of her naughtiness." Jack found Anne baf-

fling: he told Louisa that she seemed "hard to get at and yet has ideas and thoughts hidden away somewhere, which come out at unexpected moments, in the most extraordinary way." He thought time might improve her, and hoped it would hurry up.

With Pierpont monopolizing Louisa at home and abroad, Juliet filled in with Fanny—warming her mother's slippers at night, listening to her confidences, sympathizing with her "blues." She took a more sardonic view of the job than her predecessor did, reporting from London one night that Fanny had gotten herself "sort of worked up and excited and generally in a stew"—"she's been lying awake 'thinking things over' and you know what the result of that is!" Juliet escaped into her own social world as soon as she could, and as she slipped away, Fanny turned to Anne, "who has never had the same chance with me that the rest of you have had" (she told Louisa)—"so I want her, before she grows altogether away from me, to be with me, dependent on me as I on her, and it will be good for us both."

The Morgan girls were not beauties. Louisa had a tranquil sweetness in her face and Anne carried herself well, but they both inherited Pierpont's square jaw and their parents' tendency toward amplitude. Juliet was the prettiest of the three, with a slim waist and large, dark eyes. She joked about her diminutive physique, which was not the Victorian ideal: being a "ready-made size" had its consolations, she told Louisa—"I really am very inexpensive, you've no idea what a difference it makes. . . . I don't have to do half the trying on I shld otherwise."

Louisa, as the eldest, should have been the first to marry. She was twenty-four when Jack announced his engagement to Jessie. Her mother took her to balls and dinners expressly for the purpose of meeting eligible men, which resulted in a couple of eminently resistible proposals. Gossip linked her name to bachelors in America and Europe, and English newspapers referred to her as "Miss Pierpont Morgan," emphasizing her potential net worth.

Mr. Pierpont Morgan showed little interest in promoting her marital prospects. For all his fondness and material indulgence, he did not seem to imagine that his special girl might want a life of her own. He appreciated her value to him—as traveling companion, confidante, surrogate wife—and probably convinced himself, if he thought about it at all, that she derived as much benefit from the arrangement as he did. Making the social rounds with him in London one spring, Louisa plaintively told Fanny that she felt "like the heroine of a novel only that there is no sign of a hero!" and, "I sometimes think at these parties that I would like to meet some of the *young* men—they are so good-looking! This sounds ungrateful, and is entre nous."

Her father's standards did not ease the task of finding a hero. In the spring of 1889 Louisa was amused to hear rumors of her engagement to two different men, Fred Freylinghuysen and Charles Dickey. "The funny part" was that the gossips "should have hit upon the two men who would suit Papa if it *were* true—the *only* two so far as I can judge."

———

Pierpont had clear preferences among his siblings as well as his children. He saw his eldest sister, Sarah, and her husband, George, more out of duty than pleasure—they lived on East 40th Street in New York, and had a large summer "cottage" in Lenox, Massachusetts. His youngest sister, Juliet, living on the Avenue Montaigne in Paris, was almost as troubled as her mother. Erratic and emotionally unstable, she indulged in such extravagant spending sprees that Junius put her on an allowance, just as he had his wife. Fanny found Juliet's "untruthfulness" to be "rather a want of perception than anything more serious . . . perhaps a part of the general consequence of her mind."

The "general consequence" of the Lord/Pierpont genes seemed to be mood disorders. Pierpont Morgan medicated himself with hard work, ocean voyages, spa cures, and frenetic social activity, but was never able to stave off the depressions that alternated with his periods of equanimity. His mother and this sister cycled through more incapacitating extremes. Juliet's husband, the Reverend John B. Morgan, rector at the American Episcopal Church in Paris, did not play much part in the extended family. One spring Sunday Louisa described his sermon in Paris as "*awful*": "Uncle John is trying to preach extemporaneously. . . . It reminded me of nothing so much as Old Mother Hubbard. . . . Papa read the hymnal all the time."

Pierpont had for years been closest to his middle sister, Mary, and her husband, Walter Burns—the only family banker he wanted to work with besides Junius. Mary and Walter shared his worldliness and epicurean tastes. They had begun to collect art, and kept an apartment on the Champs Élysées after Burns joined J. S. Morgan & Co. In England they bought a country estate called Copt Hall in Essex, and two neoclassical houses (which they combined into one), No. 69-71 Brook Street, on Grosvenor Square.*

The Burnses had the best marriage in the Morgan family. Jack, struck by their companionable intimacy when he visited England one summer, implicitly compared it with what he saw at home: his aunt and uncle seemed "so united and at one in their ways," he told Fanny, "that it gives one a very pleasant impression of the *ménage.*"

In the ménage at 219, midlife had expanded Fanny's already substantial frame: her adoring son applauded by mail when he heard that she had been "gaining pounds and pounds"—"I know you won't like me to say it, but you

---

* The Savile Club now occupies the former Burns house.

know yourself that you are always better in health when you weigh between 180 and 190." Junius, who had made his own accommodation to an empty marriage, left no comment on Pierpont's preference for keeping the Atlantic between himself and his wife. When Fanny and all three girls went to Europe for six months one year, with a paid companion and one of Fanny's nieces, Junius worried only that his son would be lonely in New York, and wondered why he had not kept Louisa at home.

———

If Pierpont was finding romance outside his marriage, there is no evidence for it until the 1890s. He spent most of his leisure time in the eighties with friends such as the Bowdoins, Eglestons, and Laniers, and played an increasingly prominent role in the cultural life of New York.

He had been a trustee of the American Museum of Natural History ever since its founding in 1869. Board members made up the institution's deficit—often $50,000 a year—and Morgan led fund-raising efforts even when he could not attend meetings. Museum president Morris K. Jesup would announce to the other trustees, "Mr. Morgan has pledged ten thousand dollars. I will give ten thousand dollars. Mr. Iselin, will you give five? Mr. Mills? Mr. Pyne?"

In the forty-four years of his connection with the Natural History Museum, Morgan served as treasurer, vice president, and finance-committee chairman. He donated collections of minerals, gems, meteorites, amber, books, prehistoric South American relics, American Indian costumes, fossil vertebrates, skeletons, and the mummy of a pre-Columbian miner preserved in copper salts. Sending Jesup a check in 1890 for $15,000 to help purchase a gem collection assembled by Tiffany & Co. for the World's Fair Exhibition in Paris, he did not want public acknowledgment: "The less said the better to my taste."

He may have encouraged his nephew (through Memie) Henry Fairfield Osborn to join the museum's staff in 1890. As an undergraduate at Princeton, Osborn had developed an interest in paleontology and, after graduating in 1877, organized expeditions to study fossils in the American West. He did graduate work at Princeton, Columbia, and in England, where he worked under T. H. Huxley and F. M. Balfour—and met Charles Darwin. Earning an ScD from Princeton in 1880, he taught comparative anatomy there until 1890, when he moved to New York to head Columbia's new Biology Department and serve as curator of vertebrate paleontology at the Natural History Museum. A few years later he wrote of the "rare opportunity" offered by the museum's "liberal endowments for western exploration, and for the preparation of vertebrate fossils on a large scale": its collection was already "one of the finest" in the world. In 1908, with the support of his "Uncle Pierpont," Osborn became president of the museum.

Competition among New York's young cultural institutions for essential donors and dollars was well under way by the 1880s, and the Metropolitan Museum of Art wanted a Morgan on its board. Junius in 1887 gave the Met Joshua Reynolds's large group portrait of *The Honorable Henry Fane with His Guardians, Inigo Jones and Charles Blair*, which he had bought from the twelfth Earl of Westmorland for £13,500 (about $66,000). Henry Fane was the second son of the eighth Earl, who may have commissioned the painting—in which Inigo Jones, a relative of the seventeenth-century architect, looks somewhat like the young Pierpont Morgan.

With this transatlantic gift, Junius joined a few other wealthy Americans who were beginning in the late eighties to move from building private residential "museums" to endowing public institutions. Two of the most famous paintings in America at the time—Jean-Louis Ernest Meissonier's *Friedland, 1807* and Rosa Bonheur's *The Horse Fair*—were also given to the Met in 1887.* Henry G. Marquand, appointed president of the museum in 1889, donated thirty-seven Old Master paintings, including works by Vermeer, Van Dyck, and Frans Hals.

Junius's son had little to do with the Met in the 1880s—he was more involved with the Museum of Natural History across the park—but in 1888 the art museum's director, Luigi Palma di Cesnola, asked him to become a trustee. Since the Met could not elect anyone who served on the Natural History board, Cesnola tried to persuade Pierpont to switch his allegiance: "Your taste has always decidedly been in matters pertaining to *our* museum," he argued. "You have, I know, excellent art collections, and fine paintings. . . . I know too that your excellent father would be very glad to learn that you have taken an active interest in this institution which is progressing at the rate of a thousand to one compared with the other Museum."

When Pierpont, who had stronger loyalties and more catholic interests than Cesnola knew, replied that it would be impossible for him to resign from the "other" museum's board ("I have been connected with that Institution from the beginning"), the Met bent its rules and elected him anyway. He remained closely involved with both museums for the rest of his life.

The institution that had first claim on his attention in the eighties, however, was the Episcopal Church. Morgan was treasurer and senior warden at St. George's, and played an active role in national church affairs as well, attending the triennial General Convention as a lay delegate for the first time in 1886. The Church was governed by a House of Bishops and a House of Deputies, the

---

* Both were purchased from the estate of department store magnate A. T. Stewart, the Meissonnier by Judge Henry Hilton for $66,000, the Bonheur by Cornelius Vanderbilt for $53,000. In making his gift to the Met, Vanderbilt said the painting ought to be "permanently accessible to the public."

latter made up of four clerical and four lay delegates from each diocese. In his Hartford youth, Pierpont had followed the proceedings of these conventions and collected autographs of the bishops. As an adult, he attended the conventions and collected the bishops.

In July of 1886 he wrote to his old friend John Crerar in Chicago that he would be spending much of October in that city at the General Convention with a party of friends, and wanted "the best [hotel] accommodation that can be had"—a large parlor with six or eight bedrooms, as "there will be quite a number of ladies in the party, as well as Bishops." Crerar booked them into the Grand Pacific Hotel. Morgan quietly prepaid the bills.

Although he could not spare half an hour in Boston for his son, he set aside all obligations for three weeks every three years to sit among rectors and bishops, listening to dry ecclesiastical debates. Rainsford thought it was the "very archaic element" of this aspect of church life, "its atmosphere of complete withdrawal from common every day affairs of men," that answered "some need of [Morgan's] soul"—and that associating with the guardians of a "beautiful and venerable" religious tradition "had for him an attraction stronger than any other gathering afforded."

Unlike the intellectuals, from Jack's Harvard professors to William Morris and John Ruskin, who feared that industrialization was undermining spiritual values, Morgan saw no conflict between the moral and the material world, and apparently neither did his friends in the clergy. He transported parties of "ladies, as well as bishops" to Episcopal conventions in private railroad cars, putting them up for weeks at hotels or rented houses, much the way other millionaires treated friends to the horse races at Saratoga.

His religious life was not an attempt to justify or atone for his wealth, since he did not think he had anything to atone *for*. He regarded himself as doing honorable public service on Wall Street, and if the disintegration of his marriage troubled him on moral grounds, he left no indication of it. His sense of sin was abstract: Dr. Tyng had assured him in 1861 that to "come with a deep sense of your own guilt" and trust in Christ promised "entire forgiveness."

As late-nineteenth-century rationalists turned to science and history to fill the place once taken by religion, Morgan acknowledged no challenge to the authority of the Church. Its rituals gave form to his powerful, inchoate sentiments, and its worship of what Henry Adams called "silent and infinite force . . . the highest energy ever known to man" gave traditional context to his experience.

If the Church met private needs of his soul, he supplied many of its practical necessities. He was appointed in 1886 to a committee responsible for revising the Book of Common Prayer, which he knew practically by heart. He bought rare early editions of the prayer book for the committee, had 500 copies of the revised volume privately printed for the members of the 1892 Convention, and ordered another 250 bound in vellum for each American diocese and libraries in England and the United States. When the Convention met at St. George's in New York in 1889, he played secular host, arranging for the delegates' meals, housing, and entertainment. The mediator of railroad wars also arbitrated among factions in the councils of Church conventions, serving as unofficial broker of ecclesiastical peace.

Among the many individual clergymen he supported was Henry Codman Potter, appointed diocesan bishop of New York in 1887. Morgan privately supplemented Potter's salary with $12,500 a year, and raised $50,000 to insure him an income for the future. An immensely popular figure in Manhattan society, known as "pastor to the 400," the Right Reverend Potter was the son of a bishop (Alonzo Potter of Pennsylvania), and the nephew of another (Horatio Potter, his predecessor in New York, who had presided over Morgan's confirmation in 1861). He was also a social reformer who opposed child labor and sweatshops, and issued a pastoral letter objecting to workers being treated like commodities "to be bought and sold as the market shall decree." In 1887 Potter joined a Church Association for the Advancement of the Interests of Labor, which the unions welcomed. Once again, Morgan was subsidizing a clergyman who sided with labor against what Rainsford called the "tyranny of wealth."

Henry Potter's uncle, Horatio, had hoped to build an Episcopal cathedral in New York, and Morgan joined a board to raise funds for the project in 1886. "Oh that we had cathedrals in America," Nathaniel Hawthorne once sighed in a notebook, "were it only for the sensuous luxury." After the elder Potter's death, his nephew reconceived the cathedral as an American Westminster Abbey—an ecumenical Protestant house of worship for the city and the nation, to be called St. John the Divine. Morgan thanked Cornelius Vanderbilt for contributing $100,000 in January 1888, and gave hundreds of thousands himself over the next twenty-five years—$500,000 in 1892 alone. In 1887 the diocese and trustees chose a site on the rocky escarpment of Morningside Heights, far north of the populated city, although Rainsford wanted a more convenient location downtown. Columbia College, then on 49th Street between Madison and Park, purchased neighboring property at 116th Street in 1892, with the help of $100,000 from Pierpont Morgan.

Morgan also helped run the cathedral's architectural competition. Sixty-six firms submitted plans, including McKim, Mead & White, Carrère & Hastings, Richard Morris Hunt, Richard Upjohn, Peabody & Stearns, and Renwick, Aspinwall & Russell. The range of styles in these proposals reflected the ravenous eclecticism of the late Gilded Age, with references to everything from English Gothic to Egyptian pharaonic. The monumental size featured in most of the plans prompted a visiting English architect to wonder whether religious sentiment or "a craving for a tall cathedral by a people of everyday tall ideas, was the underlying motif in this undertaking." The commission went to George Louis Heins and Christopher Grant LaFarge, both trained by America's great proponent of the neo-Romanesque, Henry Hobson Richardson. Heins & LaFarge proposed to follow the Byzantine models of St. Mark's in Venice or St. Front in Périgeux for the interior, and to give the exterior the Gothic verticality of the Church of England. Construction began at Amsterdam Avenue and 112th Street in December 1892. Over a hundred years later it is still under way.

———

In another effort to bring "new blood" into the enclaves of patrician privilege, Morgan nominated John King, the president of the Erie Railroad, for membership in New York's exclusive Union Club in 1889. The club's governors rejected King, "owing to some unknown spite," Morgan reported to Levi Morton. One chronicler of the tale blamed King's table manners, and quoted Anatole France: "*Il est plus malaisé de manger comme un gentilhomme que de parler comme lui*" (it is harder to eat like a gentleman than to talk like one).

Unconcerned by King's table manners—and further annoyed at the blackballing of his friends Austin Corbin and William Seward Webb—Morgan organized a hundred Union members to walk out in protest, and commissioned Stanford White to build a new club. He is said to have told the architect, "Build a club fit for gentlemen. Damn the expense!"

At their first meeting, the Union secessionists elected Morgan president of the new club. Other founding members were Levi Morton (now Vice President of the United States), Charles Lanier, William C. Whitney, Cornelius and William K. Vanderbilt, W. Watts Sherman (son of Pierpont's first employer), James A. Roosevelt (uncle of Theodore, Jr.), Odgen and Robert Goelet, George Peabody Wetmore, and Adrian Iselin. The press dubbed it the Millionaire's Club. The founders named it the Metropolitan Club, and paid $480,000 for a site on Fifth Avenue at 60th Street. By the time Stanford White finished the palatial colonnaded Italian Renaissance clubhouse in 1894, it had cost nearly $2 million. On opening day, Morgan and White greeted members at the grand courtyard entrance on 60th Street. The club's soaring central hall had stained-glass windows, marble walls, scarlet carpets, velvet ropes, a coffered ceiling, and a spectacular double staircase leading to a second-story loggia. Someone said the gilded letter "M," set into plaques on the staircases' forged-iron balustrades, stood for Morgan.

John King, Austin Corbin, and W. Seward Webb joined the Metropolitan, but the new club rejected its founding patron's rector. Rainsford was proposed for membership early in 1894, but withdrew his name once it became clear that he would be blackballed—apparently (shades of John Pierpont) for "the extreme frankness of [his] utterances on certain social and economic questions."

―――

Morgan helped build not only monuments to high culture, Anglican religion, and masculine privilege, but also an enormous facility for popular entertainment in New York. When a syndicate set up by the National Horse Show Association bought an arena at Madison Avenue and 26th Street in 1887—originally Commodore Vanderbilt's train sheds, converted to a concert garden by P. T. Barnum in 1873—Morgan took the largest block of shares, and became president of the corporation that would erect Madison Square Garden. Other shareholders included Andrew Carnegie and Stanford White. As it became clear that the economics of the space required more than equestrian usage, the Garden developed into a multi-use pleasure palace with restaurants, theaters, recreations of Shakespeare's house, the Globe Theatre, Dickens's Old Curiosity Shop, and an amphitheater for horse, dog, and flower shows.

The Spanish-Renaissance fantasia designed by Stanford White and completed in 1890 took up an entire city block. It was mostly brick with white terra-cotta trim, Roman colonnades, tall arched windows, eight domed belvederes, and a 341-foot tower inspired by the Giralda on the Spanish cathedral at Seville. At the top of the tower, White placed an eighteen-foot copper statue of Diana with a bow and arrow by Augustus Saint-Gaudens; when the tower opened in November 1891, searchlights revealed a gloriously naked Diana against the evening sky.* The *New York Daily Graphic* pronounced the Garden "unrivalled . . . a permanent ornament to the city," and another trade journal called it a "masterpiece" that had no parallel in the United States. The capitalists who had brought about this "architectural triumph" did not see much return on their investment. Three years after the Garden opened, the corporation had paid no dividend, and its organizers considered putting the building up for sale. Instead, they rented the amphitheater to the tenant they originally had in mind, the wealthy Horse Show Association, for five years.

―――

Junius's old friend Sir John Rose collapsed and died while stalking deer in Scotland in August 1888. Alexander Duncan, Pierpont's first employer, died in his sleep in October of 1889. Perhaps prompted by these events, Junius that fall re-

―――

* White soon decided that this Diana was too large, and commissioned a smaller one. The original went on exhibition at the 1893 Chicago World's Fair—after a noisy controversy over whether or not to dress her.

vised his will. He also renewed the five-year partnership agreement he had drawn up in 1884, specifying that he would leave £1.5 million of capital in J. S. Morgan & Co. if his son chose to continue the business after his own death.

In November, Junius went to Monte Carlo with Alice Mason. Pierpont sent him Cragston apples for Christmas. The guests at the Villa Henrietta early that winter included Fabbris, Grenfells, Cunards, Whartons, Drexels, Roosevelts, and Duncans. At the beginning of March, Junius extended the lease on the house until 1898. An old friend wrote: "I heard that your son was such a wonderful businessman he was thought to be worth one hundred millions of dollars. That is the story in New York."

At the beginning of April 1890, Pierpont, who was not yet worth anywhere near $100 million, sailed with Louisa on the White Star's *Teutonic* to join his father as usual for their birthdays: he was about to turn fifty-three, Junius seventy-seven. Suffering from eczema and gout, he planned to go on after Monte Carlo to take the waters at Aix-les-Bains. He was on the Atlantic in early April when Junius set out one afternoon for Beaulieu in a light, four-wheeled victoria. A train passing along the route startled the horses into a run. No one saw exactly what happened next—the driver was facing forward—but Junius, probably standing up to look, fell out of the carriage and hit his head on a stone wall. When the driver finally stopped the horses 150 yards down the road, he looked around to see the coach empty, and drove back to find his employer lying by the wall, unconscious. Two strangers helped him lift the inert body into the carriage.

Walter and Mary Burns were summoned from London by cable. They crossed to Paris and took the *train rapide* to Monte Carlo, where they found Junius still unconscious. Though he had a concussion, a broken left hand, and cuts on his forehead, nose, and lips, his skull had not been fractured, his pulse was strong, and he showed no sign of paralysis. Three physicians, two nurses, and his valet-butler, Thomas Hand, took turns tending him. The doctors thought there was no permanent brain damage.

Pierpont at sea knew nothing of these events. When the *Teutonic* reached Queenstown, Ireland, on April 8, a White Star agent came on board with two cables from Walter Burns. The first, dated April 6, told of the accident but held out hope—"symptoms improving general strength maintained." The second, sent on the seventh, was bleaker: "Father had very restless night and has lost ground since yesterday feel very anxious but not hopeless."

"Papa bore the shock wonderfully," Louisa told Fanny. "He came to me as we were leaving Queenstown, and he was crying and sobbing poor Papa! But I think it was a little relief. He did not sleep much of course."

As soon as the *Teutonic* docked at Liverpool on April 9, another agent handed Pierpont a telegram from Burns: "Your father passed away at quarter before one on morning of April eighth he never recovered consciousness and doctors say was never aware of pain there is no need your coming Monte Carlo unless you specially desire Mary myself Hand will do everything necessary am having remains embalmed do you know whether your father left any directions about burial if not wire your wishes they will be strictly complied with by us warmest love and profound sympathy in the great loss."

Later that day Burns cabled again to say he had learned from London that Junius wanted his remains taken to Hartford for burial, along with those of Juliet and little "Doctor."

Father and daughter spent a night at the Charing Cross Hotel, then went straight through Paris to Monte Carlo. "Papa was wonderfully calm on the journey," wrote Louisa, "and though he broke down when he met Aunt Mary—still I think the being able to cry has been a great thing for him." His sister Juliet came from Paris. Sarah was in the United States.

Almost thirty years earlier, in another seaside villa nearby, Pierpont had suffered his first great loss. Now he had to relinquish the man who had dominated his existence for fifty-three years—much of that time with reproach, recently with overwhelming pride, always with fierce concentration.

The body had been embalmed and kept at the Villa Henrietta in an open coffin until Pierpont could take his final leave. The fall had damaged the lower part of Junius's face, but the cuts in his handsome forehead were superficial.

Two clergymen came from Menton to read a short service. Afterward, Alice Mason and Juliet left for Paris. The full funeral would take place in Hartford. Pierpont and Louisa stayed on with Mary and Walter Burns, arranging for Hand to accompany the body by special train to Le Havre, then home on a French steamer.

America had received the news by cable on April 8. Anne, now sixteen, sent her father a loving note: "My own dearest Papa, How, oh how I wish we were all together today, the ocean does seem such a big thing to have between one and the people one loves. We all did so long not to have the end come until you arrived there, so as not to have the dreadful shock all at once."

Fanny wrote: "I do so long to be with you in this terrible trial, and find myself going over and over and over again the different things that I would like to say and do to help you if I were only there." She wanted to join him at once, with the younger girls, and then "all come home together, when you are ready." Aware that he might not like this plan, she added, "Still I want to do the thing that will really be the best help to you, and if that is to stay on quietly here I will do that cheerfully as I may."

Many friends had called at 219 with offers of help and love. Fanny named them, then went on: "I feel how much heavier is this than any loss that has come to you since I have known you—and how vain are all attempts to make it less. It means the turn quite out of youth, and that, too, while losing your wisest friend out of your sight. It must be a comfort to you to realize your Father's loving pride in you. I think no son ever more fully satisfied his Father's ambition than you!" In closing, she repeated, "Remember that I want to help you in your own way—by going to you—or by staying here—only let me know."

Later that day, she sent another urgent offer: "These times of sorrow draw closer those that are left, and now, if ever, the girls and I can help you bear the burden of grief. You know how truly we share it with you—the loss for me is greater than I can put into words—and there will be a certain moral support to you in our presence I think. But do just what seems best to you, and I will carry out your wishes as perfectly as I can. Always your loving Frances."

Pierpont did not ask his wife to join him. He sailed for New York with Louisa on April 20, and planned to bring her back alone after the funeral in mid-May, when he would take the cure at Aix and see to his London business. Fanny begged to be included. Louisa had to explain: "I am afraid dear Mother that he won't be able to arrange it. He shrinks from looking after so big a party, when he has so much business on hand."

Letters from relatives and friends told of the extraordinary pleasure Junius had taken in his son's accomplishments. S. Endicott Peabody, who had long ago worked with the London bank, wrote: "Your chief solace will be the consciousness that for many years you have been to him the one upon [whom] he relied above all others, that no son could have been more loving and devoted than you, that no act of yours has ever caused him pain"—which was not true—"and that his affection was rewarded by a confidence and pride in you that few sons could inspire."

Abram S. Hewitt, former congressman and mayor of New York, reported that Junius had recently spoken with "pardonable pride" of all his son's achievements—"you seemed to be the chief subject of his conversation and hopes for the future." An English friend described Junius as having been "overjoyed at the prospect of seeing you. . . . What a bond it was between you. He was so proud of you: over and over again he has said to me 'that's a son to be proud of'—or words to that effect."

Pierpont arrived in New York at the end of April. George MacCulloch Miller, who had known him since the sixties, called at 219 a few days later. Having watched his old friend grow into a reserved middle age in which he was "much less accustomed than in the early days to outward manifestations of his feelings," Miller was surprised and moved by his "deep, almost uncontrolled grief," his evident "tenderness [and] very deep sense of loss."

The funeral took place at Hartford's Christ Church on May 6 in a warm rain. The Morgan family brought dozens of friends by special train from New York— among them Chauncey Depew, William C. Whitney, Oliver Hazard Payne, William Butler Duncan, the George Bowdoins, and the George MacCulloch Millers. A train coming the other way brought more friends from Boston. Bishop Williams of Connecticut performed the service, assisted by Bishop Potter and Dr. Rainsford. The honorary pallbearers included Anthony Drexel, Levi Morton, Cyrus Field, Charles Lanier, Jacob Rogers, Cornelius Vanderbilt II, and Roland Mather. Flags all over Hartford flew at half-mast.

White roses and lilies of the valley covered Junius's casket, and floral tributes filled the church—one, made entirely of roses, was a huge cross of red set in a crown of white encircled with crimson. The choir sang hymns chosen by Pierpont—"Asleep in Jesus, Blessed Sleep," "Lead Kindly Light," and "For All the Saints Who From Their Labors Rest." The clergymen preceded the coffin out into the gray morning. A tent stood over the Morgan plot at Hartford's Cedar Hill Cemetery to protect the mourners from rain. The bodies of Junius's wife and younger son were reburied alongside him.

The next day, *The Hartford Courant* wondered whether "half so much wealth was ever before gathered under one roof in Connecticut as was represented in the audience at Christ Church yesterday."

———

In his will, Junius left legacies to relatives, servants, and friends. To his daughters, Sarah and Mary, he gave several works of art, £100,000 each, and another £600,000 (about $3 million) each in trust, from which they could draw income for life. He left nothing outright to the prodigal Juliet; she would have the income from £400,000 held in trust, and the "use and enjoyment" of paintings that would go to her children after her death. For Alice Mason he had set up a fund, to be managed by Pierpont, which would yield £1,000 a year for the rest of her life. His total estate was worth about $23 million.

Most of it went to his son. Pierpont received £600,000 outright, as well as the capital Junius had in J. S. Morgan & Co., the houses in London and Roehampton, investments (primarily American securities), personal effects, and several paintings—including Gainsborough's *Miss Wilbraham*, a Romney portrait of Emma Hamilton, and Turner's Italian landscape. Excluding the art, his inheritance amounted to nearly £3 million ($15 million), equivalent to roughly $225 million in the 1990s. Neither the United States nor England taxed inheritance in 1890.

Junius's death severed the most powerful emotional bond of Pierpont's life. Unlike Memie's death, however, it did not violate the natural order of things. The elder Morgan had lived long and well, enjoyed a distinguished career, retired voluntarily, and bequeathed his work and sense of high calling to his son. In his youth, Pierpont had chafed under paternal restraints. In his thirties, finding sense in the homilies about "character" and "reputation," he had curbed some of his impulses, but continued to propose ventures Junius was loath to accept. Slowly, over the course of three decades, the younger Morgan had demonstrated his own ability and integrity as banker to the federal government and "doctor" to the nation's railroads, and in the process had gained the unqualified respect of his harshest critic. For the rest of his life he carried the assurance of that hard-won benediction, and maintained reverent attachments to everything connected with his father.

In the fall of 1890 he ordered an immense red granite monument representing the Ark of the Covenant to mark the Morgan family plot at the Cedar Hill Cemetery. He carried out all of Junius's professional and philanthropical commitments, bought books, paintings, manuscripts, jewelry, and cigars for which his father had contracted, and continued the lease of the Villa Henrietta for three years. In 1901 he gave $1 million for three buildings at the Harvard Medical School in honor of Junius, and several years later $1 million to the Wadsworth Atheneum in Hartford for a Junius Morgan Memorial Wing. He hung Frank Holl's picture of Junius in his office at 23 Wall Street and another portrait in his library at home.

In May of 1890, at fifty-three, Pierpont took his father's place as the head of J. S. Morgan & Co. The firm still did not have the international stature of Rothschilds and Barings—"Morgans" was seen in London financial circles as essentially an American bank—but Junius had long predicted that America would dominate the economic future. Tony Drexel, who turned sixty-four in 1890, had for some time served his New York partner more as colleague and consultant than supervising sentinel. On both sides of the Atlantic, Pierpont was now "the Senior" at the house of Morgan.

PART III

—

SENIOR

[New York] is a place where things "hum," and they have been humming a good deal . . . since I have been over here. . . . It is extremely interesting to find oneself in the very heart of Wall Street excitement and combinations, and to note the prodigious amount of nervous excitement and energy the Americans throw into their work. . . . Few of them live through it to advanced years except physical and intellectual giants like Morgan who has something Titanic about him when he really gets to work.

Morgan's British partner Clinton Dawkins
to Alfred Milner, July 13, 1901

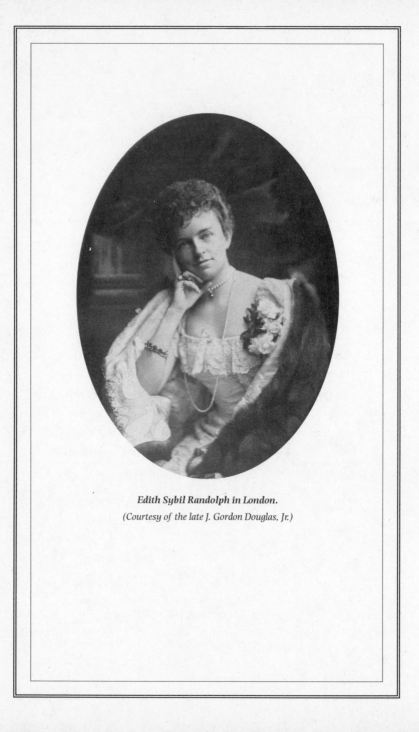

Edith Sybil Randolph in London.

(Courtesy of the late J. Gordon Douglas, Jr.)

Chapter 15

IN PRIVATE

Pierpont had intended to return to Europe with Louisa for the cure at Aix immediately after his father's funeral, but Fanny persuaded him that she, too, needed a dose of foreign waters. He sent her off with Anne and a hired companion to the spa at Royat in the Auvergne in mid-May. He would leave two weeks later. At Royat, Fanny noted that her "poor elderly legs" could barely manage the prescribed walks.

The Morgans' twenty-fifth wedding anniversary passed on May 31, 1890, with Fanny ailing in France while Pierpont crossed the Atlantic with Louisa, Juliet, and a beautiful young widow named Edith Sybil Randolph. He was fifty-three years old, she thirty-six—ages and circumstances much like those of Junius and Alice Mason.

It is not clear when Pierpont met the willowy, dark-haired Edith Randolph, but he had probably known *about* her for a long time. Her father, a Washington surgeon named John Frederick May, had removed a tumor from the neck of John Wilkes Booth, and in 1865 identified the actor's body by the scar. Edith's mother, the former Sarah Mills, was related to New York's socially prominent Oelrichs, Jays, Winthrops, and Kanes, and the Mays had moved from Washington to New York in the late sixties. As Edith came of age she moved easily into Manhattan's "smart set."

In 1878, at twenty-four, she married Arthur B. Randolph, a British military captain. The couple settled on an estate belonging to friends in Douglaston, Queens, about twenty miles east of New York City. They had two children,

Arthur, Jr., and Adelaide, before Randolph died in the late eighties. The society gossip sheet *Town Topics* described the marriage as "not over happy, and as [the Captain] resigned his commission soon after and had comparatively little means, she was obliged to lead almost a retired life in a little country cottage at Douglaston." The widowed Edith moved to Manhattan, slowly resumed an active social life, and spent summers with her parents in Maine.

"The sauciest of the lively set sped out over the Riverside Drive last Thursday with spring colors flying," reported *Town Topics* in April 1890, "and flocked through Mr. Edward Stokes' tavern with the feathery fairness of young birds." Among those who "ornamented" Claremont Avenue that afternoon were Mrs. Arthur Randolph, Mrs. Cornelius Vanderbilt, Mrs. Elliot Roosevelt, and the Chicago heiress Mary Leiter. Edith appeared in the first listing of the New York "400," where beauty ranked second to gold as a qualification.

Pierpont Morgan called on her after her husband died. He brought her to Cragston in the summer of 1889, while Fanny traveled abroad, and that fall sent her flowers, jewelry, and cases of his favorite whiskey. His courtly attentions had probably begun earlier in the year: as he prepared to leave for Europe in March, his private secretary wrote to the fashionable New York florist J. E. Thorley that Mr. Morgan wanted his regular order of violets continued in his absence: "See that there are plenty—among others four bunches of white violets for Easter Sunday." The secretary would pay all bills, and concluded discreetly, "He [Morgan] said you'd understand what he meant. I beg you'll see his instructions faithfully carried out."

Edith joined St. George's Church when she moved into the city, and worked on charitable committees with Pierpont's wife and daughters. As soon as she learned of Junius's death in April 1890 she called on Fanny at 219, and sent messages of condolence to Pierpont in Monte Carlo. She was among the friends who accompanied the Morgans to Hartford for the funeral.

A month later she and her children traveled with Pierpont, Louisa, and Juliet to Europe. Fanny, still at Royat, told Louisa she was "ready to jump with joy" at the idea of a family reunion: "Oh it is *too* delicious to think of seeing you all three so soon!"

On landing, Edith went off with other friends. Pierpont stopped briefly to see his wife, then took Louisa and Juliet for a separate cure at Aix-les-Bains, 140 miles away. Fanny, learning that Mrs. Randolph would join the Morgans to tour Scotland in July, hoped this plan would help her husband "give up the idea of going home until he has had a restful pleasure trip." She was used to his attentions to beautiful women, and probably told herself he was simply being kind to a lonely widow.

In early July a party of six—Louisa, Juliet, Pierpont, Edith, and her children—met in London and went by train to the Lake District, arriving at Windermere Station several days before Fanny was due. Louisa at twenty-four observed her father and Edith with a cognizant eye. She took Juliet (called Laily) off each morning to see towns, churches, and meadows, and noted in her diary, with an eloquent pair of quotation marks: "Papa & Mrs. Randolph too 'tired' to go for a drive this morning. Laily and I spent an hour on the lake rowing. This afternoon we all drove down the east side of the lake. Mother and Annie arrived this p.m."

Fanny wrote in *her* diary that night: "All seem so well and bright! JPM especially." The next day the entire party went on to Scotland, stopping at Birnam, north of Perth. "JPM" spent most of his time walking and driving with Edith. "After lunch P., who felt very down and cross, walked off with Mrs. Randolph," recorded Fanny. "After dinner all but Juliet & I walked to Birnam Falls. . . ." The pattern continued all week: "Others all to Crieff – I stayed quietly here, wrote, drove with the 2 Randolph children, dined alone. . . . P. drove with Mrs. R. and I with the girls to the Rumbling Bridge."

After a circuit of Scotland that took in castles, monasteries, villages, and lakes, the Randolphs left for Nottingham. The next day Fanny noted, "Pierpont slept all evening." Two days after that he went to London.

At some point that summer—perhaps on this trip to London—Pierpont found the letters he had written to his father twice a week, every week, for over thirty years. Junius had carefully preserved them in bound volumes, arranged in chronological order. They constituted an invaluable record of the two men's professional and personal lives. Too personal for anyone else to see, Pierpont apparently concluded. He burned them.

On August 18, the Morgans and Randolphs met again at Liverpool to sail home on the White Star's *Majestic*. Fanny found her stateroom "luxurious." Pierpont's was on another deck.

———

Perhaps Fanny was not worried about "P. and Mrs. R." that summer because she knew the gossip about Mrs. R. and another man—former Navy Secretary William C. Whitney. Now in the street railway business, this tall, good-looking, politically ambitious Democrat was married to the former Flora Payne, heiress to a Standard Oil fortune. During Whitney's four-year tenure at the Navy (1884–88), Flora was said to have received sixty thousand guests at their Georgetown mansion. Her husband tolerated her large social ambitions but preferred quieter forms of recreation, and often stayed in town while Flora joined the fashionable crowd at Lenox, Bar Harbor, and Newport.

The gossip column in *Town Topics*, which was as avidly read by *haute* New York as it was disavowed, had announced in April 1890—just after Junius died—that Edith Randolph was engaged to Flora Whitney's wealthy brother, Colonel Oliver Hazard Payne. A few weeks later the anonymous columnist retracted this erroneous news and came up with a racier assertion: since the widow, the colonel, and the Whitneys were "very much together now," the only possible inference was that "Col. Payne is playing the part of gooseberry" for his sister's husband. "As for Mrs. Randolph," concluded the writer—referring to her new St. George's affiliation, and dropping a risqué hint—"I understand that she has of late become a religious devotée, which does not, however, interfere to any great extent with her passion for horseback riding, to which exercise Mrs. Whitney is also devoted." Flora Whitney had no aptitude for riding.

The Whitneys went to Europe in the early summer of 1890, at the same time as the Morgans and Randolphs. Edith traveled with them in June while Pierpont took the cure at Aix. Mr. Whitney took daylong excursions alone with the handsome widow (just as Morgan would in England two weeks later), complaining that his wife's temper drove him away. Flora claimed she was cross *because* of her husband's attentions to Mrs. Randolph. When Edith rejoined the Morgans in July, Whitney left for New York. He told his wife: "you have done [Mrs. Randolph] a great injury. Scandal wags its tongue at every pretty woman almost . . . and your manner and words have injured her. She was companionable, and bright spirited and I enjoyed her socially. Why shouldn't I?" He insisted that "nothing of what you thought happens to be true."

Fanny Morgan made no such fuss that summer, and forced her husband to no explanation or denial, although she noted in her diary that one of her children (probably Anne) complained: "You constantly ask me to decide between Papa and you."

———

In May of 1890, shortly before he left for Europe with Edith, Pierpont ordered a new yacht. His fortune had more than doubled after his father's death, and his pleasure in *Corsair* had exceeded his high expectations. Yachting was now the Gilded Age's premier form of sport. There had been twenty-nine boats in the New York Yacht Club fleet when Morgan acquired *Corsair* in 1882; eight years later there were seventy-one, their increasing opulence and size measuring the rise in their owners' means.

Morgan invited a young yacht designer named J. Frederic Tams to his office, and announced that he was thinking of building a new *Corsair*: would Mr. Tams take on the job? Tams, who wrote an account of this interview years later, was nonplussed; he had no experience with such a large assignment, and wanted a few days to think it over.

Morgan had thought it over. "What are you doing tonight?" he asked. "Can't you come to dinner and let me know then? I am sailing in a few days to be away some time and want her to be ready by the time I get back."

Amused and impressed by the banker's dispatch with a matter of this magnitude, Tams considered the proposition for a few hours, and agreed over dinner at 219 to accept.

What, he asked, did Mr. Morgan have in mind as to materials, size, speed, interior decor?

"I have no time to think about all that"—Morgan waved the question away. He simply needed a bigger yacht—though not too large to turn around in the Hudson at Highland Falls—as much like the existing *Corsair* as possible.

Tams, having sailed on *Corsair*, said he thought it would be a mistake to reproduce her, as she was slow, dark belowdecks, and not very good at sea. He had not counted on his host's proprietary pride. "I shall never forget the expression that came over his face," Tams recalled. "He looked at me for some appreciable moments with those eyes of his and I suddenly became aghast at my temerity. I thought he might explode or order me out of the room."

Morgan looked away, perhaps weighing the prospect of a more advanced, better-designed yacht against the insult to the old one, and then, "turning back, said in the gentlest sort of voice, 'You are right; go ahead on that basis.' "

A few days later Tams returned to 23 Wall Street to work out details. Who would handle the payments while Morgan traveled? he wanted to know. The banker rang a bell on his desk and asked a clerk to bring him a Drexel, Morgan checkbook. When it arrived, he handed it across the mahogany desk.

Who should sign? Tams inquired.

Morgan: "Don't you know how to draw and sign checks?"

Tams: "Yes."

"Well, you draw until you are stopped."

As he had with Rainsford, Fabbri, Coster, Stetson, and Edison, Morgan chose a man whose skills had impressed him, and gave him the means to do an expert's job. He would not interfere unless things went wrong.

Though he wanted the new yacht ready by the time he returned from Europe, the process of building her took a year and a half. The hull and engines were designed by John Beavor-Webb, an Irish-born engineer who had built two of England's America's Cup contenders, and had recently married Alice May, one of Edith Randolph's sisters. Tams, supervising the project, designed the interior and fittings. The new steam yacht *Corsair*—241 feet in length, weighing 560 tons, with single screw, triple-expansion engines, 2,000 horsepower, wide wooden decks, striped awnings, two masts, auxiliary sails, a gilt clipper bow, black hull, and a gracefully sweeping sheer—was ready for use in the fall of 1891. The hull of the first *Corsair*, built in 1880, had been made of iron. The second, in 1891, was steel.

Jack accompanied his father on an inaugural sail to Cragston early that October. Forward, the second *Corsair* had two staterooms, a bath, and a large dining saloon with oak paneling and banquettes upholstered in dark green plush. There were six more staterooms aft, including Morgan's, each with its own bath. Tams had "thought things out and arranged details as I thought only a woman could do," reported Jack to his traveling mother. There were "little places to put your watch at night," sponge hooks in the bathrooms, real fireplaces, wardrobes in every room, full sets of "Corsair" china, glass, silver, and linen, a storage room for trunks, and steam heat.

"You cannot imagine anything more splendid in the way of construction, or tasteful in decoration," Jack concluded. His father was "delighted"—"I never saw him express such entire satisfaction with anything before. He went so far as to declare that there was nothing which he wished changed in any way."

No one stopped Mr. Tams from writing checks. Morgan didn't have to ask. He sold his first yacht for $70,000 once the second was built. His private "Corsair" accounts in the nineties ran well over $100,000 a year.

———

On personal items as well as yachts, Morgan remained exigent about quality and detail. He ran a steady tab with the Savile Row tailor Henry Poole & Co., clothiers to the courts of England and France, and when a shipment of dishes he bought in London reached New York, he complained that it included eighteen salad plates, "about the ugliest things I ever saw and certainly none that I ever ordered."

One unwelcome task that had come with his inheritance was managing the finances of his sister Juliet. He told her at the end of 1891 that he would not increase her income above $40,000 a year: "on the scale that you live it is absolutely impossible for you to wisely expend any more," although he would take up emergencies as they arose. Judging by his own considerably greater expenses, he went on, and by the amount he gave Fanny for hers, he could not understand Juliet's having any trouble managing on $40,000 (roughly equivalent to $600,000 in the 1990s). Furthermore, her husband was "quite able to pay a portion of the house expenses, & it is proper that he should do so."

He himself was giving away more than Juliet's annual income. At the end of 1891 he sent Connecticut's Bishop Williams a case of whiskey and a check for $2,000, to be used "for your own *personal* comfort in any way—with my dear love," and donated $30,000 to Yale's Divinity School for a Bishop Williams Scholarship Fund. When the New York Botanical Garden, founded in the spring of 1891 on East Fordham Road in the Bronx, could not procure city funding until private sources had been tapped, Morgan joined Cornelius Vanderbilt and Andrew Carnegie to produce ten subscriptions for $25,000 each, including their own.

He was also expanding his collections of books and manuscripts, though with no clear plan or direction. Junius had given him Sir Walter Scott's manuscript of *Guy Mannering* in 1881. Ten years later, long before it became popular to collect Victorian fiction, Pierpont bought some of the most important authors' manuscripts of the period—Trollope's *He Knew He Was Right* and Wilkie Collins's mysteries, *The Moonstone* and *The Woman in White. Guy Mannering* served as the cornerstone for this collection, and Morgan eventually acquired fifteen more Scott manuscripts.

He worked primarily through two London book dealers in the early nineties— J. Pearson & Co. and Henry Sotheran & Co. F. W. Wheeler at Pearson sent him lists of items for consideration: Morgan crossed some out, ordered others, and complained (with regard to a Wilkie Collins MS) "price altogether too high," and (a Byron) "don't want at any such price." He also bought printed books, among them James Bryce's *American Commonwealth*, John Lothrop Motley's *Correspondence*, Tolstoy's *Kreutzer Sonata*, Kipling's *Light that Failed*, Dickens's *Pickwick Papers*, several sets of Scott's novels, Thomas Gray's poems, biographies of Dickens, Wellington, Constable, Gainsborough, and Fanny Burney, and a volume called *Love & Marriages of Distinguished Men.*

The dealers catered to his interest in literary first editions, armorial bindings, Bibles, liturgies, royal signatures, and collections of documents relating to eighteenth-century historical events, such as the "Junius Letters,"* the trial of Warren Hastings, and the repeal of the Stamp Act. In the early nineties he purchased a collection of letters by the Kings and Queens of England from the time of Richard III, as well as a bound series of more recent date containing a wisp of the Duke of Wellington's hair and a note from the rakish Edward Albert, Prince of Wales, with a suggestive postscript: "My dear Francis . . . How did you find the lady in Chester Street?"

Morgan rarely said anything about what he purchased or why, although writing in 1892 to a man from whom he bought a second set of autographs by the signers of the Declaration of Independence—an enormously popular genre among collectors of Americana, and this set was exceptionally fine—he suggested that he had something other than private possession ultimately in mind: "I must certainly congratulate you upon the condition in which I find [the collection], as well as its character," he wrote, "and I trust it will give great pleasure to me, as well as to those who in after years may enjoy it." He later gave a third set to the Library of Congress.

---

* A series of political letters published in London's *Public Advertiser* between 1769 and 1772, under the pseudonym Junius, had attacked George III and other members of the British aristocracy. Speculation attributed the identity of the exceedingly well-read and articulate author to, among others, Gibbon, Burke, Lord Temple, Lyttleton, and William Gerard Hamilton, but Macauley claimed he was Sir Philip Francis—Gibbon's schoolteacher, later a foreign service officer in India, and assistant to Burke in the impeachment trial of Warren Hastings, the governor-general of British India. Macauley's identification of Francis as "Junius" was later endorsed by William E. Lecky and Leslie Stephen, but did not end the controversy.

———

While Morgan was assembling great works of world literature on his library shelves, for pleasure he read minor Victorian novels—the literary equivalent of his narrative salon paintings. According to Louisa, his favorites were *Geraldine Hawthorne* (whose anonymous author, Beatrice May Butt, specialized in tales of women in romantic distress); Edward George Earle Bulwer-Lytton's four-volume survey of English provincial life, *My Novel*; Mary Cholmondeley's *Sir Charles Danvers*, an entertaining romance that follows a pair of aristocratic lovers through secret yearnings, missed opportunities, noble renunciations, and high heroics to a happy end; and a little antisocialist tract and love story called *Fraternity, A Romance of Inspiration*, published anonymously in 1888 by a Miss M. M. Holland Thomas.

Morgan read *Fraternity* when it first appeared, gave copies to friends, and arranged to meet the author in London. Set mainly in Wales, the novel portrays a young Oxford graduate named Edmund Haig, orphaned and raised by priests, who devotes his life to teaching the children of the poor. He falls in love with a local girl named Blodwen in the tiny Welsh town of Llanfairydd, but can't marry her because he has no money. Forcing himself to give up personal happiness, he sets off to spread the gospel of Christian fraternity to the world.

Edmund believes that the French Revolution went wrong in stressing liberty and equality over fraternity, and tells Welsh miners to renounce their demands for better wages and working conditions in favor of brotherly love and hard work. Edmund "was a strange kind of Socialist," notes Miss Thomas, "devoid of envy, hatred, malice, and all uncharitableness. He was a fraternal Socialist, the only right kind." Stepping out of her story, the author mounts a soapbox: "You, who love the poor, who influence the poor, teach them not that the rich with-hold from them their rightful heritage; that they are victims of injustice be-cause they are poor. . . . We have no more *right* to be all equally wealthy than we have to be equally healthy." And she urges: "Come, let us take up poverty cheerfully, young Wales! Is not education open to all, science eternally true, and art forever beautiful? . . . Is not the sleep of the laboring man sweet? . . . Love each other . . . and control of self shall make you equal with the highest gentleman in the world!"

Edmund eventually learns that he is the elder son of a rich man and free to marry Blodwen after all. He tells her that deep inequalities of soul, mind, and moral beauty create more problems than differences in worldly wealth: "And we who are the elder children, so to speak, of the human family—we who are educated, and who are sensitive to the bad habits and disagreeable customs of the ignorant younger children—we must instruct and enlighten, and cheer and refine them till inequality is conquered, through Fraternity and for Frater-nity." Their students will teach other children, and "the day shall come when all the spheres shall move in harmony," and "to be rich shall no longer be counted man's chief good."

Morgan so admired this fairy tale about a benevolent, paternalistic elite refining its "ignorant younger children" until everyone lives happily ever after that he later subsidized its republication. (See Chapter 19.) More surprising than his endorsement of a shallow, patronizing screed on the problems of inequality is that he chose to read about this subject in his spare time.

Jack did not share his father's enthusiasm for *Fraternity*. He liked the love story, he told Fanny, but "as for the new Socialism, I cannot get on with it entirely. . . . It has taken nineteen centuries for one perfect life to change in as much as it has been changed at all, the nature of one small part of the world; why expect a purely human system, built on a divine idea but simply human after all, to change that nature in a hurry?"

———

Pierpont's youthful sermon to Jim Goodwin from Göttingen on the virtues of wifely domesticity and selflessness had been entirely in the prospective abstract. Thirty years later, his wife was not exactly selfless—she required more attention than anyone seemed able to provide—but as it turned out, he found domesticity stifling, and preferred consorts who did not fit his early ideal of feminine "duty" after all. He was drawn to bright, self-possessed women with a touch of champagne in their veins—women who met him on his own ground, felt at home in the world, shared his social instincts and hedonistic tastes.

At Göttingen he had also pronounced it wonderful that the Drapers continued to like him even after he and Jim had made fools of themselves in Hartford. Women always liked him, even with his forbidding visage—about which, in the right circumstances, he had a sense of humor.

Margot Tennant, who later married H. H. Asquith, met Morgan in the late 1880s, and reported in her diary that he asked her: "What wd you do if you were me with all my riches yet having this terrible nose?" ("He is cursed," she graphically explained, "with a Cyrano nose of vast blue oozing glands a hideous deformity.")

She replied, "I sd. not mind so much if I were you as you can never have been very good-looking," and concluded: "this seems to have pleased him & he tucked me into a cosy corner of his heart & has seen me about a doz. times since." Twenty-five years later he gave her £3,000 to restore a country house she and her husband were buying near Oxford; in return, she sent him a signed first edition of Carlyle's *Sartor Resartus*.

Lady Victoria Sackville, with whom Morgan had a romantic skirmish late in his life, wrote in *her* diary: "I have never met anyone as attractive; one forgets his nose entirely after a few minutes, as his eyes are either twinkling or full of kindness and expression. . . . He is . . . a wonderful man." That he was also a rich and powerful one added immeasurably to the appeal.

Edith Randolph apparently forgot his nose as well. She became very much part of his life in the early 1890s, dining at 219, visiting Cragston, joining the parties on his yacht, while Morgan kept his wife on the other side of the Atlantic. In February 1891 Juliet escorted Fanny abroad. She complained of the chore to Louisa, but reflected, "it isn't as bad as if she were at home with all the rest of the scrimmage going on outside," and begged: "Oh Isa, do get Papa to telegraph a little more often. Mother gets into such a [state] not hearing, and he needn't say anything more than—all well love—only it makes a great difference to her."

Fanny stayed in Europe all that spring and summer. She wrote from Germany that she was storing up "big supplies of health for the home-life and duties, when they come again," and worried about her husband in New York's summer heat. Hearing in July that he had been to two Hartford funerals, then gone off on the yacht with Edith, she hoped he "enjoyed his visit with Mrs. Randolph after his hard days at Hartford." Edith's father had recently died, and Fanny continued to Louisa: "You do not tell me whether her father's death leaves her any better off, in money matters—and you know that subject of people's means of support is my besetting curiosity!"

Her curiosity was somewhat misplaced. Having been banished to Europe for nine months with no idea when she would be summoned home, she learned her fate in October: "Cable from Pierpont deciding that we must stay over here all winter."

Jack told her "it hurt us all to have the cable go," but he feared New York "in the gay and busy season would undo all the great gain you have . . . made," and urged her not to feel that "we love you . . . any the less because we are driven to the opinion which Father expressed in his cable."

Pierpont engineered a change of companions a month later, bringing Louisa to join Fanny for the winter and taking Juliet home. He could not, however, consign his wife to permanent exile. When she finally returned to New York in the autumn of 1892, after nearly two years abroad, the discord in their marriage was an open secret. Jack told his brother-in-law Ned Grew that a recent dinner party had been "quite a success. . . . Papa & Mamma are behaving with strict propriety"—which implied that often they did not.

In New York, Fanny recorded Edith's visits in her diaries, but said nothing about the fact that "P." constantly arrived and left with his beautiful friend. Everyone was treating the presence of Mrs. Randolph with studied equanimity, and Morgan included enough other people in his parties to muffle the truth.

———

Divorce was not an option. Like his father, Pierpont regarded marriage as permanent, no matter how difficult. Not only religious vows but professional utility and social propriety bound the Morgan men to their wives. Divorce would shatter a banker's image of conservative decorum, and in the upper reaches of their late-Victorian world, a divorced woman would be an object of scandal even if she had done nothing wrong. Pierpont had too strong a sense of duty to abandon his wife to that fate and too much sense of entitlement to his own pleasures to abandon his extramarital pursuits.

People in their circle did get divorced. Alice Mason, ostracized for her "outrageous" behavior by puritanical Boston, had removed herself to Europe. And Fanny's old friend Adele Stevens—who so admired Pierpont's "grand noble scale"—left her husband in 1886 to travel in France with the Marquis Charles Maurice Camille de Talleyrand-Périgord. She sold her Newport and New York houses, and divorced Fred Stevens on grounds of nonsupport—an odd claim, as she had brought the fortune to their marriage. (Colonel Oliver Hazard Payne bought the Stevens mansion at 57th Street and Fifth Avenue for $600,000, and gave it to his sister, Flora Whitney.) The Marquis divorced *his* inconvenient spouse—another American heiress, the former Elizabeth Curtis—and married Adele in January 1887. His father, the third Duc de Dino, conferred his title on the groom at Adele's request, perhaps because Bessie Curtis insisted on remaining the Marquise de Talleyrand-Périgord.*

Americans from Cape May to Bar Harbor cut Adele off, and most of her former friends sided with her first husband. Fanny told Louisa in April that Fred Stevens had not been out in society since the "bad news" of Adele's remarriage, and she was giving him a dinner: "I am glad to be the person to break the ice for him." She also stayed in touch with Adele's daughter, her namesake, and urged Louisa to see the girl in Paris, but "do *not* accept any invitation to lunch or dinner or *anything* from her Mother." Louisa replied, "Of course I should not think of going to Aunt Adele—even if Papa allowed me to. I doubt if she asks me though."

Her "Papa" would probably have allowed her to see Adele. Like his own father, he took a more European view of other people's private lives than many of their compatriots did, and had little use for bourgeois convention. Both Morgan men carried on substantial affairs outside their marriages, and were not overly concerned with Old Testament Thou Shalt Nots.

Whatever strictures Pierpont imposed on his associates had to do not with morality but with discretion. In a famous, probably apocryphal anecdote that

---

* *The New York Times* on January 27 described society's "utmost sensation and surprise" at Mrs. Stevens's desertion of her family for "a Frenchman of no particular attractions, being short and rather stout and decidedly ordinary looking, and being moreover supposed to be deeply in debt." Not quite as inconsequential as the *Times* made him sound, Adele's Duke was the author of several books, a discerning collector of armor, and a descendant of Comte Edmond de Talleyrand-Périgord, nephew of the statesman-diplomat Talleyrand.

nonetheless captures the essence of his attitude, he is said to have called a young partner at the bank into his office one day and reproved him for having been caught in an adulterous affair.

"But sir," objected the sinner in surprise, "you and the other partners do the same thing yourselves behind closed doors."

"Young man"—Morgan shot him an icy stare—"*that* is what doors are for!"

He had the resources to close all the doors he liked—on his yacht, in European hotels, at the houses of friends—and he surrounded himself with people he trusted not to talk. A hundred years later, the nonagenarian offspring of his confidants refuse to discuss this aspect of his life. Smiling discreetly, they honor the code of silence required for his friendship with their parents. If he tried to reconcile his religious beliefs with his violations of the Seventh Commandment, reflects one, it would have been "with his tongue in his cheek—amused at the fact that he could do naughty things and still be part of the church. He felt perfectly justified in whatever he chose to do."

Still, people who were not bound to him by friendship did talk, others wrote things down, and Morgan himself left traces he never thought anyone would find. Given his growing prominence and the curiosity of the public and press, it would have been impossible to conceal his affairs altogether. And though he firmly shut the doors, there was nothing furtive in his conduct.

Gossip exaggerated his exploits. People talked of illegitimate children, prostitutes in Westchester apartments, an affair with the actress Maxine Elliott.* One legend, crediting him with Priapean prowess, said he built New York's Lying-In Hospital to take care of all the pregnancies he was responsible for—which probably amused him: there was a less lurid explanation for his connection with the Lying-In.

Edith Randolph introduced him to several of her friends in the early 1890s, among them an attractive obstetrician named James W. Markoe. Morgan had always taken a special interest in maternity and childbearing—when Fanny was miserable at the beginning of her unwanted fifth pregnancy, he had wished "I could do it for you." He quickly made a friend of Dr. Markoe, who had earned his MD at the College of Physicians and Surgeons in New York, trained in surgery at New York Hospital, and studied obstetrics at Munich's Frauenklinic.

At P&S, as at other American medical schools, obstetrics students attended didactic lectures and "never came within a mile of touching a patient," re-

---

* Morgan allegedly built her a theater and gave her financial advice, while she made him redesign the rooms on his yacht. Given the resistance Mr. Tams encountered to altering *Corsair,* this last detail is difficult to credit. Maxine Elliott's niece/biographer found no evidence of the reputed romance, and Morgan himself left none. When Lady Sackville asked him about the stories in 1912, he denied even knowing Miss Elliott: he had, he said, spoken to her exactly twice. In public, he told the press: "The only interest I have in Maxine Elliott's theatre is that I'd like to get a free ticket on opening night."

called one of Markoe's associates. Most never even witnessed childbirth as part of their training. Midwives handled nearly half the births in New York in the eighties, and Markoe had learned obstetrics on manikins. In Germany in 1887, however, he and a colleague, Samuel W. Lambert, went into women's homes to observe and assist at deliveries, and returned to New York determined to make experience with childbirth mandatory for American obstetrical students.

When P&S rejected their proposal to set up a clinic for outpatient care and physician training, Markoe and Lambert went ahead on their own. In 1890 they opened a midwifery dispensary in a tenement at 312 Broome Street in lower Manhattan for immigrant women who had no access to medical care. They raised the initial money themselves, and studied the example of the Boston Lying-In.

Shortly after the dispensary opened, Markoe invited local policemen in for supper. They thought he was running an abortion clinic and looking to pay them off, but once they heard his plans and toured the facilities, they sent neighborhood women for free obstetrical services. Except in complicated cases, the births still took place in the women's homes, with doctors and students attending. The dispensary treated 199 patients its first year, 955 the next, and 2,582 in 1892, when it expanded into a second building next door. Just as Markoe and Lambert had hoped, it also succeeded as a training facility: in 1893, 360 students completed its two-week course in clinical obstetrics.

Edith Randolph helped run the dispensary kitchen, giving out milk, cereal, bread, coffee, and tea to young mothers, most of them unmarried. At some point she brought Morgan to meet Dr. Markoe. The two men liked each other immediately, and before long the obstetrician agreed to become the banker's personal physician. Since medical specialties were just being established in the late-nineteenth century, doctors who treated diseases "peculiar to women" often had general practices on the side. Markoe saw male patients, including New York City firemen, in his private office after hours at home.

One night in 1893, Markoe arrived late at a dinner party uptown, having spent most of the day performing a rare Caesarean section. Morgan questioned him about the operation in detail. Markoe was less concerned about the surgical procedure than about the woman herself, who had no money and needed more sophisticated care than the dispensary could provide. Morgan told him to get her whatever she needed: he would pay the bills.

In the wake of this incident, doctor and financier agreed that the work of the clinic ought to be expanded, and Morgan made an extraordinary offer: You give up your private practice, he told Dr. Markoe, and I'll pay for a new hospital and your salary. That way, you can give your time entirely to the hospital and to me. "Mr. Morgan could be very domineering," recalled Dr. Markoe's daughter, rubbing an imaginary point under her thumb in illustration, "and Pa was devoted to him."

Morgan lent Markoe $90,000 in 1893 to buy land for a hospital site at Second Avenue between 17th and 18th streets, a block from St. George's Church. Four years later he gave $1 million for the new building, then $350,000 more, and sent Markoe abroad to study hospital construction. After the New York Lying-In opened its doors in 1902, Morgan contributed roughly $100,000 a year to its operating costs, and made up the annual deficit for the rest of his life. Someone with a sense of humor installed a sign over the maternity hospital's entrance that said PUSH.

The bargain was vintage Morgan: he chose a highly competent, activist expert, and backed him unconditionally. Both parties got what they wanted. Markoe had a first-class modern hospital, which consolidated women's health-care services under one roof, united the previously separate fields of obstetrics and gynecology, and provided women with the best available treatment, while giving medical students and obstetrical nurses excellent training and facilities for research. Moreover, by helping establish childbirth as the province of (male) doctors rather than (female) midwives, he was part of a larger movement to professionalize obstetrics, raising its stature in the medical world. Morgan, for his part, had the pleasure of endowing a project that fascinated him and observing its progress at firsthand; he also secured the exclusive professional care of an intimate friend. He addressed the doctor in letters as "My dear Jim," and signed himself "Devotedly yours."

Markoe treated Morgan's depressions as well as his head colds. According to the doctor's daughter, "whenever Mr. Morgan achieved something tremendous, he felt simply great—at the absolute top of the world. Then at other times he would go into these terrible blue slumps, and Pa was the only person who could cheer him up. A call would come, often late at night or early in the morning, for him to go down to see Mr. Morgan. In the early years, a carriage would be sent to fetch him, later a car and chauffeur. Pa would go down to 219 and work on [Morgan], tell him stories, make him laugh. I remember him coming home one day saying, 'Whew! *That* was a session!' " The content of these "sessions" remained private.

Markoe probably provided his eminent patient with contraceptive expertise and perhaps on occasion with abortions. Edith Randolph was young enough to bear more children in the 1890s, and she managed not to.*

* For all the Malthusian talk about self-control and "moral restraint" in the nineteenth century, contraceptives had been available to people with access to medical information for a long time. In the nineteenth century B.C., an Egyptian papyrus listed three prescriptions for vaginal contraceptive suppositories, and artificial means of preventing conception were discussed by medical writers in ancient Greece and Rome. Prophylactic sheaths made of linen, animal intestines, and skins were said to have been invented by an English Dr. Condom (or Conton) early in the eighteenth century. The American inventor Charles Goodyear vulcanized rubber in 1839, and five years later took out a patent on a contraceptive for men. By 1850, adults in the

Morgan turned to various kinds of men for help over the years—business colleagues, lawyers, nautical experts, art dealers, scholars, clergymen, physicians—but Dr. Markoe was the one he came to rely on most intimately. Like Dr. Rainsford, Markoe was devoting his primary professional energies to the poor—people whom Morgan, according to his son-in-law, "really did not understand." The banker had more personal interest in Markoe's pregnant mothers than he did in Rainsford's urban slum dwellers: taking care of women, especially sick women (pregnancy at the time was considered a kind of illness), had been a constant theme in his own life, and in a curious way he identified with women's suffering—he had experienced Memie's symptoms when he went abroad a few years after her death, and had always been, like his mother and Fanny, vulnerable to physical ailments and depression. Markoe's work, however, dealt with the miraculous business of childbirth, not with the "nerves" and consumption that had caused such pain in the Morgan family.

In taking care of people he liked, most of what Morgan could provide was material. What he wanted in return was of another order. The two men to whom he was closest had chosen professions—one medical, the other spiritual—that tended to human suffering. In exchange for being able to depend on Markoe and Rainsford in his own moments of need, he underwrote their attentions to others.

A fourth member of the Morgan-Randolph-Markoe circle in the early 1890s was a slender beauty with sculptured cheekbones named Annette Wetmore. She had married one of her cousins, William Boerum Wetmore (which made her Annette Wetmore Wetmore), but he turned out to be a "bad lot," recalled one of her daughters—a gambler, idler, and bully. Annette left her husband in the early nineties, taking their three children to the Shelburne, Vermont, farm of Lila (Vanderbilt) and William Seward Webb. In 1892 she divorced Wetmore, whom the family referred to from then on as "the unmentionable."

Even under these extreme circumstances, New York society frowned on divorce, and Mrs. Wetmore took refuge among a few close friends. Morgan gave her financial advice and loans. Many people said he fell in love with her as well. Perhaps he did, but in 1894 Annette Wetmore married James Markoe.

United States and Europe could buy rubber condoms and pessaries. Morgan would have had recourse to medical advice, books, and birth control technology all his life.

The Drexel Building at 23 Wall Street.
(Archives of The Pierpont Morgan Library, New York)

Chapter 16

CONSOLIDATIONS

In early July of 1890, while Morgan toured the Lake District with Edith Randolph, Congress passed an antitrust law.

Political opposition to the railroads and giant industrial corporations had intensified throughout the eighties, and legislatures in twenty-one states and territories, mainly in the South and West, had outlawed agreements to fix prices and limit output. For both legal and practical reasons, however, the states were significantly limited in their ability to regulate business conducted across state lines, and the 1887 Interstate Commerce Act was concerned exclusively with railroads; it did not apply to industrial concerns such as Standard Oil, Carnegie Steel, or the lead-smelting, sugar-refining, and whiskey-distilling monopolies. Both political parties wrote antitrust provisions into their platforms in the 1888 election campaign, and that August, Senate Finance Committee chairman John Sherman—shortly after losing the Republican presidential nomination—introduced a bill to outlaw trusts. He proposed to prohibit all agreements between individuals or companies that prevented "full and free competition" or raised consumer prices.

The word "trust" technically referred to one of the legal mechanisms used during this period for bringing competing companies under common control—the transfer of their stock to a single board of trustees—but the term had come to stand for big-business consolidations in general, and for everything about concentrated economic power that Americans hated and feared.* The radical changes that had taken place in the U.S. political economy in just one generation gave new force to the long-standing conflict over the nature and direction of American democracy.

On one side were those who saw the market dominance and ruthless efficiency of the new corporate giants as a sinister threat to individual liberty. Railroads and industrial leviathans were charging monopoly prices, driving competitors out of business, removing control of local enterprise from resident communities, ignoring labor's demands for fair wages and humane working conditions, and earning enormous amounts of money. Flagrant abuses of corporate power, such as the rebates Standard Oil exacted from railroads for carrying its rivals' oil and the steady flows of commercial cash that purchased political favors, substantiated the popular conviction that big business violated the natural order of exchange in a free society.

On the other side were those who saw the natural order of things in a different light. The United States was no longer a Jeffersonian nation of farmers and small producers working in "perfect" competitive markets. Post–Civil War revolutions in transportation, communications, and industrial productivity had created the largest domestic marketplace, with the richest natural resources, in the world. Mass production and distribution facilities were radically increasing operating efficiency as well as bringing down manufacturing costs and consumer prices. With no governmental guidance or regulation, private enterprise was opening up jobs and fostering social mobility on an unprecedented scale, and private bankers were raising previously unimaginable amounts of money. The industrialists and financiers who were shaping this new economic order regarded it as natural and inevitable, and wanted freedom to continue. Some of them opposed federal regulation simply to protect their power and profits. Others resisted it out of the conviction that "the politicians" had little understanding of modern capital markets.

The conflict did not sort out along traditional party lines. It was the Republican Senator Sherman, Wall Street's former ally, who denounced the power of the trusts as "a kingly prerogative inconsistent with our form of government," and went on: "If anything is wrong, this is wrong. If we will not endure a king

---

* The nineteenth-century uses of the financial term "trust," according to the economic historians Thomas R. Navin and Marian V. Sears, include the following: "If a man trusted another, he placed his money in a *trust fund* in the other man's care. When the other man established a company to handle a number of trust funds, he called it a *trust company*. . . . When the owners of a group of industrial enterprises surrendered their securities to a committee of so-called trustees, they called the resulting combination a 'trust.' . . . Laws set up to deal with large industrial combinations, of which the 'trusts' were the earliest examples, were called *antitrust laws*. There is still another use of the word *trust* to mean any large industrial combination, but this use is careless and inappropriate."

as a political power we should not endure a king over the production, transportation, and sale of any of the necessaries of life. If we would not submit to an emperor, we should not submit to an autocrat of trade, with power to prevent competition, and to fix the price of any commodity."

In the other camp, Democratic Senator Orville Platt of Connecticut declared that the Sherman bill proceeded on "the false assumption that all competition is beneficent to the country," and Representative John W. Stewart (Dem. Ga.) thought it "just as necessary to restrict competition as it is to restrict combination." The chairman of the House Judiciary Committee, George F. Edmunds (Rep. Vt.), said the term "monopoly" did not apply to the ingenious Texas cattle rancher who, through "superior skill and intelligence . . . got the whole business," even if it allowed him to charge monopoly prices—which seemed to say that the crucial issues were not restriction of competition or consumer price but optimal efficiency and fair play.

After two years of debate, Congress passed a heavily amended Sherman Antitrust Act on July 2, 1890—unanimously in the House, 52 to 1 in the Senate. Titled "A bill to protect trade and commerce against unlawful restraints and monopolies," it did not mention competition or consumer prices, but outlawed "every contract, combination in the form of trust or otherwise, or conspiracy, in restraint of trade or commerce," and made it a crime to "monopolize, or attempt to monopolize, or combine or conspire with any other person or persons, to monopolize any part of trade or commerce among the several States, or with foreign nations."

This vague wording left almost everything to the construction of the judiciary, and initiated a century of argument about the economics, politics, implementation, and aims of government regulation. Even supporters of the bill disagreed as to whether the real nature of the problem was too much competition or not enough. Some thought all trade restraints should be ruled illegal, including the hypothetical Texas cattle monopoly; others wanted to outlaw only "unfair" ones—but who would decide what was fair, and fair to whom? Was *bigness* per se bad? What should the government regulate—price-fixing? mergers? cartels? vertical integration? destruction of small firms? What kinds of agreements were actually restraints of trade, and what kinds of acts related to monopoly should be ruled illegal?

———

Morgan left no record of his response to the Antitrust Act or to Senator Sherman's "defection." In a mix of what would later be regarded as conservative and liberal views, he believed in the efficacy of industrial consolidation and also in the need for *administered* markets, but had no faith in the government's ability to do the administering. The country, in his view, ought to leave control of its commercial and financial resources to qualified experts. He told a friend in 1912 that the consolidation of industry was "the only thing to do": the government was "crazy to fight it. That's because they are politicians instead of statesmen."

An unlikely figure agreed. The young journalist Walter Lippmann, looking back in 1912, thought wise statesmanship should have prepared the country for the trust movement of the eighties: "Here was an economic tendency of revolutionary significance," Lippmann wrote, "the organization of business in a way that was bound to change the outlook of the whole nation." The worldwide movement toward industrial concentration had been "made possible at first by mechanical inventions, fostered by the disastrous experiences of competition, and accepted by business men through contagion and imitation." It had "vast potentialities for good and evil—all it wanted was harnessing and directing. But the new thing did not fit into the little outlines and verbosities which served as a philosophy for our political hacks. So they gaped at it and let it run wild, called it names, threw stones at it. And by that time the force was too big for them."*

Morgan had regarded himself as statesman without portfolio—as taking a larger view than the men Lippmann called "political hacks"—in helping to refund the Civil War debt and put the United States back on the gold standard in the seventies, and in safeguarding the country's railroads and international credit in the eighties. Like the men who gathered to honor his father at Delmonico's in 1877, he assumed that his financial expertise conferred political prerogatives, and that his large concerns took precedence over the interests of people who opposed him—especially with regard to the struggle over the currency, which had resurfaced in the late eighties as proponents of "easy" money lobbied the government to resume coining silver.

The combination of monetary stringency imposed by the gold standard after 1879 and explosive growth in national productivity had driven prices steadily down and the dollar's value up. This long-term deflation was good for wealthy people who owned dollars and dollar-based assets, and hard on borrowers such as farmers and small-scale entrepreneurs. Debtors watched their incomes decline as they had to repay loans with money worth *more* than what they had borrowed. An inflationary increase in the money supply would reverse that

---

* That Lippmann later revised his views is characteristic of this controversial field. Harvard Law professor Philip Areeda, summing up a distinguished career in antitrust law, said not long before he died in 1995: "Like all fields of law, antitrust ebbs and flows, sometimes with greater populist concern for protecting small firms from big ones. At other times, the emphasis is on economic efficiency. The major change in the field has been in the growing awareness that business affairs are more complex than they might seem initially, and that motivations for what initially appears to be a restraint of trade might in fact be a more subtle way to promote competition."

painful trend, making dollars easier to borrow and over time worth *less*. It seemed to agrarians in the South and West that Wall Street plutocrats had taken silver out of circulation in the "Crime of '73" in order to squeeze powerless have-nots for their own private gain.

Throughout the eighties, Farmers' Alliance groups—successors to the Granger movement—demanded the remonetization of silver, and at the end of the decade they joined with the Knights of Labor to form a National Farmers' Alliance and Industrial Union. This group set up marketing cooperatives, and formulated a broad-based political program that called for free coinage of silver, a graduated income tax, greater regulation of railroad, telegraph, and telephone lines, the abolition of national banks, and federal warehouses for storing crops until market conditions improved. In the summer of 1890 Alliance men in Kansas founded a People's Party, which, with agrarian Democrats, scored impressive victories in the midterm elections that fall. In October, Congress passed a second law bearing John Sherman's name—a Silver Purchase Act requiring the Treasury to buy 4.5 million ounces of silver a month.

To Morgan the idea of reintroducing silver currency was about as welcome as a biblical plague. Foreigners held over $3 billion worth of American securities in 1890—roughly ten times the federal government's annual budget. They stood to lose heavily if the United States devalued the dollar by increasing the money supply, and they would not sit idly by to watch. Throughout the summer of 1890 nervous British investors, anticipating the impact of silver, sold off American securities and shipped gold home.

Railroad rate wars in the West were also eroding securities values. Early in November, Union Pacific Railroad president Charles Francis Adams reported "a regular financial gale blowing in the street, and, if not a panic, something very like one." His hugely indebted UP led the declines. Wall Street suspected Jay Gould, who had been ousted from the UP board in 1885, of driving down the price of its stock. On November 11, the "gale" turned into a hurricane with the failure of three brokerage houses and a bank.

Four days later, cables from London announced that Baring Brothers had been ruined by the collapse of a speculative bubble in Argentina. Charles F. Adams had been borrowing short-term money from Barings to keep the Union Pacific afloat, and the London bank's failure heralded his own. Railroad stock prices collapsed. Jay Gould bought up huge blocks of shares, and told Morgan on November 17 that he wanted control of the UP. On the nineteenth, a defeated Adams gave it to him.*

In mid-December, Morgan once again summoned western railroad officials to meet at his house. The trade group organized there two years earlier, with

---

* The Bank of England led the rescue of the Barings, who shared the Argentina bond market with the Morgans after 1890.

the blessing of the ICC, had failed to stop rate and traffic wars, and rates had continued to decline: at the end of 1890 railroad officials reported net earnings down 30 percent. This second meeting at 219 produced a "simple but comprehensive" plan for a new Advisory Board made up of the president and a director of each road, to maintain rates and arbitrate disputes.

Morgan proudly told the press: "I am thoroughly satisfied with the results accomplished. The public has not yet appreciated the magnitude of the work. Think of it—all the competitive traffic of the roads west of Chicago and St. Louis placed in the control of about thirty men! It is the most important agreement made by the railroads in a long time, and it is as strong as could be desired."

RAILROAD KINGS FORM A GIGANTIC TRUST, announced the *Herald* the next day. The public's failure to appreciate "the magnitude of the work" did not detract from Morgan's sense of purpose. Writing to railroad officers who had not attended these meetings, he explained that he had been prompted to act by the recent "demoralization" in rates and the "shrinkage" in stock values—and also by political opposition in the West: "The granger legislatures doubtless have power for injury," he told T. B. Blackstone of the Chicago & Alton road, "and it may be that they will use it, but it should not necessarily follow that well-considered, business-like harmony among the railroads should add materially to the spirit of hostility which may be exhibited."

Morgan genuinely did not think reasonable people would object to what seemed to him so constructive—the imposition of "well-considered, business-like harmony" on the national arteries of transport. His conviction that he not only was right but was acting in the national interest extended even to using the new agreement for political ends: he told Mr. Blackstone that the Advisory Board, "representing to a degree never before secured in one body ownership of the properties, should I think be able to accomplish much good for the railways by co-operating from time to time in all matters of joint interest, including possibly that of threatened legislation."

His optimism was misplaced. When the Western Advisory Board, like all its predecessors, proved unable to enforce its sanctions, Morgan finally gave up on the tactics of "gentlemen's agreements" and cartel control.

———

The political struggles of the early nineties generated a range of efforts to regulate industry and finance. In the spring of 1891, when a bill to impose state supervision on private banking came before the New York legislature, Morgan sent a note to his old friend Vice President Levi P. Morton in Washington. "My dear Mr. Morton," he began: "I suppose the objectionable features of the Stein Bill, which has been introduced at Albany, and on which there is to be a hearing in Committee about the middle of next week, are known to you." The bill would, Morgan explained, require private bankers to make deposits with a state banking department, take out certificates in exchange, and be subject to state supervision, and he was writing "to suggest that—through Mr. Platt or otherwise—you doubtless could prevent the passage of such a measure. It is needless for me to say that it would be very harmful to all private banking interests here."

The New York State Assembly's committee on banking reported twice in favor of the bill that spring, but three weeks after Morgan wrote to Morton the measure was "laid aside" and not proposed again. Whether or not the Vice President, through Boss Platt, helped quash the bill, there would, for the moment, be no state regulation of private banks in New York.

———

Jack came down from Boston to join Drexel, Morgan in January 1891, shortly after his wedding. He and Jessie rented quarters in Murray Hill while they built a house near his parents, at 8 East 36th Street.

Drexel, Morgan in 1891 had four active partners (Pierpont, J. Hood Wright, George Bowdoin, and Charles Coster), a clerical staff of eighty, and no typewriters; only Pierpont had a secretary; the office had a private telegraph line to Drexel & Co., and got its first telephone in 1886. A long-standing rule that all papers, checks, letters, and bills had to be signed by a partner meant that the four senior men were constantly interrupted. Jack eased their load by signing papers as he learned the business.

He reported to the traveling Fanny in the summer of 1891 that his father had been " 'saving the community again' as the *Finance News* puts it." The country was recovering from the depression that followed the 1890 panic, but the Union Pacific Railroad, once again in Jay Gould's hands, was on the verge of bankruptcy, and the prospect of its failure threatened to reverse the upturn. Though Gould had lent the road $1.3 million, it wasn't enough, and he was dying. He went west in July to try cold mountain air for his consumptive lungs.

At the beginning of August the UP's worried creditors called in their loans, and the stock price plummeted on rumors of failure. Gould sent his son, George, to see Morgan. Together, the senior Morgan and the junior Gould worked out a plan for the road to offer creditors three-year 6 percent notes secured by collateral deposited with Drexel, Morgan. "Again Mr. J. P. Morgan steps in to avert a disaster," announced the *Commercial and Financial Chronicle.* "Everyone breathes easy again," Jack told Fanny on August 21, "and the railroads in the West will be able to get good business instead of fighting a bankrupt which would steal all the business there was."

Morgan had stepped in not for his own immediate profit but as custodian of the railroad industry and the recovering economy as a whole, and it was in this

context that he saw his interests as larger and higher than those of his antagonists. Jack underscored the point: "The best of it is, it is all done for nothing, except what we make in common with the other creditors, as an inducement to
them to put the plan into operation." He was thrilled to have witnessed the rescue at first hand: "I am so glad it didn't come up during my vacation."

Pierpont upgraded his son's status in the firm at the end of the year. Juliet
wrote to Fanny on New Year's Day, 1892: "The new partner of Drexel, Morgan
& Co. came home to dinner. Isn't it too beautiful and delightful to think of?"
Jack was "so pleased and proud he doesn't know whether he is on his head or
his heels." Her father seemed pleased as well: "he was going to cable you about
it but finally decided not to steal Jack's thunder."

Jessie gave birth to a son, Junius Spencer Morgan, in March 1892, and the
junior J. P. Morgans moved into their new house on 36th Street that summer.

———

At 23 Wall Street, the senior J. P. Morgan worked in a large back office with
glass walls and an open door, in plain sight of his partners and clerical staff.
Close associates found him exacting but congenial; outsiders often found him
terrifying.

Lincoln Steffens, a young reporter for Villard's *Evening Post*, did a stint on
Wall Street in the early nineties, and years later recalled asking the president of
another bank to put a question to Morgan.

"Not on your life," said the banker.

"Why not?" asked Steffens.

"You try it yourself and see."

Steffens went down to 23 Wall Street, walked into the famous glass-walled
office, and stopped before the large, neat desk where Morgan was examining a
sheet of figures. "I stood for two or three long minutes," he wrote in his autobiography, "while the whole bank seemed to stop work to watch me, and he did
not look up; he was absorbed, he was sunk, in those figures. He was so alone
with himself and his mind that when he did glance up he did not see me; his
eyes were looking inward. . . ." Soon, without registering the presence of his
visitor, Morgan dropped his eyes back to the page, and Steffens edged out.

As he left the bank one of the partners asked him what had happened.
"Nothing," replied Steffens. "He didn't even see me."

"You're lucky," volunteered the partner with a laugh. "You have to call him
to wake him up. If you had said, 'Mr. Morgan,' he would have come to. And
then—"

"What would have happened?"

"Oh, then you would have seen—an explosion."

On another occasion, Steffens did interrupt the Morgan trance. The bank had sent the *Post* a statement about a recent bond issue that the city editor found incomprehensible. He assigned Steffens to find out what it meant.

The reporter headed back to the bank in high trepidation. His account of this event years later resembles many of the stories told about Morgan, in which a brave young Daniel marches into the lion's den, faces him down, and triumphs. That so many people felt called upon to report standing up to him this way was a measure of Morgan's stature. Meeting him, certain men were inclined to measure their prowess, as it were, against his, when his was universally acknowledged to be gigantic. Intellectuals in particular tended to belittle him, especially in retrospect—to be at best baffled by and at worst contemptuous of a sensibility so alien to their own.

Steffens, according to Steffens, once again walked into the glass-walled office and across to the immaculate desk, and this time the banker looked up. "He threw himself back in his chair so hard," recalled Steffens, "that I thought he would tip over."

" 'Mr. Morgan,' I said as brave as I was afraid, 'what does this statement mean?' and I threw the paper down before him.

" 'Mean!' he exclaimed. His eyes glared, his great red nose seemed to me to flash and darken, flash and darken. Then he roared. 'Mean! It means what it says. I wrote it myself, and it says what I mean.'

" 'It doesn't say anything—straight,' I blazed.

"He sat back there, flashing and rumbling; then he clutched the arms of his chair, and I thought he was going to leap at me. I was so scared that I defied him.

" 'Oh, come now, Mr. Morgan,' I said, 'you may know a lot about figures and finance, but I'm a reporter, and I know as much as you do about English. And that statement isn't English.'

"That was the way to treat him, I was told afterward. And it was in that case. He glared at me a moment more, the fire went out of his face, and he leaned forward over the bit of paper and said very meekly, 'What's the matter with it?'

"I said I thought it would be clearer in two sentences instead of one and I read it aloud so, with a few other verbal changes.

" 'Yes,' he agreed, 'that is better. You fix it.'

"I fixed it under his eyes, he nodded, and I, whisking it away, hurried back to the office. They told me in the bank afterward that 'J.P.' sat watching me go out of the office, then rapped for [one of his partners] and asked what my name was, where I came from, and said, 'Knows what he wants, and—and—gets it.' "

Steffens's artful story amounts to a lesson in how to treat an intimidating tycoon as well as a tribute to the author's own skill and courage, since he reduces the "great man" to meek respect. (Never mind that the bank's partners never called their senior "J.P."—always "Mr. Morgan.") The portrait also captures several things it does not highlight. For all his imperious force, Morgan was surprisingly flexible, especially in relation to people who had competence he lacked. Much of the time, as in this sketch, he was inept with language—the instrument of Steffens's expertise. Of more consequence than Morgan's acceptance of journalistic help is how little his power had to do with words: his authority—in his office, over railroads, in the world's capital markets—came not from what he said but from what he did.

———

When Junius Morgan noted in 1887 that the United States had the best market in the world for its own "high-priced securities," patterns of American investment were shifting. For most of Junius's career, people with money to invest in the United States had bought real estate, New England textile stocks, and railroad bonds. By the end of the eighties, however, the railroads' huge demand for capital had declined, and investors were looking to other kinds of enterprises for profitable returns. There was as yet no financial market for "industrial" securities—the term did not come into use until 1889, to describe the stocks and bonds of companies involved in manufacturing, distribution, extraction, and processing.

There were relatively few industrial concerns worth more than $10 million by 1889, while the ten largest railroads had a net worth of over $100 million each (led by the giant Pennsylvania, at over $200 million). Still, almost as much capital had been invested in industry as in railroads: the 1890 census estimated the fixed and current assets in manufacturing alone—leaving out distribution, extraction, and processing—at $6.5 billion; for railroads, the figure was $10 billion. Most of the industrial firms were privately held, and investors considered them risky. With relatively little demand, "industrial" shares sold at about three times earnings, while reputable railroad stocks sold for seven to ten times earnings. Railroad securities had been trading on organized public exchanges for decades; they brought higher prices because of the greater liquidity and lower risk involved.

Although spectacularly successful industry leaders such as Standard Oil and Carnegie Steel generated so much income that they never had to turn to capital markets the way railroad builders did, less dominant firms had trouble raising money for expansion in the absence of an industrial securities exchange. Some borrowed short-term from commercial banks, hoping to repay the loans out of profits—which worked when the economy was booming, but not when it turned down. In the capital-intensive electrical industry, among others, trusts had evolved partly in response to this shortage of funds, as managers tried to secure steady supplies of income through consolidation.

In 1884 the Dow Jones Company, a financial news agency founded two years earlier, began to publish the average closing price of several actively traded stocks considered representative of the broader market. This first average, which appeared in a two-page *Customer's Afternoon Letter*, precursor to *The Wall Street Journal*, was made up of nine railroads, plus Western Union and Pacific Mail Steamship (it had been Pierpont's purchase of Pacific Mail shares in 1858 that elicited a paternal tirade against speculation). Conservative investors were not ready to venture out of railroads into industrial securities; first, they wanted assurances about quality and safety, as well as the liquidity afforded by public exchanges. At the end of the decade, Morgan would provide warranties and other mechanisms to open up this new investment field, but in the early nineties he remained preoccupied with railroads, and moved into the industrial marketplace with extreme, Junius-like caution.

He was first drawn in this direction through his connection with the Edison business. By the late eighties, Edison had two hundred central power stations and fifteen hundred isolated plants in operation across the United States. Morgan no longer needed a private generator behind his house in New York: electrical power for 219 came from the circuits of the Illuminating Company. Edison's was not the only entry in the electrical-industry sweepstakes, however. Like all the promising enterprises of the Gilded Age, this one stimulated fierce competition.

Some of Edison's rivals devised systems of their own, others adapted or copied his ideas. The wizard of Menlo Park spent years in court fighting over who invented what when, and once complained that taking out a patent was simply "an invitation to a lawsuit." He also maintained that his electrical inventions had brought him no profits—only forty years of litigation. In fact they made him a millionaire several times over, but he never managed to hold on to his gains.

His low-voltage, direct-current system worked well in densely populated cities, where the high costs of copper conductors could be spread out among hundreds of customers, but it proved prohibitively expensive for long-distance use. When a transformer patented in England in 1883 made it possible for high-voltage, alternating current carried over long-distance lines to be safely "stepped down" for ordinary household use, Edison's competitors responded. George Westinghouse bought the American rights to the AC transformer, and used alternating current for incandescence, industrial motors, and street trolleys. The Thomson-Houston Electric Company in Lynn, Massachusetts, expanded to produce and sell both kinds of current and a wide range of products—arc lights, motors, trolley systems, generators, and transformers. Run by a brilliant manager named Charles A. Coffin, Thomson-Houston secured financing for this expansion through the Boston bankers Lee, Higginson, & Co.

Edison dismissed alternating current as inefficient (it lost power in transformation), expensive, and dangerous: he electrocuted stray dogs and cats to demonstrate AC's lethal power, and coined a verb for the electrical execution of criminals—"to Westinghouse." Convinced that his lower-cost DC system would prevail on its own merits, he turned his attention to new projects.

Henry Villard, an early Edison backer, had returned from Germany in the fall of 1886 eager to build an international electrical-industry cartel. He had made a careful study of Germany's leading electrical firms, the vertically integrated Siemens & Halske and Allgemeine Elektrizitäts Gesellschaft, and advised Edison in the winter of 1888 to consolidate his companies on the German model. The inventor wavered, torn between his desire for autonomy and his need for outside capital. His colleague E. H. Johnson promised that the merger would be good for their interests and bad for the competition: "We shall speedily have the biggest Edison organization in the world with abundant capital when goodbye Westinghouse et al."

In May of 1889, with the help of Charles Coster and the backing of the Deutsche Bank, Villard combined the original Edison Electric Light Company and several manufacturing concerns into Edison General Electric, incorporated in New Jersey and capitalized at $12 million. New Jersey had just passed a law that allowed corporations to own controlling interests in the corporations of other states. Drexel, Morgan managed the initial $3.63 million stock offering.* The Deutsche Bank took the largest share—62.2 percent, or $2,259,000. Morgan's firm kept $600,000, gave $400,000 to Kuhn, Loeb, and divided the rest among people connected to the Edison business; none of the stock was offered to the general public. Villard, with the blessings of the Deutsche Bank, appointed himself president of Edison General Electric, put Edison's personal secretary, Samuel Insull, in charge of daily business, and began to centralize operations with headquarters in Schenectady, New York.

Edison did not have much to do with the new concern. He was preoccupied with his phonograph and an electromagnetic machine that would separate iron from low-grade ore. Thomson-Houston, meanwhile, had continued to expand: it built twice as many central power stations as Edison General, earned twice the profit, dominated the street railway business, and hired the best sales force in the industry.

At the end of 1890, Villard proposed to end the industry's "ruinous" competition through price- and output-agreements. Westinghouse flatly turned him down. Coffin at Thomson-Houston made a counterproposal—to consolidate

---

* Villard and Coster set the values at which constituent companies were brought in. The Morgan bank and its partners had invested over $1 million in the Light Company since 1878, and Coster made sure that EELC shareholders were amply rewarded in the reorganization: each $100 share was exchanged for new stock and trust certificates worth $266.66.

Edison General and Thomson-Houston into a single corporate unit, since building integrated facilities to take advantage of central distribution networks, economies of scale, and strategic, long-range planning required such enormous amounts of money that it was wasteful for similar properties to compete. In this kind of capital-intensive industry, consolidation could eliminate duplication as well as price- and patent-wars; it could also concentrate major product lines in the best-equipped plants, combine sales forces and distribution systems, and secure a steady stream of income for research, development, and expansion.

Morgan, busy trying to control railroad competition for exactly these reasons—greater efficiency and stability, an end to price wars, adequate profits—did not at first see the advantage of consolidating the electrical firms. When Coffin's banker Henry Lee Higginson suggested a merger early in 1891, Morgan wrote back: "The Edison system affords us all the use of time and capital that I think desirable to use in one channel. If, as would seem to be the case, you have the control of the Thomson-Houston, we will see which will make the best result. I do not see myself how the two things can be brought together."

A year later he had changed his mind—perhaps because Thomson-Houston was winning the marketplace war. Coffin bragged that he was "knocking the stuffing out of them all along the line." Morgan wrote to Higginson's associate T. Jefferson Coolidge in March of 1892: "I entirely agree with you that it is desirable to bring about closer management between the two companies."

Edison hated the idea of cooperating with his enemies, and began selling his holdings in Edison General Electric as the Boston and New York bankers worked out terms for consolidation. He and Villard expected EGE to take over Thomson-Houston, but the architects of the merger decided on just the opposite plan: Thomson-Houston, clearly the stronger, better-managed company, had earned 50 percent more per share than EGE in 1891. Villard resigned, and later said he disapproved of the whole thing.

Morgan told Coolidge in March that Villard's resignation would take effect on April 1, and urged that Coffin "be then elected President of the Edison General Company." When the new firm was chartered in New York on April 15, 1892, however, with Coffin as president, it was called not Edison General but General Electric.

Each Edison share was converted into one share in the new company, while three Thomson-Houston shares brought five in GE. The bankers capitalized the consolidation at $50 million: $15 million went to the Edison stockholders, $18 million to Thomson-Houston's, and $17 million (in stock) into the GE treasury. Drexel, Morgan underwrote the company's first security offering—$4 million of 5 percent convertible bonds, sold entirely to the stockholders. Morgan and Coster took seats on the GE board, as did Higginson, Coolidge, and Edison. Furious at the removal of his name and the subordination of his interests to those of his rival, Edison attended one board meeting, then gave up in disgust to pursue other interests. Still, he continued to use the services of the Morgan Bank.*

The pioneers in the electrical industry had had to turn to financiers for funding, just as capital-intensive railroads did. As a result, bankers played a central role in shaping the financial structure of the business. Morgan had no overarching design for the Edison enterprises, and did not initiate their consolidation: making his way through uncharted territory, he was following what seemed to work. With even less intimate knowledge of this industry than he had of railroads, he relied for information on Coster, and on experts such as Edison, E. H. Johnson, and Charles Coffin.

As long as individual managers did well, he left them alone. "I always make it a rule," he told a colleague in the early nineties, "unless something is radically wrong, to follow the wishes of those who are in the management of the properties in which I am interested, and refrain from pushing my views unduly." When things did go wrong, however—when the stock market was "demoralized," or the Union Pacific about to go bankrupt, or the Edison companies losing competitive ground—he felt called on to step in.

Finding the right specialist to run a given property was crucial to its long-term success, and fourteen years after Edison invented the lightbulb, it seemed clear that he was not the man to lead the electrical industry into the twentieth century. Coffin was. As president of General Electric, Coffin proceeded to rationalize its

---

* Leaving the electrical industry behind, Edison worked on the phonograph, the iron-ore machine, a storage battery, and a motion-picture projector. He spent his GE profits on the iron-ore device. On being told what the stock would have been worth had he held on to it, he shrugged, "Well, it's all gone, but we had a hell of a good time spending it." His studio in West Orange, New Jersey, produced the world's first feature film, *The Great Train Robbery*, in 1904, and a patent-pooling movie monopoly earned the inventor $1 million a year between 1907 and 1917.

One night at a dinner in 1896, he met a young engineer from the Detroit Edison Company named Henry Ford. Ford talked about an internal combustion engine he had devised for automobiles, when most people thought the future belonged to electric cars, and Edison offered enthusiastic encouragement. Ford never forgot it. Soon, he was making millions in Detroit, and bailed Edison out every time he got the chance. When Edison's West Orange headquarters burned down in 1914, Ford gave the aging inventor a $750,000 interest-free loan. When Edison retired in 1926, Ford and the tire magnate Harvey Firestone put up $93,000 for an Edison Botanic Research Company, and quietly fed in money to keep the old man occupied. Edison called his young friend "Henry," though Ford always addressed him as "Mr. Edison"—and this unlikely pair built houses next door to each other in Fort Myers, Florida. They toured the Everglades, and went camping in the Great Smokies. In 1929, to celebrate fifty years of incandescent light, Ford built a museum of Edison's works, reconstructed the Menlo Park facilities in Dearborn, Michigan, and hosted a party that included President and Mrs. Calvin Coolidge, Marie Curie, Orville Wright, Jack Morgan, and all the original Edison employees who were still alive.

constituent companies into a model of integrated modern corporate enterprise. GE stock did not pay dividends during the long depression of the nineties—its bankers organized a syndicate to supply it with cash by buying $4 million worth of company assets, at a price far above the market value, and holding them in trust until the contraction eased. Coffin used the downturn to cut costs, diversify operations, develop new products, and build a pioneering research lab. Earnings rose again at the end of the decade, and GE and Westinghouse shared a global oligopoly with Germany's leading electrical firms until after World War II.

———

All kinds of businesses tried to put together industry-dominating combinations at the end of the nineteenth century—in sugar, flour, leather, glue, cottonseed oil, linseed oil, whiskey, thread, hay, tobacco, meatpacking, lumber, salt, ice, lead, steel—and national anxiety about "monster" trusts obscured the fact that more of them failed than succeeded. A century later, General Electric, the Standard Oil spinoffs, and U.S. Steel (as USX) remain, but National Cordage, U.S. Leather, Laclede Gas, and American Ice have long since disappeared. The process of building efficient, powerful, industry-dominating firms worked well in certain kinds of business and not in others, but the differences are clear only in retrospect.*

Neither a succession of pro-business Presidents nor the courts did much to enforce the Sherman Act in the 1890s. The federal government lost seven of

* Alfred D. Chandler, Jr., has compared the companies that grew to industry dominance with those that did not. Successful *center firms*, capital-intensive and technologically advanced, were able to take advantage of processes and equipment that made possible enormous economies of scale and scope. They integrated backward into resource acquisition and forward into product distribution; they devised managerial hierarchies to run complex operations, maximized their productive and allocative efficiency, and developed long-range planning strategies suited to their markets. By contrast, companies that were labor-intensive and relatively small did not gain significant scale economies; they tried to control prices and markets through cartels, did not integrate vertically, developed no managerial hierarchies, and paid more attention to short-term profits than to long-term planning. These *peripheral firms*, in modern economic terminology, did not grow to dominate their industries, and most did not survive.

The major center firms that evolved during the period from 1880 to 1920 had extraordinary stability and longevity: Chandler compared the two hundred largest U.S. manufacturing firms (measured in assets) for 1917 and 1973, and found that the dominant companies remained concentrated in the same areas (petroleum, chemicals, food products, transportation equipment, rubber), and were mostly the *same* companies. He found an identical pattern abroad, with large center firms providing the stable, dominant group in Germany, France, Britain, and Japan, in the same industries as in the United States. That these firms survived for so long, in spite of intense domestic and foreign competition, leads to the conclusion that it was not simply a matter of monopoly or price control, but productive efficiency and the eight cases against corporations between 1890 and 1893. In 1895 the Attorney General charged that the "Sugar Trust"—H. O. Havemeyer's American Sugar Refining Company, which had acquired the stock of four Philadelphia refineries—constituted a monopoly of production in restraint of trade. The Supreme Court dismissed the case, called *U.S.* v. *E. C. Knight,* ruling that the states, not the federal government, had jurisdiction over production, and that since the sugar industry mergers concerned *manufacture,* they did not fall under the Sherman law's strictures against restraint of interstate *commerce.*

The Court's construction of the Sherman Act in the nineties tended to rule out loose cartel associations and price-fixing agreements, but not large-scale mergers or consolidations. According to the historian Thomas Cochran, the lesson seemed to be that "buying up of rivals and merging them into one big company" was lawful, while "efforts by small companies to control markets by cartels or agreements were illegal." Ironically, the Court's proscription of certain kinds of trade restraint under the Sherman law fostered not increased competition but stronger forms of consolidation, culminating in the great merger movement of the late 1890s.

In the decade that followed the appearance of the first Dow Jones average, made up primarily of railroad stocks, the American investment landscape radically changed. Dow Jones began to publish *The Wall Street Journal* in July 1889, and when it inaugurated an industrial average in 1896, General Electric was on the list. Though it dropped out twice, in 1898 and 1901, GE is the only one of the original twelve companies that remains in the average one hundred years later.* Its cumulative performance over the century, excluding dividends and adjusted for stock splits, shows a rise of 21,999 percent, compared to the Dow Jones average performance of 10,120 percent. As of May 1997, it was the largest company in the United States, and the first to be valued at more than $200 billion.

———————

nature of the industries themselves that determined success. According to Chandler's Harvard Business School colleague Thomas K. McCraw, the striking cross-national similarities "suggest strongly that *the inherent economic and technological characteristics of given industries almost force them to assume either a center or peripheral configuration and to maintain that configuration over a long period of time. These inherent characteristics seem much more important than different legal systems or different national cultures in determining the relative size and organizational structure of firms within those industries. This is a fact of surpassing importance in assessing the historical record of big business in the United States and the conceptualization of the trust question from the late nineteenth century to the present day* [his italics]."

* The twelve stocks in the first industrial average were American Cotton Oil, American Sugar Refining, American Tobacco, Chicago Gas, Distilling & Cattle Feeding, General Electric, Laclede Gas Light, National Lead, North American (which financed street railways and gas and electric companies), Tennessee Coal, Iron & Railroad, U.S. Leather (preferred), and U.S.

———

Outside the boardroom, Morgan served as ambassador-at-large for GE. He had helped bring Edison's light to the attention of European and American capitalists in the early eighties; ten years later he recommended GE bonds to wealthy friends, and in September of 1893, when Boston was about to build a new railroad terminal—the Union (later North) Station—he sent a note to Lucius Tuttle, president of the Boston & Maine.

"I don't want favoritism," he began, with his standard disclaimer about exercising undue influence, but hoped Mr. Tuttle would defer a decision on the electrical contract for the station until they could confer, "as I think that on an impartial examination you will find that the General Electric Company can suit you better than any of its competitors. I should like to feel sure that it got a chance on equal footing with the others. If you will do what you can in this direction I should be much obliged."

There was nothing improper in this request—it was the sort of promotional work Morgan did for many of his clients, and no doubt GE would "suit" the new station at least as well as its competitors. Yet the letter came from a uniquely powerful quarter. In the fall of 1893, Morgan had just negotiated peace between Tuttle's Boston & Maine and its chief regional rival, the New Haven Railroad. This agreement to divide New England rail traffic, north and south, proved more effective than those made between western roads in 1889–90, because this time Morgan had financial control. He was a director of the New Haven, was in the process of reorganizing (yet again) the Philadelphia & Reading, which owned the Boston & Maine, and his bank was financing both roads: he had secured a $2 million loan for the Boston & Maine in 1891, and issued $13 million in New Haven securities in April 1893. When he wrote to Tuttle about the Union Station contract in September 1893, his bank was about to purchase another $6 million of Boston & Maine bonds. Yet in the end, Westinghouse supplied the pneumatic switch and signal system for the new station, and probably its electrical generators as well. The General Electric archives have no record of contracts for this station in the 1890s. Contrary to popular perception, Morgan did not dictate the decisions of his clients, even when he controlled their access to capital.

———

Rubber. Several of the original twelve companies have survived in some form into the late twentieth century, but only GE has retained its membership in the Dow and its name. The early average was unweighted: Charles Dow simply added up the closing prices of the stocks (which came to 491.28 on May 26, 1896) and divided the total by 12, for an opening average of 40.94. He continued to publish a separate railroad listing, and frequently reconfigured both averages according to the fortunes of the corporations.

—

For the 1892 election, the Republicans renominated Benjamin Harrison, but replaced Levi Morton with Whitelaw Reid, owner of the New York *Tribune*. The Democrats called Grover Cleveland back from his New York law practice to run with Adlai E. Stevenson of Illinois, grandfather of the Illinois Democrat who ran for President in the 1950s. Agrarian reformers, having scored significant victories in 1890, put up their own Populist candidate in 1892—General James B. Weaver, on a platform demanding free silver and government ownership of railroads. At the Populist convention in Omaha that July the renowned orator Ignatius Donnelly denounced the corrupt corporate "interests" to thirty minutes of applause. In November the Populists earned a million popular votes—8.5 percent—but Cleveland won the election with 5.5 million (46 percent) to Harrison's 5.2 (43 percent). He was the only President ever returned to the White House after a term out of office.

Though Morgan probably voted Republican, he had no objection to Cleveland, who had spent the last four years working with Stetson's law firm. In March 1893 Harrison returned to Indiana, Morton to New York, and Cleveland to Washington with close friends and colleagues in the Morgan camp.

The conservative Democrat had just taken the oath of office when a new stock market panic touched off one of the worst depressions in U.S. history: banks failed; factories, mills, and railroads went bankrupt; thousands of people lost jobs; and the price of farm crops, already in long-term decline, fell even further. The Dow Jones twelve-stock railroad average stood at 90 in January 1893; by July it had fallen nearly 30 percent, to 61.94.

When a friend asked Morgan about General Electric, he replied that the stock had "tumbled so I do not know what to do about executing a discretionary order." Bullish about the long run—he himself would "not hesitate" to buy GE—he was conservative with other people's money: "these industrials have so fluctuated, without regard to their dividends, that I am loth to purchase it for another person without a direct order. If you are willing to take the risk, please let me know or if you prefer something that is absolutely sure with half the income."

A major factor in the 1893 panic was the Sherman Silver Purchase Act, which had had exactly the effect Morgan and his colleagues feared: as the dollar's value plummeted in the early nineties, foreigners in a "flight to quality" cashed in American securities and shipped gold home. At the end of 1892, the *Commercial and Financial Chronicle* had deplored "the lack of confidence which our policy is causing Europe to feel in our financial stability. No more foreign capital comes to the United States and as fast as Europeans can dislodge their holdings in America they take their money away."

Treasury officials had tried since 1879 to maintain a $100 million gold reserve, and though there was no legal mandate for that figure, $100 million had become a measure of public confidence in government solvency. Morgan told the managing editor of *Harper's Weekly* in February 1893 that repeal of the Silver Act was "essential to the sound financial policy of the government." In April the Treasury reserve fell below $100 million, and in May the failures of the National Cordage Company and the Philadelphia & Reading Railroad sparked the stock market crash.

President Cleveland shared Morgan's view that silver was largely to blame. In August, as banks and businesses across the country failed and gold drained out of the Treasury, he told Congress that the crisis had been brought on largely by the Silver Purchase Act, and urged the legislature not only to repeal the law but to require the government to honor its obligations "in money universally recognized by all civilized countries"—i.e., gold.

The administration's clear intent to press for repeal of the Silver Act temporarily slowed the Treasury drain. Congress debated repeal in August, and William Jennings Bryan, the newly elected representative from Nebraska, delivered an eloquent three-hour oration that would echo through the nation's political debates for years: "On the one side stand the corporate interests of the United States," Bryan declared, "the moneyed interests, aggregated wealth and capital, imperious, arrogant, compassionless. . . . On the other side stand an unnumbered throng. . . . Work-worn and dust-begrimed, they make their mute appeal, and too often find their cry for help beat in vain against the outer walls, while others, less deserving, gain ready access to legislative halls."

Bryan notwithstanding, a majority of the House voted to repeal, the Senate followed suit, and at the beginning of November the government rescinded the Silver Purchase Act—to Morgan's relief and the Populists' dismay. Still, Europe worried about the U.S. commitment to gold. The Treasury drain continued. The lines of a class struggle over the politics of gold had been clearly drawn.

—

The panic and crash of 1893 brought major corporations to 23 Wall Street for help. National Cordage, called the "rope trust," had been using the bank's international services for years. Reorganized as a holding company after the passage of the antitrust law—a holding company owns enough voting stock in subsidiary companies to control their management and operational policies—Cordage had embarked on an expansion spree that made its stock the most actively traded industrial on Wall Street in the early nineties and the talk of the financial town. When a stock market dip in May of 1893 caused lenders to call in their short-term loans, the overextended "rope trust" failed—hanged itself, mordant humorists said.

At the time of the failure, Cordage had over $1 million in outstanding credits with J. S. Morgan & Co., and Pierpont helped set up a syndicate to refinance the company with $5 million of first mortgage collateral trust bonds. Drexel, Morgan took a small ($250,000) share. By keeping the company's mills working, the loan enabled Cordage to repay some of its debt—J. S. Morgan & Co. recouped $1 million in February 1894. Pierpont told his London partners that these "satisfactory" results had come "after the hardest fight we have had in some time."

Nonetheless, Cordage failed again in 1895. Its initial default and the depression that followed cast a four-year pall on the market for industrial securities, which reinforced Morgan's caution. Besides, bankrupt railroads were demanding his time.

More roads defaulted during the 1890s than at any other time in American history. A year after the panic, 192 lines operating 40,000 miles of road and capitalized at $2.5 billion had fallen into the hands of receivers. By 1898, a third of the nation's track mileage was in foreclosure, and the impact of these failures on the national economy was catastrophic: a single rail system employed more workers and used more capital than the Post Office or the entire U.S. military service, and the railroads' bonded debt dwarfed the Treasury's.

The repeated failures of Morgan's efforts to stabilize what was still the country's most important industry had led him finally to give up on voluntary agreements and negotiated peace. He concluded after 1890 that only tighter forms of consolidation would work, and other experts agreed: John Moody had predicted that protecting investment capital from the "gigantic waste and fraud and duplication" of the American railroad system would require concentration in a "few strong hands," and Charles Francis Adams had wondered whether Morgan had the force to become a "railroad Bismarck." As bankruptcy delivered rail properties all over the country into Morgan's hands, he built huge regional consolidations that definitively answered Adams's question.

The technicalities of the bank's railroad work in the nineties were largely managed by Coster, Stetson, and Samuel Spencer, a special adviser to the firm who had years of experience as vice president of the Baltimore & Ohio and president of the Elgin, Joliet & Eastern. Describing Spencer some years later, *The New York Times* said, "there was no man in the country so thoroughly well posted on every detail of a railroad from the cost of a car brake to the estimate for a terminal."

The first big "Morganization" of the nineties involved a weak agglomeration of roads in the Southeast called the Richmond & West Point Terminal and Warehouse Company, which connected Washington, D.C., to major cities in the South, including Richmond, Atlanta, Birmingham, and New Orleans. The Richmond Terminal had been mismanaged for years by speculators interested mainly in their own profits, and a group of its investors applied to the Morgan bank for rescue in May of 1892. Knowing that the road had been used as "football of speculation," Morgan refused to take the case unless he had full control. He invited three of the principal stockholders to his office and asked them to surrender their shares. Two agreed, the third did not. According to Jack, William P. Clyde lounged on the partners' sofa at 23 Wall Street and said, "in a queer drawling tone with considerable smacking of the lips"—"Well, Mr. Morgan, I've bought the Richmond Terminal at 7 or 8 and sold it at 15 twice in the last few years—and see no reason why I should not do it again."

Morgan showed his visitors out. They shopped the property around until the onset of the 1893 panic brought them back to the Morgan bank. This time, Clyde agreed to surrender his shares. Coster drew up a radical plan for a new company, the Southern Railway, to take over the Richmond Terminal and its profitable subsidiaries but not the less successful roads. He was able to dictate terms because the Richmond Terminal had no choice—it could either work with Morgan's experts or fail. To cut down on fixed charges, the bankers refinanced some of the road's debt at lower rates, and replaced the rest with preferred stock; to raise new capital for the floating debt and future expansion, they assessed stockholders for cash and issued new securities.

Years of experience with bankrupt railroads had convinced Morgan that high fixed costs were a greater danger than large capitalization, and the hallmark of his reorganizations came to be the reduction of obligatory charges to little more than a road's minimum earning capacity; with less debt to service, the company would be able to avoid bankruptcy even in stringent times. Morganization tended to shift the balance of a firm's securities from debt to equity—from mortgage bonds requiring annual interest payments to stocks that depended on company earnings. To persuade investors to trade their relatively safe, high-interest notes for riskier equity instruments, the bankers relied heavily on *preferred* stock, which took precedence over common: companies had to pay dividends on the preferred stock first, at a specified rate.*

The financial restructuring of the Richmond Terminal was just the beginning. The bankers put all the new company's stock into a voting trust headed by Morgan, George Baker, and Charles Lanier, which would oversee the Southern Railway's management and balance sheets for five years, or until the preferred shares began paying an annual 5 percent dividend. In its first major decision, the trust appointed Samuel Spencer president of the company.

---

* In terms of investor safety, bondholders come first and holders of common stock last. Regular interest on bonds has to be paid at a specified rate, regardless of earnings. Common stock dividends are issued at the discretion of the directors, and vary with earnings. Preferred shares fall in between: they generally bear a set dividend rate, but it is paid only when earnings are sufficient. If the company defaults, the same order prevails in liquidation: bondholders take precedence, followed by preferred shareholders, then holders of common stock.

With the ongoing help of the Morgan bank, Spencer took over a badly structured, unprofitable consortium of roads and turned it into a smoothly functioning regional system. The Southern Railway added new track miles, bought back some of the roads it had sold, doubled its rolling stock, and spent millions on other improvements. Earnings over the following decade tripled.

Almost everyone connected with the Southern Railway did well. Shippers and passengers got continuous, efficient service; bondholders earned regular interest; the reorganization syndicate took payment in $750,000 of Southern common stock (5 percent of the first $15 million issued), and Drexel, Morgan earned additional management and underwriting fees.*

That the syndicate took its fee in common stock was a measure of Morgan's confidence in the railway's long-term profitability. He would be charged in the coming decade with overcapitalization, or "watering" his companies' stock. In fact he was basing his financings on future earning capacity rather than on the traditional measure of asset value, and in most cases the "water" in the stock was eventually absorbed. By taking its own payment in common stock, the syndicate assumed the highest level of risk.

Contemporary observers called the Richmond Terminal rescue "one of the noteworthy achievements of American railroad history," and predicted a "new era" for transportation in the South. The Morgan bank emerged from its twenty months of work with a secure hold on all future Southern Railway business, control of the system's management, and enhanced prestige. The combination of Morgan's reputation and his strong affiliate firms in Europe enabled him to sell the railroad's bonds even at the height of the 1890s depression.

———

Other major roads on which the bank performed reconstructive surgery in the mid-nineties included the long-troubled Erie, the Philadelphia & Reading, and the Northern Pacific. Morgan had rescued the latter two lines before, and these repeat failures, after the expiration of banker-dominated voting trusts, strengthened his commitment to vigilant, protracted control.

The New York, Lake Erie & Western—once run by Jay Gould, who died of tuberculosis in December 1892—declared its fourth bankruptcy the following July. The Morgan firms had sold millions of dollars' worth of Erie securities, and proposed a draconian reorganization that would reduce debt, raise cash, and consolidate the line's subsidiary roads into one tightly managed system. It took two years and another bankruptcy, but in November 1895 the bankers

---

* Largely because of its high capitalization, the Southern did not pay dividends on the preferred stock until 1897, and then less than the 5 percent required to terminate the voting trust; it finally paid 5 percent in 1902. By 1906, when Samuel Spencer died, the company had not paid dividends on its common shares.

(chiefly Coster) brought the main line and its affiliates into a fully integrated network called the Erie Railroad Company—two thousand miles of track running through New York, Pennsylvania, Ohio, Indiana, and Illinois. To fund the plan three months before it went into effect, Morgan sold $25 million of new Erie bonds through syndicates in London and New York: frankness about the road's condition, and capitalization based on realistic projections of earnings, helped assuage investor anxiety. The syndicates sold the entire issue in a month—an astonishing feat in a depression, and "an impressive show of confidence in Morgan's business judgment and financial strength," since no one trusted the Erie.

For two years of work, Morgan charged the road $500,000, payable in $5 shares of common stock, plus expenses. His New York and London houses split the fee, each dividing its half with the members of its syndicate. Walter Burns wanted payment in cash, but Morgan insisted on the material and moral value of equity: "We have always taken reimbursement in common stock," he cabled—"first, because think it desirable, more valuable in itself," and also because it publicly demonstrated "our belief in property when reorganized." He offered to buy London's allotment for $250,000 if Burns held out for cash, but his brother-in-law accepted the shares. In July, at the time of this exchange, the stock was trading at 8 in New York, its low for the year. By the end of December, when both syndicates closed their accounts, the price was 15¾.

Morgan rejected the railroad's candidate for president as "useless," and installed Eben Thomas, an Erie executive who had worked on the reorganization with Coster and on other "Morgan" roads as well. The men appointed to the new Erie board for long-term supervision included Coster, Stetson, Spencer, Jim Goodwin, and J. Lowber Welsh. Morganization imposed financial stability on the Erie for the first time in forty years.

It was the failure of the Philadelphia & Reading, along with National Cordage, that had started the 1893 panic. Morgan's rescue of the Reading coal roads in 1886 had earned him Wall Street's respect and extravagant praise, but seven years later his voting trust had disbanded and the conservative Austin Corbin had been replaced as president by Alexander A. McLeod, a reckless expansionist who preferred rate-cutting warfare to Morganatic cooperation. Drexel, Morgan refused to take on a second Reading rehabilitation unless McLeod resigned, and the holders of the road's securities rejected several proposals before accepting a tough reorganization plan in the summer of 1895. It followed the usual Morgan pattern, and split the road's rail and coal properties into independent entities under one corporate umbrella. *The Commercial & Financial Chronicle* called the plan not only "drastic and radical," but "thorough and effective." It was also expensive: in the fifteen months the Morgan firms spent on the second Reading rescue, they earned commissions amounting to $2.76 million, plus $650,000 in management fees.

Morgan was slowly imposing order on the "gigantic waste and fraud and du-plication" of the American transport system. When the economy had fully re-covered at the beginning of the new century, one Wall Street analyst said Morgan had made railroad bonds among the country's "safest investments." Henry Clay Frick compared them to Rembrandts.

However, a writer in the *Machinists' Monthly Journal* asked, "When J. Pier-pont Morgan, the patron of bishops and exalted pillar of the church, is at his devotions; when with a gilt-edged prayer-book in his hand he wiggles himself into a more comfortable position in his satin-lined pew . . . does he think of the starving miners who are suffering through his efforts and that of his col-leagues of the coal trust? When he reads the lessons of charity and good will toward men, does he think of the tyrannous system that reduces wages to the subsistence point, or is he figuring some new combination whereby he can augment his plethoric fortune? When the organ peals forth does not his con-science supply a discord with the wails and cries of those whose lives are sacri-ficed to the voracious demands of his class?"

———

In July of 1893, as the stock market hit its postpanic nadir, Anthony Drexel died in Carlsbad, Germany. Pierpont reported himself "stunned" by this new loss: Mr. Drexel was "very dear to me," he told a friend, "and I am at a complete loss to know how I am going to get along without him." He cabled the same message to Walter Burns in London after the funeral, still feeling "dazed and staggered in deciding what best for future." Perhaps Burns would come over to "help me decide."

Morgan's sense of paralysis had more to do with mourning than with basic doubts about his ability to carry on. The economic indicators echoed his mood: "Everything here continues as blue as indigo," he wrote in late July as the country slid from panic into depression: "hope we shall soon have some change for the better, for it is very depressing and very exhausting."

He virtually lived on board his yacht that summer, anchored in the Hudson River off 23rd Street or cruising up the Atlantic Coast to Newport and Maine with Edith Randolph. After consultation with Walter Burns, he arranged for Drexel's estate to leave the partnerships as they were for a year, so that he would not have to close out the holdings in an economic downturn.

Chapter 17

ROMANCE

Fanny had spent most of the summer of 1893 at Cragston, although she went to Bar Harbor for two weeks in late July, noting the presence of "Mrs. Randolph" in her husband's *Corsair* parties without comment. She left many of her diary's pages blank in the first months of 1894, but reported from time to time, "Pierpont dined home," "Pierpont dined out," "had a treatment . . . & book keeping lesson." On April 15 she wrote: "Spoke with P. about Mrs. R."

Whatever she said to her husband that day, she never mentioned Mrs. R. in her diary again. She went to Europe for the summer of 1894 with Louisa and Anne, and after she returned, Pierpont no longer saw Edith in her presence.

"Why does the wife of a certain wealthy man always go to Europe about the time he returns home, and *vice versa?*" wondered *Town Topics* in July of 1895. The editorship of this gossip chronicle had passed in 1891 from its publisher/owner, Eugene Mann, to his brother, Colonel William D'Alton Mann, a Civil War hero and cheerful swindler who used the paper to blackmail prominent men. The colonel's method was to detail some illicit behavior without specifying the transgressor, print the name in a paragraph nearby, and wait to be paid for silence. When he posed his question about the wife of a wealthy man in July 1895, he mentioned Mr. and Mrs. Pierpont Morgan and Edith Randolph in unrelated stories on the preceding page.

Mann knew that his success as journalist and blackmailer depended on getting facts right—he once fired an assistant for leaving the "h" out of Rhinelander. His network of informants included social climbers, servants, waiters, and chauffeurs. The names of men who had paid him off came out when he was sued for libel in 1906. Among them were William K. Vanderbilt ($25,000) and his brother-in-law, W. Seward Webb ($14,000), steelmaster Charles M. Schwab ($10,000), California railroad magnate Collis P. Huntington ($5,000), Pierpont Morgan ($2,500), and William C. Whitney ($1,000).

At his trial, Mann said these sums were simply loans that had not been repaid. Asked why a man of Morgan's stature and character would "lend" $2,500 to a virtual stranger without security, the colonel replied: "I went to Mr. Morgan the same as I did to the other men of prominence, and asked them because I felt they were of such standing that if they accommodated me there would be no occasion for me to criticize them."

Although Morgan no doubt took good financial care of Edith Randolph (all such matters were off the books), she was still relatively young, and once Fanny "spoke to P. about Mrs. R." there was no getting around the fact that the beautiful widow might have a more satisfying future with someone else. Colonel Mann's stories over the summer and fall of 1895 indicate how the couple solved this problem.

Former Navy Secretary Whitney had also courted Edith in 1890, but his wife had put a stop to it. Then in 1893 Flora Payne Whitney died. Her husband inherited her large fortune, and emerged from the requisite period of mourning as a leading candidate for the 1896 Democratic presidential nomination. In August of 1895 he sailed his new yacht, *Columbia*, up the Atlantic coast to Bar Harbor. Edith was there with her mother and children, as was Morgan on *Corsair*. On August 15, *Town Topics* reported the "first of the autumn nor'westers" whirling down the coast from Bar Harbor—"a tale of the devoted attentions paid by a former member of the Cabinet and a possible Democratic presidential candidate to a charming widow, one of a family noted for the superb physique of both its women and men, and even of his probable engagement to her."

The well-informed Colonel Mann continued: "The presence on the scene in his handsome steam yacht of an eminent financier who has long been a warm friend and supposed adviser of the widow in question has added still more to the piquancy of this Bar Harbor breeze and made the tale a more complicated one—dividing, indeed, the gossips into two hostile camps regarding it. Meanwhile, the prominent politician . . . pursues the even tenor of his ways, and the eminent financier takes the widow and her friends a-sailing o'er the blue waters of Mount Desert on his yacht." On the next page appeared the inevitable item naming notable members of the Bar Harbor colony that summer—including ex-Secretary Whitney, Edith Randolph's brother, Fred May, Levi P. Morton (elected governor of New York in 1894), and "Mr. Pierpont Morgan, on *Corsair*."

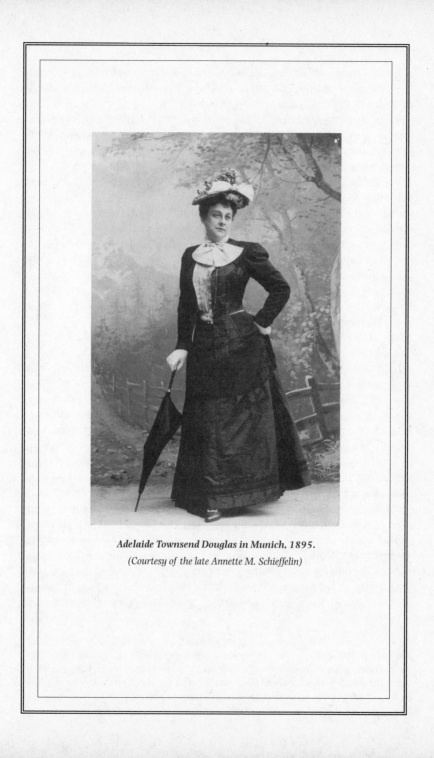

Adelaide Townsend Douglas in Munich, 1895.

(Courtesy of the late Annette M. Schieffelin)

Henry Adams wrote to an American friend from London that fall—referring to Whitney's presidential prospects—"As for our situation at home, it is wholly in the hands of Mr. Morgan and Mrs. Randolph."

Mr. Morgan's hands were in fact quite full. Colonel Mann reflected philosophically on September 19 that "It has become more and more not only a luxury but a necessity for married women in the 'smart set' to have, each one, her own private and devoted slave, selected from among the men, married or single, of the same class." Dropping a pointed reference to Morgan's work with the bankrupt National Cordage Company, Mann reported having heard over the summer about "one particular affair of this kind that is now 'on,' in which the admirer is a very well-known father of a family, who has been all too well acquainted with the woes of Cordage. His devotion is so marked as to entitle him to a certain amount of praise for frankness. The fair object of his cult is a young matron, full of fun and dash, whose object in life is apparently to have a good time, and to that end she devotes her energies, which are conspicuous. She and her family are, I hear, to spend the winter in the country at a not too great distance from the abode of the languishing swain."

The "fair object" of the "languishing swain's" attentions was Edith Randolph's best friend, Adelaide Douglas. Elegant and handsome although not conventionally pretty, she had blue eyes under hooded lids, a throaty alto laugh, and, as Mann observed, an energetic pleasure in living that matched Pierpont Morgan's. She also had a husband and two children.

Born Adelaide Louisa Townsend in 1853, she had grown up at 120 Fifth Avenue and in Bayside, Queens. Her father, descended from English Quakers who settled on Long Island in the early seventeenth century, was Effingham Lawrence Townsend, the head of a prominent auction house, Townsend & Montant. In 1879 Adelaide married William Proctor Douglas at New York's Grace Church, in a ceremony conducted by the Reverend Henry Codman Potter.

Adelaide's husband had inherited a substantial fortune and a mansion with three hundred acres of land on Little Neck Bay, Long Island.* In 1873 his family had leased their house on 14th Street to the Metropolitan Museum of Art while the Vaux-Mould building was under construction on upper Fifth Avenue. William donated a building on his Long Island estate to serve as the local railroad station in 1876, on condition that the town be called Douglaston. Eleven years older than Adelaide, with curly dark hair parted in the middle, a waxed

---

* His father, George, had come to America from Scotland in the early nineteenth century and made his fortune in the East India trade. George Douglas built a house at 55 Broadway on the Battery when fashionable New Yorkers lived downtown, then moved with the northward migration to a larger house on West 14th Street. Later, he bought the Van Zandt estate on the east side of Little Neck Bay in Queens, where he built the mansion he left to his son.

mustache and a thick beard, he figured conspicuously in the leisured masculine society of the Gilded Age. He spent his days playing polo, organizing
Coaching Club races, and sailing: his yacht *Sappho* had defeated a British challenger for the America's Cup in 1871. He and Adelaide spent a yearlong honeymoon in France, where his close friend James Gordon Bennett, Jr., was
running a Paris edition of the *Herald.*

On returning from their travels the couple settled at Douglaston, and gave
Edith and Arthur Randolph a house on the estate. The Douglases named their
son James Gordon, after Mr. Bennett, and their daughter Edith Sybil, for Mrs.
Randolph. The Randolphs had already named *their* daughter Adelaide.

The Douglases joined St. George's Church in 1883, shortly after Dr. Rains-
ford began drawing wealthy families back to the parish, even though they con-
tinued to live on Little Neck Bay. In 1888, they built a large summer house in
Southampton, which is now the Bath and Tennis Club. Their entry in the New
York *Social Register* for 1888 describes Mr. Douglas as belonging to the Union,
Racquet, Tuxedo, and New York Yacht clubs.

Exactly when Morgan shifted his affections from Edith to Adelaide is not
clear, and neither are the dynamics of the Douglas marriage. At some point,
according to Adelaide's grandson, an errant polo mallet hit Mr. Douglas in the
head, after which he was never quite "right." And gossip imputed something
more than friendship to the relations between Mrs. Douglas and Mr. Bennett—
rumors fueled by her son's having been named James Gordon rather than
William Proctor.

Adelaide was sixteen years younger than Pierpont Morgan in 1895—forty-
two to his fifty-eight—and more like Memie than Fanny. Bright, curious, animated, and self-confident, she had no aversion to society, no trouble with her
"nerves," no puritanical disapproval of the *luxe* with which he liked to adorn
women, no squeamishness about nudity in sculpture. More than conversant
with the fine arts, she became a useful accomplice in Morgan's collecting. Her
high spirits offset his tendency toward depression, and she moved easily in his
sophisticated world.

In the fall of 1896 Colonel Mann reported triumphantly on the marriage of
Edith Randolph and William C. Whitney, which he had predicted. The chief ob-
stacle to this renewed romance had been Whitney's brother-in-law, Oliver Hazard Payne, whose own name had been all too intimately linked to the first hints
of Whitney/Randolph trouble. Colonel Payne, outraged by Whitney's 1890
flirtation with Edith—if that is all it was—remained fiercely loyal to Flora's
memory. Having no heirs of his own, he was planning to leave his large fortune
to Flora's children, and threatened to disinherit those who refused to disown
their father. Two of them did side with him—Pauline, now married to the Englishman Almeric Hugh Paget, and Payne, still a student at Yale; the other

two—Harry Payne, who married Gertrude Vanderbilt in November 1895, and Dorothy, who was only nine years old—remained loyal to Whitney.

In reporting on the private wedding from afar, Colonel Mann observed that "Mr. Whitney has not been able to conceal the fact of his affection for Mrs. Randolph from his intimates from the beginning of his devotion to her, and her close friends, notably Mr. and Mrs. William Douglas and Mr. Pierpont Morgan, have doubtless felt assured, for some time, that her marriage to Mr. Whitney would certainly occur. . . . She has been almost the idol of a small set of people at Douglaston, L.I., and Bar Harbor, for some years, and her marriage will make quite a gap in this small circle." Mann surely knew that for two people in Edith's "circle," the gap had already been filled.

The ceremony took place in Bar Harbor. None of Whitney's children attended. Mann imagined that "Secretary Whitney and his bride must have made a handsome couple, for she is quite as tall as her new husband, and her fine physique and rich brunette beauty must have made her an effective bride"—then added a sly fillip: "I do not notice the name of Mr. and Mrs. Pierpont Morgan among the guests."

Colonel Mann dropped the subject of Morgan and Mrs. Douglas after 1896. His first broad hint about a "well-known father of a family . . . well acquainted with the woes of Cordage" probably amounted to a bid for money—he managed in the very next paragraph, in an unrelated story, to use the name J. Pierpont Morgan. Perhaps it was on this occasion that Morgan made the $2,500 "loan" that later came out in court testimony. *Town Topics* continued in the late nineties to mention the financier in its business columns, usually with praise.

———

Although extramarital liaisons were a salient feature of New York's Gilded Age society, certain strictures applied. Edith Wharton observed in *The Age of Innocence* that fashionable young men who had affairs with married women emerged "with calm consciences and an undisturbed belief in the abysmal distinction between the women one loved and respected and those one enjoyed—and pitied." The matriarchs of old Gotham, abetting these arrangements, agreed "that when 'such things happened' it was undoubtedly foolish of the man, but somehow always criminal of the woman." Wharton's partially awakening Newland Archer suspects that "in the complicated old European communities . . . love-problems might be less simple and less easily classified."

Morgan had spent much of his life in the complicated old European communities, and made no such "abysmal distinctions." In his attitudes and behavior he had more in common with the British aristocracy—and with his father—than with the social arbiters of the American drawing room. In England, Edward Albert, Prince of Wales, had been conducting semipublic affairs for years. During his long wait to inherit the Crown—he was fifty-nine by the time Queen

Victoria died—amorous adventure became his favorite form of entertainment: Henry James called him Edward "the Caresser," and the British regent was "never happier," wrote one of his secretaries, "than in the company of pretty women." Pretty *married* women. The rules of conduct in upper-class Victorian society, and particularly in the Prince's Marlborough House set, dictated that women remain virgins until marriage, but after they crossed that threshhold were free to carry on affairs with almost the same impunity as their husbands and brothers. At the end of the century, the Prince's "favorite" was Alice (Mrs. George) Keppel.

The heir to the British throne stayed at the Hôtel Bristol in Paris, and put his mistress up at the Vendôme a few doors away. Morgan had been staying at the Bristol for decades. Traveling with Adelaide in the early 1900s, he installed *her* at the Vendôme—and, according to her grandson, had a special suite of rooms entirely redecorated for her every spring. Art dealers billed him for eighteenth-century French furniture, porcelains, and decor "to be delivered in Paris," along with fittings, hangings, and alterations carried out in that city, every spring between 1904 and 1908; the bills were charged to a special account.

Perhaps because Fanny had spoken to him about Mrs. R., he saw Mrs. D. largely in private for several years. He took her to Cragston one July weekend in 1899 while his wife was abroad. The following spring he arranged to meet her and her daughter in London—Fanny noted that "Mrs. Douglass [*sic*] & Sybil" came to dinners and teas at Princes Gate—then stayed on in Europe with Adelaide and Sybil after Fanny returned to the United States.

The problem with Edith Randolph had been, at least in part, that she needed a husband. Adelaide Douglas did not. She and Mr. Douglas moved to 28 West 57th Street in 1899. Eventually they separated, and she renounced all claim to his estate, but he did not in the end hold their complicated situation against her. When he died in 1919, worth about $1 million, he left her a stipend and a third of his property, insisting that she accept them even though she "may have signed an Instrument of Agreement renouncing and releasing her dower rights in my real estate."

Adelaide had resources of her own, and Morgan provided for her as well. In 1897 he set up trust funds for her children of $120,000 each, the interest to go to their legal guardians until they reached maturity. To Adelaide herself he gave jewelry, works of art, antique furniture, books, catalogues of his collections, clothing, a house, and a trust fund worth about $500,000. Probably for her entertainment he bought items that had belonged to royal and aristocratic Adelaides, including a missal of 1739 containing prayers written out in the hand of Louis XV's favorite daughter, Princesse Adélaïde, and one of her beautifully bound prayer books; three prayer books used by the Duchesse d'Orléans, daughter of Louis XIV and Madame de Montespan, whose name was erroneously represented to Morgan as Louise Adelaide; and nearly two dozen letters written in the 1870s by Mary Adelaide, Duchess of Teck.

———

Morgan in middle age assumed avuncular responsibility for a number of friends, among them a widow living in Vermont named Mary McIlvaine and her son, Clarence, who had graduated from Princeton in 1885 with Memie's nephew Jonathan Sturges.* Morgan managed the McIlvaines' finances and gave them the use of a cottage on his property near Cragston. In 1887 he recommended Clarence to Whitelaw Reid, publisher of the *Tribune*, as "one of the most promising young men I know," with "strong leanings toward journalism," but that fall, with or without Morgan's help, Clarence took a job at the publishing house of Harper & Brothers. Three years later he moved to London to set up an English branch of Harper's, and spent much of his free time with Jonathan Sturges. At the end of 1891 he asked Pierpont's middle daughter, Juliet, to marry him.

Juliet reported the proposal to Louisa on New Year's Day, 1892: "Of course I don't care for him in that way at all, but I am very fond of him and hate to hurt him." Not inexperienced in affairs of the heart, the prettiest of the Morgan girls wondered why men must "always go and spoil a nice comfortable friendship by perfectly unnecessary sentiment." She told Clarence that she was much too fond of him ever to fall in love with him—which can't have cheered him up— and added to Louisa: "I'd make him miserable in two years if I did marry him."

Clarence's ill-fated attachment had no apparent effect on Juliet's father, who wrote to him six months later about financial and family matters ("I left your mother this morning looking finely"), and urged, "keep me advised from time to time how things are progressing—above all things do not break down—as a lever, do not smoke cigarettes—Excuse my saying this but I feel very deeply the necessity of cautioning you on that point."

Instead of making Clarence miserable, Juliet brought another banker into the family. In April 1894 she married a descendant of Alexander Hamilton named William Pierson Hamilton. The ceremony took place at St. George's Church and the wedding breakfast at 219, with flowers by Thorley and catering by Louis Sherry. Pierpont gave her a house in Tuxedo Park—the six-hundred-acre private community northwest of Manhattan created by Pierre Lorillard in 1886— and an income of $10,000 a year. He also took her husband into his firm.

———

Adelaide Douglas, like Edith Randolph, belonged to the intimate circle of friends who had protected Annette Wetmore between her divorce and her mar-

---

* The son of Memie's brother Fred, this Jonathan Sturges had been crippled in early childhood by polio. After graduating from Princeton he tried law school, then moved to England, where he worked as a literary journalist and became a close friend of Henry James's.

riage to Jim Markoe. The Markoes moved in 1897 to 12 West 55th Street—the house was probably a gift from Morgan, as were a sedan chair and a suit of armor that stood in the front hall. Annette expected a baby that fall.

Morgan stopped to see the Markoes almost every day after work. He would arrive in the late afternoon, head straight back to his doctor's home office on the ground floor, and take a seat on a sofa. After the two men finished their informal medical appointment, others joined them for drinks—Charles Lanier, George Bowdoin, the lawyer Lewis Cass Ledyard, the Lying-In's architect Bob Robertson. Later, more friends would come for dinner, among them Adelaide Douglas, Bessie (Mrs. Stanford) White, Edith and William C. Whitney, Mrs. Ledyard, Adelaide's sister Emily Woodbury, and Edith's sister Alice with her yacht-designer husband, J. Beavor-Webb.

These friends saw aspects of Morgan few outsiders did. He had "a very feminine streak in his nature," recalled Annette Markoe: "his tenderness and sympathy, his emotional nature, his love for beautiful things and pretty clothes were as intense as a woman's." According to the Markoes' daughter, "he loved to trade stories and make everyone laugh, but had no patience with people who bored him, and could be wickedly funny about anyone he found puritanical or pompous." He found his daughter-in-law, Jessie, boring and puritanical: he called her "cold roast Boston." She no doubt disapproved of his philandering—Jack was an entirely faithful husband—and Pierpont generally gave the younger couple wide berth.

Annette Markoe held her own in the otherwise all-male afternoon gatherings on West 55th Street. She never hesitated to challenge Morgan: "They argued madly about the Bible," continued her daughter—"he considered himself a great authority, but she matched him, chapter and verse. They'd bet on who was right before they looked something up."

Morgan spent far more time at the Markoes' house than at his own. He also took the couple on *Corsair* cruises and trips abroad—often with Adelaide—sent them art objects and antique furniture from Europe, lent them his car and driver when he went away, and provided them with a country house called Ondaora just north of Cragston. The rumor mill churned out gossip: people who didn't subscribe to the theory that Morgan built the Lying-In Hospital to accommodate all his mistresses' *accouchements* said the gift was a form of payment for his attentions to Markoe's wife.

If Morgan took a romantic interest in Annette Markoe, it appears not to have been reciprocated. The talk of a love affair between the financier and his closest friend's wife may have derived from her beauty and from the amount of time the Markoes spent first with Morgan and Edith Randolph, then with Morgan and Adelaide Douglas, supplying companionship and cover for his unorthodox social life. The gossips were not wrong about his womanizing, but probably, in this case, about its object.

When the Markoes' baby, Annette, was born in November 1897, the couple chose as her godparents Adelaide Douglas and Pierpont Morgan.

———

In the aftershock of Anthony Drexel's death in the summer of 1893, Morgan had postponed reorganizing his partnerships until the economic crisis and his own sorrow had subsided. The net earnings of Drexel, Morgan & Co. in 1892 had reached $1.6 million, but the year of the panic yielded $1.1 million in losses. Profits recovered in 1894, to almost $1.3 million, and by October Morgan had decided what to do.

He invited all ten of his Philadelphia and New York partners to dinner at the Metropolitan Club. The group included Edward T. Stotesbury and George C. Thomas from Philadelphia, and the New Yorkers Charles Coster, J. Hood Wright, George Bowdoin, and Jack. Bowdoin's son, Temple, a lawyer and bank accountant, had been made a partner in the New York firm at the beginning of 1893. Tony Drexel's son, Anthony Jr., who had more interest in society than in business, had retired a few months after his father died. The bankers met in a private dining room with a marble fireplace and clustered milk-glass chandeliers. Jack later said it was the first time all the American partners had been in one room at the same time. After the dishes were cleared, the senior Morgan outlined his plans for the future.

The two American houses would reorganize under a new partnership agreement at the beginning of 1895. The name of the New York firm would change to reflect what it had in fact been for some time—J. P. Morgan & Co. Philadelphia's Drexel & Co. would keep its name, but there would be no Drexel among its partners. Morgan would head both banks, and hold their combined capital in New York. The Paris house, renamed Morgan, Harjes & Co., would have Morgan as its senior partner and an infusion of new capital. The London house alone, presided over by Pierpont in conjunction with Walter Burns since Junius's death, would remain for the time being unchanged, and would not share the profits and losses of the other firms.*

———

* Pierpont and Walter Burns each took a 40 percent share of J. S. Morgan & Co.'s profits, and Robert Gordon the remaining 20 percent. The combined capital of J. P. Morgan & Co. and Drexel & Co. at the beginning of 1895 amounted to $7.1 million. Morgan contributed $4.6 million—nearly 65 percent; five other partners supplied the remainder. For the five-year term of the new partnership, 35 percent of the profits would go to Morgan, 14 percent each to Stotesbury and Thomas in Philadelphia, 11 percent each to Coster and George Bowdoin, and smaller percentages to the junior partners—2 percent each to Jack and Temple Bowdoin. Net earnings for the two American firms in 1895, the first year under the new arrangement, came to about $2 million—largely from railroad reorganizations—and rose steadily from $2.3 million in 1896 to $4.3 million in 1897, $5.8 million in 1898, and $8.1

The partners filing out into the night through the Metropolitan Club's colonnaded courtyard in October of 1894 faced a new kind of future. Between 1871 and 1890, Junius Morgan and Anthony Drexel had shared jurisdiction over their affiliated houses. On January 1, 1895, Pierpont took single-handed charge of the dynasty his predecessors had established, and consolidated its leadership in his own hands.

———

Among investment banking houses, Morgan's in the 1890s had a reputation for driving its partners harder than most. Charles Coster was chronically exhausted from overwork, and in November 1894, just a month after the meeting at the Metropolitan Club, J. Hood Wright dropped dead. He was fifty-eight—exactly Pierpont's age.

Jack did not figure in the inner councils at 23 Wall Street. Entrusted with neither the firm's secrets nor its lethal workload, he often had to appeal to others for information about what was going on. His father, perpetually on the lookout for professional heirs, offered a partnership in the fall of 1894 to an attractive young Harvard graduate named Robert Bacon.

At the time, Bacon was working with the Boston bankers Lee, Higginson & Co., and Morgan had probably met him during the organization of General Electric. Harvard Class of '80, Bob Bacon had starred as an undergraduate in football, baseball, track, boxing, and crew, graduated in the top third of his class, and made a lifelong friend of his classmate Theodore Roosevelt, Jr. Everyone liked this affable and extraordinarily good-looking young man. A Yale athletic rival never forgot his freshman encounter with the "tall crinkly haired blond giant, handsome as an Adonis." According to Roosevelt, Bacon was "the handsomest man in the Class and . . . as pleasant as he is handsome." The lawyer and politician Elihu Root later compared the pleasure of seeing the physically "superb" Bacon to looking "upon any natural object which approaches the perfection of beauty." Railroad baron James J. Hill, in a bizarre compliment, considered the younger man so trustworthy that one could "go to sleep with one's thumb in his mouth." One of the Morgan partners said that Pierpont had simply "fallen in love." Bacon and his wife, Martha, spent a weekend at Cragston in June of 1892, and another in October 1893.

In the masculine precincts of Gilded Age Harvard and private banking, only Bob Bacon inspired talk of beauty and falling in love. He had been planning to take a year off in France with his wife and children when the Wall Street pro-

———

million in 1899. By comparison, National City, which James Stillman was beginning to transform from an old-fashioned merchant bank into the largest and strongest commercial bank in the country, had $4.2 million in capital in 1895, and net earnings of $400,000; by 1900 the figures were $15.5 million in capital and earnings of $1.2 million.

posal came, and had no intention of leaving Boston, but Morgan's powers of persuasion proved as effective with prospective partners as they did with beautiful women.

Offered not only a coveted position in what was now one of the world's premier banks but a 5 percent interest in its profits and Morgan's warm personal friendship, Bacon said yes. Henry Lee Higginson, who initially opposed the move, wished his young colleague well in terms more applicable to a courtesan than a banker: "If Pierpont Morgan gets as much pleasure out of you and as many pleasant words and looks as I have had . . . he will be a lucky fellow. And why shouldn't he," added the Boston Brahmin, having worked closely with the Wall Street titan whom strangers found difficult and brusque, "for he deserves it, and is kind and pleasant to people." Yet knowing of the herculean labors Morgan exacted from his partners, Higginson warned Bacon: "Don't overwork like Coster just because you can and like to do it. He is wonderful—and unwise—to do so. Trade with me when you can."

Bob Bacon joined J. P. Morgan & Co. at the beginning of 1895, and his advent probably gave rise to the Wall Street maxim "When the angels of God took unto themselves wives among the daughters of men, the result was the Morgan partners."

The newest Morgan partner did not take Higginson's advice about overwork. After three months in New York he told his wife that he could not join her for a vacation in France: "I am really working for perhaps the first time in my life. I almost feel as if I were just beginning to find a use for the poor substitute which I am pleased to call my brain." Pierpont Morgan was about to leave for Europe, "and I assure you that I shudder a little to think of the responsibility which I feel. . . . My life is simply engrossed in this maelstrom, and I have no moments for any other thought except thoughts of you."

———

The wage cuts and layoffs that came with the long depression of the 1890s led to a new round of strikes—1,400 in 1894, when more than 660,000 people lost their jobs. "It is probably safe to say that in no civilized country in this century, not actually in the throes of war or open insurrection, has society been so disorganized as it was in the United States during the first half of 1894," wrote the editor of *Railroad Age*—"never was human life held so cheap; never did the constituted authorities appear so incompetent to enforce respect for the law."

America's best-selling books that summer were Henry Demarest Lloyd's attack on predatory trusts, *Wealth Against Commonwealth*, and William Hope Harvey's influential brief for silver, *Coin's Financial School*. The populist leader Jacob Coxey of Ohio organized the unemployed to march on Washington in the spring to demand an increase in the money supply and a federal work relief program. When Coxey's Army of five hundred arrived at the capital on April

30, police arrested the leaders and broke up the crowd. Nonetheless, hundreds more people marched on Washington that year—their "living petitions" for federal aid putting the human costs of the depression on graphic display.

In May, factory workers in George M. Pullman's "model" company town outside Chicago went on strike. They had been forced to absorb four wage cuts in twelve months, with no offsetting reduction in the prices of housing or food, when Pullman fired a third of the workforce and cut wages by another 30 percent. Eugene V. Debs, president of the American Railway Union, called for the strike after Pullman refused to negotiate. When other railroad managers backed Pullman, Debs expanded the local action into a general railroad strike, which affected virtually all roads west of Chicago by the end of June. Responding to an appeal from the railroads, the federal government decided to intervene—ostensibly to protect the U.S. mail, though it was not the union but the managers who refused to attach mail cars to trains that did not include Pullman coaches. Attorney General Richard Olney issued an injunction to the union to return to work. Debs defied it. On July 4 President Cleveland sent two thousand federal troops to Chicago to break the strike, which had until then been nonviolent. The arrival of the troops set off a riot that left twelve people dead; dozens were arrested.

The Pullman strike had failed, and Debs went to jail for disobeying the Justice Department's injunction. That federal authorities had sided with management against labor—and that a Democratic President had chosen to protect the railroads but not to provide work or aid to the unemployed—exacerbated the social conflicts of the era. The marches and strikes had strengthened the pro-labor positions of liberal reformers and intensified conservative fears of socialism and mob rule. Debs emerged from his six-month jail term convinced that trade unionism could not solve the economic problems of working people. He led the American socialist movement for the next two decades.

Morgan left no record of his response to these struggles. He was directing his professional energies to reorganizing bankrupt railroads in the expectation that restoring their health would promote general economic recovery. He was also keeping a watchful eye on the Treasury, and when it failed to resolve a currency crisis at the beginning of 1895, he appointed himself unofficial chancellor of the American exchequer.

Grover Cleveland.
(Culver Pictures, Inc.)

Chapter 18

POLITICS OF GOLD

Morgan's defense of the gold standard in the 1890s, hugely unpopular in the anguished South and West, established his image there as a "great financial Gorgon." As in the currency fights of the seventies, each side from its own point of view was right. Farmers, workers, and small businessmen who suffered under economic stringency were desperate for easier money simply to survive. Eastern bankers and government officials, guarding the European sources of capital for the still-emerging U.S. economy, were determined to protect the westward flow of money by keeping the dollar strong.

The United States was running a trade deficit in the early nineties, and the repeal of the Silver Purchase Act had not stanched the flight of gold: foreign investors, worried about rising U.S. demand for cheap money, continued to sell American securities and take the proceeds home. "Few people have any idea of the amount of property of every description in this country that is held by foreigners," wrote National City Bank president James Stillman to a Treasury official in July of 1894. Between 1890 and 1894, nervous creditors unloaded $300 million worth of American securities and transferred gold abroad.

By the end of 1893 the Treasury's $100 million gold reserve had fallen below $60 million. Since there was no income tax and the government had no power to issue money, the Treasury had to buy or borrow gold in order to maintain its reserve—and its ability to borrow depended on foreign confidence in the dollar.

President Cleveland and his Treasury Secretary, former Kentucky Senator and Speaker of the House John G. Carlisle, had tried in 1894 to shore up the gold supply by selling bonds. Several New York commercial banks took a $50 million issue in January, which restored the reserve to $107 million, but by November $46 million of it had disappeared. Another bond issue in November—this one sold through Drexel, Morgan—raised $50 million more.

By the end of the year it was clear that the concerted efforts of Cleveland and Carlisle could not keep the government in gold. In what amounted to an international run on the Treasury, an estimated $84 million left the country in the last three months of 1894. At the beginning of 1895 the nation watched in fascination as its gold reserve fell to $68 million on January 24 and $45 million a week later. Stock prices plummeted as Europeans sold American holdings. By early February the Treasury was losing over $2 million a *day*. At that rate, the government would have to stop payment in gold and default on the national debt in three weeks.

Cleveland tried to get congressional authority for a new issue of gold bonds, but at the height of the depression, sentiment in both houses was running high for silver and against the "goldbugs" on Wall Street and in the White House. Congress refused to authorize a bill that would strengthen gold.

Morgan had seen this crisis coming for years. If the Treasury reneged on its debt, he expected the financial markets to collapse and U.S. borrowing costs to soar. To avoid that disaster he had been quietly working with Treasury officials all along. Connecticut Representative Louis Sperry, on the House Banking and Currency Committee, asked him on January 1, 1895, whether a new bond issue would restore confidence and relieve the Treasury of the present emergency: "If so," Sperry wrote, "I'll say so to the House of my own information, knowing you don't like to be quoted, and would not use your name."

The head of the house of Morgan did not like to be quoted in part because any mention of his name in connection with these matters would heighten public antipathy to Wall Street. Cleveland told Congress on January 28 that regardless of the ongoing silver debate, the only way to restore urgently needed public confidence was to pay the Treasury's obligations in gold, and the only way to procure the necessary gold was to sell bonds. Silverites, convinced that the entire "supposed emergency" had been trumped up by eastern plutocrats, demanded to know why the shortage could not be made up in silver.

Perhaps to keep Morgan's name out of the public eye—and because any successful bond sale appeared to require foreign capital—Cleveland asked the English Rothschilds through August Belmont, Jr. (the senior Belmont had died in 1890), about syndicating a $100 million Treasury loan. Nathaniel Mayer Rothschild immediately called in Walter Burns, who cabled Morgan, and on January 30, Assistant Treasury Secretary William Edmond Curtis took a train to New York to confer with Belmont and Morgan. Lord Rothschild insisted, and the Morgan firms agreed, that in order to succeed abroad a new loan would have to be payable in gold or pounds sterling, but the administration could not sell gold bonds without authority from Congress, which it was unlikely to get.

Morgan cabled Burns of the unfolding drama: "situation . . . is critical & we are disposed do everything our power to avert calamity." He felt sure that another domestic bond issue would not work, since Americans would simply withdraw Treasury gold to buy the new government paper, leaving the Treasury with more debt and no more gold. Only a new supply of gold from Europe could restore confidence in the Treasury and stop the drain. If all these conditions could be met, Morgan concluded, an international loan would be "most creditable all parties & pay good profit. We can secure cooperation best parties this side including leading National Banks."

As he saw it, his efforts to stem the drain, avert default, and restore confidence in the dollar would protect the billions invested in the United States and reopen the channels for foreign capital: "We all," he reminded his brother-in-law, "have large interests dependent upon maintenance sound currency U.S."

———

While the bankers and Treasury officials conferred, rumors reported on default and secret rescue plans. A broker who saw Morgan emerge from the New York Subtreasury building with Curtis ran onto the floor of the Stock Exchange shouting, "The Treasury is negotiating a loan." The panic subsided at the hint of Rothschild/Morgan action, and withdrawals stopped. Nine million dollars in gold taken out for shipment abroad one night was actually returned to the Treasury coffers the next morning.

As in his railroad reorganizations, Morgan was not willing to take full responsibility unless he had full authority. When other bankers put in for participation in these negotiations, he wired Treasury Secretary Carlisle that his own house and Rothschilds would underwrite the new issue alone.

For the next few days, Assistant Secretary Curtis shuttled between Washington and New York discussing rates and terms for a bond sale that would bring in $100 million worth of gold, while Congress and the press grumbled about "dark-lantern financiering" and a conspiracy between the Treasury and Wall Street. Grumbling notwithstanding, the fact of the bankers' negotiations continued to assuage public anxiety. Morgan cabled Burns on February 3: "Effect of abandonment upon all interests would now be worse than if never begun."

Then suddenly on Monday, February 4, when he thought everything was firmly settled except the exact amount of the loan and price of the bonds, Morgan got a letter by special messenger from Secretary Carlisle canceling the negotiations. The Secretary, a former silverite who had all along been reluctant to deal with Wall Street, declared the syndicate's terms too harsh: the President would force Congress to authorize gold bonds for sale directly to the public instead.

Whether Carlisle was angling for a better deal or seriously meant to cancel, Morgan thought this news would bring on a crisis in public confidence and a crash in the markets. He telephoned the Treasury to ask for a day's delay in announcing the change: he and Belmont would go to Washington to confer personally with the Secretary and the President.

Belmont left immediately. Morgan followed a few hours later accompanied by Bob Bacon and Frank Stetson, the President's former law partner. Just before leaving, he sent Burns a gloomy wire: "We consider situation critical, politicians appear to have absolute control. We shall make strongest possible fight for sound currency, if fail & European negotiations abandoned it is impossible over estimate what shall be result U.S. . . . Must admit am not hopeful."

———

War Secretary Daniel S. Lamont, one of Cleveland's closest advisers, met the Morgan party at Washington's Union Station. He said the President was determined to force an issue of public bonds through Congress and would not meet with the bankers.

Although it was late, Morgan dropped his bags at the Arlington Hotel and went with Lamont, Bacon, and Belmont to see the Attorney General, Richard Olney, at home. "All were much wrought up," recalled Olney, a former Massachusetts corporate lawyer who had known Bob Bacon in Boston, "and anticipated, apparently with reason, that unless something were done the next day to save the situation, great financial and commercial calamities must follow." Morgan told the Attorney General he had a plan, but if Cleveland refused to see him he would return in the morning to New York.

Olney telephoned the President and persuaded him to set up a meeting with the bankers at nine-thirty the next morning. Returning after midnight to the Arlington, Morgan cabled Burns: "Still some hopes but small, have strong allies in Cabinet but greatest fear Secy Treasury[;] will do our best." He sat up alone in his hotel room for another hour, smoking a large Rosa de Santiago Celestiale and playing out rounds of solitaire.

Right after breakfast on Tuesday morning, flanked by Stetson and Bacon, Morgan crossed a chilly Lafayette Park to the White House. Ushered upstairs to the library that served as the President's workroom, the representatives of J. P. Morgan & Co. found Cleveland, Treasury Secretary Carlisle, Attorney General Olney, War Secretary Lamont, and August Belmont.

The banker, his "Attorney General," and the President knew each other well, but Cleveland greeted his guests with formal reserve. He had Olney settle the New Yorkers in a corner of the room.

While the President's men conferred among themselves, Morgan sat silent, rolling an unlighted cigar between his fingers. Every few minutes a message came in for Carlisle. One telephone call reported just $9 million of gold left in the New York Subtreasury.

After what seemed like hours, Cleveland rose from his desk with a distracted air and crossed the room to address the bankers. Standing before them with his hands in his pockets, he insisted once again that he would not discuss a bond issue. Congress was holding him up, he said, and he wanted the public to know exactly where the blame for the present crisis lay.

Morgan replied that there were outstanding drafts on the New York Subtreasury for $12 million, against $9 million in gold: if the drafts were presented that day, the government could not pay—it would have to default on its debt and destroy its credit. There was no time for congressional approval or a public sale of bonds, he said. Something had to be done.

"Have you anything to suggest?" Cleveland asked at last.

Accustomed to taking charge at moments of crisis, Morgan had been holding himself back all morning with great effort. Now, he quickly sketched out a plan. A new public issue of bonds, which Congress probably would not authorize, could not in any case work, since it would simply recycle domestic gold. Instead, a syndicate of international bankers could provide the Treasury with a new $100 million reserve.

Morgan reported that a statute enacted in 1862 had authorized Civil War Treasury Secretary Salmon Chase to buy coin with U.S. bonds as an emergency measure in the public interest. If the loan he had in mind were considered a purchase of coin rather than a sale of bonds, it would not require congressional approval. Under the 1862 law, Carlisle ought to have the same power Chase had had to buy gold.

Cleveland sent Olney out to look up the statute, and the Attorney General returned a few minutes later to read aloud the Act to Authorize the Purchase of Coin of March 17, 1862, from Section 3700 of the Revised Statutes. It provided exactly the authority Morgan described, and it was still in force. Cleveland asked his chief law officer whether the act would allow the Treasury Secretary to buy gold in the present emergency and replenish the federal reserve. Olney thought it would.[*]

The tension that had held the room in its grip all morning suddenly broke. Cleveland, Carlisle, and Morgan immediately started to work out terms, al-

---

[*] Accounts of this meeting differ as to whether it was Morgan or a member of the administration who proposed the 1862 statute as a solution. Some claim that Morgan simply recalled the law as he sat in the President's library with the minutes ticking down, although that scenario seems unlikely. He had been worrying for months about the impending crisis, and had told Olney on Monday night that he had a plan. It seems more likely that Stetson or one of his partners had found the old law on the books and provided Morgan with the

though the President insisted that they keep the negotiations secret, since Congress was scheduled to vote two days later on the issue of public bonds. No one present expected the measure to pass, but given the politics of 1895, Cleveland had to avoid any appearance of collusion with what the silverites considered "goldbuggery and Shylockism." The government could turn to Wall Street only after it had exhausted every other remedy.

The crucial feature of the negotiations concerned the continuing gold drain. Could Morgan guarantee that the new metal would not immediately be shipped abroad? the President asked.

He could, nodded the banker, without consulting London or even Belmont across the room. In the past, his father had excoriated him for making instantaneous, autocratic decisions. Now, Pierpont had only himself to answer to, and he promised to protect the Treasury from further withdrawals—in effect, to control the international markets for gold and foreign exchange during the life of the contract. It was an extraordinary warranty, and it substantially strengthened his hand.

The bankers and administration agreed that the government would buy 3.5 million ounces of gold coin from the syndicate at $17.80 per ounce, in exchange for $62 million worth of thirty-year bonds paying 4 percent interest— bonds that could ultimately be redeemed in gold or silver coin at the discretion of the government. Since the value of gold at the time was $18.60 per ounce, the bankers were selling the government $65.1 million in gold in exchange for $62.3 million in bonds; in effect, they paid a $3 million premium, buying each $100 bond for $104.5, at a yield of 3¾ percent.*

---

information he brought to the White House; that, after all, was what Morgan had first-class lawyers for. A week after the meeting, Stetson sent Cleveland a list of references to the 1862 debate "out of which has emerged the present section 3700 of the Revised Statutes."

What was there to gain from telling the story as if Morgan simply remembered the obscure law on the spot? It clearly made for better drama, and also indicated no premeditation on anyone's part. Both the bankers and the White House came under fierce attack for the 1895 loan, and participants on both sides had every reason to emphasize in retrospect the improvised nature of the proceedings. In March, after the first round of censure, Stetson told Cleveland that "your last public service is beginning to be seen aright; were it otherwise I should not cease to regret that even incidentally I was the occasion of drawing upon you criticism where you should have had only grateful praise."

* Morgan had expected to make a $100 million loan in exchange for bonds paying 3⅝ percent. Cleveland and Carlisle ultimately agreed to the higher 3¾ percent rate, but not on a full $100 million. Over Morgan's protest they reduced the amount of the loan to $65 million— just enough to restore the reserve to $100 million. Cleveland later said he thought Morgan had been right: the government should have taken the full $100 million to give the Treasury a healthy surplus—"and I have always since regretted that [Morgan's 'wise suggestion'] was not adopted."

Morgan was able to get a lower purchase price (i.e., a higher yield) than he expected because he knew exactly how desperate the situation was, had access to the capital that offered a solution, and could promise, at least in theory, to make the solution work. The Treasury agreed to give the bankers a large spread—the difference between the price the syndicate paid and the price it could charge the public—in exchange for urgently needed gold and protection of the federal reserve. The syndicate would have six months to complete the contract, and would procure half the new gold abroad at a rate not exceeding 300,000 ounces a month.

The meeting ended at 2:00 P.M.—it had lasted four and a half hours—and when Morgan stood up, a fine brown powder drifted from his lap to the floor. He had all morning been grinding the unlit cigar in his hand into dust. Cleveland laughed and handed around a box of fresh cigars.

———

"Impossible convey any just idea of what I have been through today," Morgan cabled Burns from the Arlington Hotel later that afternoon, "but we have carried our point & are more than satisfied." The new plan "will we think inspire confidence & act as an indicator that the U.S. Govt will buy gold when & where needed to maintain its Credit."

He took an evening train to New York, arriving late Tuesday night. Two days later, as expected, Congress defeated the bill to issue public bonds. Morgan returned to Washington on Thursday, February 7, in a heavy blizzard, to conclude the negotiations. He wired Burns on Friday: "Have just left Treasury Department, homeward bound. Could not have better document." He and Belmont would have "absolute control sales U.S." The Rothschilds and J. S. Morgan & Co. would have the same in London.*

———

* In a retrospective account of these events, Cleveland dated his initial meeting with Morgan three days later than it actually took place, making it seem as though he had negotiated with the bankers only after Congress rejected the public bond issue on February 7. In fact he had carefully worked out terms for the private loan before the congressional vote.

On Friday, the eighth, he sent a message to Congress announcing the terms of the deal. He had reserved the right to substitute 3 percent gold bonds at par for the 4 percent coin bonds selling at a premium—bonds that might ultimately be redeemed in silver—if he could get congressional authority within ten days of signing the contract. The full 1 percent difference in yield indicated that investors would have been willing to earn substantially less interest for guaranteed payment in gold. Substituting a gold bond bearing lower interest would have saved the government $16 million, but congressional silverites rejected the alternative and gave up the $16 million. Morgan would have been delighted to substitute a 3 percent bond payable in gold for precisely the reason Congress refused it—it would have substantially strengthened the country's commitment to gold.

London and New York each took half of the $62 million issue, and applications for syndicate participation were overwhelming. In the United States, Morgan and Belmont allotted their own firms about $2.7 million each, and gave large shares to George Baker's First National Bank, James Stillman's National City Bank, the United States Trust Co., and Harvey Fisk & Sons. They allotted lesser amounts (under $1 million each) to Standard Oil, the Mutual and the Equitable life insurance companies, and private banks including Winslow, Lanier; Kuhn, Loeb; Lazard Frères; Kidder, Peabody; Brown Brothers; and Morton, Bliss. The life insurance companies and Standard Oil, the only industrial firm in the syndicate, had so much available capital that they acted like banks.

On February 20, twelve days after signing the contract with the government, J. P. Morgan & Co. offered the bonds for sale at 112¼—nearly eight points above the syndicate's purchase price—and sold out the entire issue in twenty minutes. "Subscriptions something enormous," Morgan cabled his London partners. The issue was heavily oversubscribed, with a total bid of almost $200 million. J. S. Morgan & Co. in London had the same experience, closing its books after two hours with bids amounting, not including Rothschild's figures, to $100 million.

"We are quite overwhelmed by success of transaction," continued Morgan to Burns the next day. "We send you our deepest heartfelt congratulations. You must appreciate the relief to everybody's minds for the dangers were so great scarcely anyone dared whisper them."

A week later the price of the bonds in New York climbed to 124, which suggested that the initial offering could have been priced higher. Yet as it was, the public objected to unconscionable Wall Street profits; the criticism would have been even louder had the opening price been higher.

———

Morgan's messages to Burns recall Junius's remark about duty being a word whose definition could be made to conform to almost anything one *wants* to do. Pierpont preferred to have railroad companies and national economic affairs run smoothly on their own, and when they didn't—they often didn't—he complained of the responsibilities thrust onto his shoulders by a troublesome world. He rarely acknowledged how much he enjoyed being the man to whom other people turned in an emergency. Some years after the gold crisis, discussing his various rescue operations with his librarian, he highlighted this view of himself as reluctant hero, observing: "Sometimes I had to *take* command but it was always because there was no one else to do it."

"Perhaps there was no one else who *could* do it," she obligingly suggested.
He nodded: *"Vous avez raison."*

———

With the 1895 bond issue placed, gold on its way to the Treasury, and congratulations exchanged, Morgan turned to the harder part of his job—protecting the new reserve from withdrawals. The day before the bonds went on sale he had cabled Burns: "Whole transaction promises large profit but what is much more essential now that profit secured is to show public that our promises made at the time of the negotiations will be fulfilled & that our influence is powerful enough to maintain so far as possible Treasury gold reserves."

He could not reverse the trade deficit or stop the legitimate payment of gold for imported goods. He could and did, however, sustain the reserve by other means. At the outset he had set aside $3 million in bonds to sell as necessary to protect the exchange market, and a reserve of $10 million in gold to cover Treasury withdrawals. When people traded paper currency for gold, the syndicate replaced the gold, effectively providing the government with another $25 million—$15 million more than Morgan had anticipated with his $10 million reserve. The bankers took paper notes in exchange, but since the notes did not pay interest, the syndicate lost income on these substitutions. Morgan also set up a credit fund in Europe so that American traders buying foreign products could pay for them on credit rather than ship gold from New York.

And he intervened in the foreign-exchange markets, borrowing pounds in London and selling them in New York to prop up the dollar. Having allotted syndicate participation to the major traders in foreign exchange on condition that they not sell gold below a set price, he managed temporarily to offset the law of supply and demand. It was a classic Morgan consortium, with each party having a vested interest in a common end—in this case, protecting the Treasury against further loss of gold.

Morgan was in his element with the foreign-exchange campaign. Ever since his first trip abroad at age fifteen, he had been fascinated with the prices of money in different markets. Clerks at his Wall Street office brought him hourly reports of currency quotations, and at home over breakfast he got the figures from London by wire or phone. He monitored exchange markets the way a doctor takes a pulse, gauging the pressure in the financial arteries of nations. Through this information he could predict roughly what was going to happen to various currencies, and, reported his son-in-law Herbert Satterlee, "personally conducted considerable operations in exchange"—arbitrage operations, buying money in one market and immediately selling it in another to profit from the discrepancy in price. He used these diagnostic skills in 1895 to keep other people from speculating in Treasury gold.

To the surprise of skeptics on both sides of the Atlantic, his strategy worked. The $32.5 million in gold pledged by the American syndicate was delivered within a few weeks. The dollar's value held. Gold not only stopped leaching out of the Treasury—throughout the spring of 1895 it flowed steadily in. By the end of June the Treasury's reserve stood at $107.5 million. And as Morgan had hoped, the loan's success brought European capital back into U.S. markets.

It also amplified public perceptions of his power. The New York *Sun* attributed the restoration of foreign faith in America's credit entirely to Morgan. When he returned from his annual spring trip abroad that June, he not only had sold millions in U.S. securities through his own firms, reported the *Sun*, but had "revived a confidence in the wealth and resources of this country that has made a market for issues of securities of corporations with which he has no connection."

———

"I support Pierpont Morgan for President on a distinct gold monometallic platform," announced Henry Adams that June. To this Cassandra of America's economic politics, the country in 1895 consisted of two elements—borrowers and lenders of money—with the latter incontrovertibly in command. Adams, whose private income depended on the lenders, saw Morgan as the incarnation of capital, the gold standard, and America's financial dependence on England—all of which he regarded with antic dismay: "As a man of sense," he continued by mail to his brother Brooks, "I am a gold-bug and support a gold-bug government and a gold-bug society. As a man of the world, I like confusion, anarchy, and war."

On the sidelines Adams kept switching sides, concluding one minute that "the gold-bugs are not likely to lose the fight. They can't"—and the next that the syndicate would not be able to fulfill its obligations under the government contract, much less carry the country through the 1896 election.

With regard to the contract, Adams was partly right. The syndicate failed to provide the government with the full $32.5 million in gold it had pledged to deliver from Europe. During the six-month life of the contract, some of the foreign investors who had agreed to buy bonds reneged on their commitments—probably because of the depression, unresolved U.S. currency questions, and new corporate bankruptcies. When the bankers made their final gold delivery to the Treasury on June 24, they had imported just $15.75 million, less than half the amount promised. Secretary Carlisle allowed them to modify the contract and eliminate the import requirement. Syndicate members made up the difference from their own domestic reserves.

Morgan had insisted in February that public confidence could be restored only if half the coin came from abroad. As it happened, everyone *thought* the gold was coming from Europe, which in itself restored public equanimity. In financial markets, confidence can be as good as gold.

The sale of gold to the government involved significant risk. If the markets had not taken the bonds at or above the purchase price, syndicate members would have had to hold or sell them at a loss. Had the bankers failed to come up with $65 million in gold, had Morgan been unable to protect the reserve, had the trade deficit grown, a renegade currency trader broken ranks, or the country repudiated the gold standard, the whole operation could have gone off track.

To Morgan, those risks were worth taking because of the greater danger posed to the national economy by government default and the related threat of currency devaluation. All the foreign investment in the United States—much of it represented by the house of Morgan—depended on gold's disciplinary "rule of law." Morgan couldn't afford *not* to take the action he did in 1895. As he had cabled Walter Burns at the outset, "We all have large interests dependent upon maintenance sound currency U.S."

The people who suffered most under the economic stringency of the nineties were outraged by the bankers' gold bond issue. Rumors put the syndicate profits at $5 million to $18 million. A Farmers' Alliance publication denounced the "great bunco game" that had cheated the American people out of more than $8 million in bankers' profits while adding another $62 million to the national debt, and called for a revolution against the vampires of the financial trust.

The Rothschilds' participation provoked a display of the anti-Semitism that has animated xenophobic populism of the left and right throughout American history, reflexively linking issues of money and credit with Jews. William Jennings Bryan ordered the House clerk to read Shylock's bond, then demanded "that the Treasury shall be administered on behalf of the American people and not on behalf of the Rothschilds and other foreign bankers." Pulitzer's *World* complained that a "Wall Street conspiracy" of foreign aliens and bloodsucking Jews had robbed the country of millions in twenty minutes. Mary E. Lease, a populist writer who advised farmers to "raise less corn and more hell," denounced Cleveland as "the agent of Jewish bankers and British gold."

With the archfiend Rothschild far away across the Atlantic, his accomplice in New York took the brunt of American wrath. "The abuse poor Morgan has received, is receiving, and is likely to receive," wrote a Brown Brothers partner to his London office at the beginning of March, "is both outrageous and discouraging." In mid-March, exhausted by the syndicate work and public attacks, Morgan reported himself to Walter Burns as "completely worn out hardly fit for business."

No President for two decades forgot the intensity of public outrage at Washington's deal with Wall Street. Cleveland published an account of the episode nine years later, using the language of his accusers with heavy irony: "Without shame and without repentance, I confess my share of the guilt" in the "crime charged," he wrote, "and though Mr. Morgan and Mr. Belmont and scores of other bankers and financiers who were accessories in those transactions may be steeped in destructive propensities, and may be constantly busy in sinful schemes, I shall always recall with satisfaction and self-congratulation my collusion with them at a time when our country sorely needed their aid."

Some of the press took a sympathetic line. Villard's *Evening Post* said in February of 1895 that the bankers and the President had acted to allay an unprecedented "emergency in public finance," while Congress stood by "like a lot of boys playing with dynamite." *The New York Times* reported that "the admiration of the financial world is turned upon [Morgan's] masterly management of the loan": no other banking house "could have pledged the power now behind the contract, to keep the Treasury reserve intact, and investors large and small would not have trooped so willingly for possession of the bonds except for the safeguards thrown about them and about the gold reserve." The syndicate had earned its profits, concluded the *Times*—no corporation could have "put the business of the country on its feet for $5,000,000."

In fact, the syndicate earned far less than $5 million on the transaction. It had pledged to deliver $65 million in gold in exchange for $62 million in bonds. The American group as a whole netted about $1.5 million—just under 5 percent of the $31 million U.S. half of the issue—plus roughly $500,000 in interest (not generally calculated as profit) on the securities. J. P. Morgan & Co.'s share of the American profits came to $131,932; the firm's total earnings from the operation, including interest and half of the U.S. management fee, were $295,653.*

In view of the amounts these bankers regularly handled and the specter of federal default, the American syndicate's $1.5 million earnings were relatively modest, yet even that figure would have been seen by their political opponents as robbery. When the Senate investigated the transaction the following year, Morgan refused to discuss his fees. He regarded a private banker's earnings and losses as private. Testifying in June 1896, he was questioned first by the pro-business New York Republican boss (now Senator), Thomas Collier Platt, and then by an ardent silverite, George Vest of Missouri.

* The Morgan and Belmont firms earned a ¾ percent commission for managing the loan, paid out of the syndicate account, which came to $116,841 each. Pierpont also received 40 percent of the London house's profits. Total figures for the European syndicate are not available, but J. S. Morgan & Co.'s earnings came to £18,400, or about $89,424.

Platt, endorsing Morgan's declaration that he had acted out of large, public motives, concluded: "And so your real purpose, as I understand you, in this transaction was not the idea that you could take this bond issue and make money out of it, but that you could prevent a panic and distress in the country."

Morgan: "I will answer that question, though I do not think it necessary, in view of all that I have done. I will say that I had no object except to save the disaster that would result in case that foreign gold had not been obtained."

Senator Vest asked, "If that was your sole object, why did you specify in your telegraphic communication to Mr. Carlisle that your house, or you and Mr. Belmont, were to have exclusive control of the matter?"

Morgan: "Because it was absolutely impossible for more than one party to negotiate—to make the same negotiation for the same lot of gold. It would only have made competition."

A skeptical Vest: "If the gold was abroad I take it for granted that anybody could get hold of it who had the means to do so. If you were actuated by the desire to prevent a panic, why were you not willing that other people should do it, if they wanted to?"

Morgan. "They could not do it."

Theoretically, investors with access to good information buy securities on the merits. Yet taking into account the condition of the Treasury in 1895, unresolved currency questions, and the weakness of the Executive Office, Morgan thought large numbers of investors would buy bonds only if his name was on the deal.

He did what he did. It made sense to him. He insisted on control. He would not go into particulars. To his antagonists at the time and since, this reasoning seemed arrogant and self-serving. Yet his claim in response to Vest's last question—that other people "could not do it"—was probably true. Another banker might have raised $65 million in gold, but probably no one else could have managed the markets and the men involved in them for six months as effectively as Morgan did. His power lay in his willingness to take on this kind of risk and responsibility, his knowledge of markets, his access to capital, and the record that had earned him the confidence of the world's leading financiers.

Grover Cleveland years later recalled that when the syndicate contract expired he asked Morgan how he had known he could "command the cooperation of the great financial interests of Europe?"

"I simply told them that this was necessary for the maintenance of the public credit and the promotion of industrial peace," Morgan replied, "and they did it."

An inadvertent witness at the time testified both to the dubious profitability of the loans and to the unquestioning trust the international financial community now placed in Morgan. The London firm of C. J. Hambro & Son, on being offered a share in a new bond issue in January of 1896, told the Morgan bank that under present circumstances it did not have much hope of profits on the business, but would nonetheless "readily subscribe if you in any way wish."

Other bankers did what Morgan told them to do because he was working for them all, to maintain the dollar's value and the international credit of the United States. The President had not been able to stop the gold drain or calm the agitated markets in 1895, and Congress wouldn't. Morgan alone seemed to have the power, motive, and will to end this crisis.

Contrary to his assertions before the senators, he had been careful from the outset to secure the syndicate's profits—partly because he was in business for profit, and partly to offset the expenditures he would, and did, have to make to protect the reserve. In the political climate of 1896, however, he could not make that obvious point in public.

Once again, he did not question the equation of his own and the country's best interests. The acute distress of farmers and workers probably seemed to him an unfortunate but inevitable side effect of business-cycle downturns, tight money, and rapid industrialization, and he was trying on several fronts to get the entire economy back on course. His own short-term profits in issuing the 1895 loan were immaterial next to the long-term growth that depended on stable U.S. credit, and it was in that light that he saw himself as having averted national disaster.*

———

Just a few weeks after the syndicate contract expired in the summer of 1895— as Colonel Mann reported on the swirling Atlantic "nor-wester" involving a beautiful widow (Edith Randolph), a potential Democratic presidential candidate (Whitney), and an eminent financier (Morgan)—gold exports and the flight from the dollar resumed: further railroad bankruptcies and the prospect of more struggle over the U.S. currency prompted European investors once again to sell American stocks. The syndicate supplied the Treasury with an-

---

* It is impossible to say what would have happened if Morgan had not intervened in 1895. Going off the gold standard would probably have escalated the flight of foreign capital, as he feared, leading to a market collapse, a deeper depression, and an increase in unemployment, but it probably would not have derailed the essentially vital U.S. economy for more than a few years. Milton Friedman and Anna Schwartz have characterized the 1893 panic and subsequent depression as "at bottom simply the way in which an adjustment, forced by other considerations, worked itself out." World gold prices dropped 11 percent between 1891 and 1897, and as long as the United States remained on the gold standard, it had to reduce prices and income accordingly. Unlike Morgan, however, Friedman and Schwartz do not think it would have been economically undesirable for the United States to abandon the gold standard: "On the contrary, our own view is that it might well have been highly preferable to the generally depressed conditions of the 1890s. We rule it out only because, as it turned out, it was politically unacceptable."

other $2 million in gold, but a dejected Morgan cabled Walter Burns from Newport: "We must acknowledge defeat[,] accept the situation and lose prestige attained. Subject deepest regret to me for unfortunately I seem to be personally held [responsible] by public for whole business."

Burns replied, with unintended comic understatement, "You cannot control US balance trade"—and tried to cheer his brother-in-law up: "Do not feel unhappy, our prestige firmly established by what you have done already."

The gold reserve fell from $93 million in late September to $50 million by the end of January 1896. Morgan met quietly with Cleveland and Carlisle at the White House the day before Christmas, 1895, to discuss ways of protecting the money supply. Returning to New York that night, he began organizing a new international group to furnish the government with gold. The press, led by Pulitzer's *World,* promptly attacked him and his syndicate of thieving "sharks."

On January 4 Morgan wrote to the President "with great hesitation," but "the gravity of the situation must be my excuse." His recent visit to Washington had convinced him that Congress would not act, as he delicately put it, to "improve the methods at the disposal of the Executive." Since Cleveland's hands were tied, Morgan offered to raise another $200 million in gold: "I do not hesitate to affirm, in fact to urge that such a contract would in every way be for the best interests of the Government and the people." Still, he knew that political opposition might prohibit another private loan. If Cleveland had to resort to a public bond issue, Morgan would "pledge to you every influence and effort in my power to assist the Government" and make the sale succeed.

Cleveland's potential successor, William C. Whitney, urged the administration to work with Morgan on a new loan: "Personally," he told War Secretary Daniel Lamont, "I think it very fortunate there is such an alliance to be had by the Government as Morgan & his great power. . . . If I were the President whatever I did I should do with Morgan—It will fail of the effect otherwise."

———

Public sentiment that winter ran higher than ever against the syndicate. Henry Adams, writing at the end of 1895 to his brother Brooks, lumped together "Lombard Street, Wall Street, State Street, and all the other Judengassen" now running the world. Brooks in turn denounced Wall Street as "the final result of the corruptest society which ever trod the earth. I tell you," he wound up, in a tirade that might have made Morgan, had he seen it, chuckle— "Rome was a blessed garden of paradise beside the rotten, unsexed, swindling, lying Jews, represented by J. P. Morgan and the gang who have been manipulating our country for the last four years."

Even men who might have been expected to trust Morgan sided with his critics. The Reverend Endicott Peabody, the Groton headmaster who had enlisted the financier's help in the founding of his school, did not "at all like Cleveland's giving out this new loan to Mr. Morgan," he told a friend early in 1896: "Nothing is more calculated to bring out dissatisfaction in the West—and it does not seem to me altogether above suspicion. I can't quite understand a man like Mr. Morgan making money out of his country's need. . . . The fewer of such men we have in this country the better I say. Dullness which is contented with smaller profits is better in the long run."

As the din of condemnation swelled to a roar, Walter Burns cabled his brother-in-law from London: "I cannot bear thought your incurring such obloquy and annoyance as you had before for profit which at best doubtful and mostly reaped by others. Only object doing business is patriotism and gaining national credit."

Morgan replied: "You have no idea situation here personal to myself from certain classes politicians others who desire wreck everything. Am watched & followed attacked papers—hence necessary very careful."

Cleveland and Carlisle decided against a second private contract. On January 6 they announced a public sale of bonds to raise $100 million in gold. Morgan dissolved his new syndicate and, as if he were the head of an allied independent state, urged its members to subscribe to the government's loan: "I desire to sustain the Executive to the fullest extent in his efforts to maintain sound currency and the credit of the country," he told them, "for which every loyal citizen should hold him in gratitude."

When an irate Walter Burns declined to share in the loan, Morgan warned that they could not play Achilles: "In view our position here we cannot withdraw and appear to sulk." He put together a smaller consortium to bid for the entire $100 million issue; the government awarded a third to his group. The bonds sold well, which Burns saw as likely to have "great influence restoring general confidence."

Morgan went briefly to Europe that May. Louisa left Fanny in Germany to meet him in Paris on the ninth, noting in her diary, "Father arrived this morning looking very well & seeming cheerful." Morgan *père et fille* dined with friends and shopped at Worth's, then crossed to London. Louisa accompanied friends to Scotland for two weeks while her father tended to his London business. On June 3 she returned to her mother, he to New York: "Dearest Father!" she wrote in her diary, "he has seemed like his old self these last days. The queer strain of this spring was quite gone."

The new gold did not stay in the Treasury. As the fight over the currency continued, the reserve dropped from $128 million at the end of March to $101 million by July, when the Democrats met to nominate a presidential candidate.

———

The 1896 election generated greater national excitement than any since the Civil War, and most of it centered on the economy. The Republicans had taken control of Congress by a large majority in 1894, promising economic recovery from the Cleveland-era depression, while Democrats and Populists across the country were voted out. Still, the Populists' numerical tally rose 42 percent between 1892 and 1894. In 1896, the Democratic Party split along sectional lines, just as it had in 1860: this time, agrarian Democrats in the South and West allied with Populists to support silver and oppose the "conspiracy" of goldbugs, led by the apostate Cleveland, in the conservative Northeast.

The leading candidate for the Republican nomination was William McKinley, a former congressman and two-term governor of Ohio. Courtly, heavyset, and handsome—the wide V of his eyebrows gave him the look of an amiable falcon—McKinley had a formidable asset in his friend Mark Hanna, a wealthy Ohio industrialist turned political boss. For more than a year, Republican Party chairman Hanna had been spending all of his time and much of his own money in the effort to put McKinley in the White House.

Because the candidate from Ohio was willing to work for international bimetallism—a double standard of silver and gold—the eastern wing of the party judged him a "Straddle-bug." Hanna called him the "advance agent of prosperity." To Morgan, a president not firmly committed to gold looked like the advance agent of disaster.

Shortly before the Republican convention in June, Ohio banker and state party leader Myron Herrick called on Morgan and found the banker "violent" in his views. According to Herrick, Morgan declared McKinley's waffling on the currency question "nauseating," and said that if the candidate did not have a "backbone of jelly" he ought to come out squarely for gold.

Herrick pointed out that the election was not entirely up to Wall Street: politicians had to answer to larger constituencies, and the country was sharply divided over gold. Political expediency dictated that McKinley hedge now in order to get elected. "If the bankers are on one side and the politicians on the other," warned Herrick, "you will divide the country at the Mississippi, and we shall lose."

To help get the bankers and the politicians on the same side, Herrick arranged for Mark Hanna to meet Morgan on board *Corsair* that night. In the yacht's oak-paneled dining saloon, Morgan delivered an impromptu lecture on the gold standard. Hanna in turn made out the case for McKinley, promised to stiffen the candidate's backbone on gold, and asked his host to help underwrite the campaign. By the time the trio left the yacht late that night, Morgan had agreed to raise money for the Republican ticket. McKinley won the nomination on the first ballot in June, on a Hanna-engineered platform committed to protectionism and gold.

A month later, silver Democrats took over their party's convention in Chicago. They overwhelmingly rejected the Old Guard represented by Cleveland and Whitney, with speeches denouncing gold, the trusts, national banks, the Morgan loan, and the Supreme Court. The "new" Democrats nominated the relatively unknown William Jennings Bryan, on a platform committed to unlimited coinage of silver.

It was at this convention that Bryan delivered his famous speech: "We have petitioned, and our petitions have been scorned; we have entreated, and our entreaties have been disregarded; we have begged, and they have mocked when our calamity came. We beg no longer; we entreat no more; we petition no more. We defy them. . . . Having behind us the producing masses of this nation and the world, supported by the commercial interests, the laboring interests, and the toilers everywhere, we will answer their demand for a gold standard by saying to them: You shall not press down upon the brow of labor this crown of thorns, you shall not crucify mankind upon a cross of gold."

The "Cross of Gold" speech brought the convention to its feet—delegates cheered, cried, shouted, and applauded for thirty-five minutes. Two weeks later, in St. Louis, the Populists also nominated Bryan, with a different vice presidential candidate. Gold Democrats bolted their party. The day after the Chicago convention, 150 Democratic members of the New York Stock Exchange waving American flags marched to the rostrum and put on McKinley buttons, shouting "Down with the red flag" and "up with the Stars and Stripes." The *World* somewhat prematurely concluded that "the sceptre of political power has passed from the strong certain hands of the East to the feverish, headstrong mob of the West and South."

———

One Southern Democrat who believed in "the strong certain hands of the East" was a young German-Jewish newspaperman from Chattanooga, Tennessee, named Adolph Simon Ochs. His *Chattanooga Times* had come out squarely for gold, and in the summer of 1896, Ochs made a bid for the country's leading metropolitan newspaper, *The New York Times.* Founded in 1851, the *Times* had been staunchly Republican during and after the Civil War; when its "Mugwump" editors backed Cleveland against Blaine in 1884, however, Republican readers and advertisers defected in droves. Democrats took over the paper, but with poor management and lively competition—especially from the new, scandal-mongering "yellow" press such as Pulitzer's *World* and Hearst's *Journal*—it had gone deeply into debt. By 1896 its paid circulation had fallen to nine thousand and it was losing $2,500 a week.

The combination of Ochs's success in Tennessee, his credible ambitions, his stalwart support of gold, and a letter of endorsement from Grover Cleveland persuaded the owners of the *Times* to sell him a controlling interest in the paper for a quarter of the stock's face value. Next, Ochs asked the principal bondholders, including Morgan, to exchange their securities for new ones paying lower interest. He later recalled his terror at the prospect of approaching the formidable financier. To his amazement, when he arrived at the inner sanctum at 23 Wall Street, Morgan—who specialized in refinancing debt—rose to greet him, shook his hand, and said warmly, "So you're the young man I have heard about. Now, where do I sign the papers?"

In his first issue as publisher of the *Times* on August 19, 1896, Ochs announced that he would publish the news "impartially, without fear or favor, regardless of party, sect, or interests involved," and would not depart from the policies that distinguished the *Times* as a "non-partisan newspaper—unless it be, if possible, to intensify its devotion to the cause of sound money and tariff reform, opposition to wastefulness and peculation in administering public affairs, and in its advocacy of the lowest tax consistent with good government, and no more government than is absolutely necessary." It was a measure of the moment's moral absolutism that an honest proponent of sound money and small government could call them nonpartisan issues.

Morgan, Belmont, and Jacob Schiff each held $25,000 worth of the *Times*'s $600,000 debt, which the new owners eventually bought back and retired. That the men involved in the resuscitation of the paper shared a commitment to gold was taken for conspiracy. Rumors that Morgan owned *The New York Times* haunted the paper and the banker for years.

———

The Populist movement, growing out of the Grange associations, Greenback Party, and Farmers' Alliances, tried to redirect the course of American economic development. According to one of its leading historians, Lawrence Goodwyn, it was "the largest democratic mass movement in American history." Relentlessly squeezed by falling crop prices, high railroad rates, and the rising cost of debt, America's farmers and their urban allies had in the early nineties proposed a range of measures to take power away from the "money centers" and giant corporations of the Northeast, and to expand government authority over finance, transportation, and land. The United States eventually adopted many of those measures, but in 1896 silverites gained control of the Populist/Democratic "fusion," and focused the campaign on a single panacea.

Throughout the summer and fall, Bryan traveled across the country speaking to large crowds. In clear, powerful language he denounced a complacent plutocracy that appeared to be governing the country in predatory self-interest, and promised more money to people who did not have enough—higher crop prices, easy credit, cheaper (silver) dollars available in abundance. His appeal was personal as well as ideological. Ellen Maury Slayden, the wife of a Democratic congressman from Texas, found Bryan's conversation "easy, unpretentious, and amazingly humorous for such a dead-in-earnest person." She thought his hair too long ("the usual weakness of Western statesmen") and his clothes "queer, but I didn't notice them until he was on the stage. I saw only his clear, steel-blue eyes with black brows and lashes, very Irish, his straight un-compromising mouth, and well-kept teeth." He addressed a crowd of Texans with "the most perfect voice I ever heard," continued Mrs. Slayden. "The audi-ence went wild. When he finished people swarmed around him, shaking his hands, touching his shoulders, almost kissing the hem of his garment. How can a man retain his sanity amid such adulation?"

The double nomination of Bryan and his single-minded commitment to sil-ver united the formerly bipartisan conservative establishment. In what amounted to a twentieth-century fund-raising effort orchestrated by Mark Hanna, wealthy individuals, banks, railroads, insurance companies, and cor-porations contributed roughly $7 million to the McKinley campaign, while the Populist national treasurer took in about a dozen letters a day containing "twenty-five cents to a dollar." Brooks Adams claimed that Hanna got $2 mil-lion out of one Boston office building in the first week of August.

Hanna also ran a modern publicity campaign in 1896. He distributed pro-paganda by the ton—posters, pamphlets, leaflets, banners, buttons—and sent Republican speakers, including former President Benjamin Harrison and New York City police commissioner Theodore Roosevelt, out to rally voters all over the country. McKinley refused to go on the stump, partly on account of his wife's poor health, but also, he said, because "I might just as well put up a trapeze on my front lawn and compete with some professional athlete as go out speaking against Bryan. I have to *think* when I speak." Instead of sending McKinley to the voters, Hanna brought the voters to the candidate's front porch. Pro-McKinley railroads offered such low rates to Ohio that over 750,000 people made the trip—somebody quipped that visiting the Republi-can nominee was cheaper than staying home.

While the Democrats fanned popular fears of malevolent foreign bankers, Republicans played up the specter of revolutionary anarchy and appealed to widespread anxieties about radical foreign ideas. At the Chicago Coliseum in October, Roosevelt warned an audience of thirteen thousand against people who read Tolstoy, Marx, and Proudhon—and against anyone who "believes that at this stage of the world's progress it is possible to make everyone happy by an immense social revolution."

Just the word "revolution" was enough to unhinge the stock market and renew the Treasury drain. The new Dow Jones average of twelve industrial stocks had opened at 40.94 on May 26, 1896. By the end of August it had fallen over 30 percent, to 28.28.

The day after the Populists nominated Bryan in July, Morgan put together an informal combination of New York's leading international bankers to restrict gold shipments and stabilize the markets for foreign exchange, just as he had done under the 1895 Treasury contract. In effect, he appointed himself ex-tragovernmental Secretary of the Treasury, and Assistant Secretary Curtis applauded his efforts in a private letter home: "The New York people have come up well," Curtis wrote, "& we see the curious spectacle of the U.S. finances being controlled by a committee, of which J. P. Morgan is the Chairman, & the majority of whom are Hebrews, while the Secretary of the Treasury sits, practically powerless, in his office."*

To the Republicans' delight, Bryan focused on silver to the exclusion of all other issues: he did not press for agricultural loans, railroad regulation, or an income tax, nor did he address the troubles of the urban working class. Hanna exulted that the Democratic/Populist candidate was "talking silver all the time, and that's where we've got him." Henry Demarest Lloyd, the author of *Wealth Against Commonwealth*, pronounced free silver "the cow-bird of the reform movement. It waited until the nest had been built by the sacrifices and labour of others, and then it laid its eggs in it, pushing out the others which lie smashed on the ground."

On November 3, McKinley defeated Bryan by 610,000 on the popular ballot, and 271 to 176 in the electoral college. Bryan had won 6,493,000 votes—more than any previous presidential victor—but carried no state north of Virginia or east of Missouri, and not a single industrial urban state. The Republicans won majorities in the Senate and House, and in many state legislatures as well. "If the primary purpose of the old [Democratic] party was a national victory for silver," concludes the historian C. Vann Woodward, "the campaign was a failure. If on the other hand the purpose was the destruction of the Populist party, it was a success." The sweeping Republican victory meant a return to conservatism, an uncontested gold standard, and the dominion of big business, but many of the issues that animated the Populist revolt resurfaced in the Progressivism of the early twentieth century.

The day after the 1896 election, Morgan cabled Walter Burns: "Have won glorious victory—from present returns McKinley has secured 310 Electoral votes at least. Heart full thankfulness."

Burns replied: "Result most gratifying, gives great satisfaction here as evidencing determination maintain country's credit. We congratulate you most heartily & we feel you have contributed largely to the result." Ironically, just as the hard-money men were winning their fight against silver, huge deposits of gold were discovered in Colorado, Alaska, and South Africa. The doubling of the world's gold supply between 1890 and 1914 brought about the monetary easing that Bryan and his supporters desperately wanted. Moreover, a combination of crop failures abroad and a bumper U.S. harvest in 1897 helped

---

* Once again, Morgan created sufficient capital inflow to forestall a flight from the dollar. Just the formation of a Morgan syndicate virtually stopped the gold drain. At the end of August, when the seasonal export of agricultural produce began to bring in new supplies of gold, the syndicate dissolved without having made a single transaction.

American farmers and ended the trade deficit, bringing in a steady flow of European gold: at the end of that year the Treasury reserve stood at $137 million, and by mid-1898 at $245 million.

From the edge of bankruptcy the U.S. economy recovered, and the country embarked on a new period of expansion. Farm prices rose steadily in the first decade of the twentieth century, as did the price of land—without the benefit of silver, and without the loss of national credit that Morgan had fought to prevent in his long defense of gold.

Chapter 19

ACQUISITIONS
AND LOSSES

M organ turned sixty in 1897. He had emerged from the Treasury gold
crises as one of the most influential bankers in the world, to applause in
some quarters and vilification in others. The complicated arrangements of his
private life were bringing him more pleasure than his marriage had in decades.
And he was making a great deal of money. The profits of his American firms
rose from $2 million in 1895 to over $8 million in 1899, and his share of those
earnings came to nearly $8 million. For the same period in London, J. S. Mor-
gan & Co. posted profits of £622,000, or $3,110,000, to his account. Not in-
cluding investment returns, he earned about $11 million in five years—nearly
half of what his father had accumulated in a lifetime.

The explosion of activity in Morgan's public and private lives over the
decade that followed Junius's death would have been remarkable in a man half
his age. During the closing years of the Victorian century he extended his railroad consolidations, began organizing industrial trusts, bought four more
country properties, built a new yacht, and started in earnest on his second career as collector of art.

In the fall of 1895, a month after *Town Topics* first reported on his liaison
with Adelaide, Morgan bought a "fishing box" in Newport. Fanny apparently
never saw it. Louisa described it to her many years later as "quaint, and so entirely different from anything suggested by the name 'Newport' that it amuses
me greatly." It amused her father to hear that drivers of tour buses stopped

there after showing off the nouveaux châteaux of the Vanderbilts, Belmonts, Wetmores, and Astors to announce, "And *this* is the Newport residence of Mr. Pierpont Morgan."

Mr. Morgan's Newport residence consisted of six small wooden buildings on fifteen acres of coast at Graves Point. Everywhere else he hired white servants, but at Newport he had a cook named Lizzie, whom Louisa described as "a big, fine negress and a real cordon bleu," married to "a well trained butler of the days 'fo de war' beginning to be a bit shaky on his pins, but with all the old ideas and ways." Sadie, the assistant cook, was "a more modern darkey with an amiable smile and her frizzy hair in *curl papers.*" The man in charge of fishing, "a native New Englander" named Eugene, had "never been off the island of Rhode Island in his life!"

Morgan stopped at Newport once or twice a summer, usually with Adelaide and the Markoes, Bowdoins, or Laniers. The women took walks and paid calls in town while the men, not including their host, fished from wooden stands set on jagged shelves of rock. As a joke for friends who said Morgan did nothing at Newport but play cards and eat, Lanier posed him one day for a photograph with someone else's catch: in a yachting cap, white pants, and a navy blue jacket buttoned across his ample girth, the resolute nonsportsman sits beside a string of large bass with a fishing rod in one hand and a Pekinese on his lap.

In 1897, two years after acquiring the Newport "box," he bought an apartment on Jekyl Island, a former plantation turned into a resort off the coast of Georgia. Incorporated in 1885, the Jekyl Island Club drew half of its original members from Manhattan's Union Club, and *The New York Times* predicted that it would become a winter Newport. (Residents spelled Jekyl with one *l* until 1929, then changed it to two.) The attractions of the island resort included a racecourse, stocked fish and game, wide beaches, ocean views, salt marshes, live oaks draped in Spanish moss, and a past populated by Indians, Spanish missionaries, and French planters. In 1904, *Munsey's Magazine* called Jekyl the "richest, the most exclusive, the most inaccessible" club in the world.

Several members built houses on the island, and five of them constructed a six-apartment complex called Sans Souci in 1896. Morgan bought the sixth unit the following year. He saw it for the first time in 1898, and after that brought Adelaide and other friends down for occasional respite from New York winters.

He acquired property in the Adirondack Mountains in the late 1890s as well. Dr. Thomas Clark Durant, one of the promoters of the Union Pacific Railroad, had built a short rail line from Saratoga Springs to North Creek in the central Adirondacks in 1865, and bought up tracts of surrounding land. In the seventies he enlisted his son, William West Durant, to develop the heavily wooded wilderness. By the early nineties, W. W. Durant had brought in telegraph lines, a post office, a general store, and Episcopal and Catholic churches.

From left: Alice Beavor-Webb, Pierpont Morgan, Adelaide Douglas,
J. Beavor-Webb, and Annette Markoe at Camp Uncas in the Adirondacks.
(Courtesy of the late Annette M. Schieffelin)

He also built private camps, using local white pine and inventing the style—part log cabin, part Swiss chalet—that has defined Adirondack architecture ever since. After he sold his first camp to the railroad magnate Collis P. Huntington in 1895, Durant moved into the second, on Lake Mohegan, which he named Uncas after the hero of James Fenimore Cooper's *Last of the Mohicans.* He had borrowed money from Morgan, and at the beginning of 1896 he offered Camp Uncas as partial payment of the debt.

Morgan went up to see the property in February. From the train station he drove by sleigh through miles of dense forest, past frozen lakes banked with drifts of snow; the only sounds to break the winter silence were an occasional animal cry and the snap of trees cracking in the cold. He took one look at Camp Uncas, recalled one of his granddaughters, "and decided that he wasn't interested, as he was not at all an outdoor gentleman." The following year he changed his mind, taking title to the camp in July of 1897 on the theory that his family and friends might enjoy it.

They did. His Adirondack property consisted of fifteen hundred wooded acres with its own iron foundry and sugarhouse, just south of Raquette Lake. Two of Durand's peeled-log cabins had been named Chingachgook and Hawkeye, after other characters in *The Last of the Mohicans.* The main lodge, built on a stone foundation, had polished pine beams, built-in bureaus, wraparound banquette window seats, and enormous stone fireplaces. In the summers, tame bears named Ursula and Uncas came to the cabins for handouts.

Morgan held no romantic notions about the virtues of roughing it in the woods. He kept Durant's Adirondack "stick" furniture, guide boats, earthenware crockery, and Franklin stoves, but installed fully equipped modern bathrooms, long-distance telephones, and a twelve-griddle kitchen range. He eventually sent two Steinway pianos up to Camp Uncas, along with three dozen champagne glasses, blue and white china, thick fur sleigh rugs, embroidered linens, iron beds, brass lamps, horsehair mattresses, feather pillows, ice cream molds, asparagus kettles, angelfood-cake tins, jardinières, a white polar-bear rug, and 125 Plymouth Rock hens. He retained Durant's cook and caretaker, along with carpenters, stable hands, farmers, gardeners, and maids.

He visited his northern preserve only in the winter. In the summers he preferred yacht cruises and European travel to this isolated retreat, but his children took their friends to the Adirondacks in all seasons.

Shortly after he bought Camp Uncas, Morgan financed construction of a winter access road through the forest from Durant's North Creek railroad terminal. Then in 1898 he and his Adirondack neighbors built an eighteen-mile rail line linking their properties to the New York Central branch station at Clearwater. Among the other directors of the new Raquette Lake Railway were W. W. Durant, Bob Bacon, William C. Whitney, Collis Huntington, Chauncey

Depew, and W. Seward Webb (who owned property on both sides of Lake Champlain). For its size, this tiny road probably had the wealthiest board of directors in the world.

Construction proceeded quickly, and in the fall of 1899 Huntington took an inaugural run up to Raquette Lake on his private train, *Genesta*. More impressive to the locals than his extravagantly appointed cars was his Japanese staff, imported from California. Morgan chartered Pullman Palace coaches for his own visits to the Adirondacks, creating another kind of sensation by keeping an engine waiting at the station twenty-four hours a day, steam up and ready to go, in case he wanted to leave on a moment's notice for New York.

He rarely spent more than a few days at any of his rural preserves, and often did return to the city on short notice. Sometimes professional crises called him back, but usually it was his own restlessness that kept him in constant motion. He found little pleasure in nature or bucolic life; only on ocean liners and at European spas did he fully relax. As soon as he finished setting up and fitting out each new country "barony," from Cragston to Camp Uncas, he tended to lose interest and move on.

———

He embarked on an unusual venture in the fall of 1896 when the publishing house of Harper & Brothers asked for his financial help. Harper's was one of the oldest publishers in the United States, including among its authors Dickens, Macauley, the Brontës, Thackeray, George Eliot, Wilkie Collins, Thoreau, Melville, William Dean Howells, Mark Twain, and Henry James. In addition to its trade book division, the company owned the illustrated family newspaper *Harper's Weekly*, a children's journal called *Harper's Round Table*, the weekly fashion magazine, *Harper's Bazar* [sic], and *Harper's New Monthly Magazine*, which serialized many of its novels. It also published textbooks.

Cultural distinction had not translated into profit, and Harper's was nearly bankrupt when one of its directors, William Mackay Laffan, asked Morgan to engineer a rescue. Laffan was an Irish-born journalist and arts connoisseur, formerly an editor with Harper's, now publisher of the New York *Sun* and one of Morgan's advisers on art. (He had published a book about *Engravings on Wood* in 1887 and would bring out another on *Oriental Ceramic Art* in 1897.) J. P. Morgan & Co. reorganized the seventy-nine-year-old Harper's partnership as a corporation in November 1896, issuing $2 million of stock and $3 million in bonds. The Harper family bought most of the stock, and Laffan earned a $100,000 commission. Over the next three years the house of Morgan lent the house of Harper $850,000.

Morgan did not impose new management on Harper's the way he did on bankrupt railroads, and in 1899 the publishers again faced default. The book division was earning no profit, the English office had closed (Clarence McIl-vaine, Juliet's rejected suitor, stayed on as Harper's London representative, hiring a young associate named Jonathan Cape), and the magazine was losing advertising and circulation. A rival monthly called *McClure's*, which cost 15¢ to *Harper's* 35¢, had drawn authors away with the prospect of wider distribution through its affiliated newspaper syndicate. Samuel S. McClure was publishing Ida Tarbell, Lincoln Steffens, Stephen Crane, William Allen White, Ray Stannard Baker, Frank Norris, O. Henry, Booth Tarkington, Theodore Dreiser, and Jack London; he was also publishing books in partnership with Frank Doubleday.

McClure was to the Harpers what Charles Coffin was to Thomas Edison—an astute manager who had figured out how to run the business more effectively than his rivals—and at Laffan's suggestion, Morgan invited McClure to take over the ailing house of Harper at a bargain price: two thirds of the $2 million in stock for roughly half its nominal value, or $692,000, payable over ten years. McClure wired an associate: "I have got the earth with several things thrown in, and am eager to see if you don't want one or two kingdoms for yourself." He could not raise money for the purchase, however, partly because of Harper's large debt.

Morgan offered to increase his loan in the fall of 1899, but the Harper directors decided to put the company into receivership. They hired George M. Harvey, a former managing editor of Pulitzer's *World*, to reorganize and run it. Morgan approved, telling the board that "the downfall of the House of Harper would be a national calamity." When William Dean Howells learned of the Harper default, he said, "It was as if I had read that the government of the United States had failed." In the early years of the twentieth century, people said the *Weekly* had become more Harvey's than Harper's.*

Morgan never asked the publisher to repay his loan, and advanced additional sums over the next several years for a total of almost $2.5 million, much of which was still on the books at the time of his death. He did not expect profit or editorial influence—he really thought "the downfall of the House of Harper

---

* His regime was as notable for its public relations campaigns as its literary successes. Harvey gave lavish publication parties at Delmonico's and Sherry's, courted the American Booksellers Association, and treated his staff to white-tie dinners. To keep Mark Twain at Harper's he made a prescient if theatrical gesture in 1900, proposing to store the author's memoirs in a bank until the year 2000, when they would be reissued "in whatever modes should then be prevalent, that is by printing as at present, or by use of phonographic cylinders, or by electrical methods, or by any other method which may then be in use." He also offered to give a dinner at which he and Twain would publicly sign a contract and sell autographed copies for $50 each. Nothing came of these plans, but Harper's secured exclusive rights to all of Twain's work, guaranteeing the author $25,000 a year for five years; by 1914, it had paid him and his heirs over $300,000.

would be a national calamity." Nonetheless, Harvey knew exactly how in-debted he was to the banker, whose picture hung on his office wall. It was Har-vey who reissued the novel *Fraternity:* on the flyleaf of the first copy off the press, he wrote, "Republished for Mr. Morgan with the compliments of George Harvey. October 6, 1910."*

As Morgan entered his seventh decade, several of his contemporaries died. His sister Sarah suffered sudden heart failure at Bad Nauheim, Germany, in July of 1896. And in November 1897 Walter Burns collapsed in London and died.

Pierpont had been closer to Mary's husband than to any other colleague ex-cept Junius or Tony Drexel, and had trusted him with the management of the London firm. Now, he would assume responsibility for his sister's family—she had two children, Mary Ethel, called May, and Walter Spencer Morgan Burns—and have to make new arrangements for J. S. Morgan & Co.

As a first step, he sent Jack to England at the beginning of 1898 to represent the family and learn the professional ropes. Crossing the Atlantic on the RMS *Teutonic* with his wife and three young children, Jack reported to Fanny: "Everyone treats us as if the Morgan family owned the earth which makes it very pleasant for us."

His father had preceded them to England, and "laid himself out to make us comfortable," continued Jack. The junior Morgans stayed at Princes Gate and Dover House until they found a house of their own at No. 2 South Street in Mayfair, between Florence Nightingale and Earl Grey. Pierpont remained in En-gland for several weeks to settle the Burns estate, take charge of affairs at J. S. Morgan & Co, and introduce his son to City bankers, the Lord Chief Justice, the Prime Minister (Lord Salisbury), Joseph Chamberlain (head of the Colonial Of-fice), and the political journalist James Bryce. Both Jack and Walter S. M. Burns were made partners in J. S. Morgan & Co. on January 1, 1898.

---

* After Morgan died, his partners replaced Harvey with managers who had a stronger al-legiance to the Morgan bank than to literary quality, and major writers left the firm. The ed-itors Cass Canfield and Eugene F. Saxton restored its reputation in the twenties, eventually bringing in J.B.S. Haldane, J. B. Priestley, James Thurber, E. B. White, Richard Wright, Glen-way Wescott, and Julian and Aldous Huxley. In 1932 Saxton refused to accept his friend John Dos Passos's radical montage of fiction and fact, *1919*, unless the novelist revised his portrait of Morgan as the "boss croupier of Wall Street"—a "bullnecked irascible man with small black magpie's eyes and a growth on his nose," who used the country's financial crises for personal gain. Dos Passos refused to alter his text. Harcourt, Brace published the book. Thirty years later Dos Passos had changed his politics and his mind. He told a biographer in 1965: ". . . looking back on it I realize now that the Morgan piece was a prejudiced piece of work. If I were to write the book over I would modify it. Actually, old man Morgan, before his death, worked hard to avert the coming war."

Most evenings in London after dinner, Jack told Fanny, Pierpont and his sister challenged the next generation at dominoes: "Father & Aunt M. winning amid triumphant cheers—from themselves," and two weeks later, "It is too funny to see Father & Aunt Mary gravely sitting down to play that imbecile game." Though the elder Morgan complained of a head cold, giddiness, and liver trouble, he struck Jack as "more cheerful and contented than I've seen him for a long time," especially after "the biggest medical man around" pronounced him eligible for life insurance.

If Morgan privately made fun of his daughter-in-law's "cold roast Boston" propriety, he appreciated her attractive appearance and social skills. Neither he nor Junius had had a wife who was an asset in London society, and he showed himself (to Jack's surprise) as "immensely interested in Jessie's social *career*!" When Morgan the elder arranged to have Jessie presented to the Queen, Jack reported to his mother in mock complaint that "Louisa's friend Victoria R. won't receive any young married women whose husbands haven't been to a [royal] Levee so I am booked for Feb. 21, with court dress & all, sword and cocked hat too, I believe, to go and see *my* friend Albert Ed. Prince of Wales. It will make me feel like seven kinds of jackass but Jessie must go to court at all hazards, & at any cost. Sad isn't it."

Earlier in the century, presentation at court had been restricted to the titled and landed British aristocracy, but by the 1890s Victoria Regina had opened her receptions to women from wealthy families in Britain, the empire, and the United States. Jack's formal introduction to the Prince of Wales went off without a hitch, and Jessie was presented to the Queen in the Buckingham Palace throne room three days later. Others attending the event included the Duke and Duchess of Marlborough (formerly Consuelo Vanderbilt of New York), Lord and Lady Churchill (the former Jennie Jerome of Brooklyn), the Dukes of Richmond, Norfolk, and Devonshire, Lady Spencer, and Lady Cadogan. The Queen wore black robes and brilliant jewels.

London's *Daily Mail* the next day confused the senior and junior Morgans in concluding that "Quite the most beautiful dress in the whole room was the one worn by Mrs. Pierpont Morgan, whose husband is one of the big American financiers, and who is herself a pretty woman—tall, slender, with fair hair and blue eyes, and a very charming smile." The striking feature of her dress, made of muslin and lace over a white satin slip, was a satin train falling from the shoulder, lined with pale blue miroire velvet and edged with pink roses.

The younger Morgans were, as the elder intended, taken up by London society, and they became ardent Anglophiles. Pierpont accepted his association with British aristocrats as a matter of course. Jack, always less sure of himself, gave it a snobbish turn. After he and Jessie had tea one day at Windsor Castle with Lady Antrim, who was "in waiting" to the Queen, he told Fanny: "Jessie and I feel much more at home with the swells who are *real* swells, not wildly gay ones but the very best, than with almost anyone."

After seeing Jessie out in royal London, Pierpont went off to Monte Carlo and Rome—probably with Adelaide—but rumors that the United States might go to war with Spain cut his trip short. Ninety miles off the Florida coast, Cuban insurgents had been fighting Spain's colonial misrule for years, and American sympathy for the rebels intensified in the late nineties when more than two hundred thousand Cubans died of hunger and disease. Humanitarians urging American intervention were joined by imperialists who wanted the United States to conquer new territories, open foreign markets, and test its military strength. The "yellow press" *World* and *Journal* heightened the country's bellicose mood by playing up Spanish atrocities and Cuban anguish. Early in 1898, U.S. religious and political leaders joined the chorus calling for war with Spain.

The American business community opposed the impending conflict as likely to disrupt international trade and jeopardize the recent economic recovery. Cleveland in his second term had resisted congressional pressure to intervene in Cuba, and pro-business Senators Mark Hanna and Nelson W. Aldrich tried to help McKinley avert war in 1898. Jingoists ridiculed all opposition to the prospective fight as unpatriotic. Theodore Roosevelt, now Assistant Secretary of the Navy, announced that "this country needs a war" as he condemned the "flabby, timid type of character, which eats away the great fighting qualities of our race," and accused the "money power" of being more interested in profit than in principle.

In mid-February, the sinking of the American battleship *Maine* in Havana Harbor (probably the result of an internal malfunction, not a Spanish torpedo) edged the overwrought nation closer to war. Morgan had planned to spend the winter in Rome. The news from the United States changed his mind. He stopped in London on the way home. Jack found him "so worried and bothered by the number of things on his mind and the annoyance of war rumors" that he was "not feeling very well & is rather down about himself but probably Markoe will be able to set that all right."

As the senior Morgan sailed for New York at the end of March, the junior offered his own analysis of the political situation to his mother by mail: "Personally I do not like to see a civilized nation taking up the cause of the Cuban insurgents who are of so low a kind as to shoot a man under a flag of truce, as they did the other day. I am sorry for the poor starving wretches and should be glad to help by sending food, but they are not fit to govern themselves and we shall be responsible in the eyes of the world for such a state of things as now exists in Hayti, or worse. That is not a pleasant prospect."

Pleasant prospect or not, McKinley was moving toward military intervention. In mid-April he blockaded the Cuban coast, and on the twenty-fifth Con-

gress declared war. The Navy immediately requisitioned *Corsair*, rechristened
her the USS *Gloucester*, and turned her into a gunboat. Jack, hearing rumors to
that effect in London, asked Fanny whether or not they were true, "and if so,
what is Father going to do for a summer home this year? Personally, I believe it
would pay the Government to keep him in yachts and thereby in health; his services would be more valuable to them when well."

The government paid Morgan $225,000 for his yacht, leaving him to build
a new one on his own. The *Gloucester*, née *Corsair*, joined three other U.S. ships
to blockade the Spanish admiral Cervera at Santiago Harbor on July 3, and in
the course of a few hours the Americans destroyed his entire fleet.* On July 16,
the Spanish command surrendered. The "splendid little war," as John Hay
called it, lasted about ten weeks—just long enough to fire the national imagination with half-fictional tales of manly heroics, including Teddy Roosevelt's
highly publicized Rough Riders' charge up San Juan Hill, and not long enough
to bring on an extended political debate or sacrifice many American lives.

Morgan was not so concerned with the economic consequences of the war
that he neglected another kind of crisis. Years later, when a friend asked about
the provenance of a fine cigar, he said: "You remember the time of the break-
out of the Spanish war, how the declaration hung in the balance for a long
time? I knew that if we had war, that would be the last of the Havana cigars. I
had somebody in Washington ready to cable me of the declaration of war. I received my cable before it was made public, got into a hansom and drove to every
cigar store which I knew sold those cigars, paid cash and gathered the boxes
into my hansom, for I did not dare to trust them to send them after war was declared, and after two or three trips in the hansom I had enough to last me until
now."

The Spanish-American War did less damage to the economy than Wall
Street had feared, and the quick victory—bringing with it over the next few
years acquisitions in Guam, Puerto Rico, the Philippines, Wake, and Hawaii—
reinforced the imperialists' determination to compete for foreign "spheres of
influence" with the other great powers in the West. Even before the treaty with
Spain was ratified by the Senate, leading opponents of America's global reach
formed an Anti-Imperialist League; among them were Grover Cleveland,
Charles Francis Adams, George Boutwell, John Sherman, Andrew Carnegie,
Charles W. Eliot, William Dean Howells, William James, and Mark Twain.

Morgan probably sided with the Anti-Imperialists. He had told a friend in the
early eighties of his "strong opposition to government giving any aid to . . . any

---

* The *Gloucester* later defended the harbor of Guanica, Puerto Rico, firing off 3- and 6-
pound cannons while a landing party went ashore to capture the town. After the war she
made a victory sail to Gloucester, Massachusetts, and remained with the Navy through
World War I. Sold to a commercial line in 1919, she was eventually wrecked in a hurricane
off Pensacola, Florida.

enterprise outside the U.S." with regard to the Panama Canal, and responded with caution as the country began in the nineties to seek greater access to foreign markets. He underwrote government bond issues in Argentina, Mexico, China, and Japan, but did not begin to lend to foreign states or to finance remote railroads on a large scale until he had men he trusted in Latin America and the Far East.* A decade went by before he warily cooperated with politicians eager to establish "dollar diplomacy" abroad.

———

Less than a month after the second *Corsair* was converted into a gunboat, Morgan commissioned her engineer, J. Beavor-Webb, to design a third. The new yacht, built by T. S. Marvel at Newburgh, New York, and completed in December 1898, measured 304 feet, 63 feet more than her predecessor. She was also stronger and faster, but had the same gleaming black hull, gilt clipper bow, elegantly curved sheer, raked stack—and carpet pattern: since the mill that had made the 1890 rugs had gone out of business, Morgan ordered new ones custom-made.

As well equipped as a Gilded Age town house, the third *Corsair* also had polished maple panels lining her engine room, a library the width of the hull, a player piano, lace curtains in every stateroom, capes, cloaks, parasols, perfume

———

* His New York firm's small offering of Mexican government bonds in 1899 was hailed as a major turning point in the history of American finance. London's *Daily Mail*, praising this "first appearance" of an American banking house on a foreign loan prospectus, reported that New York was "flapping its wings over the new departure of Messrs J. P. Morgan & Company, who well deserve to be congratulated on their courage and enterprise." In Argentina, Morgan's London house became a leading provider of capital to both government and private enterprise after the 1890 Baring crisis—particularly to the Great Western Railway Company, which it restored to financial health. Japan, rapidly modernizing and hoping to decrease its financial dependence on London, approached J. P. Morgan & Co. in 1898 about issuing bonds for a government-chartered industrial bank. Morgan declined, since some of his London experts considered the issue risky and Japan would not put up the security he required. The Japanese regarded the good faith of their government as "equal to any in the world," explained the head of the American Trading Company in Japan, and "it hurts their pride to be classed with the Chinese" by having to furnish collateral. In China, which was far less economically and industrially advanced than Japan, J. S. Morgan & Co. accepted shares in government loans sponsored by other bankers in the nineties. As the West began to fight over access to commercial opportunities in China—called the "slicing of the melon"—Morgan subscribed along with Jacob Schiff, James Stillman, and Levi P. Morton to the stock of an American China Development Company. Chartered in New Jersey in 1895, this corporation staked U.S. claim to railroad and mining concessions in China. Early in the new century Morgan became the largest shareholder in the ACDC, and played a quasi-diplomatic role in a struggle between the U.S. and Chinese governments over the Canton–Hankow railroad. (See Chapter 26.)

vials, and powder puffs for female guests, silver-backed hairbrushes, cut-glass inkstands, leather portfolios filled with "Corsair" stationery, cases of vintage wine and brandy, fifty pounds of "Morgan" tea (a blend of Earl Grey and Lapsang Souchong), and humidors filled with Cuban cigars. In the linen closet were 68 blankets, 116 sheets, 177 pillow cases, and 670 towels. The kitchen pantry accommodated several sets of "Corsair" china, silver baskets for almonds, candy, and fruit, fish forks and oyster forks, menu holders, champagne glasses, pearl-handled fruit knives, nut picks, sugar sifters, flower vases, marrow scoops, cocktail shakers (one marked "JPM"), julep strainers, grape shears, gold spoons, asparagus tongs, 84 linen tablecloths, 800 napkins, and 47 finger bowls. One spoon-and-fork set bore the name of Admiral Cervera, the Spaniard whose fleet had been demolished at Santiago Harbor with the help of the USS *Gloucester.* On dozens of coffee cups, saucers, and spoons were the initials "A.D.," for Adelaide Douglas.

Morgan's third yacht could carry enough coal to cross the Atlantic, and he often sent her and the crew ahead while he sailed to Europe on White Star liners. He took friends cruising in the Mediterranean or along the Italian coast, and joined Europe's crowned heads for sailing races at Cowes and Kiel. At the ends of these trips, *Corsair* preceded him home, then steamed out to pick him up in New York Harbor.*

———

While Morgan was introducing his son and daughter-in-law to London in February 1898, Edith Sybil Randolph Whitney suffered a gruesome accident at her husband's estate in Aiken, South Carolina. Riding a tall horse under a covered bridge one day, she failed to duck low enough, smashed her head into the overhang, and fell to the ground bleeding and unconscious.

When she woke up three days later she was in a cast from head to hip, with a broken cervical vertebra and both arms paralyzed. She and Whitney and their daughters, Adelaide Randolph and Dorothy Whitney, stayed in South Carolina for two months, then took a private train to New York. There, confined to her

* On the inevitable question of what it cost, the third *Corsair* was valued for estate purposes after Morgan's death in 1913 at $135,000, although the government had paid him $225,000 in 1898 for the second. In 1917 Jack turned *Corsair* (III) over to the Navy to fight in the Great War, and that May complained to Franklin Delano Roosevelt, Assistant Secretary of the Navy, that the Naval Board had originally valued the yacht at $400,000 but the figure had just been reduced to $325,000 and he wanted to know why. A month later he told FDR it would cost him $850,000 to replace the hull alone. The Navy returned the yacht in 1919, and Jack sailed her until 1930, when he sold her to the U.S. Coast and Geodetic Survey for a dollar, and commissioned a fourth, 343-foot *Corsair* from the Bath Iron Works in Maine. In 1942, the third *Corsair*—now the USS *Oceanographer*—was drafted for military service, and sailed with the Navy until 1944.

bed and in constant pain, Edith read, dictated letters, and saw close friends such as the Markoes, Adelaide Douglas, and Morgan. In the early summer, Whitney moved her to his property at Westbury, Long Island. Edith refused to give up. She asked Whitney to keep his box at the opera so she could use it as soon as she could walk. A friend wrote in his journal: "This is the cruelest thing I ever knew. Nature made this incomparable woman and then ruthlessly destroyed her."

Whitney had built stables and a racetrack at Westbury, and in the spring of 1899 Edith sat up in bed to watch the races of the Meadow Brook Steeplechase Association through a window. She must have known she was losing ground, for she called twelve-year-old Dorothy Whitney in for a confidential talk about the facts of life. A few days later she slipped into a coma, and died on May 6. Among those who sent flowers to her funeral were President McKinley, former President Cleveland, Theodore Roosevelt—now Governor of New York—and Pierpont Morgan from Aix-les-Bains.

———

Morgan had been elected Commodore of the New York Yacht Club in 1897, which meant among other things that *Corsair* presided over club races and cruises. At the NYYC annual meeting in 1898 he announced that he would donate $150,000 to buy land for a new clubhouse on 44th Street. The architects Warren & Wetmore completed a voluptuous Beaux Arts building at 37 West 44th in 1899, with curved-glass bay windows shaped like the sterns of eighteenth-century ships.

When Ireland's Royal Ulster Yacht Club issued a challenge for the America's Cup on behalf of the multimillionaire tea magnate Sir Thomas Lipton in 1899, Morgan formed a syndicate to commission a defender from America's premier yacht designer, Nathanael Herreshoff. Most U.S. Cup contenders had been owned by individuals, but in the nineties Yacht Club members adopted Wall Street syndicating methods to spread the building expenses and the risk. Morgan went into this venture with the elite of American yachting—C. Oliver Iselin, a textile industry banker and fanatical racing sailor well able to handle his own boat (unlike most New York Yacht Club members), and Edwin Denison Morgan, Jr., a cousin of Sarah's husband, George, who was said to think "no more of buying a yacht than the average man does of picking up a paper as he passes a newsstand."

The America's Cup had been in competition since 1870. Under the rules, a foreign club challenged the New York Club and sent a boat to sail against its host-defender. The race did not take place every year, but by 1899 New York had won it eight times, and it had become a major international event as well as a gauge of Anglo-American relations, since most of the challengers were British. A bitter controversy over the 1895 match intensified interest in the 1899 race: the losing

British challenger in 1895, the Earl of Dunraven, had accused the American team of cheating, and a blue-ribbon panel that included Morgan, William C. Whitney, and the U.S. naval strategist Alfred T. Mahan investigated the charges, found them false, and barred Dunraven from further competition. That the judges were American may not have struck the British as entirely fair, but they needed a new contender, and Lipton, with Ulster backing, seemed made to order.

The son of Irish grocers, Lipton had come to the United States at fifteen in 1865 and studied marketing and advertising. Returning to Britain four years later, he built a chain of grocery stores, then moved into tea by buying bankrupt plantations in Ceylon on a trip to the Far East. He was well known on both sides of the Atlantic—millions of people drank Lipton's tea, and he owned enormous stockyards and farms in the American West. Queen Victoria knighted him in 1898 after he made a large contribution to a favorite charity of the Princess of Wales.

When Lipton learned that Morgan would be in London in early 1899, he asked a mutual friend to introduce them. Jack reported to Fanny in New York: "Tonight I am going to dine with Father at Mr. Panmure Gordon's to meet Sir Thomas Lipton and a lot of old Admirals . . . to discuss the yachting prospects for next summer. . . . P. Gordon says, 'Ah you'll like Lipton; he's one of Nature's noblemen. I love him—of course I do, he brings me business.' It will probably be amusing."

Whether or not the elder Morgan found Lipton to be one of Nature's noblemen (Jack did not issue a follow-up report), the contestants for the America's Cup met off Sandy Hook, New Jersey, that fall. Lipton had spent about $450,000 on his 128-foot cutter, *Shamrock*, painted green in honor of his heritage and Ulster sponsor. The American group of Morgan, Iselin, and Morgan had spent $250,000 on their 131-foot sloop, *Columbia*, the longest Cup defender yet built. Her designer, Nathanael Herreshoff, was Morgan's kind of nobleman—an engineering genius who was making naval architecture into a science; his firm in Bristol, Rhode Island, designed and built every Cup defender between 1893 and 1920. Morgan paid for the rebuilding of an earlier Herreshoff contestant, *Defender*, to serve as *Columbia*'s trial horse.

As the competition got under way in early October, U.S. Coast Guard cutters patrolled the crowded bay, and Guglielmo Marconi reported directly from the course with his new wireless telegraph. Iselin sailed with *Columbia*'s crew. Morgan watched from the deck of his own yacht with a large party of friends.

The Cup would go to the boat that won three out of five thirty-mile races. For a frustrating two weeks, seven starts had to be canceled on account of bad weather. Finally on October 16, the contestants completed their first race in easterly winds, light fog, and a sloppy sea. *Shamrock* started well but slowed down in the chop; *Columbia* passed her and won the race by ten minutes. The second day the rivals stayed more or less even on a thirty-mile triangle until

Shamrock's topmast broke; *Columbia* completed the course alone. She needed one more victory to win. The third race started on schedule on the nineteenth, then both boats drifted to a halt for lack of wind. On the morning of the twentieth, *Shamrock* crossed the starting line a minute ahead of *Columbia*, and the two crews fought for the lead with spinnakers set as they ran before the wind for fifteen miles; returning to windward, *Columbia* outpaced her opponent to win the race and the Cup by six minutes, thirty-four seconds.

As soon as *Columbia* crossed the finish line, "Commodore J. P. Morgan and a party of women came over from *Corsair* in a launch," reported the *Tribune*. Morgan and Iselin threw their arms around each other "with a shout of delight . . . and danced about with joy." It must have made quite a sight, the 210-pound Commodore gamboling across the deck with Iselin in his arms.

Morgan's banking partners were not as pleased as his yachting comrades with the amount of time he spent that fall on this personal/national triumph. From London, Jack wrote to Charles Coster, "If the Senior did have to wait a long time for his yacht race, he had a very good one when he got it, so I suppose we must not complain even if his earning powers are somewhat prejudiced by [Jack wrote "the delay," then crossed it out for] his voyage."

Lipton sent four more *Shamrock*s across the Atlantic to compete for the America's Cup between 1901 and 1930, but never won it. The silver trophy remained in New York until 1983. Morgan concluded his two-year term as commodore of the NYYC in 1899, and was succeeded by his friend Lewis Cass Ledyard, a corporate lawyer and member of the Corsair Club. He did not care about cutting into his "earning powers," but had something else he wanted to do with his free time. Former heads of yacht clubs tend to be called Commodore for the rest of their lives—which in Morgan's case was singularly apt.

———

His taste for beautiful objects had been educated by what the historian Neil Harris has called "a lifetime of organized self-indulgence." From the kid gloves, leather boots, and copies of Roman statues Pierpont had bought on his first trips abroad, to vintage wines, Herter furnishings, Savile Row suits, French couture, English roses, Steinway pianos, regal yachts, a Stanford White clubhouse, a Herreshoff racer, and several houses, he had always been able to acquire whatever he wanted. In his sixties, he wanted rare books, manuscripts, and art.

As the center of world finance shifted from London to New York in the late nineteenth century, economic necessity was bringing great European collections into the art market, and aristocratic families long on ancestry but short of cash sought to trade with the new American merchant princes who had exactly the opposite problem. Most U.S. collectors earlier in the century had shied away from Old Masters as too risky and expensive, confining themselves to academic genre paintings and sets of books by famous authors. In the nineties, however, encouraged by art dealers and scholars who promised to vouch for quality and value, they ventured into more rarefied realms.

Leading European dealers opened galleries in New York and flattered novice American collectors. The best of them, presiding over a massive transfer of cultural wealth from the Old World to the New, shaped and refined American tastes. Scholarly experts also advised the new collectors, sometimes working in conjunction with dealers, sometimes superseding them. Popular American critics in the early eighties had shown more enthusiasm than critical judgment (Earl Shinn called the gaudy Vanderbilt house "a more perfect Pompeii"), but well-educated, enormously energetic European scholars were beginning to devise rigorous standards for judgments about art. In the 1870s, the German-educated Italian art historian Giovanni Morelli, trained in medicine and comparative anatomy, substituted scientific methodology for subjective feeling in evaluating art. Discerning specific sets of characters in the language of form, he proposed that individual artistic signatures could be recognized in the execution of details—an earlobe, for instance, or a fold of drapery. Morelli published a study of Italian works in German galleries in 1880. His method of searching for significant, revealing particulars, often compared to Freud's, influenced all fields of art history. His disciples included Bernard Berenson, Gustavo Frizzoni, the archaeologist J. D. Beazley, and the Leonardo scholar Jean-Paul Richter.

Acting on the belief that knowledge could and should be codified, art historians also began to compile extraordinarily thorough catalogues raisonnés on the works of major artists—Wilhelm von Bode, director of the Kaiser Friedrich Museum in Berlin, published an eight-volume *Complete Works of Rembrandt* with C. H. de Groot between 1897 and 1906. De Groot completely revised the Dutch section of the standard reference work on Flemish, Dutch, and French painters—publishing ten volumes on forty artists—and assembled an archive of photographs on Dutch paintings. Ulrich Thieme and Felix Becker published an authoritative lexicon of artists, with contributions from the leading art historians of the early twentieth century.

Photography made it possible for the first time to compare works of art in different locales. New scientific techniques helped determine date and place of origin for individual objects. A surge in the publication of art journals and books made all this information widely available and stimulated further ideas and research. Yet there remained wide margins of error in the rudimentary "science" of attribution, with fine shades of distinction between what was genuine and what "workshop," "school of," copy, or fake. Even experts with the best of intentions could not avoid honest mistakes, and as the American demand for European treasures drove prices up, the risk of fraud radically increased. Skillful forgers made works that passed as genuine for decades. Since collectors with more ambition than knowledge wanted big names (among the biggest in late-Victorian America were Raphael and the Florentine goldsmith and sculptor Benvenuto Cellini), shady dealers assigned undistinguished works to those artists, and even reputable experts occasionally opted for the more prestigious attribution in the face of doubt, especially when they stood to earn commissions from the dealers.

Partly to guard against fraud, Morgan did not pay for his purchases until the end of the year, and he put them on display at Princes Gate where visiting experts could pass judgment. Wise dealers realized that securing him as a steady client would be far more profitable than cheating him once.

On Wall Street he was a firm believer in professional expertise, constantly on the lookout for qualified men to do specialized work. In risky financial markets *he* was the connoisseur of quality and value. In the art markets he was an avid amateur. He knew that he did not have a scholar's deep knowledge of literary or visual culture, and relied much of the time on experts. Still, with his "good eye," lifelong attraction to beautiful things, and passion for collecting, he wanted to see himself as an authority on artistic merit. When one of his acquisitions was pronounced a forgery, he allegedly said, "Bring me anything else this talented gentleman has made."

In March 1897 he sent the Metropolitan Museum an enameled shrine he had just bought for $10,000 as a "Chapel Altar Piece." It stood two feet high, was studded with precious stones, and appeared to represent four saints, including Catherine and her wheel. The museum's director, Luigi Palma di Cesnola, thought it was a pax—an "osculatory" tablet used for the kiss of peace in the celebration of Mass. Thanking Morgan for this "very fine enamelled pax in silver gilt," Cesnola pronounced it the "best enamel and niello work I have seen in this country." He had found the initials "BC MDXXIII"—possibly Benvenuto Cellini, 1523—engraved under the enamel on Catherine's wheel.

Morgan replied: "As regards its authenticity, I have no doubt myself that the initials BC MDXXIII trace its origin to Cellini." With a deferential nod—"Of course I am not expert enough to decide"—he thought it "well worth a place in the Museum and as such I beg its acceptance."

Director Cesnola quietly began to check with experts about the object's provenance and authenticity.* Morgan's commitment to the museum meant far more than the actual gift, as American's young cultural institutions depended almost entirely on the sponsorship of wealthy patrons. When the banker tried to resign from the Met board during the depression in 1894 be-

---

* Cellini's virtuoso style and widely translated *Autobiography* had made him enormously popular with Americans, and it would not have taken an especially clever forger to engrave "BC MDXXIII" into the piece. The museum listed Morgan's gift in its Annual Report for 1898 as a "sixteenth-century Italian altarpiece," declared it a nineteenth-century forgery in 1933, and deaccessioned it in 1956.

cause he had so many other demands on his time, Cesnola refused to let him go, invoking the memory of "the friendship which your good father had for me," and insisting that "the Museum needs you." Morgan resigned from the Executive Committee but stayed on as trustee.

In March of 1897, Cesnola told Morgan he was "happy to see you taking so much interest in our often abused Museum but which even Boston is obliged to recognize as the greatest . . . in the new world." By the late nineties, the Met was indisputably America's greatest art museum, and New York the country's ranking metropolis. When the city's five boroughs officially consolidated on January 1, 1898, the *Tribune* announced, "The sun will rise this morning upon the greatest experiment in municipal government that the world has ever known." Encompassing 359 square miles, with aggregate wealth of nearly $4.5 billion and a population of 3.4 million, Greater New York suddenly became, after London, the second-largest city in the world. The benefits of consolidation may have been less apparent to the inhabitants of Lower East Side tenements than to the upper echelons of the sovereign American city, but in finance, architecture, music, science, education, and art, New York now measured itself not against its domestic rivals but by the gauges of London, Paris, Berlin, and Rome.

As a supporter of the city's Metropolitan Opera, Museum of Natural History, and art museum, and as a private collector, Morgan was bringing cultural as well as monetary capital across the Atlantic. Like Catherine the Great of Russia, who once said, "I am not a lover of art. It is voracity. I am a glutton," and like Napoleon who swept through Italy and Egypt taking cartloads of classical art for France, he set out to acquire as much as he could in a relatively short time, often buying entire collections en bloc. As he told a business colleague, his strength lay more in the consolidation of existing projects than in the promotion of new ones—an observation that also held true in the arts.

Fanny, who had little interest in art, once said that her husband would buy anything from a pyramid to Mary Magdalene's tooth. He *did* acquire a reliquary monstrance (a receptacle for the Host), probably made in late-fifteenth-century Florence, containing a molar allegedly from the Magdalene's jaw; two feet tall and made of rock crystal, copper-gilt, silver-gilt, and *verre églomisé*, this ornate object with its glass-encased tooth is now in the medieval galleries at the Metropolitan Museum of Art.

Along with a few other wealthy patrons at the turn of the century, Morgan regarded himself as endowing the United States and its leading cities with artistic treasure appropriate to its rising stature in the world—as educating the country's tastes to European ideals, and introducing the rich patrimony of the past to its American heirs. To expedite this encyclopedic project, he commissioned experts to find him the best works of art and literature in the world. One of the first and most influential of his scholarly advisers was his nephew Junius Spencer Morgan—Sarah's son. Two years younger than Jack, Junius often stayed at Cragston or 219 while his parents traveled, and developed an easy, affectionate rapport with his uncle. He went to Princeton, where he studied classics, and by the time he graduated in 1888 had become a connoisseur of rare books, manuscripts, drawings, and prints. That year he was elected to New York's prestigious society of bibliophiles, the Grolier Club; Pierpont did not become a member until 1897.

Jack had been unattractively pleased, when he and Junius visited their grandfather in the summer of 1887, to find that the Dover House servants treated *him* as the "heir presumptive," while his cousin "being only a daughter's son is comparatively left out." Of all the men who supplanted Jack as Pierpont's "heir presumptive," Junius had the lowest profile and the longest tenure.

In 1891 he married Josephine Adams Perry, a descendant of Oliver Hazard Perry and Commodore Matthew Perry. He had probably met her through her sister, Lucretia, who was married to his close friend (and another of Pierpont's nephews), Henry Fairfield Osborn—Princeton, '77. The Junius Morgans spent their honeymoon in England, and in 1897 built a thirty-room Jacobean mansion called Constitution Hill on ninety-two acres in Princeton. Junius worked as a partner in the Wall Street firm of Cuyler, Morgan & Co., but earned a master's degree at Princeton in 1896, cared more about books and art than business, and spent as much time abroad as he could.

From London on July 4, 1899, he advised his uncle by cable to buy a medieval illuminated manuscript owned by the Earl of Ashburnham. The message, like all international Morgan wires, went in code: "Tambales solmites [can obtain for you] famous gospels ninth or tenth centuries gold and jewel binding of time treasure of great value stomachers [and interest] reported unequalled england or france ashburnhams cogote [price] asked rebullir [£10,000] am told been offered postulante [£8000] parsees triturar [strongly recommend] mailing full description."

The volume was a late ninth-century Latin text of the four Gospels in Latin, preserved within two of the finest surviving Carolingian jeweled covers in the world. Having first come to light in the sixteenth century at the Benedictine monastery of St. Gall, then somewhat mysteriously migrated to a convent in Lindau, Germany, it was known as the Lindau Gospels. The British Museum wanted it but could not meet Lord Ashburnham's price. Morgan could: he paid £10,000—nearly $50,000—for a volume that would be valued at millions if it came on the market a century later. The Lindau Gospels, numbered M1 once Morgan's librarian began to organize and catalogue his acquisitions, served as the foundation for his outstanding collection of 630 medieval and Renaissance illuminated manuscripts. The Grolier Club had mounted an exhibition of illuminated manuscripts in 1892, but the art historian Walter S. Cook later observed that before the formation of Morgan's library no American scholar had "specialized in the field of illuminated manuscripts or recognized their place and importance in the history of painting." The scholar Charles Rufus Morey said no phase of medieval archaeology could be fully illustrated or understood without reference to the Morgan manuscripts.

There is, unfortunately, little surviving correspondence between Pierpont and his erudite nephew, but Junius appears to have initiated most of Morgan's important early manuscript purchases. The appeal of these volumes to their new owner probably lay in their sumptuous materials (vellum, gold leaf, brilliant pigments) and religious significance, in the complementary relations between text and decoration, and in the unimpaired quality of the original artwork, rendered with dazzling virtuosity. Unlike frescoes, panel paintings, and canvases, which deteriorate through exposure to light and air, the miniatures of medieval manuscripts tend to be well protected from the elements by their bindings, and to have lost none of their original splendor.

On the eve of the twentieth century, as machine presses and automated typesetting spread the printed word to much of the world, Morgan began with Junius's guidance to assemble a record of the physical history of the book. His collections eventually documented an evolution that began with Egyptian, Greek, and Latin papyrus rolls, went on to the medieval vellum codex and the first volumes printed with the invention of movable type by Johann Gutenberg, to later literary first editions and masterpieces of fine printing and illustration. The Latin Bible produced by Gutenberg in Mainz in about 1454–55 is universally acknowledged to be the greatest monument in the history of printing. Morgan acquired his first Gutenberg Bible in 1896 from Sotheran & Co. for £2,750 (about $13,500)—a fine copy printed on vellum. On Junius's recommendation in 1899 he purchased the private library of the London dealer James Toovey, which included a series of books printed by the fifteenth-century Venetian scholar Aldus Manutius, and the Mainz *Catholicon* of 1460, a massive Latin dictionary that was probably the last book Gutenberg printed. Toovey's collection, including its examples of European fine bindings from the Renaissance onward, was the most important of its kind to come to America, and provided the broad framework for Morgan's subsequent book collecting.

In 1900, also at Junius's urging, Morgan bought the eclectic library of Theodore Irwin of Oswego, New York. It brought him a second Gutenberg Bible—the Old Testament only, on paper, containing unique typesettings of many early leaves. Irwin's collection also included the first edition in Greek of the *Iliad* and the *Odyssey* (Florence, 1489), three volumes printed by Gutenberg's English counterpart, William Caxton, 270 Rembrandt etchings, a notable collection of Dürer prints, a French Apocalypse manuscript produced in about 1415 for Jean, Duc de Berry, and the priceless seventh-century *Golden Gospels of Henry VIII*, written in gold letters on purple vellum, thought to have been presented to Henry in 1521 by Pope Leo X when he anointed the English king "Defender of the Faith." Morgan kept it on a special stand in his manuscript vault. Out of gratitude to his nephew-adviser, he gave Junius the Dürer prints; Junius eventually gave them to the Metropolitan Museum.

There are forty-nine surviving copies of the Gutenberg Bible in varying states of completeness. Between 1896 and 1911 Morgan acquired three of them, making his library the only institution in the world to have so many.

———

He never confined himself to a single scholarly adviser, a specific period, an artistic genre, or a uniform aesthetic. From the London bookseller Pearson, he bought in 1897 the manuscript of Keats's *Endymion,* with its famous opening line: "A thing of beauty is a joy for ever." From the heirs of Byron's mistress, the Countess Guiccioli, he purchased the original autograph manuscripts of *Don Juan, Marino Faliero, Manfred,* and several shorter poems. And at about this time he acquired the original manuscript of Charles Dickens's *A Christmas Carol,* written in 1843. The most renowned Christmas story in the English language made the name Scrooge synonymous with "miser," although the bitter old skinflint is dramatically converted by the Spirits of Christmas and belated self-knowledge into a warmhearted, generous man. If Morgan intended any satirical self-reflection with this important literary prize, he left no record of it.

At Cartier's in Paris between 1899 and 1901 he spent $200,000 on jewelry, portrait miniatures, jardinières, vases, and Sèvres porcelain. From the Frankfurt antiquities dealers J. & S. Goldschmidt in 1896 he bought a richly embossed silver cup said to be by Cellini (it wasn't), from the collection of the Earl of Warwick, for £8,000 ($40,000). Morgan especially liked the ornate objects in which Goldschmidt specialized, and through this dealer he bought Limoges enamels, a reliquary casket allegedly containing an arm bone of Catherine of Braganza, sixteenth- and seventeenth-century German drinking vessels, a Louis XV chatelaine, a silver tazza said to have been owned by the Aldobrandini family, jewelry, faience, bottles, and bonbonnières.

At the galleries of Duveen Brothers in London and New York, he worked primarily with Henry Duveen, uncle of the more famous Joseph. One day, Joseph reportedly decided that Henry was not taking full advantage of the Morgan millions, and asked permission to try his own hand. He made up a tray of thirty portrait miniatures—six masterpieces, the rest mediocre—and offered them to Morgan. The banker looked them over quickly, then asked, "How much for the lot?" Joseph shot Uncle Henry a look of triumph and named a sum. Morgan selected the six good items off the velvet tray and slipped them into his pocket. He divided the figure Joseph had named by thirty, multiplied by six, said he would pay that price, and left. Uncle Henry smiled. "Joe," he said, "you're only a boy. It takes a man to deal with Morgan."

Morgan knew a great deal about portrait miniatures, and assembled one of the finest private collections of the modern era. First popularized in France at the court of Francis I (1515–47), these tiny paintings served as pledges of loyalty and love, centuries before the invention of photography. They appealed to Morgan's taste on several counts—artistic merit, historical value, royal associations, rarity, and romance. Usually painted on vellum and set in gold frames or in ravishingly beautiful gold, enamel, glass, and ivory boxes, they were worn in lockets and pendants, kept on mantels and bedside tables, and in secret drawers. Lord Nelson died with an image of Emma Hamilton around his neck. George IV did the same for his secret (Catholic, commoner) wife, Maria Fitzherbert.

Morgan owned a portrait of Emma Hamilton by Richard Cosway, the fashionable English miniaturist of the eighteenth century, and several of George IV and Mrs. Fitzherbert. In the course of a decade he acquired roughly eight hundred portrait miniatures, dating from the sixteenth to the nineteenth centuries, by most of the important artists in the field—among them Nicholas Hilliard, Hans Holbein the Younger, Jean Baptiste Isabey, and the leading sixteenth-century French painter on a large and small scale, Jean Clouet. Their subjects included Mary, Queen of Scots, Henry VIII, Sir Thomas More, Napoleon, Sir Walter Scott, Georgiana, Duchess of Devonshire (the fetching subject of the painting stolen from Agnew's before Junius could buy it), and dozens of portraits of French courtesans—Madame de Montespan (mistress of Louis XIV), Ninon de l'Enclos (whose admirers were said to have included Richelieu, Racine, Molière, and La Rochefoucauld, and whose conquests continued past the age of sixty), Madame de Maintenon, who succeeded de Montespan in the affections of Louis XIV, Madame de Pompadour, *maîtresse* to Louis XV, and Madame Du Barry, *her* successor.

Probably the most famous of the Morgan miniatures was a profile bust of Queen Elizabeth I in relief on an oval gold pendant, called the Armada Jewel. It was unsigned but closely associated with Nicholas Hilliard, and thought to have been presented by the Queen to one of her statesmen after the defeat of the Spanish Armada in 1588. Fascinated since childhood with European history and royalty, Morgan now owned objects once intimately handled by Elizabeth, Henry VIII, Napoleon, Lord Nelson, and the ladies of the French court.

The late nineties mark the beginning of a love affair with the hedonism, delicacy, and artifice of ancien régime France that lasted the rest of Morgan's life. Perhaps to complement his miniature collection, he bought autograph letters by several of the figures featured there—Madame de Maintenon, Madame de Pompadour, Marie Antoinette—and marriage contracts for all of the French kings from Louis XIII to Louis XVIII. He commissioned Duveen to furnish an entire Louis XVI drawing room at Princes Gate in 1898, with tables, andirons, tapestry screens, chairs, stools, and a Sèvres bust of the King himself. The following year he bought a commode and secrétaire en suite made in 1790 for Marie Antoinette by Jean-Henri Riesener, the finest French cabinetmaker of the period, and later a superb *bleu turquin* marble side table with neoclassical mounts made by Pierre Gouthière in 1781 for the Duchesse de Mazarin.

—

Morgan's strength as a collector lay in the decorative arts. Not what art historians irreverently refer to as a "flatware" man, he had a greater appreciation of craftsmanship, gorgeous materials, and three-dimensional objects than of painting's more conceptual pleasures. Joseph Duveen *was* a flatware man, and in advising buyers such as Benjamin Altman, Jules Bache, and Henry Clay Frick in the early twentieth century, he helped establish major collections of European paintings in the United States. The young, Harvard-educated scholar Bernard Berenson worked closely with Isabella Stewart Gardner, who built a Venetian Gothic palazzo on Boston's Fenway to house her collection of European paintings. Morgan went his own autocratic way, relying not at all on Berenson and on Duveen chiefly for decorative objects. He acquired several fine paintings through other dealers, but they amounted to a miscellaneous assemblage rather than a coherent collection.

In the late nineties, as wealthy Americans turned from relatively safe and available salon pictures to the work of great masters, Otto Gutekunst at the Colnaghi gallery in London divided paintings into two categories—"angel food and *big*, BIG, *BIG* game." Morgan was now out for *BIG* game, but he bought cautiously at first, staying close to the landscapes and decorative styles with which he was already familiar.

In 1894 he acquired through Agnew's (the firm was still pursuing the stolen *Duchess of Devonshire*) a landscape by John Constable (1776–1837) called *The White Horse, A Scene on the River Stour.* The artist considered this serene, naturalistic painting of a tow-horse being ferried across a river on a quiet summer morning "one of my happiest efforts on a large scale." Morgan lent the picture to the Royal Academy in 1895.

Three years later, also through Agnew's, he bought a series of decorative panels called *The Progress of Love,* by Jean-Honoré Fragonard. They had been commissioned in 1771 by Madame Du Barry for the new dining pavilion in her château at Louveciennes—a gift from Louis XV. Fragonard's witty, erotic narrative follows a pair of young lovers from first "Pursuit" to "The Lover Crowned," but the King's mistress rejected the paintings once they were completed. Cynics said she did not like the allusion to her own romantic adventures, but a more likely explanation is that the stylistic fashion in France had shifted from the rococo to a more formal neoclassicism, and Fragonard's sweet young shepherd-lovers looked distinctly passé. Whatever the reason for the rejection, the artist installed the four original paintings at his cousin's house in Grasse in 1790 and added several more. They remained there until 1898, when Morgan bought all fourteen for £62,000, roughly $300,000. Enchanted by the subject, style, and history of these panels, he had an entire room designed for them at Princes Gate.

He never bargained for things he wanted, and his acquisitions helped drive the art market to new heights. From the London dealer Charles Wertheimer in 1898 he bought a Rembrandt portrait of Nicolaes Ruts, a wealthy Dutch merchant in a white ruff and fur-trimmed cloak, for £6,000 (about $30,000). Dated 1631, the painting had remained in the Ruts family for nearly two centuries, but somehow by 1850, when it was sold from the collection of King Willem II of the Netherlands, it was known as *Portrait of a Rabbi*. Wilhelm von Bode had identified it as the Dutch trader from a watercolor copy of the original.*

In 1899 Morgan bought a Frans Hals *Portrait of a Lady* (£5,720), Henry Morland's *The Lady Ironing* for £3,767, a John Russell pastel of *Mrs. Topham and Her Three Children* (£4,400), and Hogarth's *The Lady's Last Stake* for £8,250. These prices suggest how dramatically art-market values change over time. The Rembrandt did not cost significantly more than canvases by artists later considered far less important, and its price was just half of what Morgan paid Duveen in 1899 for a set of Rose du Barri "Coventry Vases."

———

Throughout Europe the news that Morgan was in town now brought art dealers, booksellers, and *antiquaires* flocking to see him. Louisa reported from London one spring to Fanny in New York that "Father gets into the hands of dealers more and more, and his taste and knowledge grow in the most wonderful way." Her own knowledge, by her own account, did not keep pace. His "curios" did not interest her, she confessed—"I'm not educated up to them." At a Rembrandt exhibition in London she found some of the paintings "glorious, but you do get *so* bored with his many likenesses of his coarse and ugly self!"

Louisa proved more useful as social reporter than as art critic. At the end of 1898, Morgan's niece May Burns announced her engagement to Lewis Harcourt, son of the Liberal Party leader Sir William George Granville Venables Vernon Harcourt. "May radiantly happy," noted Louisa in her diary, "engagement really pleases Aunt Mary." It pleased Louisa's father as well.

* After Morgan died in 1913, the appraisers of his estate valued the Fragonard panels at $750,000. In 1915, Joseph Duveen bought them from Jack and sold them to Henry Clay Frick for $1.25 million. The Frick Collection also acquired *Nicolaes Ruts*, most of the sculpture and decorative arts objects from Morgan's Fragonard room, the Marie Antoinette commode and secrétaire, the blue marble Gouthière side table, Constable's *White Horse*, several more paintings, Renaissance bronzes, other choice tables, exquisite clocks, and a collection of Limoges enamels that is one of the finest in the United States.

The Harcourts traced their lineage back to the Plantagenets and lived primarily at Nuneham Park, the family seat in Oxfordshire. Lewis, known as Loulou, worked as his father's private secretary. His mother had died giving birth to him in 1863. In 1876 Sir William had married the widowed Elizabeth Cabot Motley Ives, daughter of the American historian John Lothrop Motley and an old friend of Pierpont's from Vevey. When Sir William reformed Britain's death duties as Chancellor of the Exchequer in 1894 by imposing a graduated estate tax, he had famously sighed, "We are all Socialists now." In December 1898, writing to Joseph Chamberlain (who also had an American wife) about Loulou's forthcoming marriage to Morgan's niece, Sir William sighed again— "It is another link in the American alliance. We are all Americans now!"

The celebrated weddings that joined American heiresses to titled if often impoverished Europeans in the closing decades of the nineteenth century—exemplified by Maggie Verver and her Italian prince in Henry James's *Golden Bowl*—represented another aspect of the transatlantic traffic in wealth and culture, and the announcement of the Harcourt-Burns engagement elicited widespread reflection on the conquest of London by American girls. Queen Victoria's son-in-law, the Marquess of Lorne, exclaimed to Loulou: "How the American alliance is getting on!" London's *Daily Chronicle* described May Burns as "one of the victorious army of Columbia's daughters which seems to be threatening to carry off the flower of fashionable London's eligible young men."

In the winter of 1899, Pierpont and Louisa entertained the Harcourt/Burns clans at Princes Gate and Dover House, and visited Nuneham Park and the Burnses' estate in Hertfordshire, North Mymms Park. One night at dinner, Sir William boasted that he had been "the first Englishman who *dared* to marry an American woman!"

Amused, Morgan reminded him that "there *had* been early cases." Harcourt insisted: "Oh that was long *long* ago! It was I who *revived* the fashion."

Whatever Morgan thought of Harcourt as historian or reformist politician, he gave May a diamond chain for her engagement and a string of pearls for her wedding, which took place at St. Margaret's, Westminster, on July 1, 1899.*

After Sir William died in 1904, May's uncle gave her, and England, a more significant gift. Nuneham Park needed major repairs, and the young Harcourts did not have enough money to do the work. Morgan opened a £52,000

---

* Pearls were in short supply and great demand at the turn of the century, before the development of cultivation techniques. In a dramatic example of changes in value over time, the heir to a railroad fortune sold his house at Fifth Avenue and 52nd Street to the jeweler Cartier for $1.2 million in 1917; as payment, he accepted a two-strand Oriental pearl necklace valued at $1.2 million. According to the financial journalist John Steele Gordon, the Cartier building in the 1980s was worth over $20 million, while a similar strand of pearls would not bring more than $200,000.

($260,000) line of interest-free credit in May's name at his London bank, telling her not to worry about paying back the loan: "What I want is that you & Loulou should enjoy the place. Life is short & one never knows what may happen." The couple carefully restored Nuneham's handsome old buildings and grounds; among the guests at their first house party in 1907 were Pierpont Morgan and Edward VII.

Two years later, Morgan retrieved another piece of Nuneham's past. Henry Clay Frick owned a portrait of Mary, Countess of Harcourt (1751–1833), by Sir Joshua Reynolds, who had written to the Second Earl Harcourt in September 1778: "I thought my holydays were over for this summer, but Nuneham is so pleasant both indoors and outdoors that it is irresistible." Frick was reluctant to part with his Countess, but Morgan prevailed and gave the painting to May and Loulou in August 1909.

———

In the midst of the Harcourt-Burns engagement celebrations early in 1899, Morgan met an Oxford-educated foreign service officer named Clinton Dawkins. A protégé of Alfred Milner, the British high commissioner in South Africa whose group of Oxbridge disciples was known as "Milner's kindergarten," Dawkins had been Under-Secretary of State for Finance in Egypt in 1895, and in 1899 was about to be posted to India as a financial adviser to the viceroy, his Oxford contemporary George Curzon. Louisa considered Dawkins's imminent departure unfortunate, as he was not only good-looking but "most interesting and really charming." He and his "very pretty" wife made "great acquisitions to our circle."

Morgan had been looking for someone to replace Walter Burns as senior resident in London for over a year. Dawkins was forty, just eight years older than Jack, and had no experience in banking. He did have wit, intelligence, and excellent political connections—and Morgan now wanted an Englishman to head his London office. Louisa, not usually in on her father's business secrets, confided to her diary in February that she expected "for many reasons" to see more of Dawkins in the future.

In July the British government released him from the India assignment. The London *Times* reported that though government officials wanted Dawkins in India, they "considered it still more important that he should meet the wishes of Mr. Morgan." An Anglo-American banker in London told colleagues that Morgan had tried and failed to find a partner in the City, then fallen back on "a capable Treasury official, who has his work to learn"—an account that echoed Pierpont's complaint to Junius from Wall Street twenty-five years earlier about how difficult it was to find men of character, ability, and brains, just before he hired Fabbri.

On March 31, 1900, Dawkins started work at J. S. Morgan & Co. He would have 25 percent of the firm's annual profits and losses, Pierpont 50 percent; Jack and Walter S. M. Burns would split the last 25 percent. No one had much confidence in Burns: Dawkins found him "capable" but "young, fat, and lazy."

After seven months as a banker, Dawkins described himself as "happy enough in the City, but there is not enough to do." Eventually he found enough to do, but never relinquished his primary allegiances to Milner, politics, and the British Empire. He hoped to finance his own and Milner's political careers with his banker's earnings, which a City journal estimated at £25,000 ($125,000) a year. Meanwhile he chaired a War Office Reorganization Committee, which took him away from Old Broad Street for long stretches of time and eventually earned him a knighthood. He told Milner that his American partners had been "more patriotic than Englishmen in facilitating the War Office inquiry," and added a few weeks later—reflecting the Morgan bank's sense of itself as peer to states—that the firm had let him take on the political work "since the Government acted well in releasing me from India so promptly."

Morgan hired another Englishman as well in the spring of 1900. He wanted someone to take charge of daily operations at the London office, and this time he chose a man with a background in banking. Edward Charles Grenfell had read history at Trinity College, Cambridge, and worked with two financial firms before joining Morgan's at the age of thirty. He was the son of Henry Riversdale Grenfell, the MP and director of the Bank of England whom Pierpont and Fanny had visited in Kent in 1876, when "Teddy" was six. At the end of 1900 a Barings partner reported that Morgan intended, "without regard to expenditure of money, to make the position of [his English] firm unrivalled for the next generation."

———

When Morgan gave May Burns pearls for her wedding in 1899, he presented Louisa with a strand as well, saying (she reported) " 'he meant to give it me when I married and as I didn't seem to *get* married it didn't seem worth while to wait!' " Louisa was thirty-two at the time, and though she longed to "meet some of the *young* men" at the parties she attended with her father, rarely did. Then, in 1900, a man she had known for some time proposed. He was Herbert Livingston Satterlee, a graduate of Columbia College and Law School, and a partner in the New York law firm of Ward, Hayden & Satterlee. He asked her to marry him just before she sailed for Europe with her father at the end of March. The offer took her by surprise—she thought he was interested in her sister Anne—but she promised to consider it carefully and reply from London by cable. Crossing the Atlantic, she wailed to Fanny, "Why *why* did 'he' ask me that question *just* before I left? I can't keep him waiting . . . but it is hard to settle it all from so *far* away."

With some trepidation she discussed the situation with her father. "He knew of no reason he could have against it," she reported to her mother. "He only wants me to wait and think whether I am sure that it is 'essential to my happiness.' As I have lived very happily without it for years it seems difficult to realize that it is essential now! . . . Only I am perfectly sure that I *can't* give it all up." She did not give it up, and cabled her answer to Mr. Satterlee early in April. "I am *really really* happy," she told Fanny, "a little shaky and breathless when I remember what it means!"

Her fiancé was also worried about what it meant—especially about how she would like living on $10,000 a year, "not as J. P. Morgan's daughter but as Herbert Satterlee's wife." He could not, he warned her, afford "the kind of house in the kind of neighborhood you ought to have."

Morgan asked the couple not to announce their engagement at first, for reasons he did not explain, but in May he took Louisa to Worth's to order a wedding dress and trousseau—Satterlee wondered from New York, "Don't you fear that Mr. Worth will let out the secret?" The prospective father of the bride completely commandeered the plans. Satterlee wanted a summer wedding; Morgan chose November. Satterlee liked the idea of a small ceremony; Morgan insisted on hundreds of guests. In New York one night in July, the two men stayed up late discussing details. Herbert reported to Louisa: "It was like a game of cards—I gave him the first trick, expecting that he would let me take the second—but he played the hand out, at least, he is still holding on to his cards! However, he was in a perfectly good humor about it and is quite satisfied with the way that *he* came out of the argument."

Satterlee soon took the measure of his future father-in-law's tyrannical generosity and formidable negotiating skills: "He is almost impossible to argue with, because he puts things in a way that make it seem a favor to *him,* as it were, and states not what might, could, would or should be done, but what *he will do!*" What he would do was give Louisa a house and $10,000 a year, matching Satterlee's annual income. "I tried to head him off," Satterlee protested, "but it was no use! He . . . gave me no opportunity or excuse for doing so." Even silken shackles required getting used to: "if he had been anyone else or had put the matter differently, I suppose I would have shown what would have been foolish pride and unreasonable rebelliousness because I am so accustomed to having my way about my own plans that the Commodore is a new sensation for me."

The Commodore entirely got his way about the wedding. He invited more than two thousand people to the service at St. George's Church on the afternoon of November 15, 1900. Dr. Rainsford and the bridegroom's cousin, Bishop Henry Yates Satterlee of Washington, performed the ceremony. The florist Thorley draped garlands of red and white roses over the chancel rail, and banked the altar with roses, palms, and ferns.

Louisa came down the aisle on her father's arm. She wore Worth's gown of heavy white peau de soie under point d'Alençon lace, and carried a bouquet of white roses, orchids, and lilies of the valley. Diamond ornaments held her rose-point veil in place and glittered in the folds of lace on her bouquet. After the ceremony the couple received guests in the drawing room at 219. Thorley had hung a curtain of pink roses tied back to one side at the entrance to the room. On the landings above the front hall stood arches of Bridesmaid roses, orchids, and asparagus fern; pink bougainvillea and clusters of white rose were woven into the banisters all the way to the third floor.

For dinner the wedding party filed through the house to a temporary 75- by 55-foot wing Pierpont had built off the conservatory for the occasion: Gobelin tapestries lined its dark red walls, and clusters of electric lights hung from a pleated white silk ceiling. Louis Sherry's waiters served a buffet of oysters, lobsters, sweetbreads, Yorkshire pudding, quail, pheasant, Virginia ham, salmon, chicken breasts, pâté de foie gras en croûte, ramequins, ice cream, wedding cake, and champagne.

Among the six hundred guests invited to both the ceremony and the reception were the Robert Bacons, Alexander Barings, Joseph Choates, Grover Clevelands, Ogden Codman, Jr., the Clinton Dawkinses and Robert W. deForests, Chauncey Depew, Adelaide and William Proctor Douglas, the David Eglestons, Egisto Fabbris, E. L. Godkins, several Goodwins, Secretary of State and Mrs. John Hay, James H. and J. Bruce Ismay (the owners of Britain's White Star Line), the Charles Laniers and Lewis Cass Ledyards, the just reelected President and Mrs. William McKinley, Dr. and Mrs. James W. Markoe, Alice Mason, the Junius Morgans, Professor and Mrs. Henry Fairfield Osborn, the Reverend and Mrs. Endicott Peabody, the Right Reverend and Mrs. Henry Codman Potter, the Reverend and Mrs. William S. Rainsford, Miss Adelaide Randolph, the Whitelaw Reids, the William Rockefellers, the new Vice President and Mrs. Theodore Roosevelt, the Secretary of War and Mrs. Elihu Root, the Francis Lynde Stetsons, Fred Stevens, the James Stillmans, Waldo Storys, Louis Comfort Tiffanys, several Vanderbilts, the W. Seward Webbs, and William C. Whitney.*

In giving his favorite daughter away to be married, Morgan had no intention of letting her go far. He presented the newlyweds with a house near Cragston at

---

* Those invited to the ceremony but *not* the reception included the Robert Brownings of Venice, Italy, the Andrew Carnegies, John J. Chapman, Edward S. Curtis, Richard Harding Davis, General Luigi P. di Cesnola, Harris Fahnestock, Mrs. James T. Fields and Sarah Orne Jewett, Hamilton Fish, Mrs. Ulysses S. Grant, the E. H. Harrimans, Mrs. Christian Herter, the Richard Morris Hunts, Morris K. Jesups, the Right Reverend and Mrs. William Lawrence, Columbia University president and Mrs. Seth Low, the Levi P. Mortons and Thomas Collier Platts, Augustus Saint-Gaudens, the Benjamin Strongs, J. Frederic Tams, Luther Terry, the Stanford Whites, and the Harry Payne Whitneys.

Highland Falls, and eventually built them another next to his own in town. Satterlee adapted to his father-in-law's peremptory ways, and came to share Louisa's solicitude for his health and state of mind. Morgan saw Louisa constantly in New York, but needed a new partner for his travels. After 1900 he turned to his youngest daughter, Anne, and to Adelaide Douglas.

Chapter 20

THE DYNAMO AND
THE VIRGIN

With the economy booming, incomes rising, prices falling, a relatively painless recent military victory, eight thousand new "motorcars" driving around the country, and a proud sense of international stature, much of the United States was in an ebullient mood on the eve of the twentieth century. At the Republican National Convention in June of 1900, Senator Chauncey Depew, former president of the New York Central Railroad, declared, "There is not a man here that does not feel 400 per cent bigger in 1900 than he did in 1896, bigger intellectually, bigger hopefully, bigger patriotically, bigger in the breast from the fact that he is a citizen of a country that has become a world power for peace, for civilization, and for expansion of its industries and the products of its labor."

Outside the Republican Convention hall, there were plenty of people who did not feel 400 percent bigger and more hopeful in 1900. Although the ferment over silver had died down, the impetus for social change and radical reform had not. Progressive activists and journalists were beginning to focus national attention on the widening gap between rich and poor, on the problems of cities, political corruption, the rights of women, the depletion of natural resources, continuing racial inequality, and the power of big business. The new Governor of Wisconsin, Republican reformer Robert M. La Follette, gained national prominence pledging to tax corporate property, regulate railroads, and manage public resources in the public interest.

Henry Adams, who felt more at home in the twelfth century than in the twentieth, did not share Depew's centennial triumphalism. After touring the 1900 Paris World's Fair, he genuflected in sardonic awe before the power of technology: "As he grew accustomed to the great gallery of machines," wrote Adams of himself in "The Dynamo and the Virgin," "he began to feel the forty-foot dynamos as a moral force, much as the early Christians felt the Cross. The planet itself seemed less impressive, in its old-fashioned, deliberate, annual or daily revolution, than this huge wheel, revolving within arm's length at some vertiginous speed, and barely murmuring,—scarcely humming an audible warning to stand a hair's breadth further for respect of power,—while it would not wake the baby lying close against its frame. Before the end, one began to pray to it; inherited instinct taught the natural expression of man before silent and infinite force."

Adams then compared this "occult mechanism" for the conversion of motion into energy to an older and higher power: at the Louvre and at Chartres, "the force of the Virgin" was "the highest energy ever known to man, the creator of four-fifths of his noblest art, exercising vastly more attraction over the human mind than all the steam-engines and dynamos ever dreamed of. . . . All the steam in the world could not, like the Virgin, build Chartres."

Unlike Adams, Morgan experienced no moral shock at the force of the new machine. On the contrary, his own energies had for years been helping to drive the industrial dynamo. What little he said about the changes he was setting in motion contained no modernist note of irony or ambiguity and no question about their ultimate meaning. If he perceived conflicts beneath the surface of life at the beginning of the new century, he did not seem to find them irreconcilable. He was subsidizing commerce and art, the modern and the medieval, railroads and Rainsford, the ideas of Darwin (at the Museum of Natural History) and the idea of God.

He left no reflections on the state of the union in 1900, nor on the death of Queen Victoria in January 1901. She had begun her reign the year he was born, and had ruled over the world he knew, as monarch and metaphor, all his life. H. G. Wells said she had sat on England like a great paperweight, and after her death things blew all over the place.

Political conservatives, including Morgan, were relieved to see McKinley re-elected in November 1900, with 51.7 percent of the vote. William Jennings Bryan had run again on a Democratic/Populist ticket, but did less well (45.5 percent) than he had four years earlier: a Prohibition Party candidate and Eugene Debs, running as a Social Democrat, took a few points off the Bryan vote. Morgan was not sure what to make of McKinley's Vice President, the reform-minded young Governor of New York, Theodore Roosevelt. The Republican insider Mark Hanna had warned the party's nominating convention, "Don't any of you realize there's only one life between this madman and the Presidency?"

Andrew Carnegie.

(Culver Pictures, Inc.)

From London early in 1901, Clinton Dawkins sketched for Alfred Milner in South Africa a picture of his employer that surpassed Junius Morgan's dreams. "Old Pierpont Morgan and the house in the U.S. occupy a position immensely more predominant than Rothschilds in Europe," Dawkins reported. The New York and London firms combined "probably do not fall very far short of the Rothschilds in capital, are immensely more expansive and active, and are in with the great progressive undertakings of the modern world." The next twenty years should "see the Rothschilds thrown into the background, and the Morgan group supreme," but Dawkins thought the head of it all must finally be winding down: "Old Pierpont Morgan is well over 60, and no human machine can resist the work he is doing much longer."

Dawkins radically underestimated the force still left in the aging Morgan machine. Visiting New York six months later, he took more of an insider's view: "This is a place where things 'hum,' " he wrote, "and they have been humming a good deal . . . since I have been over here. . . . [I]t is extremely interesting to find oneself in the very heart of Wall Street excitement and combinations, and to note the prodigious amount of nervous excitement and energy the Americans throw into their work. . . . Few of them live through it to advanced years except physical and intellectual giants like Morgan who has something Titanic about him when he really gets to work."

Charles Coster, Morgan's master of detail, did not live through it. He collapsed with pneumonia and died in March of 1900, at forty-seven. *The New York Times* blamed his early death on a workload "far heavier than any one man ought to bear." John Moody echoed Dawkins in noting how many Morgan partners "succumbed to the gigantic, nerve-wracking business and pressure of the Morgan methods and the strain involved in the care of the railroad capital of America." Only " 'Jupiter' Morgan" himself managed to "come through that soul-crushing mill of business, retaining his health, vigor, and energy."

James J. Hill, head of the Great Northern Railway, feared that Coster's death would leave the railroad end of Morgan's business "unprotected." Morgan wasted no time replacing the partner he most relied on: at Coster's funeral he persuaded an astute railroad lawyer named Charles Steele to join the firm.

Thinning white hair, occasional trouble hearing, and use of a silver-tipped mahogany walking stick were the chief signs of Morgan's advancing years. Dawkins described his senior partner's face as "delightful in spite of his beastly nose; it is so lit up with intelligence and quickness." The Markoes' daughter recalled that when "the Commodore" entered a room "you felt something electric: he wasn't a terribly large man but he had a simply tremendous *effect—he* was the king. He was *it*." The bishop of Massachusetts said that a visit from Morgan left him feeling "as if a gale had blown through the house."

The gale that blew through the American economy early in 1901 was the creation of U.S. Steel. Financial historians nine decades later called it "the deal of the century." The century was three months old.

———

Somewhat to the surprise of the financial community, industrial securities had come through the depression of the nineties in better shape than railroad stocks, and several of the biggest corporations had suffered least. As business confidence picked up in 1897–98, that performance helped persuade investors to venture into the market for industrial stocks and bonds. It helped persuade Morgan as well. His firm had handled just a few non-railroad issues in the past—for the Atlantic Cable, the Illinois & St. Louis Bridge, James Scrymser's Mexican Telegraph Co., a French company trying to build a canal across Panama—and had not played a major role in the mergers of the early nineties. Morgan had just managed to recoup his loan to National Cordage, the overextended "rope trust," before its second failure, but had been more involved in the organization of General Electric, which used the long contraction to cut costs and broaden operations, and emerged at the end of the decade strong, diverse, and profitable.*

Enforcement of the Sherman Antitrust Act hit a "low water mark" during McKinley's first term. In *E. C. Knight* and *Hopkins* v. *U.S.*, the Supreme Court created the impression—short-lived, as it turned out—that the Sherman Act would not be applied to mergers among local manufacturing concerns, since the government had failed to show that they restrained interstate commerce. These judicial decisions, combined with a surge in economic activity, the

---

* Early in 1901 Morgan advanced $150,000 to Nikola Tesla, an eccentric Croatian-born electrical engineer who had developed an alternating-current motor, worked briefly for Edison in the mid-1880s, and sold his AC patents to Westinghouse, Edison's chief rival, in 1888. Tesla's system provided the basis for the first major harnessing of power at Niagara Falls. Like Edison, Tesla worked on a wide range of projects, including high-frequency currents, an air-core transformer called the Tesla coil, wireless communication, and artificial lightning. He attended Louisa Morgan's wedding, and there were rumors (entirely false) of his engagement to Anne. With Morgan's funding in 1901—for which he assigned the banker a 51 percent interest in his patents—Tesla set out to develop a worldwide communications system, and built a 200-foot transmission tower at Shoreham on Long Island. At the end of 1904, he asked his patron for another $75,000—"Since a year, Mr. Morgan, there has been hardly a night when my pillow was not bathed in tears," he wrote. The banker replied through his secretary that he could not "do anything more in the matter"—nothing came of the Shoreham project—and declined to fund other Tesla proposals, but Jack lent the inventor $25,000 after Pierpont died.

surprisingly strong performance of industrial securities during the depression, and Wall Street's sky's-the-limit mood, created a tidal wave of industrial combinations between 1897 and 1904. Virtually overnight, in the most intense merger activity in American history, 4,277 firms consolidated into 257. The hundred largest concerns quadrupled in size and took control of 40 percent of the country's industrial capital. "Every conceivable line of manufacturing had its trust," wrote the financial historian Arthur Stone Dewing—"conservative bankers, shrewd business men, and doctrinaire economists became infected with the virus of large-scale production. People condemned the trusts one moment and bought their securities the next. It was the harvest time of promoters."

Steel, which had succeeded railroads as the country's most important industry, seemed to Morgan a natural next step. Even in the context of the long-term postwar expansion, American steel productivity had been phenomenal. World output rose from roughly half a million tons in 1870 to almost 28 million in 1900—a 56-fold increase. U.S. output grew from 22,000 tons in 1867 to 11.4 million by 1900, increasing 520-fold. The new machinery and production processes that made this spectacular growth possible fueled competition as well, and in the boom that followed the depression of the nineties the steel industry was faced with overcapacity, price cuts, buccaneer profiteering, hostile takeovers, and speculative raids—all familiar to Morgan from the railroad wars.

Andrew Carnegie remained the uncontested sovereign in steel. He had combined his operations into the Carnegie Steel Company, Ltd., in 1892, capitalized at $25 million, although in fact it was worth far more; three years later he acquired exclusive rights to the richest iron-ore deposits in the country—the Mesabi Range in Minnesota—from John D. Rockefeller, whom he referred to as "my fellow millionaire."* Carnegie Steel made money throughout the depression, and its earnings doubled yearly as the economy recovered, from $11 million in 1898 to $21 million in 1899 to $40 million in 1900.

Carnegie's personal control of this gigantic business was a rarity by the nineties, when most large corporations had outgrown the ability of their founders to finance and run them. Converting private companies into publicly held corporations had helped establish the market for industrial securities, and also a class of professional managers. Unlike the new corporate officers,

---

* In leasing this land, Carnegie did not have to put up a cent. Instead, he agreed to pay 25¢ per ton of ore extracted, and to ship at least 1.2 million tons a year for fifty years on Rockefeller's railroad and shipping lines. The magnitude of his operations enabled him to promise huge annual volumes, which brought him essential raw materials and transport at minimal cost. No small competitor could have made such a promise.

Carnegie could plow his earnings back into the company rather than pay them out as dividends to investors.

Even though he dominated the industry from Pittsburgh, there were successful steelmakers in other parts of the country, and the merger mania of the late nineties brought new contenders into the field. Among the most flamboyant were the Chicago brothers James and William Moore, and the notorious gambler John W. Gates, a burly man with a bullet-shaped head who allegedly once bet $1,000 on which of two raindrops would reach the bottom of a windowpane first. The Moores cobbled together combinations of companies—primarily makers of finished products such as wire, nails, hoops, and tubes—and embarked on competitive price-slashing sprees. "Bet-a-Million" Gates had built a barbed-wire trust in the eighties with the help of a loan from Morgan, and in 1895 became president of Illinois Steel, the largest producer west of Pittsburgh. Two years later he asked the Morgan bank to finance a consolidation of steel and wire companies. Morgan entertained the idea for several months, then—partly because of the Spanish-American War and partly because he did not trust Gates—said no.

Gates enlisted Elbert Gary, general counsel for Illinois Steel, and put together a $90 million combination called American Steel and Wire in April of 1898. Gary was a corporate merger expert and former county judge from Illinois who looked like "a Methodist bishop—benign, suave, cordial and earnest." Morgan preferred the Methodist bishop to the speculative plunger, and when Gary approached 23 Wall Street late that spring with a meticulous proposal for combining Illinois Steel with raw-material suppliers and transport systems into one self-contained, low-cost, centrally managed firm, Morgan assigned his partners to study the figures, then said yes.

Over the summer of 1898, Gary and Bob Bacon worked out the details. In September they contracted to buy controlling interests in Illinois Steel, the Lorain Steel Companies of Ohio and Pennsylvania, the Minnesota Iron Company (the second largest producer in the northern ore country), and two railroads, and to bring them all into a holding company called Federal Steel. It did not include Gates's American Steel & Wire. The *New York Commercial* described the Gary/Morgan combine as "the beginning of one of the greatest contests for supremacy that the world has ever seen. It is a fight between a new concern and the Carnegie interests, both backed by almost unlimited capital."

Carnegie was generating "almost unlimited capital" through his spectacularly remunerative steel operations, while the bankers for the new concern had to raise money in markets that were still wary of industrials. Morgan's name on the deal assured investors that Federal would issue "investment quality" securities, in contrast to those of the fly-by-night promoters.

The organizers of Federal Steel issued $100 million each of preferred and common shares. Since there are few surviving records of this deal, exactly how the financing worked is not clear, but it probably went like this: Morgan exchanged about $100 million of Federal shares for the stock of the properties he was bringing into the merger. At the same time, he organized a syndicate to provide the consolidation with $14 million in immediate cash. Syndicate members put up $4.8 million of this commitment right away, and pledged to furnish the rest pending the outcome of a public sale of Federal stock. The Morgan bank offered the second $100 million of stock for purchase—first to the shareholders of the constituent companies, then to the public, although not a very wide segment of the public. The buyers of industrial securities were still an elite group of wealthy institutions and individuals; small investors did not enter the capital markets in large numbers until the 1920s. The stock sold so well that the syndicate never had to produce the rest of its $14 million commitment. During the first year of operations, Federal Steel paid dividends on its preferred and common shares, and produced about 15 percent of the country's steel ingots.

"Bet-a-Million" Gates, who made half a million dollars selling Illinois Steel stock to Federal, wanted to run the new consolidation, but Morgan had a better idea. As soon as the deal was complete he called Elbert Gary to his office.

"Judge Gary," he said, "you have put this thing together in very good shape. We are all very well pleased. Now you must be president."

Surprised, Gary said no.

"Why not?" asked Morgan.

"I have a law practice worth $75,000 a year," Gary explained, "and I cannot leave it."

"We'll take care of that," Morgan assured him. "We must make it worth your while."

Gary wanted time to think it over. Morgan, as always, wanted an answer right away.

Who, asked Gary, would be the directors of the new concern?

Morgan shrugged: "You can select the directors, name the executive committee, choose your officers and fix your salary."

Twenty-four hours later, Gary said yes.

Like the head of the house of Morgan, the new head of the second largest steel producer in the United States knew little about making steel—one adversary said that Gary didn't see the inside of a blast furnace till the day he died. Gary did know about law and corporate organization, and he believed, with Morgan, in rationalizing competitive and overlapping enterprises through administrative consolidation and coordination of production and pricing. Since both men also believed that corporations issuing publicly traded securities had to account for their financial performance, Federal took the then unusual step of issuing quarterly reports.

Andrew Carnegie did not think Gary and Morgan could make the consolidation work. Now in his mid-sixties, with his close-cropped beard and hair gone white, the diminutive Scot took an entirely different approach to the market, and in 1898 he dismissed his new rivals out of hand: "I think Federal the greatest concern the world ever saw for manufacturing stock certificates," he said, ". . . but they will fail sadly in steel."

Carnegie represented the pure type of autocratic free-market competitor—capitalism in its most effective, ruthless form. Unlike the railroad pirates whom Morgan had been trying all his adult life to control, the steelmaster was not a profligate wrecker. He concentrated on primary steel and heavy products—ingots, rails, billets, sheets, bars, and beams—and he dominated the industry by making a better, cheaper product than anyone else, keeping tight control over costs, supplies, and output, and holding workers' wages down. One of the worst labor-capital conflicts of the 1890s had taken place at Carnegie's steelworks in Homestead, Pennsylvania.

The Amalgamated Association of Iron, Steel, and Tin Workers had already organized the plant when Carnegie bought it in 1883, and after a strike in 1889, the Amalgamated leaders accepted a sliding wage scale that would parallel industry profits in exchange for union recognition. Although Carnegie, born into poverty and reared among radical Scots Chartists, liked to see himself as an enlightened champion of workingmen, he opposed organized labor, and his hardheaded instincts won out over his benevolent ideals when the Homestead contract came up for renewal in 1892. The man in charge of the Homestead works in 1892 was the president of Carnegie Steel, Henry Clay Frick, an enormously successful coke producer who shared Carnegie's antipathy to unions but not his avowed compassion for individual workers. Since the steel markets were in decline in 1892, Carnegie and Frick proposed to reduce the minimum wage in the new contract and to abolish the bargaining power of the union. Just before the old contract expired, Carnegie went to Scotland for the summer, leaving the situation in Frick's hands. He knew that his own sympathies would be divided, and that Frick would use draconian measures to win the fight. He may not have realized just how draconian.

Frick built a stockade around the Homestead works, fortified with barbed wire and rifle slits, and hired three hundred men from the Pinkerton Detective Agency to stand by. On July 1, he offered union officials conditions they could not accept. The Amalgamated called a strike. Five days later the Pinkertons came down the Monongahela River on barges in the middle of the night to take over the plant, but steelworkers surprised them with an armed counterattack. The battle raged all day, until the heavily outnumbered Pinkertons surrendered and the workers seized control of the plant. Nine strikers and seven guards had been killed, and hundreds of others wounded. The governor of Pennsylvania sent eight thousand troops to occupy Homestead while strikebreakers operated the plant. An anarchist who tried to assassinate Frick succeeded only in wounding him—and in eroding sympathy for the walkout. Frick made no concessions to the union. When the strike ended in November, the company imposed lower wages and longer hours. Carnegie said nothing in public at the time. He continued to talk about his friendly relations with workers, but he knew where the fault for this hideous confrontation lay, and that it undermined all his pious claims. Years later he wrote, "No pangs remain of any wound received in my business career save that of Homestead."

———

Once the Illinois/Federal consolidation of raw-material suppliers, basic-steel producers, and transportation facilities was complete, Judge Gary began to aggregate makers of finished products as well, aiming to build a "steel republic" that would reach around the world. With Morgan's backing he organized companies called National Tube (a consolidation of 14 large manufacturers, capitalized at $80 million) and American Bridge (25 companies, $60 million). Early in 1900, according to his biographer Ida Tarbell, he suggested to Morgan that they buy the gigantic Carnegie Steel as well, which would give them the "capacity to develop a systematic foreign trade." Morgan replied, "I would not think of it. I don't believe I could raise the money." When a market downturn later that year reduced demand, the Gary/Morgan group and the more speculative Moore brothers' trusts decided to economize by expanding their manufacture of basic steel and reducing their dependence on Carnegie's firm.

To Carnegie, these canceled orders amounted to a declaration of war. If his rivals were integrating backward to encroach on his territory, he would move forward to take over theirs. "The situation is grave and interesting," he wrote from Scotland to the new president of his company, Charles M. Schwab. "A struggle is inevitable and it is a question of the survival of the fittest." There was no question as to who would survive. No one could beat Andrew Carnegie at the steel game.

He asked Schwab how much more cheaply they could make tubes, if they built a new manufacturing plant, than Gary's National Tube could. "At least $10 per ton," reported Schwab.

"Well," said Carnegie, "go ahead and build the plant then." Schwab started work on a $12 million factory at Conneaut Harbor, Ohio, with its own ore source, cheap transportation on Lake Erie, and the technology to make a new type of seamless tube.

Carnegie outlined to Schwab what he would do to run the steel industry "if I were czar"—pretty much what he already was doing—which prompted his biographer Joseph Wall to remark that "his use of the subjunctive . . . was an amusing conceit. He was czar."

If Morgan wanted to win this contest and prevent a hugely disruptive battle in the country's basic industry, it would have to be with dollars, not tubes, and an opening appeared on December 12, 1900. That night he attended a dinner in honor of Charles Schwab at the new University Club designed by Charles McKim on Fifth Avenue at 54th Street. Schwab was just thirty-eight, two decades younger than most of the men who had come to pay him tribute— among them Jacob Schiff of Kuhn, Loeb, E. H. Harriman of the Union Pacific Railroad, Standard Oil president H. H. Rogers, and Bishop Henry Codman Potter. He had started out at seventeen carrying leveling rods at Carnegie's Edgar Thomson plant in Braddock, Pennsylvania, and worked his way up through the ranks to become president of Carnegie Steel by the time he was thirty-five, in 1897. Dark and strapping, with a clean-shaven, pudgy face that made him look even younger than he was, he knew almost as much about the industry as Carnegie himself. He also knew that Carnegie intended to stop work at some point in order to give away his fortune, and would be willing to sell out under the right circumstances.

For the testimonial dinner at McKim's formal Renaissance palazzo in December 1900, Morgan was seated next to the guest of honor. After coffee had been served, Schwab gave a speech that outlined his hopes for American steel. Carnegie's hard-driving methods had brought production costs down as far as they could go, noted Schwab, but there were large economies still to be gained at the distribution end. If a giant, centrally managed, superefficient firm could run specialized plants that concentrated on single products, it should be able to rationalize and almost infinitely expand the markets for steel. Locating plants near the buyers of products would cut delivery costs. Combining competing sales forces into one streamlined unit could match supply to demand. Coordinating product shipments would eliminate "crosshaul" duplications. Evaluating comparative plant performance would enable the firm to concentrate resources on the best producers and managers, and to strengthen or eliminate stragglers. Executives would cooperate on pricing and production in mutual self-interest. Research would find better ways of making and using steel. If this kind of consolidation could be achieved, concluded Schwab, the premier enterprise driving the American economy would continue to grow, ensuring stable markets and ample profits for producers, lower prices for buyers, and pride of place in the modern industrial world for the United States.

This picture of industrial/national order was tailor-made for Morgan, who listened closely. He and Schwab talked briefly before the evening broke up, and agreed to meet again. Bob Bacon described his "Senior" as "very much impressed by the new light that had been thrown on the whole steel situation, its growth and possibilities, and for the first time he indicated to me that it seemed a possible thing to undertake the purchase of the Carnegie Company."

Early in January 1901 Morgan and Schwab resumed their conversation over dinner, then met Bacon in Morgan's mahogany-paneled study at 219. Fanny was in New York that winter—she had stayed for Louisa's wedding in November, and would not go abroad until early March—but her husband's guests did not see her or any other member of his family that night. The three men talked until 3:00 A.M., and agreed that they would try to put together a giant combination in steel. Its pillar would have to be Carnegie's firm. A few days after the midnight meeting at 219, Schwab brought down to 23 Wall Street a list of all the companies he thought should be included. Morgan, glancing over it quickly, said, "Well, if you can get a price from Carnegie, I don't know but what I'll undertake it."

Carnegie apparently knew nothing of these plans. He and Morgan had worked together in the early seventies, and though they never became intimate, their enmity has been exaggerated. Carnegie participated in several Morgan underwritings, called on Junius whenever he visited England, and later said that after Pierpont bought out a $60,000 Carnegie interest in a railroad for $70,000—showing a "nice sense of honorable understanding as against mere legal rights"—he "had in me henceforth a firm friend." Carnegie joined a party Morgan took to Philadelphia in December 1891 to celebrate the opening of the Drexel Institute. Still, he had not been pleased when the West Shore Agreement interfered with his attempt to break the Pennsylvania Railroad's monopoly in the coal regions in 1885, and he had far more faith in competitive action than in negotiated "communities of interest."

Schwab had no idea whether or not Carnegie would sell to Morgan. It depended in part on how eager the steel czar was to get on with dispersing his fortune. It also depended on his puritanical streak. Schwab had taken care to conceal certain facts of his own life from his uncompromisingly straitlaced boss—estranged from his obese, childless wife, he had an illegitimate daughter by her nurse—and he suspected that Carnegie's misgivings about Morgan had more to do with the banker's womanizing than with his manufacture of stock certificates. According to Schwab's biographer, Robert Hessen, "Carnegie could not fault Morgan for no longer being sexually attracted to his wife, but he was appalled by the rumors that Morgan kept a steady succession of mistresses, as many as seven at a time, and he was revolted by the rumor that Morgan had made a gift of land, buildings, and funds for the New York Lying-In Hospital in order to have some place to accommodate the women whom he was alleged to have made pregnant. To Carnegie's mind, these rumors far outweighed the well-known facts that Morgan was an active layman in the Episcopal Church and a patron of the arts." The rumors also outweighed the truth.

In early February, Schwab called on Carnegie's wife, Louise, at home on 51st Street, for advice. She suggested that he broach the subject of selling out to

Morgan over golf, which usually put "Andy" in a good mood. Accordingly, Schwab joined his chief for a round of golf on a dry, wintry day in Westchester County, and let him win. He presented the proposition over lunch: Carnegie could name his price.

Carnegie deliberated overnight. The next day—apparently disregarding moral qualms—he handed Schwab a single sheet of paper with his terms spelled out in pencil: the price he wanted for the Carnegie Company and all its holdings was $480 million.* Since the company made approximately $40 million a year, the purchase price amounted to about twelve times earnings. Schwab drove downtown and presented the paper to Morgan, who took one look and said, "I accept this price."

Thirty years earlier, Carnegie had been enthralled when Junius agreed "to move into the market the necessary gold to heat the foundries in Pittsburgh and put iron beams across a muddy river 5,000 miles away." The necessary gold in 1870 was £1 million. In 1901, Junius's son promised with a nod of his head to move half a billion dollars into the market.

A few days after accepting "this price," Morgan drove up to 51st Street to congratulate Carnegie on becoming the richest man in the world. The owner of over 50 percent of Carnegie Steel stood to make $240 million at one stroke, in addition to the fortune he had already earned. According to Wall Street lore, Carnegie several months later sidled up to Morgan on board a steamer headed for Europe and, clearing his throat, said, "Mr. Morgan, I believe I should have asked you for another $100 million." Morgan allegedly replied, "If you had, I'd have paid it."†

Although he had been skeptical about the "manufacturers of stock certificates," Carnegie wrote to one of his partners at the end of February 1901: "Morgan has succeeded as I felt he would. Now we are all right"—and he added

---

* Carnegie specified:

$160,000,000 of Carnegie Company bonds to be exchanged at par
for bonds in the new company $160,000,000

$160,000,000 stock, each $1000 Carnegie Company share to be
exchanged for a $1500 share in the new concern $240,000,000

Profits for the past and coming year (estimated): $80,000,000

Total: $480,000,000

† In prosaic fact, Carnegie told a congressional committee in 1912 that he had named his price and Morgan considered it fair: "I have been told many times since by insiders that I should have asked $100,000,000 more and could have got it easily. Once for all, I want to put a stop to all this talk about Mr. Carnegie 'forcing high prices for anything.' " Adding $100 million to the deal would have implied a price/earnings ratio of 14.5.

to a friend a week later, "It is a marvel . . . the new company will make such enormous profits it can afford to pay Carnegie Company what it has."

———

Less than twelve weeks had elapsed between the Schwab dinner and Morgan's announcement on March 3, 1901, that he was organizing the largest corporation in the world. United States Steel would be capitalized as a New Jersey holding company at $1.4 billion. Hardly anyone thought in terms of billions in 1901. The federal government was spending about $350 million a year— $130 million less than Carnegie's selling price. As Dawkins observed, things were indeed "humming" at 23 Wall Street.

Working with his partners and lawyers, Morgan bought up the other properties on Schwab's list, mostly without haggling over prices—he wanted them in the new combination, and took their own measures of their value. (One exception was John W. Gates, who tried to hold up the combination for far more than Morgan thought his American Steel and Wire company was worth, and had to back down.) The bankers contracted to pay for shares in the old companies with stock in the new. They also acquired rights to additional Lake Superior iron-ore deposits from the Rockefellers; when Gary balked at the price ($30 million), Morgan said: "Judge Gary, in a business proposition as great as this would you let a matter of $5,000,000 stand in the way of success?"

The giant holding company would own steel mills, blast furnaces, coke ovens, ore mines, barges, steamships, thousands of acres of coke and coal land, and several railroads. It would control nearly half of America's steelmaking capacity, and produce more than half its total output—7 million tons a year. The $1.4 billion figure was equivalent to 7 percent of the U.S. gross national product in 1901. A comparable percentage in the 1990s would come to roughly $400 billion.

Power over this colossal enterprise would be concentrated in the hands of a few men, all appointed by Morgan. Charles Schwab resigned from Carnegie Steel to become president of U.S. Steel—Morgan had asked Carnegie about the younger man's ability to run the new corporation, and the steelmaster had recommended him "unreservedly." Elbert Gary was made chairman of the Executive Committee, Bob Bacon the head of Finance. Morgan himself would sit, with three of his partners, on the twenty-four-man board of directors, and also, with his friend George Baker of the First National, on the Finance Committee. He refused to give Bet-a-Million Gates a seat on the board.

The formation of U.S. Steel captured headlines all over the world, and reactions to the "Billion Dollar Trust" overshadowed reports of the ceremonies ushering in the McKinley-Roosevelt administration. Senator Albert Beveridge of Indiana called Morgan "the greatest constructive financier yet developed among mankind." A writer in Hearst's *Cosmopolitan* magazine announced that "the world, on the 3rd day of March, 1901, ceased to be ruled by . . . so-called statesmen" and had been taken over by "those who control the concentrated portion of the money supply." The journalist Ray Stannard Baker, who published a study of the new corporation in *McClure's* magazine, concluded that U.S. Steel was "planning the first really systematic effort ever made by Americans to capture the foreign steel trade," and that it was virtually "a republican form of government, not unlike that of the United States." Yale's president Arthur T. Hadley predicted that unless the government checked the advancing power of the trusts, the United States would see "an emperor in Washington within twenty-five years." The inimitable Henry Adams said, "Pierpont Morgan is apparently trying to swallow the sun."

Some of the criticism was surprisingly good-humored. William Jennings Bryan's populist *Commoner* quoted Morgan as saying, "America is good enough for me," and replied: "Whenever he doesn't like it, he can give it back to us." Finley Peter Dunne described Morgan's power in the voice of his fictional Irish saloonkeeper, Mr. Dooley: "Pierpont Morgan calls in wan iv his office boys, th' president iv a national bank, an' says he, 'James,' he says, 'take some change out iv th' damper an' r-run out an' buy Europe f'r me,' he says. 'I intind to re-organize it an' put it on a paying basis,' he says. 'Call up the Czar an' th' Pope an' th' Sultan an' th' Impror Willum, an' tell thim we won't need their savices afther nex' week,' he says. 'Give thim a year's salary in advance. An', James,' he says, 'ye betther put that r-red headed book-keeper near th' dure in charge iv th' continent. He doesn't seem to be doin' much,' he says."

In London, bizarre rumors said that people were insuring Morgan's life at 3 percent a month for £2 million—not true, Jack told Fanny, but one man *had* taken out a policy at 3 percent a year for £50,000: "It's a curious idea," reflected Jack, "but this man considered it the wise course, as Father is in the same category with Queen Victoria and other rulers on this side of the Atlantic!" Since Victoria had just died, Jack's analogy was as curious as the idea of insuring Pierpont's life.

Compared with the high-rolling speculators, Morgan looked like the Rock of Gibraltar, but he was using unfamiliar financial procedures and techniques. Investors were accustomed to bonds—loans mortgaged by "hard" assets of physical plant, real estate, and equipment—and critics of U.S. Steel, noting by how much the new securities exceeded the assets of the constituent companies, accused the bankers of "watering" the stock. The corporation issued $304 million in 5 percent gold bonds, and $1.1 billion in stock—$550 million in 7 percent convertible preferred shares, $550 million in common—for the $1.4 billion total. Even the experienced banker Isaac Seligman pronounced it "enough to take one's breath away." The Bureau of Corporations, a fact-finding agency in the Department of Commerce and Labor, later estimated that the tangible value of the properties in the combination was somewhere between $676 million and $793 million.*

U.S. Steel easily had enough tangible assets to back its $304 million issue of bonds, and even at the low estimate, nearly enough to cover its $550 million of convertible preferred shares as well. The value of the common stock depended on the company's future earnings, which, as in Morgan's railroad reorganizations, were expected to rise because of increased efficiencies, economies of scale, and administrative rationalization. To the extent that the consolidation worked, it would create value for the $550 million of common stock.

Since this financial structure did not differ in kind from those Morgan devised for railroads, it was apparently the sheer *size* of the consolidation that took Wall Street's breath away. The pro-industry *Iron Age* praised the stabilizing Morganization of steel in February, but in April criticized the company as "an aggregate of large consolidations, each liberally dosed at the time it was formed with *aqua pura*," plus "additional quantities of water . . . sprinkled in to cement the amalgamation." *The Wall Street Journal* acknowledged a certain "uneasiness over the magnitude of the affair," wondering whether the company would ever pay dividends, and warning that the extraordinary transaction might be "a turning point in the market: The high tide of industrial capitalism."

The organization of U.S. Steel *did* mark the high tide of the turn-of-the-century merger movement, but Morgan entertained none of his critics' doubts. Experience with the railroads' high fixed charges had led him to prefer equity to debt. Regarding what others called "water" as capitalized future earnings, he expected the benefits of consolidation to enable the corporation to service its debt and pay dividends, probably without raising the price of steel. In a circular issued on March 2, 1901, he said: "Statements furnished us . . . show that the aggregate of the net earnings of all the companies for the calendar year 1900 was amply sufficient to pay dividends on both classes of the new stocks, besides making provision for sinking funds and maintenance of properties. It is expected that by the consummation of the proposed arrangement the neces-

---

* The $117 million difference between these figures suggests the difficulty of measuring an industrial property's net worth. One way would have been to add up the securities of the constituent companies, but since the stock of Carnegie Steel had never traded on the market there was no reliable estimate for its preconsolidation value. Another method, calculating the value of U.S. Steel's tangible property, raised questions about what exactly to measure—the price historically paid? replacement value? probable price if offered for sale? According to William T. Hogan, who wrote an economic history of the American steel industry in 1971, the difference between the bureau's $700 million to $800 million figures and U.S. Steel's $1.4 billion lay in the value assigned to the ore lands—$100 million by the bureau, $700 million by the corporation. Hogan concluded that "the years since have tended more to justify the $700 million figure than the smaller estimate."

sity of large deductions heretofore made on account of expenditures for improvements will be avoided, the amount of earnings applicable to dividends will be substantially increased and greater stability of investment will be assured, without necessarily increasing the prices of manufactured products."

Morgan organized a syndicate to secure at least 51 percent of the stocks of the constituent companies (by exchanging them for shares of U.S. Steel), and also to underwrite $200 million of the new corporation's securities to meet immediate cash needs.* He had done the same thing on a smaller scale for Federal Steel. U.S. Steel, too, would offer shares to the public, and whether or not it had to call for the full $200 million pledged by the syndicate would depend on how the public offering went. By March 21, the merger had acquired over 90 percent of its constituents' stock, and four days later, J. P. Morgan & Co. asked the syndicate to raise $25 million in cash—12.5 percent of its $200 million commitment. Morgan hired Wall Street floor-operator James R. Keene to manage the offering on the Stock Exchange, and demand was huge. Keene reportedly made $1 million in commissions. The new shares sold so well that the remaining $175 million of syndicate cash never had to be called.

The Billion Dollar Trust raised with fresh urgency all the country's objections to financial concentration and gave new force to a range of questions: Did corporate size per se threaten competition and individual freedom? Did consolidation in fact promote efficiency over the long run? Would Morganization stifle not only destructive conflict but also the creative energy that stimulates innovation and economic growth?

Some of the consolidation's critics at the time argued that it was wildly reckless—composed of so much *aqua pura* that it would never pay dividends. Others condemned it as a monopolistic restraint of trade. Since it cannot have been both a foolhardy issue of worthless paper *and* an instrument of tight market control, these arguments suggest, again, that it was the size of the deal that elicited instinctive abhorrence.

The speed with which U.S. Steel had been put together left critical considera-

---

* Unlike Morgan's railroad and government bond syndicates, which were made up largely of banks, the three hundred members of the Steel syndicate included wealthy individuals. J. P. Morgan & Co. took a $6,457,000 participation, John W. Gates $6 million, E. H. Gary $4.5 million, James Stillman, William Rockefeller, H. H. Rogers, and George Baker's First National $3,125,000 each. P. A. B. Widener subscribed for $2,875,000, Kidder, Peabody for $2.5 million, and Thomas Fortune Ryan for $1,875,000. In at $1 million each were William C. Whitney, Levi P. Morton, Henry Clay Frick, D. O. Mills, Morgan, Harjes & Co., and Kuhn, Loeb. Among those who took under a $1 million share were E. H. Harriman, Charles Schwab, Mark Hanna, August Belmont & Co., Lazard Frères, Francis Lynde Stetson, H. M. Flagler, Daniel Lamont, Robert Lincoln, George Bowdoin, S. Endicott Peabody, Bob Bacon, and Chauncey Depew. The largest subscribers by far were the Moore brothers and two of their associates, who as a group subscribed for almost $75 million—about 38 percent of the total.

tions about its structure and direction unresolved (see Chapter 22), but time proved Morgan right about the financing. The corporation created real value for its investors, earning $60 million in net profit between March and December 1901, and $90 million in 1902—enough to pay a 7 percent dividend on the preferred stock and 4 percent on the common, and still have a sizable surplus. Over the next quarter of a century, its stock performed better than that of all other American steel companies except Bethlehem. Morgan seemed to be turning everything he touched to gold.

———

Even more controversial than the size of the merger were the syndicate's earnings—about $50 million, paid in shares of U.S. Steel preferred and common stock at then current market valuations. For the first year of the corporation's existence the preferred shares traded at around 94, the common at 44. After reimbursing participants for the $25 million put up in cash and deducting $3 million incurred as expenses, the syndicate paid $40 million to its members and $10 million as management fee to J. P. Morgan & Co.

The Bureau of Corporations in 1911 called these charges "greatly in excess of a reasonable compensation," and *The Wall Street Journal* looking back in 1988 concluded that they "represented a level of greed probably without contemporary parallel." Fifty million 1901 dollars would be roughly equivalent to $750 million in the 1990s.

Entries in the U.S. Steel syndicate book indicate that the $40 million paid to the subscribers in four installments during 1902 was 5 percent of the $800 million worth of securities the syndicate underwrote—$200 million pledged in cash, plus about $600 million in new shares traded for stock of the constituent companies. The Morgan bank's $10 million management fee brought the total to 6.3 percent—not "greatly in excess of a reasonable compensation" at a time when underwriting commissions ranged from 2.5 to 10 percent. (In the 1990s, neither a gross fee of 6 percent for an initial public offering nor a 20 percent management fee would be out of line.)

The syndicate's defenders at the time pointed out that it had helped float the entire deal, providing well over 51 percent of the merging companies' stocks; that it would have been liable for $200 million in cash had the launching not gone so well; and that the main reason it *did* go well was the credit furnished by its organizers, specifically by the house of Morgan. Investors knew that if anything went wrong, the bank would provide the necessary capital and "stand by its goods."

U.S. Steel stock prices fluctuated for the first few years: during a contraction in 1903–4, the preferred traded below 50, the common as low as 8⅜, and the directors had to suspend dividends on the latter. If the syndicate's $50 million profit had been calculated at these prices (it was based on market values), it would have amounted to slightly over $16 million.

Morgan was confident that the corporation would create value for its paper certificates over the long run, and it did. The stock performed so well, argued economist George Stigler years later, that the formation of U.S. Steel should be seen as "a master stroke of monopoly promotion," and critics were "churlish" to complain at the syndicate's earnings. The Morgan bank argued when the merger came under attack that the properties were fully worth the value of the securities, and that since the transaction was "unique" in character and scope, it could not be judged by the standards of "ordinary experience." Virtually everyone not connected with the deal judged it monstrous.

—

In early March 1901, as Morgan was about to announce the formation of U.S. Steel, he hired a new partner. George Walbridge Perkins, first vice president at the New York Life Insurance Company, was a trim man with protruding ears, a thick brush of mustache, and a gift for making deals. Between 1892 and 1899 he had transformed New York Life from the smallest of the three big insurance companies (called "the racers"—the other two were the Equitable and Mutual Life) into the largest. Under his guidance New York Life had begun to function as an investment bank, using its immense financial resources to underwrite corporate securities and foreign government loans; by 1900 its assets seemed likely to exceed a billion dollars within a decade.

Competition among "the racers" was fierce, and though Perkins outperformed his rivals, he believed that the competitive struggle for power had more costs than benefits. "The entire path of our industrial progress is strewn with the white bones of . . . competition," he declared, and the conflicts had become "too destructive to be tolerated. Co-operation must be the order of the day." He tried to impose regulation and self-discipline on insurance-industry warfare. A moralistic, second-generation insurance agent who wanted to eliminate irresponsible practices and stabilize his sales force, he also took steps to improve New York Life's relations with its workers: he set up pension plans, death benefits, and cash bonuses for workers. The bonuses were given not in relation to volume, which might have encouraged reckless expansion, but for steady performance, and Perkins was delighted with the results: he told a friend in 1897 of his pride at having linked the interests of managers and workers in "a corporation that is composed of nearly 300,000 members."

Perkins was also an adroit politician, friendly with President McKinley, Vice President–elect Theodore Roosevelt, and Senators Beveridge and Hanna. Wall Street took note of Perkins's skills, especially once he negotiated loans to the governments of Germany and Russia. In November 1900 James Stillman made him a director of the National City Bank, and commended him to Morgan. In December Morgan asked Bob Bacon, who also sat on the City Bank board, to bring the insurance man to 23 Wall Street.

Perkins welcomed the invitation. He was raising money to save the eroding cliffs on the western bank of the Hudson—he lived in Riverdale, just north of Manhattan, and Roosevelt as Governor of New York had made him chairman of a Palisades Interstate Park Commission; Perkins wanted Morgan to contribute. As soon as he took a seat in the famous glass-walled office, he started to explain his mission. Morgan cut him short.

"I know all about that," he said. "You are chairman of the Commission. What is it you want?"

Perkins: "I want to raise $125,000."

Morgan: "All right, put me down for $25,000. It is a good thing. Is that all?"

Somewhat flabbergasted, Perkins managed to ask who else might subscribe. Morgan suggested John D. Rockefeller. Perkins thanked him and was rising to leave when Morgan said: "I will give you the whole $125,000 if you will do something for me."

"Do something for you?" repeated Perkins. "What?"

"Take that desk over there," said Morgan, pointing to the room in which his partners worked. He was offering a coveted position at his right hand to a man he had just met.

Perkins stalled: "I have a pretty good desk up at the New York Life."

Morgan made it explicit: "No, I mean come into the firm."

Like everyone who got these imperious invitations, Perkins asked for time to think it over. "Certainly," said Morgan. "Let me know tomorrow if you can." As Perkins was leaving, Morgan stipulated that of course he would give up his work at New York Life if he came to 23 Wall Street, since the big insurance companies had become large buyers of securities sold by the Morgan bank.

Perkins quickly canvassed his influential friends—Senator Beveridge warned him that Morgan was a partner killer; President McKinley advised him to stay at New York Life—and declined Morgan's offer, although not without using it to raise his salary from $30,000 to $75,000 a year.

Two months later, at the end of February 1901, Morgan invited Perkins to breakfast. He explained that he was about to launch U.S. Steel, and would soon be organizing similar ventures in other industries. He knew that Perkins shared his views on excessive competition. He also knew that some of the hostility to his own work came from the "occult mechanisms" of high finance, and thought that if people understood what he was doing they would see it the way he did— as a national service. Probably he was aware as well of Perkins's popular worker-benefit programs, at a time of escalating conflict between capital and labor. He said he wanted help with the social and political problems created by the trusts, and according to Perkins's biographer, John A. Garraty, this appeal worked: Perkins believed that "size and business efficiency went hand in hand, and that the most challenging problems of the modern world were to be found in the relationships that were developing between the giant corporations and their workers, and between these corporations and the public."

The terms of Morgan's offer added incentive. Perkins would earn $250,000 a year, plus a share of the bank's profits. As to the condition Morgan mentioned at the end of their first interview—resignation from New York Life—Perkins refused, since he wanted exactly what his new employer did not, a direct link between the buyers and sellers of securities. Morgan was concerned about what a later era would call conflicts of interest, and gave in to Perkins against his better judgment: "if you . . . believe you can carry out this dual position, which I do not believe you can," he said, "I am willing to try it temporarily."

"Temporarily" turned out to be ten years. That Perkins, age thirty-nine, got his way on this critical point indicates again that Morgan's legendary power was not as absolute as people thought. In need of Perkins's skills, he put prudent objections aside.

To James Stillman at the City Bank, Perkins said he hoped "when I find my place down the street I will not, in any way, disappoint you." Stillman sent back "heartiest good wishes. You have the most splendid opportunity in being so closely associated with the greatest financier, in spite of his peculiarities, this or any other age has ever seen, and one which I am free to say I envy you."

Perkins quickly became a one-man department of public relations at the Morgan bank, holding press conferences, publishing articles and pamphlets, and giving speeches on the advantages of industrial consolidation. Appointed to the Finance Committee and board of directors at U.S. Steel, he issued such rhapsodic statements that his friend Beveridge warned him to "Go slow . . . about Mr. Morgan's philanthropic motives in Steel Trust or the public will think you protest too much."

As Morgan and Gary had done at Federal Steel, Perkins lifted the veil of corporate secrecy: in the fall of 1901 he began to publish quarterly financial reports for U.S. Steel. *The Commercial & Financial Chronicle* praised this first accounting as "the fullest and frankest earnings statement ever submitted . . . by a great industrial concern," and welcomed Big Steel's recognition of the "public's right to know." From London, Jack described the report as well received in spite of skeptics who called its figures "impossibly good," the product of "expert bookkeeping": he hoped it would force other companies to follow suit, and help dispel the prejudice against industrial securities.

In March of 1902, Pulitzer's New York *World* announced that "George W. Perkins now does all the talking . . . for the firm of J. P. Morgan and Co. . . . [He] has the facility of saying just enough and not too much on any subject." Perkins acted so consistently as the bank's ambassador to Washington over the next decade that he became known as Morgan's Secretary of State.

—

At the beginning of April 1901, Morgan sailed for Europe on the White Star's *Teutonic*—to avoid reporters, photographers, and curious crowds he had to duck up the second-class gangway. He would from now on find privacy only behind closed doors. For the first time in years, Louisa, four months pregnant, did not accompany him. He traveled with his sister Mary Burns instead.

He played solitaire and slept most of the way across the Atlantic. Henry Adams wrote to his friend Elizabeth Cameron: "Wall Street goes quite wild, while Lombard Street is dead broke. . . . London and Berlin are standing in perfectly abject terror, watching Pierpont Morgan's nose flaming over the ocean waves, and approaching hourly nearer their bank-vaults."

For the moment, Morgan had more interest in Europe's art markets than its bank vaults. He did not see Fanny, who was touring Italy with Anne, for several weeks. Shortly after he arrived in London he bought the *Duchess of Devonshire*, the Gainsborough portrait that Junius had been about to acquire in 1876 when it was stolen from Agnew's Bond Street gallery. The thief, Adam Worth, unable to unload his renowned white elephant all these years and now seriously ill, had finally handed it over to a Pinkerton agent and William Agnew's son Morland at a Chicago hotel in March 1901, in exchange for an undisclosed sum and probably immunity from prosecution.

Although the canvas was dirty and cut, the Duchess's face and voluptuous figure were intact. Agnew took the picture to London, where Morgan agreed to buy it sight unseen, asking the dealer to have it restored and to charge whatever he considered fair. London papers buzzed with the story, but never managed to learn the price. Morgan told a friend: "Nobody will ever know. If the truth came out, I might be considered a candidate for the lunatic asylum."

He paid £30,000 (nearly $150,000) for the well-traveled Georgiana—five times what he paid for Rembrandt's *Nicolaes Ruts* three years earlier. William Agnew, who had retired, congratulated him on "possessing the finest Gainsborough in the world," which was a proprietary stretch. Another Agnew son, Lockett, said later that he thought the "*réclame*" [publicity] aspect of the acquisition probably appealed most to Morgan, since seven weeks elapsed between his purchase of the painting and the first time he saw it. Sentiment played a role as well: Junius had wanted the picture, and Pierpont carried out his father's wishes without regard to content or cost.*

---

* The painting remained in the Morgan family until July 1994, when it was sold through Sotheby's to the Chatsworth House Trust for £265,500. It is now at Chatsworth, seat of the Dukes of Devonshire. With regard to long-standing doubts about the painting's authenticity, the present Duke told the London *Times*, "I personally think that it is a Gainsborough," then shrugged, smiled, and added, "To me it's a very jolly picture."

In Paris two weeks after he secured the Duchess, he made a far more significant purchase. By 1901 no painter was held in higher esteem in the United
States than Raphael. Nineteenth-century American artists and connoisseurs
traveled to Europe explicitly to study the High Renaissance master's work. They
especially admired his Madonnas—paintings that combined grandeur with
tenderness, flawless execution with sensuous color and form. The Sturgeses
owned a print of Raphael's *Sistine Madonna,* and made a pilgrimage to see the
original in Dresden on their European tour in 1859. As American collectors'
taste for Old Masters developed toward the end of the century, and as American
artists and architects looked increasingly to Renaissance Rome for cultural
models, Raphael came to represent the supreme moral and aesthetic ideal. According to David Alan Brown, the curator of an exhibition on *Raphael and
America* at the National Gallery of Art in 1983, Raphael was "the only artist
whose prestige had endured all changes of taste and fashion up to the end of
the nineteenth century," and was "referred to by Berenson without exaggera-
tion as the 'most famous and most beloved name in modern art.' Indeed, his
name was synonymous with Art."

There was not a single painting by Raphael in the United States in 1897, and
the scarcity of the artist's work in a rising market had driven its prices beyond
the reach of most collectors. In 1898, at the urging of her adviser, Bernard
Berenson, Isabella Stewart Gardner bought Raphael's portrait of *Tommaso Inghirami,* a fat, wall-eyed Roman prelate in a red robe and cap, shown writing at
his desk.* Two years later, also through Berenson, she purchased for £5,000 a
Lamentation by Raphael, part of an altarpiece predella. These works did not satisfy her, however: like other major collectors at the time, she wanted the
supreme trophy—"a *heavenly* Raphael *Madonna*"—and to Berenson's dismay
she refused for a time to buy anything else, insisting that "My remaining pen-
nies must go to the greatest Raphael. . . . Nothing short of that. I have tasted
blood you see."

Mrs. Gardner never acquired a Raphael Madonna, but Morgan did. He
crossed the English Channel at the end of April 1901, and on a quick visit to the
Charles Sedelmeyer gallery in Paris bought an early Raphael altarpiece known
as the *Colonna Madonna,* painted in 1504–5 for the convent of Sant' Antonio of
Padua in Perugia. Mrs. Gardner's predella panel was originally part of it.

Vasari described the altarpiece as a "truly marvellous and devout" work,
"much extolled by all painters." It had a royal pedigree, having been owned by

* Mrs. Gardner's painting came from the Inghirami Palace in Volterra, but there was another version at the Pitti Palace. For most of the twentieth century, scholars considered the
Gardner picture the earlier of the two, but a careful restoration and scientific examination of
the Pitti Palace portrait in the 1980s led most experts to accept it as the prime version, and
attribute Mrs. Gardner's to "Raphael and School."

the Colonna princes in Rome and successive kings of Naples. Ruskin, who did not particularly admire Raphael, had urged Liverpool's merchants to buy this painting in 1874, and French critics had commended it to the Louvre as a "work of the highest order, which every European Gallery should be eager to secure." A brochure printed by Sedelmeyer quoted some of these assessments, traced the work's provenance, called it the "richest and most important composition of all the various Madonna pictures of Raphael," and compared it favorably with the *Ansidei Madonna*, which London's National Gallery had bought from the Duke of Marlborough in 1885 for £70,000 ($350,000), then the highest price ever paid for a painting.

Not all the experts agreed. The Louvre and the National Gallery had declined the painting—known as the "Madonna of a million" in the seventies because of its million-franc price tag—and it had been on display at the South Kensington Museum, where Morgan had probably seen it, from 1886 to 1896 without finding a buyer. The dealer Martin Colnaghi finally bought it in 1896 for $200,000, less than half the price then asked, and sold it to Sedelmeyer, who had it restored and cleaned. Morgan probably did not know that Sedelmeyer had offered it to Mrs. Gardner in 1897, or that Berenson had denounced it to her as only partly painted by Raphael, its composition devoid of "that spacious eurhythmy, that airy buoyancy which Raphael gives you in the *Sposalizio,* in the *Belle Jardinière,* in his Stanze. . . ." After Morgan bought the painting, Berenson went even further, lumping it with "pictures Raphael barely looked at."

Berenson exaggerated the picture's faults—he tended to disparage anything he had not authenticated—but art historians at the time and since have found the *Colonna Madonna* puzzling, lacking the elegance, lucidity, and coherence of Raphael's great work. Now at the Metropolitan Museum of Art, the panel is given to Raphael but described as "more primitive" than his other work of the period—the *Ansidei Madonna* and a fresco in San Severo, Perugia—and valued more highly for its place in the artist's development than for its aesthetic caliber.

Morgan acquired the altarpiece the day he saw it in Paris, for 2 million francs ($400,000), along with paintings by Rubens, Titian, Nattier, and Morland, paying $600,000 in all. (He later returned the Titian, probably as not genuine.) He did not hesitate to spend nearly half a million dollars for a single work by the "Prince of Painters," any more than he flinched at committing half a billion for Carnegie Steel. When he wanted something, he paid little attention to critics or price, and he wanted a Raphael Madonna.

He responded less to abstract qualities in works of art than to subject, history, rarity, provenance. The subject of the Raphael panel was what Henry Adams called "the highest energy ever known to man," and Morgan later complemented this acquisition with other Renaissance depictions of the Virgin and Child, filling his private study with Italian Madonnas. The history and rarity of the altarpiece were not in doubt. David Alan Brown has described the *Colonna*

Madonna as "the most ornate of Raphael's pictures," and guessed that it appealed to Morgan's taste for "decorative richness": when the painting was cleaned at the Metropolitan in the 1970s, restorers found that marble veining and gilding had been added. Critical reservations notwithstanding, the *Colonna Madonna* was "*BIG* game"—a grand, costly prize by an incontrovertibly great artist, which would confer distinction on the collection and country to which it belonged. Since Morgan had set out to furnish America with exceptional cultural treasures, this one was irresistible.

He did not pay for it until the end of the year, as was his practice with large acquisitions. If it turned out to be "wrong," he would return it, as he did the "Titian" he had bought the same day. It did not turn out to be wrong. When Morgan paid Sedelmeyer's bill through his London office in December 1901, Clinton Dawkins cabled Jack from London (using the code name "Flitch" for the senior Morgan), "I hope, though we cannot hint it, that Flitch will not buy the National Gallery at the end of the year." In early January 1902 the *New York Herald* announced: MR. J. PIERPONT MORGAN GIVES RECORD SUM FOR RAPHAEL! Mr. J. Pierpont Morgan lent his Raphael to London's National Gallery, had it featured in a sumptuous hand-printed catalogue, and grew steadily prouder of it as the years went by. When he died in 1913, it was considered the most important painting in his collection.

At the end of April 1901, after acquiring the *Colonna Madonna* in Paris, he went off to Aix-les-Bains for a rest.

Morgan at Dover House, 1902.
(Courtesy of the late Annette M. Schieffelin)

Chapter 21

RAID

Morgan had reserved the suite of rooms he always took at the Grand Hôtel in Aix. Mary Burns accompanied him to the spa in 1901, and his daughter Anne left Fanny in Paris to join them—Fanny went on with her maid to visit Jack and Jessie in London.

The hot springs in the hills of southeastern France, famous for its mountain views and Roman ruins, had been attracting European royalty for centuries. In recent decades Aix's eminent visitors had included Queen Victoria (who traveled, hardly incognito, as the "Countess of Balmoral"), her cousin Belgium's King Leopold II, the Emperor of Brazil, George I of Greece, and the Empress Elizabeth of Austria. Illicit love affairs carried out under the pretext of medical necessity had made the spa's *chronique scandaleuse* as renowned as its cure. Morgan's daily regimen there consisted of thermal baths and long massages in the morning, followed by lunch with his companions; in the afternoon he answered letters and cables, and took a drive through the countryside— over the years he had visited every beautiful spot within twenty miles. After dinner he played cards until bedtime. Although he enjoyed the attentions of the spa physicians, he adamantly refused the exercise and foul-tasting mineral waters they prescribed. He once told a reporter that the secret of health was "contentment, cheerfulness, and not to expect too much from others"—implicitly attributing his ailments to depression. On arriving at Aix in the spring of 1901 he made a large contribution to the local hospital. The mayor presented him with a bouquet as official thanks, and the town eventually named a street the Boulevard Pierpont Morgan.

On Saturday, May 4, Morgan was settling into his spa routine when a messenger brought him a cable from New York. Slicing it open, he learned that hostile raiders had launched a secret attack on one of "his" railroads, the Northern Pacific.

Events, it seemed, were not going to concede him a vacation. He had been connected with the Northern Pacific for twenty years, having raised $40 million for the last phase of its construction in 1880, and three years later rescued the road from bankruptcy. Like the Reading, the NP had gone on an expansion spree after its five-year, banker-controlled voting trust expired, and had loaded itself up with so much debt that it had defaulted again in the summer of 1893, requiring Morgan to step in once more.

James J. Hill, head of the Great Northern Railway, had been watching the NP closely. Born in Canada, he had moved to Minnesota in the 1850s, and by 1893 his Great Northern ran from Duluth to Puget Sound. His entrepreneurial gifts and short, stocky build had earned him the moniker Little Giant. Like many Gilded Age tycoons, he saw himself as an American Napoleon, and had commensurate dreams. None of the big east–west roads yet reached all the way across country, but Hill hoped to build a truly transcontinental system from coast to coast that would link up with shipping lines for trade with Asia and Europe. If his well-managed Great Northern cooperated with the Northern Pacific, two hundred miles to the south, they could construct an efficient, low-cost system of trade between America's breadbasket and the markets of the Pacific; their competition would be not with each other but with foreign transport systems as the United States laid claim to international commerce.

Hill and his financial backers, the Deutsche Bank and New York's Kuhn, Loeb, proposed to Morgan that they end competition between the two big northwest roads by merging them into a single system to be managed by Hill. The Little Giant from St. Paul with his bushy beard and shoulder-length gray hair was another unlikely Morgan ally: he looked as though he would be happier in buckskins than dinner jackets, yet his expertise spoke for itself and his aims coincided with those of 23 Wall Street. Morgan and Coster cabled their London associates in July of 1895: "proposed plan in every way desirable all interests."* The proposed plan was not in fact desirable to Morgan's lawyers. Stetson thought it would constitute an illegal restraint of trade. He was right: Minnesota's Supreme Court invalidated the plan, and in March of 1896 the U.S. Supreme Court rejected a constitutional challenge to the state statute that prohibited mergers between parallel or competing railroad lines.

---

* The Great Northern agreed to guarantee an issue of Northern Pacific mortgage bonds up to $175 million and, in return, to take half of Northern Pacific's capital stock and appoint five of the road's nine directors.

A month later, representatives of the Great Northern and Northern Pacific met in London and agreed privately to "form a permanent alliance defensive, and in case of need offensive" to avoid competition and protect their common interests: neither road would encroach on the other's territory by building or buying control of competing lines. Hill and his associates purchased about $16 million of Northern Pacific stock—roughly 10 percent of the total; these shares, combined with those held by Morgan's people, brought the two groups effective joint control of the NP.

A voting trust reorganized the Northern Pacific in 1896, changing its name from Railroad to Railway.* J. P. Morgan & Co. formed a syndicate with the Deutsche Bank to take $45 million of new NP securities, and the road prospered after its second Morganization, paying a 4 percent dividend on its preferred shares by 1898, and 2 percent on the common a year later.

Hill turned out to be a political power broker as well as an expert railroad manager. As the NP reorganization got under way in May of 1896, Coster forwarded him a telegram from a Washington informant reporting that one of the fifteen members of Congress who lived along the NP route had "declined to sign the request that the federal reorganization bill be taken up immediately": the holdout was Representative Joel P. Heatwole of Minnesota, "whose district lies largely on the line of the Great Northern, and he is in doubt as to whether you would approve his signing. Please wire him to do so."

Hill apparently authorized the congressman to sign. He earned a large profit from the NP reorganization, since he had bought nearly 260,000 shares of stock (par value $26 million) in the bankrupt road for $4 million. He had, however, hoped to control this resuscitated rival. Instead, Morgan ran the new voting trust, put Bacon, Coster, and Stetson on the board, and appointed two presidents of the NP whom Hill did not like—first Edwin Winter, then Charles S. Mellen. From 1896 until 1901, the Great Northern and the Northern Pacific abided by their peace treaty, but Hill wasn't satisfied.

The cable that reached Morgan at Aix on May 4, 1901, informed him that a combination of bankers and railroad men had secretly managed to buy up

---

* The name change had to do with raising money. The original NP charter stipulated that the road could issue bonds only for equipment and construction, not for new financing. To get around that provision, Morgan's lawyers found an unbuilt road in Wisconsin with a more liberal charter, the Superior & St. Croix; they bought the St. Croix, changed its named to the Northern Pacific Railway, and had it buy the NP Railroad.

Testifying about the road a few years later in court, Morgan needed help remembering its name. He said, "I made up my mind that it was essential that the Northern Pacific Railroad Company—railway, or whatever you call it—what is it?"

Mr. Stetson: "Railway."

Morgan (continuing): "Railway . . ."

more than half of Northern Pacific's stock on the open market. Leading the raiders in this "battle of financial giants" was Edward H. Harriman, a diminutive former stockbroker with a droopy mustache, wire-rimmed glasses, a penchant for stock manipulation, and a history of conflict with Morgan. He now controlled the Union Pacific, which ran from Kansas City and Omaha to Promontory Point, Utah (where it had met the Central Pacific in 1869). Like Hill, Harriman considered himself an American Napoleon and was known in railroad circles as a Little Giant. Also like Hill, he wanted to build a worldwide network of railroads and shipping lines based on his own companies. Unlike Hill, Harriman did not play by the Morgan rules: he favored guerrilla warfare over cooperative covenants.

He had taken charge of the Union Pacific by stealth. In 1895, when the bankrupt UP appealed to Jacob Schiff at Kuhn, Loeb for reorganization, Schiff deferred to Morgan, who had been one of the road's bankers and part of an earlier reorganization plan: "That is J. P. Morgan's affair," said Schiff. "I don't want to interfere with anything he is trying to do." Only after learning that Morgan wanted nothing further to do with the UP but was willing to help did Schiff take on the job.

While the Morgans had been channeling British capital to U.S. railroads, the German-Jewish firm of Kuhn, Loeb had been doing the same thing with money from Germany and France, and though the top Yankee and Jewish investment houses did not work together, they maintained gentlemanly agreements not to invade each other's territory. Schiff's plan for the Union Pacific was about to go into effect late in 1896 when things mysteriously began to go wrong among shareholders, journalists, and politicians. A baffled Schiff checked with Morgan, who knew nothing about the disturbance but promised to find out, and reported a few weeks later, "It's that little fellow Harriman. . . . you want to watch him carefully."

When Schiff confronted "that little fellow," Harriman said he was fighting Schiff's plan because he wanted to reorganize the UP himself, and he soon maneuvered his way onto the railroad's board and executive committee. Over the next few years he managed to turn the bankrupt UP into a strong, profitable line. Once he secured connections to the Pacific coast, his system posed a threat to the NP and GN. And in 1901 he acquired control of the huge Southern Pacific, running from Los Angeles to New Orleans.

Meanwhile, he was fighting with the other Little Giant, Hill, over a 7,911-mile rail network called the Chicago, Burlington, & Quincy. Both men wanted this dense web of midwestern roads for its access to Chicago, which offered connections to the Atlantic seaboard. Harriman had tried and failed to buy the CB&Q in 1900. Hill and Morgan acquired it for the joint account of the Great Northern and Northern Pacific in late March 1901. The road's Boston Brahmin owners explicitly chose Morgan over Harriman: "if Hill means also Mor-

gan and the Northern Pacific, as he says it does," they explained, "that would
be the stronger and safer place for us to land." Harriman demanded a third of
the deal, but Hill and Morgan turned him down. They did not want this bel-
ligerent spoiler "butting in."

Harriman, of course, did not regard himself as butting in. He saw Hill and
Morgan as filching the CB&Q out from under him—the new combination
would be much stronger than the UP—and he quickly came up with a
Napoleonic plan for revenge: to secure the CB&Q he would take over the giant
Northern Pacific.

Buying stock out from under Morgan's formidable nose would be next to impossible, however. Harriman was going to need a great deal of luck and even
more cash, and to assure himself of the latter he turned to Kuhn, Loeb and to
the commercial National City Bank. Between 1891, when James Stillman became president of the City Bank, and 1901, the amount of its deposits had
multiplied nearly ninefold, and its total assets had risen from $22 million to
$194.5 million. William Rockefeller, John D.'s brother and chief financial offi-
cer, had chosen the City as the Standard Oil bank, and he and Stillman had
been helping Schiff and Harriman refinance the Union Pacific.*

Morgan's lofty manner and dominant position on Wall Street had not en-
deared him to his rivals, and Hill later claimed that what came next had more
to do with banks than with railroads—that the "City Bank crowd" backed Harriman in order "to show the world that Morgan was not the only banker in
America," and to challenge his assumption "that all other Banking Houses
were nothing more than his clerks." Stillman, said Hill, talked of "cutting
[Morgan's] wings."

———

Schiff, working for Harriman, began to buy Northern Pacific shares as soon as
Morgan left for Europe at the beginning of April. McKinley's second election
had promised more heady times for Wall Street, and bullish investors were
pushing volume and prices on the New York Stock Exchange to new highs. In
January 1901 the market had its first 2-million-share day. In April, millionaires created by the steel merger, called the "Pittsburgh crowd," descended on
New York ready to gamble, which provided perfect cover for Harriman's raid.

Morgan and his associates controlled the Northern Pacific board but owned
less than half of its common stock; they assumed that no one would dream of
trying to take over a $155 million railroad. NP common had ranged in price
from 45 to 86 in 1900. It closed at 96 on April 1, 1901, on a heavy volume of
437,000 shares, and continued to climb all month. Kuhn, Loeb occasionally

* National City and the First National merged in 1955 to become the First National City
Bank of New York, predecessor of Citibank.

sold shares to modulate the rise and allay suspicion, attributing the run-up to Northern Pacific's increased value after the CB&Q acquisition. The stock hit 103 on April 22, and 105 three days later. On April 30, volume on the Stock Exchange soared to a record 3.3 million shares.

Harriman had calculated that the Morgan partners in their Senior's absence would not take alarm at the unusual activity in NP stock. The unsuspecting Bob Bacon actually sold 20,000 of Morgan's own shares to profit from the rise, which seemed to confirm Hill's prediction a year earlier that Coster's death would leave the railroad end of Morgan's business "unprotected." John W. "Bet-a-Million" Gates told a reporter in May, "It looks as though the little boys . . . commenced while the big boy was away. If Mr. Morgan had been here this never would have happened." By Wednesday, May 1, NP common was trading at 115, and on Sunday, the *New York Herald* looked back at "the most colossal week of speculative trading in the world's history."

Hill was in New York that week, and though he had noticed the upward pressure on Northern Pacific, he did not know that Harriman was behind it—until Schiff told him.

Schiff had been Hill's own banker until 1897, when Harriman demanded Kuhn, Loeb's exclusive attention, and Hill began to work more closely with Morgan. Both Kuhn, Loeb and the Great Northern had offices at 27 Pine Street, a block north of J. P. Morgan & Co., and it was there on Friday, May 3, that Schiff explained the situation to Hill. According to Hill, the banker invited him to join the effort to "throw Morgan overboard," promising him the presidency of the Northern Pacific and "all manner of things by way of control of the Union and Southern Pacific as well." Schiff said his group had spent $79 million, and held 420,000 of the NP's 750,000 preferred shares and 370,000 of the 800,000 common—in other words, nearly majority control of the road. Adding Hill's stock to this inventory would give Harriman a huge margin of victory, but Hill, on his own account, refused to "abandon Morgan" and join this "plan of piracy." Hill may have embellished the story he told, but he did not invent its most surprising feature—that Schiff was mounting a brazen attack on the reigning lord of American finance.

Schiff may have shared Stillman's desire to clip Morgan's ample wings, but his formal manners, German accent, white goatee, and refined tastes spoke more of Old World *haute banque* restraint than of hostile takeovers and secret stock raids, and he had been careful not to "interfere" with what Morgan was trying to do in the UP reorganization. Perhaps in 1901 he had succumbed to pressure from Harriman and the "City Bank crowd," hoping that Hill would join them in a bloodless coup.

Hill disguised his shock at this astonishing information on Friday, May 3, then left Schiff and raced down Broad Street to 23 Wall. There, poring over stock-transfer books, he and Morgan's partners discovered to their immense relief a hitch. Since the road's directors—virtually all Morgan men—could retire the preferred shares as of January 1, 1902, the common stock was the controlling factor, and Harriman did not yet have fully half of it. It was at this point that Bacon cabled his senior partner, and from Aix late Saturday afternoon Morgan wired instructions to buy 150,000 shares of NP common.

In New York that Saturday morning, Harriman was in bed with a cold and vaguely uneasy about not having 51 percent of the NP common. He sent a message to Schiff to acquire another 40,000 shares (the Stock Exchange was open on Saturdays till noon). Schiff got the order but decided not to carry it out. Perhaps he thought he already had a majority of the stock—or perhaps, having tipped his hand to Hill, he had belatedly realized the implications of trying to outfox Morgan, and determined not to deliver the coup de grâce. Had he bought 40,000 more shares on May 4, his group would have taken control of Morgan's road.*

———

On Monday, May 6, brokers for the Morgan/Hill group went onto the exchanges in London and New York to buy all the Northern Pacific stock they could. They used cash supplied by the big life insurance companies—chiefly, Perkins's New York Life. Northern Pacific shot up to 127½ by the end of the day in New York, and closed on Tuesday at 149¾. When Hill ordered his London associates not to sell NP common, one of them replied: "Friends here will stand firm. Much surprised Schiff should join in attempt to wrest control of NP from you. Keep me posted." Not even the railroad's managers knew what its bankers were doing. From St. Paul on Tuesday, NP president Charles Mellen wired his vice president in New York, "Cannot you give me some idea what is transpiring, to explain tremendous movement our stock?"

Short speculators had for days been selling into the rise, certain that it could not continue, and expecting to make a killing by contracting to deliver at $140 stock they would buy more cheaply as the price came down. On Tuesday, however, when the Morgan traders stopped buying at $146, the price did not come down. The market had gone berserk.

The risk for a buyer of stock has a boundary of zero—a share bought at $100 cannot lose more than 100 percent of its value. For short sellers, how-

* Schiff was at synagogue when the message reached him on Saturday, and most versions of this story say he did not execute the order out of obedience to Jewish laws forbidding work on the Sabbath. Yet if he could not buy stock on Saturday, he could have instructed the partner who brought him the message to do the job. Instead, he told the man not to buy the shares, since it was not necessary, and said he would take full responsibility for the decision.

ever, the risk is boundless, since the price can go up indefinitely and the seller is obligated to deliver what he has pre-sold regardless of what he has to pay. On May 7 and 8, 1901, other stock prices crashed as the NP shorts dumped everything they had to cover their sales, and on "Blue Thursday," May 9, NP leaped to a preposterous $1,000 a share. Speculators grimly realized the market was effectively cornered: they had sold 100,000 more shares than had ever been printed, and could not buy the stock at any price.

The Morgan/Hill group had acquired 150,000 shares in two days. If they paid an average of $129 a share, they had spent nearly $20 million. They had also precipitated a major Wall Street panic. Aware on Blue Thursday that countless brokers and stockholders would be ruined and the markets ravaged if the panic was not contained, the bankers at J. P. Morgan and Kuhn, Loeb agreed to postpone delivery of stock they had bought, and to sell enough shares at $150 to allow the shorts to cover. Hill and Harriman made a public promise to negotiate peace, with Morgan appointing a new board of Northern Pacific directors. The panic subsided.

It had actually been the short sellers, not the buyers, who drove the market to the frenzied heights of Blue Thursday, and it had been the Harriman group's raid, not the Morgan defense, that had set the action in motion. Still, what the world saw was Wall Street bankers diving like great white sharks after their prey, and Morgan took responsibility for repairing the damage. He had issued instructions by cable from Aix all week, but on Blue Thursday he abandoned his holiday and went to Paris, then London, where the crisis was threatening to derange the English markets. At Princes Gate, Fanny noted in her diary: "Pierpont is coming tomorrow. . . . Tremendous excitement in Wall Street, over Union & Northern Pacific."

Morgan found the City anticipating a "disastrous" panic, but once he and Kuhn, Loeb's English associates offered London brokers the same terms advanced in New York, the British markets calmed down.

When Hill and Morgan's New York partners counted up their NP stock, they learned that they had only 394,830 shares of the common, and needed 400,001 for a majority. They quietly bought more, mainly in London, and by May 18 had 420,000 shares, 52.5 percent of the total.

From New York on May 15, Hill cabled a partner at Baring's, using the code name "Feejee" for Morgan: "everything clearing here . . . feejees strength increasing daily general feeling city and country runs high against Schiff's conduct all our friends firm enemy making overtures."

The next day, Schiff wrote Morgan a long, self-justifying letter, explaining that he had bought Northern Pacific stock in order to protect the Union Pacific with regard to the CB&Q—"not with a view of actually taking away the control and management of the property from those in whose possession it was," but only to secure a position of influence on its board—and that he had told Hill of the purchase in order "to bring about the harmony and community of interest which other means and appeals to him had failed to produce." Blaming most of the trouble on Hill, Schiff assured Morgan that the "Union Pacific interests" had never intended "to do aught meant to be antagonistic to you or your firm," and that he and his banking partners had "at all times wished, as we continue to do, to be permitted to aid in maintaining your personal so well deserved prestige." Both Kuhn, Loeb and the Union Pacific were

> entirely ready to do anything in reason that you may ask or suggest, so that permanent conditions shall be created which shall be just to all interests and not bear within them the seed of future strife, discord, and possible disaster. Trusting, then, dear Mr. Morgan, that you will understand the spirit in which this letter is written, and hoping that the rest of your stay abroad may be pleasant and not interrupted by any unsatisfactory events, I am, with assurances of esteem,
>
> > Yours most faithfully,
> > Jacob H. Schiff

———

Morgan considered interrupting his European trip to deal with the "unsatisfactory events" that had just occurred, but the recovery of market equanimity persuaded him he could remain abroad. There is no record of his response to Schiff, or to the partners who almost lost a property he had been working on for twenty years—a road he thought he controlled, but had had to pay top dollar on the open market to secure, with horrendous consequences.

On May 15, Fanny's birthday, he left London at 10:00 A.M. for Paris. He met Adelaide and her daughter there, and brought them back to England two weeks later. Fanny noted in her diary on June 2 that Mrs. Douglas and Sybil joined a dinner party at Princes Gate, and on the fourth that the Douglases came to call with Annette Markoe and her elder daughter, Dagmar Wetmore. On the fifth, Fanny sailed for home.

The uncrowned king of American finance was invited to lunch early that June with the new King of England (who would not be officially crowned until 1902). The royal family was still in mourning for Queen Victoria; Morgan, Jack, George Bowdoin, and Morris K. Jesup drove down to Windsor Castle in black frock coats and top hats. Edward VII gave them a tour of the palace art collections and lunch in the Orangery.

A few weeks later Morgan had another royal encounter, with Edward's second cousin Leopold II of Belgium. He had declined an invitation to meet Leopold in Brussels in May, writing from the Hôtel Bristol of his "extreme" regret. With the panic on both sides of the Atlantic under control, he was probably more interested in seeing Adelaide than Leopold (whose chief historical distinction, unconscionable exploitation of the Congo, had mired him in debt). On June 21, Jack reported to Fanny: "Father . . . went down to Gravesend last night with Dawkins and dined with the King of the Belgians who wanted to see them about some business and brought his yacht over because Father could not go to Brussels. Rather amusing; they spent the night on board."

Henry Adams had described with delight the "abject terror" of London and Berlin as Morgan's nose "approached hourly nearer their bank vaults" in early April. Two months later, Swiss newspapers reported that the American *Trust-meister* was planning to take over Switzerland's watch industry to protect New England watchmakers from competition. Morgan, still trying to take a vacation, was probably buying watches, not factories.

Jack reported to Fanny in mid-June that his furloughed father had spent a full day on the Thames ("I did not ask who were the party") and "actually came to the office yesterday where he lunched and left almost at once." Morgan surprised his son even more three days later. Just before leaving New York that spring he had received a call from two Boston doctors, Collins Warren and Henry Bowditch, who were raising money for a new Harvard Medical School campus near the Fenway. As the Bostonians laid out architectural sketches, Morgan in a characteristic hurry pointed to three structures and asked how much they would cost. Dr. Warren said he did not yet know the exact costs. "When you have gotten your plans and estimates," said Morgan, "let me know." Warren sent him the figures in London that June. Morgan wired back that he would give $1 million for three buildings in memory of his father. He called Jack into his office at Old Broad Street and showed him the cable without a word. "You had better believe I was pleased," Jack told his mother. "I don't know that there is anything he could have done which would have pleased me more, though I realize it was not done with that object!"

The senior Morgan returned to New York on the *Deutschland,* sailing June 28, with Charles Lanier, Waldo Story, and Mr. and Mrs. Clinton Dawkins. Adelaide and her daughter stayed on in England—in July they signed the Visitors Book Morgan had just begun to keep for people who came by private invitation to see his collections at Princes Gate.

———

For years Hill and Morgan had been trying to create a solid "community of interest" among the northwest roads, and the 1901 crisis provided both occasion and urgent motive. In the wake of the panic, Hill told his friend Lord Mount Stephen, a Canadian banker and railroad president now living in England, that he was spending all his time trying to unite "the Great Northern, NP, and CB&Q under one control. This will give us within five years the best railway property in America with larger annual income for dividends than the Pennsylvania and the New York Central combined. Had we delayed the opportunity would never again have arisen. . . . With the large fortunes of this country it is absolutely necessary for permanent safety to lock up control." Morgan was thinking along the same lines. Mount Stephen cabled Hill on June 6: "Have just seen Morgan. . . . Wants prompt unification of 2 roads. Delay might lead to serious consequences." Hill replied the next day: "Nothing more can be done [in the United States] until Morgan arrives."

Once Morgan did arrive in early July, he installed a new board of Northern Pacific directors that included parties from both sides of the recent conflict—Harriman, William Rockefeller, and Hill—"in order," he said later, "to show there was no hostility." And as announced in May, the former adversaries devised a plan for permanent railroad peace in the Northwest—a giant holding company that would control the securities of the Northern Pacific, the CB&Q, and the Great Northern. Morgan was so impatient to wrap up this consolidation, and so cavalier about the antitrust law, that one of his attorneys snapped, "What do you want to do? Do you want to go to jail?"

While Stetson and his associates worked out details of the unification plan, Morgan turned his attention to another urgent conflict—a strike at U.S. Steel. The Amalgamated Association of Iron, Steel and Tin Workers had steadily lost membership after the Homestead strike of 1892, and its leaders saw the formation of the giant steel trust as an opportunity to revitalize the union. The corporation had recognized the Amalgamated where it was already established in April 1901, but refused to allow it to organize nonunion mills. The labor leaders moved quickly, convinced that if they did not act before U.S. Steel solidified its position, the union "would be virtually banished from the industry."

That spring, Amalgamated president T. J. Shaffer demanded a union wage scale and recognition in all the mills of two U.S. Steel subsidiaries, and when the two companies rejected the plan for plants not previously under union contract, he called a strike against them. By July 10, thirty-six thousand steelworkers had walked out, and Shaffer was threatening to shut down U.S. Steel. He expected railroad and miners' unions to join the fight.

At the end of July, when Amalgamated leaders met with U.S. Steel officials, Morgan proposed a compromise: the corporation would pay union wages across the board, but hold the line against organizing nonunion mills. He said he was not opposed to organized labor, and expected all U.S. Steel plants to have union contracts within two years; for the moment, however, it was impossible to impose a single policy on the subsidiaries. At the urging of other labor leaders, Shaffer agreed to Morgan's proposal, but his executive board rejected it, and on August 10 the Amalgamated called for a general strike against U.S. Steel. While other unions debated sympathy walkouts, the corporation hired strikebreakers. In late August, John Mitchell, head of the United Mine Workers of America, persuaded Shaffer to reconsider Morgan's initial proposal plus reinstatement for all strikers. This time, Shaffer managed to get his board's approval, partly because its members thought that Mitchell's UMW would join the strike if the new negotiations failed.

When Mitchell, Samuel Gompers of the AFL, and other labor representatives took the recycled Morgan proposal to U.S. Steel headquarters on September 4, however, Charles Schwab rejected it. He said he would not sign union contracts for nine of the mills that had been union the preceding year, but would take no action against anyone who participated in the strike; he proposed to leave this offer on the table for twenty-four hours. Mitchell urged Shaffer to accept it and end the strike. Shaffer asked for a day's extension to consult his board, but produced no answer twenty-four hours later. Neither the UMW nor the AFL joined the strike. On September 14, the Amalgamated was forced to accept far harsher terms than either Morgan or Schwab had proposed, and lost fourteen mills that had been unionized when the strike started. According to the labor historian Philip Taft, the outcome of the steel strike was "disastrous" to the Amalgamated "and to the labor movement generally."*

A year after the strike, George Perkins put into effect a plan that would allow rank-and-file U.S. Steel workers to buy its preferred stock on installment at special prices. His aim was to provide employees with a stake in the corporation's productivity and profits—to "people-ize" the industry, he said, as well as to forestall unionization and offset public antipathy to corporate giants.

Profit sharing was not a new idea at the beginning of the twentieth century. Albert Gallatin, Treasury Secretary from 1801 to 1814, had tried it at his Pennsylvania Glass Works in 1795, and sharecroppers and fishermen had always taken portions of their yields. By 1900, U.S. companies with profit-sharing plans included the Illinois Central Railroad, Procter and Gamble, the National Biscuit Company, New York Life, Pittsburgh Coal, and Carnegie Steel.

The program Perkins devised at the largest corporation in the world went further than its antecedents, offering preferred stock at a discount to every employee, with payment on an installment plan and bonus incentives for long-term employment. Those most able to take advantage of the plan were executives and skilled workers at the highest salary levels, but 10 percent of the company's 122,000 unskilled workers, earning an average of $550 a year, signed up as well. Gary claimed that the plan made "the wage earner an actual partner." The journal *Finance and Commerce* predicted that employee stock ownership would turn the country into "a nation of conservative Bourbons."

---

* In the aftermath of these events, Gompers accused Shaffer of rejecting "the good will and kindly assurances of J. P. Morgan that the steel corporation might recognize the unions in a few years if the union would not now 'attempt to drive him further than it was possible for him to go.' "

Not surprisingly, it didn't, although it tended to take the pressure off wage questions and to undermine union bargaining power. The *American Mining Congress Journal* called employee stock ownership "a prophylactic against government ownership," and Samuel Gompers dismissed it as a genteel surrogate for factory police and strikebreaking Pinkertons. Thousands of people dropped out of the U.S. Steel plan in its first few years, unable to afford even discounted shares, yet in 1911 over 30,000 workers owned company stock, and 42,258 by 1918.

Perkins, sounding a little like the author of *Fraternity*, regarded the program as "socialism of the highest, best and most ideal sort." He stressed the moral and psychological investment that came with stock ownership, criticizing managers who used similar programs not in "a true, an honest, and a fair spirit of cooperation," but simply to exact higher returns from labor. He also claimed that this program had reduced the "strike menace to almost nothing." Though he was offering what the unions regarded as paternalistic tokens, Perkins genuinely thought he could replace worker-management conflict with mutually beneficial accord—just as he and Morgan thought corporate cooperation could supplant "ruinous" warfare.*

———

Sir Thomas Lipton sent a second *Shamrock* to challenge New York for the America's Cup in 1901, and that August—just as Shaffer called for the general strike against U.S. Steel—Morgan went by yacht to Bar Harbor to watch the trials. He returned to New York when Louisa's baby arrived a week early. Satterlee wrote to his mother on September 1: "The Commodore has come several times and held the baby [named Mabel] to his and also her great satisfaction. He says that 'barring Louisa' she is the prettiest baby he has ever seen."

At the end of September the Commodore took a party of friends to Sandy Hook, New Jersey, on *Corsair* to watch the first race between the new *Shamrock* and *Columbia*, the defender. *Columbia* won by seconds. As soon as she crossed the finish line, Morgan left the course, sailed up the East River, boarded a launch for shore, and was driven to Grand Central Station, where a train was waiting to take him to San Francisco for the Triennial Episcopal Convention.

Signalmen from New York to California routed trains to side tracks so the Morgan "special" wouldn't have to stop. Among those on board were Bishops

---

* Most early experiments with "welfare capitalism" collapsed during the depression of the 1930s. The evidence from more recent employee stock-ownership, profit sharing, and management-participation plans suggests that under the right circumstances they effectively increase worker income and satisfaction as well as productivity and innovation. (See Roger Alcaly, "Reinventing the Corporation," *The New York Review of Books,* April 10, 1997.)

Henry Potter and William Doane, Jim Goodwin, Adelaide's cousin Amy Townsend, and Frank Stetson. Morgan's Attorney General, also an active lay member of the Episcopal Church, had the plans for the northwest railroad consolidation so firmly under control that before leaving New York he had given an associate the *minutes*—not the agenda—of a forthcoming Northern Pacific stockholders meeting.

In San Francisco, Morgan put his friends up for three weeks at a house he had leased from the railroad builder and banker Charles Crocker, and consigned all culinary arrangements to the New York restaurateur Louis Sherry, whom he had imported for the occasion. During the ecclesiastical councils at San Francisco's Trinity Church, messengers brought him telegrams about the yacht races taking place off Sandy Hook. Morgan read these bulletins aloud, and the night *Columbia* won the Cup he held a Sherry-catered dinner for the votaries of church and yacht.

After the convention he took his party up the coast to Oregon and Washington, where he bought them all furs. Northern Pacific Railway president Charles Mellen met the group in Portland—a friend teased him about "entertaining Bishops and other ecclesiastical dignitaries and escorting them in their beautiful lawn sleeves along the bottom of copper mines." In late October, Morgan escorted the dignitaries home.

———

Adelaide Douglas moved from 28 West 57th Street to 4 East 46th in 1901, and as soon as Morgan returned to New York that fall he bought objects for her new house at the Duveen Brothers gallery on Fifth Avenue. The New York City street directories list Adelaide and her husband at 46th Street and Douglaston, Long Island—she may have stayed primarily in town, he in the country. A clerk at Duveen's annotated the lists of Morgan purchases in 1901, marking some pieces as going to "House" (219), some to "Museum" (the Metropolitan), some to 55th Street (the Markoes); the items sent to "4 East 46th" in the fall of 1901 included Chelsea porcelains, Dresden candlesticks, a silver lamp bracket, a green velvet embroidered coverlet, antique Italian gilt and carved wood candlesticks, and a Louis XIII armchair. Adelaide apparently encouraged Morgan's interest in the decorative arts of the French court, for among the objects he gave her over the next few years were a "coffret de mariage de Marie-Antoinette," Riesener furniture, a Louis XV secrétaire, groups of Sèvres and Meissen porcelain, books on *Les Femmes de Versailles* and *Napoléon et les Femmes*, and a silver-plated "Temple of Love" by the Parisian silversmith André Aucoc. Working in the late-nineteenth century, Aucoc was well known for closely copying eighteenth-century models, and the neoclassical "Temple" Morgan gave to Adelaide—standing seventeen inches high on a ten-inch solid-silver base—is reminiscent of table centerpieces used for royal occasions in late-eighteenth-century France. She kept it in the center of her dining table.

———

On November 12, 1901, lawyers for Morgan and Hill chartered a New Jersey holding company called Northern Securities, authorized to issue $400 million of capital stock. The next day the new, Morgan-appointed board of the Northern Pacific Railway voted to retire its preferred stock at par, and to pay for it with a $75 million issue of convertible bonds; since Harriman sat on the board and owned a majority of these shares, his assenting vote put a final full stop to the raid. Also on November 13, J. P. Morgan & Co. bought Harriman's NP common shares and sold them to the Northern Securities Company. The new corporation quickly acquired 76 percent of all Northern Pacific stock and 96 percent of the Great Northern's, issuing its own shares in exchange; it gave Harriman's Union Pacific group a $9 million premium for trading in their shares. Although the GN and NP would remain separate entities, Northern Securities created the huge regional community of interest that Morgan and Hill had been trying to establish for years.

Hill headed the Northern Securities board. Among the other directors were Morgan partners Bacon, Perkins, and Steele, First National Bank president George Baker, Northern Pacific officers Charles Mellen and Daniel Lamont, and the erstwhile raiders, Harriman, Stillman, William Rockefeller, and Schiff. In addition to the NP, GN, and CB&Q, the holding company acquired steamships, land grants, timberlands, coal properties, and iron mines. Hill thought $200 million a low estimate for the value of the nonrailroad assets.

Morgan, questioned five months later about his motives for organizing Northern Securities, talked about securing "moral control." When news of the raid reached him at Aix, he said, he had instantly realized what was at stake: "I feel bound in all honor when I reorganise a property and am morally responsible for its management to protect it, and I generally do protect it; so I made up my mind that it would be desirable to buy 150,000 shares of stock, which we proceeded to do, and . . . that actually gave us the control."

He had done an enormous amount of work on the Northern Pacific since 1880. "Protecting" it in 1901 had meant buying nearly $20 million of its stock on the open market, then combining it with the Great Northern into a holding company so large and closely held that it would not be susceptible to hostile raids: "We didn't want convulsions going on," he explained. Since the court he addressed in 1902 was considering whether or not Northern Securities violated the antitrust law, Morgan stressed *size* as the key to "protection," even though his long experience with railroads (and the raid on Northern Pacific) had convinced him that only majority stock ownership guaranteed control. He had thought the $155 million NP safe from "being absorbed by a competing line without our knowledge or consent," he said. When it turned out not to be, he concluded that greater size would ensure stability: "The capital of the Northern Securities Company was so large [at $400 million, that] I did not believe in a night or week anybody would ever be able to get control of it."

What he wanted was to be able to "go to Europe and not hear next day that somebody had bought it for the Boston and Maine, or I don't know what other company. I wanted the Northern Pacific stock put where nothing could interfere with the policy I had inaugurated and for the carrying out of which we were perfectly satisfied and morally responsible."

To people concerned about railroad monopolies and the stifling of competition, these statements sidestepped the essential problem: that parallel and competing carriers had been brought together under one corporate roof. Morgan was looking at a different set of problems, and he regarded the outcome in this case—the ending of regional warfare, the inclusion of former enemies on one corporate board, the promise of steady transport between the country's agricultural interior and its ports, and the positioning of U.S. commercial interests to compete with Europe—as an ideal solution.

Yet he and his associates had also taken steps to protect their consolidation which he could not have called "moral," and would not have been willing to discuss in public. On November 18, 1901, six days after the incorporation of Northern Securities, Minnesota Governor Samuel R. Van Sant invited the governors of neighboring states to join him in an effort "to fight the great railway trust." For various reasons the other governors declined, but they passed a resolution on December 31 declaring the consolidation "contrary to sound public policy" and approving Minnesota's challenge. On January 7, 1902, Minnesota asked the Supreme Court for leave to file a complaint against Northern Securities as an illegal combination in restraint of trade—a request the Court denied. Minnesota's attorney general brought suit in state court.

Hill had assured Van Sant that since neither the GN nor the NP controlled the other and each remained independent, "no law of the State of Minnesota is being avoided or violated." Still, criticism mounted in the local press. Suspecting that rival railroads were behind it, Hill instructed his son to "try to get Minnesota Journal & Tribune, Pioneer Press and Globe" to tell his side of the story: "You should spend Forty or Fifty or Seventy-five thousand, if necessary, to good advantage. . . . It may be best to smoke out the opposition of the other roads."

Charles Mellen, who hated Hill, urged Morgan to keep the Great Northern and its president "in the background." The Northern Pacific, Mellen claimed, was far more popular in Minnesota than Hill's GN, and could "do many things without much expense that can only be done by the other party through such a lavish use of money as borders on scandal." Since Mellen himself was engaged in bribing public officials, it seems to have been the amount rather than the fact of corporate payoffs that justified calling the kettle black.

In late January 1902, two weeks after Minnesota moved against Northern Securities, Mellen told Morgan in a letter marked STRICTLY CONFIDENTIAL that Van Sant was about to recommend to a special session of the state legislature new laws regarding railroad rates "of a nature we should term retaliatory, and it is my belief that he can be dissuaded from such a course, and his message be made wholly silent on the subject."

Though "not prepared to say definitely that this can be done," Mellen thought he had an avenue "by which it can be accomplished, and my object in writing you is to ask if you will personally place at my disposal a modest sum of money, available, in my descretion [*sic*], in case I secure the desired result." Practically blushing and scraping the floor with his toe, he said he had in mind "no unreasonable sum; my experience in such matters has been of a modest character; and I feel sure the amount will meet your entire approval." It turned out to be $5,000. Mellen was appealing to Morgan in order to disguise the fact that the money would be coming from the Northern Pacific, he explained: once the "desired result" was accomplished, the banker could recover the sum from the NP "in ways that will occur to you, and that have been used before, and keeping the matter wholly a confidential one between you and myself."

Mellen assured Morgan that none of the money would "either directly or indirectly, ever reach the Governor" himself, "for I think he is beyond anything of the kind." Mellen's coy rectitude—he claims "modest" experience with these matters, and appears to respect a politician who is "beyond" bribery: paying off those who were *not* beyond it (probably members of the governor's staff) might be dirty work, but somebody had to do it—suggests that he was worried about someone else's scruples. "Should this matter appeal to you," he concluded to Morgan on January 25, 1902, "I beg you will telegraph me yes or no."

Four days later, Morgan replied, "Yes."

On February 1, Mellen reported the matter "well in hand," although the governor was "weak . . . suspicious" and "unreliable." On the third he wired Morgan, "We are all right, message will be satisfactory." He elaborated by mail that it would be "silent on the question of legislation as to railroad rates," and would recommend "no legislation on the merger question other than an appropriation to continue the [antitrust] litigation."

With this mission accomplished, Mellen turned immediately to another. The Minnesota legislature was now likely to "attack us through rate bills" on its own, he told Morgan, and also to impose a heavy new tax on iron ore, "in which [he hardly needed to remind his correspondent] the United States Steel Corporation is greatly interested. Sub rosa we are advised bills have been prepared, attacking in this direction." Mellen thought he could head off *this* threat for a sum that would be "inconsiderable as compared with our former experience with legislatures here." And in what amounted to a fine illustration of Saint Jerome's lesson about "strong men in controversy . . . justifying the means by the end," he went on: "I assume you want success, or rather, in this instance, immunity, and the method is not so important as the result."

Two weeks later Morgan wired, "Quite approve your going ahead; would like to know maximum amount required."

Mellen: "Not in any event to exceed twenty five."

Morgan: "All right, do whatever is necessary."

At the beginning of March, Mellen reported that he had put $25,000 "in the hands of a third party" and arranged for there to be no "adverse legislation" regarding railroads or steel. He asked Morgan to credit $25,000 to his account: the Northern Pacific, Great Northern, and US Steel would "equitably" repay the advance.

Although the sums involved in these purchases of political inaction were relatively small—"inconsiderable as compared with our former experience with legislatures," volunteered Mellen—they would have confirmed the public's worst fears about Wall Street and the corrupt use of corporate cash, had they or their predecessors come to light. Morgan probably did not much like these activities—several things he would not have wanted posterity to see *did* escape the censors, and there are few instances of outright graft—but accepted them as the cost of doing business. He had a capacious definition of "moral responsibility" that covered what seemed necessary to achieve the goals he had in mind: "the method," as Mellen obligingly put it, was "not so important as the result"—"immunity" from rate regulation, ore taxes, and legislation hostile to the Morgan clients' interests.

Even without knowing about the Minnesota transactions, nervous democrats saw in Morgan a symbol of everything they feared about the imperious power of Wall Street. In his *annus mirabilis* (also *horribilis*), he had organized the steel trust, halted the Northern Pacific panic, and set up a giant monopoly of railroads in the Northwest. The business community applauded Northern Securities as a constructive extension of Morganatic harmony. Most of the country condemned it as another nefarious trust, and feared that Morgan was indeed, as Henry Adams quipped, trying to swallow the sun. From London at the end of December, Clinton Dawkins condoled with his American partners about the "disagreeable and exasperating" time they were having, and sympathized "with Flitch [Morgan] over the interminable bother and trouble that the villainous raid on NP has brought in its train."

Chapter 22

TROUBLE

D isagreeable and exasperating" times for the house of Morgan were just beginning. On September 6, 1901, an anarchist named Leon Czolgosz had shot President McKinley at the Pan-American Exposition in Buffalo, New York. According to *The New York Times*, Morgan was about to leave his office late that afternoon—he was glancing over a ledger at a clerk's desk, hat on, cane in hand—when a reporter ran in with the news. "What?" Morgan demanded, seizing the man's arm and searching his face. The journalist repeated the story. Morgan dropped his cane, returned to his own desk, and asked an associate to confirm the report. For several minutes he sat in his office, staring at the carpet, until another newspaperman came in with an "extra" on the attempted assassination. Morgan read it slowly, then told the journalists, "This is sad, sad, very sad news. . . . There is nothing I can say at this time."

Responding to rumors that he would call a conference of financiers that night, reporters stationed themselves outside his bank, Delmonico's, the Fifth Avenue Hotel, and the Union, Metropolitan, and New York Yacht Clubs. The country's unofficial central banker spent the night on *Corsair*, anchored in the Hudson. Police authorities were afraid that Czolgosz was part of a larger anarchist plot, and when Morgan arrived at 23 Wall Street the next morning he found the building guarded by half a dozen detectives. Later in the day he issued a statement to the press: "The financial situation is absolutely good. There is nothing to derange it. The banks will take care of that. You need not worry about it."

On September 14, McKinley died.

Mark Hanna had warned the Republicans against putting Theodore Roosevelt on the ticket in 1900. A year later the man he called "that damned cowboy" was President of the United States.

Morgan had known and admired the senior Theodore Roosevelt, and supported the junior at the New York State Assembly in the early eighties. The Harvard-educated Knickerbocker from Oyster Bay had turned in a heroic performance for the Republican ticket and the gold standard in 1896, and Morgan reportedly gave $10,000 through Easy Boss Platt to Roosevelt's 1898 gubernatorial campaign. Once in the Albany State House, Roosevelt made it clear that he, not Mr. Platt, would govern New York, and began to challenge the comfortable alliance between big business and party bosses that had come to be known as the "invisible government"—pushing through a corporate franchise tax over Wall Street's protest and publicly criticizing the trusts. Platt promoted Roosevelt for Vice President in 1900 largely to get him out of New York.

A month after the Republican victory that fall, well aware that he alarmed his party's "respectables," Roosevelt made a gesture of deference to the Old Guard by giving a dinner in Morgan's honor. He wrote to the Secretary of War, Elihu Root, on December 5: "I hope you can come to my dinner to J. Pierpont Morgan on the 29th inst. at the Union League Club. . . . You see it represents an effort on my part to become a conservative man, in touch with the influential classes, and I think I deserve encouragement. Hitherto I have given dinners only to professional politicans or more or less wild-eyed reformers. Now I am hard at work endeavoring to assume the Vice Presidential poise."

Writing to the honoree about the event, Roosevelt addressed him as "My dear Mr. Morgan," signed his note "with great regard," then added that Jack was invited as well—"I have always known him as 'Jack' and I am not certain whether he is J. Pierpont Morgan Jr. or not."

Morgan left no account of the dinner at the Union League Club, nor of his thoughts on TR as the country's second in command, but the "Vice Presidential poise" in December 1900 was one thing, the presidential nine months later altogether another.

With McKinley in the Executive Office, Morgan had known more or less what to expect: minimal antitrust prosecution, regular consultation between Wall Street and Washington, virtual carte blanche to promote the market stability and economic policies favored by the conservative elite of both parties. As Morgan finished up the organization of U.S. Steel in 1901, Senator Beveridge of Indiana reported to George Perkins on a "bully talk" he had recently had with President McKinley, in which both men agreed that Morgan was "not only a financier but a statesman."

From Roosevelt, however, widely regarded on Wall Street as a "bucking bronco," Morgan had no idea what to expect. The new President was six weeks

Theodore Roosevelt.
(Culver Pictures, Inc.)

shy of forty-three when he took the oath of office—the youngest man yet to occupy the Executive Mansion. Radiating energy and determination, he had been
a sickly, asthmatic child who schooled himself in strenuous altheticism. A
moral idealist who had mastered pragmatic politics, he adored public life and
glorified war (coming upon a dying Rough Rider at San Juan Hill, he grasped
the man's hand and said, "Well, old chap, isn't this splendid?"), but was also
drawn to remote wilds of nature, and was passionately devoted to his family.
Romantic jingoist, militant imperialist, soldier, scholar, naturalist, hunter, author, crusader, dealmaker, dude—he had so many interests and facets that one
friend called him "polygonal."

Roosevelt kept his distance from the plutocrats. During the 1896 Republican
victory celebrations he told his sister he could see "all of Brooks Adams'
gloomiest anticipations of our gold-ridden, capitalist-bestridden, usurer-
mastered future" coming true. In 1897 he criticized the cozy relations between
"corrupt wealth . . . the Pierpont Morgan type of men" and "powerful, un-
scrupulous politicians" such as Platt: "I am glad I am out of it." He was not entirely out of it. He knew how to use Platt's machine, accepted campaign
contributions from Perkins's New York Life and "the Pierpont Morgan type of
men," and courted Morgan himself as soon as he was elected Vice President.

Part of what made for Roosevelt's political success was an unusual combination of intelligence, personal conviction, supple principles, superhuman energies, an instinct for centrist popular sentiment, and a conspicuous love of the
limelight. "He would go to Halifax for half a chance to show off," said Mark
Twain, "and he would go to hell for a whole one." Oliver Wendell Holmes, Jr.,
thought TR had the talent "of a first class megaphone." With his glinting spectacles, barrel chest, toothy grin, upper-class accent, and rasping, articulate
voice (someone said he "used adjectives like hammers"), Teddy was a favorite
subject for cartoonists, which only increased his prominence. The English historian John Morley described him as "an interesting combination of St. Vitus
and St. Paul," as much a "wonder of nature" as Niagara Falls. Henry Adams
reflected: "Power when wielded by abnormal energy is the most serious of
facts, and all Roosevelt's friends know that his restless and combative energy
was more than abnormal. Roosevelt, more than any other man living within
the range of notoriety . . . was pure act." Adams admired thought more than
action, but Roosevelt became the first President since Lincoln whose stature
was commensurate with the office.

As Governor of New York he had advocated the regulation of big business,
and the major question at the start of his presidency was whether he would
continue McKinley's laissez-faire policy toward the trusts. In early October
1901, with the country in mourning and Morgan attending the Episcopal
Convention in San Francisco, Bob Bacon and George Perkins called on the new

President at the White House. Roosevelt liked both men, especially Bacon, whom he had coaxed into the boxing ring at Harvard, reporting gleefully that he might have landed a punch if only his arms had been longer—or Bacon's shorter. The sparring match at 1600 Pennsylvania Avenue in early October 1901 concerned the trusts. U.S. Steel had just issued its first quarterly report.

According to Roosevelt, Perkins asked him to retract various proposals he had made to turn a "searchlight" on the trusts, since corporations financed by the Morgan bank had voluntarily begun to disclose their earnings and losses: "Perkins wanted me to do nothing at all, and say nothing except platitudes," the President told his businessman brother-in-law, Douglas Robinson, "accept the publication of what some particular company chooses to publish, as a favor, instead of demanding what we think ought to be published from all corporations as a right." Although he considered the ambassadors from the house of Morgan to be men "of the highest character . . . genuine forces for good as well as men of strength and weight," he thought "on this particular occasion they were arguing like attorneys for a bad case, and at the bottom of their hearts each would know this if he were not personally interested; and especially if he were not the representative of . . . so strong and dominant a character as Pierpont Morgan."

Roosevelt, adept at playing both sides of the street, wrote a second letter to Douglas Robinson that day, marked "to give to Mr. Perkins." In it he said he was "delighted to see the publication made by the steel company. It is in every way a good thing. I much enjoyed the visit from Perkins. I am particularly desirous to see him and Bacon as often as possible."

When Mark Hanna and other Republican leaders urged TR to "go slow" about the trusts, he promised to follow McKinley's lead. He showed a draft of his first message to Congress to Hanna, who took out a section on overcapitalization, but the speech as delivered on December 2, 1901, did address the problem of the trusts. Ignoring the Perkins-Bacon request, Roosevelt said that in order to protect the public's general welfare, "the Government should have the right to inspect and examine the workings of the great corporations engaged in interstate business." Still, he praised businessmen who were promoting economic stability and national prosperity, and insisted that he did not aim to "do away with corporations"—"on the contrary, these big aggregations are an inevitable development of modern industrialism, and the effort to destroy them" would be likely to "work the utmost mischief to the entire body politic." He wanted to *regulate* big business, not annihilate it: "We draw the line against misconduct, not against wealth."

Finley Peter Dunne's Mr. Dooley immediately mocked the President's temporizing: " 'The trusts,' says [Roosevelt], 'are heejous monsthers built up be th' inlightened intherprise iv th' men that have done so much to advance progress in our beloved counthry,' he says. 'On wan hand I wud stamp thim undher fut; on th' other hand not so fast.' "

Eager to assert Washington's power over Wall Street, however, Roosevelt did move "fast." He took direct aim at what one historian has called "the very Sanhedrin of the nation's financial oligarchy"—Morgan, Schiff, Stillman, William Rockefeller, Harriman, and Hill—the men responsible for the Northern Pacific panic and the latest giant trust. Working quietly with his Attorney General, Philander Knox, the President did not even consult the other members of his cabinet before he announced in February 1902 that his administration would prosecute the Northern Securities Company under the Sherman Act as an illegal restraint of trade.

The stock market shuddered. Morgan was stunned. His lawyers had put together Northern Securities with a careful eye on the antitrust law. He thought the President should have conferred with him, given him a chance to resolve their differences and make whatever adjustments might be in order, before publicly branding him an outlaw.

From London, Clinton Dawkins wondered by mail how the President reconciled his "brutal assault" on Northern Securities with "his fine language about 'leaving unhampered the strong, forceful man, upon whom the success of business operations rests[.]' " Jack, also in London, pronounced himself "very sorry that Teddy did not stop to ask the opinion of someone interested before making an announcement of that sort," as it had made things "extremely uncomfortable over here."

In Washington, Henry Adams hooted to Elizabeth Cameron that "our stormy petrel of a President" had "suddenly, this week, without warning . . . hit Pierpont Morgan, the whole railway interest, and the whole Wall Street connection, a tremendous whack square on the nose. The wicked don't want to quarrel with him, but they don't like being hit that way." Although Morgan was invited to a dinner at the White House for Prince Henry of Prussia, the brother of Kaiser Wilhelm, "the Wall Street people are in an ulcerated state of inflammation," and "Pierpont has declined the White House dinner."

Adams, who was no great admirer of Morgan and unable to resist any opportunity to make fun of his nose, nonetheless credited him with having more than self-interest at heart: "Pierpont is furious," he told Mrs. Cameron, "because Theodore, suddenly, without warning, at a critical moment of the market when very large amounts of money were involved and borrowed on collateral, had hit him an awful blow square in the face. . . . Pierpont says that Roosevelt should have given him warning so that he could have had time to support the market."

Morgan went immediately to Washington to confer with the President and the Attorney General. He arrived at the White House on February 23, accompanied by Senators Hanna and Depew. According to Roosevelt, who left the only surviving account of this meeting, Morgan wanted to know why he had not been warned.

Warning Wall Street, said Roosevelt, was "just what we did not want to do."

Morgan: "If we have done anything wrong, send your man [Knox] to my man [Stetson] and they can fix it up."

Roosevelt: "That can't be done."

Knox: "We don't want to fix it up, we want to stop it."

Northern Securities was not the most vital concern at 23 Wall Street, and Morgan wanted to know how far the President intended to go. "Are you going to attack my other interests," he asked, "the Steel Trust and the others?"

Roosevelt: "Certainly not, unless we find out . . . they have done something that we regard as wrong."

The President, by his own account, told Knox as Morgan and his companions left the White House: "That is a most illuminating illustration of the Wall Street point of view. Mr. Morgan could not help regarding me as a big rival operator, who either intended to ruin all his interests or could be induced to come to an agreement to ruin none."

The two men *were* essentially "big rival operators," each convinced that he had the country's long-term best interests at heart, and ready to use any means in his considerable arsenal to bring about the future he had in mind. One of them was President of the United States, looking forward to imperial dominance abroad and intent at home on publicly subjugating the "mighty industrial overlords of the country" to governmental authority. The other was a private banker who looked exclusively to economic efficacy, confident that military and political questions would take care of themselves if the United States had stable markets and steady productive growth.

From Morgan's point of view it was wildly irresponsible of "the politicians" to interfere with the delicate financial mechanisms over which he was unofficially presiding as the balance of economic power shifted from the Old World to the New. Half a century after his father moved to England to funnel European capital to America, two decades after Morgan syndicates sold U.S. government bonds abroad, and five years after Morgan himself secured foreign gold for the Treasury, the British government was raising capital in the United States.* In putting together Northern Securities and U.S. Steel, Morgan was, as he saw it, building unassailable systems to compete in world markets and launch an American century. If his enterprises succeeded, they would benefit steelworkers and coal miners as well as bankers, and he counted on intelligent men in government to back him up.

---

* J. P. Morgan & Co., acting as agent for the Bank of England, had taken $12 million in subscriptions to a British loan for the Boer War in March 1900. Two months later the firm joined Drexel & Co., Kidder, Peabody, and Baring, Magoun in New York to handle a $30 million Ex-

By 1902, however, relatively few of Morgan's compatriots shared his point of view. The country now objected so strenuously to the dominion of big business that groups who traditionally feared state authority—labor, farmers, small businessmen, the growing middle class—began looking to the government for protection. It was a political moment to which Theodore Roosevelt could not have been more perfectly suited. He wrote later that "the absolutely vital question" of the government's power to control corporations "had not yet been decided." The Supreme Court decision in the 1895 case against the sugar trust (*E. C. Knight*) "had, with seeming definiteness, settled that the National Government had not the power." TR was determined to prove that it did.

After meeting with the President on February 23, Morgan dined at Chauncey Depew's with Wayne MacVeagh, who occasionally worked with Stetson's law firm.* "The whole party was black," reported Henry Adams, "in spite of dear Wayne's efforts to cheer it up. Pierpont sulked like a child. From the White House came a telephone [call] inviting the party to come over. Pierpont refused but they made him go. There the President was very cordial, and they sat about for a while and went home. The [Morgan] party had come on to see whether some arrangement could be made so that they could go on with their consolidation-scheme, but as far as Wayne saw, not a beginning of a step had they made."

Morgan reluctantly attended the President's dinner for Prince Henry the next evening after all, then returned to New York. Early in March he took Adelaide, the Markoes, and his daughters Anne and Juliet to Jekyl Island for a week in the sun (Fanny was touring Italy with her sister Clara). He stopped in Washington on the way down and back to confer with Hanna as the administration built its case against his railroad trust.

Henry Adams's antic running commentary on the Morgan-Roosevelt clash that spring cast the banker as competent adult and the President as obstreperous child. On March 2: "Theodore's vanity, ambition, dogmatic temper, and cephalopodic brain are all united on hitting everybody, friend or enemy, who happens to be near. . . . He has knocked the stockmarket silly, and has made enemies of pretty much every man in Congress."

---

chequer loan, and in 1901 the Bank of England authorized this same group plus Rothschilds to take subscriptions for another $300 million. The British government was worried about turning to the United States for help (just as Grover Cleveland had worried about relying on Britain and Wall Street in 1895), but ultimately decided it had no choice. Morgan shared in a last issue of £32 million in April 1902, just a month before the end of the Boer War.

* An influential Philadelphia Republican who had been Garfield's Attorney General and represented the Pennsylvania Railroad in the West Shore deal, Wayne MacVeagh was the father of Stetson's partner, Charles, and a close friend of Henry Adams. Called "one of the knightliest figures in the courtroom," he joined Bangs Stetson Tracy & MacVeagh for three years in the eighties, and later was "of counsel" to the firm.

March 4: "Theodore is blind-drunk with self-esteem. He has not a suspicion that we are all watching him as we should watch a monkey up a tree with a chronometer. Cleveland was a mere donkey beside this bucking broncho [*sic*]. . . . Luckily for him, all his . . . friends and enemies hate each one the other worse than they hate him. . . . What he would never enjoy or forgive is to become seriously conscious that his father's old friends look at him with precisely the same curious interest with which they regard . . . a naughty boy who breaks china when his mother isn't looking."

March 11: "I do not know whether Pierpont Morgan can once more hold up the market and save a panic."

On April 6, as the markets grew increasingly bearish: "Wall Street is in a desperate state of mind since Roosevelt so nastily struck it his foul blow on the Northern Securities; and Pierpont Morgan and Hanna insist that, at any cost, Hay and Root [the Secretaries of State and War] must stay. Until they have worked Roosevelt into harness, or he has fairly kicked over the traces, the old machine has got to be kept running. You can see how necessary it is for Wall Street to lose no more ground here."

April 7: "Hanna [who maintained his interests in Ohio steel mills] says that not an order has been booked in Cleveland beyond November, and all on account of the Northern Insecurities."

———

Conflict with the government did not slow the pace or diminish the scale of Morgan's consolidations, but trouble was erupting on other fronts as well. Early in 1902 the "gigantic, nerve-wracking business and pressure of the Morgan methods" took their toll on another partner—Bob Bacon. After a year of work on the organization of the steel trust, the Northern Pacific panic (for which he bore some responsibility), White House communications, and the controversy over Northern Securities, the former all-star athlete suffered a nervous breakdown. He took a leave of absence at his physician's insistence.

He hoped to return to 23 Wall Street after an extended rest in Europe, but the doctors warned him he would "smash up completely" if he did. During his young friend's recuperation, Morgan put him on the board of U.S. Steel and visited him in Europe. The Boston Adonis withdrew from the firm at the end of his leave.

As Governor of New York in 1900, Roosevelt had urged Bacon to give up banking for politics. As President in 1905, he appointed Morgan's former partner Assistant Secretary of State under Elihu Root, and when Root resigned in 1909, Bacon served as Secretary for the final weeks of Roosevelt's second term. The federal government was apparently an easier taskmaster than the house of Morgan, since Bacon's health held up well. Pierpont and Jack stayed in close touch with their former partner at the State Department and after he became William Howard Taft's ambassador to France.

———

Things were not going well at U.S. Steel when Bacon left for Europe early in 1902. Having outraged public opinion with the size of its initial capitalization, the corporation found after less than a year that it needed another $50 million in cash—primarily to repay construction loans incurred by the constituent companies before the merger; though consolidation had made the additional building largely unnecessary, the companies could not cancel their commitments. Perkins, who replaced Bacon as chairman of the Steel Finance Committee, came up with a plan to retire $200 million of the company's preferred shares in exchange for $200 million of 5 percent second mortgage bonds, and to sell an additional $50 million of bonds for cash. Since the preferred shares paid a 7 percent dividend, the exchange was expected to decrease the company's annual charges by $1.5 million.

Morgan, busy with other projects, assented to this plan even though he generally opposed increasing debt—and just about everything possible went wrong. Jack paraphrased the reaction he expected from London: "Here is the greatest company in the world, with the largest capital ever known, only running 9 months, and which has got to call for 50 million of new capital. We do not understand, but feel were fully justified in mistrusting at the beginning." Shareholders were reluctant to trade stock paying 7 percent for bonds paying 5 percent, even though bonds carried less risk. When J. P. Morgan & Co. organized a syndicate in March to underwrite the conversion, Perkins had such trouble securing participants that he had to promise matching commitments from the Morgan bank.* In May and June, two groups of minority shareholders sued to stop the exchange, objecting to the syndicate's 4 percent commission and the increase in bonded debt, among other things. (One litigant offered to drop the suit if Perkins gave him a call on 20,000 shares each of Steel preferred and common.) The lawsuits held up the conversion until February 1903, when a court ruled them groundless, but by that time the steel business had entered a decline, share prices and earnings had plummeted, and it was impossible to effect the exchange. The conversion offer expired in May with only $45 million

---

* In April 1902 the syndicate agreed to offer shareholders the right to trade preferred stock for bonds, and to buy (also with stock) whatever bonds the shareholders did not take. It guaranteed subscriptions to $100 million of the bonds, with $80 million payable in preferred shares and $20 million in cash. Syndicate members put up the $80 million of preferred shares in the spring of 1902, promising to hold them until October 1903, then effect the exchange: J. P. Morgan & Co. and John D. Rockefeller started things off by each depositing $10 million worth of shares in a joint account. Syndicate earnings were set at 4 percent on the aggregate amount of bonds sold or delivered; Perkins thought it would not be a "particularly profitable" contract.

of stockholders' shares (separate from the syndicate's commitment) converted into bonds and a mere $12,000 raised in cash. A desperate Perkins extended the syndicate's term to June 1904, but in the fall of 1903 the corporation called the whole thing off.*

————

Internal conflicts at U.S. Steel were as troublesome as its finances. There had been two distinct groups with potentially clashing aims all along—the Gary/Morgan lawyers and bankers, interested chiefly in industry stability, steady profits, and staying out of court, and the production-oriented steel men

---

* In the end, only about $170 million of the proposed $250 million in bonds were issued in exchange for stock and cash. Of that total, the syndicate subscribed for roughly $125 million—$114 million in the stock conversion, $11 million bought with cash. J. P. Morgan & Co., acting for the syndicate, delivered approximately $7 million in cash in 1903, and another $4 million early in 1904—slightly over half of its $20 million cash commitment. Gary's second annual report, in March 1904, said the corporation could call for the remaining $9 million at any time, but that "in order to avoid the unnecessary burden of interest upon bonds issued for money not immediately needed," it would not call the remainder "except when and as the cash shall be needed by the Corporation."

There is no accurate record of the syndicate's profit or loss on this transaction, nor can there be, in part because it is impossible to say what the members would have done with the preferred shares had they not pledged them to the conversion. When the plan was set up, the bonds were selling at about 95 and preferred shares at 94. By March of 1903, when the plan went into effect, the bond price had fallen to 88, the preferred to 85, and the gap continued to widen: by November the bonds were trading as low as 65, the preferred under 50. As a result, the syndicate had to exchange shares it had furnished at 94 for bonds worth far less (in November 1903 the paper loss would have been $29 per share, or a total of $23.2 million on the $80 million pledged in preferred stock). Still, that loss was smaller than what the members would have sustained had they *held* the preferred as its value declined from 94 to 50—a loss on paper of $44 per share, or a total of $35.2 million.

The syndicate offset some of its losses in the fall of 1903 by buying about 250,000 preferred shares on the open market and exchanging them for the higher-priced bonds, at a gain of about $10 per share (roughly $2.5 million). Since the conversion plan was proving no more advantageous to U.S. Steel than to the syndicate, the Finance Committee asked the Morgan bank on November 19 to terminate the contract, which it immediately did.

All told, the syndicate delivered *more* than the $100 million it had guaranteed, but in different proportions—not $20 million cash and $80 million in preferred shares exchanged for bonds, but $11 million cash and $114 million converted preferred; the additional shares probably came from the open market operations in the fall of 1903. If the syndicate did lose roughly $23.2 million on its delivery of preferred shares, if it gained back $2.5 million by buying shares in the fall of 1903 and trading them for bonds, and if it earned a $6.8 million fee (4 percent of $170 million), its total loss would have been about $14 million. Over the long run, the preferred stock sold at much higher prices than the bonds, which meant that stockholders and syndicate members who traded shares for bonds had sacrificed significant potential profit.

represented by Schwab. Schwab's dream of a centralized, superefficient firm never came true, and he blamed its failure largely on Gary's opposition to the aggressively competitive policies that had made Carnegie Steel a success. Yet Schwab's own actions and imprudence contributed to his undoing.

As president of U.S. Steel, Schwab alienated colleagues already worried about the company's image by attracting exactly the kind of notoriety they did not want. When he announced to the graduating class of a New York City trade school in May of 1901 that boys going into business did not need college educations, speakers and writers all over the country fulminated against him, Big Steel, the decline of American culture, and a "delirium of material drunkenness." After he told an industrial commission that unions reduced their members to the "level of the cheapest workman, instead of the most capable and highest priced," Hearst's *Journal* reported that the Steel Trust was planning to destroy unions once it had tricked the public into buying its worthless stock. Executive Committee chairman Gary had to deny rumors that Schwab earned $1 million a year, saying, "He is a very wealthy man, a large holder of the stock of the company, and does not need and would not accept an extravagant salary." Schwab apparently did need an extravagant house, for he began in 1901 to build a multimillion-dollar mansion, modeled on Chenonceaux in the Loire, with ninety bedrooms, six elevators, a 116-foot tower, a sixty-foot swimming pool, a bowling alley, a gymnasium, and its own power plant. It took up an entire city block at 73rd Street and Riverside Drive.

These crimes against conservative decorum paled next to the scandal that erupted when reporters spotted Schwab at a Monte Carlo casino in January 1902. SCHWAB BREAKS THE BANK read the headline in the New York *Sun*, and newspapers played up the story for days. Carnegie was so outraged that he cabled his former protégé: "Public sentiment shocked. . . . Probably have [to] resign. Serves you right," and wrote to Morgan: "I feel . . . as if a son had disgraced the family. . . . He is unfit to be the head of the United States Steel Co.—brilliant as his talents are. . . . I recommended him unreservedly to you. . . . I have had nothing wound me so deeply for many a long day, if ever."

Morgan did not share Carnegie's rhadamanthine views. When Schwab offered to resign "if Morgan thinks I should," Perkins replied that the uproar had not made "the slightest impression on Mr. M. Do not give the matter any further thought. . . . Go ahead and have bully good time."

"Many thanks," wired back Schwab, "appreciate Mr. Morgan attitude more than possible to express," and continued by mail: "Steel Co. first—me second . . . I'll do anything Mr. Morgan wants. He's my idea of a great man. Carnegie has condemned me without a hearing. Mr. Morgan a new friend is broader gauged by far. I'm his to command."

When Morgan saw Schwab for the first time after this episode, in March

1902, he told him to "forget it, my boy, forget it." The press, however, was not willing to forget the "moral delinquency" of the head of the Steel Trust, nor was the narrow-gauged Carnegie, who subjected his former understudy to such a barrage of condemnation that Schwab had a nervous breakdown. In August 1902 he retreated to Aix-les-Bains (probably at Morgan's urging) and stayed abroad for nearly a year. When he finally decided to resign from U.S. Steel in 1903—having also been charged by a New York court with "ruinous extortion" in connection with a shipbuilding trust—Morgan helped him make a graceful exit, praising his "unequalled powers as an expert in the manufacture of steel," attributing his departure entirely to ill health, and keeping him on as a member of the Steel board and Finance Committee.

Carnegie's prodigal son may not have been the right man to run the Morgan/Gary consolidation, but Morgan had correctly assessed his expertise. In 1904 Schwab took over management of Bethlehem Steel, a small Pennsylvania producer of rails and specialty items, and over a decade built it up into the second largest firm in the country, the chief rival to U.S. Steel.*

After Schwab's departure, his assistant, William E. Corey, became president of U.S. Steel, but it was Gary who effectively set company policy for the next twenty-five years. He did not follow Schwab's prescription for geographic rationalization, unified sales facilities, and innovative research, nor did he carry forward Carnegie's hard-driving, cost-cutting, price-slashing lead. Instead, he presided over a loose holding company of intact subsidiaries, and created a structural umbrella that allowed the giant firm and its smaller competitors to maintain steady prices even in fluctuating markets. He and Morgan wanted primarily to stabilize the country's fundamental industry—and secondarily to avoid antitrust prosecution—and under their governance U.S. Steel squandered the advantages it inherited from Carnegie. Its share of the American steel market declined from about two thirds in 1901 to one third by the 1930s.

———

The presidential waffling that Finley Peter Dunne lampooned ("On wan hand I wud stamp [the trusts] undher fut; on th' other hand not so fast") accounted for much of Morgan's consternation at the move against Northern Securities.

---

* Schwab had bought Bethlehem Steel in June 1901 for roughly $7 million. He sold it to the U.S. Steel syndicate at that price, then bought it back in 1902 for $7.2 million and sold it to his U.S. Shipbuilding Company for $30 million of its stock and bonds. He gave the Morgan syndicate 50,000 shares of the stock as profit on the resale, but the shipping venture failed in July 1903. In December 1904 Schwab secured a New Jersey charter for the Bethlehem Steel Corporation, sold off extraneous facilities, and concentrated on making commercial steel.

Roosevelt had recently given a dinner in honor of the country's "Railroad Bismarck," and even as he filed suit against the northwest rail consolidation in February 1902 he was encouraging Morgan to organize a giant international shipping trust (see Chapter 23).

In the fall of 1902, TR welcomed Morgan's help in settling a major labor-management dispute. Workers in Pennsylvania's anthracite coal mines—most of which were owned by Morganized railroads such as the Erie and the Reading—had gone on strike in the late summer of 1900 for a wage increase (which they had not had in twenty years), an eight-hour day (instead of ten), better working conditions, an end to excessive charges at company stores, and union recognition. UMW President John Mitchell negotiated a settlement that fall with the help of Morgan and Mark Hanna, who convinced the railroad presidents that a prolonged strike would hurt Republicans in the last weeks of a presidential election campaign (the party slogan was a "Full Dinner Pail" for American workers). The settlement included a 10 percent wage increase, recognition of workers' grievance committees, and two related promises— Mitchell would guarantee a year of no strikes in the coal regions, and Morgan would try to get the mine operators to recognize the union.

Neither side proved able to keep its promise: local, unauthorized strikes continued, and the coal-road presidents adamantly opposed union demands. The conflict came to a head again early in 1902. Mitchell, who had meanwhile tried to mediate between workers and executives in the 1901 U.S. Steel strike, met with Morgan in February 1902, and reported to Hanna that the banker said he would "do what was right when the opportunity for action came"— that "if the railroad presidents were wrong he would not sustain them; if the miners were wrong he would not help them." Ralph Easley, head of the National Civic Federation, a group of industrialists and labor leaders organized to head off violent confrontations and promote industrial peace, told Mitchell that Morgan was "a good deal in the same fix with these coal roads, as he was last summer with the Steel Corporation. He has a lot of unruly presidents on his hands who are willing to resign any minute if he undertakes to coerce them. He has not got a lot of men standing around to put in their place." Easley counseled patience, assuring Mitchell that in time "we will have friendly men instead of hostile old cranks at the head of [the coal roads]."

In May, after a futile meeting between Mitchell and the railroad presidents, 140,000 miners went on strike. Over the next few months Mitchell earned the union widespread popular support by curtailing violence and emphasizing to the press the strikers' honesty, reasonable demands, and willingness to negotiate. The mine owners, by contrast, were arrogant and harsh. Easley considered them "forty years behind the times in their attitude toward organized labor," which seemed an understatement when the Morgan-appointed president of the Reading Railroad, George F. Baer, answered a clergyman's appeal for settlement by saying that the "rights and interests of the laboring man" would best be protected "not by labor agitators, but by the Christian men to whom God in his Infinite Wisdom has given control of the property interests of the country." After Baer's letter was published in the press, Clarence Darrow pronounced him "George the Last," and the *Chicago Tribune* said that the "real subverters of law and order" were not the strikers but the coal-road presidents.

The striking miners supplied new words to the popular song "Just Break the News to Mother":

> *Just break the news to Morgan that great official organ,*
> *And tell him we want ten per cent of increase in our pay,*
> *Just say we are united and that our wrongs must be righted,*
> *And with those unjust company stores of course we'll do away.*

When Morgan returned from Europe in August, Mitchell, Easley, Hanna, and Chauncey Depew tried to get him to arbitrate between the owners and strikers—Samuel Gompers and James Duncan at the AFL told National Civic Federation leaders that they believed "in the absolute integrity and fairness of Mr. Morgan." According to Herbert Satterlee, Morgan thought the two sides should reach an agreement on their own, and if they couldn't, it should be the government, not he, who stepped in. Nonetheless, Mitchell said Morgan began working for settlement behind the scenes in August. Between May and October the price of coal rose from $5 to $30 a ton. Morgan helped set up, supply, and pay for a depot on the Lower East Side of Manhattan, where people could buy coal below cost.

In September, New York's Democratic State Convention endorsed nationalization of the mines, and a rally of ten thousand people in Madison Square supported the strikers. A Socialist organizer in Pennsylvania said the coal strike had "done more for the cause of Socialism than all the events that ever happened in the United States before." Jacob Riis warned Roosevelt that if he did not find a remedy, "the arrogance of the money power will bring a revolution."

Roosevelt feared the democratic "mob" even more than he disliked "corrupt wealth." His speeches against Bryan and other radical extremists had come from the heart, as had his early opposition to organized labor. He believed in the rights of property owners, but in 1902 the coal barons' "wooden-headed obstinacy and stupidity [TR's terms]," the threat of social upheaval, and the rising price of coal as cold weather and the midterm election approached, induced him to intervene.

He invited the mine owners and Mitchell to meet at the White House on October 3. Mitchell agreed to accept arbitration by an independent commission, but Baer refused to "waste time negotiating with the fomenters of this anarchy," and demanded that the President use the army to end the strike. Roosevelt, who already had ten thousand troops in the coalfields, considered using them to take over the mines instead. News of the owners' inflexibility increased public support for the miners, who voted on October 8 not to end the strike.

It was at this point that the administration turned to Morgan. On October 11, Secretary of War Elihu Root took a train to New York, and on board *Corsair* that afternoon he and Morgan drafted a statement for the coal-road presidents to sign. Morgan negotiated with these men all the next day—they insisted on several changes (probably adding bombast about labor's "reign of terror" and protests about their own small profits and fair practices), but ultimately adopted the proposal, which Morgan delivered to Roosevelt in person on October 13. The presidents agreed to arbitration by an independent commission, but not to negotiations with the union. They named five categories of men to arbitrate the dispute—an engineer, a judge, an "eminent" sociologist, a military officer, and a mining expert. Mitchell the next day objected to their rhetoric and attempt to pack the commission, but agreed to arbitration if Roosevelt would add two more mediators—a priest (most of the miners were recent immigrants and Catholic) and a union man.

Root telephoned Morgan with this news. On October 15, George Perkins and Bob Bacon, just back from his recuperation in Europe, went to Washington to say that Morgan could not get the owners to accept the two extra men. "A most comic incident ensued," wrote Roosevelt a few days later. "For two hours I talked with Bacon and Perkins, both of whom were nearly frenzied." While agreeing with the President on the imminent dangers of "anarchy and war," they insisted that the owners would never admit a labor representative to the board. Finally, Bacon said nobody would care *who* the arbitrators were as long as they came under the categories named—and Roosevelt realized that the mine owners' "mighty brains . . . had formulated the theory that they would rather have anarchy than tweedledum, but that if I would use the word tweedledee they would hail it as meaning peace. In other words . . . they had not the slightest objection to my appointing a labor man as 'an eminent sociologist.' " He proposed exactly that, and "to my intense relief this utter absurdity was received with delight by Bacon and Perkins, who said they were sure the operators would agree to it!" The President promptly named a commission that was accepted by both sides.

"My dear Morgan," he wrote the next day: ". . . it really does begin to look as if there was light ahead. And now, my dear sir, let me thank you for the service you have rendered the whole people. If it had not been for your going into the matter I do not see how the strike could have been settled at this time, and the consequences that might have followed upon its being unsettled when cold weather set in are in fact dreadful to contemplate. I thank you and congratulate you with all my heart." By October 23 the miners were back at work.*

Morgan had waited until the government asked for his help—perhaps because it gave him a stronger hand with the "unruly" presidents—but he was accused of forcing the owners to the table simply to protect his "personal" interests. John Mitchell came to his defense. "To my personal knowledge," Mitchell told a reporter, "Mr. Morgan has been trying to settle the coal strike ever since he came back from Europe two months ago. If others had been as fair as Mr. Morgan was, this strike would have been settled a long time ago. . . . Mr. Morgan could not very well have been forced to do something which he had been trying to achieve for several weeks."

Morgan's interest in ending the strike had to do not with personal profits but with averting a national fuel shortage and containing the conflict the owners' egregious behavior provoked. Richard Hofstadter has noted the irony that it was Morgan and Hanna, "paramount symbols of the bloated plutocracy," who helped Roosevelt end this crisis. Where previous Presidents had intervened on the side of management—Hayes in the railroad strikes of 1877, Cleveland in the 1894 Pullman Strike—Roosevelt in 1902 made labor a full party to the settlement, and his action underlined the new status of the federal government as objective authority, broker of the "square deal." Hofstadter could not "refrain from adding that it ill accorded with the stereotypes of Progressive thinking that 'Dollar Mark' Hanna and J. P. Morgan should have attended as midwives at the birth of the neutral state."

———

Articulating the fears of a nation in dramatic flux, Roosevelt was the first chief executive to address the complex problems created by a modern industrial economy, and the first to pose old federalist questions about the relations between government and business in this new context. That the United States by 1902 had become the leading industrial nation in the world was due more to private enterprise than to government policy. Could Washington begin to exercise a measure of control over the stupendously powerful "interests" and still maintain the country's economic momentum? How did private property rights weigh against public responsibilities in the operation of vast transportation systems and industrial enterprises? Could the government define and protect the interests of "the common man"? Could it effectively impose public accountability and regulatory restraints on the trusts? Roosevelt actually had no

* Five months later the commission gave them a 10 percent raise and a nine-hour day, but did not recognize the union; instead, it created a conciliation board with worker representation. It also allowed the owners to raise coal prices 10 percent. Radical leaders denounced Mitchell for selling out the union.

quarrel with Morgan's objectives of industrial consolidation, economic stability, and U.S. dominion in world markets; he wanted chiefly to check abuses of financial power and end government subservience to Wall Street. Although the Northern Securities prosecution established his reputation as a trustbuster, neither he nor Knox meant to stop industrial combinations. They were trying to work out a "right" balance between competition and consolidation, with government as the judge of what was right.*

The President appreciated Morgan's assistance in settling the coal strike, and over the next few years he often worked closely with the bankers at 23 Wall Street. In 1903 George Perkins from the heart of trust country helped set up government agencies to regulate private industry—a Department of Commerce and Labor, with a fact-finding branch called the Bureau of Corporations. Judicious railroad executives had for years seen federal regulation as likely to help stop rate declines and cutthroat competition, as well as to override restrictive local measures, and they greeted the 1903 Elkins Act, which finally made the granting of rebates to big shippers such as Standard Oil and Carnegie Steel

---

* Many years later, in his autobiography, Roosevelt offered an analysis of the questions he had faced, and laid out the case for regulation. The nineteenth century in America, he wrote, had witnessed a "riot of individualistic materialism," and the "total absence of governmental control had led to a portentous growth in the financial and industrial world both of natural individuals and of artificial individuals—that is, corporations. . . . In no other country in the world was such power held by the men who had gained these fortunes. . . . The power of the mighty industrial overlords had increased with giant strides, while the methods of controlling them, or checking abuses by them, on the part of the people, through the Government, remained archaic and therefore practically impotent. . . .

"One of the main troubles was the fact that the men who saw the evils and who tried to remedy them attempted to work in two wholly different ways, and the great majority of them in a way that offered little promise of real betterment. They tried (by the Sherman law method) to bolster up an individualism already proved to be both futile and mischievous; to remedy by more individualism the concentration that was the inevitable result of the already existing individualism. They saw the evil done by the big combinations, and sought to remedy it by destroying them and restoring the country to the economic conditions of the middle of the nineteenth century. This was a hopeless effort, and those who went into it, although they regarded themselves as radical progressives, really represented a form of sincere rural toryism. . . .

"On the other hand, a few men recognized that corporations and combinations had become indispensable in the business world, that it was folly to try to prohibit them, but that it was also folly to leave them without thoroughgoing control. These men realized that the doctrines of the old *laissez-faire* economists, of the believers in unlimited competition, unlimited individualism, were in the actual state of affairs false and mischievous. They realized that the Government must now interfere to protect labor, to subordinate the big corporation to the public welfare, and to shackle cunning and fraud exactly as centuries before it had interfered to shackle the physical force which does wrong by violence."

illegal, with relief. In December 1904 *The Wall Street Journal* found it "noteworthy" that, contrary to expectations, the "financial interests in control of the railroads and the industrial corporations" *favored* regulatory laws that would, "if carried into effect, deprive them of so much of their present power. . . . [T]his is of vast significance. . . . [S]ome of the foremost railroad men of the country are at this time at work in harmony with the President for the enactment of a law providing for federal regulation of rates which shall be equitable both to the railroads and the public."

Roosevelt had made his symbolic move against Northern Securities. As the case made its way through the courts, he did not even shake a regulatory stick at Morgan's combinations for the remainder of his time in the White House.

———

Far more problematic for Morgan than TR early in the new century was a profound national shudder of revulsion against big business—the widespread clamor for reform that came to be known as progressivism. Encompassing a range of impulses and ideologies, this latest wave of antipathy to the "money power" had a broader, less radical, more urban, middle-class base than the agrarian and silver movements, and stronger moral and intellectual leadership.

Some progressives, hoping to restore the moral cohesion of earlier times, looked back in what Roosevelt called "sincere rural toryism" to the small-scale antebellum economy with its relatively free markets and individualistic values. At the same time, urban reformers tackled the social consequences of industrialization head-on. Lay and clerical activists made national issues of child labor laws, industrial safety, workmen's compensation, public housing, and public health. Moral hygienists tried to outlaw alcohol and prostitution. Political theorists who believed with Roosevelt that the United States could have the benefits of an advanced industrial economy *and* a humane society raised searching questions about the public interest and the nature of democracy in a modern corporate state. To the left of the mainstream, Socialist Eugene V. Debs won 3 percent of the vote in 1904, 2.8 percent in 1908, and 6 percent in 1912.

Dramatic economic changes contributed to the national sense of unease. Americans accustomed to declining prices and a steady increase in the purchasing power of the dollar during the long period of post–Civil War deflation suddenly found prices going up. The increase in gold production after 1897 had led to monetary expansion and price inflation in all the gold standard countries, including the United States, and the cost of living for American families rose about 35 percent between 1897 and 1913. Cheaper dollars made life easier for farmers and other borrowers, but people on fixed incomes were able to buy less, the value of dollar-based assets declined, and wages for skilled labor did not rise nearly as quickly as costs. AFL membership went from 548,000 in 1900 to more than 1.5 million by 1910.

A newly aggressive cultural realism gave urgent force to the pressure for reform, as did a talented group of investigative journalists who focused national attention on the disparity between what America promised and what it had become. With the success of mass-circulation magazines in the late nineteenth century, information had become big business, and editors competing for readers simultaneously created and fed the public's appetite for human interest stories, moral crusades, and political exposés.

The literature of exposure had its unofficial inauguration in *McClure's* magazine at the beginning of 1903. Samuel S. McClure, whom Morgan had invited to take over Harper's in 1899, had continued his own publishing ventures, and his stable of skillful, meticulous writers was making journalism glamorous. McClure announced in his editorial for the January 1903 issue of the magazine that three of its articles, revealing a contempt for law at all levels of society, amounted to such an "arraignment of the American character as should make every one of us stop and think." At once enunciating the era's challenge to corrupt authority and appealing to its new ethos of personal responsibility, McClure concluded: "There is no one left; none but all of us."

Lincoln Steffens led off with "The Shame of Minneapolis," an exposé of municipal corruption that chronicled flagrant collusion between politicians, criminals, and the police—including photographs of a ledger listing specific bribes. A piece on the 1902 anthracite coal strike by Ray Stannard Baker, called "The Right to Work," indicted the UMW for its treatment of the seven thousand workers who did *not* join the walkout. And Ida M. Tarbell, the leading female journalist in the country, published an installment of her carefully researched, devastating portrait of Rockefeller's Standard Oil.

Appearing in book form in 1904, Miss Tarbell's *History of Standard Oil* proved to be one of the most influential accounts of business ever published in America. Tarbell had grown up in the Pennsylvania oil regions, where her father, an independent oil producer, had been ruined by the Rockefeller trust. When Franklin Tarbell learned what his daughter was undertaking, he warned her, "Don't do it, Ida. They will ruin the magazine." She did it anyway, bringing to her task both special knowledge and an obvious bias. She gained access to company officials and their archives, studied affidavits, legislative records, and judicial proceedings, interviewed people all over the country who had dealt with Standard Oil. What she found, and serialized in riveting detail month after month in *McClure's*, was "as nearly a perfect machine, both in efficiency and monopolistic power, as ever has been devised"—and a shocking record of bribery, espionage, special privilege, ruthless tactics, and industrial deceit. "Mr. Rockefeller has systematically played with loaded dice," Miss Tarbell concluded, "and it is doubtful if there has ever been a time since 1872 when he has run a race with a competitor and started fair."

Her exhaustive indictment briefly made her the most famous woman in America. It made Rockefeller, for considerably longer, the most hated man. Most reviewers praised her documentation and dispassion, although *The Nation* issued a notable dissent. Still the voice of high-minded reform, the magazine criticized her for recklessly stirring up "popular hatred," for using insinuation rather than proof, for painting her villain too black and her victims (the independent producers) too white: "We need reforms badly enough, but we shall not get them until we have an electorate able to control its passions, to reserve its condemnation, to deliberate before it acts. When that time comes, a railing accusation will not be accepted as history."

Rockefeller never responded directly to Tarbell's charges. A neighbor described his attitude as "that of a game fighter who expects to be whacked on the head once in a while. He is not the least disturbed by any blows he may receive. He maintains that the Standard has done more good than harm."

The Tarbell study eventually led to local and federal prosecutions of Standard Oil, and to an increase in Rockefeller's philanthropy. In its wake came a flood of further exposés, some painstaking and serious, others inaccurate and sensationalistic—of the insurance industry, meatpacking, railroads, child labor, racial discrimination, slum housing, patent medicines, high finance, and the Senate. Novels by Theodore Dreiser, Frank Norris, Jack London, and Upton Sinclair added to the graphic picture of a nation ravaged by predatory capital, as did the speeches of Robert La Follette, paintings by members of New York's urban-realist Ashcan School, and the photographs of Jacob Riis. When Sinclair's best-selling 1906 novel about conditions in the Chicago stockyards, *The Jungle,* led to passage of the country's first serious consumer-protection measure, the Pure Food and Drug Act, the author complained: "I aimed at the public's heart, and by accident I hit it in the stomach."

Investigative journalists documented abuses of power at all levels of American society, but the paramount villain in the popular imagination was Big Business and its apotheosis, the Trust. Ray Stannard Baker's articles on the coal strike and U.S. Steel did not vilify Morgan, but later pieces by other writers and cartoonists did. Morgan left no response to his critics, and paid little attention to the country's striking shift in sensibility. He probably would not have changed course even if he had been more in touch with the progressive national mood, since he did not think he was doing anything wrong.

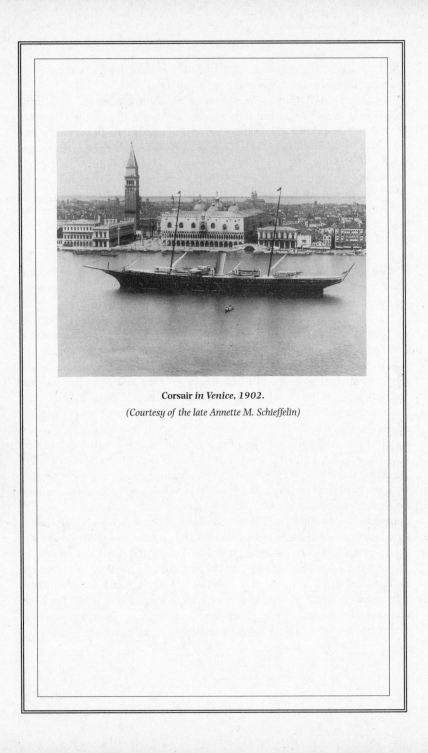

Corsair *in Venice, 1902.*
(Courtesy of the late Annette M. Schieffelin)

Chapter 23

COMMUNITY OF INTEREST ON THE ATLANTIC

Pierpont Morgan . . . is carrying loads that stagger the strongest nerves," wrote Henry Adams in April 1902. "Everyone asks what would happen if some morning he woke up dead."

It was a good question. Morgan had just turned sixty-five, and though he had no intention of waking up dead, he was beginning to ease out from under his nerve-staggering load. When he left for Europe as usual that April, he was organizing the U.S. Steel bond-conversion syndicate, the defense of Northern Securities, and a gigantic international shipping trust.

None of the ideas for his major consolidations originated with him. Charles Coffin and Lee, Higginson & Co. had proposed the merger that became General Electric, Judge Gary broached the idea of Federal Steel, Charles Schwab sketched out the initial plan for U.S. Steel, and James J. Hill first argued for the union of competing northwest railroads that developed into Northern Securities. The maritime trust was no exception. It started at the instigation of men in the shipping trade.

A Philadelphian named Clement A. Griscom was the dominant figure in American transatlantic transport in 1900. His International Navigation Company, chartered in New Jersey, owned U.S., British, and Belgian lines that ran merchant ships between the eastern seaboard and Europe. Like E. H. Harriman and James J. Hill, Griscom had dreams of stretching America's transportation empire around the world—of rail-ship links that would make it possible to send American grain on American carriers all the way from the midwestern plains to Liverpool and Hong Kong.

In the 1830s the United States had carried 90 percent of its relatively small international trade under its own flag, but high construction and operating costs, as the industry shifted from sail to steam, had caused a dramatic decline in domestic shipbuilding after 1850. By 1900 only 10 percent of U.S. foreign trade moved on U.S. ships. Griscom, aiming to expand the American merchant marine and free the richest country in the world from dependence on foreign carriers, had procured a federal subsidy for mail in 1891, and lobbied throughout the nineties for further government aid. Then the Boer and Spanish-American Wars stimulated shipbuilding, and a tremendous surge in U.S. exports between 1898 and 1900 won political as well as commercial support for greater American participation in oceangoing trade.

In this auspicious climate, Griscom decided to refinance some of his debt and build new ships. He engaged Drexel & Co. to float a $13 million loan for his INC in 1899. The ink on the bonds was barely dry when he learned that the largest freight carrier in the North Atlantic, Britain's Frederick Leyland & Co., was about to acquire his only domestic rival, the Baltimore-based Atlantic Transport Company. British ownership of the ATC would threaten not only the INC but also the prospect of a strong U.S. presence in North Atlantic shipping—which was probably how Griscom described the situation to Morgan.

Exactly when and how he secured Morgan's interest is not clear. The Leyland-ATC deal fell apart in May of 1900. When other bankers, possibly representing Leyland, approached Morgan about a "large shipbuilding combination" that July, he told his English partners, "I do not think favorably of entertaining shipbuilding business." By the end of the year he had changed his mind. The highly competitive shipping industry had earned record profits in 1900, which may have helped persuade him that if a "large combination" could reduce rate wars, consolidate operations, and build fast new ships, it would be able to stabilize international trade and yield even greater returns.

In December 1900, Morgan agreed to finance a merger of the INC and the ATC, to advance cash for building new ships, and to bring in two more lines. He expected Congress to subsidize a U.S.-based merchant marine that would service the busiest trade route in the world.

One of the additional companies brought in under this agreement was Leyland & Co. Just months after the prosperous British freight line threatened to take over America's oceangoing transport, the direction of the takeover reversed. Early in 1901, as Morgan worked on the organization of U.S. Steel, his associates in London negotiated for Leyland. Its chairman, John R. Ellerman, was an experienced financier who held out for three times the Americans' initial $3.5 million offer—his shareholders got $11 million, in *cash*. The house of Morgan advanced the $11 million, since the merger's funding was not yet in place.

Before the Leyland purchase, Morgan had been acting simply as banker for Griscom's plan—issuing credit, preparing to sell securities, organizing the merger. Once his bank committed $11 million, however (roughly equivalent to $165 million in the 1990s), he had an investment in transatlantic shipping. At some point in 1901, ownership of the Leyland shares was divided equally among the INC, the ATC, and J. P. Morgan & Co.

The fourth company the combination set out to acquire early in 1901 was not a cargo carrier but White Star, the most profitable and prestigious of Britain's luxury passenger lines, and Morgan's personal favorite. By June—after the formation of U.S. Steel, the Northern Pacific raid and panic, Morgan's aborted vacation at Aix, and his lunch at Windsor with Edward VII—men acting for him in London had arranged to purchase the White Star line for $32 million. They negotiated chiefly with William J. Pirrie, the second-largest holder of White Star securities and head of the prominent Belfast shipbuilding company, Harland & Wolff. The president of White Star, and the largest shareholder, was J. Bruce Ismay, son of its recently deceased founder.*

———

Rumors about these secret negotiations circulated immediately, but the British took nearly a year to panic over U.S. acquisition of their major freight and passenger lines. Germany reacted at once. Two Germans in particular were keeping a wary watch on Britain's maritime fortunes and Morgan's oceanic ambitions—Kaiser Wilhelm II and Albert Ballin, head of the Hamburg-Amerika line (HAPAG).

The Kaiser had embarked in 1898 on a program of aggressive naval expansion intended to challenge Britain's long-term supremacy at sea, and to consolidate the plans for a German Empire set in motion by Otto von Bismarck in 1871. Wilhelm's admirals worked quickly, as did the owners of Germany's commercial fleets: by 1900, HAPAG was the largest steamship company in the world. Ballin called it "the embodiment of the national purpose of a 'greater Germany' and of imperial power."

Although Germany's military and industrial growth dwarfed that of Great Britain in the last third of the nineteenth century, England expected the blood ties between the Prussian Hohenzollerns and the largely Germanic British royal family (Saxe-Coburg-Gotha until 1917, when George V changed the

---

* The privately held White Star had no market price in 1901: $32 million amounted to ten times its record 1900 earnings. Ten times earnings was not an unusual price for a transportation company at the turn of the century, but the basis itself (earnings of $3.2 million) was extremely high—almost a third larger than White Star's average earnings for the previous five years, which included no recessionary time. The Americans had expected to pay $24 million, wisely basing their estimates on average rather than peak earnings.

name to Windsor) to ensure peace. The Kaiser was Queen Victoria's grandson: his mother, Princess Victoria, had married Crown Prince Friedrich of Prussia in 1858. Wilhelm, however, managed to infuriate Buckingham Palace as soon as he succeeded his father in 1888, when his "Uncle Bertie" was still Prince of Wales. Willful, grandiose, and insecure, he complained that the Prince treated him "as an uncle treats a nephew" instead of recognizing him as an emperor. The Queen dismissed this grievance as *"perfect madness"*—"it is really too *vulgar* and too absurd." Prince Edward said his nephew ought to learn that he was living at the end of the nineteenth century, not in the Middle Ages.

Queen Victoria's death at the beginning of 1901 brought personal hostilities to a temporary halt, although the poet and diplomat Wilfrid Scawen Blunt predicted that it would "mean great changes in the world, for the long understanding among the Emperors that England is not to be quarrelled with during the Queen's lifetime will now give place to freer action. The Emperor William does not love his uncle, our new king."

The Emperor William soon raised the stakes in his quarrel with England. Hearing the rumors about an Anglo-American alliance in the North Atlantic, and fearing that Morgan railroads would give preferential rates to Morgan ships, he dispatched Mr. Ballin to London to investigate. Ballin, a German Jew, had been trying to control competition in the transatlantic lanes for years. He met with Pirrie, the temporary spokesman for the trust, and suggested establishing a "community of interest" between the Anglo-American combination and Germany's major shipping companies, HAPAG and North German Lloyd. Negotiations proceeded slowly. In February 1902 Ballin went to New York to meet with Morgan.

He had noted in his diary six months earlier that the American financier was reputed to combine "the possession of an enormous fortune with an intelligence which is simply astounding"—a view he endorsed when he and Morgan saw eye to eye in New York. On Thursday, February 20, the Germans and Americans signed agreements to divide Atlantic traffic geographically for ten years, to stay out of each other's waters, cooperate on rates, and share certain profits and ventures—including the purchase of the British Cunard and Dutch Holland-America lines. Ballin reported that Morgan gave a dinner in honor of his new friends "at his private residence which abounds in art of all descriptions." After the two men cabled news of their agreement to Berlin, the Kaiser awarded Ballin the Order of the Red Eagle, and invited Morgan to meet him on the imperial yacht at Kiel in June.

It was in the midst of these negotiations that Roosevelt announced the prosecution of Northern Securities. Morgan went to Washington as soon as he could leave the Germans. He divided his time in the capital between trying to defend his railroad trust against the President's "attack" and trying to secure federal support for his maritime trust, with the President's approval. Roosevelt, who took an internationalist view of America's new manifest destiny, was waving his antitrust banner with one hand and beckoning Wall Street to promote a stronger U.S. presence at sea with the other. Other champions of the shipping trust in Washington included the Secretaries of War and State, Elihu Root and John Hay, the influential naval historian Alfred T. Mahan, and Senators Hanna, Depew, Nelson Aldrich, and Henry Cabot Lodge. Congress that February was debating a shipping subsidy bill. Morgan partner Charles Steele reported to London on February 26 that he, Morgan, and Griscom had just returned from Washington where "Senators in charge of Shipping Bill" were "enthusiastic about general plan [for the merger] but request delay publishing for three weeks within which they predict final action will be taken by U.S. Congress."

On March 17 the shipping subsidy bill won Senate approval and went to the House.* The impending maritime merger gave Morgan until April 30 to form an underwriting syndicate—he had the right to withdraw from his commitment at any time before that date, although the sellers did not: all parties were waiting to see whether Congress would authorize the subsidy. Planning to go abroad at the beginning of April, he organized a provisional syndicate pledged to raise cash in exchange for bonds of the as yet unnamed transatlantic trust. He had no trouble finding participants: men profiting from the U.S. Steel syndicate eagerly signed on.

Morgan gave testimony to a U.S. Circuit Court in the case against Northern Securities on March 26—a special examiner had been sent to depose witnesses in New York—then sailed for Europe on April 2 with his daughter Anne. In London he conferred with the owners of White Star and its chief rival, Cunard, while his American partners kept him posted on the subsidy measure. Western congressmen, adamantly opposing what they saw as yet another Wall Street swindle, amended the bill to *prohibit* U.S. assistance to foreign-built ships, which included most of those in the proposed combine. On April 10, Perkins and Steele reported that their friends in the Senate were "willing we should go ahead to bring out shipping combination" without waiting for the House vote. Perkins had "talked freely with President of U.S. on subject," and found him reluctant to sign the radically weakened bill even if it passed. Morgan's resourceful Secretary of State suggested that announcing the combination might help

---

* With popular hostility to Wall Street running high, Senate positions on the subsidy divided sharply along East/West lines. Of the four senior conservative Republicans who usually acted as a unit—Nelson Aldrich of Rhode Island, Orville Platt of Connecticut, William Allison of Iowa, and John Spooner of Wisconsin—the easterners voted for the bill, the westerners against.

defeat the now unwelcome legislation, a plan that "appealed strongly to President and he was most enthusiastic in urging such a course." The bankers had little to lose by making the combine public, counseled Perkins, especially as it "would help materially with President in disposing of Northern Securities case"—presumably by doing him a favor on the high seas.

Morgan replied, "fully agree your views"—he thought Cunard more likely to join later in any case—and added after a week, "quite willing go ahead now and form Syndicate."

The decision not to wait for federal aid proved in one sense wise, since the subsidy bill died in the House. Going ahead without government assistance, however, meant that the combine would have to bear the full cost of building and operating expensive new ships—and the economics of the industry had radically changed between 1900 and 1902. The shortages created by the Boer and Spanish-American Wars had produced unprecedented earnings and a shipbuilding boom. Over 4 million tons of new ships entered the water between 1896 and 1900, their owners following the prevalent if improvident practice of adding to capacity at the end of an upturn. Then, in 1901–2, tonnage commandeered for the Boer War returned to compete for trade, a depression on the Continent reduced freight traffic, the American corn crop failed, and U.S. immigration began to wane. Freight rates fell 30 percent during 1901, and profits were cut in half. Passenger lines suffered as well: Cunard's earnings plummeted 50 percent in 1901, and in March of 1902 Cunard paid out more than it had earned to issue half of its expected dividend.

Morgan was free to withdraw his commitment in April 1902. If he had simply dissolved the provisional syndicate, the deal would not have gone through. He knew that with shipping profits down and no federal subsidy, the prospects for selling the combine's securities looked bleak. On the other hand, his firm had invested nearly $4 million (a third of the $11 million paid for Leyland) in the merger, plus additional funds for building new ships, and a great deal of time and work. Also weighing in on the side of proceeding were the agreement he had negotiated with the Germans, the earnings history of White Star and Leyland, the inclusion of the Belfast shipbuilders, Harland & Wolff (whose costs were 30 percent lower than those of American yards), and political support from the U.S. President, cabinet, and Senate.

Still, it is surprising that he did not try to renegotiate terms with the shippers in 1902, given the industry downturn. Perhaps he thought the terms didn't really matter, since the sums involved were small compared with U.S. Steel—or perhaps he expected the combination to help solve the industry's problems. The purveyors of conventional wisdom had been skeptical about his ability to float securities for U.S. Steel, and the market had proved them wrong. In mid-April, he decided to go ahead.

On the nineteenth, his London partners leaked news of the shipping combine to the press. The next day, Morgan went to Paris with Anne, and on the twenty-second Henry Adams reported people wondering what would happen "if some morning he woke up dead."

———

Morgan met his wife, the Laniers, and the Bacons in Paris at the Hôtel Bristol on April 20. Three days later, Fanny left for London and New York with her hired companion, a Miss Janes. Anne stayed on with her father in Paris.

London was in an uproar over his transatlantic trust. Just before the semi-official announcement in the press, Ballin had told Germany's London embassy that the Morgan bankers would try to present the combination "in the light of a big Anglo-American 'community of interest' agreement . . . the fact that it virtually cedes to the United States the control of the North Atlantic shipping business will be kept in the background, as far as it is possible to do."

It wasn't possible at all. The British government and House of Commons were "*boulversé* [bowled over] by Morgan's latest little combination," reported Dawkins to Alfred (now Viscount) Milner, who was still British high commissioner in South Africa, on April 25: "Ships this time." Britain's politicians, preoccupied by the Boer War, had taken considerably longer than the Kaiser to recognize the "American peril" on the Atlantic, and by the time they woke up to the danger, three of their greatest maritime assets—Leyland, White Star, and Harland & Wolff—were disappearing into the maw of the Morgan trust.

Dawkins ruefully explained the situation to Lord Milner in light of England's incontrovertible decline: "I don't like it and wish that it were we who exported across the Atlantic and controlled the transportation from a vast hinterland to the coast," but "the facts are that the Americans say [']we raise the wheat and cotton ferried over, we haul it thousands of miles to the Seas, we insist on a large share in carrying it further, and we back our claim with more spare money than you have, and that money can be realized and disposed of by a commanding genius at these games[']"—i.e., by Morgan. The essential point, Dawkins thought, was that "under Morgan's auspices the great railways and growing shipping lines in the U.S. have become as thick as thieves. The railways control all the Atlantic ports except New York, which remains an old-fashioned entrepôt port. Consequently the railways had begun to give and threatened to go further in giving preferential rates to cargo taking American boats, and our boats might have been squeezed out of all ports but New York."

Berlin's *National Zeitung* pointed out with more than a hint of schadenfreude that "The blow to England is all the greater since the German companies have been able to keep out of the trust and maintain their independence."

Dawkins had discreetly tried to warn his friends in the government ahead of time—as had the chairman of Cunard, Lord Inverclyde—to no avail. In a nice display of outrage over information they had had for some time, ranking members of His Majesty's government denounced Morgan's "latest little combination" in April on grounds of national security and honor: the Royal Navy, they declared, had to be able to requisition freighters and passenger liners in times of crisis, and under no circumstances would English vessels fly the American flag. Having dominated world shipping for two hundred years, Britain was not about to let Morgan rule the waves.

The financial community was more pragmatic. Gaspard Farrer at Baring Brothers told James J. Hill: "If the U.S. have the money and desire to own ships assuredly nothing we can do will prevent her: & I would rather JPM bought our old ones at high prices than build new ones when prices are low."

———

As of April 23, "JPM" was on vacation. Cables about the shipping trust followed him to Paris and then Aix, where news of the Northern Pacific raid had cut his holiday short the previous spring. In 1902 he issued occasional instructions as he traveled, but turned most of the wired queries back to his partners. On April 24, when Dawkins asked for advice about the combination's capitalization and voting trust, Morgan replied from Paris: "Difficult in fact impossible for me to instruct or act at this distance without papers and agreement before me, all questions must be decided in NY unless some questions asked me direct." The next day, informed that costs for White Star's new tonnage were far higher than estimated—the calculations had been based on "conjecture" since the line's president, J. Bruce Ismay, had "refused to give us figures"—he wired, "Have no suggestions make quite satisfied you all can adjust it without me, but if needed will come to London for the purpose of further meeting."

Steele and Dawkins tried to adjust it without him, but Ismay kept coming up with new conditions and demands. Appealed to again at Aix, Morgan advised, "It does not seem to me safe to continue make concessions placing ourselves at mercy of Ismay in the management for which we are personally morally responsible"—he was even willing to leave White Star out of the combine.

The consolidation as it tentatively took shape in May kept White Star in, along with Griscom's INC, the ATC, Leyland, and another British freight carrier, the Dominion line. It did not include Holland-America, as Ballin had wanted, but acquired a controlling interest in its stock. Griscom would be president of the still-unnamed enterprise, with headquarters in Philadelphia, and the bankers took familiar steps to insure supervisory control: Morgan himself would sit on a five-man voting trust, along with Steele, the Philadelphia streetcar magnate P.A.B. Widener (a major INC stockholder and a participant in the U.S. Steel syndicate), Ismay, and W. J. Pirrie of Harland & Wolff. Dawkins would be vice president in London. Griscom, Widener, Steele, and Perkins would sit on the board of directors.

Capitalization for the consolidation was calculated at $170 million—$60 million each of preferred and common stock, and $50 million in cash, to be raised through syndicate bond sales. The Morgan partners had hoped to purchase most of the constituent properties with securities of the new trust, just as they had for U.S. Steel, but the shipping industry downturn, the dubious prospect of dividends, and the subordination of the equity to $50 million of bonded debt meant that the shares were expected to sell well below face value ($100) by the spring of 1902—the preferred at about $85, the common at $35—and the bankers proceeded to sweeten parts of the deal.

White Star's shareholders had agreed in 1901 to take 75 percent of their price ($24 million) in preferred stock of the new trust and $8 million in cash. In 1902 the line's owners insisted on an additional $7 million in cash, plus a bonus of half a share of new common stock with each share of preferred. As a result, exactly at the moment Morgan might have been expected to renegotiate terms more favorable to the consolidation—asking the sellers to take a lower price in a worsening market—he did the opposite: he gave White Star *more* than he had initially promised. Since the $24 million in preferred had a market value of about $20 million in 1902, he made up the difference with common stock worth about $4 million (face value $12 million), plus $7 million cash. In addition, the combine bought the partnership that managed White Star for an additional $2.5 million in cash and stock worth about $2.4 million.

The size of the syndicate's $50 million underwriting was determined by the need for three major outlays of cash: $17.5 million to the White Star owners and managers; $11 million to repay the money advanced to purchase Leyland in 1901, plus interest; and $17 million for new ships—the combine took over the shipbuilding loans made by the Morgan bank in 1901, as well as commitments other lines had made to buy new tonnage. The cash requirements amounted to $46.5 million, and at the end of April 1902—a week after the Morgan bank set the deal in motion—syndicate members were asked to put up 25 percent of the $50 million they had pledged in exchange for bonds.

Critics in the English financial press said the trust had based its prices on the most prosperous year in the history of shipping, which yielded healthy profits to the British companies but so inflated the value of the combination that most of its stock represented *aqua pura*. The bankers had heard these charges before.*

* At the end of 1903, the independent auditors Price, Waterhouse, & Co. estimated the actual depreciated value of the constituent companies to be about $65 million, not including Leyland. Thomas Navin and Marian Sears, whose 1954 analysis of the shipping merger remains the best existing account, noted that the $65 million figure also did not include roughly $10 million for "other physical assets and net working capital," and they concluded that a "conservative valuation" of the properties in the merger as of December 1902 was about $75 million—again, not including Leyland: "This figure should be compared not with $170,000,000 but with $83,700,000, the cost in cash plus the anticipated opening market

The financial problems of the new trust were quickly relegated to the background by its political problems. Dawkins and Jack cabled Morgan at Aix in early May that British Cabinet ministers were determined to prevent "English lines passing under American control": the politicians had "every confidence in you and spoke of you in highest terms," but were worried about the future, and wanted the English lines "put on same basis as German." Morgan's partners had said no change was possible now that the contracts were signed, but suggested "some way could be found" of meeting British objections once the merger went into effect. To "the Senior" they reported, "[We] said we are quite sure you will gladly see them on your return. This they welcomed."

Morgan kept the British government waiting while he completed his spa cure, but appeared in London for dinner with the Colonial Secretary, Joseph Chamberlain, toward the end of May. He had known Chamberlain and his Bostonian wife, the former Mary Endicott, for years.* They lived at No. 40 Princes Gardens, just down the Exhibition Road from Princes Gate, and Morgan had watched with interest as his neighbor, the wealthy owner of a screw factory, moved into national politics—first as the Liberal Unionist heir apparent to Gladstone, more recently as a militant imperialist appointed to the Conservative Colonial Office. Chamberlain was strongly in favor of an Anglo-German alliance, a cause that was not helped when the Kaiser denounced British ministers as a set of "unmitigated noodles."

---

value of the securities issued in payment. Although higher by 10 per cent than the $75,000,000 valuation, the price paid for the component properties . . . was not unreasonably out of line with the depreciated cost."

A second way to appraise the value of the merger was the method the bankers used—earning power. The companies going into the combination, including Leyland, had earned an average of $6.5 million a year before depreciation for the previous five years. After subtracting for depreciation, the earnings came to about $4 million, a figure the bankers expected to increase through consolidation—they thought net income from new ships alone would amount to roughly $3 million a year. The merger was committed to pay fixed charges of about $3 million a year on its $50 million issue of bonds. Navin and Sears thought that even if the level of earnings did not increase, "interest would be 'covered' about twice by earnings before depreciation. Earnings anticipated on the increased tonnage would have covered interest about three times. The Morgan partners must have considered this coverage sufficient, though it was hardly enough for a high-grade bond."

* Mary was Chamberlain's third wife. His six children included a future Prime Minister, Neville, and a future Foreign Secretary, Austen; both his previous wives had died in childbirth. Mary's father, William Crowninshield Endicott, had been a justice of the Massachusetts Supreme Court and Secretary of War in the first Cleveland administration; her mother, Ellen, was a cousin of Junius's former partner, S. Endicott Peabody. When the Endicotts visited London in the early 1880s, they called on the Morgans at Dover House and Princes Gate.

The slim, stylish Secretary, who invariably wore a monocle in his eye and a fresh orchid in his lapel, met Morgan in London "hot" with rage—partly at British shipowners for putting business above patriotism, partly at the Germans for having negotiated an independent treaty with the trust, and partly at the Americans for jeopardizing Britain's national interests. Over dinner, Morgan promised to commit the new company not to transfer British ships to any foreign register for fifty years, and offered to meet most of the remaining political objections. To his surprise, Chamberlain rejected all his proposals, hinting that the British government might simply buy the White Star line's best ships.

In that case, Morgan said, the government would have to pay up to 40 percent more than the liners were worth, which would only put money in the combination's pockets for building better, faster ships. (That the combination was paying more than the companies were worth apparently did not enter the discussion.) The loss would not even temporarily set the trust back, since its German and Dutch partners could lend ships.

Then, apparently speaking not only for America's commercial interests but for its foreign policy as well, Morgan "went on to say impressively," reported Dawkins, "that while no formal alliance between [the British] and the U.S. could take place[,] nothing would do more to establish a good understanding and feeling between the two countries than community of business interests"—and that evidence of British hostility, such as buying White Star ships, would induce the American government "to exert itself." Whether or not Morgan had authorization to issue this threat is unclear.

Chamberlain did not back down. According to Dawkins, the American financier left the dinner "very sore and astonished and inclined to withdraw all his offers." Though a skillful diplomat with men in high places who fundamentally agreed with him, Morgan was tone-deaf to the sensitivities of people whose interests did not coincide with his own, and Britain's intransigence in 1902 genuinely took him by surprise. He "expected to have been received with open arms on his arrival," observed one of his English friends a few days later, "as the man who had done our country a good turn. Instead of this, he had been everywhere cold-shouldered, having been suspected of filching our mercantile ships."

The deal with the Germans granted them partnership status in the maritime trust. Instead of treating the British as partners, Morgan was forcing them to surrender sovereignty at sea, and had not taken into account how they would hate acknowledging the economic superiority of the United States.

Dawkins and Jack quashed a suggestion from New York in late May that the name of the new combine reflect "American control." The only way to prevent defensive British government action, they warned, was "to suppress as much as possible the national aspect of the matter and emphasize the commercial advantages only." In early June, Morgan named the trust the International Mercantile Marine.

———

He returned to Paris immediately after his unsatisfactory dinner with Chamberlain, to meet Adelaide and Sybil Douglas, the Markoes, Charles Lanier, and Anne. The last unmarried Morgan child, Anne had replaced Louisa as both parents' preferred traveling companion. She was the least conventional of the siblings, and bore a strong resemblance to her father—tall, square-jawed, and beautifully dressed at a hefty 170 pounds. She also had his energy and strength of will. Like Louisa, she learned to manage the often-conflicting demands of her estranged parents. In New York she brought some of her social life home to entertain Fanny at 219 and Cragston. Abroad, her presence in Pierpont's entourage helped allay Fanny's anxieties about his other female companions (Anne's letters home never mention Adelaide). It also gave her more freedom and experience of the world than a single young woman could otherwise have.

The Morgan party left Paris on May 28, 1902, traveled quickly through Switzerland, stopped in Verona to see Juliet's tomb, and went on to Venice to meet *Corsair* and her crew. Crowds lined up to see the magnificent yacht anchored in the Grand Canal opposite the Piazza San Marco, hoping for a glimpse of "Il Morgan." The Americans explored Venice for two days, then sailed down the Dalmatian coast and through the Isthmus of Corinth to Athens. Living aboard *Corsair,* they toured Byzantine churches and the Erechtheum. At the National Museum they inspected the fabulous gold treasure discovered by Heinrich Schliemann at Mycenae and one of the famous bronzes recently recovered from the sea near the island of Antikythera. Then they proceeded to Delphi, Corfu, and across the Strait of Otranto to Brindisi. "Quiet day on *Corsair,*" noted Anne in her diary on June 8: "Father leaves 5:30 for London."

Her father left for London to dine with the King. Dawkins had continued trying to placate the British Government—"I've talked my tongue nearly off," he moaned to Milner—and decided to enlist a higher authority: "I hoicked my old man over from Venice to dine with Edward Rex." At dinner with the British monarch on June 11, Morgan said he thought he could get the United States to enter into an Atlantic convention with Britain to guarantee the IMM's merchant ships against third-party competition, and repeated the offer he had made to Chamberlain in May—that no British ships built by the combine would be transferred to foreign registry. The King was due to be crowned in two weeks. He left Morgan "quite reassured and comforted for the moment," judged Dawkins. "But to bulldoze E.R. for the moment is perhaps no great feat."

Morgan returned to Venice on June 13. His party sailed down the Italian coast to Naples, then went by train to Rome. Dawkins complained to Steele that "JPM . . . shows a marked inclination for the present at any rate, to pull out of business more and more and any arguments or facts to be put before him have to be compressed into small concentrated doses like patent medicine."

———

Junius Morgan had not begun to "pull out of business" until he was over seventy, then ceded complete control of the bank to his eager, competent heir. He had so carefully directed Pierpont's education and professional training that he did not seem, when he finally retired, to be giving anything up. He simply handed his authority on, and regarded his son's ascent with uncommon pride.

Pierpont was taking no comparable steps to fashion his son into an instrument of dynastic succession. He delegated authority to other men—Coster, Bacon, Perkins, Dawkins, Steele—but as he turned his attention away from work in the early years of the new century, he did not set up an alternate chain of command. His partners had to beg him, not always successfully, for direction and advice.

That a man so intent on shaping the American future should have done little to prepare for his own decline seems both paradoxical and fitting. He lived entirely, almost carelessly, in the present, and if he followed his anxieties about his health to their logical conclusion—that someday he was going to "wake up dead"—it fueled his sense of how much he still had to do. He had always wanted to do more than work. In his twenties and thirties he had taken periodic years off to explore Europe and restore his "nerves." Even in good health he insisted on annual sojourns abroad. In his sixties he had begun to direct his "Titanic" energies to collecting art, but he only partly wanted to let go of affairs at 23 Wall Street. After George Perkins rescued a railroad in the South from manipulation by Bet-a-Million Gates in April 1902, Jack noted shrewdly that "the Senior pretends to feel disgusted that JPM & Co. should be called upon always when there comes a question of saving the situation." Morgan wanted the huge responsibilities he had shouldered all his life, along with the acclaim they brought; he also wanted freedom to do as he pleased.

In New York that summer, with minimal guidance from "the Senior," Perkins put together another big consolidation. The sons of Cyrus Hall McCormick, inventor of the reaper, had asked him to help end competitive warfare between farm-equipment makers in the Middle West—chiefly, Deering Harvester and McCormick Harvesting Machine. (The William Deering family had no relation to John Deere & Co., which made steel plows.) Morgan did not think the bank needed this business, but agreed by cable from Europe to take it on if the other partners approved. Perkins merged the two rivals into the International Harvester Company, for a $3 million fee, and reported: "The new company is to be organized by us; its name chosen by us; the state in which it shall be incorporated is left to us; the Board of Directors, the Officers, and the whole outfit left to us."

Morgan's response was lukewarm: "Plan seems satisfactory and safe. Approve signing preliminary contract if you all agree."

Perkins had in fact engineered a coup. This combination controlled nearly 85 percent of the American reaper and harvester market, and began earning profits once it fully centralized operations in 1906. When a threat of antitrust prosecution arose in 1907, Roosevelt headed it off, convinced (partly in response to adroit lobbying from Perkins) that Harvester represented the "good" kind of trust.

———

Roosevelt had appointed Jack first secretary of a Special American Embassy for the coronation of Edward VII, scheduled to take place at Westminster Abbey on June 26, 1902. Noting the younger Morgan's taste for all things royal, Dawkins sighed to Steele, "How you Republican gentlemen like a King!"

Jack was bitterly disappointed when a precoronation ball at Windsor Castle had to be canceled at the last minute because "the inconvenient old King of Saxony had to go and die. . . . [R]eally its hard to forgive," he told his mother. "There has not been a ball at Windsor for something like 70 years." The republican Anglophile was not impressed with the royal family's organizing skills: no one seemed to be in charge of the coronation preparations, invitations were going to the wrong people, the King refused to delegate responsibility and kept making last-minute changes—Jack thought "what they need is a sort of British JPM to arrange all the details for them."

The American JPM arrived from Paris with Anne on June 20 to celebrate the crowning of his friend Edward Rex. Jack stopped grousing when a shocking piece of news interrupted the dress rehearsal at Westminster Abbey on June 24: court physicians had just performed an emergency royal appendectomy. The King was recovering, but the coronation had to be indefinitely postponed.

———

The senior Morgan remained in London for a few days, then went off to Kiel to keep his long-standing appointment with Kaiser Wilhelm. Anne described the trip to her mother by mail. On Tuesday, July 1 their party (which probably included the Markoes and Adelaide) left Dover on *Corsair* in a cold fog, sailing north. That night they ran into a "nasty sea and rolled so hard we almost came up the other side. As a result the boat which had been put in apple pie order got soaked through & through," and the passengers stayed in their cabins till noon. In calmer weather, *Corsair* steamed up the Elbe River and through the Nord-Ostsee Canal, arriving at Kiel around midnight.

"The next morning Mr. Ballin of the Hamburg American appeared and Father received his orders to go in the [Kaiser's new yacht] *Hohenzollern* for an audience at ten which he proceeded to do." The American financier and the German Emperor had not previously met. Wilhelm was the smaller and slighter of the two, at five feet nine and 155 pounds. A birth injury had left him with a withered left arm—photographs and portraits invariably show him from the right, with his weak hand tucked into a pocket or behind his back—and the crushing right handshake with which he greeted guests seemed designed, like Morgan's defiant glare, to override his deformity.* Wilhelm wore a heavily decorated military uniform, tall black boots, and his mustache waxed up into stiff points.

The British royals were not alone in finding him pompous, intemperate, and obnoxious. His cousin the Russian Empress Alexandra loathed him, as did the aged Bismarck. His mother, whom he had repudiated and deprived of her palace and fortune, did not want him at her deathbed. Still, the German diplomat Count Eulenberg thought "his artlessness and disinterested friendliness give him a quite peculiarly fascinating charm, and he is one of those people who by their very nature arouse spontaneous sympathy." Others said he brought out the best in people to whom he directed his attention, and had "magnetic power" in conversation.

Morgan, reported Anne, was "most impressed by the Kaiser who, however, walked him up & down the deck for an hour and a half while he was talking." She added the "however" because she knew exactly how little her father liked physical exertion, though he could hardly refuse to keep pace with his host. Striding up and down the broad *Hohenzollern* deck, Wilhelm held forth all morning on the International Mercantile Marine. He acknowledged that he had not thought it "unfair to make a little trouble" between Britain and the United States over ships: "We must all woo your great Republic," he said, "and the English thought they had advanced so far in your regard over the Spanish War that it was fair to disturb [the] attachment."

Dawkins, reporting this conversation to Milner (he probably had it directly from Morgan), reflected: "I think that they understand these things in America. They keep a very close watch and a not unapprehensive watch on Germany in Washington where they seem to be well posted in foreign affairs in spite of (or because of) having no regular diplomatic service."

Morgan for the moment constituted the irregular diplomatic service. He left the imperial yacht at 11:30 A.M., and returned for lunch at one. Two other American representatives of the IMM, Clement Griscom and P.A.B. Widener, had come to this informal summit conference as well, and while Morgan con-

---

* The traumatic birth that had damaged his arm had probably also deprived his brain of oxygen for several crucial minutes, which medical experts suggest may have caused his "hyperactivity and emotional lability."

tinued his discussions with the Kaiser, Alfred Ballin took the Widener, Griscom, and *Corsair* parties to lunch at the Kiel Yacht Club. Traveling with the Griscoms, reported Anne to her mother, was "Mrs. Nat Goodwin Maxine Elliott!!!!!!" The exclamation points probably had to do with the actress's celebrity, for if Anne suspected, as other people did, that her father was having an affair with this famous beauty, she would not have gushed about it to Fanny.

Anne soon had an even more thrilling encounter. "At three o'clock the Kaiser, Von Bülow, his aide de camp and an admiral all came on board the Corsair and stayed an hour and a half, and no words can say how perfectly delightful he made himself. Of course we were all scared to death and didn't know what to do, but he hates ceremony of any kind when he is off that way and insisted upon doing everything as if he was one of us. As to his looks, he isn't a bit like his photographs or portraits there isn't one of them that begins to be strong enough. His eyes are perfectly marvelous[,] very blue & they look you through and through. Well I tell you it was the shortest hour and a half I ever spent."

If the Kaiser had not thought it unfair to "make a little trouble" between Britain and the United States over ships, Morgan clearly did not think it unfair to put a little pressure on the British with this display of friendship between the American architects of the IMM and the German high command.

The next morning the entire American contingent, traveling as the Emperor's guests, left Kiel for a tour conducted by Ballin. "You must have seen some account of it in the papers," wrote Anne to her mother, "but no description could half tell you how funny it was. All the party driving around Hamburg in about seven landaus—an enormous lunch of thirty at the smart restaurant & a really beautiful dinner and fête at the Ballins" in honor of the American Fourth of July, with speeches and fireworks. "Then the next morning a special steamer around the harbor—brass band on board & all the Hamburg line boats dressed with flags. Then the train to Berlin – another unending banquet there . . . and finally to bed."

In Berlin, Morgan called on Wilhelm von Bode, the director of the Kaiser Friedrich Museum, which Wilhelm II had dedicated to the memory of his father. Bode was an expert on Western European art from the medieval period through the seventeenth century, especially early Italian sculpture and Dutch Baroque painting. For Prussia's new imperial museum he was building encyclopedic collections of masterpieces from all over the world, like those at the Louvre and the Kunsthistoriches Museum in Vienna—also models for the patrons of the Metropolitan in New York. Bode took Morgan on a tour of the Berlin museum that July, with special attention to its early Raphael Madonnas, and agreed to provide his guest with occasional scholarly advice.

On Sunday, July 6, continued Anne, "we were up and doing about 9:30 for Potsdam—did all three castles there & out all afternoon which had been mapped out by the Kaiser and came back to Berlin total wrecks." There the tour ended, and Morgan's party went back through Paris to London.

Anne worried that this "wild jag" had tired her father, "though I know he has enjoyed it all very much and seems very well."

Meeting them in London, Jack thought the trip had *not* done his father much good—"He is always imprudent in his eating habits and his liver has been somewhat upset which naturally makes him rather blue. Moreover he thinks he has lost some weight which always alarms him."

Neither fatigue from the trip nor alarm about his weight curtailed Morgan's London social life. He gave lunch and dinner parties when he was not dining out, and took friends to see his Raphael altarpiece at the National Gallery and his Fragonards at the Guildhall. Dawkins, trying to get him to focus on the IMM, complained to Perkins in mid-July that "the Senior . . . refuses to attend to business. We never see him & it is difficult to get hold of him. He spends his time lunching with Kings or Kaisers or buying Raphaels."

The coronation of Edward VII had been rescheduled for August 9. Morgan rented a house along the procession route, planning to watch the spectacle from there with a party of friends, including the Markoes. Then he received an invitation to the service itself. At the end of July, the Satterlees arrived in London for the occasion with two-year-old Mabel. "Nan [Anne] and Father engaged up to the eyes," Louisa reported to Fanny, who remained in New York. Jack and Jessie would attend the ceremony as part of the official American delegation, and at the last minute English friends secured a ticket for Anne.

On the eve of the coronation, Morgan gave a small dinner at Princes Gate, and tried on the court suit he had "with much sorrow of mind induced himself to get," reported Anne—black velvet breeches and jacket with silver buttons, silk stockings, pumps, and a silver-hilted sword. Bereft of the three-piece suit and wide wing collar he wore like a uniform, he "fussed like mad" over the breeches, recalled the Markoes' daughter, Annette, and minded the sword, noted Anne, "worst . . . of all."

Early the next morning he once more decked himself out in velvet and silver while Anne's maids arranged her hair. Father and daughter left Princes Gate before eight, and proceeded by carriage to Westminster Abbey. Crowds had been gathering along the route all night. The Satterlees, Markoes, and Morgan's other guests watched from the house he had rented on Piccadilly—twenty to thirty people outside fainted in the August heat, reported Louisa. Inside the abbey Morgan took his seat in a gallery above the peeresses, with a clear view of the pageant; Anne was further back behind a choir screen, near Jessie and Jack.

Edward arrived at eleven-thirty. He had reserved a box for his female friends (court wits called it the King's Loose Box), including Sarah Bernhardt, Mrs. Arthur Paget, Lady Kilmorey, Feo Sturt, and his mistress, Alice Keppel. He later said that what impressed him most all day was "the simultaneous movement of the peeresses in putting on their coronets," since "their white arms arching over their heads" looked like "a scene from a beautiful ballet." Morgan was perfectly situated to appreciate the choreography.

The Abbey released the crowned monarch at three. Morgan paid calls all afternoon, and the next day gave a lunch at Dover House, an afternoon reception, and a dinner. Louisa, out of practice after two years of marriage, told Fanny that "Father's presence brings so much hurry and pressure it is really extraordinary!" Pierpont and Anne sailed for home on August 13, taking Dover House melons, peaches, and cream to supplement the White Star fare.

———

For a change—and for exactly the reasons it aroused foreign alarm—Morgan's shipping combine proved popular in the United States. *Scientific American* reported in July that "irrespective of the attitude of the American people toward trusts in general," news of the IMM had been greeted with "a distinct feeling of pride and satisfaction." Adding several hundred thousand tons to the U.S. merchant marine would give the country "a position of pre-eminence such as it has not enjoyed since the decadence of shipbuilding" after the Civil War.

Popular favor never turned into political support for a federal subsidy, however, and the Northern Securities case haunted the IMM. The Roosevelt administration was still "anxious to help us," cabled Steele from New York, but Attorney General Knox would not "make any suggestion" as to what form of organization would protect the new combine against antitrust prosecution. Though the bankers were sanguine about the ultimate outcome of Northern Securities—wrongly, as it turned out—they feared that organizing the IMM along similar lines would invite "attack" from the government and the press. Steele wired Morgan in August: "We are very anxious have benefit your views in every aspect business."

Morgan had put together U.S. Steel in twelve weeks. The negotiations over the IMM had dragged on for nearly two years. Impatient finally to set this deal in motion, he saw no point in equivocation: while he favored any measure "which will leave us less liable to attack, still everybody knows what we are trying to do, & nothing that we can do will ever hide it from them."

Objections to what Morgan was generally "trying to do" came from several quarters that summer. Gaspard Farrer at Barings, who had fatalistically accepted the shipping trust in the spring, told Hill in July that "our friend JPM" had "set a bad example in his big paper capitalizations of recent years & a worse one in exacting commissions for his firm on deals in which he is really the dominant factor on both sides of the table." Still, Farrer added, "he is a leader among men & worth the whole lot of that miserable mean money grubbing clique of slanderers who are incessantly on the watch to ruin him."

William Nelson Cromwell, a partner in Sullivan and Cromwell, the New York law firm hired by the McCormicks to assess their harvester deal, said that Morgan recklessly inflated securities for his own profit, and warned his clients to take care lest "you be uchred [*sic*] out of your boots."

An American not worried about his boots gave himself a sixty-seventh-birthday party at the Metropolitan Club that December. He made up place cards with an engraved self-portrait, and wrote on one: "J. Pierpont Morgan. For financial advice apply without diffidence to Mark Twain."

———

The British government accepted the IMM over the summer of 1902, reluctantly concluding that it had no choice. Its minister in Washington, Sir Julian Paunceforte, warned in June—Dawkins told Milner—that without the Morgan trust an "avowedly hostile combine" would have been formed in the United States "to run our ships off the Atlantic and squeeze them . . . by cooperation with the railways, out of U.S. ports." At the same time, the Liberal Party leader Sir Edward Grey advised (again paraphrased by Dawkins) that "we had better go into partnership with [Morgan] and through him with the American people." In August, the leading Conservative opponents of the trust—Joseph Chamberlain, Lord Selborne, the head of the Admiralty, and Gerald Balfour, president of the Board of Trade—urged the government to "avoid unnecessary friction with the Morgan Combination, and in particular to abstain from action likely to stir up national animosities." The Conservative Prime Minister, Lord Salisbury, resigned in early August, and was succeeded by his nephew, Arthur James Balfour. At the beginning of September, Dawkins went to Scotland for a weekend with the "brothers Balfour"—the new Prime Minister and the president of the Board of Trade—to draw up an agreement between the house of Morgan and His Majesty's government.

The Morgan bank promised to protect British interests in the shipping trust for fifty years—on roughly the terms Morgan had promised Chamberlain and "Edward Rex."* Gerald Balfour told the bankers as he prepared to present this "treaty" to the public at the end of September that he had "every desire make announcement in terms satisfactory to JPM." He succeeded. The firm replied,

---

* The agreement stipulated that British ships in the combine would continue to sail under British flags and carry British crews; that half of all new IMM tonnage would be built in Britain by Pirrie's Harland & Wolff; that no British ships, including new ones built by the combine, would be transferred to foreign registry without the consent of the president of the Board of Trade; and that the Admiralty could draft IMM ships on thirty hours' notice. The Americans agreed not to grant preferential rates to the U.S. rail freight carried on IMM ships. In exchange for all this, the government agreed to give the British lines in the combine the same mail and freight privileges it granted to other British carriers.

"JPM & CED [Dawkins] much gratified by [Balfour's] speech. . . . JPM has every confidence that HM Government will derive increasing satisfaction from establishing of community of interest on Atlantic between two countries." Parliament approved the agreement. The IMM was finally incorporated as a New Jersey holding company in early October 1902—as Morgan helped Roosevelt settle the anthracite coal strike.

The Anglo-American trust owned nearly one fifth of the scheduled tonnage in the North Atlantic trade. It controlled 136 ships and 1,074,884 gross register tons, and was allied with another 329 ships and 1,736,091 gross tons through the Germans. Operating forty-five routes between Europe and North America, and running freight carriers from England to South Africa, Australia, New Zealand, and the West Indies, it owned London office buildings, Liverpool repair shops, and docking facilities in major European and American ports. In 1902 it began to build five new piers on the Hudson River.

Though the British government acceded to this spectacular assertion of American economic prowess, it held out in one crucial respect: it paid Cunard, White Star's chief rival for transatlantic passenger service, *not* to join the combine. Cunard received a £2.4 million loan at low rates, and a subsidy of £150,000 a year to build the largest new passenger steamships in the world, the *Lusitania* and the *Mauritania*, with modern turbine engines and hulls built to the specifications of the Royal Navy. To match this challenge, White Star commissioned three expensive "big ships" of its own in 1907: the *Olympic*, the *Britannic*, and the *Titanic*.

———

In trying to create a community of interest on the Atlantic, Morgan and his partners failed to take into account not only the national self-interest of foreign states but also the economics of the seasonal, cyclical shipping trade—which one contemporary analyst called about "as shifting and unstable as the sea"—and their timing could not have been worse. The IMM bought its expensive components just as maritime transport headed into a decline that ended only with World War I. Leyland's managers, probably gauging the excess capacity and foreseeing a downturn, had sold out at the top of the market for $11 million *cash*. The expansion-minded managers of the other lines, gaining access to the bankers' deep pockets, leaped at the chance to order new tonnage.

Having based the combine's financial structure "largely on conjecture" since they could not get accurate accountings from White Star, the Morgan partners immediately found themselves saddled with huge "unforeseen commitments." Dawkins complained to Steele early in 1903 that "what threatens to swamp us is this monstrous indebtedness for shipbuilding, and I don't feel satisfied that we are not putting more big ships into the Atlantic than it can bear." Pirrie, whose yard got the commissions, had "dilated a great deal on the earning capacity of these new boats," but Dawkins was inclined to agree with those who had dubbed IMM "the Pirrie Relief-Bill."

The drop in shipping revenues that coincided with the organization of the IMM persuaded its backers not to apply for listing on the Stock Exchange. Brokers traded some of the stock off the Exchange, at prices far lower than those factored into the deal: in December 1902 the preferred opened at 55, the common at 15. And the increased earnings Morgan had expected from consolidation never materialized. White Star alone showed a profit in the IMM's first year of operation; steep losses on all the other lines forced the trust to forgo dividends on both classes of its stock.

Severe stringency in the U.S. money markets made the situation worse. In 1902 Treasury Secretary Leslie Shaw pumped $57 million into circulation, but his central-bank-style intervention failed to avert a contraction. The end of the year saw heavy liquidation in the stock market as banks called in loans. Morgan remained bullish in public, assuring *The New York Times* in March 1903 that the lack of confidence was "not justified by the facts" but had to do with a surfeit of "undigested securities." In private, he arranged with George Baker and James Stillman to set up a $50 million reserve fund in case of a crisis.

In April the U.S. Circuit Court sitting in St. Paul declared Northern Securities an illegal combination in restraint of trade; the company's lawyers immediately appealed to the Supreme Court.* Morgan's assurances did not halt the dumping of stocks, and the market crashed that fall in what came to be known as the "Rich Man's panic." Banks and businesses failed; railroads cut back on orders for iron and steel; U.S. Steel common fell to $10 a share (its high for the year had been $39⅞) and stopped paying dividends.

Roosevelt, coming up for reelection in 1904 and probably eager to burnish his antibusiness reputation, blamed the market unease on "the speculative watering of stocks on a giant scale in which Pierpont Morgan and so many of his kind have indulged during the last few years." The banker/publisher Henry Clews agreed, citing "revelations of fraud, chicanery, and excessive capitalization," but pointed out that the bankers' aggressive mergers had launched the country on "an unprecedented industrial boom." *The Commercial & Financial Chronicle* attributed the crash to the recent Northern Securities decision, which threatened "the prosperity of by far the greatest industry in the land." As usual, no one really knew what caused the panic, and everyone assigned rea-

---

* In September the judge in the Minnesota lawsuit held that the company violated no state laws. That decision, too, was appealed to the Supreme Court.

sons of his own. The contraction hit bottom in August 1904, after which the economy embarked on a new expansion.*

———

The IMM syndicate had put up 25 percent of its $50 million cash commitment at the end of April 1902, and the calls continued all year, amounting to 100 percent by July 1903. There was no market for the bonds. Morgan kept extending the syndicate's life, but when he finally closed the account in July 1906, its members held almost 80 percent of the $50 million in bonds. His firm tried to dull their pain by calling for IMM payments right after disbursals of Steel syndicate earnings, since many subscribers belonged to both groups. To people who thought Morgan operations involved easy profit and no real risk, the IMM—like the failed Steel bond-conversion plan—was vivid evidence to the contrary.

The Morgan bank had set the IMM syndicate fee at 25,000 shares of preferred and 250,000 shares of common stock, and its own management fee at one fifth of that—5,000 preferred, 50,000 common. In the markets of May 1902, with the stock expected to trade at 85 and 35, the fees were theoretically worth about $11 million; when the stock opened later that year at 55 and 15, the earnings had fallen to $5 million, and no one was buying shares. By the end of 1903, the preferred was quoted at 18, the common at 5. When Morgan closed the syndicate account in 1906, his firm made up a $17,000 deficit.

J. P. Morgan & Co. had earned nearly $23.3 million in 1902, largely from launching U.S. Steel; that figure remained the record during Pierpont's lifetime. In the contraction of 1903, the firm posted a loss of over $3.5 million, with the IMM accounting for nearly two thirds ($2.3 million) of the deficit. There is no record of the bank's IMM losses over the long term. A rough guess would be that, net of fees, it lost under $3 million—not an inconsiderable sum, but not, for Morgan, nearly as damaging as the injury to his reputation.

George Perkins's New York Life Insurance Company had taken a $4 million share in the IMM syndicate. At the end of 1903, the investment was worth only about $3 million, and Perkins was not eager to have the decline appear on the company's books; he also did not want to sell the bonds at a loss. He therefore "sold" $800,000 of New York Life's IMM bonds to J. P. Morgan & Co. at his

———

* In early October 1903, two months after he denounced Morgan's speculative stock-watering, Roosevelt sent a note to "My dear Mr. Morgan," asking him to stop in at the White House when he next came to Washington, as "I should very much like to see you to talk over certain financial matters." Morgan replied from New York that "I should like extremely to have an interview with you," but in "the serious condition of affairs in this City"—the crash and its immediate consequences—"it is absolutely impossible for me to leave." Roosevelt said there was no hurry—"I wished to speak to you about certain matters of financial legislation," but it could wait.

purchase price on December 31; a few days later, safely into 1904, he bought them back for the same price. As a result, New York Life's 1903 annual report showed only $3.2 million in IMM bonds and an $800,000 increase in cash. This sleight of hand was not lost on Charles Evans Hughes, the lawyer for a New York State committee that investigated the insurance business in 1905.

———

The IMM never gained control of shipping. It owned 20 percent of the scheduled North Atlantic tonnage, and its German allies owned another 47 percent—about the same share of the market U.S. Steel had. In shipping, however, 67 percent did not restrain price wars or dominate the market. The large investment required to build a fleet of ships created a barrier to entry but not an insuperable one, largely because there were no rights of way or tracks to confer control, and other lines were already servicing the Atlantic trade. The British government twice handicapped the trust—by prohibiting the use of preferential rates on U.S. cargo, and by subsidizing Cunard, which forced the IMM to spend vast sums it was not earning to build competitive ships. And finally, the IMM was set up as a loose holding company that never managed to cut costs by integrating its constituent parts or rationalizing operations.

Dawkins had been urging such economies for months, and at the end of 1902 he angrily pointed out how little was being done to make the new enterprise work. "Apparently none of us can arrive at being credited with the understanding that the mere fact of the IMMCo. being organized does not provide an inexhaustible source of revenue," he protested to his New York partners, and struck the note Morgan himself had sounded often before: "If we cannot grasp the urgency of economy it is perhaps easier to understand [that we have a] certain moral responsibility for the success of the business owing to the fact that we are in many ways connected with it." The managers of the companies were "not disposed to go well in harness," and someone—clearly Griscom was not doing the job—had to take charge.

Stepping up his sarcasm, Dawkins went on: "It is comforting to find that there is no need to trouble about the theory of the business, all that is sufficient being to realize that 'the IMMCo. is a great and good institution.' Such simple medicine is, however, not good enough for all children, including the unintelligent Government here which wants to know, as does [the firm's solicitor] Mr. Crisp, exactly where things stand." And he concluded: "I have no doubt we shall be able to fix matters up, but I fear it would be difficult to ask the Government merely to fold its hands and rest content, as I have much pleasure in doing, with an apostolic assurance that the 'IMMCo. is a great and good institution.' "

Perhaps something more than apostolic assurance could have been applied to the problem if Morgan had been attentively minding the store. By 1902 he was more interested in Raphaels than in balance sheets, and he believed so firmly in the efficacy of combination and the power of abundant capital that he failed to come to terms with recalcitrant facts.

In June of 1903, Dawkins wrote to Gerald Balfour about the wording of the IMM agreement. Their "New York friends" had taken alarm at its "phraseology" in light of that spring's Northern Securities decision: "To put it plainly," said Dawkins, "the blessed word 'combination' is what frightens them, as to use the word . . . in America causes as much disturbance now as the singing of the Marseillaise did under the Third Empire." Morgan shared this apprehension, but was "quite certain that the Government would never wish to cause him any difficulty by insisting on a mere matter of phraseology if the substance can be as well expressed in another manner."

Morgan's certainty that Washington would not cause him trouble over wording may have come from high sources, but the government in this case was not the problem. By the end of 1903 the international financial world recognized the shipping trust as a disaster. Jack reported to his father from London that the air was "thick with rumors about your retirement," and early in 1904 Henry Adams wrote, "Pierpont Morgan's collapse is greatly to be regretted—says Oliver Payne—because he is the last Christian banker in exchanges." Dawkins told Steele that "if the [IMM] *cannot* come right . . . we may as well put up our shutters." He thought it *would* come right in the end, but signed himself, "Yours truly & of a desperate courage."

Early in 1904 Morgan tried what had worked for other troubled corporations—hiring better management. He asked Albert Ballin, who he surely knew was Jewish, to take over as president of the trust; the Hamburg-Amerika director declined the offer "chiefly on account of my relations with the Kaiser," while noting that Morgan was finding it "impossible to get the right men to take their places." Morgan finally replaced the ineffectual Griscom with the difficult White Star chairman J. Bruce Ismay, saying that he "did not mind losing money, but he did object to doing so owing to poor organisation." Shouldering "moral responsibility" for the floundering combine, he promised Ismay that if the company did not earn enough to pay its fixed charges, he would make up the deficiency for the next three years.

With Griscom out, Morgan moved the company headquarters from Philadelphia to New York. He did make up the deficits, but neither his subsidy nor Ismay's presidency saved the IMM.

Ironically, the existence of the American-dominated trust *stimulated* foreign competition, and for the next ten years the ships of rival nations—not only Cunard, but the scheduled freight lines and tramp steamers of other countries as well—vied with the IMM for traffic in the North Atlantic lanes. *The Wall Street Journal* concluded: "The ocean was too big for the old man."

The old man refused to believe that the IMM would not "come right." Three months before he died, he objected to a description of the shipping trust as "ill-fated." "It's *not* ill-fated," he told his librarian. "They say that because they can't see beyond their noses or the daily ticker. America's future is international and the Mercantile Marine is part of that future. . . . Speaking of the ticker, some day you'll see this stock at *par*. Maybe I will too, but *you* watch."

America's future *was* international, but the Mercantile Marine never became part of it. The company defaulted on its bonds in 1914, and went into receivership a year later. Saved temporarily by World War I, it eventually sold off its foreign holdings, reorganized as the United States Lines, ceased to exist as an operating company in 1937, and went bankrupt again in 1986.

PART IV

PATRON

[Morgan's] urge for collecting came naturally to him and had nothing to do with a concern to improve his social standing, as was the case with Frick, since Morgan already belonged to the elite. He was really interested in all kinds of art . . . especially those not readily accessible to the general public, such as early manuscripts, medieval jewelry, enamels, Chinese porcelains, etc. Paintings, usually the most obvious field for a collector, interested him least, although in his library he was surrounded by masterpieces of the early Renaissance.

Reminiscences of William R. Valentiner

This afternoon I visited J. P. Morgan's [London] house. It looks like a pawnbroker's shop for Croesuses.

Bernard Berenson to Isabella Stewart Gardner,
November 1906

*Rendering of Mr. Morgan's Library (now The Pierpont Morgan Library),
from the office of the architects McKim, Mead & White, about 1902.*
(Archives of The Pierpont Morgan Library, New York)

Chapter 24

—

COLLECTOR

Clinton Dawkins had sketched a vivid picture of Morgan's "inclination to pull out of business" in the summer of 1902: all facts had to be put before him in "small concentrated doses like patent medicine." Leaving his partners to do most of the firm's work in London and New York, Morgan was fully caught up in a romance with art that combined his cultural nationalism, interest in history, sensuous response to beauty, and love of acquisition. Operating on an imperial scale in the early twentieth century, he seemed to want all the beautiful things in the world. There was what the French cultural critic Jean Baudrillard has called "a strong whiff of the harem" about this kind of collecting—a sense of intimacy "bounded by seriality," a wish to stand alone surrounded by exquisite objects like the "sultan of a secret seraglio."

There was also a charged relationship to past and future. Ownership of art, like intense romantic love, is inherently transitory. As Morgan appropriated treasures of the world's great civilizations, he seemed to be engaged in a drama of rescue, gathering works that had been widely dispersed and giving them orderly new contexts under his own name. Royal patrons and the Church had owned these objects in the past; in the twentieth century they would be housed in American galleries and museums. Inscribing himself into the lineage of art, Morgan followed Medicis, Chigis, Hapsburgs, Bonapartes, pharaohs, popes, and kings. The objects he acquired would be known as Morgan's Gutenbergs, the Morgan Apocalypse, the Morgan Fragonards—until someone else acquired them. The fleeting nature of possession enhanced its potent appeal.

His choices for acquisition seemed modeled to some extent on the Royal Library at Windsor and the Wallace Collection. The library of the British royal family had taken its modern form in the 1830s, when William IV concentrated on early printed books (Caxton's 1484 edition of *Aesop's Fables*, the Mainz Psalter of 1457), maps, portrait miniatures, herbals, watches, clocks, Old Master drawings, and Napoleonic memorabilia. The Wallace Collection, formed largely by the fourth Marquess of Hertford (1800–1870) and supplemented by his illegitimate son, Sir Richard Wallace, opened to the public in 1900, but Morgan had probably seen it earlier; exhibited at Hertford House on London's Manchester Square were room after room of paintings, porcelains, tapestries, Renaissance bronzes, eighteenth-century French furniture and decorative arts, majolica, ivories, portrait miniatures, arms and armor, and gold- and silversmiths' work. The Windsor and Wallace collections had been assembled by many hands over the course of decades. Morgan amassed his collections, with the help of scholarly advisers, in twenty years.

He bought with such avidity that there was no time, even had he had the inclination, for studious contemplation of individual pieces. One winter he came across a receipt for a bust of the infant Hercules, ostensibly by Michelangelo, for which he had paid £10,000. He sent the bill to his librarian with a note asking where the sculpture was. "This bronze Bust is in your library," she wrote in green ink across the bill, "and faces you when sitting in your chair. It has been there about a year."*

Beyond the "lifetime of organized self-indulgence" that found its fullest expression in collecting was Morgan's larger project—to harvest "the best" of the world's cultural past for the American future. In stocking U.S. institutions with great works of literature and art, he was providing historical records, setting scholarly standards, and marking directions for future research.

———

In the early 1900s Morgan kept most of his acquisitions in England—some on loan to museums, others at Princes Gate. He had opened the house for private viewing in 1901: among the first visitors to see his collections were Lady Victoria Sackville-West, the Duchesses of Wellington and Westminster, Baron Rothschild, the Duke of Marlborough, the Harcourts, Alice Mason, John Singer Sargent, Joseph Duveen, P.A.B. Widener, George Baker, and James Bryce. In the 1870s Morgan had toured the art galleries of England's great country houses, including the Sackvilles' Knole Park in Kent; thirty years later he invited British aristocrats to examine his own collections in town.

* It turned out not to be by Michelangelo, and is now on display at the Morgan Library as probably seventeenth-century Flemish.

He had financial as well as cultural reasons for keeping the collections abroad. The U.S. government's 1897 Revenue Act had imposed a 20 percent tariff on imported works of art. After the Treasury charged Isabella Stewart Gardner $200,000 on $1 million worth of art she brought to the United States in 1898, other collectors and the dealers who sold to them went to great lengths to avoid the customs "dragnet."*

The Revenue Act contained a significant exception, however. Books and manuscripts could come to America duty-free as long as they were used for religious, educational, scientific, philosophical, or literary purposes. Not more than two copies could be listed in any one invoice, and the items could not be offered for sale. Since Morgan was buying single copies of rare books and manuscripts that he did not intend to sell, he could bring his literary collections to the United States without paying the import tax.

His scholarly nephew, Junius, may have encouraged him to concentrate his New York holdings on manuscripts and books. Though Morgan probably regarded himself as heir to the Italian Renaissance patrons who commissioned illuminated manuscripts and built magnificent libraries to house their collections of classical, humanistic, and religious texts, he had American predecessors in book collecting as well—among them the Drexels, Theodore Irwin (whose library he had bought in 1900), Robert Hoe, Henry Walters, James Lenox, and Samuel Tilden.[†]

By the turn of the century Morgan had brought to New York more books and manuscripts than his study at 219 could hold. He stored some of them in his cellar and others at the Lenox Library uptown, but saw no point in having all these precious materials locked inaccessibly away. In 1900 he had begun to think about building a private library, and asked Whitney Warren, the designer of the New York Yacht Club, to draw up plans. When Warren submitted a set of florid Beaux Arts sketches, however, Morgan shelved the project.

---

* The Revenue Act of 1897 exempted works of art that were exhibited for educational purposes to the public, and Mrs. Gardner tried to claim that exemption. The Customs Office ruled against her in 1904 on the ground that severe restrictions on admission to her museum—she allowed a limited number of people to view her collections four days a month—disqualified it as a "public" institution.

† Lenox had in 1870 commissioned Richard Morris Hunt to design a library for his rare books and manuscripts at Fifth Avenue and 70th Street (now the site of the Frick Collection). Former New York Governor Tilden at his death in 1886 had left twenty thousand books and the bulk of his estate to establish a free library and reading room in New York. These two collections merged with a third, endowed by the will of John Jacob Astor, to form the New York Public Library in 1895. Between 1897 and 1911 the firm of Carrère & Hastings built the Public Library on the former site of the Croton Reservoir at 42nd Street and Fifth Avenue, a few blocks from Morgan's house.

Then one night in late March 1902—as he was in the midst of lobbying Congress for a shipping subsidy, putting together the provisional IMM syndicate, testifying about Northern Securities, and authorizing Perkins to set up the bond-conversion plan for U.S. Steel—he telephoned Charles Follen McKim, the leading proponent of Italian Renaissance architecture in the United States, and asked him to stop by 219 the next morning.

McKim lived nearby, at 9 East 35th Street. When he arrived at Morgan's for breakfast on Thursday, March 27, his host said that he had bought most of the land on the north side of 36th Street between his own house and Park Avenue, and wanted to build a private library in the middle and a house for the Satterlees at the far end. The library should be a simple, classical structure set in a garden, with ample space for his growing collections and a study in which he could meet with business colleagues, art dealers, and friends. Would McKim design both buildings?

Like countless other sudden Morgan commissions, this one took its recipient by surprise. McKim had been expecting to discuss a project of his own, the fledgling American Academy in Rome, for which he had just secured the banker's patronage. Still, he accepted the double assignment. "You can imagine my pleasure," he wrote to a friend that night, "not so much for this expression of confidence on [Morgan's] part, as for the assurance which it gives of his support of the Academy."

Morgan chose McKim, whom he had only recently met, over his partner, Stanford White, although White had designed two previous "Morgan" projects, Madison Square Garden and the Metropolitan Club. By 1902 McKim was widely regarded as the dean of American architecture: his style infused classical discipline with measured grandeur and opulence—perhaps better suited to Morgan's evolving taste than White's buildings, which gave rein to a lyrical, exuberant imagination. White's failing health (kidney disease) and extravagant lifestyle may have influenced Morgan's decision as well. The diligent, sober McKim had designed the Harvard Club, the University Club, and the new Columbia University campus on Morningside Heights; in 1902 he contracted to build a monumental Pennsylvania Railroad Terminal at Seventh Avenue and 33rd Street in New York, and to restore the White House for the Roosevelts (who changed its name from Executive Mansion to the term most Americans already used). Moreover, his aims for America's cultural education were very much in line with Morgan's own.

Having been been trained in the language of classical architecture, McKim wanted to establish a residential colony in Rome at which American artists and scholars could study the aesthetic achievements of the past. "We were starving for standards within reach to stimulate our taste and inspire emulation," he told a friend. "It is a pity that more artists will not consent momentarily to become students, and endeavor to grasp the spirit that produced Rome." The colony of American artists that made William Wetmore Story's Palazzo Barberini its informal headquarters had been studying the "spirit that produced Rome" for decades, sometimes with Morgan's financial help. Germany, France, Belgium, and Spain all sponsored academies in Rome—Louis XIV had established the French Academy at the Villa Medici in 1666. Unlike its nationally subsidized predecessors, however, the American study center would have to be privately financed, which was why McKim had asked Charles Lanier for an introduction to Morgan.

Morgan added his name to that of the Baltimore art collector Henry Walters on a fund-raising letter for the academy late in 1901. By the time he had breakfast with McKim in March of 1902, the list of supporters included John Hay, Elihu Root, Marshall Field, Charles Francis Adams, Jr., John LaFarge, Augustus Saint-Gaudens, the presidents of Harvard, Yale, Princeton, Cornell, Pennsylvania, Johns Hopkins, and the University of Chicago.

On April 2, five days after Morgan made his proposal to McKim, he sailed to Europe with Anne. Junius would oversee the library plans in his absence. Morgan stayed abroad for nearly five months, traveling with Adelaide and the Markoes, negotiating over the IMM, visiting the Kaiser and Bode, attending the coronation of Edward VII.

In Paris that April he bought a rare and magnificent longcase regulator clock made by the finest artisans of eighteenth-century France—the *ébéniste* Balthazar Lieutaud, the *horloger* Ferdinand Berthoud, and the bronzemaker Philippe Caffiéri, whose plaques and sculpture on the case represent Ovid's story of Apollo.* In May, through the Frankfurt dealers J. &. S. Goldschmidt, he purchased a collection of works by seventeenth-century German goldsmiths— including a sumptuously whimsical nautilus shell with a silver-gilt mount in the shape of a snail and an ostrich-shaped ewer with an ostrich egg for the belly, elaborate feathered goldwork for the neck, wings, and tail, and a detachable head for pouring wine. Goldschmidt assured Morgan that the owner of this collection, a director of the Dresdener Bank in Berlin named Gutmann, "never would have consented to sell . . . to such a low price except to Mr. Morgan, on account of the ready money, because dealers or Museums are not able to pay at once as Mr. Pierpont Morgan!" The "ready money" in this case was £75,000 ($375,000).

From Duveen in London that spring Morgan bought a tapestry that had belonged to Cardinal Mazarin for $340,000, a marble bas-relief of the Virgin and Child attributed to Donatello ($74,000), Dresden figures, and Louis XV and XVI gold and enameled snuffboxes. He acquired another Gainsborough por-

---

* It is now in the Frick Collection.

trait, *Mrs. Tennant,* from Charles Wertheimer for $150,000, and from Durlacher Brothers a Dürer drawing dated 1509, a Clodion statuette, and a superb collection of bronzes, for about $64,000. From the publisher George Allen he purchased major Ruskin manuscripts, including *The Stones of Venice,* for $82,000.

His forays in the cultural markets met with no more favor in England than his acquisition of shipping lines. During the uproar over the IMM that May, Gaspard Farrer at Barings wrote to James J. Hill: "Curiously enough [Morgan's] operations in pictures, tapestries & curios have done him more harm with the general public than steel or shipbuilding. Of the value of the latter they do not pretend to judge: but their imagination is struck when they hear of 2 to 10 times as much being given for curios as has ever been paid before. It is pathetic to see a man who has proved himself a real big man losing the respect of those to whom he should be a guide. One can only explain his recent operations on the ground that 'summat has gone wrong i' his head.'"

Morgan did not care how much he had to pay for important works of art— he once said that the three most expensive words in any language were *unique au monde.* He *was* throwing large sums of money around. He was also acquiring extraordinarily fine things. Just when his British critics concluded there was "summat wrong" with his head in June of 1902, he made the greatest of his en bloc book purchases (once again on the advice of Junius), the library of William Bennett of Manchester, for $700,000. Bennett himself had built on the work of other collectors, assembling incomparable illuminated manuscripts and six hundred early printed books—including thirty-two Caxtons and the Abbeville edition of Augustine's *City of God* (1486)—largely from the libraries of the Earl of Ashburnham and William Morris. Morgan eventually had a four-volume illustrated catalogue of this collection printed by the Chiswick Press in London, with commentary by scholar-experts: the palaeographer, medievalist, and biblical scholar M. R. James edited the volume on manuscripts, and the keeper of Printed Books at the British Museum, Alfred W. Pollard, prepared three volumes on early printed books.

———

Given the interest Morgan took in his possessions and surroundings, it is surprising that he never commissioned a house. Instead, as in his business consolidations and collecting, he built on foundations established by others. He completely remodeled Cragston and 219, closely supervising the architects and interior designers. For properties he did not use often—Camp Uncas, the Newport "fishing box," the apartment at Jekyl Island—he assumed ownership without much modification. The two English houses he inherited from his father he eventually altered to suit his own tastes. He did not even commission the initial design for his yachts, but hired engineers who gradually improved on the model of the first *Corsair.* The only structures he built de novo were his private library and Louisa's house.

For the library, as for the renovations at 219 and Cragston, he proved to be an exacting client who paid close attention to every detail of execution and design. Junius explained to McKim in May 1902 that his uncle wanted low bookcases with space for "bric-a-brac" on top and a librarian's office fitted out with shelves for catalogues and reference books. The building would not house a "reading library" but a collection of rare volumes—about ten thousand as of 1902, with more to come.

McKim sent preliminary sketches to England with the Satterlees when they left for the coronation in late July. Inspecting the drawings in haste, Morgan said that he wanted more light and air between the library and its surroundings, no part of the structure more than forty feet high, and greater use made of interior space, since he had twice as many books as initially calculated and might bring some of his art collections to the library as well—although he explicitly did *not* want it designed as a "picture gallery." Satterlee apologized to McKim for his "brutal brevity" in relaying these instructions, adding that Morgan "liked the dignity of your building & its purity of design & your ingenuity."

After Morgan returned to New York that August, he conferred regularly with his architect over breakfast at 219. McKim proposed to grind and file the structure's Tennessee marble blocks so that they fit together without mortar, like those of the Erechtheum on the Athenian Acropolis, which Morgan had just seen. Dry mortice and tenon joints would enhance the building's strength and durability, he told his client, but would be invisible and more expensive than conventional joints.

How much more expensive? Morgan asked.

Fifty thousand dollars, said McKim.

Fine, Morgan nodded: go ahead.

In the end, the extremes of the New York climate required McKim to introduce a film of lead one sixty-fourth of an inch thick into the horizontal beds, which made the seams somewhat more conspicuous than those of the Erechtheum. Still, the architect pronounced the vertical joints almost as good as "the best of the Greek, it being impossible to insert a knife blade into them."

Early estimates set the library's cost at about $850,000, but by the time the building was completed in 1906 the total came to $1.2 million. Morgan wanted the finest materials and techniques, and McKim was impressed at the "extraordinary and unexpected manner in which . . . Mr. Morgan closed his contracts for everything" from an antique wooden ceiling and Roman marble floors to lapis lazuli columns, bronze bookcases, Istrian marble mantelpieces, and a pair of sixteenth-century Paduan andirons. McKim himself went to Rome to find the mantelpieces and ceiling. When he could not travel, he relied on his and Morgan's mutual friend Waldo Story, who ordered antique marble slabs and a large porphyry disk for the library's floor, reported in detail on measurements, prices, and varieties of stone, and photographed the gardens and Roman buildings McKim was using as models.

Morgan kept making adjustments. He ordered a balustrade lowered, issued "blasts on the subject of the rear cornice," demanded the removal of five stones from the outer edge of the steps. Regarding the Satterlee house at 37 East 36th Street, Louisa noted in her diary at the end of 1903, "Father much upset by plan of stairs at 37. McKim apologetic as usual."

Augustus Saint-Gaudens warned McKim "not to allow J.P.M. to bully you; I think if you were to sass him back, he would respect you more . . . that's been my experience and you will thereby be more able to work in peace."

McKim probably never "sassed" his imperious client—whom he referred to as Lorenzo the Magnificent—but did on occasion curtail his eclecticism. He diplomatically reminded the traveling banker of their aesthetic theme by cable in the spring of 1904: "While fully recognizing great merit of Chateau D'Arnay chimney piece we should strongly recommend consistent Italian marble example in building of Italian Renaissance design."

One sweltering day that August, McKim took Morgan to the University Club to see the murals being painted on its ceiling by an American artist named Henry Siddons Mowbray. McKim had sent Mowbray to study in Rome, then persuaded him to stay on for a year as temporary director of the new American Academy. In May 1904 he commissioned the artist to paint the ceilings in Morgan's library, somewhat along the lines of the work in progress at the University Club. Morgan surveyed the painted bays and scaffolding at the University Club without a word. McKim finally broke the silence: "White is crazy over this work."

Morgan: "He is always crazy."

There was another long wait as the banker continued to scrutinize the ceiling. At last, reported McKim, he "expressed his admiration and entire satisfaction with the work, calling it both 'magnificent' and 'superb.' " Mowbray began work on the Morgan library ceilings that fall.

———

Henry Adams reported to Mrs. Cameron on one of his favorite topics early in 1903: "Pierpont's face is now too terrible to look at; the nose has spread. How our summer-roses fade!"

Morgan was no longer taking pains to keep his wife and Adelaide Douglas on opposite sides of the Atlantic. Adelaide had quietly separated from her husband—she remained at the house on East 46th Street when Mr. Douglas moved in 1903 to 71 Central Park West on the Upper West Side, far from "Morgan Hill." Morgan took her to Cuba that March, along with the Markoes, Anne,

Charles Lanier, and several other friends. Fanny accompanied the party by train to Washington, then went on with her maid and a companion to California.

Cuba had remained an occupied American protectorate between 1898 and 1902, when it signed a treaty granting the United States extensive political and economic control. Morgan, arriving by boat from Key West, told the Havana press he had come for a vacation, but once journalists learned he was staying with the owner of the Havana Steamship line they reported that he must be acquiring Cuban shipping companies for the IMM, buying railroads, or negotiating a government loan.

His bank did become the New York representative of the Banco Nacional de Cuba at about this time. He had a private interview one day with the new, American-educated Cuban President, Tomás Estrada Palma, and the following night dined with high-ranking Cuban politicians at the presidential palace. He and his friends saw a jai alai game and toured the island. No doubt he also stocked up on Cuban cigars. On March 6 he paid a long farewell visit to the President, who assured the Associated Press that there had been no discussion of an impending loan. That night Morgan took his party to a restaurant called El Louvre, and later stuck the menu, with the signatures "Adelaide T. Douglas" and "J. Pierpont Morgan" running down the fold between the wines on the left and food on the right, into a recipe book.

On the way north, the group stopped at Jekyl Island for several days, then went to Washington, where Morgan conferred with President Roosevelt for half an hour. He met as well with Senators Aldrich and Hanna, and lobbied Treasury Secretary Leslie Shaw for a reduction of the import duties on art, pointing out that it would cost him $3 million to bring his collections from London to the United States.

As workmen began construction on his library and the Satterlee house early that April, Morgan bought the Dodge mansion next door to his own, 225 Madison Avenue, for Louisa and Herbert to live in until their new quarters were ready. He celebrated his sixty-sixth birthday at home on April 17—Fanny was still in California—then sailed for Europe with Adelaide and Anne.

At Aix that May he purchased from the firm of the Frankfurt dealer Goldschmidt a manuscript that would become one of the treasures of his collection. It was a small illuminated book of hours by the miniaturist Giulio Clovio, finished in Rome in 1546, for Cardinal Alessandro Farnese, a grandson of Pope Paul III. Goldschmidt probably realized that everything about this masterpiece would appeal to Morgan: famous, sacred, exquisitely painted, and rich in historical associations, it had taken nine years to complete, and was encased in a dazzling gold and silver cover attributed to Cellini (though later found to be by Antonio Gentili). Vasari had described it in effusive detail as one of the "sights of Rome," an achievement "with the brush . . . so stupendous, that it does not appear possible to go so far with the eye or with the hand." Vasari anointed Clovio "a new, if smaller, Michelangelo."

According to William Voelkle, curator of medieval manuscripts at the Morgan Library, the Farnese Book of Hours—"justly regarded as the last great Italian manuscript"—is also "a superb mirror of Mannerist art," with "the *figura serpintinata* of Michelangelo and the elongated and sinuous forms of Pontormo. Mannerist, too, are the seemingly indefatigable love of surprise, the novelty, ingenuity, virtuosity, rampant complexity, scintillating color, and spatial effects." Twenty-six full-page miniatures offer pairs of Old and New Testament themes—a scene of the Magi adoring Christ faces the Queen of Sheba on her knees before Solomon. Into the latter page, Clovio has painted a portrait of Cardinal Farnese as Solomon, and another of himself looking out at the viewer as a dwarf in painter's clothes—a visual pun, Mr. Voelkle points out, since Clovio was a "miniature" painter. Morgan paid Goldschmidt £22,500 ($112,500) for the Farnese Hours and several pieces of Italian majolica. He so prized this new volume that he carried it home himself, and brought it out to show special guests in New York.

———

Buying more works of art and literature than he could house or even see, Morgan began to donate some of them to American public institutions. In 1899 he gave the nascent New York Public Library a collection of manuscripts, letters, and books that included correspondence by Noah Webster, Horace Greeley, Andrew Jackson, and James Monroe. Two years later he bought three collections of antique textiles for the new Cooper-Hewitt Museum, founded by the daughters of his old friend Abram Hewitt. And in 1902 he gave two thousand Chinese porcelains to the Metropolitan Museum of Art. This collection, assembled by the banker James A. Garland with the help of the Duveens, had for years been on loan to the Met. Museum officials hoped the loan would become a gift, but when Garland died in 1902 making no such bequest, Henry Duveen bought all two thousand pieces from the estate for $500,000. Morgan immediately repurchased them for $600,000, asked the dealer to fill out incomplete sequences, and left the Garland—now Morgan—Collection of Chinese porcelains on deposit at the museum without a single vase having been moved. His bills from Duveen Brothers in 1902 list over $200,000 worth of additional Chinese porcelains sent to the museum.

He was elected first vice president of the Met at the beginning of 1904, and immediately helped secure another important collection. That winter, his and Fanny's old friend Adele Stevens left her second husband, the Duc de Dino. On learning that this high-living French aristocrat, no longer supported by Adele's fortune, was looking to sell his famous collection of armor, Morgan cabled Rutherfurd Stuyvesant, a museum trustee and armor collector who lived half the year in Paris. Stuyvesant promptly called on Dino, agreed to a purchase price of $240,000, and made out a check, although he did not have that much money in his French bank. He wired Morgan, who called a meeting of the Met board in New York, solicited pledges for the necessary funds, and transferred $240,000 to Stuyvesant's account in time to cover the check. (The museum eventually repaid the trustees.) In April, Morgan's English partners shipped forty-three cases of the Duc de Dino's armor to the Metropolitan at freight rates, labeled "hardware."

The Metropolitan board elected Morgan president of the museum that fall, formalizing his position as one of the country's leading patrons of the fine arts. Well aware of the value of expertise in markets where risk ran high, Morgan immediately hired a young scholar named Bashford Dean to install and catalogue the Dino armor.

Dean was an authority on the evolution of fish. At Columbia University he had studied with the patriarch of North American paleontology, John Strong Newberry, and worked closely with Pierpont's nephew Henry Fairfield Osborn. Together, Dean and Osborn had founded Departments of Zoology at Columbia and of Vertebrate Paleontology at the American Museum of Natural History. As knowledgeable about arms and armor as he was about prehistoric fins, Dean specialized in the armored fishes of the early and middle Paleozoic age, particularly the gigantic Devonian *Dinichthys,* whose articulating, overlapping plates made it look like a direct ancestor of the medieval knight. He recognized the quality of the Dino collection as he began to unpack it in the basement of the Metropolitan, and congratulated Morgan on securing an exceptional prize at low cost.

Morgan assigned Dean to prepare a catalogue of all the armor at the Met, appointed him curator of Arms and Armor in 1906, and supported his courtship of an eccentric expatriate named William H. Riggs, whose armor collection was even larger and finer than Dino's. Riggs had been a classmate of Morgan's at Vevey (his father, Elisha, was an early partner of George Peabody's in Washington), and spent his life in Europe collecting armor. Morgan's accession to the Metropolitan presidency encouraged Riggs to regard the museum as the ultimate repository for his collection. The board made him an honorary trustee, and Morgan offered him a "magnificent" gallery in a new wing. Nonetheless, Riggs toyed with the Met for years.

In Paris in 1912, on the verge of finally making the gift, Riggs told Dean he was too preoccupied with a hotel he owned at Luchon in the Pyrenees to proceed. Dean crossed the Channel to consult Morgan in London, and reported the conversation to a colleague at the museum. The banker restated the curator's report: " 'So Mr. Riggs can't pack his collection and catalogue it because his mind is upset by troubles with his hotel property at Luchon?' (He took his cigar in his fingers, and his eyes blazed). 'How much would it cost to buy the property at once?' " Dean thought it would cost five to six hundred thousand francs ($25–30,000). "Well, buy it," Morgan ordered: "I'll take it and lose a couple of hundred thousand francs. Not a bad investment if the Museum gets a collection worth three millions of dollars!" Dean bought the hotel for 400,000 francs—in the end, Morgan charged the property to the museum—and Riggs gave the Met his unparalleled collection in 1913, largely, he said, out of admiration for Morgan.*

The development of the Arms and Armor Department under Morgan was characteristic of his administrative style—he hired an outstanding scholar, secured two choice collections, and established the department in 1912 (until then Arms and Armor had been part of Decorative Arts). Morgan had in 1907 bought for himself a black steel helmet made in 1543 by the Milanese Filippo Negroli, called the "Michelangelo of armorers." Jack Morgan gave this burgonet to the museum after his father died, and it ranks among the Arms and Armor Department's finest single pieces.

———

During Morgan's presidency the Metropolitan radically changed its orientation and scope. Its 1905 annual report announced that it would no longer accept random gifts that did not measure up to professional scholarly standards—as many of Morgan's own early gifts did not—nor would it display copies, casts, or amateur accumulations of unrelated objects. The aim of the institution would be "not merely to assemble beautiful objects and display them harmoniously . . . but to group together the masterpieces of different countries and times in such relation and sequence as to illustrate the history of art in the broadest sense."

The museum's operating budget, not including art purchases, rose under Morgan from $185,000 in 1904—most of which was covered by a $150,000 appropriation from the city—to $363,000 in 1913, which, even with larger city contributions, ran the museum $70,000 into the red. Morgan led the trustees in making up the annual deficit and packed the board with friends and colleagues, which assured him general cooperation, sage advice, and virtually unlimited access to cash.† He oversaw the professionalization of the administrative and curatorial staffs, the creation of new departments, the funding of archaeological excavations, the development and improvement of existing col-

———

* The Met did not manage to sell the Grand Hôtel de Luchon et du Casino until 1920, for just 150,000 francs.

† During his tenure George Baker, William Laffan, Henry Clay Frick, Henry Walters, George Blumenthal, John G. Johnson, William Church Osborn, Edward S. Harkness, and

**Junius Spencer Morgan, 1889
(nephew of Pierpont Morgan).**
*(University Archives. Department of Rare Books and
Special Collections. Princeton University Library)*

Dr. James W. Markoe, about 1897.
(Courtesy of the late Annette M. Schieffelin)

Annette B. Wetmore at Shelburne, Vermont (1889?).
(Courtesy of the late Annette M. Schieffelin)

Clockwise from top left: Charles H. Coster, Robert Bacon, Henry P. Davison, George W. Perkins.
(Archives of The Pierpont Morgan Library)

"Hold on Boys!"
(Morgan trying to prevent
a clash between capital
and labor, 1901).
(Culver Pictures, Inc.)

"The Break in the Coal
Strike." (Roosevelt and
Morgan meeting to resolve
the 1902 anthracite
coal strike).
(Culver Pictures, Inc.)

"The Field Marshall of Industry," 1902.
(The Granger Collection, New York)

Morgan and Mabel M. Satterlee at Dover House, 1902.
(Archives of The Pierpont Morgan Library)

Adelaide Townsend Douglas.
(Courtesy of the late J. Gordon Douglas, Jr.)

A dinner at Delmonico's. Clockwise from Morgan (third from left, rear): Adelaide Douglas, Lewis Cass Ledyard, Annette Markoe, Richard Young, Emily Woodbury, Charles Lanier, Kate Blaque, Isaac Townsend, Polly Iselin, Townsend Irvin, Sybil Douglas, Ernest Iselin, Tibbe Keene, George Pollock, unidentified woman and man, Isabel Ledyard.

(Courtesy of the late Annette M. Schieffelin)

219 Madison Avenue, with the Library at the far right.
(Archives of The Pierpont Morgan Library)

The Rotunda of the Library, with the Jean Barbet angel at left.
(Archives of The Pierpont Morgan Library)

Rembrandt, *Nicolaes Ruts*. Purchased by
Pierpont Morgan, 1898.
(Copyright The Frick Collection, New York)

Albrecht Dürer, *Adam and Eve*. Purchased by
Pierpont Morgan,1910, I, 257d.
(The Pierpont Morgan Library, New York)

Giulio Clovio, *Adoration of the Magi* and *Solomon Adored by the Queen of Sheba*, from
the Farnese Hours. Purchased by Pierpont Morgan, 1903, M.69, ff. 38v-39.
(The Pierpont Morgan Library, New York. Photo: David A. Loggie)

Two portraits of Morgan by Edward Steichen, 1903.
(Archives of The Pierpont Morgan Library, reprinted with permission of Joanna T. Steichen)

Richard T. Greener in New York (late 1880s?).
(Courtesy of the Harvard University Archives)

Elsie de Wolfe (upper right)
and Elisabeth Marbury at the
James Hazen Hyde Ball at
Sherry's, January 31, 1905.
*(Courtesy of the Museum
of the City of New York, Byron
Collection)*

House party at the Harcourts' Nuneham Park, 1907 (Morgan standing
on stairs, fourth from top; Edward VII seated at center).
(Archives of The Pierpont Morgan Library)

"The Magnet," *Puck* magazine.
(Archives of The Pierpont Morgan Library)

At the White Star pier, 1912.
(Archives of The Pierpont Morgan Library)

News photograph of Morgan (left) and William Howard Taft (right) receiving honorary degrees at Yale in June 1908. *(Copy furnished by Oliver Jensen)*

In Egypt, February 1912. From left: Lucy T. Lythgoe, Albert Lythgoe, Mrs. William Lawrence, Dr. John Kinnicut, Mrs. John "Tilly" Markoe, Pierpont Morgan, John L. Cadwalader, Bishop Lawrence. *(The Metropolitan Museum of Art. Photograph by the Egyptian Expedition)*

Morgan's funeral leaving St. George's Church, April 1913.
(Culver Pictures, Inc.)

lections, and a major architectural expansion designed by McKim, Mead & White. His own gifts substantially added to the Met's holdings, accentuating the need for more gallery space, and encouraged other donors to follow suit.

Henry James, who visited America in 1904–5 for the first time in nearly a quarter of a century, took note of the new spirit at the museum: "Education, clearly, was going to seat herself in these marble halls . . . and issue her instructions without regard to cost. The obvious, the beautiful, the thrilling thing was that, without regard to cost either, they were going to be obeyed." Taking a somewhat facetious view of America's purchasing power, James went on: "Acquisition—acquisition if need be on the highest terms—may, during the years to come, bask here as in a climate it has never before enjoyed. There was money in the air, ever so much money. . . . And the money was to be all for the most exquisite things—for *all* the most exquisite except creation, which was to be off the scene altogether. . . . The Museum, in short, was going to be great."

General Cesnola, who had been director of the Met since 1879, died just before Morgan assumed the presidency in the fall of 1904. To replace Cesnola early in 1905, the board hired the director of London's South Kensington Museum, Sir Caspar Purdon Clarke. Against the background of the IMM and Morgan's cultural raids, this acquisition gave rise to tales of British chagrin. The secretary at the South Kensington, returning from a leave of absence that winter, is said to have asked whether some porcelains the museum wanted had arrived. "No, sir," answered a clerk. "J. P. Morgan bought them." What about a set of tapestries bid on at the same time? "Mr. Morgan got them," was the reply. "Good God," said the secretary, "I must talk to Sir Purdon." "Sorry, sir," returned the clerk, "Mr. Morgan bought him also."

A second Englishman with whom Morgan opened negotiations early in 1905 was the art critic Roger Fry. As an undergraduate at Cambridge in the late 1880s, Fry had belonged to the Apostles, the secret discussion society whose past and future members included Tennyson, Arthur Hallam, Bertrand Russell, John Maynard Keynes, Lytton Strachey, E. M. Forster, and Leonard Woolf. Fry decided at Cambridge to "take up art" as a profession, and after a postgraduate trip to Italy began to write and lecture on the subject, as well as to paint. As his friends Russell, R. C. Trevelyan, and Max Beerbohm launched brilliant careers, Fry grew increasingly dissatisfied with his own: "I loathe art criticism more and more," he announced, "and long to create." Lukewarm responses to his paintings sent him back to criticism, however, and by 1905 he was struggling to support two children, a wife who suffered from mental illness, the travel necessary to write about art, and a fine-arts journal he had

---

Charles Follen McKim joined a board that already included Whitelaw Reid, Elihu Root, E. D. Adams, John Bigelow, Joseph Choate, John Cadwalader, Harris Fahnestock, John S. Kennedy, Darius O. Mills, and Rutherfurd Stuyvesant.

founded in 1903, the *Burlington Magazine*. At the urging of Morgan's friend William Laffan, Fry went to New York to raise money for the *Burlington* and to be interviewed for a position at the Metropolitan Museum.

At first he felt an exhilarating sense of possibility in America—especially the possibilities open to money: "I am having a roaring good time among these millionaires," he told his wife in early January, "and what's more, I find them a sympathetic, agreeable sort." After touring the Met on January 8, he pronounced Morgan's Chinese porcelains "marvellous" but the museum's pictures "a nightmare." Americans, he concluded, "have a desperate desire to get at real things. They have been kept in the dark so long by dealers and others, and they jump at enlightenment."

Morgan offered Fry a job as assistant director of the museum—Purdon Clarke "will be more or less of a figurehead," Fry reported: "I am offered the second place with reversion of headship if I succeed." He would have £1,600 (about $8,000) a year, plus expenses to travel in Europe half the year and freedom to write and lecture. He felt inclined to accept.

Morgan had invited him to Washington "to dine with him and the President of the U.S.A. It's alarming and interesting." The occasion for this trip was an American Institute of Architects dinner at the Arlington Hotel for the American Academy in Rome. McKim, now president of the AIA, hoped the event would pressure Congress to incorporate the academy as a national institution. Henry Walters had pledged $100,000 to start a $1 million endowment fund at the end of 1904, and Morgan had agreed to match it.

The Morgan party leaving New York on January 11 included Adelaide, Anne, Elihu Root (who had resigned from the cabinet in 1904 and gone back to the practice of law in New York, accepting a retainer as counsel to Morgan), and Fry, who described the scene to his wife: "I travelled down in the most luxurious way imaginable, that is to say in Pierpont Morgan's own private car tacked on to the end of a special express. . . . as it was cold & snowing we had a fire lit in the car. The whole thing is fitted up like a private house in the grandest style and an immaculate luncheon was served on the way." Morgan was "the most repulsively ugly man with a great strawberry nose," who would "make a splendid portrait like Ghirlandaio's Strozzi man in the Louvre."* He be-

---

* The figure in Domenico Ghirlandaio's *Portrait of an Old Man and a Boy* had, like Morgan, a grotesque rhinophymous nose. Another observer several years later noticed the resemblance as well. When Wilhelm von Bode took his daughter to see the Morgan collections at Princes Gate, their host personally showed them around. At one point during the tour several grandchildren rushed in, and one climbed into the old man's lap. Miss Bode, recognizing the scene, whispered, "Ghirlandaio, Father," but she did not speak softly enough, for Morgan looked up and said, "What's that about Ghirlandaio, miss?" Bode got them out of this embarrassing moment by saying they were discussing the "magnificent" Ghirlandaio portrait of Giovanna Tornabuoni that Morgan had recently acquired.

haved "not like a host but like a crowned head. There's no doubt he's a very remarkable and powerful man, and everyone says his ambitions are too big for
him to be other than quite straightforward."

The crowned head/host, surrounded by "lots of smart women," was in a
jovial mood, continued Fry—"making jokes, which I parried, about my becoming an American. After lunch a cigar called the Regalia de Morgan." In a brief
business talk on the train, the banker promised the scholar "a free hand with
the [museum's] pictures," as well as money for the *Burlington*—"pretty much
whatever I wanted. . . . I felt, as I sat next him, like a courtier who has at last got
an audience, and, as though, for a few minutes, I wielded absolute power." A
little discomfited by his audience with power, Fry went on: "I think I behaved
tactfully and indeed why should I not be able to manage, for they've not got
anything but money to intimidate you with. There's precious little distinction
or cachet about the whole lot, so one ought to be able to hold one's own. Really,
[Morgan] strikes me as a big man all the same and too big in his ambitions to be
low or mean or go back on his word. He has guaranteed my salary for five
years, but the fact is that they are determined to have a great boom in art here
and my salary ought to be indefinitely extensible."

On arriving in Washington, Morgan checked his guests into the New Willard
Hotel. A few hours later the entire party proceeded to the AIA dinner in
evening dress. The Arlington did not admit women at formal events, but
McKim had persuaded its management to improvise a special ladies' "box,"
which he placed at the disposal of the President's wife. When Edith Roosevelt
and her guests, including Anne Morgan and Adelaide Douglas, arrived, a male
quartet sang "Hail to the Fairest."

The dining room had been draped in white, with green festoons and
branches of palm. Morgan sat at the high table with Roosevelt, Root, the
French Ambassador Jules Jusserand, and the Secretaries of State and War,
John Hay and William Howard Taft. McKim had "dragooned" John LaFarge
and Augustus Saint-Gaudens into attending, and crowed to the latter in his excitement, "Henry James is coming; in fact, *everybody*, and *more* than we want!"
"Everybody" included Finley Peter Dunne; Charles Dana Gibson; Henry Siddons Mowbray; McKim's partners Mead, White, and William Kendall; the
architects Thomas Hastings, Charles Lang Freer, and Charles Moore; Pennsylvania Railroad president Alexander Cassatt; Columbia University president
Nicholas Murray Butler; University of Chicago president William Rainey
Harper; Senators Nelson Aldrich, George Peabody Wetmore, and Henry Cabot
Lodge; House Speaker Joseph Cannon; Supreme Court Justice James Harlan;
and Navy Secretary William H. Moody.

The evening's theme was the marriage of high culture and nationalist
ideals. Root, the principal speaker, surveyed America's architectural history
and praised his contemporaries who, touring Europe to see "the great examples

of art in the ancient and modern world, have come back with new standards." No longer content to let wealthy individuals and institutions "be the sole inheritors" of beauty and art, Americans and their political representatives wanted "the art of our fathers, the art of our private citizens . . . to be the art of . . . our whole people." To that end, Root announced, McKim had secured a site for the American Academy in Rome, the Villa Mirafiori on the Janiculum, and Walters and Morgan had each given $100,000 to start an endowment: "It was one of Jefferson's cherished ideas that young men of America might become saturated with the ideas of classical art by study in Rome; and now we are beginning the enterprise through which America will no longer be obliged to take her ideas of classic art at second hand, but will go directly to the fountain source at the home of art, under the direction and cherishing care of an American institution maintained by American munificence."

Henry James described the evening to a friend as a "big success and beautifully done," but found its flagrant chauvinism "quaint and queer. . . . The Eagle screamed in the speeches as I didn't know that that Fowl was still (after all these years and improvements) *permitted* to do."

Roger Fry expressed no such reservations. To his wife he reported that "The journey back [to New York] in a special train crowded with the big architects of the country was full of importance . . . really fine intelligent men all working together with a big idea of the future of art, full of enthusiasm and good sense and with the knowledge that they can carry out their schemes without any difficulty." What impressed him even more than American money was this "real power to shape things"—and also the American response to *him:* "It is extraordinary to find oneself looked up to and one's opinion regarded as it is here. I think that is really the thing that inclines me most."

Fry's sense of his own importance got him into trouble. Having been offered £1,600 a year to serve as assistant director at the Met, plus traveling expenses abroad and support for the *Burlington,* he decided that "for so big a job for which I am fitted, and for which they couldn't well get anyone else so fitted, I ought to be paid really well." He asked for £2,400. Morgan dropped the negotiations. Fry's appraisals of the "big man" tended to rise and fall with the tides of his own fortunes, and when the job offer was withdrawn his enthusiasm turned to contempt. "I don't regret that I stood up to Morgan," he told his wife. "He's not quite a man; he's a sort of financial steam-engine and I should have been in the position of watching the cranks work and dancing attendance."

Fry was wrong about fitting the job better than anyone else. Later that year the Met board hired Edward Robinson, director of the Museum of Fine Arts in Boston, to serve as assistant director and curator of classical art in New York. Purdon Clarke *was* "only a figurehead." Robinson quietly did the director's real work for five years, then took over the position after Clarke retired in 1910, and ran the museum brilliantly until 1931. Early in 1906 Roger Fry accepted a lesser post at the Met, as curator of paintings for £500 a year, and worked uneasily around Morgan.

Congress voted to charter the American Academy in Rome seven weeks after the AIA dinner, and in New York that spring McKim hosted another celebratory evening, at his University Club. Unable to resist addressing his audience as "Friends, Romans, Countrymen," he proposed a toast "To Mr. Morgan, who headed the list and became our first founder, and those who followed him, all honor, and I ask you to rise once again and drink with me the health and long life of these Medicean benefactors."

———

Public responsibilities at the Met did not slow the progress of Morgan's private acquisitions, and in the spring of 1904 he ventured off in a new direction with an expert who suited him better than Roger Fry. The Oxford-trained art historian and former Anglican clergyman Robert Langton Douglas, author of a *History of Siena* (1902), had just mounted a major exhibition of Sienese paintings at the Burlington Fine Arts Club, and when Morgan arrived in London with Adelaide that April he asked Langton Douglas to take them on a tour of the galleries.

Unlike Florentine artists of the early fourteenth century, Giotto in particular, the painters of Siena had not rejected the Byzantine tradition; instead, following Duccio (1278–1318), they gave graceful, emotional dimension to medieval forms. After seeing the Burlington exhibition, Morgan commissioned Langton Douglas to find him works from Siena, and gave the scholar £1,000 for his own research.

Langton Douglas thanked his new patron for "enabling me to continue and complete my historical and artistic researches," and ten days later sold him several Sienese paintings for £1,705, some of them out of the Burlington show; they included a Duccio triptych of the Crucifixion, four predella panels depicting scenes from the life of Saint John the Baptist by Giovanni di Paolo, and a Virgin and Child by Matteo di Giovanni, which Morgan hung in his bedroom.

When word of this purchase got out, the price of Sienese art soared. A delighted Langton Douglas continued to advise his American patron—among the works he procured for him over the next several years were a Romney portrait (*Mrs. Scott Jackson*) and a Lorenzo Costa *Annunciation* in 1905, a Perugino *Virgin and Child with Two Saints* from Sir George Sitwell in 1911, and a bronze *Virtue Overcoming Vice* attributed to Cellini.* Langton Douglas also counseled

———

* Morgan did not substantially add to his Sienese holdings after 1904. The paintings he purchased through Langton Douglas remained in his collection until his death, and most were eventually sold by his heirs. The Duccio is now at the Museum of Fine Arts in Boston, the purchasing committee at the Metropolitan Museum, and eventually inherited Fry's advisory role.

From London in May of 1904, Morgan went as usual to Paris, where Adelaide served as his collecting accomplice. He ordered several objects from Cartier at 13 Rue de la Paix, including a porcelain flask, "*vieux Saxe, representant 'Les trois Grâces,'* " and a little porcelain box, "*Mennecy, 'Femme couchée.'* " When they arrived at Princes Gate in June, he did not recall having bought them. Cartier's clerk wrote: "I take the liberty to remind you that Mrs. Douglas, who was present when you were purchasing the two articles you refer to, made a jocular remark about the word 'Mennecy' and that she also greatly advised you to add the said articles to your collection of boxes and flacons."

That spring Morgan also acquired the ink-smudged manuscript used by Milton's printer to set type for Book I of *Paradise Lost*—the only surviving manuscript of the poem. And he made the first of several diplomatic gestures designed in part to counter Europe's concern about American appropriation of its cultural heritage. He had bought a beautiful embroidered textile, reportedly for $15,000, and lent it to the South Kensington Museum, where scholars recognized it as a thirteenth-century ecclesiastical cloak that had been given to the Italian cathedral at Ascoli by Pope Nicholas IV and recently stolen. In 1904 Morgan returned the "Ascoli Cope" to Italy. In Rome the following spring, King Victor Emmanuel gave a dinner in his honor as official thanks, and Pope Pius X granted him a private audience in the Vatican Library; pontiff and banker conversed through a translator about paintings and books, and Morgan was invited to call at the Vatican whenever he visited Rome.

———

In order to make room for his growing collections of paintings and objects of decorative art, Morgan bought the house next door to No. 13 Princes Gate in 1904 and opened the interior walls to join the two buildings, converting the first two floors into galleries. Jack told Fanny the following summer: "Father has got the new French rooms furnished properly and they are most entirely satisfactory to him and to everyone. I haven't seen the bedroom and housekeeping part of the house but presume it is not as good as the show part."

For his "new French rooms" Morgan had ordered voluptuous furnishings from Duveen Brothers. There were four Louis XVI X-frame benches with

———

the Giovanni di Paolo panels—among the artist's best-known works—at London's National Gallery. The Romney, purchased from the Morgan family by Andrew Mellon, is now at the National Gallery of Art in Washington. The Perugino remains at the Pierpont Morgan Library. The bronze *Virtue*, now in the Frick Collection, is not by Cellini.

matching armchairs covered in blue silk and a pair of Louis XV andirons for the Fragonard Room; in a Louis XVI Drawing Room were Beauvais tapestries, a marquetry commode by Riesener, tables and secrétaires decorated with Sèvres porcelain plaques, and candlesticks made by Pierre Gouthière. In addition, the "show part" of the house featured a Regency Room, a Louis XV Sitting Room, and a Louis XVI Marble Hall.

A few years later Morgan's friend William Lawrence, the bishop of Massachusetts (and the son of Junius's Boston landlord, A. A. Lawrence), stayed at Princes Gate and described its interior in his memoirs. "As one entered the front door, he was still in a conventional London house," wrote Lawrence, "until passing along three or four yards, his eye turned and looked through the door on the left into the dining-room—in size an ample city dining-room, but in glory of color such as few other domestic dining-rooms ever enjoyed. The visitor was amazed and thrilled at the pictures: Sir Joshua Reynolds' masterpiece, *Madame Delmé and Children*, a great full-length portrait of a lady by Gainsborough, another by Romney [*Mrs. Scott Johnson*]. One's eye seemed to pierce the wall into the outer world through the landscapes of Constable [*The White Horse*] and Hobbema. Behind Mr. Morgan's chair at the end of the table hung a lovely Hoppner of three children [*The Godsall Children*], a beautiful boy standing in the center, full of grace."

Lawrence wondered why Morgan had placed this last picture behind him until he noted that a narrow mirror between two windows on the opposite wall enabled the financier to see the figure in reflection. He did not point out that Morgan would see *himself* in the mirror as well—"portrait of beautiful boy with owner"—or that anyone facing Morgan would see him in conjunction with Hoppner's figures.

Upstairs in a large drawing room on the second floor hung Gainsborough's well-traveled *Georgiana, Duchess of Devonshire*. "Turning from her," Lawrence continued (accepting the attributions assigned by his host), "one's eye glanced about the room and recognized portraits made familiar through prints and engravings of a Rembrandt, a Frans Hals, a child by Velázquez, and the magnificent Van Dyck *Woman in Red and Child*. . . . Across the hall to the front, we entered the Fragonard Room, whose walls were drawn in by the builder to meet the exact dimensions and designs of the panels." The bishop's survey took in more Gainsboroughs and Raeburns, Louis XV furniture, Sèvres porcelain, objects from Egypt and Rome, glass cabinets filled with jeweled boxes, drawers of fine portrait miniatures by Holbein, Nicholas Hilliard, Isaac Oliver—and Juliet Pierpont Morgan's collection of china pug dogs.

One night at Princes Gate, Lawrence's dinner companion, the wife of the bishop of Southwark, remarked, "What a mass of interesting things are in this house!"

"Mrs. Talbot," replied Lawrence, "the most interesting thing in this house is the host."

The most eminent visitor who came to see the new galleries at Princes Gate was Edward VII. Morgan showed his guest through the house in July of 1906—the King recognized several portraits as having belonged to his friends—then offered him iced coffee and cigars in the library. A portrait of Junius hung over the mantel between Sir Thomas Lawrence's *Miss Croker* and Romney's *Lady Hamilton*. Across the room was Lawrence's full-length portrait of the beautiful actress Elizabeth Farren dressed in white silk and furs, which Morgan had just bought from Agnew's for $200,000.* The King, speaking as one connoisseur of femininity to another, objected that Miss Farren looked cramped: "The ceiling is too low in this room for that picture," he observed. "Why do you hang it there?" Morgan looked at the portrait for a long time, then said, "Because I like it there, sir."

A more critical observer than Edward VII or Bishop Lawrence toured No. 13–14 Princes Gate later that year. "This afternoon I visited J. P. Morgan's house," reported Bernard Berenson to Isabella Stewart Gardner in November, 1906—implicitly comparing Morgan's collections to her own, largely selected by him: he liked one of Morgan's Van Dycks, and loved the Fragonard Room, but thought the house looked "like a pawnbroker's shop for Croesuses."

Morgan's ecumenical appetites did give the house a look of expensive jumble, but Berenson's scorn was partly designed to reinforce his own intellectual distinction. Relatively new at what he called "expertising," he was earning a living by working as both dealer and critic, and the lines between aesthetic judgment and commerce were not always clear. Other scholars accused him of "selling" attributions. The American journalist and arts editor August Jaccaci reported with relief in 1903: "I have actually found an apparently honest man—Langton Douglas; he is a dealer, though an art critic, and frankly says so. No Berenson business about him."

Taste and knowledge constantly revise valuations in art, and the combination of steep prices and questionable authenticity creates an uneasy mutual dependence between wealthy collectors and scholarly experts. Knowledge, as Henry Adams bitterly pointed out all his life, brings one kind of power, but generally not the kind that makes things happen in the world or moves art from one continent to another. Scholars such as Berenson and Roger Fry—but apparently not Langton Douglas, Bode, or Bashford Dean—tended to denigrate money and worldly power as ranking far below knowledge on the scale of ulti-

---

* The daughter of a surgeon, Elizabeth Farren sat for Lawrence in 1790, just three years after he was admitted to the Royal Academy. She retired from the stage when she married the twelfth earl of Derby in 1797. The painting is now at the Metropolitan Museum of Art.

mate values, especially when collectors did not do their bidding. Morgan wielded the power of his checkbook, while Berenson and Fry plied their educated intelligence and sometimes used connoisseurship as a weapon. If they had to suffer the humiliation of kowtowing to wealth, they exacted revenge by sneering at its taste.

———

Charles McKim had a nervous breakdown in the summer of 1905, just a few months after thanking his "Medicean benefactors" for funding the American Academy in Rome. His doctors ordered him to rest. Almost finished with the library on 36th Street, he suggested that Stanford White complete the job. Morgan told McKim to take a vacation and forget about the building: "When you go, work on the library will stop until you return. No one else shall touch it."

McKim did not stay away long, and early in 1906 he reported to White with relief that his client seemed pleased: "The sky is blue and there is no cause for worry. [Morgan] expressed great pride and satisfaction in the building."

On a quiet side street in Murray Hill, McKim had built an Italianate villa that paid gracious tribute to the High Renaissance, drawing on the palaces and churches of sixteenth-century Rome. Everything about the building expressed its owner's sense of grandeur and aesthetic privilege, his deliberate, personal enunciation of America's claim to a place among the great cultures of the world. Known as Mr. Morgan's Library, it had a luxurious formal gravitas, and spoke with silent authority of high scholarly standards and patrician tastes.

A private underground tunnel connected the library to Morgan's house. At the entrance on 36th Street a flight of broad marble stairs led up between a pair of lionesses (sculpted by E. C. Potter, who later created the famous lions on the steps of the New York Public Library) and two sets of Ionic columns to an august Palladian portal. Heavily ornamented bronze doors opened from this recessed portico into a vaulted rotunda. Inside, above lapis columns and Roman marble floors, Mowbray's ceiling decorations invoked the literary arts and the library's identification with the Italian Renaissance.

More interesting for its iconography than for its aesthetic qualities, the ceiling drew heavily on quattrocento compositions, particularly on Pinturicchio's representations of the seven liberal arts in the Borgia Apartments, and on Raphael's vault decorations for the Stanza della Segnatura—both in the Vatican. Mowbray had proposed a general design for these decorations, but Morgan made several alterations. As completed, the ceiling's elaborate schematic allegory combines reverence for learning—four female figures represent philosophy, religion, science, and art—with a literary history of love.* If Morgan

———

* I am indebted to William Voelkle, curator of medieval manuscripts at the Morgan Library, for his detective work concerning the ceilings in the rotunda and East Room.

as collector was writing himself into the record of beautiful objects, he may with these images have been placing himself in a lineage of famous lovers—and humanizing the library's baronial solemnity by paying sly homage to the anarchic vitality of Eros and art.

Three painted lunettes over the doors leading out of the rotunda contain figurative references to great works of literature from classical antiquity, the Middle Ages, and the Renaissance. Among the lovers represented here are Orpheus and Eurydice, Odysseus and Circe, Lancelot and Guinevere, Tristan and Isolde, Dante and Beatrice, Petrarch and Laura, Tasso and Leonora d'Este: only the first pair are married to each other, and Eurydice, like Memie Sturges, died shortly after her wedding. Behind Dante and Beatrice, in the lunette referring to romances of the Middle Ages, Paolo reads to Francesca da Rimini, his lover and his brother's wife, about the first kiss of Lancelot and Guinevere (who was married to King Arthur). Paolo and Francesca were put to death for their transgression and consigned to the second circle of Hell ("they suffer here who sinned in carnal things"). In the fifth canto of the *Inferno*, Francesca tells Dante how the story of the Arthurian lovers prompted her fall: "One day, for pleasure, / We read of Lancelot, by love constrained." She and her own "constrained" lover sometimes looked up from the book into each other's eyes—

> "But one particular moment alone it was
> Defeated us: *the longed-for smile,* it said,
> *Was kissed by that most noble lover:* at this,
> This one, who now will never leave my side,
> Kissed my mouth, trembling. A Galeotto* that book!
> And so was he who wrote it; that day we read
> No further."

Perhaps Morgan "read" his own experiences with love in the context of these celebrated tales—or read stories of earlier lovers with Adelaide, the way Paolo and Francesca did.

The ceiling in the East Room, the library itself, extends the play of personal reference. Above triple-tiered bookcases made of bronze and Circassian walnut, Mowbray had painted into the ceiling a series of twelve hexagonal panels pairing the signs of the zodiac with Roman gods. The idea and some of the layouts were based on ceilings with astral motifs at the Villa Farnesina in Rome, designed by Raphael and painted by Baldassare Peruzzi and Giulio Romano in

---

* Galeotto, or Gallehault, served as messenger between Lancelot and Guinevere, and the French word came to serve as a synonym for "pander" or "go-between."

about 1508–11 for the Roman banker Agostino Chigi. (The villa was acquired by Alessandro Farnese after Chigi's death; Morgan had acquired the Farnese Book of Hours in 1903.) The constellations in the Farnesina relate to Chigi's horoscope, and the signs in the East Room apparently refer to Morgan's. His birth sign, Aries, accompanied by Venus and Cupid, appears above the entrance to the East Room next to Gemini, which may stand for his marriage to Fanny; across from Gemini over the lunette for Tragedy is Aquarius, the sign under which Memie died. And references to Olympian adultery appear in the lunette representing Virgo (Adelaide was born on September 16): Juno tries to seduce her husband, Jupiter, whose attentions have wandered, by exposing her breast, and in the next panel is Vulcan, the lame and ugly god of the forge, who caught his wife, Venus, in bed with Mars.

Above the mantel in the East Room, Morgan hung a sixteenth-century Brussels tapestry, *The Triumph of Avarice.* One of a series on the Seven Deadly Sins designed by Pieter Coecke van Aelst, it portrays a winged female Avarice emerging from a flaming Inferno. In the foreground is King Midas, who wished that everything he touched would turn to gold, then found that he could neither eat nor drink and retracted the wish. A Latin inscription at the top reads, "As Tantalus ever thirsts in the midst of water, so the miser hungers always for wealth," and an angel points a warning finger at the mouth of Hell.

Morgan left no explanation for his choice of this subject. It may have been ironic, since he did not regard himself as avaricious although he knew others did. On the other hand, he probably also knew that in the Middle Ages the Sins were represented to invoke their opposing virtues—in this case, generosity. He intended to leave his collections for the "instruction and pleasure" of the American people, and asked in his will that they be made "permanently available" to the public. His decision to build a library for the manuscripts and rare books meant that the rest of the objects would go elsewhere.

Once the library was complete, Morgan spent part of every day in his private *studiolo,* the West Room. McKim had installed a sixteenth-century Italian wooden ceiling, stained-glass window panels, red damask walls bearing the Chigi coat of arms, a mantelpiece from the studio of Desiderio da Settignano, a pair of candelabra in the form of kneeling Florentine angels, and a broad Italianate desk, custom-made for the room in England. Over time, Morgan lined the study's walls with Italian Renaissance paintings and reliefs attributed to Perugino, Botticelli, Cima da Conegliano, Francesco Francia, Antonio Rossellino, and Raphael (neither of the two "Raphaels" he bought after the Colonna altarpiece turned out to be genuine).

In this setting, he placed himself at a distinct remove from the modern industrial world, and from the familial and social discord that lay just beyond his sanctuary's doors. He held his first meeting at the library in November 1906—of the Metropolitan Museum's purchasing committee. George Perkins reported to a colleague at the end of February 1907 that "the Senior" had not been to 23 Wall Street since mid-December: "[He] is taking a good deal of comfort in his Library, which we youngsters have dubbed 'The Up-Town Branch.' "

Chapter 25

SINGULAR
WOMEN

As the work on his library neared completion, Morgan decided he needed someone to organize and manage his literary collections, and the indispensable Junius found the right person. Junius served in an advisory capacity at the Princeton University Library, where a young clerk named Belle da Costa Greene had impressed him with her quick intelligence and eager aptitude for knowledge about books. Late in 1905 he introduced her to his uncle. There is no record of that first meeting, but a recommendation from Junius was all Morgan needed. He hired Miss Greene for $75 a month. She had been earning $40 at Princeton.

Small and slender, with dark hair and olive skin dramatically set off by light green eyes, Belle Greene had an extraordinary allure that appealed to both men and women. Men in particular. Bernard Berenson, who met her in 1908, later described her as "the most vitalizing person I have ever known."

Her middle name and exotic looks came, she said, from her maternal Portuguese grandmother, Genevieve da Costa Van Vliet. Her parents had separated when she was a child, and her mother, "a native of Richmond, Va., and a proud and cultivated lady of old-fashioned dignity, [had] moved with her children to Princeton, New Jersey, where she gave music lessons to support them while they attended local schools." Belle later told the *Evening Sun*: "I knew definitely by the time I was twelve years old that I wanted to work with rare books. I loved them even then, the sight of them, the wonderful feel of them, the romance and thrill of them. Before I was sixteen, I had begun my studies, omitting the regular college courses that many girls take before they have found out what they want to do."

She quickly joined the ranks of gifted deputies to whom Morgan gave large authority and freedom to spend his money. The unique advantages of being female and willing to devote herself almost entirely to his collecting helped her become his agent, accomplice, and personal confidante as well. Returning from Europe one year, she smuggled several of his acquisitions through customs in her suitcase. She let the inspectors find a few things of her own, "with great seeming hesitation," she told a friend—acting "*very* indignant" and protesting "to their great joy." The examiners never noticed the more important items, and "when I landed at the library with all of JP's treasures—a painting—three bronzes—a special kind of watch he had asked me to get in London & several other things, well he & I did a *war* dance & laughed in great glee."

Though young and inexperienced, Miss Greene assumed with Morgan's backing and her own growing expertise a prominent position in the world of rare books and manuscripts. She met leading art scholars, assimilated their advice, and walked off with the best items at European auctions. Far more voluble and articulate than the man she called (behind his back) her "Big Chief," she gave offhand glimpses of their shared sensibility—describing an exhibition of "our" medieval illuminated manuscripts as radiating color and light, an effect that emphasized "the luxury and gorgeous barbaric beauty of the Church in the early days."

Presiding over rare books of hours and Gutenberg Bibles at "Mr. Morgan's Library," she added her own insouciant sense of style to the decorous tone of the place. "Just because I *am* a librarian," she reportedly once announced, "doesn't mean I have to *dress* like one": she wore couturier gowns and jewels to work. In London she stayed at Claridge's, and in Paris at the Ritz. She disciplined dealers who tried to charge too much or offered less than top-quality items, and she directed Morgan's voracious impulses into systematic, scholarly channels. Her one aim, she told him a few years after she settled in, was to make his library "*pre-eminent,* especially for incunabula, manuscripts, bindings and the classics." She thought their only rivals were the British Museum and the Bibliothèque Nationale, but hoped "to be able to say some day that there is neither *rival* nor *equal.*" No young American library could surpass the great European repositories of culture, but Morgan and Belle Greene in a relatively few years secured individual masterpieces and scholarly collections of the highest quality. In the decades after her patron's death, Miss Greene became known as "the soul of the Morgan Library."

And virtually all the information she gave out about her life was false.

Some of the inventions had to do with personal vanity—she was twenty-six when she came to work for Morgan, not, as she said, twenty-two. But forty

Belle da Costa Greene, 1911.
(Berenson Archive, reproduced by permission
of the President and Fellows of Harvard College.
Photograph by Clarence White)

years after the end of the Civil War, she had a far more compelling motive than feminine guile for obscuring the biographical facts. Her given name was not Belle da Costa Greene but Belle Marion Greener, and she was the daughter of the first black man to graduate from Harvard.

The matrilineal Portuguese/Dutch descent was pure fiction. Belle's mother, Genevieve Ida Fleet, came from Washington, D.C., not Richmond, Virginia, and was the daughter not of Genevieve da Costa Van Vliet but of the former Hermione C. Peters and a music teacher named James H. Fleet. The 1845 Fleet-Peters wedding appears in a registry of *Blacks in the Marriage Records of the District of Columbia*, and the 1850 Washington census lists the family as mulattoes. Belle's birth certificate identifies her as the daughter of Genevieve Fleet and Richard Theodore Greener. Place of birth: 1462 T Street, Washington, D.C. Date: November 26, 1879. Color: "Colored."

W.E.B. Du Bois considered Richard Greener one of America's most gifted black intellectuals, a representative of the upper echelon of character and intelligence that Du Bois called the "talented tenth." Belle Greene belonged to that meritocracy as well, although few people knew she was black. Father and daughter both earned listings in the *Dictionary of American Biography*, under different names, with no cross-referencing *q.v.*

Richard T. Greener was born in Philadelphia in 1844 to Richard Wesley Greener and the former Mary Ann Le Brune. His paternal grandfather, Jacob, ran a "colored" school in Baltimore. Richard W. left work as a ship steward in 1853 to dig for gold in California, and never came back. Mary Ann, the daughter of "a Spaniard from Puerto Rico" and a "negress" (her son wrote later), moved in 1853 to Cambridge, Massachusetts, where the light-skinned nine-year-old Richard went briefly to school, then worked to support her as an office boy, porter, and clerk. He read constantly, and so impressed one of his Boston employers that the man sent him to a preparatory school at Oberlin, one of the few white colleges to admit black students before the Civil War. Greener wanted to join the first Ohio regiment of black Union army soldiers, but he was underage and his mother refused consent. He spoke at his graduation on "Colorphobia," then returned to Massachusetts for a senior high school year at the Phillips Andover Academy.

Harvard admitted him in 1865 as an experiment in the education of a Negro. He was twenty-one, and his appearance in Harvard Yard just five months after Appomattox and Lincoln's death probably seemed to abolitionist Boston a vivid emblem of the victory just won.

Greener had to repeat his freshman year, but his senior dissertation on land tenure in Ireland earned him Harvard's Bowdoin Prize. In a long essay he wrote just before graduating in 1870, he gave a detailed account of his life to answer rumors that had circulated throughout his undergraduate career—

that he had escaped from slavery, come straight from the cotton fields to college, served as a Union army scout, been fathered by a rebel general. He had few pleasant memories of Harvard, he said, and hoped not to hear of the unpleasant incidents ever again. Looking ahead, he wanted not wealth but intellectual distinction—the area in which his race had been most denigrated: "My chief desire is to lead a purely literary life in my own way. I have a great fondness and some knowledge of art, I am particularly interested in metaphysics, general literature, and the Greek and Latin classics when divested of grammatical pedantry. My plans in life are to get all the knowledge I can, make all the reputation I can, and 'do good' and make a comfortable competence as the corollaries of the other two."

Du Bois, who became the first black man to earn a PhD at Harvard in 1895, wrote in *The Souls of Black Folk* (1903) a famous passage about the double experience of the Negro in America—"a world which yields him no true self-consciousness, but only lets him see himself through the revelation of the other world. It is a peculiar sensation, this double consciousness, this sense of always looking at one's self through the eyes of others, of measuring one's soul by the tape of a world that looks on in amused contempt and pity."

Greener looked back at the white world with a combination of ambition and defiance, and resolved to make his own way in the fields of higher learning. During the Reconstructionist 1870s he taught Greek, Latin, mathematics, and constitutional history at the University of South Carolina—the only institution of higher education in the South to attempt integration—while earning a law degree. Though it is hard to imagine how he had time, he also worked as university librarian, arranging and classifying the library's twenty-six thousand books. He married Genevieve Ida Fleet in 1874, and moved with her to Washington when Reconstruction came to its inconclusive end.

The Greeners took a house next door to Genevieve's mother, now a dressmaker, and had six children by 1887—Mary Louise, Russell Lowell, Belle Marion, Ethel Alice, Theodora Genevieve, and a son who died in infancy. While Morgan helped Treasury Secretary Sherman refund the Civil War debt and restore the gold standard in the late seventies, Greener worked as a Treasury clerk. In 1879 he was appointed dean of the Howard University Law School, and over the next few years he taught, practiced law, lectured, wrote, and recruited blacks for the Republican Party. As a reward for political work, Republican officials in 1885 sent him to New York to be secretary of the Ulysses S. Grant Monument and chief examiner of the Municipal Civil Service Board. Greener wrote to a friend from Manhattan: "For the first time in my life I feel that I am working up to something like my ability."

It took his family a long time to find a home in New York, but they finally settled at 29 West 99th in 1892. Greener was having professional and personal troubles. A New York social reformer described him to Booker T. Washington that summer as "a colored (nearly white) gentleman, a Harvard graduate and lawyer," who "has a wife & family, and is hard pressed for a living. He has all the ability and education that ought to secure competence, but political influence being against him, has suffered severely."

After some sort of breakdown, Greener himself reported to Mr. Washington in 1894: "I am devoting myself now to literary work, what I always should have done." Although he had for a time "disappeared beneath the waters," he was in excellent health and spirits "for real work, and there is much to be done. Neither the white nor the Black Problem will be settled in our day." Washington was apparently looking to help Greener, for another observer reported to him that summer from the nation's capital: "In regard to Professor Greener's family I have ascertained that Mrs. Greener is a native of this city—being a Miss Fleet before marriage. She is colored and never passed for anything else while here. It is understood . . . however that she associates only with whites in New York. They are poor and in very straitened circumstances."

In a photograph taken at about this time, Greener looks like a revolutionary or a poet: his hair has begun to recede, he wears scholarly wire-rimmed glasses, a wing collar turned up, a goatee and a wide mustache. He described himself in his Harvard Class Report for 1895 as engaged in reformist Republican politics, committed to the Irish Republican cause (he helped raise $150,000 for Parnell and Gladstone), and "devoted . . . entirely to literary work." His elder children were attending school in New York, Belle Marion at Teachers College.

In 1898 Booker T. Washington helped secure Greener a consular appointment under President McKinley—the Republicans gave foreign jobs to a few prominent blacks as a means of attracting the Negro vote. The State Department sent Greener first to Bombay, which he found too hot, then to Vladivostok. He stayed in that remote Russian outpost until 1905, when the Roosevelt administration recalled him after getting reports that he had drifted into alcoholism and debt. Greener denied both charges, insisting that they were brought by an official who had never visited Vladivostok and confused him with someone else. He was exonerated, but never held another political job.

In the context of America's turn-of-the-century racial politics, Greener's posting to southeastern Russia looked to many of his contemporaries like exile, and seemed to mark the failure of his early promise. Convinced that a democratic society would open up to accommodate black achievements, Greener refused to define himself only as a Negro leader, championing Irish Catholics in their struggle against England, advocating women's rights, and arguing for labor unions as instruments of worker independence. Years later he wrote: "I still believe and preach the doctrine that each man who raises himself, elevates the race." He may have accepted his geographical and metaphorical consignment to Siberia in that spirit, but his long absence probably had to do with the dissolution of his marriage as well.

The New York City street directories until 1897 list Richard T. Greener, lawyer, with an office at 27 Chambers Street and home at 29 West 99th. For 1897–98, the directory places him at Chambers Street only, and has a separate entry for Genevieve I. Greener at 29 W. 99th. After his assignment overseas, the family disappears from the records for a few years, and when Mrs. Greener turns up again on West 99th Street in 1901–2, she has dropped the final *r*, calling herself "Genevieve Greene, teacher." The following year, 1902–3, she appears as "Genevieve I. Greene, widow"—so much for Mr. Greener—and then vanishes from the listings. She probably moved to New Jersey when Belle began work at the Princeton Library. By the time Belle took the job with Morgan late in 1905, she was calling herself Belle da Costa Greene. Her mother does not appear in the New York directories again until 1908–9, at which point the transformation is complete: Genevieve V. V. [Van Vliet] Greene, widow, is listed at 403 West 115th Street with her son, Russel da Costa, a civil engineer. She had been associating "only with whites" in the early nineties, when she was still living with Greener. From about 1905 on, she and her children "passed."

What happened within this family, and whether Greener had any contact with his wife and children after 1898, may never be known. In 1906 he attended a meeting of the pro–Du Bois Niagara Movement at Harpers Ferry as a spy for Booker T. Washington, then retired to Chicago, where he continued writing and lecturing to "advance the race." He died in Chicago in 1922. Although he did not want to see himself only in terms of race, his Republican patrons probably saw little else. Bob Bacon at Roosevelt's State Department, considering a consular service appointment for another black diplomat in 1907, asked a colleague, "Would he be better than some new coon?"

The light-complexioned "Greenes" expunged Richard Greener from the record, and with him all acknowledgment of their race. Belle may not have completed the course at Teachers College, as its alumni office has no record of her. She later said she had studied art at the Pratt Institute in Brooklyn, founded in 1887, but Pratt's student records do not go back that far. On her own initiative she moved into a rarefied, cosmopolitan world that excluded even the top tenth of the "talented tenth," and with Morgan's patronage created for herself an independent, heady, precarious life that few women of her time, black or white, could have imagined.

If "passing" freed her from the public burden of having to represent her race, it also brought her an even more complex self-consciousness than the double vision described by Du Bois. While her father had the "peculiar . . . sense of always looking at one's [black, male] self through the eyes of [white] others," Belle had the sense of looking at her black, female self through the eyes of peo- .

ple who thought she was white. Her hunger for learning and intellectual distinction seems directly derived from her father's. In her case, however, it also had to do with claiming for a black (whom most people didn't recognize) woman (whom they clearly did) a place in the universally exalted realms of literature and art—a share in what George Eliot called "the hard-won treasures of thought, which generations of painful toil have laid up for the race of men."

If Morgan knew about Belle's background he left no indication of it. Once she became indispensable at his library, he might not have cared. He entrusted her not only with his literary masterpieces but also with intimate secrets. She ghostwrote some of his letters, ran his private errands, helped him draw up guest lists, bought flowers and wedding presents on his behalf, saw to it (she claimed) that he was regularly shaved, manicured, and pedicured, opened his mail—except when the handwriting looked unmistakably "blonde"—and arranged the schedule of his female callers at the library so that one wouldn't run into the next.

Many people suspected that she was his mistress—asked if they had had an affair, she reportedly replied, "We tried"—but all the evidence suggests not. He tended to get involved with women from his own social class, and somewhat closer to his own age (Belle was twenty-six and he sixty-eight when they met—Adelaide was fifty-two); and the chatty, intimate tone Belle took with her lovers is entirely different from the voice in which she addressed Morgan. She alternately worshiped and railed against her autocratic "Chief" to others, but treated him with fond, somewhat awed respect. He made her feel, as he made many women feel, that she was the only person who truly understood him, and partly in response to this seductive compliment she gave him her best work and fierce allegiance.

As flirts, they were in the same league. One night he asked her whether she would like him better "if he were thirty years younger," she reported, "& I said no, I'd leave the library—he would be too dangerous—which seemed to please him & then he said he never wanted to be younger except when he was with me & thought of me. I don't doubt he has said that to every woman he knows but I love him just the same."

From behind the closed doors of Morgan's library, Belle Greene proved refreshingly indiscreet, writing to one of her own lovers at entertaining length between 1909 and 1913 about the collecting and amorous activities of her beloved "Boss." (See Chapters 29 and 30.) The recipient of these confidences was Morgan's resolute critic Bernard Berenson, who lived with his wife, Mary, on a handsome hillside estate outside Florence, the Villa I Tatti. Morgan invited the Berensons to see his library when they visited New York in December 1908. Afterward, "BB" described himself to Isabella Stewart Gardner as "duly impressed" with the illuminated manuscripts but divided about the *objets*—some "tremendously fine," others "what they call in Venice 'Musica.' "

Berenson was more than duly impressed with Belle Greene. They saw each other and exchanged notes several times over the next two months. She addressed him at first as "Dear Mr. Berenson," but on March 9, 1909, began a letter "Dear thou of my heart," and went on (he had gone to Boston): "I have been with you in thought every moment since you left me—have wished for you at dinners—at the theatre & opera, in the morning afternoon and night—My thoughts have been wrapped around you as I should have wished to be and my absorbing occupation has been to chop off, day by day, the long weary hours that lie between us. How I wish I might gather them all up in my hand and throw them over the edge of the world! How I wish that *you* might gather *me* up & take me to the wood beyond the World where we two might learn to know Life and each other." Berenson was forty-three, and Belle thirty when they met (though she claimed to be twenty-five); she moved her birth date around like a potted plant. Before he returned to Europe in mid-March, he sent her a set of his favorite books, sixteen volumes of *The Thousand and One Nights,* in French. "I am *so* excited by possessing them," she wrote: "I was all alone in *my* library when they arrived." She canceled her evening plans and resolved to stay home (she lived with her mother on West 115th Street) in her "most comfortable peignoir & go off into les nuits enchantées – I shall take you with me & we won't come back at all – never." Above all she desired his knowledge: "How I should love to be with you in London – to see those wonderful things with your eyes. I am sure that I could amount to something with you to help me – but *who* is there here to teach one? Be *sure dear* and tell me every thing you do and all the wonderful things you see. . . ."

Berenson had had affairs outside his forgiving marriage before, but according to his biographer Ernest Samuels, this one "would stand apart from all others in depth and intensity." Its transatlantic heat lasted several years, and its underlying friendship for decades. Berenson carefully preserved the hundreds of letters Belle sent him; she destroyed the hundreds he wrote to her.

Urbane, widely traveled, witty, charming, and one of the world's leading experts on Italian art, Berenson was a Lithuanian Jew whose family had immigrated to Boston in 1875. He graduated from Harvard in 1887—two years before Jack Morgan—and made his way into the international art world through a combination of his own acute intelligence and the support of his patroness, Isabella Stewart Gardner. Belle probably knew about his background, but it apparently did not inspire her to let him in on her secret. He later reflected that her mysterious origins were "Malay." Still, other people whispered about her bloodline.

Mrs. Gardner reported a "nasty" story to the Berensons at the end of 1909, having no idea that BB was wildly in love with its subject. Miss Greene had

written to ask if she could see the collections at Fenway Court in Boston, and
"of course I said yes. She came, stayed not quite an hour, was very exuberant."
A week later, at a dinner party in New York, Belle discussed the visit with a man
who turned out to be a friend of Mrs. Gardner's. She said (Mrs. G told the B's)
that "I had invited her to come, and had charged her $1 for coming, that she
had spent the night here at Fenway Court and hoped to the Lord never to do
such a disgusting thing again." Under skeptical questioning from her dinner
companion, who said he knew Mrs. Gardner well, Belle grew flustered but continued, saying that Fenway Court was full of forgeries, that its Maria Strozzi
bust was a laughingstock in New York, and that Berenson didn't trust his
Boston patroness. Shocked, Mrs. Gardner asked the Berensons: "What do you
think of it, and incidentally of her, as all her account of her visit here was a lie.
She probably does not know either of you at all. . . . It turns out she is a half-
breed, and I suppose can't help lying. But let me know what you think."

That offhand assumption—that other races "can't help lying"—probably
had a good deal to do with the "Greenes'" decision to lie about who they were.
Not recognized as black, they no doubt heard countless remarks such as those
Louisa made to Fanny about the "darkies" her father had hired in Newport.

Belle asked Berenson by mail to tell Mrs. Gardner "that I told you I loved her
collections as some villain has told her to the contrary and she wrote me a
rather bitterly plaintive letter."

Berenson temporized, describing the tale to Mrs. Gardner as "incredible."
Miss Greene had impressed him at first as "a very competent young woman,
absorbed by her job, and devoted to her employer," and he had found no reason
since to change his mind.

Unfortunately, the tale was not incredible, although it made no difference to
Berenson. Belle took considerable liberties with the truth, in her reporting on
Morgan as well as for dinner-party effect, and was as prone as BB to self-
aggrandizing derision of other people's art (Fenway Court was full of forgeries;
Raphael had "barely looked at" the Colonna Madonna).

Whatever Belle did tell Berenson about her background, her letters to him
made constant, deeply conflicted reference to blackness and her physical appearance—reflecting a painful consciousness of a world that defined beauty in
features that were not her own. She alluded casually to her Portuguese descent, her mother's "grand Southern blood," her sister's "stunning complexion
and beautiful golden brown hair." Joking about her own "dusky" coloring and
jealousy of blondes, she anticipated a dinner party at which "*I* shall probably
look like a huckleberry in a bowl of milk!" Sending Berenson photographs
of herself, she told him to tear up the ones he didn't like—"I am sure the
'Esquimaux-nigger-Burmese' one will appeal to you." When her maid died in
1910, she mourned "that poor little black thing who had been more than a

mother to me . . . almost the first person I saw when I opened my eyes to this world, and my faithful and adoring slave for 26 years." (It was thirty-one years, and it would be surprising if the Greeners had servants when Belle was born; calling the maid her "slave" seems a pointed obfuscation.) She decided one winter not to attend a conference in Montreal because, she told BB, "I am so damned black that it is impossible for me to go anywhere . . . without being identified."

Mary Berenson, who also wrote and lectured about art, showed a Blooms-buryian tolerance for her husband's extramarital adventures, and had several of her own. She described Belle after their first meeting as "a most wild and woolly and EXTRAORDINARY young person." A year later she wished her husband (in her Philadelphia Quaker prose) all happiness with his new companion: "I hope thee will make this into something lasting and agreeable . . . for I love her youth, her *élan*. I find her remarkably attractive, too." When BB took Belle on an art tour of Europe in the summer of 1910—she had come to buy things for Morgan, who did not know about the liaison—he reported to Mary: "I am all in a whirl, for she is the most incredible combination of sheer childishness, hoy-denishness," mixed with "sincerity, cynicism and sentiment." From Ravenna he described her as "incredibly and miraculously responsive and most of all to the things I really care most about."

Mary urged him to "make the most of it," but BB was as baffled as he was aroused. Belle seemed "much more cerebral than sensual," he told his wife. "Of the erotic there is little in her and under the mask and manner and giggle there is something so genuine, so loyal, so vital, so full of heart . . . that . . . my impressions vary from minute to minute." He closed this odd marital confidence: "Goodbye my darling. Even though polygamous I am not the less yours."

The equally polygamous Belle attached herself intellectually and often romantically to a series of distinguished scholar/experts, beginning, she told Berenson, with "a terrific *crush*" on Junius Morgan, "which I secretly gloated over as the tragedy of my young life." She *was* more cerebral than sensual, and her promiscuity probably had to do with longing to absorb what these men knew, as well as with a need to see reflected in their eyes again and again that she was not only *visible* to the arbiters of high cultural authority, unlike many others of her race, but dazzling, desirable, unique.

Among the other men with whom she claimed to have had romantic liaisons were Sidney Cockerell, director of the Fitzwilliam Museum in Cambridge, the editor and Morgan art adviser William Laffan, and William M. Ivins, curator of prints at the Met. She regaled Berenson with tales of her flirtations—with John D. Rockefeller ("one of the very greatest men America has ever known"), "Benny" Altman, "my dear Charles Lanier," Alfred Pollard, the Keeper of Printed Books at the British Museum (who "quite loved my library"), Pollard's

British Museum colleague Charles Hercules Read ("it was only sheer will power—aided and strengthened by a lukewarmedness on his part [—] that prevented my falling desperately in love with him"), and many more.

Her wandering attentions made Berenson deeply unhappy, and Mary soon took alarm at the depth of her husband's feeling. She told her sister Alys (Mrs. Bertrand Russell): "I really do not mind what seems his greatest folly [Belle] for there is always something big and fine when a person of character and feeling falls in love—the generosity of the impulse (he who is very selfish about his own things is giving some of his loveliest pictures etc. to her)— . . . but it is a dreadful blackness and bitterness of spirit that hangs around him."

When the heartsick BB sent a friend to ask Belle whether she was simply making use of his mind without really caring for him—a poignant turn on the conventional female version of the question—she vehemently denied it. "[T]hat is one of the few things you could say that could really hurt me," she replied, then went on in her disarmingly frank way: "I really had to laugh at your last letter complaining of all the scandal you were hearing about me—I suppose they say everything from calling me the daughter of J.P. *à la main gauche*, to . . . the mother of triplets—but what difference does it make? . . . I've come to the conclusion that I really must be grudgingly admitted the most interesting person in New York, for it's about all they seem to talk about—*C'est à rire*—You know perfectly well BB . . . that I get 'hipped' on some man, regularly every six months and I suppose it will be so until I die—but I get over it all so very quickly that it does not really disturb the actual current of my life at all—And BB . . . these men and this talk and all is so stupidly unimportant and irrelevant—the only time I was really 'scandalous' was in your own dear company so if I guarantee that I will be really wicked only with you isn't it alright? . . . I don't want to be 'in society' and I do want to really know things—so you see I don't need many people in my life."

———

Belle did not see much of Morgan's family during his lifetime—they bored her "to extinction," she complained to Berenson, and after her "Big Chief" died she added, "More and more do I understand why JP loved to be away from his 'nearest and dearest.' " Belle's scorn apparently precluded interest in the one Morgan daughter whose life had anything in common with her own.

Anne had always stood out as more spirited and rebellious than her siblings: Louisa once described her as "irresistibly funny . . . in spite of her naughtiness," and Jack had found her puzzling, with ideas and thoughts that came out "at unexpected moments, in the most extraordinary way." In serving as her father's official traveling companion, Anne had grown close to Adelaide— they were thrown together constantly, and sometimes met alone for lunch or tea—but she had to keep everything connected with Mrs. Douglas from her mother. She also had to arrange her own life around her parents' separate demands. When the Henry Fairfield Osborns invited her to join them on a trip to the West in the summer of 1903, Anne told Mrs. Osborn there was not "the shadow of a chance" that she could: "Between Mother's summer & the yacht races, two things which mustn't meet & yet both of which I must join in," it was impossible for her "to make any further plans," although missing out on the western expedition was "the biggest kind of disappointment I could have."

Still living at home at age thirty, Anne had an allowance of $20,000 a year and no apparent inclination to marry. At the beginning of February 1904 she met her father, Adelaide, and the Markoes for a tour of Canada (Fanny was in Italy), a stop at Camp Uncas—where it was too rainy to sleigh in—and a train ride home.

She spent much of her time in New York that winter organizing a club for women with her friends Helen Hastings, wife of the architect Thomas Hastings, Helen Barney, daughter of the banker Charles T. Barney, and Daisy Harriman.* They had set out in 1902 to provide themselves and their friends with the same kinds of social resources and athletic facilities that the Metropolitan and Union Clubs afforded their fathers, husbands, brothers, and sons—Anne specifically requested a swimming pool and a squash court. They named it the Colony Club, and encountered considerable resistance: a German newspaper denounced it as "the swan-song of the American home and family," and Grover Cleveland advised that woman's "best and safest club is her home."

Anne's father supported the enterprise, serving on the men's advisory committee, but its organizers wanted to show the world what women could do on their own. They raised money, bought land at the corner of 30th and Madison, commissioned Stanford White to build a clubhouse, enrolled 550 members, and assigned the interior work to a novice decorator named Elsie de Wolfe. When the luxurious six-story Federal Revival building finally opened, one mother of eminent sons announced: "I've waited for this evening all my life. I've just telephoned the boys, 'Don't wait dinner. I'm dining at my club.' "† Anne made full use of the Colony facilities, but what became more important to her than the club itself was a new friendship with Elsie de Wolfe and her companion, Elisabeth Marbury.

---

* The former Florence Jaffray Hurst, whose father was head of a steamship company and president of the New York Yacht Club, had been schooled with the Morgan girls at 219, and married J. Borden Harriman, a banker and first cousin of E. H. Harriman, in 1889. Active in Democratic politics, Daisy Hurst Harriman was appointed U.S. minister to Norway by Franklin Roosevelt in 1937.

† The Colony Club moved uptown to a building designed by Delano & Aldrich at 560 Park Avenue in 1924.

This pair, who lived together at 122 East 17th Street, opened up to the well-traveled but relatively sheltered Anne a wide new world. Unlike most of the women in the Morgans' circle, they worked for a living. Elsie—slender, chic, vain, and socially ambitious—had spent years trying to build an acting career on little talent. *Town Topics* referred to her as "Miss de Lamb," and in 1887 ran a fictional sketch called "After the Matinee," in which Maud asks her friend Ethel as they leave the theater, "What did you think of Miss de Wolfe?" Ethel: "I thought she was splendid in the second dress." At the turn of the century, Elsie was becoming the first woman to make a career in interior design. She had fallen in love with the decorative arts of eighteenth-century France on summer trips abroad, and sent home trunks full of inexpensive furniture, mirrors, dishes, and lamps. Heavily influenced by Edith Wharton and Ogden Codman's 1897 *Decoration of Houses* (Mrs. Wharton hated the "sumptuary excesses" of the Gilded Age, and saw its overstuffed interiors as a branch of dressmaking), Elsie began clearing out New York's Victorian clutter and opening rooms up with sunlight, chintz, white paint, and fresh air. One of her first notable achievements was the sunny, trellised tearoom at the Colony Club.

She had been living with the mannish, deep-voiced, thoroughly unfashionable Elisabeth Marbury, called Bessie, since 1892. They made an unlikely couple—Bessie as heavyset and plain as Elsie was lithe and attractive—and according to Elsie's biographer, Jane Smith, were "almost certainly" lovers. The literary editor of *McClure's* said of Bessie, "If she chewed tobacco she would be complete." Henry Adams after a dinner party in Paris described the Misses Marbury and de Wolfe as "the only men of the lot."

Like Anne Morgan, Bessie came from a prominent New York family. She had grown up on Irving Place, spent summers at Oyster Bay, and traveled abroad with her lawyer-father, Francis F. Marbury.* As a child she read Horace, Kant, Plutarch, Tasso, Shakespeare, and Ruskin, gave lectures on the solar system to her friends (admission: 5¢), and converted to Roman Catholicism. Early on she decided that people were either wasters, mollusks, or builders—and that she was a builder. She had a brief, successful run as a poultry breeder on the third floor of her parents' house, and once said she had missed her true vocation by not becoming a grandmother.

She was wrong. She found her true vocation as a theatrical agent, and by 1895 had offices all over Europe. She represented Oscar Wilde, George Bernard Shaw, J. M. Barrie, Beerbohm Tree, Frances Hodgson Burnett, Arthur Wing Pinero, Victorien Sardou, Rostand, Feydeau, Halévy, Richepin, and the entire French Society of Dramatic Authors. "Rapacious Elisabeth Marbury," complained the Socialist Shaw: "What do you want me to make a fortune

---

* One of his relatives was party to the famous 1803 case, *Marbury* v. *Madison*, which established a precedent for the Supreme Court to rule on the doctrine of judicial review.

for? . . . The next time you have so large an amount to remit, please send it to me by installments, or you will put me to the inconvenience of having a bank account." After Wilde's sensational trial and imprisonment on charges of "gross indecency" in 1895, Bessie tried to save his American royalties for his family, and in 1898 sold American syndication rights for *The Ballad of Reading Gaol*. Wilde told his British publisher that he knew "as much about business as a chrysanthemum!" but had "full confidence in Miss Marbury, a brilliant delightful woman, who is anxious to help me."

Elsie decorated their town house at 17th Street and Irving Place in the style of 18th-century France, and there she and Bessie—called "the Bachelors" by their friends—held court. Henry Adams told Mrs. Cameron in 1901: "I went to see the Marbury salon and found myself in a mad cyclone of people. . . . I was struck blind by the brilliancy of [Elsie and Bessie's] world. They are grand and universal." Mrs. Astor, head of "the 400," decided to upstage these new rivals with a "bohemian" party of her own. Asked whom she planned to invite, she provoked hilarity in the Bachelors' set by replying, "J.P. Morgan and Edith Wharton."

Elsie flirted with men—Berenson once described her hugging and kissing him "in a way that was not exactly sisterly"—and in 1926, at the age of sixty, she married Sir Charles Mendl, an Englishman attached to the British embassy in Paris. Bessie, however, was interested only in women—specifically, in 1904, in Anne Morgan.

When Anne sailed for Europe as usual that April with her father, Adelaide, and Charles Lanier, she arranged to meet Bessie in Paris. Her party stayed in London about a week, celebrating Pierpont's sixty-seventh birthday at Princes Gate—it was on this trip that Langton Douglas showed him through the Sienese exhibition at the Burlington Fine Arts Club—then went on to Paris, where Anne reported in her diary, "Miss Marbury ill bronchitis." She had lunch with John Singer Sargent and James McNeill Whistler, visited her aunt Mary Burns, tried on dresses at Worth's, and spent every free minute with "E.M.": "Afternoon saw Miss Marbury . . . Quiet dinner with Miss Marbury . . . lunch E.M."

Bessie had just bought an abandoned villa on the Boulevard Saint-Antoine in Versailles, the "Villa Trianon," built in the early nineteenth century by the French royal family, but left vacant after the Revolution of 1848. The outbuildings of this elegant ruin dated to the eighteenth century, and were full of associations with Marie Antoinette, the ancien régime, and the Trianon palaces at Versailles—Pierpont might well have bought it for Adelaide. The "Bachelors" had discovered it in 1903 while renting a house nearby from Alice Mason, and Elsie decided she couldn't live without it. The indulgent (and solvent) Bessie paid $13,000 for the house and two acres of land in the winter of 1904, and took Anne to see it on May 1. Anne wrote in her diary: "Versailles with E.M.!!

Villa Trianon—drive through park. Short walk. Tea reservoir heavenly drive home. Beginning of perfect things."

Anne had to go to Aix with her father and Adelaide on May 3. On the second she saw Sarah Bernhardt perform and spent a "perfect afternoon with E., even with leaving—tea talking a joy." ("E." in Anne's diaries is Bessie; when she meant Miss de Wolfe, she wrote "Elsie.") She lunched with Bessie on the third—"All happiness except that it is the end of Act I"—and left at 2:00 P.M. At Aix, her mood rose and fell with the reception of news from "E"—"perfectly satisfactory letter to think over . . . no letter rather depressed till wire came . . . better letter than ever. Father and Mrs. D. in auto to Cluny." She accompanied her father and Mrs. D. to northern Italy in mid-May, found "wonderful letters waiting" when she returned to Paris, and was ecstatic to meet up again in London with "E!" in early June. They lunched, dined, went to the theater, and took an overnight trip to Oxford: "Colleges all morning," wrote Anne, "afternoon . . . rain . . . Quiet and happiness." At the end of June she returned to New York with her father and Adelaide—Bessie must have stayed abroad, for she does not appear in Anne's diary again until October.

Anne was in love. She had been spurning marriage proposals for years, apparently resigning herself to the difficult task of tending both parents as the price of independence. It is impossible to say what she had known of her sexuality before she met Bessie, or what went on behind closed doors once she did—probably what goes on behind closed doors between most people who are passionately drawn to each other. Under the tutelage of the astute E.M., who was seventeen years her senior and bore distinct physical and managerial resemblances to Pierpont Morgan, Anne began to escape from the strictures of Madison Avenue spinsterhood to a brilliant international demimonde of aesthetic appreciation, social activism, and female independence.

The domestic arrangements at Irving Place appear not to have been disturbed by the addition of a third party. In the fall of 1904 Anne took walks, drives, and teas with E.M., but often noted the presence of "E. de W." as well. She spent much of her time at 17th Street when she was in New York, and in summers at the Villa Trianon the three women became known as the Versailles Triumvirate. Anne eventually bought land for the Trianon gardens and added an entire "Morgan Wing." The erotic intensity of her new alliance appears to have passed unnoticed at 219—an unmarried daughter would inevitably spend most of her time with other women, and Fanny welcomed the addition of the Misses Marbury and de Wolfe to her cloistered world.

———

Anne continued to travel with her father. In September 1904 Fanny stayed at Cragston while Pierpont, Anne, and Adelaide entertained the archbishop of Canterbury in Maine. Morgan had persuaded the leader of the Anglican

Church to come to Boston for the Triennial Episcopal Convention that fall, and had been planning the arrangements for months. On Friday, September 9, he and Anne escorted Archbishop Randall Davidson and his wife to Bar Harbor. Adelaide was already there, as was *Corsair.*

Early Sunday morning, Morgan took a large party by yacht to Northeast Harbor, where the archbishop was to give the morning sermon. Bishop Lawrence and his family boarded at 8:30 A.M., joining Adelaide, Anne, the Davidsons, and several other Morgan friends. Marian Lawrence, the bishop's daughter, noted in her diary that she and her parents had already had breakfast, and "would have liked to have sat on deck and enjoyed the lovely sail, the fresh air, and fine day, but fate and Mr. Morgan decreed that we were to go down into the close dining room where a sumptuous repast of nine courses was set before us. Mr. Morgan [ate] it all heartily and slowly, from melons, oatmeal, eggs, and bacon to buckwheats and fruit again, and all the time I was getting dizzier and more of a headache. Pride alone kept me to my seat. Papa . . . sought the deck and fresh air about half way through, and *none* of us [ate] a thing except a nibble of toast and coffee."

By the time Morgan finished his breakfast it was time to land. Miss Lawrence continued: "the church was overflowing but the front seats had been kept for our party. . . . Directly behind us was Mr. Morgan singing lustily. Of course they were the observed of all observers. North East was simply agog with curiosity and excitement."

After the service, the archbishop greeted parishioners "while Papa & J.P. Morgan &c stood aside!" reported Marian. The men went on to lunch with Northeast Harbor's Bishop Doane, while Marian and her sister "were expected to lunch on the *Corsair* with Anne Morgan, Molly Coles, Mrs. Douglas & Mrs. Wright. I didn't jump at the idea of another meal in that rolly, stuffy cabin." She escaped. Over the next few days Anne lunched with Adelaide, and played tennis with Marian Lawrence, Adelaide Randolph, and Sybil Douglas while her father occupied himself with the bishops. There were receptions and dinners every night.

On September 22 Morgan took Archbishop Davidson to Washington to dine with Roosevelt at the White House, and the next day back to New York for a *Corsair* cruise and a visit to Cragston. Herbert Satterlee found the Davidsons "very unprepossessing—not at all distinguished looking, & badly dressed, but agreeable."

At the beginning of October the "unprepossessing" couple and Morgan's other guests—this time including Fanny—went to Boston for the convention. As usual, Morgan rented a house with full staff, and put Louis Sherry in charge: he had fifty-six people to dinner one night. Another night, Fanny joined her husband for a small dinner with Bishops Lawrence, Davidson, Potter, and Doane. What the clergymen made of the alternating presence of Mrs. Douglas and Mrs. Morgan they did not record. Fanny attended a convention session on divorce.

Morgan's overbearing generosity did not always take into account the actual preferences of his friends, as Marian Lawrence's description of the *Corsair* breakfast suggests. Bishop Lawrence one day asked the Davidsons whether they would like a rest, a walk, or a drive. "Oh, a walk," they eagerly replied. "Mr. Morgan has carried us everywhere, and we have not felt the American soil!"

———

After Anne returned from Bar Harbor in the fall of 1904 she saw Bessie Marbury virtually every day, including Thanksgiving and Christmas. She took her to lunch with Adelaide at the end of November, to Boston with Fanny in early December, and to Uncas with Pierpont and Adelaide early in the new year. On March 1, 1905, the day she was to leave with her father on their annual trip to Europe, she spent the morning at 17th Street, and two weeks later was exultant to find "flowers from E." waiting at her Paris hotel. In mid-May, returning from two months of Morgan/Douglas travel, she arrived in Paris early one morning—"lunched Versailles! dined alone Father [Café] Anglais—long talk." Perhaps in this long talk she asked permission to stay on in Paris, for her father took Adelaide and Sybil Douglas to Aix without her. The next day Anne wrote in her diary: "E. arrived to spend night. Mr. [Henry] Adams to dinner." Anne spent most of that summer in Paris and Versailles with "E." They took motor trips through France, and entertained Adams, Edith Wharton, Sardou, Pierre de Nolhac (the curator at Versailles who was undoing Louis-Philippe's atrocious modernization and advising Elsie on decorative art), and Count Robert de Montesquiou, the orchidaceous aesthete/dandy who was one of the models for Baron Charlus in Proust's *Remembrance of Things Past.*

Late that fall, after Anne and her father had returned to the United States, another French aesthete was mesmerizing the New York art world. Morgan hired this man, a Monsieur de Beauvoir, to give private art lectures for two at Adelaide's house on 46th Street. De Beauvoir was also giving evening classes at the residence of Ogden Codman, Edith Wharton's collaborator, for "everybody interested in art in New York." Roger Fry described him as a ruined French aristocrat "who knows everything, [and] has the most perfect taste and manners of the Ancien Régime. Instead of being my rival, and he was already installed as arbiter elegantiarum when I came, he has done all he can to befriend me and been in fact all that one doesn't expect from a cher confrère."*

———

* According to Fry, the Frenchman in New York so longed for London "that he goes close to the subway exits parce que c'est la même odeur que celle du Tuppeny Tube." Fry had found a kindred spirit: "Like all other Europeanised people here we make signals of distress to one another in this weltering waste of the American people. It is strange what an invariable bond of sympathy this instinctive hatred of America as it exists to-day is—tho' many believe in the future. I suppose I do, as I'm investing so much in it. . . ."

Elsie de Wolfe, persuaded by a friend to see de Beauvoir for ten minutes, gave him two hours: "He thrilled me," she reported, opening up "vistas of knowledge of all the things I was trying to learn about." She, Bessie, and Anne entertained M. de Beauvoir early in 1906, and Fanny gave a dinner party for him.

New York's art dealers were mystified by the unfamiliar Frenchman who was charming the likes of Fry, Ogden Codman, Morgan, and the "Bachelors." Elsie tried several times to introduce her erudite expert to Henry Duveen, but de Beauvoir invariably failed to appear. Then one day she and Codman took him to see the Widener collection in Philadelphia, and by chance ran into Duveen there. De Beauvoir succumbed to a sudden coughing fit, holding his handkerchief over his face, but the dealer had recognized him. A few days of research confirmed the impression, and Duveen reported his findings to Morgan.

This paragon of knowledge and taste turned out to be an ingenious con man named Maurice Bosdari who had crossed Morgan's path before. Calling himself a count, he had sold the banker several *objets* in August 1902 for £11,500 ($57,000), and Morgan had confirmed the purchase in writing—"a bronze statuette of Ganymede by Cellini, now at the South Kensington Museum, a French Commode Louis XV, and 40 English mezzotint portraits." The bronze, needless to say, was not by Cellini, and the sale set in motion Bosdari's larger plan: with Morgan's signature in hand, he forged it on bills that he persuaded high-ranking British politicians, manufacturers, and financiers to discount, instructing them under no circumstances to show the bills to J. S. Morgan & Co., by express command of Morgan himself. When two of the bills, for £11,500 each, showed up at Old Broad Street early in 1903 and were recognized as fakes, Morgan's partners found it "inconceivable that businessmen should have accepted such a story" and not informed them: "The bill brokers gave as the excuse for their silence that they were afraid of being told to mind their own business if they discussed JPM's transactions with his firm."

As soon as the fraud was detected Bosdari disappeared. The London police posted notices for his arrest, describing him as forty-five years old, five feet six inches, Italian by birth, fluent in French, German, English, and Spanish, respectable in appearance, and well known to the principal art dealers of London. When his clothes and personal effects were found on the deck of a steamer to Dieppe, people concluded that he had drowned. Officially dead, he secured money and a transatlantic ticket from a friend, went to Canada, entered a monastery, and two years later emerged as de Beauvoir in New York.

After the encounter with Duveen at Widener's, Bosdari once again disappeared—this time to Italy, where he was arrested and briefly detained, then to France.* The picture of Morgan in Adelaide's parlor listening to private lectures

---

* Anne noted running into "Bosdari & de Beauvoir" in France in the fall of 1907, and he was listed, with Morgan, Charles Eliot Norton, James Russell Lowell, and Joseph Choate as a

on art given by the imaginative huckster who had robbed official London in his name probably afforded Bosdari some retrospective diversion. Most likely it did not cause Morgan to lose any sleep.

———

Bessie Marbury took full credit for the education and emancipation of Anne. Morgan's daughter had been "young for her age," she wrote in a memoir, and not "allowed to grow up." Using an image that would never have occurred to the Madison Avenue ladies, Bessie went on: "Her mind was ready for the spark plugs to be adjusted"—and there happened to be an able mechanic at hand. After their first visit to Versailles, Anne began "to draw her own conclusions, to develop her own opinions, to select her own interests, in other words to stand on her own feet."

Miss Marbury noted strong similarities between Anne and her father. He was "a man of marvelous energy, of infinite courage, and of concentrated opinions. Once he believed in anyone or in any cause, no outside influence would have the slightest effect upon him"—and the same could be said of his daughter. Morgan held a position in the world that no woman could attain, however, and Bessie took a shrewd measure of his strengths: while they "drove him into leadership, as he grew older it was evident that he suffered from their very defects. To acknowledge defeat was foreign to his temperament. He was always loyal to his mistakes."

Bessie may have exaggerated her role in Anne's metamorphosis, but it was in the context of this amorous friendship that Morgan's youngest daughter discovered strengths of her own, and ventured to defy him. He had begun moving the departure dates for his European trips back from spring to winter, and lengthening his stays from weeks to months. When he sailed in February 1906, Anne did not accompany him for the first time since Louisa's marriage. She had decided no longer to travel with him and his mistress.

No one challenged him this way, and especially not on this subject. Though apparently furious, he was helpless to force compliance in a young woman whose will was as strong as his own. He remained abroad from February till July. Louisa, who had always accommodated herself to his schedule and demands, took her family to London in June (she had had a second baby girl), perhaps partly to offset her sister's defection.

Anne followed with Fanny at the end of the month, meeting up with "E. and Elsie" in London the day she arrived. On June 30 she wrote in her diary:

———

member of the American Dante Society in 1908. He was finally caught in London as an unregistered alien under the name of Brémont in 1917, and sentenced to three years in jail. Jack professed himself "highly pleased" that Bosdari had been "found, tried, and convicted, even after all these years."

"Lunch Carlton E. . . . opera Faust Aunt M[ary]—strong talk!" And on July 1: "E. in a.m. Lunch and dinner Dover House. Long hot talk Herbert." This strong, hot talk was probably about her defiance, but Anne did not change her mind. Not only was she no longer willing to serve as paternal helpmeet and chaperone; she now had a rich social world of her own.

On July 3, she went to France with Elsie and Bessie. She noted in her diary that "Father arrived" in Paris on the tenth. The next day "dined home with Father." She did not say what they discussed. Then the "Triumvirate" moved to Versailles. On July 28, Marcel Proust came to the Villa Trianon for tea.

Morgan went on with his own summer—he dined at the Harcourts' with Edward VII on July 14, gave his royal confrère the tour of Princes Gate on the sixteenth, and two days later sailed back to New York.

Anne stayed in France until the end of September, and after 1906 moved into a life that had little except its energetic drive to do with her father's. She made friends with Ida Tarbell and other members of the new investigative-journalist crowd, and visited Hull House, Jane Addams's social-work settlement in Chicago. She opened a temperance restaurant for workers in the Brooklyn Navy Yard, engaging Mrs. Andrew Carnegie and Mrs. Elbert Gary as waitresses. After watching the Wright brothers demonstrate their flying machine at Le Mans in August 1908, she went up in a plane with Elsie and Wilbur Wright. With Bessie and Daisy Harriman, she tried to interest the Senate in a woman who was developing industrial training programs for impoverished young people in Georgia. Discussing this project over lunch at the White House early in 1909, she told a Roosevelt aide: "there are such opportunities for [women's] careers in America now that it makes one restless . . . With the money that we have back of us and the energy we have stored up in us one hardly knows where to begin." She *had* begun.

In 1909 she joined a group of society women known as "the mink brigade" to support an International Ladies Garment Workers Union strike. Thirty thousand strikers, mostly teenage girls, walked off sweatshop jobs on New York's Lower East Side and stayed out for thirteen weeks, forcing three hundred manufacturers to settle with the union. Anne met with the "shirt waist girls," helped raise money for them, and attended meetings of the Women's Trade Union League. She also raised money for the ILGWU after 146 women died in a fire at the Triangle Shirtwaist sweatshop in Greenwich Village in 1911.

Dr. Rainsford reported to Louisa from France one spring on a confidential talk he had with Anne (clearly not confidential enough), and offered to exercise his influence over her in any way he could: "Surely the time will come when bitterly she will regret allowing anything *any friend to separate her from her father. She should be now his constant companion—Oh life is so short! its opportunities so soon [gone]! and they come not again.*"

In the fall of 1910, Belle Greene was returning from her Berensonian tour of

Europe via the White Star's *Oceanic* when she learned that Anne and Bessie were on board. Anne "got me aside for a long talk," she reported to BB, and "asked me to use all of my influence to show 'Father' he was pursuing the wrong course with her. I lied quite boldly and calmly and said JP never discussed his family affairs with me. She seemed disappointed and a bit incredulous." Anne repeated her request the next day, "but I told her it was *absolutely* impossible for me to do." The two women rarely crossed paths in New York, and Belle distrusted this "sudden amiability—besides I want to avoid meeting Miss Marbury if possible. . . . She may be mighty interesting but she certainly is horrid to look at. She has a strong resemblance to some of the portraits of Antinous."

Belle succeeded in avoiding Anne's horrid-looking friend in 1910, and referred disparagingly two years later to the "tiresome female house of Morgan Marbury & Co." When she finally did meet Bessie, early in 1913, she fell (she told Berenson) "immediately in love." The older woman's "breeziness, frankness, and sincerity drew me irresistibly"—Belle was sorry they could never be friends, presumably because of the warfare over Anne. A month later she continued: "Your friend Miss Marbury seems really to like me, but I'm a gent's lady!!! Tell me all she says about me." Anne's sister Juliet "*hates* Bessie Marbury," and would do anything to "injure her and Elsie de Wolfe," Belle informed BB: "You might tip them off if they don't already know." Juliet spoke of Bessie as if she were a "leper" from whom Anne had got a disease.

Juliet probably reflected the general family view, and a document at the New York-Historical Society describes Morgan taking revenge on the person he blamed for Anne's desertion.

Ever since Bessie had begun her work on behalf of the French theater, her friends had expected her to receive the Légion d'Honneur. Sardou wrote a letter of recommendation, as did Rostand, Richepin, three American ambassadors, the French Ambassador Jusserand, Theodore Roosevelt, and William Howard Taft. "I want the Legion of Honor for Bessie Marbury," Henry Adams told John Hay in September 1904—Hay had recently received the Legion's Grand Cross for his work on behalf of world peace: "Sardou is superintending the affair, and all the French literarers are in it, writing letters for her. Please write somebody a letter saying how glad you would be to have her under your command. . . . I will get La Farge to march in your regiment too, and Falstaff never had two funnier recruits than La Farge and Bessy Marbury.

"Miss Marbury has only one thing against her . . . —she has done more than everyone else together to get for America a real grip on French interests. She has the whole French literary, theatrical, class in her pocket. She is the only Legionary,—or will be,—of the American lot, (including yourself) who has done real service."

After World War I there was further reason to honor Miss Marbury, as she had raised money for French charities and given the Villa Trianon to be used as a hospital between 1914 and 1918. Moreover, both Anne and Elsie had received the Croix de Guerre—Anne for organizing an American Committee for Devastated France, with offices in Paris and Blérancourt, that provided housing, food, clothing, clinics, and medical supplies throughout the war; she was awarded the Legion of Honor as well. In 1920 Bessie wrote to her friend James Hazen Hyde, a wealthy American living in Paris, to find out why she had never received a medal.

Hyde left among his papers a memorandum saying that in response to Bessie's letter he had called on his friend Bob Bacon and learned the answer. Bacon, appointed ambassador to France by President Taft at the end of 1910, had arrived with a specific nongovernmental mission: "J. P. Morgan, Sr., to whom he was under great obligation, had asked him to do only one thing when he went abroad as Ambassador," wrote Hyde—and that was "to block [Elisabeth Marbury's] getting the Legion of Honor. Morgan said she had stolen his daughter, Anne, away from him and prejudiced her against him. Marbury [had] said to Miss Morgan that her father compromised her by using her as a chaperone when he travelled with his mistress, Mrs. Douglas."

This story may well be true, but its foundations are shaky. Bacon was ambassador for less than two years, in 1911–12, and it seems unlikely that his veto would have been sustained for another decade. Moreover, Hyde said that Bessie's letter, written on April 7, 1920, had prompted his informative call on Bacon. Bob Bacon died on May 29, 1919.

Jack Morgan.
(Archives of The Pierpont Morgan Library, New York)

Chapter 26

—

BACK NUMBER?

In the winter of 1901, news of the U.S. Steel deal had prompted talk of an imperial Morgan ruling the world, and a 1902 cartoon portrayed him as "the Field Marshall of Industry" with his arms circling the globe. By late 1903, a combination of the Northern Securities suit, the failure of the U.S. Steel bond-conversion plan, and the difficulties of the IMM had bred rumors of Morgan's imminent retirement and collapse. As more trouble followed, financial insiders on both sides of the Atlantic concluded that "the old man" was over the hill.

On March 14, 1904, the U.S. Supreme Court ruled five to four that the Northern Securities Company constituted an illegal combination in restraint of trade and would have to be dissolved.

The range of judicial opinion in this case, in which two lower courts had come to opposite conclusions, reflected the country's abiding confusion about competition, monopoly, and regulation under the antitrust law. Writing for the majority, Justice John M. Harlan contended that the combination of previously competing roads *in itself* violated the Sherman law, even if the combination did not have greater market power than the individual roads and did not commit illegal acts. "If Congress has not, by the words used in the [Sherman] Act, described this and like cases," argued Harlan, "it would, we apprehend, be impossible to find words that would describe them." Without this kind of judicial interpretation, he continued, "the efforts of the national government to preserve to the people the benefits of free competition among carriers engaged in interstate commerce will be wholly unavailing, and all transcontinental lines, indeed the entire railway systems of the country, may be absorbed, merged and consolidated, thus placing the public at the absolute mercy of the holding corporation."

Oliver Wendell Holmes strongly disagreed. Appointed to the Court by Roosevelt in 1902, Holmes began his first dissent with an argument for the judiciary's independence of politics in words that have become famous: "Great cases like hard cases make bad law," he wrote, for "great cases are called great not by reason of their real importance in shaping the law of the future but because of some accident of immediate overwhelming interest which appeals to the feelings and distorts the judgment. These immediate interests exercise a kind of hydraulic pressure which makes what previously was clear seem doubtful, and before which even well-settled principles of law will bend."

The "accident of immediate overwhelming interest" exerting pressure on the law in 1904 was the country's hatred of the trusts. Holmes did not think that one company's ownership of previously independent companies violated the Sherman Act, since the act said nothing about competition or numbers of competitors—it ruled out only agreements that restricted commerce, and if it were to be construed in such general terms as those argued by the government, Holmes could "see no part of the conduct of life with which on similar principles Congress might not interfere." To make his point clearer, he suggested imagining that the parties in the case were small grocers rather than giant railroads: "There is a natural feeling that somehow or other the [antitrust] statute meant to strike at combinations great enough to cause just anxiety on the part of those who love their country more than money, while it viewed such little ones as I have mentioned with just indifference." In other words, Holmes would not rule out combinations on grounds of *size:* he thought the legal question ought to concern their effect on commerce.

Roosevelt had set out to establish the federal government's power to control corporations, and had just won a major, popular victory over Morgan and Wall Street, eight months before a presidential election. He felt betrayed by Holmes. Having expected this intellectual Bostonian, his first appointment to the Court, to agree with him, he fumed: "I could carve out of a banana a judge with more backbone than that." Holmes dined at the White House two weeks after the decision was announced, but the subject of the case did not come up. Many years later, he told a friend that his *Northern Securities* dissent "broke up" his "incipient friendship" with Roosevelt, who saw it as "a political departure (or, I suspect, more truly, couldn't forgive anyone who stood in his way). We talked freely later but it never was the same after that."*

* Holmes never revised his view of the Sherman law. Years after *Northern Securities* he asked Solicitor General John W. Davis: "Mr. Solicitor, how many more of these antitrust cases have you?"

Jack Morgan was in New York when the decision came down. He cabled Dawkins that it was "almost as bad as possible. . . . Dissenting opinions very strong and by best men. Impossible at present say anything about effects," and he added a few days later by mail: "The Senior is having endless conferences with the various gentlemen interested in the property, and I presume a scheme for liquidation will be arrived at before long."

On March 22 the "gentlemen interested in the property" approved a plan, over the objections of E. H. Harriman, to distribute its assets to shareholders pro rata. Harriman wanted the combination to return the exact number of shares each owner had put in, which would give him the huge Northern Pacific position he had acquired in 1901, and when the vote went against him he sued to prevent distribution. The federal circuit judges who had heard the original case ruled unanimously against his petition on April 19, but he appealed all the way to the Supreme Court, and lost there as well in 1905.

With the dismantling of Northern Securities, the big Northwest railroads returned to the competitive status quo of 1901, with the Hill/Morgan group controlling the Northern Pacific, Burlington, and Great Northern, and Harriman the Union Pacific and Illinois Central.

U.S. merger activity had declined as the contraction of 1903 and the disappointing performance of new consolidations left "undigested securities" on the market. By the time the Court ordered Northern Securities dissolved in 1904, the country's first great merger movement was over.

———

Even before the *Northern Securities* case was decided, Morgan apparently considered four years of Theodore Roosevelt quite enough. In May of 1903, he, Mark Hanna, and other leading Republicans tried to draft Grover Cleveland for a third term, announcing that they would switch parties to support the Democrat "with all their power." Cleveland declined to run. Hanna died in February 1904. Dawkins wrote to Jack that it "will have been a blow to your father. I suppose [Hanna's] removal makes Roosevelt's nomination certain and that the chances of a Republican majority are good."

He was right. The Democrats nominated a conservative New York judge

———

Davis: "Quite a number, Mr. Justice."

Holmes: "Bring 'em on and we'll decide 'em. Of course I know and so does every other sensible man that the Sherman Law is damned nonsense, but if my country wants to go to hell I am here to help do it."

John W. Davis was solicitor general from 1913 to 1918, when Woodrow Wilson appointed him ambassador to the Court of St. James; after he returned to the United States in 1921 he became head of the "Morgan" law firm, formerly Stetson, Jennings and Russell, eventually Davis, Polk & Wardwell.

named Alton Parker who had all "the salient qualities of a sphere," said the New York *Sun*. Parker didn't bother to campaign against the charismatic advocate of the Square Deal and the busted trust. At the beginning of October, Pulitzer's *World* breathed life into a stultifying race by implying that Republican Party chairman George Cortelyou, formerly Secretary of Commerce, was blackmailing corporations for campaign funds. Roosevelt denounced the story in a rage, and it quickly died. Cortelyou didn't have to blackmail the corporations: wealthy Republicans with no viable alternative supported the party on their own.

Morgan's friend William Laffan at the *Sun* announced the paper's reluctant support of the President in a five-word editorial: "Theodore, with all thy faults———."

Morgan, Frick, and Standard Oil each contributed $100,000 to the campaign, and Harriman raised an additional $300,000. Testifying before a Senate investigation into campaign finance several years later, Morgan said he had given $100,000 in cash in October, and then another $50,000 through the Harriman Fund in early November, because party officials thought they might not carry New York State. Senator Thomas H. Paynter of Kentucky, pointing out Morgan's "very liberal" initial contribution, asked whether the banker had been surprised to be called on for a second installment.

Morgan: "No: I got accustomed to it."

Paynter: "Did [party fund-raisers Cortelyou and Cornelius Bliss] express . . . their gratitude that you had given . . . $100,000 and had consented to give another $50,000?"

Morgan. "No. Gratitude has been rather scarce in my experience."

Roosevelt had become president by virtue of McKinley's assassination, and hated jokes about "His Accidency." He won his first presidential election in 1904 by a landslide—57 percent of the vote to Parker's 38 percent. During the victory celebrations that night, for reasons no one has ever fully understood, he announced that he would follow the "wise custom which limits the President to two terms" and not run again. It was, according to his biographer William Harbaugh, "the worst political blunder" of his career. Years later TR told a friend, "I would cut my hand off right there"—pointing to his wrist—"if I could recall that . . . statement."

———

When Morgan went to Europe in the spring of 1904—the spring of the Sienese art exhibition and Anne's first trip to Versailles with Bessie—he was worried about his English firm. He had predicted in 1900 that it would be "unrivalled" for the next generation, but since then it had steadily lost caste. Jack and Dawkins had put together a disastrous consolidation of Scottish coal mines called United Collieries in 1902,* the IMM was a fiasco, and the partners were a decidedly mixed lot. Teddy Grenfell proved to be the only clear success: having started out in charge of routine internal operations, he worked well with clients and other bankers and became a partner, with a 4 percent share of the firm's profits, in 1904. Jack showed few signs of distinction. The junior Walter Burns, whom Dawkins had described in 1900 as young, fat, and lazy, spent little time at work. And Morgan now reluctantly concluded that Dawkins had been a mistake. In April 1904 he began to confer in secret with Baring Brothers about a merger that would close down J. S. Morgan & Co.

That step would erase the name of Junius Morgan and broadcast a momentous failure. Pierpont had terminated ailing partnerships before, but hated to confront people who disappointed him. He did not let Dawkins in on his deliberations. Meeting with Lord Revelstoke (John Baring) in mid-April, he talked only of Northern Securities as long as Dawkins was in the room. The instant his partner left, however, he "plunged into more personal questions" about the future, reported Revelstoke.

After Barings' near failure in 1890, the house of Morgan had taken the lead in their long-standing rivalry. When James Stillman at the National City Bank asked Barings to join in a British government loan in 1900, Cecil Baring had advised against it: "we take it absolutely for granted," he told his brother, Revelstoke, "that we are committed to [Morgans]." He thought the City Bank *ought* to be included in big issues, but when "the time comes J.P.M. will be the man to offer Stillman the business." The Barings worked well in Boston with Kidder, Peabody, but their New York office, Baring, Magoun, was faring as poorly as Morgans in London. In 1904, Morgan and Revelstoke discussed closing their weaker branches and relying on each other's strengths—J. P. Morgan & Co. would represent Barings in New York while Baring Brothers handled Morgan's London business.

According to Revelstoke, Morgan hoped not only to solve his London problem but to defend his interests against increasingly aggressive competition from other American banks, particularly Stillman's and Kuhn, Loeb: he "inveighed bitterly against the growing power of the Jews and of the Rockefeller crowd, and said more than once that our firms and his were the only two com-

---

* When the London firm organized an underwriting syndicate to subscribe for £1 million of 5 percent Collieries debentures and sell them to the public, the New York partners declined participation, but Perkins's New York Life took £125,000 of the bonds. Suffering from bad management and declining coal prices, the Collieries trust earned no profit and its bonds never sold. J. S. Morgan & Co. loaned it hundreds of thousands of dollars over the next two years, and by the spring of 1904 faced several lawsuits. Morgan was furious. The London firm cabled Jack in New York that April: "We talked matter over with JPM who declined to go into details but said we had got into bad business with which we must deal."

posed of white men in New York." Age, and the pressure of his recent difficulties, brought out an anti-Semitism Morgan had not shown before.

Kuhn, Loeb was the only Jewish firm powerful enough to pose a threat to the "white" men in New York. It had alliances with Harriman's railroad interests, Stillman's "Rockefeller" bank, and the Equitable Life Assurance Society. Moreover, it had taken the lead, after Morgan's financing of the Boer War, in sponsoring U.S. international loans. Other German-Jewish houses in the early years of the new century, still largely dependent on European affiliates, were more willing than Yankee firms to meet the financial needs of small business, light industry, and retail stores, and began through those channels to gain a foothold in underwriting. Not until 1906, however, did Lehman Brothers and Goldman, Sachs float successful loans for Sears, Roebuck and United Cigar. Although Jacob Schiff was regarded as the second most powerful banker in America after Morgan, Jews were not about to take over Wall Street in 1904.

Morgan held several more discussions with Barings that April, then went off with Adelaide and Anne (who had not yet decamped) to Aix. Dawkins was taking his own measure of the London "débacle." Now Sir Clinton (he had been knighted for his War Office work), he told Milner: "Morgan has done some bad business for which I am not really responsible"—probably the IMM. "Other bad or unfortunate business has been entered upon for which I am in a large measure responsible"—probably United Collieries—"in the direction rather of not having stopped it than of having originated it. Much the same thing." He predicted that Morgan would not recover his "former position" in England, and that his own political career would suffer: "Any criticism or detractions for having engaged in unsound finance will be accentuated in my case because, as an Englishman, I am engaged in operations offensive to national susceptibilities."

That the house of Morgan had engaged in "unsound finance" seemed to be common knowledge. In New York that fall, James Stillman pronounced Morgan a "back number."

As Morgan escorted the archbishop of Canterbury from Maine to Washington in October 1904, he was vacillating about the alliance with Barings. Impulsive in his choice of people and decisive about starting new ventures, he had a terrible time making up his mind when things went wrong. In the 1870s he had wanted to retire rather than sort out unsatisfactory partnerships. Now, in the fall of 1904, he brought Bob Bacon and George Perkins into his deliberations, although not together: Bacon agreed in principle to head a reorganized Morgan-Baring New York office—on condition that Perkins go back to New York Life. Morgan asked Barings not to discuss the negotiations with his London partners, and said it was "absolutely essential nothing be said to Jack."

Dawkins had observed in 1901 that few men lived through the crushing pressure of the firm's work "except physical and intellectual giants like Morgan." Late in 1904 Dawkins himself, at forty-eight, developed heart trouble, and Morgan retreated from the Barings confederation on the ground that "it might kill Dawkins if any change were made." Early in 1905 Dawkins had a heart attack. He went off on doctors' orders to his country house in Surrey, then to Italy.

Morgan continued to put off closure with Barings for fear, he claimed, "of inflicting a mortal hurt on Dawkins." As Bessie Marbury noted, he was always loyal to his mistakes. He finally decided *not* to liquidate J. S. Morgan & Co., and in August of 1905 the Barings, referring to him as "the Old Man," gave up. Revelstoke reflected that the "London lot [of Morgan partners], as at present constituted, are so entirely useless and so out of touch with anything which is of value in English financial and commercial life that Morgan's people will find their power constantly decreasing on this side. They have made several serious and expensive blunders, and carry no sort of confidence in the City." He thought the real difficulty all along had been not Dawkins but Jack: "I expect there is little sympathy and less confidence between father and son. JPM told me Jack did not know a word of what had been mooted." Dawkins died at the end of the year.

It may have been at about this time that Morgan said to Rainsford, "My first choice of a man is sometimes right—my second never is." His choices of Fabbri, Coster, Stetson, Baker, Bristow, Edison, and Coffin had been first-rate, but lately, as Ballin said with regard to the IMM, he was finding it "impossible to get the right men to take their places."

Instead of dissolving his English partnership, Morgan rearranged it. He hired a new associate, a friend of Jack's and a cousin of Grenfell's named Vivian Hugh Smith, whose father had been governor of the Bank of England. He left Walter Burns in place but summoned Jack to New York. If Dawkins had been a poor choice, Teddy Grenfell had not: the Bank of England made him a director in 1905, and at the end of the year Morgan appointed him resident senior in London. Grenfell in six years had seen only the taciturn side of his chief. From Aix early in 1906, he told his sister: "JPM is placid but he is an impossible man to have any talk with. The nearest approach he makes is an occasional grunt."

———

In preparation for Jack's return to New York, Morgan bought the last of the three houses built by the Phelps family on Madison Avenue between 36th and 37th Streets, No. 229, and gave it to his son. Jack reflected to Fanny from London in January 1905: "It is extra nice of Father to let us have it. . . . It will be perfectly charming to be so near 219 and [Louisa at] 225. Certainly Father has managed to get his family close about him this winter at any rate."

Over the next year, Jack and Jessie entirely remodeled the house. When completed, it had forty-five rooms, twelve bathrooms, twenty-two fireplaces, a silver vault, a two-thousand-bottle wine cellar, and a formal ballroom. Jack decided he didn't like the number 229—perhaps it was too similar to 219—and changed it to 231. When the Satterlees moved to their new house at 37 East 36th Street in 1906, the senior Morgan tore down 225 and turned the space between his house and Jack's into a garden.

Depressed and anxious about his health, he sailed for Europe at the beginning of March 1905 with Adelaide, Sybil, and Anne. He celebrated his sixty-eighth birthday in Rome, where the Pope and the King thanked him for returning the Ascoli Cope. Staying at Rome's Grand Hotel, he wrote to an American physician in Florence, William W. Baldwin: "I want very much to see you myself," and "some of the ladies are also under the weather and need your care."

From Aix in early June, Morgan's French physician, Dr. Léon Blanc, reported to Jim Markoe that their shared patient was quite depressed, and the tension in his arteries "so high that a cerebral congestion was to be feared. For this reason I . . . ordered some artificial Nauheim baths with strong rubbing after and some electricity to try to give him better sleep. After a few days of treatment the arterial tension which was at the beginning 27 fell to 23 and sometimes less." Morgan cut back his caloric intake during spa cures: "He was careful not to eat and drink so much," continued Blanc—"the only thing that I was not able to diminish is the use of cigars, but on this point he will not admit of a contradiction." The Frenchman urged Markoe to prescribe Nauheim waters ("brine baths with carbonic acid") for Morgan in New York, and to pay "great attention to the regular function of the bowels. If he will be prudent enough to continue the diet and the baths he will enjoy a long life so useful to his country."

———

Roosevelt's second inauguration took place in March of 1905, while Morgan was en route to Europe. Putting aside the Northern Securities case and the Republican Old Guard's attempt to unseat the White House incumbent, the house of Morgan and the chief executive worked out a wary mutual accommodation between 1905 and 1908. Roosevelt accepted the general efficacy of industrial consolidation and, in trying to distinguish between "good" and "bad" trusts, tended to place Morgan's combinations in the former camp. Refusing to endorse what he saw as a reactionary antipathy to bigness per se, he aimed to penalize *conduct* rather than size. And he continued to consult Morgan on matters of finance.

Shortly after the banker returned from Europe in July 1905, he heard from the President about China. Anti-American sentiment in that country was running high: nationalists led by Sun Yat-sen, eager to promote China's economic independence, were threatening to boycott American goods, and the Chinese government wanted to buy back the stock of the American China Development Company, which granted railroad-building and mining concessions to the United States (see page 371). Only 28 of a proposed 1,000 miles of track had been laid for the first U.S.-owned railroad, the Canton–Hankow, and Chinese opposition to the project had dimmed its prospects. The ACDC directors had voted to accept Peking's offer of nearly $7 million for the concession, pending shareholder approval. Morgan, the largest shareholder in the company, saw no reason not to sell, but Roosevelt wanted to maintain a strong U.S. commercial presence in China. On July 18, the President quoted to Morgan a letter on the subject from Henry Cabot Lodge.

According to Senator Lodge, Morgan had said that the amount of money involved in the railroad was not "serious enough to make him at his age enter on a struggle with the Chinese," especially since it was not clear the U.S. government would support him. Lodge argued to TR that the loss of "this great line of railway" would be "a blow to our prestige and to our commerce in China which we want to foster in every way." In his own voice, the President went on: "Now, my dear Mr. Morgan, it is not my business to advise you what to do. From the standpoint of our national interests, I take entirely Lodge's view. I cannot expect you or any of our big business men to go into what they think will be to their disadvantage. But if you are giving up this concession, if you are letting the railroad slip out of American hands, because you think that the Government will not back you up, I wish to assure you that in every honorable way the Government will stand by you and will do all that in its power lies to see that you suffer no wrong whatever from the Chinese or any other Power in this matter. . . . My interest of course is simply the interest of seeing American commercial interests prosper in the Orient."

Two days later, Chinese nationalists started a boycott of U.S. goods that quickly spread to Hawaii, the Philippines, and parts of Japan. In August Morgan had lunch with Roosevelt at Oyster Bay, and the President said he was prepared to "insist that China shall carry out its side of the agreement regarding the concession. . . . Can your company delay action for a few weeks longer? If so, I'll call a halt in emphatic terms to the Chinese Government." At the end of August, however, for reasons that do not appear in the correspondence, Roosevelt agreed that Morgan should accept the Chinese government's $6.75 million settlement for canceling the concession.

With regard to corporate policy, Roosevelt's fact-finding Bureau of Corporations, set up with the help of George Perkins in 1903, was providing Morganized companies with an invaluable testing ground. When the bureau threatened to investigate U.S. Steel in 1905, Judge Gary went to the White House and worked out an agreement to open the corporation's books in exchange for confidentiality: U.S. Steel would correct any violations of the law the bureau found, and would submit disputed questions about the use or publication of "trade secrets" to Roosevelt.

This kind of private negotiation was roughly what Perkins and Bacon had proposed to TR in October of 1901, and the Morgan associates found it infinitely preferable to protracted legal and political battles. Gary regarded federal supervision as "a strong safeguard . . . to the prevention of violent attacks on private rights in general that might otherwise come," and, sounding not unlike his banker, reported that U.S. Steel "had been absolutely satisfied with the treatment it had received from the Bureau." Perkins proudly told Morgan when the Justice Department brought suit against Standard Oil in 1906 that he and Gary had "anticipated a great many questions and situations that might have been unpleasant and that the [Steel] Corporation is looked upon in Washington with more favor than perhaps any other concern. There has been a great deal of a favorable nature in the papers during the last two or three weeks, comparing us with the Standard Oil and its companies."

Early in 1907, on learning that the Bureau of Corporations was turning to International Harvester next, Perkins and Cyrus McCormick held a two-day conference with its commissioners at Judge Gary's Waldorf suite in New York, to work out another nonaggression pact. Roosevelt asked Perkins in the course of this investigation whether Harvester would be "satisfied with whatever the [bureau's] findings were[.]" Perkins said he expected the officers would "frankly come to us and point out any mistakes or technical violations of the law; then give us a chance to correct them, if we could or would, and that if we did, then we would expect the Attorney General not to bring proceedings." As the bureau concluded its work, Deputy Commissioner Herbert Knox Smith told Roosevelt that he had found no "moral ground" for a Harvester prosecution, and warned that it would be politically foolish to attack the Morgan interests over a case in which no "substantial" wrong had been found—it would only make enemies of strong men who "up to this time have supported the advanced policy of the administration."

When these agreements between the administration and the house of Morgan came to light, they provoked outrage reminiscent of the response to the Cleveland gold deal. Critics charged that the bankers and industrialists had used privileged information to avoid prosecution, and that the White House, ostensibly trying to eliminate corporate corruption and impose government regulation on the trusts, had given virtual carte blanche to giant monopolies affiliated with the reigning lord of Wall Street. The businessmen seemed at least consistent in their pursuit of self-interest. The President looked two-faced.

Roosevelt was in fact transforming the executive branch of government from a weak adjunct of Congress into a powerful force in national and international affairs. Working with men he trusted on Wall Street, he had begun, clumsily, to define a relationship between strong government and big business—to check egregious abuses of corporate power while preserving what he regarded as industrial progress, confident that he could discipline the "captains of industry" and protect the American public from rapacious trusts. To the cumbersome machinery of punitive lawsuits, he preferred prior government approval of "rational" corporate policy—as did the Morgan bank.

———

George Perkins was turning out to be a decidedly mixed blessing for the Morgan bank. While his political skills had helped secure useful agreements in Washington, his arrogant manner and divided professional loyalites—to which Morgan had objected from the outset—alienated many of his partners. Bob Bacon had agreed to head a Morgan-Baring New York office only if Perkins went back to New York Life. The problem of the dual affiliation assumed public proportions when a wealthy Boston stockbroker and speculator named Thomas W. Lawson published a series of articles in *Everybody's Magazine* on the connections between Wall Street and the insurance industry. Lawson reported that the three big life insurance companies, called the "racers"—the Equitable, Mutual, and New York Life—had systematically bribed politicians and regulators, used "captive" trust companies to conduct illegal financial operations, and put policyholders' money into risky ventures. The specter of Wall Street "money kings" gambling with the savings of widows and orphans, plus a bitter public fight over ownership of the Equitable, prompted the New York State legislature to investigate the insurance industry.

Traditionally, life insurance companies had put most of their portfolios into government bonds, but the yields on those securities had declined in the deflation of the nineties, and insurers had begun seeking higher returns for their enormous surplus capital just as investment bankers needed steady sources of domestic cash for industrial underwritings. As a result, the racers had supplied the great turn-of-the-century merger movement with cash. They each had $1 billion of insurance in force by 1899, and their total annual premium income came to more than 75 percent of the gross income of America's nationally chartered banks.

When the Equitable's founder, Henry Hyde, died in 1899, he left 51 percent of its stock in trust to his twenty-three-year-old son, James, a Harvard-educated Francophile who wore silk shirts, bow ties, yellow gloves, and violets in his buttonhole. (It was James Hazen Hyde who wrote the 1920 memo about Morgan's making sure Bessie Marbury never got the Legion of Honor.) Uninterested in the technicalities of the insurance business, he had a shrewd eye for new investment opportunities, and put much of the society's surplus capital into corporate securities, largely through Kuhn, Loeb. The Equitable had lent millions to Harriman and Schiff in their attempt to take over Northern Pacific in 1901, while New York Life furnished millions to Morgan.

James Hyde stood to assume majority control of the society in 1906. The Equitable's conservative president, James W. Alexander, profited from Hyde's policies but insisted that life insurance was a "sacred trust," not "a monster money-making scheme," and feared that Hyde would sell out once he turned thirty and inherited his shares. Potential buyers, alert to this internal power struggle, began circling overhead.

On January 31, 1905, Hyde gave a costume ball at Sherry's restaurant. Oblivious to the public's increasing distaste for the excesses of the rich, he hired Whitney Warren to turn Sherry's grand ballroom into the Hall of Mirrors at Versailles, engaged the Metropolitan Opera orchestra and the French actress Gabrielle Réjane for entertainment, invited prominent friends from all over the world, and set up a special gallery for photographers and the press. Elsie de Wolfe came as a dancer from the court of Louis XV. When the press reported that the "orgy" had cost the Equitable $200,000 and that Hyde was having an affair with Mme. Réjane—neither of which was true—the battle for control of the company turned into front-page news.

Both Hyde and Alexander lost the confidence of the board, and in February the directors appointed a panel of lawyers headed by Elihu Root to mutualize the company, which would vest control in its policyholders. Root was preparing to argue the Morgan/Hill case against Harriman before the Supreme Court— defending the pro rata plan for the liquidation of Northern Securities—but decided that the insurance crisis required immediate attention, since a collapse of confidence in companies that had millions invested in the industrial economy could bring on a general panic. He asked the Court to delay its hearing of Northern Securities arguments, and the judges granted his request.

Root scotched the mutualization plan. Over the next few weeks a committee of Equitable board members found the company's management guilty of "moral obliqueness" and financial misconduct. Those who wanted to buy the Equitable included E. H. Harriman, William Rockefeller, and George Gould, but Root arranged for one of his own clients, the financier and street-rail magnate Thomas Fortune Ryan, to acquire Hyde's majority holdings—on condition that control of the society be turned over to a voting trust. New York State law required the Equitable to maintain the stock price and dividend rate set at its founding in 1859. As a result, in 1905, 51 percent of the shares in a company with over $400 million in assets—a combination of cash in hand, premium income, investments, and real estate—had a par value of $51,000, and paid a 7 percent dividend of $3,570. Mutual Life had reportedly offered to buy out Hyde in the early 1900s for $10 million. Ryan paid him $2.5 million in 1905, which was a large premium over the par value of the stock but significantly less than the company's apparent market value.*

Ryan's claim years later that he had bought the company in order to protect America's financial stability did not find many subscribers. Wall Street suspected that Morgan had engineered the sale—he was abroad between March and July of 1905, but Root could easily have consulted him by cable. The banker surely shared Root's fear that a major insurance-industry struggle could precipitate a panic; he would not have wanted Harriman to control the $400 million life insurance company; and he might well have insisted on a voting trust to keep Ryan from playing fast and loose with the Equitable assets. Harriman, once again snookered out of a deal, was enraged: "He shook the tree for months and months," wrote the new chairman of the Equitable board, Navy Secretary Paul Morton, "and Ryan walked off with the plums."

Secretary of State John Hay died in July of 1905, and Elihu Root accepted Roosevelt's invitation to return to Washington as head of the State Department, with Bob Bacon as his assistant. The new Equitable board fired James Alexander at the end the year. James Hazen Hyde, not yet thirty, retired from business and moved to France. Elsie de Wolfe declared his infamous ball one of the last great parties of the Gay Nineties.

In the fall of 1905 an investigative committee headed by New York State senator William W. Armstrong and his chief counsel, a red-bearded reformer named Charles Evans Hughes, began to take evidence about the insurance scandals. The appearance before the committee of George Perkins (dubbed "Gabby George" by Finley Peter Dunne) riveted attention on the house of Morgan. Examining transactions in which Perkins had acted as both buyer and seller of securities—purchasing the bonds of railroads, U.S. Steel, and the IMM for New York Life from the Morgan bank—Armstrong asked him, "When, in your judgment, are you acting for the New York Life?"

Perkins: "All the time."

Armstrong: "When are you acting for J. P. Morgan & Company?"

Perkins: "It depends on what the actual case is."

Pressed on this point, he protested: "Mr. Chairman . . . I know when a transaction comes to me, whether it is in J. P. Morgan & Company, or the New York Life or the Steel Corporation, or whatever it may be, I take up that question and dispose of it as I see my duty."

The public did not share Perkins's confidence in his sterling sense of duty, especially after Hughes brought out the details of his "parking" $800,000 of

---

* Ryan had started out as an errand boy in Virginia, and built a financial empire worth over $1 billion; by 1905 he was personally worth about $50 million. William C. Whitney, with whom he had organized American Tobacco and New York's Metropolitan Traction Company, described him as "the most adroit, suave, and noiseless man" he knew, and said that if Ryan lived long enough he would "have all the money in the world."

IMM bonds with J. P. Morgan & Co. on December 31, 1903, and buying them back a few days later in order to hide the extent of New York Life's loss for its annual report. The *Chicago Tribune* ran a cartoon of Perkins milking a cow labeled "New York Life" for Morgan while policyholders fed money into the animal's mouth. Pulitzer's *World* pictured a bloated, top-hatted Morgan as Dickens's Bill Sykes, with a rolled-up paper labeled "Ship Building Trust" in his pocket, hoisting tiny "Oliver" Perkins through the window of New York Life to steal "policy holders dough."

Hughes documented collusion between insurers, legislators, and banks, and offered specific recommendations for reform. Among the regulatory measures passed by the New York State legislature in April 1906 were laws barring life insurance companies from underwriting securities issues and from investing in corporate stock and bonds. As a result, investment bankers changed the structure of their financings after 1906. Morgan made larger allotments to other syndicate partners, but the reduced demand for securities following the "Armstrong laws" contributed to a general market decline. The investigation's disclosures heightened public awareness of financial corruption and stepped up the demand for change: in the fall of 1906 Charles Evans Hughes, the Armstrong Committee's highly effective counsel, was elected governor of New York with a mandate for economic reform.

———

A month after Gabby George testified about banking and insurance in 1905, Morgan sent him on a special mission to Russia. Officials in the government of Czar Nicholas II had been trying for years to enlist Morgan's help in opening U.S. markets to Russian bonds. The director of the International Bank of Commerce in St. Petersburg had sent the U.S. financier an extravagant plea in 1898, calling him "the King of America" and insisting that no one else could "so successfully take in hand the Russian flag." Russia's Finance Minister, Sergei Witte, also tried to engage the American "King" on almost any terms, but Morgan had repeatedly declined: in the late nineties he did not think U.S. markets would take up the bonds of this unstable economy, and there was no one he trusted to look out for his interests halfway around the world. Still, he stayed in touch with Russia's leading financiers.

George Perkins had been less cautious. Before joining the Morgan bank he had arranged for New York Life to set up branch offices in Russia, invested some of his company's profits in Russian railroads, and handled the first large sale of Russian securities in the United States. Between 1885 and 1914 New York Life was the most successful American commercial venture in imperial Russia.

Although Russia's internal turbulence and war with Japan in 1904–5 seemed to justify Morgan's prudence, he began at this unlikely moment to change his mind. Political unrest under fiercely repressive local and national regimes had been building in Russia for years. When two hundred thousand St. Petersburg factory workers carrying religious icons and singing "God save the Czar" gathered in front of the Winter Palace with a petition for fair wages, reasonable hours, universal suffrage, and a democratically elected government one Sunday in January 1905, the Czar's ministers called out troops who shot into the crowd, killing hundreds of people. "Bloody Sunday" led to strikes, assassinations, riots, attacks on property and the gentry, calls for armed insurrection, the formation of councils, or "soviets," of workers in Moscow and St. Petersburg, and struggles over the leadership of all this revolutionary activity.

The war that broke out in 1904 between Russia and Japan was partly a czarist effort to shift popular attention abroad, and partly a Great Power conflict over spheres of influence in the Far East. France financed the Russian imperialists who wanted to secure control of Manchuria and protect their East Asian border, especially Korea and the remote Pacific port at Vladivostok (where Richard Greener was serving as American consul), from aggressive, newly westernized Japan. England had a military alliance with Japan, which saw Korea as essential to *its* national security, and also wanted to control raw materials and markets on the Asian mainland, deploy its modernized armed forces, and gain recognition from the West. The Barings quietly underwrote £35 million in Japanese war loans, but kept their name off the issues, since they had also been lending to Russia. They found an enthusiastic American partner in Jacob Schiff, who opposed Russia's anti-Semitic pogroms and was urging the world's influential Jewish bankers *not* to finance the Czar. J. P. Morgan & Co. took a $500,000 share in Kuhn, Loeb's first $50 million Japanese loan.

The Warburgs and Rothschilds participated in this underwriting as well, but most of the world thought Japan was being financed by the United States. Barings concealed their role so well that Morgan knew nothing about it. In July 1905 he told Revelstoke that his own house could have handled the Japanese loan as well as Kuhn, Loeb, and guessed that it had come to Schiff through the British financier Sir Ernest Cassel. Revelstoke said nothing. One of his partners reflected: "It is curious that the Old Man should not be better posted."

Like Barings, Morgan did business with both sides in this war. In March of 1905, after the Japanese won the largest land battle ever fought at the time, at Mukden, he sent a representative to Russia proposing to build battleships with money raised by an American bond syndicate, perhaps to generate business for the IMM's Harland & Wolff. Two months later, in the "greatest sea battle since Trafalgar," Japan destroyed an entire Russian squadron at Tsushima Strait, and with it all Russian hope of winning the war.

In July 1905, a few days after Roosevelt urged Morgan not to sell the Canton–Hankow Railroad back to China, he hosted a peace conference between Russia and Japan in Portsmouth, New Hampshire. The President sympathized with Japan, but wanted to prevent a wider war and maintain a strategic balance of power in the region to safeguard U.S. commercial interests.* The Czar's chief negotiator at the Portsmouth Conference—which produced a peace treaty and won Roosevelt a Nobel Prize—was his former Finance Minister, Sergei Witte. As soon as the conference ended, Witte went to see Morgan in New York.

The banker took his guest up the Hudson on *Corsair* to West Point. Having lunched with Roosevelt at Oyster Bay and found the fare "almost indigestible," Witte said he got the only decent meals of his entire American trip on Morgan's yacht. He had come to ask for help in liquidating Russia's war debt, but first he ventured to bring up a delicate personal subject—his host's nose. Witte himself was no beauty: Robert Massie has described him as "a huge, burly man with massive shoulders, great height and a head the size of a pumpkin."

Seizing a moment with Morgan alone, Witte said (he later recalled) that he had been treated for a skin disease by a celebrated Berlin professor named Lassar. He had seen patients in the doctor's office with "morbid nose formations such as yours," the Russian minister told the American banker: Dr. Lassar surgically removed the growths and restored his patients' noses to normal.

Morgan said he knew all about the professor and his operations, but could not possibly undergo such an operation—if he did, he could never return to the United States.

Why not? Witte asked.

Because, replied Morgan, "if I come to New York with my nose cured, every street boy will point at me and split his sides laughing. Everybody knows my nose and it would be impossible for me to appear on the streets of New York without it."

Being "King of America" had its price.

On questions of finance, Witte found Morgan at last willing to sponsor a Russian government loan. Witte proposed that the Americans lend $400 million to Russia as part of an international syndicate. Morgan agreed in principle but radically scaled the American share down, offering $50 million to $100 million. The Russians had also approached Stillman and Schiff, but Morgan insisted that his own house manage the American issue alone. He specifically asked that "the Jewish group of bankers headed by Jacob Schiff" have no part in the deal, according to Witte. In fact, Schiff was refusing to raise money for Russia because of its "shameful policy" toward Jews, and claimed that the American people shared his abhorrence.

The Russian government and its European bankers wanted Morgan's partic-

---

* TR wrote to a friend that July: "when I feel gloomy about democracy I am positively refreshed by considering the monstrous ineptitude of the ideal absolutism [in Russia]," and "the more I saw of the Czar and the Kaiser the better I liked the United States Senate."

ipation because selling bonds for a defeated, virtually bankrupt country at a time of violent political turmoil seemed nearly impossible. Although cognoscenti on Wall Street and in London considered the old man a "back number," his name still inspired more confidence than any other banker's in the world.

In early October Morgan delegated Perkins to negotiate for him in St. Petersburg, and to carry out a second assignment as well: the rails of the Trans-Siberian road needed replacing, and U.S. Steel hoped to get the contract. Gary and Frick accompanied Morgan to see Perkins off on the *Kaiser Wilhelm II* (called Rolling Billy by those who knew her motion at sea) on October 10.

Morgan asked Jack, who was visiting London that fall, to go to Russia as well. "Our scheme there is a broad one which GWP will explain," he cabled—"think most important you accompany [Perkins] to Russia not only for your information but the experience." The other parties to the negotiations would be France, Germany, England, Holland, the Russian Finance Minister Vladimir Kokovtsoff, and Witte, who had just been made a count for his work at Portsmouth.

Perkins and Jack were on their way to Petersburg on October 17 when Morgan wired a change of heart. He had consulted George Baker and "reluctantly" concluded that in the unsettled condition of U.S. money markets it would be "absolutely impossible make successful issue here for some time." Other factors darkening prospects for the loan were the "imbroglio" over the life insurance investigation and a report that "the Jews are combining in opposition."

The Americans took rooms at the Grand Hôtel d'Europe in St. Petersburg, and conveyed this news to the Russians. Witte and Kokovtsoff wanted Morgan in the group so badly, "even if for nominal amount," that they were "willing make any and all concessions they can," reported Perkins and Jack.

Cables flew back and forth between Petersburg and New York for the next few days, with the Russians offering steadily easier terms, and Morgan insisting that an unsuccessful issue "would have very injurious effect in future on what we so much desire—to open American market to Russian loan."

His envoys invoked patriotism and "moral responsibility": "Please do not think we fail to appreciate your point of view and arguments," they urged, "but when the choice is between facing a temporary non-successful issue of small amount and seriously hampering Russian Government in their plan of an international issue undertaken largely because of your advice, we feel your name and credit, and credit of USA, so much involved that we are most unwilling drop business and thereby show ourselves so weak that we disappoint Russian Government and strongest financial group ever formed in Europe."

That did it. Morgan warned the Russians once again of his pessimism about the issue's success, but authorized his partners to take $20 million of a $250 million loan. Two days later a Russian railroad strike turned into the October Revolution of 1905. The bankers called off negotiations.

Train service stopped. Factories, hospitals, newspapers, schools, food delivery, and electrical generators shut down. Crowds marched through dark city streets hoisting red flags. Witte persuaded the Czar that the only way to stop the rebellion was to grant liberalizing reforms—a constitution, civil liberties, a democratic constituent assembly—and Witte himself drew up a manifesto announcing these promised changes.

"What a time to be in Russia!" Jack wrote to Fanny on October 31. He had come in late the night before after calling at the British embassy, and was getting ready for bed "when I heard a triumphant shout from the street." Running outside, he found people reading the Czar's (actually, Witte's) proclamation, which someone translated for him into German. "For about an hour the whole town . . . was shouting and cheering. The people cheered even the Cossack patrols and the policemen! . . . It was really an historic moment and gave me quite the proper thrill." He sent his mother a copy of the manifesto.

To his father, he and Perkins cabled: "We have seen death of old and birth of new Russia . . . business postponed for the present."

With rail transport at a halt, the Americans left by boat. Jack went back to London. Perkins, arriving in Berlin on the same day as the King of Spain, wired Morgan: "Have changed government of Russia, separated Norway from Sweden* and welcomed the King of Spain to Germany. Am leaving for France tonight. If there is anything you think needs attention there cable me at Paris."

The "birth of new Russia" was still a long way off. The Czar refused to yield power to the constituent assembly. The country's internal struggles continued. Witte tried to hold the international banking consortium together. In April 1906 he found Morgan willing to take part in a $500 million loan, but this time Perkins and Jack objected: it would, they said, be "impolitic and very injurious" to issue the bonds in New York in view of uneasy U.S. money markets, the opposition of the financial world, and public hostility to Russia. The house of Morgan did not take part in the 1906 Russian loan. Witte borrowed two billion francs ($500 million) from France.

Morgan's indecision and conflicting instincts regarding a Russian loan are striking. He said no for years, then at a peculiar moment said yes, only to change his mind after consulting colleagues in New York, then change it again under pressure from his partners and foreign politicians. External circumstances took matters out of his hands in October, but a few months after the 1905 revolution he was once again willing to proceed, until the son he usually ignored persuaded him not to. It was curious, as a Baring partner observed on a related question, "that the Old Man should not be better posted."

Only half attending to business as he devoted most of his energies to travel and art, he appears to have been operating more on past principles and innate

---

* Norway, having been ruled by Sweden since 1814, had just claimed independence.

bullishness than on a careful gauge of political or economic facts. The Old World's premier private banks had built financial empires on their relations with royal courts, and Junius Morgan had earned prestige and profit with an audacious loan to France at the end of the Franco-Prussian War. Moreover, the Russian empire had come to Pierpont Morgan essentially on its knees. He may have hoped to counter speculation about his "collapse" by scoring an international coup: if the liquidation of Russia's war debt and the opening of American markets to Russian bonds went well, the house of Morgan stood to play a leading role in the economic future of a vast, resource-rich country and to secure new markets for its corporate clients. Morgan apparently did not credit the force of political opposition to ancien régime despotism abroad any more than he accommodated to the progressive spirit in the United States.

By the end of 1905 Roosevelt was as concerned about domestic radical social unrest as he was with checking corporate corruption. The Socialist Party led by Eugene Debs had won 3 percent of the vote in 1904, and violent conflicts between labor and capital in the West continued to alarm the "respectables" (now including TR) in the East. In December 1905 Idaho's former Governor Frank Steunenberg was killed by a bomb in his own front yard; the man charged with the murder claimed to be working for the militant Western Federation of Miners.

Convinced that investigative journalists reporting on the country's social and political ills were no longer working in a sober spirit of reform but instead whipping up national hysteria, Roosevelt wrote that fall to Samuel S. McClure, the leading publisher of exposés. TR praised the editor's "crusade against corruption," but wished "very much that you could [also] have articles showing up the hideous iniquity of which mobs are guilty, the wrongs of violence by the poor as well as the wrongs of corruption by the rich." Could not McClure's journalists put more "sky in the landscape"—give a sense of perspective rather than "encourage people to believe that all crimes are connected with business, and that the crime of graft is the only crime"?

Early in 1906, partly in response to sensational charges made by David Graham Phillips in an article on "The Treason of the Senate," the President launched a series of attacks on the "scandal-mongering" press. Speaking at a Gridiron Club dinner in January, he declared that certain journalists had become like "the Man with the Muck-Rake" in Bunyan's *Pilgrim's Progress* "who could look no way but downward . . . [who] continued to rake to himself the filth of the floor . . . [who] consistently refuses to see aught that is lofty, and fixes his eyes with solemn intentness only on that which is vile and debasing." This man "speedily becomes, not a help to society, not an incitement to good, but one of the most potent forces for evil."

Roosevelt himself did not look in only one direction as he assigned blame for the country's troubles. In March he told his Secretary of War, William Howard Taft, that the greed, arrogance, and "dull, purblind folly of the very rich men" was combining with the muckrakers' evidence of corruption in business and politics to produce "a very unhealthy position of excitement and irritation in the popular mind, which shows itself in part in the enormous increase in the socialistic propaganda" and the building up of "a revolutionary feeling."

Roosevelt's opposition had little effect on either journalists or the public response to abuses of power, and his derogatory sobriquet, "muckraker," became to liberals and the left a term of praise.

Wall Street was more concerned with uneasy financial markets than with presidential denunciations, although a number of people on and off the Street blamed Roosevelt for undermining business confidence with his "attacks." After the economy recovered from the 1903–4 contraction, the Dow Jones average had more than doubled, rising from a low of 42 in November 1903 to 103 in January 1906. This surge in economic growth created an enormous demand for capital, but world gold production had not kept pace with industrial output, and money everywhere, pegged to gold, was in short supply. Morgan and his colleagues had been worried since the 1890s that the antiquated, decentralized U.S. banking system could not meet the needs of a modern industrial economy. At the beginning of 1906 Jacob Schiff warned a group of financiers that "if the currency conditions of this country are not changed materially . . . you will have such a panic . . . as will make all previous panics look like child's play."

Chapter 27

"MORE COLOSSAL THAN EVER"

Though Morgan kept an eye on the unsettled U.S. money markets in 1905–6, he was directing most of his attention to art. At the end of 1905 he purchased through Junius an outstanding collection of Rembrandt and Dürer prints assembled by George W. Vanderbilt. The youngest son of William Henry Vanderbilt was, like Junius, the scholar/aesthete in a largely mercantile family. He told Junius that both collections were "as complete as is possible. Many examples are unique, and I only secured them at auctions by bidding against museums & Baron Rothschild, & the latter is now the only private collection which can rank with mine as a whole, for quality of impressions." With this acquisition, for which he paid $150,000, Morgan added 112 Rembrandt etchings to the 272 he had bought from Theodore Irwin in 1900, to create what became the finest collection of Rembrandt prints in the United States.

He continued to acquire individual works as well as collections en bloc. Early in 1905 he bought a Thackeray manuscript from the children of Leslie Stephen. Stephen's first wife had been Thackeray's daughter, Minny, who died in 1875. A few years later Stephen married the widowed Julia Duckworth, who already had three children, and had four more with him—Vanessa, Thoby, Virginia, and Adrian. Julia Stephen died in 1895, her husband in 1904. At the beginning of 1905 Jack reported to his father from London that he was in the process of acquiring Thackeray's draft of *Vanity Fair*—"the family are disposing of the manuscript for their benefit so if you get it you may be quite sure of its pedigree." Jack sent George Duckworth (Julia's son) £1,600 for the manuscript in January, regretting "that there was not a great deal more of it preserved." A month later he told Teddy Grenfell, "It may interest you and Duckworth to know that we got ahead of the man who offered JPM the Vanity Fair Ms. for £5,000!"

In July of 1906, Morgan bought another Thackeray manuscript from the Duckworth/Stephen clan. Virginia told her friend Violet Dickinson: "Thoby made £1,000. *one thousand pounds* by selling 10 pages of Thackerays Lord Bateman. George sold it to Pierpont Morgan. . . . I wish my manuscripts would sell for more than their meaning!"*

The collector of Rembrandt and Thackeray also struck out in an entirely new direction in 1906. Edward Sheriff Curtis, who lived in Seattle and had been taking hauntingly beautiful photographs of American Indians for eight years, had come East in 1905 to raise money for his documentary study of the "Vanishing American." Theodore Roosevelt endorsed the project: "There is no man of great wealth with whom I am on sufficient close terms to warrant my giving a special letter to him," he wrote to Curtis on White House stationery in December 1905, "but you are most welcome to use this letter in talking with any man who has any interest in the subject."†

Curtis probably used the letter to help secure an interview with Morgan in January 1906, since there is a copy of it in the Morgan archives. Just before the meeting he sent the banker detailed descriptions of his current work and plans to publish twenty large-format volumes of photographs, text, and drawings, portraying the surviving Indian tribes in the North American West, and using the finest paper, binding, and photogravure work available; in addition, he proposed to publish seven hundred separate portfolios containing large prints of

---

* *Lord Bateman* was an anonymous ballad that Dickens and George Cruikshank had published in 1839; Thackeray wrote it out and illustrated it that year. Virginia later said of the rambling house her family lived in at 22 Hyde Park Gate, "One never knew when one rummaged in the many dark cupboards and wardrobes whether one would disinter Herbert Duckworth's barrister's wig, my father's clergyman's collar, or a sheet scribbled over with drawings by Thackeray which we afterwards sold to Pierpont Morgan for a considerable sum." In 1909, Morgan bought additional Thackeray manuscripts and drawings from Vanessa Stephen Bell for £2,000.

† The President praised Curtis's work for its artistic merit and historical and ethnological value, then went on, with no acknowledgment of his own culture's responsibility for what he described: "You have begun just in time, for these people are at this very moment rapidly losing the distinctive traits and customs which they have slowly developed through the ages. The Indian, as an Indian, is on the point of perishing, and when he has become a U.S. citizen, though it will be a much better thing for him and for the rest of the country, he will lose completely his value as a living historical document." It evidently did not occur to Roosevelt that the native American culture destroyed by railroads and western expansion might have value to *itself,* or that it should be preserved for reasons other than "the rest of the country's" romantic nostalgia.

Morgan leaving his house at Princes Gate in London.
(Archives of The Pierpont Morgan Library, New York)

his most important pictures. Morgan agreed to fund Curtis's fieldwork with $75,000 ($15,000 a year for five years) in exchange for twenty-five sets of the books and five hundred prints.

"I congratulate you with all my heart," Roosevelt wrote to the photographer on February 6: "That is a mighty fine deed of Mr. Morgan's."

At Morgan's suggestion, Curtis submitted his proposal to Harper & Brothers, who said they could not publish the books unless Morgan supplied the capital and guaranteed their firm against loss. When other publishers said much the same thing, Curtis and Morgan decided that the photographer ought to produce the volumes himself, charging $3,000 each for five hundred sets.

Curtis went back to work in the West, sending Morgan occasional news of his progress, inviting editorial criticism of his introduction to the first volume, and asking how his patron would like to be acknowledged. Morgan's secretary replied that the banker had no textual changes to suggest, and would leave "the matter of mentioning his connection with the work entirely to you: he says, 'the less said the better.' "

The first two volumes of *The North American Indian* were published at the end of 1907, with a Foreword by Theodore Roosevelt, to scholarly and popular praise. Morgan gave sets to Edward VII, the Metropolitan Museum, the Museum of Natural History, the Guildhall Library in London, and several American libraries that could not afford them.

Self-publication of these exquisite volumes proved to be even more difficult and expensive than the photographer and his backer had expected. Some potential donors refused to contribute on the assumption that Morgan would. Curtis secured more money from Morgan ($60,000 more in 1909), and sold $3,000 subscriptions to many of the banker's friends. After Morgan died, Jack supported the project. Complete publication of the twenty volumes took twenty-three years and cost about $1.2 million, of which the Morgans contributed $400,000.

———

One of Morgan's most significant and least conspicuous art advisers was his friend William M. Laffan, whose fields of expertise included engravings and Oriental ceramics—he had compiled the catalogue of Morgan's Chinese porcelains. Morgan helped Laffan buy the New York *Evening Sun* in 1902, and three years later appointed him to the Metropolitan Museum board. In 1906 Laffan encouraged Morgan to set up a Department of Egyptian Art at the Met, and to sponsor archaeological field excavations.

Western interest in the ancient Near East had steadily grown after the Napoleonic invasion of Egypt. Schliemann had captured the public's imagination with his claim to have found treasures from Homeric Troy, and other archaeologists discovered cuneiform tablets, buried Sumerian cities, mummies, papyri, and early Christian texts. Arguments about the theory of evolution, between biblical fundamentalists and the intellectual heirs of Darwin, added to late-nineteenth-century interest in the literary and material evidence that lay buried in the countries of the eastern Mediterranean, and American academic journals devoted to biblical archaeology, classical studies, Oriental studies, and Semitic languages and literature began to appear in the 1880s. The University of Pennsylvania sponsored an expedition to the biblical Babylon (now Iraq) in 1888, and a group of U.S. universities set up the American School of Oriental Research in Jerusalem in 1900.

In Egypt, local thieves who looted pharaonic-period tombs found avid markets in the tourist trade, while the rise of western "Orientalism" created a huge traffic in forgeries. German scholars and a British Egyptologist named William Flinders Petrie, aided by new scientific techniques and the professionalization of archaeology, began to set standards for excavation in the nineties. The Egyptian government tried to impose a measure of control by outlawing unlicensed digging and granting concessions to qualified foreign excavators on condition that they offer half of what they found to the Cairo Museum (the Boulaq Museum's collections had been transferred to the Cairo Museum, which opened in 1902). This policy only slightly reduced the flow of objects to foreign institutions—the Cairo Museum rarely took more than a third—and it fostered intense competition among museums and collectors in the West.

Archaeological studies were expensive. They entailed setting up excavation facilities, sending researchers to live and work at remote sites, and publishing scholarly findings. Most of the American cultural institutions that developed first-rate departments of Near Eastern art had wealthy private patrons behind them. In the 1890s a San Francisco widow named Phoebe Apperson Hearst—the mother of William Randolph Hearst—sponsored an expedition in Egypt for the University of California at Berkeley. John D. Rockefeller financed an Oriental Exploration Fund for the University of Chicago in 1903, and later endowed the Oriental Institute there. Jacob Schiff helped pay for Harvard's Semitic Museum, dedicated in 1903. Gardiner Martin Lane, a partner at Lee, Higginson & Co., supported archaeological work in Egypt for Boston's Museum of Fine Arts, and Harvard published the scholarly findings.

Early in 1906 Laffan visited the site of a prolific MFA/Harvard excavation at the Giza pyramids, and in Paris that April had no trouble persuading Morgan that the New York museum ought to fund expeditions of its own. They hired the Boston project's chief field officer, Harvard professor Albert M. Lythgoe, to come to the Met as curator of Egyptian art.

From Paris in April Laffan wrote to the editor of the *Sun*, Edward Page Mitchell: "I see Morgan daily and have spent a million or more of his money since I arrived. . . . What a whale of a man! . . . the Egyptian business is all due to his big way of looking at things and doing them."

Lythgoe urged his New York patrons to hurry, since the combination of other excavators clearing ancient sites and raids by local thieves meant that the best material would be gone in fifteen years. Morgan set up a $16,000 fund for a Metropolitan Museum expedition, and at the beginning of 1907 Lythgoe began work in Egypt. Morgan visited the project for the first time in 1909. (See Chapter 29.)

In addition, he fostered the study of ancient civilizations at his own library, Princeton, and Yale. He personally gave $25,000 on the Met's behalf to a Princeton expedition at Sardis. For the Met in 1908 he bought 1,157 ancient Mesopotamian cylinder seals that had been assembled, probably on his account, by the American collector William Hayes Ward. These tiny, potent artifacts of the first civilizations in the Near East to invent a form of writing record a history that dates from about 5000 to 330 B.C. When the Metropolitan's trustees rejected the seals as beyond the museum's scope, Morgan purchased them for his own library; its collection of cylinder seals is now one of the best known in the world.*

Morgan was also acquiring ancient cuneiform tablets, and through Laffan in 1907 he hired a British Assyriologist named C.H.W. Johns to advise him. Morgan had apparently been cheated on a recent purchase, and Johns told Laffan, "I hope that little deal will not put you and Mr. Morgan off Babylonian things. I think them most important for the study of early humanities and if you follow my advice and buy through me, you will pay top price as is right to get the plums, but you will not be 'had' again."

Through Laffan, Morgan commissioned Dr. Johns—an Anglican minister, master of Queens' College, Cambridge, and canon of Norwich—to edit the catalogues of his "Babylonian things." After Laffan died at the end of 1909, Johns questioned Belle Greene by mail about Morgan's intentions with regard to his own work; then in the spring of 1910 he came to the United States, demanded more money, and resigned as editor of the catalogues. Belle told him in a huff that Morgan's interest was "only to place material here at the service of Assyriological scholars," and that her employer would bear the entire expense involved, "including your time and eminent knowledge. . . . I am so devoted to Mr. Morgan myself, and have such an admiration for his unselfish, and too often unappreciated, efforts to further knowledge in every way, that I assume

---

* The earliest seals were flat, used to stamp motifs on clay pots or tags. Around 3500 B.C., just before the invention of writing, the Mesopotamians devised round stones shaped like spools, incised with designs that made an impression in soft material such as damp clay. Rolled out, a cylinder covers more surface than a stamp, and conveys more information— abstract designs, animals, human beings, monsters, inscriptions, gods. These seals, the largest source of visual information about the ancient Near East, were carefully carved, often of valuable stone, to tell symbolic stories of daily life, religion, and myth; they also served as amulets, to bring their owners the protection of the gods.

(perhaps unwarrantably) that every one else who is at all lifted above the plane of mere money making, feels the same way, and that we are all anxious to help in so far as we are able." From France, Morgan cabled Belle: "Perhaps as well pay him what he asks and have done with him. Will settle with him very quickly when I reach London if he appears."

To replace Johns they hired Professor Albert T. Clay, an Assyriologist at the University of Pennsylvania (who told Belle that Johns had come "to work the Americans, as so many foreigners do, for the yellow-metal"). Morgan endowed a chair and purchase fund at Yale in Laffan's memory, with $100,000 of U.S. Steel stock. Albert Clay, the first Laffan Professor of Assyriology and Babylonian Literature, built Yale's Babylonian Collection into one of the finest in the world. He also prepared a catalogue of Morgan's cuneiform inscriptions. One of the inscriptions, on a tablet made of sun-dried Mesopotamian river mud, is the earliest surviving version of a flood myth, from 1966 B.C.—antedating the story of Noah in the Book of Genesis by about a thousand years.

————

Several of Morgan's gifts to the Metropolitan, like his sponsorship of the Egyptian expeditions, reflected his personal tastes. In 1906 he gave the museum an exceptional collection of decorative arts made in eighteenth-century France, which he bought from a Parisian architect and designer named Georges Hoentschel. The museum set up a Department of Decorative Arts to accommodate this gift of ornately carved woodwork, furniture, porcelains, ormolu, and faïence, and McKim designed a new north-central wing for it. (In 1911 Morgan bought and lent to the museum a set of six Italianate landscape paintings by Hubert Robert. Completed in 1779, they had been commisioned for the brother of Louis XVI, the count of Artois, and formed part of the decoration at Bagatelle, his pavilion near Paris.)

A second collection Morgan bought from Georges Hoentschel in 1906, of medieval art works, included superb Gothic sculptures, choir stalls, tapestries, church columns, ivories, Limoges enamels, and a bronze angel of 1475 by Jean Barbet from the Château du Lude. The Met did not yet have a medieval collection, and Morgan installed these objects in the museum's galleries as a loan. He paid about $1.5 million for both Hoentschel collections, which came with illustrated catalogues documenting their caliber and provenance. Jack Morgan converted the loan of medieval objects into a gift after his father's death.*

Morgan also gave the museum its first medieval tapestry—five handsome fragments from a large mid-fifteenth-century south Netherlandish work, *The*

————

* Jack kept Barbet's bronze angel at the library; after his death, in 1943, it was acquired by the Trustees of the Frick Collection.

Story of the Seven Sacraments and their Prefiguration in the Old Testament—immediately after he bought it from a New York dealer early in 1907.

He had refused to give up his support of the Natural History Museum to join the Met board in 1888, and continued to play a vital role in the "other" museum's affairs. When its long-term president, Morris K. Jesup, died in 1908, the trustees appointed Henry Fairfield Osborn, Morgan's vertebrate-paleontologist nephew, to succeed him. Morgan contributed $16,000 a year to Osborn's fossil department, and set up a fund for the publication of Osborn's two-volume monograph on *Proboscidea,* which weighed forty pounds and cost $280,000 to produce, partly because of its lavish illustrations, partly because of the author's proclivity for rewriting in page proof. Running the museum for the next twenty-five years, Osborn enlarged its building, staff, endowment, and attendance, and made its collection of fossil vertebrates—especially dinosaurs—the finest in the world.* The value of Morgan's lifetime gifts to the American Museum of Natural History amounted to more than $700,000.

———

Morgan's social landscape was changing as he aged. Between 1904 and 1908 William C. Whitney, Grover Cleveland, and Henry Codman Potter died—the Reverend David H. Greer succeeded Potter as bishop of New York—and Dr. Rainsford resigned from St. George's Church.

Dr. Markoe had replaced Rainsford as Morgan's closest male confidant in the 1890s, and over the next few years the rector's contentious character, religious doubts, and alternating spells of depression and "superabundant" energy had intensified. Rainsford suffered a nervous breakdown in 1903. After he recovered, he went off to Africa on a tour that was probably funded by Morgan. He submitted his resignation to the St. George's vestry from Cairo in January 1906.

This news came as a "painful surprise" to Louisa, but her father had probably seen it coming. Rainsford went back to Africa on safari ("quite alone," he said—except for seventy-five black porters and a missionary-trained transla-

* Among Osborn's major trade publications were *The Age of Mammals in Europe, Asia, and North America* (1910), and *The Earth Speaks to Bryan* (1925), a Darwinian answer to William Jennings Bryan after the infamous Scopes trial. In 1910 Osborn wrote to one of his trustees that the museum ought to add "an agreeable Hebrew" to the board, since "the Zoo, the Metrop[olitan Museum], the Public Lib. have all done so, and our atti[tude] is becoming conspicuous." The trustees elected banker Felix M. Warburg. After Pierpont Morgan died, Jack took his place on the board, and refused in 1916 to attend any meeting at which Warburg was present: Jack was convinced, contrary to the facts, that German Jewish bankers were supporting Germany in World War I. "I cannot stand the German Jews," he wrote to Osborn in October 1916, "and will not see them or have anything to do with them. . . . In my opinion they have made themselves impossible as associates for any white people for all time. I am sorry to bother you but there it is."

tor), then traveled in Europe with his wife. He returned to the United States early in 1910. Morgan was at Aix that April when his secretary asked him by cable whether Rainsford should be invited to preach at St. George's. "Would advise talk matter over confidentially with Bishop Greer," Morgan replied. "Cable result to me."

Two years later Rainsford was deposed from the Episcopal Church. He *had* been suffering from depression and nervous exhaustion before he left New York, but he had also been having an affair with a parishioner, and it somehow came to light. This was not a sin at which Morgan would cast stones, even in a man of the cloth, but it required discretion.

Rainsford's affair had probably been the cause of his resignation. At the rector's request, Bishop Greer deposed him at the See House of the Cathedral of St. John the Divine in May 1912. Church canon held that if a minister resigned for reasons not having to do with morality, the Bishop would suspend him for six months, and at the end of that period announce that the deposition was "for causes which do not affect the man's moral character." Rainsford received no six-month suspension and no tribute to his moral character.

Gossip for the rest of the century said that he had taken up with one of Morgan's women. That seems possible but unlikely, as the woman in question played no apparent role in Morgan's life, and after the deposition Morgan helped underwrite another Rainsford expedition to Africa, through the Museum of Natural History. He cabled Jack that though the cost of the trip appeared to be twice the figure originally proposed, "am willing myself to pay as much as all others subscribe."

Six months after Rainsford resigned in 1906, Stanford White was murdered. Morgan had not chosen White to design his library, and had kept his distance as the increasingly ill and improvident architect went so deeply into debt that he gave up his partnership with McKim and worked as a salaried employee. White's notorious sexual conquests had included a chorus girl named Evelyn Nesbit, who later married the Pittsburgh millionaire Harry K. Thaw. Her retrospectively jealous husband tracked White down on the roof garden of Madison Square Garden one night in June 1906 and shot him. The press played up the story for months: STANFORD WHITE, VOLUPTUARY AND PERVERT, DIES THE DEATH OF A DOG, ran a headline in *Vanity Fair*. New York high and low followed every word of the "trial of the century." Thaw was found not guilty by reason of insanity and sent to a New Jersey hospital. Elsie de Wolfe pronounced Evelyn pretty but not worth dying for.

———

A different kind of sensation upset New York's cultural elite in January of 1907 when the Metropolitan Opera first performed Richard Strauss's *Salome,* based on the play by Oscar Wilde. This sexually explicit tale about Herod's daughter and John the Baptist had already caused an uproar in Europe. Its controversial features included the erotic "Dance of the Seven Veils" and Salome's lustful fondling of John's severed head. The premiere took place on January 22. Four days later the Opera's board, on which Morgan sat, notified its director that the production was "objectionable and detrimental to the best interests of the Metropolitan," and asked that it not be performed again.

According to front-page news stories that occasionally appeared next to items about Harry Thaw, the instigator of this protest was "a daughter of J. Pierpont Morgan" (Louisa), who saw the premiere from her father's box, and urged him "to get the Opera House Directors" to cancel its run. On January 27 the *Times* reported that Morgan had called a meeting of the directors and persuaded them to order the performances stopped. The next day the *Times* said there had been no meeting, just a telephone call from board president George G. Haven polling members about terminating the production. The Met canceled the remaining performances of *Salome.* Oscar Hammerstein staged a new production at the Manhattan Opera House in 1909, with Mary Garden in the title role.

Morgan was not puritanical about culture, but if Louisa came to him horrified at the spectacle of Salome embracing the severed head, and if the Met board shared her alarm (its members included George Bowdoin, George Baker, Charles Lanier, D. O. Mills, William K. Vanderbilt, and August Belmont), he may well have advocated the production's termination. There is no mention of the incident in the Morgan family papers.

———

Morgan's usual winter depression was especially acute that January. He had come down with influenza after Christmas, and "the poison seems to have got into his spirit worse than I have ever known it to do," Jack reported to Walter Burns: "I am in great hope that he will shortly go away as he does not seem able to shake off the depression." The junior Morgan had broached the subject of his father's heavy spending for art, observing that it reduced the bank's available capital and prevented "our making as much as we might otherwise have done. I was not asking for apologies or excuses on his part," Jack told Walter Burns, "but I think he fully appreciated the point. At any rate he did not object to my mentioning it, which surprised me somewhat."

The conversation had no effect on Morgan's purchases of art. A month later he paid $100,000 for a painting by Johannes Vermeer—*A Lady Writing*—in which a young woman in a yellow jacket with white fur trim looks up from her writing table. The exquisitely lucid, deceptively simple work of this enigmatic seventeenth-century Dutch master, with its brilliant effects of color, stillness, and light, had been in eclipse for nearly two centuries until the French critic Étienne-Joseph-Théophile Thoré rediscovered Vermeer in the 1860s. Henry

Marquand had given *Young Woman with a Water Pitcher* to the Met in 1889, Isabella Stewart Gardner bought *The Concert* in 1892, Collis P. Huntington gave *Woman with a Lute* to the Met in 1900, and Henry Clay Frick acquired *Girl Interrupted at her Music* in 1901. There are about thirty-five known paintings by Vermeer; with Morgan's acquisition in 1907, the United States had five.

Morgan seemed no more willing to resolve the problems created by his semi-retirement than to cut back on his "heavy spending." Jack complained to Grenfell in January 1907 that "it makes work a little complicated to have [father] out of the office when he wishes to decide many questions himself." Though the elder Morgan cheered up later in the month, he refused to leave his library. He had not been downtown in ten weeks, when, at the end of February, his partners began calling the library "the Up-Town Branch."

Certain things were going well without his full attention. A notable success for the firm during this troubled period was the resuscitation of the ailing American Telephone and Telegraph Company, which had been financed primarily by Kidder, Peabody in Boston. The manager of the predecessor Bell Company, Theodore N. Vail, had argued for structural centralization and vertical integration in the eighties, and when his conservative New England investors rejected those changes, Vail resigned. In 1902 AT&T's Boston bankers turned for new financing to a consortium led by J. P. Morgan & Co. and Baker's First National. The New Yorkers brought Vail back and, following his advice, began a major expansion in 1906: they underwrote a $100 million issue of bonds, and reorganized the company to operate on a national scale. Jack described it as "the best business I've seen in a long time." After 1906 the house of Morgan served as principal banker to AT&T.

In the wake of the 1904 Northern Securities decision, large systems of allied roads had continued to extend their territorial dominion. Men approved by Morgan managed major rail networks in the South, the Northwest, Pennsylvania's anthracite coal territory, and New England—Charles Mellen had left the Northern Pacific for the New York, New Haven, & Hartford in 1903, to build a community of transportation interests in the Northeast. By 1906 two thirds of the country's total track mileage was under the control of seven groups, and Morgan played a supervisory role in the affairs of four of the Big Seven—his own, and the systems headed by the Vanderbilts, the Pennsylvania Railroad, and James J. Hill.

The government's major antitrust and regulatory actions of 1906 did not seriously disturb the Morgan bank. When Attorney General Charles Bonaparte brought suit against Rockefeller's Standard Oil, Perkins crowed about the wise preventive measures taken at U.S. Steel. And after Congress passed a new bill to regulate railroads—the Hepburn Act, authorizing the ICC to prescribe just and reasonable rates for the future—the bankers once again hoped that federal regulation would impose the stability they had been seeking for decades. Perkins told Morgan in June 1906 that "while the treatment is mighty heroic, it is going to work out for the ultimate and great good of the railroads. There is no question but that rebating has been dealt a death blow."

That the ICC did not aggressively attack railroad rates over the next few years disappointed the roads' opponents, but the Hepburn Act did limit fare increases, which cut into the railroads' profits, lowered the value of their securities, and restricted their access to capital for improvement, expansion, and equipment.

The U.S. economic picture had grown darker since Schiff's prediction in January 1906 that without currency reform there would be "such a panic . . . as will make all previous panics look like child's play." The Boer and Russo-Japanese Wars had absorbed much of the West's capital reserves. England and Germany raised their interest rates in the fall of 1906, to attract funds. As cash drained out of U.S. markets, the Treasury had no means to expand the money supply.*

Princeton University president Woodrow Wilson attributed the country's economic troubles of 1906–7 to the government's "aggressive attitude toward the railroads, that made it impossible for them to borrow." Much of the business community agreed, and urged Roosevelt to ease up on regulatory measures and antitrust prosecutions. Instead, TR threatened at the end of 1906 to subject all large trusts to federal control. He declared that Americans were enjoying "a literally unprecedented prosperity."

Morgan planned to leave for Europe in mid-March 1907, but the combination of monetary shrinkage and a rumor that Roosevelt would make some dramatic new move against the railroads called him out of his "Up-Town Branch." He went to Washington on March 12 and spent two hours discussing "the present business situation" with the President. As he left the White House he told the press that Roosevelt would soon meet with the heads of leading railroads to see what might be done to "allay public anxiety." On March 14, the day after Morgan sailed for Europe, the stock market crashed in

---

* Treasury Secretary Leslie Shaw, who tried informally to adjust the money supply to seasonal fluctuations in demand, wrote at the end of 1906: "If the Secretary of the Treasury were given $100,000,000 to be deposited with the banks or withdrawn as he might deem expedient, and if in addition he were clothed with authority over the reserves of the several banks, with power to contract the national-bank circulation at pleasure, in my judgment no panic as distinguished from industrial stagnation could threaten either the United States or Europe that he could not avert. No central or Government bank in the world can so readily influence financial conditions throughout the world as can the Secretary under the authority with which he is now clothed." According to Milton Friedman and Anna Schwartz, this large claim contained "much truth": "The Treasury's monetary powers were very great indeed. If they had been expanded as Shaw requested, the Treasury would have been clothed with effective power different from but not clearly inferior to that later assigned to the Federal Reserve System."

spite of record corporate earnings. Prices collapsed, brokerage houses closed, interest rates soared. Roosevelt called off his meeting with the railroad men. The Dow Jones average lost nearly 25 percent of its value, falling from 96 in January to 75 in March. Morgan's New York partners cabled their London colleagues that the "underlying cause" of the "enormous drop" was impossible to discern.

An impromptu emergency committee consisting of Harriman, Frick, Schiff, William Rockefeller, and H. H. Rogers called at 23 Wall Street to suggest that the house of Morgan and Kuhn, Loeb organize a pool of $25 million to intervene in the markets and stop further declines. Jack cabled this proposal to his father, but said it might be safer to do nothing: he had heard from George Baker that the Treasury Secretary was about to step in.

Morgan, concerned in equal measure with propriety and feasibility, urged restraint: "Think plan suggested would be unwise," he replied from London—"entirely at variance with all policies we have ever adopted being at the head of a declared Stock Exchange manipulation which do not think we are competent undertake." He could imagine circumstances that "might make it imperative at any cost," but "so long as parties in Washington have power to checkmate any good we might do the danger is still greater. I feel this is all I can say and must leave you deal with situation. Show this George F. Baker you can have no better counsellor."

To help meet the demand for money, Roosevelt's new Treasury Secretary, George Cortelyou—former Commerce Secretary and Republican Party chairman—deposited $12 million with national banks in New York. At a similar moment in the "Rich Man's" panic of 1903, Morgan had put together a reserve of $50 million. Now, four years later, his colleagues took his advice against intervening in the market, but the ten largest New York banks pledged $2.5 million each to a new pool in case the crisis grew worse. The Treasury cash and the widely advertised fact of the bankers' reserve calmed the markets briefly, but throughout that spring stock prices continued to slide, businesses and brokerages to fail, and bank reserves to decline. Wary investors on both sides of the Atlantic sold securities and hoarded gold.

———

Morgan celebrated his seventieth birthday at Aix on April 17 with Adelaide and his sister Mary. Jack's cable for the occasion went a bit far: "As Jesus the Son of Sirach says let us praise famous men and our Fathers that begat us leaders of the people by their counsels and knowledge, rich men furnished with ability living peacably in their habitations, merciful men whose righteousness has not been forgotten. This with loving birthday greetings."

From Aix the Morgan party went to Paris and London, then in late May met Roger Fry in Perugia for a tour of Italian art. Fry had continued to work as curator of paintings at the Met, and his estimations of its president continued to fluctuate. In June of 1906 he took Morgan to see Degas's *Le Viol* (*The Rape*) in Paris, for possible acquisition by the museum, and offered a rare firsthand glimpse of "the big man's" response to modern art. The anti-vice crusader Anthony Comstock had just raided the Art Students League in New York and confiscated paintings of nudes. The president of the Met had to take American puritanism into account, although his own instincts before the Degas seemed appreciative. Fry reported: Morgan felt "that, in spite of its beauty, [*Le Viol*] would be open to objection from the Comstockians, and that we ought not at present to face that particular music."*

A year later Fry complained to the Philadelphia collector John G. Johnson that Morgan had just skimmed three paintings for himself from a group of Italian works offered to the Met, "and expressed a pious hope that the Museum might be able to buy the rest! When I think that you [Johnson], who have nothing to do with our Museum, always generously stand aside when we are in for things, I confess this from the President of the Museum surprises me. However he is, I believe, quite friendly with me so that this anecdote had better not get abroad."

Fry was counting on Morgan's friendliness in the spring of 1907. He hoped to change his title at the Met to European adviser on paintings, with no cut in salary, which would leave him free to spend more time abroad, and when Morgan invited him to Perugia to see an exhibition of Umbrian art and tour the region, the critic took it as a good sign: "You may guess from this," he told his wife, "that Morgan has become very affable to me and seems quite willing that I shall have my own terms with the Museum. As he is omnipotent, that is everything."

In Italy, Fry found himself pleasantly surprised by the "affable" potentate's character and taste. He met Morgan, Adelaide Douglas, and Mary Burns in Perugia on May 27. The next day the group went through the Exhibition, "where [Morgan] was received like royalty without any notice of his coming being given," Fry wrote to his wife. "It's quite curious whenever we go to a church there's a little crowd of young men gathered to watch and at the Exhibition all the chief people come to offer their services. It astounds me that here they should know and feel about him like that. Somehow he has touched the imagination of people as no other millionaire has. He enjoyed himself hugely and really loves to go about to the churches and to see things that he can't buy, which I like in him. Indeed, I've got on wonderfully with him in this mood."

---

* The painting was given to the Philadelphia Museum of Art with the Henry McIlhenny Collection in 1986, and is now called *Interior* (*The Rape*). It depicts a man and woman in a room just after the event described: he stands, fully clothed and facing her, with his back to a wall; turned away from him, her torn dress exposing one shoulder, she appears to be crying, though her face is obscured in shadow.

From Perugia the travelers motored to Assisi. Fry described their reception as "incredibly comic": the town was "in a state of frenzied excitement, all the Franciscan monks hoping to get [Morgan] to give them money to buy back their convent, bowing and scraping and opening up their sacredest treasures . . . poor St. Francis's marriage with Poverty seemed to have brought forth a strange offspring. But the thing was not so crude after all because to my surprise Morgan was deeply impressed by the lower church. Thought Giotto's *Raising of Lazarus* the finest picture he had ever seen and generally displayed a kind of intelligence which I hadn't expected."

Bernard Berenson happened also to be at Assisi, and Fry dined with him that evening. "We laughed," Fry wrote home, "over my position as bear leader to the great man."

In Florence a few days later, Morgan bought the autograph manuscript of Beethoven's last violin sonata (Opus 96 in G Major) from the Florentine rare-book dealer Leo Olschki, and Fry dined with the Berensons at the Villa I Tatti, where the hospitality was mixed with intellectual one-upmanship: "B.B. quite absurd wanting to catch me out over his pictures," Fry complained. He declined to play the attribution game, pleading fatigue, but his host persisted in trying "to make my ignorance as apparent as he could."

Berenson reported to Mrs. Gardner: "Fry burst in upon us . . . looking dead tired. He had left Morgan for a day or two, Morgan and his Mrs. Douglas, and gave the most interesting account of them." BB was not impressed: "It seems Morgan's desire now is to re-value the masterpieces of Italian art. The worst of it is he will succeed. The fact that he liked a picture will probably be remembered for years. Such are people," sighed the critic/connoisseur. "No critic, no connoisseur affects them . . . [but] the whole public will go see a picture that Morgan's nose has corruscated over approvingly. These by the way are my reflections, not Fry's. Fry really admires Morgan very much—as doubtless should all of us if we only could."

Fry's admiration continued to grow. The party went on to Siena and San Gimignano, then boarded Morgan's "marvellous yacht greeted from the shore by the whole population of Ancona and its brass band." From Paris ten days later Fry reported buying "some fine things for the Museum and some superb ones for Morgan. He's more colossal than ever in his purchases but also much more intelligent. He's mighty pleased with me."

In the sunlight of the "great man's" pleasure, Fry did manage to change his job at the Met to European adviser on paintings, with no loss of recompense.

Morgan made other magnificent purchases in the summer of 1907 as well. Through Duveen Brothers he acquired a selection of paintings from the estate of the French collector Rodolphe Kann. He had put up half of the $4.5 million Duveen paid the Kann estate, on condition that he have first choice of about thirty pictures. The paintings he chose included Ghirlandaio's *Giovanna*

Tornabuoni, Portrait of a Young Man by Andrea del Castagno, a Roger van der Weyden *Annunciation,* two panels by Memling, and works by Gerard David, van Ruysdael, Metsu, and Terborch—but not, surprisingly, Rembrandt's *Aristotle Contemplating the Bust of Homer.**

Proceeding to London in June, Morgan spent a weekend at Nuneham Park in Oxfordshire—the country estate he had helped May and Loulou Harcourt restore—with a party that included Edward VII, Alice Keppel, Prime Minister Henry Campbell-Bannerman, and Mr. and Mrs. Leopold Rothschild. He also reviewed page proofs for an illustrated catalogue of his paintings prepared by W. Roberts and T. Humphry Ward, authors of a 1904 catalogue raisonée of the works of Romney.

By 1907 Morgan had commissioned catalogues for several of his collections. Joseph Sabin had published an inventory of the library at 219 in 1883, and Earl Shinn listed Morgan's early paintings in the *Art Treasures of America* in 1879. As the scope of his collecting expanded, Morgan hired specialists to assess and classify what he had acquired, and to present the information in beautifully produced volumes—leatherbound elephant folios with scholarly text and fine color plates, printed on vellum or high-quality paper. Many of his predecessors had published similar registers—Morgan had bought catalogues of the Wallace and Alfred de Rothschild collections from Sotheran in 1902–3, and presented scholarly inventories of the Hoentschel collections to the Met. He gave copies of his own catalogues as they were completed to royal friends in Europe (including Edward VII and Kaiser Wilhelm), as well as to scholars, dealers, museums, libraries, and universities.

---

* Duveen had promised to reserve the Castagno for Isabella Stewart Gardner, and Morgan reluctantly agreed to let the dealer offer it to her. Berenson urged her to buy it for £12,500. Formerly in the Torrigiani Collection, the painting ranked among the "highest achievements of Italian art," said BB, and was "the grandest surviving work of one of the greatest figures in Italian art . . . an overwhelming masterpiece." The stock market's 1907 troubles had reduced Mrs. Gardner's income, however, and she declined the picture: "Woe is me!" she wailed to BB. "Why am I not Morgan or Frick? I am wretched about it."

Morgan kept the Castagno. Berenson tried and failed to buy it from his estate in 1914. Then in 1932, in his *Italian Pictures of the Renaissance,* BB changed the attribution to Antonio Pollaiuolo. He had apparently considered Botticelli as well. Belle Greene asked him whether, "in memory of our long and hectic devotion, you could find time to let me know *why* our Castagno-Botticelli is now Pollaiuolo? I have tried my hardest to understand this, but my feeble and ageing mind refuses to do so." Andrew Mellon bought the picture in 1935, and it is now—attributed to Castagno—in the National Gallery of Art in Washington. Morgan's Vermeer, *A Lady Writing,* also now belongs to the National Gallery. The Ghirlandaio from the Kann Collection is part of the Baron Thyssen Collection in Madrid, and the Memlings are at the Morgan Library. The Van der Weyden *Annunciation,* Metsu's *A Visit to the Baby,* and the Terborch, *Young Girl at Her Toilet,* are at the Metropolitan Museum.

These volumes at once located Morgan in relation to the objects' previous owners, and somewhat offset the transitory nature of possession: although he currently owned bronze sculptures, portrait miniatures, the Colonna Raphael, the Grasse Fragonards, and Rembrandt's *Nicolaes Ruts*, someone else might acquire them after he died. The catalogues preserved his collections under his name.

Catalogues also made it possible for people who could not visit the collections to examine the works described. Morgan asked George C. Williamson, who compiled the volumes on his watch, jewel, and portrait miniature collections, to present the illustrations in such a way that students could use them. According to Williamson, when the catalogue of watches was completed, Morgan said, "in some respects, it was more pleasant to see the illustrations than the originals, because, in the former, one could look at every side of the watch . . . at a glance, whereas the original had to be opened and turned over."

The medievalist M. R. James, who had edited the illustrated Chiswick Press volume on the Bennett collection, produced a catalogue of some of Morgan's medieval and Renaissance illuminated manuscripts in 1906. William Laffan had compiled the catalogue of Chinese porcelains, Albert Clay prepared the volumes on Babylonian tablets, and Wilhelm Bode in Berlin finished two volumes on Morgan's Renaissance bronzes in 1909. In an introduction, Bode wrote that Morgan—"the greatest collector of our time"—owned "the most comprehensive and probably the most important collection of bronzes to be found in private possession, a collection moreover exceptionally rich in Italian small bronzes of the Renaissance."

Bode then sketched a picture of Morgan's general method: "Beginning to collect bronzes at a time when it was thought that they had almost disappeared from the market, he proceeded upon lines very similar to those which he had followed when forming his collection of books, miniatures, and other objects; first securing certain notable collections *en bloc* and then gradually adding any good examples which happened to come under his notice. Thus in less than a decade he has succeeded in bringing together a collection superior even to many which have taken a lifetime to form."

———

Roger Fry had described Morgan at the end of their 1907 Italian tour as "mighty pleased with me." After changing his job at the Met, probably with its president's blessing, Fry rarely came to New York, and the board ignored most of his recommendations. In June of 1909 he found a Fra Angelico *Virgin and Child*, from the King of Belgium's collection, in a Paris gallery, and asked permission to buy it for the museum for £10,000. Board secretary Robert W. de Forest wired back authorization, subject to the approval of Morgan or Laffan, but Morgan in the meantime saw and bought the painting for himself.

Fry had been outraged before at Morgan's appropriation of items on offer to the Met. Others at the museum, beholden to its president for major collections and dozens of individual gifts, maintained a discreet silence whenever he bought something out from under them. Not Fry. In 1909 he fired off a letter of reproach. Morgan wrote across the top, probably to de Forest, "This is the most remarkable letter I ever received. I do not propose to answer it until I see you. Bring it back."*

Over the next several months, Fry entirely lost the confidence of the Met trustees: asked to come to New York to save his job, he stayed in London and protested his ill treatment. In late December 1909 the Met's assistant director, Edward Robinson, told Fry that his services had "not been up to expectations" for some time, and let him go. Belle Greene told Berenson early in 1910 that she was "up in the air" about what had actually happened: Fry had done "several inexplicable and erratic things" recently, "but no one seems to know or is willing to tell just what was the last straw."

Fry blamed his dismissal on Morgan but continued trying to sell him things—a Persian astronomical treatise, Macauley manuscripts, bronze doors, several paintings, a little bronze "Cellini"—and at the end of 1912 he personally designed the cover for bound copies of a *Burlington Magazine* series on Morgan's Byzantine enamels, sending the issues to New York with a note: "I hope you will think them not unworthy of the splendid objects they treat of. . . . I was very sorry to hear you had been ill but hope that you are quite recovered, and that I may wish you a very happy New Year." (At some point between 1905 and 1912, Morgan had bought 1,000 shares of preferred stock in the *Burlington* for £1 a share. In the inventory of his estate they were listed as having no value.)

Many years later, Fry wrote an account of the 1907 Italian trip and gave it to Virginia Woolf, who published it in her 1940 biography, *Roger Fry*. In witty detail Fry told of Morgan "sleeping upstairs in the arms of the elderly and well preserved Mrs. Douglas," of shady Levantine dealers and provincial Italian aristocrats desperate to sell their wares to "il Morgan," and of Mary Burns, "Mrs. Douglas' chaperone," who was "entirely unnoticeable" except when she "uttered little shrill mouse-like squeaks of admiration at pictures, scenery, or Mr. Morgan's remarks."

---

* Berenson jeered to Mrs. Gardner that "Morgan . . . has just bought on Fry's advice the King of Belgium's Fra Angelico. It is a most beautiful picture. It was offered to me for eight, and I am confident I could have had it for six; but the next day it was sold to Morgan thro' Fry for twelve thousand pounds! What a world the dealers' is, what a goose Fry, and what a lamb am I!" Morgan's heirs sold the painting, *Virgin and Child Enthroned*, shortly after his death. It is now in the Baron Thyssen Collection, attributed to a follower of Fra Angelico.

In 1907 Fry had been struck by Morgan's intelligent responses, "huge enjoyment," appreciation of Giotto, and interest in things he could not buy. In retrospect he said exactly the opposite: "Morgan . . . didn't know how bored he was going to be with the frescoes at Assisi where . . . there was nothing one could buy. . . . Assisi was a failure. Mr. Morgan was displeased with the condition of the frescoes. . . . Mrs. Douglas would like to have improved her mind by pumping me on the history of the church and Giotto but we were hurried away since Morgan [was not] enjoying [himself]."

Continuing at length in this vein, Fry delivered a summary judgment that has defined Morgan as collector for generations of scholars and readers: "A crude historical imagination," the critic wrote, "was the only flaw in his otherwise perfect insensibility [to art]."

History is subject to a tyranny of the articulate, and Fry had the weapon of artful words in his contest with "the big man"—a contest Morgan barely noticed. Flummoxed by an implacable force he could neither sway nor disconcert, the aesthete resorted long after the fact to scorn.

In 1940, after Virginia Woolf's *Roger Fry* was published in England, Jack Morgan asked the author (through one of his London partners) to delete two sentences for the American edition—the one about Morgan sleeping with Adelaide, and Fry's reflection "I always wondered that his mistresses in New York got such substantial subsidies as they did." Mrs. Woolf wrote to her American publisher: "As he [Jack Morgan] says that [the two sentences] give him and the Morgan family great pain, I have had to agree. . . . Privately, I think the objection is unreasonable, but of course I did not like to refuse." The book had already been printed, and the changes were never made.

Wall Street during the panic of 1907.
(Archives of The Pierpont Morgan Library, New York)

Chapter 28

—

PANIC

Morgan remained abroad for five months in 1907, from mid-March until mid-August. His major interests had not been hurt by the market turmoil in the spring: "The bank is fine," noted Fanny in her diary on April 28, and on May 4: "The bank is glorious." Jack reported that U.S. Steel earnings for the quarter ending June 30 would be the largest in its history—$45.5 million—and that the company was spending $10 million a month on expansion, which should increase earnings further. "The figures are so enormous that one hardly believes them possible," Jack told his London partners, "but there they are."

The worldwide credit shortage had not eased. The city of San Francisco had been unable to float a loan in New York that spring, and the Egyptian Stock Exchange crashed. The Bank of England sent $3 million in gold to Alexandria to stop the slide, then found itself short of cash. As stocks plummeted on the Tokyo Exchange, banks failed all over Japan. French investors sold American stocks to buy gold and ship it home, which further depleted U.S. reserves. Over the summer, large new bond offerings for Westinghouse and the cities of Boston and New York did not sell. New York's Metropolitan Traction Company and a major iron-manufacturing house went bankrupt. On August 10, the American stock market crashed again. *The New York Times* estimated the losses at $1 billion. Morgan sailed for home on August 21.

The Roosevelt administration had not checked its regulatory course. That summer, Federal District Court Judge Kenesaw Mountain Landis fined Standard Oil $29 million on fourteen hundred counts of illegal rebating,* and Jack echoed much of Wall Street in ascribing the market crash to government "attacks" on big business—"everyone is frightened to death by the action of people like our fool Attorney General," he told his London partners. Roosevelt defended himself to the Boston banker Henry Lee Higginson: pointing to recent breaks on foreign stock exchanges, and to declines in British government and railroad securities, the President found it "difficult to believe" that the worldwide financial crisis was "due to distrust of my policies, reasonable or unreasonable." A few days later he leveled a charge of his own: "certain malefactors of great wealth" were inducing panic to force a "reversal" of his policies, "so that they may enjoy unmolested the fruits of their own evil-doing."

The first explanation made more sense than the second. Europe's troubles critically affected the international flow of money, and it was the currency supply more than the antitrust law that chiefly worried the elder Morgan. The rapidly expanding American economy, requiring enormous amounts of capital, faced a liquidity crisis: world gold production had declined relative to industrial growth, recent wars had absorbed western cash reserves, foreign governments had raised their interest rates, and the United States had no central bank to adjust supply to demand. The worst crises always came in the autumn, when rural banks drew money out of New York to meet agricultural demand. America's obsolete banking system was like an immense tangle of dry brush and timber waiting for a spark.

There were in 1907 nearly twenty-one thousand state and national banks across the country, with no coordinated management or pool of common reserves. Most of them lent their surpluses to correspondent banks in New York, the national money center, and the New Yorkers lent the money out to the Stock Exchange, individuals, and business. Banks beyond the Hudson could call in the loans at a moment's notice, however, and New York's large national banks, required to keep 25 percent of their deposits in cash, could not possibly meet demand if all the correspondents suddenly demanded their money at once.

The weakest institutions in the system were trust companies, chartered by the states to handle individual trust funds, wills, and estates. Entirely different from industrial "trusts" such as Standard Oil and U.S. Steel, the trust companies operated like commercial banks—accepting deposits, issuing loans, financing speculative ventures—but they had no mandated reserves or regulatory supervision. Thomas W. Lawson, author of the muckraking articles on "Frenzied Finance" that helped bring on the Armstrong insurance investigation, described the trust company as "the irrigating canal of Wall Street, the insurance company as the reservoir."

---

* The judgment against Standard Oil was eventually overturned. Landis became the first commissioner of baseball.

At the beginning of October 1907, Morgan went to Richmond, Virginia, with a party of friends to attend the Triennial Episcopal Convention. While he was gone, an attempt by two speculators to corner the stock of a copper company failed, bankrupting a mining concern, two brokerage houses, and a bank. The speculators, F. Augustus Heinze and Charles W. Morse, had induced several New York trust companies to fund their venture—including the Knickerbocker Trust, headed by Morgan's acquaintance Charles T. Barney. As reports of Barney's involvement in the copper scheme swept through New York, terrified Knickerbocker depositors began drawing their money out.

Morgan's partners kept him posted on the situation by messenger and wire, but insisted that he not come back early since a sudden change of his plans would increase the sense of panic. The Richmond convention ended on Saturday afternoon, October 19. Morgan immediately left by train for New York, arriving early Sunday morning. He went straight to his library, where his partners were waiting.

They quickly filled him in. The Knickerbocker depositors' demands had been met for two days with help from the National Bank of Commerce, which acted as clearinghouse for the Trust, but the run was likely to resume on Monday and the panic certain to spread.* Stocks were broadly down, and cash was in short supply. If country banks and individual depositors all tried to get their money out of New York in the next few days, the result would, as Schiff had predicted, "make all previous panics look like child's play." Morgan smoked cigars as he listened. He had told Walter Burns during the 1895 gold crisis that "We all have large interests dependent upon maintenance sound currency U.S." Twelve years later he had even larger interests dependent on the maintenance of the U.S. banking system, currency supply, and Stock Exchange.

---

* Morgan had been a director of the National Bank of Commerce since 1875, when it participated in the Treasury refundings, and a vice president from 1893 to 1904. The Commerce had merged with several other bank and trust companies to become the second largest bank in the country by 1904, and also one of the most stable. It managed enormous sums of money and acted as a clearinghouse for half the money flowing through New York's financial institutions, including the three big life insurance companies. New York's official Clearing House Association settled bank transactions at the end of each day, totaling up checks and drafts and coordinating transfers of funds; it also served as lender of last resort for member banks that needed help during panics, issuing loan certificates—paper that could be used as currency among the banks—secured by sound but temporarily illiquid assets. After 1903, when the Clearing House insisted that trust companies keep 10 percent of their deposits on reserve, most of them resigned from the association and cleared through the National Bank of Commerce. Though Morgan stepped down as vice president of the Commerce early in 1904, he remained a director and a member of its executive board. Because of his long-term affiliation, the Bank of Commerce was often referred to as J. P. Morgan's bank. In fact it was owned by the Equitable Life Assurance Society, which, as of June 1905, was owned by Thomas Fortune Ryan.

As soon as word got out that he had returned to New York, reporters stationed themselves across from the library on 36th Street. Bankers and government officials dropped by all Sunday afternoon and evening as the old man marshaled information and resources. He had managed the 1895 crisis with the aid of his lawyers, August Belmont, and President Cleveland. In 1907, seventy years old and facing a far more complex set of problems, he was going to need a wider network of help.

President Roosevelt was hunting in the Louisiana canebrakes. He told a reporter on Sunday: "We got three bears, six deer, one wild turkey, twelve squirrels, one duck, one opossum, and one wildcat. We ate them all, except the wildcat."

In New York that night Morgan lined up two groups of men. The first consisted of himself, George Baker of the First National, and James Stillman at the City Bank—a high command that could review information, raise money, and decide on allocations as the country's provisional lender of last resort. Baker had worked closely with Morgan for thirty years. This crisis induced Stillman to join forces with the man he had recently dismissed as a "back number." The second group was made up of George Perkins, Henry P. Davison (a protégé of Baker's and a vice president at First National), and Benjamin Strong: Davison had organized the reputable Bankers Trust Company in 1903, and he recommended Strong, the secretary of Bankers Trust. These six men would try to ascertain which trust companies were hopelessly overextended and should be allowed to fail, and which were essentially healthy and could be saved. Somehow they would find ways to supply liquidity where it would do the most good. Late Sunday night other New York financiers pledged to support any plan Morgan might devise. Treasury Secretary Cortelyou sent word that he would deposit $6 million in New York's banks, and more if necessary.

It was after midnight by the time the meetings at the library broke up. Jack was in London. Anne and Fanny had recently returned from Europe and gone straight to Cragston. No. 219 Madison was closed for cleaning after the summer. Morgan stayed with the Satterlees in their new house.

On Monday, October 21, he held a strategy session over breakfast with Perkins before heading downtown. The pressure on the Knickerbocker Trust had increased: it had $60 million on deposit but just $10 million in cash. Its directors reported to 23 Wall Street shortly after Morgan arrived that they had forced Charles Barney to resign, but were afraid this news would accelerate the panic. While they talked, word came in that the National Bank of Commerce would no longer clear for the Knickerbocker—a decisive vote of no confidence. The Morgan and Knickerbocker people conferred all afternoon and evening, moving from 23 Wall to the library to a private dining room at Sherry's. They adjourned at 2:00 A.M. with no clear plan except that the Trust Company would open in the morning, and Davison and Strong would examine its books: if the younger men found it financially sound, Morgan would find money to keep it afloat.

Long lines formed outside the Knickerbocker Trust at Fifth Avenue and 34th Street overnight. Early Tuesday morning, as Morgan's lieutenants pored over accounts in a back office, depositors clamored for information and cash. The streets of the financial district "reflected the panicky feeling indoors, in the worried faces and the unusual crowds of hurrying men," reported *The New York Times*. By noon the Knickerbocker had paid out $8 million, and Davison and Strong told Morgan they could not determine whether it had enough assets to secure a loan without more time. Morgan decided not to intervene, even though he had known Charles Barney for years. At 2:00 P.M. the Knickerbocker closed its doors.

Secretary Cortelyou took the afternoon train to Manhattan as banks around the country began withdrawing their reserves from New York. Stock prices tumbled. The annual interest rate of money on the exchange—"call" money lent briefly by banks to brokers to finance their trades—reached 70 percent.* As Morgan left his office, he told waiting reporters: "We are doing everything we can, as fast as we can, but nothing has yet crystallized."

"Knickerbocker troubles everywhere," wrote Anne in her diary on Tuesday, October 22: "Terrible day downtown."

Late that night, the bankers met with Cortelyou at his hotel—the Manhattan, at Madison Avenue and 42nd Street—and at 1:00 A.M. Perkins told reporters that a syndicate would furnish money to the healthy trusts. The hardest hit, after the Knickerbocker, had been the Trust Company of America, with assets of $100 million. Hoping to ease public fears, Perkins promised specifically to buttress the TCA, but naming any institution in an atmosphere of panic turned out to be a mistake.

"All hands are leaning on the Senior," Perkins cabled Jack in London before he went home—"he is in fine form." The old man *was* in fine form, although he had come down with a heavy cold. He had had no time for lunch and barely touched his dinner on Tuesday. Instead of food he was consuming cigars.

The next morning—Wednesday, October 23—the Satterlees had trouble waking him up. When they finally succeeded, he had no voice and seemed to be in a stupor. Dr. Markoe came and dosed him with lozenges, gargles, and sprays.

John D. Rockefeller, at the urging of his philanthropic adviser, told the Asso-

---

* At the "money post" on the Stock Exchange floor, banks furnished "call loans" to brokers for anywhere from a minute to a few days. If a bank suddenly called in its loan, a broker could usually turn around and borrow the same amount from someone else, but in volatile markets interest rates fluctuated wildly according to the money supply.

ciated Press on October 23 that he would give half his fortune to sustain the country's credit in this crisis. When reporters asked him if he was really willing to put up half his securities to stop the panic, he said, "Yes, and I have cords of them, gentlemen, cords of them."

On arriving, late, at 23 Wall Street, Morgan found Harriman, Frick, and Thomas F. Ryan waiting to ask him how to stop the spreading disaster. He said he did not yet know. He called several trust company presidents to his office at noon, settled them in a back office, and told them to come up with a plan.

That morning's headlines—AID TRUST COMPANY OF AMERICA: J. P. MORGAN IS TO HELP—spooked the TCA depositors, who lined up to get their money out. At 1:00 P.M., TCA president Oakleigh Thorne told Morgan he had only $1.2 million in cash left. Without a loan he could not stay open until closing time at 3:00. As Thorne left the Morgan bank, Ben Strong arrived with a preliminary report on the TCA finances. He and Davison had stayed up all night studying the accounts. Strong later recalled that as he presented his findings to the senior trio (Morgan, Baker, and Stillman), Morgan said little: the old man wanted no details, just general facts and results. Several times he asked, "Are they solvent?" Strong said the TCA surplus was gone but its assets were more or less intact.

Would the bankers be justified in seeing this company through? Morgan wanted to know.

Strong said he thought they would.

Morgan turned to Baker and Stillman: "This is the place to stop the trouble, then."

He dismissed the trust company presidents, and asked Thorne to come back with securities TCA had accepted as collateral for its loans. By 2:15 Thorne's cash was down to $180,000, and his employees were trooping into 23 Wall Street with leather boxes and sacks full of certificates. Morgan, Strong, and Thorne sat down around a big table to add up the value of the stocks and bonds. Stillman got on the phone to his bank. Morgan, coughing and sneezing, took notes on a pad, and as soon as he had enough collateral for an advance, told Stillman to send that amount around to the Trust. By 3:00, about $3 million had been delivered and the Trust Company of America had, for the moment, survived. The advance from Stillman's till would be shared in equal parts by First National, National City, the Hanover National, and J. P. Morgan & Co. The securities went down to the Morgan vault.

Strong spent the rest of that day and night confirming his appraisal of the TCA's assets. Baker trusted Davison; Davison trusted Strong. The key figure supplying Morgan with crucial information during this crisis was a man he had just met.

Though the TCA had pulled through until closing time on October 23, it was not yet in the clear, and other institutions were getting clobbered. Westinghouse had gone into receivership, a run had started on the Lincoln Trust Company, and the Pittsburgh Stock Exchange had suspended trading—which would probably precipitate a stock market panic in New York. The interest rate on call money loaned by banks to brokers on the Exchange had risen to 90 percent. The entire credit structure of the country was under siege.

Morgan told the heads of the trust companies to meet him, Baker, and Stillman late that night at the Union Trust, on Fifth Avenue at 38th Street. Once they had assembled, he announced that a *trust company* panic was at the root of all the trouble: the TCA was going to need $10 million the next day, and if the solvent trusts pledged money, the commercial banks and Morgan's firm would help. The presidents talked. Nothing happened. Prepared for this impasse, George Baker directed the head of Bankers Trust to commit $1 million. The others made no move.

Sick and worn-out, Morgan fell asleep in his chair, cigar in hand. Talk continued around him for half an hour. When he woke up, he asked Strong for a pencil and paper. "Gentlemen," he said, "the Bankers Trust Company has agreed to take its share." Turning to one of the men near him, he asked, "Mr. Marston, how much will the Farmers Loan and Trust Company subscribe?" Marston agreed to match the Bankers Trust pledge. Morgan went around the room until he had $8.25 million. He committed the commercial banks to make up the rest, and left with Stillman to bring Cortelyou up to date.

After conferring with the bankers, the Treasury Secretary told reporters that the government would deposit another $25 million in New York to ease the crisis. He himself would stay in Manhattan, working out of the Subtreasury. If the public would "reflect on the real strength of our banking institutions," he advised, confidence would quickly return.

Morgan went home. Perkins cabled Jack in London: "We have had tremendous day; whole financial district thronged with people. . . . As far as human foresight can tell, believe we have passed the crisis; Thursday will decide. All well!"

———

CORTELYOU PUTS IN $25 MILLION, announced *The New York Times* on Thursday morning, and MORGAN'S BANK LEAGUE WILL DO FOR THE TRUST COMPANIES WHAT THE CLEARING HOUSE DOES FOR THE BANKS. As Morgan drove down to his office at ten, people shouted, "There goes the Old Man!" and "There goes the Big Chief!" He pretended not to notice, recalled Satterlee, "but it was evident that he was pleased."

John D. Rockefeller provided $10 million to support the trust companies on Thursday, but the panic had spread to the Stock Exchange. Financial institutions calling in loans were choking off the market's money supply. Every few minutes a broker came into J. P. Morgan & Co. from the Exchange across the street to report on plummeting stock prices. By 12:30 cash was so scarce that the call rate reached 100 percent. At 1:30, Stock Exchange president Ransom H. Thomas told Morgan he would have to suspend operations before the 3:00 P.M. close.

Shutting down the Exchange was out of the question, Morgan said. It would destroy public confidence. He would find money to lend the brokers.

Because of the Armstrong laws, he could no longer borrow cash from the big life insurance companies. Instead, he telephoned the presidents of New York's major commercial banks, and by 2:00 they were gathered in his office. He said he needed $25 million to lend to the Exchange or fifty brokerage houses would fail. Stillman pledged $5 million from the City Bank. Minutes later, Morgan had $23.5 million. When he sent word of relief to the trading floor, euphoric traders ripped the messenger's coat off. The market took up $19 million in half an hour, at rates ranging from 10 to 60 percent. "The rebound was instantaneous," reported the *Times*. The Exchange stayed open till 3:00.

Thursday had been the fourth straight day of panic. As the hysteria spread, banks across the country stepped up their withdrawals from New York. Perkins cabled Jack at 4:30 A.M.: "Situation appears very desperate . . . several New York State banks probably cannot get through tomorrow. . . . All things considered I am very apprehensive and yet there is chance still to get through."

On Friday morning, Morgan, Baker, and Stillman announced that they would furnish more money to the Stock Exchange and the trusts, but by noon the call-money rate had soared to 150 percent. Morgan gathered the commercial bankers at the Clearing House and raised another $10 million to be lent to the Exchange at 25 to 50 percent. He marched back to his office to notify the floor: "With his coat unbuttoned and flying open, a piece of white paper clutched tightly in his right hand, he walked fast down Nassau Street," reported Satterlee. "His flat-topped black derby hat was set firmly down on his head. Between his teeth he held a paper cigar holder in which was one of his long cigars, half smoked. His eyes were fixed straight ahead. He swung his arms as he walked and took no notice of anyone. He did not seem to see the throngs in the street, so intent was his mind on the thing that he was doing. . . . He simply barged along, as if he had been the only man going down the Nassau Street hill past the Subtreasury. . . . Not more than two minutes after he disappeared into his office, the cheering on the floor of the Stock Exchange could be heard out in Broad Street."

As Morgan left his office late that afternoon, he told reporters that if people would leave their money in the banks, everything would be all right. Perkins cabled Jack: "We have successfully passed another day and feel much encouraged. This gives us till Monday in which to try to restore confidence. All well."

The Stock Exchange had weathered its siege, and most of the trusts were still open. No money would be lent over the weekend. Before the Morgan teams took a recess, however, they set up a public relations committee to give out encouraging information to the press, and a spiritual relations committee that urged city clergymen to counsel calm.

Lord Rothschild in London praised "the unselfish, remedial action of Mr. Morgan. Before now it has been generally recognized and agreed that he is worthy of his reputation as a great financier and a man of wonderful resources. His latest action fills one with admiration and respect." Jacob Schiff told an English friend that no one else "could have got the banks to act together, and to join hands in the work, as [Morgan] did, in his autocratic way."

Saturday's newspapers reported that $5 million in gold would be sent from London, that confidence had returned to the French Bourse, "owing to the belief that the strong men in American finance would succeed in their efforts to check the spirit of the panic," and that "J. P. Morgan has a cold." With liquidity still New York's chief problem, the senior trio on Saturday authorized a $100 million issue of Clearing House certificates—temporary paper loans that would expand the currency in circulation.*

Morgan, who had not had more than five hours' sleep any night that week, took a Saturday-afternoon train to Cragston and slept most of the way. "Very quiet evening," wrote Fanny in her diary. "[P.] says he feels that the end of the trouble has come." All day Sunday it rained. From pulpits throughout the city, religious leaders told people not to panic.

Roosevelt had been on the sidelines all week. In Nashville on Tuesday, October 22, he insisted that his policies had not caused the panic, and promised to pursue them "unswervingly." He paid a visit that afternoon to Andrew Jackson's Hermitage—perhaps to align himself with another president who had challenged a financial elite, although October 1907 was a poor moment to highlight the parallel: Jackson's destruction of the Second U.S. Bank had left the country with no national monetary authority and therefore dependent on men like Morgan. After TR returned to Washington Wednesday night and conferred with Bob Bacon and Elihu Root, he changed his tune. He sent Cortelyou a letter designed for publication—the newspapers printed it on Sunday—congratulating the Treasury Secretary and "those conservative and substantial business men who in this crisis have acted with such wisdom and public spirit." The fundamentals of the American economy were essentially sound, the Pres-

---

* These certificates, secured by collateralized obligations, could be used as currency among banks that belonged to the Clearing House Association.

ident wrote, and the actions taken in New York to check the panic should "produce entire confidence in our business conditions."

Late Sunday afternoon, Morgan returned to the city. Perkins cabled Jack that night: "The week's work has been one of the greatest of all the Senior's triumphs. He is being showered with congratulations. Believe we have the situation well in hand. All well here, but very shy on sleep."

———

By Monday nearly $20 million of European gold had started for New York, but the bankers did not yet have the situation in hand. The next domino to totter was New York City. Mayor George B. McClellan (son of the Civil War general) came to see Morgan, Baker, and Stillman on Monday afternoon. The city needed $30 million to meet its payroll and interest obligations, and there was no money to borrow. Without help, New York would be bankrupt by the end of the week. The trio put together a syndicate to take $30 million in municipal revenue bonds paying 6 percent—Morgan traded them for new Clearing House certificates credited to the city's accounts at the First National and City Banks—and New York did not default.

On Tuesday, U.S. Steel reported third-quarter earnings of almost $44 million—second only to the figures reported in June—and holdings of $76 million in cash. Judge Gary made an explicit point of the corporation's strength, hoping to offset the current "delirium."

For the rest of the week the battle-fatigued Morgan troops continued to shore up trusts, plug holes in the banking system with cash, scan the financial horizon for more signs of trouble, and try to steady shattered nerves. When one banker reported to 23 Wall Street that he was worried because his reserve had dipped below the legal limit, Morgan snapped: "You ought to be ashamed of yourself to be anywhere near your legal reserve. What is your reserve for at a time like this except to use?"

Morgan's men met at the library every day and issued optimistic reports each night, but on Friday, November 1, the probable failure of a brokerage house called Moore & Schley threatened to set off a new round of panic.

This firm, headed by Grant Schley, had played a leading role in the promotion of industrial mergers between 1898 and 1902—second in prominence only to the house of Morgan. It was for years the largest brokerage on Wall Street. In the fall of 1907 Moore & Schley owed about $35 million to various banks, and among the securities it had used to guarantee its loans were shares of the Tennessee Coal, Iron & Railroad Company, an independent steel producer with headquarters in Birmingham, Alabama. The brokerage house did not actually own this stock. Grant Schley had helped organize two syndicates in 1905–6 to buy a controlling interest in TC&I shares. His firm had lent money to members of both syndicates, taking TC&I stock as collateral, and then pledged the shares again to secure its own bank loans. A prominent member of the syndicates was John W. "Bet-a-Million" Gates, who controlled Republic Iron & Steel in Birmingham, and was hoping to build a steel empire in the South.

What happened with TC&I in 1907 provoked more controversy than any other aspect of the two-week panic, and became the subject of congressional investigations in 1909 and 1911. Witnesses gave testimony at the second hearing that directly contradicted what they said at the first, and made statements that bore little relation to facts recorded at the time. There has been so much dispute about these events, and so many conflicting retrospective claims on all sides, that it is nearly impossible to reconstruct the complete story.

The problem in late October 1907 had to do at first not with Moore & Schley but with Schley himself and one of his syndicate partners, a wine merchant named George Kessler. Both had been speculating in TC&I stock and using the shares as collateral for large loans. Kessler was vastly overextended, with accounts at ten different houses. When his brokers asked him to pay off his loans and take back the stock, he could not come up with cash.

The banks that autumn refused to accept more TC&I stock as collateral, Schley said later, partly because the bankrupt Kessler's "name had been mixed up with it." Another reason was that the value of the shares had fallen far below $130, the price Schley's second syndicate had paid. There were no transactions at the asking price of 135, and steel industry experts considered the shares worth only about 60. Asked again what had caused the banks' objection to TC&I, Schley this time answered: "Chiefly its position marketwise . . ."

Schley himself was also hugely leveraged in 1907. He owed money to his firm, his friends, and several banks—about $1 million to J. P. Morgan & Co., and more than $2 million to First National—and he could not cash out on the unmarketable TC&I stock. At the beginning of the panic he had taken his case to Morgan, who arranged for U.S. Steel to lend him $1.2 million worth of its own bonds for eighteen months, taking $2 million worth of TC&I shares valued at 60 as security. No one else would lend against TC&I even at 60, less than half the 135 asking price. The Steel loan was a drop in a draining bucket.*

Two weeks of panic intensified the pressure on Schley. He had been discussing his troubles all along with another TC&I syndicate member, Oliver Hazard Payne, a director of American Tobacco and Standard Oil (and brother-in-law of the recently deceased William C. Whitney), who had large loans out to Schley and his firm. On Friday, November 1, Payne suggested that the syndicate sim-

---

* Schley was married to George Baker's sister. He had worked at the First National from 1874 to 1880, and became a stockholder in the bank at the insiders' price ($300 a share, when $700 was bid, none offered) in 1901.

ply "sell the Tennessee Coal & Iron [company] and be done with it." There was, both men agreed, only one potential buyer—U.S. Steel. Accordingly, Schley sent for Payne's lawyer and Morgan's friend, Lewis Cass Ledyard, to open negotiations for the sale of TC&I. Earlier in the year, George Kessler had tried to interest Morgan in buying TC&I for $130 a share. Morgan had consulted U.S. Steel officials Gary and Frick, who thought the company was not worth that price. At the end of October, Ledyard went over the Moore & Schley books, and asked Schley what would pull him out. Schley said he and the majority of shareholders would be willing "to sell that [TC&I] stock at par [$100]. . . . It had to be disposed of if it could be."

The next morning Ledyard took this information to Morgan. Kessler had just defaulted, and it looked as though Schley would be next. Morgan, having navigated through two straight weeks of crisis, was determined to forestall further panic, and thought Schley's failure likely to wreck the incipient recovery. In addition to the brokerage's $35 million of outstanding debt in Boston, Chicago, Philadelphia, and New York, Schley had borrowed millions on his own. If he went bankrupt and the banks auctioned off his securities, other financial firms would fail as well, returning public confidence would erode, and it would be impossible to raise more money for the still-foundering trusts.

Morgan called in Gary and Frick. If U.S. Steel bought TC&I, he proposed, it could substitute its own highly rated gold bonds for the unmarketable TC&I stock as collateral at the banks. The bonds would act like money in the market, bank portfolios would not lose value, and Moore & Schley would not need a huge infusion of cash, just when it looked as though the trusts were going to need another $25 million. Morgan may not have known much about TC&I— he had not been to a Steel directors' meeting between January and October— but he thought this trade would work.

Neither Frick nor Gary liked it. They knew that TC&I had high costs and inefficient operations: Gary had declined to include it in the 1901 U.S. Steel consolidation because of its unprofitable record and inept management. In 1907 he was also worried about the antitrust law. He had been careful all along to keep U.S. Steel's constituent properties and market share at levels that would not invite prosecution.

The U.S. Steel Finance Committee met at Morgan's library for several hours on Saturday, November 2, and late that afternoon Frick and Gary called on Schley with two offers: the corporation would either lend the brokers $5 million or buy the TC&I stock at $90 a share. Schley said no. He needed far more than $5 million, and his associates would not take less than $100 for the stock.

That night Morgan's accountants began going over the TC&I books, and on Sunday Schley and the company's officers tried to impress on the Steel men "the value of the property"—its ore and coal reserves. George Perkins noted dryly that TC&I had owned those reserves for twenty years, "but it didn't prevent the stock selling at 30." The overall picture presented to the U.S. Steel Finance Committee at Morgan's library on November 3 was decidedly mixed.*

As in 1895, Morgan was not acting out of altruism. He and people he represented all over the world had billions of dollars invested in the United States, but it was not only rich capitalists and industrial corporations who would suffer if the markets collapsed as they had in 1893 and the country slid into a long depression. In recent economic downturns, corporate giants had generally trimmed their sails and pulled through, often buying up competitors at bargain prices. Those hit hardest by a prolonged contraction would be farmers, workers, immigrants, small businessmen, and the unemployed.

Once Morgan convinced the Steel executives that trading their bonds for TC&I stock would avert a further crisis in 1907, they took care not to make it a commercial sacrifice. TC&I, they apparently concluded, had enough potential

---

* TC&I had been one of the industrials that made up the first Dow Jones average in 1896, and it remained on the list in 1907. It had, however, severe technical and managerial problems, high production costs, poor local markets, and insufficient capital. A northern steel man who became chairman of its board in 1901 found "scarcely any of the property that was right, if it was possible for it to be wrong," and estimated five years later that the company would need $25 million to bring it up to northern standards. TC&I's outlook had improved in 1906, when the Schley-Gates syndicate installed new management and supplied $6.2 million to modernize the facilities. The company reported its highest earnings in 1906—$2,753,160—or about $9.40 per share. Gary and Frick thought TC&I possibly worth the $60 a share on which Morgan had based his October loan, but Schley was holding out for $100—ten times peak earnings.

TC&I did own large iron ore, limestone, and coal properties in close proximity to its plants, whereas the big northern steelmakers had to ship raw materials in from distant mines. The company estimated that it had 300 million to 700 million tons of ore, and close to a billion of coal, but not all that acreage was productive, the facilities had inadequate water supplies, and the ore was of a lower quality than that of mines in the North. U.S. Steel in 1906 had leased the rights to more than half of James J. Hill's Great Northern ore lands on the Mesabi Range in Minnesota; the high-quality ore in Hill's 65,000 acres was estimated at 400 million to 500 million tons.

The TC&I plant at Ensley, Alabama, was by 1907 manufacturing open-hearth steel rails. Birmingham's high-phosphorus ore was better suited to open-hearth than to cheaper Bessemer processing, and the new rails were stronger, though more expensive to make, than the old. It was clear that American roads would be switching to the superior rails, and U.S. Steel was constructing a large new integrated mill of its own at Gary, Indiana, on Lake Michigan, with open-hearth capacity of over a million tons a year. In the spring of 1907, E. H. Harriman ordered 157,000 tons of rails from Ensley for his Union and Southern Pacific roads—an apparent coup for southern steel. Production costs proved so high, however, and the technology still so problematic, that TC&I manufactured the Harriman rails at a loss of $4 a ton, and many had to be returned as defective.

to outweigh its liabilities: it could provide U.S. Steel with significant mineral resources, control of an unstable company, new productive capacity, and a stronghold in the South. Over the long run, Morganization and large infusions of cash might turn it into a profitable asset.

Early Sunday evening the Finance Committee offered to trade about $30 million worth of U.S. Steel bonds for about $30 million in TC&I stock valued at $100.* Schley accepted these terms, and his associates agreed to the exchange. Gary, however, would not proceed without Roosevelt's approval: he did not want to risk prosecution under the Sherman Act. He telephoned the White House on Sunday at 10:00 P.M. to set up an appointment for the next morning, and took a midnight train to Washington with Frick.

———

On Saturday, November 2—the day the Steel Finance Committee met at the library to consider taking over TC&I—Morgan's town house reopened, and Fanny and Anne moved back to the city. Fanny wrote in her diary that night: "Town. P. dined at home with us quietly at *219 Madison*."

Crisis had followed crisis for two long weeks. The senior trio had manufactured liquidity for desperate markets, coming up with funds by persuasion, fiat, threat, and loan. Night after night they had deliberated while their lieutenants supplied them with facts, and everyone from bankers to trust company presidents, stockbrokers, and account clerks was exhausted.

Davison and Strong remained on twenty-four-hour research duty as rumors continued to fly around town. On Saturday afternoon they reported that the Trust Company of America and the Lincoln Trust held mostly solid assets but needed more cash. On Sunday, November 3, bankers and steel men were in and out of the library all day and most of the night. To the press Morgan said only that they were discussing the general financial situation. The trust company officers held meetings of their own at the Waldorf-Astoria, on Fifth Avenue between 33rd and 34th Streets, sending occasional messages to Morgan's headquarters. At 9:30 P.M. more than fifty men gathered at the library. One of them later recalled the "anxious throng of bankers, too uneasy to sit down or converse at ease, pacing through the long marble hall and up and down the high-ceilinged rooms" filled with Renaissance bronzes, Gutenberg Bibles, and tiers of books. A fire blazed in the study. Morgan told the trust company presidents that he was working on a solution to the Moore & Schley problem, but they had to raise another $25 million on their own.

* The corporation would put up second mortgage bonds, then quoted at 84, which had a face value of $35,407,000 and a market value of about $29,742,000. It would take in exchange 297,420 shares of TC&I valued at 100, nominally worth $29,742,000. The corporation would pay an additional $632,655 in cash.

Then he retired with Ledyard, Gary, and Frick to Belle Greene's office (the "North Room") off the rotunda. At 10:00 Gary phoned the White House and left for Washington with Frick. Ben Strong, waiting to make a report on the trusts, fell asleep. When he woke up, Stillman asked him when he had last been to bed. Not since Thursday night, admitted Strong. Stillman said the country would not collapse if Strong went home, but at that moment Morgan asked for the figures on the TCA. At 3:00 A.M., after Strong finished his report, he headed to the library's front doors and found them locked. Morgan had the key in his pocket. No one would leave until this crisis was resolved.

The trust company presidents continued to talk in the West Room. At 4:15, Morgan walked in with a statement providing for each trust company to sub-scribe its share to a new $25 million loan. One of his lawyers read it out loud, then set it down on a table. "There you are gentlemen," Morgan said.

No one moved.

Morgan went over to Edward King, head of the Union Trust, and drew him to the table. "There's the place, King," he said, "and here's the pen." King signed. The other presidents followed suit. A committee of five large trusts, led by King, was appointed to handle the loan and supervise the final-stage rescue of Lincoln and the TCA. The library's brass doors swung open at 4:45 to let the bankers out.

———

Four hours later, Gary and Frick had breakfast at the White House with Roo-sevelt and Elihu Root. They quickly sketched in the outlines of the situation. As a pure business proposition they did not want TC&I, they said: it would be of dubious benefit to U.S. Steel. Moreover, the purchase was likely to arouse pub-lic antagonism and invite antitrust proceedings, which was why they wanted clearance from Washington. They had deliberately not acquired more than two-thirds of the country's steel properties, and the TC&I takeover would not bring the total over that limit.

Roosevelt, by this time aware of the dangers just averted, desperate to pre-vent further trouble, and grateful for Morgan's expertise, approved the proposi-tion. Root undoubtedly concurred. The President drafted a note to his Attorney General. The steel men felt, he wrote,

> that it is immensely to their interest, as to the interest of every responsible businessman, to try to prevent a panic and general industrial smashup at this time, and . . . are willing to go into this transaction, which they would not otherwise go into, because it seems the opinion of those best fitted to express judgment in New York that it will be an important factor in pre-venting a break that might be ruinous; and that this has been urged upon

them by the combination of the most responsible bankers in New York who are now thus engaged in endeavoring to save the situation. But they asserted they did not wish to do this if I stated that it ought not to be done. I answered that while of course I could not advise them to take the action proposed, I felt it no public duty of mine to interpose any objection.

Minutes before the stock market opened at 10:00 A.M., Gary telephoned Perkins from the White House with news of Roosevelt's assent. Perkins relayed word to the Exchange, and the panic finally did, after two harrowing weeks, stop. The stock market had its best day since the trouble began. News of the all-night Morgan Library conference, with its assurance that Lincoln and the Trust Company of America would be "taken care of," began to restore general confidence. Millions of additional dollars in gold were shipped from Europe. Fanny wrote in her diary that night: "P. dined with Nan and me and dozed in his big chair and slept all night till 8 a.m."

On Tuesday, November 5, the city's leading bankers and industrialists once again gathered at Morgan's library. By 11:30 A.M. carriages and automobiles lined 36th Street from Madison to Park. Meetings went on all day and into the night as these men worked out details of the final trust company relief and the sale of TC&I. Shortly before midnight, a wagon from the Waldorf pulled up to the library's front door, and waiters carried coffee urns and hampers of food inside. At 3:00 A.M., Edward King issued a signed statement: the TCA and the Lincoln Trust would pay their depositors in full, and would for the time being be controlled by his new committee of five trustees.

On Wednesday the stock market opened "buoyantly," Perkins later recalled: "A tremendous change for the better had taken place . . . and all talk of failure and collapse ceased." The first $7 million in gold arrived from Europe, which began to ease the money supply.* U.S. Steel's directors approved the takeover of TC&I, and over the next few days the exchange of Steel bonds for non-negotiable TC&I shares relieved the pressure on banks, brokers, markets, and on Grant Schley. He used the bonds to pay off $12 million in personal debts, and his firm began to redeem its loans from the banks. The Roosevelt administration, reported Perkins, was anxious to help in any way it could.

Charles Barney, the ex-president of the Knickerbocker Trust whose involvement in the copper speculation had touched off the panic, killed himself on November 14.

Bernard Berenson wrote to Mrs. Gardner that "Morgan should be repre-

---

* The Bank of England and the Imperial Bank of Germany, anxious to protect their own reserves and prevent large-scale exports of gold, raised their rates to 7 percent and 7½ percent, respectively—higher than at any time since 1873.

sented as buttressing up the tottering fabric of finance the way Giotto painted St. Francis holding up the falling Church with his shoulder."

———

After the gold crisis of 1895, populists had accused Morgan and Cleveland of conspiring to squeeze the stricken nation for private profit and to "crucify mankind upon a cross of gold." The panic of 1907 generated even greater animosity—especially the "deal" between the President and U.S. Steel over TC&I. Morgan was charged with having created the panic in order to grab a threatening rival on the cheap, and Roosevelt with having succumbed to a Wall Street trick.

Few observers of these events at the time or since accepted U.S. Steel's portrait of itself as reluctant saint. The executives' stance of moral rectitude, taken in anticipation of the "attack" that inevitably followed, seemed rank hypocrisy to a public on the lookout for abuses of corporate power. "There has been so much trickery and dishonesty in high places," Roosevelt wrote to his brother-in-law on November 16—"the exposures about Harriman, Rockefeller, Heinze, Barney, Morse, Ryan, the insurance men, and others have caused such a genuine shock to people that they have begun to be afraid that every bank really has something rotten in it. In other words, they have passed thru the period of unreasoning trust and optimism into unreasoning distrust and pessimism."

Wisconsin's Senator Robert M. La Follette charged the "group of financiers who withhold and dispense prosperity" with having "deliberately brought on the late panic, to serve their own ends." Upton Sinclair's 1908 novel, *The Money-Changers*, portrayed a Morgan-like figure orchestrating the crisis to devastate ordinary people for private gain. John Moody, who had left banking in 1900 to start his *Manual of Industrial Securities*, said that if the bankers "checked the panic" in acquiring TC&I, "they did it by taking a few dollars out of one pocket and putting millions into another."

U.S. Steel had paid $30 million for a company that critics now claimed was worth anywhere from $90 million to $2 billion—estimates that far exceeded those of the company's shareholders in 1907. Even if Morgan had paid Kessler's asking price of $130 a share, the total would have come to just $39 million, less than half of the lowest retrospective valuation.

A 1909 Senate Judiciary Committee investigation of the TC&I takeover concluded that the "Morgan banks" in New York had squeezed Moore & Schley, and forced the brokers to "surrender" the TC&I stock. According to the committee's report, TC&I was worth several hundred million dollars, and it brought U.S. Steel control of the country's iron-ore supply and open-hearth rail production, as well as a monopoly of the iron and steel trade in the South and elimination of a "strong and growing competitor." The Steel trust had absorbed TC&I in violation of the Sherman Act, declared the committee, and Roosevelt had no business authorizing nonenforcement of the law.*

Two years later, a House investigation of the steel industry led by Augustus Stanley of Kentucky made newspaper headlines for months. Schley, who had instigated the sale of TC&I and testified as to its urgent necessity in 1909, told the Stanley Committee that his firm might have survived without the sale, and that a $5 million loan could have saved it—an offer he rejected at the time. One of the committee's most popular witnesses was the furious John W. Gates, who had wanted TC&I for his Republic Iron & Steel. Gates was abroad in the fall of 1907—he did not return until November 5, to find that Schley had sold TC&I out from under him. Having been on the Atlantic did not prevent him from testifying in colorful detail about events that took place during his absence, nor from doubling the estimates of TC&I mineral reserves and concluding that U.S. Steel had got "the best property in the country and at a bargain price."

Theodore Roosevelt, no longer President, appeared before the committee in August 1911, and took full responsibility for having authorized Frick and Gary to proceed. What mattered in early November of 1907, he said, was to stop the panic, and his approval of the steel merger had done just that. He had known perfectly well that once the "imminent and too appalling" danger had passed, he would be subject to attack. "If I were on a sailboat," he explained, "I should not ordinarily meddle with any of the gear; but if a sudden squall struck us and the main sheet jammed so that the boat threatened to capsize, I would unhesitatingly cut the main sheet even though I were sure that the owner, no matter how grateful to me at the moment for having saved his life, would a few weeks later, when he had forgotten his danger and his fear, decide to sue me for the value of the cut rope."

Representative Martin Wiley Littleton wanted to show that Gary and Frick had hoodwinked Roosevelt, but the former President flatly denied it. "I was then thoroughly satisfied, and after events made me more thoroughly satisfied, that what was done was absolutely necessary to save the situation," he testified. "A good many of your questions enter into the hidden domain of motives. I never supposed they were going to take action that would be damaging to themselves. . . . Using the same simile I used before, if I think it necessary to haul on a rope on a boat to prevent its going over, I welcome help from any

---

* The Satterlees spent a "thrilling" day with Roosevelt on the USS *Mayflower* early in 1909, Louisa told Fanny. She was "extremely interested" in hearing the President talk:. "His egotism is something overwhelming. I really believe that since Congress is attacking him about the Tennessee Coal & Iron deal . . . he is beginning to think that *he*—by permitting it—was the one who stopped the panic!! . . . the barefaced, fulsome flattery dished out to him by his friends is really worse and more blatant than what I hear bestowed upon Father!"

husky individual who hauls. I don't worry about his altruistic motives toward me. I want him to pull on the rope."

Littleton, who lived near Roosevelt on Long Island and had recently crewed for Thomas Lipton in a race against the Kaiser, supplied a nautical trope of his own: "Doesn't it make a difference," he asked, "whether the rope is attached to the sail or is one of the guy ropes attached to the mast? The question is whether you are led to pull on the right rope."

The question was whether the President had been duped. Roosevelt replied: "No man would do such a thing as you suggest during a storm. It is not human. The supposition is preposterous. We were pulling on the rope attached to the one sail that was in danger. No human being who knew the facts doubted it, and the result has made it clearer."

When George Perkins took the witness stand, Congressman Charles L. Bartlett of Georgia suggested that Morgan had brought on the panic in order to destroy trust companies that competed with his bank. "What do you say to the statement that the panic was started to get rid of certain undesirable bankers, and that you gentlemen later were unable to manage it?" asked Bartlett.

Perkins stood up in high theatrical dudgeon and slammed his fist on the table. "I say that there never was a more infamous lie started than that. There is not a scintilla of truth in it. You might just as well say that a certain group of gentlemen made a contract with Mrs. O'Leary's cow to kick over the lamp that set Chicago on fire."

Witness after witness denied that the bankers had squeezed Moore & Schley, that U.S. Steel had hammered TC&I to force down its price, that Morgan had cooked up the panic. Even Grant Schley could point to no evidence of diabolic design. The committee's inquiry struck an unintentionally comic note when Chairman Stanley examined Percival Roberts, Jr., a director of the Pennsylvania Railroad and a former steel man. It was one thing to blame America's complex ills on Big Business and the trusts; it was another to give evil a personal face. "Is there in the financial world today," asked Stanley, "a man of infinite power and vast interests whose example is regarded in a way as the law by big business men?"

"No," replied Roberts. "I think there are certain new ideals of co-operation which govern us all, ideals that may be personified in certain individuals."

"Is there such an individual in America?" continued Stanley.

"Yes, I think so."

"Where does he reside?"

Roberts: "I think his name is legion."

Apparently, nobody laughed.

"At least," continued Roberts, "that is the hope for the future of this country. If we destroy individualism we surely will get into trouble."

"Who is the example in the steel industry?"

"I think no one man in particular."

Stanley: "Is there not one man whose example business men of the Nation follow, on account of his immense grasp of modern conditions, his touch which potentiates the railroads of the nation, the steel manufacturing business, the establishment of banks, and extends to all the multifarious ramifications of business of the country, and who can not only frame business conditions, but change them by the mere press of a button?"

Roberts, smiling: "I suppose I have in mind who you mean."

In the fall of 1911, President Taft's Attorney General brought suit against U.S. Steel under the antitrust law, partly in response to the absorption of TC&I. "A desire to stop the panic was not the sole moving cause" of the takeover, read the charge; the corporation had also aimed to acquire "a company that had recently assumed a position of potential competition."

If anyone in the drama of late 1907 can be retrospectively identified as Mrs. O'Leary's cow, it is Grant Schley. He was fighting to save himself, and, fortunately for him, the prospect of his firm's failure just as the panic was easing did represent a threat to the tenuous recovery. That Schley had an asset U.S. Steel might use was a stroke not of conspiratorial genius but luck. There were no other takers for TC&I in November 1907. In the 1911 investigation, Littleton asked Schley: "Was there any particular reason why the TC&I should be made the subject of a trade between you and the Steel Corporation?"

"It relieved my needs," answered Schley frankly. "It relieved every friend I had and relieved my office."

Morgan had been worried in the fall of 1907 not about a potentially competitive steel producer in the South but about sustaining the U.S. economy. Weighed against the enormous, long-range interests he had appointed himself to guard, TC&I scarcely tipped the scale. He and his colleagues were pragmatic men. If they had really wanted to force down TC&I's price and pick the company up for a song, why didn't they simply watch Moore & Schley fail, let the banks unload the shares, and pay far less than $30 million? U.S. Steel paid off $3 million in TC&I debts right away, and by 1913 had spent another $23.5 million on long-term improvements—almost exactly the amount its board chairman thought would be required—which effectively brought the acquisition price to $56.5 million, or twenty times TC&I's 1906 earnings. Even if the takeover turned out to be a great deal for U.S. Steel, and it didn't, Morgan had not substantially underpaid. He was negotiating during a crisis, and paid a far higher price than his associates advised. If TC&I was a steal, why were there no other buyers when all Wall Street knew it was on the table?

Some of the leading champions of the takeover were in Birmingham, Alabama. What northern politicians and journalists denounced as an act of invidious corporate imperialism, Birmingham saw as likely to bring greater output, more jobs, and higher profits. Absorption into the steel trust would "make the

Birmingham district the largest steel-making center in the universe," announced the *Birmingham News* in 1907. Six years later, the *Age-Herald* scolded the "demagogues and enemies of the corporation" who "have tried to make it appear that greed was the motive and the only motive."*

———

That the U.S. economy had grown far beyond one man's control was an irony Morgan's critics missed. His American firms lost $21 million in 1907.†

John D. Rockefeller, reflecting on his and Morgan's support of seventy banks during the panic, asked a senator: "Now, wasn't that a pretty nice thing for two such very, very bad men to do?"

The 1907 crisis was relatively brief, but despite Morgan's efforts it brought on a severe nationwide contraction that destroyed not only speculative enterprises but healthy banks and businesses as well, and threw people all over the country out of work. The *Commercial and Financial Chronicle* called the "industrial paralysis and prostration" of 1907–8 "the very worst ever experienced in

* At the end of 1907, producing open-hearth rails at the TC&I mill in Ensley, Alabama, cost $29 a ton, just $1 below the nominal market price—a small margin of profit that disappeared if the rails sold at a discount. Between 1907 and 1909, U.S. Steel cut the tonnage loss in rail manufacture from 40 percent to 10 percent. The corporation opened new local mines, built by-product ovens, imported water, and increased Ensley's steel capacity from 60,000 to 600,000 tons. Still, by 1910 the Alabama mill was turning out open-hearth rails for $19.24 a ton, while the cost at northern plants was $17.53. In 1913 it still cost $2 a ton more to make rails in Birmingham than in Pittsburgh, and the new president of TC&I, southerner George G. Crawford, concluded: "The Birmingham district is one that cannot be made like the rosy pictures I have heard described, but it can develop into a reasonably good business proposition." Most of the steel industry had operated under a "basing point pricing" system since 1880. Because of Carnegie Steel's undisputed dominance, Pittsburgh prices served as the industry's point of reference: other mills sold steel at the Pittsburgh price plus transportation charges to a given buying point. In 1905 TC&I had sold finished products at "Pittsburgh Plus" prices, although rails were exempt. After U.S. Steel acquired TC&I in 1907, Crawford persuaded the corporation to replace "Pittsburgh Plus" with a smaller "Birmingham differential"—a charge of $3 per ton above Pittsburgh prices, to account for TC&I's higher production costs. Another southern U.S. Steel subsidiary, American Steel and Wire, had to charge $15 a ton over Pittsburgh prices. The TC&I differential, which rose from $3 to $5 in 1920, has often been cited as evidence of U.S. Steel's attempt to stifle competition from the South; in fact the corporation's policy *favored* TC&I, and was less an attempt to throttle its own subsidiary than to "manage" industry-wide competition and maintain national price stability. According to the historian Kenneth Warren, at the 1914 Iron and Steel Institute meetings in Birmingham, "U.S. Steel was widely praised for putting southern steel-making firmly on its feet at last."

† The net profits for J. P. Morgan & Co. and Drexel & Co. had fallen from $12 million in 1905 to $1.2 million in 1906. The 1907 loss came to $21.5 million. Profits rose in 1908 to $13.2 million, and to $19.4 million in 1909.

the country's history." Those who did not blame these troubles on Morgan attributed them to the antiquated U.S. banking system, and the disaster seemed to confirm what Schiff, Morgan, and Baker had been saying for some time—that the country urgently needed a monetary policy, new banking legislation, and currency reform. Morgan and Baker went to see Roosevelt late in November 1907 about creating a more elastic money supply. Frank Vanderlip, Stillman's vice president at the City Bank, reported to a colleague in December that "sentiment is unquestionably growing in favor of a central bank," especially in the West (though some of the eastern bankers who "favored it at first now begin to suspect that their self interest will be conflicted with. . . . Very few people rise above their self interests in considering the whole subject").

Those who regarded Morgan as a national hero after the 1907 panic wondered what would happen when he was no longer around to take charge, and for the first time he showed signs of anticipating his demise. In late February 1908, George Baker called at 219 as Morgan prepared to leave for Europe. Walking his guest to the door at the end of their interview, Morgan put his hands on Baker's shoulders and said, "If anything happens to me, I want you to know that my association with you has been one of the most satisfactory parts of my life, especially the last six months. I have had many pleasant things in my life, but none more than this. I want you to remember it always."

Congress in 1908 passed a Currency Act authorizing banks to form reserve associations that could issue money temporarily in emergencies, and setting up a National Monetary Commission to study the nation's financial structure. Nelson W. Aldrich, chairman of the Senate Finance Committee, was appointed to head the commission. He promptly hired Henry P. Davison and the Harvard economist A. Piatt Andrew as his advisers. George Perkins cabled Morgan in July that Davison would soon be "meeting you London or elsewhere for conference regard to matter. . . . It is understood Davison is to represent our views and will be particularly close to Senator Aldrich."

Aldrich represented "our" views as well. He had become one of Morgan's key political allies after Mark Hanna died in 1904. Having started out in the wholesale grocery business, Nelson Wilmarth Aldrich entered the Senate in 1881 with about $50,000 in net worth; he retired three decades later worth about $7 million. In 1897 he had bought the Warwick, Rhode Island, estate of Fanny's Hoppin in-laws, and his daughter, Abby, married John D. Rockefeller, Jr., in 1901. Lincoln Steffens in 1905 called Aldrich the "boss of the United States." David Graham Phillips devoted a whole article to him in his series on "The Treason of the Senate." Aldrich made most of his fortune in 1906, when he sold his Rhode Island street-rail systems to Charles Mellen at the Morganized New Haven Railroad for several million dollars.

Morgan arranged for the Aldrich Commission to meet with the heads of leading banks in London, Paris, and Berlin in the summer of 1908. Most

British financiers were out of town when the Americans arrived that August. Teddy Grenfell asked U.S. Ambassador Whitelaw Reid to set things up for the visiting delegation: "Mr. Morgan thinks very desirable you give dinner Tuesday," Grenfell wired. ". . . I understand that Lord Rothschild, Sir George Murray, the Governor of the Bank of England, and Mr. Huth Jackson have accepted your kind invitation." The following winter, Aldrich added three more men to the commission: Paul Warburg of Kuhn, Loeb; Frank Vanderlip, who had been a journalist and assistant Secretary of the Treasury under Lyman Gage (1897–1901) before joining Stillman at City Bank; and Charles Conant, treasurer of the Morton Trust and a financial writer whose *Principles of Money and Banking* had been called "the standard work on the subject" by *Bankers Magazine* in 1906.

Morgan had functioned in the crisis of 1907 as the country's de facto central banker, supplying liquidity as necessary to forestall more widespread collapse. The specter of a New York plutocrat taking charge of the nation's economic equilibrium elicited more fear than admiration among the general public, but on Wall Street and in international finance the old man emerged from this trial with greater stature than ever. Over the next few years, as the Aldrich Commission conducted its investigation, Morgan worked with former rivals to manage, insofar as it was possible, America's principal banks and money supply. His chief partners in this entente cordiale were Baker and Stillman. After 1907, they called themselves the Trio.*

From London at the end of 1909 Teddy Grenfell told a friend that Morgan's "position to-day in America is not due to his riches. There are 20 richer men there. It is due to the fact that in the dark days of 1907, he knew no fear, he believed in the country & himself & imparted pluck & spirit to others & infused strength & hope into men 20, 30 & 40 years younger than himself. If he had given way, the whole house of financial cards would have fallen. . . .

"[T]he popular idea of this man is very wide of the truth. He is neither hard nor cunning. Outwardly he is rough because he is very strong & yet very shy &

---

* After the United States passed legislation establishing the Federal Reserve System in 1913, Ben Strong became the first governor of the Fed Bank in New York. Milton Friedman and Anna Schwartz, pointing out the "striking contrast" between Morgan's effective handling of the 1907 crisis and the failure of the Federal Reserve to contain the 1929 panic and limit the consequent depression of the thirties, speculate about what might have happened had Strong not died in 1928: "Strong, more than any other individual, had the confidence and backing of other financial leaders inside and outside the [Federal Reserve] System, the personal force to make his own views prevail, and also the courage to act upon them. . . . If Strong had still been alive and head of the New York Bank in the fall of 1930, he would very likely have recognized the oncoming liquidity crisis for what it was, would have been prepared by experience and conviction to take strenuous and appropriate measures to head it off, and would have had the standing to carry the System with him."

has no command of words. He will run rather than make a speech. He sees clearly enough but his explanations in words are quite incoherent. He sees the goal & makes straight for it. He has made big mistakes & even when his schemes are well conceived, he runs big risks of being tripped up or attacked in flank by meaner or smaller men. . . .

"To-day in New York his old rivals Stillman & Kuhn Loeb, remembering 1907, offer him absolute obedience. They will share all with him, knowing that he will take no advantage. . . . Thinking of him as my senior, you can well believe I am proud to be his colleague. His shortcomings are so patent that they almost add to his attraction."

Chapter 29

TRIO

Once the panic was over, Morgan, Baker, and Stillman worked together to forestall any possible recurrence. Morgan and Baker had collaborated for years. The City Bank was the newcomer to the alliance. After seeing Stillman at Aix in April of 1908, Morgan cabled Jack: "Inform [Baker] that [Stillman] said he was unwilling do anything except with cordial endorsement of the trio, nor anything which would change permanency or joint efforts for public welfare already established and recognized throughout country, and to which he was unchangeably pledged."

Morgan himself had been "unchangeably pledged" to what he regarded as "efforts for public welfare" all his professional life. He had raised money in Europe to refinance the Civil War debt and build railroads, secured gold for the Treasury in 1895, assured investors and bankers on both sides of the Atlantic that the enormous amounts of money they put up for his industrial underwritings would be relatively safe, and furnished liquidity to stop the recent panic. In 1877 Junius had announced to the country's financial elite that "the future is in our own hands." Thirty years later, the events of 1907 convinced Pierpont more than ever that the country's economic welfare was in the hands of his own generation's leading financiers, and that he had a mandate to consolidate control of its industrial and capital resources. The same events convinced other people, however, that the country's economic welfare could no longer be left to private bankers, and that Morgan's extraordinary authority endangered the public welfare. Between 1908 and 1912, the progressive movement united radical dissidents, liberal reformers, and a range of conservatives in opposition to the concentrated power of Wall Street and the trusts. Morgan paid no attention.

There were threats against his life. At the end of January 1908, Jack forwarded to New York's police commissioner a letter promising to eliminate New York's "High Financiers, Trust Magnates, and Trust Builders" by "causing them to pass out of the world without anyone suspecting foul play." Jack asked the commissioner to reply to him and not his father, "whom we generally do not allow to be bothered with such matters if it can be avoided."

A month later Morgan was on his way to Europe when Minnesota Senator Knute Nelson scoffed that U.S. Steel officials had "bushwhacked" Roosevelt over TC&I, and that "the only way the bankers stopped the panic was by violating the law and holding up depositors."

In London that March the American banker showed Queen Alexandra and her sister, the Dowager Empress of Russia, through his collections at Princes Gate. In Rome in April he met with Italy's royal family and the Pope, who wrote in Italian: "We hope that God will impart every prosperity to J. P. Morgan and his family." At Aix Morgan secured Stillman's "cordial endorsement of the trio," then met Adelaide in Paris in May, and returned home in time to receive an honorary degree from Yale in June. Fanny, touring the American West that spring, was in the care of a "nerve specialist" named M. Allen Starr.*

At the Republican convention in Chicago on June 19, Roosevelt resisted a 49-minute ovation and refused to run again. The party nominated his designated successor, the conservative, genial, three-hundred-pound Secretary of War, William Howard Taft. A graduate of Yale, Taft had been solicitor general, a federal judge, and governor of the Philippines before TR appointed him to take Root's place at the War Department in 1904. Cynics said that the candidate's last name stood for "Take Advice from Theodore."

Five days after the convention, when Yale awarded honorary degrees to Morgan and Taft, *The New York Times* reported that the financier attracted as much attention as the Republican candidate. Journalists joked about Morgan's LLD (££D, £.s.d, LL$). The professor who conferred it compared the recipient to Alexander the Great—"but for the fact that Alexander was a free trader"—and went on, to cheers from the crowd: "Great governments lean upon him in military and financial crises; his consolidations of industrial and transportation properties cover continent and ocean; his art collections vie with those of royal houses. . . . But his colossal power is both honorable and beneficent. . . . It was

---

* A professor of neurology at the Columbia College of Physicians and Surgeons, Dr. Starr had studied in Heidelberg, Vienna, and Paris (under Jean-Martin Charcot). He wrote extensively about nervous disorders, and was an editor of the *Psychological Review* and the *Journal of Mental and Nervous Diseases.*

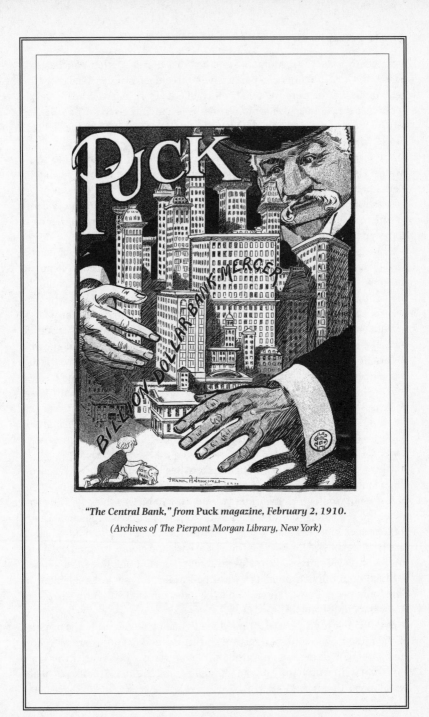

"The Central Bank," from Puck *magazine, February 2, 1910.*

(Archives of The Pierpont Morgan Library, New York)

but recently given to Mr. Morgan—another Sheridan at another Winchester—to stay the fury of a financial panic which threatened disaster. He did not forget, nor did we, the words of a man who had not where to lay his head, and yet spake as never man spake: 'Unto whomsoever much is given, of him shall be much required; and to whom men have committed much, of him they will ask more.' "

A few months later the London *Times,* calling Morgan's library "one of the wonders of the world," compared the American banker to Lorenzo the Magnificent, and announced that in the current age of millionaires, "one out of ten has taste; one out of a hundred has genius. Mr. Frick, Mr. Altman, Mr. Widener in America, and the late Rodolphe Kann in Paris, come under the former category; but the man of genius is Mr. Pierpont Morgan."

Analogies to Alexander the Great, Sheridan at Winchester, and Lorenzo de' Medici were only a notch less extravagant than the biblical allusions, some humorous, some in earnest, now piling up—Berenson's Saint Francis holding up the falling Church, Jack's "let us praise famous men," Yale's "Unto whomsoever much is given," and Percival Roberts's "I think his name is legion."

With such encomia at hand it was easy for Morgan to shrug off his detractors. The extremity of both the praise and the attacks after 1907, along with his distrust of politics, his age, and his sense of high calling, increased the distance he had always kept from the American public. While he acknowledged that business in the twentieth century would have to be conducted with "glass pockets," he remained reluctant to display the contents of his own pockets—or his mind. Toward the end of 1908 his refusal to address a dinner held in his honor in Chicago prompted the *Tribune* to announce, MONEY TALKS BUT MORGAN DOESN'T.

The next day, however, in an uncharacteristically expansive mood, he gave a statement to *The New York Times:* "My father told me to follow my own bent in business but whatever that business was to work hard. One thing he said I was always to remember, not to discount the future of America. 'Remember my son,' he said, 'that any man who is a bear on the future of this country will go broke. There may be times when things are dark and cloudy in America, when uncertainty will cause some to distrust and others to think there is too much production, too much building of railroads, and too much development in other enterprises. In such times and at all times remember that the growth of that vast country will take care of all.' "

By 1908 many people in the United States had more interest in the troubles of the present than in the promise of the future, and did not share Morgan's Hamiltonian faith in economic growth. What he said about himself was true, as far as it went, but so stiff and sanctimonious, and so alien to the skeptical national mood, that it invited derision.

———

The Democrats that summer once again nominated William Jennings Bryan—this time on a reformist platform that proposed stronger antitrust laws, lower tariffs, increased railroad legislation, and strong pro-union measures, which secured an endorsement from the ordinarily nonpartisan AFL. Campaigning against the East Coast plutocracy, Bryan repeatedly denounced Roosevelt's assent to the TC&I deal. Herbert C. Pell, later a Democratic congressman from Manhattan, refused to vote: "I couldn't see much difference in the candidates," he recalled. "One had a big head and no brains, and the other had a big belly and no guts." The Morgan bank contributed $30,000 to Taft's campaign, and the man with the big belly won with 52 percent of the vote, as against 43 percent for Bryan, and 3 percent for Eugene Debs. Taft's margin of victory over Bryan (9 percent) was much smaller than TR's over Alton Parker in 1904 (20 percent); the Republicans lost three House seats, as well as several state and local elections.

Morgan telegraphed Taft on November 3: "I wish to express to you my heartfelt congratulations on to-day's splendid results." The London Morgan partners cabled 23 Wall Street on the fourth: "Heartiest congratulations Presidential Election. Hope now we can have peace quiet and good business." Roosevelt went to Africa to hunt.

Republican insider George Perkins informed Morgan in February 1909 that Taft's inaugural address would be "in all respects conciliatory and harmonizing in its tone." Five months later, Perkins added that he personally had chosen key members of the new cabinet—Chicago banker Franklin MacVeagh for Treasury Secretary, New York corporate lawyer George Wickersham for Attorney General—and that "other places are filled to our entire satisfaction."

Jack had a cheerful suggestion for Perkins in the midst of all this wheeling and dealing. Worried about the increasing strength of German Jews on Wall Street, Jack wrote, "I think that if we are going on with business, some of us will have to turn Jew, and as you are such a good politician you are sure to be elected to that position, so you might as well choose your surgeon now."

Perkins's optimism was misplaced. Taft sought Wall Street's help with dollar diplomacy ventures abroad, but refused to "take advice from Theodore" about the trusts. Roosevelt had brought fifty-seven antitrust prosecutions in the course of two terms; Taft would bring ninety in just one. And though the new chief executive had none of his predecessor's political skill or charismatic personality, he went further than TR did in establishing government authority over economic affairs: he endorsed stringent new railroad legislation, expanded the powers of the ICC, imposed federal regulation on telephone and telegraph companies, and authorized an income tax.

In November 1909, Henry Cabot Lodge reported to the traveling Roosevelt that Morgan was "very much disappointed in Taft," although Lodge did not think there was "anybody in the country who is more anxious for Taft's success than Morgan." The financier made a quiet visit to the President's summer cottage in Beverly, Massachusetts, one July afternoon in 1910—he arrived by motorboat, dressed for yachting, "and seemed as anxious to avoid publicity as did the President," recalled a Taft aide. "They had a talk for nearly an hour, but I have not heard as yet what the old fellow wanted. The President has more regard for him than any man of his class and set, but thinks it bad policy to see him often."

Even the Republican Old Guard now supported some form of corporate accountability and government regulation. Colleagues who had dismissed Morgan as a "back number" had changed their minds after the 1907 panic, but popular antipathy to Wall Street was running so high that a President who conditionally respected "the old fellow" considered it bad politics to see him.

————

The most valuable asset Morgan gained from the panic of 1907 was not TC&I but Henry Pomeroy Davison. Throughout the two long weeks of the crisis, and afterward as an adviser to Aldrich on the National Monetary Commission, Davison appeared uniquely qualified to become Morgan's professional heir. The official position had of course to go to Jack, but Davison shared more of the senior Morgan's instincts and abilities than the junior Morgan did.

According to Satterlee, at a bankers' dinner one night in 1908, Morgan turned to Baker and said, "George, will you do something for me?"

Baker: "Of course, yes—anything you want."

Morgan: "All right—I want you to let me have Harry Davison for my firm."

Davison left First National at the end of 1908 to join J. P. Morgan & Co. He had worked his way up from small-town Pennsylvania origins to prominent positions in white-shoe New York firms, and was as much at ease shooting rhinos in the Sudan as he was consulting the heads of European banks and dining on Morgan's yacht. Personally trained by Baker, he had a reputation for conservative straight dealing, and shared his new senior partner's faith in industrial consolidation and banker control. He once dreamed he was still a bank clerk in Pennsylvania, unable to balance the books. Told he would be horsewhipped if he failed to get the figures right, he broke out in a cold sweat. "What happened then?" asked his wife when he woke up. "I finally solved the problem," he said. "I bought the bank."

Morgan finally solved the problem of his succession by adopting George Baker's professional "son." He took Davison fully into his confidence, summoning him to conferences in Europe and cruises in Maine, granting him round-the-clock access to the Up-Town Branch in New York, seeking him out for companionship as well as professional talk. Although the scope of the bank's work had grown tremendously since the formation of J. P. Morgan & Co. in 1895, the number of partners had increased only from ten to eleven. And with Davison, Morgan for the first time had a lieutenant he was willing to place in a position of real command as he directed most of his own energies back to travel and art.

The other two members of the Trio at the beginning of 1909 also turned management of their banks over to younger men. Baker, age sixty-eight, ceded the presidency of the First National to Francis L. Hine, and took a new title as chairman of the board. Stillman stepped down as the City Bank president and became chairman of *its* board, moving to Paris—where Mary Cassatt was advising him about collecting art; Frank Vanderlip, who had been the City's vice president since 1901, moved up to become president.

The Trio had agreed in 1908 that the originating house in any new issue of securities would take 50 percent and give 25 percent to each of the other two. Between 1898 and 1908, the City Bank had shared in just one underwriting with J. P. Morgan & Co. and none with First National. From 1908 to 1912, the three houses acting together bought or underwrote 36 new issues—for the Interborough Rapid Transit Company, New York Central, U.S. Steel, and the Atchison Topeka & Santa Fe, among others—amounting to nearly $500 million. Acting with other banks, they sponsored another 51, for a total of 87 new issues worth over $1.3 billion. The Trio's reach horrified the opponents of financial concentration, yet the value of the new issues sponsored by the three houses over four years came to slightly less than Morgan's 1901 capitalization of U.S. Steel.

Morgan was compressing all his New York activities into the few months between his summer yacht cruises and long sojourns in Europe. "He is the most *exhausting* person I know," Belle Greene complained to Berenson in August of 1909: "He often tells me he 'likes my personality,' and yet when I leave him I feel utterly divested of it—as of a glove one draws off and gives to a friend because he likes it."

The ailing E. H. Harriman asked Morgan to come see him that August, and the two men worked out some sort of peace just before Harriman died. The Morgan bank bought his majority interest in the giant Guaranty Trust, which Davison quickly merged with the Fifth Avenue and the Morton Trusts to create the largest trust company in the country, with capital resources of $26 million and deposits of $147 million.

When the Guaranty moved to take over the Morton Trust, Levi Morton— now eighty-six years old and "mentally breaking up very fast," according to the company's vice president Charles H. Allen—objected to the loss of his name. According to Allen, Morgan said: "This is the thing for you to do, Morton. We will make you 'Chairman of the Board,' and you will become associated with one of the greatest financial institutions in the world. I'll make that stock worth $1000 a share." Allen observed: "The last delicate allusion to the sentimental side of the question dried his tears, and he thereafter—for a few hours—became an enthusiastic advocate of the plan."

Also that fall Morgan took control of the Equitable Life Assurance Society. He bought some of the stock from Harriman's estate and the rest from Thomas Fortune Ryan. Ever since the fight over the Equitable that had led to Ryan's purchase, the society had been in the hands of conservative trustees. One of them—Grover Cleveland—had died in 1908, another had retired, and the five-year voting trust was due to expire in 1910. Moreover, Ryan's reputation had not improved. Many of his street-rail interests had gone bankrupt, and Robert La Follette told the Senate that one of them had "cleaned up" at least $100 million "by methods which should have committed many of the participants to the penitentiary." According to Belle Greene, Morgan called Ryan to the library and told him: "Your name won't do [in conjunction with the Equitable]—right or wrong, it spells distrust." She confided to Berenson that she had always had a "sneaking fondness" for "Tommy" Ryan—"although it is a mystery to me how he has managed to keep out of States Prison all this time . . . he is so gentle & mild & kind hearted that if I did not positively *know* of his atrocities I should never believe them."

Morgan's purchase of Ryan's Equitable stock, for the price Ryan had paid ($2.5 million) plus 4 percent interest since 1905, inevitably came under attack. Questioned about it later, Morgan said he had bought the Equitable not for control in the ordinary financial sense, but "to take it out of the situation." Like most of his explanations, this one failed to clarify his motives. He probably meant that he wanted to take the company out of Ryan's hands and "protect" it from ownership struggles, takeover attempts, and the market gyrations that had proved hazardous to share- and policyholders, as well as to the broader financial markets, in the past. As always, he saw himself performing a large public service in preserving national economic order—and as always these days, few people outside his immediate circle believed him. He tried to sell the Equitable stock back to the company at his cost plus interest, in order to mutualize it, but the society did not have enough money to buy the shares; the Equitable finally mutualized with the help of the Morgan bank in 1925.

With Davison as his heir apparent in New York, the seventy-two-year-old Morgan reorganized his London firm at the end of 1909 in another preparation for the succession. Junius had asked that the English bank retain his own name only during Pierpont's lifetime, and any wish of his father's was "a law unto JPM, who is above all a sentimentalist," Grenfell told a friend. Young Walter Burns had finally resigned, to everyone's relief, and J. S. Morgan & Co., led by the Englishmen Grenfell and Vivian Smith, was renamed Morgan Grenfell & Co. in 1910.*

Jack was visiting London in December 1909 when a slightly manic Perkins sent him a cable marked "Denkstein"—code for top secret, to be translated only by the person addressed: "We have concluded purchase of Guaranty Trust Co. . . . Stock will be put in Voting Trust. . . . We have sold all the Steel Common of the Paris syndicate and closed the account . . . profits . . . average something over 90. Newspapers have commented most favorably on Senior's purchase of Equitable stock, even to the extent of favorable editorial in New York Evening Post. . . . Have concluded negotiations with Telephone Co. by which you and HPD to go on [the AT&T] Board. . . . HPD will be elected a Director in Chemical Bank next week. This is all for today thank you."

To which Jack replied: ". . . unless you feel it very desirable hope you will not buy the earth."

———

Echoing Perkins at the end of 1909, Belle Greene told Berenson that her Big Chief had "succeeded in acquiring all the world here now and most of the world without and it keeps us very busy every minute. I cannot understand his unfailing energy and grasp." Morgan was deploying cultural experts for his own and the Met's collections much the way he had utilized the junior trio during the 1907 panic.

Belle had begun to discipline dealers accustomed to her patron's liberality about price. She rejected scores of items offered by the Florentine bookseller Leo Olschki, marking "price too high," "do not want," and "have already" in the margins of his lists. Olschki's fawning manner annoyed her, and his fractured English didn't help. When she turned down a 1468 copy of Cicero's *De Oratore* as too expensive (8,000 francs—$1,600), the dealer protested: ". . . I permit to say that I am always endeavoring to content in the best possible manner Mr. Morgan whom I consider now my most influential customer, and to be worth of his esteem I should never try to make for him higher prices than for any other one." He got around Belle by selling directly to Morgan in Europe, reporting to her triumphantly in the spring of 1908 that his latest offerings had "enthusiasmed [Morgan] very much."

Belle warned Morgan by mail one spring about charges that he was throw-

---

* Before 1910, Pierpont and Jack had been partners in J. S. Morgan & Co., which was independent of the other Morgan banks. With the reorganization, Morgan Grenfell would have no individual American partners: the American firms, J. P. Morgan & Co. and Drexel & Co., acted as a single partner, putting up £1 million in capital and entitled to 50 percent of the London profits.

ing money recklessly around, and put her own loyalty on display: "I know perfectly well, as I write this, that it will hurt you almost as much as it hurt and angered me, also that you in your 'bigness,' which I adore, will ignore it, but really *I* could not. . . ." He did ignore it, just as he ignored criticism of his "overcapitalized" trusts. He *was* spending large amounts of money.

London's leading book dealer, Bernard Quaritch, learned in the spring of 1907 that Lord Amherst of Hackney was willing to sell a library that Quaritch had helped him assemble, and Belle forwarded the news to Morgan in Paris. The collection included a number of books from the press of William Caxton, which Belle described as "most *exceptional* as they are perfect copies (almost unheard of) and would make your Caxton collection *unique au monde!*" Junius, who had seen the library, sent his uncle a copy of its catalogue with marks next to books he "would like you to have."

Belle went to London for the Amherst Library auction in December 1908. The London *Times* reported that the Chancellor of the Exchequer would contribute £30,000 (roughly $150,000) to the British Museum for the purchase of Lord Amherst's books. Morgan authorized Belle to bid £32,500 for the Caxtons. Instead, she made a private offer through Quaritch of £25,000 cash, payable at once. At a dinner with some of her competitors from the British Museum the night before the sale, she learned that Amherst had accepted her offer. One scholar asked her not to bid against him for a particular volume the next day. She promised: she had already secured it. With the help of Quaritch and Junius, she took home seventeen extraordinarily fine Caxtons for Morgan's library, including the first two books printed in English, *Recuyell of the Historyes of Troye* and *The Game and Play of Chess* (1474).

———

As president of the Metropolitan Museum in 1907, Morgan asked Wilhelm Bode in Berlin to find a man who could organize and install the Hoentschel collections. Bode nominated "the most gifted and best equipped young student of art that I have ever had in the [Kaiser Friedrich] Museum," William R. Valentiner. Bode said he hated to lose this promising scholar, an authority on Rembrandt and the early Dutch and Flemish schools, but liked giving him the opportunity to work at the Met, "where works of art are now coming together more than anywhere else."

Valentiner arrived in New York to become the museum's first curator of Decorative Arts early in 1908. Morgan immediately invited him to dinner with Edward Robinson, the Met's de facto director. (Purdon Clarke did not leave until 1910—Belle Greene called him "Sir Burden.") Exhausted from his trip and worried about his "bad English," Valentiner was reassured to learn from Robinson that their host spoke German. It turned out not to matter, he later recalled: "After shaking hands with me—[Morgan] had very soft, big hands—in a very hearty way, he did not utter a single word, sitting like a big and powerful Buddha at the head of the table, saying at intervals a couple of unfinished sentences I could not understand. This silence was characteristic of him—it sufficed to impose his will on those around him, who were numb with awe."

The new curator began to arrange the medieval objects from the Hoentschel collection in the Met's entrance hall, and hung early French tapestries behind magnificent sculptures of the *Entombment* and *Pietà* from the Château de Biron. Morgan often stopped by with Adelaide to watch. One day he observed, "It looks like a junk shop" (which was just what Berenson had said to Mrs. Gardner about the house at Princes Gate). Valentiner changed nothing. He got along well with Morgan, whose wide-ranging interests he appreciated, and whom he called "the most important art collector I ever met."* Hoping to bid $60,000 for an important group of early Oriental rugs owned by Charles Tyson Yerkes (the model for the central character in Theodore Dreiser's 1912 novel, *The Financier*), Valentiner secured the museum president's approval, and "it was done, although at that time Morgan was probably the only one [on the Met board] who had an inkling of their value."

When Valentiner described a recent museum acquisition—a bronze putto by the fifteenth-century Florentine sculptor, painter, and goldsmith, Andrea del Verrocchio—as the first authentic work by that master in the United States, "Morgan told me irritably that I was wrong," that there were several Verrocchio pieces in his own library. Morgan also observed, not inaccurately, that "museum curators believe only those things to be genuine which they themselves have purchased." Valentiner decided that a pair of andirons at Morgan's library were not in fact by Verrocchio, but that a female terra-cotta bust was—and made amends by publishing an article about it.†

* Valentiner thought Morgan's "urge for collecting came naturally to him and had nothing to do with a concern to improve his social standing, as was the case with Frick, since Morgan already belonged to the elite. He was really interested in all kinds of art . . . especially those not readily accessible to the general public, such as early manuscripts, medieval jewelry, enamels, Chinese porcelains, etc. Paintings, usually the most obvious field for a collector, interested him least, although in his library he was surrounded by masterpieces of the early Renaissance."

† He compared the profile of the bust with a drawing by Verrocchio's greatest student, Leonardo, at Windsor Castle, and suggested that teacher and pupil had used the same model. Later, other experts dismissed this work as a fake, or as a study of a nineteenth-century figure in Renaissance dress. In 1997, however, it turned up at a London auction room, having been tested by a process called thermoluminescence, which established that it had been fired in about the fifteenth century. "Whatever it was," wrote James Fenton in *The New York Review of Books* in 1998, "there was no reason to call it a fake. And if it was not a fake, perhaps Valentiner's opinion might merit further consideration." After Valentiner left the Met, he worked at the Detroit Institute of Arts and in various capacities with the Los Angeles County Museum of Art. He helped start the J. Paul Getty Museum in Malibu, and was director of the North Carolina Museum of Art in Raleigh from 1956 until he died in 1958.

Early in February 1909, while the Senate Judiciary Committee heard testimony about the U.S. Steel takeover of TC&I, Morgan went to Egypt to see the excavations he was sponsoring for the Met. He took along Mary Burns, his middle daughter, Juliet, and Charles Hercules Read, the British Museum's keeper of Medieval Antiquities and Ethnography. Albert Lythgoe, who was supervising this work as the Met's curator of Egyptian art, served as tour guide. Edward Robinson urged Lythgoe not to be modest about recommending purchases once Morgan arrived in Egypt, and to remember "that nobody enjoys the fun of buying more than he when he is in the right mood."

Lythgoe skillfully coordinated the work of his scholars in the field with the interests and resources of his patrons in New York. He liked Morgan, whom he saw not only as a source of artifacts, money, and organization, but also as a key figure in the international competition over the study of Egypt's past. Lythgoe and his wife met the travelers at Shepheard's Hotel in Cairo in late February 1909. The American minister, Lewis Iddings, had made arrangements as if for a visiting head of state—he gave a dinner one night for Morgan to meet various European ministers, and introduced his guest to the Khedive. Morgan called on the French director-general of the Egyptian Antiquities Service, Gaston Maspero, and went twice to the Cairo Museum to examine the collections of the Newport millionaire Theodore M. Davis, who had been financing excavations in the Valley of the Kings since 1903.*

In early March he rented a large houseboat called a *dehabiyeh*—the word means "thing of gold"—and took his party thirty-five miles up the Nile to see the museum's excavations at Lisht. Lythgoe showed the group the site of the pyramid of Senwosret I, where three hundred men were clearing away mounds of debris and sand, gradually exposing wall remains and brilliantly painted, scattered temple relief blocks dating back to almost 2000 B.C. The following day, at the pyramid complex of Senwosret's predecessor, Amenemhat I, Morgan watched the work for some time (Lythgoe reported to Robinson) and listened intently to explanations about digging methods, equipment, the recording of scientific findings, and the project's general aims. That night he said, "It was perfectly magnificent. I don't think I ever enjoyed anything so much before in my life."

From Lisht the party went on another hundred and twenty miles south and then west to the Great Oasis at Khargeh. They rode donkeys up to the expedition camp built on the slope of a ridge, with a wide view of palm trees, villages,

---

* Davis's men had recently found a cache of items bearing the name of Tutankhamun, but did not realize what it was—a sacred pit for materials gathered up after the burial of the famous god-king. Not until 1922 did the British archaeologists Lord Carnarvon and Howard Carter discover the actual tomb of Tutankhamun nearby. In the spring of 1909 Davis gave the cache of jars, linen bags of powdered natron, and dried floral wreaths to the Metropolitan.

and cultivated fields. Museum archaeologists were finding remnants of the great temple at Hibis, which was thought to have been built by the Persian Emperor Darius in the fifth century B.C., as well as evidence of Egypt's early Christian era at Khargeh—domed tomb-chapels decorated with frescoes of biblical scenes, and houses datable to the period of the Roman Emperor Constantine the Great, who adopted Christianity in the early fourth century A.D. Morgan said to Lythgoe as they boarded the train the next day, "I don't like to leave all this. I never imagined I would see so many interesting things in my life." He cabled Jack when they reached Luxor: "Returned from desert all well, trip most extraordinarily delightful." Lythgoe was delighted as well. He told Robinson the trip had been "perfect from beginning to end," and that Morgan's interest in the Met's work "so vigorous that it has put things on the best possible basis."

———

In the spring of 1909, Congress debated a tariff bill sponsored by Senator Aldrich and Representative Sereno E. Payne that would, among other things, eliminate the 20 percent import duty on works of art more than a hundred years old. Jack sent news of its terms to his father in Cairo that March, and Davison reported the passage of the bill in June. The customs collector for the Port of New York told an Assistant Treasury Secretary that Aldrich had "put the free art paragraph in the tariff bill especially in the interest" of the Morgan collections.*

In May, out of gratitude to Wilhelm Bode for preparing the catalogue of his bronze collection (and perhaps for the "gift" of Valentiner as well), Morgan gave Berlin's Kaiser Friedrich Museum a predella by Fra Angelico, but did not want his name as donor known. Bode wrote back: "I need not mention that we are, in spite of your incognito, very much obliged to you for your noble gift."

Morgan returned to the United States in mid-July, and was in Maine on *Corsair* when his nephew Junius told Josie, his wife of eighteen years, that their situation had become "impossible," and moved to Europe. Louisa reported to Fanny the gossip about Junius's "unnatural" behavior, and predicted that if he stayed in Europe he would "fall into the hands of some woman," though she didn't think there had been one yet. Belle told Berenson that Junius confided more of his troubles to her than to anyone else, "yet I knew nothing."

If Pierpont Morgan "knew" anything he left no record of it. Once Junius settled in Europe he divided his time between Paris and Fiesole, outside Florence. His uncle continued to consult him about purchases, but after Junius decamped, Morgan relied more on other advisers, including Valentiner, Lythgoe, Bode, Hercules Read, and Belle.

---

* The 1909 Payne-Aldrich Act also modestly reduced other tariffs, set a 2 percent tax on corporate income, and authorized a constitutional amendment for a personal income tax.

For his library that fall he acquired for £50,000 ($250,000) an outstanding collection of Old Master drawings that had been assembled by the English connoisseur and artist Charles Fairfax Murray. It was the first great European drawings collection to come to the United States, and the addition of these fifteen hundred sheets to works Morgan already owned made his library the finest American repository of drawings for the Italian Renaissance and eighteenth-century schools, and for seventeenth-century Holland (Rembrandt in particular) and Flanders. Morgan had rejected this collection, however, at a lower price, two years earlier. The dealer Sotheran had offered him Murray's "remarkably fine and well known" Old Master drawings at the beginning of 1907 for £45,000, but Belle Greene, in the first year of her employment at the library, replied: "Mr. Morgan wishes me to say . . . that he does not care to purchase the Murray Fairfax [*sic*] collection." When the collection was offered again in 1909, she consulted Berenson and Hercules Read at the British Museum. Read replied: "as to Fairfax Murray . . . If it is the *whole* of his collection of drawings, it is certainly well worth having. He is about the best judge of such things here, and has been buying quietly for years past."

Also in 1909 Morgan bought the manuscripts of *Pudd'nhead Wilson* and *Life on the Mississippi* directly from the author. Twain told him, "One of my highest ambitions is gratified—which was, to have something of mine placed elbow to elbow with that august company which you have gathered together to remain indestructible in a perishable world."*

And for the Metropolitan Museum that fall, Morgan presided over a month of celebrations honoring Henry Hudson's discovery of the "North" River and Robert Fulton's first commercial steamboat. The museum mounted two major loan exhibitions for the occasion—one of seventeenth-century Dutch masters drawn from collections in the United States, the other of American paintings, furniture, and industrial arts. The latter show went up only after a controversy within the museum, but proved enormously popular with the public. The Old Masters exhibition, organized by Valentiner, honored New York's Dutch her-

---

* The company was more august than he knew. After Twain died in 1910, a magazine editor offered Morgan a private edition of the author's "Conversazione at the Court of Queen Elizabeth," with the warning that it was "frankly and appallingly vulgar." Belle Greene replied, "frankly and confidentially," that "there are two men whom I have been endeavoring for several years to give a clean slate for posterity—one is George Washington, and the other is Mark Twain. I have very often been asked to buy vulgar outpourings of these two men, and I have refused to do so because I thought that they did not typify the men themselves and would only give rise to nasty and unjust statements in future biographies. Since Mark Twain's death I have been appalled at the amount of such stuff of his that has been offered me, and, as the books in this Library will be preserved for all time, I felt that it would be an injustice to him to hand this side of him on to posterity." The Washington material she felt called on to clean up for posterity apparently had to do with stockbreeders' language.

itage and new stature as a center of world art. Morgan headed the Exhibition Committee, and contributed $25,000 to the production of a catalogue written by Valentiner. Among the 149 works shown, according to the 1909 attributions, were 37 by Rembrandt, 20 by Frans Hals, and 6 by Vermeer. Three of the Rembrandts belonged to Morgan, as did four works by Hals, Vermeer's *Lady Writing*, two Hobbemas, a Cuyp, and paintings by Gabriel Metsu, Jacob van Ruisdael, Pieter de Hooch, and Dirk Hals.* Foreign visitors were impressed, and not entirely pleased: Max Friedlander of the Prussian Royal Art Museums complained that America had more paintings by Frans Hals than Germany did, and 70 of the world's 650 known Rembrandts.

"We are launched on the Hudson-Fulton delirium," Belle told Berenson with a characteristic mix of irreverence and exhilaration, "and I am already a wreck. We receive daily delegations of all sorts of 'furriners' at the Library—Saturday I spent on the Corsair from ten in the morning until the wee small hours. The River was *enchanting* at night – all the foreign & our own warships were decked out in electric lights from bow to stern. There were eighty yachts in line with the Corsair leading & tugs, floats & excursion boats galore. Even although I find the whole performance *disgusting* I was perforce amused & a tiny wee bit excited by the electrical display. Every building in NY & the entire Fifth Avenue is draped in a hideous combination of orange & blue & red white & blue and at night it is a fairyland thoroughfare of electric lights. The Exhibition of Dutch masters at the Museum is a great success."

Though Belle regaled Berenson with gossip about Morgan's "dames" (see Chapter 30), she had little to say about Adelaide Douglas. Perhaps she did not consider Adelaide a "dame." Perhaps she knew less than she thought she did about her Big Chief's private life. Or perhaps this affair, begun in about 1895, had cooled into friendship.

At Morgan's request between 1907 and 1909, Belle sent Adelaide magazines, opera tickets, pictures of paintings from the Wallace Collection, framed mezzotints and engravings of Morgan's own paintings, and books—on Fragonard, Raeburn, Watteau, on tapestries, English porcelains, old English silver, a volume of Queen Victoria's letters, a history of portrait miniatures, the cata-

---

* Five of the Vermeers in the Hudson-Fulton exibition are still ascribed to that artist. They are, in addition to Morgan's, *Young Woman with a Water Pitcher* and *Woman with a Lute* (both at the Met), *Girl Interrupted at Her Music* (at the Frick Collection), and *A Woman Asleep* (from the collection of Benjamin Altman, who gave it to the Met by bequest in 1913). The sixth canvas was John G. Johnson's *The Guitar Player*, now in the Philadelphia Museum of Art as an excellent copy. The 1909 exhibition did not include Isabella Stewart Gardner's *The Concert*, which was stolen in 1990.

logue of the Siennese exhibition Adelaide and Morgan had seen with Langton Douglas in 1904, and catalogues of the Morgan collections printed on vellum. Belle had charge of the dealers' bills that recorded Morgan's larger gifts to Adelaide—a Louis XV secrétaire with ormulu mounts, signed "Migeon," the little red morocco casket that had been a wedding gift to Marie Antoinette, and objects that had belonged to historical Adelaides. From Cartier in Paris there was a blue and green enameled box with a garland of gold laurels laced through the initials "ADL" (her middle name was Louise), and a circle brooch with kittens surrounding the letter "A."

Adelaide's last trip to Europe with Morgan appears to have been in the spring of 1908. Her son, J. Gordon Douglas, married that year and moved out of his mother's house on East 46th Street. In 1909, Adelaide's husband moved from 71 Central Park West to 12 West 76th, and the couple's separation was finally acknowledged by separate listings in the Social Register. (Douglas's move to the Upper West Side in 1903 appeared only in the New York City street directories.) Then, in 1910, Adelaide began to build a house near Morgan's, on Park Avenue between 37th and 38th Streets, for herself and her daughter, Sybil. According to her grandson, Morgan paid for it.

The architect was Horace Trumbauer of Philadelphia, who had designed Peter Widener's Lynnewood Hall and was just beginning his most important decade of work, on the Free Library of Philadelphia, the Philadelphia Museum of Art, Duke University, and a mansion for James B. Duke at 1 East 78th (now the Institute of Fine Arts). Trumbauer built Adelaide's house at 57 Park Avenue in the style of eighteenth-century France.* Six stories high and 25 feet wide, faced with granite and limestone, it has a quiet, feminine elegance—Louis XVI in New York—with wrought-iron railings, French doors, casement windows, colonnades, balconies, sculptured spandrels, a mansard roof, pedimented dormers, copper coping, and decorative flowers, urns, and swags. Behind the marble entrance hall and wide staircase on the first floor was the dining room, with Morgan's silver-plated "Temple of Love" at the center of the table. Two eighteenth-century French salons occupied the second floor, and on the third were the master bedroom in the rear and a library facing Park Avenue. Mr. Morgan had a private entrance at the back of the house, reported Adelaide's grandson, and the children were instructed to vanish when their grandmother's eminent friend arrived.

———

President Taft may have thought it bad policy to see Morgan often, but did not hesitate to enlist the "old fellow" when he could be useful. The administration

---

* It was designated a New York City landmark in 1979, and is now the Guatemalan Mission to the UN.

wanted to enlarge America's economic and political presence in China, partly to compete with European spheres of influence there, and partly to offset the imperialist designs of Russia and Japan. Morgan never liked operating in unpredictable foreign markets where he had no representative. He had given up on one venture in China—the Canton–Hankow Railroad—in spite of Roosevelt's pleas about America's "national interests."

The Chinese government had approached Morgan and Kuhn, Loeb about a loan late in 1908, and the discussion expanded early the following year to include other financiers and the White House. In the spring of 1909, Taft's Secretary of State, Philander Knox (who had brought suit against Northern Securities as Roosevelt's Attorney General), asked the four leading New York banks—the Trio plus Kuhn, Loeb—to form an American Group that would share a new Chinese railroad loan with a consortium of German, French, and British banks. The liberal journalist Herbert Croly later wrote that the Americans went into the Group "not because they were seeking Chinese investments but in order to oblige the administration."

The bankers probably decided that obliging the government would give them leverage on other issues, and hoped the venture would be profitable over the long term. Schiff told his partner Otto Kahn that the initial Chinese transaction had "very little attraction for American capitalists. . . . But sooner or later China and her finances must be thoroughly reorganized, and it is as well to pave the way now for participation at that time."

Jack cabled news of these developments to his father at Dover House in June. Kuhn, Loeb was sending a man to represent them all in China, a former U.S. consul general at Mukden named Willard Straight: "On the whole," Jack reported, "idea strikes us favorably and Robert Bacon highly recommends Strait [*sic*]." The senior Morgan, sounding like his father in the 1870s, replied: "Strikes me favorably, but strictly confidential and for your own use only, important JPM&Co. take lead and name mentioned first. Suppose fact already recognized but must not be overlooked."

The house of Morgan took the lead but it did them no good. In the four years the Group served as America's financial representative in China, the Morgan partners spent more time mediating between the U.S. government and their European colleagues than they did on the actual loans—and they hated taking orders from the State Department. Davison asked Grenfell early on to let the Europeans know that a certain sticking point was "a proposition of the Government and not of the bankers," and on another occasion told Jack, "you can hardly appreciate embarrassing position we in due delay on part U.S. Govt approving our proposed Pekin cable. It seems perfectly ridiculous we should be held up in this matter."

A Chinese official deftly helped Davison out of another "embarrassing position" at a dinner in Berlin in 1911. Seated next to this man and knowing no

Chinese, Davison spent the evening talking to the diplomat on his other side—until the Peking minister interrupted to ask him in perfect English who was pitching for the White Sox.

The twenty-nine-year-old Willard Straight was a key figure in the bankers' undertaking. Tall, handsome, outgoing, and ambitious, he had traveled to the Far East after graduating from Cornell, studied Mandarin, worked as a journalist in Korea and Japan, and assisted Roosevelt in China. He hoped the American presence would save China from exploitation by other foreign powers, but the State Department's confused policies and the inherent difficulties of the political situation—opposition from Russia and Japan, Chinese nationalist hostility to the reign of foreign finance, and China's own internal struggles—doomed the U.S. venture. The administration's effort to promote American interests in the Far East failed, and the bankers did not even cover their costs.

Straight was new to the bankers' *hauteur.* After Morgan told Davison in the summer of 1910 to "make it clear that when we want to discuss things with the United States Government we want [the Secretary of State] and not [the Assistant Secretary]," Straight observed, "It was not difficult to see where the real power lies in this country." The following spring, Morgan informed Davison that Straight would like a diplomatic post as first secretary in Peking—"will you take up matter with State Department?" Davison said he would, though he was surprised Straight wanted a government job, "as regard it step down rather than up."*

By this time, Straight had something other than work on his mind. Shortly before he left for Peking in 1909, he had fallen in love with William C. Whitney's youngest daughter, Dorothy. Among the obstacles he faced were two rival suitors, the junior Bob Bacon and the Harvard economist who was working with Davison on the Aldrich Monetary Commission, A. Piatt Andrew. More-

---

* In 1935 the English diplomat Harold Nicolson reflected on the Morgan bank's attitude toward government. Nicolson was writing a book about Morgan partner Dwight Morrow, and the bank, now headed by Jack, objected to certain passages of the manuscript. Nicolson told his wife, Vita Sackville-West, that the conflict boiled down to the difference between his own conception of banking and Morgan's: "I had written, in describing the immense expansion assumed by Morgan's bank at the outbreak of [World War I], 'It ceased to be a private firm and became almost a Department of Government.' I meant that as a compliment. Old J. P. Morgan [Jack] appears to have regarded it as an insult. He has added a little note on his own, 'I have no right to ask you to alter this, but it will be interpreted as if we were reduced to the status of a department subordinate to the Government.'

"This is characteristic of both of us," continued Nicolson. "*I* feel it the highest compliment to compare Morgan's to the Foreign Office. *They* regard it as an insult to suggest that they have any connection with the Government, or any Government. But you see, the whole point of view is different. I regard bankers and banking as rather low-class fellows. They regard officials as stupid and corrupt."

over, Dorothy's family considered him a fortune hunter. (They had grounds for suspicion: Straight had courted Harriman's daughter, Mary, and the daughter of a wealthy senator from West Virginia, before he met Dorothy.) A nod from Morgan would be invaluable.

Dorothy called on the financier just before he left for Europe early in 1911, and reported to Straight: "Mr. J.P.M. was lovely to me. . . . He laughed and said he wished I would go there every single week—so I warned him I might. . . . Dear Mr. J.P. he's such a sweetie underneath the sternness!" Whether or not Morgan put in a word for her suitor, Dorothy accepted Straight's proposal that spring and married him in September.

The couple returned to a China torn apart by revolution. The Euro-American consortium had been financing the corrupt Manchu dynasty, and a republican revolt in 1911 forced the six-year-old emperor, Pu-yi, to abdicate. One night the Straights got caught in a riot and had to be rescued by U.S. Marines.

The American bankers shared loans to the new Chinese Republic with England, France, Germany, Russia, and Japan, but Woodrow Wilson's 1912 election put an end to dollar diplomacy in China. Opposed to U.S. intervention in foreign affairs, Wilson revoked the American Group's mandate in March 1913, and the United States withdrew from the consortium.

The China experience increased both the bankers' aversion to politicians and the country's aversion to bankers. Once again, the Trio was on center stage—only this time at the government's request, for virtually no reward. Opponents of big business, imperialism, and "the money power" nonetheless concluded that Wall Street had used the State Department to exploit a weak foreign nation for selfish gain. "Patriotism," cheered La Follette when Wilson terminated the connection in 1913, "is to be given precedence over profits." Taft's China venture yielded neither political nor material profit.*

———

An equally unsuccessful and unpopular venture for the Morgan bank during this period was a consolidation of New England transportation properties headed by Charles Mellen, the president of the New York, New Haven, & Hartford Railroad. Mellen had left the Northern Pacific in 1903 largely because he couldn't stand James J. Hill, and set out to build a system for the Northeast that would include intercity trolley and coastal steamship lines as well as railroads.

———

* Recalled to New York, Willard Straight went to work at the Morgan bank and stayed four years, but never really fit in. He and Dorothy supported Roosevelt in 1912, and in 1914 they financed a new left-liberal magazine about politics and the arts edited by Herbert Croly, *The New Republic*. Straight left the Morgan bank in 1916, and died in 1918. Dorothy subsidized *The New Republic* for the next forty years.

Morgan financed Mellen's ambitious plans for New England, hoping to halt the region's industrial decline. Over the next ten years, however, Mellen proceeded to quadruple the New Haven's capitalization, increase its bonded debt from $14 million to $242 million (strictly against the usual Morgan rules), overpay for new properties, and antagonize shippers, politicians, journalists, and reformers. In 1906 he paid $21 million for a combination of street-rail and gas companies controlled by the Philadelphia traction barons, W. L. Elkins and P.A.B. Widener. Senator Aldrich, who had sold his Rhode Island trolley interests to the combination, helped negotiate the deal.

When Mellen bought 36 percent of the Boston & Maine Railroad in 1907, corporate lawyer Louis Brandeis launched a campaign to dismantle the Morganized monopoly of New England transport. Known as "the people's attorney," the southern-born, Harvard-educated Brandeis was a champion of labor and an outspoken adversary of big business. In 1910, after Mellen testified about the merger of the New Haven and the Boston & Maine, Senator La Follette announced that everyone was mistaken about Mellen and the other parties to the deal: "these men . . . are but hired megaphones through which a beefy, red-faced, thick-necked financial bully, drunk with wealth and power, bawls his orders to stock markets, Directors, courts, Governments, and Nations. We have been listening to Mr. Morgan."

Mellen did tremendous damage to the New Haven and to the reputation of the Morgan bank: his overpayments and escalating debt kept the road from improving its facilities, which affected its credit in the markets; and earnings steadily declined. Morgan attended meetings of the New Haven board, but his preoccupation with other matters left the "moral responsibility" for the property in Mellen's hands. It was more than curious, in this case, that "the Old Man should not be better posted." (See Chapter 31.)

———

Roosevelt, kept apprised by mail about American politics as he traveled abroad, was furious with Taft for betraying his legacies on conservation, progressive reform, and the trusts—and he hated his self-imposed retirement. When TR returned to the United States in June of 1910, Woodrow Wilson, still president of Princeton, warned that "We have a very erratic comet sweeping across our horizon." The fifty-two-year-old Roosevelt organized an insurgent Republican movement in 1910 that split the party between radical dissidents and the conservative Old Guard. Democrats capitalized on the country's disgust with political and financial corruption, gained strength among farmers and workers, and swept the gubernatorial and congressional elections, winning a majority of seats in the House for the first time since 1892.

Morgan was out of town that November, but Belle Greene said he would have voted Democratic had he been there. "We are all very pleased" with the sweep, she told Berenson: "I think we need fear nothing from [TR] at the next Presidential election. It seems to me to be a clear field for Woodrow Wilson."

It might have surprised Brandeis and La Follette to learn that the "beefy, red-faced, thick-necked financial bully" was supporting the Democratic Wilson. This former law and history professor had transformed the alma mater of Junius Morgan, Henry Fairfield Osborn, and Jonathan Sturges into one of the country's major centers of higher learning. Pierpont Morgan had attended Wilson's Princeton inauguration in 1902, along with Grover Cleveland, Booker T. Washington, William Dean Howells, and Mark Twain. In November 1907, shortly after the panic, Wilson described Morgan to *The New York Times* as "a man of brains" who might lead a "common council, a sort of people's forum" that would be above national politics. Two years later, Morgan pledged $25,000 to Princeton University, to be paid over five years; he sent Wilson the first installment ($5,000) on November 1, 1909, and the second a year later, just days before the scholar was elected governor of New Jersey.* Though Wilson had criticized Roosevelt's antitrust prosecutions, denounced William Jennings Bryan, and condemned excessive government regulation, he ran for governor as a reformer in 1910, proposing to protect workers from hazardous conditions and to regulate big business.

———

Death continued to take its toll among Morgan's contemporaries. Charles McKim died in September 1909—Morgan served as pallbearer at his funeral, and helped persuade the American heiress Clara Jessup Heyland to leave a handsome seventeenth-century estate on the Janiculum, the Villa Aurelia, to the American Academy in Rome. Edward VII died in May of 1910.

Morgan himself seemed to be in good health, and took no more notice of the exhausting effect he had on others than he did of political opposition to his power. When Belle warned him that he had a reputation for wearing people out, he was (she told Berenson) "as astonished and angry as if it had been untrue."

He was in London attending the funeral of Edward VII in June 1910 when he learned that his son had become the latest partner to give way under the nerve-racking pressure of the bank's business. Jack reported to his father from New York that the doctors had found "nothing organic wrong," just "fatigue" and nervous strain. Davison added a few days later that the physicians had simply prescribed "a good rest."

Jack, now forty-three, had been trying all his life to overcome self-doubt and

* Morgan sent $5,000 to Princeton presidents John Aikman Stewart in 1911 and John Grier Hibben in 1912. The gifts were recorded in a diary of expenses and appointments kept by Morgan's secretary; there is no diary for 1913, the year Morgan died.

win paternal approval. The timing of his trouble—eighteen months after Davison's arrival and six months after Morgan handed the London office over to Grenfell and Vivian Smith—suggests that it may have had to do with his status at the bank. Jack liked all three of these men, and after Pierpont's death they worked well together, with Jack serving as formal head of the house of Morgan while Davison largely ran it. In 1910, however, Jack's "nervous strain" may have resulted from conclusive proof, in the agreeable presences of Davison, Grenfell, and Smith, that he had been judged not worthy of the kingdom.*

The elder Morgan returned to the United States in time to receive an honorary LLD from Harvard at the end of June: Jack proudly presented his father with the award before going off to Scotland for a rest cure.

———

Morgan added several exceptional works to his art and rare-book collections in 1910–11. From Durlacher Brothers in May of 1910, on the advice of Hercules Read, he purchased the Stavelot Triptych, a twelfth-century Byzantine reliquary said to contain a piece of the True Cross, for £40,000. Taking its name from the Benedictine Abbey of Stavelot in what is now Belgium, this luxuriantly beautiful triptych made of gold, copper gilt, silver, enamel, vernis brun, and precious stones depicts scenes from the Legend of the True Cross. Its illustrative stories, Byzantine hagiography, European narrative, and use of cloisonné and champlevé enamels bring together Eastern and Western traditions in art. As the earliest cross reliquary with scenes from the Legend of the True

---

* One of the physicians Jack consulted was Austen Fox Riggs, to whom he referred years later as "my much admired and beloved" Dr. Riggs. In 1919 Jack pledged $20,000 to the Austen Riggs Foundation for the study and treatment of nervous disorders in Stockbridge, Massachusetts. Born in Cassel, Germany, Riggs had come to the United States with his parents as a child, graduated from Harvard in 1898, and trained at the Columbia College of Physicians and Surgeons. He specialized in pulmonary tuberculosis for several years in New York, then in 1907 gave up his practice because of an illness and moved to Stockbridge. After a year off he went back to work specializing in nervous disorders, and was in Stockbridge when Jack saw him in 1910. A quiet pioneer in the nascent field of psychiatry, Riggs published an article on the "Treatment of Neurasthenia" in 1916, and a book called *Just Nerves* in 1922. His foundation, incorporated in 1920 and capitalized at $125,000, was designed especially for patients who could not afford treatment. Riggs served as consulting neurologist at hospitals in Massachusetts and Connecticut, and was appointed clinical professor of neurology at Columbia in 1922. Jack sent him several patients, including one of his own daughters in 1917 and one of his partners—Harry Davison—in 1921. Riggs's cure, Jack explained to his mother on the latter occasion, "means beside health a power to take life in such a way as not to fall down so far again. What Davison has lacked has been a certain moderation of mental outlook which Riggs teaches how to cultivate." Davison may have lacked mental moderation, but he also had a brain tumor, and died the following year.

Cross, it is an uncontested masterpiece and the most important art object now at the Morgan Library.

Morgan acquired his third Gutenberg Bible in London in 1911—a paper copy, more simply decorated than the two he already had, but complete and unusually large and fresh; as a pure representative of Gutenberg's achievement, it is the finest of the three.

And in the spring of 1911, as he traveled abroad, he authorized Belle Greene to bid for several items from the library of the American bibliophile Robert Hoe, who had died in 1909 leaving one of the greatest book collections of the modern era. Belle wanted above all to secure a unique Caxton on vellum, Malory's *Morte d'Arthur*—one of two copies known to exist (the other was in England) and the only perfect one. When Belle wrote to Morgan in March that the price might go as high as $20,000, he wired her to "buy Caxton price at your discretion," and to spend $75,000 more on other items she considered essential.

Leading foreign book dealers came to New York for the sale, as did a representative of the British Museum, and news of Morgan's interest drove the market up. Belle cabled her Chief at Aix on April 28: "Prices absurd and evidently made with you in mind. . . . Fear cannot buy Caxton under forty thousand. . . . Shall I buy at any price? Please answer immediately."

He replied: "Use your discretion would give seventy five or even a hundred rather than lose."

In the early days of the sale a dealer named George D. Smith dominated the bidding, making most of his purchases for the California collector Henry Huntington, Collis Huntington's nephew. When the Caxton came up on May 1, other buyers entered the competition but dropped out one by one as a small, dauntless woman steadily raised Smith's bids. The volume went to Belle Greene for $42,700, and her "victory evoked a hearty round of applause," reported *The New York Times*.

Belle cabled Morgan the news: she had bought about forty items altogether, spending slightly over $100,000. Furious at Smith for paying "ridiculous" prices, she doubted that he would "find any market save Huntington and Hearst hereafter . . . he has made of the Hoe sale a very disgusting and undignified performance."

The prospect of Morgan's deep pockets had moved prices up as well, but confirmation of Belle's view came from Albert Clay, the new Laffan Professor at Yale: he told Morgan that Miss Greene had made "a profound impression" at the sale "by her dignified demeanor, and for refusing to pay unreasonable prices for what she desired to purchase for the library," even though everyone knew she had "unlimited means back of her. It seems her course met with the hearty approval of all because of the ridiculously high prices paid by Mr. Huntington. I understand people were generally disgusted with his doings."

In terms of both quality and price, the Hoe sale was a major event in the evolution of American book collecting. It lasted nineteen months, and brought nearly $2 million.

———

Exactly two years after Davison arrived at 23 Wall Street, George Perkins left. Although he had done useful work for the firm, he had also caused considerable trouble. He never really fit the bankers' mold, beginning with his refusal to leave New York Life when Morgan asked him to. Since then, he had engineered his own deals and nurtured his own political influence. The corruption disclosed by the Armstrong Committee in 1905 had justifiably exacerbated public antipathy to the insurance business and tainted the Morgan bank. And though Morgan himself no longer wanted to monitor the daily operations of his firm, he did want partners who shared his style and aims, played by his rules, and deferred to his expertise. When Perkins negotiated financing for the Studebaker Company and B. F. Goodrich Rubber without sufficient clearance from his senior partner late in 1910, the old man decided the prima donna had to go.

As always, however, Morgan hated to deliver bad news. "He tried to make his partners do it," recalled Satterlee. "Then he tried to get Mr. Baker to do it. Finally he told George to be at the Library [one day] at 5 p.m. Ledyard went up there at 5:15 and passed George going out. When [Ledyard] went into the West Room Pierpont got up and cried out—'He's going to leave January 1st'—and executed a hornpipe."

According to Belle, at 1:00 A.M. that New Year's Eve, Morgan breathed a sigh of relief, "Thank God—no more Perkins!"

Once again, the popular image of Morgan as Wall Street commando barking orders to his minions was wide of the mark: he had not been able to impose his will on Perkins from the outset, had kept him on for longer than he wanted to, couldn't get any of his partners or friends to do the firing, and did it himself only when he thought he had no choice.

It was Davison who found an effective replacement for Perkins—Thomas W. Lamont, a Harvard graduate ('92) who had worked briefly as a reporter before making a career on Wall Street. Davison had brought Lamont to Bankers Trust in 1903, enlisted him to work for the junior trio during the 1907 panic, promoted him as his own successor at Baker's First National in 1909, and then to Morgan late in 1910. At the end of October, Morgan summoned Davison's candidate to 23 Wall Street and said, "Lamont, I want you to come down here as a partner on January 1st"—he had already talked to George Baker, who was again willing to give up one of his top young associates. On January 1, 1911, Lamont joined the Morgan bank.

One of his chief attractions was his knowledge of journalism and publishing. Although Morgan made few concessions to popular opinion, the younger members of his firm were acutely aware of the need for an effective public relations campaign, specifically for ways to answer the muckraking press. Lamont owned stock in several magazine ventures, including the steel industry's *Iron Age*, and had a controlling interest in the Crowell Publishing Company. Early in 1911 the Crowell company bought the progressive *American Magazine*, which had a circulation of 1.7 million and a list of contributors that included Ida Tarbell, Finley Peter Dunne, Lincoln Steffens, Ray Stannard Baker, and William Allen White. Several of these writers had grown disillusioned with the literature of exposure, and left *McClure's* in 1906—shortly after TR coined the term "muck-rake"—to start the *American*. They described their aim as neither utopian nor cynical: the new magazine would be "wholesome, hopeful, stimulating, uplifting." Ida Tarbell observed years later, "The idea that there was something fundamentally sound and good in industrial relations, that in many spots had gone far beyond what either labor or reformers were demanding, came to the office as a new attack on the old problem."

Reporting on the Crowell/Lamont acquisition of the *American* in 1911, *The New York Times* announced the birth of a "Magazine Trust," and noted rumors that "the interests" were swallowing up the muckrakers. Morgan's publishing trust, said the New York *Press*, planned to control editorial policy and increase magazine profits, as well as to build an empire that would include the Morgan-financed Harper publications and perhaps *Munsey's* magazine. Among the opponents of this latest Morganization were Condé Nast, the conservationist Gifford Pinchot, Robert Collier of *Collier's Weekly*, and S. S. McClure.*

Over the next two years, as opposition to the Morgan "interests" ratcheted up, Lamont bought newspapers, syndicates, and reporters in an attempt to disseminate what he termed "proper" facts.

No thanks to Lamont's rearguard action, some of journalism's leading muckrakers concluded on their own that popular antagonism to Morgan had gotten out of hand. Lincoln Steffens mocked the national hysteria about the banker's power one afternoon as he walked along a railroad track with his young assistant, Walter Lippmann. Gauging their footsteps, Lippmann noted that the ties had not been designed for an ordinary man's stride. Of course not, Steffens explained: "You see, Morgan controls the New Haven and he prefers to make the people ride."

Lippmann himself observed that as monopoly became the "New Devil" in the United States, "Big Business" with its "ruthless tentacles" served as mate-

---

* McClure entertained an offer of several hundred thousand dollars from Lamont a few months later, as he tried to reorganize his financially strapped company. Fearing Wall Street control, he turned Lamont down and found financing elsewhere, but the new owners quickly forced him out. He later told the editor of the *American* that he had made a mistake in not selling to Lamont.

rial for "feverish" popular fantasies: with "everything askew—all the frictions of life are readily ascribed to a deliberate evil intelligence, and men like Morgan and Rockefeller take on attributes of omnipotence that ten minutes of cold sanity would reduce to a barbarous myth."*

———

If the Morgan bankers hoped that cooperating with the Taft administration in China would give them leverage on the trusts, they were wrong: in the spring of 1911, the President ordered his Attorney General to cooperate with the Stanley Committee's investigation of U.S. Steel. Also that spring the Supreme Court found Standard Oil and American Tobacco to be in violation of the Sherman law, and ordered them dissolved.†

Morgan remained abroad for the first eight months of 1911. The Stanley Committee's "revelations" about his role in the 1907 panic made front-page news all summer. Belle Greene told him by mail in June that she was "very

---

* Lippmann also gave an acute analysis of Morgan's role in modern capital markets—in which giant corporations are owned by thousands of diverse shareholders who exercise no direct control: "to-day the central condition of business is that capital shall be impersonal, 'liquid,' 'mobile.' The modern shareholder is a person of no account whatever. It mattered very much what kind of people the old landlords were. But it matters not at all what kind of person the shareholder is. . . . He cannot fulfill any responsibility to the property he owns." As a result, it mattered very much what kind of person did take responsibility for supervising industrial managers and answering to the shareholders. Morgan's "enormous power," continued Lippmann in 1914, lay in his "ability to direct the flow of capital." The financier headed what was "no doubt a colossal autocracy," and great efforts had been made "to break it up, to decentralize the power that concentrated about Morgan. But no one proposes to put back into the hands of the investor the decision as to the financing of industry. . . . The question of where money is to be applied is a matter for experts to answer. And so reform of the credit system does not consist in abolishing the financial expert. It consists in making him a public servant."

And when Ida Tarbell wrote essays that did not expose corruption in high places, she was surprised to learn that her readers wanted only "attacks"—"they had little interest in balanced findings." In 1925 she published a book about Elbert Gary that did not portray him or U.S. Steel as evil incarnate, and former admirers dismissed her as having been bought. The flood of ugly revelations produced during the Progressive Era led the public to believe, Tarbell wrote in her autobiography, "that the inevitable result of corporate industrial management was exploitation, neglect, bullying, crushing of labor, that the only hope was in destroying the system."

† The Court in the Standard Oil case formulated a "rule of reason," under which only contracts that *unreasonably* or *unduly* restrained trade could be held unlawful. This principle more or less upheld Roosevelt's view that the Sherman law should apply to specific illegal conduct rather than to size or the mere fact of combination—his Northern Securities suit notwithstanding.

much disturbed over this disgusting political exhibition, which is called an 'investigation'. . . ." Other people said "there is too widespread respect and admiration for you, as the biggest man in the country, to permit you to be called to the witness-stand in this miserable affair," she reported. "However, I do hope for your sake and for all of us who feel this way toward you, that you will not return here until this matter is well over."

When Roosevelt was called to testify about the acquisition of TC&I, neither the committee nor the public believed his version of events. Jack evoked genealogical superiority as he denounced to Fanny the "insinuations made about Father by a lot of curs who want to make people think he is the same breed as they are. . . . There is no country in the world except this where Father would not have had the highest honour and the greatest respect and affection for what he has [done] all his life. . . . Here the press and the legislature and the public only say 'he probably found it profitable to cause the panic.' "

Morgan returned to New York in mid-August. Fanny left for Europe three weeks later. In October, Attorney General George Wickersham—although handpicked by Perkins—filed suit against U.S. Steel. The government charged, among other things, that Gary and Frick had tricked Roosevelt into permitting the purchase of TC&I, in violation of the Sherman Act.

Satterlee read the charges to his father-in-law aloud. Morgan sat silent for several minutes, then said, "Well, it has come to this!" He seemed baffled and "very much depressed" by the lawsuit.

Two weeks after the acquisition of TC&I, on November 20, 1907, Steel Chairman Gary had held a famous dinner meeting in New York. He told his guests—executives representing 90 percent of the industry—that the business needed "a friendly exchange of views rather than [the] unreasonable and destructive competition" that had led to "violent fluctuations" in price and had injured manufacturers, customers, and workers. For the next two years U.S. Steel officials met regularly for dinner with independent producers to set prices at levels that enabled them all to survive. U.S. Steel's bankers and lawyers supported this policy, but its steel experts hated it, since they steadily lost market share to the independents: one of them complained to Schwab's successor, William Corey, "it is better by all odds to make . . . profit on a full output at competitive prices than by half output at artificial prices."

Gary and Morgan wanted specifically to control competitive prices in the interest of steel-industry stability. "It is not at all certain that if the management that was in force [in 1900] had continued," Gary testified in 1911, "the Carnegie Company would not have driven entirely out of business every steel company in the United States." The executives at U.S. Steel also wanted to avoid prosecution under the antitrust law, however, and largely for that reason they abandoned the "Gary dinners" in 1909. Price stabilization did create an umbrella under which the 40 percent of the industry that was not part of the trust could survive, and Big Steel rarely engaged in the kind of pricing that would ruin its rivals. Gary took as much care to secure Washington's approval of his "friendly intercourse" with the independents as he had for the takeover of TC&I, but what he and Roosevelt considered friendly intercourse the Taft administration regarded as price-fixing.

Morgan sailed for Europe again at the end of December. His partners told *The New York Times* that the Stanley Committee had made no attempt to require his appearance: "His departure for Europe at this time was not hastened or affected by the Committee's activities." Belle confided to Berenson, however, that "JP went a fortnight earlier than he expected and we were *all* glad to get him off—on account of the Steel investigation and the cold weather." Jack told Grenfell: "the Senior's leaving early was a great coup, as he thereby avoided even the least appearance of running away."

In Paris in early January, Morgan stayed with U.S. Ambassador Bob Bacon, spent several evenings with James Stillman, then went on to Monte Carlo. Stillman cabled his son that the old man (code name "Zorew") seemed "optimistic, but I think was whistling to keep his courage up. . . . I have just returned from lunching with Zorew at Monte Carlo. He sails tomorrow for Egypt. He had no news, but was very genial."

An outraged Roosevelt denounced the U.S. Steel suit in private letters and in the press—Taft had endorsed the TC&I takeover in 1907, TR said, and "a succession of lawsuits" was about as likely to solve the complicated problem of the trusts as "a return to the flintlocks of Washington's Continentals." Roosevelt believed more in administrative regulation than judicial prosecution, saw U.S. Steel as a "good" trust, and thought his political enemies were out to embarrass him about the 1907 "deal" over TC&I. They were. These charges, reinforcing the antagonism between the former president and his former protégé, helped bring Roosevelt into the presidential ring for 1912, as the Morgan lawyers prepared to defend U.S. Steel.*

---

* In the case against U.S. Steel, many of the corporation's customers and rivals testified that it had not abused its pricing power, but had kept prices low in rising markets and high in declines, which enabled smaller firms to survive business-cycle fluctuations. A West Coast steelmaker told the court: "I have always found the competition of the United States Steel company and its subsidiaries fair; its existence has been beneficial to the steel and iron trade of the country." The federal district court ruled unanimously in 1915 that U.S. Steel did not violate the Sherman Act. The judges found no evidence of the competitive "oppression" that had appeared in the cases against American Tobacco and Standard Oil, and concluded that insofar as competing steel companies had united "in testifying that the business conduct of the Steel Corporation has been fair, we can rest assured that there has been neither monopoly nor restraint." The court also discovered no evidence for "that most injurious feature of monopoly's wrong to the public"—increased prices or deteriorating quality of products. A

Although Morgan was not listening to his critics, his partners, lawyers, and friends tried to play down the image of the Trio's power. When, prompted by three decades of habit, Morgan suggested via cable from Europe that Baker and Stillman be appointed to the new Equitable voting trust in May 1910, Baker warned of "probable public feeling . . . that Wall Street would have too much to do with Equitable," and Stillman concurred. The board appointed Ledyard and Perkins (six months before he left the bank) instead; though no less affiliated with Wall Street than Baker and Stillman, these men had somewhat lower profiles.

Ledyard, a senior partner in the firm of Carter, Ledyard, & Milburn, was counsel to the New York Stock Exchange and a director of dozens of banks and railroads. He had been at Morgan's right hand during the 1907 panic, the way Stetson had been in 1895; he did not supplant Stetson as attorney for the bank, but handled many of Morgan's legal affairs, and belonged to the intimate group that met almost daily at the Markoes'.

When Morgan tried to dictate the timing and outcome of a new presidential election at the Equitable in April 1911, Jack, recovered from his breakdown, wired Davison that Ledyard thought it "most unwise for Trustees or Flitch [Morgan] make any effort dominate the situation or control election of President. . . . It is impossible to exaggerate importance there should be no possibility of criticism of Flitch's actions all through this matter, and that no opportunity for suggestion of Wall Street domination be given. . . . Have not kept Flitch informed from day to day of this matter, understanding that Trustees were in charge acting for him, and as long as no action was called for by him he did not want to be bothered."

Morgan did not need to be bothered. Financial consolidation was proceeding smoothly in Davison's hands. In 1910–11, when the Equitable and Mutual Life insurance companies divested themselves of their controlling interest in the National Bank of Commerce—the country's second-largest bank, after National City—the Trio banks bought the shares. They had considered the Commerce stock just as well off in the insurance companies' vaults as in their own, but once it came onto the market, Davison arranged for them to acquire it and

---

concurring opinion held that U.S. Steel had intended to restrain trade, but that since it had not tried to ruin its rivals or drive them out of the market, since price controls were efficient only when cooperatively deployed, and since the company had been "conspicuously free from that business brutality, meanness, and unfairness" that characterized other large corporations found guilty under Sherman Act, "a decree of dissolution should not be entered against it." The Supreme Court upheld this result in 1920.

share control: "decidedly in the interest of Bank, of Group [Trio], and of general situation," he cabled Morgan.* The "Group" appointed its own representatives to the Commerce finance committee and board.

In 1912 Davison arranged further trust-company mergers, absorbing the Manhattan Trust into the Bankers Trust, and buying the Standard Trust for the Guaranty, which brought the Guaranty's capital to $33 million and its deposits to almost $190 million.

Meanwhile, Aldrich's National Monetary Commission and its allies in politics, journalism, banking, and the universities were trying to explain the need for financial reform. Charles Conant published a series of articles on "A Central Bank of Issue" in *The Wall Street Journal* in the fall of 1909, giving a concise account of the "requirements of modern commerce" and proposing a detailed plan for national economic stabilization. President Taft that fall urged the country to "take up seriously the problem of establishing a central bank." Paul M. Warburg pointed out in articles and speeches that modern financial markets could no longer regulate themselves but required periodic intervention by experts: "Our present scandalous system, of attempting to regulate the money market of the entire country by first pouring money into the stock market, and then withdrawing it, creating inflation and exorbitant security prices, followed in due course by stringency and unnecessary price depression, will [under a central reserve bank] give place to more orderly movements, as our discount markets develop." Most of the country's financiers were in favor of a central bank, reported Warburg, as long as it was not controlled by " 'Wall Street' or any monopolistic interest."

In mid-November 1910, several members of the Aldrich Commission went down to the Millionaire's Club at Jekyl Island, probably courtesy of Morgan, to work out a specific plan. The expedition included Aldrich, Davison, Vanderlip, Warburg, A. Piatt Andrew, and Ben Strong, now a vice president at Bankers Trust. Eager to deflect public suspicions of a Wall Street cabal drawing up plans for the country's economic future, they told reporters they were going duck hunting, and on their way south in Aldrich's private railroad car addressed each other by first name only. Davison and Vanderlip went so far as to call each other Orville and Wilbur, though a sighting of the famous Wright brothers was unlikely to forestall gossip among the porters.

Over the next two weeks, these men drew up plans for a national system of regional reserve banks led by a central board of private bankers. They hoped that

---

* Stillman had vetoed the idea of merging the Commerce with Chase National, thinking it "better at present not to call attention to the great power of trio, which might increase public sentiment against that power throughout the United States," Jack reported to his father. Stillman also did not want to lose his position as the "first bank in US"—if the Commerce had merged with Chase, the resulting combination would have been larger than City Bank.

coordinated regulation of the money supply would prevent drastic contractions, check impulses toward "overheated" expansion, forestall panics, and establish an official lender of last resort. And by giving control to bankers rather than government officials, they meant to take finance out of politics. Like Morgan, these men saw themselves not as serving their own interests, but as devising a financial system that would benefit the country as a whole.

The Democratic Congress did not agree, and over the next two years it rejected the "Aldrich plan" as giving too much power to private banks. When the Federal Reserve Act finally passed in December 1913, it provided for a governing board in Washington, appointed by the President, to represent the public interest.*

Convinced after 1907 that the country could not wait for government action on the Aldrich Committee's plans for a monetary policy—and that the government would not police vast flows of capital as well as they themselves could—Morgan, Baker, and Stillman were constructing a private regulatory system of their own. The Trio's concerted actions as the nation's self-appointed central bankers brought on charges that they were running a "money trust." Charles A. Lindbergh, a progressive Minnesota congressman (and the father of the future aviator), called in 1911 for an investigation of "financial combinations in restraint of trade." The United States so urgently needed monetary control, said *The Wall Street Journal*, that if a money trust didn't exist somebody ought to invent one.

---

* Woodrow Wilson thought this mix of public and private interests would give government the upper hand and effectively turn banks into "the instruments, not the masters, of business, and of individual enterprise and initiative." Louis Brandeis disagreed, claiming that there could be no compromise with the devil—that "Concessions to the big-business interests must in the end prove futile." The journalist William Greider has concluded that Wilson probably did strike the "right moderate balance," since the Federal Reserve legislation was attacked by extremists on both sides. Populists in the West saw it as serving the interests of big business, while the New York *Sun,* speaking for Wall Street, denounced it as "covered all over with the slime of Bryanism." The Federal Reserve Act provided for regional reserves from which money could be delivered quickly to local banks in times of crisis, and an "elastic" national currency that would expand and contract to meet perennially shifting demand. Despite its founders' hopes, the Fed has been only partly successful at controlling the contractions and expansions of the business cycle, and it failed spectacularly in 1929–41. Just how "disinterested" the system actually turned out to be has been subject to debate ever since.

*Lady Victoria Sackville in the early 1900s, at
about the time she met Pierpont Morgan.
(Courtesy of Nigel Nicolson)*

Chapter 30

PORTRAITS

Morgan left so few records in his own voice for the last years of his life that it is possible to see him mainly through other people's eyes. Biography inevitably includes elements of triangulation—locating an unknown point on a triangle by reference to its two known points—but the known points for the aging Morgan rarely yield straight lines. His wealth and power so affected people's perceptions that he could not tell whether they were responding to him or to what he could do for them. Neither could they.

Since discretion was a prerequisite for membership in his inner circle, few of his close friends left public assessments of his character, and those who did were so intent on defending him against the myth of his satanic majesty that their accounts tend to be numbingly pious and banal. According to Satterlee, Morgan loved children, dogs, and the Fourth of July. Tom Lamont: "I have never visioned a man with such a strong sense of community responsibility as Mr. Morgan had." New York's Bishop Greer said Morgan "was the possessor of a big brain, a sincere heart, and honesty was the one secret of his success."

More incisive sketches came from colleagues who were not writing for posterity, such as Dawkins to Milner on Morgan's dinners with Joseph Chamberlain and "Edward Rex," or Grenfell on Morgan as outwardly "rough because he is very strong & yet very shy. . . . He sees clearly enough but his explanations in words are quite incoherent."

Belle Greene's delightfully uncensored letters to Berenson raise the question of witness reliability. Just as Dr. Rainsford, Lincoln Steffens, and Roger Fry told stories that emphasized their own intellectual or moral superiority to "the great man," Belle offered up accounts that were at least as much about herself as they were about her Big Chief. She saw more of the private Morgan than most people who gossiped about him did, but constantly imposed her own profile on the picture. And while she professed interest only in his unadorned self and the high scholarship he was underwriting, she, like everyone else, had other motives as well.

In the inner sanctum of the library on 36th Street, she learned how much her patron wanted to be admired. He did not know about her affair with Berenson, and once when the two men were about to meet in Europe, she advised BB to "remember that [Morgan] *never* tires of flattery—he can swallow the most barefaced kind & *loves it . . . don't* be afraid to let him see that you admire & like him *very much* personally. It will be all for our good later on."

She herself dispensed lavish doses of adulation. As Morgan traveled abroad one spring, she wrote: "you must know that my admiration and esteem, above all knowledge of you, makes me feel that whatever of value my little life has, is simply its devotion to you and your interests, and I am willing to fight on to the end, if necessary, in that idea." The library's garden, just coming into bloom, "would enchant your soul which loves the beautiful so passionately."

Rich as this draft was, it did not compare to the defense she mounted when Berenson ventured to criticize Morgan's taste in June of 1909. Earlier that spring Morgan had bought a *Madonna and Child,* ostensibly by Raphael, from the Italian dealer Ezra Volpi on the recommendation of Dr. Bode, for $200,000. Otto Gutekunst, director of the Colnaghi Gallery in London, wrote to Berenson that he had "called on Morgan the other day and . . . could have cried with rage and disappointment, seeing how delighted he was with some awful rubbish various people—robbers!—must have palmed off on him quite lately! And at phenomenal prices too & there I was unable to tell him the truth because I did not dare make him feel ashamed of himself. Amongst other things he showed me a small Italian picture quite passably pretty & I pretended to like it. But when he began talking about Raphael, I felt funny."*

That Berenson and Gutekunst considered Bode wrong might have been grounds for humility—some acknowledgment that the science of attribution was inexact, and that the best scholars made mistakes (Berenson himself was wrongly assigning the canvas to Pintoricchio). Instead, other people's mistakes tended to breed gloating disdain. Writing to Mrs. Gardner that summer about

---

* Berenson attributed the picture to Pintoricchio in 1909, and pronounced it worth $25,000 to $30,000 at most. Later, he labeled it a fake. Morgan hung the painting in his West Room, and though Bode listed it as one of four authentic Raphaels in America at the end of 1911, it turned out not to be. Morgan's heirs sold it at auction in 1944 as "School of Raphael," for $2,500.

the "Raphael" and the Fra Angelico Morgan had just bought out from under Roger Fry, Berenson claimed to be above the fray: "Sometimes it amuses me to see all these fabulous great art merchants tear their hair with envy and spite at each other. But on the whole it disgusts me." He repeated Gutekunst's critical remarks about Morgan to Belle Greene.

Though perfectly capable of sneering at Morgan's taste herself, Belle took immense pride in him—as well as in her intimate understanding of him—and she replied to BB: "I am going to . . . beg of you on my knees, if you have any spark of friendship—affection or love for me *please* don't jeer at my dearly-beloved Boss—You can't know how your perhaps thoughtless words hurt me—they cut like a whip and make me physically—mentally and at heart sick—

"You see I have a peculiarly tender feeling for him—for many reasons—but most of all perhaps because he has shown himself to me (in the *all* too *few* years I have known him) in a unique way. He has been so absolutely like a *child* in his confidences—in the expression of his thoughts and feelings. . . . There is an honesty of thought between us—a soul-oneness which makes it possible for him to tell me things which, as he has often said, he has told no other living being—and I rejoice to hear him, *not* because it flatters me, but because I cannot help but feel that it affords him a certain relief."

Of course it flattered her. This "soul-oneness" made her his partner and the keeper of his secrets. Belle took her place in a long line of interesting women—beginning with Mrs. Hoffman in Vevey—to whom Morgan turned for the pleasure and relief of intimate talk. To BB, she constantly highlighted her stature as chosen confessor, as uniquely able to engage this immensely powerful man.

Joining the chorus of voices that exalted Morgan with biblical allusions, she went on with no flicker of irony to portray him as the Man of Sorrows: ". . . by some unerring instinct he remains pre-eminently *human*," she told BB—"in him I touch, as it were, the ultimate symbol of humanity and yet he has the Christ-like *genius* of suffering—though he gazes at one with smiling eyes (his *wonderful* eyes!) one's heart is smitten through and through by the pain back of the smile—by the pity of it all—I feel him Royal and Compelling and yet while my heart praises him, it yearns for him."

For all her hyperbole, Belle accurately saw Morgan's isolation, depression, and soreness at being used for what he could give: "I wonder how many other people know, as I do, of the utter *loneliness* of his life?" she continued. "It seems to me that he is bound to a perpetuity of pain . . . the ever-recurring bitterness of knowing that his kindness, friendship, and rare affection [have] met with a base or at best a poor return. He gives *all* and gets what? Only a sickening realization of his money and the world-power it brings him."

She also saw some of his conflicts and aspirations: "The night before he sailed . . . he told me bits of his life—of his unfulfilled hopes—of his failures and disappointments—(never a word of what the world knows as his successes!)—of how he had always sought to be a builder—not a wrecker in the world of things—of how he had tried to put ambition, as such, behind him and accomplishment in the betterment of mankind and things before him—and how it had been indelibly burned in upon his belief that in every phase of action, joy, and love there is fulfillment *only otherwhere*—and so lost was I in him, so completely attuned to him—that I did not realize until long after I reached home and could not sleep through the rest of the night—that my hand was aching and sore from his grasp.

"And this you see is how *I* know him, and love him and reverence him and ache with pity for him," she wound up, lapsing back into humbuggery. "He is the hero of my soul and the child of my heart. It may seem queer and hysterical and far fetched to you . . . who know him as the Power to whom all, even kings, bow down—& whose path *seems* to be strewn with roses—and to whom all joys *seem* to come—It is because of my knowledge of him that I can't bear to have you sneer at him in his relation to art. . . . For the things he stands for, are *not* his art collections, be they good, bad or indifferent—they are after all but his amusement, as are his yachts, his Belles-dames, his game of solitaire and his game of finance."

What he actually stood for she did not say, but portrayed the hero of her soul as the ultimate symbol of humanity, bound to a perpetuity of pain with a Christlike genius for suffering.

Belle's peroration temporarily silenced Berenson's scorn. After calling at Princes Gate a month later, he reported to Mrs. Gardner that he found Morgan "as usual affable, simple, as proud and eager as a nice schoolboy, and a thoroughly life-enhancing person."

When Morgan returned from Europe that August, he took Belle, Charles Lanier, and a couple named Dixon to Newport and Bar Harbor on *Corsair.* Belle explained to Berenson that Dr. George Dixon was Morgan's "attending physician" whenever Jim Markoe was unavailable. She pronounced Lanier "a dear & comfortable friend . . . 70 or thereabouts & one of my 'senile' lovers"—and Mrs. Dixon "an incomparable bore . . . & as such a superb chaperone." Fanny Morgan was already at Newport: "thank God I am stopping with a crowd which knows her not. She bores and irritates me continuously which is of course to my discredit as she is famed for being good as gold and tries to be kindly but I am certain that if I were a man and tied to her I should commit all sorts of indiscretions."

On the subject of Morgan's indiscretions, Belle was generally amused, taking a line of high detachment that pointed up her own superiority. "Why is it," she rhetorically asked BB, "that every woman who comes within a mile of JP immediately loses her head, all sense of dignity and becomes, to all appearances desperately enamoured of him & a willing candidate for the harem[?] He seems to bowl them over completely[;] they lose all sense of discretion modesty & even common decency. It disgusts me thoroughly with my sex. It surely is not his fault, for all he does is to sit like a reviewing general & they flock to him all day long in rapid and sickening succession. Each one pluming her feathers and thinking she is the hen pheasant, when in reality she is forgotten before her successor appears."

At other moments, however, she professed herself disgusted by her Chief's amorous adventures, reporting that "all his wonderful points seem to fall away & this one festering sore seems to fill one's vision." Like Scheherezade in the stories Berenson had given her, Belle embellished her tales for reasons of her own, and mixed splashes of fiction in with the facts. Still, the picture she draws is of an indefatigable Don Juan.

Early in 1910, she described Lady Alan Johnstone, the former (American) Antoinette Pinchot, as "extremely attractive. The Big Chief thinks the same. . . . Needless to say she sees that her attractiveness is properly rewarded—but I do not blame her and really prefer her to most of the others, besides she is neither *fat* (which I loathe) nor a fossil. What I can never understand is how any one of them can feel *flattered* since as all the world knows of the *others* they must also. I never could see much distinction in sharing the delights of a harem. It is a truly discouraging aspect of the dear man that I am *so* fond of. . . ."

A few months later she complained that Morgan was running her ragged with meetings "all day long of his different interests. I wonder if there will ever come a time when I can be left alone for an hour a day even, with my beloved books and not be bothered with financiers, dealers and *ladies*—the last named bother me more than all the rest—they are such *damned fools*. . . ."

Lady Johnstone reappeared that fall: "I had an awfully funny time getting her to see JP," Belle reported. "Three of his other pets were in the library at the same time & he laughed heartily over my attempts to keep them away from each other."

In the spring of 1911, Belle told Berenson that Morgan was not buying much art in Europe, "as he wrote me the other day that he had not seen anything (except a couple of dames) that interested him. I wrote him in reply to stick to the dames and avoid the masterpieces of art."

———

Morgan had taken a tour of Egypt early that winter with a scholar who might have said much the same thing. When Albert Lythgoe could not escort the banker through the Nile Valley in 1911, the job fell to his assistant, Herbert Winlock. An unusually gifted young archaeologist who had been Lythgoe's student at Harvard, Winlock would succeed his mentor as the Met's curator of Egyptian art in 1929 and become director of the museum in 1932. His letters to Lythgoe are frank, self-assured, and witty—Winlock shuddered when he learned of his assignment to Morgan's 1911 tour, and hoped a financial crisis would forestall it. He had been digging for a year in the ruins of the palace of Amenhotep III at Thebes, and Lythgoe had warned him that Morgan was "not interested the least little bit" in that site. The twenty-six-year-old Winlock wanted to concentrate on his work, not play factotum to a visiting tycoon.

The first few days on the Nile in a rented *dehabiyeh* went "splendidly," Winlock reported to Lythgoe: Morgan, traveling with Mary Burns and his friends the Morton Patons, was "in very good health & spirits" and "sometimes quite jolly—the other night at dinner he recited reams of French poetry—and he usually has a joke on hand about something." Still, the archaeologist objected to the financier's extravagance. When Morgan bought two Persian walking sticks for $2,500, Winlock said nothing, though he thought them not worth nearly that much. He did veto an Armenian book and a Ptolemaic bronze cat, and found his judgment accepted "without a murmur—to my great surprise!" He approved of several other Morgan purchases, including a black granite bust of Rameses II: "He says with a twinkle in his eye he arrived in Egypt too late & found everything had been bought up by the Metropolitan but he was able to find a few little things & then he looked at his bust of Rameses II. For goodness sake," Winlock instructed Lythgoe, "admire it when you see it. I think it is an ideal thing for [Morgan]—and he does too."

At Asyut a few days later, Morgan fell in love with two very fine model funeral boats, each about three feet long, for which a dealer was asking £2,500. Winlock pronounced them unique but the price ridiculous. Morgan offered £1,000 each, which Winlock also thought ridiculous. The dealer understood enough English, however, to reject Winlock's offer of £750. Winlock took Morgan back to their boat, returned to the shop, and argued for two hours but could not get the price down to £1,000; he refused to pay more. At dinner that night, Morgan told his friends: "I know Mr. Winlock thinks I am a fool but I want the boats & I don't want the £1000."

He had a point—a thousand pounds meant nothing to him—but Winlock had his way. He *did* think Morgan foolish, and also inept, having "spoiled it all by blurting out his price." Winlock's professional pride, and his concern to keep the antiquities market in reasonable line with value, led him to hold out against the dealer's demands. The party sailed without the boats, "and everybody has suffered," Winlock told Lythgoe.

When Maspero, the director of the Cairo Museum, identified Morgan's black granite head of "Rameses II" as from another period altogether, Winlock, having called it "Ramesside," told Lythgoe that "Morgan likes it as a Rameses the Great and doesn't like it as anything else. When you see it don't try to wean him too suddenly." And reporting that Morgan had asked Thomas Cook to submit designs for a *dehabiyeh* of his own because "he likes it all so much he wants a boat" permanently on the Nile, Winlock groaned: "You may accept this letter of mine as a tentative resignation from the M.M.A. if he is going to continue to come out & if I have got to [be] going through Cairo" doing his errands.

At the end of the tour, Winlock complained that he was worn-out and fed up. Still, Morgan had given the Met a group of extraordinarily important XIX Dynasty reliefs, the greater part of a chapel from Abydos dating back to the time of Seti I; Winlock thought them among the finest reliefs the museum had, and wanted them put on prominent display.

The following winter, Morgan took the Lythgoes, Mary Burns, and Bishop and Mrs. Lawrence up the Nile in his own *dehabiyeh,* which he named *Khargeh**—and managed to buy the model boats Winlock had held out against in 1911 after all, for £1,000. He refused to let them out of his sight during the cruise, but afterward gave them to the Met, along with a complete XII Dynasty burial that Lythgoe praised as "the most superb thing of its kind in any museum." Morgan also in 1912 commissioned an expedition house for Winlock's work at Deir el-Bahri and in the Asasif Valley on the western bank of the river at Luxor, ancient Thebes. This area proved enormously productive over the next twenty years. Morgan helped choose the furnishings and design for the expedition house, which was built to resemble a Coptic church; it had domes, arcades, missionary furniture, twelve bedrooms, a shaded veranda, thick walls to keep in cool air, and a high-ceilinged living room—luxurious accommodations for archaeologists accustomed to life in the rough.

Both Winlock and Lythgoe recognized Morgan's ingenuous excitement over the archaeologists' finds, but what the younger man characterized as bumbling and childish seemed to the elder a genuine—and extraordinarily useful—passion. In 1912, when Winlock's workmen at Luxor uncovered a bronze Coptic incense burner with a lioness attacking a boar on top, Lythgoe reported to Robinson that "Morgan was able to lift it out of the ground with his own hands, and he carried it back in triumph to the steamer. He was delighted, and it is now his most treasured possession. His only fear is that Maspero will take it away from him, but I have assured him that we can arrange the matter. . . ."[†]

Bishop Lawrence later sketched in another dimension of Morgan's fascination with Egypt. As they sailed along the Nile in 1912, Lawrence recalled, Morgan pointed to the shore and said, "There is the place where Moses was hidden in the bulrushes. It doesn't look it now; critics may say there never were any bulrushes or any Moses, but I know that there was a Moses and that he was

---

* With a shallow draft and steep sides, this steam-powered houseboat had been fitted out in Morgan style: 130 feet long, it had a glass forward observation deck, a dining room and three staterooms on the main deck, and seven more staterooms as well as servants' quarters below. It had cost about $60,000.

[†] The piece is now in the Metropolitan Museum.

hidden in the bulrushes, for there is the spot. It must be so." As post-Darwinian rationalists questioned the fundamental assumptions of theology, Morgan insisted that Egypt's ancient geography confirmed the literal truth of the Bible. Lawrence reflected: "It was in this somewhat humorous but serious way that his religious conservatism met the onslaughts of the critics."

———

From Egypt each winter Morgan went on to Italy and France. In Rome in 1911, after the trip with Winlock, he made several visits to the site of the new American Academy on the Janiculum. He had bought additional property nearby, and proposed to transfer ownership to the academy once its directors came up with detailed plans. In Paris, he gave the French government a reliquary head of Saint Martin that turned out to have been stolen from a village church; the grateful President of France installed a plaque honoring Morgan in the Galérie d'Apollon at the Louvre.

In London at the end of May 1911, the American financier was presented to the new King, George V, and the next day went to Belfast with J. Bruce Ismay, president of the IMM and chairman of the White Star line, for the launching of the 46,000-ton RMS *Titanic*.

In June, he took Charles Lanier to Kiel for a German-American yacht race. At lunch on board the Kaiser's yacht, *Hohenzollern,* Morgan gave his host a letter written by Martin Luther to Charles V, the sixteenth-century Holy Roman Emperor, which he had bought for $25,000 the previous spring. "Emperor very pleased," reported Lanier, "and presented to Mr. Morgan the decoration of the Red Eagle—a high honor." The Americans won the yacht race, and the Kaiser gave Morgan and Lanier use of a royal railroad car for the return trip to Calais.

In London in July, Morgan ordered himself a claret-colored Rolls-Royce with a six-cylinder, 50-horsepower engine, custom-equipped with an electric cigar lighter, silver flower vases, mother-of-pearl trays, brass fittings, a Frodsham clock, hat racks, velvet carpets, leather hassocks, silk curtains, a long trumpet horn, and "JPM" on the doors. The cost came to £1,455 ($7,275). He liked it so much, when it was delivered to him in London the following spring, that he ordered an exact duplicate sent to New York, and gave a third to his friend Lewis Cass Ledyard for Christmas.

Also in July of 1911, Morgan embarked on a new romance, with Lady Victoria Sackville. He had visited Knole, her uncle's estate in Kent, with Fanny in 1876, but did not meet Victoria herself until 1900. After that, she had often come to see his collections at Princes Gate. The illegitimate daughter of the Honorable Lionel Sackville-West and a Spanish dancer named Pepita, Victoria had been educated in a French convent, served as her father's hostess when he headed the British Legation in Washington in the 1880s, and married her cousin, another Lionel Sackville-West, in 1890.* For about ten years she and her husband "adored" each other, she later wrote. They had a daughter, Vita, and divided their time between London and Knole, the complex of gray stone buildings covering six acres that Lionel inherited from his father. Given to the Sackvilles by Queen Elizabeth I, it was the largest house in England still in private hands. It had seven courtyards, a hundred chimneys, crenellated turrets, four-hundred-year-old gardens, vast parklands, galleries hung with ancestral portraits, dozens of tapestries, a Poet's Parlour (where Pope, Dryden, and Congreve had dined with Charles Sackville, sixth Earl of Dorset), a King's Bedroom (James I), heraldic leopards everywhere, hothouses, a carpenter's shop, and a forge. Vita, who once met up with a stag taking shelter from the cold in the Great Hall, called it a medieval town.

The estate yielded an income of about £13,000 a year, which was enough to maintain Knole but not to support the Sackvilles' expensive tastes. Finding that Lionel had more interest in sporting expeditions than in managing his property, Victoria took over the family finances. She speculated on the Stock Exchange (probably on advice from male friends), modernized the running of Knole, and opened a shop on South Audley Street called Spealls, which sold candles, stationery, and sachets. When, after a decade of marriage, Lionel's affections began to wander, she turned to a series of older men. According to her grandson, Nigel Nicolson, "she made a corner in millionaires and lonely elderly artists." Her admirers were said to include Rudyard Kipling, Lord Kitchener, W. W. Astor, Auguste Rodin, Sir Edward Lutyens, Gordon Selfridge, Cecil Spring-Rice, Sir John Murray Scott, Henry Ford—and Morgan. Spring-Rice told her: "You are an accomplished mistress in love. You play with it and use it and manage it, like a seagull in the wind, on which he floats but is never carried away."†

Lady Sackville was forty-nine when she took up with Morgan in the summer of 1911, and still quite beautiful, with flawless skin, blue eyes, and masses of

---

* A famous political scandal forced Victoria's father to leave Washington in 1888. A man who signed himself Charles Murchison and claimed to be English wrote from California to ask the British minister which candidate in the upcoming U.S. election would be better for England. Sackville-West foolishly replied that he favored the incumbent Democrat, Cleveland, for a second term. "Murchison" turned out to be a Republican, and the minister's letter was leaked to the press ten days before the election: BRITISH LION'S PAW THRUST INTO AMERICAN POLITICS, declared the headlines, and the State Department demanded Sackville-West's recall. Victoria's father became the second Lord Sackville when his brother, Mortimer, died a month later. He held the title until his own death in 1908, at which point the younger Lionel and Victoria became Lord and Lady Sackville.

† Spring-Rice, a British diplomat and close friend of Theodore Roosevelt's, wrote the lyrics to "I Vow to Thee My Country," which became the favorite hymn of Diana, Princess of Wales, and was played at her wedding and funeral.

softly curling dark hair drawn up in a thick knot; loose, it fell almost to her knees. Speaking French-accented English, this "accomplished mistress in love" was also vain and self-dramatizing. She made up legends about Knole as if its legitimately grand heritage were not enough, wrote out her admirers' compliments, endearments, and entire conversations, and was given to exclaiming in her diary, *"Quel roman est ma vie!"* Her daughter preferred Lionel, and later described Victoria as "ruthless and completely unanalytical"—also "adorable . . . tiresome . . . wayward . . . capricious, and thoroughly spoilt; but her charm and real inward gaiety enabled her to carry it all off."

Victoria's principal beau in the first decade of the twentieth century was Sir John Murray Scott, the wealthy bachelor-trustee of the Wallace Collection at Hertford House. Their intimate friendship had grown out of a shared appreciation of beautiful things and her appreciation of his ample bank accounts. It probably did not include sex. Nicolson thought his grandmother "enjoyed adulation, but in her middle age was repelled by physical lust."

Scott—whom Vita nicknamed "Seery" because his French servants called him "Seer John"—gave Victoria about $400,000 over the course of ten years, and made generous provision for her in his will. Her husband encouraged this profitable connection, handling the negotiations when Seery paid for a Sackville house in Mayfair. The "capricious" Victoria fought constantly with her patron, however, and in 1911 he was threatening to cut her out of the will: "it would be a terrible thing for you," he warned, "if I were to die suddenly and you were to find all your hopes shattered."

Her precarious economic balance had already been thrown off when Lloyd George, the new Liberal Chancellor of the Exchequer, put through a budget in 1910 that sharply increased inheritance, land, and income taxes—in order, he said, to "wage implacable warfare against poverty and squalidness."* Winston Churchill, president of the Board of Trade, supported what the Liberal press called "the People's Budget." Conservatives denounced it as revolutionary and socialist, and London bankers warned Prime Minister H. H. Asquith that it would cripple business, employment, and wages. It had an immediate effect on landed gentry such as the Sackvilles, who early in 1911 determined to evade the death duties and raise cash by selling off some of their heirlooms.

The first item to go was a Gainsborough portrait of *Miss Linley and her Brother*, sold to a dealer in February for £36,000. "Alas! Miss Linley is gone!" mourned Victoria in her diary: "We suppose some American will buy it eventually—alas, alas!" The American who bought it in London that spring was

---

* Estates worth more than £1 million would be taxed at 25 percent, a supertax would be imposed on incomes over £5,000, and a 20 percent land tax levied on the unearned gain in value when land changed hands.

Morgan. When Victoria saw him at a party in July, she avoided him "most carefully," she noted, "as we have got tapestries to sell, and I did not want him to think I was running after him." Fluent in the language of covert glances and studied disregard, she was all innocent surprise when he followed her to her car and said (according to her): "Why did you not tell me direct & not through dealers that you had some heirlooms to sell!? I *must* see you—Give your own time and come. You know that I have always taken great interest in you so you must come and tell me your troubles."

Three days later Lady Sackville called at Princes Gate, and recorded the experience in her diary. She found it "rather a shock" to be ushered into the room where *Miss Linley* was hung, but thought the painting had been overcleaned and "lost its mellow look, so I did not feel as miserable as I might have." Her host kept her waiting for over an hour while he met with the Crown Prince of Sweden—he came in at one point to ask her not to be impatient, and gave her the catalogue of his Chinese porcelains to read. Finally free, he showed her into the room in which he kept his miniatures, with a view of the gardens, and settled her on a sofa. Now, he asked, why did she want to sell? The Lloyd George taxes, she explained.

Morgan: "Damn Lloyd George! What a shame to spoil a place like Knole and you who have taken so much trouble about it all. I want to help you. What have you got to get rid of?"

Lady S: "Tapestries."

JPM: "I don't want any tapestries; let me come down to Knole and look around."

Lady S: "No, Mr. Morgan, we have nothing else to sell; it is a case of take it or leave it."

He considered for a few moments, reported his guest, then said he would take the tapestries, "to help you, as I have always had the greatest admiration and esteem for you all at Knole." How much did she want for them?

Negotiation being first cousin to flirtation, Lady Sackville was an expert. Though she had an offer of £40,000 for twenty-nine tapestries and £10,000 for two seventeenth-century carpets, she coolly informed Morgan that the figures were £45,000 and £20,000, and that she had the offer in her pocket: would he care to see it?

Morgan said, "No, I trust what you say and I'll take your tapestries and your 2 carpets for £65,000."

He had just agreed to pay $325,000 for objects he had not seen. He did not, however, take much risk with this purchase: the provenance of the Knole treasures was gilt-edged, and buying directly from the family avoided dealers' prices and fees. Lady Sackville congratulated him on having made the best bargain of his life, claiming that dealers would have charged him £100,000.

When he rose to show her out, saying again how glad he was to be able to help, she asked him to put the agreement in writing. He obligingly wrote out £65,000 payable within a year (she happened to have brought stationery), but warned that he could not pay at once, as he was "quite dry." Then he walked her to the door. There, she reported, "to my utter astonishment, he folded me in his arms and said I hope you don't mind, but I feel such respect & affection for you. I hope you are happy now over this transaction and go home happy. I respect you so much; you have always behaved so well."

She did not mind, and over the next few weeks this autumnal courtship blossomed. Morgan went to see the tapestries at Knole, and was delighted with a series on the Seven Deadly Sins. Victoria invited him to dinner with former Prime Minister Lord Rosebery, the art collector and critic Sir Hugh Lane, the banker Montagu Norman, Lord Northcliffe, owner of the London *Times*, the French ambassador, and Lady Paget (formerly Minnie Stevens of New York, the mother-in-law of Pauline Whitney). Somehow Victoria managed to escape her other guests for "a long talk with P. Morgan in the garden," she wrote later that night: "he told me many of the bothers of being very rich, that the great thing was to have personality which he has to an infinite degree; he is very *sympathique* to my nature; he said I had done wonders here." She showed him through the house—he wanted to buy several silver dogs from the King's Bedroom and the Great Hall, and so admired a doorstop figure of "Shakespeare" that she gave it to him. "I have never met any one as attractive," she concluded: "one forgets his nose entirely after a few minutes, as his eyes are either twinkling or full of kindness and expression; he said he will be 75 next April! He is full of life and energy, a wonderful man."

In early August, Morgan took delivery of the tapestries and invited Lady Sackville to call on him twice more at Princes Gate. She wailed about *Miss Linley* in her diary but found her host "most friendly": "I really hope I have secured a good friend in him. He does not like everybody & he seems to like me & is most kind & considerate & says charming little compliments which may come from the heart." She resented people coming in with questions and papers for him to sign, and constantly reminded herself that she had no interest in his money.

Reading her diaries is a little like watching a woman make herself up in a mirror when she thinks she is alone: Lady Sackville constantly touches up unattractive spots and strikes poses to catch herself at the best angle. Yet unlike the woman in the mirror, who knows she is improving on reality, Victoria does not admit what she is up to. She lies to her own diary.

She was "really tempted" by Morgan's amber Chinese vases, but "hardly pretended to look at them & hardly admired them, as I hate cadging & he is the last person in the world from whom I shd like to cadge, because he has been so nice & spontaneously generous about the tapestries." Though disappointed that he had not produced the £65,000 check, she professed: "I *hate* talking about money with Mr. Morgan or the Stock Exchange, or anything that is not art or friendship, pure & simple."

He was about to leave for New York. She sent him a note asking for her "Shakespeare" doorstop back (it had been a loan), and offering to *buy* some of his amber Chinese vases. She also asked for a photograph of him, "looking at me full face." She wanted "no money no presents," just "your friendship"—and promised never to become *"une femme gênante"* [troublesome]. I know and understand your nature very well because I have so much sympathy for you and have always had it."

He sent her a wire from the SS *Olympic* at Queenstown. *"Ces petites choses là font plaisir,"* she reflected, *"venant d'un homme aussi occupé"* [These little things give pleasure, coming from such a busy man]."

In Paris that fall, Anne Morgan lunched with the Sackvilles and Sir John Murray Scott. Fanny had Lady Sackville to tea. By the end of the year, Morgan had paid for the Knole tapestries.

———

The combination of Lloyd George's death duties, the Payne-Aldrich Act eliminating the American import duty on old works of art, and Morgan's sense of mortality finally prompted him to begin transferring his collections to the United States. In November 1911 he told William Loeb, Jr., the chief customs officer for the Port of New York, that he planned to bring the "extensive art collection which I have been gathering during the past forty years" across the Atlantic. Since all the works were more than one hundred years old, they should be entitled to free entry under the tariff law, but he had two requests regarding procedure. First, the law required certification from sellers as to the objects' age and value, but Morgan did not have invoices for most of what he had bought; he proposed to furnish a complete inventory, and asked that the requirement of sellers' certificates be waived. Second, he planned to have the collections sent directly to the Metropolitan Museum. He hoped the prospect of exhibiting them all together would induce New York City officials to fund the building of a new wing. In the meantime, the objects would have to be stored indefinitely, and Morgan proposed to avoid the "almost certain loss and injury" that would result from having customs inspectors open and examine shipment cases in New York by hiring at his own expense a U.S. customs officer to inspect the art works as they were packed in London.

"I feel justified in asking that this course be taken," he explained, "because this collection is really a matter of great public and educational interest, and a large part of the articles could not be replaced if lost or injured, and the Metropolitan Museum of Art, which is specially concerned in having the arrangement, is a public institution upon which many millions of dollars have been spent by the city Government. . . . If your examiner wishes anything further than his own judgment upon the question whether these articles are over 100 years old, I suppose that after my long experience I am qualified to testify, as an expert, and my opinion would be sustained by the fact that I was willing to pay for the articles, and that in practically every case I took the advice of competent experts who were satisfied of their genuineness."

Art and legal authorities might have rejected Morgan's offer to testify in his own defense, but for the most part he *had* sought the advice of scholarly experts, the objects *were* old, and the collection *was* "a matter of great public and educational interest." Mr. Loeb reported on these proposals to Washington, and Treasury Secretary Franklin MacVeagh approved both parts of the plan. He wrote to Morgan: "I am greatly interested as a citizen in the coming of your great collections, and it will give me sincere satisfaction to render all permissible official assistance to importations by which the entire country is to be eminently benefited."

At the end of 1911, Morgan commissioned the French art dealer Jacques Seligmann to supervise the packing and transatlantic shipping of the paintings, miniatures, furniture, silver, sculpture, and other objects from Princes Gate, the remainder of the Hoentschel collection from Paris, paintings borrowed by the National Gallery, and everything Morgan had lent to the South Kensington Museum (Queen Victoria at the end of her life had directed that its name be changed to the Victoria and Albert)—in all, several million dollars' worth of bronzes, ivories, majolica, enamels, porcelains, metalwork, and jewelry. Though they would be sent to the Metropolitan, the collections were not designated a gift. Morgan had not decided about their ultimate disposition.

The process of packing up and shipping the art to New York took an entire year. Morgan ordered the bronzes on loan at the V&A to go first, to delay the dismantling of his rooms at Princes Gate. In January 1912, as objects began to disappear from British exhibitions, the London press blamed the "disastrous" removal of Morgan's "magnificent" collections on "official shortsightedness." Hercules Read at the British Museum and the independent scholar J. H. Fitzhenry wrote letters to the *Times* insisting that Morgan had always intended to take his collections to New York, had made "princely" gifts to British institutions, had been completely satisfied with the consideration shown him by English authorities, and wanted to protect his heirs from the "very large sum" that would be due on his estate if he left his collections in England.

As promised, the U.S. Customs Office sent an art specialist named Michael Nathan to conduct the inspections in London—he told *The New York Times* that no amount of money could now buy Mr. Morgan's collections—and the first shipment crossed the Atlantic safely in February 1912. Morgan insisted on using only White Star ships.

Everything was proceeding according to plan when Nathan unexpectedly returned to the United States at the end of March. Morgan ordered all shipments stopped, and asked Seligmann to meet him at Aix in mid-April.

On Monday, April 15, a shocking piece of news reached him at the spa. "Have just heard fearful rumor about *Titanic* with iceberg without any particulars," he wired Jack: "Hope for God sake not true." His partners kept him posted by cable. The reports were wildly contradictory at first. Everyone was saved. Everyone had drowned. The *Titanic* was unsinkable. The *Titanic* had sunk. White Star vice president Philip Franklin announced in New York Monday night that the ship had gone down at 2:20 A.M., with a "horrible loss of life."

On Wednesday, the seventeenth, Morgan's partners and family sent subdued greetings for his seventy-fifth birthday. He wired his thanks, "but greatly upset by loss Titanic"—"my heart . . . very heavy." A *New York Times* correspondent sent to Aix to convey the newspaper's respects found the financier sunburned and hale after his sojourn in Egypt, and inundated with birthday messages from royal heads of state, but "exceedingly grieved at the appalling disaster." Morgan had no comment for the press, saying that at a moment of such public excitement he preferred to wait for an accurate report of the full story.

Anne Morgan joined the *Titanic* relief committee in New York, and met the survivors as they reached port. More than fifteen hundred people had died, among them Colonel John Jacob Astor; George Widener and his son, Harry; Mr. and Mrs. Isador Straus; Taft's military aide, Archie Butt; the artist Frank Millet, executive secretary of the American Academy in Rome; and hundreds who did not have famous names. "JP has been keeping all wires hot," Belle reported to Berenson a week after the event, "& I have gotten out of bed & dressed several nights in order to send him answers."

The shipping trust had been a financial fiasco for years. Now it was a human catastrophe as well. Although most of the officers and crew gave their lives to save women and children, IMM president J. Bruce Ismay had jumped into a lifeboat, and his survival seemed an outrage. The Senate immediately opened an investigation. Jack cabled his father on the nineteenth: "Newspapers, which are unspeakably bad, and Congress which is worse, seem to have made up their mind . . . [Ismay] is to blame for whole thing." To the elder Morgan, the treatment of Ismay sounded "infernally brutal."

The U.S. naval expert Admiral Mahan said that Ismay could not be held responsible for the collision, but the shortage of lifeboats meant that "so long as there was a soul that could be saved, the obligation lay on Mr. Ismay that that one person and not he should have been in the boat." Brooks Adams went further, claiming that Ismay *was* responsible for the captain's reckless speed, the lack of lifeboats, the crew's lack of discipline: "In the face of all this he saves himself, leaving fifteen hundred men and women to perish," Adams wrote to Senator Francis Newlands. "I know of nothing at once so cowardly and so brutal in recent history. The one thing he could have done was to prove his honesty and his sincerity by giving his life. I hope that you gentlemen will make it plain that such men cannot be kept in control of passenger ships if we can help it."

The Senate's investigation, and another by the British Board of Trade, found an appalling series of human and technical errors, but brought no charges against Ismay or the IMM. Shipowners in the United States and Britain were protected by limited liability laws, and private damage claims against White Star amounting to $16 million were eventually settled out of court in 1916 for $664,000. Ismay had been planning to retire before the loss of the *Titanic*. Now, he wanted to stay on and fight back, but he had become an unlimited liability. That fall, the Morgan partners firmly eased him out.*

———

The Treasury Department sent a customs agent named Lorenzo Chance to replace Mr. Nathan, and the packing and shipping of Morgan's art collections, supervised by Seligmann, resumed. By the end of the year, 351 cases had been stored, unopened, in the Metropolitan basement.

Morgan stayed at Aix longer than usual that spring. He went to Venice at the end of April for the dedication of a new Campanile di San Marco, which he had helped pay for (the old one collapsed in 1902), then returned to the spa for an additional fortnight. In mid-May he traveled up to London and phoned Lady

---

* The death of Harry Elkins Widener on the *Titanic* provided an unexpected benefit for Harvard. Looking to build a new library, the university had asked Jack in 1910 whether his father might be inclined "to help us out on a big scale." Jack said he never approached his father about financial gifts, but over the next two years he conferred regularly with Harvard president A. Lawrence Lowell about the project, discussing such potential donors as Frick, Carnegie, Mrs. Russell Sage, Peter Widener, and Isador Straus ("whose people are very high class," Jack wrote, "and who might help us with the Hebrew fraternity here").

In February of 1912, Jack reported that Joseph Choate was opposed to asking Carnegie, since the College was "too dignified to have a Carnegie Library" and would not want "inevitably attached to Harvard for all time Mr. Carnegie's name." Early in April, Jack suggested that Bishop Lawrence "speak to Father about the Library"—it would help to say that George Baker might contribute, as "he likes to do things with that gentleman."

Two weeks later, Harry Widener drowned. A graduate of Harvard ('07) and a serious book collector, this grandson of Peter Widener had just bought a 1598 edition of Francis Bacon's *Essaies* from Bernard Quaritch in London, remarking that he planned to take it with him on the *Titanic*—"if I am shipwrecked it will go with me." His mother reached New York with the other survivors on April 19. The Philadelphia book and art dealer A.S.W. Rosenbach told Belle Greene that Mrs. Widener had known "nothing of the fate of her husband and Harry until informed of it on the dock. The shock was overwhelming as she thought they were in another boat." That summer, Eleanor Elkins Widener agreed to build Harvard's library in memory of her son. The architect, whom she designated as a condition of the gift, was Horace Trumbauer.

Sackville as soon as he arrived—she was thrilled. He asked her to call on him the following day.

Sir John Murray Scott had died in January without, in the end, cutting Victoria out of his will. He left her £150,000 in cash, various valuable *objets,* and the contents of his house on the Rue Laffitte in Paris, estimated to be worth £350,000. His family was contesting the will, charging the Sackvilles (whom they called "the Locusts") with having used undue influence to alienate his affections. The case would not come to trial until 1913. If she won the lawsuit, Lady Sackville would have Seery's Paris collection to sell, but in the summer of 1912 she was still in financial straits.

She told her diary when Morgan phoned in May that she hated "to appear nice and friendly to get things out of him, as I don't really want to. He respects me & I like being a friend of his & to know well such a great & clever man."

When she arrived at Princes Gate on May 20, he was in the midst of meetings about the China loan, but set aside half an hour for her. "He came in like a whirlwind & crushed me," she reported breathlessly, "saying he had longed for this moment to see me again . . . he had told nobody of his return but wanted to see me at once. Nothing could be more affectionate than the welcome he gave me, and I went away with mixed feelings of friendship & apprehension of what may follow from this great friendship, as I am so straight."

At home, she told her husband she was thinking of putting a stop to the whole thing, but "L. made me change my mind," saying it would be unkind to a man who had asked her "to become the friend of his old age." Since Morgan was seventy-five, both Sackvilles apparently thought him "safe," and Victoria had deftly secured Lionel's permission for another lucrative dalliance. "So now *le sort en est jeté!* [the die is cast]," she exclaimed: "I can think of nothing else; that man has such marvellous personality & attraction for me."

Two days later, Morgan called on her in Mayfair punctually at five, "beaming with joy to be quietly alone with me." He told her several times (she reported) that he had cared for her "for ever so long" but had not dared tell her. He remembered all the occasions on which they had met, and referring back to their talk in her garden the previous July, said "how much he was in love that day & that I must have seen it or guessed it (but I really did not!)." He promised to care for her even if she got "ill, ugly, or an invalid"—and he talked of Memie. As he recalled that he had only been married to her for sixty days (actually, four months), "two great tears came in his kind eyes."

Then without missing a beat—although it is not clear whether the elision is an artifact of Morgan's narrative or Victoria's—"He said there was nothing in the world like the sort of affection he had for me & he felt I cared for him not for his money or things and he had watched that for a long time in me. (How true it is, as it is the man himself who attracts me so. . . .)" Intimacy established, he made himself at home, smoking (with her permission) a big cigar, and taking "a little snooze." He told her he was "*very very* shy with strangers (on acct of his poor nose, which I do not mind a bit)," asked her about Lionel and Vita and Seery, and made a date to bring Senator Aldrich to see Knole. After he left, Victoria reflected on how "touchingly loving" he had been: "I can't get over his rough gentleness & his affectionate little ways. . . . Rue Laffitte subject [i.e., the lawsuit over Seery's estate] hardly discussed today."

Each party to this elaborate *folie à deux* played out the flirtation while calmly pursuing more practical ends: ready cash on one side, authentic treasures on the other. It is hard to say which half of the well-matched pair comes off worse—Victoria in her silly narcissism, feigned innocence, and spurious claims of financial disinterest, or Morgan in his (hardly unique) professions of undying love, crocodile tears over Memie, and eagerness to believe that Victoria was not after his money.

He was "most amusing" the day he brought Aldrich to Knole, reported Lady S.—"Vita says she liked him immensely; he . . . talked such a lot & sat down on all the best chairs! & ordered us about & went where he liked. . . . As he did not want Senator A. to notice anything" about their secret, he spent little time with her alone. He *did* want two paintings by Hoppner, the best Persian carpet in her Reynolds Room, some tapestries from the Venetian Room, and the silver dogs—"but he won't get them." When he hurried off to finish up a £35 million bond deal ("What a wonderful personality!"), Aldrich stayed behind to see the gardens.

Morgan returned the next day at four, alone. "I made him send away his big Rolls-Royce which he ordered back at 5:30. People must not notice his visits." Bringing up Seery's will, Victoria asked whether, if she became rich, she could buy *Miss Linley* back, since she missed the picture terribly.

Her seasoned admirer was not about to be hornswoggled by a pair of pretty eyes: "I don't think, dear, I shld like to part with it now."

Lady S: "Then do you like Miss Linley better than you like me?"

JPM: "No, dear, I don't; and I shall think about your proposal; but I hate parting with her."

Victoria crossed the room to pick up a book. When she returned, Morgan took her hand and promised not to take the painting to America. It would not go to his son, he said, or to the Metropolitan; it would never leave his hands except to come into hers. She silently held out the book—it was a biography of him—opened to a passage that said Mr. Morgan never breaks his word.*

---

* Carl Hovey, the editor of *Metropolitan Magazine*, had written a series of articles on Morgan, and published them as a book in 1911. When the publisher, Sturgis & Walton, advertised the volume as an "authorized" biography, Morgan complained: "As you know," he wrote, "this statement is false, as I have never seen the person who wrote the book nor had anything whatever to do with it." Hovey's portrait was, on the whole, flattering. Belle Greene probably read the book aloud to Morgan, for in 1912 she recorded some of his comments in the margins of her copy.

On the subject of his art, he asked her whether she thought it better than the Wallace Collection, which had been managed until recently by Seery: "Of course it is better," she agreeably replied. When he told her he had been religious all his life, and firmly "believed," she was surprised. He parried a suggestion that she come to America, saying it would be "too dangerous"—"He is very careful not to get me talked about." Then "the big cigar came out and he tells me little phrases now & then, so brusquely and so nicely, too, and holds my hand with so much affection and said he wd never care for me in any way I shld not approve of, that he was very sorry to be so old (and yet he is so vigorous) but I was the one woman he loved & wld never change." She urged herself not to "talk about Miss Linley or money with him. I hate it. Our friendship must be free from any sordid motive."

At a dinner given by the Whitelaw Reids a few days later, Morgan sat with Lady Sackville all evening, and surreptitiously held her hand. The whole party seemed to revolve around him, she reported. When the conversation turned to love, one of the guests announced that no one ever stayed in love with the same person for more than two years—at which Morgan shot Lady Sackville a look, and said: "On the contrary, when it is sincere, love increases all the time, especially if much sentiment is mixed up with it."

She noted that night, "He deplores all the time being so old, but I don't mind."

They saw each other every few days. When he asked her what people thought of him, and whether she considered his manner rough and brusque, she replied: "Yes, *very*, but corrected by great kindness; and that made him smile." He often alluded to his death, especially in connection with shipping his art to New York, a subject that made Victoria "tremble for Miss Linley. I must screw up my courage & speak to him about her returning to Knole some day! But how horrid for me to ask for any favour from him. But I *must*."

Once she had secured Morgan's affection, she concentrated on getting *Miss Linley* back. Her septuagenarian lover put her off by saying that returning the painting would give them away: "he wants to protect me against gossip and scandal of which he has a morbid fear; he says, [']I am so much discussed that we must take every precaution.[']" In the days of his confidential correspondence with Jim Goodwin and his engagement to Fanny, Morgan's sense that the world's eyes were trained on his romantic interests signaled his youthful self-importance; now, the world's real avidity for such news helped him keep Lady Sackville at bay. She offered to buy the Gainsborough when she got her legacy from Seery's estate. That, he said, would not be for a long time. Perhaps he might give it to her anyway, she calculated in private: "I see how utterly devoted he is to me and he knows that I never make up to him for any presents etc. I have certainly become very dear to him"—then reminded herself, "after all, his friendship is much more precious than Miss L."

———

Morgan went off on *Corsair* in late June with Teddy Grenfell, the Markoes, and the Morton Patons, to attend the Kiel regatta at the invitation of Kaiser Wilhelm. Grenfell found the German Emperor "most attractive & manly & up in everything . . . & does not show the mailed fist. He turned up [on board *Corsair*] at 9:45 this morning as we were finishing breakfast which was rather disturbing." On June 26, Morgan sailed with the Kaiser in a five-hour race, which they won by twenty seconds: "They got so excited in a tight place rounding the buoy," reported Grenfell, "that the Emperor & old JPM were hauling on the main sheet with the crew like boys & sweating at every pore. . . . As the Emperor had lost 7 races before, he looked on JPM as a mascotte & was as elated as a child."

At the end of this trip, Grenfell reflected: "To an artist of humour, the games of JPM & his surroundings wd provide endless food. He is the most thoughtful of hosts & though appearing not to notice things, he sees everything & a chance remark with a twinkle in his eye makes one find the old fox has not missed a trick in the game. He is splendid & at 75 years of age can tire out the youngest."

That fall, the Kaiser sent Morgan a life-size marble bust of himself in full military decorations. "Unaccountably," noted Satterlee later with no apparent sarcasm, "it disappeared in 1914."

From Germany, in July, Morgan went to Rome. He had transferred title to his properties on the Janiculum to the American Academy, and raised money for a building, designed by McKim's firm, to house the fellows, a library, and a small museum. He turned the soil for the new building.

While he was on the Continent, Lady Sackville took friends to see his silver at Princes Gate. She found most of the art being packed up, and learned from the butler that even *Miss Linley* was under "marching orders" for America: "I could have fainted," she told her diary. Instead of fainting, she refused to see Morgan when he returned to town. Running into him at a Court Ball—he said he had come hoping to find her there—"I asked him not to call again, which seemed to distress him; but I know in my heart of hearts that . . . goodbye in public is much better." She promised to write. "I could see he was extremely *gêné* [upset] . . . but we parted the *very best* of friends. I wore green dress & emeralds."

In mid-July, Morgan sailed for New York on the *Titanic*'s sister, the *Olympic*, taking with him the *Duchess of Devonshire* and several other paintings. Just before he left, he sent Victoria a book about his life (no doubt the Hovey volume, which she already had), inscribed "To Lady Sackville from J. Pierpont Morgan with his affectionate regards." She concluded: "So this judgment is closed and we remain the very best of *friends*, bless him."

She never saw him again. A few days after Morgan left London, an artist named Philip Lazlo came to Knole for lunch. He wanted to paint Morgan's portrait, and asked Victoria to intercede. She refused, she noted in her diary, "as he wants to do my old friend's nose true to life!! which is really an exaggerated idea of faithfulness to his art."*

The painters who did get commissions to immortalize Morgan's features knew better than to display any such "exaggerated faithfulness" to art. A German portraitist named Fedor Encke produced an idealized image in 1903 that gave Morgan more hair, larger eyes, a smaller nose, and darker mustache than he actually had, taking ten years off his age—only the eyebrows and clothes look true to life. (The painting is now at the Metropolitan Club in New York.)

John Singer Sargent agreed to paint Morgan's portrait a few years later, then changed his mind, saying in answer to an inquiry from the banker's partners in 1909 that he had "entirely given up portrait painting, which I hate. I hope Mr. Morgan will let me off, he probably knows I have refused commissions for two years past."† The artist had in fact sworn to a friend in 1907: "No more paughtraits. . . . I abhore and abjure them and hope never to do another especially of the Upper Classes." He made exceptions—notably for his good friend Henry James (1913) and John D. Rockefeller (1915).

By far the best-known portrait of Morgan came about by chance. When the financier would not sit still for the Encke painting in 1903, the artist's friend

---

* Morgan left *Miss Linley* to Jack in his estate. It was eventually sold, and now belongs to the Sterling and Francine Clark Institute, Williamstown, Mass. Lady Sackville won the lawsuit brought by the Scotts in June 1913, partly by virtue of her star performance in the witness box. At one point she scolded a cross-examining lawyer, "You don't seem to realize, Mr. Smith, that Knole is bigger than Hampton Court." The judge told the members of the jury that if the "influence" Victoria had exercised over Sir John was that of friendship, "the influence arising out of a community of tastes, out of the affinity of natures . . . it was perfectly legitimate, and you ought to say so in your verdict." They did. The judgment made Lady Sackville rich. She got £150,000 outright, and sold off the contents of the Paris house for £270,000. "This," observed her grandson, "was perhaps the only shameful part of the affair, for Seery (as she well knew) had hoped she would use his 'fine things' to enrich the Knole collection, not sell them to provide her with pocket money."

† Sargent had done a portrait of Jack's wife, Jessie, in the spring of 1905. He asked her to bring a box of dresses to the first sitting so that he could decide what looked best in his studio's light, and set up a mirror in which she could watch him paint. She found it "thrilling. . . . He is very agreeable. I had 13 sittings." As the portrait neared completion, Jack asked Sargent whether, "as you are an American, it might be possible that your pictures could come in to America free of duty." A few weeks later, the banker urged the artist "to do whatever is necessary at the Consulate to see that the picture comes through free of duty, and I shall be very much obliged to you for all your trouble." The portrait, for which Jack paid £1,050—about $5,000—is now at the Pierpont Morgan Library.

Alfred Stieglitz, leader of the avant-garde Photo-Secession group, recommended that the young Edward Steichen take a photograph for Encke to work from. Steichen agreed to do the job if he could also make a negative for himself.

On the appointed day he set up his shot with a janitor in the banker's chair. When Morgan arrived and assumed his usual pose, Steichen quickly snapped the first exposure. Then, putting a new plate into the camera, he suggested that his subject slightly move his head and hands. Morgan complied, but said he was uncomfortable. Steichen asked him to find a natural pose. According to Steichen, Morgan then settled on his own into the posture the photographer had proposed, "but his expression had sharpened and his body posture became tense, possibly a reflex of his irritation at the suggestion I had made. I saw that a dynamic self-assertion had taken place, whatever its cause, and I quickly made the second exposure, saying 'Thank you, Mr. Morgan,' as I took the plate holder out of the camera.

"He said, 'Is that all?'

" 'Yes, sir,' I answered.

"He snorted a reply, "I like you, young man. I think we'll get along first-rate together.' Then he clapped his large hat on his massive head, took up his big cigar, and stormed out of the room." On his way to the elevator, Morgan peeled off five $100 bills and told Encke to give them to "that young man."

Steichen claimed that in the studio he saw only Morgan's riveting eyes, and did not notice the "huge, more or less deformed, sick, bulbous nose" until he developed the negatives. He retouched the one he had taken for Encke. On the second shot, his own, he made the nose just "a little more vague," and removed "spots that were repulsive."

The differences between the two photographs have to do with more than Morgan's nose. In the first, "official" head-and-shoulders shot, Morgan looks like a big ship about to embark under triumphant sails. The light picks up the rich textures of his jacket, silk cravat, starched white collar, and gold watch and chain. His face, half in shadow, has an imposing force, and with his body angled slightly to the right, head left, he gazes past the camera—we can't really catch his eye. When Steichen showed him the proofs, Morgan liked this one immediately, and ordered a dozen prints.

The second exposure, taken from another angle, captures the "dynamic self-assertion" Steichen was after. Unsettled by the change in posture, Morgan seems to have puffed out his feathers like an angry eagle. His eyes glare straight at the viewer with terrifying intensity, eyebrows arching, jaw tense. As his body disappears in the blackness, the light catches only his head, the watch and chain, and his hand on the gleaming metal arm of his chair: this last detail looks like the blade of a dagger, and Morgan appears about to stride out of the frame slashing—the ruthless capitalist pirate of popular myth.

According to Steichen, the banker took one look at this picture, pronounced it "Terrible," and tore it up. The photographer was understandably furious. He sent Morgan twelve copies of the first shot, and made an exquisite print of the second. Eventually he gave the latter to Stieglitz, who published it in a special "Steichen Supplement" of his magazine, *Camera Work,* in 1906 (which helped launch Steichen's career), and three years later exhibited the original at his gallery, "291" Fifth Avenue. Belle Greene saw it there in the fall of 1909.

She considered it the finest portrait of Morgan she had ever seen, and asked Stieglitz for copies: "I think Mr. Steichen and yourself are to be much congratulated," she wrote, "on the impetus you have given to photography in America." She apparently changed her Big Chief's mind about the "dagger" photo as well, since Morgan offered to buy the original for $5,000. Stieglitz refused to sell, and Steichen kept the banker waiting three years for an order of new prints—"my rather childish way of getting even with [him] for tearing up that first proof."*

Photographs did not satisfy Morgan's desire for "the real thing," however, and after Sargent turned him down in 1909, the banker commissioned a Peruvian named Carlos Baca-Flor to paint another official portrait. Since Baca-Flor, like Encke, could not get his subject to sit still, he also worked from the Steichen photo (in *Camera Work*). Depicting Morgan in a stately academic pose, with gleaming black satin lapels, one hand resting on leather-bound books, the other hooked in his waistcoat pocket, the painting is utterly empty and stiff. An aspiring young artist named George Biddle described it as "built up with many timid brush strokes—like the encrusted Christmas cards which had a renewed vogue some years ago—until it had achieved an undulating papier-maché vulgarity, the more incredible for its very lifelike unreality."

---

* Belle, of course, became friends with both men. Steichen loved writing out her name in full, "Belle da Costa Greene, for it sounds great"—which was even more of a compliment than he intended, since she had made some of it up. Stieglitz in 1914 asked her to contribute an essay to a special issue of *Camera Work* on "291." He was inviting people to whom it "seems to have meant something very much out of the ordinary," he explained, "to put down their *feelings.* . . . You often gave me to understand that the little place did mean something to you. . . . I am not looking for any personal adulation. Nor am I desirous of any theorizing. I am primarily after the recording of a few real heart-beats, if there be any heart-beats for the little garret. If you would, in as few words as possible, put down on paper what '291' meant to you I would appreciate it immensely." The issue (XLVII, July 1914), was published in January 1915, titled "What is 291?" The respondents included Mabel Dodge, Hutchins Hapgood, Djuna Barnes, Charles Demuth, Marsden Hartley, Arthur Dove, Eugene Meyer, Jr., Agnes Meyer, Abraham Walkowitz, Man Ray, Edward Steichen, John Marin, Francis Picabia, and Belle Greene.

Biddle, brought by a friend to have tea with Morgan at his library, where the recently completed portrait hung, later recalled that for a while "the great bear of a financier sat staring at his effigy, which stared back dully at the original." Then the original announced: " 'It is the finest portrait he has ever painted, and Baca-Flor is the most significant portrait painter since Romney.'

"Never," concluded Biddle, "did a great man open his guard more completely to an art student's scorn."

Morgan paid Baca-Flor $56,000 for this canvas and two replicas—he gave one to the Metropolitan Museum and one to the Wadsworth Atheneum in Hartford—and an additional $23,000 to paint portraits of his friends John Bigelow and Joseph Choate. He was not alone in admiring his likeness. President Taft came to the library to see it early in 1910 and went away, Belle told her traveling Chief, "most enthusiastic"—he wanted Baca-Flor to paint him at the White House that spring. A former president of the Stock Exchange pronounced the Morgan canvas "the work of a reincarnated Velasquez," and said no finer piece of portraiture or painting had "been given to the world for 200 years"—to which Belle added a fervent "Amen!" She herself, Henry Walters, and Jack Morgan signed up for sittings.*

———

The most interesting of the writers who drew literary sketches of Morgan during his lifetime are E. M. Forster and Henry James. The art drain that was transferring the contents of ancestral English houses to the collections of American millionaires reached a peak in 1909–10—the value of exported art works that year exceeded £1 million—and the "larger morality" of this international drama fascinated James.

Late in 1909, a British public protest prevented the sale of the Duke of Norfolk's Holbein masterpiece, *The Duchess of Milan,* to Henry Clay Frick. The English raised £72,000 to buy the painting for the National Gallery, and the incident gave James the idea for a play he wrote that fall called *The Outcry.* It was never produced. Two years later he turned it into a novel. Slight, witty, charming (James called it an "inferior little product"), and far more successful

* Three years after the Peruvian "Velasquez" finished his portraits of Morgan, they started to melt. He had mixed a tar-based bitumen into his oils, and loaded the paint so thickly on the canvas that it was highly susceptible to heat. In the summer of 1914, a streak of brown from the coat sleeve ran down over the cuff on the copy at the Met, and the whole surface exuded a sticky sweat. Baca-Flor took the canvases back and tried to restore them, but in 1928 Belle, who had long since revised her opinion of the artist, found the Hartford copy in the "same deplorable condition as all the other portraits of the late Mr. Morgan which were executed by the thoroughly unreliable . . . Baca-Flor." In 1939 Jack Morgan sent the Met a replica, and asked that the original be destroyed.

with the public than his serious late work, it went through five printings within weeks of publication.

James's fine comic sense plays in this novel over questions of *value*—as discerned by the "new" connoisseurship in art, as accruing more to the names of certain artists than to others, as contained (or not) in aristocratic lineage, as measured by large sums of cash, as inherent in intelligence, imaginative perception, and unselfish love.

There is no record of a meeting between Henry James and Pierpont Morgan, but the author often visited Junius at Dover House in the 1880s, usually with Alice Mason, sometimes with his friend Jonathan Sturges, occasionally on his own. He toured the art collections at Princes Gate by invitation in 1906, and visited Morgan's library in New York early in 1911. In *The Outcry* he drew an oblique portrait of Morgan as Breckenridge Bender, a rich American collector with two last names. The physiognomy of this character seems unmistakable, although James pointedly omitted the glaring, overgrown nose and substituted a face remarkable for its *lack* of feature.

Mr. Bender, writes James,

had six feet of stature and an air as of having received benefits at the hand of fortune. Substantial, powerful, easy, he shone as with a glorious cleanness, a supplied and equipped and appointed sanity and security; aids to action that might have figured a pair of very ample wings—wide pinions for the present conveniently folded, but that he would certainly on occasion agitate for great efforts and spread for great flights. These things would have made him quite an admirable, even a worshipful, image of full-blown life and character, had not the affirmation and the emphasis halted in one important particular. Fortune, felicity, nature, the perverse or interfering old fairy at his cradle-side—whatever the ministering power might have been—had simply overlooked and neglected his vast wholly-shaven face. . . . Nothing seemed to have been done for it but what the razor and the sponge, the tooth-brush and the looking-glass could officiously do. . . . It had developed on the lines, if lines they could be called, of the mere scoured and polished and initialled 'mug' rather than to any effect of a composed physiognomy; though we must at the same time add that its wearer carried this featureless disk as with the warranted confidence that might have attended a warning headlight or a glaring motorlamp. The object, however one named it, showed you at least where he was, and most often that he was straight upon you.

Prowling England for treasures, Bender temporizes with the lovely, "hard up" Lady Sandgate, who urges on him Lawrence's portrait of her great-grandmother—"the most beautiful woman of her time," she insists, "and the greatest of all Lawrences." Bender is after bigger game—some "*ideally* expensive thing"—and when he tours Dedborough Place, the country estate of Lady Sandgate's friend Lord Theign, he particularly wants the great *Duchess of Waterbridge* by Joshua Reynolds. Theign, however, refuses to "traffic."

"People *have* trafficked," observes Theign's daughter Lady Grace—the acute Jamesian observer at the story's moral center: "people do; people are trafficking all round."

"Ah," cries her new friend Hugh Crimble, a young art scholar who bears strong resemblances to Roger Fry and to James's friend Hugh Walpole: "that's what deprives me of my rest and, as a lover of our vast and beneficent art-wealth, poisons my waking hours. . . . Precious things are going out of our distracted country at a quicker rate than the very quickest—a century and more ago—of their ever coming in."

England's precious things, Lady Grace points out, don't really belong to England: "I suppose our art-wealth came in—save for those awkward Elgin Marbles!—mainly by purchase too, didn't it? We ourselves largely took it away from somewhere else, didn't we? We didn't *grow* it all."

This pulls Hugh up short for a moment, then: "We grew some of the loveliest flowers—and on the whole to-day the most exposed. Great Gainsboroughs and Sir Joshuas and Romneys and Sargents, great Turners and Constables and old Cromes and Brabazons, form, you'll recognise, a vast garden in themselves. What have we ever for instance more successfully grown than your splendid 'Duchess of Waterbridge'?"

Which brings them to the subject of Mr. Bender. James draws him in caricature—a booming, energetic American with a big checkbook and bigger ideas, who is more interested in what he wants than what he has, and uses native locutions such as "ain't," "I guess," "anyhow," and "hey." The others refer to him as "a money-monster," "a terror," "you dreadful rich thing," "the wretch who bagged Lady Lappington's Longhi," the avatar of "such a conquering horde as invaded the old civilisation, only armed now with huge cheque-books instead of spears and battle-axes." Yet Bender is far less malignant a presence than the brutal and stupid Lord Theign of Dedborough (listen to the names), bloated with an empty sense of his own "noble" value, more willing to sell his daughter than one of his heirlooms.

James describes Bender as "all genial and all sincere," with a "voracious integrity," "always easy, but always, too . . . aware of everything." Bender takes the perceptive measure of Hugh's real intelligence. He displays a "dangerous" knowledge of Dutch painters. And he has a far more expansive sense of value than most of his British counterparts. Discussing a portrait by Moretto of Brescia—which Hugh now thinks may be an exceedingly rare Mantovano—

Grace's repugnant suitor, Lord John, wants to know whether a Mantovano would be "so much greater a value" than a Moretto.*

Hugh asks, "Are you talking of values pecuniary?"

Lord John: "What values are *not* pecuniary?"

"Hugh might, during his hesitation, have been imagined to stand off a little from the question. 'Well, some things have in a higher degree that one, and some have the associational or the factitious, and some the clear artistic.'

" 'And some,' Mr. Bender opined, 'have them *all*—in the highest degree.' "

Bender has a sense of humor about himself. When he asks Hugh how much "higher under the hammer" the picture would come as a Mantovano, Hugh turns to Lord Theign: "Does Mr. Bender mean come to *him,* my lord?"

Theign looks hard at them both—"I don't know *what* Mr. Bender means!"—and turns away.

Bender continues: "Well, I guess I mean that it would come higher to me than to any one! But how *much* higher?"

"How much higher to you?"

"Oh, I can size *that.* How much higher as a Mantovano?"

And when Theign asks why he can't simply make the Moretto as expensive as he likes, Bender sounds positively Jamesian: "Because you can't do violence to *that* master's natural modesty."

Theign finally determines more out of spite than generosity to give the authenticated Mantovano to the National Gallery, and forces Lady Sandgate to donate her Lawrence in kind. Bender goes away empty-handed, having inadvertently effected this happy (for England) outcome. In the "larger morality" of James's drama, he comes off relatively well.

———

Whereas James drew on aspects of Morgan for his fictional Breckenridge Bender, E. M. Forster referred to the financier by name in his 1910 novel, *Howards End.* Roger Fry, who was a friend of Forster's and had recently been dismissed by the Metropolitan Museum, probably served as a source of information, and Virginia Woolf may have as well; but Morgan was a familiar figure in England, and the novelist no doubt had impressions of his own.

The events in *Howards End* turn on matters of money—who has it, who doesn't, how it has shaped England and her empire, what it makes possible in

* James thought he had invented the name—"the Mantuan"—and was embarrassed to learn in 1912 that there was a sixteenth-century artist, Rinaldo Mantovano, whose works were at the National Gallery: "*my* Mantovano was a creature of mere (convincing) fancy," he told the friend who pointed out his mistake, "and this revelation of my not having been as inventive as I supposed rather puts me out!"

the Bloomsbury group's ideal life of humane values and moral imagination, and how cruelly its power can be abused by those who have no such values or imagination. In Forster's portrait of Edwardian England, the wealthy Wilcox men "seemed to have their hands on all the ropes," and they live in a world of "panic and emptiness," "telegrams and anger"—at a far remove from the intellectual Schlegel sisters with their passionate commitment to an ethos of personal relations.

Helen Schlegel, talking with a bank clerk named Leonard Bast whose life has been inadvertently ruined by Mr. Wilcox, is enraged at the rich man's refusal to take responsibility for what he has done. "I believe in personal responsibility. Don't you?," she asks Leonard. "And in personal everything. I hate—I suppose I oughtn't to say that—but the Wilcoxes are on the wrong tack surely. Or perhaps it isn't their fault. Perhaps the little thing that says 'I' is missing out of the middle of their heads, and then it's a waste of time to blame them. There's a nightmare of a theory that says a special race is being born which will rule the rest of us in the future just because it lacks the little thing that says 'I.' Had you heard that?"

Leonard: "I get no time for reading."

"Had you thought it, then? That there are two kinds of people—our kind, who live straight from the middle of their heads, and the other kind who can't, because their heads have no middle. They can't say 'I.' They *aren't* in fact, and so they're supermen. Pierpont Morgan has never said 'I' in his life."

Leonard tries gamely to engage Helen's argument. " 'I never got on to Nietzsche,' he said. 'But I always understood that those supermen were rather what you may call egoists.'

" 'Oh, no, that's wrong,' replied Helen. 'No superman ever said 'I want,' because 'I want' must lead to the question 'Who am I?' and so to Pity and to Justice. He only says 'want.' 'Want Europe,' if he's Napoleon; 'want wives,' if he's Bluebeard; 'want Botticelli,' if he's Pierpont Morgan. Never the 'I'; and if you could pierce through him, you'd find panic and emptiness in the middle.' "

———

If Morgan was in the unusual position of being a hero to his literary valet, he was many other things as well. Though Belle Greene leaped to defend him from other people's scorn, she herself often disparaged his taste, partly to flaunt her recently acquired own. "JP is so well trained now," she boasted to Berenson early in 1911, "that he *rarely* ever buys a book or manuscript without consulting me." She cheered when her "Boss" sent six "exquisite manuscripts," a Perugino, and the Memlings from the Kann Collection to the library, but she wished all his purchases "were of that quality," and dismissed some of his acquisitions as "punk," "truck," and "trash." Still, the verbal pictures she drew to enhance her own image also captured Morgan's tyrannical possessiveness and some of the less attractive ways in which he used the power of his money.

Belle on occasion defied him, and their worst battles came when he suspected she might leave him for another man. In the fall of 1911, he heard a rumor that she was engaged, "which made him rave & foam at the mouth," she told BB. "He really was so ridiculous that I became disgusted and angry & told him that had it been true it was none of his business which caused our relations to be somewhat strained for a day or two. Finally he came to me with tears & crocodile heart breakings beseeching me *not* to leave him, *not* to marry any one & *not* to look at any man. I confess that in spite of my really sincere love and admiration for him, I was thoroughly annoyed & disgusted and I could hardly keep from telling him so."

They repeated the scene a month later—"he went into a *towering* rage. I really thought he was going to have an apoplectic fit. I just stood & looked at him & listened to him in *disgust* especially when he wound up with 'the day you get married will be the last day I shall set eyes on you & you *won't get anything from me if you do* (I daresay I told you that he put me in his will). Well, I was *mad* (as he so often makes me feel nowadays) and I told him that in the first place I had no intentions of marrying *anybody any time*—but that if I had, not all his anger or all his threats of 'disinheritance' would bother me in the slightest, that I not only did not care a damn . . . for his money but there were many times when it *disgusted* me—that he could buy a great deal with his gold but *not* me or my affections. I really was *so* furious that I got it all out in one breath & then *he* was aghast—& said 'I don't like you to speak to me that way.' Said I—'I don't like it either but you make me lose (temporarily) the real respect I have for you when you talk to me as you did, as if I was something you had bought & paid for.' Then I went out of the room still so mad that I almost murdered two or three dealers who were waiting to see me. *But* in about half an hour he came out & apologized at great length. He is much too accustomed to talking to people as he pleases and I certainly am not going to let him start that with me. Even if I have to leave him. I suppose no one else would pay me the salary he does but I can live on less if necessary at any rate I will *not* be talked to as he might to a mistress or a chamber maid. . . ."

For Labor Day weekend of 1912 Morgan planned to go off on *Corsair* from Sunday to Tuesday, and Belle told him she would be visiting friends on Long Island. (No longer living on 115th Street uptown, she had an apartment near the library.) When she arrived in the country Sunday afternoon, she found a telegram from him telling her to be at the library "without fail" at nine-thirty Monday morning. Thinking something important must have happened, she drove back to town early on Monday. "He just *laughed* when I saw him—calmly announced that the important business was to see me, and sat here until 7 o'clock when he went away to dress for a dinner engagement." He had wanted to reel her in. "That is the sort of thing that makes me lose my high reverence for him—because it *means* nothing—simply a cussed desire to *demand* my presence and to show that he has a right to—in spite of all of which I am deeply and truly devoted to him and would and will do all I can for him. In his heart he is fond of me and loyal and I know that were I ever in any trouble he would speed to the rescue."

He often reminded her that she could do anything she liked except leave the country for six months of the year while he was away, and "it seems but little that you be with me as much as I wish for the other six." Reflecting on this deal to Berenson, she said, "not for *one* instant would I grumble were it not for you." She suspected that Morgan now opposed her going abroad because he had heard about her relations with BB, "and for that reason . . . I (a *tiny* bit) despise him—And when you think of his 75 years of affaires du coeur!

"However, aside from my affection for him, I must submit for a reason I believe I have not told you before." Actually, she had told him before. "That is, he put me into his will, at a fairly good figure, contingent upon the agreement that I would never leave him while he was alive—now that will make me seem pretty mercenary to you—but it means a number of things which may be important to both you and me. For instance it means that after his death I shall be in a certain small way *independent*, that I can adopt what line of work I want . . . that I can travel and that I can provide for my family and so not have them hanging around my neck—

"You see what I mean dear—and it cannot *be* a *very* long time (I *hate* to write that). . . ."

Chapter 31

—

TRUST AND
MONEY

At the beginning of 1912, Morgan had traveled from Paris to Monte Carlo (where Stillman pronounced him "optimistic" but "whistling to keep his courage up") to Egypt with the Lawrences and Lythgoes. In February, as he cruised the Nile and had the first of his art collections shipped to New York, a congressional subcommittee headed by Louisiana Representative Arsène Pujo began to investigate the "money trust." The New York lawyer Samuel Untermyer, who helped initiate the inquiry, defined its subject as a "money oligarchy"—a "system, vicious and dangerous beyond conception," through which a few groups of men in New York controlled the nation's banks, corporations, railroads, insurance companies, and Stock Exchange. "Within the past five years," Untermyer declared, "there has been a concentration of this money power greater than that known in the preceding fifty years," and it was stifling the free play of industrial and financial competition.

The Washington Post urged Congress to "settle once for all the question whether a small group of men control the financial and business destiny of the nation." *The New York Times* described the coterie of bankers as "the trust of trusts, without whose favor all other trusts must languish to a lingering death." *The Wall Street Journal,* calling the "money trust" simply another name for Morgan, did not see cause for concern: "The condition which has developed in Wall Street in the past fifteen years is to a considerable extent a personal one, and the authority which centers in the hands of Mr. Morgan, a man 75 years of age, is by no means something which can be passed down to his successors.

Such men have no successors; and their work is either left undone after they are dead or the world devises other means and other work to take its place."

Morgan's partners and attorneys conferred about the investigation all spring. In March, Steele and Jack cabled "Flitch" that it would be "advantageous to general situation testify in general way as to our own affairs, declining answer any questions in regard to our relations with depositors or as to our clients' interests in syndicates etc." Handled well, the inquiry might "help dissipate present public apprehension." Then in April the committee appointed Untermyer its chief counsel, and the House passed a resolution enlarging the investigation's scope. Jack wired his father in Venice ten days after the sinking of the *Titanic* that the inquest would probably be as "unpleasant" as possible.

Samuel Untermyer was an experienced trial lawyer and lifelong Democrat who specialized in corporate finance. In the late eighties and nineties, he had made a fortune organizing financial syndicates and industrial consolidations. He raised orchids and bred dogs on his Hudson River Valley estate, and once said that a young lawyer starting out in practice needed $5 million to ensure his independence. Untermyer had also worked in the nineties for the Boss of New York's Tammany Hall, Richard Croker. Two years after Adolph Ochs took over *The New York Times*, in 1898, Untermyer called on him with a message from Croker: the *Times* could have all the city's advertising if it agreed to hire "a certain well-known newspaper man" for $10,000 a year. Ochs refused the bribe. Early in the new century, Untermyer began to criticize corporate trusts, and gave a series of speeches in 1911 calling for government action to break up or regulate monopolies.

A week after the Pujo Committee appointed Untermyer, Harry Davison met Morgan, Senator Aldrich, and AT&T president Theodore Vail at Aix, and cabled Jack: "most delighted appearance Flitch who in spite of 'Titanic' and NY annoyances seems in good spirits and philosophical." On May 3 he and Morgan wired their New York office that the bank and its associates ought to be represented by "best counsel obtainable," and also by the best publicist, to see that "correct facts" about the investigation "reach the public in their true and proper light."

The Morgan bank already had the best available counsel, including Stetson, Ledyard, Joseph Choate, former Wisconsin Senator John C. Spooner, and Richard Lindabury, who was working on the U.S. Steel case. With regard to publicity, Tom Lamont had taken charge. He replied from New York, referring to himself in the third person, that "TWL's man" C. T. Brainerd, the former manager of a subscription book business in Boston, had just bought the McClure newspaper syndicate from McClure's successors for $75,000: "Lamont is delighted. Thinks it will eventually prove source of great strength." Brainerd was already doing "good work" through a journalist named E. J. Edwards, who wrote syndicated financial letters under the pseudonym "Holland" and was

Morgan in Algeciras, Spain, January 1913.
(Archives of The Pierpont Morgan Library, New York)

taking "proper and valuable attitude on money enquiry." Brainerd planned to move "very slowly and cautiously so as to . . . retain confidence of newspapers" as he supplied them with information about the money trust investigation "strictly sub rosa." If word of this arrangement leaked out, concluded Lamont, the news syndicate could be acknowledged as an information pipeline or "bureau of facts."

Davison reported that Morgan, Aldrich, and Vail "enthusiastically approve bureau plan. All agree it is of the utmost importance and should be most effective and great power for good."

In late May, Lamont sent Brainerd to Washington to work with the managing editor of *The Washington Post*, William P. Spurgeon, and told Davison: "Are furnishing [the *Post*] with proper literature" for urging the Senate to restrict and perhaps even stop the Pujo investigation. "Are hopeful of strong opposition developing naturally, but politics are so controlling outcome is uncertain." With "politics" and the liberal press winning the battle for public opinion, Lamont fought back, but his efforts to influence the press only heightened popular perceptions of the Morgan bank as a monster extending its tentacles in all directions.*

———

As Lamont dispatched Brainerd to *The Washington Post* in May of 1912, New Haven Railroad president Charles Mellen in Boston was defending himself

* Elaborating on his plan for a publishing trust, Lamont thought Brainerd could buy leading newspapers in Washington, Chicago, and New York, as well as associations that sold packaged inserts to country papers, and that as a result the bankers would openly "control powerful and widespread outlets for distribution of facts." Including *Harper's Weekly*, which Morgan was already supporting, the entire operation, "with the unusual journalistic talent with which we are in close touch and can command, can be made into an exceedingly profitable enterprise." Things did not work out that way, but Lamont did buy New York's *Evening Post* in 1917. Decades later he was still trying to sweep back the sea of critical public statements about Morgan. After Henry Steele Commager wrote about the Pujo investigation in *The New York Times Magazine* in 1938, Lamont sent him a letter of corrections; he sent similar dispatches to Endicott Peabody (who criticized Morgan's handling of the 1895 gold crisis in the *Groton Quarterly* in 1945), Morgan biographer Frederick Lewis Allen (1949), and H. G. Wells, who published an interview with Joseph Stalin in the *Herald Tribune* in 1934. Lamont took issue with Wells's description of Morgan as a "parasite upon society" who "only thought about profit," but he failed to change the author's mind. Morgan, however, had a more interesting advocate than Tom Lamont. Stalin, in his interview with Wells, observed: "In speaking of the capitalists who strive only for profit, only to get rich, I do not want to say that these are the most worthless people capable of nothing else. . . . We Soviet people learn a great deal from the capitalists. And Morgan, whom you characterize so unfavorably, was undoubtedly a good, capable organiser."

against the charge of being Morgan's puppet: "To hear the self-appointed guardians of the public interest, one would think I was simply Mr. Morgan's lieutenant and stood ready to cut throats whenever he gave the order," Mellen told *The New York Times*. Asked why he had gone to Wall Street rather than State Street to raise money for a New England road, he replied, "Because I can get the money in New York when it is needed and I can't get it in Boston."*

The Stanley Committee hearings on the steel industry had taken a spring recess. When the investigation resumed at the end of May, Belle hoped it would "not frighten JP and keep him abroad longer than he intends."

Morgan was traveling on the Continent when the heir to the Hapsburg empire, Archduke Francis Ferdinand, toured his house at Princes Gate. An official at the Austro-Hungarian embassy in London reported to him by mail on May 27 that the Archduke had "enjoyed it immensely. . . . I regret very much that there has been no opportunity for His Imperial Highness to meet you personally as he has so many interests in common with you and would certainly have enjoyed a talk with you very much." Morgan never met the man whose assassination by a Bosnian Serb terrorist in 1914 precipitated World War I.†

———

Responding to the rising U.S. demand for reform, insurgent Republicans led by Wisconsin Senator La Follette had organized a "Progressive Republican

---

* Mellen made highly contradictory statements about his relations with Morgan. Though he denied to the *Times* that he was just following orders in May of 1912, he had told Clarence W. Barron of the Boston *News Bureau* in 1911: "I wear the Morgan collar, but I am proud of it." To another reporter in 1912 he said: "If Mr. Morgan were to order me tomorrow to China or Siberia in his interests, I would pack up and go." After Morgan died, Mellen was forced to resign from the nearly bankrupt New Haven road. Louis Brandeis ascribed the company's troubles to "banker mismanagement," and congressional investigations found serious ethical and financial abuses. The New Haven failure bears some resemblance to that of the IMM. Vincent Carosso, after examining the former in detail, concluded: "It does not serve Morgan's reputation to excuse his lack of vigilance by attributing it to old age or long absences from the office. . . . The inescapable fact is that he erred seriously in several respects. He had misjudged Mellen, failed to keep adequately informed of his policies and methods, and had overestimated New England's future growth and the New Haven's capacity to earn enough money to meet the fixed charges on the huge debt imposed upon it, much less maintain its regular dividend payments. Morgan also discounted too readily the potential for competition from the growing automobile and trucking industries, about which he appears to have been poorly informed. Not the least of his mistakes was his inability to appreciate the extent to which the Progressive protest had changed the nation's mood, especially the public's growing suspicion of big business."

† The Morgan bank in 1912 hoped to end hostilities between Turkey and the Balkan states by issuing loans to both sides, on condition that they accept American mediation. The plan

League" that called for increased regulation of transportation and the trusts, an end to corporate and political corruption, and a candidate to run against the conservative Taft. When Roosevelt, the obvious choice, turned them down, La Follette himself launched a campaign. In February 1912, however, TR decided that only he could heal the breach in the party ranks and give the country a rational program for change. At a constitutional convention in Ohio, he told a reporter, "My hat is in the ring."

He quickly eclipsed the infuriated La Follette, promising to protect the country's natural resources and individual rights, to promote "the fair distribution of prosperity," and to "prevent the waste of human welfare which flows from the unfair use of concentrated power and wealth in the hands of men whose eagerness for profit blinds them to the cost of what they do." Though Roosevelt would need conservative support to win the nomination, he had apparently left his pragmatic instincts in Africa: these proposals, along with an attack on the judiciary as "an instrument for the perpetuation of social and industrial wrong," drove the Old Guard into the arms of Taft. The battle between the former President and his former disciple raged all spring. One night, a reporter found Taft in the lounge of a train "with his head between his hands." When the President looked up, he said, "Roosevelt was my closest friend," and started to cry.

TR had a huge popular mandate going into the convention that June, but the Republican National Committee gave a majority of contested seats to Taft, which secured the nomination. This "crime," Roosevelt announced to his outraged supporters, "strikes straight at the heart of every principle of political decency and honesty. . . . We fight in honest fashion for the good of mankind; . . . we stand at Armageddon, and we battle for the Lord." Seven weeks later, declaring that he felt "strong as a bull moose," he accepted the nomination of a third, "Progressive" Party. His supporters included Walter Lippmann, Herbert Croly, Jane Addams, Henry Wallace, Felix Frankfurter, Dean Acheson, Herbert Satterlee, and George Perkins.

The Democrats nominated Woodrow Wilson in July. William Jennings Bryan sponsored a resolution opposing any candidate "who is the representative or under any obligation to J. Pierpont Morgan, Thomas F. Ryan, August Belmont, or any other member of the privilege-hunting and favor-seeking class"— clearly unaware of Wilson's connections to Morgan. Wilson appointed Louis

---

originated with Morgan's partner Herman Harjes in Paris and the U.S. ambassador to France, Myron Herrick. Jack finally decided against it, thinking the money would be used to continue rather than stop the war. John dos Passos later said that "old man Morgan, before his death, worked hard to avert the coming war," but the effort appears to have come largely from his partners.

Brandeis, the "people's attorney" who was an outspoken critic of big business, to serve as an economic adviser to his campaign.

Taft never won much support. According to the historian John Milton Cooper, the fight between Roosevelt and Wilson pitted "the most vivid political presence since Andrew Jackson against the most accomplished political mind since Thomas Jefferson. It was a grand moment in American politics." Several issues figured in the campaign, but progressive Democrats and former Republican Progressives focused largely on the question of the trusts.

Wilson accused TR of collaborating with the architects of monopoly, and promised to resuscitate competition: his program, which he called "the New Freedom," would promote liberty, as against the Progressives' "regulation." The former president of Princeton announced, somewhat inscrutably, "I am for big business, I am against the trusts."

Roosevelt charged that *his* program, "the New Nationalism," contained "definite and concrete" plans to "correct real abuses and achieve real results," while his opponent's "assault on monopoly" was "make-believe." The Bull Moose candidate had always credited his own ability to distinguish between "good" and "bad" trusts. He sought to punish *conduct*, not size, and to check abuses of corporate power with the power of government. Wilson pointed out the aristocratic paternalism in TR's view that America's problems could be solved only by professional experts (a view Morgan shared), and contrasted it with his own belief that if the people could not "understand the job, then we are not a free people."

Morgan stayed abroad until late July 1912, courting Lady Sackville, negotiating over the last China loans, and helping the Kaiser win his sailing race at Kiel. When he returned to New York, he gave no statement to the reporters who thronged the dock. Belle found him in a "*most* angelic frame of mind, at peace with all the world except Taft, Roosevelt and Perkins."

Dissension in the Morgan ranks reflected the Republican rift. Lamont told a friend in August that he and Morgan would vote for the "secure, careful, intelligent, and broad-minded" Taft, who seemed likely to promote the country's "happiness and prosperity." Satterlee and Willard Straight—and the departed Perkins—were firmly in the Roosevelt camp. Louisa wrote to her traveling mother in October: "I am having a very hard time just now! My *natural* male advisers (my Father and my husband) are on different sides of the fence and I am not even *on* the fence between them. Isn't it dreadful? I think they are *both wrong*! How do you feel about it? . . . O! I'm *so* thankful that I am *not* a man!! *and* that women do not yet have the vote!"

Anne, probably not so delighted not to be able to vote, attended Progressive Party meetings that fall.

When George Harvey, the editor of *Harper's Weekly,* came out for Wilson, the

Democratic nominee feared the endorsement would hurt his campaign, since Harper's was publicly identified with Morgan. Harvey promptly criticized Wilson in an interview with *The New York Times.*

The Pujo Committee hearings had begun briefly in June, then adjourned until after the fall election. In September, Henry Morgenthau, a major Wilson supporter and chairman of his campaign finance committee, called on Frank Vanderlip at the City Bank. Vanderlip described their wide-ranging conversation to Stillman, and one aspect of it in detail: "Morgenthau tells me that Untermyer is preparing for a thorough going campaign to begin after election . . . and has got a lot of men working on it now. His whole ambition is to, in some way, get a whitewash for his character. He has offered a hundred thousand dollars (all of this is quite confidential, of course), if he can be assured of a foreign mission. Indeed, he would give any amount for an important one, and has even the audacity to think that he might possibly be appointed to England. Wilson will make no promises whatever and they have accepted only $10,000 as yet and probably will accept no more. [Untermyer] would also like to be Attorney General. Morgenthau says that, of course, is quite impossible, although he could imagine that he might be sent to some post of about the grade of Italy."

In early October, a Senate committee investigating political campaign contributions called Morgan to Washington. The senators wanted to know whether Morgan's gifts to Roosevelt's 1904 campaign—$100,000 outright, and $50,000 through the fund organized by Harriman—had "bought" the President's complicity in the U.S. Steel acquisition of TC&I. It was at these hearings that Morgan said, when asked whether party fund-raisers had expressed gratitude for his having given the additional $50,000, "No. Gratitude has been rather scarce in my experience." Ledyard told Grenfell that the "Senior" had been "rather dreading the ordeal of testifying," but "proved a very good witness." Massachusetts Governor Thomas R. Marshall did not agree. The day after Morgan testified, Marshall declared that the contribution showed him up as a "tightwad": "President Roosevelt gave him the right in violation of the law to amalgamate the Tennessee Coal and Iron Co. with the Steel Trust. That deal netted Morgan $69,000,000. I repeat that if he only gave back $100,000 of it he is a tightwad."

If Morgan had dreaded appearing before the campaign finance committee, he dreaded the "Money Trust" ordeal even more. Belle described him to Berenson at the end of October as "very blue . . . due to that underbred, disgusting and scoundrelly friend of yours, Sam Untermyer . . . it's like a nasty little Italian flea attacking a mountain lion . . . it takes all my physical and mental strength to keep JP cheered up and optimistic." She read to him, sat with him while he played solitaire, and sometimes just perched "quietly on a little stool at his knee while he sits and thinks and shakes his great head in anger."

To no one's surprise, the Republican split gave the election to the Democrats in November. Wilson carried forty of forty-eight states, and 42 percent of the popular vote—to Roosevelt's 27 percent, Taft's 23 percent, and 6 percent (nearly a million votes) for the Socialist Eugene Debs. The first Democrat to occupy the White House since Cleveland would have Democratic majorities in both houses of Congress.

The Pujo Committee resumed its hearings in mid-November.*

Stetson had assured Untermyer that his clients would cooperate with the committee and supply the documents requested, but would disclose no information about the affairs of *their* clients. Moreover, they would not agree that the country's financial system needed a thorough overhaul—on the contrary, the bankers thought it had never before been "as sound and good as it is to-day, and that improvements have been and are being worked out steadily and naturally through practical experience." Stetson asked that the examination of Morgan be completed as quickly as possible, since the old man was planning to go abroad.

On Tuesday, December, 17, Jack wired Grenfell: "Going Washington today with Flitch who in splendid form, entirely ready for the very probable difficulties which may occur. He has never been better so am not at all apprehensive." "Flitch" in fact had a cold, and was exhausted when his party—which included Davison, Lamont, Jack, Louisa, and fifteen lawyers—reached the capital by special train that night.

Louisa was watching him closely for signs of strain. He stayed up late playing solitaire in his room at the Willard Hotel. "Spent a.m. in uncertainty," Louisa wrote in her diary the next day: "Finally went at 2 p.m. to House Office Building to Rooms of Money Trust Committee." She and Jack rode to Capitol Hill with their father. The lawyers and other partners followed in separate cars. Untermyer expedited his examination of the statistician, Scudder, in order to call Morgan at 3:00. "The financier showed weariness as he took the stand," reported *The New York Times* on the nineteenth: "He did not have that spruce look that characterized him when he appeared before the Senate committee investigating campaign funds last October. At times his voice was low, but his answers could be heard distinctly."

For half an hour, Untermyer elicited general facts about the Morgan bank from his witness. At 3:30, when the congressmen were called to the House, Chairman Pujo adjourned the hearing until the following morning.

---

* Jack told President Wilson in 1914 that the investigation had been "offered" to the Morgan Bank for $40,000, through "underground channels"—and the Stanley Committee steel inquiry to Judge Gary for $10,000—but that "we had never bought anybody yet and did not propose to begin with that sort of person."

At 9:00 A.M. on Thursday, before a packed hall, Untermyer began by asking Morgan about his control of railroads. He established that the voting trustees for the Southern Railway were Morgan, Baker, and Lanier, and that these men were also the road's principal bankers. Would it not be better for interstate railroad corporations to sell their securities in open competition, asked Untermyer, than be tied to one banking house, "however just its methods?"

Morgan said, "I should not think so." He explained that the securities issued by railroads did not always "prove good."

Untermyer: "But the banking house assumes no legal responsibility for the value of the bonds, does it?"

Morgan: "No sir, but it assumes something else that is still more important, and that is the moral responsibility which has to be defended as long as you live."

Untermyer sarcastically submitted that "moral responsibility never materializes into money, does it?"—meaning money for the bankers.

Morgan took him to mean money for investors: "Yes, because the company is reorganized, bonds are issued, and people get their money and interest."

Untermyer observed that bankers never lose money—the first thing provided for in reorganizations was banker profit.

Morgan: "Not always—only if the reorganization goes through."

Untermyer asked him to name one instance in which a banker who advanced money on defaulted securities failed to get his money back in the reorganization.

Morgan: "I cannot recall it now, sir, but I am sure there are cases." Many of his own reorganizations had in fact failed after their voting trusts expired. In some cases, he lost money. In others, he went back and reorganized the companies a second and third time. Because of his long-term commitment, most "Morganizations" eventually did yield profit to their investors and bankers— but their author was seventy-five years old, not adroit with old details, and not about to deliver a lecture on railroad finance.

Moving on to the recent consolidations of financial institutions in New York, Untermyer asked about the relations between J. P. Morgan & Co., Baker's First National, and Stillman's National City Bank. He had no idea that they referred to themselves as "the Trio." The committee's final report would show that the combined financial resources of the Trio banks amounted to over $630 million, and that the partners and officers of these banks and their affiliated trusts held directorships in companies with aggregate capital resources of $25 billion—a concentration of private wealth that staggered the national imagination.

At the hearing, Untermyer asked Morgan: "You have made many issues or purchases jointly with First National—Mr. Baker's bank?"

Morgan: "Yes."

Untermyer: "You and Mr. Baker have been old and close friends and associates for many years, have you not?"

Morgan: "For a great many years; yes."

Untermyer: "Almost since you began business?"

Morgan: "Well, since 1873, at least."

When Untermyer asked whether the two banks had not made joint purchases and issues, and invited each other to participate in offerings—implying insidious collusion—Morgan answered frankly: "I always offered them anything I had."

Because the old man did not recall exactly who sat on which boards, Davison volunteered that Whitelaw Reid was not on the executive committee of the First National. Morgan agreed with Davison. Untermyer did not, and proposed to look the matter up.

Morgan: "I think I am right, Mr. Counsel."

Untermyer: "Mr. Davison says you are right, does he not?"

Morgan: "Yes."

Untermyer: "That is the reason you think so?"

Morgan: "I always believe anything Mr. Davison says."

He had been spending six to eight months a year in Europe lately, while Davison effected most of the financial consolidations, and age had dimmed his once phenomenal memory. In addition, his partners and lawyers had finally convinced him that in the current political climate it would be better if he was not seen as playing a commanding role in the country's economic affairs—that his adversaries would read only nefarious intent in the financial control the Trio had assiduously secured. Not at ease with shades of gray, Morgan proceeded to disavow every inference about his power, which led to a certain amount of unnecessary dissembling.

Untermyer asked: "You spend probably half the year abroad of late years?"

Morgan (although a truthful "Yes" would have helped explain his fogginess about details): "No, not generally; about four or five months."

At another point, discussing Bob Bacon's 1898 negotiations for the acquisition of anthracite coal roads, Untermyer asked: "Who was Robert Bacon?"

Morgan: "Who was Robert Bacon?"

Untermyer: "Yes."

Morgan: "At what date?"

Untermyer: "1898."

Morgan: "He may have been a partner of mine."

This literal-minded answer—"may" referring to the date (Bacon had been Morgan's partner from 1894 to 1902, but held other positions after that)—seemed a superfluous dodge.

Untermyer then took Morgan in detail over the purchase of the Equitable Life Assurance Society in 1910. Baker and Stillman had each agreed to accept a quarter-interest in the company if Morgan asked them to, but he had not asked. "You may explain, if you care to, Mr. Morgan, why you bought from Messrs. Ryan and Harriman $51,000 par value of stock that paid only $3,710 a year, for approximately $3,000,000, that could yield you only one-eighth or one-ninth of 1 per cent."

Morgan: "Because I thought it was a desirable thing for the situation to do that."

Untermyer: "That is very general, Mr. Morgan, when you speak of the situation. Was not that stock safe enough in Mr. Ryan's hands?"

Morgan: "I suppose it was. I thought it was greatly improved by being in the hands of myself and these two gentlemen [Baker and Stillman] provided I asked them to do so."

Untermyer observed that the acquisition of stock paying one eighth of a percent did not make business sense when the current rate of return on money was 5 percent.

Morgan: "I am not talking about it as a question of money."

Untermyer again asked why Morgan bought it.

Morgan: "For the very reason that I thought it was the thing to do, as I said."

Untermyer: "But that does not explain anything."

Morgan: "That is the only reason I can give."

Untermyer: "It was the thing to do for whom?"

Morgan: "That is the only reason I can give. That is the only reason I have, in other words. I am not trying to keep anything back, you understand."

Untermyer: "I understand. In other words, you have no reason at all."

Morgan: "That is the way you look at it. I think it is a very good reason. . . . Some of these days you will agree with me."

Untermyer: "You can never tell what may happen. Some of these days"—he turned it around—"you may agree with me, Mr. Morgan."

Morgan: "Very well. That may be. If I do, I shall wait for a good reason."

After this droll exchange, Morgan repeated that he had not bought the Equitable to make money, but wanted the stock "where it could not be divided up into small lots." Harriman had died, Ryan had sold half his shares, and there was no telling who would take control of the company, with assets now worth $500 million: "Those are the things I had in mind. I am trying to show you some of the things that went through my mind."

A few minutes later, when Untermyer again asked about the eighth-of-a-percent return, Morgan said: "My friend, if I should attempt to tell you where the money is in every transaction I make, I would have a very hard time of it."

Untermyer: "You would not be able to do it?"

Morgan: "I have given you, from my heart, the exact facts."

Untermyer: "I know you have, Mr. Morgan, and I am trying to find out the real reason for this thing."

Morgan *was* actually trying to show "some of the things that went through" his mind—an effort he rarely made. He had wanted to keep the Equitable safe from market-disrupting takeover attempts, which was all the reason he needed. That there might be a difference between "good" and "real" reasons for his actions was a modernist concept entirely alien to his sensibility.

He was as certain that he had been doing the country great service all his life as Untermyer was certain that the Money Trust was up to no good, and the gulf between their positions came out plainly on the subject of monopoly concentration. What to Untermyer represented an oligarchical "system, vicious and dangerous beyond conception" had for Morgan evolved as a practical solution to a range of economic problems.

The consolidation and amalgamation of railroad systems, industries, and banks "does not look to any concentration?" asked the lawyer in open disbelief.

"No sir."

A dubious Untermyer: "It looks, I suppose to the dispersal of interests rather than to concentration?"

Morgan: "On no; it deals with things as they exist."

———

When the questioning ended on Thursday afternoon, December 19, Morgan walked up to the rostrum, shook hands with the members of the committee, thanked them for their courtesy, and said it had been a pleasure to offer his testimony. His party returned to New York by train, arriving in time for dinner. "Father made a magnificent showing," Louisa wrote in her diary that night: "Untermyer *nowhere!*"

Congratulations poured in to 23 Wall Street and 219. Jack told Herman Harjes that his father had "in no way suffered from the strain, because he feels that he has done a good thing, and we hope now he will sail on January 7th and get a good holiday in Egypt, which he has earned mighty well."

Belle described her Chief as feeling very much better and looking "about seventy years younger" than when he left for Washington. Fanny returned from Europe on December 24 to find "All well, Pierpont especially so." On Christmas morning, reported Belle, he marched into the library singing "O Come All Ye Faithful" at the top of his lungs—"throwing his hat and cane into the nearest receptacle (a porphyry sarcophagus) and putting both arms around me and kissing me on both cheeks." He asked her to go to Egypt with him, she told BB. When she said they should not both be away from the library at once, he invited Louisa. He sent his usual Christmas greetings to friends, including Bishops Lawrence and Doane, Ladies Sackville, Johnstone, and Dawkins, and Margot Asquith, the wife of the Prime Minister, at No. 10 Downing Street.

Harper's editor George Harvey called at the library and reported that Morgan regarded Wilson's presidency with "honest apprehension" but remained as "optimistic as ever" about the American future. As his guest prepared to leave, the old man rose from his chair "with difficulty, for he was then quite feeble," and said, " 'When you see Mr. Wilson, tell him for me that if there should ever come a time when he thinks any influence or resources that I have can be used for the country, they are wholly at his disposal. . . .' "

The Metropolitan Museum was mounting an exhibition of 29 paintings Morgan had recently brought to America from London. As he considered leaving several of his collections to the museum, he hoped that the city would fund the building of a new wing, but New York officials had made no move, and the Met had a policy of not accepting conditional bequests. In 1909, however, Benjamin Altman had offered his collection to the museum if it could be kept together in one gallery, with a curator he appointed and paid for, and Morgan as president of the Met had agreed in that case to bend the rules. When the Altman bequest finally came to the museum at Altman's death in 1913, it was valued at $15 million. Robinson described it as "without question the most splendid gift that a citizen has ever made to the people of the city of New York." According to the art critic Calvin Tomkins, Morgan's collection was to Altman's "as the ocean to an inland sea." Had it belonged to someone else, Morgan would surely have found a way to secure it for the Met.

In November 1912, with no prospect of city funding, Morgan told Edward Robinson, now the museum's director, that he had no intention of leaving his art to the Met: "He said that the value of these collections at the present time was about $50 million," Robinson reported in a memo, "and he regarded this as much too large an asset to take out of his estate in case it might ever be needed." The director added, "This is the first indication Mr. Morgan has ever made to me of his ultimate intentions with regard to his collections."

In late December, after the Pujo hearings, Morgan brought up the subject again. Although the exhibition of his paintings would open in January, he asked Robinson not to have any of his other collections unpacked, on the theory that if the city found out they were on display it would not fund the new wing. When Robinson assured him that the Board of Estimate promised to appropriate funding soon, Morgan replied "with some vehemence" that whether or not the money was granted, nothing was to be done with any of his art until he issued further instructions.

He had just that December bought from Duveen, with an endorsement from Bernard Berenson, a Filippo Lippi altarpiece called *St. Lawrence Enthroned with*

Saints. It was, Berenson wrote to Morgan, one of Filippo Lippi's "suavest, sanest, completest, and most characteristic works," with a "flower-like beauty so worthy of the master of Botticelli"; it ranked with "the hundred best pictures painted in Florence during its gloriously creative fifteenth century." Described by Vasari, these panels of tempera on wood with gold ground had been painted in about 1440 for the chapel of the Alessandri family villa near Fiesole. Berenson, who had a contract with Duveen for 25 percent of the profit on works he authenticated for sale, pointed out the paintings' "immense historical interest," since Alessandro degli Alessandri had been "obviously . . . very friendly to the nascent power of the Medici." He urged Morgan to "conceive how startingly rare it is to get hold of a work of art" that in the course of its four hundred seventy-two years had "changed hands only on falling into yours."

Morgan paid $215,000 for the altarpiece. Belle told BB on December 31 that "JP wanted to send it to the Museum but I would not let him. So I am going to hang it in the Library as soon as he goes" abroad. It went to the museum.*

Duveen and Berenson had also offered Morgan a small painting by Crivelli that fall—Belle told BB she would leave Morgan if he didn't buy it. He didn't buy it, and she didn't leave. At the end of the year she reported that "a man named Lehman" had bought it for $450,000. She had just met his son, a Yale student, at the George Blumenthals', and when she told him the painting had been refused by Morgan he seemed "crestfallen," but cheered up after she explained that the shame was Morgan's, not the picture's. "He was," she told BB, "merely a nice amiable Jewish little boy of no charm or interest." He was Robert Lehman, who later became a vice president and trustee at the Met as well as head of Lehman Brothers. His collection forms the nucleus of the Met's Lehman Wing.

Morgan took Belle to the Met to see his paintings on January 5, before the exhibition opened. To BB she reported: "He seemed anxious to swap opinions with me and fortunately there were about a dozen upon which we could agree—the big Raphael from the National Gallery looks *wonderful* and the Filippi Lippi more beautiful than ever. . . . *How* I wish that the little Crivelli could have been with them! Then we went to look at the Persian things and I was really amazed by his intuitive appreciation of the right thing—Oh! he's learning and fast. He thinks that he could not stand the pace if I were with him in Europe because I want to look at everything and walk too fast . . . —I felt like telling him that I was sure *you* would give me a good recommendation! But he

---

* In 1932, Belle read in BB's *Italian Pictures of the Renaissance* that he had demoted the work, rating it only "G.P."—"in great part" by Filippo Lippi. She wrote: "To me-ow and scratch, I must say that the 'G.P.' after our Fra Filippo Lippi would have saved us much money had it been contained in your original letter to Duveen." The Metropolitan Museum bought the altarpiece in 1935, and attributes it to Filippo Lippi.

was very sweet & fatherly and amused and treated me as if I were an untamed kitten most of the time. I am glad he is sailing on Tuesday but know I shall be desolate for a while. . . ."

Morgan's exuberance after his Pujo "ordeal" alternated, as often before, with darker moods. He seemed nervous and exhausted in early January—Jack pronounced him "very much overdone . . . by all the Washington business."

For years friends had been urging Morgan to choose an official biographer. Satterlee brought the subject up that January, after watching his father-in-law destroy several "exceedingly personal" papers. He knew of the letters Morgan had burned after Junius died, and pointed out that the grandchildren would want some kind of record. According to Satterlee, Morgan replied, "Well, if you feel that way about it, why don't you write it?" Could he talk freely to friends, partners, and relatives? Satterlee asked. Morgan nodded, but said, "be sure that you do not publish anything as long as I am alive." Satterlee: "And read all your letters and correspondence?" Morgan smiled: "Yes, if you can find them."

The next day, he sailed for Egypt with Louisa, the Aldriches, the Lythgoes, and his favorite Pekinese, "Shun," on the White Star's *Adriatic.*

He seemed fine most of the way across the Atlantic, reported Louisa, but as they approached Madeira he grew agitated and depressed. Brief trips ashore at Algeciras and Monaco seemed to revive him. The party reached Cairo on January 26, and took suites at Shepheard's Hotel. Morgan and Louisa had lunch with the legendary British colonial officer Herbert Kitchener, who talked at length about raising cotton in Egypt, and "*rather sharply* about the antiquities taken out of the country by Americans," noted Louisa in her diary.

Joined by a physician from Cairo named Tribe, the Americans started up the Nile on board *Khargeh* on January 31. Three days later Morgan suffered an acute breakdown. The intermittent agitation and anxiety he had been experiencing all month intensified into paranoid, suicidal delusions. His companions reported that he was afraid he would jump out a window or off the deck of the boat. He could not eat. Nightmares and "distorted business ideas" interrupted his sleep. He thought he was going to die, that there was a conspiracy against him, that Egyptians would kill him. Dr. Tribe sedated him with bromides and ordered him to bed. When his party reached the Metropolitan expedition house at Deir el-Bahri, Morgan, too tired for lunch, went back to the boat.

News from New York upset him, as did not receiving news. Louisa told Jack to send cheerful items only, and she edited what arrived. Morgan had planned to continue south to Khartoum in the Sudan, but his companions decided in mid-February to return to Cairo. In a cable marked "Denkstein" (to be decoded only by the addressee), Louisa reported to Jack, using the family code name "Charcoal" for their father: "Charcoal in very nervous condition . . . result months strain apparent now. . . . We return down river, doctor thinks greater quiet would be better for him than travel. Tell Markoe."

Dr. Markoe, familiar with his patient's hypochondria, sent reassurance: he thought this "trouble" only natural after the "tremendous strain in Washington." "Charcoal," he reminded Louisa, had been in excellent physical condition when he left.

Davison testified before the Pujo Committee in February. At the hearings, and in a letter he wrote to the committee on behalf of the bank, he pointed out that large amounts of capital had been concentrated in New York in response to "economic laws which in every country create some city as the great financial centre." A few prominent bankers had taken it upon themselves to monitor the capital supplies of the country's expanding industrial economy, in view of America's antiquated banking system. The picture drawn by the committee, of these financiers controlling the boards of companies with resources of $25 billion, was misleading, Davison continued: much of that money was invested in factories, land, and equipment—it was not available as cash "subject to the selfish use or abuse of individuals." And the presence of bankers on corporate boards had to do not with a desire to manage daily operations or buy securities at insider prices, but with a sense of their "moral responsibility," as sponsors of the corporations' securities, to keep an eye on policy and protect investors' interests: "For a private banker to sit upon such a directorate is in most instances a duty, not a privilege."

These explanations did not affect the committee's conclusions, but they delighted Morgan, who was lucid enough in mid-February to read the reports and wire Davison: "Perfectly splendid. I am deeply grateful to you myself for all you have done. Love to you and Mrs. Davison. I feel quite seedy myself, but Doctor says I am improving."

Davison replied: "Greatly delighted your cable being, of course, most anxious that my testimony should please you." To cheer the old man up, he added: "our House stands higher and better today than ever before, which is also true, if possible, of yourself."

Neither that message nor Markoe's reassurances eased Morgan's despair. He asked Satterlee to come to Egypt, to help Louisa and relieve his own mind. He also wanted Markoe or his backup physician, George Dixon, since they understood his condition "better than a stranger can."

Satterlee and Dr. Dixon left for Egypt at once. Markoe himself was ill. Jack wanted to join them, but his father reminded him through Louisa "how much depends upon your being on the spot in NY—how many interests are in your hands." Though this directive assigned new authority to Jack, it also kept him thousands of miles away.

Morgan had a sharp attack of chest pain on February 14. Dr. Tribe called it anginal, and it disappeared with medication, but the patient was anxious to get back to Cairo.

A trained nurse was waiting when the travelers reached Shepheard's Hotel. Lythgoe turned away reporters and dealers.

From Cairo, Tribe cabled Markoe a detailed description of Morgan's symptoms. "Fickle appetite and slight bladder irritation . . . aggravated depressed apprehensive, anorexia, insomnia, slight stomatitis and throat irritation. No physical sign chest or abdomen or laryngoscopic. No fever . . . Mouth and bladder condition improved under treatment but nervous depression and insomnia obstinate with varying phase . . . anginal attack yielding quickly treatment but patient very upset. Blood pressure hundred and fifty. Pulse regular . . . Diagnosis—general physical and nervous exhaustion resulting from prolonged excessive strain in elderly subject."

The stock market slumped on February 17, reacting to rumors about Morgan's health. Jack announced that his father had merely had an attack of indigestion and was resting comfortably, which worked for about forty-eight hours. Then *The New York Times* reported the seriousness of the illness, and began to issue daily bulletins: Satterlee heading for Egypt; Morgan confined to room; Morgan goes out for drive; fresh eggs and butter shipped from Cragston; Morgan improving; Pope hopes to see him.

"How I wish we could get rid of this desperate depression," sighed Louisa. She cabled Jack: "Charcoal wishes you tell mother he sure of her sympathy as she understands suffering from nervous depression better than anyone else."

"Charcoal" was also having trouble with his teeth. At some point in the last few years he had been fitted with dentures, which now caused him so much discomfort that he refused everything except milk and broth.

On warm mornings he sat on the hotel piazza; in the afternoons he went out for drives. The Kaiser sent a diplomatic agent with a personal message. Senator Aldrich came to call. Markoe wired further messages of reassurance and love.

In early March, Jack relayed the news (vetted as sufficiently cheerful by Louisa) that Woodrow Wilson's cabinet was not as bad as they had expected. Brandeis was not in it, although William Jennings Bryan would be Secretary of State. Attorney General J. C. McReynolds seemed "honest though somewhat radical." The President's inaugural address indicated that matters might be "quieter than heretofore."

Dixon and Satterlee arrived in Cairo on March 3. They found Morgan thin, exhausted, terrified of losing his mind, obsessed with the idea that he was about to be subpoenaed or cited for contempt of court, convinced that the Khedive was going to harm him, and that he was dying. He asked the same questions over and over, like a child, and felt "acutely the persecutions he has been subjected to," reported Dixon, "with the intense desire to impress the world that he has never knowingly done a business wrong in his life."

For over seventy years Morgan had ignored his critics. He shrugged off parental admonition as a boy. Punished by a schoolteacher, he turned the tables and scolded *her.* After the partners at Duncan, Sherman warned him about his "sharp" and "contracted" manner, he thanked them for the advice but did not change his behavior. Early notes of public disapproval had sounded over his Civil War gun deal and gold corner. After that, choruses of voices had objected in succession to the refunding of the Civil War debt by private bankers and foreign Jews, to the reimposition of a rigid gold standard, to the "Morganization" of railroads, the "collusion" between Wall Street and Cleveland's White House over the 1895 gold deal, the formation of the billion-dollar trust in 1901, the Northern Pacific panic, the failure of the IMM, the role played by Wall Street titans in 1907, and the power of the "money trust." Morgan's sense of calling, his father's final unqualified benediction, his insulation from people who did not see the world as he did, the trust accorded him by the world's leading bankers, and his sincere conviction that he was doing indispensable work for the American future, in finance and in the arts, all shielded him from the cumulative force of popular outrage.

The attacks on him that followed the 1907 panic had been so extreme that they strengthened his inclination to listen only to praise. Always tone-deaf to the claims of his adversaries, he was at the end of his life literally hard of hearing as well. By 1911–12, however, the nation's fury had grown too loud and insistent to ignore—in the Stanley Committee hearings, the prosecution of U.S. Steel, accusations of "banker mismanagement" in the New Haven Railroad mess, the uproar over the loss of the *Titanic*, the campaign-finance inquiry, and the charges of the Pujo Committee.

During his lifelong struggle with depression, Morgan had often reported feeling "way down," worthless, paralyzed, "completely used up and unfit for anything." More than once he had concluded that "the best thing would be for me to give up" work—"I don't feel good for much anyway." The few people with whom he discussed his private anguish revealed little about it. Dr. Markoe maintained complete professional silence. Dr. Rainsford reported that when the famous reserve broke down, the "profound emotionalism of his nature had its way with him," and in his hours of "despairing despondency," he "deeply doubted himself." Belle Greene relayed to Berenson the fact but not the content of her Chief's ruminations about his "unfulfilled hopes . . . his failures and disappointments." She also saw the "utter *loneliness*" of his frenetic social life, and his aim always "to be a builder—not a wrecker in the world of things."

In January 1912, Stillman had thought Morgan was "whistling to keep his courage up." By early 1913, a military marching band could not have drowned out the din of reproach. Probably it was a combination of age, physiological deterioration, a long-standing vulnerability to depression, and the experience of being forced to explain himself to hostile inquisitors that tore down Morgan's bulwarks and brought on this collapse.

His companions in Cairo assured him that he was not going insane and would get well. Dixon told Jack he had found no organic trouble, and that the old man's vitality seemed "remarkable" but "his business life is finished."

With the arrival of Satterlee and Dixon, Morgan felt "less absolutely, steadfastly, *sure* that the country was going to ruin, that his race was run, and his whole life work going for naught!" reported Louisa. Still, he longed to "get out of Egypt and into a 'Christian country.' " On March 10 they went to Rome.

There, they took the royal suite at the Grand Hotel, with eight bedrooms and two parlors. Morgan recovered enough to direct his chauffeur on a drive up the Janiculum, where he showed Louisa and Herbert the building in progress at the American Academy. An American dentist named A. T. Webb fitted him for new dentures. Satterlee warded off art dealers and the press. Flowers arrived from friends on both sides of the Atlantic.

All the doctors urged Morgan to return to New York, but he wanted to go on as usual after Rome to Aix. "I have assured him," Satterlee told Jack, "that whenever he goes home he will be absolutely immune from being put in the witness chair again, for the rest of his life, as [a doctor's] certificate would excuse him." Morgan was "much relieved" by this opinion, but Jack did not agree. He thought his father likely to be subpoenaed the minute he returned. And since "Charcoal" would not be able to "stand many appearances such as he would have to make in the Steel suit, possibly also the Harvester suit, New Haven matters, New York Central matters," and all sorts of questions before the ICC, Jack advised the sentinels in Rome to keep him abroad: "He will always play any game he is in up to the limit of his power to play, therefore he must not be allowed to use himself up in these futile things."

The Grand Hotel looked like a besieged fortress, reported London's *Daily Mail.* Waves of art dealers and amateurs with bundles of things to sell descended on the hotel "from early morning to late at night and are repulsed with the regularity of surf on the beach."

Since uncertainty about Morgan's condition was once again unsettling the financial markets, Satterlee arranged for Dixon to issue a statement to the Associated Press. The doctor announced that Morgan had suffered a nervous prostration brought on by digestive upsets, a head cold, and years of business strain that had "culminated in the vexatious investigations of the so-called Pujo Committee last December. . . . He is not, and has not been, dangerously ill, and with the absolute rest he is now having his complete restoration to perfect health is assured." Privately to Jack, Dixon added: "I wish Untermyer and the Pujo Committee were where I would like them to be!"

Though eager to quell rumors about his father's decline, Jack disliked giving the Pujo hearings any credit. "We have all here maintained the note which [Father] struck so well in Washington," he told Satterlee, "that he was much too big to be annoyed by miserable little things like that. The admission that it was vexatious called further attention to the feeling that already existed, but which the public throughout the country did not know of, and the statement was to that extent unfortunate." Jack asked that anyone issuing medical statements in the future check with New York first: "There is no use in letting that little rascal Untermyer smile a happy smile and say, 'I brought it off after all.' " In private, Jack now referred to Untermyer as "the beast."

Public denials notwithstanding, Morgan *was* "dangerously ill"—irrational, incoherent, furious when others did not understand him. One day he said, "Has Dr. Phelps done with the horrors?" meaning "Has Dr. Webb finished my teeth?"—a transposition Satterlee found "not inapt" but difficult to read. The old man was affectionate and malleable when depressed, but during "nerve storms," Satterlee had to hold him while Louisa administered sedatives. Morgan took food and medicine only from her.

He now feared that the Italian King would prevent him from leaving Rome, and complained of being "watched and directed." To be reduced from indomitable command to childlike dependence and paranoid delusion was as frightening to him as it was painful for his companions to see. He withdrew from everything that once engaged him, refusing even to play solitaire. Most days he lay on a sofa near the fire in the flower-scented suite, with all the windows closed and the thermometer at eighty, smoking a cigar. At night Dixon slept in his room with Satterlee on call next door.

Learning that Fanny's "nerve specialist," M. Allen Starr, was in Italy, Dixon asked him to come to Rome. Starr arrived for twenty-four hours on March 21. Morgan took the doctor by car to see the American Academy. "For ten minutes," Starr reported, he "was as interested and as active mentally as ever," then lapsed back into indifference. Since this diversion seemed briefly beneficial, Starr urged the others to let their patient do what he wanted whenever they could.

On Easter Sunday, March 23, he wanted to go to church. His caretakers assented, but the outing brought on a new collapse. Dixon, fearing that "the Commodore was getting out of our control," ordered him to bed for a complete rest in a darkened room with nurses around the clock, and asked Louisa not to spend so much time there. "Father sleepy & heavy with bromide & veronal," she wrote in her diary the next day. Removing Morgan's last shreds of autonomy and pleasure directly contravened Starr's advice, but a more liberal regimen probably would have made no difference.

"We are out of woods," Dixon wired New York on Wednesday. Morgan would not eat, though he liked his new dentures. He stopped recognizing people. One night he insisted on getting up and going to school. Dixon gave him codeine and morphine. Starr came back, and in view of the patient's deterioration, advised moving the entire entourage to Dover House. On Saturday, March 29, Satterlee ordered an ambulance and special train for Monday morning.

On Sunday, however, Morgan was delirious and too weak to be moved. "Very little hope favorable turn," Louisa cabled Jack: "Comfort in fact he is unconscious and does not suffer. Dearest sympathy for you all so far away. Everything possible being done."

MORGAN'S DOCTORS ADMIT CONDITION IS "MOST CRITICAL," reported *The New York Times,* and the *Sun* announced: J. P. MORGAN SINKING FAST. Jack reminded Satterlee and Dixon to clear all public statements through New York.

On Monday, March 31, Morgan's temperature went up to 104½ and his pulse to 140. He slept quietly. Louisa held his hand all morning. She cabled Jack shortly after noon: "Charcoal died today twelve five."

That evening a young American woman wrote to her fiancé from Rome: "Dr. Dixon has been in here a great deal and told us in so many words on Fri-day that the old man was dying, and also told us about lots of the facts of his illness. It seems terrible to me that a man like Mr. Morgan – a man with his mind – should have to end his life in that state. He was without doubt a wonderfully big man and I don't think there's anything fine enough we can say about him. Generous to a degree and the most public spirited man in America, I've heard hundreds of people say, and even if he had a great many bad points, his good ones certainly out-balance them by a great deal. Dr. Dixon said that the man who said this Untermyer affair would kill Mr. Morgan . . . struck it right. The insult and humility [she probably meant *humiliation*] of it all has been on the poor old man's mind day and night and has resulted in the nervous prostration that made him fail as quickly as he has during the last week or ten days. To think of the smallness of that horrid Jew [Untermyer] to cause so much trouble and ignominy for the most respected people. . . . [Morgan] died at 12:30 and they tried to keep it quiet until the stock exchange closed at home, but I suppose they couldn't. . . .

"All the parties here for to-night have been given up and the place seems to be very much shocked. . . . All the Embassies are closed and his death is as much of an event as it must be at home. He was a great deal more than just a private citizen, wasn't he?"

———

A certificate filed by an Italian physician in Rome attributed Morgan's death to "dispepsia psichica." Psychic dyspepsia is a wonderful description of the old man's condition during his last few weeks, but the physiological cause of his death was never ascertained. His physician at Aix, worried about his high blood pressure in 1905, had feared a "cerebral congestion." In 1913 Morgan probably suffered a series of small strokes, beginning on the Nile or even earlier, followed by a massive stroke at the end. Whatever the physical mechanism, and regardless of what Jack wanted the public to think, the clash of ideologies on the floor of the Pujo Committee hearing room, and the crescendo of public cynicism about the values by which Morgan had conducted his life's work, contributed to his demise.

The stock market went up the day after he died—it had discounted the news in advance—and flags on Wall Street flew at half-mast. Condolences and tributes streamed in to the Grand Hotel from all over the world, nearly four thousand overnight. Pope Pius told the press, "He was a great and good man." Kaiser Wilhelm sent a personal message to the family through his ambassador in Rome and a wreath to place on the coffin. Secretary of State William Jennings Bryan instructed the American ambassador to assist the Morgan family in any way he could. Charles Thorley, Morgan's New York florist, wired his Roman counterparts to buy up all the orchids and lilies of the valley in the Eternal City ("because I knew Mr. Morgan's taste for quiet colors") to fill the orders that would come.

The Satterlees held a private service at the hotel, then accompanied the body by train to Paris and Le Havre. *Le Figaro* described the accumulating tributes—the Italian army in Rome marching before Morgan's coffin as before a king's, mourners in Paris covering it with orchids, carnations, roses, and palms, French soldiers at Le Havre saluting it with high honors—and concluded: "No other American citizen would have received such marks of respect from Europe—and no other would have merited this homage."* On April 5, the Satterlees sailed with the casket for New York on the *France*.

Frank Vanderlip wrote to James Stillman: "The king is dead. All New York is at half-mast. There are no cries of 'Long live the king,' for the general verdict seems to be that there will be no other king; that Mr Morgan, typical of the time in which he lived, can have no successor, for we are facing other days."

Belle Greene cabled Berenson, "My heart and life are broken."

———

A few hours after Morgan died, Dr. Dixon wired for Jack's approval a draft of a new medical bulletin for the press, mentioning the severe strain of 1907 and other harassing pressures leading up to December 1912 as having precipitated

———

* These accolades did not satisfy Morgan's survivors. The Satterlees were hurt that the Italian King did not pay his personal respects to the memory of "one who had rendered Italy no inappreciable services," reported Herman Harjes, who had raced down from Paris to help out in Rome. And they were all "a little put out" that the British ambassador had not called, especially in light of the "exceedingly courteous" message and tribute from the Kaiser. To prevent a similar slight in France, Harjes telegraphed the American ambassador in Paris to see that the French government rendered some honor—which it did "in a very handsome way" at Le Havre. Harjes told Grenfell he hoped the European governments' recognition of Morgan's "great work and personality" would "counteract in some way the antagonistic and unsympathetic attitude of our Government in America."

the banker's decline. Jack told him to omit these references, and the statement as published two days later said nothing about financial panics or congressional hearings. Information proved as difficult to control as money, however. Dr. Starr told reporters that the emotions aroused by the Pujo investigation had brought on Morgan's breakdown, and the story circulated widely in the United States. Surprised members of the committee recalled the old man's apparent ease on the witness stand, and denied that they had had anything to do with his death.

The *France* reached New York on April 11. Morgan's casket, surrounded by flowers, was laid out in his library on 36th Street under the white pall that had covered Junius's body twenty-three years earlier. The Commodore had left explicit instructions for his funeral: it was to be exactly like his father's. Specifying the clergymen who would preside, the order of the hymns, and the trains that would carry mourners from New York to Hartford, he was stage-managing his own burial. Even he could not have arranged for it to take place on Junius's one hundredth birthday.

On Monday, April 14, the New York Stock Exchange was closed in his honor till noon. At 9:23 A.M., the bronze doors of the library swung open and six men carried the coffin down the steps to a waiting hearse. Five thousand jacqueminot roses left a trail of red petals behind. Four carriages followed the hearse through streets cleared by New York City police to St. George's Church at Second Avenue and 16th Street.

An all-male choir led the procession into the church at 10:00. There were fifteen hundred people inside, and estimates of the crowd gathered in Stuyvesant Park went as high as thirty thousand. The clergymen followed the choir, with Bishop Lawrence reading, "I am the resurrection and the life, saith the Lord; he that believeth in Me, though he were dead, yet shall he live. . . ." The honorary pallbearers came next—George Baker, Jim Markoe, Elihu Root, Bob Bacon, Lewis Cass Ledyard, Henry Fairfield Osborn, Robert W. de Forest, Joseph Choate, Elbert Gary, George Bowdoin, Morton Paton, Seth Low. As the coffin entered the church ahead of Morgan's family, the choir sang "Lord, let me know my end and the number of my days."

Flowers banked the chancel. The Kaiser had sent a giant cross of orchids, the government of France a spray of palms. From James Bryce, British ambassador to the United States, there was a garland of violets and lilies of the valley, and from the Italian King a wreath of American Beauty roses tied in ribbons of red, white, and green. The Morgan family accepted only a fraction of the floral tributes, sending the rest to the Lying-In and other hospitals around New York.

Bishops Lawrence (Massachusetts), Greer (New York), and Chauncey Brewster (Connecticut), and Karl Reiland, the rector of St. George's, conducted the simple service. Among those attending were Sturgeses, Chauncey Depew, James J. Hill, Mrs. E. H. Harriman, Thomas Fortune Ryan, the Beavor-Webbs,

H. L. Higginson, W. K. Vanderbilt, Endicott Peabody, Andrew Carnegie, Thomas Edison, Charles Coffin, August Belmont, Jr., Henry Clay Frick, Mr. and Mrs. John D. Rockefeller, Jr., George Cortelyou, Frank Vanderlip, Charles Mellen, Otto Kahn, Mortimer Schiff, Isaac Seligman, Anson Phelps Stokes, Henry Walters, Edward Robinson, Benjamin Strong, George W. Perkins, the Morgan bank's partners and staff, the *Corsair* crew, and representatives of the clubs, corporations, charities, religious and genealogical societies, and cultural institutions with which Morgan had been affiliated. His surviving sisters, Mary and Juliet, were both in Europe.

According to Morgan's instructions, there was no eulogy. The choir sang his favorite hymns—"Asleep in Jesus" and "Lead, Kindly Light." Dr. Reiland read from First Corinthians 15. Bishop Greer led the creed and prayers. Then the black baritone from St. George's choir, Harry Burleigh, sang a solo, "Calvary." Bishop Brewster pronounced the benediction. To the sounds of "For all the Saints who from their labors rest," the pallbearers carried the coffin out to the hearse. Morgan's family and close friends drove directly from the church to Grand Central Terminal, where they boarded a private seven-car train for Hartford.

Flags in Hartford were at half-mast under a gray April sky when the funeral train arrived at 2:00 P.M. City and state government offices had closed for the afternoon, as had all of Hartford's schools and the businesses along its main streets. A large crowd was gathered at the station, and people three-deep lined the sidewalks as the cortège drove three and a half miles through town, past the black-draped house in which Morgan had been born, to the Cedar Hill Cemetery. The city fire bell tolled seventy-six times—the old man would have been seventy-six in three days. He had selected his burial spot, directly opposite his parents in the Morgan family plot at the crest of a hill. As at Junius's interment in May of 1890, a large white tent protected the mourners from rain. Flowers from the library and church encircled the mourners, and red roses lined the grave.

Bishop Brewster opened the brief service—"We therefore commit his body to the ground, earth to earth, ashes to ashes, dust to dust. . . ." The red-granite monument Pierpont had ordered to mark the family plot after Junius died bore an inscription from Romans 6:5: "For if we have been planted together in the likeness of His death, we shall be also in the likeness of His resurrection." The rain held off.*

Memorial services were held that day in London and Paris. The Canon of

---

* Designed for Morgan by the Hartford architect George Keller in 1892, this imposing rectangular monolith of hand-polished stone, carved with a mix of medieval, Christian, and ancient symbols, stands at the center of the plot surrounded by maples and oaks. Headstones for four generations of Morgans face the points of the compass—Joseph and Sarah north, Junius and Juliet east, Pierpont and Fanny west, Jack and Jessie south.

Westminster, William Boyd Carpenter, conducted the Anglican service at Westminster Abbey. King George and the Queen Mother sent representatives, as did the governments of Italy, Germany, and Argentina. Among the others present were Prime Minister and Mrs. Asquith, Leopold Rothschild, Junius Morgan, the Harcourts, E. C. Grenfell, Vivian and Lady Sybil Smith, Lady Dawkins, Sir Thomas Lipton, Sir Ernest Cassell, Almeric Paget, and Sir Hercules Read. At the American Church of the Holy Trinity in Paris, draped in black cloth lined with silver, those who came to honor Morgan included James Stillman, Senator and Mrs. Aldrich, Ambassador and Mrs. Myron Herrick, Jacques Seligmann, William Riggs, Mrs. Rutherfurd Stuyvesant, and Dr. and Mrs. Bashford Dean.

The day after the funeral, Fanny wrote in her diary: "Pouring . . . Spent morning in bed & Pierpont [she meant Jack] read us Pierpont's beautiful & wonderful will."

Newspapers published the contents of the will a week later. Morgan had left most of his estate to his son, just as his father had done. He gave Fanny $1 million in trust, specifying that the income, combined with that of a trust Junius had set up for her ("which fund has been very largely increased during my lifetime"), should yield $100,000 a year—equivalent to roughly $1.5 million in the 1990s. He also left her Cragston and the house at 219 Madison, with all their contents, for the rest of her life. He had set up a $3 million trust for each of his daughters, and gave $1 million each to his sons-in-law, Herbert Satterlee and Will Hamilton. To Jack, he left $3 million outright and everything else— the library, his art collections, English houses, *Corsair*, Camp Uncas, the Newport "fishing box," other real estate holdings, his interests in the Morgan banks, securities, bank accounts, positions in New York cultural institutions, wine cellars, and cigars. The total value of the estate would be calculated three years later at $80 million.

Morgan named Jack, Satterlee, Hamilton, and Ledyard as his executors. He directed them to set aside for Jim Markoe a sum that would yield $25,000 a year for the rest of the doctor's life, and the same amount to Annette if she survived her husband. To Belle Greene he left $50,000, and asked his heirs to keep her on at a salary not less than what she was earning at the time of his death. He gave $600,000 in trust to St. George's Church; $250,000 outright to his friend and yacht designer, J. Beavor-Webb; $100,000 to the House of Rest for Consumptives in Spring Lake Beach, New Jersey, designated "The Amelia Sturges Morgan Memorial Fund"; $100,000 each to Fanny's sisters; and £1,000 a year to Alice Mason (who had, it turned out, died two months before he did). Adelaide had long since been taken care of by a trust fund that had no bearing on the estate. Morgan gave smaller amounts to other friends, the *Cor-*

sair captain, his private secretary, and people who worked at the library, his houses, and the bank. He directed his executors to continue his charitable contributions, and to follow a number of other specific instructions. The will ran to thirty-four pages.

His art collections, which were eventually valued for estate purposes at $20 million, were in fact worth far more—possibly three to four times more. Morgan had estimated their value in November 1912 at $50 million. He said in his will: "it has been my desire and intention to make some suitable disposition of [the collections] . . . which would render them permanently available for the instruction and pleasure of the American people. Lack of the necessary time to devote to it has as yet prevented my carrying this purpose into effect." He hoped Jack would make some such disposition, and suggested that the Wadsworth Atheneum in Hartford be part of it, but expressly did not intend his wishes to impose binding obligations. He did not mention the Metropolitan Museum of Art.

He had assumed full responsibility for virtually everything that interested him all his life—from account books, banks, railroads, government fundings, industrial corporations, the Episcopal Church, and New York's major cultural institutions, to his guests' country weekends, Memie's failed cure, French couturiers' designs, the roses in his English garden, the pattern on his salad plates, and the details of his own funeral. Yet when it came to the works of art he had accumulated with such passion over the course of decades, he simply opened his hands and let them go. Two days after he died, the newspapers announced that New York City's Board of Estimate would appropriate $750,000 to build a new wing for his collections at the Met. It was too late.

The will opened with a vivid declaration of the Evangelical doctrine Morgan had believed in all his life—that it is not man's works but only Christ's death on the Cross that offers atonement for sin. "I commit my soul into the hands of my Saviour," he wrote, "in full confidence that having redeemed it and washed it in His most precious blood He will present it faultless before the throne of my Heavenly Father; and I entreat my children to maintain and defend, at all hazard, and at any cost of personal sacrifice, the blessed doctrine of the complete atonement for sin through the blood of Jesus Christ, once offered, and through that alone."

Newspapers across the country quoted this passage approvingly on Saturday, April 20. The press response was "not a matter of chance," Lamont told Davison: "We worked over the matter with a good deal of care, and prepared a 2,000 word summary of the will, which the A.P. used without change and telegraphed all over the country. I also prepared a brief summary to assist the New York papers, and further memoranda for the New York editors whom we knew, pointing out certain striking features."

Nonetheless, an irreverent editor in Texas ran the story that Saturday under the headline MORGAN GIVES SOUL TO MAKER, MONEY TO SON. Ministers quoted the will in their sermons the next morning, and on Monday, New York's *Evening Post* warned: "it is perhaps a little unwise for clergymen to seize upon this, in the way in which so many of them did in the pulpit yesterday. Their praise could easily be perverted into an apparent belief that what the world most needs is . . . an overwhelming demonstration that godliness is profitable. There are other Christian doctrines more in need of emphasis just now."

———

Teddy Grenfell was in New York when he learned of his senior partner's death. Returning to England on board the White Star's *Olympic*, he wrote to his fiancée that for Morgan more than for most people, "a sick old age would have been full of misery. His life had been one of fight, he had no taste for reading nor gifts of conversation, & a life of inactivity, bittered by illness, would have been a living torture to himself & his friends. . . . It is rare that the obituary notices of an American financier can be written without unpleasant criticism of methods & intentions & yet, though he was almost brutally independent of the press, the notices of JPM were uniformly pleasant. . . .

"He filled a great place & on two occasions especially saved America from disaster. It may be that his work was finished & that no occasion will again arise for treatment of a crisis in the peculiarly masterful manner that he adopted.

"Probably that is for the general good. The one man power may bring evils unless the agent is entirely single-minded & with human nature as it is, ambition jeopardizes single-mindedness." If Grenfell meant that self-interest jeopardized objectivity, he echoed the concerns of the American editorialists who praised Morgan's Pujo testimony with the reservation, "It will never do to say that unchecked power is a good thing because it is in the hands of good men."

Assuming "moral responsibility" for the growth of the strongest economy in the modern world, Morgan had earned the trust of leading international financiers and statesmen. His brusque exterior notwithstanding, he did care about what people thought of him, but he neither looked for popular favor nor altered course in the face of opposition. He could no more give up what he had been doing all his life than he could explain it. As he said, he thought it was the thing to do.

AFTERWORD

Belle Greene told Berenson in April 1913 that Morgan's $50,000 bequest would take care of her alone but not her family. She was earning $10,000 a year, she wrote, and could not afford to quit: "If some day by hook or by crook—(I guess it would have to be by *crook*!)—I could put together $100,000 for my family I could get up and leave with a clear conscience. I might as well dream of a million." Still, she may not altogether have wanted to leave. For the next three decades, as she and Jack added to the library's collections, she played a major role in international scholarship concerning manuscripts and rare books. Her relations with Berenson gradually subsided into friendship. She retired in 1948, and died two years later.

Jack put his father's art collections, with the exception of the materials at the library, on exhibition at the Metropolitan Museum in 1914—it was the only time they were all on view together (Morgan himself never saw them assembled in one place), and the museum drew a record number of visitors that year. Jack also had the collections quietly appraised, primarily by Fairfax Murray and Hercules Read. He hoped to raise $10 million to $15 million to fulfill his father's cash bequests and cover the New York State inheritance tax. As word of potential sales got out, *The New York Times* announced, ALL THE WORLD SEEKS MORGAN ART—and reported that experts in Paris, London, and New York considered it "the finest private collection" in existence.

To Duveen Brothers early in 1915, Jack sold the Chinese porcelains (for $3 million), the Fragonard panels (for about $1 million—Henry Clay Frick promptly bought them for $1.25 million), and much of the eighteenth-century French furniture, for $2 million. Also leaving the Metropolitan Museum in 1915–16 were Morgan's tapestries (sold to P. W. French & Co.) and his Renaissance bronzes and Limoges enamels (most of both collections were bought by Duveen and sold to Frick). When the director of the museum, Edward Robinson, expressed regret at the withdrawal of these works, Jack replied: "I am very sorry that there should be anything in what I do to make the Museum unhappy, and very much regret that you should have been made unhappy too." He said he had warned Robinson that the collections would be "probably very materially reduced," and "I am sure that you will realize the difference between loans and gifts."

In his father's name, at the beginning of 1916, Jack gave the Met Raphael's Colonna altarpiece and the superb medieval part of the Hoentschel collection (including the two sculptures, the *Entombment* and *Pietà*, from the Château de Biron). A year later (also as from his father) he gave the museum approximately 7,000 additional objects, estimated by Belle to be worth about $8 million—among them Assyrian, Egyptian, and classical antiquities; collections of Byzantine, Romanesque, and Gothic enamels and ivories; medieval and Renaissance metalwork, sculpture, jewelry, and amber; French pottery of the sixteenth to the eighteenth centuries; the Negroli helmet; a collection of snuffboxes and other small jeweled and ornamented caskets; several paintings; and works of Asian and Islamic art. Most of these objects were exhibited in the new Pierpont Morgan Wing until 1943, when, with the permission of Morgan's heirs, they were dispersed throughout the museum.

Morgan had said in his will that he hoped Jack would include the Wadsworth Atheneum in the disposition of his collections, and in 1917 Jack gave about 1,300 fine objects to the museum in Hartford, including ancient bronzes and glass, Italian Renaissance majolica, silver-gilt works and ivories from the seventeenth and eighteenth centuries, Venetian glass, English ceramics, and porcelains from Germany and France.

Among the Morgan paintings, Lawrence's portrait of Miss Farren—the beautiful silver-haired actress dressed in silk and fur—aroused the greatest popular interest. John D. Rockefeller, Jr., asked Jack in April 1915 whether he might buy the picture directly, and whether, if the paintings were to be sold as a group, Jack might not be willing to give him "first call" on the Lawrence. Frick also offered to buy *Elizabeth Farren* and Reynolds's *Lady Betty Delmé*: "I would like very much to have two full lengths for my dining room, and would be willing to pay you $500,000 prompt cash for these two pictures." In the estate, the Lawrence was valued at $125,000, the Reynolds at $175,000.

Jack decided to keep *Elizabeth Farren* himself. Once the estate was settled in 1916, each of Morgan's children chose several paintings (Louisa took Reynolds's *Lady Delmé*, Gainsborough's *Duchess of Devonshire*, and a Canaletto). Jack sold many of his father's paintings through M. Knoedler & Co. between 1935 and 1943: Vermeer's *Lady Writing* was eventually given by the Havemeyer family to the National Gallery in 1966; the Metropolitan Museum of Art bought the Filippo Lippi *Saint Lawrence Enthroned with Donors* in 1935, and received *Elizabeth Farren* with the bequest of Edward S. Harkness in 1940; the Trustees of the Frick Collection bought Rembrandt's *Nicolaes Ruts* through Knoedler in 1943.

In 1919 Jack offered his house at Princes Gate to the U.S. government for use as the American embassy, and the offer was accepted in 1922. Among the ambassadors who lived there were Andrew Mellon, Robert Worth Bingham, and Joseph P. Kennedy. The house now serves as headquarters for the Royal College of General Practitioners. Jack sold Dover House to the London County Council for £120,000 in 1920, and Cragston to a real-estate development syndicate in 1927; the house at Cragston was destroyed by fire in 1948.

Jack gave the McKim library and its contents to New York City as a public museum and research facility early in 1924, with an endowment of $1.5 million. After Fanny died that fall, the brownstone at 219 Madison Avenue was torn down, and in 1928 an annex designed by Benjamin Wistar Morris extended the library all the way to Madison Avenue: the new exhibition hall and reading room were connected to the original building by a "cloister" gallery.

Dr. James Markoe was shot and killed at St. George's Church in 1919 by an assassin who mistook him for Jack.

Jack remained head of the bank until he died in Boca Grande, Florida, at the age of seventy-five, in 1943.

SELECT
BIBLIOGRAPHY

BOOKS

Aaron, Daniel. *Men of Good Hope.* New York: Oxford University Press, 1961.

Adams, Henry. *The Education of Henry Adams.* New York: The Library of America, 1983 [1918].

———. *The Letters of Henry Adams.* Ed. J. C. Levenson, Ernest Samuels et al. Cambridge, Mass.: The Belknap Press of Harvard University Press, 1982–88. Six volumes.

Addison, James Thayer. *The Episcopal Church in the United States, 1789–1931.* New York: Charles Scribner's Sons, 1951.

Adler, Cyrus. *Jacob H. Schiff, His Life and Letters.* Garden City, N.Y.: Doubleday, Doran and Co., Inc., 1928. Two volumes.

Ahlstrom, Sidney. *A Religious History of the American People.* New Haven, Conn.: Yale University Press, 1972.

Allen, Frederick Lewis. *The Big Change, America Transforms Itself 1900–1915.* New York: Harper and Brothers, 1952.

———. *The Great Pierpont Morgan.* New York: Harper and Brothers, 1949.

Aronson, Theo. *The King in Love.* London: Corgi, 1989.

In August Company, The Collections of the Pierpont Morgan Library. New York: The Pierpont Morgan Library, 1993.

Baker, Paul R. *The Gilded Life of Stanford White.* New York: The Free Press, Macmillan, 1989.

Balfour, Michael. *The Kaiser and His Times.* Cambridge, Mass.: Houghton Mifflin Co., 1964.

Behrman, S. N. *Duveen.* New York: Random House, 1951, 1952.

Berenson, Bernard, and Isabella Stewart Gardner. *The Letters of Bernard Berenson and Isabella Stewart Gardner, 1887–1924.* Ed. Rollin Van N. Hadley. Boston: Northeastern University Press, 1987.

Berenson, Mary. *Mary Berenson, A Self-Portrait from Her Letters and Diaries.* Ed. Barbara Strachey and Jayne Samuels. New York: W. W. Norton & Co., 1983.

Bishop, Joseph Bucklin. *Theodore Roosevelt and His Time.* New York: Charles Scribner's Sons, 1920.

Blum, John Morton. *The Republican Roosevelt.* Cambridge, Mass.: Harvard University Press, 1977.

Boller, Paul F., Jr. *Presidential Campaigns.* New York: Oxford University Press, 1984.

Brady, Kathleen. *Ida Tarbell, Portrait of a Muckraker.* New York: Seaview/Putnam, 1984.

Brandes, Stuart. *American Welfare Capitalism, 1880–1940.* Chicago: University of Chicago Press, 1976.

Brown, David Alan. *Raphael and America.* Washington, D.C.: National Gallery of Art, 1983.

Brownlee, W. Elliot. *Dynamics of Ascent: A History of the American Economy.* New York: Alfred A. Knopf, 1974.

Bruchey, Stuart. *Growth of the Modern American Economy.* New York: Dodd, Mead & Co., 1975.

Bryce, James. *The American Commonwealth.* New York: Macmillan Co. Revised edition, 1912 [1896].

Burk, Kathleen. *Morgan Grenfell 1838–1988, The Biography of a Merchant Bank.* Oxford and New York: Oxford University Press, 1989.

Carlson, W. Bernard. *Innovation as a Social Process, Elihu Thomson and the Rise of General Electric, 1870–1900.* New York: Cambridge University Press, 1991.

Carnegie, Andrew. *The Autobiography of Andrew Carnegie.* Boston: Houghton Mifflin Company, 1920.

Carosso, Vincent. *Investment Banking in America.* Cambridge, Mass.: Harvard University Press, 1970.

———. *The Morgans, Private International Bankers, 1854–1913.* Cambridge, Mass.: Harvard University Press, 1987.

Carson, Ralph. *Davis Polk Wardwell Sunderland & Kiendl.* Privately printed, 1965.

Cecil, Lamar. *Albert Ballin, Business and Politics in Imperial Germany.* Princeton, N.J.: Princeton University Press, 1967.

Chandler, Alfred D., Jr. *Scale and Scope, The Dynamics of Industrial Capitalism.* Cambridge, Mass.: The Belknap Press of Harvard University Press, 1990.

———. *The Visible Hand, The Managerial Revolution in American Business.* Cambridge, Mass.: The Belknap Press of Harvard University Press, 1977.

———, and Richard S. Tedlow. *The Coming of Managerial Capitalism.* Homewood, Ill.: Richard D. Irwin, Inc., 1985.

Chernow, Ron. *The House of Morgan, an American Banking Dynasty and the Rise of Modern Finance.* New York: Atlantic Monthly Press, 1990.

———. *Titan, The Life of John D. Rockefeller, Sr.* New York: Random House, 1998.

Cleveland, Harold van B., and Thomas F. Huertas. *Citibank 1812–1970.* Cambridge, Mass.: Harvard University Press, 1985.

Cochran, Thomas. *The American Business System, 1900–1955.* New York: Harper and Row, 1962.

———, and William Miller. *The Age of Enterprise.* New York: Macmillan Co., 1943.

Colnaghi in America. Ed. Nicholas H. J. Hall. New York: Colnaghi, 1992.

Conot, Robert. *A Streak of Luck, The Life and Legend of Thomas Alva Edison.* New York: Seaview Books, 1979.

Cooper, John Milton, Jr. *The Pivotal Decades, The U.S. 1900–1920.* New York: W. W. Norton and Co., 1990.

———. *The Warrior and the Priest: Woodrow Wilson and Theodore Roosevelt.* Cambridge, Mass.: Harvard University Press, 1983.

Cotter, Arundel. *The Authentic History of the U.S. Steel Corporation.* New York: The Moody Magazine and Book Co., 1916.

Croly, Herbert. *Willard Straight.* New York: Macmillan Co., 1924.

Doctorow, E. L. *Ragtime.* New York: Random House, 1975.

Donald, David Herbert. *Charles Sumner and the Rights of Man.* New York: Alfred A. Knopf, 1970.

———. *Lincoln.* New York: Simon & Schuster, 1995.

Dos Passos, John. *1919.* New York: Harcourt Brace & Co., 1932.

Duveen, James Henry. *The Rise of the House of Duveen.* New York: Knopf, 1957.

Edel, Leon. *Henry James.* Philadelphia: J. B. Lippincott & Co., 1953–1971. Five volumes.

Emerson, Ralph Waldo. *The Letters of Ralph Waldo Emerson.* Ed. Ralph L. Rusk. New York: Columbia University Press, 1939. Six volumes.

Exman, Eugene. *The House of Harper.* New York: Harper & Row, 1967.

Foner, Eric. *Reconstruction 1863–1877.* New York: Harper & Row, 1988.

Foner, Philip S. *The History of the Labor Movement in the United States.* New York: International Publishers, 1964.

Forster, E. M. *Howards End.* New York: Alfred A. Knopf, 1946 [1921].

Friedel, Robert, and Paul Israel. *Edison's Electric Light, Biography of an Invention.* New Brunswick, N.J.: Rutgers University Press, 1986.

Friedman, Milton, and Anna Schwartz. *A Monetary History of the United States 1867–1960.* Princeton, N.J.: Princeton University Press, 1963.

Fry, Roger. *The Letters of Roger Fry.* Ed. Denys Sutton. New York: Random House, 1972. Two volumes.

Galbraith, John Kenneth. *Money.* Boston: Houghton Mifflin Co., 1975.

Garraty, John A. *Right-Hand Man, The Life of George W. Perkins.* New York: Harper and Brothers, 1957.

Glendenning, Victoria. *Vita.* New York: Alfred A. Knopf, 1983.

Goodwyn, Lawrence. *The Populist Moment, A Short History of the Agrarian Revolt in America.* New York: Oxford University Press, 1978.

Grant, James. *Bernard M. Baruch.* New York: Simon & Schuster, 1983.

———. *Money of the Mind.* New York: Farrar, Straus & Giroux, 1992.

Harbaugh, William Henry. *The Life and Times of Theodore Roosevelt.* New York: Collier Books, 1963 [1961].

Harris, Neil. *The Artist in American Society: The Formative Years, 1790–1860.* New York: George Braziller, 1966.

———. *Cultural Excursions: Marketing Appetites and Cultural Tastes in Modern America.* Chicago: University of Chicago Press, 1990.

Havighurst, Alfred F. *Twentieth-Century Britain.* New York: Harper & Row, 1962.

Hellman, Geoffrey. *Bankers, Bones & Beetles.* Garden City, N.Y.: The Natural History Press, 1968.

Herter Brothers, Furniture and Interiors for a Gilded Age. Ed. Katherine S. Howe, Alice Cooney Frelinghuysen, Catherine Hoover Voorsanger et al. New York: Harry N. Abrams, Inc., 1994.

Hessen, Robert. *Steel Titan, The Life of Charles M. Schwab.* New York: Oxford University Press, 1975.

Hicks, John D. *The Populist Revolt.* Minneapolis: University of Minnesota Press, 1931.

Hofstadter, Richard. *The Age of Reform.* New York: Vintage Books, 1955.

———. *The American Political Tradition.* New York: Vintage Books, 1948.

Hogan, William T. *An Economic History of the Iron and Steel Industry in the U.S.* Lexington, Mass.: Lexington Books, 1971. Five volumes.

Hovey, Carl. *The Life Story of J. Pierpont Morgan.* New York: Sturgis & Walton Co., 1912.

Hoyt, Edwin P., Jr. *The House of Morgan.* New York: Dodd, Mead & Co., 1966.

Hughes, Jonathan. *The Vital Few: The Entrepreneur and American Economic Progress.* New York: Oxford University Press, 1986 [1965].

Hughes, Thomas P. *Networks of Power, Electrification in Western Society 1880–1930.* Baltimore: Johns Hopkins University Press, 1983.

Hulderman, Bernard. *Albert Ballin.* London: Cassell and Co., 1922.

James, Henry. *The American Scene.* New York: The Library of America, 1993 [1907].

———. *The Outcry.* New York: Charles Scribner's Sons, 1911.

———. *Henry James Letters.* Ed. Leon Edel. Cambridge, Mass.: The Belknap Press of Harvard University Press, 1974–1984. Four volumes.

Jefferson, Thomas. *The Writings of Thomas Jefferson.* Ed. Paul L. Ford. New York: G. P. Putnam's Sons, 1894. Ten volumes.

Josephson, Matthew. *The Robber Barons, The Great American Capitalists 1861–1901.* New York: Harcourt Brace & Co., 1934.

Kenny, Kevin. *Making Sense of the Molly Maguires.* New York: Oxford University Press, 1998.

Klein, Maury. *Jay Gould.* Baltimore: Johns Hopkins University Press, 1986.

———. *Union Pacific,* Vol. II. *The Rebirth 1894–1969.* New York: Doubleday, 1990.

Kohlsaat, H. H. *From McKinley to Harding.* New York: Charles Scribner's Sons, 1923.

Kolko, Gabriel. *Railroads and Regulation, 1877–1916.* Princeton, N.J.: Princeton University Press, 1965.

———. *The Triumph of Conservatism.* New York: The Free Press, 1963.

Kuklick, Bruce. *Puritans in Babylon, The Ancient Near East and American Intellectual Life 1880–1930.* Princeton, N.J.: Princeton University Press, 1996.

Lamont, Thomas W. *Henry P. Davison: The Record of a Useful Life.* New York: Harper & Brothers, 1933.

Lamoreaux, Naomi R. *The Great Merger Movement in American Business, 1895–1904.* New York: Cambridge University Press, 1985.

Lawrence, William. *Memories of a Happy Life.* Boston: Houghton Mifflin Co., 1926.

Letwin, William. *Law and Economic Policy in America, The Evolution of the Sherman Antitrust Act.* New York: Random House, 1965.

Lewis, Arnold, James Turner, and Steven McQuillin. *The Opulent Interiors of the Gilded Age.* New York: Dover Publications, 1987.

Lincoln, Abraham. *The Collected Works of Abraham Lincoln,* Ed. Roy P. Basler. New Brunswick, N.J.: Rutgers University Press, 1953. Eight volumes.

Lippmann, Walter. *Drift and Mastery.* Westport, Conn.: Greenwood Press, 1978 [1914].

———. *A Preface to Politics.* New York: Mitchell Kennerley, 1913.

Livesay, Harold C. *Andrew Carnegie and the Rise of Big Business.* New York: Harper-Collins, 1975.

Livingston, James. *Origins of the Federal Reserve System: Money, Class, and Corporate Capitalism 1890–1913.* Ithaca: Cornell University Press, 1986.

Logan, Sheridan A. *George F. Baker and His Bank, 1840–1955.* Privately printed, 1981.

Lyon, Peter. *Success Story: The Life and Times of S. S. McClure.* New York: Charles Scribner's Sons, 1963.

Madrick, Jeffrey. *The End of Affluence.* New York: Random House, 1995.

Magnus, Philip. *King Edward the Seventh.* New York: E. P. Dutton & Co., Inc., 1964.

Marbury, Elisabeth. *My Crystal Ball.* New York: Boni & Liveright, Inc., 1923.

Martin, Albro. *James J. Hill and the Opening of the Northwest.* St. Paul: Minnesota Historical Society Press, 1991 [1976].

Massie, Robert K. *Dreadnought, Britain, Germany, and the Coming of the Great War.* New York: Random House, 1991.

———. *Nicholas and Alexandra.* New York: Atheneum, 1972.

McCraw, Thomas K. *Prophets of Regulation.* Cambridge, Mass.: The Belknap Press of Harvard University Press, 1984.

McElroy, Robert. *Levi Parson Morton.* New York: G. P. Putnam's Sons, 1930.

McPherson, James M. *Battle Cry of Freedom.* New York: Oxford University Press, 1988.

Moody, John. *The Masters of Capital.* New Haven, Conn.: Yale University Press, 1919.

J. Pierpont Morgan, Collector. European Decorative Arts from the Wadsworth Atheneum. Ed. Linda Horvitz Roth. Hartford, Conn.: Wadsworth Atheneum, 1987.

Moore, Charles. *The Life and Times of Charles Follen McKim.* Boston: Houghton Mifflin Co., 1929.

Morris, Edmund. *The Rise of Theodore Roosevelt.* New York: Coward, McCann & Geoghegan Inc., 1979.

Mott, T. Bentley. *Myron T. Herrick, Friend of France: An Autobiographical Biography.* Garden City, N.Y.: Doubleday & Co., 1930.

Nevins, Allan. *Grover Cleveland, A Study in Courage.* New York: Dodd, Mead & Co., 1932.

Nicolson, Nigel. *Portrait of a Marriage.* New York: Atheneum, 1973.

Parker, Franklin. *George Peabody*. Nashville, Tenn.: Vanderbilt University Press, 1971.

Passer, Harold C. *The Electrical Manufacturers, 1875–1900*. Cambridge, Mass.: Harvard University Press, 1953.

Peritz, Rudolph J. R. *Competition Policy in America 1888–1992*. New York: Oxford University Press, 1996.

Phelan, Craig. *Divided Loyalties, the Public and Private Life of Labor Leader John Mitchell*. Albany: State University of New York Press, 1994.

Pringle, Henry F. *Theodore Roosevelt, A Biography*. New York: Harcourt, Brace & Co., 1931.

Rainsford, William S. *A Preacher's Story of His Work*. New York: The Outlook Company, 1903.

———. *The Story of a Varied Life*. Garden City, N.Y.: Doubleday, Page & Co., 1922.

Reitlinger, Gerald. *The Economics of Taste, The Rise and Fall of the Picture Market 1760–1960*. New York: Holt, Rinehart & Winston, 1961.

Ripley, William Z. *Trusts, Pools and Corporations*. Boston: Ginn and Co., 1916.

Roosevelt, Theodore. *Autobiography*. New York: Charles Scribner's Sons, 1920.

———. *Works*. Ed. Hermann Hagedorn. New York: Charles Scribner's Sons, 1926. Twenty volumes.

———. *Letters of Theodore Roosevelt*. Ed. Elting E. Morison and John M. Blum. Cambridge, Mass.: Harvard University Press, 1951–54. Eight volumes.

———. *Selections from the Correspondence of Theodore Roosevelt and Henry Cabot Lodge, 1884–1918*. Ed. Henry Cabot Lodge. New York: Charles Scribner's Sons, 1925. Two volumes.

Rousmaniere, John. *The Life and Times of the Equitable*. New York: The Equitable Companies, Inc., 1995.

Saarinen, Aline. *The Proud Possessors*. New York: Random House, 1958.

Samuels, Ernest. *Bernard Berenson*, Vol. II, *The Making of a Legend*. Cambridge, Mass.: Harvard University Press, 1987.

Satterlee, Herbert L. *J. Pierpont Morgan, An Intimate Portrait*. New York: Macmillan Co., 1939.

Schlesinger, Arthur M., Jr. *The Age of Jackson*. Boston: Little Brown and Co., 1947.

———. *The Crisis of the Old Order, 1919–1933*. Boston: Houghton Mifflin Co., 1957.

Scott, James Brown. *Robert Bacon—Life and Letters*. Garden City, N.Y.: Doubleday, Page & Co., 1923.

Sherman, John. *Recollections of Forty Years*. Chicago: The Werner Company, 1895.

Sklar, Martin J. *The Corporate Reconstruction of American Capitalism, 1890–1916*. New York: Cambridge University Press, 1988.

Smalley, George W. *Anglo-American Memories*. New York: G. P. Putnam's Sons, 1912.

Smith, Adam. *The Wealth of Nations*. New York: Random House Modern Library, 1937.

Smith, Jane S. *Elsie de Wolfe, A Life in the High Style*. New York: Atheneum, 1982.

Sobel, Robert. *Panic on Wall Street*. New York: Collier Books, 1968.

Steel, Ronald. *Walter Lippmann and the American Century*. New York: Vintage, 1981.

Steffens, Lincoln. *The Autobiography of Lincoln Steffens*. New York: Harcourt, Brace & Co., 1931.

Stern, Robert A. M., Gregory Gilmartin, and John Massengale. *New York 1900: Metropolitan Architecture and Urbanism 1890–1915*. New York: Rizzoli, 1995 [1983].

Sterne, Margaret. *The Passionate Eye, the Life of William R. Valentiner*. Detroit, Mich.: Wayne State University Press, 1980.

Stigler, George J. *The Organization of Industry*. Chicago: University of Chicago Press, 1968.

Swanberg, W. A. *Pulitzer*. New York: Charles Scribner's Sons, 1967.

———. *Whitney Father, Whitney Heiress*. New York: Charles Scribner's Sons, 1980.

Tarbell, Ida M. *The History of the Standard Oil Company*. Gloucester, Mass.: Peter Smith, 1963 [1904].

———. *The Life of Elbert H. Gary, The Story of Steel*. New York: D. Appleton & Co., 1925.

Taylor, Francis Henry. *Pierpont Morgan as Collector and Patron*. New York: The Pierpont Morgan Library, 1970.

Temin, Peter. *The Jacksonian Economy*. New York: W. W. Norton & Co., Inc., 1969.

Tomkins, Calvin. *Merchants and Masterpieces, The Story of the Metropolitan Museum of Art*. New York: E. P. Dutton and Co., Inc., 1973 [1970].

Vasari, Giorgio. *Lives of the Painters, Sculptors and Architects*. Trans. Gaston du C. de Vere. New York: Everyman's Library, Alfred A. Knopf, 1996. Two volumes.

Wall, Joseph Frazier. *Andrew Carnegie*. Pittsburgh: University of Pittsburgh Press, 1989 [1970].

Warren, Kenneth. *The American Steel Industry 1850–1970, A Geographical Interpretation*. Oxford: The Clarendon Press, 1973.

Webb, Ross A. *Benjamin Helm Bristow*. Lexington: University of Kentucky Press, 1969.

Werner, Morris R. *William Jennings Bryan*. New York: Harcourt, Brace and Co., 1929.

Wharton, Edith. *The Age of Innocence*. New York: Charles Scribner's Sons, 1968 [1920].

Wilkins, Mira. *The History of Foreign Investment in the United States to 1914*. Cambridge, Mass.: Harvard University Press, 1989.

Wilson, John A. *Signs and Wonders Upon Pharaoh*. Chicago: University Press of Chicago, 1964.

Woodward, C. Vann. *Origins of the New South, 1877–1913*. Baton Rouge: Louisiana State University Press, 1951.

Woolf, Virginia. *Roger Fry*. New York: Harcourt Brace Jovanovich, 1968 [1940].

Yarmolinsky, Abraham, trans. and ed. *The Memoirs of Count Witte*. Garden City, N.Y.: Doubleday, Page & Co., 1921.

Ziegler, Philip. *The Sixth Great Power, Barings, 1762–1929*. London: Collins, 1988.

ARTICLES, DISSERTATIONS, GOVERNMENT REPORTS,
LAW CASES, UNPUBLISHED MANUSCRIPTS

Alcaly, Roger, "Reinventing the Corporation," *The New York Review of Books*, April 10, 1997.

Baker, Ray Stannard. "What the U.S. Steel Corporation Really Is." *McClure's Magazine*, Vol. VIII, No. 1, November 1901.

Blakely, Allison. "Richard T. Greener and the 'Talented Tenth's' Dilemma." *Journal of Negro History*, Vol. LIX, No. 4, October 1974.

Cleveland, Grover. "The Cleveland Bond Issues." *Saturday Evening Post*, May 7, 1904.

Conant, Charles A. "Saving the National Credit." Unpublished memorandum about the 1895 gold crisis at the Pierpont Morgan Library, HLS Box 7, folder 7.

Davis, Richard W. " 'We Are All Americans Now!' Anglo-American Marriages in the Later Nineteenth Century." *Proceedings of the American Philosophical Society*, Vol. 135, No. 2, 1991.

Dell, Theodore. "J. Pierpont Morgan, Master Collector: Lover of the 18th-Century French Decorative Arts." *The International Fine Arts and Antique Dealers Show*, Seventh Regiment Armory, New York, October 1995.

de Wolfe, Elsie. "Story of Mr. De Beauvoir." Unpublished manuscript. The Pierpont Morgan Library.

Edison, Thomas A. Papers: A Selective Microfilm Edition. Ed. Thomas E. Jeffrey et al. Four parts to date. Bethesda, Md.: University Publications of America, 1985–.

Garber, Peter M., and Vittorio U. Grilli. "The Belmont-Morgan Syndicate as an Optimal Investment Banking Contract." *European Economic Review* 30, 1986.

Hidy, Muriel Emmie. "George Peabody, Merchant and Financier, 1829–1854." Radcliffe PhD thesis, 1939.

Lawrence, William. "Memoir of J. Pierpont Morgan," 1914. Unpublished manuscript. The Pierpont Morgan Library.

Logan, Andy. "That Was New York: Town Topics." *The New Yorker*, August 14 and 21, 1965.

McCraw, Thomas K. "Rethinking the Trust Question." *Regulation in Perspective*. Ed. Thomas K. McCraw. Cambridge, Mass.: Harvard University Press, 1981.

————, and Forest Reinhardt. "Losing to Win: U.S. Steel's Pricing, Investment Decisions, and Market Share, 1901–1938." *Journal of Economic History*, Vol. XLIX, No. 3, September 1989.

Meade, Edward S. "The Capitalization of the International Mercantile Marine Company." *Political Science Quarterly*, Vol. XIX, 1904. Reprinted in William Z. Ripley, *Trusts, Pools and Corporations*, pp. 360–71.

————. "The US Steel Corporation's Bond Conversion." *Quarterly Journal of Economics*, Vol. XVIII, 1903. Reprinted in Ripley, pp. 228–68.

Meyer, Balthasar H. "A History of the Northern Securities Case." *Bulletin of the University of Wisconsin*, No. 142, Madison, 1906.

Moody, John, and George K. Turner. "Masters of Capital." *McClure's Magazine,* November 1910.

Navin, Thomas R., and Marian V. Sears. "The Rise of a Market for Industrial Securities, 1887–1902." *Business History Review,* Vol. 29, June 1955.

———. "A Study in Merger: Formation of the International Mercantile Marine Company," *Business History Review,* Vol. 28, December 1954.

Pope-Hennessy, John. "Roger Fry and the Metropolitan Museum of Art." *Oxford, China and Italy: Writings in Honor of Sir Harold Acton on his 80th Birthday.* Ed. Edward Chaney and Neil Ritchie. London: Thames & Hudson, 1984.

(Pujo Committee) *Money Trust Investigation.* Testimony of J. Pierpont Morgan. Printed from the stenographic transcript taken in Washington, D.C., December 18–19, 1912. The Pierpont Morgan Library.

Rainsford, William S. "Personal Recollections." Unpublished manuscript. The Pierpont Morgan Library.

Ravitz, Abe C. "John Pierpont: Portrait of a Nineteenth Century Reformer." PhD dissertation, 1951, Department of English, New York University.

Roosa, Ruth A. "Banking and Financial Relations between Russia and the U.S." *International Banking 1870–1914.* Ed. Rondo Cameron and V. I. Bovykin. New York: Oxford University Press, 1991.

Rousmaniere, John. "Called into Consultation, The History of Davis Polk & Wardwell, 1849–1992." Unpublished manuscript. Davis Polk & Wardwell.

Simon, Matthew. "The Morgan-Belmont Syndicate of 1895 and Intervention in the Foreign-Exchange Market." *Business History Review,* Vol. 42, No. 4, Winter 1968.

Smith, George David, and Richard Sylla. "The Transformation of Financial Capitalism: An Essay on the History of American Capital Markets." *Financial Markets, Institutions and Instruments,* Vol. 2, No. 2, May 1993.

Soukoup, Nancy Hamlin. "From Orthodoxy to Liberalism: The Theology and Ministry of William Stephen Rainsford (1850–1933)." Master of Divinity thesis, 1983, The Episcopal Divinity School.

US v. Northern Securities Company et al., U.S. Circuit Court, District of Minnesota, Third Division. Special Examiner's Transcript, Complainant's Testimony, Vol. I (1902).

U.S. Senate Committee on Judiciary Report on Absorption of Tennessee Coal and Iron, to Accompany S. Res. No. 243. Washington, D.C., 1909, 60th Cong., 2nd Sess., Report No. 1110.

Valentiner, Wilhelm R. Papers. "Reminiscences." Unpublished manuscript. Archives of American Art, Smithsonian Institution, Washington, D.C.

Wiebe, Robert W. "The House of Morgan and the Executive." *American Historical Review,* Vol. 65, 1959–60.

NOTES

MANUSCRIPT COLLECTIONS

Barings—The Baring Archive at ING Barings, London
Bodleian—The Bodleian Library, Oxford University
CHS—The Connecticut Historical Society, Hartford, Conn.
Columbia—Rare Book and Manuscript Library, Columbia University, New York
Cornell—Division of Rare and Manuscript Collections, Cornell University Library,
    Ithaca, N.Y.
HBS—Historical Collections, Baker Library, Harvard University Graduate School of
    Business Administration, Boston, Mass.
Huntington—The Huntington Library, San Marino, Calif.
I Tatti—Villa I Tatti, The Harvard University Center for Italian Renaissance Studies,
    Florence, Italy
JJH—The James Jerome Hill Reference Library, St. Paul, Minn.
King's—King's College Library, Cambridge University
LC—Manuscript Division, Library of Congress, Washington, D.C.
Lilly—The Lilly Library, Indiana University, Bloomington, Ind.
MGCo.—Morgan Grenfell Archives, the Guildhall Library, London
MGCo. (GWS)—Morgan Grenfell at Great Winchester Street (now Deutsche/Mor-
    gan Grenfell), London
MHS—The Massachusetts Historical Society, Boston, Mass.
MMA—The Metropolitan Museum of Art Archives, New York
MMA Egypt—The Metropolitan Museum of Art, Egyptian Art Department archives
NHHS—The New Hampshire Historical Society, Concord, N.H.
N-YHS—The New-York Historical Society, New York
PEM—Phillips Library, The Peabody Essex Museum, Salem, Mass.
PML—The Pierpont Morgan Library, New York
PML, MSI—the Mabel Satterlee Ingalls papers at The Pierpont Morgan Library
Princeton—Manuscripts Division, Department of Rare Books and Special Collec-
    tions, Princeton University Library, Princeton, N.J.
Schieffelin—private papers of the late Annette Markoe Schieffelin
St. Just—private papers of the Estate of the First Lord St. Just

TAEM—Thomas A. Edison Papers: A Selective Microfilm Edition. Edited by Thomas E. Jeffrey et al. Four parts to date. Bethesda, Md.: University Publications of America, 1985–

Valentiner—William R. Valentiner, "Reminiscences," Archives of American Art. Microfilm reel D31, frames 410–433.

INDIVIDUALS

AC—Andrew Carnegie
AJD—Anthony J. Drexel
AL—Albert Lythgoe
AMS—Annette Markoe Schieffelin
AS/ASM—Amelia Sturges, Amelia Sturges Morgan
ATM—Anne Tracy Morgan
BB—Bernard Berenson
BG—Belle da Costa Greene
CED—Clinton E. Dawkins
CFM—Charles Follen McKim
CHC—Charles H. Coster
CS—Charles Steele
ECG—Edward C. Grenfell
EPF—Egisto P. Fabbri
ER—Edward Robinson
FLT/FTM—Frances Louisa Tracy, Frances Tracy Morgan
GP—George Peabody
GWP—George Walbridge Perkins
HA—Henry Adams
HCS—Henry Cady Sturges
HFO—Henry Fairfield Osborn
HJ—Henry James
HLS—Herbert L. Satterlee
HPD—Henry Pomeroy Davison
ISG—Isabella Stewart Gardner
Jack—J. P. Morgan, Jr.
JJG—James Junius Goodwin
JJH—James J. Hill
JM—Joseph Morgan
JP—John Pierpont, Jr.
JS—Jonathan Sturges
JSM—Junius Spencer Morgan (father of JPM)
JSM2—Junius Spencer Morgan (nephew of JPM)
Juliet—Juliet Pierpont Morgan (mother of JPM)
Juliet(d)—Juliet Pierpont Morgan (daughter of JPM)

Juliet(s)—Juliet Pierpont Morgan (sister of JPM)
LPM/LMS—Louisa Pierpont Morgan, Louisa Morgan Satterlee (daughter of JPM)
LS—Lady Victoria Sackville
MCS—Mary Cady Sturges
MLP—Mary Lord Pierpont
RJP—the Reverend John Pierpont
RF—Roger Fry
TAE—Thomas Alva Edison
TR—Theodore Roosevelt
TWL—Thomas W. Lamont
VHS—Vivian Hugh Smith
VSO—Virginia Sturges Osborn
WHB—Walter Hayes Burns
WSR—Willam S. Rainsford

D after any individual's initials (as in JPMD) indicates diary entries.

L before or after initials indicates published letters (*LHA* = *Letters of Henry Adams*; *HJL* = *Henry James Letters*).

BG notes in Hovey: Morgan's librarian, Belle Greene, probably read him Carl Hovey's *Life Story of J. Pierpont Morgan* (1912) aloud, because she made notes of his comments in the margins of her copy; it is at The Pierpont Morgan Library.

INTRODUCTION

Page

ix "There were": Frederick Lewis Allen, *The Great Pierpont Morgan*, p. vii.

ix "Unto whom": *Yale Alumni Weekly*, Commencement Number, 1908. "financial Moses": B.C. Forbes, *Men Who Are Making America* (New York: B.C. Forbes Publishing Co., 1916), p. 252.

x "beefy": NY *Times*, April 13, 1910. "boss croupier": John Dos Passos, *1919*, p. 337. " 'imperiously' ": Matthew Josephson, *The Robber Barons*, p. 319. "a burly": E.L. Doctorow, *Ragtime*, p. 114.

xi "peculiarly": Josephson, *Robber Barons*, pp. 440–41.

xii "most important": William R. Valentiner "Reminiscences." "a crude": in Virginia Woolf, *Roger Fry*, p. 141.

xii "This ridiculous": A.M. Lindbergh to author, July 2, 1987.

xii "JPM"—St. Just: ECG to Maud Grenfell, May 19, 1906. "MONEY TALKS": *Chicago Daily Tribune*, Dec. 10, 1908.

xiii "pure act": Henry Adams, *The Education of Henry Adams*, p. 1101.

xiii "you felt": AMS interview, May 9, 1993. "as if": PML—William Lawrence, "Memoir of JPM," p. 68. "the most": I Tatti—BG to BB, Aug. 24, 1909.

xiii "[T]he popular idea": St. Just: ECG to Mrs. Willy Buckler, Dec. 4, 1909.

xiv a "land": Walter Lippmann, *Drift and Mastery*, pp. 23–25.

Page   CHAPTER 1: MONEY AND TRUST

4 $25 billion: "Final Report from the Pujo Committee," Feb. 28, 1913. *House Report No. 1593*, 62nd Cong., 3rd sess., 2.

4 "Napoleon": *Economist*, April 5, 1913.

5 "glass pockets": William S. Rainsford, *The Story of a Varied Life*, p. 291.

7 "I hope": MGCo., Ms 21,800—CED to Jack, Dec. 10, 1901.

7 "We never": MGCo. Ms 21,800—CED to GWP, July 19, 1902.

8 "One out of": London *Times*, Dec. 4, 1908.

8 "the blessed": MGCo. Ms 21,800—CED to Gerald Balfour, June 8, 1903.

9 "behave" & "Investigation": PML—Jack to JPM, March 22 & April 25, 1912.

9–10 "So I can hear": NY *Post*, Dec. 20, 1912.

10 "No, thanks" & ff.: NY *Times*, Dec. 20, 1912.

10–11 "Oh no": NY *Times*, Dec. 20, 1912.

11 "What I say": *Money Trust Investigation*, Testimony of JPM (1264), Dec. 18 & 19, 1912, p. 53.

11 "Your idea" & ff.: Ibid., pp. 54–56.

11 "I do not": NY *Times*, Dec. 20, 1912.

11 "suddenly": NY *Post*, Dec. 20, 1912.

12 "Your power" & ff.: *Money Trust Investigation*, pp. 67 ff.

13 "The basis" & ff.: Ibid., pp. 92–93.

13 "We are": NY *Times*, Dec. 21, 1912.

13 "quite": PML—Jack to ECG & VHS, Dec. 20, 1912.

13 "If impressions": NY *Times*, Dec. 21, 1912.

14 "uncommon": NY *Post*, Dec. 20, 1912.

14 "the country": PML—LMS to Jack, March 6, 1913.

14 "HOW WEALTHY": NY *Herald*, April 2, 1913.

15 "rugged": NY *Press*, April 1, 1913. "sincerity": *The Outlook*, April 12, 1913, p. 816. "first-class": WSJ quoted in *Literary Digest*, April 12, 1913. "distinctly": London *Times*, April 1, 1913. "embodiment": NY *Evening Sun*, March 31, 1913.

15 "commanding" & ff.: NY *World*, April 1, 1913.

15 "Whatever": NY *Post*, March 31, 1913.

                          CHAPTER 2: PIERPONTS AND MORGANS

18 "the vinegar": RJP to Samuel Hitchcock, June 22, 1806, in Abe Ravitz, "John Pierpont" p. 9.

18 "perfectabilitarian": Sidney Ahlstrom, *A Religious History of the American People*, pp. 399–401.

18 "his eyes": PML—Joseph H. Choate interview with HLS, Jan. 1916.

19 "an irritating": PML—RJP to JP, Oct. 26, 1857. "and when": Ibid., Aug. 26, 1855.

19 "do all": PML—RJP to MLP, March 31, 1836.

Page
19   "as I": PML—JSM to RJP, Feb. 13, 1836.
19   "beautiful": PML—JSM to JPM, March 1 [1884].
19   "a perfect": PML, HLS Papers—Mary Beach interview.
19   "the most": George W. Smalley, *Anglo-American Memories*, p. 219.
20   *fn.*: PML—JMD, 1809–12.
21   "Locomotive": Ibid., Dec. 14, 1839.
21   "Those who": "Notes on the State of Virginia," in *The Writings of Thomas Jefferson*, Vol. III, pp. 268–70.
22   "Was introduced": PML—JMD, Feb. 8, 1832.
22   "Abroad": Ibid., Dec. 31, 1832.
23   "whether": Arthur M. Schlesinger, Jr., *The Age of Jackson*, p. 108.
23   "might": Ibid., p. 91.
23   "The Bank": Ibid., p. 89.
23   "altho' ": PML—JSM to RJP, Feb. 13, 1836.
24   *fn.*: F. Perry Close, *History of Hartford Streets* (Hartford: The Connecticut Historical Society, 1969).
24   "Junius came": PML—JMD, May 11, 1836.
24   "I leave": in John Kenneth Galbraith, *Money*, p. 108.
24   "This day": PML—JMD, March 3, 1837.
24   "roughly": Galbraith, *Money*, p. 21.
24–25 "Don't" & ff.: PML—Howe, Mather to JSM, May 8, 13, & 18, 1837.
25   "Our own" & "We are": Ibid., May 8 & 13, 1837.
25   "Self &": CHS, Ms 72547—JSM Correspondence.
25   "young Mr. Morgan" & ff.: PML—JMD, Feb. 19, March 2 & 24, 1838.
25   "Child" & "Boy": Ibid., April 29 & July 28, 1838.
25–26 "Master" & "Bub": PML—JSM to RJP, Nov. 14, Dec. 8, 1838.
26   "Whatever": PML, HLS Box 6, folder C-12—"Personal Anecdotes," Nov. 6, 1913.
26   "your *beautiful*": PML—JM to JSM, June 13, 1839.
26   "quite troubled: PML—JSM to RJP, Dec. 27, 1839.
26   "he had not": Rev. E.C. Towne, "A Discourse in Commemoration of the Life and Character of Rev. John Pierpont," Medford, Mass., Sept. 2, 1866.
27   "very long": PML—JMD, Dec. 21, 1838.
27   "he was": PML—Mary E. Pierpont to RJP, May 13, 1860.
27   "My ideal" & "Dear Father": PML—JP to RJP, June 6, 1852, April 11, 1854.
27–28 "too busy": in Ravitz, pp. 140–46, 280.
28   "indignant": PML—JSM to RJP, Oct. 11, 1839.
28   "*every*" & ff.: in Ravitz, pp, 283, 227.
28   "I think": RWE to TP, July 17, in Ralph Rusk, *Letters of Ralph Waldo Emerson*, Vol. III, pp. 70–71.
28   "I hope": PML—JSM to RJP, Feb. 21, 1842.
28   "ecclesiastical" & ff.: in Ravitz, pp. 285–97.
29   "James K. Polk": PML—JMD, March 4, 1845.

Page

29   "church . . . only": Ahlstrom, *Religious History*, p. 630.

30   "Without" & ff.: JMD—Dec. 13, 1846; April 9, 1847.

CHAPTER 3: A MORAL EDUCATION

31   "the very": PML—JPM to RJP, Jan. 3, 1848.

31   "I am": Ibid., March 14, 1848.

32   "Pierpont goes": PML—JSM to RJP, April 10, 1848.

32   "I noticed": PML—JSM to JPM, April 17, 1848.

32   "twice glad": PML—Juliet to JPM April 23, 1848.

32   "It only shows": PML—Juliet to RJP, June 15, 1860.

32   "very careful": PML—JSM to JPM, March 1, 1851.

34   "I think": PML—in Juliet to JPM, Feb. 23, 1851.

35   "more than any": Joseph P. Thompson, *Young Men Admonished* (Buffalo: Phinney & Co., 1852), pp. 10–32.

35   "full of": PML—J.B. Burbank to HLS, April 4, 1914.

35   "Miss Stevens": PML, MSI—JPM to Sophia Stevens [1850].

36   "lofty": PML—JPM to JJG, June 17, 1856.

36   "I promised": *An Introduction to Geometry*, James Munroe & Co., 1846.

36–37   "the celebrated" to "I expect": PML—JSM to JPM, May 16 & 30, [1850].

38   "Sleighing" & ff.: PML—JPMD, Jan.–June 1850. "Glad to" & ff.: Ibid., Aug. 26, 1850; March 7 & Nov. 29, 1851.

38–39   "It is": Jared Sparks, *Life of George Washington* (Boston: Tappan and Dennet, 1843), Vol. I, abridged, pp. 4–9.

39   Math problems: PML Base Family Collection Box III.

39–40   Essays: PML, Base Family Collection Box II.

40–41   "Did you," "I would," & "to see": PML—JPM to JJG, Jan. 23 & 30 & Oct. 1, 1852.

41   "change": PML, HLS A-3—JJG to HLS, Oct. 31, 1914.

41–42   "Wind" to "woefully": PML—JPM Journals, and letter to his parents Nov. 23, 1852.

42   "O!" & "in order": PML—JPM Journal, Dec. 25 & 18, 1852. "I get": to parents, Jan. 8, 1853.

43   "according" & "The people": Ibid., Nov. 23, 1852.

43   "These lazy": Ibid., March 4, 1853.

43   "I don't": PML—Journal, Jan. 3, 1853. "I wish": to parents, Jan. 24, 1853.

43   "It seems" to "no more": PML—JPM to parents, Jan. 8–Feb. 23, 1853.

44   "I continue," "I miss," & "as fast": Ibid., Feb. 23, April 2, March 6 & 22, 1853.

45   "I held": PML—JPMD, May 19, 1853.

45   "Had 1st": Ibid., Aug. 19, 1853. "Father thinks": PML, MSI—JPM to JJG, Sept. 13, 1853. "Have to": JPMD—Sept. 16, 1853.

45   "very dull" & "hardly": PML—JPM to JJG, Sept. 20 & Oct. 6, 1853.

Page

46   "it would": Transylvania University, Jefferson Davis Papers, JPM to
      Jefferson Davis, Sept. 20, 1853.

46   "We went": A.A. Lawrence to Giles Richards, June 1, 1854, in James
      McPherson, *Battle Cry of Freedom*, p. 120.

46   "Great excitement": PML—JPMD, June 2, 1854.

46   "I should" & "positively": PML, MSI—JPM to JJG, Dec. 6, 1853.

47   JPM's Napoleon essay: PML—Base Family Collection.

47   *fn.*: Albert Guérard, *Reflections on the Napoleonic Legend* (New York:
      Charles Scribner's Sons, 1924) p. 101; Howard Mumford Jones &
      Daniel Aaron, "Notes on the Napoleonic Legend in America," *The
      Franco-American Review*, Vol. II, No. 1, Summer 1937, p. 18.

CHAPTER 4: FOREIGN AFFAIRS

50   "We believe": PEM, George Peabody Papers—George Peabody to DS&Co.,
      April 2, 1852, in Muriel E. Hidy, "George Peabody," p. 343.

52   "a very": PML, MSI—JPM to JJG, Sept. 5, 1856.

52   "a secluded": Franklin Parker, *George Peabody*, pp. 29–33.

53   "we naturally": A.M. Chadboone to JSM, April 28, 1854. "If Mr.":
      Samuel G. Ward to Baring Bros & Co, Oct. 27, 1854. Both in Vincent
      Carosso, *The Morgans*, p. 36.

53   "a splendid": MGCo.—GP to JSM, May 5, 1854.

53   "the advantage": CHS, Ms 72263—JSM to JJG, April 7, 1857.

53   "my heart": PML—Delmonico's dinner pamphlet, Nov. 8, 1877.

54   "Father commenced": PML—JPMD, Oct. 2, 1854.

54   "docile": PML—T.J. Scalé to JSM, Nov. 2, 1854.

54   "Imagine": PML—JPM to RJP, June 15, 1855.

55   "In a room" & ff.: PML—JPM to Pars., Nov. 19 & Dec. 30, 1854.

55   "dear Pierpont" & "Adapts": PML, MSI—Sillig to JSM, Nov. 10, 1854, &
      Feb. 21, 1855; also in HLS, A-13.

55   "I never": PML—JPM to Pars., Dec. 30, 1854.

55   "the very": CHS, Ms 72263—JPM to JJG, Dec. 4, 1855.

56   "it has": PML—JPMD, Dec. 31, 1854.

56   "pantaloons" & ff.: PML—JPM account books 1854–57.

56   "an eruption" & ff.: PML—JPM to JJG, July 30, 1855.

57   "plenty of" & ff.: CHS, Ms 72263—JPM to JJG, Sept. 7, 1855.

57   "In every": Ibid., Nov. 3, 1855. "If . . .": PML, MSI—JPM to JJG, March 1,
      1856.

57   "don't it": CHS, Ms 72263—JPM to JJG, Nov. 20, 1855. "Why" & "it is":
      PML, MSI—JPM to JJG, March 1, 1856.

58   "I was": CHS, Ms 72263—JPM to JJG, Sept. 7, 1855. "In all labor":
      PML—Base Family Collection, II; June 1855. "little short": PML—
      William Riggs to HLS, Nov. 20, 1913.

Page

58 "How pleasant": CHS, Ms 72263—JPM to JJG, Dec. 16, 1855. "that uneasiness": PML, MSI—JPM to JJG, Oct. 14, 1856. "I tell you": CHS, Ms
72263—JPM to JJG, Dec. 4, 1855.

58–59 "tip top" & "Grandmother": PML, MSI—JPM to JJG, Feb. 16 & March 1,
1856.

59 "The whole": CHS, Ms 72263—JPM to JJG, Oct. 1, 1855.

59 "When one": PML, MSI—JPM to JJG, April 15, 1856.

60 "situated" to "for he": Ibid., April 29, June 17, & July 1, 1856.

61 *fn.,* "I can": PML—RJP to JP, April 6, 1855.

61 "a capital": PML, MSI—JPM to JJG, June 17, 1856.

61–62 "Although" to "dull": Ibid., May 10 & July 1, 1856.

63 "little": PML—RJP to JP, Oct. 26, 1857. "constitution" & "imaginative":
JP to RJP, March 3 & 26, 1857.

63–64 "consider" to "Between": PML, MSI—JPM to JJG, Sept. 5 & Oct. 14, 1856.

64 "famously" & ff.: PML—JSM to GP, Nov. 14, 18, 25, 1856, & Jan. 9, 1857.

65 "Columbus": JSM to Cyrus Field, Aug. 10, 1858; quoted in *Cyrus W. Field,
His Life and Work,* edited by Isabella Field Judson (New York: Harper &
Brothers, 1896), p. 104. "None": PML—JSM to JPM, August 6, 1858.

65 "You do": PML—JSM to Cyrus Field, Dec. 28, 1860.

65 "great sorrow": PML, HLS Box 2—W. Parker Prentice to HLS, Feb. 10,
1914.

65 "It is" & "interfered": CHS, Ms 72263—JPM to JJG, March 15, & JSM to
JJG, April 7, 1857.

66 "Mother objects": Ibid.—JPM to JJG, July 13, 1857.

66 "We none": PML—JSM to F.P. Corbin, March 25, 1857.

66 "the economic": quoted in Havighurst, *Twentieth-Century Britain,* p. 14.

66 "It was" & "sound": PEM, George Peabody Papers—W.W. Sherman to GP,
July 18, 1857, & GP to Wm. Tiffany, April 27, 1850. "I look": MGCo.: GP
to JSM, April 14, 1854.

67 "for some": PEM, GP Papers—WWS to GP, July 18, 1857.

67 "I want": PML—JSM to JPM, July 24 [1857].

CHAPTER 5: NEW YORK

70 "fine style": CHS, Ms 72263—Sarah Goodwin to JJG, Oct. 13, 1857.

70 "one of": George Lockwood, *Manhattan Moves Uptown* (Boston: Houghton
Mifflin Company, 1976), p. 175.

70–71 "There is" & "I am": PML—JSM to JPM, Oct. 29 & 8, 1857.

71 foreign investment figures: Mira Wilkins, *The History of Foreign Investment in the U.S.,* pp. 76, 95–96.

71 "season": PML—JSM to F.P. Corbin, Oct. 2, 1856.

72 "We are easy" & "You are": PML—JSM to GP, Oct. 7, & to JPM, Oct. 8
[1857].

Page

72   "What a pity": Ibid., to JPM, Oct. 29, 1857.

72   Dun & Co.: in Carosso, *Morgans*, p. 65.

73   "It pained": PML—JPM to JSM, Dec. 4, 1857.

73   profit: MGCo. Ms. 21,761—GPCo. P&L Statements, 1854–64.

73   "reliable": in Carosso, p. 69.

75   "the prince": *Dictionary of American Biography* (Tyng).

75   "come": PML—Stephen H. Tyng, "The Vow Assumed" (New York: John A. Gray, 1858).

75   "in great need": PML—Juliet to RJP, Feb. 3, 1857.

75   "much the most" to "perfect": PML—RJP to JP, Oct. 26, 1857, & Jan. 7, 1858.

76   "strange": PML—Juliet to RJP, Jan. 8, 1858.

76   "The poor": PML—in Juliet to JPM, March 14, 1858. "his gentle" to "I cannot": JSM to JPM, March 25, 1858.

77   *fn.:* David McCullough, *The Path Between the Seas* (New York: Simon & Schuster, 1977), pp. 34–36.

77   "I do not" & "I judged": PML—JSM to JPM, March 25 & April 16, 1858.

77–78 "Be true" & "Do not let": Ibid. (March 25 & April 16).

78   "little improvement": PML—JSM to RJP, July 2, 1858.

78   "I don't know": PML—JSM to JPM, Aug. 6, 1858.

79   "the most": PML—"To Her Majesty Queen Amelia from Her Grateful and Obliged Lord Chancellor" (New York: Century Association, 1858).

79   "even if": PML—AS to MCS [summer 1858].

79   *fn.: The Century, 1847–1946* (New York: Century Association, 1947).

80   "Father was out": N-YHS, Henry Fairfield Osborn Papers, Box XXIV—Virginia Sturges Diary, April 16, 1851.

81   "Our cottage": PML—AS to MCS, July 17, 1856. *fn.,* "an entirely": *Harper's Weekly,* 1867, in *American Paradise, The World of the Hudson River School* (New York: Metropolitan Museum of Art, 1987), p. 42; "Heart of the Andes": PML—JPMCo. Ledger C, Jan. 20, 1863; Kevin J. Avery, *Church's Great Picture, The Heart of the Andes* (New York: Metropolitan Museum of Art, 1993).

81   "in a laughing": N-YHS, Osborn Papers—AS to "Aunt" [Elizabeth Murray], Feb. [probably Jan.] 10, 1859.

82   "We feel": Ibid., MCS to [Elizabeth Murray], Jan. 29, 1859.

82   "Sea": PML—ASD, Feb. 9, 1859. "full": CHS, Ms 72263—Sarah Goodwin to JJG, March 4, 1859.

82   "You are": PML—JSM to JPM, March 15, 1859.

82   "low-spirited," "We young," & "She is": CHS, Ms 72263—Sarah Goodwin to JJG, March 4 & 28, 1859.

82–83 "Having been": PML—JPM to JS, April 11 [1859].

83   "an excellent" & "raptures": PML—ASD, May 17, 1859, & AS to [Elizabeth Murray], July 9, 1859.

Page

83   "miserable": PML—ASD, Sept. 14, 1859.

83   "voluntary": PML—DS&Co. to JPM, Sept. 24, 1859.

84   "I cannot": PML—JPM to DS&Co., Sept. 24, 1859.

84   "in walked": PML—HCSD, Nov. 11, 1859.

84   "Returned" & a "delicious": PML—ASD, Nov. 14 & 24, 1859.

CHAPTER 6: A HOUSE DIVIDED

87   "tremendously" & ff.: CHS, Ms 75347—JPM to JJG, Jan. 9, 1860.

88   "all the shame": quoted in McPherson, *Battle Cry of Freedom*, pp. 199–201.

88   "Of all the": CHS, Ms 75347—JPM to JJG, Jan. 9, 1860.

88   "1000" & ff.: PML—JPMD, Jan. 6–26, 1860.

89   *fn.*, "get taken": Huntington, BW Box 34 (41)—JSM to Samuel Barlow, Feb. 7, 1860.

89   "& others": PML—JSM to JPM, May 8, 1860.

89   "A house divided": *Collected Works of Abraham Lincoln,* edited by Roy P. Basler, Vol. II, p. 461.

89   "into a higher": *Speech of William H. Seward Delivered at Rochester, New York, Oct. 25, 1858* (Washington, D.C.: Buell & Blanchard, printers, 1858).

90   "I feel": PML—JSM to JPM, July 11, 1860.

90   "something": PML—AS to HCS, Sept. 28, 1860.

90   "You see": PML—JSM to AS, Feb. 22, 1861.

90   "for Memie": N-YHS, Osborn Papers, Box I—VSO to Aunt [Elizabeth Murray], Jan. 31, 1861.

90   "some difficulty": PML—JSM to AS, Feb. 22, 1861.

91   "nothing short": PML—JSM to JVL Pruyn, Jan. 5 [1861].

91   "terrible state": PML—JSM to AS, Feb. 22, 1861.

91   "bright": N-YHS, Osborn Papers, Box I—MCS to her mother, March 2, 1861.

92   "a long": Adams, *Education,* p. 817.

92   "it would be": N-YHS, Osborn Papers, Box I—VSO to Lucy Wheeler, May 6, 1861.

92   "the Gallant": PML—HCSD, April 19–20, 1861. "one out of": N-YHS, Osborn Papers, Box I—VSO to Lucy [Wheeler], May 6, 1861.

92   "Well done": PML—JP to RJP, May 7, 1861.

92   " 'the seceded' " & ff.: PML—RJP to JP, Oct. 18–31, 1861.

93   "familiar": Reports of Committees of the House of Representatives, 37th Cong., 2nd sess. 1861–62 (Washington, D.C., Government Printing Office, 1862), Vol. I, p. 238.

94   "hurry up": *U.S.* v. *Simon Stevens,* Appeal from the Court of Claims (No. 2,524), Supreme Court of the United States, No. 343. Filed Dec. 7, 1867, pp. 1–2.

Page
94   *fn.,* "How are books": Parker, *George Peabody,* p. 161.
94–95   payments & earnings: War Department Investigation of Hall Carbine Affair, Vol. II: Arms Purchase Report, p. 472.
95   "in good order" & ff.: *U.S.* v. *Stevens,* pp. 3–4.
95   "no public": House Reports, Vol. II, p. lxviii.
95   "Mr. Morgan had": War Dept. Investigation, Vol. II, p. 472.
95   R. Gordon Wasson, *The Hall Carbine Affair, A Study in Folklore* (New York: Pandick Press, Inc., 1948).
96   "dreadful": PML—ASM to MCS, Oct. 1, 1861.
96   "at this": PML—JSM to JS, August 30, 1861.
96   "violent": PML—AS to MCS, Oct. 1, 1861.
96–97   wedding dress: at the Fairfield, Conn., Historical Society.
97   "Memie is": PML—JPM to [JS, Oct. 9, 1861].
97   "came upon": Ibid., Dec. 15, 1861.
97–98   "quite tasteless" to "Now don't": PML—ASM to MCS, Nov. 15, 1861.
98   "I think" & "but I believe": PML—ASM to MCS, Dec. 5 & 9, 1861.
99   "*he* is very": PML—JS to "sister," Jan. 1, 1862.
99   "I do not wish" & "I cannot hide": PML—JPM to JS, Dec. 21 & 28, 1861.
100   "We miss": PML—MCSD, Feb. 6, 1862.
100   "Whenever" & ff.: PML—VSO to ASM, Feb. 18, 1862.
100   "tell Ed": PML—JS to MCS, Feb. 7, 1862.
100   "threw" & ff.: PML—MCS to VSO, Feb. 18, 1862.
101   "Mr. Morgan": PML—MCSD, Feb. 19, 1862.
101   "I cannot" & "It is not": PML—JSM to JPM, Feb. 17 & 18, 1862.
102   "We would": PML—Juliet to JPM, March 12, 1862.

CHAPTER 7: QUESTIONS OF CONTROL

105   "absolutely": PML—in MCS to JS, March 20, 1862. "together": PML—JPM to JJG, March 21, 1862.
105   "Pierpont took" & "Heard": PML—MCSD, May 11 & 12, 1862.
106   "I was": PML—JJG Recollection to HLS.
106–7   "tremendous traffic" to "My place": PEM, George Peabody Papers—JPM to JSM, Sept. 12–19, 1862.
107   "Once a": PML—JPM Box 6, Nov. 15, 1862.
108   "the sweet": PML—MCS to her mother, Dec. 20, 1862.
108   "Dissatisfaction": PEM, GP Papers—JPM to GPCo., Sept. 12, 1862. "disasters": CHS, Ms 75347—JSM to JJG, Sept. 20, 1862.
108   "demented": Adams, *Education,* p. 838.
108   "All are against": PML—MCSD, Nov. 11, 1862. "If there is": in McPherson, *Battle Cry,* p. 574. "somewhere": Adams, *Education,* p. 874.
109   "Down with" & "There goes": in McPherson, *Battle Cry,* p. 610.

Page

110   millionaires: Robert Sobel, *Panic on Wall Street*, p. 117. *fn.*, 1863 for-
       tunes: Alfred D. Chandler, Jr., and Richard S. Tedlow, *The Coming of Man-
       agerial Capitalism*, p. 260.

110   *fn.*, price of gold: Milton Friedman and Anna Schwartz, *A Monetary His-
       tory of the United States*, p. 85.

110   "which governs": PEM, GP Papers—JPMCo. to GP Co., Sept. 12, 1862.

110–11 Profit on gold corner: PML—JPMCo. Ledger C, pp. 171–75; Carosso,
       Morgans, p. 102; Allen, *Great Pierpont Morgan*, p. 27.

111   "a young": NY *Times*, Oct. 12, 1863. *fn.*, gold prices: PML—JPMCo.
       Ledger C, pp. 172–75, & NY *Times*, Oct. 13–17, 1863; "first-rate": Dun
       & Co. "Credit Ledgers," CCCXLVII, 882, in Carosso, p. 103.

111   "disappointed": CHS, Ms 75347—JSM to JJG, Jan. 31 [1864].

112   Shares of capital & profits: PML—Dabney, Morgan & Co. Private
       Ledger, 1864–1879. *"just right"*: CHS, Ms 72263—JSM to Maj. James
       Goodwin, Dec. 17, 1864.

112   "fiery trial": Abraham Lincoln, Second Annual Message to Congress,
       Dec. 1, 1862, in *Collected Works*, Vol. II, p. 688.

113   "As you may": PML—BG to H.B. Ledyard, Jan. 11, 1910. copy: HBL to
       BG, Jan. 29, 1910.

113   "obvious": PML, HLS Box 2, A-4—JPM to George W. McCrary, May 15,
       1877.

114   *fn.*, "princely": in Parker, *Peabody*, pp. 147–49.

114–15 "without" to "fearful": PML—JPM to FLT, March 17, 19, & 20, 1865.

115   "curiosity" & ff.: Ibid., March 20, 1865.

116   "warmest": PML—JSM to JPM, April 11 & 15, 1865.

116   "to allow": PML—JPM to FLT, April 17, 1865.

116   "being nurse": PML—JPM to MCS, June 22 [1865]. "She has": PML—
       VSO to MCS, Aug. 15, 1865.

117   "startling": NY *Times*, Aug. 16, 1865.

117   "the most": CHS, Ms 75347—JSM to JJG, Sept. 2, 1865.

117   loss to Ketchum: PML—DMCo. Ledger A, p. 582, and Private Ledger
       (1864–79), second set. p. 80.

117   "Nothing will": CHS, Ms 75347—CHD to JJG, Sept. 15, 1865.

118   "where she is": PML—RJP to JP, Oct. 27, 1864.

119   "when his": CHS, Ms 75347—CHD to JJG, April 10, 1866. "in his new":
       PML—JSM to JS, July 1, 1866.

119   "didn't want" to "I condoled": PML—JPM to FTM, Feb. 26–March 4, 1867.

119   "You don't" to "It will": Ibid., July 5–8, 1867.

120   "as the bell" & ff.: PML—Fred Sturges to Henry Sturges, Aug. 16, 1867.

120   "fearfully" to "the most": PML—JPM to FTM, Aug. 17–20, 1867.

121   "I have no": PML—JSM to JVL Pruyn, Dec. 11, 1885.

121   "in greater danger": E. Foner, *Reconstruction*, p. 24.

Page
122   "happily": PML—JPM to FTM, Dec. 8, 1867.
122   *fn.*, "By the time": Galbraith, *Money*, pp. 88–89.
123–24   "seemed to be" & "though he": PML—JPM to FTM, Dec. 12, 1867, & Aug. 2, 1868. "could have": in E. Foner, *Reconstruction*, p. 340.
124–25   "most agreeably" to "Father was": PML—JPM to FTM, July 12–Aug. 18, 1868.
126   "thin aesthetic": Robert Hughes, *The Culture of Complaint* (New York: Warner Books, 1994), p. 174.
126   "every important" & *fn.*: Nicholas Hall, "Old Masters in a New World," *Colnaghi in America*, pp. 9–10.
126   "rival": Ibid., p. 26. "I think": HJ to Thomas S. Perry, Sept. 20 [1867], *Henry James Letters*, Vol. I, p. 77.
127   "I get" & "*far* more": PML—JPM to FTM, July 26 & Oct. 30, 1868.

CHAPTER 8: NEW DIRECTIONS

129–30   Economic figures: Jonathan Hughes, *The Vital Few*, pp. 400–401; Jeffrey Madrick, *The End of Affluence*, p. 54; Stuart Bruchey, *Growth of the Modern American Economy*, p. 84.
130   "the wonderful": PML—JSM to F.P. Corbin, March 25, 1857. Foreign investment: Wilkins, *History of Foreign Investment in U.S.*, pp. 109 & ix.
131   Railroad capital: Alfred D. Chandler, Jr., *The Visible Hand*, p. 90.
131   "Such comfortable" & ff.: PML—FTMD, July 19–Aug. 26, 1869.
136   "carrying things": CHS, Ms 72254–72263, Letterpress Vol. JJG 1865—JJG to JSM, Aug. 20, 1869.
137   "waged not": NY *Times*, Jan. 24, 1873.
137   "consd. of": in Chandler & Tedlow, *Managerial Capitalism*, p. 261.
137   net worth: Carosso, *Morgans*, p. 141.
137–38   "lost his" to "Please do not": CHS, Ms 72254–72263 Letterpress Vol. JJG 1865—JJG to JSM, Dec. 20, 1869, & Feb. 3, 1870.
138   "masterly": MGCo.—JSM to M. K. Jesup, Jan. 22, 1870.
138   Carnegie's worth: Joseph Frazier Wall, *Andrew Carnegie*, pp. 222–23.
138    $7 million: David McCullough, *The Great Bridge* (New York: Simon & Schuster, 1972), p. 183.
138   "toll-gate": Andrew Carnegie, *Autobiography*, p. 155–57; "novel": MGCo. Ms 21,795—JSM to DMCo., March 24, 1870.
138–39   "that was all": Wall, *Carnegie*, p. 272. "already smaller": MGCo.—JSM to DMCo., April 2, 1870.
139   "we have": AC to JSM, June 6, 1876, in Wall, p. 329.
140   "There are": in Philip Ziegler, *The Sixth Great Power*, p. 10.
140   "signed": MGCo.—JSM to S.T. Dana, July 16, 1870.
140–41   Junius decision: Smalley, *Anglo-American*, p. 216.

Page

141 "I feel": PML—JPM to JJG & GHM, Jan. 3 [1871].

142 "largely": MGCo. Ms 21,760—AJD to JSM, Jan. 27, 1871.

143 "timely notice": PML—JPM to CHD, JJG, GHM, March 10, 1871.

CHAPTER 9: ILL WINDS

145 "my beloved": PML—JPM to FTM, Jan. 18, 1882.

146 "Cooks": Nissan Perez, *Focus East* (New York: Harry N. Abrams, Inc., 1988), p. 46.

146 "a sort": in Leon Edel, *Henry James*, Vol. II (*The Conquest of London*), pp. 91–92.

147 "my pocket" & "overdo": PML—JPM to FTM, May 3 & 7, 1872.

147 Cragston: PML, MSI—Charles Tracy to FTM, April 26 & July 18, 1872.

147 "We each": PML—FTM to MCS, June 26, 1872.

149 "head and": Robert McElroy, *Levi Parsons Morton*, p. 53.

149 "While we": MGCo.—JSM to LPM & JPM, Feb. 8, 1873.

149 "no questioning": PML—JPM to JSM, July 24, 1873.

150 "amber": Ibid., June 8, 1877.

150–51 "which can" to "nothing harassing": Ibid., March 28, April 17 & 18, June 7, & July 24, 1873.

151 $1.5 billion: Wilkins, *History Foreign Investment*, pp. 90–91. "Affairs": PML—JPM to JSM, Sept. 20, 1873. "cyclone": Ibid., to Rodewald, Oct. 30, 1873.

151–52 "Everything": PML—JPM to JSM, Sept. 20, 1873. "No anxiety": MGCo. Ms 21,760—JPM & AJD to JSM, Sept. 26, 1873.

152 "People of": Adam Smith, *The Wealth of Nations*, p. 128. "The tendencies": Thomas K. McCraw, *Prophets of Regulation*, p. 66.

153 "general principles": in Chandler, *Visible Hand*, p. 125.

153 "great principle": J.W. Garrett to JSM, March 9, 1877, in Carosso, *Morgans*, p. 228.

154 "The market is": Harold Livesay, *Andrew Carnegie*, p. 105.

155 "To imagine": Richard Hofstadter, *The American Political Tradition*, p. 165.

155–56 "Its powers": NY *Times*, Oct. 14, 1876.

156 "they divided": Hofstadter, *APT*, p. 169.

156 "as if": Henry Demarest Lloyd, in Daniel Aaron, *Men of Good Hope*, p. 151. "an auction": in Thomas C. Cochran and William Miller, *The Age of Enterprise*, p. 158.

157 "not merely": in E. Foner, *Reconstruction*, p. 523.

157 "I don't": PML—JPM to JSM, Feb. 13, 1874.

157 "Fanny": PML, MSI—Adele Stevens to FTM, Nov. 20, 1873.

157 "The competition": PML—JPM to JSM, Jan. 29, 1875, #2. "a great": Ibid., to Rodewald, Aug. 11, 1875.

Page

158 "sweep": NY *World,* June 1874. Hamilton Fish Diary, June 5, 1874. Both in Ross A. Webb, *Benjamin Helm Bristow,* pp. 136–37.

158 "pleasure": MGCo. Ms 21,802—JSM to BHB, Jan. 28, 1875; "clear-headed": PML—JPM to JSM, March 24, 1875.

158 "I am": MGCo. Ms 21,760—JPM to BHB, Feb. 8, 1876; "I need": BHB to JPM, Feb. 9, 1876; "to beg": JPM to BHB, Feb. 23, 1876; "I beg": BHB to JPM, Feb. 28, 1876.

159 "as if" & "He is": PML—JPM to JSM, March 3 & 30, 1875. "rough": Joseph Seligman in Carosso, *Morgans, n.* 26, p. 693.

159 "a capital" & "strongly": PML—JPM to JSM, March 30 & Sept. 10, 1875.

159–60 "he bounded": Ida Tarbell, *A History of the Standard Oil Company,* Vol. I, p. 43.

160 "extra stout": PML—JPM to C. Turner, June 23, 1886.

160 "must depend," "unexceptionable," & "like a duck": PML—JPM to JSM, Sept. 10 & Oct. 19, 1875, & Jan. 10, 1876.

161 "although I": Ibid., Jan. 10, 1876.

161 "liberal patron": Luigi Palma di Cesnola, "In Memoriam Junius S. Morgan," *Philadelphia Evening Bulletin,* April 11, 1890.

162 *fn.,* "I don't": Gerald Reitlinger, *The Economics of Taste,* pp. 187–88.

163 "another": PML—FTMD, July [5–9], 1876.

163 "The King": PML—JPM to FTM, July 7, 1876.

163 "After dinner": PML—FTMD, Aug. 8–9, 1876.

163 "strict": MGCo.—EPF to JSM, July 12–14, 1876.

164 "a third-rate": E. Foner, *Reconstruction,* p. 567. *fn.,* "Bristowism": Webb, *Bristow,* p. 220.

164 *very great*": MGCo.—EPF to JSM, July 12–14, 1876.

164 "just such": PML, MSI—LPM to FTM, March 18, 1913.

165 "Such contributions" & "looking": MGCo.—DMCo. to JSMCo., Sept. 15 & JSMCo. to DMCo., Sept. 18, 1876.

165 "Oh!" & "Though the": PML—FTMD, Jan. 8 & 11, 1877.

166 "that potentate": Ibid., April 6, 1877.

CHAPTER 10: "THE FUTURE IS IN OUR OWN HANDS"

167 "Pierpont brought": PML—FTMD, Oct. 2, 1878.

168 "all the high": Ibid., Aug. 20, 1877.

168 "I hope" & "I wish it": PML—JPM to FTM, Aug. 23, 1877.

168 "a hideous": PML—FTMD, March 28, 1878.

170 to "drain": in E. Foner, *Reconstruction,* p. 557.

172 "a nation's": John Sherman, *Recollections,* II, pp. 604–5.

173 Molly Maguires: Kevin Kenny, *Making Sense of the Molly Maguires.*

Page

174   "It takes": Henry James, *The American Scene*, p. 495.

174   "it contains": in Calvin Tomkins, *Merchants and Masterpieces*, p. 43.

174   "desolate": Albert S. Bickmore, in Robert M. Peck, "The Museum That Never Was," *Natural History*, July 1994, p. 66.

176   "one of": NY *Times*, Nov. 9, 1877, p. 8.

176–79   Speeches: PML—"JSM Testimonial Dinner, Nov. 8, 1877."

179   "interested": PML—JPM to JSM, Jan. 17, 1878.

179   "we should" & "alarming": Ibid., Feb. 8 & March 4, 1878.

180   *fn.*, "suitable" & $10,000: MGCo. Ms 21,760—DMCo. to JSMCo., Sept. 3 & DMCo. to Belmont, Oct. 23, 1878.

180   "Thanks for": McElroy, *Morton*, p. 81.

180   "I never was": PML—JPM to WHB, Oct. 30, 1878.

181   "such that": PML—JPM to J. Rogers, Feb. 10, 1879.

181   "very much": PML—JPM to WHB, Oct. 30, 1878.

181   Edison patents: Robert Friedel and Paul Israel, *Edison's Electric Light*, pp. 1, 224.

181–82   "never so" & "The only answer": in J. Hughes, *Vital Few*, pp. 173–76. "I have it": in Friedel and Israel, p. 13. gas stock prices: PML—JPM to WHB, Oct. 30, 1878.

182   "All I want": TAE to GPL, Oct. 3, 1878, in Friedel and Israel, p. 22.

182   strengths: JPM to Francis Lynde Stetson, in John Rousmaniere, "Called Into Consultation," p. 34.

182   "to the world": PML—JPM to WHB, Oct. 30, 1878.

182   "enough money" & ff.: TAEM—GPL to TAE, Oct. 18 & 23, & Dec. 10, 1878.

183   "extreme secrecy": PML—JPM to WHB, Nov. 19, 1878. *fn.*, agreements: TAEM—GPL to Gouraud, Dec. 31, 1878, GPL to DMCo., March 25, 1880.

183   "good enough": in J. Hughes, *Vital Few*, p. 177. "I cannot": PML—JPM to JSM, Dec. 26, 1878.

184   "honor and": in McElroy, *Morton*, p. 88.

185   "all [our]" to "It seemed": PML—JPM to WHB, Jan. 21, 1879.

185–86   "cutting" & "I have rarely": N-YHS, BV Morton, Bliss & Co., Letterpress Vol. III—George P. Bliss to L.P. Morton, April 8, 1879. "We accept": MGCo. Ms 21,760—JSMCo. to DMCo., April 9, 1879.

186   "our Mr.": MGCo.—DMCo. to JSMCo., April 22, 1879.

186   "turned over" & Fort Sherman: James Grant, *Money of the Mind*, pp. 58, 41.

186   "We have": N-YHS, BV Morton, Bliss & Co., Letterpress Vol. III—George P. Bliss to C.D. Rose, May 27, 1879.

187   "undertake": MGCo.—JPM to WHB, June 28, 1881.

187   "secure": PML—JPM to F. Wood, Dec. 6, 1880.

187   "single": J. Moody and George K. Turner, "Masters of Capital," *McClure's Magazine*, No. 1, Nov. 1910, pp. 13–14.

Page	CHAPTER 11: FAMILY AFFAIRS AND PROFESSIONAL ETHICS

189 "He was powerless": Family papers of Thomas P. Cook—"Highland Falls," memoir of Grace Bigelow Cook, p. 3.

189 "Felt forlorn" & ff.: PML—FTMD, May 17–21, 1879. "Good bye": JPM to FTM, April 26, 1879.

190 "I wish you could see": Ibid., May 7, 1879.

190 "Everything," "altho' " & "it makes": PML, MSI—JPM to LPM, May 7 [1880], [spring 1883?], & Dec. 22 [1881].

190 "touched": PML—JPM to Gov. W.W. Hoppin, Dec. 16, 1879.

191 "tête-à-tête": PML—JPM to FTM, Feb. 29, 1880.

191 "I can scarcely" & "I dread": Ibid., March 22, 1880.

191–92 "I felt" to "joyful": Ibid., April 11, 1880.

192 "enjoyed": Ibid., April 20, 1880.

192 "which also": PML, MSI—JPM to LPM, May 7 [1880]. "No. 5": PML—JPM to FTM, April 26, 1880.

192–93 "swallowed" to "And darling": Ibid., May 5, 1880.

193 "Hard a port!": PML—JPM to JSM, June 9, 1880.

193–94 "loneliness" to "come back": PML—JPM to FTM, July 16–19, 1880.

194 "little high": MGCo. Ms 21,802—JPM to JSM, Feb. 10, 1880.

194–95 "I certainly": PML—JPM to JSM, March 10, 1880. "Tell Mama": (MSI) to LPM, May 7, 1880. "just the house": to FTM, April 30, 1880.

196 "our friends" & ff.: MGCo. Ms 21,802—JSMCo. to DMCo., Dec. 6, 13, & 14, 1873, & Jan. 10, 1874.

196 "We all know": PML—JPM to JSM, Dec. 8, 1875.

197 "We have had": PML—JPM to Mr. Pierson, Nov. 26, 1877.

198 "attacked": PML—JPM to JSM, Feb. 4, 1880. *fn.*, "we did": PML—JPM to JSM, March 10, 1880; "I never": PML—JPM to S.E. Peabody, June 24, 1884.

198 "between continuing": Maury Klein, *Jay Gould,* p. 242.

198 "with a view," "I had," & ff.: PML—JPM to JSM, Feb. 4, Aug. 27, & Oct. 19, 1880.

199 "navigating" & ff.: Ibid., March 1, 1881. "you just": Sheridan A. Logan, *George F. Baker,* p. 77.

199 "about as" & "If it were": PML—JPM to JSM, March 1, 1881, & to JJG, Feb. 27, 1880.

200 "Mrs. Sumner" to "natural feelings": David H. Donald, *Charles Sumner and The Rights of Man,* pp. 276–77, 290, 314. "a pathological": Adams, *Education,* p. 950.

201 "Ladies": Howe to Sumner, Feb. 14, 1868, in *The Selected Letters of Charles Sumner,* edited by Beverly Wilson Palmer (Boston: Northeastern University Press, 1990), Vol. II, p. 420. *fn.*,* "women are": Violet Paget, July 16, 1885, in *Vernon Lee's Letters,* edited by Irene Cooper Willis (privately printed, 1937), pp. 177, 222; "like a": Donald, *Sumner,* p. 320.

Page

201 "outrageous": HA to Elizabeth Cameron, Sept. 25, 1895, in *Letters of Henry Adams*, Vol. IV, p. 332. "her great": Edel, *HJ*, Vol. II, p. 106.

201 *fn.*†, "intrinsically": HJ to Mrs. HJ Sr., Jan. 18 [1879], in *HJL*, Vol. II, p. 212.

202 "There it": PML—in FTM to MCS, Jan. 10 [1882].

202–3 "protected" to "My next": PML—JPM to FTM, Jan. 14–18, 1882.

203 "Man intends" to "there is": Ibid., Jan. 23, 1882.

203 "it would seem": in John A. Wilson, *Signs and Wonders Upon Pharaoh*, p. 73.

204–5 "Egyptomaniac" to "one of the most gorgeous": PML—JPM to FTM, Jan. 23–Feb. 11, 1882.

205 "I must leave" to "you pass": Ibid., Feb. 18, 1882.

206 "Steam yacht": PML—Van Heerden: Cragston Guest Book.

206 "Fairylike": Paul R. Baker, *The Gilded Life of Stanford White*, p. 212. "Pneumonia" & "robber baron": John Parkinson, Jr., *The History of the New York Yacht Club* (New York: The New York Yacht Club, 1975), pp. 111–12.

206 "You have": Bill Robinson, *Legendary Yachts* (New York: David McKay Co., 1971) p. 11. "If it makes": PML, HLS Box 6, folder C-12—Bonbright to HLS, May 20, 1927. Sale for $70,000: PML—JPM to William Moore, Oct. 3, 1891.

207 "great decision": PML—FTMD, July 20, 1882.

207 "I can't": PML—JSM to JPM [May 1881?].

208 "Please come" & "O you": PML—Jack to FTM, March 9 & Nov. 15, 1883. "How nice": (MSI) to LPM, Oct. 28, 1883. "you will be" to "Do you think": (PML) to FTM, April 4–15, Oct. 4, Nov. 15, & May 6, 1883.

209 "Papa hates" & ff.: Ibid., Nov. 23 & Oct. 23, 1885, & Feb. 18, 1883.

209 "I cannot" & ff.: Ibid., Feb. 7, June 10, Nov. 30, 1883, & June 4, 1884.

209 "plain living": PML, MSI—FTM to LPM, May 16, 1886.

210 "[I] trust" to "I wish": Ibid., July 27 & August [n.d.] 1886, & April 16 & May 13, 1883.

210 "When you" to "I suppose": Ibid., May 9 [1883]; Sept. 6 [1886]; April 18, 1884; Aug. 30 & 13, 1886.

210 "I note": Ibid., JPM to FTM, Sept. 23, 1886.

211 "Of course": Ibid. LPMD, April 12, 1889. "she was" & ff.: LPM to FTM, [April], April 24, & May 18, 1883.

212 "like the": PML—JSM to JPM, March 1 [1884].

212 "very much": PML—JPM to J. Rogers, March 17, 1884. "To the glory": JPM to Thomas Dana, March 28, 1884.

212 "Grandpa and": PML, MSI—LPM to FTM, May 18 [1884].

CHAPTER 12: "THE GILDED AGE"

215–16 annual incomes: Thomas G. Shearman, "The Owners of the United States," *The Forum*, Vol. VIII, Nov. 1889, p. 265.

Page

216   "decent people": Edith Wharton, *The Age of Innocence*, pp. 125–66.

217   "only about": *The "400"* (New York: Melville Publishing Co. [1892]).

217   "Scarcely": Adams, *Education*, p. 1037.

218   "tight little": Wharton, *Age of Innocence*, p. 31.

218   "a little too": MGCo. Ms 21,802—JPM to JSMCo., Aug. 31, 1907. "white": Barings—Lord Revelstoke to Gaspard Farrer, April 19, 1904. *fn.*, "By which": PML—ATM to FTM, July 27 [n.d.].

218   "deep-chested": *Evening Sun*, May 1888, in Nancy Hamlin Soukoup, "From Orthodoxy to Liberalism," p. 90.

219   "the wrong side": Rainsford, *Story of a Varied Life*, pp. 64–65.

219   "a dirty": Ibid., p. 210.

219–20   "Done," "No man," & "I am not": PML—Personal Recollections of Dr. W. S. Rainsford, pp. 4–8.

220   "hive": James T. Addison, *The Episcopal Church in the United States*, p. 282. "Isn't it": PML, MSI—Jack to LPM, March 11 [1883].

221   "great work": PML—JPM letter, in WSR Recollections, pp. 12–13.

221   "so that": PML—JPM to J. Hickson, Jan. 15, 1883. "Don't work": Rainsford, *Story of a Varied Life*, p. 278.

221–22   "wide and": PML—WSR Recollections, p. 16. "I do not," "intemperate" & ff., & "extraordinarily": Rainsford, *Story*, pp. 292, 284–89, 287–89; *fn.*, "very": PML—Jack to FTM, Oct. 6, 1922.

222   "Many love": Rainsford, *Story*, p. 289.

223   "an American artist" & ff.: *The Century Magazine*, Nov. 1884 to April 1885, Vol. XXIX, new series Vol. VII.

223   "humanize" & ff.: Tomkins, *Merchants and Masterpieces*, pp. 17–24.

224   "the present": M.E. Sherwood, in Arnold Lewis, James Turner, and Steven McQuillin, *The Opulent Interiors of the Gilded Age*, p. 18.

224   "an almost indiscriminate": *Herter Brothers*, p. 200.

225   "just beginning": Edward Strahan in Lewis, Turner, McQuillan, *Opulent Interiors*, pp. 17–18.

225   "I wish": EW to OC, May 2, 1897, in Pauline C. Metcalf, *Ogden Codman and the Decoration of Houses* (Boston: Boston Athenaeum, 1988), p. 149. "either bizarre": in Peter Thornton, *Authentic Decor, The Domestic Interior 1620–1920* (New York: Viking, 1984), p. 309.

225–26   "That house": *World*, Jan. 6, 1884, in W.A. Swanberg, *Whitney Father, Whitney Heiress*, p. 70.

227   "*himself*": Lewis, Turner, McQuillan, *Opulent Interiors*, p. 147.

230   "funds" & ff.: Friedel and Israel, *Edison's Electric Light*, pp. 22, 38. "had been": TAEM—GPL to TAE, Dec. 23, 1878.

231   "Mr. Fabbri looked" & ff.: Ibid., Jan. 25, 1879.

231–32   "that you agreed": Ibid., Oct. 24, 1879. $480,000: Harold C. Passer, *The Electrical Manufacturers*, p. 88. "Friend": TAEM—EPF to TAE, Dec. 26, 1879.

Page

232 "I think": PML—JPM to W.W. Hoppin, March 23, 1881. *fn.* "to relieve": TAEM—DMCo. to TAE, April 19 & 27, 1881.

232 exhibitions: Friedel & Israel, pp. 213–14, and Thomas P. Hughes, *Networks of Power,* pp. 50–57.

232–33 "The greatest": Friedel & Israel, p. 230. "begin[n]ing": Edison National Historic Site, LM-003—Samuel Insull to E.H. Johnson, Jan. 8, 1882.

233 "showed": NY *Times,* Sept. 5, 1882; NY *Herald* & NY *Sun* in Friedel & Israel, p. 222.

233 "If it was": PML, HLS A-10—E.H. Johnson Recollections, Nov. 1914.

233–34 "great pains" & "I must": PML—JPM to James M. Brown, Dec. 1 & 8, 1882, & to S.B. Eaton, Dec. 27, 1882.

234 "The house" & ff.: PML—Johnson Recollections.

234 "Certainly": PML, MSI—Jack to LPM, Nov. 18, 1883. "the spirit": *Herald,* April 1 [n.d.].

235 "league-long": HJ to E. Wharton, Feb. 8, 1905, in *HJL,* Vol. IV, p. 346.

235 "These steps" and "Mr. M.": Peabody and Stearns drawings, Peabody and Stearns Architectural Collection, Fine Arts Department, Boston Public Library.

236 "asks $50": PML, MSI—FTM to LPM, April 15, 1887.

236 "going ahead": PML—JPM to Peabody & Stearns, Oct. 24, 1887. "but Papa": PML, MSI—LPM to FTM, April 12, 1883.

236 "eggs": PML—JPM to W.W. Story, Nov. 21, 1884.

237 "If you" & "My dear": PML—JPM to Elizabeth Darling, Oct. 24, 1887, & Sept. 2, 1893.

237 "I do not" & "sorry": PML—JPM to William J. Graves, Dec. 8, 1887, & Jan. 5, 1888.

CHAPTER 13: A RAILROAD BISMARCK?

239 "Your road": MGCo., Ms 21,760—"Reorganization of Northern Pacific Railroad Co.," May 20, 1875. "the largest": Chandler & Tedlow, *Managerial Capitalism,* p. 271.

239 "Nothing": MGCo. Ms 21,760—DMCo. to JSMCo., Dec. 18, 1880. "Warmest" & "We reciprocate": Ibid., Jan. 5, 1881.

240–41 "with which": PML—JPM to JSMCo., Oct. 17, 1883. "made radical" to "it is a": to WHB, Dec. 18, 1883. Net $2 million: to T. Jefferson Coolidge, July 2, 1884.

241 "Whatever": Ibid., to WHB, Dec. 18, 1883.

241 "politicians" & ff.: James Bryce, *The American Commonwealth,* Vol. II, pp. 56, 67.

242 "laughed": Theodore Roosevelt, *Autobiography,* p. 56.

242 "to lower": Hofstadter, *APT,* p. 176.

242 Grover the Good & ff.: Paul F. Boller, Jr., *Presidential Campaigns,* pp. 149–53.

Page
242–43   "(1) He is": W.A. Swanberg, *Pulitzer*, p. 82.

243   "Result": MGCo. Ms 21,795—JPMCo. to JSMCo., Oct. 13, 1884.

244   *fn.*, "not sufficient": PML—JPM, AJD, George Childs, Nov. 9, 1880; "although": JPM to US Grant, Dec. 4, 1882.

244   "Many of": Sobel, *Panic*, p. 255.

245   "nice" & ff.: PML—JSM to JPM, Dec. 20, 1884.

245   "a mind in": John Moody, *The Masters of Capital*, p. 20. "Where shall we" & "Morgan's right arm": PML—Jack Box 93, folder 36-A.

246   "absurd": MGCo.—JSMCo. to DMCo., Oct. 4 [1884?].

246   "I don't": PML, MSI—LPM to JPM, May 1 [1882].

247   "My dear Charlie": PML, HLS Box 3, folder A-10. Lanier quits: NY *Sun*, Jan. 10, 1884.

247   "There is": NY *Tribune*, July 21, 1885.

248   "not very": MGCo. Ms 21,795—JSM to WHV, May 27, 1885. "how fast": PML, MSI—JPM to LPM [n.d.]. JPM-WHV conversation: reported in NY *Sun*, July 20, 1885.

248   "I will": PML, HLS Box 2, folder A-4—Memorandum from Chauncey Depew, Nov. 29, 1913.

249   "To railroads": *C&FC*, Sept. 10, 1887, in Chandler & Tedlow, *Managerial Capitalism*, p. 274.

250   "Papa enjoyed": PML, MSI—LPM to FTM, May 3, 1885.

250   "as here" & "delicate": Ibid., April 21, & [spring] 1886.

251   "systematically": MGCo. "Private Telegrams," IV—AJD to JSMCo., Sept. 30, 1882; in Carosso, *Morgans*, p. 259.

251   Reading reorganization: Carosso, pp. 259–61.

252   "scarcely" & achievement: PML—JPM to JSM, Jan. 28 & 30, 1886. "We ourselves": JPM to WHB, March 2, 1886.

252   "I created" & "The best": PML, MSI—JPM to FTM, Sept. 23, & LPM to FTM, Sept. 19, 1886. "Papa is": PML—Jack to FTM, Sept. 19 & 26, 1886.

253   "you have": PML—JPM to AC, Oct. 12, 1888.

253   "I cannot": PML—JPM to J. Lowber Welsh, Dec. 6, 1887.

253–54   "heartily" & ff.: PML—JSM to JPM, Dec. 29, 1887.

254   "peace and": NY *Sun*, Feb. 15, 1886.

254   "My dear": PML—JPM to Charles A. Dana, Feb. 15, 1886.

255   "What can": Mrs. Frederick Bellamy, in Allan Nevins, *The Evening Post* (New York: Boni & Liveright, 1922), p. 546.

255   "I am not": PML—JPM to ELG, July 24, 1886. "Pierpont Morgan seems": ELG to Frederick Sheldon, Sept. 19, 1886, in William M. Armstrong, ed. *The Gilded Age Letters of E.L. Godkin* (Albany, N.Y.: SUNY Press, 1974), p. 347–48.

255   "railroad organ" & "no money": ELG to H. Villard, June 7 & 21, 1893, ibid., pp. 447–48.

256   "God's time": Chandler & Tedlow, *Managerial Capitalism*, p. 552.

Page

257   freight revenues: Gabriel Kolko, *Railroads and Regulation, 1877–1916*, p. 7.

257   "a delusion": Hofstadter, *APT*, p. 178. "a disturbing": MGCo.—JSM to DMCo., Dec. 12, 1888.

258   "money kings": Boller, *Presidential Campaigns*, p. 150.

258   "Providence": Hofstadter, *APT*, p. 172.

259   "The feeling" & "make the": The New York Public Library, Astor, Lenox and Tilden Foundations, Manuscripts and Archives Division, Levi P. Morton Papers—Morton to Harrison, Feb. 4, & Harrison to Morton, Feb. 8, 1889.

259   $1,000: PML—JPM to George E. Lemon, Jan. 25, 1889.

260   "This is not": Carl Hovey, *The Life Story of J. Pierpont Morgan*, pp. 139–41. If the railroad: PML—Depew Memo to HLS, Nov. 29, 1913.

260   "rope" & ff.: MHS, Charles Francis Adams II Papers—CFA II Memorabilia, Dec. 23, 1888, pp. 5, 12. "remove" & "sanction": in Kolko, *Railroads*, p. 60.

261   "revolution": NY *Sun* in Herbert Satterlee, *J. Pierpont Morgan*, p. 250. "few strong": John Moody & George K. Turner, "Masters of Capital."

261   "to a hill" & "Is it worth": in Klein, *Gould*, p. 440.

261   "Will Pierrepont": MHS, Charles Francis Adams II Papers—Memorabilia, pp. 8–9.

CHAPTER 14: FATHERS AND SONS

263   "We are" to "The Americans": MGCo. Ms 21,795—JSM to DMCo., Jan. 27, 1887. *fn.*: W. Elliot Brownlee, *Dynamics of Ascent*, p. 191.

264   "the best": PML—JSM to JVL Pruyn, April 10, 1889.

264   "I wish": PML, MSI—LPMD, April 10, 1889.

264   "According": Ibid.—LPM to FTM, May 18 [1884].

265   "nothing that": Reitlinger, *Economics of Taste*, p. 156. "lopsided": PML—Jack to FTM, July 17, 1887.

265   "late" & "the top": PML—JPM Letterpress Vol. 2, p. 127, Oct. 12, 1888, & p. 50, March 6, 1888.

266   "I wish" & "It makes": PML—Jack to FTM, Feb. 25 & Sept. 26, 1886.

266   "stray": George Santayana, *Persons and Places*, edited by William C. Holzberger and Herman J. Saatkamp, Jr. (Cambridge, Mass.: MIT Press, 1986), Vol. I, p. 349.

266   "a little": Ronald Steel, *Walter Lippmann and the American Century*, p. 13. "rather die": PML—Jack to FTM, Feb. 25, 1886.

266   "intellectual": Samuel Eliot Morison, *Three Centuries of Harvard University, 1636–1936* (Cambridge, Mass.: Harvard University Press, 1936), p. 322. "disgusted": PML—Jack to FTM, Dec. 11, 1887.

267   "nurse and": PML, MSI—EPF to FTM, July 12, 1886.

267   "and had": PML—Jack to FTM, March 18, 1889.

268   "If Papa" & "I cannot": PML—Jack to FTM, Feb. 1 & Sept. 26, 1886.

Notes ❀ 723

Page
268   "I do not": TR to TR Sr., Oct. 22, 1876, *Letters of Theodore Roosevelt*, Vol. I, p. 18.
268   "causes," "heir," & "belle": PML—Jack to FTM, July 2 & 12, 1887.
268   "Tell Papa" & "tone": Ibid., Jan. 13 & March 24, 1889.
269   "Nothing" & "attitude": Ibid., March 6 & 7, 1889.
269   "sickening": PML, MSI—FTM to LPM, March 24 [1889].
269–70 "irresistably" & "hard to": Ibid.—LPM to JPM, May 4 [1881?], & Jack to LPM, Sept. 29 [1889].
270   "sort of" & "who has never": Ibid.—Juliet(d) to LPM, March 10, 1891, & FTM to LPM, April 7, 1891.
270   "ready-made": Ibid.—Juliet(d) to LPM, Sept. 12, 1886.
270–71 "like the heroine" & "The funny": Ibid.—LPM to FTM, June 4, 1887, & March 15, 1889.
271   "untruthfulness": Ibid.—FTM to LPM, Oct. 12, 1886.
271   "Uncle John": Ibid.—LPM to FTM, April 18, 1885.
271   "so united" & "gaining": PML—Jack to FTM, July 18, 1887, & Nov. 28, 1889.
272   "Mr. Morgan has": Geoffrey Hellman, *Bankers, Bones & Beetles*, p. 78.
272   "The less said": Ibid., p. 77.
272   "rare opportunity": Henry Fairfield Osborn, "After Twenty Years," Princeton Class of 1877.
273   *fn.:* "permanently"—in Lewis, Turner, McQuillen, *Opulent Interiors*, p. 23.
273   "Your taste": MMA Archives—Cesnola to JPM, March 16, 1888. "I have": PML—JPM to Cesnola, March 27, 1888.
274   "the best" & bills: PML—JPM to John Crerar, July 16 & 24, 1886.
274   "very archaic" & "beautiful": Rainsford, *Story of a Varied Life*, p. 285, & (PML) Recollections, pp. 5–6.
274   "silent": Adams, *Education*, pp. 1067, 1071.
275   "to be bought": Addison, *Episcopal Church*, p. 286.
275   "Oh that": Nathaniel Hawthorne, *The Works of Nathaniel Hawthorne*, Standard Library Edition (Boston, 1863, 1891), Vol. II, p. 335; in Neil Harris, *The Artist in American Society*, p. 148.
276   "a craving": Alexander Graham, quoted in Robert A. M. Stern, Gregory Gilmartin, John Massengale, *New York 1900*, p. 398.
276   "owing": PML—JPM to L.P. Morton, Nov. 4, 1889. "*Il est*": Paul Porzelt, *The Metropolitan Club of New York* (New York: Rizzoli, 1982), p. 9.
277   "the extreme": *Town Topics*, March 1, 1894, pp. 6–7.
277   "unrivalled" & "architectural triumph": Baker, *Stanford White*, pp. 155, 159.
278   "I heard": MGCo. Ms 21,760—L. Chadwick to JSM, March 31, 1890.
278   "symptoms" & ff.: PML—WHB to JPM, April 6–7, 1890. "Papa bore": PML, MSI—LPM to FTM, April 9 [1890].
278   "Your father": PML—WHB to JPM, April 8, 1890.

Page

279   "Papa was": PML, MSI—LPM to FTM, April 13, 1890.

279   "My own": PML—ATM to JPM, April 8, 1890.

279–80   "I do so" & ff., & "These times": PML—FTM to JPM, April 8, 1890 (1) & (2).

280   "I am afraid": PML, MSI—LPM to FTM, April 19, 1890.

280   "Your chief": PML—SEP to JPM, April 8, 1890; "pardonable"—A.S. Hewitt to JPM, May 6, 1890; "overjoyed"—Emma Stirling to JPM, April 14, 1890.

280   "much less": PML, HLS Box 2, folder A-4—G.M. Miller Personal Recollections.

281   "half so": *Hartford Courant,* May [7], 1890.

281   JPM inheritance: PML, Jack Box 116—JSM Will (Epitome), and Carosso, *Morgans,* p. 276.

CHAPTER 15: IN PRIVATE

285   "poor": PML—FTMD, June 15, 1890.

286   "not over" & "The sauciest": *Town Topics,* Oct. 1, 1896, & April 24, 1890.

286   "See that": PML—G.W. Knight to J.E. Thorley, March 20, 1889.

286   "ready" & "give up": PML, MSI—FTM to LPM, June 19 & 27, 1890.

287   "Papa &": Ibid.—LPMD, July 21, 1890.

287   "All seem" & ff.: PML—FTMD, July–Aug., 1890.

287–88   "very much": *Town Topics,* May 15, 1890, p. 2.

288   "you have": Swanberg, *Whitney Father, Whitney Heiress,* pp. 87–90.

288   "You constantly": PML—FTMD, Oct. 20, 1890.

288   "What are" & ff.: PML—Memorandum of J. Frederic Tams, Feb. 27, 1925.

290   "You cannot": PML, MSI—Jack to FTM, Oct. 7, 1891.

290   "about the": PML—JPM to Daniell, Aug. 12, 1891.

290   "on the scale": PML—JPM to Juliet(s), Dec. 23, 1891.

290   "for your": PML—JPM to Williams, Dec. 30, 1891.

291   "price" & ff.: PML—JPM to Pearson, Jan. 27 & Aug. 12, 1891.

291   "I must": PML—JPM to Col. Charles C. Jones, Jr., Dec. 22, 1892.

292   "was a strange" & ff.: *Fraternity, A Romance of Inspiration* (New York: Harper & Brothers, 1910).

293   "as for the": PML—Jack to FTM, Feb. 8, 1889.

293   Diary of Margot Asquith, Nov. 13, 1911 (privately owned).

293–94   "I have never": Lilly—Sackville-West manuscripts, LSD, July 30, 1911.

294   "it isn't" & ff.: PML, MSI—Juliet(d) to LPM, March 10 & April 8, 1891.

294   "big supplies" to "you do": Ibid.—FTM to LPM, July 19 & July 27, 1891.

294   "Cable from": PML—FTMD, Oct. 6, 1891. "it hurt": PML, MSI—Jack to FTM, Oct. 7, 1891. "quite a": PML—Jack to Edward W. Grew, Nov. 11, 1892.

295   "bad news" & "do *not*": PML, MSI—FTM to LPM, April 29 & March 27, 1887. "Of course": LPM to FTM, April 11, 1887.

Page
296   "with his tongue in his cheek": AMS interview.
296   *fn.* "The only": Diana Forbes-Robertson, *My Aunt Maxine, The Story of Maxine Elliott* (New York: Viking, 1964), p. 200.
296–97 "never": Dr. Lewis A. Conner in James A. Harrar, M.D., *The Story of the Lying-In Hospital of the City of New York* (New York: The Society of the Lying-In Hospital, 1938), p. 74.
297   "Mr. Morgan": AMS interview.
298   "whenever" & ff.: Ibid.
299   "really did": Satterlee, *JPM*, p. 372.
299   "bad lot": AMS interview.

CHAPTER 16: CONSOLIDATIONS

302   *fn.* "If a man": Thomas Navin & Marian Sears, "The Rise of a Market for Industrial Securities," p. 119, *n.* 21.
303–4 "a kingly": March 21, 1890, in Theodore S. Burton, *John Sherman* (Boston & New York: Houghton Mifflin Co., 1906), p. 359.
304   "the false" & ff.: Rudolph J.R. Peritz, *Competition Policy in America 1888–1992*, pp. 16–23.
304   "the only": PML—BG notes in margins of Hovey, *Life Story of JPM*, p. 225.
304   "Here was": Lippmann, *A Preface to Politics*, pp. 22–31. *fn.* (Areeda) "Like all": NY *Times*, Dec. 27, 1995.
305   "a regular": in Maury Klein, *Jay Gould*, p. 454.
306   "simple but": Ibid., p. 460.
306   "I am": Satterlee, *JPM*, p. 257. "Railroad Kings": NY *Herald*, Dec. 16, 1890, in Klein, *Gould*, p. 460.
306   "The granger": PML—JPM to T.B. Blackstone, Dec. 26, 1890.
306–7 "My dear": PML—JPM to L.P. Morton, March 16, 1891.
307   "laid aside" &c.: *New York State Assembly Journal*, 1891, Vol. I, pp. 588, 658; Vol. II, pp. 1076, 1083, 1231, 1239.
307   " 'saving' ": PML, MSI—Jack to FTM, Aug. 21, 1891.
307   "Again Mr.": in Klein, *Gould*, p. 469.
308   "The best": PML—Jack to FTM, Aug. 21, 1891. "The new": PML, MSI—Juliet(d) to FTM, Jan. 1, 1892.
308–9 "Not on your" to "I fixed": Lincoln Steffens, *Autobiography*, pp. 188–90.
310–11 industrial securities market: Navin & Sears, "The Rise," pp. 106–9.
311   "an invitation": J. Hughes, *The Vital Few*, p. 151.
312   "We shall": Robert Conot, *A Streak of Luck*, p. 277.
312   EGE figures: Carosso, *Morgans*, pp. 272–73.
313   "The Edison system": PML—JPM to HLH, Feb. 3, 1891.
313   "knocking": W. Bernard Carlson, *Innovation as a Social Process*, p. 294. "I entirely": PML—JPM to TJC, March 24, 1892.
313   "be then": Ibid., JPM to TJC.

Page

313–14 GE figures: Carlson, p. 294, & Carosso, p. 391. *fn.*, "Well": J. Hughes, *Vital Few*, pp. 204–5.

314 "I always": PML—JPM to Charles T. Barney, Jan. 18, 1893.

315 GE nineties: John W. Hammond, *Men and Volts, The Story of General Electric* (Philadelphia: J.B. Lippincott Co., 1941), pp. 407–8.

315 Ice: David Hemenway, "The Ice Trust," *Prices and Choices* (Lanham, Md.: University Press of America, 1993), pp. 189–203.

315–16 *fn.*: Alfred D. Chandler, Jr., *Scale and Scope*, pp. 21–23; "suggest": Thomas K. McCraw, "Rethinking the Trust Question," p. 24.

316 "buying up": Thomas Cochran, *The American Business System*, p. 54.

316 GE performance: *Wall Street Journal*, "A Century of Investing," May 28, 1996, & NY *Times*, May 14, 1997.

317 "I don't want": PML—JPM to Lucius Tuttle, Sept. 8, 1893.

317 systems for Union Station: HBS—Boston & Maine Railroad Annual Reports, 1892–93 and 1893–94.

318 "tumbled": PML—JPM to E. Coles, July 10, 1893.

318 "the lack": *C&FC*, Dec. 12, 1892, in Sobel, *Panic*, p. 243.

319 "essential": PML—JPM to R.R. Sinclair, Feb. 13, 1893.

319 "in money" & "On the one": Allan Nevins, *Grover Cleveland*, pp. 534, 540.

320 "satisfactory": MGCo.—DMCo. to JSMCo., Feb. 12, 1894.

320 "there was no": NY *Times*, Nov. 30, 1906.

321 "in a queer": PML—Jack memorandum in JSM Box 5, folder 4.

321–22 Southern earnings, "one of," & "new era": Carosso, p. 372.

323 "an impressive": Ibid., p. 376.

323 "We have": MGCo.—JPM to WHB, July 31, 1895.

323 "drastic" & earnings: Carosso, pp. 382–83.

324 "gigantic": Edward S. Meade, "Mr. Morgan as Financier," *The Independent*, Dec. 11, 1902. "safest": in James Grant, *Bernard Baruch*, p. 54.

324 "When J. Pierpont": "A Case of Conjecture," *Machinists' Monthly Journal* [n.d.], reprinted in the *Eight Hour Herald* (Chicago), Sept. 2, 1897.

324 "stunned": PML—JPM to Edward Coles, July 10, 1893; "dazed"—to WHB, July 19, 1893; "Everything"—to Coles, July 21, 1893.

CHAPTER 17: ROMANCE

325 "Pierpont dined": PML—FTMD, Jan. 1894. "Why does": *Town Topics*, July 25, 1895.

326 payoffs & "I went": Andy Logan, "That Was New York," Vol. II, pp. 66–72.

328 "As for": HA to Elizabeth Cameron, Oct. 4, 1895, *LHA*, Vol. IV, p. 336.

330 "Mr. Whitney" & ff.: *Town Topics*, Oct. 1, 1896.

330 "with calm" & ff.: Wharton, *Age of Innocence*, p. 97.

331 "the Caresser": HJ to Oliver Wendell Holmes, Jr., Feb. 20, 1901, *HJL*, Vol. IV, p. 184. "never happier": Theo Aronson, *The King in Love*, p. 65.

Page

331   "to be delivered": PML—Duveen Brothers files.

331   "Mrs. Douglass": PML—FTMD, June 2 & 4, 1900.

331–32   "may have signed": Last Will and Testament of William P. Douglas, May 23, 1910. Trusts & gifts: Interview with James Gordon Douglas, Jr., Sept. 27, 1987. Indenture Feb. 3, 1897, between JPM and the Central Trust Co. of New York.

332   "one of": PML—JPM to WR, July 19, 1887.

332   "Of course": PML, MSI—Juliet(d) to LPM, Jan. 1, 1892.

332   "I left": PML—JPM to CM, June 11, 1892.

333   "a very": PML—HLS Box A-9, Annette W. Markoe, June 19, 1924. "loved to": AMS interview.

334–35   *fn.*, Morgan figures: Carosso, *Morgans*, pp. 303–7, 432. City Bank: Harold van B. Cleveland & Thomas F. Huertas, *Citibank*, p. 320.

335   "tall" & ff.: James B. Scott, *Robert Bacon*, pp. x, 28–29, 70, 86.

336   "If Pierpont": Ibid., p. 71—HLH to RB, Nov. 23, 1894.

336   "I am": Ibid., p. 72—RB to MB, March 26, 1895.

336   "It is probably": in Sobel, *Panic*, p. 260.

CHAPTER 18: POLITICS OF GOLD

339   "Few people": LC, Grover Cleveland Papers—James Stillman to William E. Curtis, July 31, 1894.

340   1894 bond issues: Matthew Simon, "The Morgan-Belmont Syndicate," p. 388.

340   "If so": PML—Louis Sperry to JPM, Jan. 1, 1895.

340   "supposed": Hovey, *Life Story of JPM*, pp. 159–60.

341   "We all": MGCo. Ms 21,802—JPM to JSMCo., Feb. 1, 1895.

341   "The Treasury is": PML—Charles A. Conant, "Saving the National Credit," p. 12.

341   "dark-lantern": Nevins, *Cleveland*, p. 659.

341   "Effect of": MGCo. Ms 21,802—JPM to JSMCo., received Feb. 4, 1895.

342   "We consider": Ibid., received Feb. 5, 1895.

342   "All were": PML—Olney to HLS, April 15, 1914.

342   "Still some": MGCo. Ms 21,802—JPM to JSMCo., received Feb. 5, 1895.

342–43   Cleveland to bankers: Conant, p. 19, and James A. Scrymser, *Personal Reminiscences* (privately printed, 1915), p. 56.

343   "Have you": Hovey, p. 178.

343   Morgan on statute: Conant, pp. 21–23.

343–44   *fn.*, "out of which" & "your last": LC, Cleveland Papers—FLS to GC, Feb. 9 & March 18, 1895.

344   "goldbuggery": Carosso, *Morgans*, p. 327.

344   *fn.*, "and I have": Cleveland, "The Cleveland Bond Issues," *Saturday Evening Post*, May 7, 1904.

Page

344–45 Syndicate terms: Peter M. Garber and Vittorio U. Grilli, "The Belmont-Morgan Syndicate," pp. 658–60.

345 "Impossible" & "Have just": MGCo. Ms 21,802—JPM to WHB, received Feb. 6, & JPM to JSMCo., received Feb. 9 & 11, 1895.

346 "Subscriptions" & "We are": MGCo. Ms 21,802—JPMCo. to JSMCo., Feb. 20 & 21, 1895.

346 "Sometimes I had": PML—BG notes in Hovey, p. 227.

347 "Whole": MGCo. Ms 21,802—JPMCo. to JSMCo., Feb. 19, 1896.

347–48 control of foreign exchange: Garber & Grilli, pp. 649–77; Friedman & Schwartz, *Monetary History*, pp. 111–12.

347 "personally": PML, HLS—HLS memo, Misc. Box.

348 "revived": NY *Sun*, June 21, 1895.

348 "I support" to '96 election: HA to BA, June 5, & to Elizabeth Cameron, July 25, 1895, in *LHA*, Vol. IV, pp. 282–85.

349 "great bunco": *Industrial News*, Jackson, Mich., March 9, 1895, in Nevins, *Cleveland*, p. 665.

349 Bryan on Jews: in Nevins, p. 665, & Allen, *GPM*, pp. 117–18. "Wall St. conspiracy": in Carosso, p. 335. "raise" & ff.: Mary Lease in Richard Hofstadter, *Age of Reform*, pp. 79–83.

349 "The abuse": N-YHS, Brown Brothers Harriman Papers, Chronological File, "Private and confidential . . ."—John Crosby Brown to Howard Potter, March 1, 1895. "completely": MGCo. Ms 21,802—JPM to WHB, March 16, 1895.

350 "Without shame": Cleveland, "The Cleveland Bond Issue."

350 "emergency" & "the admiration": NY *Post*, Feb. 21, & NY *Times*, Feb. 23, 1895.

350 Syndicate profit: PML—JPMCo. Syndicates 1; Carosso, p. 339; Allen, p. 124.

351 "And so" & ff.: Hovey, p. 191.

351 "command" & ff.: Allen, p. 119.

352 "readily": MGCo. Ms 21,802—in JSMCo. to JPM, Jan. 17, 1896.

352 *fn.*: Friedman & Schwartz, pp. 110–11.

353 "We must" & "Do not": MGCo. Ms. 21,802—JPM to WHB & WHB to JPM, Aug. 2, 1895.

353 "sharks": in Carosso, p. 342.

353 "with great": PML, HLS Box 6, folder C-13—JPM to Cleveland, Jan. 4, 1896, in "Mr. Morgan and the Bond Syndicate."

353 "Personally": WCW to D. Lamont, Jan. 3, 1896, in Mark D. Hirsch, *William C. Whitney. Modern Warwick* (New York: Archon Books, 1969 [1948]), p. 482.

353 "Lombard Street": HA to BA, Dec. 27, 1895, in *LHA*, Vol. IV, p. 350. "the final": BA to HA, 1896, in Daniel Aaron, *Men of Good Hope*, p. 260.

Page

353–54 "at all": Endicott Peabody to Bishop Attwood, Jan. 5, 1896, in Frank Davis Ashburn, *Peabody of Groton* (New York: Coward, McCann, Inc., 1944), p. 116.

354 "I cannot" & "You have": MGCo. Ms 21,802—WHB to JPM, Dec. 28, 1895, & JPM to WHB, Jan. 9, 1896.

354 "I desire": PML, HLS Box 6, folder C-13—JPM to Syndicate, Jan. 14, 1896.

354 "In view" & "great influence": MGCo. Ms 21,802—JPM to WHB, Feb. 5, & WHB to JPM, Feb. 6, 1896.

354 "Dearest father": PML, MSI—LPMD, May 9–June 3, 1896.

355 "advance": Boller, *Presidential Campaigns*, p. 168.

355 "violent" & ff.: Bentley Mott, *Myron T. Herrick*, pp. 68–69.

356 "We have": Morris R. Werner, *William Jennings Bryan*, pp. 73–75.

356 "the sceptre": Ibid., p. 96.

357 "So you're": Harrison Salisbury, *Without Fear or Favor* (New York: Times Books, 1980), p. 27.

357 "impartially": NY *Times*, Aug. 19, 1896.

357 "the largest": Lawrence Goodwyn, *The Populist Moment*, p. vii. Populist program: Goodwyn, C. Vann Woodward, *Origins of the New South*, p. 250, & John D. Hicks, *The Populist Revolt*, pp. 356–62.

357–58 "easy" & ff.: *Washington Wife, Journal of Ellen Maury Slayden from 1897–1919* (New York: Harper & Row, 1962), p. 4.

358 "twenty-five cents": Goodwyn, p. 278. $2 million: Aaron, p. 261.

358 "I might": in Mott, p. 64.

358 "believes": Edmund Morris, *The Rise of Theodore Roosevelt*, p. 553.

359 "The New York people": LC, W.E. Curtis correspondence, Vol. 7—W.E. Curtis to Mary Ann Curtis, July 23, 1896, in Carosso, p. 347. *fn.*: Friedman & Schwartz, p. 113.

359 "talking silver" & "the cow-bird": in Hofstadter, *APT*, pp. 191, 189.

359 "If the": Woodward, p. 289.

359 "Have won" & "Result": MGCo., Ms 21,802—JPM to WHB, & WHB to JPM, Nov. 4, 1896.

CHAPTER 19: ACQUISITIONS AND LOSSES

361–62 "quaint": PML, MSI—LMS to FTM, Aug. 17 [1909]. "And *this*": Satterlee, *JPM*, pp. 512–13.

362 "a big": Ibid., LMS to FTM, Aug. 17 [1909].

362 "richest": in William Barton McCash and June Hall McCash, *The Jekyll Island Club* (Athens: University of Georgia Press, 1989), p. 1.

364 "and decided": PML—Frances M. Pennoyer Recollections.

364–65 Racquette Lake Railway: Harold K. Hochschild, *Life and Leisure in the Adirondack Backwoods* (Blue Mountain Lake, N.Y.: Adirondack Museum, 1962), p. 37.

Page

366   "I have got": Peter Lyon, *Success Story,* p. 167.

366   "the downfall," "It was," & *fn.,* "in whatever": Eugene Exman, *The House of Harper,* pp. 182–92.

367   *fn.,* Saxton story: Exman, 227, & Dos Passos, *1919,* p. 337; "looking back": in Melvin Landsberg, *Dos Passos' Path to USA* (Boulder, Colo.: Colorado Associated University Press, 1972), p. 253.

367   "Everyone" & "laid himself": PML—Jack to FTM, Jan. 17 & 25, 1898.

368   "Father," "more cheerful," "immensely," & "Louisa's friend": Ibid., Jan. 25, Feb. 8, 25, & Jan. 28, 1898.

368   "Quite the": *Daily Mail,* Feb. 26, 1898.

368–69   "Jessie and I": PML—Jack to FTM, June 25, 1898.

369   "this country": Henry F. Pringle, *Theodore Roosevelt,* pp. 167–68.

369–70   "so worried," "Personally," & "and if": PML—Jack to FTM, March 28 & 25, & April 26, 1898.

370   *fn.:* Erik Hofman, *The Steam Yachts, An Era of Elegance* (Tuckahoe, N.Y.: John de Graff, Inc., 1970), p. 67.

370   "You remember": PML—Lawrence Memoir, p. 59.

370–71   "strong opposition": PML—JPM to Jacob Rogers, Dec. 19, 1882. *fn.,* "first appearance": *Daily Mail,* June 8, 1899, & "equal to": James R. Morse to F.B. Jennings, April 29, 1898; both in Carosso, *Morgans,* pp. 420–28.

372   *fn.:* PML—Jack to FDR, May 23 & June 20, 1917.

373   "This is": Alexander Gunn, Sept. 12, 1898, in Swanberg, *Whitney,* p. 164.

373   "no more": in William P. Stephens, *Traditions and Memories of American Yachting* (Brooklin, Me.: WoodenBoat, 1989), p. 232.

374   "Tonight": PML—Jack to FTM, Jan. 25, 1899.

375   "Commodore": NY *Tribune,* Oct. 20, 1899. "with a shout": Satterlee, *JPM,* p. 538.

375   "If the Senior": PML—Jack to CHC, Oct. 24, 1899.

375   "a lifetime": Neil Harris, *Cultural Excursions,* p. 271.

377   "very fine" & "As regards": MMA Archives—Cesnola to JPM, & JPM to Cesnola, March 1, 1897.

377   *fn.:* MMA Archives.

378   "the friendship" & "the Museum": Ibid., Cesnola to JPM, Nov. 23 & Dec. 5, 1894.

378   "happy": Ibid., March 1, 1897.

378   "The sun": NY *Tribune,* Jan. 1, 1898.

379   "Tambales": PML, M1 file—JSM2 to JPM, July 4, 1899.

380   Cook & Morey in *Medieval and Renaissance Manuscripts, Major Acquisitions of the Pierpont Morgan Library 1924–1974* (New York: The Pierpont Morgan Library, 1974), p. xi.

381   Dürers to JSM2: PML—BG to Fritz Lugt, Jan. 17, 1917.

381   "How much" & ff.: Aline Saarinen, *The Proud Possessors.* p. 72.

Page
381–83   Duveen purchases: PML—Duveen Bros. files, & *The Frick Collection, an Illustrated Catalogue,* Vol. VI, Furniture and Gilt Bronzes, French (Princeton, N.J.: Princeton University Press, 1992).

383   "angel food": *Art Commerce Scholarship, A Window onto the Art World—Colnaghi 1760 to 1984* (London: P. & D. Colnaghi & Co., Ltd., 1984), p. 22.

383   "one of my": *The Frick Collection Catalogue,* Vol. 1, Paintings (Princeton, N.J.: Princeton University Press, 1968), p. 32.

384   "Father" & "I'm not: PML, MSI—LPM to FTM, April 19, 1900. "glorious": Ibid.—LPMD, Jan. 7, 1899.

384   "May radiantly": LPMD, Jan. 6, 1899.

385   "We are all": Havighurst, *Twentieth-Century Britain,* p. 19. "It is another": Harcourt to Chamberlain, Dec. 2, 1898, in Richard W. Davis, " 'We Are All Americans Now!' " pp. 140–41.

385   "How the" & "one of the": Lorne to Lewis Harcourt, Dec. 4, 1898, & *Daily Chronicle,* July 3, 1899, both in Davis, p. 142.

385   "the first" & ff.: PML, MSI—LPMD, Jan. 6, 1899.

385   *fn.,* pearls: John Steele Gordon, "The Problem of Money and Time," *American Heritage,* May/June 1989.

386   "What I want": PML—May Harcourt to Jack, May 16, 1913.

386   "I thought": Reynolds to Harcourt in Sotheby's Catalogue, Nuneham Park Sale, June 10, 1993, p. 4.

386   "most interesting" & ff.: PML, MSI—LPMD, Feb. 1–9, 1899.

386   "considered": London *Times,* July 22, 1899. "a capable": N-YHS, Brown Brothers Harriman Papers, Chronological File 1899–1900, "unannotated . . . partnership matters"—Mark Collett to John Crosby Brown, July 25, 1899; both in Carosso, *Morgans,* pp. 443–45.

387   "capable": Bodleian, MS. Milner deposit 213, folios 59–60—CED to Alfred Milner, Dec. 21, 1900.

387   "happy enough": Ibid., Milner dep. 213, fols. 160–61—CED to Milner, Nov. 2, 1900. "more patriotic": Ibid., dep. 213, fols. 59–60, Dec. 21, 1900. "since the": Ibid., dep. 214, fol. 42, Feb. 8, 1901. £25,000 a year: *London Stock Market Report,* May 10, 1902.

387   "without regard": Cecil Baring to Lord Revelstoke, Dec. 28, 1900, in Ziegler, *Sixth Great Power,* p. 297.

387   " 'he meant' ": PML, MSI—LPM to FTM, April 21, 1899.

387–88   "Why" to "I am": Ibid., Mar. 31–April 6 [1900].

388   "not as" & "the kind": Ibid., HLS to LPM [March] and May 4, 1900.

388   "Don't you" & "It was": Ibid., May 4 & July 9, 1900.

388   "He is": Ibid., Aug. 1, 1900.

CHAPTER 20: THE DYNAMO AND THE VIRGIN

391   "There is": *Orations, Addresses and Speeches of Chauncey M. Depew,* ed. John D. Champlin (New York: privately printed, 1910), Vol. VI, p. 45.

Page

392   "As he grew" & ff.: Adams, *Education*, pp. 1067–75.

392   "Don't any": Pringle, *Roosevelt*, p. 233.

394   "Old Pierpont" & "This is": Bodleian, MS. Milner dep. 214, fol. 42—CED
       to Milner, Feb. 8, 1901, & dep. 214, fol. 46, July 13, 1901.

394   "far heavier": NY *Times*, March 18, 1900. "succumbed" & ff.: Moody,
       Masters of Capital, p. 29.

394   "unprotected": JJH—JJH to D. Lamont, March 31, 1900.

394–95 "delightful": Bodleian, MS. Milner dep. 215, fols. 43–49—CED to Milner,
       May 9, 1902. "the Commodore": AMS interview, May 9, 1993. "as if":
       PML—Lawrence Memoir, p. 68.

395   "deal of the century": George Smith and Richard Sylla, "The Transfor-
       mation of Financial Capitalism," p. 2.

395   *fn.*, "Since a year": PML—N. Tesla to JPM, Oct. 13, 1904. "do anything
       more": C. W. King to Tesla, Oct. 15, 1904.

395–96 mergers: Smith & Sylla, p. 2; Navin & Sears, "The Rise of a Market,"
       pp. 128–29; Chandler & Tedlow, *Managerial Capitalism*, p. 554.

396   "Every conceivable": Arthur Stone Dewing, *The Financial Policy of Corpo-
       rations*, Vol. IV (1920), p. 36.

396   rise in output: H.R. Schubert, "The Steel Industry," in Charles Singer et
       al., *A History of Technology* (Oxford: Oxford University Press, 1958), Vol.
       V, p. 61.

396   "my fellow": Livesay, *Carnegie*, p. 153. Steel figures: Ibid., pp. 132–55, &
       Robert Hessen, *Steel Titan*, p. 65.

397   "a Methodist": Allen, *GPM*, p. 164.

397   "the beginning": in William T. Hogan, *An Economic History of the Iron and
       Steel Industry in the U.S.*, Vol. I, p. 266.

397–98 Federal deal & figures: MGCo., Ms 21,760. HC 3.1.1. (129); Navin &
       Sears, "Rise," pp. 133–34; Smith & Sylla, p. 16; Allen, p. 167; Chandler
       & Tedlow, p. 282.

399   "Judge Gary" & ff.: Ida Tarbell, *The Life of Elbert H. Gary*, pp. 94–95.

398   "I think": Livesay, p. 183.

400   "No pangs": Ibid., p. 144.

400   "steel republic": in Hogan, Vol. II, p. 470. "capacity to": Tarbell, *Gary*,
       p. 111.

400   "The situation": Hessen, p. 112.

400   "At least": Livesay, p. 186.

400   "if I were": Wall, *Carnegie*, p. 773.

401   Schwab speech: Hessen, pp. 115–16.

401   "very much": Scott, *Bacon*, p. 82.

402   "Well, if": Hessen, pp. 117–18.

402   "nice sense": Carnegie, *Autobiography*, pp. 165–66.

402   "Carnegie could not": Hessen, pp. 121–22.

403   "I accept": Wall, p. 789.

Page
403   *fn.** Carnegie figures: Ibid., pp. 788–89.
403   *fn.*† "I have been": Carnegie, p. 256.
403–4   "Morgan has" & "It is": LC, Andrew Carnegie Papers—AC to George Lauder, Feb. 26, 1901, & to John Walker, March 3, 1901.
404   Federal spending: James Grant, *Bernard Baruch*, p. 56.
404     $30 million: Ray Stannard Baker, "What the U.S. Steel Corporation Really Is." "Judge Gary": Tarbell, *Gary*, p. 120.
404   half U.S. capacity: Hessen, p. 123. 7 percent GNP: Smith and Sylla, p. 2.
404–5   "the greatest": LC, Albert J. Beveridge Papers—AJB to GWP, April 1, 1901. "the world": Allen, p. 184. "planning": R.S. Baker, "What the U.S. Steel Corp." "an emperor": Allen, p. 180. "Pierpont Morgan is": HA to E. Cameron, Feb. 11, 1901, *LHA*, Vol. V, p. 199.
405   "America is" & "Pierpont Morgan calls": in Allen, pp. 180–81.
405   "It's a": PML—Jack to FTM, Feb. 17, 1901.
405   Securities issued & "enough to": in Carosso, *Morgans*, pp. 470–71.
405–6   Bureau estimate: U.S. Commissioner of Corporations, Report on the Steel Industry, Vol. I, July 1, 1911, in William Z. Ripley, *Trusts, Pools and Corporations*, pp. 185–201.
406   *fn.*, "the years": Hogan, Vol. II, p. 476–77.
406   "an aggregate": *Iron Age*, April 18, 1901, in Carosso, p. 472. "uneasiness": *Wall Street Journal*, Feb. 27, 1901, in *WSJ*, Nov. 15, 1988.
406   "Statements furnished": in Hogan, Vol. II, p. 477.
407   *fn.*, syndicate members: PML—USS Syndicate Book II, p. 209, and Carosso, p. 801, *n.* 20.
408   profits 1901–2: Hogan, Vol. II, p. 477. Performance: George J. Stigler, *The Organization of Industry*, pp. 111–12.
408   earnings: PML—USS Syndicate Book II, p. 209, & Ripley, pp. 204–5.
408   "greatly in excess": in Ripley, p. 205. "represented": *Wall Street Journal*, Nov. 15, 1988.
408   average commissions: Carosso, *Investment Banking in America*, p. 75.
409   "a master": Stigler, pp. 111–12. "unique": in Ripley, p. 209.
409   "The entire": in Arthur M. Schlesinger, Jr., *Crisis of the Old Order, 1919–1933*, p. 21.
409   "a corporation": John A. Garraty, *Right-Hand Man*, p. 56.
410   "I know all" & ff.: Ibid., pp. 84–85.
411   "size and" & "if you": Ibid., pp. 86–87.
411   "when I" & "heartiest": Columbia, George Walbridge Perkins Papers—GWP to Stillman, March 2, & Stillman to GWP, March 6, 1901.
411   "Go slow": Ibid.—Beveridge to GWP, March 8, 1901.
411   "the fullest": *C&FC*, Oct. 5, 1901, in Carosso, *Morgans*, p. 488. "impossibly": PML—Jack to GWP, Oct. 10, 1901.
411   "George W.": NY *World*, March 9, 1902, in Garraty, p. 92.
412   "Wall Street": HA to E. Cameron, April 8, 1901, *LHA*, Vol. V, p. 231.

Page

412   "Nobody will": Satterlee, *JPM*, p. 353.

412   "possessing": Geoffrey Agnew, *Agnew's 1817–1967* (London: B. Agnew Press, 1967), p. 84. *"réclame"*: in NY *Herald*, April 1, 1913. *fn.*, "I personally": in London *Times*, July 14, 1994.

413   "the only": D.A. Brown, *Raphael and America*, p. 39.

413   *fn.*, Inghirami: interview with Dr. Hilliard Goldfarb, chief curator, the Isabella Stewart Gardner Museum.

413   "a *heavenly*" & "My remaining": ISG to BB, March 11, 1901, & April 1, 1902, in *Letters of Bernard Berenson and Isabella Stewart Gardner*, pp. 251, 285.

413–14   "truly marvellous": Vasari, *Lives of the Painters*, Vol. I, p. 715. Ruskin, "work of," & "richest": in Brown, pp. 66–68.

414   "that spacious" & "pictures": BB to ISG, Nov. 9, 1897, *Letters BB-ISG*, p. 97, & Sept. 25, 1902, in Brown, p. 53.

414   "more primitive": *Italian Paintings, Sienese and Central Italian Schools*, Federico Zeri (New York: Metropolitan Museum of Art, 1980), p. 73.

415   "the most": Brown, pp. 67, 105, *n.* 233.

415   "I hope": MGCo. Ms 21,800—CED to Jack, Dec. 10, 1901. "Mr. J. Pierpont" & ff.: Brown, pp. 68, 64.

CHAPTER 21: RAID

417   "contentment": NY *Times*, April 18, 1912.

418   Hill's plans: Balthasar H. Meyer, "A History of the Northern Securities Case," pp. 227–36, & Albro Martin, *James J. Hill*, p. 441.

418   "proposed plan": MGCo., Private Telegrams VIII—JPMCo. to JSMCo., July 3, 1895. Court rulings: Carosso, *Morgans*, p. 384, & William Letwin, *Law and Economic Policy in America*, p. 185.

419   "form a": NHHS, Charles S. Mellen Papers. "Memorandum of a Conference held in London on the 2nd of April 1896."

419   *fn.*, name change: Rousmaniere, "Called into Consultation," pp. 90–92; "I made": *U.S.* v. *Northern Securities*, Vol. I, p. 328.

419   "declined": JJH—CHC to JJH, May 15, 1896.

420   "That is": Maury Klein, *Union Pacific*, Vol. II, p. 21.

420   "It's that": Ibid., p. 24.

420–21   "if Hill": Ibid., p. 98. "butting in": Satterlee, *JPM*, p. 354.

421   "City Bank crowd": JJH—JJH to J.S. Kennedy, May 16, 1901.

422   "It looks": in NY *Times*, May 9, 1901.

422   "throw": JJH—JJH to J. S. Kennedy, May 16, 1901. "all manner" & "abandon": JJH to Mount Stephen, June 4, 1901.

423   *fn.*: Klein, *Union Pacific* Vol. II, p. 105.

423   "Friends here": JJH—Stephen to JJH, May 8, 1901. "Cannot": NHHS—Mellen to D.S. Lamont, May 7, 1901.

Page

424   "Pierpont is": PML—FTMD, May 11, 1901.

424   "everything": JJH—JJH to Gaspard Farrer, May 15, 1901.

424–25 "not with": PML—J. Schiff to JPM, May 16, 1901.

426   "Father . . .": PML—Jack to FTM, June 21, 1901.

426   ("I did not"): Ibid., June 18, 1901.

426   "When you have": PML—Lawrence Memoir, pp. 100–101; "You had": PML—Jack to FTM, June 21, 1901.

426–27 "the Great Northern": JJH—JJH to Stephen, May 18 & June 4, 1901. "Have just" & "Nothing more": Mount Stephen to JJH June 6–7, 1901.

427   "in order": *U.S. v. Northern Securities,* p. 341. "What do you": Ralph Carson, *Davis Polk Wardwell Sunderland & Kiendl* (privately printed, 1965), p. 34, *n.* 46.

427   "would be": in Philip Foner, *History of the Labor Movement in the United States,* p. 79.

427–28 strike: Ibid., p. 79, & Craig Phelan, *Divided Loyalties,* pp. 135–37.

428   Mitchell & Shaffer: Phelan, p. 136.

428   negotiations with U.S. Steel: Phelan, p. 139; Hogan, Vol. II, p. 443; P. Foner, p. 84. "disastrous" & *fn.,* "the good will": in P. Foner, pp. 84–85.

428   "people-ize": Schlesinger, *Crisis of the Old Order,* p. 21.

428   "the wage earner" & "a nation": in Stuart Brandes, *American Welfare Capitalism,* pp. 86–87.

429   "a prophylactic" & stock ownership: Garraty, *Right-Hand Man,* pp. 112–13. Gompers: in Brandes, p. 87.

429   "socialism": Schlesinger, *Crisis,* p. 21. "the strike menace" & "a true": in Brandes, pp. 90, 86.

429   "The Commodore": PML, MSI—HLS to Mrs. G. B. Satterlee, Sept. 1, 1901.

430   minutes of NP meeting: Rousmaniere, "Called Into Consultation," p. 115.

430   "entertaining": NHHS—R.W. Martin to C.S. Mellen, Oct. 31, 1901.

431   Hill thought $200 million: JJH—JJH to Mount Stephen, Sept. 10, 1903.

431–32 "I feel" & ff.: *U.S. v. Northern Securities,* pp. 338, 345, 356.

432   "to fight": in Meyer, "Northern Securities," p. 242.

432   "no law" & "try to get": JJH—JJH to Van Sant, Nov. 18, 1901, & to Louis W. Hill, Dec. 7, 1901.

432   "in the background": NHHS—Mellen to JPM, Feb. 3, 1902.

433   "STRICTLY CONFIDENTIAL" & ff.: NHHS—Mellen to JPM, Jan. 25, 1902.

433   "Yes": Ibid.—JPM to Mellen, Jan. 29, 1902.

433–34 "Well in hand" & "attack us": Ibid.—Mellen to JPM, Feb. 1 & 3, 1902.

434   "Quite approve": Ibid., JPM to Mellen, Feb. 15, 1902. "Not in": Feb. 16, 1902. "All right": JPM to Mellen, Feb. 18, 1902.

434   "in the hands": Ibid.—Mellen to JPM, March 4, 1902.

434   "disagreeable": MGCo. Ms 21,800—CED to Jack, Dec. 20, 1901.

Page   CHAPTER 22: TROUBLE

435   "What?" to "The financial": NY Times, Sept. 7, 8, 1901.

436   "that damned": H.H. Kohlsaat, From McKinley to Harding, p. 101.

436    $10,000 for TR, 1898: Autobiography of Thomas Collier Platt (New York:
       B.W. Dodge & Co., 1910), p. 538.

436   "I hope" & "My dear": LC, Theodore Roosevelt Papers—TR to E. Root,
       Dec. 5, 1900, and to JPM, Dec. 5, 1900.

436   "bully talk": LC, Beveridge Papers—Albert J. Beveridge to GWP, April 1,
       1901.

436   "bucking": Kohlsaat, p. 98. "polygonal": Pringle, Roosevelt, p. vii.

438   "all of": Hofstadter, APT, pp. 220–21. "corrupt wealth": TR to Henry
       Cabot Lodge, Oct. 16, 1897, Letters of Theodore Roosevelt, Vol. I, p. 287.

438   "He would go" to "hammers": Daniel Aaron, "Theodore Roosevelt as
       Cultural Artifact," Raritan, Winter 1990, pp. 112–14. "an interesting":
       in Pringle, p. 370. "Power when": Adams, Education, p. 1101.

439   "Perkins wanted" & "to give": TR to Douglas Robinson, both Oct. 4,
       1901, LTR, Vol. III, pp. 159–60.

439   "go slow" & "the Government": Joseph B. Bishop, Theodore Roosevelt and
       His Time, Vol. I, pp. 154, 162. "do away" & ff.: Hofstadter, APT, p. 226.

439–40 " 'The trusts' ": in Allen, The Big Change, p. 95.

440   "the very Sanhedrin": in Chandler & Tedlow, Managerial Capitalism, p. 554.

440   "brutal assault": MGCo. Ms 21,800—CED to Charles Steele, Feb. 22,
       1902. "very sorry": PML—Jack to GWP, Feb. 21, 1902.

440   "our stormy" & "Pierpont is": HA to E. Cameron, Feb. 23 & 24, 1902,
       LHA, Vol. V, pp. 344–47.

441   "just what" & ff.: Bishop, pp. 184–85.

441   "mighty": Roosevelt, Autobiography, p. 423.

441–42 fn.: Carosso, Investment Banking, pp. 80–81, & Morgans, pp. 512–13.

442   "the absolutely": in John Morton Blum, The Republican Roosevelt, p. 117.

442   fn., "one of": Rousmaniere, "Called Into Consultation," pp. 62–63.

442   "The whole": HA to E. Cameron, Feb. 24, 1902, LHA, Vol. V, p. 346.

442–43 "Theodore's vanity" & ff.: Ibid., pp. 349–68.

443   "smash up": PML—Jack to GWP, Feb. 15, 1902.

444   bond exchange: Edward S. Meade, "US Steel Corporation's Bond Conver-
       sion," in Ripley, Trusts, Pools, pp. 228–68.

444   "Here is": PML—Jack to GWP, Feb. 7, 1902. fn., "particularly": Meade in
       Ripley, pp. 228–39.

444–45 Lawsuits & conversion results: Garraty, Right-Hand Man, pp. 104–5.

445   fn., syndicate earnings: U.S. Commissioner of Corporations, Report on
       the Steel Industry, Vol. I, July 1, 1911, in Ripley, pp. 257–68.

446   "SCHWAB BREAKS": NY Sun, January 13, 1902, in Hessen, Steel Titan,
       p. 134. "Public sentiment" & "I feel": Columbia, Perkins Papers—AC to
       C. Schwab (copy), & to JPM, both Jan. 14, 1902, both in Hessen,
       pp. 134–35.

Page

446 "if Morgan thinks" & "the slightest": Columbia, Perkins Papers—
Schwab to GWP, Jan. 14, & GWP to Schwab, Jan. 16, 1902.

446 "Many thanks" & "Steel Co.": Ibid., Schwab to GWP, Jan. 17 & 28, 1902.

447 "forget it" to "unequalled": Hessen, pp. 137, 153–55.

447 *fn.* Schwab: Hessen, pp. 145–65; Hogan, *Iron and Steel,* Vol. II, pp. 538–40.

447 market share: Thomas K. McCraw & Forest Reinhardt, "Losing to Win,"
pp. 595–96.

448 strike settlement: P. Foner, *History Labor,* pp. 87–89, & Phelan, *Divided
Loyalties,* p. 131.

448 "do what": Mitchell to Hanna, Aug. 15, 1902; "a good deal": Easley to
Mitchell, March 5, 1902. Both in P. Foner, p. 90.

448–49 "forty years" & "rights and": in Phelan, pp. 157, 180. "George the" to
"Just Break": in P. Foner, pp. 92–96.

449 "in the absolute": MHS, Charles Francis Adams II Papers—Easley to
Charles A. Moore, Sept. 29, 1902. coal depot: Satterlee, *JPM,* pp. 388–94.

449 "done more" & "the arrogance": in P. Foner, pp. 96–97.

449 "wooden-headed": TR to Winthrop M. Crane, Oct. 22, 1902, *LTR,* Vol.
III, pp. 365–66.

450 "waste": Allen, *GPM,* p. 225.

450 "A most": TR to Crane (as above, Oct. 22, 1902). "mighty brains": TR to
H.C. Lodge, Oct. 17, 1902, *Correspondence of TR and Henry Cabot Lodge,*
pp. 539–41. "to my": TR to Crane, Oct. 22, 1902.

450 "My dear": TR to JPM, Oct. 16, 1902, *LTR,* Vol. III, p. 353.

451 "Mr. Morgan has": in Satterlee, *JPM,* p. 394.

451 "paramount" & ff.: Hofstadter, *Age of Reform,* pp. 236–37.

452 *fn.:* TR, *Autobiography,* pp. 423–25.

453 "noteworthy": *Wall Street Journal,* Dec. 28, 1904, in Kolko, *Railroads,*
p. 120.

453–54 economic changes: John Milton Cooper, Jr., *The Pivotal Decades,* pp. 82, 145.

454 "Don't do it": Kathleen Brady, *Ida Tarbell,* p. 123. "as nearly"—Tarbell,
History Standard Oil, Vol. II, pp. 29, 288.

455 "popular": *Nation,* Jan. 5, 1905, in Brady, p. 153.

455 "that of": Brady, p. 143.

455 "I aimed": in Cooper, *Pivotal Decades,* p. 86.

CHAPTER 23: COMMUNITY OF INTEREST ON THE ATLANTIC

457 "Pierpont Morgan . . .": HA to E. Cameron, April 22, 1902, *LHA,* Vol. V,
p. 377.

458 "large shipbuilding": MGCo. Ms 21,802—JPM to JSMCo., July 18, 1900.

459 "the embodiment": in Robert K. Massie, *Dreadnought, Britain, Germany,
and the Coming of the Great War,* pp. 799–800.

460 "as an uncle" & ff.: in Philip Magnus, *King Edward the Seventh,* pp. 209–11.

Page
460 "mean great": in Havighurst, *Twentieth-Century Britain*, p. 5.
460 "the possession" & "at his private": Bernard Hulderman, *Albert Ballin*, pp. 47, 56–57.
461 "Senators": MGCo. Ms 21,802—CS to JSMCo., Feb. 26, 1902.
461–62 "willing" & ff.: Ibid., CS & GWP to JPM, April 10, 1902. "fully agree" & "quite willing": JPM to CS & GWP, April 10 & 17, 1902.
462 shipping 1901–2: Thomas R. Navin and Marian V. Sears, "A Study in Merger," pp. 305–16; Edward S. Meade, "Capitalization of the IMMCo.," in Ripley, *Trusts, Pools*, pp. 360–67.
463 "in the light": Hulderman, p. 59.
463 "*boulversé*" & ff.: Bodleian, MS. Milner dep. 215, fols. 41–42—CED to Milner, April 25, 1902.
463 "The blow": May 13, 1902, in Lamar Cecil, *Albert Ballin, Business and Politics in Imperial Germany*, pp. 55–56.
464 "If the U.S.": JJH—GF to JJH, May 24, 1902.
464 "Difficult": MGCo. Ms 21,802—JPM to CED, April 24, 1902. "conjecture": CS to CED, April 25. "Have no" & "It does not": JPM to CED, April 25, & to JSMCo., May 6, 1902.
464–66 structure of deal & *fn.*: Navin & Sears, "A Study," pp. 305–14.
466 "English lines" & "every confidence": MGCo. Ms 21,802—JSMCo. to JPM, May 6, & CED to JPM, May 7, 1902. "some way": CED to JPM, May 7, 1902.
466 "unmitigated": Magnus, p. 299.
467 "hot" to "very sore": Bodleian, MS. Milner dep. 215, fols. 49–53—CED to Milner, May 23, 1902.
467 "expected": Sir Edward Hamilton Diary, June 2, 1902, in Kathleen Burk, *Morgan Grenfell*, p. 109.
467–68 "to suppress": MGCo. Ms 21,802—CED & Jack to CS, May 23, 1902.
468 "Quiet day": PML—ATMD, May 28–June 8, 1902.
468 "I've talked": Bodleian, MS. Milner dep. 215, fols. 54–55—CED to Milner, June 13, 1902.
468 "JPM . . .": MGCo. Ms 21,800—CED to CS, June 18, 1902.
469 "the Senior": PML—Jack to GWP, April 19, 1902.
469–70 "The new" & "plan seems": Garraty, *Right-Hand Man*, pp. 132–40.
470 "How you": MGCo. Ms 21,800—CED to CS, June 18, 1902.
470 "the inconvenient": PML—Jack to FTM, June 20, 1902.
470–71 "nasty sea" & ff.: PML—ATM to FTM, July 7, 1902.
471 *fn.*: in Hannah Pakula, *An Uncommon Woman, The Empress Frederick* (New York: Simon & Schuster, 1995), p. 125.
471 "his artlessness" & ff.: Michael Balfour, *The Kaiser and His Times*, p. 140.
471 "most impressed": PML—ATM to FTM, July 7, 1902.
471 "unfair" & ff.: Bodleian, MS. Milner dep. 215, fol. 60—CED to Milner, Nov. 6, 1902.

Page

472–73 "Mrs. Nat" to "wild jag": PML—ATM to FTM, July 7, 1902.

473 "He is": PML—Jack to FTM, July 12, 1902.

473 "the Senior": MGCo. Ms 21,800—CED to GWP, July 19, 1902.

473 "Nan and": PML, MSI—LMS to FTM, Aug. 7, 1902.

473 "with much": PML—ATM to FTM, Aug. 9, 1902. "fussed": AMS interview, Dec. 31, 1993.

474 "the simultaneous": Magnus, p. 299.

474 "Father's": PML, MSI—LMS to FTM, Aug. 16 [1902].

474 "irrespective": "The Shipping Trust and Higher Rates," *Scientific American*, Vol. 87, July 26, 1902.

474 "anxious to" & "We are": MGCo. Ms 21,802—CS to CED, June 24, & to JPM, Aug. 7, 1902.

474 "which will": Ibid.—JPM to CS, Aug. 1, 1902.

474 "our friend": JJH—G. Farrer to JJH, July 1, 1902.

475 "you be uchred": in Garraty, p. 136.

475 "avowedly": Bodleian, MS. Milner dep. 215 fols. 54–55—CED to Milner, June 13, 1902. "avoid": in Burk, p. 110.

475–76 "every desire" & "JPM &": MGCo. Ms 21,802—Jack to CED, Sept. 29 & CED to Jack, Oct. 3, 1902.

476 IMM scope: Navin & Sears, "A Study," p. 291; John J. & Margaret T. Clark, "The International Mercantile Marine Company: A Financial Analysis," *American Neptune*, No. 2, Spring 1997, p. 146.

476 "as shifting": Meade "IMMCo.," in Ripley, p. 368.

476 "largely on": MGCo. Ms 21,802—CS to CED, April 24, 1902. "unforeseen" & "what threatens": Ms 81,200—CED to Jack, Aug. 14, 1903, & to CS, Jan. 7, 1903.

477 "not justified": NY *Times*, March 31, 1903.

477 "the speculative": TR to H. C. Lodge, Aug. 6, 1903, *LTR*, Vol. III, p. 545. "revelations": Henry Clews, *Fifty Years of Wall Street* (New York: Irving Publishing Co., 1908), pp. 770–71.

478 *fn.*, "My dear," "I should," & "I wished": LC, TR Papers—TR to JPM, Oct. 8; JPM to TR, Oct. 12; TR to JPM, Oct. 13, 1903.

478 JPMCo. profit & loss 1902–3: Carosso, pp. 614–15.

479 "Apparently none": MGCo. Ms 21,800—CED to CS, June 16, 1902.

480 "To put": Ibid.—CED to G. Balfour, June 8, 1903.

480 "thick with": PML—Jack to JPM, Nov. 13, 1903. "Pierpont Morgan's": HA to EC, Feb. 14–16, 1904, *LHA*, Vol. V, p. 550. "if the": MGCo. Ms 21,800—CED to CS, Sept. 18, 1903.

480 "chiefly on": in Hulderman, pp. 62–63. "did not" & JPM promise: J.B. Ismay to Harold Ismay, Feb. 9, 1904, in Wilton J. Oldham, "The Ismay Line," *Journal of Commerce* (Liverpool, 1961), pp. 146–47.

480 "The ocean": in Cecil, pp. 57–58.

481 "It's *not*": BG notes in Hovey, p. 228.

485 "a strong": Jean Beaudrillard, "The System of Collecting," *The Cultures of Collecting*, edited by John Elsner and Roger Cardinal (Cambridge, Mass.: Harvard University Press, 1994), p. 10.

486 "This bronze": PML Vendors' files, Canessa—bill for Dec. 13, 1909.

487 books duty free: U.S. Revenue Act 1897, pp. 503, 609.

488 his host said: LC, McKim Papers—Charles F. McKim to W.R. Mead, April 2, 1902.

488 "You can": Ibid.—CFM to Theodore N. Ely, March 27, 1902.

488 "We were starving": in Charles Moore, *The Life and Times of Charles Follen McKim*, p. 260.

489 "never would": PML Vendors' files—Goldschmidt to JPM, May 16, 1902.

490 "Curiously": JJH—G. Farrer to JJH, May 24, 1902.

491 "bric-a-brac" & "picture gallery": N-YHS, McKim Mead & White, 1950 Collection, "Morgan Library," Box 627, folder B—JSM2 in HLS to CFM, May 19, 1902, & HLS to CFM, July 29, 1902.

491 Erechtheum joints: in Moore, *McKim*, p. 282.

491 "the best" & "the extraordinary": LC, McKim Papers—CFM to Gorham P. Stevens, June 1904, & to W.M. Kendall, May 16, 1904.

492 "blasts": Ibid., CFM to Mead, Aug. 26, 1904. "Father much": PML, MSI—LMSD, Dec. 18, 1903.

492 "not to": N-YHS, MMW, 1968 Collection, Sherman Statue file, Box M-8—Saint-Gaudens to CFM, Aug. 23, 1905.

492 "While fully": Ibid., 1950 Collection, "Morgan Library," Box 626—CFM to JPM, April 25, 1904.

492 "White is" & ff.: Moore, pp. 260–63. "expressed": LC, McKim Papers—CFM to Mead, Aug. 26, 1904.

492 "Pierpont's face": HA to EC, Feb. 1, 1903, *LHA* Vol. V, p. 448.

493 lobbies Shaw: NY *Times*, March 14, 1903.

493–94 "sights": Vasari, *Lives of the Painters*, Vol. II, pp. 851–55.

494 "justly regarded": *In August Company*, p. 110.

494–95 Dino armor: Tomkins, *Merchants*, p. 152. "hardware": MGCo. Ms 21,795—CED to JPM, April 30, 1904.

496 "So Mr. Riggs": MMA Archives—B. Dean to H. Kent, June 5, 1912.

496 "not merely": in Tomkins, *Merchants*, p. 99.

497 "Education": James, *American Scene*, pp. 513–14.

497 "No, sir" & ff.: in Tomkins, p. 102.

497 "I loathe": Virginia Woolf, *Roger Fry*, p. 119.

498 "I am having" & "will be": Roger Fry to Helen Fry, Jan. 9 & 10, 1905, in *Letters of Roger Fry*, Vol. I, pp. 228–29.

498–99 "I travelled" to "not like": RF to HF, Jan. 11, 1905. There are two different letters of this date, one in Denys Sutton's *Letters of Roger Fry*, Vol. I, p. 230, the other at King's College, Cambridge, and I am quoting from

Page

them both. *fn.*, "Ghirlandaio": in James Henry Duveen, *The Rise of the House of Duveen*, p. 235.

499 "lots of" & ff.: RF to HF, Jan. 11, 1905, *LRF*, Vol. I, pp. 230–31.

499 "dragooned" & "Henry James": Moore, p. 242.

499–500 "the great examples": Elihu Root, "Art and Architecture in America," in *Miscellaneous Addresses by Elihu Root*, edited by Robert Bacon and James Brown Scott (Cambridge, Mass.: Harvard University Press, 1917), pp. 189–96.

500 "big success": HJ to Mary Cadwalader Jones, Jan. 13, 1905, *HJL*, Vol. IV, p. 337.

500 "The journey" to "He's not": RF to HF, Jan. 13 & 21, 1905, *LRF*, Vol. I, pp. 231–33.

501 "Friends, Romans": Moore, p. 251.

501–2 "enabling" & ff.: PML—Robert Langton Douglas to JPM, May 3, 12, & 20, 1904; RLD to Jack, July 29, 1937.

502 "I take": PML Vendors' files, Cartier—J.P. Worth to JPM, June 16, 1904.

502 "Father has": PML—Jack to FTM, June 20, 1905.

503 "As one entered" & ff.: in Francis Henry Taylor, *Pierpont Morgan as Collector and Patron*, pp. 21–25.

504 "The ceiling": Satterlee, *JPM*, p. 434.

504 "This afternoon": *Letters BB & ISG*, p. 388.

504 "I have": in Denys Sutton, "Robert Langton Douglas, Connoisseur of Art & Life," *Apollo*, CIX–CX, April–July 1979.

505 "When you go": Moore, p. 282.

505 "The sky": N-YHS, MMW, 1950 Collection, "Morgan Library," Box 627, folder B—CFM to White, Feb. 1, 1906.

506 "One day" & ff.: *The Inferno of Dante*, translated by Robert Pinsky (New York: Farrar Straus & Giroux, 1994), p. 53.

507 "instruction and pleasure": PML—JPM Last Will and Testament.

508 "[He] is": GWP to P. Widener, Feb. 27, 1907, in Garraty, p. 199.

CHAPTER 25: SINGULAR WOMEN

509 BG salaries: PML—JPMD, Dec. 31, 1905, & Box 22, Trustees Records, Princeton University Archives, Seeley G. Mudd Manuscript Library, Princeton University Library.

509 "the most": PML—Bernard Berenson to Philip Hofer, Nov. 26, 1934.

509 "a native": *Notable American Women*, Vol. II. "I knew": NY *Sun*, Oct. 19, 1916.

510 "with great": I Tatti—BG to BB, Oct. 29, 1910.

510 "the luxury": Ibid., Sept. 20, 1913.

510 "pre-eminent": PML—BG to JPM, April 23, 1909.

Page

512 Fleet wedding: Virginia State Archives, Paul E. Sluby, Sr. and Stanton L. Wormley, *Blacks in the Marriage Records of the District of Columbia, Dec. 23, 1811–June 16, 1870,* Vol. I, p. 184.

512 Du Bois on Greener: in Allison Blakely, "Richard T. Greener and the 'Talented Tenth's' Dilemma."

513 "My chief desire": Harvard University Archives—"Richard T. Greener, Class Notes," May 19, 1870.

513 "a world which": W.E.B. DuBois, *The Souls of Black Folk* (New York: New American Library, 1969), p. 45.

513 twenty-six thousand books: Harvard University Archives, Class Reports—Greener, 1895.

513 "For the first": in Blakely, p. 308.

513–14 "a colored": Ellen Collins to BTW, Aug. 23, 1892. "I am devoting": RTG to BTW, May 26, 1894. "In regard": Thomas Junius Calloway to BTW, May 2, 1894. All in *Booker T. Washington Papers,* edited by Louis Harlan (Urbana: University of Illinois Press, 1972–1989), Vol. 3, pp. 258–59, 448, 415.

514 Vladivostok charges: Louis Harlan, *Booker T. Washington* (New York: Oxford University Press, 1983), pp. 89–90.

514 "I still believe": *The Freeman,* Jan. 25, 1896, in Blakely, p. 311.

515 "Would he be": R. Bacon to C.R. Dean, July 3, 1907, in Blakely, p. 314.

516 "the hard-won": George Eliot, *The Mill on the Floss* (New York: Collier Books, 1962), p. 321.

516 "blonde": I Tatti—BG to BB, Nov. 6, 1912.

516 "if he were": Ibid.—BG to BB, Jan. 19, 1911.

516–17 "duly impressed": BB to ISG, Dec. 5, 1908, *Letters of BB and ISG,* p. 426.

517 "Dear thou": I Tatti—BG to BB, March 9, 1909.

517 "I am *so*" & "How I should": Ibid., April 9 & March 17, 1909.

517 "would stand": Ernest Samuels, *Bernard Berenson,* Vol. II, p. 73.

517 "Malay": Ibid.

518 "of course" & ff.: ISG to BB, Dec. 18, 1909, *Letters BB–ISG,* p. 462.

518 "that I": I Tatti—BG to BB, Dec. 21, 1909. "incredible" & ff.: BB to ISG, Jan. 1, 1910, *Letters BB–ISG,* p. 463.

518–19 Portuguese descent: I Tatti—BG to BB, April 9, 1909. "grand": Nov. 22, 1910. "stunning": Feb. 27, 1912. "*I* shall": Oct. 29, 1910. "I am sure": Dec. 15, 1911. "that poor": Dec. 28 & 13, 1910. "I am so": Dec. 29, 1913.

519 "a most" & "I hope": MB to Ray Costelloe, Feb. 18, 1909, & MB to BB, Aug. 21, 1910, in *Mary Berenson,* eds. Barbara Strachey and Jayne Samuels, pp. 150, 160. "I am all," "incredibly," & "much more": Samuels, *BB,* Vol. II, pp. 109–11.

519 "a terrific": I Tatti—BG to BB, April 18, 1921.

519 "one of," "my dear," & "quite loved": Ibid., April 14, July 6, & July 19, 1909.

Page
520 "I really": MB to AR, May 24, 1911, in *Mary Berenson*, p. 170.

520 "[T]hat is": I Tatti—BG to BB, Jan. 9, 1912.

520 "to extinction" & "More and": Ibid., April 23, 1909, & July 9, 1913.

521 "the shadow" & ff.: N-YHS, Osborn Papers, Box XXII—ATM to Mrs. HFO, June 1 [1903].

521 "the swan-song," "best," & "I've waited: Cleveland Amory, *Who Killed Society?* (New York: Harper & Brothers, 1960), p. 222.

522 "Miss de Lamb": Jane S. Smith, *Elsie de Wolfe*, p. 56.

522 "almost certainly": Ibid., p. 24. "the only": HA to E. Cameron, Sept. 12, 1899, *LHA*, Vol. V, p. 30.

522 Bessie childhood: Elisabeth Marbury, *My Crystal Ball*, pp. 12–13, 34; J.S. Smith, pp. 26–34.

522 "If she": Brady, *Ida Tarbell*, p. 197.

522 "Rapacious": Smith, p. 57. Bessie & Wilde: *The Letters of Oscar Wilde*, edited by Rupert Hart-Davis (New York: Harcourt, Brace & World, 1962), pp. 668–69, 698–99.

523 "I went": HA to E. Cameron, Jan. 28, 1901, *LHA*, Vol. V, p. 189. "J.P. Morgan": Smith, p. 71.

523 "in a way": Samuels, *BB*, Vol. II, p. 50.

523–24 "Miss Marbury ill" to "Colleges": PML—ATMD, April–June 1904.

525 "would have liked" to "were expected": MHS, Marian Lawrence Peabody Papers—Marian Lawrence Peabody Diary, Sept. 11, 1904.

525 "very unprepossessing": PML, MSI—HLS to Mrs. Satterlee, Oct. 3, 1904.

526 "Oh, a": William Lawrence, *Memories of a Happy Life*, p. 201.

526 "everybody": PML—ATM Box 4, Elsie de Wolfe, "Story of Mr. de Beauvoir". "who knows" & *fn.*: Woolf, *Roger Fry*, p. 135.

527 "He thrilled": PML—de Wolfe, "Story."

527 "a bronze": MGCo. Ms 21,760—JPM to Bosdari, Aug. 7, 1902. "inconceivable": MGCo. Ms 21,799—ECG notebook, pp. 88–90.

527–28 *fn.* "Bosdari &": PML—ATMD, Sept. 23, 1907. "highly pleased": PML—Jack to ECG, March 12, 1918.

528 "young for" & ff.: Marbury, *My Crystal Ball*, pp. 151–53.

529 "there are such": *The Letters of Archie Butt*, edited by F. Lawrence Abbott (Garden City, N.Y.: Doubleday, Page & Co., 1924), p. 267.

529 "shirt waist": PML—ATMD, Dec. 5–15, 1909.

529 "Surely": PML, MSI—WSR to LMS, March 28, 1908.

529–30 "got me aside" & ff.: I Tatti—BG to BB, October 19, 1910, and [n.d.] "Oceanic," 1910. "tiresome": July 9, 1912. "immediately" & "Your friend": March 17 & April 21, 1913. "*hates*": July 9, 1913.

530 "I want" & ff.: HA to John Hay, Sept. 28, 1904, *LHA*, Vol. V, p. 612.

531 "J.P. Morgan, Sr.": N-YHS, James Hazen Hyde Papers, Correspondence M, Elisabeth Marbury file.

Page   CHAPTER 26: BACK NUMBER?

533   "If Congress": "*Northern Securities Co. v. U.S.,*" 193 U.S. 197, in Ripley, *Trusts, Pools,* pp. 491–92.

534   "Great cases" & ff.: "*Northern Securities Co. v. U.S.,*" in *The Dissenting Opinions of Mr. Justice Holmes,* arranged by Alfred Lief (New York: Vanguard Press, 1929), pp. 163–75.

534   "I could": William H. Harbaugh, *The Life and Times of Theodore Roosevelt,* p. 161. "broke up": OWH to F. Pollock, February 9, 1921, in *Holmes-Pollock Letters, The Correspondence of Mr. Justice Holmes and Sir Frederick Pollock 1874–1932,* edited by Mark A. DeWolfe Howe (Cambridge, Mass.: Harvard University Press, 1941), Vol. II, pp. 63–64.

534–35   *fn.,* "Mr. Solicitor": Yale University Library, Manuscripts and Archives, John William Davis Papers—John W. Davis to Herbert Brookes, Oct. 19, 1944.

535   "almost as" & ff.: PML—Jack to CED, March 14 & 21, 1904.

535   "with all their": TR to H.C. Lodge, May 23, 1903, *LTR,* Vol. II, p. 17. "will have been": MGCo.—CED to Jack, Feb. 17, 1904.

536   "the salient": in Boller, *Presidential Campaigns,* p. 184.

536   "Theodore": *Dictionary of American Biography* (Laffan).

536   "No" & ff.: "Campaign Contributions," Testimony before a Subcommittee of the Committee on Privileges and Elections, U.S. Senate 62nd Cong., 3d sess. Pursuant to S. Res. 79, 386, and 418. Vol. I, pp. 437–53, Oct. 3, 1912.

536   "wise custom" & ff.: Harbaugh, p. 224. "I would": H.W. Brands, *Theodore Roosevelt, The Last Romantic* (New York: Basic Books, 1998), pp. 515–16.

537   *fn.* "We talked": PML—JSMCo. to Jack, April 25, 1904.

537   "plunged": Barings—Revelstoke to Gaspard Farrer, April 19, 1904.

537   "we take it": Cecil Baring to Revelstoke, Nov. 27, 1900, in Ziegler, *Sixth Great Power,* p. 297.

537–38   "inveighed": Barings—Revelstoke to Farrer, April 19, 1904.

538   "débacle" & ff.: Bodleian, MS. Milner dep. 216, fol. 61—CED to Milner, May 5, 1904.

538   "back number": Barings—in Farrer to John Sterling, Sept. 22, 1904.

538   Bacon on Perkins: Barings—Sterling to Farrer, Oct. 4, 1904. "absolutely": Ibid.—JPM to Revelstoke, Nov. 4, 1904.

539   "it might": Ibid.—R. Winsor to Revelstoke, Oct. 10, 1904.

539   "of inflicting" & "Old Man" & ff.: Ibid.—Revelstoke to Winsor, March 17, 1905, & to Hugo Baring, Aug. 8, 1905.

539   "JPM is": St. Just—ECG to Maud Grenfell, May 19, 1906.

540   "It is": PML—Jack to FTM, Jan. 3, 1905.

540   "I want": Ibid., JPM to Baldwin, April 14, 1905.

540   "so high": Schieffelin—Léon Blanc to James Markoe, June 29, 1905.

541   "serious enough" & ff.: TR to JPM, July 18, 1905, *LTR,* Vol. IV, p. 1277.

Page
541 "insist": TR to JPM, Aug. 17, 1905, Ibid., p. 1303.
542 "a strong safeguard": Memorandum of First International Harvester Conference, Jan. 18, 1907, in Robert Wiebe, "The House of Morgan and the Executive," pp. 52–53. "anticipated": Columbia, Perkins Papers—GWP to JPM, June 25, 1906.
542 "satisfied" & ff.: Perkins Memorandum, Aug. 28, 1907 (Perkins Papers, Columbia), in Wiebe, pp. 53–54; "moral ground": in Garraty, *Right-Hand Man*, p. 257.
544 "moral obliqueness" & insurance industry figures: John Rousmaniere, *The Life and Times of the Equitable*, pp. 101, 75–78.
545 *fn.* "the most": Mark D. Hirsch, *William C. Whitney, Modern Warwick* (New York: Archon Books, 1969 [1948]), p. 466.
545 "He shook": Rousmaniere, *Equitable*, p. 104.
545 "When, in your" & ff.: Garraty, p. 171.
546 "the King": MGCo.—Alexander Koch to JPM, Feb. 10, 1898, in Carosso, *Morgans*, pp. 401–2. JPM declines Russian loans: Ruth A. Roosa, "Banking and Financial Relations between Russia and the U.S.," pp. 305–11.
547 "It is curious": Barings—Farrer to Winsor, July 29, 1905.
547 proposal to build battleships: Roosa, p. 313. "greatest": Robert K. Massie, *Nicholas and Alexandra*, p. 90.
548 *fn.,* "when I": TR to Cecil Spring-Rice, July 24, 1905, *LTR*, Vol. IV, pp. 1285–86.
548 "a huge": Massie, *Nicholas*, p. 101.
548 "morbid nose" & ff.: Yarmolinsky, *Memoirs of Count Witte*, p. 170.
548 Witte's proposal: Roosa, pp. 313–14. "the Jewish": Yarmolinsky, p. 169. "shameful": Adler, *Schiff*, Vol. II, p. 124.
549 "Our scheme": PML—JPM to Jack, Oct. 7 & 10, 1905.
549 "reluctantly," "even if," "would have": Ibid.—to Jack & GWP, Oct. 17; GWP & Jack to JPM, Oct. 21; JPM & CS to GWP & Jack, Oct. 22, 1905.
549 "Please": Ibid.—GWP & Jack to JPM, Oct. 23, 1905.
550 "What a time" & "We have": Ibid.—Jack to FTM, Oct. 31, GWP & Jack to JPM, Oct. 31 & Nov. 1, 1905. "Have changed": Garraty, p. 185.
550 "impolitic": PML—Jack & GWP to JPM, April 7–11, 1906.
551 "crusade": TR to McClure, Oct. 3, 1905, *LTR*, Vol. V, p. 45.
551 "the Man": TR *Works*, Vol. XVI, pp. 415–18.
552 "dull, purblind": TR to Taft, March 15, 1906, *LTR*, Vol. V, pp. 183–84.
552 "if the currency": in Sobel, *Panic*, p. 303.

CHAPTER 27: "MORE COLOSSAL THAN EVER"

553 "as complete": PML—GW Vanderbilt to JSM2, Nov. 25, 1905.
553–54 "the family": PML—Jack to JPM, Jan. 6, 1905. "that there": to G. Duckworth, Jan. 16, 1905. "It may": to ECG, Feb. 24, 1905.

Page

554 "Thoby": *The Letters of Virginia Woolf,* edited by Nigel Nicolson and Joanne Trautmann (New York: Harcourt Brace Jovanovich, 1975), Vol. I, No. 279. *fn.,* "One": Virginia Woolf, *Moments of Being* (New York: Harcourt Brace Jovanovich, 1976), p. 160.

554 "There is" & *fn.:* PML—TR to Curtis, Dec. 16, 1905.

554–56 Curtis plans & "I congratulate": PML—Curtis to JPM, Jan. 23, 1906, & TR to Curtis, Feb. 6, 1906.

556 "the matter": PML—C.W. King to Curtis, Aug. 28, 1906.

556 Curtis project costs: Barbara A. Davis, *Edward Sheriff Curtis, The Life and Times of a Shadow Catcher* (San Francisco: Chronicle Books, 1985), p. 75.

556–57 archaeological studies: Bruce Kuklick, *Puritans in Babylon,* pp. 102–5.

557 "I see Morgan": Laffan to Edward P. Mitchell, April 24 [1906] in Mitchell's *Memoirs of an Editor* (New York: Charles Scribner's Sons, 1924), p. 360.

558 fifteen years: MMA Egypt—A. Lythgoe to E. Robinson, Feb. 26, 1906.

558 "I hope": PML—Johns to Laffan, Oct. 2, 1907.

558–59 "only to," "Perhaps as," "to work": PML—BG to Johns, April 1; JPM to BG, April 29; Clay to BG, April 20, 1910.

560 Morgan gifts to Natural History Museum: *The American Museum,* April 1913, & Geoffrey Hellman, *Bankers, Bones and Beetles,* pp. 118–33. *fn.,* "I cannot": PML—Jack to HFO, Oct. 11, 1916.

560–61 "painful surprise": PML, MSI—LMSD, Feb. 4, 1906. "quite alone": Rainsford, *Story,* p. 461. "Would advise": PML—JPM to C.W. King, April 26, 1910.

561 "for causes": Canon 32, *Of Renunciation of the Ministry,* Journal of the General Convention of the Protestant Episcopal Church, 1910, in Soukoup, "From Orthodoxy to Liberalism," pp. 97–98.

561 "am willing": PML—JPM to Jack, May 29, 1912.

561 "STANFORD WHITE, VOLUPTUARY": Suzannah Lessard, *The Architect of Desire* (New York: Dial Press, 1996), p. 245.

562 "objectionable": NY *Times,* Jan. 27, 1907.

562 "the poison" & ff.: PML—Jack to WSMB, Jan. 4, 1907.

563 "it makes": PML—Jack to ECG, Jan. 11, 1907.

563 "the best": PML—Jack to JSMCo., Feb. 13, 1906.

563 seven groups: Chandler & Tedlow, *Managerial Capitalism,* p. 278.

564 "while the": Columbia, Perkins Papers—GWP to JPM, June 25, 1906.

564 *fn.:* Shaw, *Annual Report on the Finances,* 1906, p. 49, in Friedman & Schwartz, *Monetary History,* pp. 149–50.

564 "aggressive": NY *Times,* Nov. 24, 1907, in Carosso, p. 534. "a literally": in Sobel, *Panic,* p. 300.

564 "allay": Washington *Star,* March 12, 1907.

565 "underlying": MGCo.—JPMCo. to JSMCo., March 15, 1907.

565 "Think plan": PML—JPM to Jack, March 26, 1907.

565 "As Jesus": PML—Jack to JPM, April 16, 1907.

Page

566   "that, in spite" & "and expressed": RF to A. F. Jaccaci, June 18, 1906, & to JGJ, April 3, 1907, in *Letters of Roger Fry*, Vol. I, pp. 266, 283.

566–67   "You may" to "to make my": RF to HF, May 21–June 2, 1907, Ibid., pp. 284–88.

567   "Fry burst": BB to ISG, June 26, 1907, *Letters of BB & ISG*, p. 400.

567   "marvellous": King's College, RF to HF, June 7, 1907. "some fine": RF to HF, June 16, 1907, *LRF*, Vol. I, p. 288.

568   *fn.* "highest" & "Woe": BB to ISG, Aug. 14, & ISG to BB, Aug. 26, 1907, *Letters BB-ISG*, pp. 403–5. "in memory": PML—BG to BB, Feb. 26, 1932.

569   "in some": George C. Williamson, *An Experiment in Book Collecting* (London: Cassell & Co., Ltd., 1931), p. 26.

569   "Beginning": Wilhelm Bode, *Bronzes in the Collection of J. Pierpont Morgan* (Paris: Librairie Centrale des Beaux-Arts, 1909).

570   "This is the most": PML—note on RF to JPM, June 20, 1909. *fn.:* BB to ISG, July 11, 1909, *Letters BB-ISG*, pp. 450–51.

570   "up in": I Tatti—BG to BB, March 11, 1910.

570   "I hope": PML—RF to JPM, Dec. 10, 1912.

570   "sleeping" & ff.: Woolf, *Roger Fry*. pp. 140–44.

571   "As he": VW to Donald Brace, Oct. 6, 1940, *The Letters of Virginia Woolf*, Vol. VI (New York: Harcourt Brace Jovanovich, 1980), p. 438.

CHAPTER 28: PANIC

573   "The figures": PML—Jack to VHS, July 2, 1907.

574   "everyone": Ibid., Aug. 14, 1907.

574   "difficult": TR to HLH, Aug. 12, 1907, *LTR*, Vol. V, pp. 746–47. "certain malefactors": Harbaugh, *Roosevelt*, p. 297.

574   "the irrigating": in Rousmaniere, *Equitable*, p. 80.

576   "We got": NY *Times*, Oct. 21, 1907.

577   "reflected the" & "We are": Ibid., Oct. 23, 1907.

577   "All hands": PML—GWP to Jack, Oct. 22, 1907.

578   "Yes, and": in Chernow, *Titan*, p. 543.

578   "This is": PML, HLS Box 12, folder 2—Benjamin Strong recollections to T.W. Lamont, Feb. 1, 1929.

579   "Gentlemen": Ibid.

579   "reflect on": NY *Times*, Oct. 24, 1907.

579   "We have": PML—GWP to Jack, Oct. 24, 1907.

579   "There goes the" & ff.: Satterlee, *JPM*, p. 473.

580   "Situation": PML—GWP to Jack, Oct. 25, 1907.

580   "With his": Satterlee, *JPM*, p. 479.

580   "We have": PML—GWP to Jack, Oct. 25, 1907, #2.

581   "the unselfish,": NY *Times*, Oct. 26, 1907. "could have": Adler, *Schiff*, Vol. I, p. 176. "owing to" & "J.P.": NY *Times*, Oct. 26, 1907.

Page

581–82   "unswervingly": NY *Times*, Oct. 23, 1907. "those conservative": TR to Cortelyou, Oct. 25, 1907, *LTR*, Vol. V, p. 823.

582   "The week's": PML—GWP to Jack, Oct. 27, 1907.

582   "delirium": NY *Times*, Oct. 30, 1907.

582   "You ought": Allen, *GPM*, p. 266.

583   Kessler problems, Schley explanations: NY *Times*, Nov. 5, 1907, & Aug. 3, 1911.

583   U.S. Steel loan to Schley, 1907: NY *Times*, June 3, 1911.

584   "sell the" & "what would": NY *Times*, Aug. 3 & July 30, 1911. "to sell": *U.S. Senate Committee on Judiciary Report on Absorption of TC&I*, p. 6.

584   Gary declined TC&I 1901: W. David Lewis, *Sloss Furnaces and the Rise of the Birmingham District* (Tuscaloosa: University of Alabama Press, 1994), p. 291. Careful about antitrust law: Gary testimony, NY *Times*, June 3, 1911, & Kenneth Warren, *The American Steel Industry*, p. 186.

584   Schley says no: NY *Times*, June 3, 1911, & Garraty, p. 211.

585   "but it didn't": NY *Times*, Aug. 3, 1911. *fn.*, TC&I history: Warren, pp. 185–87, & Hogan, *Iron & Steel*, Vol. II, pp. 498–512.

586   *fn.*, bond-stock trade: Hogan, p. 504; Carosso, *Morgans*, p. 830, *n.* 68.

586   "anxious": Thomas W. Lamont, *Henry P. Davison*, p. 81.

587   "There you": PML—Strong to TWL, & Allen, pp. 262–64.

587–88   "that it": TR to Charles J. Bonaparte, Nov. 4, 1907, *LTR*, Vol. V, pp. 830–31.

588   "buoyantly": PML, HLS Box 12, folder 2—GWP memorandum on the Panic of 1907, Jan. 4, 1921.

588–89   "Morgan should": BB to ISG, Nov. 7, 1907, *Letters of BB & ISG*, p. 412.

589   "There has": TR to Douglas Robinson, Nov. 16, 1907. *LTR*, Vol. V, pp. 845–46.

589   "group of": *The Bankers Magazine*, April 1908, p. 480, in Carosso, p. 547. "checked the": *The Public*, Oct. 16, 1908.

589   $90 million: Julian Kennedy, in Warren, p. 186. $2 billion: J.W. Gates, NY *Times*, Nov. 7, 1907.

589   "Morgan banks": *Senate Judiciary Committee Report*, 1909, pp. 5, 14–15. *fn.*, "thrilling": PML, MSI—LMS to FTM, Feb. 22, 1909.

590   Gates in NY *Times*, Nov. 7, 1907, & May 28–30, 1911, & 1909 *Judiciary Committee Report*, p. 9.

590   "imminent and" & ff.: NY *Times*, August 6, 1911.

591   "What would": Ibid., Aug. 11, 1911.

591–92   "Is there": Ibid., June 10, 1911.

592   "A desire": in Garraty, *Right-Hand Man*, p. 252.

592   "Was there": NY *Times*, Aug. 3, 1911.

592–93   "make the": in Woodward, *Origins*, p. 310. "demagogues": July 2, 1913. *fn.*, TC&I after 1907: Warren, pp. 188–209.

593   "Now, wasn't that": NY *Times*, Jan. 25, 1908.

Page

593–94 "industrial paralysis": in James Livingston, *Origins of the Federal Reserve System*, p. 172. "sentiment is": Columbia, Vanderlip Papers—Vanderlip to George E. Roberts, Dec. 23, 1907.

594 "If anything": PML, HLS Box 3, folder A13—memorandum of G.F. Baker.

594 "meeting you": Columbia, Perkins Papers—GWP to JPM, July 23, 1908.

594 Aldrich wealth: Nathaniel W. Stephenson, *Nelson W. Aldrich* (New York: Charles Scribner's Sons, 1930), p. 323.

595 "Mr. Morgan thinks": MGCo. Ms 21,795—ECG to W. Reid, August 4 & 8, 1908. "the standard": in Livingston, pp. 159–60.

595–96 "position to-day": St. Just—ECG to Mrs. Willy Buckler, Dec. 4, 1909.

CHAPTER 29: TRIO

597 "Inform": PML—JPM to Jack, April 23, 1908.

598 "High Financiers" & ff.: PML—Jack to Theo. A. Bingham, Jan. 29, 1908.

598 "bushwhacked" & "We hope": NY *Times*, Feb. 27 & April 5, 1908.

598 "but for": *Yale Alumni Weekly*, Commencement, 1908.

600 "one of the": London *Times*, Dec. 4, 1908.

600 "MONEY TALKS": Chicago *Daily Tribune*, Dec. 10, 1908.

600 "My father": NY *Times*, Dec. 11, 1908.

601 "I couldn't": Columbia University Oral History Research Office Collection: "Reminiscences of Herbert C. Pell," p. 117.

601 "I wish": LC, William Howard Taft Papers—JPM to WHT, Nov. 3, 1908. "Heartiest": MGCo. Ms 21,802—Jack, ECG, VHS to JPMCo. Nov. 4, 1908.

601 "in all" & "other places": Columbia, Perkins Papers—GWP to JPM, Feb. 25 & July 23, 1909.

601 "I think": PML—Jack to GWP, Nov. 19, 1908.

602 "very much": Lodge to TR, Nov. 30, 1909, *Correspondence of Theodore Roosevelt and Henry Cabot Lodge*, Vol. II, p. 355. "and seemed": July 17, 1910, *Taft and Roosevelt, The Intimate Letters of Archie Butt* (Garden City, N.Y.: Doubleday, Doran & Co., Inc., 1930), Vol. II, p. 443.

602 "George, will": PML—HLS notebook, "JPM."

602 "What happened": Lamont, *Davison*, p. 121.

603 Trio: Frank Vanderlip, *Farm Boy to Financier* (New York: D. Appleton-Century Company, 1935), p. 190. Moody, *Masters*, pp. 194–95.

603 "He is": I Tatti—BG to BB, Aug. 24, 1909.

603 "mentally": LC, Elihu Root Papers—Charles H. Allen to Root, Jan. 12, 1910.

604 "cleaned up": *Congressional Record*, 60th Cong., 1st sess., p. 3568. "Your name": BG notes in Hovey, p. 285. a "sneaking": I Tatti, BG to BB, April 11, 1910.

604 "to take it": PML, Jack Box 116—W.H. Hotchkiss to Equitable Directors, April 20, 1911, p. 2.

Page

604 "a law": St. Just—ECG to Mrs. Buckler, Dec. 4, 1909.

605 "We have" & "unless": PML—GWP to Jack, Dec. 5, & Jack to GWP, Dec. 6, 1909.

605 "Big Chief": I Tatti—BG to BB, Dec. 21, 1909.

605 "I permit" & "enthusiasmed": PML—Olschki to BG, Sept. 25, 1907, & April 7, 1908.

606 "I know": PML—BG to JPM, April 19, 1910.

606 "most *exceptional*": PML—BG to JPM, May 6, 1907. "would like": Bernard Quaritch to JPM, June 17, 1907.

606 "the most": Tomkins, *Merchants,* pp. 166–67. "where works": Margaret Sterne, *The Passionate Eye,* p. 92.

606–7 "After shaking": Valentiner, "Reminiscences."

607 *fn.** "urge for": Ibid.

607 "It looks" & "it was": Sterne, pp. 94, 96.

607 "Morgan told" & ff.: Ibid., p. 95. *fn.†* "Whatever": James Fenton, "Verrocchio: The New Cicerone," *The New York Review of Books,* Feb. 19, 1998.

608 "that nobody": MMA Egypt—Edward Robinson to Albert Lythgoe, Jan. 26, 1909.

608 "It was": Ibid., AL to ER, March 5, 1909.

609 "I don't": Ibid., AL to ER, March 18, 1909. "Returned": PML—JPM to Jack, March 13, 1909. "perfect": MMA Egypt—AL to ER, March 31, 1909.

609 "put the": LC, Franklin MacVeagh Papers.—W.L. Loeb, Jr., to J.C. Curtis, Sept. 19, 1911.

609 "I need not": PML, Vendors' files—Bode to JPM, May 17, 1909.

609 "impossible": Princeton—Morgan Family Papers Box 10—JSM2 to Josephine P. Morgan, Aug. 15, 1909. "unnatural": PML, MSI—LMS to FTM, August 17 [n.d.]. "yet I": I Tatti—BG to BB, Aug. 21, 1909.

610 "remarkably" & "Mr. Morgan": PML Vendors' files—Sotheran to BG, Jan. 5, & BG to Sotheran, Jan. 25, 1907. "as to": C.H. Read to BG, Nov. 9, 1909.

610 "One of": PML—with *Pudd'nhead Wilson* MS. *fn.,* "frankly": PML—BG to Ray Brown, Feb. 2, 1911. stockbreeders: N-YHS Misc. Mss. Hughes, Rupert—Rupert Hughes to Wilmer B. Leech, Nov. 12, 1949.

611 Friedlander: in Harris, *Cultural Excursions,* p. 260.

611 "We are launched": I Tatti—BG to BB, Sept. 27, 1909.

613 "not because": Herbert Croly, *Willard Straight,* p. 340. "very little": Schiff to Kahn, June 25, 1909, in Adler, *Schiff,* Vol. I, p. 251.

613 "On the" & "Strikes me": PML—Jack to JPM, June 2, & JPM to Jack, June 3, 1909.

613 "a proposition": MGCo.—HPD to ECG, Aug. 6, 1909, in Carosso, *Morgans,* p. 554. "you can": PML—HPD to Jack, May 21, 1912.

613 "embarrassing": Lamont, p. 160.

Page
614 "make it": Swanberg, *Whitney*, p. 299. "will you" & "as regard": PML—
JPM to HPD, May 17, & HPD to JPM, May 18, 1911. *fn.:* HN to VSW, June
1, 1935, in *Harold Nicolson Diaries, 1930–1939*, edited by Nigel Nicolson (New York: Atheneum, 1966), p. 203.

615 "Mr. JPM": Division of Rare and Manuscript Collections, Cornell University Library—DPW to WDS, Jan. 30, 1911.

615 "Patriotism": in Carosso, p. 577.

616 Mellen quadruples: Ibid., p. 608.

616 "these men": NY *Times*, April 13, 1910.

616 "We have a": Cooper, *Pivotal Decades*, p. 158.

616 JPM would have voted: PML—BG to J.H. FitzHenry, Nov. 1, 1910. "We
are": I Tatti—BG to BB, Nov. 11, 1910.

617 "a man of brains": NY *Times*, Nov. 24, 1907.

617 "as astonished": I Tatti—BG to BB, Oct. 1, 1912.

617–18 "nothing organic" & "a good rest": PML—Jack to JPM, June 1, & HPD to
JPM, June 4, 1910. *fn.*, "means beside": PML—Jack to FTM, July 5, 1921.

619 "buy Caxton": PML, Vendors' files "JPM 1910–13"—JPM to BG, March
1911.

619 "Prices absurd" & "Use your": Ibid.—BG to JPM, April 28, & JPM to BG,
April 29, 1911.

619 "ridiculous": Ibid.—BG to JPM, May 5, 1911. "a profound": Clay to JPM
[May] 6, 1911.

620 "He tried": PML—HLS notebook, "JPM." "Thank God": BG notes in
Hovey, p. 309.

620 "Lamont, I": Edward M. Lamont, *The Ambassador From Wall Street* (Lanham, Md.: Madison Books, 1994), p. 41.

621 "wholesome" & "The idea": in Hofstadter, *Age of Reform*, p. 197*n.*

621 "Magazine Trust": NY *Times*, Feb. 5, 1911. Publishing trust: NY *Press*,
Feb. 6, 1911. "proper" facts: PML—TWL, CS, & Jack to HPD, May 23,
1912.

621 "You see" & "New Devil": Lippmann, *Drift and Mastery*, pp. 23–24, 83.

622 *fn.*, "to-day": Ibid., p. 46; "attacks": Tarbell, *All in the Day's Work* (New
York: Macmillan, 1939), pp. 242, 364.

623 "very much": PML—BG to JPM, June 1, 1911.

623 the "insinuations": PML—Jack to FTM, June 7, 1911.

623 "Well, it has": Satterlee, *JPM*, p. 531.

623 "a friendly": Tarbell, *Gary*, p. 211. "it is": W.B. Dickson to Corey, Feb. 16,
1909, in Hessen, *Steel Titan*, p. 187.

623 "It is not": Livesay, *Carnegie*, p. 187.

624 "His departure": NY *Times*, Jan. 3, 1912. "JP went": I Tatti—BG to BB,
Jan. 9, 1912. "the Senior's": PML—Jack to ECG, Jan. 8, 1912.

624 "optimistic": Columbia, Stillman Papers—J. Stillman to J.A. Stillman,
Jan. 19, 1912.

Page

624 "a succession": Harbaugh, *Roosevelt*, p. 380. *fn.*, "I have": *U.S. v. U.S. Steel Corporation et al.* (1915), in McCraw & Reinhardt, "Losing to Win," pp. 599–601; "in testifying" & ff.: Arundel Cotter, *U.S. Steel*, pp. 199–202.

625 "probable": PML—Jack to JPM, May 23, 1910.

625 "most unwise": PML—Jack to HPD, April 11, 1911.

626 "decidedly": PML—HPD to JPM, March 15, 1911. *fn.*, "better at": PML—Jack to JPM, Feb. 2, 1911.

626 Conant, Taft, Warburg: in Livingston, *Origins*, pp. 191–97.

627 *fn.*, "The instruments" to "covered all": William Greider, *Secrets of the Temple* (New York: Simon & Schuster, 1987), pp. 277–78.

627 Lindbergh and *Wall Street Journal*, Aug. 1, 1911, in James Grant, *Money of the Mind*, p. 124.

CHAPTER 30: PORTRAITS

629 "I have": Lamont, *Davison*, p. 126. "was the": David H. Greer, *Literary Digest*, April 12, 1913.

630 "remember": I Tatti—BG to BB, Jan. 6, 1911. "you must": PML—BG to JPM, April 19, 1910.

630 "called on": Gutekunst to BB, May 19, 1909, in Brown, *Raphael & America*, p. 69. *fn.:* Ibid., pp. 105, 70.

631 "Sometimes": BB to ISG, July 11, 1909, *Letters of BB & ISG*, p. 450.

631 "I am going": I Tatti—BG to BB, June 15, 1909.

632 "as usual": BB to ISG, July 11, 1909, *Letters BB-ISG*, p. 450.

632–33 "attending" & ff.: I Tatti—BG to BB, August 2, 1909. "Why is it" & "all his": June [28?] & Feb. 24, 1910. "extremely": Feb. 24, 1910. "all day": June [28?], 1910. "I had" & "as he": Nov. 11, 1910, & May 6, 1911.

634 "not interested": Herbert E. Winlock, *Excavations at Deir el Bahri 1911–1931* (New York: Macmillan Co., 1942), p. 1.

634 "splendidly" & ff.: MMA Egypt—Winlock to A. Lythgoe, Feb. 17, 1911.

634 "I know" & ff.: Ibid., Feb. 20, 1911.

634–35 "Morgan likes" & "he likes": Ibid., March 2–3 & Feb. 17, 1911.

635 "the most superb": MMA Egypt—AL to Caroline Ransom, March 17, 1912.

635 "Morgan was able": Ibid.—AL to ER, Feb. 19, 1912.

635–36 "There is": William Lawrence, *Memories*, p. 323.

636 "Emperor": PML—HLS Box 3, folder A-10, Lanier recollections.

637 "adored": Nigel Nicolson, *Portrait of a Marriage*, p. 54. Knole: Victoria Glendenning, *Vita*, p. 9.

637 "she made" & "You are": Nicolson, p. 55.

638 "ruthless": Glendenning, p. 16.

638 "enjoyed": Nicolson, p. 56.

Page

638   "it would": Susan Mary Alsop, *Lady Sackville* (New York: Avon Books, 1978), pp. 152–53.

638   to "wage" & "the People's": in Havighurst, *Twentieth-Century Britain*, p. 102.

638–39   "Alas" to "Why": Lilly—Sackville-West Mss., LSD, Feb. 23 & July 5, 1911.

639–41   "rather a shock" to "I *hate*": Ibid., July–Aug., 1911.

641   "looking at": PML—Vendors' files (S Misc. I), LS to JPM, Aug. 8, 1911. "*Ces petites*": Lilly—LSD, Aug. 10, 1911.

641   "almost certain" & ff.: PML Vendors' files (JPM 1910–13)—JPM to William Loeb, Nov. 14, 1911.

642   "I am": Ibid., MacVeagh to JPM, Nov. 17, 1911.

642   "princely" & "very": London *Times*, Jan. 27, 1912.

643   "Have just": PML—JPM to Jack, April 15, 1912. "horrible": Walter Lord, *A Night to Remember* (New York: Henry Holt & Co., 1955), p. 161.

643   "but greatly" & "my heart": PML—JPM to Jack, April 17, & to Stotesbury & CS, April 22, 1912. "exceedingly" & no comment: NY *Times*, April 18 & 19, 1912.

643   "JP has": I Tatti—BG to BB, April 23, 1912.

643   "Newspapers" & "infernally": PML—Jack to JPM, April 19, & JPM to Jack, April 23, 1912.

643   "so long": Walter Lord, *The Night Lives On* (New York: William Morrow & Co., 1986), p. 212. "In the face": in Wyn Craig Wade, *The Titanic, End of a Dream* (New York: Rawson, Wade Publishers, Inc., 1979), p. 251.

644   *fn.*, "to help": PML—Archibald C. Coolidge to Jack, June 9, 1910. "whose people," "too dignified," & "speak to": Jack to A.L. Lowell, Aug. 29, 1911, & Feb. 13 & April 5, 1912. "if I am": *DAB*, H.E. Widener. "nothing of": PML Vendors' files—Rosenbach to BG, April 20, 1912.

645–46   "to appear" to "No, dear": Lilly—LSD, May, 1912. *fn.*, "As you know": PML Vendors' files (S Misc. IV)—JPM to Sturgis & Walton, Sept. 9, 1911.

647   "Of course" to "after all": Lilly—LSD, May–June, 1912.

648   "most attractive" & ff.: St. Just—ECG to Maud Grenfell, June 27, 1912.

648   "Unaccountably": Satterlee, *JPM*, p. 549.

649   "marching orders" to "as he wants": Lilly—LSD, June–July 1912. *fn.**: Nicolson, pp. 71–73.

649   "entirely given": PML—VHS to Jack, May 1, 1909. "No more": Stanley Olson, *John Singer Sargent* (New York: St. Martin's Press, 1986), pp. 227–28. *fn.*[†], "thrilling": PML—Jessie Scrapbook, 1905; "as you are" & "to do": Jack to Sargent, Nov. 15, 1905, & Jan. 9, 1906.

650   "but his expression" & ff.: Edward Steichen, *A Life in Photography* (Garden City, N.Y.: Doubleday, 1963), Chapter 3.

651   "I think": PML—BG to Stieglitz, Dec. 18, 1909. "my rather": Steichen, *A*

Page

     Life. fn., "Belle da Costa": PML—Steichen to BG [n.d.], 1910; "seems to": Stieglitz to BG, July 10, 1914.

652 "the great bear" & ff.: George Biddle, *An American Artist's Story* (Boston: Little, Brown, 1939), pp. 134–35.

652 "most enthusiastic" & "the work": PML—BG to JPM, March 17 & April 19, 1910. *fn.*, "same deplorable": PML Vendors' files, Wadsworth Athenaeum—BG to Charles Goodwin, June 5, 1928; Jack to Met: MMA Archives, JPM Gifts, Paintings 1900–12—BG to William Ivins, July 6, 1939.

652 "inferior": HJ to Edith Wharton, November 19, 1911, *HJL*, Vol. IV, p. 592.

653 "had six": Henry James, *The Outcry*, p. 24.

654 "the most beautiful" to "We grew": Ibid., pp. 24–45.

655 *fn.*, "*my* Montovano": HJ to Robert C. Witt, Nov. 27, 1912, in *HJL*, Vol. IV, pp. 640–41.

655 "Are you talking" to "Because": *Outcry*, pp. 79–85.

656 "I believe" & ff.: E.M. Forster, *Howards End*, pp. 267–68.

656 "JP is" & "exquisite": I Tatti—BG to BB, Feb. 21 & Aug. 11, 1911.

657 "which made" & "he went": Ibid., Sept. 2 & Oct. 11, 1911.

657 "He just *laughed*": Ibid., Sept. 6, 1912.

CHAPTER 31: TRUST AND MONEY

659 "money oligarchy," "settle," "the trust," & "The condition": in *Literary Digest*, Feb. 17, 1912.

660 "advantageous" & "unpleasant": PML—CS & Jack to JPM, March 15 & April 25, 1912.

660 "a certain": Adolph S. Ochs to Effie Ochs, August 4, 1898, in Richard F. Shepard, *The Paper's Papers* (New York: Times Books, 1996), pp. 63–65.

660 "most delighted" & "best counsel": PML—HPD to Jack, May 2, 1912, & JPM & HPD to CS & Jack, May 3, 1912.

660 "TWL's man" & ff.: PML—TWL to HPD, May 3, & (with CS & Jack) May 23, 1912.

662 "enthusiastically": PML—HPD to T. Bowdoin, May 5, 1912.

662 "Are furnishing": Ibid.—TWL, CS, Jack to HPD, May 23, 1912. *fn.*, "control powerful": Ibid.; "parasite": HBS, Thomas W., Lamont Papers—TWL to H.G. Wells, Dec. 1, 1934, & March 28, 1935; "In speaking": *Modern Monthly*, Dec. 1934.

663 "To hear": NY *Times*, May 26, 1912. *fn.**, "I wear" & "If Mr.": Allen, *GPM*, p. 235; "It does not": Carosso, *Morgans*, pp. 610–11.

663 "not frighten": I Tatti—BG to BB, May 21, 1912.

663 "enjoyed": PML—Vendors' files (A Misc. III), Albert Mensdorff to JPM, May 27, 1912. *fn.*†, plan: Ron Chernow, *House of Morgan*, p. 183.

Page

664 "My hat" to "strong as": Harbaugh, *Roosevelt*, pp. 390–407.

664 "who is": Boller, *Presidential Campaigns*, p. 195.

665 "the most vivid" to "understand the job": Cooper, *Pivotal Decades*, pp. 175–81.

665 "*most* angelic": I Tatti—BG to BB, [August] 7, 1912.

665 "secure, careful": HBS, Lamont Papers—TWL to W.H. Oliver, Aug. 22, 1912. "I am": PML, MSI—LMS to FTM, Oct. 30 [1912].

666 "Morgenthau tells": Columbia, Vanderlip Papers—Vanderlip to Stillman, Sept. 20, 1912.

666 "rather dreading": MGCo. (GWS)—Ledyard to ECG, Oct. 16, 1912. "tightwad": NY *Times*, Oct. 4, 1912.

666 "very blue": I Tatti—BG to BB, Oct. 30, 1912.

667 *fn.*, "offered": PML, Jack Box 108 f. 378(2)—Memorandum, May 1914.

667 "as sound": HBS, Lamont Papers, "Money Trust Investigation (Pujo Committee)"—F.L. Stetson to S. Untermyer, Oct. 18, 1912.

667 "Going Washington": PML—Jack to ECG, Dec. 17, 1912.

668–71 JPM's Pujo testimony: *Money Trust Investigation* transcript, pp. 18–79.

671 "in no way": PML—Jack to Harjes, Dec. 23, 1912.

671 "about seventy": PML—BG to Mrs. Amos Pinchot, Dec. 23, 1912. "throwing his": I Tatti—BG to BB, April 12, 1913.

672 "honest": PML—George Harvey, "A Public Soul," speech delivered to American Bankers Association, May 8, 1913.

672 "without" & "as the": Tomkins, *Merchants*, p. 174.

672 "He said that" & "with some": MMA Archives, M822—E. Robinson Memoranda, Nov. 29 & Dec. 23, 1912.

673 "suavest" & ff.: PML—BB in Duveen Brothers Monograph on *Saint Lawrence Enthroned*.

673 "JP wanted": I Tatti—BG to BB, Dec. 31, 1912. *fn.*, "To me-ow": PML—BG to BB, Feb. 26, 1932.

673 "a man named Lehman" & "He seemed": I Tatti—BG to BB, Dec. 31, 1912, & Jan. 5, 1913.

674 "very much": PML—Jack to Bishop Doane, Feb. 19, 1913.

674 "exceedingly personal" & ff.: Satterlee, *JPM*, pp. 566–68.

674 "distorted": PML—George A. Dixon to Jack, March 3, 1913.

674–75 "Charcoal in" & "tremendous strain": PML—LMS to Jack, & Jack to LMS, Feb. 13, 1913.

675 "economic laws" & ff.: *J.P. Morgan & Co. to Pujo*, in Carosso, pp. 638–39.

675 "Perfectly splendid" & "Greatly delighted": PML—JPM to HPD, Feb. 13, & HPD to JPM, Feb. 14, 1913.

675–76 "better than" to "Fickle appetite": PML—LMS to Jack, Feb. 14–17, 1913 (including Tribe cable, Feb. 15).

676 "How I wish" & "Charcoal": PML—LMSD & LMS to Jack, Feb. 19, 1913.

Page

676 "honest though" & "acutely": PML—Jack to JPM, March 5, & Dixon to Jack, March 4, 1913.

677–78 "remarkable" & "less absolutely": PML—Dixon to Jack, March 4, & LMS to Jack, March 6, 1913.

678 "I have assured" & "stand many": PML—HLS to Jack, March 19, & Jack to Dixon, March 17, 1913.

678 "from early": in NY *Times*, March 2, 1913.

678 "culminated" & "I wish": PML—Dixon & HLS to Jack, March 14, & Dixon to Jack, March 23, 1913.

678–79 "We have all" & "the beast": PML—Jack to HLS, March 18, & to JPM, Jan. 11, 1913.

679 "Has Dr. Phelps": PML—HLS to Jack, March 19, 1913.

679 "watched" & "For ten": PML—M. Allen Starr to Jack, March 23, 1913.

679 "the Commodore": PML—Dixon to Jack, March 25, 1913.

680 "Dr. Dixon has": [possession of author] Florence Blair to H. Rivington Pyne, March 31, 1913.

680 "dispepsia": Carosso, p. 642.

681 "He was a great" & "because": NY *Times*, April 1–2, 1913.

681 "No other": *Figaro*, April 5, 1913. *fn.*, "one who" & ff.: MGCo. (GWS)—H. Harjes to ECG, April 4, 1913.

681 "The king": Columbia, Vanderlip Papers—Vanderlip to Stillman, April 4, 1913. "My heart": I Tatti—BG to BB, April 2, 1913.

684 "which fund" & ff.: PML—Last Will and Testament of John Pierpont Morgan, January 4, 1913.

685 "not a": HBS, Lamont Papers—TWL to HPD, April 24, 1913.

686 "MORGAN GIVES": Austin *Statesman*, April 20, 1913. "it is perhaps": NY *Post*, April 22, 1913.

686 "a sick": St. Just—ECG to Florence Henderson, April 3, 1913.

686 "It will never": NY *Evening Post*, Dec. 21, 1913.

AFTERWORD

687 "If some": I Tatti—BG to BB, April 29, 1913.

687 "the finest": NY *Times*, Jan. 27, 1914.

687 sales: PML—Jack Box 220. "I am very": PML—Jack to ER, Jan. 5, 1916.

688 "first call" & "I would like": PML—JDR Jr. to Jack, April 20, 1915, & HCF to Jack, April 20, 1915.

688 sale Dover House: MGCo. (GWS), JPM 3E, p. 144.

ACKNOWLEDGMENTS

In the process of writing about Pierpont Morgan I have had a great deal of help from many people. For the sake of brevity I will not delineate my gratitude to most of them, but there are some essential exceptions. Roger Alcaly has taught me about markets and economics with inexhaustible generosity, and I could not have written the financial sections of this book without him. To my superb editor, Jason Epstein, I am immeasurably grateful for his intellectual acuity, wise counsel, extraordinary patience, and wit. Joan R. Mertens kindly offered to read portions of the manuscript that concern art collecting, and ended up applying her wide-ranging erudition to much more. And I owe special thanks to Georges Borchardt, Jonathan Galassi, Ann Godoff, and Christopher MacLehose.

For careful readings of the entire manuscript I am indebted to Sean Wilentz and Richard Grand-Jean—and, for expertise on particular sections, to Sidney Babcock, Michael Boudin, Connie Brown, Stephanie Engel, Arthur Goldhammer, David Hemenway, Marsha Hill, Paul Needham, Ben Sonnenberg, Dan Strouse, Tom Strouse, Richard Sylla, Michael Train, and William Voelkle.

The vast majority of the papers I consulted were at The Pierpont Morgan Library. Its administration and staff have made my work there a pleasure, and I warmly thank Charles E. Pierce, Jr., Brian Regan, Robert Parks, Christine Nelson, William Voelkle, Sidney Babcock, Marilyn Palmeri, Inge DuPont, and Glory Jones. Herbert Cahoon, H. George Fletcher, Paul Needham, Bill Robinson, Charles Ryskamp, Fredric W. Wilson, and David Wright, who have left the Library, also provided invaluable assistance; Mr. Wright, the Library's former archivist, meticulously guided me through years of work on previously uncatalogued material.

I would like particularly to thank several members of the Morgan family: John P. Morgan II and Charles F. Morgan for their generous permission to quote from the Morgan papers, and the late Mabel S. Ingalls, the late Frances M. Pennoyer, Robert M. Pennoyer, Gita and Sandra Van Heerden, Anne and Constantine Sidamon-Eristoff, and Miles Morgan, for information, memories, documents, and photographs.

In addition, I am grateful to Daniel Aaron, Jonathan Alexander, Frederick H. S. Allen, Susan Mary Alsop, Bob Asahina, Jean Ashton, Louis Auchincloss, Katharine Baetjer, Gail W. Berry, Helen Bodian, Barbara Bristol, Michael Brock, Anne Taylor

Brown, Ulf Buchholz, Kathleen Burk, Larry Butler, W. Bernard Carlson, Andy Carpenter, Alfred D. Chandler, Jr., Ron Chernow, Thomas C. Cochran, Joel Conarroe, Claire Le Corbeiller, Terry Collins, Mark Crandall, Peggy and Gordon Davis, Richard W. Davis, Sharon Delano, Jean and J. Gordon Douglas III, Mary L. Douglas, Nick Egleson, Colin Eisler, Barbara Epstein, Yasmine Ergas, Eric Foner, Helen Franc, R. William Franklin, the Art Reference Library at The Frick Collection, Eugene Gaddis, Peter Galassi, Susan Grace Galassi, Dorothy Gallagher, the Reverend Stephen Garmey, John A. Garraty, Donald Garstang, Jeanne Brooks Gart, Gary Gerstle, Paul Gewirtz, Paula Giddings, Hilliard Goldfarb, Diana D. Goodrich, Leonard Groopman, Peter Grossman, Megan Hahn, Neil Harris, Robert Heilbroner, Nancy Hoppin, Elizabeth and John Horder, Glenn Horowitz, Joseph A. Jackson, Walter Kaiser, Henry L. King, Maury Klein, Bruce Kuklick, Michael Jacobs, Jeanie James, Jim Lambert, Naomi Lamoreaux, Jenny Lawrence, Judith W. Leavitt, Hermione Lee, Anne Morrow Lindbergh, Arthur Lubow, Thomas K. McCraw, Irene McHugh, Diane McWhorter, Dan Menaker, Louis Menand, Joy de Menil, the Reference Department of the Thomas J. Watson Library at The Metropolitan Museum of Art, the Reverend Edward O. Miller, Jim Miller, Ken Miller, Honor Moore, the Right Reverend Paul Moore, John M. Morris, David Mortimer, Kathleen Mortimer, Edgar Munhall, David Nasaw, Thomas Navin, Mary Wistar O'Connor, John Orbell, Sybil D'Origny, Robert M. Peck, Mark Piel and the staff of the New York Society Library, the Reverend Thomas Pike, Ben Primer, Philip Prioleau, James R. Pyne, Sono Rosenberg, Leona Rostenberg, Linda H. Roth, John Rousmaniere, Mary Rousseau, John Russell, Mariam and Edward W. Said, Martha Saxton, Sanford J. Schlesinger, Anne Schneider, Margaret M. Sherry, Caron Smith, Scott Smith, John Snyder, Nancy H. Soukoup, Peter Stansky, Madeleine Stern, Jerome Sternstein, Roger W. Straus, Joseph P. Sullivan, Paul Sweezy, Brent Sverdloff, Adeline Tintner, Geoffrey C. Ward, Betty Whiddington, W. Thomas White, William F. Whitehouse, William Wixom, Peter M. Wolf, and Mary Yeager.

I have quoted from public and private papers by permission of Barings ING; the Peabody and Stearns Architectural Drawings Collection, Fine Arts Department, Boston Public Library; Annabel Cole (letters of Roger Fry at King's College, Cambridge); the Rare Book and Manuscript Library, Columbia University; the Columbia University Oral History Research Office Collection; The Connecticut Historical Society; Thomas P. Cook ("Highland Falls," unpublished memoir of Grace Bigelow Cook); Division of Rare and Manuscript Collections, Cornell University Library; Davis Polk & Wardwell (two histories of the firm); Deutsche Morgan Grenfell; J. Gordon Douglas III (family papers); the Hon. Lady Phillips, the Hon. Natasha Grenfell, and the Hon. Mrs. Katya Middleton (letters in the Estate of the First Lord St. Just); Historical Collections, Baker Library, Harvard University Graduate School of Business Administration; Harvard University Archives; The James Jerome Hill Reference Library; Mrs. Priscilla Bibesco Hodgson (diary of Margot Tennant Asquith); Department of Manuscripts, The Huntington Library; The Lilly Library; The Massachusetts Historical Society; The Metropolitan Museum of Art; The Pierpont Morgan Library; the Warden and Fellows, New College, Oxford (letters of Clinton E. Dawkins at the Bodleian Library); The New Hampshire Historical Society; The New-York Historical Society; Manuscripts and Archives Division, The New York Public Library; Nigel Nicolson (Lady Sackville diaries); The Peabody Essex Museum; Manuscripts Division, Department of Rare Books and Special Collections, Princeton University Library; Princeton University Archives, Seeley G. Mudd Manuscript Library, Princeton University Library; James R. Pyne (letter of Florence Blair, March 31, 1913); the late Annette M. Schieffelin (family papers); Villa I Tatti and the President and Fellows of Harvard College; Special Collections, Transylvania University Library; Department of Manuscripts and Archives, Yale University Library.

For financial assistance without which it would not have been possible to complete this project, I am grateful to the John Simon Guggenheim Memorial Foundation, the National Endowment for the Humanities, the Ingram Merrill Foundation, the New York Foundation for the Arts, Jean Stein, the Kentucky Foundation for Women, and the Gilder Lehrman Institute of American History.

Annette Markoe Schieffelin, who knew Morgan and talked with me about him on dozens of occasions, urged me to finish the book in time for her to read it. To my great sorrow, she died in 1997. Others whom I can thank only in memoriam are Jean F. Block, Vincent Carosso, J. Gordon Douglas, Jr., Leon Edel, Gerald Freund, Martha and Stanton A. Friedberg, Brendan Gill, Gordon N. Ray, Tony Roth, Lady St. Just, and Frank A. Vanderlip.

INDEX

ABOUT THE AUTHOR

JEAN STROUSE won the Bancroft Prize in American History and Diplomacy for her biography, *Alice James*. Her essays and reviews have appeared in *The New Yorker*, *The New York Times Book Review*, *The New York Review of Books*, *Vogue*, and *Newsweek*, and she has held fellowships from the John Simon Guggenheim Memorial Foundation and from the National Endowments for the Humanities and the Arts. She lives in New York City.

ABOUT THE TYPE

This book was set in Photina, a typeface designed by
José Mendoza in 1971. It is a very elegant design with
high legibility, and its close character fit has made it a
popular choice for use in quality magazines and art
gallery publications.